KU-476-480

Paul and Tracey
AAA Members,
Bargain Hunters

At Days Inns our money gets the best mileage.

AAA Members: Save 10% - 30%* at 29 Days Inn® hotels in Ontario.

Just book and save at the AAA-approved Days Inn® locations listed in this Tourbook.® You'll get a free continental breakfast and a free national newspaper at most properties**. When you join TripRewards,® you can earn points that are good for an amazing selection of rewards. Not to mention special bonus offers for AAA Members all year long!

Show Your Card & Save

DAYS INN
The Best Value Under The Sun

For specific locations and reservations, call
**1-800-432-9755 or
daysinn.com**

*Discount is off published Tourbook rate and may not be combined with any other discounts or special offers.
**Discounts and amenities vary by property. See property for details. Some restrictions may apply. ©2004 Days Inns Worldwide, Inc.

Trust AAA/CAA for the Last Word on Quality ... Approved.

Choosing hotels that are AAA/CAA Approved means choosing with confidence. **AAA/CAA's professional evaluators** have been there and done the research, checking for qualities like cleanliness, service, and value — assigning a rating from one to five Diamonds.

Wherever you travel, take AAA/CAA's word for it: Approved! Choose your accommodations and Diamond ratings from the TourBook® listings, in print and on aaa.com, and look for the bright red AAA/CAA logo on billboards and signage.

For more information on AAA/CAA Lodging Diamond Ratings, turn to page 16.

Ontario

Are we meeting your travel needs?

Send written comments to:

AAA Member Comments
1000 AAA Drive, Box 61
Heathrow, FL 32746-5063

Published by:
AAA Publishing
1000 AAA Drive
Heathrow, FL 32746-5063
Copyright AAA 2005

The publisher is not responsible for changes that occur after publication. TourBook® guides are published for the exclusive use of AAA members. Not for sale.

Advertising Rate and Circulation Information
Call: (407) 444-8280

Printed in the USA by
Quebecor World, Buffalo, NY

Photo Credit: (Cover & Title Page)
Rossport
© *2004 Ontario Tourism*

 Printed on recyclable paper.
Please recycle whenever possible.

Stock #4619

Ontario

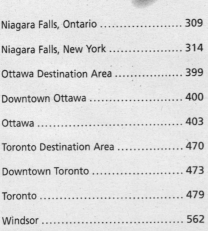

Featured Information

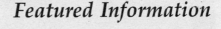
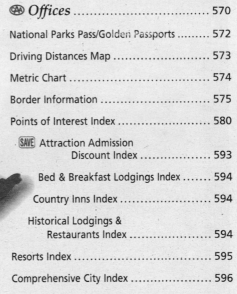

4

ALL I WANT IS...

a great start to the day and a great guarantee.
The best place to stay when you travel? Hampton® Hotels.
You'll find delightful accommodations and a staff that's
committed to pleasing you. With every stay, you'll enjoy
our complimentary breakfast and our 100% Satisfaction
Guarantee. Plus, we offer special rates for CAA members.
Visit www.hamptoninn.com or call 1-800-HAMPTON.

Kamloops, BC • Vancouver-Airport, BC • Vancouver-Downtown, BC
Langley/Surrey, BC • Surrey/Guildford, BC • Calgary-Airport, AB
Calgary University NW, AB • Winnipeg, MB • Toronto/Mississauga, ON
Toronto/Airport, ON • Windsor, ON • Niagra Falls/North, ON
Niagra Falls, ON • Ottawa, ON • Montreal/Dorval, QC

©2004 Hilton Hospitality, Inc. TheHiltonFamily

www.hamptoninn.com

© 2002 Ontario Tourism

Getting away just got better.

Sheraton
HOTELS & RESORTS

Sheraton Gateway Toronto Hotel
Sheraton Centre Toronto Hotel
Sheraton Parkway Toronto North
Sheraton Fallsview Hotel, Niagara Falls
Sheraton On the Falls, Niagara Falls
Sheraton Hamilton
Sheraton Ottawa Hotel

Four Points
Sheraton

Four Points by Sheraton Toronto Lakeshore
Four Points by Sheraton St. Catharines Niagara Suites
Four Points by Sheraton Mississauga
Four Points by Sheraton Kitchener
Four Points by Sheraton Kingston
Four Points by Sheraton London
* Four Points by Sheraton Toronto Airport

WESTIN
HOTELS & RESORTS

The Westin Harbour Castle, Toronto
The Westin Prince, Toronto
The Westin Ottawa
* The Westin Trillium House Blue Mountain

Whether you travel by plane, train, or automobile, simply
show your AAA card and receive exclusive savings at
Starwood Hotels & Resorts worldwide.
* Hotel not yet inspected by AAA.

To make reservations or to learn about
AAA special rates and member benefits call **866 782 7737**
www.starwood.com/aaa

MEMBER OF STARWOOD PREFERRED GUEST®   ©2005-2006 Starwood Hotels & Resorts Worldwide, Inc.

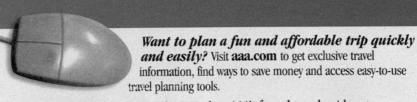

Want to plan a fun and affordable trip quickly and easily? Visit **aaa.com** to get exclusive travel information, find ways to save money and access easy-to-use travel planning tools.

Searchable TourBook®guides. Find AAA's famous TourBook travel information including: Approved hotels (get Diamond ratings, member discounts on room rates, plus online reservations), Approved restaurants, recommended attractions, local events, and detailed destination descriptions.
AAA TripTiks®. Create your own customized TripTik: get door-to-door driving directions and maps, find AAA Approved hotels and reserve a room, locate AAA recommended restaurants, and discover things to do and see at your destination and along the way.
AAA Drive Trips*. Review AAA recommended drive trips.
Vacation Getaways. Take to the skies, hit the high seas or select a tour and receive exclusive benefits from AAA's Preferred Travel Partners.
Travel Guides. Get a 5% discount on

AAA's famed travel guides at aaa.com/barnesandnoble.
Disney® Vacations. Get exclusive benefits and savings on AAA Vacations® Disney vacation packages.
Hertz Rental. Save up to 20% on car rental.
Show Your Card & Save. Search for savings on lodging, travel, entertainment, retail, and e-merchants.
AAA Travel Money. Get no-fee travelers cheques, foreign currency and prepaid cards.
AAA Map Gallery*. Know the best way to go wherever you travel.
Cash Back. Get up to a 5% rebate every time you use your AAA credit card to gas up.
AAA Approved Auto Repair. Find your nearest AAR shop to get your car ready for the road.

Travel to aaa.com to do all your vacation planning!

aaa.com

Travel With Someone You Trust®

*Products and Services available through participating AAA and CAA Clubs.

THE NAME OF THE GAME IS FUN.

At Ontario Charity Casinos and Slots at Racetracks the action is hot, the smiles are warm and the fun never stops. You'll find a wide array of exciting games, good food and much more in a casual, comfortable setting. So for an exciting change of pace and non-stop action any day of the week, go for a spin at Ontario Charity Casinos and Slots at Racetracks.

For more information, call 1-888-942-6224.

Know your limit, play within it!
The Ontario Problem Gambling Helpline
1 888 230-3505

www.**OLGC**.ca
For more information visit the Winner's Circle pour renseignements en français.

Must be 19 years of age or older. Government issued photo identification may be required. Some restrictions may apply.

Trust the AAA TourBook® guide for objective travel information. Follow the pages of the TourBook Navigator to thoroughly understand this unique member benefit.

Making Your Way Through the AAA Listings

Attractions, lodgings and restaurants are listed on the basis of merit alone after careful evaluation, approval and rating by one of our full-time, professionally trained Tourism Editors. Annual evaluations are unannounced to ensure that our Tourism Editors see an establishment just as our members would see it.

Those lodgings and restaurants listed with an (fyi) icon have not gone through the same evaluation process as other rated properties. Individual listings will typically denote the reason why this icon appears. Bulleted recreational activity listings are not inspected but are included for member information.

An establishment's decision to advertise in the TourBook guide has no bearing on its evaluation or rating. Advertising for services or products does not imply AAA endorsement.

How the TourBook is

Organized

Geographic listing is used for accuracy and consistency. This means attractions, lodgings and restaurants are listed under the city in which they physically are located—or in some cases under the nearest recognized city. The Comprehensive City Index located in the back of the book contains an A-to-Z list of cities. Most listings are alphabetically organized by state, province, region or island; city; and establishment name. A color is assigned to each state or province so that you can match the color bars at the top of the page to switch from ❶ Points of Interest to ❷ Lodgings and Restaurants.

Destination Cities and Destination Areas

The TourBook guide also groups information by destination city and destination area. If a city is grouped in a destination vicinity section, the city name will appear at its alphabetical location in the book, and a handy cross reference will give the exact page on which listings for that city begin. Maps are placed at the beginning of these sections to orient you to the destinations.

❸ **Destination cities**, established based on government models and local expertise, are comprised of metropolitan areas plus nearby vicinity cities.

Destination areas are regions with broad tourist appeal. Several cities will comprise the area.

All information in this TourBook guide was reviewed for accuracy before publication. However, since changes inevitably occur between annual editions, we suggest you contact establishments directly to confirm prices and schedules.

Points of Interest Section

Orientation maps
near the start of each Attractions section show only those places we call points of interest. Coordinates included with the city listings depict the locations of those cities on the map. A GEM symbol (✹) accents towns with "must see" points of interest which offer a *Great Experience for Members* ®. And the black ovals with white numerals (**22** for example) locate items listed in the nearby Recreation Areas chart.

Destination area maps
illustrate key travel areas defined by local travel experts. Communities shown have listings for AAA approved attractions.

National park maps
represent the area in and around the park. Some campground sites and lodges spotted on the maps do not meet AAA/CAA criteria, but are shown for members who nevertheless wish to stay close to the park area.

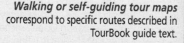

Walking or self-guiding tour maps
correspond to specific routes described in TourBook guide text.

City maps
show areas where numerous points of interest are concentrated and indicate their location in relation to major roads, parks, airports and other landmarks.

Lodgings & Restaurants Section

Destination area maps
illustrate key travel areas defined by local travel experts. Communities shown have listings for AAA-RATED® lodgings and/or restaurants.

Spotting maps
show the location of lodgings and restaurants. Lodgings are spotted with a black background (**22** for example); restaurants are spotted with a white background (**23** for example). Spotting map indexes have been placed immediately after each map to provide the user with a convenient method to identify what an area has to offer at a glance. The index references the map page number where the property is spotted, indicates if a property is an Official Appointment and contains an advertising reference if applicable. It also lists the property's diamond rating, high season rate range and listing page number.

Downtown/city spotting maps
are provided when spotted facilities are very concentrated. GEM points of interest also appear on these maps.

Vicinity spotting maps
spot those properties that are outside the downtown or city area. Major roads, landmarks, airports and GEM points of interest are shown on vicinity spotting maps as well. The names of suburban communities that have AAA-RATED® accommodations are shown in magenta type.

Featured Information Section

Driving distance maps
are intended to be used only for trip-distance and driving-time planning.

Sample Attraction Listing

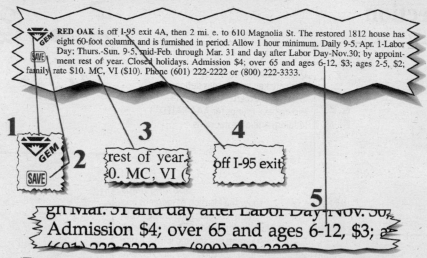

RED OAK is off I-95 exit 4A, then 2 mi. e. to 610 Magnolia St. The restored 1812 house has eight 60-foot columns and is furnished in period. Allow 1 hour minimum. Daily 9-5, Apr. 1-Labor Day; Thurs.-Sun. 9-5, mid-Feb. through Mar. 31 and day after Labor Day-Nov.30; by appointment rest of year. Closed holidays. Admission $4; over 65 and ages 6-12, $3; ages 2-5, $2; family rate $10. MC, VI ($10). Phone (601) 222-2222 or (800) 222-3333.

1

2

3 rest of year. 0. MC, VI (

4 off I-95 exit

5

gh Mar. 31 and day after Labor Day-Nov. 30;
Admission $4; over 65 and ages 6-12, $3;

1 This attraction is of exceptional interest and quality and therefore has been designated a AAA GEM—offering a *Great Experience for Members*®.

2 Participating attractions offer AAA/CAA, AAA MasterCard or AAA Visa cardholders a discount off the attraction's standard admission; members should inquire in advance concerning the validity of the discount for special rates. Present your card at the admission desk. A list of participating points of interest appears in the Indexes section of the book. The SAVE discount may not be used in conjunction with other discounts. Attractions that already provide a reduced senior or child rate may not honor the SAVE discount for those age groups. All offers are subject to change and may not apply during special events, particular days or seasons or for the entire validity period of the TourBook. Shopping establishments preceded by a SAVE icon also provide discounts and/or gift with purchase to AAA/CAA members; present your card at the mall's customer service center to receive your benefit.

3
AX=American Express	DS=Discover	MC=MasterCard
CB=Carte Blanche	JC=Japan Credit Bureau	VI=VISA
DC=Diners Club		

4 Unless otherwise specified, directions are given from the center of town, using the following highway designations: I (interstate highway), US (federal highway), Hwy. (Canadian or Caribbean highway), SR (state route), CR (county road), FM (farm to market road), FR (forest road), MM (mile marker), Mex. (Mexican highway).

5 Admission prices are quoted without sales tax. Children under the lowest age specified are admitted free when accompanied by an adult. Days, months and age groups written with a hyphen are inclusive. Prices pertaining to points of interest in the United States are quoted in U.S. dollars; prices for Canadian province and territory points of interest are quoted in Canadian dollars; prices for points of interest in Mexico and the Caribbean are quoted as an approximate U.S. dollar equivalent.

Bulleted Listings: Casino gambling establishments are visited by AAA personnel to ensure safety; casinos within hotels are presented for member information regardless of whether the lodging is AAA approved. Recreational activities of a participatory nature (requiring physical exertion or special skills) are not inspected. Wineries are inspected by AAA Tourism Editors to ensure they meet listing requirements and offer tours. All are presented in a bulleted format for informational purposes.

These Show Your Card & Save® partners provide the listed member benefits. Admission tickets that offer greater discounts may be available for purchase at the local AAA/CAA club. The discount applies to the cardholder; the attraction, at its discretion, may also offer the discount to up to five family members.

Attraction Partners

SeaWorld/Busch Gardens (aaa.com/seaworld)

[SAVE] Save $5 on general admission at the gate at SeaWorld and Busch Gardens

[SAVE] Save $3 on general admission at the gate at Sesame Place, Water Country USA and Adventure Island

[SAVE] Save 10% on select up-close dining. Reservations are required; visit Guest Relations for details

Six Flags Theme Parks

[SAVE] Save $4 on general admission at the gate

[SAVE] Save $12 on general admission at the gate each Wednesday

[SAVE] Save 10% on selected souvenirs and dining (check at main gate for details)

Universal Orlando (aaa.com/universal)

[SAVE] Save $4 on a 2-day/2-park pass or $5 on a 3-day/2-park pass at Universal Orlando's theme parks (savings apply to tickets purchased at the gate)

[SAVE] Save 10% on select dining and souvenirs at both Universal Orlando theme parks and at select Universal CityWalk Orlando restaurants (except Emeril's)

Universal Studios Hollywood (aaa.com/universal)

[SAVE] Save $3 on a 1-day Universal Studios pass (savings applies to tickets purchased at the gate)

[SAVE] Save 10% on select dining and souvenirs at Universal Studios Hollywood and Universal CityWalk

Gray Line (aaa.com/grayline)

[SAVE] Save 10% on sightseeing tours of 1 day or less

Restaurant Partners

Landry's Seafood House, The Crab House, Chart House, Muer Seafood Restaurants, Joe's Crab Shack

[SAVE] Save 10% on food and non-alcoholic beverages at Landry's Seafood House, The Crab House, Chart House, Muer Seafood Restaurants and Joe's Crab Shack and 10% on merchandise at Joe's Crab Shack. Savings applicable to AAA/CAA member and up to five additional people

Hard Rock Cafe

[SAVE] Save 10% on food, non-alcoholic beverages and merchandise at all U.S. and select Canadian and international locations. Savings applicable to AAA/CAA member and up to five additional people.

Visit aaa.com to discover all the great Show Your Card & Save® discounts in your area.

Sample Lodging Listing

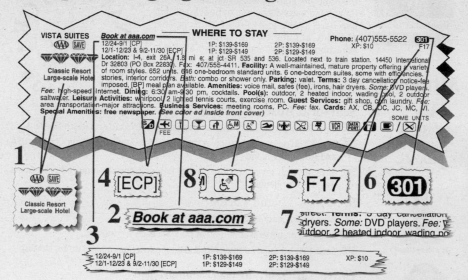

1. 🔺 or 🔺 indicates our Official Appointment (OA) lodgings. The OA program permits properties to display and advertise the 🔺 or 🔺 emblem. We highlight these properties with red diamonds and classification. Some OA listings include special amenities such as free continental breakfast; expanded continental breakfast or full breakfast; early check-in/late check-out; free room upgrade or preferred room, such as ocean view or poolside (subject to availability); free local phone calls; and free daily newspaper. This does not imply that only these properties offer these amenities. The 🔺 or 🔺 sign helps traveling members find accommodations that want member business.

   ▼▼▼ ▼▼▼ or ▼▼▼ ▼▼▼ The number of diamonds—not the color—informs you of the overall level of quality in a lodging's amenities and service. More diamond details appear on page 16.

   Classic Resort Large-scale Hotel or Classic Resort Large-scale Hotel: All diamond rated lodgings are classified using three key elements: style of operation, overall concept and service level. See pages 22-23 for details about our Lodging Classifications and Subclassifications.

Member Values

🔲SAVE Official Appointment properties guarantee members a minimum 10% discount off the standard room rates published in TourBook guides or the lowest public rate available at the time of booking for the dates of stay, for standard rooms.

🔲SD Establishments offer a minimum senior discount of 10% off the listed rates. This discount is available to members 60 or older.

🔲ASK Many properties offer discounts to members even though the lodgings do not participate in a formal discount program. The 🔲ASK is another reminder to inquire about available discounts when making your reservations or at check-in.

> Discounts normally offered at some lodgings may not apply during special events or holiday periods. Special rates and discounts may not apply to all room types. Some Member Values may not apply in Mexico or the Caribbean.

To obtain published rates or discounts, you must identify yourself as a AAA or CAA member, request AAA rates when making reservations and have written confirmation sent to you. The SAVE or senior discount may not be used in conjunction with other discounts. At registration, show your membership card and verify the room rate.

Discounts normally offered at some lodgings may not apply during special events or holiday periods. Special rates and discounts may not apply to all room types. Some Member Values may not apply in Mexico or the Caribbean.

The rates listed for approved properties are provided to AAA by each lodging and represent the regular (rack) rate for a standard room. Printed rates, based on rack rates and last room availability, are rounded to the nearest dollar. Rates do not include taxes and discounts. U.S., Mexican and Caribbean rates are in U.S. dollars; rates for Canadian lodgings are in Canadian dollars.

2 Book at aaa.com - Internet Reservations
Indicates AAA/CAA members can conveniently check room availability and make reservations in a secure online environment at aaa.com.

3 Rate Lines
Shown from left to right: dates the rates are effective; meal plan provided with rates (see Meal Plan Indicators-if no plan noted, rate includes room only); rates for 1 person or 2 persons; extra person charge (XP); and any applicable family plan indicator.

Rates Guaranteed
AAA/CAA members are guaranteed that they will not be charged more than the maximum regular rate printed in each rate range for a standard room. Rates may vary within the range depending on season and room type. Listed rates are based on last standard room availability. Rates for properties operating as concessionaires for the U.S. National Park Service are not guaranteed due to governing regulations. Rates in the Mexico TourBook are not guaranteed and may fluctuate based on the exchange rate of the peso.

Exceptions
Lodgings may temporarily increase room rates, not recognize discounts or modify pricing policies during special events. Examples of special events range from Mardi Gras and Kentucky Derby (including pre-Derby events) to college football games, holidays, holiday periods and state fairs. Although some special events are listed in AAA/CAA TourBook guides, it is always wise to check, in advance, with AAA travel professionals for specific dates.

Discounts
Member discounts will apply to rates quoted, within the rate range, applicable at the time of booking. Special rates used in advertising, and special short-term, promotional rates lower than the lowest listed rate in the range, are not subject to additional member discounts.

4 Meal Plan Indicators
The following types of meal plans may be available in the listed room rate:
AP = American Plan of three meals daily
BP = Breakfast Plan of full hot breakfast
CP = Continental Plan of pastry, juice and another beverage
ECP = Expanded Continental Plan, which offers a wider variety of breakfast items
MAP = Modified American Plan of two meals daily
See individual listing "Terms" section for additional meal plans that are not included in the room rate.

> Check-in times are shown in the listing only if they are after 3 p.m.; check-out times are shown only if they are before 10 a.m.

5 Family Plan Indicators
F = Children stay free
D = Discounts for children
F17 = Children 17 and under stay free (age displayed will reflect property's policy)
D17 = Discount for children 17 and under

6 Lodging Locators
Black ovals with white numbers are used to locate, or "spot," lodgings on maps we provide for larger cities.

7 Unit Types
Unit types, amenities and room features preceded by the word "Some" indicate the item is available on a limited basis, potentially within only one unit.

8 Lodging Icons
A row of icons is included with each lodging listing. These icons represent the member values, member services, and facilities offered by that lodging. See page 19 for an explanation of each icon.

The Lodging Diamond Ratings

AAA Tourism Editors evaluate and rate each lodging based on the overall quality, the range of facilities and the level of services offered by a property. The size, age and overall appeal of an establishment are considered as well as regional architectural style and design.

While guest services are an important part of all diamond ratings, they are particularly critical at the four and five diamond levels. A property must provide a high level of service, on a consistent basis, to obtain and support the four and five diamond rating.

These establishments typically appeal to the budget-minded traveler. They provide essential, no-frills accommodations. They meet the basic requirements pertaining to comfort, cleanliness, and hospitality.

These establishments appeal to the traveler seeking more than the basic accommodations. There are modest enhancements to the overall physical attributes, design elements, and amenities of the facility typically at a modest price.

These establishments appeal to the traveler with comprehensive needs. Properties are multifaceted with a distinguished style, including marked upgrades in the quality of physical attributes, amenities and level of comfort provided.

These establishments are upscale in all areas. Accommodations are progressively more refined and stylish. The physical attributes reflect an obvious enhanced level of quality throughout. The fundamental hallmarks at this level include an extensive array of amenities combined with a high degree of hospitality, service, and attention to detail.

These establishments reflect the characteristics of the ultimate in luxury and sophistication. Accommodations are first-class. The physical attributes are extraordinary in every manner. The fundamental hallmarks at this level are to meticulously serve and exceed all guest expectations while maintaining an impeccable standard of excellence. Many personalized services and amenities enhance an unmatched level of comfort.

The lodging listings with **fyi** in place of diamonds are included as an "information only" service for members. The icon indicates that a property has not been rated for one or more of the following reasons: too new to rate; under construction; under major renovation; not evaluated; or may not meet all AAA requirements. Those properties not meeting all AAA requirements are included for either their member value or because it may be the only accommodation available in the area. Listing prose will give insight as to why the **fyi** designation was assigned.

Guest Safety

Room Security

In order to be approved for listing in AAA/CAA TourBook guides for the United States and Canada, all lodgings must comply with AAA's guest room security requirements.

In response to AAA/CAA members' concern about their safety at properties, AAA-RATED® accommodations must have dead-bolt locks on all guest room entry doors and connecting room doors.

If the area outside the guest room door is not visible from inside the room through a window or door panel, viewports must be installed on all guest room entry doors. Bed and breakfast properties and country inns are not required to have viewports. Ground floor and easily accessible sliding doors must be equipped with some other type of secondary security locks.

Tourism Editors view a percentage of rooms at each property since it is not feasible to evaluate every room in every lodging establishment. Therefore, AAA cannot guarantee that there are working locks on all doors and windows in all guest rooms.

Fire Safety

Because of the highly specialized skills needed to conduct professional fire safety inspections, AAA/CAA Tourism Editors cannot assess fire safety.

Properties must meet all federal, state and local fire codes. Each guest unit in all U.S. and Canadian lodging properties must be equipped with an operational, single-station smoke detector. A AAA/CAA Tourism Editor has evaluated a sampling of the rooms to verify this equipment is in place.

> **For additional fire safety information, read the page posted on the back of your guest room door, or write:**
>
> **National Fire Protection Association**
> **1 Batterymarch Park**
> **P.O. Box 9101**
> **Quincy, MA 02269-9101**

Requirements for some features, such as door locks and smoke detectors/sprinkler systems, differ in Mexico and the Caribbean. If a property met AAA's security requirements at the time of the evaluation, the phrase "Meets AAA guest room security requirements" appears in the listing.

Access for Mature Travelers and Travelers with Disabilities

Qualified properties listed in this guide are shown with symbols indicating they meet the needs of the hearing-impaired or offer some accessible features for mature travelers or travelers with disabilities.

Hearing Impaired

Indicates a property has the following equipment available for hearing-impaired travelers: TDD at front desk or switchboard; visual notification of fire alarm, incoming telephone calls, door knock or bell; closed caption decoder; text telephone or TDD for guest room use; telephone amplification device, with shelf or electric outlet next to guest room telephone.

Accessible Features

Indicates a property has some accessible features meeting the needs of mature travelers and travelers with disabilities. Lodging establishments will provide at least one guest room meeting the designated criteria as well as accessible restrooms and parking facilities. Restaurants provide accessible parking, dining rooms and restrooms.

> AAA/CAA strongly urges members to call the property directly to fully understand the property's exact accessibility features. Some properties do not fully comply with AAA/CAA's exacting accessibility standards but may offer some design standards that meet the needs of some guests with disabilities.
>
> AAA/CAA does not evaluate recreational facilities, banquet rooms, or convention or meeting facilities for accessibility.

Service Animals

> No fees or deposits, even those normally charged for pets, may be charged for service animals. Service animals fulfill a critical need for their owners—they are *not* pets.

The Americans With Disabilities Act (ADA) prohibits U.S. businesses that serve the public from discriminating against persons with disabilities. Some businesses have mistakenly denied access to persons who use service animals. ADA, a federal mandate, has priority over all state and local laws, as well as a business owner's standard of business, which might bar animals from the premises. Businesses must permit entry to guests and their service animals, as well as allow service animals to accompany guests to all public areas of a property. A property is permitted to ask whether the animal is a service animal or a pet, and whether the guest has a disability. The property may not, however, ask questions about the nature of the disability, the service provided by the animal or require proof of a disability or certification that the animal is a service animal.

Note: These regulations may not apply in Canada, Mexico or the Caribbean.

What The Lodging Icons Mean

Member Values
(see p. 14)

(AAA) or (CAA) Official Appointment

[SAVE] Offers minimum 10% discount or lowest public rate *(see p. 14)*

[A$K] May offer discount

[S] Offers senior discount

[fyi] Informational listing only

Member Services

[✈] Airport transportation

[🐕] Pets allowed

[🍴] Restaurant on premises

[🍴+] Restaurant off premises (walking distance)

[24🍴] 24-hour room service

[🍸] Cocktail lounge

[🧸] Child care

Accessibility Feature
(see p. 18)

[♿M] Accessible features

[♿] Roll-in showers

[👂] Hearing impaired

Safety Features
(Mexico and Caribbean only)

[S] Sprinklers

[D] Smoke detectors

Leisure Activities

[🎲] Full service casino

[🏊] Pool

[🏋] Health club on premises

[🏋→] Health club off premises

[🎯] Recreational activities

In-Room Amenities

[✗] Designated non-smoking rooms

[AC] No air conditioning

[TV] No TV

[CTV] No cable TV

[VCR] VCR

[🎬] Movies

[DATA PORT] Data port/modem line

[✆] No telephones

[🍱] Refrigerator

[📟] Microwave

[☕] Coffee maker

Availability and Additional Fees

If an in-room amenity is available only on a limited basis (in one or more rooms), the term "SOME UNITS" will appear above those icons. Fees may be charged for some of the services represented by the icons listed here. The word "FEE" will appear below each icon when an extra charge applies.

SOME UNITS

[♿M] [👂] [VCR] [🎬] [☕] / [✗] [DATA PORT] [🍱] /
            FEE FEE   FEE

Preferred Lodging Partners

Show Your Card & Save

AAA. Every Day.

SAVINGS. SELECTION. SATISFACTION. — When contacting one of the partners listed, you will be given AAA's best rates for your dates of stay. Your valid membership card must be presented at check-in.

SATISFACTION GUARANTEE — If you are not satisfied with any part of your stay, you must provide the property the opportunity to correct the situation during your stay. If the matter cannot be resolved, you will be entitled to recompense for a portion of, or your entire, stay. Satisfaction guarantee varies by chain.

Select the chain you want and have your membership card available when making a reservation and checking in.

| **Visit** | Over 1,100 AAA Offices | **Click** | aaa.com | **Call** | 866-AAA-SAVE |

Special rates and discounts may not apply to all room types. All discounts are off full rates and vary by location and time of year. Special rates and discounts are not available to groups and cannot be combined with other discounts. Restrictions apply to satisfaction guarantees. Valid AAA/CAA membership card must be presented at check-in. Offers good at time of publication; chains and offers may change without notice. Lodging partners offering discounts to AAA/CAA members may vary in Mexico and the Caribbean.

Making Reservations

When making reservations, you must identify yourself as a AAA or CAA member. Give all pertinent information about your planned stay. Ask about the lodging's pet policy, or the availability of any other special feature that is important to your stay. Request written confirmation to guarantee: type of room, rate, dates of stay, and cancellation and refund policies. At registration, show your membership card. Note: Age restrictions may apply.

Confirm Deposit, Refund and Cancellation Policies

Most establishments give full deposit refunds if they have been notified at least 48 hours before the normal check-in time. Listing prose will note if more than 48 hours notice is required for cancellation. However, when making reservations, confirm the property's deposit, cancellation and refund policies. Some properties may charge a cancellation or handling fee.

When this applies, "cancellation fee imposed" will appear in the listing. If you cancel too late, you have little recourse if a refund is denied.

When an establishment requires a full or partial payment in advance, and your trip is cut short, a refund may not be given.

When canceling reservations, phone the lodging immediately. Make a note of the date and time you called, the cancellation number if there is one, and the name of the person who handled the cancellation. If your AAA/CAA club made your reservation, allow them to make the cancellation for you as well so you will have proof of cancellation.

Review Charges for Appropriate Rates

When you are charged more than the maximum rate listed in the TourBook guide for a standard room, question the additional charge. If management refuses to adhere to the published rate, pay for the room and submit your receipt and membership number to AAA/CAA within 30 days. Include all pertinent information: dates of stay, rate paid, itemized paid receipts, number of persons in your party, the room number you occupied, and list any extra room equipment used. A refund of the amount paid in excess of the stated maximum will be made if our investigation indicates that unjustified charging has occurred.

Get the Room You Reserved

When you find your room is not as specified, and you have written confirmation of reservations for a certain type of accommodation, you should be given the option of choosing a different room or finding one elsewhere. Should you choose to go elsewhere and a refund is refused or resisted, submit the matter to AAA/CAA within 30 days along with complete documentation, including your reasons for refusing the room and copies of your written confirmation and any receipts or canceled checks associated with this problem.

How to Get the Best Room Rates

You'll find the best room rate if you book your reservation in advance with the help of a travel professional or agent at your local AAA/CAA office.

If you're not yet ready to make firm vacation plans or if you prefer a more spontaneous trip, take advantage of the partnerships that preferred hotel chains have arranged with AAA. Phone the toll-free number 866-AAA-SAVE that has been set up exclusively for members for the purpose of reserving with these Show Your Card & Save® chain partners.

Even if you were unable to make a reservation, be sure to show your membership card at the desk and ask if you're being offered the lowest rate available for that time. Many lodgings offer reduced rates to members.

Lodging Classifications

To ensure that your lodging needs/preferences are met, we recommend that you consider an establishment's classification when making your travel choices.

While the quality and comfort at properties with the same diamond rating should be consistent (regardless of the classification), there are differences in typical décor/theme elements, range of facilities and service levels. Please see the descriptions below.

Large-scale Hotel

A multistory establishment with interior room entrances. A variety of guest unit styles is offered. Public areas are spacious and include a variety of facilities such as a restaurant, shops, fitness center, spa, business center, or meeting rooms.

Hotel Royal Plaza, Lake Buena Vista, FL

Small-scale Hotel

A multistory establishment typically with interior room entrances. A variety of guest unit styles is offered. Public areas are limited in size and/or the variety of facilities available.

Baymont Inn, Dallas/Ft. Worth-Airport North, TX

Motel

A one- to three-story establishment typically with exterior room entrances facilitating convenient access to parking. The standard guest units have one bedroom with a bathroom and are typically similar in décor and design throughout. Public areas are limited in size and/or the variety of facilities available.

Best Western Deltona Inn, Deltona, FL

Country Inn

Similar in definition to a bed and breakfast, but usually larger in scale with spacious public areas and offers a dining facility that serves at least breakfast and dinner.

Greenville Inn, Greenville, ME

Bed & Breakfast

Small-scale properties emphasizing a high degree of personal touches that provide guests an "at home" feeling. Guest units tend to be individually decorated. Rooms may not include some modern amenities such as televisions and telephones, and may have a shared bathroom. Usually owner-operated with a common room or parlor separate from the innkeeper's living quarters, where guests and operators can interact during evening and breakfast hours.

1884 Paxton House Inn, Thomasville, GA

Evening office closures are normal. A continental or full, hot breakfast is served and is included in the room rate.

Condominium

Vacation-oriented or extended-stay, apartment-style accommodations that are routinely available for rent through a management company. Units vary in design and décor and often contain one or more bedrooms, living room, full kitchen, and an eating area. Studio-type models combine the sleeping and living areas into one room. Typically, basic cleaning supplies, kitchen utensils and complete bed and bath linens are supplied. The guest registration area may be located off-site.

Sands of Kahana, Kahana, Maui, HI

Desert Rose Inn, Bluff, UT

Cabin/Cottage

Vaca tion-oriented, small-scale, freestanding houses or cabins. Units vary in design and décor and often contain one or more bedrooms, living room, kitchen, dining area, and bathroom. Studio-type models combine the sleeping and living areas into one room. Typically, basic cleaning supplies, kitchen utensils, and complete bed and bath linens are supplied. The guest registration area may be located off-site.

Lost Valley Ranch, Deckers, CO

Ranch

Typically a working ranch with an obvious rustic, Western theme. In general, equestrian-related activities are featured, but ranches may include other animals and activities as well. A variety of guest unit styles is offered in a family-oriented atmosphere.

ResortQuest, Hilton Head Island, SC

Vacation Home

Vacation-oriented or extended-stay, large-scale, freestanding houses that are routinely available for rent through a management company. Houses vary in design and décor and often contain two or more bedrooms, living room, full kitchen, dining room, and multiple bathrooms. Typically, basic cleaning supplies, kitchen utensils, and complete bed and bath linens are supplied. The guest registration area may be located off-site.

Lodging Subclassifications

The following are subclassifications that may appear along with the classifications listed above to provide a more specific description of the lodging.

Casino

Extensive gambling facilities are available such as blackjack, craps, keno, and slot machines. **Note:** This subclassification will not appear beneath its diamond rating in the listing. It will be indicated by a dice icon and will be included in the row of icons immediately below the lodging listing.

Classic

Renowned and landmark properties, older than 50 years, well-known for their unique style and ambience.

Historic

These properties are typically over 75 years of age and exhibit many features of a historic nature with respect to architecture, design, furnishings, public record, or acclaim. Properties must meet one of the following criteria:
- Maintained the integrity of the historical nature
- Listed on the U.S. National Register of Historic Places
- Designated a U.S. National Historic Landmark
- Located in a U.S. National Register Historic District

Separate criteria designate historic properties in Canada, Mexico and the Caribbean.

Resort

Recreation-oriented, geared to vacation travelers seeking a specific destination experience. Travel packages, meal plans, theme entertainment, and social and recreational programs are typically available. Recreational facilities are extensive and may include spa treatments, golf, tennis, skiing, fishing, or water sports, etc. Larger resorts may offer a variety of guest accommodations.

Sample Restaurant Listing

WHERE TO DINE

THE SEASONS RESTAURANT — *Menu on aaa.com* — Dinner: $16-$36 — Phone: 336/555-5555 ⑤
Location: On I-459, exit 13 (US 31); 0.3 mi n of jct SR 802. 1000 Ocean Blvd 35244. Hours: 6 pm-10 pm. Closed: Mon, also Tues 5/1-11/15. Reservations: suggested. Features: Guests are in for a treat at this top-notch establishment. Dining is an all-around pleasurable experience—from the wait staff's casually elegant service approach to the tranquil, oceanfront setting to the striking grounds views from the cozy dining area. The chef transforms ingredients, based on what is seasonally and regionally available, into mouthwatering dishes. Decadent desserts put an exclamation mark on the meal. Dressy casual attire; cocktails; entertainment. Parking: valet. Cards: AX, CB, DC, DS, MC, VI. Classic

Regional American

2 Dinner: $16-$36   **5** Classic   **6** ⑤

1 Regional American

3 Cards: AX, DC, DS, MC, VI.

Menu on aaa.com

4

1. ⓐⓐ or ⓐ indicates our Official Appointment (OA) restaurants. The OA program permits properties to display and advertise the ⓐⓐ or ⓐ emblem. We highlight these properties with red diamonds and cuisine type. The ⓐⓐ or ⓐ sign helps traveling members find restaurants that want member business.

   ▼▼▼ or ▼▼▼▼ The number of diamonds—not the color—informs you of the overall level of quality for food and presentation, service and ambience. Menus for red Diamond restaurants can be viewed on aaa.com.

   A cuisine type is assigned for each restaurant listing. AAA currently recognizes more than 90 different cuisine types.

2. Prices represent the minimum and maximum entree cost per person. Exceptions may include one-of-a-kind or special market priced items.

3. AX = American Express
   CB = Carte Blanche
   DC = Diners Club
   DS = Discover
   JC = Japan Credit Bureau
   MC = MasterCard
   VI = VISA

4. These three icons are used in restaurant listings. When present, they indicate: the presence of a cocktail lounge, the lack of air conditioning, and/or that the restaurant has a designated non-smoking section or is entirely smoke-free.

5. If applicable, restaurants may be further defined as:

   Classic—renowned and landmark restaurant operations in business longer than 25 years, known for unique style and ambience.

   Historic—properties must meet one of the following criteria:
   - Listed on the U.S. National Register of Historic Places
   - Designated a U.S. National Historic Landmark
   - Located in a U.S. National Register Historic District

   Separate criteria designate historic properties in Canada, Mexico and the Caribbean.

6. These white ovals with black numbers serve as restaurant locators and are used to locate, or "spot," restaurants on maps we provide for larger cities.

The Restaurant Diamond Ratings

AAA Tourism Editors are responsible for determining a restaurant's diamond rating based on established criteria.

These criteria were established with input from AAA trained professionals, members and restaurant industry experts. They are purposely broad to capture what is typically seen throughout the restaurant industry at each diamond rating level.

A one diamond restaurant must meet basic requirements pertaining to management, cleanliness and overall quality. The primary focus is on providing wholesome, straightforward and familiar food at an economical price. Generally, the menu selection is limited to a restaurant's specialty, such as hamburgers, fried chicken, pizza or tacos. Service is limited, in many instances self service, and the surroundings are often utilitarian.

A two diamond restaurant displays noticeable enhancements to food presentation such as the use of common garnishes in combination with the dishware. Typically, the menu offers a wide selection featuring familiar favorites or home-style foods often cooked to order and reasonably priced. The service, while often limited, is plain-speaking and relaxed. The surroundings, while limited in scope, typically reflect a clear theme. All elements combine to provide a familiar, often family-oriented experience.

A three diamond restaurant often employs a professional chef and a supporting staff of highly trained cooks. The menu is skillfully prepared and often reflects interpretations of the latest trends or a mastering of traditional cuisine. Typically, there are expanded offerings of beverages in compliment to the menu such as, international/regional wines, specialty beers, cocktails and soft drinks. The front of the house is headed by a professional dining room manager with a compliment of efficient service staff. The service reflects some degree of refinement such as reservations accepted, personal assistance or the ability to adapt to a guests's specific needs. The decor reflects the use of well-coordinated design mediums that provide a distinct theme and good comfort. Restaurants at this level convey an entry into fine dining and are often positioned as an adult-oriented experience.

A four diamond restaurant is geared to individuals in search of a distinctive fine-dining experience. Often orchestrated by an executive chef and an accomplished staff, menus reflect a high degree of creativity and complexity using imaginative presentations to enhance high quality, market fresh ingredients. The equally proficient service staff demonstrates a strong desire to meet or exceed guest expectations. A wine steward is typically available to provide menu-specific knowledge on wine selection. The ambiance is highly refined, comfortable and well coordinated incorporating quality materials and a variety of upscale design enhancements that give a first-class impression. The overall dining experience is typically expensive.

A five diamond restaurant is renowned and consistently provides a world-class experience. This is *haute cuisine* at its best. Menus are cutting edge, using only the finest ingredients available. Food is prepared in a manner that is highly imaginative and unique. The combination of technique and ingredients is extraordinary reflecting the impeccable artistry and awareness of highly acclaimed chefs. A maitre d' heads an expert service staff that exceeds guest expectations by attending to every detail in an effortless and unobtrusive manner.

The restaurants with [fyi] in place of diamonds are included as an "information only" service for members. These establishments provide additional dining choices but have not yet been evaluated.

YOU'RE READY...

NOW YOU'RE READY FOR ANYTHING.

Travelers Cheques
Available in US Dollars, Canadian Dollars, Euros, and Pounds Sterling; AAA VISA® Travelers Cheques are accepted worldwide.

TravelMoney® Card
Make purchases at millions of Visa debit merchants or withdraw local currency at over 870,000 Visa ATMs in the USA and around the world.

Foreign Currency
We supply over 100 different currencies and can advise which is the best for your destination.

AAA TRAVEL MONEY
Know Before You Go.

Visit Participating AAA offices **Click** aaa.com/travelmoney **Call** 866-339-3378

Savings for all Seasons

Hertz rents Fords and other fine cars. ® REG. U.S. PAT. OFF. © HERTZ SYSTEM INC., 1999/2006/99

No matter the season, Hertz offers AAA members exclusive discounts and benefits.

Operating in 150 countries at over 7,000 locations, Hertz makes traveling more convenient and efficient wherever and whenever you go. Hertz offers AAA members discounts up to 20% on car rentals worldwide.

To receive your exclusive AAA member discounts and benefits, mention your AAA membership card at time of reservation and present it at time of rental. **In addition**, to receive a free one car class upgrade, in the United States mention PC# 929714, in Canada mention PC# 929725 and in Puerto Rico mention PC# 929736 at the time of reservation. Offer available through 12/15/05.

For reservations and program details, call your AAA Travel office or the Hertz/AAA Desk at **1-800-654-3080**.

Show Your Card & Save

AAA. Every Day.

exactly.

This offer is available at participating Hertz locations in the U.S., Canada and Puerto Rico, including Hertz Local Edition locations, subject to availability. Advance reservations are required. Blackout periods may apply. Offer may be limited in some cities at some times, especially during periods of peak demand. Maximum upgrade is to a Premium (Class G) car. Coupon has no cash value, must be surrendered on rental and may not be used with any other CDP#, coupon, discount, rate or promotion. This coupon may only be used with a AAA CDP#. Hertz' standard age, driver and credit qualifications for the renting location apply and the car must be returned to that location. Taxes and optional services, such as refueling, are not included and are not subject to discount. Call for details.

Delegate Travel Planning to Someone You Trust

Visit **aaa.com** and enjoy a whole new world of travel information.

AAA's Internet TripTik® provides interactive maps and search tools that make travel planning easy. Get hotel Diamond ratings, photos, and great room rates. Find countless places to eat and play.

Trust AAA to simplify travel planning.

Travel with Confidence.
Travel with AAA.

Ontario

Royal Botanical Gardens
A stunning synergy of tamed and untamed landscapes

Ottawa
New World verve, Old World grace and manners

Hamilton
History, culture, education, festivals, shopping, greenspaces and hospitality

Toronto
A cosmopolitan city of contrasts, unified by dignity

Shaw and Stratford
Six months of the finest the stage has to offer

Black Creek Pioneer Village, Toronto
© Bill Brooks
Alamy Images

land
of many
faces

Muskoka
© 2004 Ontario Tourism

Trying to describe Ontario in a few words is like drinking water from a sieve: You're bound to miss far more than you get. The difficulty lies in the province's immense size and diversity. Larger than many nations, Ontario stretches from frigid Hudson Bay south to Lake Erie. Although the extreme north boasts far more moose and deer than people, the region bordering the Great Lakes is packed with farms, towns and cities.

Most visitors are introduced to Ontario's variety through spectacular Niagara Falls. You can't plunge over the falls in a barrel anymore, but you can travel behind, above and alongside the tumbling waters by way of tunnels, towers and tour boats.

The embodiment of diversity is cosmopolitan Toronto, where more than 80 ethnic groups come together and the culinarily curious can choose from a spectrum of cuisines. Here you'll also find the lofty, vertigo-inducing CN Tower and the Royal Ontario Museum, which combines world-renowned art, history and science collections under one roof.

Yet another facet of Ontario is Ottawa, the picturesque Canadian capital. Double-decker buses and the traditional Changing the Guard on the lawns of Parliament Hill reveal the province's British roots.

Then there's the natural beauty of Algonquin Provincial Park and Pukaskwa National Park. See all this—falls, cities and parkland—and you've taken only a small sip of what Ontario offers.

You're in a town called Stratford on the Avon River not far from London. Sitting in a large theater, you watch an actor in Elizabethan garb recite these immortal lines from William Shakespeare's "As You Like It":

"All the world's a stage, And all the men and women merely players.. ..."

Obviously you're in England, right? Not necessarily.

On this side of the Atlantic, Ontario also boasts a Stratford, an Avon River and a London that has its own Thames flowing through it. And although Shakespeare is most closely identified with his English homeland, the province's early settlers brought a love for the Bard of Avon's work with them. In 1953 this abiding appreciation gave rise to the renowned Stratford Festival, an event that draws several hundred thousand theatergoers each season.

"Full Fathom Five Thy Father Lies...."

References to the great playwright and his work appear in other parts of Ontario, too. Fathom Five National Marine Park's name, for instance, evokes a song about a drowned shipwreck victim sung by Ariel, Prospero's fairy servant in "The Tempest." Aptly named, the park protects some 26 shipwrecks—popular with divers and snorkelers—below Georgian Bay's clear surface. Those who prefer to stay dry can gaze at these sunken hulks aboard glass-bottom boats departing from Tobermory.

Inside Fathom Five's boundaries are 22 islands, including Flowerpot Island, named for its rock pillars standing like sentinels along the shore. These might remind you of lighthouses, which you'll see dotting the coast here as well.

Within nearby Bruce Peninsula National Park, the Niagara Escarpment's limestone cliffs dramatically meet Georgian Bay, producing a stunning landscape of chalk-white cliffs stacked above the water in sedimentary layers. At Georgian Bay Islands National Park, wetlands and hardwood forests provide sanctuary to a variety of birds, snakes and frogs.

Shakespeare is not the only British playwright honored with an annual event in Ontario. The Shaw Festival in Niagara-on-the-Lake showcases the works of George Bernard Shaw and his contemporaries in three different theaters.

Samuel de Champlain founds New France on the Lower St. Lawrence River.

1608

© Bettmann/Corbis

Queen Victoria decrees Ottawa the national capital.

1857

Library of Congress

The Canadian Federation is formed and Upper Canada becomes Ontario.

1867

1763

The Treaty of Paris gives England ownership of the region.

Ontario Historical Timeline

1929

Work begins on the first superhighway in North America, the New Niagara Highway (now the QEW).

No doubt Shakespeare could have penned a suitable sonnet to describe the breathtaking cascades at nearby Niagara Falls. Awesome volumes of water plunge over Niagara's precipice every minute, creating a natural wonder that has drawn legions of sightseers for centuries. The most spectacular views of the falls can be enjoyed from Skylon Tower and perfectly manicured Queen Victoria Park, which lines the Niagara River. *Maid of the Mist* boat tours take passengers—wearing waterproof coats—right up to the falls' base.

The Bard also would likely note how Ontario wears its English heritage "on its sleeve," to borrow one of his expressions. This mind-set is reflected in the provincial motto "Loyal she began, loyal she remains," and if you're wondering to whom the province remains loyal, just take a look at the regal British visage on any Canadian coin.

Particularly reminiscent of England's age-old pomp and pageantry, Ottawa's Changing the Guard on Parliament Hill features soldiers marching in meticulous formation adorned in scarlet tunics and tall fur helmets. The verdigris-tinged roofs and formidable stone walls of Canada's parliament buildings form a striking backdrop for this ceremony, and a Big Ben-style clock and tower makes the setting seem all the more European.

"O Brave New World, That Has Such People In't!"

But Ontario's British roots are only one aspect of its multifaceted character: Just consider Toronto, home to the third largest theater scene in the English-speaking world. Although the provincial capital is no stranger to Shakespeare's works, plenty of plays by home-grown Canadian writers—not to mention those from many other nations—are produced here each year. In fact, Canada's largest city is one of the most culturally diverse in the world; more than 100 different languages are spoken within its limits.

If he were alive today, Shakespeare would certainly be amazed by this "brave new world." Contemporary visitors to Ontario may be astonished as well.

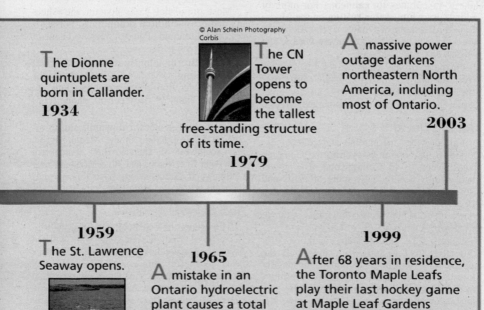

© Alan Schein Photography
Corbis

The Dionne quintuplets are born in Callander.
1934

The CN Tower opens to become the tallest free-standing structure of its time.
1979

A massive power outage darkens northeastern North America, including most of Ontario.
2003

1959
The St. Lawrence Seaway opens.

© Bob Krist/Corbis

1965
A mistake in an Ontario hydroelectric plant causes a total power blackout for the eastern half of North America.

1999
After 68 years in residence, the Toronto Maple Leafs play their last hockey game at Maple Leaf Gardens before moving to the new Air Canada Centre.

Recreation

Pedal. Schuss. Dive. Climb. Trek. Paddle. Glide. Mush. Hook. Sail. Recreation in Ontario is best described with action verbs.

Water World

Ontario, which means "beautiful lake," is almost synonymous with water. Containing literally hundreds of thousands of lakes and countless rivers, certainly there's no shortage of opportunities for water sports. **Sailing, swimming, boating** or **sailboarding** can be enjoyed in or on nearly any body of water, but gorgeous white sand dunes at Sandbanks Provincial Park provide a picture-perfect setting.

Freshwater fishing also is outstanding. A cast into one of Ontario's lakes yields walleye, whitefish, Northern pike, bass, and lake and brook trout. Lodges and fish camps sprinkle the province, especially in lake-studded northern Ontario. It's impossible to pick just one—or ten—fishing holes, but Lake Nipissing near North Bay is a good starting point. After freeze-up, bundle up and go **ice fishing.**

Rocky-ridged Killarney, vast and peaceful Algonquin and woodsy Quetico provincial parks maintain thousands of kilometres of lake-to-lake routes for **canoeing.** For more of a thrill, try **white-water rafting** on the Madawaska, Missinaibi or Ottawa rivers. Along the Missinaibi you may spot moose, bears and wolves along the shoreline.

Or head to the clear waves off Fathom Five National Marine Park, where **scuba diving** and **snorkeling** charters go to great depths to explore various submerged wrecks.

Getting Out and About

Fall provides memorable and colorful excursions. One option is **cycling** the Georgian Trail; access is in Collingwood. The gravel path climbs steadily past apple orchards and crosses the Beaver River, where you can stop for a fine view of the rushing creek. From there, it's a leisurely downhill ride to Meaford.

Hikers take to the Bruce Trail, an 800-kilometre (497-mi.) footpath alongside the spectacular Niagara Escarpment, a lengthy limestone outcrop running from Tobermory on the Bruce Peninsula to Queenston Heights Park, near Niagara Falls. Along the route, the trail encounters deep valleys, scenic waterfalls and rugged hills. The northern portion, from Tobermory to High Dump, is arguably the most scenic: About 30 kilometres (19 mi.) of the trail skirts high cliffs overlooking Georgian Bay's blue waters.

Rock climbers often are spotted dangling from the cliffs, which can reach heights of 24 metres (80 ft.). Old Baldy, Lion's Head and White's Bluff crags are challenging climbs.

The Bruce Trail terminates in Queenston Heights Park, where it meets the Niagara River Recreation Trail. The latter, a paved path perfect for **bicycling, inline skating, jogging** or **walking,** runs through Niagara-on-the-Lake, ending at the famous falls. This 25-kilometre (16-mi.) portion of the trail loosely follows the picturesque Niagara River and is lined with fruit farms and stately homes, which further enhance the view.

Icy Thrills

With all the snow Ontario receives, it's no wonder there are so many ways to enjoy it. The Muskoka area north of Toronto is termed "Cottage Country" due to the great number of city slickers who frequent the locale for vacations. A winter escape finds folks partaking in a plethora of activities: **Ice skating, tubing, tobogganing, dog sledding** and **snowshoeing** are some examples.

Ice climbing is a favored pastime in Orient Bay, north of Nipigon. The area contains about 120 climbs.

Most provincial parks contain snowshoeing and **cross-country skiing** trails. For starters, try Algonquin, Pinery, Sleeping Giant or Wasaga Beach parks.

Some 49,000 kilometres (30,449 mi.) of **snowmobiling** trails are maintained by the Ontario Federation of Snowmobile Clubs. To obtain a mandatory daily permit, phone (705) 739-7669.

Ontario's best known **downhill skiing** areas are Loch Lomond in the Mount McKay area southwest of Thunder Bay; Searchmont near Sault Ste. Marie; and Blue Mountain near Collingwood. Some resorts have lighted trails for night skiing, including Blue Mountain.

Recreational Activities

Throughout the TourBook, you may notice a Recreational Activities heading with bulleted listings of recreation-oriented establishments listed underneath. Similar operations also may be mentioned in Destination City recreation sections. Since normal AAA inspection criteria cannot be applied, these establishments are presented only for information. Age, height and weight restrictions may apply. Reservations often are recommended and sometimes are required. Addresses and/or phone numbers are provided so visitors can contact the attraction for additional information.

Fast Facts

POPULATION: 11,410,046.

AREA: 1,076,395 sq km (415,596 sq mi); ranks 4th.

CAPITAL: Toronto.

HIGHEST POINT: 693 m/2,274 ft., Ishpatina Ridge.

LOWEST POINT: sea level, Hudson Bay.

TIME ZONE(S): Eastern/Central. DST.

MINIMUM AGE FOR UNRESTRICTED DRIVER'S LICENSE: 16 years, 8 months.

MINIMUM AGE FOR GAMBLING: 19.

SEAT BELT/CHILD RESTRAINT LAWS: Seat belts required for driver and all passengers. Child restraints required for children less than 18 kilograms (40 lbs.).

HELMETS FOR MOTORCYCLISTS: Required.

RADAR DETECTORS: Prohibited.

FIREARMS LAWS: By federal law, all nonresidents entering Canada with a firearm must declare their weapon in writing and pay a fee of $50 (Canadian). Contact the Canadian Firearms Centre at (800) 731-4000 to receive a declaration form or for additional information.

HOLIDAYS: Jan. 1; Good Friday; Easter Monday; Victoria Day, May 24 (or closest prior Mon.); Canada Day, July 1; Civic Holiday, Aug. (1st Mon.); Labour Day, Sept. (1st Mon.); Thanksgiving, Oct. (2nd Mon.); Remembrance Day, Nov. 11; Dec. 25; Boxing Day, Dec. 26.

TAXES: Ontario's provincial sales tax is 8 percent. Canada's goods and services tax is 7 percent.

INFORMATION CENTERS: Provincial information centers open all year are in Barrie, Cornwall, Fort Erie, Fort Frances, Niagara Falls, St. Catharines/Niagara-on-the-Lake, Sarnia, Sault Ste. Marie, Toronto and Windsor. Information centers open from mid-May through Labour Day are in Kenora and Rainy River. The Hill Island center at Thousand Island Bridge, the Hawkesbury center, the Lancaster center, the Prescott center and the center near Pigeon River, Minn., are open mid-May through Canadian Thanksgiving (second Monday in October).

FURTHER INFORMATION FOR VISITORS:

Ontario Travel
5700 Explorer Dr.
Mississauga, ON, Canada L4W 5J3
(905) 282-1721 (English, in the Toronto area)
(905) 612-8776 (French, in the Toronto area)
TTY (905) 612-0870
(800) 668-2746 (English, in continental United States, Hawaii and Canada)
(800) 268-3736 (French)
TTY (888) 908-8825

RECREATION INFORMATION:

Ontario Ministry of Natural Resources
Ontario Parks
300 Water St., 6th floor
P.O. Box 7000
Peterborough, ON, Canada K9J 8M5
(800) 667-1940

FISHING AND HUNTING REGULATIONS:

Ontario Ministry of Natural Resources
Information Centre
Room M1-72
MacDonald Block
900 Bay St.
Toronto, ON, Canada M7A 2C1
(800) 667-1940

SPECIAL REGULATIONS: Studded tires and tinted windshields or front side windows that do not allow a clear view of the vehicle's interior are illegal.

ALCOHOL CONSUMPTION: Legal age 19.

NATIONAL PARKS: In Canadian national parks, those 65 years of age or older generally can expect a discount off fees established for adults. Visitors need not be Canadian citizens to receive this discount.

PROVINCIAL PARKS: All Ontario provincial parks allow pets on a maximum 1.8 metre (6-ft.) chained leash (not retractable/bungee leashes). Pets are not permitted on beaches or in public swimming areas.

HIGHWAY SIGNAGE: Many provincial routes are becoming county routes with new numbers. All changes may not be reflected in this TourBook. See the CAA/AAA Ontario sheet map for more current information.

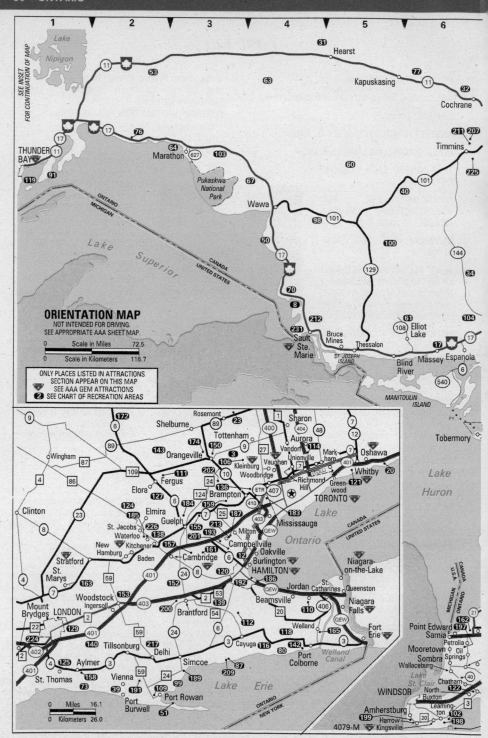

ORIENTATION MAP
NOT INTENDED FOR DRIVING.
SEE APPROPRIATE AAA SHEET MAP.

Scale in Miles   72.5

Scale in Kilometers   116.7

ONLY PLACES LISTED IN ATTRACTIONS
SECTION APPEAR ON THIS MAP
SEE AAA GEM ATTRACTIONS
SEE CHART OF RECREATION AREAS

4079-M

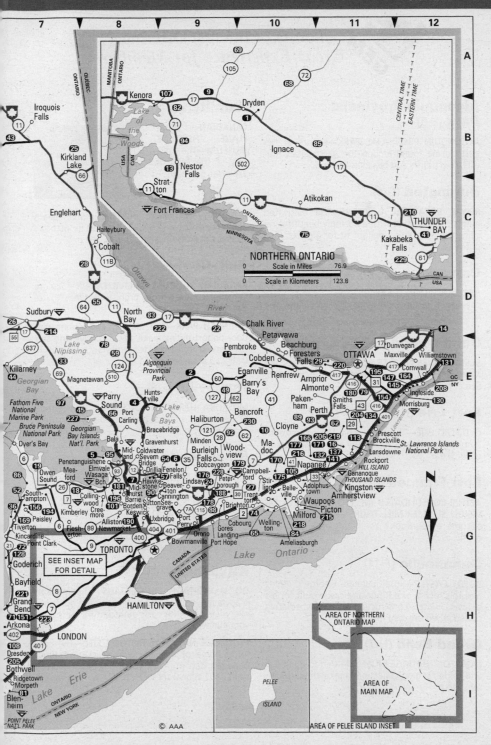

NORTHERN ONTARIO
Scale in Miles 76.9
Scale in Kilometers 123.8

SEE INSET MAP
FOR DETAIL

AREA OF NORTHERN
ONTARIO MAP

AREA OF
MAIN MAP

AREA OF PELEE ISLAND INSET

PELEE
ISLAND

© AAA

Points of Interest Offering A *Great Experience for Members*®

Algonquin Provincial Park (E-9)

ALGONQUIN PROVINCIAL PARK—Nature at her best can be found among the park's lakes, forests, rivers, cliffs and beaches. See p. 50.

Burlington (G-4)

ROYAL BOTANICAL GARDENS—The cultivated meets the untamed with amazingly beautiful results in this botanical delight fit for a queen. See p. 64.

Cambridge (G-3)

AFRICAN LION SAFARI—You won't feel cheetahed on this drive on the wild side. See p. 65.

Collingwood (G-8)

SCENIC CAVES NATURE ADVENTURES—View the Niagara Escarpment from above and beneath. See p. 69.

Fort Erie (H-5)

OLD FORT ERIE—This formidable fort echoes with long-forgotten cries for loyalty and for independence. See p. 125.

Fort Frances (C-9)

ABITIBI-CONSOLIDATED INC., FORT FRANCES DIVISION SUMMER MILL TOURS—How does a tree become a TourBook? You'll find out here. See p. 74.

Gananoque (F-11)

BOLDT CASTLE—Hotel magnate George C. Boldt had this replica of a Rhineland castle built for his beloved wife; construction was immediately halted when she died in 1904. See p. 75.

Grand Bend (H-7)

LAMBTON HERITAGE MUSEUM—Period buildings and wide-ranging collections make this a must-see. See p. 78.

Hamilton (H-8)

CANADIAN WARPLANE HERITAGE MUSEUM—The history of the RCAF is explored. See p. 81.

DUNDURN NATIONAL HISTORIC SITE—Learn about life above and below the stairs in Victoria's time at this magnificent mansion. See p. 81.

Hull, Québec

CANADIAN MUSEUM OF CIVILIZATION—Explore Canada's cultures, from prehistoric times to today. See p. 150.

GATINEAU PARK—The summer and winter outdoor opportunities make this extensive and scenic park a must-see for visitors to the Hull-Gatineau area. See p. 151.

Huntsville (E-8)

MUSKOKA HERITAGE PLACE—The 19th-century pioneers would feel at home in this living-history museum. See p. 83.

Kingston (F-11)

FORT HENRY NATIONAL HISTORIC SITE—Discover what garrison life was like in 1860. See p. 88.

Kingsville (I-5)

JACK MINER'S BIRD SANCTUARY—Honking is not impolite here in March and November. See p. 90.

Kitchener (G-2)

DOON HERITAGE CROSSROADS—Mingle with blacksmiths, tailors and bakers as they go about everyday life in this early 20th-century crossroads community. See p. 91.

WOODSIDE NATIONAL HISTORIC SITE—The boyhood home of William Lyon Mackenzie King, Canada's 10th prime minister, has been restored to its 1891 appearance. See p. 92.

Kleinburg (F-3)

McMICHAEL CANADIAN ART COLLECTION—Look at the superb landscapes on the walls, then look out the windows to see the views that inspired them. See p. 92.

Midland (F-8)

THE MARTYRS' SHRINE—The eight Jesuit missionaries who died here have been canonized. See p. 98.

SAINTE-MARIE AMONG THE HURONS—The original of this reconstructed mission was built in 1639. See p. 98.

Morrisburg (E-12)

UPPER CANADA VILLAGE—Talk with townsfolk in this 1860s village. See p. 103.

Niagara Falls, Ontario (H-5)

JOURNEY BEHIND THE FALLS—Get a behind and bottom-up view of the Horseshoe Falls from this unusual vantage point. See p. 114.

MAID OF THE MIST—You'll be grateful for the waterproof clothing on this trip in front of the falls. See p. 114.

MARINELAND—After you've seen the spectacular shows, make a spectacle of yourself on the roller coaster. See p. 115.

NIAGARA FALLS—A favorite of honeymooners, daredevils and millions of tourists, the majestic falls are a true natural wonder. See p. 115.

QUEEN VICTORIA PARK—If the falls have dampened your spirit, let these fine floral displays perk you up. See p. 120.

RIPLEY'S BELIEVE IT OR NOT! MUSEUM—Explore the outer limits of reality at this museum of the unusual. See p. 120.

WHIRLPOOL AERO CAR—Get a bird's-eye view of the Niagara Gorge and the whirlpool from this cable car. See p. 121.

WHITE WATER WALK—You'll be swept away by this up-close view of the roiling Niagara River rapids. See p. 121.

Niagara Falls, New York

CAVE OF THE WINDS TRIP—Get a topsy-turvy view of the falls from this interesting cave. See p. 130.

GOAT ISLAND—Skirt the edges of both the Canadian and American falls from mid-stream. See p. 130.

MAID OF THE MIST—Rides on these boats take visitors directly in front of the powerful falls. See p. 130.

NIAGARA AEROSPACE MUSEUM—Find out about western New York's contributions to aviation history. See p. 131

NIAGARA FALLS—Visit Niagara Falls State Park to get splendid views. See p. 131.

POWER VISTA—The electrifying story of the harnessing of the falls' power is explained at the Niagara Power Project's visitor center. See p. 132.

Niagara-on-the-Lake (G-5)

SHAW FESTIVAL—You've seen the water fall, now watch the curtain rise. See p. 127.

Oshawa (F-5)

PARKWOOD, THE R.S. McLAUGHLIN ESTATE NATIONAL HISTORIC SITE—Between the World Wars, automotive pioneer R.S. McLaughlin lived the good life here. See p. 137.

Ottawa (E-11)

CANADA SCIENCE AND TECHNOLOGY MUSEUM—Who, what, where, when, why and how are all answered here. See p. 144.

THE CATHEDRAL BASILICA OF NOTRE-DAME—The cathedral's glorious interior inspires reverence. See p. 144.

CHANGING THE GUARD—This ceremony is an impressive reminder that Canada is a member of the British Commonwealth. See p. 146.

CURRENCY MUSEUM OF THE BANK OF CANADA—Learn everything you ever wanted to know about money, except how to make it. See p. 145.

DIEFENBUNKER, CANADA'S COLD WAR MUSEUM—Originally built to shelter government officials, this bunker now is a museum. See p. 145.

NATIONAL GALLERY OF CANADA—The architecture of this building is nearly as impressive as the works it contains. See p. 145.

PARLIAMENT BUILDINGS—Allow plenty of time to explore these magnificent Gothic-style buildings. See p. 146.

Parry Sound (E-8)

30,000 ISLAND CRUISE—Explore the narrow channels of the Georgian Bay on this 3-hour trip. See p. 153.

Peterborough (G-9)

THE CANADIAN CANOE MUSEUM—The importance of canoes and kayaks to Canada's history is explored at this museum. See p. 156.

LANG PIONEER VILLAGE MUSEUM—Rural life in the Peterborough area during the 19th century is depicted courtesy of this restored village and its costumed interpreters. See p. 156.

Point Pelee National Park (I-7)

POINT PELEE NATIONAL PARK—This pocket park is so popular that even monarch butterflies summer here. See p. 158.

Sault Ste. Marie (D-4)

AGAWA CANYON TOUR TRAIN—Any time of year, this is a journey into beauty. See p. 165.

Stratford (G-1)

STRATFORD FESTIVAL OF CANADA—Find out how many playwrights it takes to fill the four theaters to "Standing Room Only." See p. 170.

Sudbury (D-7)

DYNAMIC EARTH—Learn about Sudbury's mining history both above and below the ground. See p. 172.

SCIENCE NORTH—Here you can explore the practical applications of scientific principles. See p. 172.

Thunder Bay (C-12)

CENTENNIAL PARK—Hike, bike, swim or fish for three seasons, then toboggan or ski when Jack Frost is out and about. See p. 174.

FORT WILLIAM HISTORICAL PARK—Meet the people who lived and traded in an 1815 fur trade post. See p. 175.

Toronto (G-4)

ART GALLERY OF ONTARIO—Ten centuries of artworks are a feast for the eyes. See p. 189.

THE BATA SHOE MUSEUM—You'll feel right in step after viewing the collection of footwear at this museum. See p. 189.

CASA LOMA—Between 1911 and 1914, financier Henry Pellatt spent $3.5 million building this castle. See p. 190.

CN TOWER—"As far as the eye can see" takes on a new meaning here. See p. 191.

GIBSON HOUSE MUSEUM—This carefully restored Georgian house reflects upper middle-class life in 1851. See p. 192.

HISTORIC FORT YORK—This 1793 garrison is where Toronto began. See p. 192.

HOCKEY HALL OF FAME—Here you can explore a locker room or do a play-by-play of game highlights. See p. 192.

ONTARIO LEGISLATIVE BUILDINGS—Ontario's Provincial Parliament has met here since 1892. See p. 194.

ONTARIO PLACE—You can easily spend an entire day in this sprawling waterfront complex of parks, attractions and shops. See p. 195.

ONTARIO SCIENCE CENTRE—Feed your brain and tickle your fancy here. See p. 195.

ROYAL ONTARIO MUSEUM—Explore the cultural history of man and the natural history of the planet in Canada's largest museum. See p. 195.

SPADINA MUSEUM: HISTORIC HOUSE AND GARDENS—The opulent home and gardens of four generations of the prosperous Austin family can be seen on a guided tour. See p. 197.

TORONTO ZOO—Meet inhabitants of seven geographical regions of Earth without ever leaving town. See p. 198.

Vaughan (F-4)

PARAMOUNT CANADA'S WONDERLAND—Turn your world upside down on one of the 11 roller coasters here. See p. 210.

Wasaga Beach (F-8)

NANCY ISLAND HISTORIC SITE—Realities of the War of 1812 come alive at this site. See p. 212.

Whitby (F-5)

CULLEN GARDENS AND MINIATURE VILLAGE—These superb gardens and meticulously crafted miniatures are overwhelming. See p. 213.

RECREATION AREAS

	MAP LOCATION	CAMPING	PICNICKING	HIKING TRAILS	BOATING	BOAT RAMP	BOAT RENTAL	FISHING	SWIMMING	PETS ON LEASH	BICYCLE TRAILS	WINTER SPORTS	VISITOR CENTER	LODGE/CABINS	FOOD SERVICE
NATIONAL PARKS *(See place listings)*															
Bruce Peninsula (F-7) 155 square kilometres. Nature programs. Canoeing, cross-country skiing, snowshoeing. Motorboats prohibited.		•	•	•	•			•	•	•		•			
Fathom Five National Marine Park (E-7) Historic. Scuba diving.		•	•	•	•	•		•	•	•				•	
Georgian Bay Islands (F-7) 25 square kilometres. Nature programs. Canoeing, wildlife viewing, windsurfing.		•	•	•	•			•	•	•	•		•		
Point Pelee (I-6) 15 square kilometres. Nature programs. Bird-watching, canoeing.			•	•	•		•	•	•	•	•	•	•		•
Pukaskwa (C-3) 1,878 square kilometres. Canoeing, cross-country skiing, snowshoeing, white-water rafting, wildlife viewing.			•	•				•	•	•		•	•		
St. Lawrence Islands (F-10) 600 hectares. Nature programs. Canoeing, kayaking.		•	•	•	•	•	•	•	•	•			•		
PROVINCIAL															
Aaron (B-10) 117 hectares 24 km e. of Dryden on Thunder Lake. Canoeing, cross-country skiing, snowshoeing.	**1**	•	•	•	•	•	•	•	•	•		•			•
Algonquin (E-9) 7,725 square kilometres. Scenic. Canoeing, cross-country skiing, snowshoeing, wildlife viewing. *(See place listing p. 50)*	**2**	•	•	•	•	•	•	•	•	•	•	•	•	•	•
Arrowhead (E-8) 1,237 hectares 8 km n. of Huntsville on Hwy. 11. Canoeing, cross-country skiing, snowshoeing. Motorboats prohibited.	**4**	•	•	•	•		•	•	•	•	•	•	•		•
Awenda (F-8) 2,915 hectares 11 km n. of Penetanguishene via CR 26. Nature programs. Canoeing, cross-country skiing, wildlife viewing. *(See Penetanguishene p. 154)*	**5**	•	•	•	•		•	•	•	•	•		•		
Balsam Lake (F-9) 448 hectares 8 km s.w. of Coboconk off CR 48. Canoeing.	**6**	•	•	•	•	•	•	•	•	•		•	•	•	•
Bass Lake (F-8) 65 hectares 6 km w. of Orillia off Hwy. 12. Canoeing, cross-country skiing.	**7**	•	•	•	•		•	•	•	•	•		•		•
Batchawana Bay (D-4) 169 hectares 64 km n. of Sault Ste. Marie on Hwy. 17. Playground.	**8**		•		•	•	•	•	•						•
Blue Lake (B-9) 353 hectares 8 km w. of Vermilion Bay on Hwy. 17. Canoeing; playground.	**9**	•	•	•	•	•	•	•	•	•		•	•	•	•
Bon Echo (F-10) 6,643 hectares at Bon Echo off Hwy. 41. Canoeing, wildlife viewing; Indian rock paintings. Motorboats restricted.	**10**	•	•	•	•		•	•	•	•			•	•	•

RECREATION AREAS

	MAP LOCATION	CAMPING	PICNICKING	HIKING TRAILS	BOATING	BOAT RAMP	BOAT RENTAL	FISHING	SWIMMING	PETS ON LEASH	BICYCLE TRAILS	WINTER SPORTS	VISITOR CENTER	LODGE/CABINS	FOOD SERVICE
Bonnechere (E-9) 162 hectares 45 km s.w. of Pembroke on CR 58. Canoeing, windsurfing.	11	•	•	•	•	•	•	•	•	•	•		•	•	•
Bronte Creek (G-3) 640 hectares off Queen Elizabeth Way (QEW) in Oakville. Historic. Nature programs. Cross-country skiing, tennis.	12	•	•	•				•	•	•	•	•	•		•
Caliper Lake (B-9) 147 hectares 5 km s.w. of Nestor Falls on Hwy. 71. Canoeing, wildlife viewing.	13	•	•	•	•	•	•	•	•	•					•
Charleston Lake (F-11) 2,353 hectares near Outlet, 22 km from Hwy. 401. Canoeing, hunting. Motorboats restricted	16	•	•	•	•	•	•	•	•	•	•			•	•
Chutes (E-6) 108 hectares .5 km n. of Massey off Hwy. 17. Canoeing, cross-country skiing.	17	•	•	•					•	•		•			•
Craigleith (F-7) 66 hectares n.w. of Craigleith on Hwy. 26. Canoeing, windsurfing.	18	•	•		•			•	•						•
Darlington (F-5) 209 hectares at e. edge of Oshawa off Hwy. 401 on Lake Ontario. Canoeing, windsurfing.	20	•	•	•	•	•	•	•	•	•			•	•	•
Driftwood (D-9) 422 hectares 7 km s.e. of Stonecliffe on Hwy. 17. Scenic. Canoeing, cross-country skiing.	22	•	•	•	•	•	•	•	•			•			•
Earl Rowe (F-3) 312 hectares 3.25 km w. of Alliston on Hwy. 89. Nature programs. Canoeing, cross-country skiing, windsurfing. Motorboats prohibited.	23	•	•	•	•	•	•	•	•	•	•		•		•
Emily (F-9) 83 hectares 8 km n.e. of Omemee off Hwy. 7 on Pigeon River. Canoeing, cross-country skiing.	24	•	•	•	•	•	•	•	•			•		•	•
Esker Lakes (B-7) 3,237 hectares 16 km e. of Kirkland Lake via Hwy. 66, then 21 km n. on CR 672. Canoeing, wildlife viewing. Gas-powered boats prohibited.	25	•	•	•	•	•	•	•	•	•	•		•		•
Fairbank (D-7) 105 hectares 55 km w. of Sudbury via Hwy. 17 to R.R. 4, then 21 km. n. Canoeing, cross-country skiing, scuba diving.	26	•	•	•	•	•	•	•	•	•				•	•
Ferris (F-10) 198 hectares 2.4 km s. of Campbellford on the Trent River. Canoeing.	27	•	•	•	•	•	•	•	•			•			
Finlayson Point (D-8) 37 hectares 1.5 km s. of Temagami. Canoeing.	28	•	•	•	•	•	•	•	•	•			•	•	
Fitzroy (E-10) 185 hectares 56 km n.w. of Ottawa. Canoeing, cross-country skiing.	29	•	•	•	•	•	•	•	•	•		•			•
Forks of the Credit (G-3) 282 hectares 24 km n.w. of Brampton on McLaren Rd. Cross-country skiing; fall foliage.	202		•	•				•				•		•	•
Frontenac (F-10) 5,214 hectares 26 km n. of Kingston on CR 5A. Canoeing, cross-country skiing, wildlife viewing. Motorboats restricted.	166	•	•	•	•	•		•	•	•				•	•
Fushimi Lake (A-4) 5,294 hectares 35 km n.w. of Hearst via Hwy. 11. Canoeing, wildlife viewing.	31	•	•	•	•	•	•	•	•	•					
Greenwater (A-6) 5,350 hectares 34 km n.w. of Cochrane. Canoeing. Gas-powered motorboats prohibited.	32	•	•	•	•	•	•	•	•	•					•
Grundy Lake (E-7) 2,554 hectares 21 km n. of Britt off Hwy. 69. Canoeing. Motorboats prohibited.	33	•	•	•	•	•	•	•	•	•			•		•
Halfway Lake (D-6) 4,730 hectares 90 km. n. of Sudbury on Hwy. 144. Canoeing, wildlife viewing.	34	•	•	•	•	•	•	•	•	•			•		•
Inverhuron (G-7) 289 hectares at Inverhuron on Lake Huron. Canoeing.	36		•		•	•		•	•	•					
Ivanhoe Lake (C-5) 1,589 hectares 12 km w. of Foleyet off Hwy. 101. Canoeing, wildlife viewing, windsurfing. Motorboats restricted.	40	•	•	•	•	•	•	•	•	•		•		•	•
Kakabeka Falls (C-12) 500 hectares. Scenic. Canoeing, cross-country skiing. *(See Kakabeka Falls p. 84)*	41	•	•	•				•	•		•	•	•	•	•
Kettle Lakes (B-7) 1,261 hectares 24 km w. of Matheson on Hwy. 101. Nature programs. Canoeing, cross-country skiing, ice fishing. Motorboats restricted.	43	•	•	•	•	•	•	•	•	•	•	•	•	•	•

RECREATION AREAS

	MAP LOCATION	CAMPING	PICNICKING	HIKING TRAILS	BOATING	BOAT RAMP	BOAT RENTAL	FISHING	SWIMMING	PETS ON LEASH	BICYCLE TRAILS	WINTER SPORTS	VISITOR CENTER	LODGE/CABINS	FOOD SERVICE
Killarney (E-7) 48,500 hectares. Nature programs. Scenic. Canoeing, cross-country skiing, wildlife viewing. Motorboats prohibited. *(See Killarney p. 85)*	44	•	•	•	•	•	•	•	•	•		•	•		
Killbear (E-7) 1,756 hectares 16 km n. of Parry Sound via Hwy. 69 to CR 559, then 19 km w. Scenic. Canoeing, scuba diving, windsurfing.	45	•	•	•	•	•	•		•	•	•			•	•
Lake St. Peter (E-9) 478 hectares 15 km n. of Maynooth off Hwy. 127. Canoeing.	49	•	•	•	•	•	•	•	•	•	•				•
Lake Superior (C-4) 155,646 hectares. Nature programs. Scenic. Canoeing, ice fishing, wildlife viewing; Indian rock paintings. *(See Wawa p. 213)*	50	•	•	•	•	•	•	•	•	•		•	•		
Long Point (I-2) 150 hectares 8 km s. of Port Rowan on Lake Erie. Bird-watching, canoeing.	51	•	•		•	•		•	•	•					•
MacGregor Point (F-7) 1,204 hectares 3.6 km s.w. of Port Elgin on Lake Huron. Nature programs. Cross-country skiing.	52	•	•	•				•	•	•	•	•	•		•
MacLeod (A-2) 74 hectares 10 km e. of Geraldton off Hwy. 11. Canoeing, rockhounding, wildlife viewing.	53	•	•	•	•	•		•	•	•					•
Mara (F-8) 40 hectares 1.5 km s. of Atherley on Lake Simcoe.	54	•	•		•	•		•	•	•					•
Marten River (D-8) 400 hectares at Marten River off Hwy. 64. Canoeing, cross-country skiing; logging exhibit	55	•	•	•	•	•		•	•	•		•	•		•
The Massasauga (E-7) 13,105 hectares along the coast of Georgian Bay, 15 km s.w. of Parry Sound; accessible by boat only. Canoeing, kayaking, wildlife viewing.	227	•	•	•	•	•	•	•	•	•					
McRae Point (F-9) 138 hectares 11 km e. of Orillia off Hwy. 12. Water skiing, windsurfing.	57	•	•	•	•	•		•	•	•					•
Mikisew (E-8) 138 hectares 16 km w. of South River on Eagle Lake. Canoeing.	59	•	•	•	•	•		•	•	•					•
Missinaibi (B-5) 99,090 hectares 89 km n.w. of Chapleau. Canoeing, wildlife viewing; Indian rock paintings.	60	•	•	•	•	•		•	•	•					
Mississagi (D-6) 4,900 hectares 26 km n. of Elliot Lake off Hwy. 108. Canoeing, wildlife viewing.	61	•	•	•	•	•		•	•	•		•			•
Murphys Point (F-11) 1,240 hectares 12 km s.w. of Perth off CR 1. Historic. Canoeing, cross-country skiing. Motorboats restricted.	62	•	•	•	•	•		•	•	•	•	•	•		•
Nagagamisis (A-4) 8,131 hectares. Historic. Scenic. Canoeing, wildlife viewing. Motorboats restricted. *(See Hearst p. 82)*	63	•	•	•	•	•		•	•	•					•
Neys (B-3) 3,445 hectares 26 km w. of Marathon off Hwy. 17. Canoeing, wildlife viewing.	64	•	•	•	•	•	•	•	•	•			•		•
North Beach (G-10) 89 hectares 5 km s.w. of Consecon on Lake Ontario. Canoeing.	65		•		•	•		•	•	•					
Oastler Lake (E-8) 32 hectares 8 km s. of Parry Sound on Hwy. 69. Canoeing.	66	•	•		•	•		•	•	•					
Obatanga (C-4) 9,409 hectares 32 km s. of White River on Hwy. 17. Canoeing, wildlife viewing.	67	•	•	•	•	•	•	•	•	•		•			
Ojibway (A-10) 2,630 hectares 21 km s. of Sioux Lookout on Hwy. 72. Bird-watching, canoeing.	68	•	•	•	•	•	•	•	•	•					
Pakwash (A-9) 3,993 hectares 20 km n.w. of Ear Falls on Hwy. 105. Canoeing.	69	•	•	•	•	•		•	•	•					
Pancake Bay (D-4) 490 hectares 77 km n. of Sault Ste. Marie on Hwy. 17. Nature programs. Canoeing.	70	•	•	•	•	•		•	•	•		•		•	
Pinery (H-7) 2,532 hectares 8 km s.w. of Grand Bend on Hwy. 21. Canoeing, cross-country skiing, wildlife viewing, windsurfing. Motorboats prohibited. *(See Grand Bend p. 77)*	71	•	•	•	•	•	•	•	•	•	•	•	•		•
Point Farms (G-7) 307 hectares 4.8 km n. of Goderich off Hwy. 21. Canoeing, cross-country skiing.	72	•	•	•	•			•	•	•		•	•		•
Port Bruce (I-1) 5 hectares w. of Port Bruce on Lake Erie.	73		•		•	•		•	•	•					

RECREATION AREAS

	MAP LOCATION	CAMPING	PICNICKING	HIKING TRAILS	BOATING	BOAT RAMP	BOAT RENTAL	FISHING	SWIMMING	PETS ON LEASH	BICYCLE TRAILS	WINTER SPORTS	VISITOR CENTER	LODGE/CABINS	FOOD SERVICE
Port Burwell (I-2) 231 hectares near Port Burwell off CR 19 on Lake Erie. Bird-watching, canoeing.	39	•	•	•	•			•	•	•					•
Presqu'ile (G-10) 937 hectares. Nature programs. Bird-watching, cross-country skiing, ice fishing, wildlife viewing. *(See Brighton p. 62)*	74	•	•	•	•	•		•	•	•	•	•	•		•
Quetico (C-10) 475,782 hectares. Canoeing, cross-country skiing; Indian rock paintings. Motorboats restricted. *(See Atikokan p. 53)*	75	•	•	•	•			•	•	•	•	•	•	•	•
Rainbow Falls (B-2) 575 hectares 10 km e. of Rossport on Hwy. 17. Canoeing, cross-country skiing.	76	•	•	•	•	•	•	•	•	•		•			•
René Brunelle (A-6) 3,015 hectares 13 km n. of Moonbeam on CR 581. Canoeing, windsurfing.	77	•	•	•	•	•	•	•	•	•	•	•			•
Restoule (E-8) 2,800 hectares 5 km n. of Restoule on Restoule Lake. Canoeing.	78	•	•	•	•	•	•	•	•	•		•		•	•
Rideau River (E-11) 187 hectares 5 km n. of Kemptville. Canoeing.	79	•	•	•	•	•		•	•	•	•				
Rock Point (I-4) 187 hectares 10 km s.e. of Dunnville. Bird-watching, canoeing, fossil viewing.	80	•	•	•	•			•	•	•					•
Rondeau (I-7) 3,254 hectares s. of Morpeth off CR 3 to CR 17 following signs. Nature programs. Bird-watching, canoeing, ice fishing, wildlife viewing, windsurfing. *(See Morpeth p. 101)*	81	•	•	•	•	•	•	•	•	•	•	•	•		•
Rushing River (B-9) 340 hectares 5 km s. of Longbow Corners off Hwy. 17 on Hwy. 71. Scenic. Canoeing, cross-country skiing.	82	•	•	•	•	•	•	•	•	•		•			
Samuel de Champlain (D-8) 2,550 hectares 16 km w. of Mattawa on Hwy. 17. Nature programs. Canoeing, cross-country skiing. Motorboats restricted.	83	•	•	•	•	•		•	•	•		•	•		
Sandbanks (G-10) 1,509 hectares 15 km s.w. of Picton. Canoeing, cross-country skiing, windsurfing.	84	•	•	•	•	•		•	•	•		•	•		•
Sandbar Lake (B-10) 5,083 hectares 11 km n. of Ignace on CR 599. Canoeing, wildlife viewing.	85	•	•	•	•	•		•	•	•					
Sauble Falls (F-7) 20 hectares 20 km n. of Sauble Beach. Scenic. Canoeing, cross-country skiing.	86	•	•	•	•			•		•		•			•
Selkirk (I-3) 73 hectares 8 km s. of Selkirk on Lake Erie. Canoeing.	87	•	•	•	•			•	•	•					•
Sharbot Lake (F-10) 69 hectares 5 km w. of Sharbot Lake on Hwy. 7. Canoeing.	89	•	•	•	•	•		•	•	•					
The Shoals (C-4) 10,644 hectares 50 km w. of Chapleau on Hwy. 101. Canoeing, wildlife viewing.	98	•	•	•	•	•		•	•	•					
Sibbald Point (F-8) 225 hectares 8 km e. of Sutton on Lake Simcoe. Nature programs. Canoeing, cross-country skiing; museum. *(See Sutton p. 172)*	90	•	•	•	•	•		•	•	•		•	•	•	•
Silent Lake (F-9) 1,450 hectares 18 km s.w. of Bancroft on Hwy. 28. Canoeing, cross-country skiing, ice fishing. Motorboats prohibited.	92	•	•	•	•			•	•	•	•	•		•	
Silver Lake (F-10) 43 hectares just w. of Maberley on Hwy. 7. Canoeing.	93	•	•	•	•	•		•	•	•					
Sioux Narrows (B-9) 130 hectares 7 km n. of Sioux Narrows on Hwy. 71. Historic. Canoeing, wildlife viewing. Indian rock paintings.	94	•	•	•	•	•		•		•					
Six Mile Lake (F-8) 94 hectares 10 km n. of Port Severn off Hwy. 400. Bird-watching, canoeing, cross-country skiing.	95	•	•	•	•	•		•	•	•		•	•		
Sleeping Giant (C-1) 24,400 hectares 73 km e. of Thunder Bay at Silver Islet. Historic. Scenic. Canoeing, cross-country skiing, wildlife viewing.	91	•	•	•	•	•		•	•	•		•	•	•	
Springwater (F-8) 47 hectares n.w. of Barrie on Hwy. 26. Cross-country skiing. *(See Barrie p. 55)*	181		•	•								•	•	•	
Sturgeon Bay (E-7) 14 hectares 8 km n.w. of Pointe au Baril Station. Canoeing.	97	•	•		•	•	•	•	•	•				•	•

RECREATION AREAS

	MAP LOCATION	CAMPING	PICNICKING	HIKING TRAILS	BOATING	BOAT RAMP	BOAT RENTAL	FISHING	SWIMMING	PETS ON LEASH	BICYCLE TRAILS	WINTER SPORTS	VISITOR CENTER	LODGE/CABINS	FOOD SERVICE
Turkey Point (I-3) 316 hectares 21 km s.e. of Delhi. Cross-country skiing, golf.	99	•	•	•	•	•		•	•	•		•			•
Voyageur (D-12) 1,464 hectares 16 km e. of Hawkesbury off Hwy. 417. Canoeing, cross-country skiing.	14	•	•	•	•	•	•	•	•	•		•	•		•
Wakami Lake (C-5) 8,806 hectares 64 km s.e. of Chapleau on CR 667. Historic. Nature programs. Canoeing, wildlife viewing.	100	•	•	•	•	•	•	•	•	•			•		
Wasaga Beach (G-8) 1,844 hectares. Nature programs. Bird-watching, canoeing, cross-country skiing, tennis, windsurfing. Museum. *(See Wasaga Beach p. 211)*	101		•	•	•	•		•	•	•	•	•	•		•
Wheatley (I-6) 241 hectares 1.5 km s.e. of Wheatley off CR 3. Bird-watching canoeing.	102	•	•	•				•	•	•					•
White Lake (B-3) 1,726 hectares 36 km w. of White River on Hwy. 17. Nature programs. Canoeing, wildlife viewing.	103	•	•	•	•	•	•	•	•	•		•			
Windy Lake (D-6) 118 hectares 50 km. n. of Sudbury on Hwy. 144. Canoeing, cross-country skiing, ice fishing, windsurfing.	104	•	•	•	•	•	•	•	•	•		•			•
OTHER															
Adolphustown U.E. Loyalist (F-10) 4 hectares in Adolphustown on Hwy. 33. Museum.	105	•	•		•	•	•	•	•	•					
Albion Hills (F-3) 446 hectares 8 km n. of Bolton on Hwy. 50. Bird-watching, canoeing, cross-country skiing, horseback riding. Motorboats prohibited.	106	•	•	•	•		•	•	•	•	•	•			•
Anicinabe (B-9) 17 hectares in southern section of Kenora on Golf Course Rd.	107	•	•		•	•	•	•	•	•					•
A.W. Campbell (H-7) 126 hectares 3.2 km n.e. of Alvinston. Canoeing.	108	•	•	•				•	•	•		•			
Backus (I-2) 431 hectares. Historic. Nature programs. Cross-country skiing. *(See Port Rowan p. 159)*	109	•	•	•				•	•	•		•	•	•		
Balls Falls (H-4) 567 hectares s.w. of Jordan off Hwy. 81. Historic. Cross-country skiing.	110	•						•		•		•	•		
Baxter (E-11) 68 hectares on Regional Rd. 13 (Dilworth Dr.), 3 km e. of Hwy. 416, just s. of Kars. Nature programs. Cross-country skiing.	195	•	•	•				•	•	•		•	•		•
Belwood Lake (F-2) 1,348 hectares 4 km n.e. of Fergus off Fergus-Orangeville Rd. Canoeing, cross-country skiing, windsurfing.	111	•	•	•	•	•	•	•	•	•		•			•
Big Bend (I-6) 16 hectares 3 km s. of CR 2, just e. of Wardsville on Big Bend Rd. Archeological site.	205	•	•	•	•			•	•	•					
Binbrook (H-3) 391 hectares s.w. of Binbrook on Harrison Rd. off Hwy. 56. Cross-country skiing, windsurfing.	112	•	•	•	•	•		•	•	•		•			•
Brant (H-2) 5 km w. of Brantford on Jennings Rd. Canoeing.	200	•	•				•		•	•		•			•
Brown's Bay (F-11) 65 hectares 18 km w. of Brockville on Thousand Islands Pkwy.	113		•		•	•		•	•	•	•				•
Brucedale (G-7) 48 hectares 8 km s. of Port Elgin on Hwy. 21, then w. on Concession Rd. 12/13 to Lakeshore Rd. Canoeing, hunting.	169	•	•	•	•				•	•					
Bruce's Mill (F-4) 108 hectares off Hwy. 404 on Stouffville Rd. Cross-country skiing. Golf driving range.	114		•	•					•	•		•			•
Byng Island (H-4) 190 hectares 1.6 km w. of Dunnville on Hwy. 11. Canoeing.	116	•	•	•	•			•	•	•					
Chippawa Creek (H-4) 148 hectares s.w. of Wellandport via Hwy. 20, off Hwy. 45. Cross-country skiing.	118	•	•	•				•	•	•		•			•
Chippewa (C-1) 121 hectares. Amusement park. *(See Thunder Bay p. 175)*	119	•	•		•			•	•	•				•	•
Christie Lake (G-3) 336 hectares 8 km w. of Clappison's Corners on Hwy. 5. Canoeing, cross-country skiing.	120		•	•	•	•	•	•	•	•		•			

RECREATION AREAS

	MAP LOCATION	CAMPING	PICNICKING	HIKING TRAILS	BOATING	BOAT RAMP	BOAT RENTAL	FISHING	SWIMMING	PETS ON LEASH	BICYCLE TRAILS	WINTER SPORTS	VISITOR CENTER	LODGE/CABINS	FOOD SERVICE
C.M. Wilson (I-6) 31 hectares on Hwy. 40 near Chatham, following signs. Canoeing, cross-country skiing, windsurfing. Motorboats prohibited.	122		•	•	•	•		•	•	•	•		•		•
Col. Roscoe Vanderwater (F-10) 243 hectares 27 km n. of Belleville, then 4 km e. at Thomasburg on Concession Rd. 4.	170		•	•				•		•	•	•			
Conestogo Lake (G-2) 2,347 hectares n. of Elmira on Hwy. 86 to Hwy. 11, then 3.2 km e. Canoeing, windsurfing.	124	•	•	•	•	•	•	•	•	•	•	•			•
Confederation Park (H-3) 83 hectares off Centennial Pkwy. on Confederation Dr. in Hamilton. Go-carts, miniature golf, water park. *(See Hamilton p. 81)*	192		•	•					•			•		•	•
Crawford Lake (G-3) 219 hectares on Guelph Line, 5 km s. of Hwy. 401 at Steeles Ave. in Milton. Historic. Nature programs. Cross-country skiing, snowshoeing.	201		•	•							•	•	•		•
Crowe Bridge (F-9) 9 hectares 14 km n.e. of Campbellford off CR 50 on CR 38. Miniature golf.	228	•	•	•				•	•	•					
Dalewood (H-1) 283 hectares on Hwy. 30, 1.6 km n. of St. Thomas. Canoeing; disc golf.	125		•	•	•	•	•	•	•	•					
Deer Creek (I-2) 122 hectares 6 km s. of Langton, w. of CR 59 on CR 45. Canoeing. Motorboats prohibited.	191		•	•		•	•	•	•						
Depot Lakes (F-10) 1,000 hectares 3 km n. of Verona on CR 38, then 9 km w. on Snyders Rd.	171	•	•	•	•			•	•	•	•	•			
Durham (F-2) 61 hectares in Durham on Durham Rd. Cross-country skiing.	172	•	•	•	•			•	•	•	•	•		•	
Elora Gorge (G-2) 202 hectares. Canoeing. *(See Elora p. 72)*	127	•	•	•	•			•	•	•	•	•			•
Falls Reserve (G-7) 93 hectares 6 km s.e. of Goderich on Hwy. 8 to Hwy. 1. Nature programs. Cross-country skiing.	128	•	•	•				•	•	•	•	•			
Fanshawe (H-1) 995 hectares. Historic. Cross-country skiing. *(See London p. 94)*	129	•	•	•	•	•	•	•	•	•	•	•	•		•
Farran (E-12) 36 hectares s. of Ingleside on Hwy. 2.	130	•	•	•					•	•					•
Fifty Point (H-4) 76 hectares on Baseline Rd. n. of Stoney Creek. Marina.	186	•	•	•	•	•	•	•	•	•	•	•			•
Foley Mountain (F-11) 332 hectares 1 km n. of Westport on CR 10. Cross-country skiing.	206	•	•	•				•	•	•	•	•			
Gillies Lake (B-6) 30 hectares in Timmins at jct. Hwy. 101E and R.R. 655.	207		•	•	•				•	•	•	•			
Glengarry (E-12) 25 hectares 3 km e. of Lancaster on south service road.	131	•	•	•		•		•	•	•					•
Glen Haffy (F-3) 325 hectares on Airport Rd. s. of Hwy. 9 in Caledon. Bird-watching.	3		•	•				•		•	•				
Gould Lake (F-10) 589 hectares 10 km n.e. of Sydenham on CR 19, following signs to entrance. Canoeing, cross-country skiing.	132	•	•	•	•			•	•	•	•	•			
Gray's Creek (E-12) 43 hectares just e. of Cornwall, 3 km s. of Hwy. 401 on Boundary Rd. Cross-country skiing; model aircraft runway.	208	•	•	•	•	•	•	•	•	•		•	•		•
Great Canadian Hideaway (H-7) 974 hectares n.e. of Parkhill at jct. hwys. 7 and 81. Canoeing, go-carting.	151	•	•	•	•			•	•	•	•	•		•	•
Grenville (F-11) 45 hectares 5 km e. of Prescott on Hwy. 2.	134													•	•
Guelph Lake (G-3) 1,608 hectares 10 km n.e. of Guelph on Victoria Rd. Canoeing, windsurfing. Motorboats restricted.	184	•	•	•	•	•	•	•	•	•	•	•			•
Haldimand (I-3) 56 hectares 5 km w. of Selkirk off R.R. 3 on Lakeshore Rd.	209	•	•	•	•			•	•	•					
Harrison Park (F-7) 45 hectares. Tennis; miniature golf. *(See Owen Sound p. 152)*	19	•	•	•				•	•	•	•	•			•
Hazelwood Lake (C-12) 618 hectares 14 km n. of Thunder Bay off Hwy. 102 (Dawson Rd.) on CR 589 (Hazelwood Dr.). Canoeing. Motorboats restricted.	210		•	•	•	•		•	•	•	•	•			

RECREATION AREAS

	MAP LOCATION	CAMPING	PICNICKING	HIKING TRAILS	BOATING	BOAT RAMP	BOAT RENTAL	FISHING	SWIMMING	PETS ON LEASH	BICYCLE TRAILS	WINTER SPORTS	VISITOR CENTER	LODGE/CABINS	FOOD SERVICE
Heart Lake (F-3) 169 hectares 7 km n. of Hwy. 7 on Heart Lake Rd. in Brampton. Motorboats prohibited. *(See Brampton p. 59)*	136	•	•	•	•	•	•	•	•	•	•				•
Hersey Lake (B-6) 180 hectares 5 km n. of Timmins on R.R. 655. Canoeing, cross-country skiing. Motorboats prohibited.	211	•	•	•				•	•	•		•			
Hiawatha Highlands (D-4) 848 hectares 8 km n. of Sault Ste. Marie on Hwy. 17 (Great Northern Rd.), then 2.4 km e. on Fifth Line. Scenic. Cross-country skiing.	212	•	•					•	•	•		•	•		
Hillman Marsh (I-6) 5 km e. of Leamington at jct. CR 37 and Mersea Township Rd. #2. Canoeing.	198	•	•	•				•	•	•		•	•	•	
Hilton Falls (G-3) 645 hectares 6 km w. of Milton off R.R. 25 on Campbellville Rd. Historic. Cross-country skiing.	213	•	•	•				•			•	•	•	•	•
Holiday Beach (I-5) 2 km s. of Malden Centre on CR 50. Bird-watching.	199	•	•	•				•	•	•	•				
Hope Mill (G-9) 8 km s. of jct. Hwy. 7 and CR 34 e. of Peterborough. Canoeing; interpretive programs, museum.	188	•	•						•	•					
Indian Line (F-4) 29 hectares w. of Hwy. 427 on Finch Ave. in Brampton. Canoeing. Motorboats prohibited.	183	•		•				•	•	•			•		•
Inglis Falls (G-7) w. of Owen Sound and jct. hwys. 6 and 10 on CR 18. *(See Owen Sound p. 152)*	194	•	•	•				•		•	•	•	•	•	
Island Lake (F-3) 332 hectares in Orangeville at entrance to Hurontario St., at jct. hwys. 9 and 10. Motorboats restricted.	150	•	•	•	•	•	•	•		•	•		•		
Ivy Lea (F-11) 19 hectares just w. of Ivy Lea Bridge on Thousand Islands Pkwy., 34 km w. of Brockville.	137	•	•	•	•	•		•	•	•	•	•			
Kelso (G-3) 396 hectares on Hwy. 401 s.w. of Milton. Canoeing, downhill skiing, snowboarding, snow tubing; museum.	187	•	•	•	•	•	•	•	•	•	•	•	•		•
Kiwanis (G-2) 13 hectares in Waterloo on the s. side of Grand River.	138	•	•	•				•	•	•			•		
La Fortune (H-3) 45 hectares 4.5 km w. of Caledonia off CR 54 on Onondaga Town Line Rd.	139	•	•	•				•	•	•					
Lake Laurentian (D-7) 950 hectares 8 km s.e. of Sudbury off Ramsey Lake Rd. on South Bay Rd. Nature programs. Scenic. Canoeing, cross-country skiing, kayaking.	214		•	•						•	•	•	•		
Lake Whittaker (H-2) 142 hectares on Hwy. 37, n.e. of St. Thomas via Hwy. 73. Canoeing, disc golf.	140	•	•	•	•	•	•	•	•	•			•		•
Laurel Creek (G-2) 294 hectares in Waterloo on Westmount Rd. N. Canoeing, cross-country skiing, windsurfing. Motorboats prohibited.	185	•	•	•	•			•	•	•	•	•	•		•
Lemoine Point (F-11) 135 hectares 5 km w. of Kingston via Front and Coverdale rds. Cross-country skiing.	141		•	•				•	•	•	•				
Little Bluff (G-11) 28 hectares 3 km e. of South Bay on CR 13.	215		•	•				•	•	•					
Little Cataraqui Creek (F-11) 394 hectares 2 km n. of Hwy. 401 in Kingston on Division St. Nature programs. Canoeing, cross-country skiing.	216	•	•	•	•			•	•		•	•	•		•
Little Lake (H-2) 40 hectares 4.8 km s. of Norwich off R.R. 19 on Windham Rd. 3.	217	•	•	•	•			•	•	•					
Little Trout Bay (D-12) 18 hectares 35 km s. of Thunder Bay on Hwy. 61, then e. on Little Trout Bay Rd.	229		•	•	•	•		•		•					
Long Beach (H-4) 56 hectares 8 km w. of Port Colborne via Hwy. 3. Cross-country skiing.	142	•	•	•				•	•	•			•		
Lorne C. Henderson (H-6) 135 hectares at 3653 Petrolia Line (CR 4), 2 km w. of Petrolia.	197	•	•	•				•	•	•	•				
Luther Marsh (F-2) 5,200 hectares n. of Grand Valley on Hwy. 25, then 8 km w. on concession road. Bird-watching, cross-country skiing. Motor boats prohibited.	143		•	•				•		•	•	•			
Mac Johnson (F-11) 532 hectares off Hwy. 29 n. of Brockville. Canoeing, cross-country skiing, wildlife viewing.	204		•	•	•	•		•		•			•		

RECREATION AREAS

Area	MAP LOCATION	CAMPING	PICNICKING	HIKING TRAILS	BOATING	BOAT RAMP	BOAT RENTAL	FISHING	SWIMMING	PETS ON LEASH	BICYCLE TRAILS	WINTER SPORTS	VISITOR CENTER	LODGE/CABINS	FOOD SERVICE
McGeachie (F-9) 200 hectares w. of St. Ola and 2 km w. of Hwy. 62, on the n. shore of Steenburg Lake.	230		•	•	•			•		•	•	•			•
McLaren (E-11) 40 hectares e. of Ingleside via Hwy. 2 on Long Sault Pkwy.	145	•		•	•	•		•	•	•					
Marks Bay (D-4) 103 hectares 18 km w. of Sault Ste. Marie on Regional Rd. 565 (Airport Rd.).	231			•	•		•	•	•	•		•			
Massassauga Point (G-10) 24 hectares 8 km s.e. of Belleville on Massassauga Rd. Historic. Cross-country skiing.	218	•	•	•	•			•	•	•		•			
Mille Roches (E-11) 21 hectares s. of Long Sault on Long Sault Pkwy.	147	•	•	•	•	•	•	•	•	•					•
Mill Pond (F-11) 520 hectares 10 km s.w. of Lombardy off Hwy. 15 on R.R. 38 (Briton-Houghton Bay Rd.). Canoeing, cross-country skiing.	219	•	•	•	•			•		•		•			
Monora (F-3) 19 hectares 2.4 km n. of jct. hwys. 9 and 10 at Orangeville.	174		•	•				•		•	•	•			
Morris Island (E-11) 47 hectares off R.R. 22 near Fitzroy Harbour. Canoeing, cross-country skiing.	220	•	•	•	•			•		•		•			
Morrison Dam (H-7) 43 hectares 2 km e. of Exeter on CR 3, then .5 km s. on Morrison Line. Canoeing, cross-country skiing. Motorboats prohibited.	221	•	•	•	•			•		•		•			
Mountsberg (G-3) 472 hectares on Milborough Line 4 km w. of Campbellville. Nature programs. Scenic. Bird-watching, cross-country skiing. *(See Campbellville p. 66)*	193		•	•				•		•		•	•		•
New Lowell (G-8) 57 hectares 2 km w. of CR 10 on CR 9 in New Lowell. Canoeing, cross-country skiing.	196	•	•	•	•			•	•	•	•				•
Norfolk (I-3) 19 hectares 10 km s. of Simcoe off Hwy. 24 on Lakeshore Rd.	189	•	•			•		•	•	•					•
Papineau Lake (D-9) 6 hectares 5 km s. of Mattawa on Papineau Lake Rd.	222		•		•	•		•		•					
Parkhill (H-7) 800 hectares 2 km e. of Parkhill off CR 7. Canoeing, cross-country skiing, windsurfing. Motorboats prohibited.	223	•	•	•	•			•	•	•		•			
Petticoat Creek (F-5) 68 hectares on White's Rd., 1 km s. of Hwy. 401 in Pickering.	121		•	•					•	•					
Pinehurst Lake (H-3) 115 hectares on Hwy. 24A, 6 km n. of Paris and 13 km s. of Cambridge. Canoeing, cross-country skiing.	152	•	•	•	•			•	•	•		•			
Pittock (H-2) 809 hectares n. of Woodstock on Hwy. 59 to Pittock Park Rd.	153	•	•	•	•	•		•	•	•		•			
Quinte (F-10) 130 hectares 3.2 km w. of Belleville on Hwy. 2 at Wallbridge Loyalist Rd. Cross-country skiing.	175	•	•	•	•			•	•	•		•			
Rim (G-2) 200 hectares in the n.e. section of Waterloo at 2001 University Ave. Golfing.	226	•	•	•				•		•		•	•		•
Riverside-Cedar (E-11) 69 hectares 10 km e. of Morrisburg on CR 2. Canoeing.	154	•		•	•	•	•	•	•	•				•	
Rockwood (G-3) 80 hectares off Hwy. 7, s. of Rockwood, 11 km e. of Guelph. Canoeing; miniature golf.	155	•	•	•				•	•	•		•			•
Saugeen Bluffs (G-7) 100 hectares 4 km n. of Paisley on CR 3, then 1 km w. Cross-country skiing.	156	•	•	•	•			•		•		•			•
Scanlon Creek (G-8) 282 hectares 2 km n. of Bradford, then .5 km e. on 9th Concession Rd. Cross-country skiing.	190		•	•				•		•		•			
Selwyn (F-9) 29 hectares 3 km w. of Selwyn on Township Concession Rd. 20. Cross-country skiing.	176		•	•				•	•	•		•			
Serpent Mounds (F-9) 28 hectares 10 km e. of Peterborough on Hwy. 7, then 14 km s. on CR 34. Historic. Nature Programs.	88	•	•	•	•	•		•	•	•			•		
Shades Mills (G-2) 177 hectares in n.e. Cambridge on Avenue Rd., 3.2 km e. of Hwy. 24. Canoeing, cross-country skiing. Motorboats prohibited.	157	•	•	•	•			•	•	•		•			

RECREATION AREAS	MAP LOCATION	CAMPING	PICNICKING	HIKING TRAILS	BOATING	BOAT RAMP	BOAT RENTAL	FISHING	SWIMMING	PETS ON LEASH	BICYCLE TRAILS	WINTER SPORTS	VISITOR CENTER	LODGE/CABINS	FOOD SERVICE
Sharon Creek (H-1) 48 hectares 4 km s.e. of Delaware off CR 2 on Springer Rd. Canoeing, cross-country skiing, windsurfing. Motorboats prohibited.	224	•	•	•				•	•	•		•			
Sheffield (F-10) 467 hectares 38 km n. of Napanee on CR 41.	177		•	•	•			•	•						
Springwater (I-1) 145 hectares 4 km w. of Aylmer on Hwy. 3 to Orwell, then 3.2 km s. on Hwy. 35. Canoeing, cross-country skiing.	158	•	•	•	•	•	•	•	•	•	•	•	•		•
Squirrel Creek (G-9) 111 hectares 19 km s. of Peterborough on CR 28, then 3.2 km e. on Hwy. 28.	178	•		•	•			•	•	•					
Terra Cotta (G-3) 192 hectares 1.6 km n. of Terra Cotta.	159	•	•	•				•	•	•					
Valens (G-3) 300 hectares 8 km w. of Freelton via Hwy. 97 to Hamlet of Valens. Cross-country skiing.	161	•	•	•	•	•	•	•	•	•	•	•	•		•
Warsaw Caves (F-9) 271 hectares 3.6 km n.e. of Warsaw on Caves Rd. Historic. Canoeing, cross-country skiing.	179	•	•	•	•	•	•	•	•	•	•	•	•		
Warwick (H-6) 73 hectares in Warwick, 32 km e. of Sarnia on Hwy. 7.	162	•	•		•			•	•	•	•				
W.A. Taylor (E-11) 6 hectares 8 km s. of Manotick on Regional Rd. 19.	180		•	•	•			•	•	•					
Welland Recreational Waterway (H-5) 4,199 hectares. Historical. Cross-country skiing. (See Welland p. 129)	165		•	•	•			•		•	•	•	•		
White Waterfront (B-6) 7 hectares in South Porcupine at west end of Porcupine Lake. Cross-country skiing.	225		•	•	•	•		•	•	•	•	•			
Wildwood (H-1) 1,295 hectares 6 km e. of St. Marys along Hwy. 7. Cross-country skiing.	163	•	•	•	•	•	•	•	•	•	•	•	•	•	•
Woodlands (E-12) 26 hectares e. of Ingleside on Long Sault Pkwy. via Hwy. 2.	164	•	•	•	•	•		•	•	•					•

Ontario Temperature Averages
Maximum / Minimum
From the records of the Canadian Government Travel Bureau.
Temperatures in Celsius.

	JAN	FEB	MAR	APR	MAY	JUNE	JULY	AUG	SEPT	OCT	NOV	DEC
Ottawa	-6 / -16	-6 / -16	1 / -8	10 / -1	18 / 6	24 / 12	27 / 15	26 / 17	21 / 9	13 / 3	4 / -3	-4 / -12
Thunder Bay	-8 / -19	-7 / -18	-1 / -11	7 / -3	15 / 3	20 / 8	24 / 11	22 / 11	17 / 7	11 / 1	1 / -7	-6 / -14
Toronto	-1 / -8	-1 / -8	4 / -4	11 / 2	18 / 8	24 / 13	27 / 16	26 / 16	22 / 12	15 / 6	7 / 1	1 / -5

Points of Interest

Some municipalities in Ontario have combined or soon will combine with neighboring cities. These mergers will eliminate some existing cities and may affect street names, addresses and political boundaries referenced in this guide. For further information, please contact Ontario governing agencies or the local CAA club.

ADOLPHUSTOWN (F-10)

UNITED EMPIRE LOYALIST HERITAGE CENTRE, in Adolphustown U.E. Loyalist Park on PR 33, is in an 1870s brick house. The center displays tools, documents, uniforms and other memorabilia of the Loyalists who emigrated to Canada during the American Revolution. A genealogical research library and the U.E.L. Memorial Cemetery are on the premises.

Guided tours are available. Allow 30 minutes minimum. Tues.-Sat. 10-4:30, May 1-second Mon. in Oct. Admission $3, under 4 free. Rate may vary during special events. Phone (613) 373-2196.

 **ALGONQUIN PROVINCIAL PARK (E-9)**

East of Huntsville *(see place listing p. 83)* and west of Pembroke *(see place listing p. 154)*, the park stretches across 7,725 square kilometres (2,983 sq. mi.) of wild and beautiful lakes and forests, bogs and rivers, cliffs and beaches. There are two parts to Algonquin—the vast Park Interior accessible only by canoe or on foot, and the Parkway Corridor, the 56-kilometre (35-mi.) section of Hwy. 60 running through the southwest corner of the park, where most of the facilities and services are.

The park's two main entrances, both off Hwy. 60, are the West Gate, just east of Dwight, and the East Gate, just west of Whitney. Other access points also are available—from Hwy. 17 north of the park, off Hwy. 11 from the west and from Hwy. 60 approaching from the east.

The park is a favorite with those wanting to experience Canada's wilderness. In addition to the sparkling, clear waters the park is known for, visitors might see loons, moose, deer, beavers, owls, wolves and the occasional black bear.

Canoeists can access almost 2,000 kilometres (1,243 mi.) of canoe routes in the Park Interior from 29 different access points around the park. Clearly marked portages connect the routes when waterways are not sufficiently deep for canoeing. Hikers can choose from three different overnight backpacking trails to explore the Interior; the loops range from 6 to 88 kilometres (4 to 55 mi.). Outfitting services and canoe rentals are available in the park. Outfitters also are available on the park's periphery. Algonquin offers three cross-country skiing trails during the winter as well as primitive camping.

The park's two major attractions, the Algonquin Logging Museum and the Algonquin Visitors Centre, are along the Parkway Corridor. Each has a theater and exhibit area depicting park history. Three resorts and eight organized campgrounds are along the Parkway Corridor, as are restaurants and stores, picnic areas, swimming facilities, walking trails and a mountain-bicycling trail. The Algonquin Gallery at kilometre 20 features the work of well-known wildlife and landscape artists.

Camping facilities include year-round car camping, backpacking and canoe sites in season. Reservations are highly recommended although a few sites are available on a first-come-first-served basis. The park maintains controlled-travel zones. Camping reservations and passes for backcountry travel are required.

Naturalist services, such as conducted hikes, wolf howling expeditions, canoe outings, children's programs, special events and lectures, and an information package are available. Contact Visitor

Discover

LEADING SPAS OF CANADA

1 800 704-6393 • www.leadingspasofcanada.com

Information, Algonquin Provincial Park, Box 219, Whitney, ON, Canada K0J 2M0.

West Gate open daily 8 a.m.-9 p.m., Victoria Day-Labour Day; 8-6, Apr. 1-day before Victoria Day and day after Labour Day-second Mon. in Oct.; 9-4, rest of year. East Gate open daily 8-7, Victoria Day-Labour Day; 8-4:30, rest of year. Other entrances generally open daily 7-7, Apr. 1-second Mon. in Oct. Schedule may vary; phone ahead.

Day-use admission is by $12 daily private vehicle permit. A summer pass is $70; a winter pass is $50. Vehicle campsites $22-$30. Interior primitive camping $9; ages 6-17, $4.25. MC, VI. Phone (705) 633-5572 for information or (888) 668-7275 for camping reservations and backcountry passes. *See Recreation Chart.*

ALGONQUIN LOGGING MUSEUM, near the east entrance, km 55 from the west gate, depicts life at an early Canadian logging camp. The theater shows films providing a historical look at various types of logging activities. The outdoor museum uses artifacts and equipment to recount logging from the 1830s to the present. Indoor exhibits daily 10-5, Victoria Day weekend-second Mon. in Oct. Outdoor exhibits daily 24 hours. Free with daily private vehicle or camping permit. Phone (613) 637-2828.

ALGONQUIN VISITORS CENTRE, km 43 from the west gate, provides park information and introduces visitors to the park's history through exhibits, dioramas, theater presentations and a panoramic view of the landscape.

Food is available. Daily 9-9, mid-June through day before Labour Day; daily 10-6, Victoria Day weekend to mid-June and Labour Day-second Mon. in Oct.; daily 10-5, late Apr.-day before Victoria Day weekend and day after second Mon. in Oct.-Oct. 31 (also during Spring Break and Easter weekend); Sat.-Sun. 10-5, early Feb.-late Apr.; Sat.-Sun. 10-4, rest of year (also daily 10-4, Dec. 25-early Jan.). Free with daily private vehicle or camping permit. Phone (613) 637-2828.

ALLISTON (G-8) pop. 9,679

SOUTH SIMCOE PIONEER MUSEUM is e. off King St. N. on Fletcher Crescent in Riverdale Park. The museum's buildings and galleries depict the area's history and heritage. An 1851 log cabin provides insights into pioneer life, and an 1858 barn features agricultural displays. The main building contains area memorabilia from the 1800s. Genealogical information is available. The museum hosts special events throughout the year.

Allow 30 minutes minimum. Wed.-Sun. 10-3:30, June 1-Labour Day; Tues.-Fri. 10-3:30, rest of year. Closed holidays. Admission $2; over 64 and ages 5-17, $1; family rate $5. Phone (705) 435-0167.

ALMONTE (E-10) pop. 4,659

One of the first towns in the Ottawa Valley to be settled, Almonte was once the home of Robert Tait McKenzie, whose work in rehabilitative medicine

during World War I brought him national acclaim. He also was respected as a sculptor and educator. McKenzie eventually joined the faculty of the University of Pennsylvania but frequently returned to Almonte where he restored the Mill of Kintail, named for the McKenzie fort in the Scottish Highlands.

Almonte also was the boyhood home of Dr. James Naismith, the creator of basketball. A plaque on CR 29 at Clayton Side Road commemorates the site.

MILL OF KINTAIL CONSERVATION AREA is 5 km (3 mi.) n.w. on CR 29, then 2 km (1.2 mi.) w. on Clayton Rd. and 1 km (.6 mi.) n. on Concession Rd. 8. The 1830 gristmill was restored in 1930 by Robert Tait McKenzie and served as his summer home and studio. Inside the mill, the museum contains McKenzie's original furnishings, more than 70 sculptures, a summary of his life and regional Canadian pioneer items.

Nature trails and picnic facilities are on the grounds. Afternoon tea on the lawn is served Wednesday and Saturday during July and August. Museum open daily 10:30-4:30, Victoria Day weekend-second Mon. in Oct. Admission $5 per private vehicle. Tea $2.50, children $1.50. Phone (613) 256-3610.

AMELIASBURGH (G-10)

AMELIASBURGH HISTORICAL MUSEUM, in the town center, contains a collection of buildings, including a tea room, church, log cabin, blacksmith shop, barns and carpenter's shop. Memorabilia depicting a rural community from 1850 to the present also are displayed. Other highlights include a beekeeping museum and a restored Goldie Corliss steam engine. Interpreters demonstrate various crafts on special activity days.

Food is available. Allow 1 hour minimum. Fri.-Wed. 10-4:30, Victoria Day weekend-Aug. 31; Fri.-Tues. 10-4:30, Sept. 1-second Mon. in Oct. Admission $4; over 59 and students with ID $3; ages 5-15, $2. Phone (613) 968-9678.

AMHERSTBURG (I-5) pop. 20,339

One of the oldest settlements in southwestern Ontario, Amherstburg was laid out by Loyalists after the British evacuation of Detroit in 1796. The town was named for Lord Jeffrey Amherst, commander of the British forces in America at the time of their conquest of Canada.

Amherstburg Visitor Information Centre: 116 Sandwich St. N., Amherstburg, ON, Canada N9V 2T7; phone (519) 736-8320 Apr.-Nov. For information the rest of the year contact the Town of Amherstburg Tourism and Economic Development Department, 271 Sandwich St. S., P.O. Box 159, Amherstburg, ON, Canada N9V 2Z3; phone (519) 736-3589 or (800) 413-9993.

FORT MALDEN NATIONAL HISTORIC SITE, 1 blk. w. of CR 20 at 100 Laird Ave., following signs, was built on the Detroit River after the British surrender of Detroit in 1796. A principal Upper

Canada frontier post for about 50 years, it was a rallying point for the British in the 1812 attack on Detroit.

Earthworks, restored barracks from 1819 and two exhibition buildings can be seen; of interest are original military documents and artifacts. A video presentation is shown; a resource library and archives are available by appointment. Daily 10-5, May-Oct.; Sun.-Fri. 1-5, rest of year. Closed Jan. 1, Good Friday, Nov. 11 and Dec. 25-26. Hours may vary; phone ahead. Military demonstrations are presented Sat.-Sun. Admission $3.50; over 64, $3; ages 6-16, $2.50; family rate (maximum seven persons) $10. Phone (519) 736-5416.

THE NORTH AMERICAN BLACK HISTORICAL MUSEUM AND CULTURAL CENTRE is at 277 King St. Amherstburg, at the narrowest crossing point on the Detroit River, was a popular destination on the Underground Railroad.

Exhibits in the two-story museum, cultural center, an 1812 log cabin and the adjacent 1848 Nazrey African Methodist Episcopal (A.M.E.) Church, a National Historic Site, examine African civilization, the slave trade, the migration of blacks to freedom in Canada and the contributions these refugees have made to their adopted country.

Allow 30 minutes minimum. Wed.-Fri. 10-5, Sat.-Sun. 1-5, third Wed. in Apr.-Oct. 31. Admission $5.50; over 64 and ages 2-14, $4.50; family rate (maximum five people) $20. Phone (519) 736-5433 or (800) 713-6336.

PARK HOUSE MUSEUM, 214 Dalhousie St. at Kings Naval Yard Park, was originally built in Detroit and moved to Amherstburg in 1799 after that city's American occupation. Thomas Park purchased it in 1839, and his descendants lived there until 1941. The house reflects domestic life of the 1850s. Tinsmithing, open-hearth cooking and candlemaking demonstrations are given.

Daily 11-4, June-Aug.; Mon.-Fri. 11-4, rest of year. Hours may vary during special events; phone ahead. Admission $2.50; over 64, $1.50; ages 6-16, $1; family rate $7. MC, VI. Phone (519) 736-2511.

WINERIES
• D'Angelo Estate Winery is at 5141 Concession 5. Mon.-Sat. 10-6, Sun. 11-5, May-Oct.; Wed.-Sat. 10-5, rest of year. Closed most major holidays. Phone (519) 736-7959 or (888) 598-8317.

AMHERSTVIEW (F-10)

FAIRFIELD HOUSE AND PARK, on Hwy. 33 at Loyalist Pkwy., is a 1793 house built by Loyalist refugee William Fairfield. The New England-style house was donated to the province of Ontario in 1959 for preservation as a historic site; its 1984 opening was attended by Queen Elizabeth II. The galleried veranda provides a view of Amherst Island across the St. Lawrence.

Picnicking and swimming are permitted. Allow 30 minutes minimum. Wed.-Sun. 10:30-4:30, July 1-Labour Day. Guided 20-minute tours are available. Admission $3; ages 2-12, $1; family rate $5. Phone (613) 384-2813.

ARKONA (H-7) pop. 598

Surrounded by orchards, Arkona's rolling hills and scenic points of interest beckon naturalists and families alike.

Tourism Sarnia-Lambton—Arkona: 556 N. Christina St., Sarnia, ON, Canada N7T 5W6; phone (519) 336-3232 or (800) 265-0316.

ROCK GLEN CONSERVATION AREA, 8680 Rock Glen Rd., reflects its location at a transition zone between the Great Lakes-St. Lawrence and the Carolinian Forest zones, offering abundant opportunities for fossil hunting. The 27-hectare (67-acre) recreation site includes lookouts above the 11-metre (36-ft.) falls, picnic facilities, nature trails, and the Arkona Lions Museum and Information Centre which has First Nations artifacts and fossils dating back 400 million years.

Park open daily 9-dusk, Apr.-Oct. Museum daily 9-5, June-Aug.; Sat.-Sun. 9-4, Apr.-May and Sept.-Oct.; other times by appointment. Admission $3. Phone (519) 828-3071.

ARNPRIOR (E-10) pop. 7,192

ARNPRIOR & DISTRICT MUSEUM, 35 Madawaska Blvd., is in the 1896 post office. Displays and artifacts illustrate the development of this lumbering settlement during the 19th century. A gallery of photographs of the town, local Indian artifacts and Victorian displays can be viewed. Allow 30 minutes minimum. Tues.-Fri. noon-5, Sat.-Sun. noon-4, mid-June to mid-Sept.; by appointment rest of year. Admission $2.50, senior citizens $2, students with ID $1.50, under 5 free, family rate $8. Phone (613) 623-4902.

ATIKOKAN (C-10) pop. 3,632

Atikokan derives its name from the Ojibway Indian word meaning "caribou bones." Once the home of two iron mines, Atikokan's economy now relies on a thriving forest industry, a thermal generating station and a mixture of government, retail and manufacturing services. Beneath a wilderness veneer, Atikokan is a lively town with various recreational activities and historic and cultural sites. Calling itself the "Canoeing Capital of Canada," the city is a jumping-off point for nearby Quetico Provincial Park (see attraction listing).

Atikokan Economic Development Corporation: P.O. Box 218, Atikokan, ON, Canada P0T 1C0; phone (807) 597-2757 or (888) 334-2332.

ATIKOKAN CENTENNIAL MUSEUM AND HISTORICAL PARK are at 204 E. Main St. and Legion Point. The museum has local history exhibits and displays of mining and lumbering tools. The park, across the river on Legion Point, features a restored logging train and log cabin. Museum open Mon.-Fri. 9-5, mid-Feb. to mid-Dec. Hours may vary; phone ahead. Free. Phone the museum at (807) 597-6585.

QUETICO PROVINCIAL PARK, 44 km (27 mi.) e., is a wilderness of interconnected waterways forming part of the boundary with the U. S. Quetico and its U.S. counterparts, the adjoining Boundary Waters Canoe Wilderness Area and nearby Voyageurs National Park, preserve much of the historic trade route from Lake Superior to Lake of the Woods.

A highlight is a large concentration of Indian pictographs. An information pavilion is off Hwy. 11 at French Lake. Park open Mon.-Fri. 8:30-noon and 1-4:15. Admission $10.50 per private vehicle. Phone (807) 597-2735 for information or (888) 668-7275 for camping reservations. *See Recreation Chart and the AAA/CAA Eastern Canada CampBook.*

RECREATIONAL ACTIVITIES

Fishing

- **Browns' Clearwater West Lodge** is on Hwy. 622N. Write P.O. Box 1766, Atikokan, ON, Canada P0T 1C0. Other activities are offered. Daily year-round. Phone (807) 597-2884 or (800) 900-4240.

AURORA (F-4) pop. 40,167

AURORA MUSEUM, 22 Church St., contains a schoolroom, an old-fashioned parlor, a pharmacy, antique toys and quilts. Changing exhibits depict local history. **Note:** The museum is undergoing renovations; reopening is expected late in 2005. Phone ahead to confirm availability. Allow 30 minutes minimum. Wed.-Sun. 1-5; closed July 1 and Dec. 25-Jan. 3. Free. Phone (905) 727-8991.

HILLARY HOUSE is 2 blks. n. of Wellington at 15372 Yonge St. Built in 1862, the Gothic Revival house was both home and office to four generations of physicians. The two front rooms, originally an examining room and a dispensary, exhibit medical instruments and equipment. The house is interpreted in various periods: An 1888 bathroom has many early fixtures, and a study represents the time just before World War I. Guided tours relate the history of the home and its owners.

Allow 30 minutes minimum. Wed.-Fri. and Sun. 1-5, Sat. 10-noon and 1-5; closed Dec. 25. Admission $3; over 64, students with ID and ages 6-12, $2. Phone (905) 727-4015.

AYLMER (I-1) pop. 7,126

WINERIES

- **Rush Creek Wines Ltd.** is s. on Hwy. 73, then w. on Jamestown Line following signs. Tours and tastings Mon.-Sat. 10-5, Sun. noon-5; closed Jan. 1, Good Friday, Easter and Dec. 25. Phone (519) 773-5432.

Everything Travel

Dreams Become Reality With AAA/CAA Travel

EXPLORE THE MOUNTAINS, THE DESERTS, AND THE CITIES - ANYWHERE, ANYTIME - WITH AAA/CAA, A TRUSTED NAME IN TRAVEL FOR 100 YEARS.
LET AAA/CAA TRAVEL TAKE CARE OF ALL YOUR TRAVEL NEEDS.
TO RECEIVE EXCLUSIVE AAA/CAA MEMBER BENEFITS, CALL OR VISIT YOUR NEAREST AAA/CAA TRAVEL OFFICE, OR CLICK ON www.aaa.com TODAY.

Travel With Someone You Trust.®
www.aaa.com

BADEN (G-2)

SAVE CASTLE KILBRIDE NATIONAL HISTORIC SITE is at 60 Snyder's Rd. W.; from Hwy. 7/8 turn n. onto Regional Rd. 51 and follow signs. This restored 1877 Italianate mansion was the home of James Livingston, the "Flax Mill King" of Canada. Guided tours offer details about the restoration, the antique furnishings and the life of the Livingstons.

The house is noted for its three-dimensional *trompe l'oeil* artwork. The belvedere has a small art gallery, and the Wilmot Historical Museum in the basement has exhibits of local interest and displays of township artifacts.

Allow 1 hour minimum. Tues.-Sun. 1-4, Apr. 1-Dec. 21; Sat.-Sun. 1-4, in Mar. Closed Good Friday and Nov. 11. Admission $6; over 65 and ages 13-18, $4.75; ages 5-12, $3.50; family rate $16. MC. Phone (519) 634-8444, or (800) 469-5576 in Canada.

BALA (F-8)

BALA'S MUSEUM WITH MEMORIES OF LUCY MAUD MONTGOMERY is at the corner of Maple and River sts. "Anne of Green Gables" author Lucy Maud Montgomery vacationed in Bala in 1922. Another of her books, "The Blue Castle," is based on that holiday. The museum, in the home where Montgomery dined during her stay, is restored to its 1922 appearance and contains artifacts belonging to the author, including an extensive collection of her works, as well as displays about the history of Bala.

Allow 30 minutes minimum. Tues.-Sat. 1-4, July 1-Labour Day; Sat. 1-4, Victoria Day weekend-June 30 and day after Labour Day to mid-Oct.; by appointment rest of year. Admission $2.75, family rate (maximum four people) $7. MC, VI ($10). Phone (705) 762-5876 or (888) 579-7739.

JOHNSTON'S CRANBERRY MARSH & MUSKOKA LAKES WINERY is 4 km (2.5 mi.) n. on Muskoka Rd. 169, 1 km (.6 mi.) w. on Medora Lake Rd., then 2 km (1.2 mi.) s. to 1074 Cranberry Rd. This family-owned farm has grown cranberries since 1952. During the September/October harvest, wagons are pulled through the marsh while guides provide an explanation of the cranberry harvest and the transformation of the fruit into wines, jams and dried berries.

At other times an audiovisual presentation, a guided winery tour and a self-guiding exploration of the farm are offered. Picnicking is permitted. Allow 1 hour minimum. Mon.-Sat. 9-5, Sun. 11-4; closed Jan. 1, Good Friday, Easter and Dec. 25. Free. Guided tours $3, under 13 free. Phone (705) 762-3203.

BANCROFT (E-10) pop. 4,089

The abundant minerals and semiprecious stones found in Bancroft make the town internationally renowned among mineralogists and rockhounds. The area yields examples of 80 percent of Canada's minerals, including nepheline-bearing rocks and minerals containing the radioactive elements uranium and thorium. The town's most impressive resource is blue sodalite, found almost exclusively in Bancroft.

From late July to early August the Bancroft Rockhound Gemboree offers 4 days of mineral shows, demonstrations and field trips. Also during July and August, mineral-collecting field trips are offered on Tuesday, Thursday and Saturday. Contact the chamber of commerce for details.

The chamber of commerce sponsors the Bancroft Mineral Museum, in the old station. Constructed to resemble the inside of a mine, the museum houses a display of more than 300 mineral specimens from around the world.

Eagles Nest Lookout is a picnic site 2 kilometres (1.2 mi.) north on Hwy. 62. From an elevation of 488 metres (1,600 ft.) it overlooks the village and surrounding countryside. The Hastings Heritage Trail is a recreational corridor that follows an abandoned railway bed across Hastings County, from Glen Ross to Lake St. Peter; it can be used for bicycling, hiking, skiing, dog sledding, snowmobiling, horseback riding, bird-watching and wildlife viewing.

Bancroft and District Chamber of Commerce: Box 539, Bancroft, ON, Canada K0L 1C0; phone (613) 332-1513.

ART GALLERY OF BANCROFT is at 8 Hastings Heritage Way. The museum, in Bancroft's old train station, mounts 12 shows each year featuring works by local and regional artists. The restored station retains its original stamped tin ceiling. Allow 30 minutes minimum. Tues.-Sun. noon-5, June 1-Labour Day; Wed.-Sat. noon-5, rest of year. Closed Jan. 1, Good Friday and Dec. 25. Donations. Phone (613) 332-1542.

NORTH HASTINGS HERITAGE MUSEUM is in the park on the York River, downtown on Station St. behind the post office. The museum, a log house built in 1879 for the Bronson Weston Lumber Co., was moved from its original site. Displayed are Victorian and pioneer items reflecting local history, dental and medical equipment from the old outpost hospital and an extensive mineral collection. Changing exhibits also are presented.

Daily 9-6, July-Aug.; Mon.-Fri. 9-5, Sat. 10-4, last week in June and Sept. 1-Labour Day. Admission $2; ages 12-18, $1; family rate $5. Phone (613) 332-1884.

BARRIE (G-8) pop. 103,710, elev. 221 m/725′

Originally a landing place on the west side of Kempenfelt Bay for aboriginal inhabitants and later for fur traders, Barrie was an important connection along the Nine Mile Portage, a vital supply route during the War of 1812. The site became a community in the 19th century and was named for Robert Barrie, commodore of an inactive squadron in Kingston during the 1830s.

At the first hint of summer water-skiers, swimmers, sailors and golfers converge on Barrie to bask in the sun around Kempenfelt Bay on Lake Simcoe, one of Ontario's largest lakes, with a shoreline of about 161 kilometres (100 mi.).

Activity does not end with the coming of cold weather; skiers, snowboarders and snowmobilers make use of the many trails and winter sports facilities nearby. Anglers are most fortunate, as they can pursue small-mouth bass and lake trout all year. Georgian Downs, west off Hwy. 400 Innisfil Beach Road exit at 7485 Sideroad #5, offers harness racing all year; phone (705) 726-9400.

Note: Policies concerning admittance of children to pari-mutuel betting facilities vary. Phone for information.

Barrie hosts a variety of trade and consumer shows throughout the year. Featured community events include Winterfest in early February and the street performers, midway, food and entertainment of Promenade Days in early summer. Kempenfest Waterfront Festival occurs throughout Civic Holiday weekend, ending the first Monday in August; one of the largest outdoor arts and crafts festivals in North America, it also features live entertainment, an antique show, cooking demonstrations, samples and competitions, and a sports and leisure show.

The Gryphon Theatre, off Hwy. 400 Duckworth Street exit, offers major professional productions and concerts year-round; phone (705) 728-4613. Shows, sporting events and concerts are held at Barrie Molson Centre, 555 Bayview Dr.; phone (705) 737-6850.

Springwater Provincial Park, 10 kilometres (6 mi.) northwest on Hwy. 26, has a native wildlife exhibit with raptors, black bears, coyotes, swans, ducks, deer, raccoons, gray wolves, foxes and other animals as well as picnic facilities and cross-country ski trails. Several hiking trails, including one geared to children, range in length from 2.5 kilometres (1.5 mi.) to 5 kilometres (3 mi.) and wend through various forest environments. *See Recreation Chart.*

Tourism Barrie: 205 Lakeshore Dr., Barrie, ON, Canada L4N 7Y9; phone (705) 739-9444 or (800) 668-9100.

Shopping areas: Bayfield Mall, off Hwy. 400N at 320 Bayfield St., features specialty shops and Winners. Georgian Mall, off Hwy. 400N at 509 Bayfield St., is an enclosed mall featuring The Bay and Sears. Kozlov Centre, off Hwy. 400N at 400 Bayfield St., features specialty shops and Zellers.

BARRIE BOAT CRUISES depart from the city dock at the bottom of Bayfield St. and Lakeshore Dr. Sixty- and 90-minute cruises aboard the 265-passenger *Serendipity Princess* provide narration about local sights. Dinner and lunch cruises also are available. Fall foliage cruises, also on the *Serendipity Princess*, depart from Port Severn; phone for information.

Sightseeing departures Mon.-Sat. (weather permitting) at 11:45, 1:30 and 3:30, Sun. at 1:30 and 3:30, mid-June to late Sept.; Sat. at 11:45, 1:30 and 3:30, Sun. at 1:30 and 3:30, late May to mid-June. Boarding is 15 minutes prior to departure. Fare $16; over 64, $15; students with ID $13; under 13,

$10; family rate (five persons) $42. Reservations are required. VI. Phone (705) 728-9888 or (888) 833-2628.

CANADIAN FORCES BASE BORDEN MILITARY MUSEUM—*see Borden p. 57.*

MacLAREN ART CENTRE, 37 Mulcaster St., displays a permanent collection of approximately 400 works by local and regional artists as well as changing regional, national and international art exhibits. Food is available. Allow 30 minutes minimum. Tues.-Fri. 10-6, Sat. 10-4; closed major holidays. Donations. Phone (705) 721-9696.

SIMCOE COUNTY MUSEUM—*see Midhurst p. 97.*

BARRY'S BAY (E-10) pop. 1,259

Barry's Bay, a lumbering town, also is an outfitting center in the Kamaniskeg Lake vacation region.

[SAVE] **MADAWASKA RIVER FLOAT TRIPS** (Madawaska Kanu Centre), 14 km (9 mi.) s. on Dunn St., then e. on River Rd. following signs, offers guided 2-hour white-water float trips on the Madawaska River. Life jackets and helmets are provided; swimsuits and sneakers are required. Instruction in canoe, kayak and white-water paddling also is available.

Two-hour trips depart every 2 hours Mon.-Thurs. 10-2, mid-June through Aug. 31. Fare $30; under 12, $20. Reservations are required. Passengers should arrive 30 minutes prior to departure. MC, VI. Phone (613) 756-3620, or (613) 594-5268 after Labour Day to mid-June.

BAYFIELD (H-7) pop. 909, elev. 186 m/610'

Named after British surveyor Henry Wolsey Bayfield, the village on Lake Huron began as a port for shipping grain. After the coming of railroads the port no longer was needed, and the townsfolk turned to fishing for a way of life. A full-service marina is available for boaters.

Bayfield and Area Chamber of Commerce: P.O. Box 2065, Bayfield, ON, Canada N0M 1G0; phone (519) 565-2499 or (866) 565-2499.

Self-guiding tours: A walking tour of the village's historic district features late 19th-century houses surrounded by large oak trees. Highlights of the houses include decorative woodwork, carved doors and buff-colored brickwork.

GODERICH TOWNSHIP WINDMILL, 4 km (2.5 mi.) n. off Hwy. 21, is purportedly North America's only wind-driven sawmill and gristmill. Half-hour guided tours and demonstrations are offered. Picnic facilities are available. Allow 30 minutes minimum. Daily noon-4, June 1-Labour Day. Admission $4; ages 6-12, $2.50. Phone (519) 482-5058 to verify schedule.

BEACHBURG (E-10) pop. 870

RECREATIONAL ACTIVITIES
White-water Rafting

• **Wilderness Tours Whitewater Rafting** can be reached following signs off Hwy. 17 to CR 7. Write P.O. Box 89, Beachburg, ON, Canada K0J 1C0. Other activities are offered. One-day whitewater trip departs daily, May-Aug.; Wed.-Sun., in Sept. Phone (613) 646-2291 or (800) 267-9166.

BEAMSVILLE (H-4)
pop. 20,612, elev. 108 m/354′

WINERIES
• **Peninsula Ridge Estates Winery** is s. off QEW exit 68 (Bartlett Ave.), then 1.6 km (1 mi.) e. on Main St. E. (Regional Rd. 81) to 5600 King St. W. Tastings daily 10-6, May-Oct.; Mon.-Fri. 11-5:30, Sat.-Sun. 10-5:30, rest of year. Closed Dec. 25. Tours daily at 11:30 and 3. Phone (905) 563-0900.

BEAVERTON (F-9)
pop. 3,065, elev. 236 m/774′

BEAVER RIVER MUSEUM is at 284 Simcoe St. W. at Centennial Park. Three restored 19th-century buildings—a stone jail, a settler's log cabin and a brick farmhouse—help depict local history. All contain period furniture and artifacts. Guided tours are available. Picnicking is permitted. Allow 30 minutes minimum. Wed.-Mon. 1:30-4, July-Aug.; Sat.-Sun. 1:30-4, May-June and in Sept. Donations. Phone (705) 426-9641.

BELLEVILLE (F-10)
pop. 45,986, elev. 77 m/253′

Belleville, at the mouth of the Moira River on the Bay of Quinte, was settled by United Empire Loyalists in 1784 and incorporated in 1878. Known for its yacht harbor and excellent fishing, Belleville and the surrounding area also are noted for cheese.

Thousands of roses bloom in Corby Park, and music chimes from the clock tower of city hall. Houses in Belleville range from charming old stone and clapboard buildings to ornate Victorian mansions.

Belleville and District Chamber of Commerce: 5 Moira St. E., P.O. Box 726, Belleville, ON, Canada K8N 5B3; phone (613) 962-4597 or (888) 852-9992.

GLANMORE NATIONAL HISTORIC SITE, 257 Bridge St. E., houses collections of Victorian furnishings and European art. Tues.-Sun. 10-4:30, June-Aug.; 1-4:30, rest of year. Closed Jan. 1, Good Friday, July 1, Nov. 11 and Dec. 25-26. Admission $3; over 54 and students with ID $2.50; ages 5-12, $1.50. Phone (613) 962-2329.

BLENHEIM (I-7) pop. 4,795, elev. 209 m/685′

Named after a site in Oxford, England, Blenheim had a general store by 1845, but was not incorporated until 30 years later. The town is part of a rich farming area noted for sugar beets, corn and tomatoes.

Chatham-Kent Tourism—Blenheim: 445 Grand Ave. W., P.O. Box 944, Chatham, ON, Canada N7M 5L3; phone (519) 354-6125 or (800) 561-6125.

RM CLASSIC CAR EXHIBIT is just s. off Hwy. 401 exit 90 (Hwy. 40) following signs to One Classic Car Dr. In addition to viewing a collection of vintage automobiles, visitors also can see the restoration work necessary to return these cars to their original condition. Guides explain the process and the steps taken to rebuild the cars. Allow 30 minutes minimum. Daily 9-5, Apr.-Nov. Admission $5, over 64 and students with ID $4, under 12 free. Phone (519) 352-9024 or (877) 523-2684.

BLIND RIVER (E-5) pop. 3,969

A settlement at the concealed mouth of the Mississagi River between Sudbury and Sault Ste. Marie, Blind River was so named because the approach to the river could not be seen from Lake Huron. Historically a lumbering town, it is now the site of Cameco Ltd., a uranium refinery. The importance of the forestry industry to the area is depicted by the bronze Northern Ontario Logging Memorial next to Timber Village Museum *(see attraction listing).*

A modern marina facility is available to accommodate boaters. The area also is noted for its camping, hiking trails, beaches, hunting, fishing and ice fishing, golfing, cross-country skiing, snowmobiling, and boating.

North Shore Travel Centre: Hwy. 17E, P.O. Box 640, Blind River, ON, Canada P0R 1B0; phone (705) 356-2555 or (800) 563-8719.

DID YOU KNOW

Ontario has a population of more than 11 million in an area that is more than 50 percent larger than Texas.

TIMBER VILLAGE MUSEUM, e. on Hwy. 17 at 180 Leacock St. beside the Northern Ontario Logging Memorial, consists of replicas of buildings, pioneer household items and memorabilia depicting the trade history that shaped the economy of the north shore of Lake Huron. Exhibits feature exploration and fur trade, mining, logging and commercial fishing. A gallery also displays local artworks.

Daily 10-5, July-Aug.; Mon.-Fri. 10-4, May-June and Sept.-Oct. Admission $2; over 64 and ages 13-18, $1.50; under 13, $1. VI. Phone (705) 356-7544.

BOBCAYGEON (F-9) pop. 2,854

Bobcaygeon, meaning "shallow rapids" in the Mississauga Indian language, is aptly named: It is built on three islands surrounded by rapids. Originally a lumber mill town, Bobcaygeon is now a recreational center for the Kawartha Lakes region, where boating, fishing, snowmobiling and cross-country skiing can be enjoyed.

Bobcaygeon and Area Chamber of Commerce: 21 Canal St. E., P.O. Box 388, Bobcaygeon, ON, Canada K0M 1A0; phone (705) 738-2202 or (800) 318-6173.

BOYD HERITAGE MUSEUM is on the w. side of the locks at 21 Canal St. In the building that formerly housed the M.M. Boyd Lumber Co., the museum displays artifacts and photographs from the 19th-century when the Boyd family was prominent in the lumber industry. In addition to his timber interests, Mossom Boyd also was the founder of the Trent Valley Navigation Co., which operated freight and passenger ships throughout the region.

Allow 30 minutes minimum. Daily 10-4, July-Aug.; Fri.-Sun. 10-4, Victoria Day weekend-June 30 and Sept. 1-second Mon. in Oct. Donations. Phone (705) 738-9482.

FENELON FALLS/BOBCAYGEON BOAT CRUISE —see Fenelon Falls p. 72.

KAWARTHA SETTLERS' VILLAGE is at 85 Dunn St. The 9-acre village includes restored homes and buildings dating to the 1800s. This former farm site has a barn with displays of agricultural equipment, an 1870s log home, an early 20th-century schoolhouse, an 1885 Methodist church with a pump organ, a carriage house and a general store. Special events are offered throughout the year.

Picnicking is permitted. Allow 30 minutes minimum. Guided tours are offered Wed.-Sun. 1-5, mid-June to late Aug.; otherwise by appointment. Last tour begins 1 hour before closing. Hours may vary during special events; phone ahead. Donations. Phone (705) 738-6163.

BORDEN (G-8) elev. 120 m/393′

CANADIAN FORCES BASE BORDEN MILITARY MUSEUM, on Hwy. 90, has indoor and outdoor displays of aircraft, tanks and other vehicles, artillery, uniforms and other military items. Picnic facilities and food are available. Tues.-Fri. 9-noon and 1-3,

Sat.-Sun. and holidays 1-4; closed day after Mon. holidays, Easter weekend and Dec. 25-Jan. 1. Donations. Phone (705) 423-3531.

BOTHWELL (I-7) pop. 1,002

FAIRFIELD MUSEUM AND AVENUE OF PEACE, w. on CR 2, displays items excavated from the original site of Fairfield village, which was burned by the Americans in the War of 1812. Aboriginal and pioneer relics are exhibited as well as items depicting the establishment of the Moravian church in the area.

The Avenue of Peace, on the site of the original Main Street, has plaques commemorating the first settlers and the many years of peace between the United States and Canada. Tues.-Sat. 10-5, Sun. and holidays 1-5, May-Oct. Admission $2; ages 6-12, $1. Phone (519) 692-4397.

BOWMANVILLE (G-9)

With a fine natural harbor on the north shore of Lake Ontario, Bowmanville was formerly a mill town. It now flourishes as a horticultural center. Archibald Orchards & Estate Winery, off Hwy. 401 exit 432, then 12 kilometres (8 mi.) north to 6275 Liberty St. N., produces apple wines. Pick-your-own apples, storytelling and special events also are offered as are wine tastings; phone (905) 263-2396.

Recreational activities include hiking, horseback riding, skiing and snowmobiling. The Mosport International Raceway, 16 kilometres (10 mi.) north of town, holds motorcycle competitions and automobile races; phone (905) 983-9141.

Clarington Communications and Tourism: 40 Temperance St., Bowmanville, ON, Canada L1C 3A6; phone (905) 623-3379 or (800) 563-1195.

BOWMANVILLE MUSEUM, 37 Silver St., is in a large house built in 1847. Included are 10 period rooms, Victorian costumes, furnishings, an antique doll gallery and toys. An archives reading room also is available. Special events are held throughout the year. Allow 30 minutes minimum. Daily 11-4, July-Aug.; Tues.-Sun. and Mon. holidays 11-4, rest of year. Closed Dec. 25-Jan. 2. Admission $3; over 64 and under 18, $2; family rate (five persons) $7. Archives $10. Phone (905) 623-2734.

BOWMANVILLE ZOOLOGICAL PARK is off Hwy. 401 exit 432, then 1.6 km (1 mi.) n. on Liberty St. and 1 km (.6 mi.) e. to 340 King St. E. On 45 acres of parklike land, the zoo features more than 300 animals such as elephants, lions, tigers and monkeys. Elephant rides, children's mechanical rides and picnic facilities are available. Animal shows are performed daily.

Food is available. Daily 10-6, July-Aug.; daily 10-5, in May; Mon.-Fri. 10-5, Sat.-Sun. 10-6, in June; Mon.-Fri. 10-4, Sat.-Sun. 10-5, in Sept.; Sat.-Sun. 10-4, in Oct. Admission $14; over 64 and ages 13-17, $11; ages 2-12, $8. Elephant rides $5. VI. Phone (905) 623-5655.

DARLINGTON NUCLEAR GENERATING STATION, Waverly Rd. s. to S. Service Rd., then w. to Park Rd., provides 20 percent of Ontario's electricity. The Information Centre offers interactive displays, literature and an orientation videotape about Ontario's nuclear energy. Also on the grounds is the 7.5-kilometer (4.5-mi.) Waterfront Trail. Picnicking is permitted. Mon.-Fri. 8:30-4; closed holidays and late Dec.-early Jan. Free. Phone (905) 623-7122.

TYRONE MILL is off Hwy. 401 exit 432, then 13 km (8 mi.) n. on Liberty St. to 2656 Concession Rd. 7. Built in 1846, this water-powered gristmill produces lumber and apple cider. A flour mill and woodworking room also can be visited. Flour production commences in early October.

Although open all year, the mill is most active during the cider-producing season from mid-September through May 31. Allow 30 minutes minimum. Mon.-Sat. 9-6, Sun. noon-5; closed Jan. 1, Good Friday, Easter and Dec. 25. Free. Phone (905) 263-8871.

BRACEBRIDGE (F-8) pop. 13,751

Located in the heart of the Muskoka Lakes region and at the 45th parallel, a highway sign in Bracebridge says "halfway to the North Pole," meaning halfway between the equator and the North Pole. The town overlooks Bracebridge Falls and both branches of the Muskoka River; more than 20 waterfalls are in the area.

The area's agricultural bounty is showcased at a farmers' market that operates Saturdays from June through October. Winter outdoor activities abound, with fine snowmobiling, skating, and cross-country and Nordic skiing. Summer recreation includes boating, golfing, swimming, fishing and hiking.

Bracebridge Visitor Information Centre: 1-1 Manitoba St., Bracebridge, ON, Canada P1L 2A8; phone (705) 645-8121 or (866) 645-8121 in Canada.

Shopping areas: Manitoba Street, downtown in the historic district, offers a variety of shops. Balls Flats, on Hwy. 118 west of Wellington Street, features Zellers and specialty stores.

LADY MUSKOKA **CRUISES** depart from the Riverside Inn. The 2.75-hour sightseeing cruises on Lake Muskoka on the 300-passenger boat pass islands, local landmarks, resorts and palatial summer homes. Dinner and Sunday brunch cruises also are offered. Sightseeing cruises depart daily at 11 and 2:15, July 1-Labour Day; departures vary May-June and day after Labour Day to mid-Oct. Fare $18; over 60, $17; ages 5-12, $9. MC, VI. For schedule information phone (705) 646-2628, or (800) 263-5239 in Ontario.

SANTA'S VILLAGE AND SPORTSLAND is 6 km (4 mi.) w. on Santa's Village Rd. At this forested 20-hectare (50-acre) fairyland children can meet Santa

exactly.

This offer is available at participating Hertz locations in the U.S., Canada and Puerto Rico, including Hertz Local Edition locations, subject to availability. Advance reservations are required. Blackout periods may apply. Offer may be limited in some cities at some times, especially during periods of peak demand. Maximum upgrade is to a Premium (Class G) car. Coupon has no cash value, must be surrendered on rental and may not be used with any other CDP#, coupon, discount, rate or promotion. This coupon may only be used with a CAA CDP#. Hertz' standard age, driver and credit qualifications for the renting location apply and the car must be returned to that location. Taxes and optional services, such as refueling, are not included and are not subject to discount. Call for details.

Savings for all Seasons

No matter the season, Hertz offers CAA members exclusive discounts and benefits.

Operating in 150 countries at over 7,000 locations, Hertz makes traveling more convenient and efficient wherever and whenever you go. Hertz offers CAA members discounts up to 20% on car rentals worldwide.

To receive your exclusive CAA member discounts and benefits, mention your CAA membership card at time of reservation and present it at time of rental. **In addition,** to receive a free one car class upgrade, in the United States mention PC# 929714, in Canada mention PC# 929725 and in Puerto Rico mention PC# 929736 at the time of reservation. Offer available through 12/15/05.

For reservations and program details, call your CAA Travel office or the Hertz/CAA Desk at **1-800-263-0600;** Toronto **(416) 620-9620.**

and his reindeer, visit his workshop and a petting farm, cool off in the Splash Zone, ride a miniature train, riverboat, roller coaster, merry-go-round, paddle boat, Ferris wheel and pony, and enjoy live entertainment. Sportsland has miniature golf, batting cages, video games, laser tag and go-carts. Food is available. Santa's Village daily 10-6, late June-Labour Day. Sportsland Mon.-Sat. 10-9, Sun. 10-6, late June-Labour Day. Village all-inclusive admission $19.95; over 64 and ages 2-4, $14.95. Sportsland tickets $3 each or $25 for 10 tickets. MC, VI. Phone (705) 645-2512.

WOODCHESTER VILLA, close to the center of town, following signs from Manitoba St. to 15 King St., is a restored house notable for its octagonal shape. Built in 1882 of concrete, the house boasted indoor plumbing, forced-air heating, ventilation shafts and electric lighting—all unusual features at the time. This historic house museum contains the René M. Caisse Exhibition, dedicated to this Bracebridge nurse. Tues.-Sat. 9-5, July 1-Labour Day. Admission $2; under 13, $1; family rate $5. Phone (705) 645-5501.

Muskoka Arts and Crafts, Inc. (The Chapel Gallery), on the grounds of Woodchester Villa, is housed in a reconstruction of the first Presbyterian church in Bracebridge. In addition to its permanent collection of works in various media by Muskoka artists, the gallery presents monthly exhibitions by local and provincial artists and offers workshops, lectures and other special events. It holds a spring arts and crafts show in April, a summer show in July and a holiday show in November.

Gallery open Tues-Sat. 10-1 and 2-5; closed holidays, the last week of Sept., the first 2 weeks of Oct. and Dec. 25-Jan. 2. Donations. Phone (705) 645-5501.

BRAMPTON (G-3) pop. 325,428

When John Elliott and John Scott arrived from England more than 150 years ago, present-day Brampton consisted of no more than a tavern named Buffy's Corners at two intersecting dirt roads. The two opened a store, a copper shop, a distillery and a potashery and named the new community Brampton, after Elliott's hometown in northern England.

Brampton citizens are proud of the town's many walking trails and parks; it is said to have more parkland and recreation facilities per capita than any other Canadian city. One such park is Heart Lake Conservation Area, north of Hwy. 7 on Heart Lake Road; phone (905) 846-2494. The facility takes its name from the heart-shaped lake that is the park's centerpiece; visitors can enjoy swimming, fishing, boating, picnicking and hiking *(see Recreation Chart).*

Gage Park, Wellington Street W. and Main Street S. (Hurontario Street), is home to a wading pool, skating rink and picnic facilities; phone (905) 874-2133. Professors Lake Recreation Centre, east of Hwy. 410 at 1660 North Park Dr., west of

Torbram Road, features a lakefront for swimming and boating and a 30-metre (98-ft.) waterslide as well as hiking trails; phone (905) 791-7751.

Bramalea Live Theatre performs several productions each year from September to early June at the Bramalea and Cyril Clark Library Theatre, 20 Loafer's Lake Ln., and at the Lester B. Pearson Theatre, 150 Central Park Dr.; phone (905) 458-5252 for information or (905) 874-2800 for tickets.

Although benefiting from its proximity to nearby Toronto, Brampton also retains links to its rural past. Fruit orchards, strawberry farms and livestock are still important to the economy. On Saturdays a farmers' market is held downtown late June to mid-October.

Brampton Economic Development Office: 33 Queen St. W., Brampton, ON, Canada L6Y 1L9; phone (905) 874-2650 or (888) 381-2726.

Self-guiding tours: Information about a self-guiding walking tour that includes the city's historical buildings and sites is available through the Brampton Heritage Board; phone (905) 874-2106.

Shopping areas: Two major shopping malls offer enough stores to satisfy even the most indefatigable bargain hunters. Bramalea City Centre, at the southeast corner of Dixie Road and Queen Street (Hwy. 7), has more than 250 shops and services, including The Bay and Sears. The Bay is the largest store at Shoppers World Brampton, at the northwest corner of Main Street S. and Steeles Avenue.

BOVAIRD HOUSE is at 563 Bovaird Dr. E. at jct. Kennedy Rd. This Georgian farmhouse is a reminder of Brampton's agricultural roots and traditions. Built about 1840, the two-story brick home has been restored to represent the 1850-1920 period. The grounds include a garden and a gazebo. Special events are offered throughout the year. Guided tours are available. Allow 30 minutes minimum. Wed. and Sat.-Sun. noon-4, mid-Feb. to mid-Dec. Donations. Phone (905) 874-2804.

CHINGUACOUSY PARK, Bramalea Rd. and Regional Rd. 107 (Queen St./Hwy. 7), is a 40-hectare (99-acre) park with an animal farm and petting zoo, garden teahouse, wading pool, greenhouse, miniature golf course, tennis courts, skateboarding park, a curling rink, soccer fields, baseball diamonds, track fields and a ski hill. The park is host to many city-wide events. Skiing and snowboarding equipment rentals are available.

Park open daily dawn-dusk. Teahouse and craft room open Mon.-Fri. noon-4, Sat.-Sun. noon-6, mid-May through Labour Day. Animal farm open daily noon-8, miniature golf daily 10-8, mid-May through Labour Day. Wading pool Sat.-Thurs. 10-5, Fri. 11-6, June 1-Labour Day. Closed Jan. 1 and Dec. 25. Animal farm and greenhouse free. Miniature golf $3. Wading pool $1. MC, VI. Phone (905) 458-6555.

PEEL HERITAGE COMPLEX, 9 Wellington St. E., showcases an art gallery, museum and archives in a renovated 19th-century jail and the historic Peel County Courthouse. The Art Gallery of Peel features changing displays. The Region of Peel Museum recounts the region's history and development in permanent displays; two galleries offer changing exhibits, and a small gallery relates the jail's history. The Region of Peel Archives has original records and a reading room.

Allow 1 hour minimum. Mon.-Fri. 10-4:30 (also Thurs. 6-9 p.m., Sept.-July), Sat. noon-4:30 (also Sun. noon-4:30, Sept.-July). Archives Mon.-Fri. 10-4:30. Reading room Sat. noon-4:30. Closed major holidays. Admission $2.50; over 64 and ages 13-17, $1.50; ages 5-12, $1; family rate $7. MC, VI. Phone (905) 791-4055.

WILD WATER KINGDOM, 2 km (1.2 mi.) w. of Hwy. 427N on Finch Ave. near the Clairville Conservation Area, is situated on more than 40 hectares (100 acres) of natural parkland and features more than 14 waterslides, two seven-story speed slides, a .2-hectare (.5-acre) wave pool, a 550-square-metre (6,000-sq.-ft.) Caribbean-themed swimming pool, hot tubs, tube rides, rock climbing, a children's area and a water playground, two miniature golf courses, batting cages and picnic grounds.

Dogs are allowed only in the picnic area. Food is available. Daily 10-8, July 1 to mid-Aug.; daily 10-6, mid-June through June 30 and mid-Aug. through Labour Day; Sat.-Sun. 10-6, June 1 to mid-June (weather permitting). Admission $25.50; over 64 and ages 4-9, $19. Admission after 4 p.m., $15. Miniature golf $4.50; ages 4-9, $3.50. Batting cages $1.50 for 10 pitches. Parking $7. AX, MC, VI. Phone (416) 369-9453 or (905) 794-0565.

BRANTFORD (H-3)

pop. 86,417, elev. 211 m/692'

In 1784 Capt. Joseph Brant led the Six Nations Iroquois from northern New York to Canada, where they settled on a tract of land in south central Ontario in the Grand River area. The land was granted to the Indians as a reward for their support of the British during the American Revolution; their allegiance to the British cost them their land in New York's Mohawk Valley. Brantford is named for this celebrated leader.

The city is in a valley region of the Grand River, in a pocket of Carolinian forest where popular recreational options include canoeing, rafting, fishing and bird-watching. The Trans Canada Trail meanders through Brantford along the Grand River.

The city has won national and international awards for its beautiful municipal gardens and parks. The hometown of Wayne Gretzky, Brantford showcases memorabilia of the hockey great as well as other area athletes in the Brantford and Area Sports Hall of Recognition in the Wayne Gretzky Sports Centre, 254 N. Park St. The center is open to the public at no charge; phone (519) 756-9900.

The Sanderson Centre for the Performing Arts, 88 Dalhousie St., offers entertainment year-round in a restored, 1919 vaudeville theater that seats 1,134; for ticket information phone (519) 758-8090.

During the International Villages Festival held in early July, ethnic groups set up "villages" around town and offer traditional foods, entertainment and displays of arts and crafts. Later that month in nearby Ohsweken is the Grand River Champion of Champions Powwow, which celebrates native music, dance, art, and crafts.

Brantford the telephone city

Bell Homestead National Historic Site

Kanata 17th Century Iroquoian Village

Grand River: Canadian Heritage River

Heritage and Cultural Attractions . . .
The Bell Homestead National Historic Site, Kanata - 17th Century Iroquoian Village, pow-wows, museums, galleries, and unique specialty shops.

Fascinating festivals . . .
International Villages Festival, Elvisfest, Gardens on Parade, Brant Studio Tour & The Storytelling Festival.

Grand Adventures . . .
Canoe, raft or fish the Grand River. Hike or bike our trails. Stroll through award-winning gardens.

Visit Brantford's Visitor & Tourism Centre - open year round. Free RV Waste Disposal Station.

BRANTFORD ONTARIO ◆ CANADA

www.brantford.ca/tourism 1-800-265-6299

Tourism Brantford: 399 Wayne Gretzky Pkwy., Brantford, ON, Canada N3R 8B4; phone (519) 751-9900, or (800) 265-6299 in the U.S. and Canada (except Québec). *See color ad p. 60.*

BELL HOMESTEAD NATIONAL HISTORIC SITE, 5 km (3 mi.) s.w. on Mt. Pleasant Rd., then .5 km (.3 mi.) s. at 94 Tutela Heights Rd., is the former homestead of Alexander Graham Bell and his family, and the site where the inventor conceived the idea of the telephone in 1874. Restored to the 1870s period, the house includes a working kitchen and an extensive collection of Bell family artifacts.

Next door in the Henderson House are the first Canadian telephone business office, a restored 1920s telephone exchange and displays of early telephones. Tues.-Sun. 9:30-4:30; closed Dec. 25-Jan. 1. Admission $4, over 65 and students with ID $3.25, under 6 free. Phone to confirm prices. Phone (519) 756-6220.

BELL MEMORIAL, West St., is an impressive monument dedicated to the invention of the telephone. Unveiled by Alexander Graham Bell in 1917, the memorial is surrounded by gardens.

BRANT MUSEUM AND ARCHIVES, 57 Charlotte St. opposite City Hall Square, displays Brant County history from the Six Nations settlement to the present. An archival research room also is available. Wed.-Fri. 10-4, Sat.-Sun 1-4, July-Aug.; Wed.-Fri. 10-4, Sat. 1-4, rest of year. Closed holidays. Admission $2; over 64 and students with ID $1.50; ages 6-12, $1.25. Phone (519) 752-2483.

BRANT'S FORD is at the w. end of Lorne Bridge in Lorne Park. An inscribed boulder and sundial rest near the spot where Mohawk captain Joseph Brant, the namesake of the ford and town, crossed the Grand River. Lorne Park is an award-winning horticultural area.

CANADIAN MILITARY HERITAGE MUSEUM, 347 Greenwich St., uses a collection of 10,000 artifacts to relate the history of the Canadian military from the Loyalist era of the 1700s to the present. Displays include vintage military vehicles, replicas of WW II airplanes, weapons, medals, uniforms and photographs and documents.

Allow 30 minutes minimum. Tues.-Sun. 10-4, May-Sept.; Fri.-Sun. 10-4, Mar.-Apr. and Oct.-Nov.; by appointment rest of year. Admission $4; over 64, $3; students with ID $2; under 12, $1. Phone (519) 759-1313.

GLENHYRST ART GALLERY OF BRANT, 20 Ava Rd., 2 km (1.2 mi.) s. of Hwy. 403, is in a 6.5-hectare (16-acre) park overlooking the Grand River. The gallery exhibits paintings, graphic arts, sculpture and photographs. The Trans Canada Trail runs behind the landscaped grounds. Tues.-Fri. 10-5, Sat.-Sun. 1-5. Free. Phone (519) 756-5932.

HER MAJESTY'S CHAPEL OF THE MOHAWKS, 3.2 km (2 mi.) s.w. on Mohawk Rd., dates from 1785 and is the successor to the original Mohawk Chapel, built in 1712 in the Mohawk Valley of New York. Named St. Paul's of the Mohawks, Her Majesty's Royal Chapel, it is the oldest Protestant church in Ontario and the world's first Royal Native chapel. The tomb of Mohawk captain Joseph Brant is next to the chapel.

Daily 10-6, July-Aug.; Wed.-Sun. 10-6, Labour Day-second Mon. in Oct.; Wed.-Sun. 1-5:30, May 24-June 30. Donations. Phone (519) 756-0240.

THE MUSEUM IN THE SQUARE, 1 Market St. in Market Square, features the decorative arts of the Harrison M. Scheak collection, various pottery and antique furniture and other changing exhibits. Allow 30 minutes minimum. Mon.-Sat. 10-4, July-Aug.; Mon.-Fri. 10-4, rest of year. Closed holidays. Donations. Phone (519) 752-8578.

MYRTLEVILLE HOUSE MUSEUM, 34 Myrtleville Dr., has changed little since Allen Good built this Georgian-style farmhouse in 1837. The Goods and their descendants lived in the dwelling for nearly 140 years. The heirlooms they brought from Ireland and many personal furnishings now fill the house. Other highlights include more than 2.5 hectares (6.2 acres) of lawns and gardens and a working blacksmith shop. Special events are scheduled throughout the season.

Mon.-Fri. 9-4, Sat.-Sun. noon-4, May-Sept.; Mon.-Fri. 9-4, rest of year. Admission $3; over 64 and students with ID $2.75; ages 5-12, $2.50. Phone (519) 752-3216.

WOODLAND CULTURAL CENTRE, 184 Mohawk St., offers information about the history and traditions of the First Nations People of the Woodland area through museum displays, educational programs, seminars and special events. The culture of the Iroquois and Algonkian peoples is reflected in changing exhibits about history, science, art and contemporary issues.

Facilities include the museum, a library and a language and cultural resource center. Museum Mon.-Fri. 9-4, Sat.-Sun. 10-5. Admission $5; over 65, $4; ages 6-16, $3. MC, VI. Phone (519) 759-2650, ext. 241.

CASINOS

- **Brantford Charity Casino** is at 40 Icomm Dr. Daily 24 hours. Phone (519) 752-5004 or (888) 694-6946.

BRIGHTON (G-9) pop. 9,449

Brighton was settled by United Empire Loyalists in the 1700s. By the mid-1800s the village was incorporated. The town is now in the center of an apple-growing region. Area produce is available at a farmers' market every Saturday from May to mid-October.

Brighton & District Chamber of Commerce: 74 Main St., P.O. Box 1421, Brighton, ON, Canada K0K 1H0; phone (613) 475-2775 or (877) 475-2775.

MEMORY JUNCTION MUSEUM is at 60 Maplewood St. at jct. Monck St. Housed in the town's late 19th-century train station, the museum features railway memorabilia as well as historical items from the Brighton area. An old steam locomotive, boxcars and three cabooses are on-site. Allow 1 hour minimum. Wed.-Thurs. and Sat.-Mon. 10-4, June-Sept.; hours vary in May and Oct. Donations. Phone (613) 475-0379.

PRESQU'ILE PROVINCIAL PARK, 3.25 km (2 mi.) s. via Hwy. 30, is on a peninsula jutting into Lake Ontario. "Almost an island" in French and known for its sandy beach and warm, shallow waters, the park has a variety of landscapes—forests, marshes, sand dunes and abandoned farmlands. Hiking and bicycling trails offer bird and wildlife viewing. An observation tower is on the marsh area boardwalk, and one of Ontario's oldest operating lighthouses, and its lighthouse keeper's cottage, are in the park.

Park open daily 8 a.m.-10 p.m., Victoria Day-second Mon. in Oct.; 8-4:30, rest of year. Admission $9.50 per private vehicle. MC, VI. Phone (613) 475-4324. *See Recreation Chart.*

PROCTOR HOUSE MUSEUM is at 96 Young St., on the w. side of Hwy. 30 in the Proctor Park Conservation Area just n. of town. A restored merchant's mansion dating to the late 1860s, the Italianate-style house commands a spectacular view of Lake Ontario and the countryside. The gallery and lower level feature changing exhibits. Guided 45-minute tours of the house describe its history.

Also on the property are hiking trails, a carriage shed with antique vehicles, an agricultural museum and a community theater. Picnic facilities are available. Allow 30 minutes minimum. Tues.-Fri. 10-4, Sat.-Sun. 1-4, July-Aug. Last tour begins 1 hour before closing. Fee $2.50, students with ID $1, under 6 free. Phone (613) 475-2144.

BROCKVILLE (F-11) pop. 21,357

Founded in 1785, Brockville was named in honor of Gen. Sir Isaac Brock, a hero of the War of 1812. Its location near the Thousand Islands resort area makes the city a center for tourists and boating enthusiasts. An industrial city, Brockville also is the commercial center for a large dairying region. The province's oldest newspaper, the *Recorder and Times,* has been published since 1821.

The 1842 County Courthouse and Jail at Courthouse Square is one of the oldest remaining structures of its type in Ontario. The 1860 Brockville Railway Tunnel is Canada's oldest Underground Railway tunnel. It is open for viewing mid-May through the second Monday in October. Visitors wandering the walking paths along the waterfront and through the town can learn of the development of this river city from plaques.

A variety of theatrical performances, concerts and other events are presented April through August at the Brockville Arts Centre, 235 King St. W.;

phone (613) 342-7122 or (877) 342-7122 for information and tickets. Recreational opportunities include the Brockville Trail, which stretches for 6 kilometres (4 mi.) from the St. Lawrence River waterfront into the city. The trail is popular with hikers and bicyclists.

Brockville and District Chamber of Commerce Tourism Office: 10 Market St. W., Brockville, ON, Canada K6V 4R7; phone (613) 342-4357 or (888) 251-7676.

1000 ISLANDS & SEAWAY CRUISES, departing from Blockhouse Island on the waterfront, offers 1- and 2.5-hour cruises featuring the eastern groups of the 1000 Islands, Brockville's historic waterfront and the main ship channel of the St. Lawrence Seaway. Dinner cruises also are offered.

One-hour cruises Mon.-Fri. at 11, 1 and 5, Sat.-Sun. and holidays at 11, 1, 3:30 and 6, last Mon. in June-Labour Day; Mon.-Fri. at 12:30 and 2:30, Sat.-Sun. and holidays at 11, 1 and 5, Victoria Day weekend-last Sun. in June and day after Labour Day to mid-Oct. (weather permitting). Departures for 2.5-hour cruises Mon.-Fri. at 2:30, Sat.-Sun. and holidays at 12:30 and 3, last Mon. in June-Labour Day; Sat.-Sun. and holidays at 2:30, Victoria Day weekend-last Sun. in June and day after Labour Day to mid-Oct. (weather permitting). Schedules may vary; phone ahead.

One-hour fare $13; over 59 and students with ID $12; ages 4-12, $7.50. Fare for 2.5-hour cruise $22; over 59 and students with ID $20; ages 4-12, $12. AX, MC, VI. Phone (613) 345-7333 or (800) 353-3157.

BROCKVILLE MUSEUM, 5 Henry St., features transportation artifacts manufactured in Brockville. Included are a horse-drawn buggy, an 1890s St. Lawrence skiff and a 1914 Atlas car as well as such agricultural implements as a late 1800s J.W. Mann seeder. Changing themed exhibitions also are presented. The Genealogical Library, River City Gallery and local history archives also can be visited.

Picnicking is permitted. Mon.-Sat. 10-5, Sun. 1-5, Victoria Day-second Mon. in Oct.; Mon.-Fri. 10-4:30, rest of year. Closed Jan. 1, Good Friday and Dec. 25-26. Admission $2; ages 4-17, $1. VI. Phone (613) 342-4397.

FULFORD PLACE, 287 King St. E., gives visitors a glimpse of the gracious and luxurious style of living of the newly rich at the beginning of the 20th century. This Edwardian mansion displays interesting architectural details as well as furnishings collected during the family's grand tours of the world. A summer tea room is available. Special events are held throughout the year.

Allow 1 hour minimum. Guided 45-minute tours depart as needed Tues.-Sun. 11-4, June 1-Labour Day weekend; Sat.-Sun. 11-4 (also Tues. and Thurs. at 1:30), rest of year. Closed Dec. 24-26. Last tour departs 1 hour before closing. Admission $5; over 64 and ages 6-18, $4; family rate (four persons)

$14. Narration in French is available by advance reservation. MC, VI. Phone (613) 498-3003.

BRUCE MINES (E-5) pop. 627

Situated on Hwy. 17 about 60 kilometres (37 mi.) east of Sault Ste. Marie, Bruce Mines, founded in 1846, was named after the first Governor General of Canada, James Bruce, the eighth Earl of Elgin. The first settlers were Cornish miners whose determination made the site the first successful copper mine in Canada. The town offers waterfront parks and opportunities for bicycling, boating, fishing, hiking, cross-country skiing and snowmobiling.

The full-service marina can accommodate up to 40 vessels May through September; phone (705) 785-3201, or (705) 785-3493 in the off-season.

The Corporation of the Town of Bruce Mines: 9180 Hwy. 17, P.O. Box 220, Bruce Mines, ON, Canada P0R 1C0; phone (705) 785-3493.

Self-guiding tours: Information about a self-guiding walking tour of the town is available at the Bruce Mines Museum.

BRUCE MINES MUSEUM is in the Presbyterian Church on the Rock on Hwy. 17. The church was built in 1894. The museum, which reflects the heritage of the area's Cornish settlers, displays pioneer furnishings, a Victorian dollhouse owned by the daughter of the ninth Marquess of Queensberry; a 1911 sailing canoe; an 1876 slot machine music box; an 1870s puddingstone vase; a 1905 Edison gramophone; and geological and agricultural displays. Archives also are available.

Note: The museum is temporarily closed; reopening is expected during 2005. Phone ahead to verify status and hours. Daily 10-5, July-Aug.; Mon.-Fri. 10-5, in June and Sept.; otherwise by appointment. Admission $3; over 64, $2; students with ID $1; family rate $6. VI. Phone (705) 785-3426, or (705) 785-3493 in the off-season.

SIMPSON COPPER MINESHAFT, on Hwy. 17 across from the Bruce Mines Museum, provides guided 30-minute tours of a restored pre-steam mineshaft. Displays include photographs and documents; mining equipment, including a horse-powered hoisting machine (horse whim); rocks; 1840s geology books; and replicas of the original 1848 mine office.

Note: The mine is currently closed; reopening is expected during 2005. Phone ahead to verify status and hours. Allow 30 minutes minimum. Tours depart every half-hour daily 10-5, July-Aug.; by appointment May-June and in Sept. Last tour leaves 30 minutes before closing. Admission $3; over 64, $2; students with ID $1; family rate $6. Phone (705) 785-3080, or (705) 785-3493 in the off-season.

BRUCE PENINSULA NATIONAL PARK (F-7)

Elevations in the park range from 177 metres (575 ft.) at Lake Huron to 221 metres (725 ft.) at Cyprus Lake. Refer to CAA/AAA maps for additional elevation information.

Along both sides of the Bruce Peninsula, the park encompasses 155 square kilometres (60 sq. mi.). Bruce Peninsula National Park preserves one of the last remaining wild areas in southwestern Ontario; it is the core of the Niagara Escarpment World Biosphere Reserve. The backbone of the park is a portion of the Niagara Escarpment, a 725-kilometre (451-mi.) ridge that extends from Queenston Heights on the Niagara River to Tobermory.

The waters of Georgian Bay have carved the escarpment into a spectacular series of overhanging cliffs and caves that form the park's eastern border. At the western edge of the peninsula the park assumes a different face as the terrain slides gently into Lake Huron in a series of marshlands, shallow inlets and sand dunes.

Between the rocky headlands of Georgian Bay and the gentler strand along Lake Huron are a diversity of habitats—cedar swamps, woodlands and rocky barrens. It is this diversity that nurtures the peninsula's rare abundance of orchids, one of the finest displays in eastern North America. About 40 species are found, along with wildflowers and ferns.

Traversing the park is the Bruce Trail, which weaves its way through cedar and birch forest as it skirts the cliffs along Georgian Bay. Trails from the Cyprus Lake area, that begin near the park's major campground, intersect with the Bruce Trail at several places.

Some of the geological highlights along these trails include bioherms, or ancient coral reefs, and the dramatic, sculpted features of Indian Head Cove and Natural Arch along the bay. Close viewing might uncover such orchid varieties as rattlesnake plantain and ladies' tresses, or the fossilized remains of corals, shellfish and other sea creatures.

Summer recreational opportunities include camping, picnicking, hiking, swimming, fishing, canoeing and kayaking; winter activities are snowshoeing, snowmobiling and cross-country skiing.

The park is open all year. A camping office is open daily 8 a.m.-midnight, June-Aug.; 8:30-5, rest of year. Admission $7.50 per private vehicle. For more information write the Superintendent's Office, Bruce Peninsula National Park, P.O. Box 189, Tobermory, ON, Canada N0H 2R0; phone (519) 596-2233 for information, or (519) 596-2263 for camping reservations. *See Recreation Chart.*

BURLEIGH FALLS (F-9)

STONY LAKE CRUISES, 7 km (4 mi.) n. on Hwy. 28, then 3 km (1.9 mi.) e. on Mt. Julian/Viamede

Rd., offers 2-hour narrated historical and sightseeing cruises on Lower Stony Lake and Clear Lake aboard the *Chippewa II*, a 133-passenger replica of a steamboat. Four-hour buffet dinner/dance cruises also are available.

Food is available. Departures require a minimum of 20 persons. Cruises depart Tues.-Sun. at 1, July 1-Labour Day; Sat.-Sun. at 1, early May-June 30 and day after Labour Day-second Mon. in Oct. Schedule may vary; phone ahead. Sightseeing fare $14; ages 2-9, $7.50. Reservations are required for dinner cruise and advised for sightseeing cruise. MC, VI. Phone (705) 654-5253.

BURLINGTON (G-4) pop. 150,836

In 1784 Mohawk chief Joseph Brant (known as Thayendanegea) was granted 1,441 hectares (3,561 acres) of land in what is now Burlington in repayment for his military support of the British during the American Revolutionary War. Burlington, on the shores of Lake Ontario, is midway between Toronto and Niagara Falls. The city is notable for its waterfront park, gardens, shopping and dining as well as its wide variety of architectural styles. Double-decker buses offer sightseeing opportunities.

During a guided tour visitors can view the operations of the Crossroads Centre Christian broadcast facility at 1295 N. Service Rd. or join the studio audience; phone (905) 335-7100, ext. 1281 for information.

Tourism Burlington: 414 Locust St., Burlington, ON, Canada L7S 1T7; phone (905) 634-5594 or (877) 499-9989.

Self-guiding tours: Information about walking tours of the historic downtown, the guide to Lake Ontario's Waterfront Trail and local attraction information are available at Tourism Burlington.

DID YOU KNOW

?

Ontario has about 250,000 lakes.

Shopping areas: Burlington Mall, 777 Guelph Line at Fairview, has The Bay and Zeller's. Mapleview Shopping Centre, 900 Maple at Fairview, has The Bay and Sears as anchor stores. Village Square, a turn-of-the-20th-century-style complex at 422 Pearl St., has specialty shops and restaurants.

BURLINGTON ART CENTRE, 1333 Lakeshore Rd., contains changing exhibits of paintings, photography, sculpture, pottery and textile art. The center is more than an art gallery, as it presents approximately 20 exhibitions per year and is home to seven guilds whose members work on site.

One of the largest public art galleries in Ontario, it holds a permanent collection of Canadian contemporary ceramic art. Allow 30 minutes minimum. Mon.-Thurs. 8:30 a.m.-10 p.m., Fri.-Sat. 9-5, Sun. noon-5; closed most holidays. Free. Phone (905) 632-7796.

SAVE IRELAND HOUSE AT OAKRIDGE FARM is n. of Upper Middle Rd. at 2168 Guelph Line. This living history museum portrays the life of the Ireland family 1835-1920. The house has been carefully restored and furnished to represent different periods. Allow 30 minutes minimum. Tues.-Fri. 10-4:30, Sun. 1-4:30; closed holidays. Hours may vary; phone ahead. Admission $3.25; over 64 and ages 13-18, $3; ages 5-12, $2. Phone (905) 332-9888.

SAVE JOSEPH BRANT MUSEUM, 1240 North Shore Blvd. E., is a replica of Joseph Brant's original house that was built in 1800. The museum, built 1937-38, contains Brant's personal possessions, artifacts and artwork relating to the history of Burlington and one of the finest costume and accessories collections in the province.

Tues.-Fri. 10-4:30, Sun. 1-4:30; closed holidays. Hours may vary; phone ahead. Admission $3.25; over 64 and students with ID $3; ages 5-12, $2. Phone (905) 634-3556.

GEM ROYAL BOTANICAL GARDENS, at 680 Plains Rd. W., covers more than 1,092 hectares (2,700 acres) on the great sweep of the Niagara Escarpment around the western tip of Lake Ontario. This living museum offers what is believed to be the world's largest lilac collection; more than 100,000 spring flowering bulbs; 250,000 iris blooms; 3,000 rose bushes; 30 kilometres (18 mi.) of walking trails; and Cootes Paradise, home of one of the continent's largest wetland restoration projects.

The gardens offer themed botanical displays, while protecting a wilderness of high cliffs, deep ravines and shimmering wetlands—successfully melding untamed and cultivated landscapes. RBG Centre has information about the gardens, trails and peak bloom times. The Nature Interpretive Centre is in the arboretum. A shuttle bus provides access to the various garden areas.

Picnicking is permitted. Food is available. RBG Centre open daily 9-dusk, interpretive center daily 10-4, year-round. Mediterranean Garden open daily

9-5, year-round. Outdoor gardens open daily 9:30-dusk, May-Oct. Closed Jan. 1 and Dec. 25. Phone ahead to confirm schedule. Admission $15; senior citizens, students with ID and ages 13-18, $12; ages 5-12, $3; family rate (two adults and two children) $35. Parking $1 per hour. JC, MC, VI. Phone (905) 527-1158.

CAMBRIDGE (G-3) pop. 110,372

The city of Cambridge was created in 1973 by the amalgamation of the villages of Blair and Preston and the towns of Galt and Hespeler. The Grand and Speed rivers, which wind through Cambridge, supplied power for the mills built on the banks. The city has retained much of its 19th-century architecture.

Today scenic recreation trails wind throughout the city and along the banks of the Grand River, including a 10.5-kilometre (7 mi.) stretch of the Trans Canada Trail; opportunities exist for canoeing, bicycling, horseback riding, hiking, fishing and bird-watching. A number of factory outlets are on former mill premises.

Cambridge Tourism: 750 Hespeler Rd., Cambridge, ON, Canada N3H 5L8; phone (519) 622-2336 or (800) 749-7560.

Shopping areas: Southworks Outlet Mall, at 64 Grand Ave. S., is in a 150-year-old limestone foundry. Among the mall's discount shops are Black & Decker and Corning.

AFRICAN LION SAFARI, 4 km (2.5 mi.) s. via Hwy. 8 following signs to Safari Rd., has more than 1,000 exotic birds and animals, including lions, tigers, zebras, monkeys, giraffes and rhinoceroses, roaming freely in a 303-hectare (750-acre) drive-through park. Among the denizens of the North American reserve section are bison, elk and deer.

Other highlights include the Elephant Swim, Birds of Prey Conservation Centre with its breeding and rehabilitation facilities, Pets' Corner, *African Queen* boat tour, a scenic railway tour, three bird and animal shows, Jungle Playground and Misumu Bay Wet Play.

Visitors may drive their own cars along the 10-kilometre (6-mi.) trail or take the guided safari tour bus for an additional fee. If driving, visitors must remain in their cars with doors and windows closed; convertibles are prohibited.

Height restrictions may apply in some childrens' areas. Picnic areas and food are available. Pets are not allowed anywhere on the grounds. Allow 5 hours minimum. Admittance daily 10-5:30, late June-Labour Day; Mon.-Fri. 10-4, Sat.-Sun. 10-5, late Apr.-late June; daily 10-4, day after Labour Day to mid-Oct. Grounds open until 7:30 p.m.

Admission late June-Labour Day $24.95; over 60, $21.95; ages 3-12, $19.95. Admission remainder of season $20.95; over 60, $17.95; ages 3-12, $15.95. Tour bus $4.95; over 60 and ages 3-12, $4.75. MC, VI. Phone (519) 623-2620, or (800) 461-9453 in Canada, Mich., N.Y., Ohio and Pa. *See color ad.*

WINGS OF PARADISE is 11 km (7 mi.) n. off Hwy. 401 exit 282 (Hespeler Rd.), then 6 km (4 mi.) w. to 2500 Kossuth Rd., following signs. More than 1,000 free-flying butterflies can be seen in a walk-through tropical conservatory complete with brooks and waterfalls. The conservatory also houses close to 75 species of flowering plants and trees. A museum features rare species of butterflies, moths, insects and an observational beehive. Nature trails beckon during summer and fall (weather permitting).

African Lion Safari®
Canada's Original Safari Adventure!™

- Drive through large Game Reserves
- Thrill to exciting bird and animal shows
- Enjoy a cruise on the "African Queen" boat
- Relax aboard the "Nature Boy" scenic railway
- Misumu Bay Wet Play Area (Seasonal. Height Restrictions Apply.)
- Jungle Playground, Pets' Corner, Elephant Swim
- Family Hotel Packages Available
  (No pets permitted on property. All events weather permitting).

CAA/AAA Members receive admission discount

Get close to over 1,000 exotic birds & animals!

April 30 to October 10, 2005
Call 1-800-461-WILD (9453)
Located on Safari Road between Highways 6 and 8, North of Hamilton, RR1 Cambridge, Ontario Canada N1R 5S2 • (519) 623-2620

www.lionsafari.com

Picnicking is permitted. Food is available. Allow 1 hour minimum. Daily 10-5; closed Jan. 1 and Dec. 24-26. Last admission is 1 hour before closing. Admission $7.75; over 65 and ages 13-17, $7.50; ages 3-12, $4. MC, VI. Phone (519) 653-1234.

CAMPBELLFORD (F-10) pop. 3,675

Named for an officer who fought in the Crimean War, Campbellford serves as the center of a rich dairying district. Ferris Provincial Park is on the outskirts of town *(see Recreation Chart and the AAA/CAA Eastern Canada CampBook).*

Fish and game abound in the region. The Rotary Trail, a 3.5-kilometre (2-mi.) walk, takes hikers around the Trent-Severn Canal. Boats can dock overnight at Old Mill Park on the Trent River. A series of three locks on the Trent Canal, 13 kilometres (8 mi.) north of town, bypass Healy Falls.

The Westben Arts Festival Theatre, 2 kilometres (1.2 mi.) north, presents concerts and musical plays in a reconstructed barn; phone (705) 653-5508, or (877) 883-5777 in Ontario and Québec. Local produce can be found at a farmers' market held on Wednesdays and Saturdays, May through October; the location of the market is the Canadian Tire parking lot on Grand Road.

Campbellford-Seymour Chamber of Commerce: Old Mill Park on Grand Road, P.O. Box 376, Campbellford, ON, Canada K0L 1L0; phone (705) 653-1551 or (888) 653-1556.

Self-guiding tours: Information about a walking tour of Campbellford featuring 11 heritage sites is available from the chamber of commerce.

CAMPBELLVILLE (G-3)

MOUNTSBERG WILDLIFE CENTRE, Hwy. 401 exit 312 to Guelph Line S., following signs, is a 472-hectare (1,166-acre) conservation area with an interpretive center and hiking, mountain biking and nature trails. Weekends and holidays the Douglas G. Cockburn Birds of Prey Centre offers live bird presentations. Maple syrup demonstrations are presented in March and April. Fishing, cross-country skiing and ice skating are available, as are wagon and sleigh rides.

Picnicking is permitted. Park open daily dawn-dusk. Center open daily 9-4. Admission $4.50; over 64, $3.50; ages 5-14, $3.25. Phone (905) 854-2276. *See Recreation Chart.*

CANNINGTON (F-9)
pop. 2,007, elev. 257 m/843'

CANNINGTON CENTENNIAL MUSEUM is at 80 Peace St. in MacLeod Park. Five buildings from the 1840s to the 1930s—two mid-19th-century log cabins, a community hall, a train station and a driving shed—feature changing exhibits depicting life in rural Ontario. A highlight is a loom brought from Ireland by a pioneer family.

Picnicking is permitted. Allow 30 minutes minimum. Thurs.-Sun. and Mon. holidays 1-4, July 1-Labour Day; Sat.-Sun. and Mon. holidays 1-4, Victoria Day weekend-June 30. Donations. Phone (705) 432-3136, or (705) 432-2139 in the off-season.

CAYUGA (H-3) pop. 1,643

[SAVE] **RUTHVEN PARK,** 243 Hwy. 54, is a 19th-century Greek Revival mansion overlooking the Grand River. An ongoing preservation project, including active conservation and archeological research, allows visitors to see how life changed for the five generations of the Thompson family who lived here 1845-1993. Nature trails and forests offer opportunities for hiking, bird-watching and picnicking on the estate's 607 hectares (1,500 acres).

Allow 1 hour minimum. Mansion tours are given Wed.-Sun. on the hour 11-4, June 1-Labour Day; Thurs. 1-4, rest of year. Last tour begins at closing. Grounds open daily dawn-dusk. Admission $5; over 64, $4; students with ID $2.50; ages 6-12, $2; family rate $10. VI. Phone (905) 772-0560.

CHALK RIVER (E-9) pop. 975

Settled in the mid-1800s, Chalk River was named for a tributary of the Ottawa River. Lumber, pulp and paper mills as well as the Canada Central Railway and farming sustained the town's economy until 1945, when the first nuclear reactor outside the United States began operation nearby. The village is presently known as one of the world's foremost research centers in the field of nuclear energy.

CHATHAM (I-6) pop. 44,156, elev. 101 m/331'

Chatham figured prominently in many of Ontario's major historical events. Chief Tecumseh, with General Proctor and his Imperial Army, made a stand in the city in their retreat from Detroit. Sunken British gunboats have been discovered in the area—the remains of a skirmish of the War of 1812. Chatham also was a terminus of the Underground Railroad, which allowed about 5,000 fugitive slaves to escape to Canada 1850-61.

Events include the Festival of Nations, a multi-day event taking place around the July 1 holiday, and the Tartan Sertoma Supreme Highland Games in mid-July, which features competition between pipers, drummers, dancers and athletes. Recreation activities include bird-watching, water sports, fishing, hiking and hunting.

Chatham-Kent Tourism—Chatham: 445 Grand Ave. W., P.O. Box 944, Chatham, ON, Canada N7M 5L3; phone (519) 354-6125 or (800) 561-6125.

CHATHAM CULTURAL CENTRE, 75 William St. N., includes an art gallery, a historical museum and 700-seat theater. The gallery displays changing exhibits of works by various artists, and the theater presents a variety of plays and concerts. Allow 30 minutes minimum. Daily 1-5; closed Jan. 1, Good

Friday and Dec. 25. Donations. Phone (519) 360-1998 for information, or (519) 354-8338 or (866) 807-7770 for show and concert tickets.

Chatham-Kent Museum, in the Chatham Cultural Centre, has five galleries highlighting the history of Chatham. Changing exhibits also are presented. Allow 30 minutes minimum.

MILNER HOUSE is across from Tecumseh Park at 59 William St. N. This Queen Anne-style residence was built by Scottish immigrant Robert Milner and his wife Emma in 1894. The home of the successful buggy and sleigh manufacturer has been restored to its 1905 appearance. Costumed guides provide insight into the period furnishings, art and "modern" kitchen appliances.

The second floor features an exhibit of mounted animals and birds. Allow 30 minutes minimum. Daily 1-5, Victoria Day weekend-Labour Day. Donations. Phone (519) 360-1998 or (519) 354-8338.

WILD ZONE ADVENTURES, 567 Richmond St., is an indoor amusement park with a roller coaster, a Ferris wheel, a flying bus, amusement rides, miniature golf, laser tag, video games and bowling. Outdoor rides and attractions also are available. Amusement park open daily. Hours for attractions vary; phone ahead. Single ticket prices start at 70c. Passports start at $27.50. Multi-tickets are required for some rides. Height restrictions may apply. AX, MC, VI. Phone (519) 436-5504 or (888) 467-9453.

CLINTON (F-1) pop. 7,806, elev. 285 m/935′

SCHOOL ON WHEELS, just off jct. Hwys. 4 and 8, following signs to 76 Victoria Terr. in Sloman Memorial Park, is the only one left of seven such CNR rail cars used to reach and teach children and adults living in isolated areas of northern Canada. Fred Sloman, one of the teachers, lived and traveled in this railway car 1926-65; his family lived with him for much of this time. Visitors see the schoolroom section as well as the living quarters in the renovated train car. A video about the car's history is shown.

Allow 30 minutes minimum. Thurs.-Fri. 2-5, Sat.-Sun. and holidays 1-5, Victoria Day weekend-Labour Day; by appointment rest of year. Donations. Phone (519) 482-3997 from 8:30-4:30.

CLOYNE (F-10)

BON ECHO PROVINCIAL PARK BOAT TOURS is 10 km (6 mi.) n. on Hwy. 41 in Bon Echo Provincial Park. The 27-passenger *Wanderer Too* provides 45-minute scenic cruises through Upper Mazinaw Lake. Narration provides information about Bon Echo Rock that rises 91 metres (300 ft.) above the water and about some of the 260 Algonkian pictographs painted on it. Also on the rock is a memorial to poet Walt Whitman, carved by Scottish stonemasons.

Departures daily at 11:30, 1, 2, 3 and 4 (also Wed. and Sat. at 6 p.m.), July-Aug. Fare $5; under

12, $3. Reservations are recommended. Park admission $9.50 per private vehicle. AX, MC, VI. Phone (613) 336-9863. *See Recreation Chart.*

COBALT (C-8) pop. 1,229

According to legend, one night in the fall of 1903, blacksmith Fred LaRose threw a hammer at the gleaming eyes of a fox, which turned out instead to be the glimmer of one of the world's richest silver veins. In 10 years the mines yielded some $300 million in silver, and Cobalt's population shot up to 30,000. The Great Depression ended the boom, however, and the mines did not reopen until the 1950s. Miners then began digging for cobalt, the town's namesake, in addition to silver. Originally discarded as waste, cobalt was found to be important for use in medical and military products.

[SAVE] **COBALT MINING MUSEUM,** 24 Silver St., traces the area's silver mining history. The prospector's Hall of Fame depicts an early prospector's camp, and a native silver display is said to be one of the world's finest. Tunnels carved out by early miners can be seen on an underground mine tour. The Heritage Silver Trail, a 6-kilometre (4-mi.) self-guiding driving tour, provides insights into early 20th century mining sites; a 2-hour guided trail tour also is available.

Museum daily 9-5, June-Sept.; Mon.-Fri. 1-4, rest of year. Underground mine tour departs daily at 9, 10, 11, 1, 2, 3 and 4, July-Aug.; otherwise by appointment. Museum admission $3.25; over 64, $2.75; students with ID $2.25; family rate $8.25. Underground mine tour $5. Silver trail tour $10, family rate $30. MC, VI. Phone (705) 679-8301.

COBDEN (E-10)

On June 6, 1613, French explorer Samuel de Champlain lost his astrolabe, an instrument used to determine the altitude of celestial bodies. In 1857 the 13-centimetre (5-in.) tool was found by a boy digging at the present site of Logos Land Resort. A sign on Hwy. 17 recounts the story of the astrolabe. Homecoming, a celebration in honor of the astrolabe, is held every decade when the instrument is returned to Cobden from its place at the Canadian Museum of Civilization in Hull, Québec *(see attraction listing p. 150).*

LOGOS LAND RESORT, 4 km (2.5 mi.) e. on Hwy. 17, features waterslides, two water trampolines, pedal boats, miniature golf, two mini and three giant waterslides, a lake and a playground. Nature trails and camping facilities are available. Daily 10-7, late June-early Aug.; daily 10-6, mid-June to late June and early Aug.; daily 11-6, mid-Aug. to late Aug.; Sat.-Sun. 11-6, early June to mid-June. Day pass for all activities $16; ages 3-5, $13. AX, DS, MC, VI. Phone (613) 646-9765 or (877) 816-6605.

COBOURG (G-9) pop. 17,172, elev. 91 m/299′

Cobourg, situated on a sandy stretch of Lake Ontario with the rolling hills of Northumberland as a backdrop, was founded in 1798 by United Empire Loyalists. By 1900 Cobourg was the most popular summer resort in Canada, with more than 2,000 summer residents. Many built homes here, some on a palatial scale. Cobourg continues to be a popular tourist destination.

The Economic Development and Tourism Information Centre's offices are in the house in which 1920s film star Marie Dressler was born. The offices contain Dressler memorabilia and life-size wax figures of Miss Dressler and co-star Wallace Beery.

A farmers' market featuring locally grown produce operates on Saturday from May through December; for information phone (905) 372-4881.

Cobourg Tourism: 212 King St. W., Cobourg, ON, Canada K9A 2N1; phone (905) 372-5481 or (888) 262-6874.

VICTORIA HALL is at 55 King St. W. The exterior of this imposing 1860 three-story building has Corinthian columns, a speaker's balcony and is decorated with carved symbols of the British Isles such as lyres, dolphins and shells. The deep-well courtroom, patterned after London's "Old Bailey," has been seen in films and television shows. The Art Gallery of Northumberland features changing exhibits with an emphasis on Canadian art.

Allow 1 hour minimum for Victoria Hall, 30 minutes minimum for the art gallery. Hall open Mon.-Fri. 8:30-4; closed provincial holidays and during special events. Guided tours Mon.-Fri. at noon, July-Aug. Art gallery open Tues.-Fri. 10-4, Sat. 1-5 (also Sun. 1-4, June-Aug.); closed Good Friday and Dec. 25-26. Hall free. Art gallery by donations. Phone (905) 372-5481 or (888) 262-6874 for the hall or (905) 372-0333 for the art gallery.

VICTORIA PARK, on the shores of Lake Ontario, is a 10-hectare (25-acre) recreational area with a white sand beach and marina facilities, an outdoor swimming pool and a children's splash pool, lawn bowling, miniature golf, a playground, baseball diamond, a rose garden and a floral clock. A 3.2-kilometre (2-mi.) brick promenade links the beach, campground and Heritage Harbour.

The Cobourg Royal Marine Concert Band gives summer concerts. Food and picnic tables are available. Band concerts Tues. at 8 p.m., July-Aug. Free. Phone (905) 372-5481 or (888) 262-6874.

COCHRANE (B-6) pop. 5,690

Cochrane functions as an outfitting center for hunting, fishing, snowmobiling and nature excursions into the northern wilderness and Hudson Bay region. Destroyed by fire two times 1910-16, the town has developed into a lumbering and rail center.

Economically, the railways have been the lifeblood of Cochrane since its founding at the turn of the 20th century. The Ontario Northland Railway connects it with Moosonee (see place listing p. 101), an isolated town in the roadless region near the Arctic tidewaters at James Bay as well as linking it with other cities bordering the northern wilderness.

COCHRANE RAILWAY AND PIONEER MUSEUM, 210 Railway St., n.e. of Cochrane Union Station, is in a locomotive, caboose, baggage car and coach complex. Exhibits include a trapper's cabin, photographs, a log cabin, furniture, wooden implements, a model train, railway equipment, documents and Indian crafts.

One coach is dedicated to hockey legend Tim Horton, who was born in Cochrane. Daily 8:30-8, mid-June through Labour Day. Admission $2; students with ID $1.50; over 59, $1; family rate $5. Phone (705) 272-4361.

POLAR BEAR EXPRESS departs the Ontario Northland Station, e. of Hwy. 11 on Railway St., for a 4.5-hour train trip to Moosonee (see place listing p. 101), about 300 kilometres (186 mi.) north. Other than traveling by air, foot or canoe, the express is the only way to explore this wilderness area.

Food is available. Trains leave Cochrane Tues.-Sun. at 8:30 a.m. and depart Moosonee at 6 p.m., late June-Labour Day. Round trip $95.99; over 59, $86.40; students with ID $81.60; ages 2-11, $48; family rate (parents and four dependent children under 22) $336. Reservations are recommended. AX, MC, VI. Phone (705) 472-4500 or (800) 268-9281.

COLDWATER (F-8)

COLDWATER CANADIANA HERITAGE MUSEUM, off Hwy. 12 at 1474 Woodrow Rd., is a restored 1840's log house on its original site. Exhibits include pottery and china as well as period rooms. Adjacent buildings include printing and blacksmith shops, a carriage house, a barn, a garage with two vintage fire trucks, and a railroad flagging station. Devon tea and craft demonstrations are available in summer.

Picnic facilities are available. Allow 30 minutes minimum. Tues.-Sat. 10-5, Sun. 1-5, July-Aug.; Sat. 10-5, Sun. 1-5, Victoria Day weekend-June 30 and Sept. 1-second Mon. in Oct. Tea and craft demonstrations Wed. 1-4, July-Aug. Admission $2; ages 2-12, $1; family rate (four persons) $5. Admission including Devon tea $5; ages 5-12, $2.75. Phone (705) 835-5032.

COLLINGWOOD (G-8) pop. 16,039

On the shore of Georgian Bay and at the foot of Blue Mountain—the highest section of the Niagara Escarpment—Collingwood is the center of Ontario's largest ski area. Winter activities also include snowmobiling and snowshoeing, while bicycling, hiking, fishing, boating and canoeing can be enjoyed in summer.

The town is home to Blue Mountain Pottery '87 Inc. Factory tours are available at the plant at 2 Old Mountain Rd. (Hwy. 26); phone (705) 445-3000 or

(877) 445-7776. The Gayety Theatre, 161 Hurontario St., offers year-round entertainment and is the venue for professional summer theater productions staged by Theatre Collingwood; phone (705) 445-2200 or (866) 382-2200. The theater can be reached at (705) 444-9255.

Georgian Triangle Tourist Association and Tourist Information Centre: 30 Mountain Rd., Collingwood, ON, Canada L9Y 5H7; phone (705) 445-7722 or (888) 227-8667.

BYGONE DAYS HERITAGE VILLAGE, 879 6th St., is a collection of 29 pioneer buildings and artifacts from the mid-19th century. Guided 2- to 3-hour tours provide insights into period lifestyles. Highlights include a barn with carriages and sleds, pioneer houses, a schoolhouse, church, harness shop and tractors. Special events are held throughout the season. Guests can fish in a stocked pond (bring your own rod and bait).

Allow 2 hours minimum. Guided tours are given daily 10-4, May-Oct. Last tour begins 1 hour before closing. Admission $10; over 64 and ages 12-18, $7; ages 6-11, $5; family rate (four persons) $25. Fishing $5. Phone (705) 445-4316.

THE CANDY FACTORY, 645 Hurontario St. (CR 124) opposite Collingwood Collegiate Institute, has a viewing area from which chocolate and candy making operations can be observed. Old candy making equipment and pictures also are displayed. Mon.-Fri. 9-8, Sat.-Sun. and holidays 10-8, July-Aug.; Mon.-Fri. 9-5:30, Sat.-Sun. 10-5:30, Sept.-Dec.; Mon.-Fri. 9-5:30, Sat. 10-5:30, Sun. 11:30-5:30, rest of year. Closed Jan. 1, Easter and Dec. 25-26. Free. Phone (705) 445-2400..

COLLINGWOOD MUSEUM, 45 St. Paul St. at Hwy. 26, is in The Station, a reconstruction of an 1873 Grand Trunk Rail Station. Visitors can view exhibits about community history. Mon.-Sat. 9-5, Sun. noon-5, holidays 1-5, Victoria Day weekend-second Mon. in Oct.; Mon.-Tues. and Fri.-Sat. 9-5, Sun. noon-5, rest of year. Closed Jan. 1, Good Friday and Dec. 25-26. Donations. Phone (705) 445-4811 to verify schedule.

SCENIC CAVES NATURE ADVENTURES, 6 km (4 mi.) n. on Blue Mountain Rd., then 3 km (1.9 mi.) w. on Scenic Caves Rd., overlooks the town and Nottawasaga Bay and offers a panorama of the Niagara Escarpment. Visitors can view the large, standing rock on the former site of a Huron Indian village—*Ekarenniondi*—and visit the Ice Cave and Fat Man's Misery, both carved by glaciers millions of years ago. Rare and exotic plants, including maidenhair fern also are featured.

A 126-metre-long (413-foot) suspension bridge extends over the valley floor. Other facilities include a trout pond, a miniature golf course, gemstone mining, a playground and winter recreational activities. A guided ecoadventure tour featuring treetop walking and zip cable gliding is available seasonally.

The ecoadventure tour involves stairs and steep paths; running/hiking shoes are required. Pets are not permitted. Picnic facilities and food are available. Self-guiding tours daily 9-7, late June-Labour Day; 10-5, early May-late June and day after Labour Day to mid-Oct. (weather permitting). Winter recreational activities are available daily 10-5 rest of year. Last admission 2 hours before closing.

Cave and bridge $17; over 64, $15; ages 5-17, $13. Miniature golf $4.50; ages 5-17, $4. An additional fee is charged for mining, ecoadventure tour and winter activities. Reservations are required for the guided tours. AX, MC, VI. Phone (705) 446-0256.

RECREATIONAL ACTIVITIES
Skiing

- **Blue Mountain Resorts** is 11 km (7 mi.) w. off Hwy. 26, R.R. #3, Collingwood, ON, Canada L9Y 3Z2. Other activities are offered. Daily mid-Dec. to late Mar. Phone (705) 445-0231 or (416) 869-3799.

CORNWALL (E-12)
pop. 45,640, elev. 59 m/194′

Named in 1797 after Prince George, Duke of Cornwall, Cornwall is the headquarters of the St. Lawrence Seaway Authority. One of the city's cotton mills was among the first factories to be equipped with electric lighting by Thomas Edison. The Seaway International Bridge linking the United States and Canada crosses Cornwall Island, part of the city.

A dozen outdoor heritage murals in the downtown area and in the Le Village Shopping District have been painted by artists from throughout North America. A map showing the location of each of these murals is available at the Cornwall & Seaway Valley Tourism Office, Pitt and First streets.

Cornwall Chamber of Commerce: 113 Second St. E., P.O. Box 338, Cornwall, ON, Canada K6H 1Y5; phone (613) 933-4004.

Self-guiding tours: A brochure describing a recreational path for bicycling and walking along the scenic St. Lawrence River between Cornwall and the migratory bird sanctuary near Ingleside (*see place listing p. 84*) is available from Cornwall and Seaway Valley Tourism, 100 Pitt St., Cornwall, ON, Canada K6J 3P4; phone (800) 937-4748.

RONATAHON:NI CULTURAL EDUCATION CENTRE is riverside just n. of the Canadian Customs Building. The culture of the Iroquois, Cree and Ojibway First Nations tribes is depicted through artifacts, a replica village and a gallery with artwork by local Mohawk artists. Picnicking is permitted. Allow 30 minutes minimum. Mon.-Fri. 8-8, Sat.-Sun. 11-4, July-Aug.; Mon.-Fri. 8-4, rest of year. Closed major holidays. Admission $3; over 65 and students with ID $2; under 12, $1. Phone (613) 932-9452.

CREEMORE (G-8) pop. 1,317

CREEMORE SPRINGS BREWERY, 139 Mill St., offers a tour of the brewery, which produces premium lagers, and an explanation of the brewing process. Complimentary samples are offered. Allow 30 minutes minimum. Guided tours are given daily on the hour 1-4; closed Jan. 1, Good Friday, Easter and Dec. 25. Free. Phone (705) 466-2240 or (800) 267-2240.

DELHI (I-2) pop. 4,002

In an area where French missionaries first landed in 1669, Delhi is known as the tobacco capital of Canada. Almost half of the flue-cured tobacco grown in Ontario is produced in this town.

DELHI ONTARIO TOBACCO MUSEUM AND HERITAGE CENTRE, 200 Talbot Rd. (Hwy. 3), displays equipment and tools that document the history and technology of tobacco growing and curing from Indian times to the present. Displays include a streetscape of the former township of Delhi and multicultural exhibits. A 20-minute videotape describes the growing, marketing, processing and manufacturing of tobacco.

Allow 30 minutes minimum. Mon.-Fri. 10-4:30, Sat.-Sun. and holiday Mon. 1-4, Victoria Day-Labour Day; Mon.-Fri. 10-4:30, rest of year. Closed holidays. Donations. A fee may be charged during special events and programs. Phone (519) 582-0278 to verify schedule.

DRESDEN (I-7) pop. 2,582

In the mid-1800s the Underground Railroad was a link between the slave fields in the American South and freedom in Canada. With the aid of Rev. Josiah Henson many fugitive slaves made this journey and settled in Dresden on an 81-hectare (200-acre) property purchased by Henson and a group of abolitionists. In 1841 Henson founded the British American Institute, a school and place of refuge for former slaves.

Born into slavery, Henson escaped from Kentucky in 1830 with his wife and children. After meeting Harriet Beecher Stowe in Boston, Henson became the model for the character of Uncle Tom in Stowe's novel "Uncle Tom's Cabin," published in 1852.

The Dresden Raceway, 1244 North St. (CR 21), offers live harness racing May through September; phone (519) 683-4466.

Note: Policies concerning admittance of children to pari-mutuel betting facilities vary. Phone for information.

Chatham-Kent Tourism—Dresden: 445 Grand Ave. W., P.O. Box 944, Chatham, ON, Canada N7M 5L3; phone (519) 354-6125 or (800) 561-6125.

UNCLE TOM'S CABIN HISTORIC SITE, 1.5 km (.9 mi.) w. off CR 21 and Park St. on Uncle Tom's Rd., includes Rev. Josiah Henson's home and other 19th-century buildings. The site has exhibits dealing with Henson's career and early Canadian black history. Henson's grave is next to the museum.

Picnicking is permitted. Mon.-Sat. 10-5, Sun. noon-5, July-Aug.; Wed.-Sat. and Mon. holidays 10-5, Sun. noon-5, Victoria Day weekend-June 30 and Sept. 1-second Mon. in Oct. Admission $6.25; over 64 and ages 13-17, $5.25; ages 6-12, $4.50; family rate (five persons) $20. AX, MC, VI. Phone (519) 683-2978, or (519) 862-2291 in the off-season.

DRYDEN (B-10) pop. 8,198

Dryden's natural resources offer opportunities for numerous outdoor recreational activities. Its forests are the source for the fiber that a pulp and paper mill uses to make white paper for worldwide distribution. Excellent fishing and hunting lure visitors to the region and its numerous lakes. The city's mascot, Maximillian Moose, is represented by a 5.5-metre-high (18-ft.) steel and concrete sculpture in front of the tourist information center.

Tourist Information Centre: 284 Government St., Dryden, ON, Canada P8N 2P3; phone (807) 223-2622 or (800) 667-0935.

DRYDEN AND DISTRICT MUSEUM, 15 Van Horne Ave., is housed in a late 19th-century house. Displays include some 10,000 artifacts shown on a rotating basis. Mon.-Sat. 9-5, May-Sept.; Mon.-Fri. 9-5, rest of year. Donations. Phone (807) 223-4671.

DUNVEGAN (E-12)

GLENGARRY PIONEER MUSEUM is at 1645 CR 30. Several historic buildings that depict rural life in mid-19th-century Ontario comprise the museum complex. The main building, built as a store in the 1840s, is furnished as the inn it became in the 1860s, complete with the original barroom. Other buildings include an 1869 town hall with area maps, documents and photographs; a livery shed; a cheese factory; blacksmith's shop; and log barn.

Picnicking is permitted. Allow 30 minutes minimum. Tues.-Sun. 1-5, July-Aug.; Sat.-Sun. and holiday Mon. 1-5, Victoria Day-June 30 and Labour Day-second Mon. in Oct. Admission $3, under 16 free. Phone (613) 527-5230.

DYER'S BAY (F-7)

CABOT HEAD LIGHTHOUSE AND HERITAGE BUILDING is off Hwy. 6 Dyer's Bay Rd. exit to the end of the road, then following signs on a gravel shore road to the entrance. The 1896 lighthouse houses a museum with historical exhibits about the lighthouse and the people who lived there. There also are nautical and boat displays and a nature room with information about indigenous birds and wildlife.

A walk to the top of the lighthouse offers scenic views. Nature trails also are available. Picnicking is permitted. Allow 30 minutes minimum. Daily dawn-dusk, Victoria Day weekend-second Mon. in Oct. Donations. Phone (519) 795-7780 or (800) 268-3838.

EGANVILLE (E-10) pop. 1,230

Eganville was named for John Egan, an Irish immigrant who became one of the most powerful lumber barons in the Ottawa Valley. Nearby lakes and rivers, including the Bonnechere River which divides Eganville, attract the summer vacation crowd.

BONNECHERE CAVES, 8 km (5 mi.) s.e. via Fourth Chute Rd., following signs, are twisting passages formed by water erosion in limestone believed to have been the bottom of a sea some 500 million years ago. Fossils of coral and aquatic creatures are imbedded in the cave walls. The caves are explored on 1-hour guided tours.

Wear flat shoes and a light sweater. Picnicking is permitted. Tours depart every 20 minutes daily 10-4:30, Victoria Day-Labour Day; Sat.-Sun. 10-4, day after Labour Day-second Mon. in Oct. Schedule may vary in Sept.; phone ahead. Last tour departs at closing. Admission $12; over 64, $11; ages 13-17, $9; ages 4-12, $8. MC, VI. Phone (613) 628-2283 or (800) 469-2283.

ELLIOT LAKE (D-6) pop. 11,956

Elliot Lake was born with the discovery of uranium deposits in 1954. Nestled within the Precambrian Shield on the edge of the boreal forest, the city boasts some of the most exceptional wilderness surroundings in North America. Its location on one of the hundreds of lakes in the area provides many recreational outlets, including rockhounding, camping, hiking, bicycling, boating, canoeing and sailing, golfing, curling, swimming, fishing and ice fishing, hunting, skiing and snowmobiling.

Nearby Mississagi Provincial Park *(see Recreation Chart and the AAA/CAA Eastern Canada CampBook)*, is an unspoiled natural environment park offering camping, hiking, swimming and canoeing. Sheriff Creek Sanctuary offers hiking trails along marshes and forested areas, with opportunities for bird-watching. Also, the Firetower Lookout on Milliken Mine Road offers a panoramic view of Elliot Lake, Manitoulin Island and the U.S. mainland. Picnic tables and hiking trails are available.

Elliot Lake Welcome Centre: Civic Centre, 225 Hwy. 108, Elliot Lake, ON, Canada P5A 2P1; phone (705) 461-7240 or (800) 661-6192.

Self-guiding tours: A brochure outlining a 120-kilometre (75-mi.) triangular scenic drive called the Deer Trail as well as maps for fishing, snowmobiling, canoeing and hiking are available from the welcome center.

ELLIOT LAKE NUCLEAR AND MINING MUSEUM, in the Lester B. Pearson Civic Centre on Hwy. 108, traces area history from the lumbering and trapping days through the discovery of uranium, going full circle through the mining, milling and uses of uranium to the closure of the industry. It houses the Northern Home of the Canadian Mining Hall of Fame.

The Mine Rescue exhibit, 35 miners' lamps dating from the 1890s, a minerals collection, geologists' tools and interactive exhibits are featured. Daily 9-7, Victoria Day weekend-Labour Day; Mon.-Fri. 9-5, Sat.-Sun. by appointment, rest of year. Closed Jan. 1, Good Friday, Easter Monday, second Mon. in Oct., Nov. 11 and Dec. 25-26. Admission $2.50; ages 3-16, $1; family rate $5.50. Phone (705) 848-2084.

ELMIRA (G-2) pop. 8,155

Elmira is set amid scenic rolling hills and fertile farm land. Early settlers included Mennonites from Pennsylvania; some of their descendants still use horses and carriages instead of motor vehicles.

The last of Ontario's covered bridges is in West Montrose, 10 kilometres (6 mi.) east of Elmira. The Kissing Bridge was built in 1881 at a cost of $3,100. Today the bridge is a popular subject for artists and photographers.

Township of Woolwich Visitor Information Centre: 5 First St. E., Elmira, ON, Canada N3B 2E3; phone (519) 669-2605 or (877) 969-0094.

Shopping areas: Downtown Elmira has many specialty shops featuring quilts, food, antiques, clothing, toys and other items; these shops are closed on Sunday.

ELMVALE (F-8) pop. 2,176

ELMVALE JUNGLE ZOO, on CR 27, 4 km (2.5 mi.) s. of jct. CR 92, exhibits more than 300 animals, birds and reptiles from around the world in natural surroundings. Included in the wildlife collection are lions, tigers, monkeys, cougars, jaguars, giraffes, rare and exotic birds, snakes and zebras. Animal, bird and reptile presentations are offered daily. Pony rides tempt small children, and a playground, petting zoo, walking trails are present.

Food and picnic facilities are available. Allow 1 hour, 30 minutes minimum. Daily 9:30-7, July 1-Labour Day; Mon.-Fri. 9:30-5, Sat.-Sun. and holidays 9:30-6, Victoria Day weekend-June 30; daily 10-5, day after Labour Day-second Mon. in Oct. (weather permitting). Animal presentations daily, Victoria Day weekend-Labour Day. Pony rides daily, July 1-Labour Day. Last admittance is 1 hour before closing. Admission $11.50; over 59 and ages 13-17, $9.50; ages 3-12, $5.95. Pony rides $3. MC, VI. Phone (705) 322-1112.

ELORA (G-2)

Elora is on the Grand River, where it meets the Irvine River and the Elora Gorge begins. The gorge, with its waterfall, begins in the village and extends 4 kilometres (2.5 mi.). The Grand River in the Elora area is popular for fly-fishing with anglers from eastern North America. Many of Elora's restored late 19th-century buildings are on the river and now contain craft and specialty shops and restaurants.

The legend of St. John's Anglican Church centers on its former pastor, the Rev. John Smithurst, Florence Nightingale's first cousin and true love. The church forbade their marriage, and so the two parted—she to the Crimean War and he to Elora. Neither ever married. The Nightingale communion set was sent to the pastor in 1852 by an anonymous donor—believed to have been Florence Nightingale.

Elora Information Centre: 152 Geddes St., P.O. Box 814, Elora, ON, Canada N0B 1S0; phone (519) 846-9841 or (877) 242-6353.

ELORA GORGE CONSERVATION AREA is just w. at 7400 CR 21. The park's 202 hectares (500 acres) include unusual rock formations, a lake and a limestone gorge. Camping, swimming and picnicking areas are available. Daily 8-dusk, May 1-Sun. after the second Mon. in Oct. Admission $3.75; ages 6-14, $2. Fee for camping. Phone (519) 846-9742. *See Recreation Chart.*

ENGLEHART (C-7) pop. 1,595

ENGLEHART AND AREA HISTORICAL MUSEUM, 67 Sixth Ave. in the 1909 schoolhouse, exhibits local historical memorabilia in settings that include a schoolroom, general store, post office and settler's homestead. The Industrial Heritage Gallery features homesteaders' tools and traces railway history dating from the auction of town lots in 1906. Exhibition rooms showcase art in changing exhibits.

Allow 30 minutes minimum. Tues.-Fri. 10-4, Sat.-Sun. noon-4, Mother's Day-Nov. 30; closed holidays. Admission $3.50; senior citizens $2; ages 13-17, $1. Phone (705) 544-2400.

ESPANOLA (E-6) pop. 5,449

DOMTAR INC., 79 Tudhope St., offers guided tours of the pulp and paper mill. The 2-hour tour demonstrates each step in the paper-making process as well as providing a look at the environmental laboratory and test rooms. All safety equipment is provided.

Sandals, open-toed and high-heeled shoes are not permitted. Tours depart Mon.-Fri. at 9 and 1, July-Aug. Free. Under 12 are not permitted. Reservations are required. Phone (705) 869-2035, ext. 528 or (800) 663-6342.

FATHOM FIVE NATIONAL MARINE PARK (E-7)

At the tip of the Bruce Peninsula, Canada's first national marine park protects the wealth of marine history at the bottom of the treacherous channel between the 22 islands off the Bruce Peninsula and Manitoulin Island *(see place listing p. 95).*

The only navigable passage between Lake Huron and Georgian Bay, the channel is the final resting place for numerous ships that foundered on its many submerged reefs and shoals during autumn gales.

At least 26 shipwrecks remain preserved beneath the frigid water of Georgian Bay. Twenty-two lie within the park's boundaries and can be seen by scuba divers of all levels of experience. Two wrecks—the Sweepstakes and the City of Grand Rapids—lie in the shallow waters of Big Tub Harbour in Tobermory *(see place listing p. 177).* Glass-bottom tour boats offer excellent views of these wrecks, which also are popular with novice divers.

In addition to the wealth of wrecks, there also are the islands to explore, the most accessible of which is Flowerpot Island off Tobermory. Standing on the island's eastern shore are two large white pillars of rock resembling flowerpots that give the island its name. Hiking trails with interpretive displays traverse the island, and along these footpaths numerous wildflowers and ferns can be seen as well as caves. Modern washroom facilities and primitive campsites also are on the island.

During the summer the visitor center/diver registration office in Tobermory is open Tues.-Thurs. 8-4:30, Fri.-Mon. 8 a.m.-9 p.m.; schedule varies rest of year. The center provides information about recreational opportunities available in the park. Privately operated tour boats provide regular service to Flowerpot Island during the summer and early fall. Several dive shops in Tobermory rent equipment and boats for those who want to explore the park's shipwrecks.

The park is open all year; peak season is May through October. Park admission $4.50; over 64, $4; ages 6-16, $2.25; family rate $11.25.

Address inquiries to Superintendent, Fathom Five National Marine Park, P.O. Box 189, Tobermory, ON, Canada N0H 2R0; phone (519) 596-2233. *See Recreation Chart.*

FENELON FALLS (F-9) pop. 1,874

FENELON FALLS/BOBCAYGEON BOAT CRUISE departs from the upper side of lock #34. Two-hour narrated sightseeing excursions on the Trent-Severn Waterway traveling through Lock 34 along the Fenelon River and into Sturgeon Lake are offered aboard the *Kawartha Spirit.* A sunset dinner cruise also is available.

Two-hour sightseeing cruises depart daily at 11 and 2, July-Aug.; schedule varies mid-May through June 30 and Sept. 1 to mid-Oct. Fare $15; ages 5-12, $7.50. Reservations are required for 11 a.m. departures, recommended for others. MC, VI. Phone (705) 887-9313.

MARYBORO LODGE MUSEUM is at 50 Oak St. Built in 1837 by one of the village founders, the

**Choose Well.
AAA/CAA Approved.**

Discover the secret to choosing well, every time ...
AAA/CAA Approved.

From simple motels to rustic ranches to luxury resorts, rest
assured you've chosen well. **AAA/CAA's professional
evaluators** have tested the locks and peeked under the
beds, checking for qualities like cleanliness, service, and
value — assigning a rating from one to five Diamonds.

Choose your Diamond rated accommodations from the
TourBook® listings, in print and on aaa.com, and look for the
bold red AAA/CAA logo on signage and billboards. Choose
AAA/CAA Approved.

For more information on **AAA/CAA
Lodging Diamond Ratings,** turn to page 16.

home is the oldest in Fenelon Falls. The log house depicts the region's farming and lumbering heritage through artifacts that date from pioneer days through the Victorian era. Among the items displayed are china, furniture and elaborate hair wreaths.

Picnicking is permitted. Allow 1 hour minimum. Daily 1-5 (also Mon. and Fri. 11-1, Wed. 9-1), late June-Labour Day; Tues. and Thurs. 10-2, Sat.-Sun. 1-5, early June-late June and day after Labour Day-Sept. 30; Sat.-Sun. and Mon. holidays 1-5, mid-May to early June and Oct. 1-second Mon. in Oct. Donations. Phone (705) 887-1044.

FERGUS (F-3) pop. 16,732

Originally known as Little Falls, Fergus was renamed for its Scottish founder, Adam Fergusson. Scottish architectural tradition is evident in many 19th-century buildings made of local limestone. Examples include the tannery and gristmill, the Beatty foundry and St. Andrew's Presbyterian Church. Recreational activities attract those interested in hiking, bicycling, fly fishing and water sports, such as canoeing on the Grand River.

Templin Gardens is a restored traditional English garden in the center of town. Additional places of diversion are Fergus Market and the local craft shops. The Fergus Scottish Festival and Highland Games, held the second weekend in August, features Scottish culture, music, dancing, pipes and drums.

Fergus Information Centre: 400 Tower St. S., Fergus, ON, Canada N1M 2P7; phone (519) 843-5140 or (877) 242-6353.

WELLINGTON COUNTY MUSEUM AND AR-CHIVES, 0536 Wellington Rd. 18, consists of heritage gardens and two floors of displays chronicling area history. Exhibits include period room settings, a World War I military exhibit and displays of agricultural tools, textiles, fashions, ceramics and glass as well as photographs and paintings. Exhibitions of contemporary art also are presented. Archives hold records documenting the history of Wellington County.

Allow 30 minutes minimum. Museum open Mon.-Fri. 9:30-4:30, Sat.-Sun. and some holidays 1-5. Archives open Mon.-Fri. 9:30-noon and 1-4:30, Sat. 1-5. Closed Jan. 1, Good Friday, Nov. 11 and Dec. 25-26. Admission $3; senior citizens and students with ID $2; ages 6-12, $1. Phone (519) 846-0916.

FLESHERTON (G-7) pop. 617

SOUTH GREY MUSEUM & HISTORICAL LI-BRARY is on Hwy. 10 in Flesherton Memorial Park. Permanent and changing exhibits display items of historical significance to the area and rural Ontario. Farm equipment, wartime clothes and uniforms, spinning wheels and photographs are featured. A library offers genealogical information.

Allow 30 minutes minimum. Thurs.-Sat. 10-4, Sun. noon-4, late May-Labour Day; Thurs.-Sat.

10-4, Apr. 1-late May and day after Labour Day-Nov. 30; otherwise by appointment. Schedule may vary; phone ahead. Admission $2; under 12, 50c. Phone (519) 924-2843.

FORESTERS FALLS (E-10)

RECREATIONAL ACTIVITIES

White-water Rafting

- **SAVE** **Owl Rafting Inc.** can be reached following signs from town to the base camp at 29 Owl Ln. Write P.O. Box 29, Foresters Falls, ON, Canada K0J 1V0. Trips operate mid-May to mid-Sept. Phone (613) 646-2263 Victoria Day weekend-Labour Day, (613) 238-7238 rest of year, or (800) 461-7238.

- **RiverRun Paddling Centre** is 1 km (.6 mi.) e. to Millars Corner, then n. on CR 43, following signs. Write P.O. Box 179, Beachburg, ON, Canada, K0J 1C0. Trips operate mid-May through Sept. 30. Phone (613) 646-2501 or (800) 267-8504.

FORT ERIE—*see Niagara Falls p. 125.*

FORT FRANCES (C-9) pop. 8,315

Fort Frances, in northwestern Ontario opposite International Falls, Minn., is a busy border-crossing town. On the shores of Rainy Lake and Rainy River, it was originally established as Fort St. Pierre by Pierre de La Verendrye in 1731. The town is named after Lady Frances Simpson, who traveled with her husband Sir George Simpson, governor of the Hudson's Bay Co., on a trip to the settlement in 1830.

La Verendrye Parkway, on the waterfront along Rainy River, features a walkway, a bicycle path and pavilions for picnicking. Another scenic option is Noden Causeway, 7 kilometres (4 mi.) east of Fort Frances on Hwy. 11. The 5.6-kilometre (3.5-mi.) causeway over Rainy Lake consists of three bridges that skip over several islands. Moose, deer, bears and fish are plentiful in this area.

Fort Frances Chamber of Commerce: 474 Scott St., Fort Frances, ON, Canada P9A 1H2; phone (807) 274-5773 or (800) 820-3678.

 ABITIBI-CONSOLIDATED INC., FORT FRANCES DIVISION SUMMER MILL TOURS, 427 Mowat Ave., provides guided tours of the pulp and paper mill. The guided tour includes a demonstration of each step in the paper making process from the transport of logs to the finishing and shipping operation.

Hard hats, high-visibility vests and safety glasses are provided; completely enclosed shoes are required. Allow 1 hour, 30 minutes minimum. Tours are given Mon.-Fri. at 10:30 and 1:30, June-Aug. Free. Under 12 are not permitted. Reservations are required. Phone (807) 274-5311, ext. 1878.

FORT FRANCES MUSEUM AND CULTURAL CENTRE, on Scott St. (Hwy. 11) between Mowat and Portage aves., is in an 1898 schoolhouse. The museum offers exhibits about topics ranging from early native life to the industrial development of the area. Art and traveling exhibits also are featured. Daily 10-6, June-Aug.; Mon.-Sat. 11-4, rest of year. Closed winter holidays. Donations. Phone (807) 274-7891.

GANANOQUE (F-11) pop. 5,167

A popular resort on the St. Lawrence River, Gananoque (Gan-an-OCK-way) is the chief Canadian entrance to the Thousand Islands. Twenty-one of these islands form the St. Lawrence Islands National Park (see place listing p. 162). Tours of the islands by air and boat are available.

A variety of productions is presented mid-May to early November by the Thousand Islands Playhouse at two venues: the Springer Theater at 690 Charles St. S. and the Firehall Theatre at 185 South St. Phone (613) 382-7086 for information or (613) 382-7020 for tickets.

At Half Moon Bay, in the Admiralty of the Thousand Islands, non-denominational church services are held from a rock pulpit at the edge of a natural amphitheater during July and August. The congregation remains in boats, and ushers distribute hymnals and collect offerings in canoes.

A growing collection of historical murals can be viewed downtown, including one depicting the Half Moon Bay church service. Popular area recreational activities include bicycling, golfing, boating, fishing, hiking and snowmobiling. The 1000 Islands Parkway, which runs between Gananoque and Brockville along the St. Lawrence River shoreline, offers breathtaking scenery.

Festival of the Islands, a 10-day waterfront celebration held in August, features live entertainment, historical re-enactments and displays of arts and crafts.

1000 Islands Gananoque Chamber of Commerce—Gananoque: 10 King St. E., Gananoque, ON, Canada K7G 1E6; phone (613) 382-3250 or (800) 561-1595.

Self-guiding tours: Self-guiding walking tours of the area are available. Contact the chamber of commerce for information.

Shopping areas: Historic 1000 Islands Village, a cluster of Victorian-style cottages along the waterfront, is an interesting area in which to browse or shop while you wait for a tour boat.

ARTHUR CHILD HERITAGE CENTRE OF THE 1000 ISLANDS is at 125 Water St. The two-story Victorian building on the shore of the St. Lawrence River has a gallery with works by local artists and natural and cultural history exhibits about the Thousand Islands region. Displays include history and wildlife; missionaries and fur traders; the War of 1812; First Nations People; and the "Golden Era" of elaborate cottages and summer homes.

Guided tours are available. Allow 1 hour minimum. Daily 9-9, late June-Aug. 31; 10-6, Victoria

Day weekend-late June and Sept. 1-late Sept.; 10-4, May 1-day before Victoria Day weekend and late Sept.-Oct. 31. Phone ahead to confirm hours. Admission $2; family rate $5. AX, MC, VI. Phone (613) 382-2535 or (877) 217-7391.

BOLDT CASTLE is on Heart Island, accessible by ferry service or boat tours. The turreted, stone, 120-room, six-story castle was begun in 1900 by George C. Boldt, the proprietor of New York's Waldorf-Astoria hotel and Philadelphia's Bellevue-Stratford. Intended as a summer home for his wife, it was abandoned when she died in 1904, never to be furnished or occupied.

For more than 70 years the estate deteriorated to a condition of almost complete disrepair. Restoration of the castle, yacht house, towers, service buildings and gardens has been ongoing since 1977. Exhibits, including artifacts from the era and a videotape presentation, depict the lives of the Boldts and the development of the 1000 Islands. The grounds and formal Italian garden are well-maintained.

A photo ID and proof of citizenship or a passport are required. Picnicking is permitted. Food is available. Allow 1 hour, 30 minutes minimum. Daily 10-7:30, July 1-Labour Day; 10-6:30, early May-June 30 and day after Labour Day-second Mon. in Oct. Admission $7.85; ages 6-12, $4.50. Ferry or boat tour fares are not included in castle admission. Phone (315) 482-9724, or (315) 482-2501 in the off-season.

Boldt Yacht House, reached via ferry from the castle, is on Wellesley Island. The restored yacht house features a collection of antique wooden boats. Allow 30 minutes minimum. Ferry departs every 30 minutes from the castle. Yacht house open daily 10-6:30, late May-late Sept. Fare $5.25; ages 6-12, $3.25.

GANANOQUE BOAT LINE LTD., at the Swing Bridge and Custom Dock, offers 1-, 3- and 5-hour boat trips through the heart of the Thousand Islands, affording a close view of the islands and summer homes. The 5-hour trip, offered July 1 through Labour Day, includes a stopover at Boldt Castle.

Food and drink are available on board. Five-hour trips depart daily at 10 and 3, July 1-Labour Day. Three-hour trips depart daily at 9, 10:30, noon, 1:30, 3 and 4:30, late June-Labour Day; at 9, 11, 1 and 3, mid-May to late June, day after Labour Day-late Sept. and Oct. 8-10 (weather permitting); at 9 and noon, early May to mid-May and late Sept. to mid-Oct. (weather permitting). One-hour trips depart daily at 10:30, noon, 1:30, 3 and 4:30, late June-Labour Day; at 10:30, noon and 1:30, mid-May to late June and day after Labour Day to mid-Sept. A 1-hour sunset cruise departs at 7, late June-Labour Day.

Five-hour cruise, including Boldt Castle tour, $22; ages 5-10, $7. Three-hour cruise $20; ages 5-10, $7. One-hour cruise $14; ages 5-10, $7. Photo

ID and proof of citizenship or a passport are required for the 5-hour cruise. MC, VI. Phone (613) 382-2144 to verify schedule and fares or (613) 382-2146 for the 24-hour information line.

THE LANDON BAY CENTRE is 6 km (4 mi.) e. on 1000 Islands Pkwy. at Landon Bay. Named after a pioneer church leader during the early years of Upper Canada, The Landon Bay Centre is an 80-hectare (198-acre) ecological reserve with more than 60 themed floral gardens accessible from a 1-kilometre (.6-mi.) walking trail.

Three nature trails are available for hiking, and the facility also offers a scenic lookout, camping, swimming, bird-watching (including an osprey platform) and a playground. Picnicking is permitted. Allow 2 hours minimum. Daily dawn-dusk, May 15-Oct. 15. Admission $4. MC, VI. Phone (613) 382-2719.

CASINOS

• **1000 Islands Charity Casino** is at 380 Hwy. 2 at 1000 Islands Pkwy. Mon.-Wed. 9 a.m.-4 a.m., Thurs.-Sun. 24 hours. Phone (613) 382-6800 or (866) 266-8422.

RECREATIONAL ACTIVITIES
Kayaking

• **1000 Islands Kayaking Co.** provides pickups from local lodgings. Write P.O. Box 166, Gananoque, ON, Canada K7G 2T7. Daily May-Oct. Phone (613) 329-6265.

GEORGIAN BAY ISLANDS NATIONAL PARK (F-8)

Elevations in the park range from 177 metres (580 ft.) at the south end near the shoreline, to 211 metres (692 ft.) at Beausoleil Island. Refer to CAA/AAA maps for additional elevation information.

Along the southeastern portion of Georgian Bay, Georgian Bay Islands National Park protects 59 islands or parts of islands scattered about the bay. Along this stretch of 30,000 islands, glaciers have dramatically divided the archipelago into two well-defined natural areas. The Canadian shield has gnarled pines clinging stubbornly to expanses of pink rock in the ragged northern islands. By contrast, the southern islands are softened by meadows, swamps, wetlands and forests, representing the Great Lakes/St. Lawrence Forest region of eastern Canada.

Beausoleil Island is the park's largest island. Trails traverse the island, emerging from park campgrounds, picnic and docking areas. From the walking trails visitors can see various rare species of wildlife, a variety of birds, spectacular landscapes, precious habitats and evidence of the historical past. Summer recreational activities include fishing, hiking, swimming, bicycling, boating, kayaking and canoeing.

Access to the park's islands is by boat only. Visitors may rent one at a local marina or be transported by water taxi from Honey Harbour. The park's Day Tripper boat service provides a scenic 15-minute voyage to Beausoleil Island; phone (705) 526-8907 for information and reservations. Of the 87 campsites available at Cedar Spring Campground, 39 campsites are available by reservation, two of which are accessible to the physically impaired; phone May 1 through Labour Day for camping reservations.

Most park facilities are about a 15-minute ride from Honey Harbour, at the end of Muskoka Road 5, off Hwy. 400. Information and maps are available year-round at park headquarters in Midland, at the office in Honey Harbour from Victoria Day through Labour Day and at the visitor center and information kiosk at Cedar Spring. During July and August the park also offers exhibits, slide presentations, wildlife viewing, outdoor theater presentations, guided hikes and heritage education programs on the Greater Georgian Bay ecosystem.

Admission May-Oct. $4.50; over 64, $4; ages 6-16, $2.25. Free rest of year. Rates for heritage education programs vary. For more information about the park contact the Administration Office, Georgian Bay Islands National Park, P.O. Box 9, 901 Wye Valley Rd., Midland, ON, Canada L4R 4K6; phone (705) 756-2415 Victoria Day-Labour Day or (705) 526-9804 rest of year. *See Recreation Chart.*

GODERICH (G-7) pop. 7,604; elev. 223 m/732'

Goderich (GOD-rich), the site of the largest harbor on the Canadian side of Lake Huron, was established by John Galt, the founder of the Canada Co. Galt selected the area to be the terminus of the Huron Road (Hwy. 8), which he built from Guelph to Lake Huron. The Canada Co., a British-owned land company, was responsible for the settlement of the vast area of Ontario known as the Huron Tract.

On a bluff facing westward toward the lake, Goderich has wide tree-lined streets radiating like spokes from the courthouse. Recreation includes boating; golfing; hiking; swimming; windsurfing; fishing and canoeing on the Maitland River in spring and summer; and cross-country skiing and snowmobiling in winter. The Clinton Raceway, 20 kilometres (12 mi.) southeast of town at 147 Beech St., offers live harness racing from mid-June to late September; phone (519) 482-5270 or (519) 482-7540.

Note: Policies concerning admittance of children to pari-mutuel betting facilities vary. Phone for information.

The Blyth Festival, 25 kilometres (16 mi.) east in the village of Blyth at 423 Queen St., offers professional summer theater from mid-June through early September. The productions have a decidedly nationalistic flavor—all plays are written, produced and acted by Canadians; phone (519) 523-9300 or (877) 862-5984. Closer to home, the Goderich Little Theatre presents live theatrical productions in the historic Livery at 35 South St.; phone (519) 524-6262.

Tourism Goderich: 91 Hamilton St., Goderich, ON, Canada N7A 1R1; phone (519) 524-6600 or (800) 280-7637.

Self-guiding tours: Information about architectural and historical walking tours is available at the tourism office.

HURON COUNTY MUSEUM, 1 blk. w. of Hwy. 21 at 110 North St., depicts the development of the area through such exhibits as a History Hall featuring original storefronts, pioneer memorabilia and a steam locomotive, military and furniture galleries and agricultural displays. The county archives also are on-site; appointments are recommended. Sky Harbour Gallery, a one-room display at the airport, highlights the town's aviation history.

Allow 1 hour minimum. Mon.-Sat. 10-4:30, Sun. 1-4:30, Victoria Day weekend-Labour Day; Mon.-Fri. 10-4:30, Sun. 1-4:30, rest of year. Closed Good Friday, Oct. 9-10 and Dec. 25-26. Admission $5; students with ID $4; ages 6-11, $3.50. Combination ticket with Marine Museum and Huron Historic Gaol and Governor's House $7.50; students with ID $5.50; ages 6-11, $4. Sky Harbour Gallery by donations. Phone (519) 524-2686.

Marine Museum, off West St. on the south dock at the harbor, displays navigation instruments, maritime artifacts, model ships and items dealing with regional shipping history. The museum is in a forward cabin and pilot house that once were part of a 1907 Canadian freighter, the SS *Shelter Bay.* Allow 30 minutes minimum. Daily 1-4:30, July-Aug. Admission $1. Free with paid admission to Huron County Museum or Huron Historic Gaol and Governor's House. Phone (519) 524-9091, or (519) 524-2686 in the off-season.

HURON HISTORIC GAOL AND GOVERNOR'S HOUSE, jct. Hwy. 21 and Gloster Terr. at 181 Victoria St. N., is a large, octagonal, three-story 1842 stone building with surrounding walls. Visitors view restored cell blocks, a library, bathroom, gaoler's apartment, kitchen and governor's (warden's) office. The restored governor's house next to the gaol provides a vivid contrast to the living quarters of his charges.

Allow 1 hour minimum. Daily 10-4:30, Victoria Day weekend-Labour Day. Admission $5; students with ID $4; ages 6-11, $3.50. Combination ticket with Huron County Museum and Marine Museum $7.50; students with ID $5.50; ages 6-11, $4. Phone (519) 524-6971, or (519) 524-2686 in the off-season.

GORES LANDING (F-10) pop. 10,785

RICE LAKE BOAT CRUISES departs from the dock at the Victoria Inn, 5316 Harwood Rd. Two-hour sightseeing cruises aboard the 60-passenger *Caravelle II* take visitors around glacier-created drumlin islands, Rice Lake and the Otonabee River. A narration provides information about area history.

Allow 2 hours minimum. Departures daily at 1:30, July-Aug.; schedule varies mid-May through June 30 and Sept. 1 to mid-Oct. (weather permitting). Fare $15; senior citizens $13 (Sun. only); ages 3-12, $7.50. Reservations are recommended. MC, VI. Phone (905) 342-2828.

GRAND BEND (H-7) pop. 1,949

Surrounded by beaches and forests, Grand Bend is one of the most popular resorts on Lake Huron. Campgrounds and rentals for a variety of sports are readily available. The Grand Bend Motorplex provides races on a quarter-mile drag strip and tri-oval from May to mid-October, including the Canadian Nationals in June; phone (519) 238-7223.

Huron Country Playhouse, 3 kilometres (2 mi.) east, is Ontario's third largest summer theater, offering performances mid-June to early September in 660-seat and 160-seat restored, climate-controlled barns. For theater information phone (519) 238-6000 or (888) 449-4463.

Nearby Pinery Provincial Park is southern Ontario's largest forested area, with rare Carolinian and internationally significant oak savanna regions. A year-round nature center interprets this habitat.

Within the park are some 30 species of mammals, more than 300 species of birds, 700 species

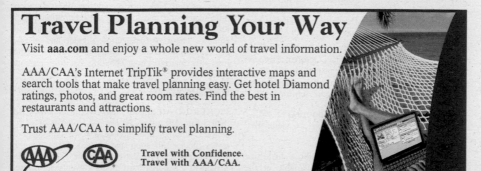

Travel Planning Your Way

Visit **aaa.com** and enjoy a whole new world of travel information.

AAA/CAA's Internet TripTik® provides interactive maps and search tools that make travel planning easy. Get hotel Diamond ratings, photos, and great room rates. Find the best in restaurants and attractions.

Trust AAA/CAA to simplify travel planning.

Travel with Confidence.
Travel with AAA/CAA.

of plants and more than 60 types of butterflies. The 2,532-hectare (6,257-acre) park offers canoeing on a slow-moving river and 10 kilometres (6 mi.) of beachfront on Lake Huron; canoe, bicycle and cross-country ski rentals are available. Hiking and cross-country ski trails are numerous. Campsites are available year-round. Phone (519) 243-2220. *See Recreation Chart and the AAA/CAA Eastern Canada CampBook.*

In mid-March thousands of tundra swans, Canada geese and ducks land near the Lambton Heritage Museum on their northward migration.

Grand Bend and Area Chamber Tourism Centre: 1-81 Crescent St., P.O. Box 248, Grand Bend, ON, Canada N0M 1T0; phone (519) 238-2001.

LAMBTON HERITAGE MUSEUM, 8 km (5 mi.) s. on Hwy. 21, exhibits collections of pressed glass, hand-colored lithographs, agricultural implements and antique carriages, including Ontario's only horse-drawn ambulance. There also are displays of domestic goods, china, fossils, Indian artifacts and other items depicting the history of Lambton County. A chapel, two barns, a slaughterhouse, an 1857 pioneer house and re-creations of a blacksmith shop also are on the premises. Special events are scheduled throughout the year.

Allow 1 hour minimum. Mon.-Fri. 10-5, Sat.-Sun. and holidays 11-5, Mar.-Oct.; Mon.-Fri. 10-5, rest of year. Closed Dec. 25-Jan. 1. Admission $5; over 64 and ages 13-16, $4; ages 5-12, $3; family rate $15. MC, VI. Phone (519) 243-2600.

GRAVENHURST (F-8) pop. 10,899

Gravenhurst, Muskoka's first town, is a Victorian town at the gateway to the Muskoka Lakes District. The downtown area, with its shops and opera house, is accented by trees and period lighting. The walls of several buildings are decorated with murals created by different artists as part of the "Picture Our Heritage" series.

Gravenhurst was the birthplace of Dr. Norman Bethune, renowned for his research in tuberculosis and for the creation of a mobile blood transfusion service on the battlefield during the Spanish Civil War. A pioneer in surgical techniques, Bethune also invented surgical instruments.

A farmers' market is held at Gull Lake Park on Wednesdays, late May to early October. Favorite summertime recreational pursuits include bicycling, fishing, golfing, hiking, swimming and boating, while winter offers skiing and snowmobiling.

Gravenhurst Chamber of Commerce: 685-2 Muskoka Rd. N., Gravenhurst, ON, Canada P1P 1N5; phone (705) 687-4432.

Self-guiding tours: Information about historical walking tours of Gravenhurst is available at the chamber of commerce office.

BETHUNE MEMORIAL HOUSE NATIONAL HISTORIC SITE, 235 John St. N., was Dr. Norman Bethune's 1890 birthplace. The ground floor and master bedroom of the late Victorian clapboard house have been restored to circa 1890. On the second floor is an exhibit that describes Bethune's life and accomplishments. A visitor center offers 1-hour guided tours, which include an audiovisual presentation. Special events are scheduled throughout the year.

Allow 1 hour minimum. Daily 10-4, June-Oct.; Mon.-Fri. 1-4, rest of year. Closed holidays. Last tour begins 1 hour before closing. Admission $3.50; over 64, $3.25; ages 6-16, $2; family rate $9.50. VI. Phone (705) 687-4261.

RMS *SEGWUN*, Muskoka Bay on CR 169 following signs for Muskoka Fleet, offers 1- to 8-hour sightseeing, specialty and dinner cruises on lakes Joseph, Muskoka and Rosseau aboard a restored Victorian-era Royal Mail Ship. Built in 1887, the *Segwun* is one of North America's oldest operating steamships. A museum on the wharf has artifacts and interactive displays about the history of Muskoka's steamboat era.

Food is available. Tours operate daily early June-second Mon. in Oct.; cruises and times vary. Fare for 1-hour cruise $11.50; ages 2-12, $7.25. Fare for 8-hour cruise $73.50; ages 2-12, $61. Museum free to boat passengers; $2 to non-passengers. AX, MC, VI. Phone (705) 687-6667 to verify prices and for schedule.

GREAT LAKES-ST. LAWRENCE SEAWAY SYSTEM

The Great Lakes-St. Lawrence Seaway System consists of a 3,768-kilometre (2,340-mi.) marine highway that extends from the Atlantic Ocean to the western shore of Lake Superior, the headwaters of the Great Lakes, at Duluth, Minn. It was completed in 1959 as a joint venture between Canada and the United States. Canada constructed canals and four locks in territorial waters between Valleyfield, Québec, and Montréal, built a canal and lock at Iroquois, and deepened channels of the Welland Canal.

The United States dredged in the Thousand Islands section and constructed the Wiley-Dondero Ship Canal and two locks in the International Rapids section between Massena, N.Y., and Cornwall, Ontario. There are opportunities to stop and observe the locks and canals in operation along the route. For information about boating facilities, phone (613) 932-5170.

GREENWOOD (F-5)

PICKERING MUSEUM VILLAGE, n. on Brock Rd. then 3 km (1.9 mi.) e. on Hwy. 7, consists of 14 restored buildings that include a town hall, general store, blacksmith shop and church. Mills, tractors and other machinery dating from the 1800s are displayed in a restored barn. Special events are offered throughout the year.

Nobody ever said you had to stay on the highlighted route.

Whether you're travelling the major highways or scenic country roads, Choice Hotels® gives you everything you need to experience Ontario. Plus, CAA members always save at any of our 100 locations across the province.* Just call to book your next stay. Then get out and hit the road.

1.800.228.1222
choicehotels.ca

Ontario
- Barrie
- Belleville (2)
- Brantford
- Brockville (2)
- Burlington
- Cambridge
- Chatham
- Cobourg
- Cornwall
- Dryden
- Gananoque (2)
- Guelph
- Hamilton
- Huntsville
- Kapuskasing
- Kenora
- Kingston (2)
- Kirkland Lake
- Kitchener

- Leamington
- London (3)
- London/St. Thomas
- Midland
- Newmarket
- Niagara Falls (9)
- Niagara Falls/Fort Erie
- Niagara Falls/St. Catharines (2)
- Niagara Falls/Welland
- North Bay (3)
- Orillia (2)
- Oshawa
- Oshawa/Whitby
- Ottawa (4)
- Ottawa/Kanata
- Ottawa/Smiths Falls
- Owen Sound
- Parry Sound
- Pembroke

- Peterborough (2)
- Port Hope
- Sarnia
- Sault Ste Marie (3)
- Simcoe
- Sudbury (3)
- Thunder Bay (2)
- Timmins
- Toronto (8)
- Toronto/Brampton
- Toronto/Markham
- Toronto/Mississauga (5)
- Toronto/North York
- Toronto/Oakville
- Toronto/Pickering
- Toronto/Scarborough
- Trenton
- Waterloo
- Windsor (5)
- Woodstock

We'll see you there.

C H O I C E   H O T E L S   C A N A D A℠

*Subject to availability. Certain restrictions may apply.
©2004 Choice Hotels Canada Inc. All rights reserved.

CAA & Choice Hotels.
No one knows Canada better.

When travelling within Canada, CAA members always save at participating Choice Hotels.

With 228 locations across Canada, Choice Hotels® fits your travel plans and your budget. To book now and save, call today and ask for CAA preferred rates,* and for hotel information visit us online.

**1.800.228.1222
choicehotels.ca**

We'll see you there.
CHOICE HOTELS CANADA℠

*Subject to availability. Certain restrictions may apply.
©2004 Choice Hotels Canada Inc. All rights reserved.

Picnic facilities are available. Allow 1 hour minimum. Wed.-Sat. 10-4:30, Sun. noon-4:30, July-Aug.; Sat. 10-4:30, Sun. noon-4:30 in June and Sept. Admission $4; over 59 and ages 13-18, $2.50; ages 5-12, $2; family rate $12. Rates may vary during special events. MC, VI. Phone (905) 683-8401.

GUELPH (G-3)
pop. 106,170, elev. 321 m/1,053'

Founded in 1827 by Scottish novelist John Galt, Guelph was named in honor of the British royal family. It is known for its architecture and picturesque setting at the junction of the Speed and Eramosa rivers. Century-old limestone buildings add to the city's distinction. In colorful contrast is the floral clock in Riverside Park which incorporates thousands of blossoms. Also in the park are gardens, a carousel, a bandshell and recreation trails.

Guelph offers a variety of music festivals ranging from classical to folk and jazz. Concerts and theatrical performances are offered at River Run Centre, on Woolwich Street beside the Speed River; phone (519) 763-3000. The city is home to the University of Guelph, known for its extensive research and involvement in the fields of agriculture and veterinary medicine.

Guelph Visitor and Convention Services: 42 Wyndham St. N., Suite 101B, Guelph, ON, Canada N1H 4E6; phone (519) 837-1335 or (800) 334-4519.

Self-guiding tours: Guelph's downtown historic district can be explored on five different walking tours. A free brochure describing each of the tours is available from the visitor and convention services office. The Guelph Arts Council offers a $5 booklet that provides details about the sites that can be seen on each tour; phone (519) 836-3280.

THE ARBORETUM is on the campus of the University of Guelph. From Gordon St. travel e. onto College Ave., s. on East Ring Rd., then e. on Arboretum Rd. Featured on 165 hectares (408 acres) are marked trails; thematic gardens, including English, Italian, Japanese and wildlife gardens; and more than 3,000 labeled trees and shrubs. Horticultural collections include dwarf conifers, roses, rhododendrons and lilacs.

Brochures for self-guiding tours are available at the information kiosk near the main entrance. Guided tours are available by appointment. Allow 30 minutes minimum. Grounds daily dawn-dusk. Free. Phone (519) 824-4120, ext. 52113.

[SAVE] **GUELPH CIVIC MUSEUM,** 6 Dublin St. S. at Waterloo Ave., is in a restored mid-19th-century limestone building. Exhibits illustrate the settlement and development of Guelph. Changing exhibits, a children's museum and special events are featured throughout the year. Allow 30 minutes minimum. Daily 1-5; closed Jan. 1, Good Friday and Dec. 25-26. Admission $4; over 64 and ages 2-18, $3; family rate $10. Family combination pass with McCrae House $12. Phone (519) 836-1221.

MACDONALD STEWART ART CENTRE, on the University of Guelph campus at 358 Gordon St. at College Ave., features seven galleries of contemporary, historical and Inuit art as well as one of Canada's largest outdoor sculpture parks. Allow 30 minutes minimum. Tues.-Sun. noon-5; closed major holidays. Donations. Phone (519) 837-0010.

[SAVE] **McCRAE HOUSE,** 108 Water St., is the 1872 birthplace of Lt. Col. John McCrae, author of the poem "In Flanders Fields," written in 1915 at the Second Battle of Ypres. Exhibits depict family history and McCrae's medical and military careers. A space for interactive and changing exhibits has videotape presentations about McCrae and World War I. The gardens have been restored to the 1850-80 time period.

Daily 1-5, June 22-Nov. 13; Sun.-Fri. 1-5, rest of year. Closed Good Friday, Easter and Dec. 25-Jan. 2. Admission $4; over 64 and ages 5-18, $3; family rate $10. Family combination pass with Guelph Civic Museum $12. Phone (519) 836-1221.

HAILEYBURY (C-8) pop. 4,543

[SAVE] **HAILEYBURY HERITAGE MUSEUM,** off Hwy. 11B at 575 Main St., contains exhibits pertaining to the Great Fire of 1922. Displays include a restored 1904 streetcar used as housing by victims of the fire, a 1922 Ruggles fire pumper and an Ontario Northland Railway caboose. Allow 30 minutes minimum. Daily 10-6, June 1-Labour Day; Mon.-Fri. 10-5, rest of year. Admission $2, over 64 and students with ID $1.50, under 12 free, family rate $5. Phone (705) 672-1922.

HALIBURTON (F-9)

Haliburton is a recreational center in the Haliburton Highlands, a region of more than 600 lakes scattered among hills, cliffs and forests. Skyline Park, .5 kilometres (.3 mi.) east on Hwy. 121, affords excellent views of the surrounding terrain. Summertime outdoor diversions include bicycling, fishing, golfing and hiking, while dog-sledding, skiing, snowboarding and snowmobiling are popular during the colder months.

The Northern Lights Performing Arts Pavilion, junction Hwy. 124 and CR 1, is the site of dramatic and musical productions year-round, including the Highlands Summer Festival from late June through early August; phone (705) 457-1235 for general information or (705) 457-9933 for festival information and tickets.

Haliburton Highlands Chamber of Commerce & Visitor Information Centre: P.O. Box 147, Minden, ON, Canada K0M 2K0; phone (705) 286-1760 or (800) 461-7677.

HALIBURTON FOREST WOLF CENTRE is 11 km (7 mi.) n. on Hwy. 118, then 17 km (11 mi.) n. on CR 7. A learning center presents videotapes with information about the history of wolves and has life-size displays showing the animals in their natural habitat. A 6-hectare (15-acre) compound has a

resident pack of grey wolves; an observatory overlooks the enclosure and allows visitors a chance
to see the animals, though sightings cannot be
guaranteed.

Allow 1 hour minimum. Daily 10-5, Victoria
Day weekend-second Mon. in Oct.; Fri.-Sun. 10-5,
rest of year. Last admission 30 minutes before closing. Admission $8; ages 7-17, $5; family rate $19.
MC, VI. Phone (705) 754-9653.

HALIBURTON HIGHLANDS MUSEUM is 1 km (.6
mi.) w. off Hwy. 118 via Bayshore Acres Rd. to
Museum Rd., following signs. The complex consists of a museum gallery with artifacts pertaining
to the area's settlement; the 1882 Reid House, filled
with furnishings of the late 19th and early 20th centuries; and several other buildings, including a
settler's cabin, barn and a forge building.

Main gallery open Tues.-Sun. 10-5, July
1-Labour Day; Tues.-Sat. 10-5, Victoria Day-June
30 and day after Labour Day-late Oct.; Wed.-Sat.
10-5, rest of year. Reid House open Tues.-Sun.
10-5, July 1-Labour Day; Tues.-Sat. 10-5, Victoria
Day weekend-June 30 and day after Labour Day-
second Mon. in Oct. Other buildings open Tues.-
Sun. 10-5, July 1-Labour Day. Closed Jan. 1 and
Dec. 25. Admission $2.50; ages 4-12, $1. Phone
(705) 457-2760.

HAMILTON (H-8)
pop. 490,268, elev. 93 m/305'

Hamilton rests at the historic Head of the Lake,
between Toronto and Niagara Falls. Although visited by French explorer Robert Cavalier, sieur de
La Salle in 1669, Hamilton's settlement began in
earnest in the late 18th century with the influx of
United Empire Loyalists leaving the American
colonies during the Revolutionary War.

When the Burlington Canal opened in 1830, linking Hamilton to Lake Ontario, the city became a
port and rail hub. Once hopeful of Hamilton's becoming the seat of provincial government, wealthy
merchants and professionals were lured to the real
estate along its lakefront. Their palatial houses and
estates still grace the heart of town; Dundurn National Historic Site *(see attraction listing)* is one of
the well-known estates from that era.

The landlocked harbor at Hamilton is one of the
largest on the Great Lakes, handling the third highest
tonnage in water traffic in the country. The home of
Canada's principal steel-producing companies, Stelco
and Dofasco, the city also is known for its preservation of green spaces and the environment.

Hamilton offers diverse arts and cultural choices
for visitors. The Ronald V. Joyce Centre for the
Performing Arts at Hamilton Place, Copps Coli-
seum and the Hamilton Convention Centre provide
concert and entertainment selections throughout the
year. The cultural scene in Hamilton also is enhanced by the Hamilton Philharmonic Orchestra,
Opera Hamilton and several theatre companies,
including Theatre Aquarius.

Bruce Trail, an ecologically sensitive trail system
that follows the Niagara Escarpment, cuts through
Hamilton and provides a pristine setting where
naturalists, bird watchers and hikers can pursue
their respective interests. The escarpment is responsible for the 26 waterfalls and cascades that are accessible to visitors and enhance Hamilton's outdoor
experience. Some 24 regional conservation areas
also offer outdoor recreation that includes boating,
fishing and swimming.

A recent amalgamation has incorporated the nearby
municipalities of Ancaster, Dundas, Flamborough,
Glanbrook and Stoney Creek into the city of
Hamilton.

Festival of Friends in early August is strictly a
Canadian festival, showcasing Canadian music,
crafts, theater and dance. In late August at the Wi-
nona Peach Festival, visitors can partake of food
and enjoy arts and crafts exhibits, live entertainment, a vintage car show and a special area for
children. Italian culture and heritage is promoted
throughout September and into October via music,
theater and food at Festitalia.

Farmers from all over southern Ontario converge
on the Hamilton Central Market at the Hamilton
Public Library, part of Jackson Square at 2 King St.

hamiltonundiscovered.com
TOURISM HAMILTON • ONTARIO, CANADA
1-800-263-8590 • 905-546-2666

W., to sell their fruits and vegetables. The farmers' market has been part of the city's history for more than 160 years. Harness racing takes place throughout the year at Flamboro Downs racetrack, west of the city on Hwy. 5; phone (905) 627-3561.

Note: Policies concerning admittance of children to pari-mutuel betting facilities vary. Phone for information.

Tourism Hamilton: 34 James St. S., Hamilton, ON, Canada L8P 2X8; phone (905) 546-2666 or (800) 263-8590. *See color ad p. 80.*

Shopping areas: Limeridge Mall, 999 Upper Wentworth St., has The Bay and Sears. For locally produced handicrafts from more than 50 artisans visit Textures Craftworks, at 236 Locke St. S. in an area of cafes and antique shops. The shop is a nonprofit artisans' cooperative that also offers demonstrations and exhibitions. Hess Village is an area of restored houses in the vicinity of Hess and George streets that provides a Victorian setting for galleries, restaurants and pubs.

ART GALLERY OF HAMILTON, 2 blks. w. of James St. at 123 King St. W., houses an outstanding collection of Canadian, American and European art. **Note:** The museum will reopen after renovation late May 2005. Phone ahead for confirmation. Allow 30 minutes minimum. Tues.-Wed. noon-7, Thurs.-Fri. noon-9, Sat.-Sun. noon-5; closed major holidays. Free. A fee may be charged for special exhibitions. Phone (905) 527-6610, ext. 200.

SAVE BATTLEFIELD HOUSE MUSEUM NATIONAL HISTORIC SITE is at Centennial Pkwy. and King St. in Stoney Creek. Costumed interpreters lead tours of the 1796 pioneer homestead Battlefield House, site of the 1813 Battle of Stoney Creek. The home is furnished with pieces from early 19th-century Upper Canada. Visitors can climb to an observation deck at the top of the 31-metre (100-ft.) monument built to commemorate 100 years of peace between the United States and Canada following the War of 1812.

Picnicking is permitted. Allow 30 minutes minimum. Tues.-Sun 11-4, June 15-Labour Day; 1-4, rest of year. Closed Jan. 1, Good Friday and Dec. 25-26. Admission $5; over 59 and students with ID $4; ages 6-12, $3; family rate $15. Phone (905) 662-8458.

CANADIAN FOOTBALL HALL OF FAME AND MUSEUM, 58 Jackson St. W. in Civic Sq., traces the history of football and honors the game's great players, coaches and executives. Tues.-Sat. 9:30-4:30; closed Jan. 1, Dec. 25-26 and Sat. before Mon. holidays. Admission $3; over 59 and students with ID $1.50; under 14, $1. Phone (905) 528-7566.

CANADIAN WARPLANE HERITAGE MUSEUM, at the John C. Munro International Airport off Hwy. 6 in Mount Hope, is **SAVE** called "Canada's Flying Museum." The history of Canadian military aviation is explained

through a collection of more than 40 vintage aircraft from World War II to the jet age, most in flying condition. Included in the collection is the only operating Avro Lancaster in North America.

The museum, housed in a distinctive wing-shaped building, also contains interactive displays, flight simulators, a theater, memorabilia and aircraft restorations. Visitors can climb into the cockpit of a World War II trainer or jet fighter. Warbird rides are available for a fee. Flying exhibitions take place weekends (weather and crews permitting).

Food is available. Allow 1 hour minimum. Daily 9-5; closed Jan. 1 and Dec. 25. Admission $10; over 64 and ages 8-18, $8; family rate (two adults and two children) $30. AX, MC, VI. Phone (905) 679-4183, or (877) 347-3359 for recorded information.

CONFEDERATION PARK, at the n. terminus of Hwy. 20, is an 83-hectare (205-acre) park with Wild Waterworks' water park as well as a 4-kilometre (2.5-mi.) waterfront promenade along Lake Ontario. Activities include windsurfing, miniature golf, go-carting, camping and swimming. Picnicking is permitted. Food is available. Daily 8-dusk. Admission $7 per private vehicle. Fees are charged for activities. Phone (905) 547-6141, or (800) 555-8775 in Canada. *See Recreation Chart.*

Wild Waterworks, in Confederation Park, has four six-story waterslides, a wave pool, a children's pool and an action river ride. Locker rooms and tube rentals are offered. Picnic facilities and food are available. Open daily 10-dusk, June 1-Labour Day (weather permitting). Admission $14.25; over 64 and ages 4-10, $9.25. Under 11 must be with an adult. AX, MC, VI. Phone (905) 561-2292, or (800) 555-8775 in Canada.

DUNDAS HISTORICAL SOCIETY MUSEUM, 139 Park St. W. in Dundas, presents glassware, furniture, clothing and other local items in period settings. The Children's Corner displays toys and dolls, and the Pioneer Store has an array of dry goods typical of a turn-of-the-20th-century general store. Allow 30 minutes minimum. Mon.-Fri. 10-4, Sun. 2-4, May-Oct.; Mon.-Fri. 10-4, rest of year. Closed holidays. Donations. Phone (905) 627-7412.

DUNDURN NATIONAL HISTORIC SITE is at 610 York Blvd. The castle is the restored 40-room Italianate villa of Sir Allan Napier **SAVE** MacNab, premier of the United Provinces of Canada 1854-56. The house's furnishings reflect the mid-19th century lifestyle of the MacNab family and the servants who lived and worked in the house. Costumed interpreters offer 1-hour tours of all 40 rooms on three floors.

Guided tours are given every 10-15 minutes daily 10-4, Victoria Day-Labour Day; Tues.-Sun. noon-4, rest of year. Closed Jan. 1 and Dec. 25-26. Last tour departs at closing. Admission, including the Hamilton Military Museum, $10; over 64 and students with ID $8; ages 6-14, $5; family rate $25. Phone to verify prices. MC, VI. Phone (905) 546-2872.

Hamilton Military Museum, 610 York Blvd., is part of Dundurn National Historic Site. An extensive collection of military artifacts dating from the War of 1812 through World War I is exhibited. Daily 11-5, Victoria Day-Labour Day; Tues.-Sun. 1-5, rest of year. Closed Jan. 1 and Dec. 25-26. Free with admission to Dundurn National Historic Site. Separate admission $2.25; over 64 and students with ID $2; ages 6-14, $1.75; family rate $7. Phone (905) 546-2872.

ERLAND LEE MUSEUM is at 552 Ridge Rd. in Stoney Creek overlooking Lake Ontario. Erland and Janet Lee's home and carriage house were built in 1808, with an addition constructed in 1873. The Lees founded the Women's Institute, the first rural women's organization, in 1897. The house has family pieces and artifacts from 1800-1930. The carriage house has agricultural items and exhibits about Stoney Creek history from 1780 to the present.

Guided tours are available. Picnicking is permitted. Open Tues.-Sat. 10-4, Sun. noon-4, Apr. 1-Dec. 24; Thurs.-Sat. 10-4 and by appointment rest of year. Admission $4.25; ages 6-12, $2.25. Phone (905) 662-2691.

GAGE PARK, Main St. E. at Gage Ave., is a 28-hectare (70-acre) botanical park known for its rose gardens. Open daily 24 hours. Free.

Hamilton Children's Museum, 1072 Main St. E. in Gage Park, encourages youngsters and their parents to participate in hands-on activities. Tues.-Sat. 9:30-3:30; closed major holidays. Admission ages 2-13, $3; over 13, $1. Phone (905) 546-4848.

HAMILTON MUSEUM OF STEAM AND TECHNOLOGY, 900 Woodward Ave., houses two 1859 steam engines. The museum has displays about the history and industrial development of Hamilton, including Hamilton's waterworks. Picnicking is permitted. Allow 30 minutes minimum. Tues.-Sun. 11-4, June 1-Labour Day; Tues.-Sun. noon-4, rest of year. Closed Jan. 1 and Dec. 25-26. Admission $6; over 60 and students with ID $4; ages 6-13, $3; family rate $15. MC, VI. Phone (905) 546-4797.

McMASTER MUSEUM OF ART, corner of Sterling and University aves. on the McMaster University campus, mounts changing exhibits of historical and contemporary art. Highlights of the 6,000-piece collection include works by Joseph Beuys, Anish Kapoor, German Expressionists and a collection of paintings from the 14th to the 20th centuries. Tues.-Fri. 11-5, Sun. noon-5; closed major holidays and Dec. 22-Jan. 4. Admission $4. A fee is charged for parking, except on Sun. Phone (905) 525-9140, ext. 23081.

   **ROYAL BOTANICAL GARDENS—** see Burlington p. 64.

SAM LAWRENCE PARK, atop Hamilton Mountain via Jolley Cut, presents an outstanding floral display and affords a panorama of the entire district. Daily dawn-dusk. Free.

WHITEHERN HISTORIC HOUSE AND GARDEN, 41 Jackson St. W., was the home of the McQuesten family 1852-1968. The family developed the town's first foundry, established the Royal Botanical Gardens *(see Burlington p. 64)*, helped relocate McMaster University to Hamilton and restored Fort Henry and the Niagara Parks. An excellent example of 19th-century Georgian architecture, the house contains original furnishings, toys, family memorabilia and ornamental gardens.

Guided tours are available. Tues.-Sun. 11-4, mid-June through Labor Day; Tues.-Sun. 1-4, rest of year. Closed Jan. 1, Good Friday and Dec. 25-26. Admission $5; over 64 and students with ID $4; ages 5-12, $3; family rate $15. Phone (905) 546-2018.

HARROW (I-5) pop. 2,935

JOHN R. PARK HOMESTEAD is 4 km (2.5 mi.) e. on CR 20, then s. on CR 50 to Iler Rd. to its end. The 1842 American Greek Revival house is the focal point of the estate, which re-creates the lifestyle of a 19th-century family. China, household items and period furniture are displayed. Outbuildings include an icehouse, a barn, a smokehouse, a blacksmith shop and a steam engine-powered sawmill.

Costumed staff demonstrate weaving, blacksmithing and cooking in summer. Sun.-Thurs. 11-4, May-Oct.; Tues.-Thurs. 11-4, rest of year. Closed Dec. 24-Jan. 1. Admission $4; ages 4-16, $2.50; family rate $12. Prices may vary during special events. MC, VI. Phone (519) 738-2029.

WINERIES

• **Colio Estate Winery** is at 1 Colio Dr. Tours daily at 1, 2 and 3; closed Jan. 1, Good Friday, Easter and Dec. 25-26. Phone (519) 738-9318 or (800) 265-1322.

HAWKESTONE (F-8)

BIG CURVE ACRES FARM, on Hwy. 11, 7.4 km (4.6 mi.) s. of jct. Hwy. 12, displays common and rare breeds of farm animals in natural settings. A petting zoo is available. Picnicking is permitted. Allow 1 hour, 30 minutes minimum. Sat.-Thurs. noon-4, July-Aug.; otherwise varies rest of year. Admission $5. VI. Phone (705) 487-2000.

HEARST (A-5) pop. 5,825

Primarily a French Canadian town, Hearst is known as a base for moose hunting and as a starting point for canoe trips to the north. A 1,000-kilometre (625-mi.) snowmobile trail originates in town.

Hearst Chamber of Commerce: P.O. Box 987, Hearst, ON, Canada P0L 1N0; phone (705) 372-2838.

NAGAGAMISIS PROVINCIAL PARK lies 64 km (40 mi.) w. via Hwy. 11, then 42 km (26 mi.) s. on

Hwy. 631. The 8,131-hectare (3,653-acre) park, on a historic fur trade route, is noted for its glacial moraines and formations. Camping, canoeing and swimming are a few of the recreational opportunities available in this secluded park. The site of an old Hudson's Bay Co. post is nearby.

Park open Sun.-Thurs. 1-10, Fri.-Sat. 9 a.m.-10 p.m., Victoria Day weekend-fourth Sun. in Sept. Admission $6.50 per private vehicle; over 64, $5.25; physically impaired $3.25. AX, MC, VI. Phone (807) 868-2254, or (705) 372-2232 in the off-season. *See Recreation Chart.*

HILL ISLAND (F-11)

SAVE **1000 ISLANDS SKYDECK** is between the spans of the Thousand Islands International Bridge. The 130-metre (400-ft.) observation tower offers excellent views of the Thousand Islands through three observation decks, one of which is glass-enclosed. On a clear day visibility is more than 64 kilometres (40 mi.). A photo ID and proof of citizenship or a passport are required. Daily 9-dusk, mid-Apr. to late Oct. (weather permitting). Admission $7.95; ages 6-12, $4.45. Bridge toll $2 per private vehicle. AX, MC, VI. Phone (613) 659-2335.

HUNTSVILLE (E-8)
pop. 17,338, elev. 319 m/1,047'

The gateway to the Lake of Bays region and the western entrance to Algonquin Provincial Park *(see place listing p. 50)*, Huntsville is a vacation and recreation center. Known for beautiful scenery and clear lakes, the region also abounds in hunting, fishing, bicycling, boating, swimming, camping, skiing, hiking, dog sledding and snowmobiling opportunities. Similar types of recreation are available in Arrowhead Provincial Park *(see Recreation Chart).*

A farmers' market, open on Thursdays from May to late October, provides an opportunity to sample local produce. Each July the town hosts the Festival of the Arts, featuring local and international performers.

Huntsville/Lake of Bays Chamber of Commerce: 8 West St. N., Unit 1, Huntsville, ON, Canada P1H 2B6; phone (705) 789-4771.

Shopping areas: Downtown Huntsville, in particular the area along Main Street between Lorne and John streets, has numerous gift, antique and craft shops; those shops devoted to wood crafts are particularly popular.

DYER MEMORIAL, 11 km (7 mi.) n.e. via Hwy. 11B and Williamsport Rd., is an impressive stone tower erected by Detroit lawyer Clifton G. Dyer in memory of his wife. The tower is built on a flagstone terrace; it is surrounded by a 4-hectare (10-acre) botanical garden and park overlooking the East River. Open daily 24 hours. Free.

MUSKOKA HERITAGE PLACE is 1 km (.6 mi.) e. at 88 Brunel Rd. The 36-hectare (90-acre) village overlooking Cann Lake is an outdoor living-history museum that re-creates the life of the area's early settlers. Among the displays are pioneer homesteads from the Huntsville area, a church, a general store, an inn, a schoolhouse, sawmill, blacksmith, First Nation's encampment, nature trails, farm animals and gardens.

Blacksmithing, pioneer baking, spinning, butter churning, candle making and sawmill operations are among the demonstrations given by costumed interpreters. The Portage Flyer, a restored steam-powered train, runs a 2-kilometre (1.3 mi.) route along the Muskoka River to Fairy Lake. The railway, which operated 1902-58, is said to be the shortest commercial railway in the world. In the re-created train station is a steam museum.

Allow 2 hours minimum. Village complex open daily 10-4, mid-May to mid-Oct. Steam train operates Tues.-Sat.; phone for departure times. Village admission $10; ages 3-12, $7. Steam train $5; ages 3-12, $3. MC, VI. Phone (705) 789-7576.

IGNACE (B-10) pop. 1,709

Once the site of two base-metal mining operations, Ignace focuses its current economy on forestry, CP Rail, natural gas transmission and tourism. Visitors can stroll down the city's Heritage Corridor to view a series of large murals depicting various themes indicative of the area.

Sandbar Lake Provincial Park *(see Recreation Chart and the AAA/CAA Eastern Canada CampBook)*, 11 kilometres (8 mi.) north of town, has opportunities for activities such as camping, swimming, fishing, boating and hiking in its 5,083 hectares (12,560 acres). The area also offers 11 canoe routes and numerous lakes and outfitters that provide anglers with excellent fishing opportunities for pike, walleye, bass and trout.

Ignace Regional Tourist Attraction Centre: 34 Hwy. 17W, P.O. Box 248, Ignace, ON, Canada P0T 1T0; phone (807) 934-2202.

INGERSOLL (H-2) pop. 10,977

INGERSOLL CHEESE FACTORY, MUSEUM AND SPORTS HALL OF FAME is 1.5 km (.9 mi.) n. of Hwy. 401 exit 218 on Hwy. 19 in Centennial Park. The six-building complex features the Cheese Factory Museum, which depicts an early 1900s cheese factory. Also on the grounds are a local history museum featuring "The Pathway of the Giants," a scene carved from wood; a sports museum that highlights outstanding area athletes and displays the speedboat *Miss Canada IV;* a blacksmith shop; and two agricultural barns.

Allow 30 minutes minimum. Daily 10-5, May 9-Labour Day; Sat.-Sun. 1-5, day after Labour Day-second Mon. in Oct.; other times by appointment. Donations. Phone (519) 485-5510, or (519) 485-0120 in the off-season.

INGLESIDE (E-12)

Ingleside is one of the access points to the Long Sault Parkway, a scenic 10-kilometre (6-mi.) drive that connects 11 islands by a series of causeways and bridges. The islands were created by the Moses-Saunders Power Dam at Cornwall *(see place listing p. 69)*. Areas along the parkway offer opportunities for swimming, picnicking, fishing, camping and bird-watching.

IROQUOIS FALLS (B-7) pop. 5,217

THE IROQUOIS FALLS PIONEER MUSEUM, 245 Devonshire Ave., exhibits books, tools, clothes and household items used by the early settlers and artifacts from the Abitibi Woodlands. The Cultural Heritage Project archival room is open to the public. Guided tours are available. Allow 30 minutes minimum. Mon.-Fri. 9-4, Victoria Day-Labour Day. Admission $2; over 59 and ages 5-12, $1. Phone (705) 258-3730.

JORDAN (H-4)

A major center of the Ontario wine industry, Jordan was once a thriving shipping point on Twenty Mile Creek.

BALL'S FALLS HERITAGE CONSERVATION AREA is off Queen Elizabeth Way (QEW) exit 57, then 6 km (4 mi.) s. on Victoria Ave. and 1 km (.6 mi.) s. on 6th Ave. (Hwy. 75). Encompassing 112 hectares (278 acres) along Twenty Mile Creek, this 19th-century industrial hamlet now serves recreational and educational purposes.

On-site structures include a gristmill, the first mill owner's house, a lime kiln, two 1790s cabins, a fruit drying shed, an 1864 church, a blacksmith shop, carriage shed and community oven. An arboretum, nature center and hiking trails are available.

Picnicking is permitted. Trails and outdoor conservation area open daily 8:30-4, Apr.-Nov. Historic area open daily 10-4, Victoria Day weekend-Labour Day; otherwise varies. Admission $3.25; over 64 and ages 5-18, $2.25; maximum rate per private vehicle $10. Phone (905) 788-3135 or (905) 562-5235.

JORDAN HISTORICAL MUSEUM OF THE TWENTY, Main St., honors the pioneers who came to this area in the early 19th century. The lives and activities of the settlers are reflected in the Jacob Fry House. A restored stone school house also is open for viewing. Of special interest are the giant fruit press built in the early 1800s and an exhibit of fraktur folk art. The Pioneer Day festival is held in October. Tues.-Sun. 10-5, mid-May through Aug. 31; Mon.-Fri. 8:30-4:30, rest of year. Donations. Phone (905) 562-5242.

KAKABEKA FALLS (C-11)

KAKABEKA FALLS, .5 km (.31 mi.) w. on Hwy. 11/17, is on the Kaministiquia River in Kakabeka Falls Provincial Park. Kakabeka's name comes from the Ojibway Indian word meaning "thundering waters." Legend says an abducted Ojibway princess pretended to guide her Sioux captors to her tribe but instead guided them over the falls.

The waterfall, 71 metres (233 ft.) wide and 39 metres (128 ft.) high, is at full force in spring and fall. Falls viewing open daily 8 a.m.-10 p.m., all year. Camping and picnic facilities open daily, Fri. before Victoria Day-second Mon. in Oct. Parking fees apply. Phone (807) 473-9231. *See Recreation Chart.*

KAPUSKASING (A-5) pop. 9,238

Kapuskasing (cap-a-SKAY-sing) derives from a Cree Indian name thought to mean "bend in the river." Founded as a company town around a pulp-processing mill, Kapuskasing was developed as a model community according to a provincial plan. Its economy later expanded to include a paper mill, which supplied *The New York Times* with newsprint for 50 years. Tembec/Spruce Falls Inc., on the east bank of the Kapuskasing River off Hwy. 11, offers mill tours in July and August; phone the Kapuskasing and District Chamber of Commerce for reservations.

The Centre de Loisirs, 7 rue Aurora, is a French Canadian cultural center containing an art gallery with free changing exhibitions. The center also has two squash courts; phone (705) 335-8461.

Kapuskasing and District Chamber of Commerce: 100 Government Rd., Kapuskasing, ON, Canada P5N 3H8; phone (705) 335-2332.

KAPUSKASING II BOAT TOUR departs from the town dock; tickets can be purchased at the log Tourist Information Bureau on Government Rd. E. Three-hour narrated trips along the scenic Kapuskasing River on the 50-passenger double-deck cruiser *Kapuskasing II* provide insights into the area's logging, trapping and river heritage. Dinner cruises are available.

Allow 3 hours minimum. Departures daily at 1, June 15-Sept. 15. Fare $19.50; over 59, $17; ages 13-18, $16; ages 2-12, $11; family rate (two adults and two children) $50. AX, MC, VI. Phone (705) 335-2332 or (800) 463-6432.

RON MOREL MEMORIAL MUSEUM, on Millview Rd. next to the train station, is housed in two coach cars and a caboose and is headed by a steam locomotive. Railroad relics and memorabilia are displayed along with a model railroad and local history exhibits. Daily 8:30-4:30, Victoria Day-Labour Day. Donations. Phone (705) 337-4274.

KENORA (B-8) pop. 15,838

On the north shore of Lake of the Woods, Kenora offers many activities including fishing, hunting and boating. The popular tourist destination also has a wide range of festivals and events during the summer and winter. A 12-metre (35-ft.) wood, steel and fiberglass statue of "Husky the Muskie" downtown is a symbol of the environment as well as the frequent record-breaking catches in this area.

Surrounding more than 14,000 islands, Lake of the Woods was originally called Lake of the Islands by the Ojibway Indians inhabiting the region. The French, who had minimal knowledge of the Indian language, misinterpreted the word "island" as "wood," and the lake's rather inappropriate name was adopted. Indian petroglyphs can be found around the lake as well as the city.

Tourism Kenora: 1500 Hwy. 17E, Kenora, ON, Canada P9N 1M3; phone (800) 535-4549.

LAKE OF THE WOODS MUSEUM, 300 Main St. S. in Memorial Park, displays aboriginal and pioneer artifacts of early Rat Portage, now Kenora, and the Lake of the Woods area. The collections focus on the years 1880-1920. Daily 10-5, July-Aug.; Tues.-Sat. 10-5, Sept.-May. Admission $2; under 18, $1. Phone (807) 467-2105.

MS *KENORA* **SIGHTSEEING EXCURSIONS** depart from the Kenora harborfront. The tours include 2-hour cruises of Lake of the Woods on a 180-passenger ship. Departures Mon.-Sat. at noon, 3 and 6:30, Sun. at 12:30, 3:30 and 6:30, mid-June through day before Labour Day; Sat.-Sun., Victoria Day to mid-June and Labour Day to mid-Sept. Schedule may vary; phone ahead.

Fare $18.95; senior citizens $17.95; ages 3-10, $11; family rate (two adults and two children) $50.90. Rates may vary; phone ahead. MC, VI. For reservations phone (807) 468-9124.

KESWICK (G-8)

On the southern shore of Lake Simcoe, Keswick is home to the Stephen Leacock Theatre, named for the author and humorist, one of Canada's most famous citizens. At 130 Gwendolyn Blvd. in the Georgina Cultural Centre, the theater is home to the Queensville Players, the South Shore Theatre and the Stephen Leacock Players. A variety of shows and events are presented year-round; phone (905) 476-0193.

GEORGINA VILLAGE MUSEUM, n. on Woodbine Ave., then e. on Baseline Rd. to 26557 Civic Centre Rd., is a heritage showcase for the pioneer days of Georgina. The collection of 11 restored buildings displays life in the 1800s and early 1900s with costumed interpreters and craft demonstrations during special events. An archives is open by appointment. Special events are featured throughout the year.

Guided tours are available. Picnicking is permitted. Allow 1 hour minimum. Tues.-Sun. and holidays 10-5, late May-Labour Day. Admission $5; over 59 and students with ID $3; ages 6-12, $2. Phone (905) 476-4305, ext. 284.

KILLARNEY (E-7) pop. 428

On the voyageur route to the west, what is now the town of Killarney was once called Shebhanoning, meaning narrow channel. Renamed in 1854, the town had become a commercial fishing center. Historical attractions such as lighthouses, oak boatbuilding sheds, a school and post office are reminders of the town's days as a fishing village.

On the shores of the Georgian Bay marking the entrance to the North Channel of Lake Huron, this area offers a range of recreational opportunities. In the summer, camping, boating, fishing and hiking are popular pursuits. In the winter, snowmobiling, cross-country skiing, ice fishing and curling are favored pastimes.

Municipality of Killarney: 32 Commissioner St., Killarney, ON, Canada P0M 2A0; phone (705) 287-2424.

KILLARNEY PROVINCIAL PARK, 61 km (38 mi.) n.e. on Hwy. 637, so inspired a generation of painters that they lobbied the government to preserve its 48,500 hectares (119,845 acres). The park's quartzite ridges, sparkling lakes and hardwood forests filled the canvases of some of Canada's renowned Group of Seven. Artists continue to paint at this site; the park is enjoyed by hikers and canoeists as well. Dozens of lakes provide a variety of water routes.

Park gates open daily 8 a.m.-9 p.m., July 1-Labour Day; 8-4, rest of year. Admission is by a $9 private vehicle day pass. AX, MC, VI. Phone (705) 287-2900, or (888) 668-7275 for camping reservations. *See Recreation Chart.*

KIMBERLEY (G-7)

Central to Beaver Valley, Kimberley is a popular skiing village. Eight kilometres (5 mi.) south of town and north of CR 4, Eugenia Falls drops 30 metres (98 ft.) into Beaver Valley. This serene area offers boating, hiking and picnicking in summer and cross-country and Alpine skiing in winter.

KINCARDINE (G-7) pop. 11,029

This Lake Huron town may be best known for its Scottish bagpipe band parade and concert, traditionally held Saturday nights from late June through Labour Day. Locals and visitors alike join the bagpipe parade as it proceeds down Queen Street, returning to the Victoria Park gazebo where the concert takes place. Also popular are the Sunday evening sing-alongs in Dunsmoor Park, early July through Labour Day weekend; Wednesday evening concerts are for those more inclined to merely listen and are offered in July and August.

For the recreation-minded, hiking, fishing, skating and cross-country skiing are available, and golf can be played at four nearby courses. The local produce scene can be checked out at the farmers' market held Mondays in Victoria Park from Victoria Day through Labour Day.

Cultural amenities include year-round performances by two theater companies, with all plays staged at the Kincardine Arts Centre, 707 Queen St. Professional performances by the Bluewater Summer Playhouse take place late June through August;

phone (519) 396-5722 or (877) 396-5722. Performances are presented by the Kincardine Theatre Guild year-round; phone (519) 396-2211 or (519) 396-9000.

Visitor Information Centre: 782 Broadway St., Box 315, Kincardine, ON, Canada N2Z 2Y8; phone (519) 396-2731 or (866) 546-2736.

KINCARDINE LIGHTHOUSE is downtown at the foot of Harbour St. directly off Hwy. 21. Built in 1881, the octagonal wooden lighthouse sits atop a two-story, six-room keeper's house. The three levels are joined by 69 steps. The lighthouse tower is topped by a red iron lantern and balcony. An exhibit about local history is in a museum at the base of the tower. Allow 30 minutes minimum. Mon.-Fri. 11-5, July 1-Labour Day. Admission $3, family rate $5. Phone (519) 396-3150 or (519) 396-4336.

PINE RIVER CHEESE AND BUTTER CO-OP, 10 km (6 mi.) s. on Hwy. 21, offers a videotape presentation about cheese making and observation areas to view the processing of Canadian cheddar.

Allow 30 minutes minimum. Visitors can view cheese being made Mon.-Fri. 9-noon. Video presentation available Mon.-Sat. 9-6 (also Fri. 6-7 p.m.), Sun. 11-6, Victoria Day weekend-second Mon. in Oct.; Mon.-Sat. 9-6, second Tues. in Oct.-Dec. 24; Mon-Sat. 9-5, rest of year. Closed Jan. 1 and Dec. 25-26. Free. Phone (519) 395-2638, or (800) 265-1175 in Ontario.

KINGSTON (F-11)
pop. 114,195, elev. 78 m/256'
See map page 87.

Kingston was founded in 1673 by Count Frontenac, governor of New France, as a fur-trading post and strategic military stronghold. The city boasts many ancient fortifications and early Canadian landmarks. Kingston's location on Lake Ontario at the junction of the Cataraqui (gateway to the Rideau Canal) and St. Lawrence rivers provides access to the Thousand Islands (*see place listing p. 173*), a vast unspoiled water playground.

Queen's University, on University Avenue, was founded in 1841 and is situated on 65 hectares (160 acres). The Grand Theatre, 218 Princess St., is an 820-seat facility offering concerts and theatrical productions. The theater also is home to the Kingston Symphony; phone (613) 546-4465 for theater information, (613) 546-9729 for symphony information or (613) 530-2050 for tickets.

The Loyalist Parkway, a scenic 100-kilometre (60-mi.) drive stretching along Hwy. 33 from Kingston to Trenton, passes through some 14 municipalities along the shoreline of Lake Ontario. Areas along the parkway offer opportunities for swimming, fishing, boating and picnicking. About 40 archeological sites and 125 historical buildings are adjacent to the highway for sightseeing.

Lake Ontario Park, 990 King St., has swimming, miniature golf, a children's playground, amusement

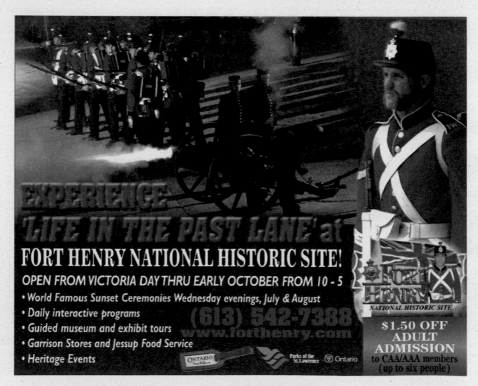

EXPERIENCE
'LIFE IN THE PAST LANE' at
FORT HENRY NATIONAL HISTORIC SITE!
OPEN FROM VICTORIA DAY THRU EARLY OCTOBER FROM 10 - 5
• World Famous Sunset Ceremonies Wednesday evenings, July & August
• Daily interactive programs
• Guided museum and exhibit tours
• Garrison Stores and Jessup Food Service
• Heritage Events

(613) 542-7388
www.forthenry.com

$1.50 OFF
ADULT ADMISSION
to CAA/AAA members
(up to six people)

ONTARIO
Parks of the St. Lawrence
Ontario

rides and picnic areas. Trips through the islands, excellent fishing, golfing, scuba diving and facilities for most water sports are available. Ferries link Kingston with Wolfe Island and Cape Vincent, N.Y.

A year-round farmers' market operates Tuesday, Thursday, Saturday, Sunday and Monday holidays behind the city hall in Market Square. A craft market joins the produce vendors from mid-April to mid-October, and an antique market is present on Sundays, late April to mid-October.

Kingston Economic Development Corporation—Tourist Information Office: 209 Ontario St., Kingston, ON, Canada K7L 2Z1; phone (613) 548-4415 or (888) 855-4555.

Shopping areas: The downtown area has several old limestone buildings that have been converted into specialty stores, including Cooke's Old World Shop, 61 Lower Brock St., and Cornerstone Fine Arts-Fine Crafts, 255 Ontario St.

The Cataraqui Town Centre, at 945 Gardiners Rd. near the junction of CR 38 and Hwy. 2, has The Bay, Sears and Zeller's among its 141 stores. Kingston Centre, bounded by Hwy. 2 and CR 33 and Sir John A. Macdonald Boulevard at 1096 Princess St., offers 80 shops and services.

1000 ISLANDS CRUISES-KINGSTON, departing from the Crawford Wharf at the foot of Brock St., offers 90-minute, 2-hour and 3- to 3.5-hour narrated tours of the Thousand Islands and Kingston Harbor aboard the *Island Queen,* a triple-deck paddlewheeler, and the *Island Belle,* a replica of a St. Lawrence River steamer. Live entertainment is featured on all 3-hour cruises. Lunch and dinner cruises aboard the glass-topped dining ship *Island Star* also are available.

Three-hour island cruises on the *Island Queen* depart daily at 10:30 and 2, late June-Labour Day; at 12:30, mid-May to late June and day after Labour Day-second Mon. in Oct. Two-hour sunset cruises depart daily at 6, late June-Labour Day. Ninety-minute harbor cruises aboard the *Island Belle* depart daily at 11, 1 and 3, mid-May through second Mon. in Oct. Boarding for sightseeing cruises is 15 minutes prior to departure.

Three-hour cruise $22.90; ages 4-12, $11.45. Ninety-minute cruise $16.85; ages 4-12, $8.40. Phone for sunset cruise fare. Reservations are recommended. AX, MC, VI. Phone (613) 549-5544. *See color ad p. 268.*

AGNES ETHERINGTON ART CENTRE is at Queen's University at University Ave. and Queen's Crescent. Changing exhibits of contemporary and historical Canadian art, consisting of almost 14,000 works, are presented throughout eight galleries. Collections also include paintings by European old masters, historic quilts and costumes, and West African and Inuit artwork.

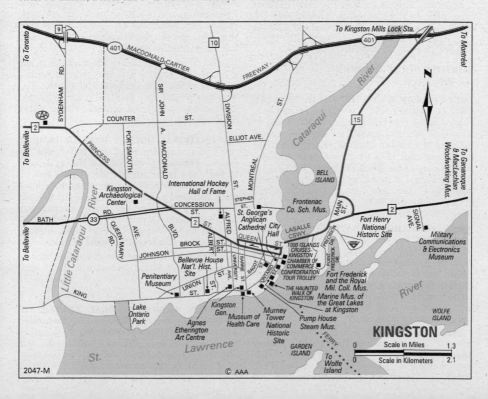

KINGSTON

2047-M   © AAA

Allow 30 minutes minimum. Tues.-Fri. 10-4:30, Sat.-Sun. and summer holidays 1-5; closed Jan. 1, Good Friday and Dec. 25. Admission $4; over 55, $2.50; free to all Thurs. Phone (613) 533-2190.

BELLEVUE HOUSE NATIONAL HISTORIC SITE, 1.5 km (.9 mi.) w. via King St. W. to 35 Centre St., was the residence of Sir John A. Macdonald, the first prime minister of Canada. Built about 1840, the Italianate villa has been restored and furnished in period style. The visitor center offers exhibits, costumed interpreters and a multilingual videotape presentation exploring Macdonald's contributions to Canadian history.

Daily 9-6, June 1-Labour Day; 10-5, Apr.-May and day after Labour Day-Oct. 31. Closed Good Friday and Easter Mon. Admission $3.50; over 64 and college students with ID $3; ages 6-16, $1.75. Phone (613) 545-8666, or TTY (613) 545-8668.

[SAVE] **CHAMBER OF COMMERCE CONFEDERA-TION TOUR TROLLEY** departs from the Tourist Information Office in Confederation Park at 209 Ontario St. A 50-minute exploration into Kingston's past lets visitors view the waterfront and many limestone buildings. Highlights of the tour include the Royal Military College, Fort Henry National Historic Site, penitentiaries, Portsmouth Olympic Harbour, Bellevue House National Historic Site and Queen's University *(see attraction listings)*.

Departures daily on the hour 10-7, July 1-Labour Day; daily 10-5, Victoria Day weekend-June 30; daily 10-2, day after Labour Day-second Mon. in Oct. Fare $11.95; over 64 and ages 6-17, $9.95. MC, VI. Phone (613) 548-4453.

FAIRFIELD HOUSE AND PARK— *see Amherstview p. 52.*

FORT FREDERICK AND THE ROYAL MILITARY COLLEGE MUSEUM is .7 km (.5 mi.) e. on CR 2. Housed in the Fort Frederick Tower, the largest of Kingston's Martello towers, the museum records the story of Canada's center of military education in existence since 1876, the exploits of its graduates and the story of the Royal Dockyard. The Douglas Arms collection is also displayed in the museum. Daily 10-5, late June-Labour Day. Donations. Phone (613) 541-6000, ext. 6664, or (613) 541-6000, ext. 6652 in the off-season.

[GEM] **FORT HENRY NATIONAL HISTORIC SITE** is e. on Hwy. 2 at Hwy. 15 (Hwy. 401 exit 623). Built during the War of 1812, the fort has been restored as a museum of British and Canadian military history. Interactive displays depict garrison life in the 1860s with rooms containing displays of militaria, clothing and artifacts. Others rooms house 19th-century military and naval arms and equipment.

The Garrison Parade is a 30-minute presentation of music, drill and artillery. The children's Military Muster Parade, offered three times daily, gives children the chance to "play soldier" with the Fort Henry Guard. The Guard also performs muster drills and military demonstrations. The Victorian schoolroom offers lessons in 1860s history and occasional opportunities to visit Fort Henry's goat mascot. Ghosts of the Fort, conducted by lantern-light, is a haunted walking tour of the fortress.

Guided tours and food are available. Fort Henry open daily 10-5, Victoria Day-early Oct. Garrison Parade daily at 3. Phone for schedule of tours, demonstrations and other special events. Admission $11; ages 13-18, $8.75; ages 5-12, $5.50; ages 2-4, $1.50. Rates may vary during special events. AX, MC, VI. Phone (613) 542-7388 or (800) 437-2233 to verify rates, or (613) 549-6366 for ghost tour information. *See color ad p. 86.*

FRONTENAC COUNTY SCHOOLS MUSEUM, 559 Bagot St., displays artifacts and archival records from the historic schoolhouses of Frontenac County. Exhibits include a turn-of-the-20th-century schoolroom complete with desks, and a gallery of artifacts including photographs, slates and books. Mon.-Fri. 9-4, July-Aug.; Mon.-Fri. 9-noon and 1-4, Feb.-June and Sept. 1-Dec. 15. Closed holidays. Admission $2; ages 6-18, $1. Phone (613) 544-9113.

THE HAUNTED WALK OF KINGSTON departs from the ticket booth in front of the Prince George Hotel, 200 Ontario St., opposite the Confederation Yacht Basin and beside City Hall. An evening tour through Kingston's historic ward is conducted by a cape-wearing, lantern-carrying guide. Stories—both ghostly and humorous—are related as the tour progresses past the district's grand old houses and little lanes of the market area.

Allow 1 hour, 30 minutes minimum. Tours are given daily at 8 and 9 p.m., July-Aug.; at 8 p.m., mid-May to late June and Sept. 1 to mid-Oct. Fee $12; over 64 and ages 13-19, $10; ages 6-12, $5. Reservations are recommended. Phone (613) 549-6366.

INTERNATIONAL HOCKEY HALL OF FAME is next to Kingston Memorial Centre at York and Alfred sts. Founded by the National Hockey League in 1943, this is the nation's oldest sports hall of fame. The game's heritage is preserved through artifacts dedicated to hockey's evolution and to those who shaped the game, in North America and around the world. Of note are Canada's first Olympic gold medal, won in 1924; an 1890s sweater; and items from the league's original six teams.

Daily noon-4, mid-June through Labour Day. Admission $4; over 54 and students with ID $3; ages 6-12, $2; family rate $10. MC, VI. Phone (613) 544-2355.

KINGSTON ARCHAEOLOGICAL CENTER, 72 Gilmour Ave., displays maps, models, illustrations and artifacts interpreting the history of Kingston and its environs from prehistoric times to the 19th century. A research library and archival collection are available by appointment. Mon.-Fri. 9-4; closed holidays. Donations. Phone (613) 542-3483.

KINGSTON CITY HALL, 216 Ontario St., was built 1843-44 and restored in 1973. The building is an excellent example of British Renaissance/Tuscan Revival-style architecture and 19th-century craftsmanship. Guided tours are available upon request. Open Mon.-Fri. 8:30-4:30; closed holidays. Guided tours are given Mon.-Fri. 10-4, late May to mid-Sept. Free. Phone (613) 546-4291.

KINGSTON MILLS LOCK STATION is 1 km (.6 mi.) n. of Hwy. 401 exit 623; go n. on Hwy. 15, then 2 km (1.2 mi.) w. on Kingston Mills Rd. (CR 21), following signs. Kingston's locks are the southernmost of 47 locks that make up the 202-kilometre (126-mi.) Rideau Canal between Ottawa and Kingston. This station has four adjoining locks that raise or lower boats 14 metres (45 ft.).

One of four blockhouses erected to protect the canal is furnished as it was in 1838 when occupied by the local militia. The lockmaster's house is the visitor center.

Picnicking at canal lockstations is permitted. Lockstations generally are open daily 8:30-7:30, late June-Aug. 31; 8:30-4:30, Victoria Day weekend to mid-June and Sept. 1 to mid-Oct. Blockhouse open daily, June 1-Labour Day. Hours may vary; phone ahead. Admission free. Parking $3. Phone (613) 283-5170 or (800) 230-0016.

MacLACHLAN WOODWORKING MUSEUM is 16 km (10 mi.) e. on CR 2 at Grass Creek Park. Housed in a 19th-century cedar log house, the museum contains more than 5,000 tools of the woodworking and other trades. On selected days in the summer demonstrations of traditional trades such as blacksmithing, candlemaking, cabinetry, spinning and baking bread in a wood-burning oven are presented.

Daily 10-5, Victoria Day weekend-Labour Day; Wed.-Sun. noon-4, Apr. 1-day before Victoria Day weekend and day after Labour Day-Nov. 30. Admission $3.75; over 64 and students with ID $3; ages 5-12, $1; family rate $8.50. Phone (613) 542-0543.

MARINE MUSEUM OF THE GREAT LAKES AT KINGSTON, 5 blks. w. of City Hall at 55 Ontario St., is in the 18th-century dry dock buildings along Kingston's historic waterfront. Exhibits about shipbuilding and shipwrecks and artifacts, engines and tools illustrate Great Lakes maritime history.

Also displayed is the 3,000-metric-ton (3,300-ton) icebreaker *Alexander Henry*; today the ship's cabins accommodate bed and breakfast guests. A library and archives are open upon request.

Picnicking is permitted. Museum open daily 10-5, May-Oct.; Mon.-Fri. 10-4, Jan.-Apr. and Nov. 1 to mid-Dec. Closed Jan. 1. Ship open daily 10-4, mid-May to mid-Oct.

A combination ticket with the *Alexander Henry* and the Pump House Steam Museum *(see attraction listing)* is available. Museum, ship or Pump House $5.25, over 60 and students with ID $4.75, family rate (two adults and up to four children under 12) $12. Two attractions $6.75, over 60 and students

with ID $5.75, family rate (two adults and up to four children under 12) $14. Three attractions $8.25, over 60 and students with ID $6.75, family rate (two adults and up to four children under 12) $17. AX, MC, VI. Phone (613) 542-2261.

MILITARY COMMUNICATIONS AND ELECTRONICS MUSEUM, 4 km (2.5 mi.) e. on CR 2 in Vimy Barracks, traces the history and development of Canadian military communication from 1867 to the present. Themed exhibits include the Riel Rebellion, both World Wars and United Nations peacekeeping missions. An archives room is available by appointment. Mon.-Fri. 8-4, Sat.-Sun. and Mon. holidays 11-5, May-Sept.; Mon.-Fri. 8-4, rest of year. Closed holidays and Dec. 19-Jan. 3. Donations. Phone (613) 541-4675.

MURNEY TOWER NATIONAL HISTORIC SITE, in Macdonald Park at King and Barrie sts., is a Martello tower built in 1846 as one of a series of coastal defenses. Now a museum, it houses a collection of historical archives and materials depicting 19th-century military life in Kingston. Daily 10-5, mid-May through Labour Day. Admission $3, under 8 free, family rate $10. Phone (613) 544-9925.

MUSEUM OF HEALTH CARE is in the Ann Baillie Building on the grounds of Kingston General Hospital on George St. In a 1904 limestone building formerly used as a nurses' residence, the museum houses more than 27,000 artifacts dating from the late 18th century to the present. Included are medical, surgical and laboratory instruments; patent medicine containers; nursing gear; patient care items; and life support machines. Guided historic walking tours of the hospital buildings and grounds also are offered.

Allow 30 minutes minimum. Museum Tues.-Sun. 10-4, June-Aug.; Tues.-Fri. 10-4, rest of year. Closed major holidays. Walking tours daily at 2, Victoria Day weekend-Labour Day. Museum by donations. Walking tour $5. Phone (613) 548-2419.

PENITENTIARY MUSEUM, 555 King St. W., with vehicle entrance off Sir John A. Macdonald Blvd., is on the grounds of the Kingston Penitentiary. Housed in the original warden's residence, the museum illustrates the history of Canadian penitentiaries through a variety of artifacts and documents. There are exhibits about methods of punishment, homemade weapons and prisoners' inventions of convenience.

Allow 30 minutes minimum. Mon.-Fri. 9-4, Sat.-Sun. and holidays 10-4, May-Sept.; otherwise by appointment. Last admission 30 minutes before closing. Donations. Phone (613) 530-3122.

PUMP HOUSE STEAM MUSEUM, 23 Ontario St., illustrates the relationship between steam and the 19th century through the interpretation of the restored 1850 waterworks plant and a large model train display. The Gordon C. Leitch Discovery Centre offers interactive displays that demonstrate the world of small machines.

Daily 10-4, Victoria Day weekend-Sept. 30. A combination ticket with Marine Museum of the Great Lakes at Kingston *(see attraction listing)* and the icebreaker *Alexander Henry* is available. Museum, ship or Marine Museum $5.25, over 60 and students with ID $4.75, family rate (two adults and up to four children under 12) $12. Two attractions $6.75, over 60 and students with ID $5.75, family rate (two adults and up to four children under 12) $14. Three attractions $8.25, over 60 and students with ID $6.75, family rate (two adults and up to four children under 12) $17. AX, MC, VI. Phone (613) 542-2261.

ST. GEORGE'S ANGLICAN CATHEDRAL, corner of King and Johnson sts., is a neoclassical domed building dating from 1825. A memorial to Molly Brant, sister of the celebrated Mohawk leader Joseph Brant and the cathedral's only female founding member, is on the right side wall of the church. Needlepoint kneelers depicting the history of the church since 1785 and a Tiffany stained glass window also are featured.

Mon.-Fri. 10-4 (also Fri. 4-7), Sat. 10-1, June-Sept.; Fri. 4-7, Sun. noon-1, rest of year. Guided 30-minute tours are available. Donations. Phone (613) 548-4617.

KINGSVILLE (I-5) pop. 19,619

Some 56 kilometres (35 mi.) south of Detroit, Kingsville is a port city rich with Victorian heritage. Situated on Lake Erie, it is one of the southernmost towns in Ontario. Pelee Island and Sandusky, Ohio, are connected to Kingsville by ferry.

The city lies directly in the migration path of Canada geese. Recreational activities include bicycling, boating, golfing, hiking, swimming and bird- and butterfly-watching.

Convention & Visitors Bureau of Windsor, Essex County & Pelee Island—Kingsville: 333 Riverside Dr. W., Suite 103, Windsor, ON, Canada N9A 5K4; phone (519) 255-6530 or (800) 265-3633.

JACK MINER'S BIRD SANCTUARY, 3 km (1.9 mi.) n. off Division Rd. and w. on Concession Rd. 3, covers 809 hectares (2,000 acres). Established in 1904 by conservationist Jack Miner, this sanctuary was the model for approximately 250 subsequent refuges in the United States. Thousands of migratory Canada geese and wild ducks can be seen during peak migration seasons.

The best time for viewing the birds is from 3 to dusk during the last 2 weeks of March and the first week of April (depending upon weather conditions), the last 2 weeks of October and all of November. A small museum has a map showing the flight course followed by the birds. Staff members demonstrate feeding and are available to answer questions. Allow 30 minutes minimum. Mon.-Sat. 8-5. Free. Phone (519) 733-4034 or (877) 289-8328.

SOUTHWESTERN ONTARIO HERITAGE VILLAGE AND TRANSPORTATION MUSEUM, w. on CR 20, then 8 km (5 mi.) n. on CR 23 to 6155 Arner Townline (CR 23), encompasses buildings dating 1826-1925 that were moved from other locations and restored, including a church, general store, doctor's office, one-room schoolhouse, barn, barber/cobbler shop, train station and several houses. A nature walk winds through natural forest.

The transportation museum has antique vehicles, including one of the only two 1893 Shamrock horseless carriages built.

Picnicking is permitted. Allow 1 hour, 30 minutes minimum. Daily 10-5, July-Aug.; Wed.-Sun. 10-5, Apr.-June and Sept.-Nov.; otherwise by appointment. One-hour guided tours are offered. Last admittance and tour are 1 hour before closing. Admission $5; over 59 and ages 13-17, $4; ages 5-12, $3; family rate (five persons) $15. Rates may vary during special events. AX, MC, VI. Phone (519) 776-6909 or (866) 776-6909.

WINERIES

- **[SAVE] Pelee Island Winery** is at 455 Seacliff Dr. (CR 20). Tours daily at noon, 2 and 4; closed Jan. 1, Good Friday, Easter and Dec. 25-26. Phone (519) 733-6551 or (800) 597-3533.

KIRKLAND LAKE (B-7) pop. 8,616

In northeastern Ontario's rich forestry and mining district, Kirkland Lake's main street, or "Mile of Gold," is built on gold-bearing rock.

Kirkland Chamber of Commerce: 6 Tweedsmuir Rd., P.O. Box 966, Kirkland Lake, ON, Canada P2N 3L1; phone (705) 567-5444.

[SAVE] MUSEUM OF NORTHERN HISTORY AT SIR HARRY OAKES CHATEAU is at 2 Chateau Dr., off Hwy. 66 at the w. end of Kirkland Lake. Sir Harry was the founder of the prosperous Lake Shore Gold Mine, and as visitors tour the chateau they learn of his rags-to-riches life and his mysterious murder in the Bahamas. Pioneer life and gold mining exhibits are presented.

Guided 30-minute tours Mon.-Sat. and holidays 10-4, Sun. noon-4; closed Jan. 1-2 and Dec. 25-26. Last tour departs 1 hour before closing. Admission $4; over 54, $3; students with ID $2; ages 5-13, $1. Phone (705) 568-8800.

KITCHENER (G-2)
pop. 190,399, elev. 336 m/1,102'

The first settlers in what is now Kitchener arrived in 1799 from Pennsylvania. In the midst of a prosperous Mennonite farming area a bustling community arose; by 1833 it was named Berlin. A large influx of immigrants from the German states of central Europe and the United Kingdom turned Berlin into a bustling industrial city by 1912. During World War I, the name was changed to Kitchener, in honor of Lord Kitchener, a British hero of that war.

As part of the twin cities of Kitchener and Waterloo *(see place listing p. 212)*, Kitchener retains the heritage of the early settlers in the many festivals that take place throughout the year. For 9 days in early October the city warms to the traditional festivities of Oktoberfest, which include festhallens, parades, dances, competitions and carnivals. This festival is reputed to be the largest Bavarian festival held outside of Munich, Germany.

KW Tourism—Kitchener: 191 King St. W., Kitchener, ON, Canada N2G 1N1; phone (519) 745-3536 or (800) 265-6959.

Shopping areas: Fairview Park Mall, King Street and Fairway Road, is the city's largest mall and has The Bay and Sears. Market Square, downtown at 79 Frederick St., has a variety of smaller shops, in addition to the Saturday Kitchener's Farmers' Market. The farmers' market at Frederick and Duke streets has operated since 1869.

For information about Kitchener's numerous factory outlet stores contact CAA Mid-Western Ontario, 148 Manitou Dr., Kitchener, ON, Canada N2C 1L3; phone (519) 894-2582.

BINGEMANS, 425 Bingemans Centre Dr., has a variety of recreational facilities, including a wave pool, wading pool, six waterslides, bumper boats, go-carts, two miniature golf courses, a nine-hole golf course, batting cages, rock climbing, a children's playhouse and a children's water park. Campsites and cabins are available.

Food is available. Daily 10-dusk, June 1-Labour Day. Admission to grounds free; fee for individual attractions. All-day pass $24.53; over 64 and ages 5-11, $21.17; ages 2-4, $7.48. Water park $14.49; over 64 and ages 5-11, $11.45; ages 2-4, $2.48. AX, MC, VI. Phone (519) 744-1555 or (800) 565-4631.

DOON HERITAGE CROSSROADS is 3 km (1.8 mi.) n.w. of Hwy. 401 exit 275 on Homer Watson Blvd. Doon Heritage Crossroads is a 1914 museum village and two farms set in 24 hectares (60 acres) of forest, marsh and farmland.

With a surge in immigration, the increasing popularity of telephones and automobiles, the availability of electricity and the onset of World War I, rural crossroads communities were no longer isolated. More than 25 buildings, period furnishings, farm animals, heritage gardens and demonstrations of daily chores re-create this time of dramatic change in Canada.

The township hall; railway station; weavery; general store; harness, print, blacksmith and tailor shops; post office; and church offer depictions of early 20th-century life.

Picnicking is available. Daily 10-4:30, May 1-Labour Day; Mon.-Fri. 10-4:30, day after Labour Day-Dec. 23. Admission $6; over 54 and students with ID $4; ages 5-12, $3; family rate $15. MC, VI. Phone (519) 748-1914.

HOMER WATSON HOUSE AND GALLERY, just off the Homer Watson Blvd. exit from Hwy. 401 at 1754 Old Mill Rd., is the home and studio of one of Canada's noted landscape artists. The studio contains Watson's original palette, easel and paint box and a frieze he painted directly on the wall in 1894. Contemporary Canadian artists' works are displayed in changing exhibits.

The park-like setting has walking trails. Allow 30 minutes minimum. Tues.-Sun. and holiday Mon. noon-4:30, mid-Jan. to mid-Dec. Donations. Phone (519) 748-4377.

JOSEPH SCHNEIDER HAUS MUSEUM AND GALLERY, 466 Queen St. S., is a restored Pennsylvania German Mennonite house that depicts life in the 1850s; outbuildings and a four-square garden also are part of the site. Costumed staff members interpret daily activities of this farming family as well as seasonal events such as quilting bees. Changing exhibits from the museum's folk art collection and from the local community are presented in two galleries.

Daily 10-5, July-Aug.; Wed.-Sat. 10-5, Sun. 1-5, Sept. 1-Dec. 24 and mid-Feb. through June 30. Admission $2.25; over 64 and students with ID $1.50; ages 5-12, $1.25; family rate $5. Phone (519) 742-7752.

KITCHENER-WATERLOO ART GALLERY, in the Centre in the Square at 101 Queen St. N., displays contemporary and historical Canadian and international art. Exhibitions of paintings, sculptures, drawings, photography, prints and video change every 8 weeks. The gallery has a permanent collection of 4,000 works, including pieces by Pablo Picasso and the Group of Seven. Workshops and lectures are scheduled throughout the year.

Guided tours and food are available. Allow 30 minutes minimum. Mon.-Sat. 10-5 (also Thurs. 5-9), Sun. 1-5; closed holidays. Donations. Phone (519) 579-5860.

SPORTSWORLD, 1.2 km (.7 mi.) n. off Hwy. 401 on Hwy. 8, is a family entertainment facility comprised of a 2-hectare (4.5-acre) water park with a heated wave pool, waterslides, two-person tube slides and a children's water play area. An amusement park offers traditional midway rides, indoor/outdoor rock climbing, go-carts, two miniature golf courses, an arcade, batting cages and an indoor driving range.

Food is available. Indoor facilities open daily 10-10, year-round. Water park open daily 10-8, July-Aug.; 10-4, in June. Midway rides open daily 10-9, June 1-Labour Day.

Grounds free. All-day pass to complex (includes unlimited midway rides and water park as well as other games and activities) $27.57; over 64 and ages 5-11, $23.59; ages 2-4, $7.95. All-day admission to water park $15.89; over 64 and ages 5-11, $11.22; ages 2-4, $1.87. Water park admission after 4 p.m. $9.81. MC, VI. Phone (519) 653-4442 to verify prices or (800) 393-9163.

WATERLOO REGIONAL CHILDREN'S MUSEUM is 2 blks w. of Market Square Mall at 10 King St. W. Pay parking ($2 for 3 hours) is available at a garage behind the museum; museum access is from the second floor of the garage. In a building formerly occupied by a department store, the museum has four floors of inventive and interactive exhibits in such themed areas as Building Blocks, Mechanical City & the Water Garden, and Energy Playground. Children can explore shadow and color, create their own fort and discover different types of energy.

Allow 1 hour minimum. Mon.-Sat. 10-5, Sun. noon-5, Victoria Day-Labour Day; Tues.-Sat. and holiday Mon. 10-5, Sun. noon-5, rest of year. Closed some holidays and first full week in Sept. Last admission 1 hour before closing. Phone ahead to confirm schedule. Admission $7, under 2 free. MC, VI. Phone (519) 749-9387.

WOODSIDE NATIONAL HISTORIC SITE, 528 Wellington St. N., is the boyhood home of William Lyon Mackenzie King, the 10th prime minister of Canada. The house, set on more than 4 hectares (10 acres) of wooded grounds, has been carefully restored and furnished to the Victorian style of 1891, guided by King's reflection on his family life.

Guided tours cover both the formal and informal areas of the middle-class home where Willie, as he was affectionately known, lived with his parents and three siblings. A video presentation provides an orientation to the house and its residents. Visitors can see the kitchen, with its cast-iron cook-stove; the dining room, which also served as a family sitting room; the library; the elaborately furnished parlor; family bedrooms; and the basement. Holiday events depict typical Victorian celebrations.

Picnicking is permitted. Daily 10-5, Victoria Day weekend-Dec. 23; closed Nov. 11. Admission $3.50; over 65, $3; students $1.75; under 5 free; family rate $8.75. Phone (519) 571-5684.

KLEINBURG (F-3)

KORTRIGHT CENTRE FOR CONSERVATION— *see Woodbridge p. 215.*

McMICHAEL CANADIAN ART COLLECTION, at 10365 Islington Ave. n. of Regional Rd. 7 (Hwy. 7), showcases 20th-century Canadian art including works by Canada's celebrated landscape artists known as the Group of Seven, and collections of First Nation, Inuit and contemporary Canadian works. Also available are outdoor sculpture, nature trails and the historic cemetery where six of the Group of Seven members were laid to rest.

The sprawling complex of galleries is situated on a 40-hectare (100-acre) tract of woodlands and meadows that provides a panorama of the Humber River Valley. The setting gives visitors the opportunity to enjoy Canadian landscape paintings in the woodland setting that inspired them. Special events include films, lectures and afternoon concerts every second Sunday.

Food is available. Allow 1 hour, 30 minutes minimum. Daily 10-5, May-Oct.; 10-4, rest of year. Closed Dec. 25. Admission $15, over 64 and students with ID $12, under 5 free, family rate (up to five persons) $30. Parking $5. AX, MC, VI. Phone (905) 893-1121 or (888) 213-1121.

LANSDOWNE (F-11)

PARKWAY BOAT LINE departs from the Front Dock at the Ivy Lea Resort and Marina on 1000 Islands Pkwy., 4 km (2.5 mi.) w. of 1000 Island Bridge. The history and ecology of the Thousand Islands are explained during 2-hour narrated cruises through this portion of the St. Lawrence River. From mid-May to mid-October an optional stopover at Boldt Castle *(see attraction listing in Gananoque p. 75)* is included, except for the last trip of the day.

Departures daily at 10, 12:30 and 3, July 1-late Aug.; at 10 and 12:30 (also occasionally at 3), mid-May through June 30 and late Aug. to mid-Oct. (weather permitting); schedule varies in early May and mid-Oct. through Oct. 31. Phone ahead to confirm schedule. Fare $25; ages 6-12, $5. There is an additional charge to tour Boldt Castle. A photo ID and proof of citizenship or a passport are required. VI. Phone (613) 659-4622.

LEAMINGTON (I-6) pop. 27,138

French *voyageurs* and missionaries visited this area in the 17th century, but the first settler, Alex Wilkinson, did not arrive until the mid-19th century. The new settlement had three different names—Wilkinson Corners, Gainsborough and, finally, Leamington, for prominent townsman William Gaines' hometown in England. Although Gaines shaped the town's early fortunes, the H.J. Heinz Co. left a greater impression when it built a factory in 1907.

Many consider Leamington the tomato capital of Canada and have enshrined this fact in the local information booth, 76 Talbot St. W., which resembles an immense tomato.

For butterfly- and bird-watchers and outdoor enthusiasts, nearby Point Pelee National Park *(see place listing p. 158)* provides opportunities for observing migrating birds, butterflies and wildfowls. A large number of shipwrecks can be found in the Pelee Passage, and scuba diving charters are available. A marina accommodates those with their own boats. Other recreational options include fishing and windsurfing.

Leamington and District Chamber of Commerce: 21 Talbot St. E., P.O. Box 321, Leamington, ON, Canada N8H 3W3; phone (519) 326-2721 or (800) 250-3336.

COLASANTI'S TROPICAL GARDENS AND PETTING FARM, 7 km (4 mi.) w. off Hwy. 3 on Third Concession Rd., has 1.4 hectares (3.5 acres) of greenhouses containing a variety of plantlife such as houseplants, tropical plants, cactuses and bonsai trees. There also are tropical birds, reptiles, jungle cats and farm animals, including a miniature horse. On the grounds are an animal exhibit and zoo, an indoor miniature golf course and an indoor playground. Special events are offered throughout the year.

Picnicking is permitted. Food is available. Mon.-Thurs. 8-5, Fri.-Sun. and holidays 8-6; closed Jan. 1 and Dec. 25. Pony rides are available Sat.-Sun. Free. Pony rides $1. Phone (519) 326-3287.

LINDSAY (F-9) pop. 17,757

Lindsay, between lakes Sturgeon and Scugog, became a farming and lumbering center following the construction of a government dock and dam completed in 1844. Now part of the Trent Canal System, Lindsay is a main gateway to the Kawartha Lakes tourist region.

Boasting the widest downtown street in Canada, Lindsay is home to the 682-seat Academy Theatre for Performing Arts, 2 Lindsay St. S., presenting plays and concerts year-round; phone (705) 324-9111 or (877) 888-0038. The Lindsay Little Theatre, 55 George St. W., presents several productions throughout the year; phone (705) 324-2445.

Visitors can browse through antique shops and art galleries, pinch the fruit at the Saturday morning farmers' market May to mid-October, or shop at three local malls. Golfers can play at six public golf courses within 20 minutes of Lindsay.

City of Kawartha Lakes Tourism: 26 Francis St., P.O. Box 9000, Lindsay, ON, Canada K9V 5R8; phone (705) 324-9411 or (866) 397-6673.

VICTORIA COUNTY HISTORICAL SOCIETY MUSEUM, 50 Victoria Ave. N., offers traveling exhibits. **Note:** The museum is closed for renovations; reopening is expected May 2005. Phone ahead to confirm schedule and rates. Mon.-Sat. 10-5, June-Aug.; Mon.-Fri. 10-5, rest of year. Hours may vary; phone for schedule. Admission $3; under 12, $2. Phone (705) 324-3404.

LONDON (H-1) pop. 336,539, elev. 259 m/850′

London's ties to the English capital are evident in the name of the city, its streets and even the river that runs through the heart of town. In 1792 Col. John Graves Simcoe founded London and lobbied to develop it as the capital of Upper Canada. Though his campaign failed, he did change the name of the river from the Iroquois name *Askunessippi* to Thames.

London, a commercial and industrial center, boasts a substantial number of parks. This, coupled with a century-old program of planting approximately 1,000 trees annually, has earned London the nickname "Forest City." Museums and galleries also are plentiful in the city, covering everything from local history to medical research and achievements. Double-decker buses departing from the downtown visitor information center tour London daily at 10 and 2 from July 1 through Labour Day.

The London Airshow & Balloon Festival takes place at the London Airport in late June; more than 75,000 attend the annual event. Beginning the second weekend in September, the Western Fair is one of Canada's largest fairs, with 10 days of exhibits, music and entertainment; more than 300,000 persons attend annually.

Tourism London: 267 Dundas St., London, ON, Canada N6A 1H2; phone (519) 661-5000 or (800) 265-2602.

Self-guiding tours: Information about London walking tours is available at Tourism London.

Shopping areas: London has three major malls, each with more than 200 department stores and specialty shops. Masonville Place, 1680 Richmond St. N. at the southeast corner of hwys. 22 and 4, has The Bay, Sears and Zellers as its anchors. Westmount can be found at 785 Wonderland Rd. S. and counts Sears and Zellers as its anchor stores. White Oaks, at 1105 Wellington Rd. S., just north of Hwy. 401, has The Bay.

The many small shops and boutiques of Richmond Row, on Richmond Street from Oxford to Carling streets, offer local crafts, antiques, clothing and gift items. For fresh produce, meats and specialty foods, visit Covent Garden Market, downtown at 130 King St.

BANTING HOUSE NATIONAL HISTORIC SITE is at 442 Adelaide St. N. at jct. Queens Ave. It was in London that Sir Frederick Banting conceived the idea that led to the discovery of insulin. Several rooms of the house in which he lived and practiced medicine 1920-21 are furnished in period.

Displays depict the development of insulin and give information about Banting who, in addition to being Canada's first Nobel laureate, was awarded the Military Cross and knighthood and was an accomplished artist. Allow 30 minutes minimum. Tues.-Sat. noon-4; closed major holidays. Admission $4; students with ID and ages 6-18, $3; family rate $8. MC, VI. Phone (519) 673-1752.

ELDON HOUSE, 481 Ridout St. N., dates from 1834 and is the oldest residence in the city. The 19th-century original family furnishings and treasures are interesting, and a large re-created 19th-century garden can be visited. Afternoon tea is served July through the last Sunday in August.

House open Tues.-Sun. noon-5, June-Sept.; Wed.-Sun. noon-5 in May and Oct.-Dec.; Sat.-Sun. noon-5, rest of year. Admission $5; over 64, $4; under 16, $1; family rate $10; by donation Wed. and Sun. Phone (519) 661-5169.

FANSHAWE PIONEER VILLAGE is in Fanshawe Conservation Area; from Hwy. 401 take Airport Rd. n., then w. on Huron St. and n. on Clarke Rd. The village, made up of 30 buildings, gardens and an orchard, depicts a 19th- and early 20th-century crossroads community typical of southwestern Ontario. Costumed interpreters demonstrate heritage crafts and skills. Special events are held throughout the season.

Village open Tues.-Sun. and holiday Mon. 10-4:30, Victoria Day-second Mon. in Oct.; special event weekends only 10-4:30, Oct.-Dec. Village admission $5; over 64 and students with ID $4; ages 3-12, $3; family rate $15. VI. Phone (519) 457-1296. See Recreation Chart and the AAA/CAA Eastern Canada CampBook.

GUY LOMBARDO MUSEUM/MUSIC CENTER, off Hwy. 2N at 205 Wonderland Rd. S., has such music memorabilia as gramophones, cylinder record players, pump organs and a player piano. Also displayed are mementos from the famous bandleader's life and his racing hydroplane Tempo VII. A 30-minute video traces the background of Lombardo and his Royal Canadians, a band best known for its New Year's Eve performance of "Auld Lang Syne" in New York City.

Guided tours are available by appointment. Allow 30 minutes minimum. Wed.-Sun. 9-noon and 1-5, mid-June through Labour Day; Sun. 12:30-4:30 and by appointment, rest of year. Donations. Phone (519) 473-9003, or (519) 652-3417 in the off-season.

LONDON MUSEUM OF ARCHAEOLOGY, 2 blks. s. of Fanshawe Park Rd. off Wonderland Rd. N. at 1600 Attawandaron Rd., depicts 11,000 years of history in southwestern Ontario. A partially reconstructed 500-year-old Iroquoian heritage village is featured and includes an excavation site with archeology demonstrations (weather permitting). Also featured are exhibits arranged according to five periods of development. An 8-minute videotape presentation focuses on the museum's collection and the excavation site.

Museum open daily 10-4:30, May-Aug.; Wed.-Sun. 10-4:30, Sept.-Dec.; Sat.-Sun. 1-4, rest of year. Archeology demonstrations May-Aug. Admission $3.50; over 59 and students with ID $2.75; ages 5-12, $1.50; family rate (two adults and four children) $8. MC, VI. Phone (519) 473-1360.

LONDON REGIONAL CHILDREN'S MUSEUM, s. of the bridge at 21 Wharncliffe Rd. S., presents three floors of hands-on, interactive exhibits for children from infants to 12 years of age. Among the nine themed galleries are Dinosaur, Street Where You Live, Arctic Adventure, Science in Your World, My Place in Space, Child Long Ago and Caves.

Daily 10-5 (also Fri. 5-8), May-Aug., Mar. break and holidays; Tues.-Sun. 10-5 (also Fri. 5-8), rest of year. Closed Jan. 1 and Dec. 25-26. Admission $5, under 2 free. Under 12 must be with an adult. MC, VI. Phone (519) 434-5726.

MUSEUM LONDON is at 421 Ridout St. N., overlooking the Thames River. This dramatically modern building, one of the country's largest art galleries, contains a collection of fine art and artifacts. Changing exhibitions by renowned artists are complemented by films, lectures, music and live

Know Before You Go

Travel plans become crystal clear in the pages of AAA TourBooks® or online at aaa.com.

Each of the advertisers makes your travel choices easier by featuring photographs, detailed descriptions, toll-free numbers and Web addresses for their hotels, restaurants or attractions.

  Travel with Confidence.
Travel with AAA.

performances. Photographs, documents and rare artifacts depict the history of the region. Tues.-Sun. noon-5; closed holidays. Donations. Phone (519) 661-0333.

THE ROYAL CANADIAN REGIMENT MUSEUM, 750 Elizabeth St. in the 1886 Wolseley Hall, contains displays illustrating the regiment's service since its formation in 1883. The museum also has other artifacts of historical interest. Guided tours are available with advance notice. Tues.-Fri. 10-4, Sat.-Sun. noon-4; closed legal holidays (except Canada Day) and week of Dec. 25. Free. Phone (519) 660-5102.

ST. PAUL'S CATHEDRAL, 472 Richmond St., is London's oldest church. Detailed canvas embroideries and four Louis Comfort Tiffany stained-glass windows are featured in the 1846 structure. Also of interest is St. Aidan Chapel, with canvas embroideries depicting the life of the saint. Guided tours are available. Allow 30 minutes minimum. Mon.-Fri. 11-4, Sun. after 11 a.m. service, July-Aug.; Mon.-Fri. 11-4, rest of year. Closed legal holidays. Free concerts are offered Tues. at 12:15. Donations. Phone (519) 434-3225.

STORYBOOK GARDENS is at 1958 Storybook Ln. in Springbank Park. This family-oriented amusement park features eight themed areas: The Castle, Storybook Valley, Slippery's Great Escape, The Village & Backwoods, Frog Pond, Pirates' Island, Old McDonald's Farm and the Enchanted Forest. A rock climbing wall, pirate ship, water habitat, farm animals, a summer water play area that becomes a winter skating area, and a maze are part of the fun.

Food is available. Picnicking is permitted. Daily 10-8, Jan. 15, May 1-second Mon. in Oct. and Dec. 2-30; 10-4, rest of year. Admission $8.25; ages 11-17, $5.75; ages 5-10, $5.25; ages 2-4, $2.50; family rate (up to two adults and four children in same household) $35.25. MC, VI. Phone (519) 661-5824.

MADOC (F-9) pop. 2,044

O'HARA MILL PIONEER VILLAGE AND CONSERVATION AREA is n.w. on Mill Rd., following signs from either Hwy. 62 or Hwy. 7. The site contains a number of restored structures dating from the 19th century, including an 1850 farmhouse, a sawmill, carriage house, blacksmith shop, carpenter's shop and a log schoolhouse. The O'Hara Mill depicts the domestic and agricultural life of the O'Hara family from the mid-1800s to the mid-1900s.

Conservation area open daily dawn-dusk. Buildings open Wed.-Sun. 10-4, July-Aug. Admission $2; ages 1-12, $1. Phone (613) 473-2084 for museum schedule or (613) 968-3434 in the off-season.

MAGNETAWAN (E-8) pop. 1,342

Formerly the midpoint of a steamboat route, Magnetawan's hand-operated dam and lock still serve pleasure boats. A painting by A.J. Casson,

who was a member of the renowned Group of Seven, depicts the town's St. George the Martyr Anglican Church as "The Church on the Rock." The painting is exhibited at the National Gallery of Canada in Ottawa.

Self-guiding tours: A self-guiding walking tour map of the town is available from the Woodland Echoes Resort, Hwy. 520 (Nipissing Road); phone (705) 387-3866. The resort also has information about a driving tour of the Ontario Ghost Trail (Nipissing Road). The ghost trail, part of the Trans Canada Trail, is lined with the abandoned cabins and barns of pioneer settlers; 23 plaques mark historical sites along the route.

MAGNETAWAN HISTORICAL MUSEUM, on Hwy. 520 at the locks, is housed in a restored 1925 hydroelectric plant and features pioneer memorabilia. A log cabin also is on the grounds. Allow 30 minutes minimum. Daily 10-4, July-Aug.; by appointment rest of year. Admission $1; under 18, 50c. Phone (705) 387-3308.

MANITOULIN ISLAND (E-5)

Believed to be the world's largest freshwater island, Manitoulin Island is 176 kilometres (110 mi.) long and 5 to 80 kilometres (3 to 50 mi.) wide. More than 100 lakes speckle the interior, including Lake Manitou—thought to be the world's largest lake within a lake. Within *that* lake are several more islands. Opportunities abound for hiking, bicycling, fishing, camping, boating and scuba diving.

Gordon's Park, near Tehkummah just north of Regional Road 542 at 18777 Hwy. 6, offers recreational activities year-round. An outdoor wildlife museum, two hiking trails, bicycling, snowmobiling, archery, astronomy and miniature golf are some of the options; phone (705) 859-2470.

Farmers' markets are held Fridays and Saturdays at several locations on the island between Victoria Day weekend and the second Monday in October. Fresh produce, baked goods and local crafts are among the items for sale; phone (705) 859-3046 for information. The island also contains five Indian reservations.

Manitoulin Island is accessible from the Bruce Peninsula by ferry from Tobermory *(see place listing p. 177)* or from Espanola via Hwy. 6 to Little Current.

Manitoulin Tourism Association: P.O. Box 119, Little Current, ON, Canada P0P 1K0; phone (705) 368-3021.

ASSIGINACK MUSEUM, in Manitowaning off Hwy. 6 on Arthur St., displays pioneer relics in an old stone building that was once the town jail. An 1880s barn, school, blacksmith shop and pioneer house are among the highlights. Daily 10-5, June-Sept. Admission $2; ages 6-12, $1; family rate $5. Combination admission for the Assiginack Museum and SS *Norisle*—Heritage Park $3; under 12, $1.50; family rate $6. Phone (705) 859-3905.

CENTENNIAL MUSEUM OF SHEGUIANDAH, 10 km (6 mi.) s. of Little Current on Hwy. 6 at Sheguiandah, includes seven buildings in a 3-hectare (7-acre) woodland setting. Artifacts dating back 9,500 years have been discovered, making it one of the oldest settlements in North America. The museum contains tools, furnishings, clothing and records of settlers.

Daily 10-4:30, mid-May to mid-Sept.; daily 1-4:30, mid-Apr. to mid-May; Wed.-Sun. 1-4:30, mid-Sept. to late Nov. Admission $4; over 54, $3.50; ages 12-16, $3; ages 6-11, $2; family rate (up to six persons) $10. Phone (705) 368-2367, or (705) 368-3500 in the off-season.

GORE BAY MUSEUM is at the w. end of Dawson St. in Gore Bay, following signs. In a stone jail operational from the 1890s to the 1940s, the museum has the original jail cells, an eating table with inmate carvings in the wood and exhibits depicting pioneer and native life and rural law enforcement. Art exhibits feature local and regional artists. Allow 1 hour minimum. Mon.-Sat. 10-4, Sun. 2-4, Apr.-Oct.; closed Labour Day weekend and Oct. 9-11. Admission $3; over 64, $2; ages 2-15, $1. Phone (705) 282-2040.

MISSISSAGI LIGHTHOUSE MUSEUM is at the westernmost tip of the island; from CR 540 at Meldrum Bay take Mississagi Lighthouse Rd. for 10 km (6 mi.), following signs. Established as a lighthouse in 1873, it is now a small museum in which rooms appear as they did when occupied by the keeper and his family. Artifacts from local shipwrecks also are displayed.

Attractive grounds provide good views of the Mississagi Strait. The area offers hiking, fishing and swimming. Food and picnic facilities are available. Daily 10-6, Victoria Day weekend-Labour Day. Phone to verify spring hours. Admission $2, under 10 free. Phone (705) 283-1084, or (705) 368-3021 in the off-season.

MS *CHI-CHEEMAUN*, docked at Hwy. 6 in South Baymouth on Manitoulin Island and in Tobermory at the tip of the Bruce Peninsula, is a large ferry whose prow swings open to accommodate 143 vehicles. The *Chi-Cheemaun*, meaning "the big canoe," connects the mainland with Manitoulin Island via 1.75-hour trips across Georgian Bay. The ship has a capacity of 638 passengers.

Four trips depart daily, late June-Labour Day; two trips daily (three on Fri. and Mon. holidays), early May-late June and day after Labour Day to mid-Oct. One-way passenger fare $12.50; over 64, $10.85; ages 5-11, $6.25; family rate $42.10. Extra charge for vehicles. Reservations are available on some trips. AX, MC, VI. Phone (519) 376-6601 in Owen Sound, (705) 859-3161 in South Baymouth, (519) 596-2510 in Tobermory, or (800) 265-3163.

SS *NORISLE*—**HERITAGE PARK,** in Manitowaning, includes the Manitowaning Roller Mills, a 19th-century grist and flour mill containing agricultural displays, and the SS *Norisle,* the last steam-powered passenger ship on the Great Lakes.

Swimming facilities are available. Picnicking is permitted. Daily 10-5, July-Aug. Admission $2; ages 6-12, $1; family rate $5. Combination admission for Assiginack Museum and SS *Norisle*—Heritage Park $3; under 12, $1.50; family rate $6. Phone the Assiginack Museum at (705) 859-3905.

MARATHON (B-2) pop. 4,416

Once known as Peninsula, the town of Marathon gained its name in 1944 when Marathon Paper Mills Co. began construction of a new pulp mill. The discovery of gold in 1983 and the modernization of the mill helped Marathon become a prosperous community.

Midway between Sault Ste. Marie and Thunder Bay, Marathon provides a variety of indoor and outdoor recreational opportunities. Neys Provincial Park, 26 kilometres (16 mi.) west off Hwy. 17; White Lake Provincial Park, 60 kilometres (37 mi.) east off Hwy. 17; and Pukaskwa National Park *(see place listing p. 160)*, 25 kilometres (15 mi.) east via hwys. 17 and 627, offer swimming, hiking, boating, fishing and camping *(see Recreation Chart and the AAA/CAA Eastern Canada CampBook).*

Marathon Tourist Information Centre: Hwy. 17, P.O. Bag TM, Marathon, ON, Canada P0T 2E0; phone (807) 229-0480 or (800) 621-1029.

MARKHAM—*see Toronto p. 208.*

MASSEY (E-6)

Settled in the 1880s during the westward push of the Canadian Pacific Railroad, Massey was a thriving lumbering center. Just 19 kilometres (12 mi.) south of the site a fur-trading post had been operated throughout the 19th century by the Northwest Co. and then by Hudson's Bay Co. The first farms were settled by riverboat along the Spanish River, and others by railroad. The town was officially organized in 1904. Today the many nearby lakes and rivers make the area a favorite with vacationers. The Tourism Information Centre is in the Massey Area Museum.

MASSEY AREA MUSEUM, center of town at 160 Sauble St. (Hwy. 17), specializes in local history. Models, tools and photographs from the logging era are displayed. Other exhibits include a general store, schoolroom, chapel, farm equipment, a 1910 fire department water pumper, pioneer domestic items, minerals, rocks and native crafts and artwork. Genealogical information also is available. Special events are held throughout the year.

Mon.-Fri. 9-6, Sat.-Sun. 10-4, July 1-Labour Day; Mon.-Fri. 11-4, Mar.-June and day after Labour Day-Nov. 30; otherwise varies. Admission $2, senior citizens and students with ID $1, under 5 free, family rate $5. Phone (705) 865-2266 to verify schedule.

MAXVILLE (E-12) pop. 864

It is said that the profusion of Scots having names beginning with "Mac" gave the town of Maxville its name. They began settling the area in the early 1800s and left their mark on more than the town's namesake. The Glengarry Highland Games held in early August constitutes one of the largest Highland gatherings in North America and is the site of the North American Pipe Band Competition.

MEAFORD (F-7) pop. 4,559

Incorporated as a town in 1874, Meaford is a waterfront community on the outskirts of Ontario's farmland. Numerous examples of late 19th century architecture can be found in the town. Memorial Park provides opportunities for camping, swimming and picnicking, and the Georgian Trail provides bicycling and hiking opportunities. Other summer recreational activities include boating, fishing and golfing, while snowmobiling and skiing are available in winter.

Beautiful Joe Park is dedicated to a dog named Beautiful Joe who was abused before being rescued and adopted by a loving family. The dog's story was memorialized by Canadian author Margaret Marshall Saunders in her 1893 novel "Beautiful Joe." The park, at Edwin and Berry streets, contains Beautiful Joe's gravesite. Animal lovers are attracted to its 3 hectares (8 acres) to view the tributes to K-9 units from around the world. For information phone (519) 538-5895.

The Georgian Theatre Festival presents summer theatrical productions at the Meaford Hall Opera House, 12 Nelson St. E., from late June through August; phone (519) 538-3569, or (888) 541-4444 in Ontario.

Meaford and District Chamber of Commerce: 16 Trowbridge St. W., P.O. Box 4836, Meaford, ON, Canada N4L 1X6; phone (519) 538-1640.

THE MEAFORD MUSEUM, in the center of town overlooking the harbor at 111 Bayfield St., is in an 1895 pump house. The museum, which depicts local history, has exhibits about area sports, such as cricket, fishing and snowshoeing; old medical tools; farm implements and equipment; marine displays; and miniature carvings. Also included is a 1938 fire truck.

Allow 30 minutes minimum. Mon.-Sat. 10-4, Sun. noon-4, July-Aug.; Fri.-Sat. 10-4, Sun. noon-4, early May-June 30; Sat. and Mon. holidays 10-4, Sun. noon-4, Sept. 1-second Mon. in Oct. Phone to verify spring and fall schedules. Admission $3, elementary and secondary school students with ID $1.50, under 6 free. Phone (519) 538-5974.

MIDHURST (G-8) pop. 617

SAVE **SIMCOE COUNTY MUSEUM,** 1151 Hwy. 26, contains exhibits illustrating area history from prehistoric times to the present. Pioneer and native relics and farm machinery are among the items displayed in the 7-hectare (16-acre) complex, which includes an indoor reconstructed Huron longhouse.

Changing exhibits also are presented. Special events are scheduled throughout the year. An archives has historical and genealogical information.

Picnicking is permitted. Allow 1 hour minimum. Museum open Mon.-Sat. 9-4:30, Sun. 1-4:30; closed Jan. 1, Good Friday and Dec. 25-26. Admission $4; over 59 and ages 14-21, $3.50; ages 6-13, $2.50. VI. Phone (705) 728-3721, or (705) 726-9331 for the archives.

MIDLAND (F-8) pop. 16,214, elev. 181 m/594'

Originally settled by the Huron people in the 14th century, the region became heavily populated by the early 1600s. French fur traders and Jesuit missionaries and their Huron converts were attracted to the growing area and became immortalized in the Jesuit Relations and Allied Documents written in the 17th century. A depiction of a Jesuit mission is among the more than 33 hand-painted murals with historic themes adorning exterior walls of downtown buildings, creating the effect of an outdoor art gallery.

Midland now is a vacation center on southern Georgian Bay. Recreational activities in the summer include boating, swimming, windsurfing, fishing, golfing and scuba diving, while winter offers ice fishing, snowmobiling and cross-country skiing.

Beausoleil Island, the principal unit of the Georgian Bay Islands National Park *(see place listing p. 76)*, is 8 kilometres (5 mi.) from Midland. Four kilometres (2.5 mi.) from Midland by water and 47 kilometres (30 mi.) by highway is the popular Honey Harbour resort. Hotels supply boats and guides.

Southern Georgian Bay Chamber of Commerce (Midland Office): 208 King St., Midland, ON, Canada L4R 3L9; phone (705) 526-7884 or (800) 263-7745.

DID YOU KNOW

The first person
to go over
Niagara Falls
in a barrel was
63 years old.

Self-guiding tours: Brochures describing a self-guiding tour of Midland's murals are available at the chamber of commerce.

[SAVE] **HURONIA MUSEUM,** at the King St. entrance to Little Lake Park, specializes in Huron Indian artifacts and history. An active art gallery features the works of Group of Seven artist Franz Johnston as well as an extensive collection of photographs, period fashions and marine exhibits depicting the history of Georgian Bay.

Picnic facilities are available. Allow 1 hour minimum. Daily 9-5, Apr. 1 to mid-Oct.; Mon.-Fri. 9-5, rest of year. Closed Jan. 1, Good Friday and Dec. 25-26. Combination ticket for museum and Huron-Ouendat Village $6; over 64, $5.50; ages 6-17, $4.50. MC, VI. Phone (705) 526-2844.

[SAVE] **HURON-OUENDAT VILLAGE,** at the King St. entrance to Little Lake Park next to the Huronia Museum, is a reconstructed village that interprets 16th-century Huron life in the region. Village features are based on archeological evidence of surrounding villages and historic documents provided by fur traders and missionaries.

Picnic facilities are available. Daily 9-5, Apr. 1 to mid-Oct.; Mon.-Fri. 9-5, rest of year. Guided tours are available July-Aug. Closed Jan. 1, Good Friday and Dec. 25-26. Combination ticket for village and Huronia Museum $6; over 64, $5.50; ages 6-17, $4.50. Tickets must be purchased at the Huronia Museum. MC, VI. Phone (705) 526-2844.

[GEM] **THE MARTYRS' SHRINE,** e. edge of town on Hwy. 12, was built in 1926 as a testimony to the faith of the Jesuit missionaries who labored among the Huron Indians 1625-50. It is a tribute to the eight pioneers who met death by martyrdom and to the Christian Hurons who accepted the faith, lived it and died for it. Among the Canadian martyrs were fathers Jean de Brébeuf and Gabriel Lalemant.

On the grounds are a prayer garden, a papal altar and a museum with a videotape theater. A lookout affords an excellent view of Georgian Bay, the Wye River and a nearby lake. Picnic facilities and food are available. Daily 8:30 a.m.-9 p.m., Victoria Day weekend-second Mon. in Oct. Admission $3, under 10 free. Phone (705) 526-3788.

[SAVE] **MIDLAND 30,000 ISLANDS BOAT CRUISES,** departing the dock on King St., offers 2.5-hour sightseeing cruises of the 30,000 Islands of Georgian Bay aboard the *Miss Midland.* Dinner cruises also are available.

Departures require a minimum of 25 persons. Trips depart several times daily, mid-June through Labour Day (weather permitting); daily departures (frequency and times vary), mid-May to mid-June and day after Labour Day to mid-Oct. Fare $20; over 64, $18; students with ID $15; ages 2-12, $10; family rate (five persons) $50. Reservations are recommended. AX, MC, VI. Phone (705) 549-3388 or (888) 833-2628.

[GEM] **SAINTE-MARIE AMONG THE HURONS,** 5 km (3 mi.) e. on Hwy. 12 opposite The Martyrs' Shrine, is a 1.2-hectare (3-acre) re-creation of the French Jesuit mission to the Hurons that stood on the site 1639-49; it is reputed to have been the first European community in Ontario. The reconstruction followed extensive excavations and more than 200 years of archeological research.

Within the palisades are an Indian mission chapel, Ontario's first permanent Christian cemetery, Huron longhouses, an Algonquin wigwam, carpenter and blacksmith shops, a cookhouse, drying and storing racks for meat and fish, Indian shelters and many other examples of 17th-century habitation.

The orientation center offers an audiovisual presentation. In July and August visitors can partake in daily activities and join a guided tour. Education tours are offered seasonally.

Pets on a leash are permitted. Food and picnic facilities are available. Allow 2 hours minimum. Daily 10-5, Victoria Day weekend-second Mon. in Oct.; Mon.-Fri. 10-5, early May-day before Victoria Day weekend and day after second Mon. in Oct.-late Oct. Last Admission 15 minutes before closing.

Admission Victoria Day weekend to mid-Sept. $11; over 64 and students with ID $9.50; ages 6-12, $8. Admission early May-day before Victoria Day weekend and mid-Sept. to late Oct. $8.50; students with ID and ages 6-12, $7.50. Family rates available. AX, MC, VI. Phone (705) 526-7838.

SAINT-IGNACE II, 1.5 km (.9 mi.) s. of Hwy. 12 between Victoria Harbour and Waubaushene, is the mission site of the martyrdom of fathers Jean de Brébeuf and Gabriel Lalemant. They were tortured and martyred by the Iroquois in 1649.

WYE MARSH WILDLIFE CENTRE is on Hwy. 12 opposite The Martyrs' Shrine. A hands-on nature discovery center, this 61-hectare (150-acre) wetland and woodland site adjoins a wilderness area that offers wildlife viewing and is home to the Trumpeter Swan Reintroduction Program; more than 100 of the birds live nearby.

Wildlife presentations; canoe trips; wildflower gardens; floating boardwalks; an observation tower; and walking and ski trails provide ways to enjoy nature. Daily 9-6, Victoria Day weekend-Labour Day; 9-5, early Apr.-day before Victoria Day weekend and day after Labour Day-early Dec.; 9-4, rest of year. Closed Dec. 25. Admission $6.50; senior citizens and ages 4-12, $5.50. Rates may increase during special events. MC, VI. Phone (705) 526-7809.

MILFORD (G-10)

MARINER'S PARK MUSEUM, s.e. at jct. CRs 10 and 13 at Lighthouse Park overlooking South Bay, encompasses several buildings, including the second oldest lighthouse in Ontario. Exhibits of the more than 3,500 artifacts include fishermen's nets, ships' logs, a map pinpointing the locations of wrecks offshore and hundreds of other relics that depict the area's seafaring history.

Picnic facilities are available. Thurs.-Tues. 10-4:30, July-Aug.; Fri.-Sun. 10-4:30, Victoria Day weekend-June 30 and Sept. 1 to mid-Sept. Donations. Phone (613) 476-8392.

MILTON (G-3) pop. 31,471

After the purchase of a tract of land from the Mississauga Indians in 1806, construction began on the York Road, encouraging settlers to enter the lands west of Toronto. Milton was the first village established in the new frontier. Due to their economic bases, these early towns were called gristmill communities.

Originally called Martin's Mills, the town later adopted the name of Milton. The first meeting of the town council was held in 1857 in the building that now serves as Milton's Town Hall. Hwy. 5 follows the route of the old York Road.

Hiking on the parklands of the Niagara Escarpment and the Bruce Trail is a popular recreational activity. The town holds the outdoor Ontario Renaissance Festival in a wooded grove off Hwy. 401 Trafalgar Road exit 328 from mid-July through Labour Day weekend. Highlights of the event set in 16th-century Tudor England include games, stage performances, musicians and wandering minstrels, jousting, taverns, crafts and food.

Milton Visitor & Community Information: 1 Chris Hadfield Way, Milton, ON, Canada L9T 5H7; phone (905) 693-1157.

HALTON COUNTY RADIAL RAILWAY, 15 km (9 mi.) n. of Hwy. 401 exit 312 at 13629 Guelph Line, offers rides on antique streetcars along 2 kilometres (1.2 mi.) of scenic track. The restoration shops can be seen. Also at the site is an original train station.

Guided tours are available. Allow 1 hour minimum. Mon.-Fri. 11-4, Sat.-Sun. 11-4:30, July-Aug.; Sat.-Sun. and Mon. holidays 11-4:30, May-June and Sept.-Oct. Admission $9.50; over 64, $8.50; ages 4-17, $6.50. AX, MC, VI. Phone (519) 856-9802.

HALTON REGION MUSEUM is w. in the Kelso Conservation Area; take exit 320 n. off Hwy. 401 to Campbellville Rd., turn w. to Tremaine Rd. and go s. to Kelso Rd. to conservation area gates. At the edge of the Niagara Escarpment, the museum is on the site of the former 19th-century Alexander Homestead. The historic Alexander Trail winds through the complex of five buildings. Exhibits depict Halton's history and heritage.

Daily noon-5, mid-May through second Mon. in Oct.; Mon.-Fri. noon-5, rest of year. Museum free. Conservation area gate fee May-Oct. $4.25; senior citizens $3.50; ages 5-14, $3. Phone (905) 875-2200.

MINDEN (F-9)

MINDEN HILLS MUSEUM, 176 Bobcaygeon Rd. N. (Main St.), offers exhibits depicting early life in Haliburton County including a furnished heritage

What Does a Perfect Vacation Sound Like?

The non-stop rhythm of a big city? The soft caress of waves on pure white sand? No matter what vacation sounds best, visit **aaa.com** before you go.

Get an internet TripTik® and find TourBook® information:

- AAA/CAA Approved hotels and restaurants
- Destination descriptions and attraction information
- Interactive maps
- Complete driving directions

Make travel planning easy with **aaa.com** CLICK! Sounds like the start of a perfect vacation.

Travel with Confidence. Travel with AAA/CAA.

home, a drive shed and replicas of the Bethel Church and Schoolhouse. Picnicking is permitted. Allow 1 hour minimum. Tues.-Sat. 10-5, Sun. noon-4, May-Oct. Admission $2; under 12, $1. Phone (705) 286-3154.

Agnes Jamieson Gallery is at 176 Bobcaygeon Rd. N. (Main St.), in the same log building as the museum. Among the gallery's permanent collection are works by artist Andre Lapine as well as changing exhibits by local and regional artists. The gallery is named for the area's mid-20th century pioneer doctor who also had a love for art. Allow 30 minutes minimum. Wed.-Sat. 10-5 (also Thurs. 5-8 and Fri.-Sat. 5-6), Sun. noon-4. Closed holidays. Schedule may vary; phone ahead. Donations. Phone (705) 286-3763.

MISSISSAUGA (G-4) pop. 612,295

Mississauga is one of Canada's largest and fastest growing cities. In the 19th century the rich farmlands along the Credit River attracted settlers, and the villages of Dixie, Clarkson, Streetsville, Meadowvale, Malton, Erindale, Cooksville and Port Credit developed. Between 1968 and 1974 these towns joined to form the city of Mississauga.

Today the metropolis is known for its innovative and colorful architecture, from the stunning 1987 brick and marble city hall to the geometrically diverse Living Arts Centre. The state-of-the-art facility, located north of the Civic Centre at 4141 Living Arts Dr., houses performing and visual arts theaters, arts studios and exhibition areas. Performances are scheduled October through May and include those by the Mississauga Symphony, Opera Mississauga and the Mississauga Choral Society. For information phone (905) 306-6100.

Hershey Centre, 5500 Rose Cherry Pl., off Matheson Boulevard E., is home to the Mississauga Ice Dogs, the city's Ontario Hockey League team. The center also hosts a variety of concerts, international skating events and family shows; phone (905) 502-9100.

Mississauga's cultural offerings are stimulating and varied. In addition to the symphony, opera and choral society, the city also has traditional, dinner and experimental theaters. For information contact the Mississauga Arts Council at (905) 615-4278.

The Art Gallery of Mississauga, in the Civic Centre, presents changing visual arts displays and has an outdoor sculpture garden; phone (905) 896-5088. The Civic Centre also houses the Mississauga Sports Hall of Fame, a conservatory and a clock tower which affords panoramas of the city. On the grounds of Civic Square are scenic gardens, a reflecting pool/ice skating rink and an amphitheater for concerts and theatrical performances.

One-hour guided tours of the Civic Centre and clock tower are available Monday through Friday; phone (905) 896-5054. The International Centre, 6900 Airport Rd., is one of Canada's largest exhibition facilities offering a wide variety of shows; phone (905) 677-6131.

The harbor is a dynamic waterfront facility with two marinas, a waterfront cycling and pedestrian trail, picnic facilities, a bandstand, children's playground and picturesque parks. It is home port to one of Lake Ontario's largest fleet of charter boats and offers anglers the chance to hook salmon, rainbow, lake and brown trout; other waterways contain trout, smallmouth bass, carp, pickerel and pike.

The city maintains more than 480 parks and woodlands whose amenities include walking, bicycling and nature trails, baseball diamonds, tennis courts, soccer and football fields and hills for tobogganing. Ice skating and cross-country skiing also can be enjoyed in the area.

Information about guided walking tours of the historic Streetsville area and of the Credit River valley is available from the Streetsville Business Improvement Association; phone (905) 858-5974.

City of Mississauga Information Centre: 300 City Centre Dr., Mississauga, ON, Canada L5B 3C1; phone (905) 896-5000.

Shopping areas: Square One Shopping Centre, just south of hwys. 403 and 10 (Hurontario Street) at 100 City Centre Dr., is eastern Canada's largest suburban shopping mall; the more than 360 shops and services include The Bay and Sears. A farmers' market is held in the parking lot on Fridays and Sundays, late June through October.

Erin Mills Town Centre, 5100 Erin Mills Pkwy. at Eglinton Avenue, offers more than 180 stores which include The Bay and Sears. With more than 130 stores and services, Dixie Outlet Mall at 1250 S. Service Rd. is a factory outlet mall that features end-of-line clearances, manufacturers' seconds and discontinued lines.

The Mississauga Chinese Centre, on a 4-hectare (10-acre) site at 888 Dundas St. E., offers more than 70 specialty shops and services relating to Chinese culture. The center also affords a look into Chinese history through architectural replicas.

BENARES HISTORIC HOUSE MUSEUM, 1507 Clarkson Rd. N. just s. of S. Sheridan Way, is a stately 1857 Georgian-style house restored to the 1918 era situated on 2 hectares (6 acres) of picturesque grounds. Guided 45-minute tours give details about the more than 2,000 original artifacts and furnishings along with the background of the four generations of the Harris family who lived there. A visitors center and interpretive gallery also are available. Special events are held throughout the year.

Allow 1 hour minimum. Wed.-Sun. 1-5, July-Aug.; Sun. 1-5, rest of year; otherwise by appointment. Closed holidays. Last tour leaves 1 hour before closing. Combination ticket with Bradley House Museum $5; over 59 and ages 13-17, $3; ages 3-12, $1.50; family rate (up to six persons) $12. MC, VI. Phone (905) 822-1569.

BRADLEY HOUSE MUSEUM, 1620 Orr Rd., a restored 1830s farmhouse staffed by costumed guides, portrays 19th-century family life. An 1830s Regency cottage has changing exhibits and offers an afternoon tea room on the last Sunday of the month. Vegetable, flower and herb gardens, a barn and a driveshed are on the grounds. The museum, on the Waterfront Trail, is within walking distance of Lake Ontario and Rattray Marsh.

Allow 30 minutes minimum. Wed.-Sun. 1-5, July-Aug.; Sun. 1-5 (also Mon.-Fri. 1-5, Sat.-Sun. 10-5, during Mar. break), rest of year; otherwise by appointment. Guided 45-minute tours are available. Last tour begins 1 hour before closing. Demonstrations end 1 hour before closing during Mar. break. Combination ticket with Benares Historic House Museum $5; over 59 and ages 13-17, $3; ages 3-12, $1.50; family rate (up to six persons) $12. MC, VI. Phone (905) 822-1569.

PLAYDIUM, w. of Hwy. 10 at 99 Rathburn Rd. W., is a physical and hands-on entertainment facility. More than 200 virtual reality and interactive games are offered, including racing, sports and flight simulators, batting cages and an IMAX Ridefilm. Outdoor activities include basketball, beach volleyball, go-cart racing, a rock-climbing wall and miniature golf.

Food is available. Indoor activities open Mon.-Fri. noon-midnight, Sat.-Sun. 10 a.m.-midnight (also Fri.-Sat. midnight-2 a.m.). Outdoor activities open daily, June-Aug.; Fri.-Sun., Apr.-May and Sept.-Oct. (weather permitting). Hours vary; phone ahead. Closed Dec. 25. Admission free. Play cards available in denominations starting at $10. AX, MC, VI. Phone (905) 273-9000.

MOORETOWN (H-6)

[SAVE] **MOORE MUSEUM,** Hwy. 40 exit Moore Line to 94 Moore Line, contains pioneer items, antique toys, musical instruments, a marine gallery and a series of re-created storefronts. A log cabin, country cottage, one-room schoolhouse, blacksmith shop, 1886 train station, 1890 range light and agricultural exhibition hall also are on the grounds.

Allow 1 hour minimum. Daily 11-5, July-Aug.; Mon.-Fri. 9-4, Sept. 1 to mid-Dec.; Wed.-Sun. 11-5, mid-Mar. through June 30. Closed Easter weekend, Labour Day, second Mon. in Oct. and Nov. 11. Admission $5; over 64, $4; high-school students $3; ages 5-13, $2; family rate $12. Phone (519) 867-2020.

MOOSONEE pop. 936

The "true north" of the Indian and fur trader is still evident in Moosonee, a village 24 kilometres (15 mi.) up the Moose River from James Bay. In contrast to nearby Moose Factory Island *(see attraction listing),* one of the oldest English-speaking settlements in Ontario, Moosonee was founded in 1903 when the Revillon Frères Trading Co. established a post. To this day no roads lead to the town; access is via an excursion train from Cochrane *(see place listing p. 68).*

Until the arrival of the railway in 1932, Moosonee was just another isolated frontier settlement, at least 8 to 10 days away from the nearest city by canoe or snowshoe. It still functions as the gateway to the Arctic and as a departure point for plane and boat excursions into the northern bush.

Polar Bear Provincial Park, in the subarctic wilderness of northern Ontario, is accessible only by charter plane. Scheduled flights are available to Peawanuck. Permits are required for aircraft landing and/or camping in the interior of the park, and are available from the Ontario Parks Superintendent, Ministry of Natural Resources, P.O. Box 730, Cochrane, ON, Canada P0L 1C0; phone (705) 272-7139.

Ministry of Northern Development and Mines: Revillion Road N., P.O. Box 307, Moosonee, ON, Canada P0L 1Y0; phone (705) 336-2991.

MOOSE FACTORY ISLAND is in the Moose River. Since 1673, when the Hudson's Bay Co. established a post, this area has been an important rendezvous point for fur traders. The English and the French engaged in bloody battles over the strategic post 1688-1730, when it was finally restored to the British. The contrasts between the present-day community and a once-rugged frontier settlement remain.

Moose Factory Centennial Museum Park, Front Rd., depicts the story of the fur trade and the development of the area. The park also has a blacksmith shop built in 1740; a powder magazine, which is the only stone building on the island; and an old cemetery where the settlement's original missionaries, traders and explorers are buried. Daily 9-5, late June-Labour Day. Free.

St. Thomas Anglican Church, on Front Rd., was built in 1860 by the Hudson's Bay Co. Highlights include beaded moosehide altarcloths, prayer books printed in the Cree language and handmade pews and pulpit. The church almost floated away in a flood in 1912, but the villagers managed to hold it on its foundation. To prevent a recurrence, holes were drilled in the floor and plugged, allowing water to fill the building rather than carry it away. Open daily 9-5. Donations. Phone (705) 658-4800.

MORPETH (I-7)

RONDEAU PROVINCIAL PARK, s. on CR 3 to CR 17, following signs, is between Lake Erie and Rondeau Bay. Ontario's second provincial park, Rondeau offers trails and boardwalks through forests and marshes for bird-watching and wildlife viewing. Swimming, windsurfing, sailing, bicycling, boating, fishing, camping and picnicking also are available. Guided hikes and interpretive programs are offered throughout the year.

Park open daily 8 a.m.-10 p.m. Visitor center open daily 10-5, in summer; hours vary rest of year. Admission $12 per private vehicle Apr.-Oct.; $9.50 per private vehicle rest of year. MC, VI. Phone (519) 674-1750. *See Recreation Chart and the AAA/ CAA Eastern Canada CampBook.*

Get More for Your Money

620 277 1234567 005
CLUB CODE / MEMBERSHIP NUMBER
MEMBER SINCE **1993**
ANNUAL MEMBERSHIP EXPIRY **JUNE 15**
CARD EXPIRY **2001**
PAT C MARTIN
DUES BILLED ANNUALLY

Get more for your money at any of the following merchants:

Stay
Call 866-AAA-SAVE
Best Western
Comfort Inn
Comfort Suites
Quality Inn
Clarion
Sleep Inn
Mainstay Suites
Econo Lodge
Rodeway Inn
Days Inn
Hampton Inn
Hampton Inn & Suites
Hyatt Hotels
La Quinta Inn
La Quinta Inn & Suites
Marriott Hotels, Resorts, Suites
Renaissance Hotels
Courtyard by Marriott
Fairfield Inn
Residence Inn
SpringHill Suites
TownePlace Suites

Play
Busch Gardens®
SeaWorld®
Sesame Place®
Water Country USA®
Adventure Island®
Hard Rock Cafe®
Hard Rock Vault®
Chart House®
Muer Seafood Restaurants®
Joe's Crab Shack®
The Crab House®
Landry's Seafood House®
Six Flags
Universal Orlando
Universal CityWalk Orlando
Universal Studios Hollywood
Universal CityWalk Hollywood

Go
Hertz Car Rental
 800-654-3080
Aloha Airlines
AAA Visa® Traveler's Cheques
AAA Cash Passport Card
Travelex Foreign Currency
Amtrak®
Gray Line Tours
 www.aaa.com/grayline

Shop
AAA Visa® Gift Cards
Casual Corner®
Petite Sophisticate®
August Max Woman®
Greg Norman Outlet Stores
Hertz Car Sales
LensCrafters
NAPA
Penske Truck Rental
Prime Outlets
Ralph Lauren Footwear Outlet Stores
Reebok Outlet Stores
Rockport Outlet Stores

Shop America VIP
Sunglass Hut
Tanger Outlets
Wal-Mart Pharmacy
Watch Station
Watch World

Click
www.ftd.com/aaa
www.aaa.com/hickoryfarms
www.aaa.com/inmotionpictures

Your AAA/CAA membership card also saves you money when you travel outside the USA and Canada.

Visit caa.ca or aaa.com/save for thousands of additional merchants near you and around the world.

Valid AAA/CAA Membership required. Not valid with other discounts or promotions. Good at participating locations only. Other restrictions may apply. Offers subject to change without notice.

MORRISBURG (E-12) pop. 2,583

Because the construction of the St. Lawrence Seaway raised the river level, a portion of the town of Morrisburg had to be moved to a higher elevation. This adjustment prompted historians to save and restore buildings left standing from the days of settlement in the early 1800s. Some of the structures in this initial restoration work became the foundation of Upper Canada Village *(see attraction listing).*

South Dundas Chamber of Commerce: P.O. Box 288, Morrisburg, ON, Canada K0C 1X0; phone (613) 543-3443.

CRYSLER PARK, 11 km (7 mi.) e. on CR 2, is a beautifully landscaped park with a beach, picnic area, rose garden, miniature railroad and marina. Queen Elizabeth Gardens features a collection of rare flowers. Monuments on the grounds honor the soldiers who fought in the Battle of Crysler's Farm, in which British and Canadian regulars defeated a much larger American force on Nov. 11, 1813.

Daily 8:30-dusk, June 15-Labour Day. Park admission $3.25; over 64, $2.75; under 12 free; maximum per private vehicle $10. Train ride $3.50; ages 5-12, $2.50; ages 2-4, $1. Phone (800) 437-2233.

PREHISTORIC WORLD, 7 km (4 mi.) e. on Upper Canada Rd., has full-size reproductions of dinosaurs and other prehistoric animals along a nature trail in a forest that simulates their natural habitat. Of the more than 50 creatures, the largest weighs 40 tons. Construction of additional figures can be observed. Daily 10-4, late May-Labour Day. Last admission is 1 hour before closing. Admission $8; over 54, $6; ages 4-15, $4.25. Phone (613) 543-2503.

UPPER CANADA MIGRATORY BIRD SANCTUARY, 15 km (9 mi.) e. on CR 2, then 2.5 km (1.6 mi.) s., following signs, is a refuge for Canada geese and other migrating birds and wildlife. The best time to view Canada geese is mid-September through October. An interpretive center has displays and nature programs are offered. A viewing tower and 8 kilometres (5 mi.) of nature trails are available.

Interpretive center daily dawn-dusk, Victoria Day weekend-last weekend in Oct. Nature trails open year-round (weather permitting). A goose feeding program takes place daily at 2:30, mid-Sept. through last weekend in Oct. Campsites are available mid-May to late Oct. Admission free. Campsites $21.25-$24.50. Phone (613) 537-2024 Victoria Day weekend-last weekend in Oct. or (800) 437-2233.

UPPER CANADA VILLAGE, 11 km (7 mi.) e. on CR 2 off Hwy. 401, depicts life during the 1860s through an active and working community. Meet the tinsmith, shoemaker,

We're Making History at

UPPER CANADA VILLAGE

Morrisburg, Ontario

See history in the making at this recreated 19th century village. Meet tradespeople and Villagers. Shop for Village-made products at the Village Store. Take a ride around town on a horse-drawn carry-all or tow scow.

Upper Canada Village ... where history is made fun!

Parks of the St. Lawrence

Ontario

CAA/AAA MEMBERS WELCOME
$2 OFF adult admission to CAA/AAA members
(up to six people)

1-800-437-2233 or (613) 543-4328 • www.uppercanadavillage.com

baker, broommaker and other townsfolk. Among the buildings are a sawmill, an 1835 tavern, a steam-powered flour mill, two churches, a cabinet-maker's shop, a woolen mill, a bakery, two farms, a schoolhouse, a blacksmith shop and a general store.

Costumed interpreters perform domestic, agricultural and commercial chores typical of the period. Horse-drawn wagon rides are available. A children's activity center is open July 1 through Labour Day weekend. Private vehicles are not allowed in the village. The Battle of Crysler's Farm Visitor Centre, just outside the village, explains the 1813 victory by 800 British, Canadian and Indian troops over far superior numbers of American soldiers.

Allow 3 hours minimum. Daily 9:30-5, Victoria Day weekend-Oct. 10. Village admission $16.95; over 65, $15.95; students with ID $10.50; ages 5-12, $7.50. Family rate (two adults and children ages 5-12) available. Visitor center $2; ages 5-12, $1. Rates may vary; phone ahead. AX, MC, VI. Phone (613) 543-4328 or (800) 437-2233. *See color ad p. 103.*

MOUNT BRYDGES (H-1) pop. 19,114

SKA-NAH-DOHT IROQUOIAN VILLAGE AND MUSEUM, in the Longwoods Road Conservation Area at 8348 Longwoods Rd., 5 km (3 mi.) w. of Hwy. 402 exit 86, is a re-created village depicting southwestern Ontario Iroquoian culture of 1,000 years ago. The Oneida word *ska-nah-doht* means "a village stands again."

The Resource Centre has displays devoted to conservation and native culture. Nature trails wind through woods, and a boardwalk allows visitors to view the marsh area. Special events are scheduled throughout the year.

Picnic facilities are available. Grounds open daily 9-dusk. Ska-Nah-Doht village and Resource Centre open daily 9-4:30, Victoria Day weekend-Labour Day; Mon.-Fri. 9-4:30, rest of year. Closed major holidays. Admission Victoria Day weekend-Labour Day $3; ages 6-17, $2. Admission rest of year by donations. Phone (519) 264-2420.

NAPANEE (F-10) pop. 7,760

In 1786 the government built a gristmill in what is now Napanee for the Loyalist settlers who fled America after the Revolutionary War. Allan MacPherson, who rented the mill, was so successful in his trade that he launched Napanee's water-powered industrial boom of the 1800s.

Numerous recreational opportunities exist in the area, including bicycling, canoeing, fishing and hiking.

Napanee & District Chamber of Commerce and Tourism Information Centre: 47 Dundas St. E., P.O. Box 431, Napanee, ON, Canada K7R 3P5; phone (613) 354-6601 or (877) 354-6601.

ALLAN MACPHERSON HOUSE AND PARK, CR 2E, following signs to 180 Elizabeth St., was built in 1826 and contains furnishings from the late 18th and early 19th centuries. Costumed staff provide guided 40- to 60-minute tours. The grounds feature heritage gardens. Special events are offered throughout the year.

Picnicking is permitted on the park grounds, by the river. House and park open Tues.-Fri. 10-4:30, Sat. noon-4:30, mid-Mar. through Nov. 30. Tea is served Thurs. 2-4, July-Aug. Last tour begins at closing.

Admission $3; over 64, $2.50; students with ID $2; under 12, $1; family rate (two adults and two children) $5. Tea is $5. Combination ticket with Lennox and Addington County Museum and Archives *(see attraction listing)* $4.50; over 64 and students with ID $3; under 12, $1.50; family rate (two adults and two children) $7.50. Phone (613) 354-5982.

LENNOX AND ADDINGTON COUNTY MUSEUM AND ARCHIVES, off CR 41S at 97 Thomas St. E., is in an 1864 limestone building that was formerly the county jail. The museum's displays pertain to local history. Extensive genealogical/local historical archives and research services are available.

Museum open Mon.-Sat. 10-4:30. Archives open Tues.-Fri. 10-noon and 1-4:30. Museum and archives closed holidays. Admission $3; over 54, $2.50; students with ID $2; ages 6-13, $1; family rate (two adults and two children) $5. Combination ticket with Allan MacPherson House and Park *(see attraction listing)* $4.50; over 64 and students with ID $3; under 12, $1.50; family rate $7.50. Phone (613) 354-3027.

NESTOR FALLS (B-9) pop. 346

Nestor Falls is 60 miles north of the border towns of International Falls, Minn., and Fort Frances, Ontario, on the eastern slopes of Lake of the Woods. It sits on the span of land separating Lake of the Woods on the west from Kakabikitchiwan and Crow lakes on the east.

The area is noted for the diversity and strength of its fishery, which includes bass, bullheads, crappie, northern and walleyed pike, lake trout and muskie. Bountiful wildlife provides photography opportunities. Mink, deer, bears and moose are commonly seen. Camping, hiking and water sports abound. In winter, ice fishing, snowmobiling and skiing are popular.

The falls of Nestor Falls, on Hwy. 71 between Kenora and Fort Frances, drop 12 metres (40 ft.) between Lake Kakabikitchiwan and Sabaskong Bay in Lake of the Woods. The falls can be seen from an overlook area on Hwy. 71.

NEW HAMBURG (G-2) pop. 7,003

The first residents of New Hamburg used the flow of the Nith River to turn the water wheels in their mills. To commemorate their past, New Hamburg residents built the Heritage Waterwheel that now turns in the river from spring to fall. The

15-metre (50-ft.) wheel is reputed to be the largest operating water wheel in North America. Walking trails and parklands can be found along the riverfront.

New Hamburg's architectural heritage is evident in the many Victorian buildings found throughout the downtown area. They house numerous arts and crafts shops. On the last Saturday in May, New Hamburg holds the Mennonite Relief Sale, where participants can bid on hand-made quilts, shop for crafts or feast on the bounty of food.

New Hamburg Board of Trade: 121 Huron St., New Hamburg, ON, Canada N3A 1K1; phone (519) 662-6628.

NEWMARKET (G-8) pop. 65,788

ELMAN W. CAMPBELL MUSEUM, 134 Main St. S., contains various local displays including artifacts, photographs, a 1924 Canadian National Railroad model, tools and toys as well as the Newmarket Historical Society Archives. Special events are offered throughout the year. Tues.-Sat. 10-noon and 1-4; closed holidays. Free. Phone (905) 953-5314.

We've been there...
Now It's Your Turn.

When you make your travel plans, the AAA/CAA TourBooks® and **aaa.com** are the first places to look to find the best in lodging, attractions and restaurants. We've done the research so you can be confident in your choice of the AAA/CAA Approved properties. So wherever your travels take you, look for the AAA/CAA Diamond rated hotels and restaurants. It's your assurance of high quality, great service and special savings for AAA/CAA Members.

Travel with Confidence.

Travel with AAA/CAA.

Niagara Falls

(including St. Catharines and Niagara Falls, New York)

There is something about Niagara Falls that appeals to the lover, daredevil and poet in everyone. Over the years Niagara Falls has been many things—a strategic military post, a prosperous trade center, a seedy carnival town—but never has it ceased to be a natural wonder, mesmerizing travelers from around the world.

The cities of Niagara Falls, Ontario, and Niagara Falls, N.Y., are connected by two bridges across the Niagara River. The river is really a strait that acts as a spillway, carrying drainage from the upper Great Lakes to Lake Ontario. At the falls its sudden drop creates one of the most spectacular waterfalls on the continent. Among the shortest rivers in the world at 58 kilometres (36 mi.), Niagara also is one of the wildest: Its rapids reach speeds of 48 kilometres per hour (30 mph).

The Canadian Falls, 54 metres (177 ft.) high, have a crest of more than 675 metres (2,215 ft.) outlining a deep curve—thus the name Horseshoe Falls. The river underneath is as deep as the cataract is high. The American Falls are higher, at 56 metres (184 ft.), but are only about 328 metres (1,075 ft.) wide in a fairly straight line. The smallest of Niagara's falls, Bridal Veil, is separated from the other falls by Luna and Goat islands. The falls are illuminated nightly. During the past 12,000 years—the approximate age of the falls—the crests have moved 11.2 kilometres (7 mi.) upstream.

Water is being diverted more evenly over all three cataracts to protect the soft shale and limestone foundations and to slow the rate of erosion. The combined flow of the river over the three falls would normally be about 3,700,000 litres (977,540 U.S. gallons) per second, but the use of the waters to generate electricity reduces the flow to about 2,842,400 litres (750,960 U.S. gallons) per second. During tourist season water is diverted only at night to ensure the beauty of the falls is maintained.

Settlement of the area began after the American Revolution when pioneers emigrated to Fort George at Niagara-on-the-Lake. The only European visitors were

Niagara-on-the-Lake / © Dennis MacDonald / Alamy Images

© Darren Greenwood / Alamy Images

French trappers, explorers and missionaries. Though admired by passers-by, the falls were not a tourist attraction. In 1795 the government of Canada declined to spend $30 to clear a trail to the falls, in the belief that "nobody wanted to see them but small boys."

Development of the area was thwarted by the War of 1812, which pitted settlers across the borders against each other. The bloodiest battle of the war occurred in Niagara Falls at Lundy's Lane. Though neither side claimed victory, this gruesome fight was the turning point of the war. Shortly afterward, the war ended in a draw: The Treaty of Ghent, signed on Dec. 24, 1814, reinstated the boundary line—creating sister cities on each side of the river.

The railroad brought the first influx of tourists about 1840, and Niagara Falls turned into a carnival of hustlers and freaks. In 1885 the Ontario Legislature established The Niagara Parks Commission to preserve the integrity of the land on the Canadian side of the falls. This agency is responsible for the well-manicured parklands along the Niagara River, which reserve the most beautiful views of the falls for the public's peaceful enjoyment.

The 20th century heralded the era of daredevils. In 1901, Mrs. Annie Taylor, a 63-year-old schoolteacher, became the first person to go over the falls in a barrel. She was fished out after 3 hours, battered and bruised but still alive. Many followed her over the brink. For the few who made it, there were many who did not. All went over the Canadian Falls, and those who died were usually trapped beneath the tons of water pouring over the crest. Fortunately the era of daredevils has largely ended; stunts on either the falls or the rapids are illegal.

There is no question that the Niagara Falls region is a mishmash of images. In some respects it resembles a sideshow with its wax museums, honeymoon specials and souvenir shops; conversely, it is a well-preserved park where man-made attractions are dwarfed by those of nature. To honeymooners, the city is an exotic destination, yet Niagara Falls is essentially a commercial metropolis.

As long as the falls exist, the tourists will keep arriving. More than 14 million people visit the Canadian side annually, and more film is sold at the falls than anywhere else in the world. On any day of the year countless shutterbugs jockey for position against the railing, just inches from the magnificent crest, in the hope of capturing the beauty, power and majesty of the falls. If they are lucky, a rainbow will appear in the mist, adding splendor to splendor.

Approaches

By Car

Most approaches to Niagara Falls are east-west oriented. The main exception is the Niagara River

(continued on p. 111)

The Informed Traveler

City Population: 78,815

Elevation: 174 m/ 571 ft.

Sales Tax: The federal Goods and Services Tax is 7 percent and applies to most goods, food/beverages and services, including hotel and motel accommodations. The Provincial Sales Tax is 8 percent on goods and restaurant food, while the Room Tax is 5 percent on most hotel and motel accommodations. The Alcoholic Beverage Tax is 10 percent.

WHOM TO CALL

Emergency: 911

Police (non-emergency): (905) 688-4111

Fire: (905) 356-1321

CAA Emergency Road Service: (905) 684-4396

Ambulance: (905) 688-2191

Weather: (905) 227-3393

Hospitals: Niagara Health System–Greater Niagara General Site, (905) 358-0171.

WHERE TO LOOK

Newspapers

Niagara Falls has one daily newspaper, the *Niagara Falls Review.* Other dailies published in the area include the *Niagara Falls Gazette,* published in Niagara Falls, N.Y., and the *St. Catharines Standard. Niagara Falls* magazine lists dining and shopping information.

Radio

The University of Buffalo's WBFO (88.7 FM) and WNED (94.5 FM) are members of National Public Radio.

Liquor Regulations

The legal drinking age in Niagara Falls, Ontario, is 19; the bars close at 2 a.m. The legal drinking age in Niagara Falls, N.Y., is 21; the bars close at 3 a.m.

Visitor Information

Niagara Falls Tourism: 5515 Stanley Ave., Niagara Falls, ON, Canada L2G 3X4; phone (905) 356-6061 or (800) 563-2557.

Ontario Travel Information Centre: 5355 Stanley Ave., Niagara Falls, ON, Canada L2E 7C2; phone (905) 358-3221.

Regional Niagara Tourist Council: 2201 St. David's Rd. W., P.O. Box 1042, Thorold, ON, Canada L2V 4T7; phone(905) 685-1571.

Currency exchange centers in Niagara Parks are at the Table Rock and Victoria Park complexes.

TRANSPORTATION

Air Travel

Four commercial airports serve the Niagara Falls area. *See Approaches by Plane for details.*

Rental Cars

Hertz, (800) 263-0600 in Canada, or (800) 654-3001 out of Canada, offers discounts to CAA and AAA members. For a complete list of agencies consult the telephone directory.

Rail Service

Via Rail serves all parts of Canada as well as Buffalo, Windsor (opposite Detroit) and Sarnia (opposite Port Huron, Mich.). The station is at 4267 Bridge St.; phone (888) 842-7245.

Buses

Daily service connects Niagara Falls with all parts of Canada and with principal cities in the United States. Canada Coach Lines, Gray Coach Lines and Greyhound Lines Inc. operate out of the terminal at 4555 Erie Ave.; phone (905) 357-2133.

Taxis

Niagara Falls taxicabs operate on the meter system. The minimum charge is $2.50, plus $1.85 for each additional kilometre (.6 mi.); there is no extra charge for additional passengers. The meter is kept running while luggage is loaded and unloaded. Major cab companies are 5-0 Taxi, (905) 358-3232, and Niagara Falls, (905) 357-4000; consult the telephone directory for others.

Destination Niagara Falls

*P*owerful. Majestic. Spectacular. Once you've heard the roar at the river's edge or gazed in awe from above, you'll want to make your own list of Niagara Falls superlatives.

*T*he breathtaking natural wonder is the undisputed main attraction; but there is much more to see and do in Niagara Falls. Parks, gardens and museums also are crowd pleasers.

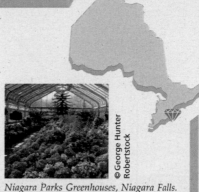

© George Hunter Robertstock

Niagara Parks Greenhouses, Niagara Falls. These hydrangeas—in full, glorious bloom—are just one of the seasonal horticultural displays presented throughout the year. (See listing page 117)

Marineland, Niagara Falls. Killer whales are the stars, and they provide a splashing good time during performances at this theme park. (See listing page 115)

© 2004 Ontario Tourism

© Earl and Nazima Kowall Corbis

Ripley's Believe It or Not! Museum, Niagara Falls. The first person to go over the falls in a barrel is memorialized at this museum of the strange and unusual. (See listing page 120)

Niagara-on-the-Lake

St. Catharines

Queenston

Niagara Falls

Niagara Falls

Welland

Port Colborne

Fort Erie

See Vicinity map page 110

© 2004 Ontario Tourism

*P*laces included in this AAA Destination City:

Skylon Tower, Niagara Falls. Rising nearly 800 feet above the falls, this multitiered observation tower is a viewing, dining and shopping destination. (See listing page 121)

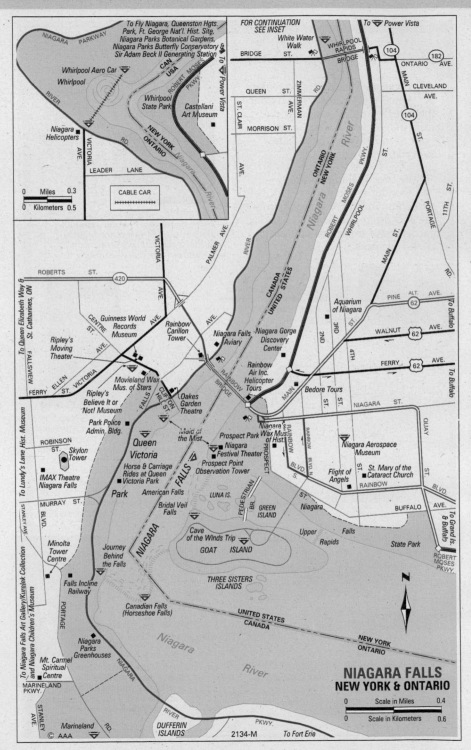

NIAGARA PARKWAY

To Fly Niagara, Queenston Hgts.
Park, Ft. George Nat'l. Hist. Site,
Niagara Parks Botanical Gardens,
Niagara Parks Butterfly Conservatory &
Sir Adam Beck II Generating Station

FOR CONTINUATION
SEE INSET

To Power Vista

White Water
Walk

WHIRLPOOL
RAPIDS

104

Whirlpool Aero Car

BRIDGE ST.

BRIDGE

ONTARIO

182
AVE.

Whirlpool

CAN
USA

ROBERT MOSES PKWY.

To Power Vista

QUEEN ST.

ZIMMERMAN AVE.

RD.

MAIN ST.

CLEVELAND
AVE.

Whirlpool
State Park

Castellani
Art Museum

ST. CLAIR

MORRISON ST.

ONTARIO NEW YORK

104

RIVER

Niagara
Helicopters

NEW YORK
ONTARIO

VICTORIA AVE.

AVE.

Niagara River

ROBERT MOSES PKWY.

WHIRLPOOL

ST.

PORTAGE

11TH ST.

LEADER LANE

RD.

0 Miles 0.3
0 Kilometers 0.5

CABLE CAR

VICTORIA AVE.

PALMER AVE.

RIVER

CANADA UNITED STATES

Aquarium
of Niagara

PINE

ALT.
62

AVE.

To Buffalo

ROBERTS ST.

420

AVE.

AVE.

WALNUT

62

AVE.

Guinness World
Records
Museum

Rainbow
Carillon
Tower

CENTRE ST.

Niagara Falls
Aviary

Niagara Gorge
Discovery
Center

2ND

3RD

4TH

FERRY

62

AVE.

To Buffalo

Ripley's
Moving
Theater

VICTORIA AVE.

RAINBOW BRIDGE

Rainbow
Air Inc.
Helicopter
Tours

MAIN

Bedore Tours

ELLEN ST.

CLIFTON HILL ST.

NIAGARA ST.

QUAY

FERRY

Movieland Wax
Mus. of Stars

FALLS

Oakes
Garden
Theatre

Niagara's
Wax Mus.
of Hist.

RAINBOW

Niagara Aerospace
Museum

ST.

ST.

Ripley's
Believe It or
Not! Museum

Park Police
Admin. Bldg.

Prospect Park

Niagara
Festival Theater

PROSPECT

RAINBOW BLVD N

Flight of
Angels

St. Mary of the
Cataract Church

BLVD.

ROBINSON ST.

Queen
Victoria

Maid of
the Mist

Prospect Point
Observation Tower

RAINBOW

Skylon
Tower

FALLS

Horse & Carriage
Rides at Queen
Victoria Park

PEDESTRIAN BR.

GREEN
ISLAND

Niagara

ST.

BUFFALO AVE.

BLVD.

IMAX Theatre
Niagara Falls

Park

American Falls

LUNA IS.

To Grand Is.
& Buffalo

MURRAY ST.

STANLEY BLVD.

Bridal Veil
Falls

NIAGARA FALLS

Upper

Falls

ROBERT
MOSES
PKWY.

Minolta
Tower
Centre

Journey
Behind
the Falls

Cave
of the Winds Trip

GOAT   ISLAND

Rapids

State Park

N

Falls Incline
Railway

PORTAGE

THREE SISTERS
ISLANDS

Canadian Falls
(Horseshoe Falls)

UNITED STATES
CANADA

NEW YORK
ONTARIO

Niagara

Niagara
Parks
Greenhouses

NIAGARA

Mt. Carmel
Spiritual
Centre

MARINELAND
PKWY.

STANLEY AVE.

Marineland

RIVER

RD.

DUFFERIN
ISLANDS

River

PKWY.

To Fort Erie

2134-M

To Fly Niagara, ...

To Queen Elizabeth Way &
St. Catharines, ON

FALLSVIEW

To Lundy's Lane Hist. Museum

To Niagara Falls Art Gallery/Kurelek Collection
and Niagara Children's Museum

© AAA

NIAGARA FALLS
NEW YORK & ONTARIO

0   Scale in Miles   0.4
0   Scale in Kilometers   0.6

Parkway, a scenic route that follows the Canadian side of the Niagara River from Lake Ontario to Lake Erie, traversing the heart of the city en route.

The primary through route is the Queen Elizabeth Way (QEW) via Hwy. 420. This modern highway originates in Toronto; skirts Lake Ontario; passes through Niagara Falls, interchanging with major streets; and terminates at the Peace Bridge, which spans the international boundary at Buffalo.

While much of the traffic coming into Niagara Falls from Canada uses at least a portion of the QEW, two other roads provide good access from Ontario's southwestern extremity: Hwy. 20, which goes directly into Niagara Falls, and Hwy. 3, from which several lesser roads lead into the city.

From the east, traffic arrives from New York and is funneled to the Canadian side via toll bridges: the Rainbow Bridge, in the heart of the sightseeing area; the Whirlpool Bridge, slightly north of downtown; the Lewiston-Queenston Bridge farther north, which completes an international expressway connection; and the Peace Bridge, linking Buffalo, N.Y., and Fort Erie, Ontario, south of Niagara Falls.

By Plane

Four commercial airports serve the Niagara Falls area. Buffalo Niagara International Airport at Genesee Street and Cayuga Road in New York is the closest to the city. ITA operates shuttle buses and cabs from this airport to Niagara Falls, N.Y., and to Niagara Falls, Ontario; phone (716) 633-8318 or (800) 551-9369 for rates and information. Shuttle service from the Buffalo airport to Niagara Falls, Ontario, is $30; to Niagara Falls, New York, the rate is $25; under 6 are free.

The Niagara District Airport, also handling commercial flights, is at Niagara Stone Road in Niagara-on-the-Lake; phone (905) 684-7447. Within 45 miles of the city is John C. Munro International Airport in Hamilton; phone (905) 679-4151. Toronto's Lester B. Pearson International Airport is approximately 2 hours from Niagara Falls. For scheduling information for terminals 1 and 2, phone (416) 247-7678; for terminal 3 information phone (416) 776-5100.

Getting Around

Street System

Traffic in Niagara Falls can be heavy during the tourist season. The main thoroughfares, the Niagara River Parkway and Falls Avenue, parallel the Niagara River. Such main streets as Clifton Hill, Victoria Avenue and Lundy's Lane run perpendicular to the falls.

Parking

Parking is a problem in the main tourist areas of Niagara Falls, especially during the summer. If your accommodations are near the falls, it is a good idea to walk or take a bus to observation points. There are parking lots at Table Rock and Rainbow Bridge.

Niagara Parks Commission Passes

The Niagara Parks Commission Passes provide savings for guests interested in visiting several Niagara Falls attractions.

The *Niagara Falls and Great Gorge Adventure Pass* includes admission to four attractions—*Maid of the Mist,* Journey Behind the Falls, the Niagara Parks Butterfly Conservatory and White Water Walk—as well as an all-day transportation pass for the People Mover and Falls Incline Railway. The pass also includes coupons, including a discount for the Whirlpool Aero Car. The passport is available May through October. Fee $34.95; ages 6-12, $21.95.

The pass can be purchased at most major Niagara Parks Commission attractions and information centers and many hotels. *See color ad p. 113.*

Cars with trailers and motorhomes should use the Rapids View Parking Lot. From Rapids View a free shuttle transports visitors to Table Rock.

Public Transportation

Public transportation in Niagara Falls, Ontario, is by Niagara Transit Commission bus service. Bus routes connect all areas of the city. Fare is $2.25, over 64 and students with ID $2, children under 53 inches tall $1. Exact change is required. Niagara Transit also operates a shuttle service providing transportation to the falls during the summer. The fare is $3; ages 5-12, $1. An all-day shuttle pass is $6, under 13 free with an adult. The Niagara Transit terminal is at 4320 Bridge St.; phone (905) 356-1179.

The Niagara Parks Commission's People Mover System is an in-park public transportation loop. Buses are spaced about 20 minutes apart and travel along the Niagara River Parkway between the Rapids View Station parking area to Queenston Heights Park and back. Service runs daily (weather permitting), mid-May to mid-October. Hours vary; phone ahead. Single all-day fare is $7.50; ages 6-12, $4.50. The loop from the Rapids View Station parking area to the falls is free. Parking at Rapids View is $10 per private vehicle. Phone (905) 357-9340.

Shuttle bus service also operates between Lundy's Lane and Niagara Falls during the summer. See *What To Do, Sightseeing for other transportation companies.*

What To See

FALLS INCLINE RAILWAY, next to Table Rock Point, operates twin cable-rail cars between the Fallsview tourist area and Table Rock Point areas. The historic railway transports visitors up and down the Niagara Escarpment. Rail cars operate daily, late Mar.-late Oct. (weather permitting). Phone ahead to confirm schedule. One-way fare $2. Phone (905) 357-9340. *See color ad p. 113.*

SAVE GUINNESS WORLD RECORDS MUSEUM, 4943 Clifton Hill, displays exhibits demonstrating world records in sports, science and nature. Videotapes depict accomplishments in outer space and high-speed travel. Daily 9 a.m.-2 a.m., June-Sept.; 10-10, Oct.-Mar.; otherwise varies rest of year. Admission $12.95; over 59 and students with ID $9.50; ages 6-12, $5.99. AX, MC, VI. Phone (905) 356-2299.

IMAX THEATRE NIAGARA FALLS, next to the Skylon Tower at 6170 Fallsview Blvd., presents "Niagara: Miracles, Myths & Magic," an exciting view of the falls on a screen six stories tall. The movie re-creates historical events that have taken place in the Niagara Falls area, including a re-enactment of Annie Taylor's 1901 tumble over the falls in a barrel. Artifacts from daredevils who have

LIVE LIKE A DAREDEVIL
FROM THE EDGE OF YOUR SEAT.

THE FALLS MOVIE
Legends & Daredevils

ONLY AT
IMAX

6170 Fallsview Boulevard, Niagara Falls, Canada
Next to Skylon Tower • 905-374-IMAX • www.imaxniagara.com

The Authentic Falls Experience.

MAID OF THE MIST

BUTTERFLY CONSERVATORY

NIAGARA FALLS
GREAT GORGE
ADVENTURE PASS

WHITE WATER WALK

JOURNEY BEHIND THE FALLS

ADULT PASS
$34⁹⁵†† CDN

YOUTH PASS
$21⁹⁵†† CDN

KIDS 5 & UNDER FREE!

Niagara Falls & Great Gorge Adventure Pass!

The Adventure Pass includes tickets to Maid of the Mist, White Water Walk, Journey Behind the Falls and the Butterfly Conservatory. You also get Priority Timed Ticketing at Journey Behind the Falls and the Butterfly Conservatory along with all day transportation on the People Mover and Incline Railway. **PLUS!** Receive valuable coupons, including a discount for the Whirlpool Aero Car. Buy your Pass on-line at **www.niagaraparks.com**, at participating Niagara Falls hotels or at the brink of the Falls.

Niagara
Parks 🇨🇦
An agency of the Government of
Ontario since 1885

††Plus tax. Pass will be valid during the time the
Maid of the Mist is sailing (approximately May to October 2005).

challenged the falls and rapids in the past are displayed. Other IMAX films also are shown.

Food is available. Films shown daily on the hour 9-9, Apr.-Aug.; 9-8, Sept.-Oct.; 10-4 (extended hours Fri.-Sat.), rest of year. Admission $12; over 64, $9.50; ages 4-12, $8.50. MC, VI. Phone (905) 358-3611 or (905) 374-4629. *See color ad p. 112.*

JOURNEY BEHIND THE FALLS, 1.6 km (1 mi.) s. of Rainbow Bridge on the Niagara River Pkwy. at Table Rock Point, contains elevators that descend to the base of the Horseshoe Falls. Three tunnels lead from the elevators and provide excellent vantage points for close-up views of the thundering falls and the Niagara River. The observation plaza is about 38 metres (125 ft.) below the gorge embankment and 8 metres (26 ft.) above the river's edge. Disposable raincoats are provided.

Saturdays and Sundays in July and August a Royal Canadian Mounted Police officer in ceremonial uniform is posted near the brink of the falls to pose with visitors for photographs. Complex opens daily at 9; closing times vary. Tunnels close 30 minutes before complex closing; phone ahead for closing times. Closed Dec. 25. Tunnel $10; ages 6-12, $6. AX, DC, JC, MC, VI. Phone (905) 354-1551. *See color ad p. 113.*

LUNDY'S LANE HISTORICAL MUSEUM, 1.6 km (1 mi.) from the falls off Hwy. 420 at 5810 Ferry St., is on the site of one of the fiercest battles of the War of 1812, the Battle of Lundy's Lane, fought here July 25, 1814. The museum, in the 1874 former Stamford Township Hall, has exhibits about the city's history. Highlights include Indian artifacts and displays about the early settlers and black history as well as a prime collection of items from the War of 1812.

Allow 30 minutes minimum. Daily 10-5, May-Oct.; daily noon-4, Jan.-Apr.; Wed.-Sun. noon-4, rest of year. Admission $3; over 64 and students with ID $2.50; ages 6-12, $2. Phone (905) 358-5082.

MAID OF THE MIST boats depart from the dock at Clifton Hill and River Rd. on the Canadian side. Since 1846 visitors have experienced the majesty and power of the falls from a series of boats, all named *Maid of the Mist.* Today's steel, double-deck, diesel-powered vessels enter the Horseshoe Basin, fight the mighty current and pass directly in front of the American and Horseshoe falls. Raincoat-clad passengers on the tossing, heaving ship are guaranteed a generous soaking from the spray of the cataract.

Trips depart daily beginning at 9, Memorial Day weekend and mid- June through Labour Day; at 9:45, mid-Apr. through day before Memorial Day weekend (depending on ice conditions in the river), June 1 to mid-June and day after Labour Day-Oct.

Lundy's Lane
Tourist Destination

Niagara Falls Canada

Over TWO MILES of fabulous Accommodation, Dining, Entertainment and Shopping only minutes from the brink of the Falls, Niagara's exciting Casinos & more!

• OVER 35 HOTELS, MOTELS, RESORTS & CAMPGROUNDS •
• MORE THAN 50 GREAT DINING OPTIONS AWAIT YOU •

Call for our Destination Guide or visit our website to make immediate room reservations

1-866-551-LANE
www.lundyslane.com

24 (weather permitting). Closing times vary; phone ahead. **Note:** These hours reflect the Canadian side; the American side runs 15 minutes later.

Fare (waterproof clothing included) $13; ages 6-12, $8. Elevator cost included. MC, VI. To confirm daily schedules phone (905) 358-5781 in Ontario or (716) 284-8897 in N.Y. *See color ad p. 113.*

◣◥**GEM MARINELAND,** 7657 Portage Rd., is known for its marine shows, which feature killer whales, dolphins, walruses and sea lions. There also are a freshwater aquarium and wildlife displays with bears, elk and buffaloes and a deer petting park. At the interactive whale habitats, Arctic Cove and Friendship Cove, visitors can touch and feed beluga and killer whales.

Several rides are available, including Dragon Mountain, a large steel roller coaster, and Sky Screamer, a triple tower ride. A few children's rides also are available.

Food is available. Daily 9-6, late June-Labour Day; 10-5, Victoria Day weekend-late June and day after Labour Day-early Oct. Show times vary according to the season. Admission $36.95; ages 5-9, $31.95. Parents should ask about height restrictions before paying admission. Phone to verify schedule and prices. AX, MC, VI. Phone (905) 356-9565. *See color ad p. 116.*

SAVE MINOLTA TOWER CENTRE overlooks the falls at 6732 Fallsview Blvd. The center rises 99 metres (325 ft.) above the ground and 203 metres (665 ft.) above the base of the falls. An indoor observation deck at the top of the center provides a magnificent view of the falls and the surrounding area.

Food is available. Allow 1 hour minimum. Daily 7 a.m.-10 p.m., with extended hours during the summer. Admission $6.95, over 64 and students with ID $4.95, under 6 free with an adult. AX, DS, MC, VI. Phone (905) 356-1501 or (800) 461-2492.

MOUNT CARMEL SPIRITUAL CENTRE, n. of McLeod Rd. at 7021 Stanley Ave., just above the falls, was founded in 1894; it is now used for religious retreats. The main altar has woodcarvings and paneling in American white oak. The center contains

Our Lady of Peace Church, built in 1827. Daily 9-4. Free. Phone (905) 356-4113.

SAVE MOVIELAND WAX MUSEUM OF STARS, 4950 Clifton Hill, displays figures of film and television personalities in scenes that made them famous. Visitors can make replicas of their own hand in the Wax Hands Emporium. Daily 9 a.m.-1 a.m., May-Sept.; 10-10, rest of year. Admission $8.99; ages 4-12, $5.99. AX, MC, VI. Phone (905) 358-3061.

◣◥**GEM NIAGARA FALLS** is on the Niagara River at the international border between Canada and the United States. The thundering falls, consisting of the Horseshoe Falls on the Canadian side and American and Bridal Veil falls in the U.S., were formed by a retreating glacier 12,000 years ago. The Canadian falls, 54 metres (177 ft.) high and 675 metres (2,215 ft.) wide, derives its name from its crescent shape.

Often heard before it can be seen, the falls have long been a favorite of honeymooners, making the city of Niagara Falls a favorite of newlyweds. In addition to scenic overlooks in Queen Victoria Park, the grandeur of the falls also can be appreciated by boat, helicopter, observation towers and bridges. The falls are illuminated at night year-round.

NIAGARA FALLS ART GALLERY/KURELEK COLLECTION AND NIAGARA CHILDREN'S MUSEUM, 1.5 km (.9 mi.) s.e. of QEW exit 27 (McLeod Rd.) at 8058 Oakwood Dr., has an outstanding collection of works by Canadian artist William Kurelek, including the series known as "The Passion of Christ."

Also noteworthy are a collection of more than 400 works of art depicting Niagara Falls and the surrounding area, and "Stepova Baba" (Grandmother of the Steppes), a work at least 2,500 years old. The gallery also houses the Niagara Children's Museum. Art gallery open Mon-Fri. 11-5, Sat.-Sun. 1-5, June-Sept.; daily 1-5, rest of year. Children's museum open Mon.-Fri. 11-5, Sat.-Sun. 1-5, June-Sept.; Mon.-Fri. 3-5, Sat.-Sun. 1-5, rest of year. Donations. Phone (905) 356-1514.

SAVE NIAGARA FALLS AVIARY, next to the Rainbow Bridge at 5651 River Rd., is a journey

Explore the tropical splendor of the rainforest as birds from all over the world fly freely all around you. Discover the mysteries of our nocturnal jungle.

NIAGARA FALLS AVIARY
BIRDS OF THE **LOST KINGDOM**

Daredevil Café • Aviary Gift Shop • Party Facilities
Authentic Javanese House • Educational Program
www.niagarafallsaviary.com

Attraction of the Year
905-356-8888   1-866-994-0090
5651 River Rd. Niagara Falls, ON.

OPEN YEAR ROUND

MarineLand ®

AAA/CAA Members Save Up to $18

Drive to Marineland and you'll see awesome beluga whales, killer whales, dolphins, walruses and sea lions. You can even feed and touch the whales. There are land animal displays and exciting rides for all ages including the world's largest steel roller coaster and the world's highest triple tower ride. Don't miss this popular Niagara attraction!

Present your membership card and receive $3.00 off regular admission. Offer is good for up to 6 people and cannot be combined with other offers.

7657 Portage Road,
Niagara Falls, Canada
905-356-9565

www.marinelandcanada.com

through a rain forest filled with more than 300 free-flying tropical birds and other animals, tropical foliage, trees and waterfalls. The conservatory, with a lost kingdom theme, features an enclosed aviary where visitors can interact with the birds. A nocturnal jungle amidst ancient ruins features bats, poison arrow dart frogs, owls and snakes.

Food is available. Allow 30 minutes minimum. Daily 9-9, July-Aug.; Sun.-Thurs. 9-6, Fri.-Sat. 9-9, rest of year. Admission $14.95; over 65, $13.95; ages 5-12, $9.95. AX, DS, MC, VI. Phone (905) 356-8888 or (866) 994-0090. *See color ad p. 115.*

THE NIAGARA PARKS BOTANICAL GARDENS, 8 km (5 mi.) n. of the falls on Niagara River Pkwy., is the home of The Niagara Parks School of Horticulture, said to be the only residential school in Canada for apprentice gardeners. Floral displays and formal and informal gardens, including 2,300 varieties of roses, are on the 40-hectare (99-acre) site.

Other gardens include rock, herb, annual, perennial and vegetable. The best viewing time is April through October, when the blooms are at their peak. Daily dawn-dusk. Guided 30-minute tours are available. Free. Phone (905) 356-8554.

Horse & Carriage Rides at The Niagara Parks Botanical Gardens depart from the gardens; timed tickets can be purchased at the Niagara Parks Butterfly Conservatory ticket booth. Forty-minute narrated tours conducted in covered, horse-drawn carriages provide an overview of the botanical gardens and a chance to see the horticulture students at work. Departures every 15 minutes daily 10-4, May-Oct. Hours may vary; phone ahead. Fare $15, children on lap free. MC, VI. Phone (905) 358-0025.

Niagara Parks Butterfly Conservatory, 2565 Niagara River Pkwy. on the grounds of the Botanical Gardens, is home to some 2,000 free-flying butterflies. Waterfalls and various tropical flora line the pathways throughout the glass-enclosed conservatory. More than 40 butterfly species can be observed in a native butterfly garden outside the conservatory.

Allow 1 hour minimum. Daily 9-5 (closing times are extended Mar. 1-second Mon. in Oct.); closed Dec. 25. Timed-tickets are available. Admission $10; ages 6-12, $6. MC, VI. Phone (905) 358-0025. *See color ad p. 113.*

NIAGARA PARKS GREENHOUSES, .8 km (.5 mi.) s. of the Canadian Horseshoe Falls, have seasonal displays of local flowers and foliage, palm trees, more than 75 tropical birds and other tropical plants and aquatic life, all set in the midst of waterfalls and pools. There also is an outdoor fragrance garden for the visually impaired. Daily 9-5 (closing hours are extended mid-June through Labour Day); closed Dec. 25. Free. Phone (905) 354-1721.

NIAGARA RIVER PARKWAY—
see Niagara-on-the-Lake p. 126.

OAKES GARDEN THEATRE, 1 km (.6 mi.) n. of the falls on the Niagara River Pkwy. at the foot of Clifton Hill, is a Greco-Roman style amphitheater in a setting of rock gardens, lily ponds, terraces and promenades overlooking the American Falls. Daily dawn-dusk. Free. Phone (905) 354-5141.

OH CANADA EH? DINNER SHOW is at 8585 Lundy's Ln. A taste of Canada's culture and traditions can be experienced at this musical production staged in a rustic log cabin decorated with Canadiana. A family-style Canadian meal is served during

Oh Canada Eh? Dinner Show
Niagara Falls

11th Year Over 2700 Shows

A Musical Celebration of Canada ... and a delicious Family Style Meal

1-800-467-2071
or 905-374-1995

AAA/CAA **SAVE $12** per
MEMBERS Some Restrictions Apply couple

www.ohcanadaeh.com

FALLSVIEW

TOURIST AREA

From Nightly Entertainment and First-Class Shopping to Dining Overlooking the Falls... Fallsview Has it All!

- 4,500 guestrooms
- More than 50 restaurants featuring gourmet, international and family dining
- The spectacular new 'Fallsview Casino' and 'Galleria Shops'
- Skylon Tower, Revolving Dining Room and Observation Deck
- SkyQuest, Niagara's largest indoor amusement arcade
- The Imax Theatre & Daredevil Exhibit

All this and more, just steps to the Falls!

WWW.FALLSVIEWTOURISTAREA.COM

NIAGARA'S PREMIER HOTELS OVERLOOKING THE FALLS

Embassy Suites - Fallsview
1-800-420-6980

Hilton Niagara - Fallsview
1-888-370-0700

Marriott Fallsview & Spa
1-888-501-8916

Radisson Hotel
& Suites Fallsview
1-877-Fallsview

Ramada Plaza Hotel Fallsview
1-800-461-2492

Renaissance Fallsview Hotel
& Conference Centre
1-800-363-3255

Sheraton Fallsview Hotel
& Conference Centre
1-877-35-Falls

*The Excitement
in Fallsview
is Reaching
New Heights!*

NIAGARA'S GREAT VALUE ACCOMMODATIONS

Best Western Fallsview
1-800-263-2580

Days Inn Fallsview District
1-800-263-2522

Fallsview Inn
1-800-263-2565

Holiday Inn by the Falls
1-800-263-9393

Horseshoe Falls Motor Inn
1-800-463-1938

Knight's Inn by the Falls
1-800-843-5644

Lincoln Motor Inn
Fallsview District
1-800-263-2575

Old Stone Inn
1-800-263-6208

Rodeway Inn Fallsview
1-866- 633-4529

Stanley Motor Inn
905-358-9238

Vacation Inn
1-800-263-2561

The World Comes to Fallsview

NIAGARA FALLS... ONE WONDER AFTER ANOTHER

the show by such Canadians as Anne of Green Gables, singing Mounties, lumberjacks, a hockey player and other performing characters.

Allow 2 hours, 30 minutes minimum. Shows are presented daily at 6:30 p.m., May-Oct.; schedule varies rest of year. Admission $51; ages 13-16, $42; under 13, $24.50. Rates may vary; phone ahead. MC, VI. Phone (905) 374-1995 or (800) 467-2071. *See color ad p. 117.*

 OLD FORT ERIE—*see Fort Erie p. 125.*

QUEENSTON HEIGHTS PARK— *see Queenston p. 128.*

 QUEEN VICTORIA PARK, on the Niagara River Pkwy. at the falls, originated in 1887. It is a 62-hectare (154-acre) landscaped park offering fine views of the falls and beautiful seasonal floral displays. The park is illuminated at night and is the site of many special events. Daily dawn-dusk. Free.

Horse & Carriage Rides at Queen Victoria Park depart from the Victoria Park Gift Shop on Niagara River Pkwy. at the falls; timed tickets can be purchased at the gift shop. Fifteen-, 45- and 80-minute narrated tours in a horse-drawn carriage provide scenic views of the cataract as well as commentary about the falls and the Niagara area.

Departures daily 4-11, mid-May through Labour Day (weather permitting). Hours may vary; phone ahead. Fare $40 per carriage for 15-minute tour; $100 per carriage for 45-minute tour; $170 per carriage for 80-minute tour. MC, VI. Phone (905) 358-5935.

RAINBOW CARILLON TOWER, at the terminus of the Rainbow Bridge, presents concerts on its 55 tuned bells. Concerts are given Fri.-Sun. at 4 and 7 and before the Friday fireworks display, early June-Labour Day. Free.

 RIPLEY'S BELIEVE IT OR NOT! MUSEUM, 4960 Clifton Hill, displays world-traveler Robert Ripley's collection of strange, odd and unusual items. Hundreds of exhibits feature curiosities and illusions such as interactive puzzles, an eight-legged buffalo and a shrunken human head.

Daily 9 a.m.-2 a.m., mid-June to mid-Sept.; 10-10, mid-Mar. to mid-June and mid-Sept. through Dec. 31; 11-7, rest of year. Admission $12.95; over 60, $9.50; ages 6-12, $5.99. A combination ticket with Ripley's Moving Theater is available. AX, MC, VI. Phone (905) 356-2238.

Ripley's Moving Theater, 4983 Clifton Hill, offers two adventure rides in a motion simulator complete with wind, mist and laser effects. **Note:** The rides are not recommended for persons with back or neck

FEAST YOUR EYES ON THIS...

The first time you visit Skylon Tower may well be for the famous view... a breathtaking 775 feet above Niagara Falls. The fabulous food is what will keep you coming back... with two levels of fine dining to choose from.

Revolving Dining Room. At the height of dining excellence... featuring award-winning continental cuisine.

Summit Suite Dining Room. The ultimate in buffet-style dining. Famous Sunday brunch. Family affordable.

Observation Deck. Spectacular indoor/outdoor viewing.

Tower Base. Distinctive specialty shops plus *SkyQuest Entertainment Centre* and the *4D Motion Theatre.*

Skylon Tower

5200 Robinson Street,
Niagara Falls, Canada L2G 2A3
Reservations: (905) 356-2651
Toll-Free: 1-888-673-7343
www.skylon.com

problems. Daily 9 a.m.-2 a.m., mid-June to mid-Sept.; 10-10, mid-Mar. to mid-June and mid-Sept. through Dec. 31; 11-7, rest of year.

Admission $12.95; over 60, $10.95; under 12, $7.69. Under 43 inches tall are not permitted. A combination ticket with Ripley's Believe It or Not! Museum is available. AX, MC, VI. Phone (905) 356-2261.

SKYLON TOWER, overlooking the falls at 5200 Robinson St., rises 160 metres (525 ft.) above the ground and 244 metres (800 ft.) above the base of the falls, providing a magnificent view of the surrounding area. Three levels at the top include a revolving dining room, a dining room featuring a buffet and an indoor/outdoor observation deck. SkyQuest, an entertainment center, and a theater showing 3-D films are at the base of the tower.

Daily 8 a.m.-midnight, May 1 to mid-Oct.; otherwise varies. Observation deck $10.50; over 64, $9.50; ages 6-12, $6. AX, DC, DS, JC, MC, VI. Phone (905) 356-2651 to verify prices or (888) 673-7343. *See color ad p. 120.*

WHIRLPOOL AERO CAR, on the Niagara River Pkwy. 3.25 km (2 mi.) n. of Horseshoe Falls, is a cable car carrying passengers 76.2 metres (250 ft.) above the Niagara Gorge and back on a 529-metre-long (1,800-ft.) cableway, affording views of the rapids and nearby hydroelectric plants. Below the suspended aero car the churning river backs up into the 24-hectare (60-acre) Whirlpool Basin.

Allow 30 minutes minimum. Car operates daily 9-5, mid-Mar. to mid-Nov. (weather permitting); closed periodically for maintenance. Closing hours are extended mid-June through Labour Day. Last car departs 30 minutes before closing. Phone ahead to confirm schedule. Timed tickets are available. Round trip $10; ages 6-12, $6. AX, JC, MC, VI. Phone (905) 354-5711.

WHITE WATER WALK is n. of the Whirlpool Rapids Bridge on the Niagara River Pkwy. After taking an elevator to the river level, visitors can stroll along a boardwalk beside the rapids of the lower Niagara River. The scenic 305-metre (1,000 ft.) pathway along the edge of the river provides a close-up view of the rapids as they rush from the falls.

Daily 9-5 (closing times are extended Sat.-Sun.), mid-Mar. to mid-Nov. Last admission 30 minutes before closing. Phone ahead to confirm hours. Admission $7.50; ages 6-12, $4.50. AX, DC, MC, VI. Phone (905) 374-1221. *See color ad p. 113.*

CASINOS

- **Casino Niagara** is at 5705 Falls Ave. Daily 24 hours. Phone (905) 374-3598 or (888) 946-3255.

- **Fallsview Casino** is at 6380 Fallsview Blvd. Daily 24 hours. Phone (888) 888-1089.

What To Do

Sightseeing

Sightseeing is *the* most popular activity in Niagara Falls. The city's enterprising businesspeople make sure that visitors can view the falls from every conceivable vantage point—from the air, from a boat, from a tower, from a bridge—and most are worth the effort.

Because of parking congestion in the vicinity of the falls and Clifton Hill, it is advisable to sightsee by bus or on foot. A people-mover system provides transportation for the 11 kilometres (7 mi.) between Queen Victoria Park and Queenston. See *Public Transportation* for details and for other transportation options.

Bus Tours

[SAVE] Gray Line offers a variety of guided sightseeing tours that cover both the Canadian and United States sides of the falls. For information phone (800) 365-3609.

Double Deck Tours offers excursions aboard a double-decker bus. Trips depart every 30 minutes beginning at 9:30 a.m. during July and August; schedule varies April through June and September through October. Phone (905) 374-7423.

Tours offered by Niagara Falls Scenic Tours (*see color ad p. 123*) include some of Niagara Falls' most popular attractions, such as *Maid of the Mist* and Journey Behind the Falls. Daily departures include hotel pick-up; phone (905) 354-6099 or (888) 325-5786. Other sightseeing companies include Niagara Airbus, (905) 374-8111. Hotels and motels also offer sightseeing tours.

Driving Tours

One of Ontario's most scenic drives, the Niagara River Parkway (*see attraction listing p. 126*) runs 56 kilometres (35 mi.) between Fort Erie and

DID YOU KNOW

Studded tires
are
illegal
in Ontario.

Niagara-on-the-Lake, paralleling the Niagara River, the falls and expanses of landscaped parkland. Picnic spots, golf courses, gardens and many other attractions border this drive. In the 1940s Winston Churchill described this as "the prettiest Sunday afternoon drive in the world."

Helicopter Tours

SAVE NIAGARA HELICOPTERS, 3731 Victoria Ave., near the Whirlpool Rapids on the Niagara River Pkwy., provides an aerial perspective of the falls and river during 9-minute flights. Headsets provide a taped narration. Daily 9-dusk (weather permitting); closed Dec. 25. Fare $100; ages 2-11, $55; couples $190; a family rate is available. AX, DC, MC, VI. For reservations phone (905) 357-5672. *See color ad.*

Sports and Recreation

Recreational activities in Niagara Falls center on the 1,720 hectares (4,250 acres) of parkland that are meticulously cared for by The Niagara Parks Commission. Included in the park system are the scenic Niagara River Parkway and its companion Niagara River Recreational Trail, golf courses, gardens, restaurants, a marina and several attractions.

The commission publishes the free *Discovery Guide* with information about attractions, a calendar of events and other helpful information. The guide is available at all Niagara Parks parking lots and attractions as well as at most tourist information centers and hotels. For more information contact The Niagara Parks Commission, Box 150, Niagara Falls, ON, Canada L2E 6T2.

Hiking is the ideal sport for the Niagara Falls area because of the Niagara River Recreational Trail. One can discover the natural beauty of the area at a slower pace along any part of the scenic trail as it winds through such major parks as Queen Victoria, Queenston Heights and the Niagara Glen. The 56-kilometre (35 mi.) paved trail meanders parallel to the Niagara River between Niagara-on-the-Lake to the north and Fort Erie to the south.

Across from The Niagara Parks Botanical Gardens, visitors can descend stairs at the Niagara Glen to trails in what is known as a "dry gorge," enjoying views of the whirlpool and rapids along the way. One of Ontario's longest trails, the Bruce Trail, intersects the Niagara River Recreational Trail at Queenston Heights Park.

Bird-watching opportunities abound in the Niagara Glen, but visitors should note that some trails are steep and climbing is necessary. Less strenuous nature trails are found at Dufferin Islands, 2 kilometres (1.2 mi.) south of the falls, where bird-watching is a popular pastime.

Camping is available in eight designated campgrounds within a reasonable distance from the falls (*see the AAA/CAA Eastern Canada CampBook*).

Fishing is a popular activity on certain sections of the Niagara River and in several parks along the river. Trout, salmon and bass are the prized catches, and fishing contests are held periodically in the summer.

In summer **boating** and **water skiing** enthusiasts head for the upper Niagara River, a safe distance away from the rapids and the falls. Several launching ramps are along the river just off the Niagara River Parkway, and the Niagara Parks Marina is south of Miller's Creek Park.

Golf season in Ontario runs from April through October, and Niagara Falls, with several public courses, provides ample opportunity for golfers to indulge themselves. There are nine-hole courses at the Queenston Golf Club, 269 Progressive Ave.,

HELICOPTER RIDES

Niagara Helicopter Rides Limited

3731 Victoria Ave.

P.O. Box 636

Niagara Falls, Ontario

Canada L2E 6V5

(905) 357-5672

www.niagara-helicopters.com

EXPERIENCE THE Wonder!

and at St. David's Golf Club, 22 Paxton Ln. An 18-hole course can be found at Beechwood Golf Club, 4680 Thorold Townline Rd. Golfers have their choice of either nine- or 18-hole courses at Niagara Falls Golf Club, 6169 Garner Rd., and at Oaklands Golf Course, 8970 Stanley Ave. S.

The Niagara Parks Commission offers golfers the Niagara Parks Golf Trail, a series of courses along 15 kilometres (9 mi.) of the scenic Niagara River Parkway beginning in the north near Queenston Heights and running south to the village of Chippawa. The largest of the sites, and also the southernmost, is Legends on the Niagara, which consists of two 18-hole courses, Battlefield and Usshers Creek, and Chippawa, a nine-hole short course. Oak Hall, a nine-hole course at 7400 Portage Rd., is on the grounds of a historic home built for a gold baron. The 18-hole Whirlpool Golf Course is south of Queenston Heights. For additional information or for reservations phone (905) 295-9595 or (866) 465-3642.

Picnicking is encouraged throughout the Niagara Parks System. Popular spots include Kings Bridge Park, 4 kilometres (2.5 mi.) south of the falls, and Queenston Heights Park, 11 kilometres (7 mi.) north of the falls. Both have picnic tables, covered pavilions, playgrounds and wading pools. Queenston Heights also has **tennis** courts and offers a view of Niagara's vineyards, while the upper river can be seen from Kings Bridge. **Horse racing** is conducted at the Fort Erie Race Track on the QEW near the Peace Bridge from late April to mid-November; phone (905) 871-3200 or (800) 295-3770.

Note: Policies concerning admittance of children to pari-mutuel betting facilities vary. Phone for information.

Shopping

If you want a Canadian souvenir, Niagara Falls has everything from T-shirts to *haute couture*. Almost every motel, restaurant and attraction has some token for sale. Most of the multitude of gift shops are privately owned, though some are run by The Niagara Parks Commission. Clifton Hill, with tree-lined brick walkways, is the main commercial street featuring stores of the souvenir variety.

An attraction with extensive shopping arcades is Skylon Tower. It has international shops selling jewelry, English china, fashions, Hummel figurines, toys, French miniatures, artwork and other items. Native crafts include wood and leather items, maple sugar products, soapstone carvings, pottery and Indian and Eskimo dolls.

The Niagara Parks Gift Shops, at Table Rock Point, The Maid of the Mist Complex, Queen Victoria Park and other locations, sell a variety of Canadian-made merchandise. A full exchange is always paid on U.S. currency.

The Niagara Square Shopping Centre, McLeod Road and the QEW, has more than 80 shops and services, making it the largest mall in the area. At

Experience **NIAGARA** WITH NIAGARA FALLS SCENIC TOURS

SAVE 10% WHEN YOU BOOK ONLINE   www.fallstour.com

2 GREAT PACKAGES

ADVENTURE PACKAGE
Mount Carmel Monastery, Whirlpool and Great Gorge, Niagara Parks Floral Clock, Minolta or Skylon Tower, Journey Behind the Falls, Maid of the Mist Boat Ride.

V.I.P. ADVENTURE PACKAGE
Mount Carmel Monastery, Whirlpool and Great Gorge, Niagara Parks Floral Clock, Skylon Tower Observation, Journey Behind the Falls, Maid of the Mist Boat Ride.

PLUS! An all-you-can-eat buffet at the Skylon Tower.
ALSO! Over 50 other scenic sights & points of interest you will see and/or hear about during the tour.

WE OFFER:
• all inclusive packages (no hidden or additional costs)
• numerous daily departures • air conditioned coaches
• complimentary hotel pick-up and drop off (Cdn. side only)
• free on site parking available
• complete package savings Adventure Pkg. only 4-5 hrs V.I.P. Pkg. only 5-6 hrs.

"The brand name of sightseeing"

WE PREFER TO LET OUR CUSTOMERS TALK...
"The tour offered us the best value in terms of time and money..."
– Norm and Lisa Anderson, Thunder Bay, Ontario

"We had a great time on the tour... visited a lot of places we wouldn't have gone on our own..."
– the Sweer Family, Rochester, New York

local **905-354-6099**
toll-free **1-888-325-5786**

RESERVATIONS REQUIRED
www.fallstour.com

VISA   ABA   NIAGARA FALLS   MasterCard

the intersection of QEW and Lundy's Lane is Canada One Factory Outlet; stores include Esprit, Guess, Levi's, Liz Claiborne, Nike, Polo Ralph Lauren, Reebok and Tommy Hilfiger.

For an interesting day of bargaining and browsing, visit the Olde Country Antiques and Flea Market on Erie Avenue. Canadian and American artworks, including oil paintings, watercolors, prints, lithographs, sculptures and Eskimo and Indian graphics, are available at the Janrielle Gallery on Portage Avenue.

Niagara Falls also has two outlets carrying discontinued or irregular patterns and products. The Dansk Factory Outlet on Ferry Street offers china, cookware, glassware and candles at discounted prices. The Oneida Factory Store on Stanley Avenue has mainly stainless steel and silver-plated items.

Niagara Duty Free Shop, *(see color ad)* on Falls Avenue near the Rainbow Bridge, offers discounted china, jewelry, fragrances, clothing and other types of brand-name merchandise; services include preshopping, a GST rebate center and a currency exchange. Official currency exchange centers are available at the Skylon Tower on the main concourse level, 5200 Robinson St., and at Table Rock Point in Queen Victoria Park.

Theater and Concerts

Niagara Falls is fortunate enough to be in the vicinity of the acclaimed Shaw Festival *(see attraction listing p. 127)*, held in Niagara-on-the-Lake only a short distance away via the scenic Niagara River Parkway. The plays of George Bernard Shaw and his contemporaries are presented at the festival from early April to early November. Performances are held Tuesday through Sunday in three theatres: the Court House and Royal George theatres, both on Queen Street, and the Festival Theatre, Picton and Wellington streets.

The Niagara Parks Commission sponsors concerts in outdoor band shells and an amphitheater. Free concerts are held on Sunday afternoons from June through August at Queenston Heights Park.

Across the border in Lewiston, N.Y., drama, musicals, operas, dances and concerts are held during the summer in the amphitheater at Artpark.

Special Events

Winter adds a spectacular dimension to the falls. It is usually in early January that an ice bridge forms in the gorge below the cataracts. To further enhance the splendor is the stunning Winter Festival of Lights, beginning in late November and extending into mid-January, during which many buildings and the trees in Queen Victoria Park are adorned with thousands of lights. Dufferin Islands nature area is a key feature, as it comes alive with dozens of motion light displays. The non-alcoholic New Year's Eve celebrations in Queen Victoria Park include concerts and midnight fireworks.

The citizens of Niagara Falls welcome the return of spring with the Spring Festival, held mid-May to the end of June. Besides the more than 500,000 daffodils that grace the city, there are parades, ethnic dances and sports contests. Every Friday and Sunday evening (also Canadian and U.S. holidays) at 10 p.m., mid-May through Labour Day, residents and visitors celebrate with Falls Fireworks. The 10-day Niagara Grape and Wine Festival begins in early September and offers 100 events. For more information phone (905) 356-6061 or (800) 563-2557.

Tax & Duty Free Savings up to 50% on brand name products.

Save every day on liquor, wine, beer, tobacco, fragrances, china, crystal, jewelry, clothing, sunglasses, specialty foods, souvenirs, gifts...

Other services include: • Currency exchange • Free instant visitor tax refunds • Pre-Shop • Multilingual assistance • Free parking...

NIAGARA DUTY FREE HORS TAXES

Niagara Duty Free, 5726 Falls Ave., (at Rainbow Bridge), Niagara Falls, Canada www.niagaradutyfree.com

1-877-642-4337

Save $5.00 with purchases over $50. Show your AAA/CAA Card. Not valid with tobacco or in combination with other offers.

The Niagara Falls Vicinity

FORT ERIE (H-5) pop. 28,143

Settled in the 1780s by United Empire Loyalists, Fort Erie is a major point of entry into Canada. The Peace Bridge, opened in 1927 by the Prince of Wales—later King Edward VIII—links Fort Erie with Buffalo. The Mather Memorial Archway and Park near the Peace Bridge was built in memory of Alonzo C. Mather, an American philanthropist. The Niagara River Parkway, a 56-kilometre (35-mi.) scenic drive, extends along the Niagara River from Fort Erie to Niagara Falls and Niagara-on-the-Lake *(see place listing p. 125).* Parks are scattered along the route.

The Gypsy Theatre and the Garrison Little Theatre offer a mix of entertainment, including comedy, drama and pantomime. Those who feel lucky can try the city's four bingo halls. Fort Erie Race Track, at Bertie Street and Concession, dates from 1897 and is one of Ontario's oldest tracks. The season runs from late April to late November; phone (905) 871-3200 or (800) 295-3770. The Prince of Wales Stakes, the second jewel of Canada's Triple Crown, is held in late July.

Note: Policies concerning admittance of children to pari-mutuel betting facilities vary. Phone for information.

Fort Erie celebrates its Friendship Festival July 1-4. Commemorating more than 175 years of peace between Canada and the United States, the event features arts and crafts exhibits, a cultural parade, equestrian jumping, concerts and fireworks. The Lake Erie Can Am Challenge Walleye Tournament, one of the top fishing events in Canada, takes place in August.

For further information contact the Ontario Travel Information Centre, 350 Bertie St., Unit 1, Fort Erie, ON, Canada L2A 6S6; phone (905) 871-3505.

Greater Fort Erie Chamber of Commerce: 660 Garrison Rd., Unit 1, Fort Erie, ON, Canada L2A 6E2; phone (905) 871-3803.

FORT ERIE HISTORICAL MUSEUM, jct. Ridge and Dominion rds. at 402 Ridge Rd., is housed in the 1874 former town hall. Exhibits trace the history of the area. The Waves of Change exhibit features the history of the waterfront. Allow 30 minutes minimum. Daily 9-5, mid-June through Labour Day; Mon.-Fri. 9-5, rest of year. Admission $1.50; under 16, 50c. Phone (905) 894-5322.

FORT ERIE RAILROAD MUSEUM, e. off Queen Elizabeth Way (QEW) Gilmore Rd. exit, then n. on Central Ave., displays railroad memorabilia in a 1910 depot. Visitors may enter the cab of a 1942 coal-fired steam locomotive. Daily 9-5, Victoria Day-Labour Day; Sat.-Sun. 9-5, day after Labour Day-second Mon. in Oct. Admission $2; under 16, 50c. Phone (905) 871-1412.

MILDRED M. MAHONEY DOLLS' HOUSE GALLERY is 2 km (1.2 mi.) n. of the Peace Bridge at 657 Niagara Blvd.; take the Queen Elizabeth Way (QEW) Central Ave. exit. The collection consists of more than 150 dollhouses built 1780-1980, all completely decorated and furnished in period, including examples from England, Holland, Japan, the United States and Canada.

The houses are displayed in Bertie Hall; the 1826 "safe house" was used to hide slaves escaping from the United States into Canada. Guided tours are available. Daily 9:30-3, May-Dec.; by appointment rest of year. Closed Easter, second Mon. in Oct. and Dec. 25-26. Admission $6; over 65, $5; ages 6-16, $4. Victorian Christmas (Nov. 15-Dec. 30) $5. Phone (905) 871-5833.

OLD FORT ERIE is on the Niagara River Pkwy. 1.6 km (.9 mi.) s. of the Peace Bridge; take the Queen Elizabeth Way (QEW) Central Ave. exit. Originally built in 1764, the fort was damaged by flooding and ice in 1779 and destroyed by a storm in 1802. A second fort begun in 1804 was still incomplete when war broke out in 1812. While garrisoned by only 170 British in July 1814, it was captured by 4,500 Americans under Gen. Jacob Brown, who strengthened the fort, defended it against assault and later abandoned it.

Restored in 1939, Old Fort Erie is an impressive structure with a dry ditch, drawbridge, bastions and guns typical of early 19th-century fortifications. It contains relics of the War of 1812 and equipment used by the British and American armies.

Battle re-enactments take place the second weekend in August. Guided tours are available. Daily 10-6, June-Aug.; 10-4, Sept. 1 to mid-Oct. Admission $7.50; ages 6-12, $4.50. AX, DS, JC, MC, VI. Phone (905) 871-0540.

NIAGARA-ON-THE-LAKE (G-5)
pop. 13,839

Niagara-on-the-Lake is a well-preserved town that was the first capital of Upper Canada 1791-96. Because of its proximity to the Niagara River and Lake Ontario, the town developed into a busy port and shipbuilding center. After the Welland Canal was completed in 1829, bypassing Niagara-on-the-Lake and damaging its port trade, the settlement declined. New industry soon arrived, however, as railroads made the area accessible to tourists.

The 19th-century aura of this quaint village is enhanced by the renowned Shaw Festival *(see attraction listing),* which offers an entire summer of superlative theater.

FLY NIAGARA
— AIR TOUR SPECIALISTS —

Enjoy the longest air tour
available in Niagara!

30 minute Deluxe Tour of
Niagara and Surrounding Region
•
20 minute Niagara Falls Tour
•
State-of-the-Art
Cessna High Wing Aircraft
•
Forward Facing Window Seats
for all Passengers
•
Fully Narrated Tours
•
Commercially Licensed
Professional Pilots
•
Customized Tours and
Private Charters available including
Niagara and Toronto packages

Fly Niagara is based out of Niagara District
Airport on Hwy 55 in Niagara-on-the-Lake.

For more information call toll free
(reservations required)

1-877-FLY-BY-AIR
(1-877-359-2924)

Visit our website at www.flyniagara.com

VISA   NIAGARA FALLS
ONE WONDER AFTER ANOTHER

MENTION THIS AD AND RECEIVE
$10 OFF OF YOUR TOUR PER PERSON

Niagara-on-the-Lake Chamber of Commerce:
26 Queen St., P.O. Box 1043, Niagara-on-the-Lake,
ON, Canada L0S 1J0; phone (905) 468-4263 or
(905) 468-1950.

Self-guiding tours: Information about walking
tours of the area is available from the chamber of
commerce.

FLY NIAGARA departs from the Niagara District
Airport at jct. Airport Rd. and Niagara Stone Rd.
(Hwy. 55); check in at the office of the St. Cathe-
rines Flying Club adjacent to the main terminal.
Half-hour flights take passengers over the Canadian
and American falls, the Welland Canal, area vineyards and Niagara-on-the-Lake. Twenty-minute
flights also are available. Flights daily 8 a.m.-dusk
(weather permitting). Fares begin at $59. Reserva-
tions are required. AX, MC, VI. Phone (877)
359-2924. *See color ad.*

SAVE **FORT GEORGE NATIONAL HISTORIC
SITE** is on the s. edge of town on Queens Parade Rd. Built 1796-99, the fort was the district's
main British post until its 1813 capture and occupation by American forces. The British retook the
fort, but abandoned it in the early 1820s. The reconstructed fort houses officers' quarters, soldiers'
barracks, the guard house, magazine, kitchen and
artificer's shop.

During July and August costumed interpreters
provide tours, musket firing demonstrations and fife
and drum performances. Open daily 10-5, Apr.-
Oct.; by appointment rest of year. Admission $10;
over 64, $8.50; ages 6-16, $5; family rate $25. AX,
MC, VI. Phone (905) 468-6614.

McFARLAND HOUSE is at 15927 Niagara River
Pkwy. Interpreters in period dress conduct guided
tours of this restored Georgian-style home, built in
1800. Insight is provided into the lifestyle of that
time and the house's use as a hospital during the
War of 1812. Allow 30 minutes minimum. Mon.-
Fri. 10-5, Fri.-Sat. 10-8, June-Aug. Admission
$3.50. Phone (905) 468-3322.

NIAGARA APOTHECARY MUSEUM, 5 Queen St.
at King St., was built in 1866. The museum has
walnut and butternut fixtures and crystal gasoliers
as well as a rare collection of apothecary glass. Allow 30 minutes minimum. Daily noon-6, mid-May
through Labour Day. Free. Phone (905) 468-3845.

NIAGARA HISTORICAL SOCIETY MUSEUM, 43
Castlereagh St., has displays about the town's role
in the War of 1812 and its status as the one-time
capital of Upper Canada. Included are military history exhibits and special collections. Daily 10-5,
May-Oct.; 1-5, rest of year. Closed Jan. 1, Good
Friday and Dec. 25-26. Admission $5; over 59, $3;
students with ID $2; ages 5-12, $1. MC, VI. Phone
(905) 468-3912.

NIAGARA RIVER PARKWAY runs along the
Niagara River from Lake Ontario to Lake Erie. The
parkway is a scenic 56-kilometre (35-mi.) drive. A

recreation trail which includes picnic areas borders the river and parkway. In the 1940s Winston Churchill described this as "the prettiest Sunday afternoon drive in the world."

SHAW FESTIVAL, held in three theaters downtown, features one of North America's largest repertory companies. One of Canada's premier theater events, the festival attracts some 350,000 theatergoers annually to its 10 plays. It is the only theater in the world that specializes exclusively in plays written by George Bernard Shaw and his contemporaries, and plays set in the period of Shaw's lifetime (1856-1950).

The 8-month celebration stages more than 800 performances of works by Shaw as well as such contemporaries as Bertolt Brecht, Anton Chekhov, Noel Coward, Henrik Ibsen and Oscar Wilde. The playbill also offers lunchtime plays and readings, seminars and brunch concerts. Phone for a brochure with schedules and ticket information.

Performances in all three theaters are offered Tues.-Sun. at 11:30, 2 and 8, Apr.-Nov. Tickets $22-$82. AX, MC, VI. Phone (905) 468-2172 or (800) 511-7429.

WHIRLPOOL JET BOAT TOURS, departing from King George III Inn at 61 Melville St., offers 1-hour trips on the lower Niagara River on 48- to 54-seat jet boats. The river can be experienced on either "wet jet" trips, where a good soaking can be expected, or a "dry" version of the trip in a domed jet boat. Features of the tours, which are half historic/scenic and half white-water adventure, include historic forts, the Niagara Gorge, white-water rapids and the whirlpool.

Note: Although a complete rain suit and wet boots are provided for the "wet jet" trip, a change of clothes is recommended. Participants should be in good health; a signed release is required. Trips are not recommended for those with heart, back or neck problems, and pregnant women may not take the tours. Allow 2 hours minimum for preparation, tour and clothing changes. Trips depart daily 10-7, Apr.-Oct. Schedule may vary; phone ahead. Arrive 30 minutes early to prepare for the trip.

Fare for either trip $54; ages 6-13, $44. Under 6 are not permitted. Reservations are recommended. Inquire about refund policy. MC, VI. Phone (905) 468-4800 or (888) 438-4444. *See color ad.*

WINERIES

• **Chateau des Charmes** is in nearby St. David's at 1025 York Rd. Daily 10-6; closed major holidays. Tours are offered at 11 and 3. Phone (905) 262-4219.

• **Hillebrand Winery** is near jct. Hwy. 55 and East-West Line at 1249 Niagara Stone Rd. (Hwy. 55). Tours and tastings on the hour 10-6; closed Jan. 1 and Dec. 25. Hours may vary; phone ahead to confirm. Phone (905) 468-7123 or (800) 582-8412.

• **Inniskillin Wines Inc.** is off the Niagara River Pkwy. on Line 3. Guided tours daily at 10:30 and 2:30, May-Oct.; Sat.-Sun. at 10:30 and 2:30, rest of year. Self-guiding tours daily 10-5. Tastings available daily 11-5:30, May-Oct.; 11-4:30, rest of year. Closed major holidays. Phone (905) 468-3554, ext. 3 or (888) 466-4754, ext. 311.

• **Joseph's Estate Wines** is near jct. Hwy. 55 and East-West Line at 1811 Niagara Stone Rd. (Hwy. 55). Daily 10-7, June-Oct.; 10-6, rest of year. Closed Jan. 1 and Dec. 25. Tours are given daily at 11, 1 and 3, May-Oct. Phone (905) 468-1259 or (866) 468-1259.

• **Peller Estates Winery** is n. on Niagara River Pkwy., then w. on East-West Line to 290 John St.

WHIRLPOOL jet boat tours

HOURLY DEPARTURES APRIL TO OCT.
TOURS DEPART FROM
NOTL, ONT. & LEWISTON, N.Y.
RESERVATIONS 905-468-4800
1-888-438-4444 • www.whirlpooljet.com
SCENIC • HISTORIC • FAMILY ADVENTURE • AGES 6+

E. Daily 10-6; closed Jan. 1 and Dec. 25. Tours are given daily every hour on the half-hour 10:30-6. Hours may vary; phone ahead. Phone (905) 468-4678 or (888) 673-5537.

- **Pillitteri Estates Winery** is 7 km (4 mi.) n. off QEW exit 38 (Niagara-on-the-Lake) to 1696 Niagara Stone Rd. (Hwy. 55). Daily 10-8, May 1 to mid-Oct.; 10-6, rest of year. Closed Jan. 1, Good Friday, Easter and Dec. 25-26. Tours are given daily at noon and 2. Phone (905) 468-3147.

PORT COLBORNE (I-4) pop. 18,450

Lying at Lake Erie's gateway to the Welland Canal, Port Colborne is a major inland port. Among the many areas where ships can be seen passing through the downtown area as they move through the canal is Fountain View Park, overlooking one of the world's longest locks. Complementing the city's commercial importance are its many popular beaches.

Port Colborne/Wainfleet Chamber of Commerce: 76 Main St. W., Port Colborne, ON, Canada L3K 3V2; phone (905) 834-9765.

PORT COLBORNE HISTORICAL AND MARINE MUSEUM, 280 King St., explores the area's marine heritage. Among the historic buildings on the grounds is an 1869 home with displays about Welland Canal history, maritime exhibits and other historical memorabilia.

Other structures include an 1870 blacksmith shop, an 1850 log home, an 1820s schoolhouse, a carriage house and a 1913 cottage that serves as a tea room. A 1901 Neff Steam Buggy built in Humberstone also is displayed. Daily noon-5, May-Dec. Free. Phone (905) 834-7604.

QUEENSTON (H-5)

FLORAL CLOCK, on Niagara River Pkwy. at Sir Adam Beck Generating Station, is one of the world's largest floral clocks. About 15,000 plants that bloom from early spring to the first frost compose the 12-metre (40-ft.) in diameter working clock.

Just north of the Floral Clock, opposite Smeaton's Cove, is the Centennial Lilac Garden. The garden's 4 hectares (10 acres) contain more than 700 shrubs with more than 200 varieties of lilacs; the plants bloom mid-May to mid-June. The Floral Clock's Westminster chimes ring every 15 minutes. Free.

THE LAURA SECORD HOMESTEAD, 29 Queenston St., is the former home of Laura Secord, a militia sergeant's wife recognized as a heroine by the Canadian government for her bravery during the War of 1812. Secord undertook a perilous 31-kilometre (20-mi.) journey on foot to alert the British of an impending U.S. invasion. Because of her warning, the Americans were defeated at the Battle of Beaverdams 2 days later. The two-story frame cottage has been restored and furnished in period.

Guided tours are offered. Food is available. Allow 30 minutes minimum. Daily 10-4, June-Aug. Admission $3.50, under 6 free. Phone (905) 262-4851.

MACKENZIE HERITAGE PRINTERY AND NEWSPAPER MUSEUM is just off the Niagara River Pkwy. following signs to 1 Queenston St. The restored home of early 19th-century firebrand editor and political reformer William Lyon Mackenzie is now a museum devoted to printing. Exhibits depict Mackenzie's life and times and the history of printing.

A collection of working printing apparatuses is featured, including what is said to be Canada's oldest printing press. Visitors can try using linotype and letterpress equipment. Allow 30 minutes minimum. Daily 10-5, June-Aug. Admission $3.50, under 6 free. Phone (905) 262-5676.

QUEENSTON HEIGHTS PARK, s. on the Niagara River Pkwy. near jct. Hwy. 405 and the Lewiston-Queenston Bridge, commemorates a crucial battle of the War of 1812. A small force of British regulars, militia and Indians under Gen. Sir Isaac Brock turned back a larger American invasion force in a stunning victory.

The popular recreation area offers tennis, hiking, picnicking, a playground and a children's splash pad. Views of the surrounding countryside can be seen from the top of the Niagara Escarpment, which dominates the park. Park open daily 9-dusk. Free.

Brock's Monument National Historic Site is in Queenston Heights Park. The 64-metre-tall (210-ft.) monument at the top of the Niagara Escarpment honors Maj. Gen. Sir Isaac Brock, British commander during the Battle of Queenston Heights in the War of 1812; he was killed in the battle. Staff in period garb lead guided battlefield walking tours; phone for schedule. Visitors can climb 235 steps to the top of the monument for scenic views of the countryside.

Note: Site maintenance during 2005 may affect the operating schedule; phone ahead to confirm hours. Allow 30 minutes minimum. Daily 10-5, mid-May to mid-Oct. Admission $2; ages 6-16, $1. Phone (905) 468-6621, or (905) 468-6614 in the off-season.

SAVE **RIVERBRINK—HOME OF THE WEIR COLLECTION** is at 116 Queenston St. at Niagara River Pkwy. In the mid-20th-century home of attorney and art lover Samuel E. Weir, the museum features his eclectic collection of art, antiques, sculpture, prints and rare books. Many works pertain to the Niagara region and the battles fought here during the War of 1812. Works exhibited include pieces by Mary Cassatt, the Group of Seven and Rockwell Kent.

Allow 30 minutes minimum. Wed.-Sun. 10-5, Victoria Day weekend-second Mon. in Oct. Admission $5, senior citizens $4, under 13 free. AX, MC, VI. Phone (905) 262-4510.

SIR ADAM BECK II GENERATING STATION is at 14000 Niagara River Pkwy., near the Queenston-Lewiston Bridge. Guided tours include an orientation about the hydroelectric station's history, a brief video presentation and a chance to see the station and its equipment in operation.

Allow 30 minutes minimum. Tours are given daily 10-4. Last tour begins 1 hour before closing. Hours may vary; phone ahead. Admission $7.50; ages 6-12, $4.50. AX, DS, MC, VI. Phone (905) 357-2379.

ST. CATHARINES (H-4) pop. 129,170

On the Niagara Peninsula along Lake Ontario and the Welland Canal portion of the St. Lawrence Seaway system, St. Catharines is the center of the Niagara fruit belt. A lookout platform at Lock 3 on the Welland Canal provides views of oceangoing ships. An information center at the lock has displays and an audiovisual presentation pertaining to the canal.

Beamsville, west of St. Catharines, was a busy and exciting place during World War I. A 121-hectare (300-acre) air field was built here to train fighter pilots. By the end of the war the Beamsville Royal Flying Corps School of Aerial Fighting had trained 1,200 pilots. Today only one of the nine flight hangars stands, the Belvedere which has long since been converted to commercial use, and a small plaque on Sann Road reminds passersby of the area's importance in "The War To End All Wars."

The surrounding area, especially beautiful during Blossom Week in early May, is interlaced with several scenic drives. Other events in St. Catharines include the Folk Arts Festival in late May and early June, the Royal Canadian Henley Rowing Regatta in early August and the Niagara Grape and Wine Festival in mid-September.

St. Catharines Tourism: 1932 Welland Canal Pkwy., St. Catharines, ON, Canada L2R 7K6; phone (905) 984-8882 or (800) 305-5134, ext. 244.

Self-guiding tours: A brochure detailing a walking tour of the Old Town section of St. Catharines is available at the Planning and Development Department.

Shopping areas: Great buys can be found at The Pen Centre, 221 Glendale Ave., one of the area's largest shopping malls. Among the anchor stores are The Bay, Sears and Zellers.

RODMAN HALL ARTS CENTRE, 109 St. Paul Crescent, is housed in a Victorian mansion that served as a private residence 1853-1959. The restored gallery now displays works of art from Canadian, American and European collections as well as changing monthly exhibits.

The center also is a forum for concerts, art classes and a lecture series. Adjoining the building are the Walker Botanical Gardens, 3 hectares (8 acres) of terraced grounds. Center open daily noon-5; closed holidays. Donations. Phone (905) 684-2925.

ST. CATHARINES MUSEUM AND ONTARIO LACROSSE HALL OF FAME & MUSEUM (Welland Canals Centre at Lock 3) is off Queen Elizabeth Way (QEW) Glendale Ave. exit, then n. on Welland Canals Pkwy. St. Catharines Museum, which tells the story of the city and the four Welland Canals, has an exhibit about Underground Railroad history and Niagara's African Canadians, a steam fire pumper and a 1912 REO automobile. An observation platform at Lock 3 provides a close-up look at ships. Memorabilia from Canada's oldest sport can be seen in the Ontario Lacrosse Hall of Fame & Museum.

Picnicking is permitted. Allow 30 minutes minimum. Daily 9-5, late Mar. to mid-Oct.; Sat.-Sun. 11-4, rest of year. Closed Jan. 1 and Dec. 25-26. Admission $4.25; over 59, $4; students with ID $3.25; ages 6-13, $2.50; family rate available. AX, MC, VI. Phone (905) 984-8880 or (800) 305-5134.

WELLAND (H-4) pop. 48,402

The 43.5-kilometre (27-mi.) Welland Canal, which crosses the Niagara Peninsula about 13 kilometres (8 mi.) west of Niagara Falls, provides passage for cargo ships between lakes Erie and Ontario. Completed in 1829, the first canal required 40 locks to close the difference between the two lakes. Successive canals were built in the 1840s and 1880s. In 1932 a new canal using "twin locks" was completed, almost 3 decades after the idea was conceived.

Eight locks now create a lift of 100 metres (330 ft.); the Twin Flight Locks and a single lock carry ships to the level of Lake Erie at Thorold. Lock 8 at Port Colborne, at 421 metres (1,380 ft.), is one of the longest in the world. The lock system can accommodate vessels up to 222 metres (725 ft.) long. Concrete tubes 7 metres (23 ft.) in diameter carry the Welland River under the ship canal downtown.

The By-Pass Channel, 13 kilometres (8 mi.) long, routes shipping through Welland's east side. The East Main Street and Townline tunnels carry vehicular and rail traffic under the By-Pass Channel.

The Welland Recreational Waterway *(see Recreation Chart)* is in the heart of the city. Water skiing, rowing, canoeing and boating contests are held during the summer.

Visitors driving Queen Elizabeth Way (QEW) from Buffalo to Toronto can view the Twin Flight Locks by taking the Thorold Stone Road exit west to the Thorold tunnel; from the tunnel take the Pine Street exit and follow signs. There is parking at all of the locks and an information facility at Lock 3.

Throughout the year an ongoing attraction is provided by the city's Festival of Arts Murals. Twenty-seven giant murals depicting historical episodes have been created by noted Canadian artists, who used the walls of downtown buildings as their canvas. Welland is the site of the Niagara Regional Exhibition, a major event held in mid-September.

Greater Welland/Pelham Chamber of Commerce: 32 E. Main St., Welland, ON, Canada L3B 3W3; phone (905) 732-7515.

WELLAND HISTORICAL MUSEUM, 65 Hooker St., is in a 1914 heritage schoolhouse and contains displays about the Welland canals and Welland's social history. Revolving exhibits also are presented. A children's museum provides hands-on activities. Guided tours are available. Open Tues.-Sat. 10-4; closed holidays. Donations. Phone (905) 732-2215.

Nearby New York

NIAGARA FALLS pop. 55,593

SAVE **AQUARIUM OF NIAGARA,** 701 Whirlpool St. at Pine Ave. (US 62), has more than 1,500 aquatic animals ranging from the Great Lakes to the coral reefs and is home to an authentic New England tide pool. Visitors can see California sea lions, sharks, piranhas and more.

Highlights include a colony of endangered Peruvian penguins and an outdoor harbor seal pool. The aquarium is the site of the 81st "Whaling Wall" by environmental marinelife artist Wyland. Open daily at 9. Closing hours vary; phone ahead. Closed Thanksgiving and Dec. 25. Penguins are fed daily at 9:30 and 2:30; seals are fed daily at 11 and 3:45; and sharks are fed on alternate days at 11:30. Admission $7.50; over 59 and ages 4-12, $5.50. AX, DS, MC, VI. Phone (716) 285-3575 or (800) 500-4609.

BEDORE TOURS departs from the Howard Johnson at the Falls at 454 Main St. near the Rainbow Bridge, and from area hotels. The U.S./Canadian Experience Tour; the All-American Adventure Tour; and an evening tour, the Canadian Illumination Tour, are among the excursions offered. Each tour visits the American, Horseshoe and Bridal Veil falls. The day tours also include sightseeing aboard the *Maid of the Mist* tour boats, the Cave of the Winds Trip and Journey Behind the Falls *(see attraction listings).*

Departures daily Apr.-Oct. During peak season there are three tours daily. Fare for either the U.S./Canadian Experience and All-American Adventure tours $59.95; ages 5-12, $32. Canadian Illumination Tour $54.95; ages 5-12, $28. Combination All-American Adventure and Canadian Illumination tours $99.95; ages 5-12, $50. Reservations are required. AX, DS, MC, VI. Phone (716) 285-7550 or (800) 538-8433.

GEM **CAVE OF THE WINDS TRIP,** on Goat Island *(see attraction listing),* follows wooden walkways to within 25 feet of the base of the falls. An elevator takes visitors 175 feet through the Niagara rock escarpment into the Niagara Gorge to view the falls from the bottom. After donning a raincoat and special footwear, visitors are guided to the Hurricane Deck, just 20 feet from the roaring Bridal Veil Falls, where a good dousing can be expected. Rainbows are generally visible day and night.

From October 30 through January 2 a gorge walk is available that takes visitors down to the first wooden structure at the base of the falls; phone for information.

Allow 1 hour minimum. Sun.-Thurs. 9-9, Fri.-Sat. 9 a.m.-11 p.m., mid-May through Labor Day; Sun.-Thurs. 9-7, Fri.-Sat. 9-8, day after Labor Day to mid-Oct. Schedule may vary; phone ahead. Admission $8; ages 6-12, $7. AX, DC, DS, MC, VI. Phone (716) 278-1730.

FLIGHT OF ANGELS is at 310 Rainbow Blvd. S. A tethered helium balloon rises 400 feet above the falls. Allow 30 minutes minimum. Daily 9 a.m.-midnight, June-Sept.; 10-10, Apr.-May and in Oct. Fare $20; under 13, $10; family rate (two adults and two or three children) $55-$60. MC, VI. Phone (716) 278-0824.

GEM **GOAT ISLAND,** in the Niagara River, separates the Canadian and American falls. Easily accessible by foot or vehicular bridge, this wooded island has paved drives and walks that offer spectacular views from the edges of both falls.

The Three Sisters Islands, which lie in the rapids, are accessible by footbridge, as is Luna Island, which lies between the American and Bridal Veil falls.

GEM **MAID OF THE MIST** boats depart from the dock at Prospect Point Observation Tower on the American side and is also listed in Niagara Falls, Ontario, where this information is included. The boats pass directly in front of the falls and enter the Horseshoe Basin.

Trips leave daily starting at 9:15, Memorial Day weekend and mid-June through Labor Day; at 10, mid-Apr. through day before Memorial Day weekend (depending on ice conditions in the river), day after Memorial Day to mid-June and day after Labor Day-Oct. 24 (weather permitting). Closing times vary; phone ahead. **Note:** These hours reflect the American side; the Canadian side runs 15 minutes earlier.

Fare (waterproof clothing included) $11.50; ages 6-12, $6.75. Elevator cost included. MC, VI. To confirm daily schedules phone (716) 284-8897 in N.Y. or (905) 358-5781 in Ontario.

NIAGARA AEROSPACE MUSEUM is at 345 Third St. Exhibits trace the development of aviation from its beginnings to recent space exploration programs, with emphasis on achievements in western New York. A hall of fame highlights contributing scientists, inventors, entrepreneurs and aviators.

Among the full-size aircraft displayed are a replica of a 1910 Curtiss bamboo and wire airframe biplane; a GA-36 experimental airplane and a Piper Cub, both built in the 1930s; a Schweitser Sailplane flown during World War II; and a rare 1947 Bell 47B-3 helicopter. Other exhibits feature engines, flight simulators, model ariplanes, photographs and aviation paraphernalia. Films of historical moments in aviation are shown in three small theaters.

Allow 1 hour, 30 minutes minimum. Tues.-Sun. 10-5, Memorial Day to mid-Sept.; Tues.-Sat. 10-3, rest of year. Admission $7; senior citizens and college students with ID $6; ages 5-18, $4. MC, VI. Phone (716) 278-0060.

NIAGARA FALLS is in the Niagara River between New York and Ontario. The falls are divided into three cataracts separated by islands. Horseshoe Falls, on the Canadian side, is the widest. Bridal Veil, the middle and smallest falls, surges between Goat and Luna islands. And the 184-foot American Falls is the highest.

While there are many opportunities to gaze at this spectacle, it was not always so. Mills and plants once blocked public access, and by the late 1860s most of the land around the falls was privately owned by entrepreneurs. In 1885 the falls were reclaimed for public enjoyment through the creation of the Niagara Reservation, the nation's first state park.

Excellent views of the river and falls are available from several vantage points within Niagara Falls State Park *(see attraction listing)*. Each night the falls are illuminated for 2.5 to 3.5 hours after dusk. A variety of guided sightseeing tours also is available *(see What to Do/Sightseeing)*.

NIAGARA FALLS STATE PARK, at Prospect Point, covers more than 400 acres. New York's oldest state park, it opened in 1885. The visitor center has information about area attractions. The Rainbow Cubs offer storytelling and interactive shows for children at various sites throughout the park. Park open daily dawn-dusk. Visitor center open daily at 8; closing time varies. Rainbow Cub performances are given Tues.-Sun. 9:30-4. Free. Phone (716) 278-1796.

Niagara Festival Theater, in the visitor center, presents a 23-minute film, "Niagara: A History of the Falls." The movie recounts the events that made the falls famous. Shows every 60 minutes daily 10-8, May 16-day before Labor Day; 10-6, Labor Day-Oct. 1; 9-5, Apr. 1-May 15 and Oct. 2-Dec. 31. Admission $2; ages 6-12, $1. Phone (716) 278-1796.

NIAGARA GORGE DISCOVERY CENTER, .5 mi. n. of the Rainbow Bridge, is accessible from the Robert Moses Pkwy. following signs. The center offers interactive displays and a multiscreen theater presentation about the natural history of the Niagara Gorge and the falls. A geological garden, scenic overlook, climbing wall and gorge trailhead are on the grounds. Guided hikes are available for a fee.

Allow 1 hour minimum. Daily 9-7, Memorial Day-Labor Day; 9-5, rest of year. Closed Jan. 1, Thanksgiving and Dec. 25. Admission $5; ages 6-12, $3. AX, DS, MC, VI. Phone (716) 278-1070.

NIAGARA SCENIC TROLLEY can be boarded at several locations on Goat Island and near Prospect Point Observation Tower *(see attraction listings)*. Thirty-minute tours follow a 3-mile route and take visitors close to the falls and other points of interest as guides provide historical narration. Stopovers are made at six sites, and passengers have the option of getting on and off the trolley as they choose.

Sun.-Thurs. 9 a.m.-11:30 p.m., Fri.-Sat. 9 a.m.-12:30 a.m., July 1-Labor Day; Sun.-Thurs. 9 a.m.-10:30 p.m., Fri.-Sat. 9 a.m.-12:30 a.m., mid-May through June 30; daily 9 a.m.-9:30 p.m., in Sept.; daily 9-9, Apr. 1 to mid-May; daily 9-6:30, Oct.-Dec.; daily 9-5, rest of year. Fare $2; ages 6-12, $1. MC, VI. Phone (716) 278-1730.

Roadtrip Perfected

Diamonds are the perfect work of nature. Make certain your next roadtrip is perfect by looking for the red hotel and restaurant Diamond ratings in AAA TourBooks® and online at aaa.com.

It's your assurance of high quality, great service and special savings for AAA Members.

**Travel with Confidence.
Travel with AAA.**

(SAVE) **NIAGARA'S WAX MUSEUM OF HISTORY,** 303 Prospect St., exhibits figures such as Princess Diana and Mother Theresa as well as famous explorers and statesmen prominent in area history. Barrels and other implements used by daredevils who attempted a tumble over the falls and a hall of presidents also are displayed. Daily 9:30 a.m.-11 p.m., May 15-Sept. 15; 10-5, rest of year. Closed Dec. 25. Admission $5.95; over 64, $5.50; ages 6-12, $3. AX, MC, VI. Phone (716) 285-1271.

(SAVE) **OVER THE FALLS TOURS** offers pick-up service at area accommodations. A variety of sightseeing tours cover highlights of Niagara Falls, N.Y., and Niagara Falls, Ontario, including opportunities to ride the *Maid of the Mist* and visit Journey Behind the Falls, Cave of the Winds, Goat Island, the Minolta Tower Centre, Skylon Tower and other key viewing areas.

Allow 4 hours, 30 minutes minimum. Tours depart daily 8-7. Hours may vary; phone ahead. Fare $64.95; ages 5-12, $39.95; under 5 on lap free. Reservations are required. AX, DS, MC, VI. Phone (716) 283-8900 or (877) 783-8900.

(GEM) **POWER VISTA** is 4.5 mi. n. of the falls on US 104; it also can be reached from Robert Moses Pkwy. N. following signs. The Niagara Power Project's visitor center features more than 50 hands-on exhibits explaining the development of hydroelectricity in the Niagara area. The Electric Lab features an operating model of a hydropower turbine. Modern energy efficiency is demonstrated in a Victorian house setting.

A large-scale terrain map provides a geographic overview of the Niagara Project, which provides one-seventh of the state's power. Just steps away, an outdoor observation deck 350 feet above the Niagara River affords views of the gorge and power plants.

Other exhibits highlight solar power, electric vehicles and local history. A mural by Thomas Hart Benton depicts Father Louis Hennepin viewing the falls for the first time. Daily 9-5; closed Jan. 1, Thanksgiving and Dec. 24-25 and 31. Free. Phone (716) 286-6661 or (866) 697-2386.

PROSPECT POINT OBSERVATION TOWER, next to the American Falls in Prospect Park, is a 260-foot structure that rises above the cliffs. Stairs lead from the tower to the Crow's Nest, an observation area beside the falls. Four elevators descend into the gorge, permitting access to the base of the falls and *Maid of the Mist* boats *(see attraction listing),* which board near the landing. Open daily at 9:30 (weather permitting), early Apr.-late Oct.; closing time varies. Admission $1, under 6 free. Phone (716) 284-8897.

RAINBOW AIR INC. HELICOPTER TOURS, departing from 454 Main St., offers views of both the American and Canadian falls. Allow 1 hour minimum. Daily 9-dusk. Fare for 10-minute tour $65. MC, VI. Phone (716) 284-2800.

RAINBOW TOURS OF NIAGARA offers pick-up service at local lodgings. The 4-to 5-hour bus tours visit either the Canadian or American sides of the falls and include a ride on the *Maid of the Mist* boat. The American tour goes to Cave of the Winds, the Whirlpool, and Goat, Luna and Three Sisters islands. Canadian tour highlights include Dufferin Island, Minolta Tower Centre, Niagara Parks Geenhouses and the Floral Clock. Other tours are available.

Daily 10-4. Hours may vary; phone ahead. Fare $62.95; senior citizens $59.95; ages 5-12, $34.95; under 5 on lap free. AX, DC, DS, MC, VI. Phone (716) 773-7087.

ST. MARY OF THE CATARACT CHURCH, 259 4th St., was built in 1847. Highlights include mosaics of American saints and 19th-century stained-glass windows. The steeple is as high as the American falls. Open daily 8-5. Free. Phone (716) 282-0059.

WHIRLPOOL STATE PARK, on the Robert Moses Pkwy. n. of the Whirlpool Bridge, is on a bluff overlooking the whirlpool that results from the Niagara River's 90-degree turn. Gorge and rim trails are available. Daily dawn-dusk. Free. Phone (716) 278-1770 or (716) 285-3892.

CASINOS

• **Seneca Niagara Casino** is at 310 4th St. Daily 24 hours. Phone (716) 299-1100.

This ends listings for the Niagara Falls Vicinity. The following page resumes the alphabetical listings of cities in Ontario.

NIAGARA-ON-THE-LAKE—

see Niagara Falls p. 125.

NORTH BAY (D-8)

pop. 52,771, elev. 195 m/640′

North Bay is a departure point for expeditions into northern Ontario. Originally a camp used by Nipissing Indians, fur traders and adventurers, today it is popular with nature lovers, anglers and hunters.

North Bay Chamber of Commerce: 1375 Seymour St., P.O. Box 747, North Bay, ON, Canada P1B 8J8; phone (705) 472-8480.

Shopping areas: The Downtown Improvement Area on Main Street contains a variety of shops. Northgate Square, 1500 Fisher St., has more than 100 stores, including Sears.

CHIEF COMMANDA II, departing from Waterfront Park off Memorial Dr., is a 300-passenger vessel with three decks providing 1.5-, 2.5- and 4-hour scenic cruises to the Manitou Islands, Callander Bay and the French River. Dinner cruises also are offered.

Food is available. Manitou Islands cruises depart Mon.-Sat. at 1, Callander Bay cruises depart Mon.-Sat. at 6:30 p.m., French River cruises depart Sun. at 1, June 1-Labour Day. Manitou Island cruises depart Sun.-Fri. at 1, Callander Bay cruise departs Sat. at 6:30 p.m., day after Labour Day-second Mon. in Oct.

Manitou Islands fare $12; over 64, $10; ages 6-12, $7.50. Callander Bay fare $18; over 64, $16; ages 6-12, $9. French River fare $25; over 64, $22.50; ages 6-12, $12.50. Family rates are available. Reservations are required for dinner and Sun. buffet cruises. AX, MC, VI. Phone (705) 494-8167 or (866) 660-6686.

[SAVE] **DIONNE QUINTS MUSEUM,** jct. North Bay Bypass and Seymour St., is the small farmhouse where the Dionne quintuplets were born in 1934. The house, moved from its original site near Callander, contains photographs and mementos of the girls' early years. Daily 9-7, July-Aug.; 9-5,

Victoria Day weekend-June 30; 9-4, Sept. 1-second Mon. in Oct. Admission $3; over 59 and ages 13-18, $2.50; ages 5-12, $1.75; family rate $7.50. Phone (705) 472-8480.

NORTH BAY AREA MUSEUM, 100 Main St. E., consists of a permanent gallery with exhibits about local history 1882-1950. Research facilities are available by appointment. Allow 30 minutes minimum. Mon.-Fri. 9-5, Sat. 10-5; closed major holidays. Admission $3. MC, VI. Phone (705) 476-2323.

NORTH BUXTON (I-6)

BUXTON NATIONAL HISTORIC SITE & MUSEUM, 21975 A.D. Shadd Rd. (CR 6), has a museum and buildings that were part of the last stop on the Underground Railroad that helped American slaves to freedom in Canada before the Civil War. Then known as the Elgin Settlement, the historically black community was founded by Rev. William King in 1849; the museum preserves artifacts and items belonging to him. An 1861 schoolhouse and an 1857 cemetery are on the grounds.

Picnicking is permitted. Allow 1 hour minimum. Daily 10-4:30, July-Aug.; Wed.-Sun. 1-4:30, Apr.-June and in Sept.; Mon.-Fri. 1-4:30, rest of year. Closed Jan. 1, Good Friday, Easter and Dec. 25. Hours may vary; phone ahead. Admission $5, under 5 free, family rate (six persons) $15. VI. Phone (519) 352-4799.

OAKVILLE (G-4) pop. 144,738

West of Toronto and east of Hamilton and Niagara Falls along the QEW highway (Queen Elizabeth Way) on the north shore of Lake Ontario, the town of Oakville takes advantage of its natural resources. With two harbors on Lake Ontario—one in Bronte and one downtown—Oakville accommodates both sail and power boaters as well as anglers. Waterfront parks and the Waterfront Trail also grace the shoreline.

Music, variety acts, comedy and theatrical productions are presented at the Oakville Centre for the Performing Arts, in the downtown/harbour area; phone (905) 815-2021.

 Rest Assured.

Enjoy the quality assurance of **AAA/CAA Approved** and Diamond rated hotels. **AAA/CAA's professional evaluators** have peeked under the beds, checked the bathroom and tested the locks – everything you'd do, and then some.

Turn to the TourBook® lodging listings, in print and on aaa.com.

For more information on AAA/CAA Lodging Diamond Ratings, turn to page 16.

Bronte Creek Provincial Park, with its working early 20th-century farm and year-round recreational facilities, is off Queen Elizabeth Way (QEW) exit 109 at Burloak Drive; phone (905) 827-6911 *(see Recreation Chart)*.

Oakville, headquarters of Ford Motor Company of Canada, also is a frequent site of the Bell Canadian Open Golf Championship. The tournament, one of the sport's premier events, is often held at the Glen Abbey Golf Course, designed by Jack Nicklaus.

Oakville celebrates the summer season with many festivals. The Oakville Waterfront Festival, generally beginning the Friday of the third or fourth full weekend in June, delights those attending with entertainment and fireworks. The Jazz Festival in mid-August has performances by international and regional jazz musicians.

Oakville Visitor Information Centre: Town Hall, 1225 Trafalgar Rd., Oakville, ON, Canada L6J 4Z5; phone (905) 815-6055 or (877) 625-8455. *See color ad.*

Shopping areas: Oakville's leading shopping mall is Oakville Place, off Trafalgar Road at 240 Leighland Ave.; among its more than 100 stores are The Bay and Sears.

CANADIAN GOLF HALL OF FAME AND MUSEUM, 1333 Dorval Dr., on the grounds of the Glen Abbey Golf Club, traces the game of golf from its origins in Scotland to the present, including the evolution of golf fashions, equipment, architecture and tournaments.

Food is available. Allow 30 minutes minimum. Daily 10-5, Apr.-Oct.; Mon.-Fri. 10-5, Sun. 11-4, rest of year. Closed Jan. 1 and Dec. 25. Admission $4; over 55 and under 18, $3; family rate $8. AX, MC, VI. Phone (905) 849-9700, ext. 411.

OAKVILLE GALLERIES is housed in two separate buildings: the Centennial Square, 120 Navy St., and the Gairloch Gardens, 1306 Lakeshore Rd. E. (Hwy. 2). Both feature exhibitions of international and Canadian contemporary art; changing special events also are offered. Centennial Square open Tues.-Thurs. noon-9, Fri. noon-5, Sat. 10-5, Sun. 1-5. Gairloch Gardens open Tues.-Sun. 1-5. Free. Phone (905) 844-4402.

OAKVILLE MUSEUM, 8 Navy St., consists of three restored buildings that contain exhibits pertaining to local history. Tues.-Sun. and Mon. holidays 1-4:30. Admission (includes all three buildings) $3.50; over 54 and students with ID $2.50; ages 5-12, $1.75. Phone (905) 338-4400.

OIL SPRINGS (I-6) pop. 758

Location of the first commercial oil well in North America (1858), Oil Springs was the site of a huge boom in the early 1860s, following the discovery of surface asphalt here in the mid-1850s.

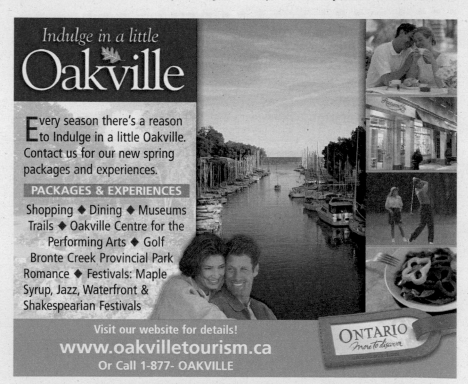

Indulge in a little

Oakville

Every season there's a reason to Indulge in a little Oakville. Contact us for our new spring packages and experiences.

PACKAGES & EXPERIENCES

Shopping ◆ Dining ◆ Museums
Trails ◆ Oakville Centre for the
Performing Arts ◆ Golf
Bronte Creek Provincial Park
Romance ◆ Festivals: Maple
Syrup, Jazz, Waterfront &
Shakespearian Festivals

Visit our website for details!
www.oakvilletourism.ca
Or Call 1-877- OAKVILLE

ONTARIO
more to discover

Even before the first well was dug, asphalt—oil that seeped to the surface and hardened—was shipped to Paris, France, in 1855 to pave its sidewalks. In 1862 the first gusher turned the area into a boom town overnight.

Within years the boom had ended and drillers moved 10 kilometres (6 mi.) north to Petrolia, where the industry has endured. More than 300 wells are still active in the Oil Springs area, many using 19th-century technology. They can be easily seen during a 5-minute drive around the perimeter of the village. Oil Springs is part of the Oil Heritage Tour, which includes signs on CR 21 (Oil Heritage Road) and on Hwy. 402.

Tourism Sarnia-Lambton—Oil Springs: 556 N. Christina St., Sarnia, ON, Canada N7T 5W6; phone (519) 336-3232 or (800) 265-0316.

SAVE **OIL MUSEUM OF CANADA,** 1.5 km (.9 mi.) s. of Main St. and .5 km (.3 mi.) e. of CR 21 on Gum Bed Line, is on the site of North America's first commercial oil well. Exhibits depict the oil industry's first 100 years with drilling equipment, geological displays and a videotape.

Outside are a reconstruction of the first commercial oil well, an 1889 railroad station, pioneer house, 1895 post office, steam drilling rig and pumping system. A driving tour of a working oil field has more than 400 wells with equipment dating from 1862.

Daily 10-5, May-Oct.; Mon.-Fri. 10-5, rest of year. Admission $5; over 64 and students with ID $4; ages 5-12, $3; family rate $15. VI. Phone (519) 834-2840.

ORANGEVILLE (F-3) pop. 25,248

In Dufferin County on the headwaters of the Credit River, Orangeville was originally called The Mills, because of the sawmill and flour mill built in 1832. The town was renamed in honor of Orange Laurence, who purchased property here in 1844. Numerous galleries, craft and antique shops are in the area as is a restored 1907 Canadian Pacific Railway Station.

The town hall, built about 1875, has been restored to its original status as an Opera House. At 87 Broadway Ave., it presents a variety of cultural events and is home to Theatre Orangeville, offering productions year-round; phone (519) 942-3423 or (800) 424-1295.

Orangeville is at the center of Headwaters Country, which includes the scenic areas of Hockley Valley, Dufferin County, the towns of Mono, Shelburne and Erin, as well as the Caledon Hills.

Island Lake Conservation Area *(see Recreation Chart)*, just east of Hwy. 10 at 673067 Hurontario St., offers opportunities for canoeing, kayaking and windsurfing as well as summer and winter fishing, hiking and cross-country skiing. The Bruce Trail along with the Caledon Trail portion of the Trans Canada Trail provide abundant hiking opportunities. Other recreational activities in the area include

boating, bicycling and horseback riding as well as snowmobiling and downhill skiing. On Saturdays a farmers' market is held in downtown Orangeville mid-May to mid-October. Special events are held throughout the year.

The Hills of Headwaters Tourism Association—Orangeville: P.O. Box 295, Orangeville, ON, Canada L9W 2L0; phone (519) 942-0314 or (800) 332-9744.

Self-guiding tours: Brochures outlining a historical walking tour of the town can be obtained from the Town Hall; phone (519) 941-0440.

ORILLIA (F-8) pop. 29,121, elev. 221 m/725´

Ancient home of the Huron Indians, Orillia was first visited by Europeans in 1615. A trading post was established in 1815 to serve Chief Yellowhead and the Ojibway Nation, who settled on the fishing grounds at the junction of Lakes Couchiching and Simcoe following their service to the British in the War of 1812. A memorial to the respected chief is in Couchiching Beach Park.

At the end of the 19th century Orillia grew rapidly into a progressive community; because of the construction of two hydroelectric plants on the Severn River, it was the first community in Canada to have electric lights.

The more than 100-year-old Orillia Opera House, 20 Mississaga St. W., is a heritage designated theater that in earlier days housed the town offices, police station, jail and farmers' market. Today the 691-seat theater is host to local theater groups, orchestras, choirs and town meetings as well as a variety of professional road shows; phone (705) 326-8011.

The Sunshine Festival Theatre Company presents a variety of shows June through mid-October featuring a summer season of classic plays and musicals as well as a holiday event in early December. An infrared system for the hearing impaired is available; phone (705) 325-2074, (800) 683-8747 or the Orillia Opera House.

Stephen Leacock turned Canada's attention toward Orillia with such endearing stories as "Sunshine Sketches of a Little Town," based on local life. Economist, historian, critic and humorist, Leacock wrote more than 61 books before his death in 1944. His house on Old Brewery Bay is now a museum where his writings are archived *(see attraction listing)*. Other notable citizens have included folk singer Gordon Lightfoot and Group of Seven artist Franklin Carmichael.

Centennial Park is home to the Port of Orillia with more than 200 slips, a beach area, children's play area, hiking trails and a boardwalk. Recreational activities in the area include fishing (both summer and winter), golfing, hiking, bicycling and boating as well as skiing and snowmobiling in the winter.

The city hosts a multitude of special events throughout the year, in addition to a Saturday farmers' market available year-round next to the opera house.

Orillia and District Chamber of Commerce: 150 Front St. S., Orillia, ON, Canada L3V 4S7; phone (705) 326-4424.

Self-guiding tours: The Orillia Museum of Art & History *(see attraction listing)* offers brochures for self-guiding walking tours of Orillia.

Shopping areas: More than 200 shops and boutiques can be found in downtown Orillia. The Orillia Square Mall, 1029 Brodie Dr., Hwy. 11 at West Street N., features more than 60 stores, including Zellers.

CHAMPLAIN MONUMENT, in Couchiching Beach Park, is a memorial to the first European explorer in this region. It is considered one of the finest bronzes on the continent. The park also contains the Aquatheatre and a rotary steam railway which operate seasonally. Park open daily dawn-dusk. Monument free. Railway admission $2.

[SAVE] **LEACOCK MUSEUM NATIONAL HISTORIC SITE,** e. off Hwy. 12B on Old Brewery Bay to 50 Museum Dr., is the 19-room Colonial-style mansion built in 1928 by one of Canada's best known humorists and authors. A national historic site, the museum contains many of his books, manuscripts, belongings and private papers. A reconstruction of the author's boathouse also is on the site.

Picnicking is permitted. Food is available. Allow 1 hour minimum. Daily 10-5, June-Aug.; Mon.-Fri. 10-5 in May and Sept.; otherwise varies. Closed Dec. 25. Admission $5; over 64, $4; students with ID $3; ages 3-12, $2; family rate (four persons) $12. AX, MC, VI. Phone (705) 329-1908.

THE ONTARIO PROVINCIAL POLICE MUSEUM is at 777 Memorial Ave., in the general headquarters building of the Ontario Provincial Police. The history of the organization is depicted through displays of uniforms, equipment, vintage cars and motorcycles, photographs and documents. A special area for children has uniforms and police gear they can try on. Allow 30 minutes minimum. Mon.-Fri. 8:30-4:30. Free. Phone (705) 329-6889.

ORILLIA BOAT CRUISES, departing from the Orillia town dock at the foot of Mississaga St., offers a variety of trips, including lunch and dinner cruises, on Lake Couchiching and connecting waterways aboard the *Orillia Island Princess,* a 200-passenger riverboat-style vessel.

Departures require a minimum of 15 passengers. One-hour cruises depart Mon.-Sat. at 10:30 (also Fri. at noon and 2:15), June 25-day before Labour Day. Two-hour cruises depart Sat.-Thurs. at 2:15, June 25-day before Labour Day. One-, 1.5- or 2-hour cruises depart daily at 2:15, mid-May through June 24 and Labour Day to mid-Oct. All cruises are weather permitting. Fares begin at $13;

ages 6-12, $6.50. Reservations are required. MC, VI. Phone (705) 325-2628, or (705) 538-0910 during the off-season.

THE ORILLIA MUSEUM OF ART & HISTORY, downtown at 11 Peter St. S., is in a late 1800s building formerly used as a post office and a police station. The museum displays historical artifacts relating to Orillia and contemporary photographs as well as art exhibits, including paintings by the Group of Seven. **Note:** The museum is at the above location through early 2005 while renovations are conducted at its permanent home at 30 Peter St. S.

Allow 30 minutes minimum. Museum open Mon.-Fri. 10-4, Sat. noon-4; closed holidays and during Christmas school break. Hours may vary; phone ahead. Donations. Phone (705) 326-2159.

CASINOS

• **Casino Rama** is 5 km. n. off Hwy. 12 on Rama Rd. Daily 24 hours. Phone (705) 329-3325 or (800) 832-7529.

ORONO (G-9) pop. 1,666

JUNGLE CAT WORLD is off Hwy. 35/115 Taunton Rd. exit to 3667 Concession Rd. 6. The 6-hectare (15-acre) wildlife park, which specializes in wild members of the cat family, allows visitors to learn about species such as Siberian tigers and Amur leopards. Guests can watch the animals being fed as well as interact with deer, goats, donkeys, sheep and peacocks that have free roam of the park. Other species on display include wolves and monkeys.

Picnicking is permitted. Allow 1 hour minimum. Daily 10-5; closed Dec. 25. Feedings daily at 1:30. Admission $12; over 59 and ages 13-17, $9; ages 2-12, $6. AX, MC, VI. Phone (905) 983-5016.

OSHAWA (F-5) pop. 139,051, elev. 99 m/325'

Oshawa, nicknamed "The City in Motion," is the center of Canada's automotive industry. The city is the site of General Motors of Canada's headquarters, the Regional Canadian Engineering Centre and Autoplex, said to be the largest automobile production facility in North America.

The McLaughlin family, who amassed a fortune in the carriage business in the 1800s, began the McLaughlin Motor Car Co. in 1907. Although the business was eventually sold to General Motors, the founder, Col. R.S. McLaughlin, remained its president.

Oshawa's Downtown Murals, a collection of 19 wall murals, depict the city's history and multicultural diversity. Painted by Canadian artists, the murals are in various downtown locations. Guided walking tours are offered June through August by reservation; phone (905) 404-2081 or (800) 663-1615.

The floral beautification that led to Oshawa's being recognized during the Communities in Bloom national competitions for several years is evident in both public and private spaces throughout the city.

McLaughlin Bay Wildlife Reserve, at the east end of Col. Sam Drive, is a natural wildlife area offering walking trails and picnic areas. Other recreational activities in the area include bicycling, fishing, bird-watching, hiking and cross-country skiing along Oshawa's trails that run along the Oshawa and Harmony Creek valleys and Lake Ontario's waterfront.

Windfields Farm, 2300 Simcoe St. N., is one of the largest racehorse breeding farms in North America and the producer of such champions as Northern Dancer, the first Canadian-bred winner of the Kentucky Derby; phone (905) 725-1195.

The city's artistic offerings include a symphony orchestra and a philharmonic choir. The Oshawa Little Theatre, 62 Russett Ave., presents theatrical performances in a 362-seat theatre; phone (905) 723-0282. A farmers' market, in the parking lot of the Oshawa Centre shopping mall, is open Fridays from mid-May through October. The city also is home to Ontario's newest university; the University of Ontario Institute of Technology, 2000 Simcoe St. N., opened in the fall of 2003.

Oshawa Tourist Information Centre: 2 Bloor St. E., Oshawa, ON, Canada L1H 8S9; phone (905) 725-4523 Victoria Day-second Mon. in Oct. For information the rest of the year contact the Greater Oshawa Chamber of Commerce, 44 Richmond St. W., Oshawa, ON, Canada L1G 1C7; phone (905) 728-1683.

Shopping areas: Five Points Mall at 285 Taunton Rd. E. offers a variety of shops and services; anchor stores include Winners and Zellers. Oshawa Centre, 419 King Street W. at Stevenson Road, has The Bay, Sears and more than 170 other stores.

CANADIAN AUTOMOTIVE MUSEUM is 1.5 km (.9 mi.) n. of Hwy. 401 via exit 417 at 99 Simcoe St. S. More than 70 displays trace the development of the automobile since the turn of the 20th century, on the site of a car dealership that dates to the 1920s. Allow 30 minutes minimum. Mon.-Fri. 9-5, Sat.-Sun. and holidays 10-6; closed Dec. 25. Admission $5; over 59 and ages 12-18, $4.50; ages 6-11, $3.50; family rate $13.50. MC, VI. Phone (905) 576-1222.

THE ONTARIO REGIMENT MUSEUM AND FERRET CLUB is off Hwy. 401 Park Rd. exit to 1000 Stevenson Rd. N., following airport signs. The museum displays wartime uniforms from around the world; weapons, medals and photographs of soldiers in the Ontario Regiment; and more than 50 restored military vehicles from World War II to Desert Storm, including locally built trucks, scout cars, jeeps and tanks. A Ferret is a type of armored vehicle used by the British and Canadian armies from the 1950s to the mid-1970s.

Allow 30 minutes minimum. Fri.-Sun. and Mon. holidays 1-5 or by appointment, Easter weekend-early Nov. Admission $4; over 64 and ages 12-17, $2.50. Phone (905) 728-6199.

OSHAWA COMMUNITY MUSEUM, in Lakeview Park at 1450 Simcoe St. S., includes the restored 19th-century Robinson House, Henry House and Guy House. Formerly the home of Thomas Henry, one of the founders of the town's Christian Church, Henry House is decorated to reflect the Victorian period. Robinson House contains galleries dedicated to local history. Guy House, the home of harbormaster James Odgers Guy, contains the community archives.

Note: Guy House is closed for repairs following a fire. Reopening is planned for May 2005; phone ahead to confirm schedule. Mon.-Fri. 8-5, Sat.-Sun. 1-5, July-Aug.; Mon.-Fri. 8-4, Sun. 1-5, rest of year. Guided tours are given Mon.-Fri. noon-5, July-Aug.; Mon.-Fri. noon-4, rest of year. Closed holidays. Admission $3; over 64 and students with ID $2; under 13, $1; family rate (four persons) $7. Phone (905) 436-7624.

PARKWOOD, THE R.S. McLAUGHLIN ESTATE NATIONAL HISTORIC SITE, off Hwy. 401 exit 417 to 270 Simcoe St. N., was the home of R.S. McLaughlin, a pioneer in the automotive industry. The site comprises a 55-room mansion furnished with antiques and original artwork and is complemented by landscaped grounds, an Italianate garden, an Oriental sunken garden, five fountains and ornamental pools. Parkwood is a rare surviving example of an estate of the inter-war years. Special events are held throughout the year.

Food is available. Tues.-Sun. and holidays 10:30-4, June 1-Labour Day; Tues.-Sun. 1:30-4, rest of year. Guided 1-hour tours are available. Last tour leaves 1 hour before closing. Admission $7; over 60, $6; ages 14-17, $5; ages 6-13, $4; family rate (two adults and two children under 10) $16. MC, VI. Phone (905) 433-4311.

ROBERT McLAUGHLIN GALLERY, at 72 Queen St., is in the Civic Centre at the foot of Bagot St., via Hwy. 401 exit 417 and Simcoe St. In addition to a permanent collection of works from the Victorian era to the present—including works by the Group of Seven and Painters Eleven (Ontario's first abstractionists)—the gallery presents changing exhibits of the works of contemporary Canadian artists. There also is an art reference library.

Food is available. Mon.-Fri. 10-5 (also Thurs. 5-9), Sat.-Sun. noon-4; closed Jan. 1, Dec. 25 and between exhibitions. Donations. Phone (905) 576-3000.

WAR MEMORIAL, in Memorial Park near the jct. of John and Simcoe sts., is a monument dedicated to Canadians who served in World War I. It was built using stones from the battlefields where Canadians served and from the countries of all the World War I Allies. Daily 24 hours. Free.

Ottawa

Take away the bicycle paths, the flower gardens and even the legendary Changing of the Guard ritual, and one would still be left with the heart and soul of Ottawa—the federal government. The city is not only an arena for debate but also a livable place where people skate and bicycle to work, lunch in nearby parks and bask in the regal aura given off by the capital of Canada.

The area was initially a rendezvous site for fur traders, explorers and lumbermen. Because of its position at the confluence of the Ottawa and Rideau rivers, Samuel de Champlain established a base camp in 1613 for future expeditions from Québec to Lake Huron and other points. For 2 centuries the Ottawa River remained the only means of travel to the interior for many.

The area's first settler was Philemon Wright, a New England Puritan who in 1796 moved his family into what is now Hull, Québec, a part of metropolitan Ottawa. He was joined in the 1800s by Nicholas Spark, who cleared a farm in what is presently downtown Ottawa. These pioneers were followed in 1815 by veterans of the Napoleonic Wars and by British Loyalists fleeing the results of the American Revolutionary War.

Lt. Col. John By, accompanied by the Royal Engineers, arrived in 1826 to carve the Rideau Canal out of the rugged north. Originally intended as a safe passageway for British gunboats facing possible American bombardments along the St. Lawrence River, the canal instead became one of the city's most successful commercial ventures. Pulp and paper mills soon rose and log booms jammed the Ottawa River, creating a prosperous lumbering village eventually called Ottawa, after the Outaouac Indians.

When Queen Victoria chose the settlement as the capital in 1857, the decision was met with outrage. But the queen—bored with the petty debates between Toronto, Kingston and Montréal, and inspired by romantic watercolor sketches of the area—insisted that the distinction go to Ottawa. Canadians, with a certain amount of tongue-in-cheek, dubbed their new capital "Westminster of the Wilderness."

It is hard to believe that cosmopolitan Ottawa was once considered a poor sister of other major Ontario cities. Ottawa is noted for more than 70 municipal parks, tree-lined streets and noble landmarks. The city's aesthetic inclinations result from the fact that government is the chief employer, leaving Ottawa relatively free of the scars that often accompany industrialization.

Development and beautification is the sole purpose of the National Capital Commission. One spectacular project is the conversion of the Rideau Canal into the world's

Winterlude / © 2004 Ontario Tourism

Rideau Canal / © Gary Neil Corbett / SuperStock

longest ice-skating rink. On any day in January and February, federal workers in gray flannel and Carleton University or Ottawa University students in blue jeans skate off to work or classes, stopping occasionally to chat, sharpen skates or warm up with a cup of coffee from one of the many vendors stationed along the canal.

As soon as the ice melts, bicyclists and joggers emerge to pound the more than 10 kilometres (6 mi.) of pathways bordering the canal, and canoeists replace the skaters on the water. Spring officially arrives when thousands of tulips and daffodils burst into bloom along the canal and around the government buildings, creating a festival of color.

The Department of Agriculture's 500-hectare (1,235-acre) Central Experimental Farm is just minutes away from historic and impressive government residences and embassies along the Mile of History (Sussex Drive). The 1,619 hectares (4,000 acres) of farmland and green space surrounding the city limits are part of the NCC Greenbelt, designed to limit urban sprawl. Trees, fresh air and Mother Nature are only a short drive from the center of the city.

Steeped in elegance and grace, Ottawa epitomizes a dignified capital. Residents have the luxury of parks, farms and a non-industrial environment while reaping the benefits of city life. Visitors will find that many Ottawans are natives, for with beauty, boundless recreational facilities, international cultures and a special *joie de vivre,* who needs anything else?

Approaches

By Car

The major east-west arteries along the south side of the Ottawa River are Hwy. 17 (a segment of the Trans Canada Highway) and Hwy. 417 (Queensway). Hwy. 417 provides freeway driving in the metropolitan area and good connections with main intersecting thoroughfares. Along the north side of the river is lightly traveled Hwy. 148. This highway, along with Hwy. 50, provides east-west access.

To the north, hwys. 5 and 105 funnel traffic coming down from the woods and lakes of Québec, providing good bridge connections from Hull, just across the river.

Approaching from the south and southwest, Ottawa-bound motorists usually traverse at least a portion of Hwy. 401 (Macdonald-Cartier Freeway), a route that skirts the north shores of the St. Lawrence River and lakes Ontario and Erie. From this thoroughfare a number of connecting routes provide good options.

Hwys. 16/416 and 31 head north directly into the city, combining on Bronson Avenue within the Ottawa city limits. A number of roads lead north from

(continued on p. 143)

The Informed Traveler

City Population: 774,072

Elevation: 87 m/285 ft.

Sales Tax: The federal Goods and Services Tax is 7 percent and applies to most goods, food/beverages and services, including hotel and motel accommodations. The Provincial Sales Tax is 8 percent on goods and restaurant food; a 5 percent Room Tax is levied on most hotel and motel accommodations. The Alcoholic Beverage Tax is 10 percent.

WHOM TO CALL

Emergency: 911

Police (non-emergency): (613) 236-1222

Fire: (613) 580-2860

Weather: (613) 998-3439

Road Conditions: (877) 401-8777

Hospitals: Montfort Hospital, (613) 746-4621.

WHERE TO LOOK

Newspapers

Metropolitan Ottawa has three daily papers: *The Ottawa Citizen; The Ottawa Sun;* and *Le Droit* (French). The monthly magazine *Where* has information about events, dining, shopping and nightlife.

Visitor Information

Ottawa Tourism and Convention Authority: 130 Albert St., Suite 1800, Ottawa, ON, Canada K1P 5G4, phone (613) 237-5150.

National Capital Commission: 40 Elgin St., Ottawa, ON, Canada K1P 1C7; phone (613) 239-5000 or (800) 465-1867.

The National Capital Commission walk-in information center is at 90 Wellington St.

For additional visitor information contact CAA North and East Ontario, 2525 Carling Ave., Ottawa, ON, Canada K2B 7Z2, (613) 820-1880; or Ontario Travel, (800) 668-2746.

Emergency phone numbers include CAA Emergency Road Service, (613) 820-1400; Canadian Customs, (613) 993-0534; Legal Aid, (613) 238-7931; Ottawa Distress Center, (613) 238-3311; Services for the Handicapped, (613) 724-5886; and the U.S. Embassy, (613) 238-5335.

TRANSPORTATION

Air Travel

Ottawa International Airport is 20 minutes from downtown. For airport information phone (613) 248-2000 Mon.-Fri. 8-4:30. National Sightseeing and Shuttle Service Ltd. offers shuttle bus service from the airport to downtown hotels. The one-way fare is $12; round-trip is $20. The shuttles operate daily every 30 minutes 5 a.m.-1 a.m.; phone (613) 260-2359. Westway Airport Taxi, (613) 523-1234 from the airport, or (613) 727-0101 elsewhere, provides transportation from the airport; the approximate charge to downtown is $22.

Rental Cars

Hertz, (613) 521-3332 or (800) 263-0600, offers discounts to CAA and AAA members. For a complete list of rental agencies consult the telephone directory.

Rail Service

Via Rail's terminal, 200 Tremblay Rd. off Queensway (Hwy. 417), can be reached by city buses from Confederation Square; phone (888) 842-7245.

Buses

Voyageur-Colonial Ltd. serves Montréal, Toronto, Mirabel Airport and other cities in Ontario, Québec and the United States. Its terminal is at 265 Catherine St.; phone (613) 238-5900. City buses also serve the terminal.

Taxis

Cabs operate on the meter system, with a minimum charge of $2 plus $1.19 for each additional kilometre. In excess of four passengers and asking the driver to load and unload baggage costs extra.

Destination Ottawa

*D*ignified and stately Ottawa balances the overwhelming presence of government—and the implied self-importance of it all—with cultural variety.

*B*y all means tour the Parliament Buildings. Then take in museums devoted to art, aviation, money, nature, photography, science, skiing and war.

Jacques Cartier Park, Hull, Québec.
When Old Man Winter transforms the park into an icy wonderland, all ages come out to play.

National War Memorial, Ottawa.
In commemoration of Canada's war dead, the memorial features bronze figures emerging through an arch, symbolizing the transition from war to peace. (See listing page 146)

© Patrick Bennett
Corbis

See Vicinity
map page 142

Canada Science and Technology Museum, Ottawa.
Learning firsthand about the wonders of science can be a hair-raising event, as this young lady has just discovered. (See listing page 144)

Canadian Museum of Civilization, Hull, Québec.
The history of Canada is explored from its earliest beginnings to the present. (See listing page 150)

*P*laces included in this AAA Destination City:

Nearby Québec

Some municipalities in Ontario have combined or soon will combine with neighboring cities. These mergers will eliminate some existing cities and may affect street names, addresses and political boundaries referenced in this guide. For further information, please contact Ontario governing agencies or the local CAA club.

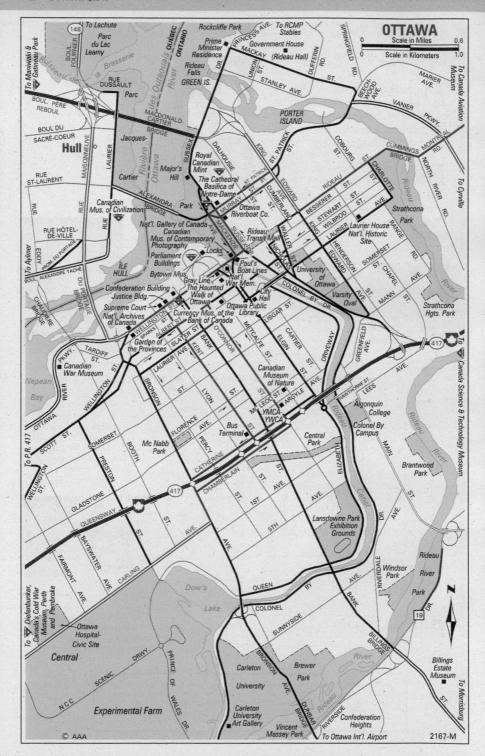

OTTAWA

Scale in Miles
0   0.6

Scale in Kilometers
0   1.0

Central

© AAA

2167-M

Hwy. 401 to intersect Hwy. 7 (also part of the Trans Canada Highway), which heads toward the city, terminating at the Queensway just a few miles from the municipal limits.

Getting Around

Street System

When negotiating the city, keep in mind that the Parliament Buildings and the Château Laurier Hotel, the city's most famous landmarks, are at the northern border of Ottawa with their backs to the Ottawa River—the dividing line between Ottawa and the province of Québec. Directions are often given in relation to these structures. The Rideau Canal, which runs north to south through the heart of the city, also can help visitors get their bearings.

Avoid the morning rush hour (7:30-9), the lunch crunch (noon-1:30) and the evening rush hour (4-6:30).

The main east-west artery is the Queensway (Hwy. 417). The Queen Elizabeth Driveway parallels the Rideau Canal on the western side, while the Colonel By Drive follows the canal on the eastern side. The Ottawa River Parkway, curving along the Ottawa River, leads from downtown into the western section of the city, where a number of government buildings and residential sections are. The Rockliffe Parkway leads to the eastern section of the city, parallel to the Ottawa River.

The Colonel By Drive and the Ottawa River Parkway are both closed Sunday 9-1, Victoria Day through Labour Day, for the exclusive use of bicyclists and joggers.

Parliament Hill, the Château Laurier Hotel and the U.S. Embassy are on Wellington Street, which becomes Rideau Street on the northeastern side of the canal. Between the two streets is the Rideau Transit Mall. Another road whose name changes for no apparent reason is Baseline Road, which suddenly becomes Heron Road.

The Mile of History, or Sussex Drive, is a boulevard that follows the contours of the Ottawa River in the northeastern section of the city. The prime minister's and governor-general's residences as well as many embassies are along Sussex Drive. The main bridge spanning the Ottawa River and connecting the cities of Ottawa and Hull, Québec, is the Macdonald-Cartier Bridge.

Left turns on red from a one-way street to another one-way street and right turns on red are permitted unless otherwise posted. Wearing seat belts is mandatory in both Québec and Ontario. All speeds and distances are in metric measurements. Most gas stations in the downtown area close every evening at 7 p.m., but a few in the environs are open 24 hours.

Parking

On-street parking in Ottawa is limited, though persistence may be rewarded. When and where on-street parking is permitted, regulations are strictly enforced; visitors should be careful to note the time limits on parking meters and signs.

Various lots and garages around the city charge $2-$4.50 per hour or $7-$18 per day. There also are public parking garages at the National Arts Centre and World Exchange.

Public Transportation

Public transportation in Ottawa means OC Transpo. Both inexpensive and convenient, the buses are used by the majority of Ottawans to get to and from work. The system has Park & Ride lots and extensive routes throughout the region, and it has a bus-only rapid transit system called the Transitway; buses operate daily 6 a.m.-2 a.m.

OC Transpo uses a computerized telephone information service that provides riders with specific schedules. To find out the destination and arrival time at a certain bus stop up to 6 days in advance, dial 560 and the four-digit bus stop number prominently displayed on each bus stop sign. Black numbers indicate standard routes; red numbers indicate rush-hour routes; green numbers indicate rush-hour express routes.

Most OC Transpo buses in Ottawa are red and white, while Québec buses, which also use some Ottawa routes, are blue and white. Basic fare is $2.50; express routes are $3.50. Exact change is required. Maps of OC Transpo routes are free from OC Transpo offices, where tickets are sold. Tickets also are available at other outlets. For information phone (613) 741-4390.

What To See

BILLINGS ESTATE MUSEUM, s. on Alta Vista to Pleasant Park, following signs to 2100 Cabot St., was built in 1828 by pioneer Braddish Billings. The neoclassical house, formerly called Park Hill, is on 3 hectares (8 acres) overlooking Ottawa and the Rideau River. Displays of furniture, textiles, photographs and other documents detail the history of the estate and the five generations of the Billings family that occupied it. Special events are offered on Sunday.

Picnicking is permitted. Allow 30 minutes minimum. Tues.-Sun. noon-5, May-Oct. Admission $2.50; over 64, $2; ages 5-17, $1.50. Phone (613) 247-4830.

BYTOWN MUSEUM, off Wellington St. at the bottom of Ottawa Locks behind the Château Laurier Hotel, is in the former commissariat used by the Royal Engineers and Lt. Col. John By during the building of the Rideau Canal. This is the oldest masonry building in the city and contains exhibits and displays about the history of Bytown and Ottawa. There also is a Parks Canada exhibit about the building of the Rideau Canal.

Mon.-Fri. 10-5, Sat.-Sun. 10-4, mid-May to mid-Oct.; Mon. and Wed.-Fri. 10-2, Apr. 1 to mid-May and mid-Oct. through Nov. 30; by appointment rest of year. Admission $5; over 64 and students with ID $3; ages 4-12, $2. Parks Canada exhibit free. VI. Phone (613) 234-4570.

CANADA AVIATION MUSEUM, at Rockcliffe and Aviation pkwys., houses a collection of more than 115 aircraft, 50 of which are displayed in a Walkway of Time that explains successive periods of aviation history from the early 20th century to the present. Engines, propellers and other aeronautical relics also are displayed.

Daily 9-5 (also Thurs. 5-9), May 1-Labour Day; Wed.-Sun. 10-5 (also Thurs. 5-9), rest of year. Closed Dec. 25. Admission $6; over 65 and students with ID $5; ages 4-15, $3; family rate (one or two adults with children) $14; free to all daily 4-5. MC, VI. Phone (613) 993-2010, or (800) 463-2038 in Canada.

CANADA SCIENCE AND TECHNOLOGY MUSEUM, 2.6 km (1.2 mi.) s. of the Queensway at 1867 St. Laurent Blvd., is devoted to the history, principles and applications of science and technology. The historical displays include steam locomotives, domestic appliances, antique automobiles and communications and space equipment. Canada's largest refracting telescope is among the featured hands-on exhibits. Special programs include workshops, stargazing and demonstrations.

Picnicking is permitted. Food is available. Daily 9-5, May 1-Labour Day; Tues.-Sun. 9-5, rest of year. Closed Sept. 13-17 and Dec. 25. Admission $6; over 64 and students with ID $5; ages 4-14, $3; family rate (two adults and three children) $14. MC, VI. Phone (613) 991-3044.

CANADIAN MUSEUM OF CONTEMPORARY PHOTOGRAPHY, 1 Rideau Canal, features the works of Canadian photographers. A theater and research center also are available. Daily 10-5 (also Thurs. 5-8), May-Sept.; Wed.-Sun. 10-5 (also Thurs. 5-8), rest of year. Free. Phone (613) 990-8257.

SAVE **CANADIAN MUSEUM OF NATURE,** 240 McLeod St. at Metcalfe St. in the Victoria Museum Memorial Building, depicts a journey through nature from the vanished world of dinosaurs to the habitats of contemporary birds, mammals and plants. Displays include hands-on exhibits, live animals and audiovisual presentations.

Note: An expansion project has begun that is expected to last until 2009. The museum will remain open during the renovations, though some exhibits may be closed. Daily 9:30-5 (also Thurs. 5-8), May 1-second Mon. in Oct.; Tues.-Sun. and Mon. holidays 10-5 (also Thurs. 5-8), rest of year. Closed Dec. 25 and 1 week in Jan. Admission $4; over 64 and students with ID $3.50; ages 3-12, $1.75; family rate (up to five members with a maximum of three adults) $9; free to all Thurs. 5-8. AX, MC, VI. Phone (613) 566-4700 or (800) 263-4433.

CANADIAN SKI MUSEUM, 1960 Scott St. above the trail head, traces the development of skiing from its European beginnings 5,000 years ago to its introduction into Canada more than 100 years ago.

Equipment displayed ranges from twisted birch bindings to present-day racing skis.

The library and archives have photographs, clippings, periodicals, books and other records detailing the sport's evolution. Canadian athletes who have triumphed in competition are honored. Sun.-Fri. 9-5, Sat. 11-5; closed holidays. Donations. Phone (613) 722-3584.

CANADIAN WAR MUSEUM, 1 Vimy Pl. on LeBreton Flats, contains war medals, paintings, photographs, uniforms, vehicles, weapons and other items relating to Canada's military history since the early 1600s. Dioramas and displays depict the old fortress of Québec, fighter airplanes and battle scenes from various conflicts including the Battle of the Atlantic and the 1943 invasion of Sicily.

Note: The museum's move to its new location on Vimy Place is scheduled for May 2005; phone ahead for confirmation. Food is available. Daily 9-6 (also Thurs.-Fri. 6-9 p.m.), July 1-Sept. 6; daily 9-6 (also Thurs. 6-9 p.m.), May 8-June 30 and Sept. 7-second Mon. in Oct.; Tues.-Sun. 9-5 (also Thurs. 5-8), rest of year. Closed Dec. 25.

Admission $10; over 64, $7; students with ID $6; ages 3-12, $4; family rate (up to four members with a maximum of two adults) $22. MC, VI. Phone (819) 776-8600 or (800) 555-5621, or TTY (819) 776-7003.

CARLETON UNIVERSITY ART GALLERY is in St. Patrick's Building at 1125 Colonel By Dr. on the Carleton University campus. Parking is available in Lot 6 near the Bronson Ave. entrance to the university. The museum's permanent collection concentrates on Canadian art created since the mid-1900s, European prints and drawings from the 16th- through 19th centuries and Inuit art. Temporary exhibits are presented throughout the year.

Allow 1 hour minimum. Tues.-Fri. 10-5, Sat.-Sun. noon-5; closed major holidays. Free. A parking fee applies Tues.-Fri.; parking free Sat.-Sun. Phone (613) 520-2120.

THE CATHEDRAL BASILICA OF NOTRE-DAME, 385 Sussex Dr., was built in 1839 and not completed until 1885. Restored to its original glory, highlights include its painted and carved neo-Gothic interior, stained-glass windows, a gilded statue of the Madonna and child, intricate wall paneling, faux marble pillars and hundreds of statues. Its two prominent spires make the Gothic Revival cathedral a local landmark.

Allow 30 minutes minimum. Mon.-Fri. 9-4. Guided tours are available July-Aug. Donations. Guided tour $2. Phone (613) 241-7496.

CENTRAL EXPERIMENTAL FARM, on the Driveway at Maple Dr., consists of 500 hectares (1,200 acres). Established in 1886, the farm is the headquarters and research station of Agriculture and Agri-Food Canada. Flowerbeds, ornamental gardens, an arboretum and a tropical greenhouse are showcased. The Canada Agriculture Museum features a barn re-creating the atmosphere of a 1920s farm. The museum also has bread and tractor exhibits.

Grounds open daily dawn-dusk. Exhibits open daily 9-5, Mar.-Oct. Animal barns open daily 9-5; closed Dec. 25. Grounds admission free. Animal barns and exhibits $6; over 65 and students with ID $5; ages 3-14, $3; family rate (two adults and three children) $13. MC, VI. Phone (613) 991-3044.

CITY HALL is at 110 Laurier Ave. W. A 45- to 60-minute guided tour is conducted of the two buildings that make up City Hall—the Ottawa-Carleton Centre and the Heritage Building. The history of both buildings is reviewed (one wing of the Heritage Building dates to 1875), and the buildings' design and artwork are explained. Tours are given Mon.-Fri. 8-4:30. Free. Underground parking $12. Reservations are required. Phone (613) 580-2400 for tour reservations.

CURRENCY MUSEUM OF THE BANK OF CANADA, 245 Sparks St. in the Bank of Canada Bldg., has seven galleries of exhibits illustrating the origin, history and development of Canadian currency dating back to wampum and beaver pelts.

Artifacts and maps describe the currencies of the early Chinese dynasties, ancient Greek civilization, the Roman and Byzantine empires, the Middle Ages, the Renaissance and North America at the time of its settlement. The museum also presents changing exhibits. Guided tours, in English and French, are available early July to mid-October by appointment.

Mon.-Sat. 10:30-5, Sun. 1-5, May 1-Labour Day; Tues.-Sat. 10:30-5, Sun. 1-5, rest of year. Closed Jan. 1, Good Friday, Nov. 11 and Dec. 25. Free. Phone (613) 782-8914, or (613) 782-8852 for tour reservations.

DIEFENBUNKER, CANADA'S COLD WAR MUSEUM is off Hwy. 417 exit 144, then 13 km (8 mi.) n. to 3911 Carp Rd. Nicknamed for Prime Minister John Diefenbaker, the bunker was built 1959-61 to house Canadian government and military officials in the event of a nuclear crisis. Visitors can see a Canadian Broadcasting Company (CBC) radio studio, a Bank of Canada gold-storage vault, the prime minister's suite, living quarters and cooking and dining areas. Archival photographs detail the construction of the shelter, which was built entirely in secret.

Allow 2 hours minimum. Daily 10-3. Guided tours are given daily at 11, noon, 1, 2 and 3 (French tour at 1), July 1-Labour Day; Mon.-Fri. at 2, Sat.-Sun. at 11, 1 and 2 (French tours by appointment), rest of year. Admission $14; over 65 and students with ID $12.50; ages 6-17, $6. Reservations are required. AX, VI. Phone (613) 839-0007, or (800) 409-1965 for reservations.

GARDEN OF THE PROVINCES, Wellington and Bay sts., contains flagpoles that fly flags of the provincial coats-of-arms. Provincial flowers are depicted on enameled bronze plaques set in stone balustrades along upper and lower terraces. Flags are flown from May through October. A tree-fountain is striking under night illumination. Daily 24 hours. Free.

GOVERNMENT HOUSE (Rideau Hall), 1 Sussex Dr. at the entrance to Rockcliffe Park, has been the official home and workplace of Canada's governors-general since 1867. The original residence was built in 1838 by Thomas MacKay, a Scottish stonemason who worked on the Rideau Canal; it was called Rideau Hall—a name still used unofficially. The building is on 32 landscaped hectares (79 acres). Costumed guides are available, and The Ceremonial Guard performs the Relief of the Sentries.

Grounds daily 8-dusk. Guided tours of the residence are offered daily 10-4, June 24-Labour Day; Sat.-Sun. 10-4, May 11-June 23; Sat.-Sun. 10-4, day after Labour Day-Oct. 31; by appointment rest of year. Guided grounds tours are given daily 10-4, July-Aug.; by appointment rest of year. Sentries relief performed daily on the hour 9-4. No tours during official functions. Free. Phone (613) 991-4422 or (866) 842-4422.

LAURIER HOUSE NATIONAL HISTORIC SITE, 335 Laurier Ave. E., was the residence of Sir Wilfrid Laurier and of Rt. Hon. William Lyon Mackenzie King. The house contains historical exhibits and personal memorabilia of both men. The contents of the study of Rt. Hon. Lester B. Pearson also are displayed. Mon.-Sat. 9-5, Sun. 1-5, mid-May through second Mon. in Oct.; Mon.-Fri. 9-5, Apr. 1 to mid-May. Admission $3.75; over 64, $3.25; ages 6-18, $2.25. Phone (613) 992-8142.

NATIONAL ARCHIVES OF CANADA, 395 Wellington St. opposite the Garden of the Provinces, houses documents relating to Canadian history. There are films, recordings, prints, paintings, engravings, photographs and maps. Exhibits open daily 9-9. Reading room Mon.-Fri. 8 a.m.-11 p.m., Sat.-Sun. and holidays 8-6. Reference room Mon.-Fri. 8:30-5. Free. Reservations may be required for some exhibits. Phone (613) 996-5115 or (866) 578-7777.

NATIONAL GALLERY OF CANADA, 380 Sussex Dr., is in a dramatically modern building highlighted by expanses of glass, skylights and interior courtyards. Incorporated in the building is the reconstructed and historic Rideau Chapel, which presents some of the museum's collection of sacred art and silver pieces.

The Canadian Galleries are the museum's centerpiece and display works from the early 19th century to the present, including paintings by the Group of Seven. In the upper-level galleries are works by such masters as Paul Cézanne, Jean Chardin, Edgar Degas, Thomas Gainsborough, El Greco, Claude Monet, Pablo Picasso, Rembrandt and Vincent Van Gogh. Photographs, prints, sculpture, videotapes and films as well as special exhibits complete the museum's extensive displays.

Food is available. Daily 10-5 (also Thurs. 5-8), Victoria Day weekend-Sept. 30; Wed.-Sun. 10-5 (also Thurs. 5-8), rest of year. Closed Jan. 1 and Dec. 25. Guided 1-hour tours are given daily at 11 and 2, June-Sept.; Wed.-Sun. at 2, rest of year. Admission $6; senior citizens and students with ID $5; ages 12-19, $3; family rate (two adults and three children) $12; free to all Thurs. after 5). Additional fees apply to some special exhibitions. Audio guides for permanent collection $3. Phone (613) 990-1985.

NATIONAL WAR MEMORIAL, on Confederation Sq. at jct. Wellington and Elgin sts., is a memorial arch dedicated in 1939 to honor the Canadian soldiers who fought in World War I. It was rededicated to all those who have served Canada in time of war.

PARLIAMENT BUILDINGS dominate the city from Parliament Hill. Centre Block tours depart from the ground floor Visitor Welcome Centre, under the Peace Tower. The three Gothic buildings with green copper roofs were built 1859-66. The Centre Block, destroyed by fire in 1916, was rebuilt to the original design, minus the wood-paneled interior. The only section left undamaged after the fire was the library.

This central building is crowned by the 92.2-metre (302.5-ft.) Peace Tower with its 53-bell carillon. Dedicated to Canadians killed in World War I, the tower has national memorials, the Memorial Chamber with its Books of Remembrance and an observation deck. Statues and monuments are at the building's sides and rear.

Centre Block tours visit the Senate and the House of Commons (unless Parliament is in session) and the Hall of Honour. East Block tours show what government offices looked like at the time of Confederation. Sound-and-light shows play against the backdrop of Parliament.

Note: Centre Block tour schedules vary, especially when Parliament is in session; phone ahead to confirm availability. When either the Senate or House of Commons is in session, visitors may watch the debates or listen to audio guides in the Public Galleries (space permitting). Guided 30-minute tours of the Centre Block are conducted in English and French Mon.-Fri. 9-7:20, Sat.-Sun. and holidays 9-4:20, mid-May-Labour Day; daily 9-3:20 (also Tues. 3:20-7:20, day after Labour Day-early Oct.), rest of year. Closed Jan. 1, July 1 and Dec. 25. East Block tours are given in English and French daily 10-6, July 2-Labour Day. Sound-and-light shows daily, May-Sept.

Free. Phone (613) 992-4793, (613) 996-0896 for building tour reservations, or (613) 239-5000 or (800) 465-1867 for outdoor tour information.

Changing the Guard takes place on the lawns of Parliament Hill. The traditional military ceremony is performed by "ceremonial guards." The ceremony includes inspection of dress and weapons, the Trooping of the Colors and the exchange of compliments between the old and new guards. After the ceremony, guards execute sentry duties at Rideau Hall.

The members of the governor-general's Foot Guards and the Canadian Grenadier Guards perform daily at 10 a.m., late June-late Aug. (weather permitting). Free. Phone (613) 993-1811.

ROCKCLIFFE PARK, 4 km (2.5 mi.) n.e. of Parliament Hill via Sussex Dr., is a scenic recreation and picnic area overlooking the Ottawa River. Daily 24 hours. Free.

ROYAL CANADIAN MINT, 320 Sussex Dr., offers guided tours of the coin-manufacturing plant. Since 1976 foreign and domestic coinage have been produced in Winnipeg, but Ottawa continues to strike special commemorative coins, tokens, medals and bullion investment coins.

Allow 1 hour minimum. Guided tours (alternately in English and French) every 15 minutes Mon.-Fri. 9-8:30, Sat.-Sun. 9-5, Victoria Day-Labour Day; daily 9-5, rest of year. Closed holidays. Phone to confirm language schedule in the off-season. Mon.-Fri. tour $5; ages 4-15, $3; family rate (two adults and up to four children) $13. Sat.-Sun. tour $3.50; ages 4-15, $2; family rate (two adults and up to four children) $10. Reservations are recommended. Phone (613) 993-8990, (613) 993-8997 or (800) 276-7714.

ROYAL CANADIAN MOUNTED POLICE STABLES, n. end of St. Laurent Blvd., offers guided half-hour tours of the premises. At times it is possible to watch the training of both members and horses for the Musical Ride, a ceremonial equestrian display. Daily 9-4, May-Oct.; Mon.-Fri. 10-2, rest of year. Free. Phone (613) 993-3751, or (613) 998-8199 for tour information.

THE SUPREME COURT OF CANADA is just w. of Parliament Hill at 301 Wellington St. Guided tours of the judicial branch of the Canadian government are provided by law students. The Supreme Court is the highest court of appeal for criminal and civil cases. Two statues, representing truth and justice, are on either side of the entrance to the Art Deco building.

Allow 30 minutes minimum. Tours are given Mon.-Fri. 9-5, Sat.-Sun. 9-noon and 1-5, May-Aug.; Mon.-Fri. 9-5, rest of year. Closed major holidays. Free. Tours are by reservation only Sept.-Apr. Phone (613) 995-4330 or (888) 551-1185, or (613) 995-5361 for tour reservations.

VALLEYVIEW LITTLE ANIMAL FARM, s. on Hwy. 416, then w. to 4750 Fallowfield Rd. in Nepean, is a petting farm with a play area and a train ride. Picnicking is permitted. Allow 1 hour, 30 minutes minimum. Tues-Sun. 10-4, July-Aug.; Tues.-Fri. 10-3, Sat.-Sun. 10-4, mid-Apr. through June 30 and Sept.-Oct. Admission $5, under 2 free. MC, VI. Phone (613) 591-1126.

VINCENT MASSEY PARK, at Heron Rd. on the Rideau River 7 km (4 mi.) s., offers picnic areas and large open spaces for recreation. Facilities include softball diamonds, horseshoe pits, a bandstand, barbecue grills and washrooms. Drinking fountains are throughout the park. Daily 7 a.m.-9 p.m., mid-Apr. to mid-Oct. Free. Parking $4, May-Sept. Reservations are required for use of some facilities. Phone (613) 239-5335 for reservations Apr. 1-Labour Day.

What To Do

Sightseeing

Boat Tours

OTTAWA RIVERBOAT CO. cruises depart from both behind Parliament Hill at the Rideau locks (Ottawa) and from Jacques Cartier Park adjacent to the Canadian Museum of Civilization (Hull). The 60-minute sightseeing cruises on the Ottawa River aboard the *Sea Prince II* include a narration describing various points of interest. Other cruises also are available.

Food is available. Sixty-minute cruises depart from Ottawa daily at 11:30, 1, 3:30 and 4:45, late June-Labour Day; daily at 11:30, 1 and 3 (also Sat.-Sun. at 5), early May-late June; daily at 1, 2:15 and 3:30 (also Sat.-Sun. at 4:45), day after Labour Day to mid-Oct. Departures from Hull are 20 minutes earlier. Fare $16; over 59 and students with ID $14; ages 6-12, $8. MC, VI. Phone (613) 562-4888.

PAUL'S BOAT LINES cruises depart from behind the Conference Centre for the Rideau Canal and from the Hull Marina for the Ottawa River; Ottawa River cruises also pick up passengers at the foot of the Ottawa Locks. The boat line offers approximately 90-minute scenic river and canal cruises. Many of the city's attractions can be seen.

River and canal cruises depart daily, early May-second Mon. in Oct. Evening cruises by appointment after Labour Day. Schedule may vary; phone ahead. River cruise $15; over 59 and students with ID $13; ages 5-14, $8; family rate (two adults and two children) $35. Canal cruise $14; over 59 and students with ID $12; ages 4-12, $8; family rate $30. Rates may vary; phone ahead. AX, DC, MC, VI. Phone (613) 225-6781, or (613) 235-8409 in summer (dock).

Bus Tours

[SAVE] **GRAY LINE** departs from jct. Sparks and Metcalfe. Fully-narrated excursions aboard both English double decker and replica trolley buses are among the tours offered. The Discover the Capital tour, stopping at 20 points of interest, allows passengers to disembark, explore an attraction or area and then reboard a later bus. A 2.5-hour tour of Gatineau Park is available in the fall. Other tours also are available.

Discover the Capital tour departs daily every 30 minutes 9-4, June 27-Sept. 1; on the hour 10-3, May 1-June 26 and Sept. 2-Oct. 13; at 10 and 1, in Apr.; schedule varies rest of year. Discover the Capital tour $30; over 59 and students with ID $25;

ages 5-12, $20; family rate (two adults and two children) $80. AX, MC, VI. Phone (613) 565-5463 or (800) 297-6422.

Walking Tours

The National Capital Commission has a visitor information center at 90 Wellington St. that is open daily 8:30 a.m.-9 p.m., May 7-Labour Day; 9-5, rest of year. The center is closed Jan. 1 and Dec. 25-26. Information about local sightseeing tours and self-guiding walking tours is available; phone (613) 239-5000 or (800) 465-1867.

THE HAUNTED WALK OF OTTAWA departs from the ticket booth at the corner of Sparks and Elgin sts. Ninety-minute ghost tours conducted by lantern light recount local ghost stories and Ottawa's dark history. The Original Haunted Walk features tales about the Bytown Museum and the Fairmont Château Laurier, and the Ghosts and the Gallows tour explores the murder of D'Arcy McGee and supernatural encounters that emanate from the old Carleton County Jail. Other tours also are available.

Tours also are available in French. Allow 1 hour, 30 minutes minimum. The Original Haunted Walk departs daily at 8 and 9 p.m., late June-day before Labour Day; daily at 8 p.m., early May-late June and Labour Day-late Oct. Ghosts and the Gallows walk departs daily at 8 and 9 p.m., late June-day before Labour Day; daily at 9 p.m., early May-late June and Labour Day-late Oct.; Fri.-Sat. at 8 p.m., Jan. 1-early May and late Oct.-Dec. 31. Closed July 1 and Dec. 25.

Fee for The Original Haunted Walk $12; over 65 and ages 13-18, $10; ages 6-12, $5. Ghosts and the Gallows $14; over 65 and ages 13-18, $12; ages 6-12, $7. The Ghosts and the Gallows tour includes stairs and is not recommended for young children. Reservations are recommended. Phone (613) 232-0344.

Sports and Recreation

Ottawa has the distinct advantage of being a large city in the middle of lush farmlands, forests and river country. As a result, tennis courts, pools and golf courses are not far away from ski slopes, canoe routes, hiking trails, lakes and beaches.

One of the most popular recreational facilities in Ottawa is the Rideau Canal. Originally built for military purposes, this attractive waterway is now available to the public all year. **Canoeing, inline skating** and **bicycling** are the dominant sports in and along the canal during the summer. With the arrival of winter, the frozen water becomes a haven for **ice skating**, and the bicycle paths are transformed into trails for **hiking** and **cross-country skiing**. Boats can be rented at many establishments along the canal.

Dow's Lake in the southern section of the city is part of the Rideau Canal. Arrangements for pedal boats and canoeing or bicycle and skate rental can be made; contact Dow's Lake Pavilion, (613) 232-1001, or Hogs Back Marina, (613) 731-6583.

Gatineau Park *(see attraction listing p. 151)*, a 35,600-hectare (87,965-acre) wilderness across the

Ottawa River in Hull, Québec, is just 15 minutes from the Parliament Buildings. The entrance to the park from Ottawa is via the Gatineau Parkway, a 35-kilometre (22-mi.) scenic drive. The park has some 40 lakes for **fishing, swimming** and **boating.**

The most popular recreational lakes are Lac Phillipe, Meech Lake and Lac la Pêche. Anglers must obtain a Québec fishing license, available at sporting goods and hardware stores in Hull. There also are **camping** and **picnicking** facilities throughout the park. For those not interested in sports, the beautiful scenery makes a visit worthwhile; phone (819) 827-2020 for park information or reservations.

Skiing, both cross-country and downhill, is best in the heart of the Outaouais Region. The downhill ski clubs include Camp Fortune, Edelweiss, Mont Cascades and Vorlage. On the Ontario side is Mount Pakenham, 90 kilometres (56 mi.) west of Ottawa, and Mont Ste.-Marie, 85 kilometres (53 mi.) north of Ottawa in the Province of Québec.

Nearly 200 kilometres (124 mi.) of cross-country ski trails wind through Gatineau Park, and most of the public parks and pathways in Ottawa become available for the sport as well.

Canoeing is readily available on numerous lakes and rivers within and around Ottawa. Dow's Lake, Mooney's Bay and the Rideau Canal are popular spots. Rentals range from $9 per half-hour to $16 per hour, while charges for complete outfitting average $23 to $45 per day. In addition to canoes, options include pedal boats, kayaks and rowboats. Canoe rentals are available at Trailhead, 1960 Scott St., (613) 722-4229, and Dow's Lake Pavilion, 1001 Queen Elizabeth Dr., (613) 232-1001.

White-water rafting trips along the Ottawa River are conducted by experienced guides; river equipment, lunches, dinners and camping facilities are provided. Wilderness Tours Whitewater Rafting operates excursions out of Beachburg *(see place listing p. 56).* Madawaska River Float Trips in Barry's Bay *(see attraction listing p. 55)* and Owl Rafting Inc. and RiverRun Paddling Centre in Foresters Falls *(see place listing p. 74)* offer 1- and 2-day tours with a broad range of difficulty. White-water season generally runs from May through September.

Swimming can be enjoyed at the many lakes in Gatineau Park in Ottawa; at Mooney's Bay Beach, Riverside Drive and Ridgewood Avenue; at Westboro Beach off the Ottawa River Parkway; and at Britannia Beach off Britannia Road. A number of public swimming pools also are available.

Golf season runs from April through October. Public golf courses include the 18-hole Capital Golf Course, (613) 521-2612; Manderley Golf and Country Club, (613) 489-2066; and the nine-hole Richmond Centennial Golf Course, (613) 838-4791. Many other popular courses are within a short driving distance from the city.

With 130 kilometres (81 mi.) of bicycle paths stretching from downtown Ottawa to the suburbs,

bicycling is both a practical and enjoyable sport. Pedaling along the Rideau Canal and the Rideau River are two popular routes. Some other pleasant sections for bicycling are the Colonel By and Rockliffe parkways, which are closed to motorized traffic on Sunday 9-1, Victoria Day through Labour Day; the westbound lane of Ottawa River Parkway also is closed Sunday 9-1. The National Capital Commission provides maps of the various trails at the visitors center at 90 Wellington St. Bicycle rentals are available from Rent-a-Bike, (613) 241-4140.

Hiking trails are found along the Rideau Canal and in Gatineau Park. Special paths for the elderly and physically impaired also are available. **Birdwatching** trails originate at the Stony Swamp Interpretation Centre on Moodie Drive. Contact the National Capital Commission for maps and information *(see The Informed Traveler box).*

Public **tennis** courts are in the many parks and school grounds throughout the city, including the Elmdale Tennis Club at Holland and Byron avenues, (613) 729-3644, and the West Ottawa Tennis Club in Britannia Park, 300 Greenview Ave., (613) 828-7622. Courts are available for a fee for 45-minute sets on a first-come-first-served basis.

Ice skating becomes a popular mode of transportation when an 8-kilometre (5-mi.) stretch of the Rideau Canal freezes, forming one of the world's longest skating rinks. Extending from the Parliament Buildings to Carleton University, the canal is used by many of the city's residents to skate to work.

Ottawa also plays host to a variety of spectator sports. As in many Canadian cities, residents are avid **hockey** fans. Two junior A teams are based in the metropolitan area: The Ottawa 67's play at the Civic Centre at 1015 Bank St. at Queen Elizabeth Driveway, (613) 232-6767, and the Hull Olympiques play at Robert Guertin Arena in Hull, Québec, (819) 595-7700. Ottawa also has an NHL franchise team, the Ottawa Senators, who play at the Corel Centre, 1000 Paladium Dr. in Kanata, (613) 755-1166 or (800) 444-7367.

Baseball fans can see the Ottawa Lynx, the AAA farm team of the Montréal Expos, play April to mid-September at their stadium, Lynx Stadium, 300 Coventry Rd.; phone (613) 747-5969, or (800) 663-0985 in Canada.

Harness racing is offered March through December at the Rideau-Carleton Raceway at 4837 Albion Rd. in Gloucester, (613) 822-2211.

Note: Policies concerning admittance of children to pari-mutuel betting facilities vary. Phone for information.

Shopping

Shopping in Ottawa runs the gamut from bustling markets to sleek department stores. Byward Market, a colorful shopping district established in the 1830s, has been preserved as a reminder of Ottawa's urban past. Farmers, fishermen, artisans and cooks congregate at the market, 1 block north of Rideau Street between York and George streets, to sell a variety of fresh fruits and vegetables, fish, meat, cheese, pastries, hand-made crafts and Canadian artwork.

Interesting boutiques specializing in china, furs, antiques, second-hand books, clothing and crafts are along the Bank Street Promenade which runs for several blocks downtown. McIntosh and Watts, Ltd. specializes in china and glassware; five branch stores are within the Ottawa area. And don't miss the boutique at the Royal Canadian Mounted Police Stables at the north end of St. Laurent Boulevard.

Place de Ville, 320 Queen St., is an underground arcade connecting the Crowne Plaza and Radisson hotels. Another downtown shopping center is L'Esplanade Laurier, 171 Bank St., with boutiques, restaurants and craft shops in the lower level of an office complex. Elyseé at World Exchange Plaza, two blocks from the Parliament buildings, offers a variety of shops and boutiques, movie theaters and restaurants.

The Bayshore Shopping Centre, on Bayshore Drive at the Queensway/Richmond Road interchange; Place d'Orleans, on Place d'Orleans Drive just off Hwy. 17 in Orleans; and St. Laurent Shopping Centre, on the Queensway at St. Laurent Boulevard, are three large shopping malls.

The 5.6-hectare (14-acre) Rideau Centre, a convention complex in downtown Ottawa, has a hotel, several movie theaters and many shops, including The Bay.

Theater and Concerts

Just steps from Parliament Hill, the National Arts Centre (NAC) celebrates the achievements of Canadian performing artists and plays a dynamic role in the development and presentation of the performing arts. The NAC presents plays from across Canada and abroad in English and French, innovative contemporary dance and ballet programs from national and international dance companies, and classical and contemporary orchestral music with the National Arts Centre Orchestra. The NAC co-produces and commissions new works and produces a range of educational and in-school activities. For NAC performances information phone (613) 947-7000; the box office is open Monday through Saturday 10 to 9, and Sundays and holidays from noon to 15 minutes after curtain time.

The visitor center, open July 1 to Labour Day, is a journey through time, with original set and costume displays from NAC productions, poster exhibits and memorabilia. Guided tours offer a behind-the-scenes look at the performing arts.

Various smaller theaters and companies offer fine productions at reasonable prices. Some of these include the the Centrepoint Theatre, (613) 727-6650; Great Canadian Theatre Co., (613) 236-5196; Kanata Theatre, (613) 831-4435; Odyssey Theatre, (613) 232-8407; Ottawa Little Theatre, (613) 233-8948; and Théâtre de l'Île in Hull, Québec, (819) 595-7455.

Special Events

Three major events enliven Ottawa. The Canadian Tulip Festival is the most celebrated. It centers on the millions of tulips—some a gift from the Netherlands' government in recognition of the refuge granted to the Dutch royal family during World War II—and other flowers, which are at their peak when the event is held in early to mid-May.

The flowers are planted in masses along the banks of the Rideau Canal and Dow's and Commissioners lakes as well as at Government House (Rideau Hall) and Parliament Hall, forming a wonderful background for the events held at 16 festival sites. Tulip Time, culminating with the Canadian Tulip Festival, features special events each weekend in May.

In addition to the profusion of blossoms, there is a giant flotilla of decorated boats on the Rideau Canal as well as a children's area, a marketplace, a flower and garden promenade, a multicultural village, concerts, the National Capital Marathon and a fireworks display. For more information about the Canadian Tulip Festival phone (613) 567-4447.

The 10-day Central Canada Exhibition in Lansdowne Park is in August. Agricultural and industrial exhibits, horse shows, games, top-name entertainment, craft shows and a carnival atmosphere are all part of the fun.

Paying homage to the games and rites of winter is a Canadian national pastime, and Ottawa celebrates them with an event spread over three Friday-Sunday weekends in February—Winterlude. Parades, fireworks, sleigh rides and snow sculptures as well as snowshoeing, cross-country skiing and speed skating competitions, are the main activities held in and around the Rideau Canal area during this spectacular winter carnival.

DID YOU KNOW

Ontario accounts for more than one-half of Canada's industrial output.

The Ottawa Vicinity

Nearby Québec

CANTLEY pop. 5,898, elev. 1,348 m/4,424'

MONT CASCADES, 7 km (4 mi.) w. on Hwy. 307 to 448 Mont Cascades Rd., is a downhill ski area in the winter and a water park in the summer. Water park highlights include a speed slide, raft rides, activity pools and children's rides. Food is available. Allow a full day. Water park open daily 10-5, mid-June through Labour Day. Admission $20.95, under 48 inches tall and spectators $13.95. Reduced rates after 2 p.m. MC, VI. Phone (819) 827-0301, or (888) 282-2722 in Canada.

HULL pop. 66,246

Part of the National Capital Region, Hull, Québec, is one of the oldest settlements in the area. In 1800 Philemon Wright arrived from Woburn, Mass., with his family and a number of townspeople and soon established the timber trade that sustained the region for more than a century. The E.B. Eddy Co., a pulp and paper products factory that is the city's main industry, was built then.

Several parks offer recreational facilities and picnic areas *(see the AAA/CAA Eastern Canada CampBook)*. Ski centers abound in the region. Of historical interest are a monument to Saint-Jean de Brébeuf, a Jesuit missionary and martyr, and an original timber slide that cuts through a wall of solid rock.

Outaouais Tourism Association: 103 rue Laurier, Hull, QC, Canada J8X 3V8; phone (819) 778-2222 or (800) 265-7822.

Shopping areas: Three shopping malls serve the Hull area: Les Galeries de Hull, 320 St. Joseph Blvd. in Hull; Les Promenades de l'Outaouais, 1100 W. Maloney Blvd. in Gatineau; and Place du Centre, 200 Promenade du Portage in Hull. With 200 stores, including Eaton's, Les Promenades de l'Outaouais is the largest mall; Place du Centre has 60 stores; Les Galeries de Hull has 70 stores.

CANADIAN MUSEUM OF CIVILIZATION (Musée Canadien des Civilisations) at 100 rue Laurier, directly across the Ottawa River from the Parliament Buildings, illustrates Canada's history from the continent's prehistoric beginnings through successive periods of migration, native settlement, exploration, fur trading, immigration and the modern era.

Life-size reconstructions such as a West Coast native village and other historic sites present a dramatic interpretation of the country's past. Other highlights include the Canadian Children's Museum, the Canadian Postal Museum and an IMAX theater.

Food is available. Sat.-Wed. 9-6, Thurs.-Fri. 9-9, July 1-Labour Day; Fri.-Wed. 9-6, Thurs. 9-9, May-June and day after Labour Day-second Mon. in Oct.; Tues.-Wed. and Fri.-Sun. (also Easter Mon.) 9-5, Thurs. 9-9, rest of year. Extended evening hours do not apply to the children's museum. IMAX schedule does not always correspond with museum schedule; phone ahead for show times. Closed Dec. 25.

Even More Ways to Travel With Someone You Trust®

AAA's automotive guides offer comprehensive, helpful information pertaining to each stage of your vehicle's life. With these guides, you can learn about financing, basic maintenance, how to handle all types of driving situations, and much more.

MAKING SENSE OF CAR CARE

AAA Auto Guide

BUYING OR LEASING A CAR

AAA Auto Guide

DRIVING SURVIVAL
How to stay safe on the road

Purchase AAA publications at participating AAA club offices, on www.aaa.com/barnesandnoble and in fine book stores.

Museum admission $10; over 64, $7; ages 13-17, $6; ages 3-12, $4; family rate (four persons with maximum of two adults) $22; museum half-price to all Sun. IMAX film $9.50; over 64 and ages 13-17, $8; ages 3-12, $7. Ask about reduced rates for a second film. Combination museum admission and one film $17; over 64, $14; ages 13-17, $13; ages 3-12, $10. Free to all Thurs. 4-9, July 1 and Nov. 11. Phone to verify prices. MC, VI. Phone (819) 776-7000, (800) 555-5621, TTY (819) 776-7003, or (819) 776-7010 for show times.

GATINEAU PARK, (Parc de la Gatineau), is just n. between the Gatineau and Ottawa rivers. Hwys. 5, 105, 148 and 366 provide access from Hull to the park's recreation areas. The park encompasses about 36,300 hectares (89,661 acres) of the rocky, wooded Laurentian Mountains.

In the southern section, the scenic Gatineau Parkway links the lac des Fées and lac Meech areas. Along with a bicycle path the route provides access to many picnic grounds and lookouts. Farther north the lac Philippe area offers fine beaches and fringe areas. In the northwestern section the lac La Pêche area provides more wilderness, a beach and canoe-camping facilities.

Meech, Philippe and La Pêche lakes provide bass fishing. Alpine skiing is available at Camp Fortune. There are 200 kilometres (125 mi.) of cross-country ski trails with day-use and overnight shelters. During the summer ski trails become hiking trails.

Anglers must have a valid Québec fishing license. Park open daily 24 hours. Camping is permitted year-round. Park free. Access fees to the beach and picnic areas at lakes Meech, La Pêche and Philippe are $8 per private vehicle, mid-June through Labour Day. Access fee to the cross-country ski network is $9 per person over age 17 per day. AX, MC, VI. Phone (819) 827-2020.

Moorside—Mackenzie King Estate, rue Barnes, was a summer residence of three-time prime minister Mackenzie King. The first floor is now a tearoom. Historical interpreters and audiovisual presentations give an overview of the 1921-48 era during Canada's longest-governing prime minister. Presentations are available in English. The formal gardens are restored and gardener-historians describe King's gardening techniques.

Guided tours are available. Food is available. Allow 1 hour, 30 minutes minimum. Mon.-Fri. 11-5, Sat.-Sun. 10-6, mid-May to mid-Oct. Admission $8 per private vehicle. Phone (819) 827-2020.

HULL-CHELSEA-WAKEFIELD STEAM TRAIN (Train à vapeur de Hull-Chelsea-Wakefield) departs Hull Station at 165 rue Deveault for a 5-hour, 64-kilometre (40-mi.) steam-powered round-trip rail excursion through the scenic Gatineau Valley. A 2-hour stay in the picturesque village of Wakefield is included. A sunset dinner train and Sunday brunch trains also are available.

Food is available. Departures daily at 10, July 1-Labour Day; Tues.-Wed. and Fri.-Sun. at 10, in June; Tues.-Wed. and Sat.-Sun. at 10, May 10-22 (also May 23 and 31), Sept. 10-17 and 20-21; daily at 1:30, Sept. 24-30; Mon.-Fri. at 1:30, Sat.-Sun. at 8:30 and 1, Oct. 1-23. Sun. brunch trains depart at 10:30, May 8, Sept. 18 and Oct. 30. Arrive 30 minutes prior to departure. Phone to confirm schedule.

Fare May 7-Sept. 21, $39; over 60, $36; students with ID $35; ages 3-12, $19; family rate (two adults and two children) $99. Fare Sept. 24-Oct. 23, $45; over 60, $41; students with ID $40; ages 3-12, $23; family rate (two adults and two children) $115. Reservations are required. AX, JC, MC, VI. Phone (819) 778-7246 or (800) 871-7246.

CASINOS

- **Casino du Lac-Leamy** is at 1 boul. du Casino. Daily 9 a.m.-4 a.m. Phone (819) 772-2100 or (800) 665-2274.

This ends listings for the Ottawa Vicinity.
The following page resumes the alphabetical listings
of cities in Ontario.

OWEN SOUND (F-7) pop. 21,431

Known to the Ojibway Indians as the "beautiful valley," Owen Sound lies in the Sydenham River Valley and is flanked on both sides by the cliffs of the Niagara Escarpment. Some 30 fern varieties and 40 species of orchids are found in the area. Its natural harbor and location have made Owen Sound a center for vacationers visiting Georgian Bay, the nearby Blue Mountains and Bruce Peninsula.

Owen Sound is the birthplace of two notable Canadians—Tom Thomson, an innovative Canadian landscape artist who was the forerunner of the Group of Seven, and Billy Bishop, a World War I ace who shot down 72 enemy planes.

The Mill Dam, off 2nd Avenue W. at 6th Street., is one of Ontario's first fish ladders. In April and May visitors can watch rainbow and brown trout swim upstream to spawn; chinook salmon can be seen migrating from August to October.

Harrison Park, on 2nd Avenue, embraces 45 hectares (114 acres) of rolling meadows and hardwood forests along the Sydenham River as well as a large bird sanctuary. *See Recreation Chart and the AAA/CAA Eastern Canada CampBook.*

Farther upriver is the Inglis Falls Conservation Area *(see Recreation Chart)*, one of 10 principal parks along the Bruce Trail. Besides hiking and cross-country skiing opportunities, the park's major highlight is an 18-metre (59-ft.) waterfall created as the Sydenham River cascades over the Niagara Escarpment. Jones Falls, also on the Bruce Trail in the Pottawatomi Conservation Area, flows 12 metres (39 feet) over the Niagara Escarpment.

Indian Falls Conservation Area, 5 kilometres (3 mi.) north of town on CR 1, encompasses 12 hectares (30 acres) of recreational parkland. The 15-metre (49-ft.) horseshoe shaped Indian Falls got its name from the area's Newash Indians. Birdwatching and hiking are just a few of the activities available. Eugenia Falls Conservation Area is home to 30-metre (98-ft.) Eugenia Falls. Some 23 hectares (57 acres) of parkland include hiking trails and picnic areas.

North of town on CR 26 is Bruce's Cave Conservation Area, home to caves that illustrate the ancient weathering processes and the magnitude of post-glacial lake levels. The area is open for summer and winter recreation.

Other recreational activities available in the area include boating, fishing, golfing, hiking, swimming, Nordic and cross-country skiing, ice fishing and snowmobiling.

The Georgian Bay Symphony presents a variety of musical performances throughout the year at various venues; phone (519) 372-0212. The Roxy Theatre, 251 9th St. E., was originally built as an Opera House. It is now a 400-seat year-round performing arts venue and is home to the Owen Sound Little Theatre group; phone (519) 371-3425 for information or (519) 371-2833 for tickets.

Among the many special events offered throughout the year is the Summerfolk Music and Crafts Festival in August, featuring contemporary, traditional and blues performers from around the world. From mid-November to mid-January enjoy more than 200 colorful light displays in downtown along the Sydenham River and in Harrison Park during the annual Festival of Northern Lights.

Owen Sound Visitor Centre: 1155 1st Ave. W., Owen Sound, ON, Canada N4K 4K8; phone (519) 371-9833 or (888) 675-5555.

Self-guiding tours: Brochures detailing both a walking tour of the city and a driving tour of the area are available from the visitor center.

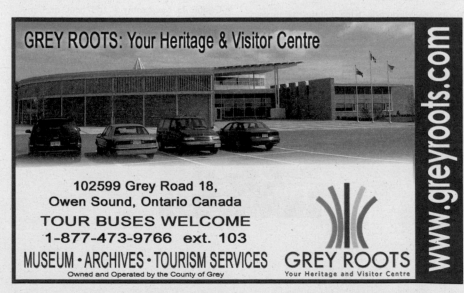

GREY ROOTS: Your Heritage & Visitor Centre

www.greyroots.com

102599 Grey Road 18,
Owen Sound, Ontario Canada
TOUR BUSES WELCOME
1-877-473-9766 ext. 103
MUSEUM • ARCHIVES • TOURISM SERVICES
Owned and Operated by the County of Grey

GREY ROOTS
Your Heritage and Visitor Centre

Shopping areas: Heritage Place, at 1350 16th St. E., is home to Sears, Zellers and more than 75 other stores. A farmers' market at 114 8th St. E. operates on Saturdays year-round.

BILLY BISHOP HERITAGE MUSEUM, downtown at 948 3rd Ave. W., is the boyhood home of the Canadian war hero who served in both world wars. The national historic site celebrates Bishop's life and career as well as the efforts of other Canadian aviators. Highlights include period antiques, Victorian furnishings, military and aviation displays, along with Bishop family pieces.

Allow 30 minutes minimum. Daily 10-4, July-Aug.; Tues.-Fri. noon-4 (also Sat.-Sun. noon-4, Mar.-June and Sept.-Dec.), Feb.-June and Sept.-Dec.; otherwise by appointment. Closed Dec. 25-31. Admission $4; ages 2-16, $2; family rate $10. MC, VI. Phone (519) 371-0031.

(SAVE) **GREY ROOTS: YOUR HERITAGE AND VISITOR CENTRE** is s. on Hwy. 6/10, then w. to 102599 Grey Rd. 18 at jct. Inglis Falls Rd. This multipurpose center contains Grey County's museum, archives and tourist information center. The museum provides exhibits and interactive displays about county history, especially as it pertains to natural resources. Local heroes also are remembered. A film about the area's history, culture and recreational activities is shown throughout the day.

Picnicking is permitted. Allow 30 minutes minimum. Museum and visitor center daily 10-5 (also Fri.-Sat. 5-7); closed Jan. 1 and Dec. 25. Phone ahead to confirm hours. Archives Mon.-Sat. 10-5, July-Aug.; Mon.-Fri. 12:30-5, rest of year. Closed holidays. Visitor center free. Admission to museum and archives $6; ages 5-13, $3.50; family rate (two adults and up to three children) $18. VI. Phone (519) 376-3690 or (877) 473-9766. *See color ad p. 152.*

OWEN SOUND MARINE & RAIL MUSEUM, 1165 1st Ave. W., 1.5 blks. n. of 10th St. in the former CNR station on the waterfront, demonstrates the role each industry played in shaping the area's economic history. Exhibits include uniforms, tools, pictures and models of trains and boats, flags, charts, propellers and ship wheels. Interactive stations and a working "G" scale model train are featured. A library is open to the public.

Allow 30 minutes minimum. Daily 10-4, Victoria Day weekend-second Mon. in Oct.; Tues.-Sun. 10-4, rest of year. Closed Dec. 25-Jan. 1. Admission $3; over 64 and ages 5-15, $2; family rate (two adults and up to three children) $6. Phone (519) 371-3333.

(SAVE) **STORY BOOK PARK,** 2 km (1.2 mi.) s. on Hwy. 6/10, then 2 km (1.2 mi.) e. on Story Book Park Rd., is an animal farm and nursery rhyme park in a wooded setting. Included are amusement rides, two waterslides, a haunted house, children's rides, a wading pool, an 18-hole miniature golf course and a train ride through the park.

Picnicking is permitted. Food is available. Allow 1 hour, 30 minutes minimum. Daily 10-6, Victoria Day weekend-Labour Day. Admission (including all rides) $14; over 64, $9.50; under 3 free. Miniature golf $1. MC, VI. Phone (519) 376-2291.

TOM THOMSON MEMORIAL ART GALLERY, 840 1st Ave. W., features a permanent exhibition of paintings by native son Tom Thomson as well as works by other Group of Seven artists. Historic and contemporary works by various Canadian artists also are displayed. Allow 30 minutes minimum. Mon.-Sat. 10-5 (also Wed. 5-9), Sun. noon-5, July-Aug.; Tues.-Fri. 11-5 (also Wed. 5-9), Sat.-Sun. noon-5, rest of year. Closed Jan. 1 and Dec. 25-26. Admission $5. Phone (519) 376-1932.

PAISLEY (G-7) pop. 1,033

THE TREASURE CHEST MUSEUM, 407 Queen St., has displays of lanterns dating to the 1800s, farm tools and machinery, glassware, period clothing, clocks, furniture, lamps, kitchenware and porcelain pieces, all collected by a local businessman to preserve examples of past lifestyles. Allow 30 minutes minimum. Mon.-Sat. 11-4, Sun. 1-4, Victoria Day weekend-second Mon. in Oct.; by appointment rest of year. Admission $3, over 64 and students with ID $2, under 4 free with adult, family rate $7. Phone (519) 353-7176.

PAKENHAM (E-10)

FULTON'S is n. off Hwy. 29 following signs. Visitors can tour 162 hectares (400 acres) of sugar bush and watch maple syrup being produced in the spring. Other highlights include hiking trails, a playground, wagon and sleigh rides, dogsledding and displays about maple sugaring. Food is available. Mon.-Fri. 10-4, first Sat. in Mar.-last Sun. in Apr. Free. A fee is charged for hayrides. Phone (613) 256-3867.

PARRY SOUND (E-8)
pop. 6,124, elev. 209 m/686'

A resort area on Georgian Bay named for Arctic explorer Sir William Edward Parry, Parry Sound is an access point to the 30,000 Islands. Fishing, boating, swimming and golfing are popular pastimes. A spectacular view of the islands, lakes and forests awaits those with the stamina to climb the 12 sets of stairs to the top of Tower Hill, built in the 1920s as a fire lookout.

Parry Sound Area Chamber of Commerce: 70 Church St., Parry Sound, ON, Canada P2A 1Y9; phone (705) 746-4213 or (800) 461-4261.

(GEM) **30,000 ISLAND CRUISE** departs the town dock for a 3-hour trip along some of the most remote and scenic waterways of Georgian Bay's 30,000 Islands. Passengers aboard the 550-passenger triple-decker *Island Queen* have close-up views of the rugged, pristine wilderness as the ship winds through narrow channels and shallow waterways. Large viewing windows and open sun decks provide ample opportunities for sightseeing as a narration describes points of interest along the way. The ship is heated for fall color cruises.

Three-hour cruise departs daily at 10 and 2, July-Aug.; at 1 in June and Sept. 1-second Mon. in Oct. Fare $25; ages 6-12, $12.50. MC, VI. Phone (705) 746-2311 or (800) 506-2628.

MV CHIPPEWA, 99 Champagne St., offers sightseeing cruises aboard a 65-foot Georgian Bay tug formerly called *Maid of the Mist #1.* Dinner and special event cruises also are scheduled. Food is available. Two-hour sightseeing cruises daily, May-Oct.; phone for schedule. Fare $16; over 59, $14; ages 6-12, $9. Reservations are recommended. AX, MC, VI. Phone (705) 746-6064.

WEST PARRY SOUND DISTRICT MUSEUM is in Tower Hill Park at 17 George St. Area history is recounted through exhibits about trapping, First Nations People, shipping, logging and agriculture. Two galleries feature changing exhibits and displays of art. An interactive children's museum is available in summer.

Picnicking is permitted. Allow 1 hour minimum. Daily 10-5, July 1-Labour Day; Thurs.-Sun. 10-4, rest of year. Closed major holidays. Admission $5; over 65, $4; ages 6-16, $2.50; family rate $12. MC, VI. Phone (705) 746-5365 or (888) 624-9005.

PELEE ISLAND (I-6) elev. 175 m/574′

RECREATIONAL ACTIVITIES
Kayaking

- **The Pelee Paddler** is at 271A North Shore Rd., Pelee Island, ON, Canada N0R 1M0. Other activities are offered. Thurs.-Sun. 10-5, July-Aug.; Sat.-Sun. in June and Sept. Phone (519) 724-2002, or (519) 258-8933 in the off-season.

PEMBROKE (E-10) pop. 13,490

The history of Pembroke is entwined with that of the lumber trade, and a portion of the city's industry still relies on the reserves of this forest region. One of Ontario's largest totem poles, carved by Pat Patterson, is in Riverside Park. The Pembroke Heritage Murals, a collection of 27 murals painted on downtown buildings, depict the history of the area.

Pembroke and Area Chamber of Commerce: 2 International Dr., Pembroke, ON, Canada K8A 6W5; phone (613) 732-1492.

CHAMPLAIN TRAIL MUSEUM AND PIONEER VILLAGE, 2.5 km (1.6 mi.) e. via old Hwy. 17 at 1032 Pembroke St. E., beside the Pembroke Mall, depicts the history and environment of the Ottawa Valley. Displays include crafts, items relating to local sports, farming tools, a water wheel, Algonquin Indian artifacts and a Corliss steam engine. Other sections examine the exploration and fur trade eras and the lumber industry. Restored buildings include a one-room schoolhouse, a log dwelling, a blacksmith shop and a pioneer church.

Picnicking is permitted. Allow 1 hour, 30 minutes minimum. Mon.-Fri. 9-5, Sat. 10-3, Sun. 1-4, June-Aug.; Mon.-Fri. 9-5 in May and Sept. 1 to mid-Oct. Admission $5; over 64, $4; students with ID $3; ages 6-12, $1. Phone (613) 735-0517.

PENETANGUISHENE (F-8) pop. 8,316

Penetanguishene (Pen-e-tang-WISH-ene) is an Abenaki Indian word meaning "place of the rolling white sands." The town has a rich and colorful history reflecting its native, French and British cultures. Strolling through town, visitors can imagine themselves back in the 18th century while costumed interpreters tell stories of yesteryear. Of interest are a variety of boat cruises, theater performances and concerts, art galleries and quaint shops as well as such craft demonstrations as glass blowing.

Awenda Provincial Park, 11 kilometres (7 mi.) northwest off CR 26 on Awenda Park Road, has significant geological and historical features; the park also offers numerous hiking and cross-country ski trails. *See Recreation Chart.*

Other recreational activities available in the area include bicycling, fishing, snorkeling, scuba diving, sailing, hiking, camping and miles of beaches for swimming. Winter brings opportunities for snowmobiling and skiing. In the spring visitors can watch maple syrup demonstrations.

Southern Georgian Bay Chamber of Commerce (Penetanguishene Tourist Information Centre): 2 Main St., Penetanguishene, ON, Canada L9M 1T1; phone (705) 549-2232 May-Sept. For information the rest of the year, contact the Midland office of the Southern Georgian Bay Chamber of Commerce, 208 King St., Midland, ON, Canada L4R 3L9; phone (705) 526-7884 or (800) 263-7745.

DISCOVERY HARBOUR is at 93 Jury Dr., following the blue ship logos from CR 93. Built just after the War of 1812, this military facility was active until 1856. Now a marine heritage center, the site has 15 reconstructed buildings including the 1845 Officers' Quarters. Costumed guides are available, and interactive activities take place in summer. An archeological dig is ongoing. King's Wharf Theatre presents live shows. Replicas of two 19th-century schooners are docked at King's Wharf.

Guided tours are available. Pets on leash are allowed. Food is available. Allow 1 hour, 30 minutes minimum. Daily 10-5, July 1-Labour Day; Mon.-Fri. 10-5, late May-June 30; otherwise varies. Last admission is 30 minutes before closing. Admission $6.50; over 64 and students with ID $5.50; ages 6-12, $4.50; family rate (four persons) $20. An additional fee may be charged for some activities. AX, MC, VI. Phone (705) 549-8064, or (705) 549-5555 for the theater.

MS GEORGIAN QUEEN, sailing from the town dock at the n. end of Main St. (Hwy. 93), offers 3-hour sightseeing cruises through the 30,000 islands of Georgian Bay with commentary about local sights and history. Dinner cruises also are available.

Food is available. Cruises depart daily at 2, mid-June through Labour Day (additional departures available Wed.-Thurs., July-Aug.); schedule varies late May to mid-June and day after Labour Day to mid-Oct. Fare $20; over 54, $18; ages 13-19, $15; ages 5-12, $10; family rate (two adults and up to three children under 12) $50. Reservations are required. VI. Phone (705) 549-7795, or (800) 363-7447 in Ontario.

PENETANGUISHENE CENTENNIAL MUSEUM & ARCHIVES, 13 Burke St., depicts the community's history. The museum contains a general store with original counters and floors, collections of early industrial and pioneer materials and a sports hall of fame. Concerts are given in a band shell on the grounds Sunday nights during the summer.

Allow 1 hour minimum. Mon.-Sat. 9-4:30, Sun. noon-4:30, May 1-second Mon. in Oct.; otherwise varies. Admission $4.50; over 64, $4; students with ID $3.50; under 5 free with an adult. Phone (705) 549-2150.

ST. ANN'S ROMAN CATHOLIC CHURCH, 18 Robert St. W., is a late Romanesque church built of stone 1886-1902. Its bells date from 1799. Paintings on the ceiling, wall plaques and two statues memorialize the Canadian Jesuit missionary martyrs. A replica of the grotto of Lourdes is on the grounds. Allow 30 minutes minimum. Daily 8-8. Free. Phone (705) 549-2560.

ST. JAMES GARRISON CHURCH-ON-THE-LINES (Anglican), 223 Church St., was built in 1836 to serve local civilian and military residents. Notable features include an extra-wide aisle designed to allow four soldiers to march abreast and a bell taken from an American schooner sunk during the War of 1812. Daily 9-4, Victoria Day-second Mon. in Oct. Free. Phone (705) 549-5816 or (705) 549-2223.

PERTH (E-11) pop. 6,003

Named after the city in Scotland, Perth was established as a military settlement. The last recorded fatal duel in Ontario was fought at Perth in 1833.

Perth Chamber of Commerce: 34 Herriott St., Perth, ON, Canada K7H 1T2; phone (613) 267-3200.

PERTH MUSEUM, at 11 Gore St. E. in the 1840 Matheson House, has an enclosed Scottish garden and three rooms reflecting the lifestyle of an 1840s upper-class family. The parlor represents the 1890s. Exhibits include Canadian whiskey history; a preserved piece of the Mammoth Cheese, a block of cheese made by eastern Ontario dairy farmers for the 1893 Chicago World's Fair; the pistols used in Ontario's last fatal duel; minerals; and Rideau Lakes Indian artifacts.

Allow 30 minutes minimum. Mon.-Fri. 10-5, Sat.-Sun. 1-5; closed Jan. 1, Good Friday and Dec. 25. Admission $4, senior citizens $3.50, over 6 and students with ID $2, family rate $8. Phone (613) 267-1947.

PETAWAWA (E-10) pop. 14,398

CANADIAN AIRBORNE FORCES MUSEUM AND C.F.B. PETAWAWA MILITARY MUSEUM are 2 km (1.2 mi.) w. on the grounds of Canadian Forces Base Petawawa. The Airborne Forces Museum has exhibits about the history of Canada's airborne units from World War II to the present. The adjacent C.F.B. Petawawa Military Museum traces the history of the base and includes an outdoor display of 25 military vehicles. Mon.-Fri. 1-4, Sat.-Sun. and holidays 11-4. Donations. Phone (613) 588-6238.

PETERBOROUGH (G-9) pop. 71,446

As a major link in the Trent-Severn Waterway and at the heart of the Kawartha Lakes region, Peterborough is well-known as a recreational center. The full-service marina, between Locks 19 and 20 on George Street, can accommodate 100 vessels. Canoe and kayak championships are held along the Trent-Severn Waterway throughout the year.

Riverview Park and Zoo, covering 20 hectares (50 acres), is at 1230 Water St. N. A small zoo, a miniature railway that operates during the summer, a children's playground, orientation center and picnic area are in the park; phone (705) 748-9301, ext. 2304.

Peterborough's history is evidenced by the 19th-century houses in the residential section and the more than 2,000-year-old Iroquois Indian burial ground in Serpent Mounds Park *(see Recreation Chart)*, 10 kilometres (6 mi.) east on Hwy. 7, then 14 kilometres (9 mi.) south on CR 34.

Peterborough's cultural offerings include the Showplace Performance Centre, 290 George St. N., offering musical and theatrical performances year-round; phone (705) 742-7089 for information or (705) 742-7469 for tickets. The Peterborough Theatre Guild entertains audiences in July and August from their home at 364 Rogers St.; phone (705) 745-4211.

Local produce can be enjoyed year-round courtesy of the farmers' market held each Saturday at Morrow Park, Lansdowne and George streets. Recreational activities include boating, bicycling, fishing, golfing and swimming in the summer, while winter offers downhill and cross-country skiing and snowmobiling. Kawartha Downs, 15 kilometres (9 mi.) southwest of the city in Fraserville at 1382 CR 28, offers harness racing year-round; phone (705) 939-6316.

Note: Policies concerning admittance of children to pari-mutuel betting facilities vary. Phone for information.

Peterborough and the Kawarthas Tourism: 175 George St. N.; Peterborough, ON, Canada K9J 3G6; phone (705) 742-2201 or (800) 461-6424.

Shopping areas: More than 500 specialty shops and boutiques as well as shops specializing in antiques and crafts can be found in downtown Peterborough. Lansdowne Place, at 645 Lansdowne St.

W., has some 70 shops and services, including Sears. Whetung Ojibwa Crafts and Art Gallery, on Curve Lake Indian Reservation 20 minutes north of town, offers authentic Indian arts and crafts.

THE ART GALLERY OF PETERBOROUGH is at 2 Crescent St. In addition to its permanent collection of historical and contemporary art, the gallery has changing exhibits of works by local, regional and international artists. Guided tours are available by appointment. Allow 30 minutes minimum. Tues.-Fri. and Sun. 1-5 (also Mon. holidays 1-5 and Wed. 5-8), Sat. 10-5, Victoria Day-Labour Day; Tues.-Fri. noon-4, Sat. 10-5, Sun. 1-5, rest of year. Closed Jan. 1, Victoria Day, July 1 and Dec. 24-26. Donations. Phone (705) 743-9179.

THE CANADIAN CANOE MUSEUM, 910 Monaghan Rd., traces the importance of canoes and kayaks in the exploration and development of Canada. A large map shows the province's long coastline and extensive network of lakes and rivers. Examples from the museum's collection of more than 600 watercraft include several versions of traditional birch bark canoes, a Pacific whaling dugout, wooden canoes, Inuit kayaks and canvas-covered vessels.

Visitors can observe canoes being preserved or constructed by master craftsmen in a replica of an 18th-century workshop and go inside a re-creation of an 1876 Hudson's Bay Co. trading post. Reflections: The Land, The People and The Canoe features former Canadian prime minister Pierre Trudeau's canoe and buckskin jacket. Paddling as a recreational pastime also is examined.

Allow 1 hour, 30 minutes minimum. Mon.-Sat. 10-5, Sun. noon-5, May-Oct.; Wed.-Fri. and Sun. noon-4, Sat. 10-5, rest of year. Closed Jan. 1, Good Friday and Dec. 25-26. Last admission is 1 hour before closing. Admission $6.50; over 64 and ages 5-17, $5; family rate (maximum of four persons) $18. AX, MC, VI. Phone (705) 748-9153 or (866) 342-2663.

HUTCHISON HOUSE MUSEUM, 3 blks. w. of George St. at 270 Brock St., was built by the community 1836-37 for pioneer physician Dr. John Hutchison and his family. Furnished in the 1840s style, the house has medical instruments, books, kitchen items and historical and herb gardens.

Guides in 1840 period costumes offer tours, and baking and cooking demonstrations are given on an open hearth. Special events take place throughout the year.

Allow 1 hour minimum. Tues.-Sun. 1-5, May-Sept.; Mon.-Fri. 1-5, rest of year. Scottish tea served Tues.-Sun. 1-4, July-Aug.; Sat.-Sun. 1-4 in June and Sept.; by appointment rest of season. Admission $2; ages 6-17, $1. Scottish tea $5; under 10, $4. VI. Phone (705) 743-9710.

INDIAN RIVER REPTILE ZOO is 16 km (10 mi.) e. on Hwy. 7 at jct. CR 38. The zoo houses more than 200 exotic reptiles and offers visitors a chance

to handle a boa constrictor. A rattlesnake exhibit and a venomous snake display also are included, as are demonstrations and videotape presentations. Guided tours are available. Allow 1 hour minimum. Daily 10-5, Mar.-Aug.; Sat.-Sun. 10-5, rest of year. Closed Jan. 1 and Dec. 25. Admission $8.50; over 64 and ages 13-17, $7; ages 4-12, $6. MC, VI. Phone (705) 639-1443.

LANG PIONEER VILLAGE MUSEUM, 10 km (6 mi.) e. on Hwy. 7, then 6 km (4 mi.) s. on CR 34 (Heritage Line), following signs, is a re-created pioneer village with more than 20 restored 19th-century buildings. The complex on the Indian River recalls the early settlement days of the area and includes log houses, a general store, print and carpenter shops, a hotel, blacksmith shop, tinsmith shop and school.

Costumed interpreters demonstrate such period tasks as baking and weaving, and the Lang Grist Mill has been operating since 1846. A museum/visitor center is on the grounds, which also feature herb and vegetable gardens and farm animals. Special events held throughout the year include corn roastings, cider making, harvest Thanksgiving and heritage Christmas. Special days feature folk groups, dancers, musicians and craftspersons.

Picnicking is permitted. Allow 1 hour, 30 minutes minimum. Village and museum open daily 11-4, Victoria Day weekend-early Oct.; open some weekends for special events, rest of year. Hours and rates may vary; phone ahead. Admission $6; over 64 and students with ID $5; ages 5-14, $3; family rate (two adults and up to four children under 14) $15. MC, VI. Phone (705) 295-6694 or (866) 289-5264.

LIFTLOCK AND THE RIVER BOAT CRUISES departs from the Peterborough Marina on Little Lake at jct. Rink and George sts., next to the Holiday Inn. A 2-hour narrated sightseeing cruise on the *Island Princess* informs passengers about the history of the Trent-Severn Waterway. Other cruises also are available.

Allow 2 hours minimum. Departures daily at 11 and 1:30, mid-June through Aug. 31; Mon.-Fri. at 10 and noon, Sat.-Sun. at 11 and 1:30, mid-May to mid-June and Sept. 1 to mid-Oct. Phone ahead to verify schedule. Fare $16; over 59 and ages 13-17, $14; under 13, $8. Parking $1 per hour. Reservations are recommended. MC, VI. Phone (705) 742-9912 or (888) 535-4670.

PETERBOROUGH CENTENNIAL MUSEUM AND ARCHIVES, on Armour Hill overlooking the lift lock at 300 Hunter St. E., is one of the highest points in the area. The Early Settlement and Pammett galleries depict the history of the First Nations, the early settlers and the Robinson Irish Migration of 1825. The Victorian Gallery takes a look at Peterborough as it grew from a frontier town to a bustling city. Industry, agriculture, homelife and society are traced. The Heideman Gallery offers changing exhibits.

Museum open Mon.-Fri. 9-5, Sat.-Sun. and holidays noon-5; closed Jan. 1, Good Friday and Dec. 25. Admission $5 per family. Phone (705) 743-5180.

PETERBOROUGH HYDRAULIC LIFT LOCK is on the Trent Canal; the Peterborough Lift Lock Visitors Centre is at Hunter St. E. at Ashburnham Dr. The lock, with a lift of 20 metres (66 ft.), is said to be the world's highest. The lock is operated during the Trent-Severn Waterway season, May through October, as canal traffic warrants. A film about the waterway and the construction of the lock can be seen at the Peterborough Lift Lock Visitors Centre.

Visitor center daily 9-6, July 1-first week in Aug.; 10-5, Apr.-June and second week in Aug. to mid-Oct. Donations. Parking $2. Phone (705) 750-4950 for the visitor center.

PETROLIA (H-6) pop. 4,849, elev. 229 m/750'

One of Canada's first boom towns, Petrolia supplied 90 percent of Canada's oil needs prior to 1900. When oil flow from local fields slowed, drillers left for 87 countries around the globe, exporting Canadian technology.

Today the town reflects the early wealth of the community, with grand Victorian houses and the Victoria Playhouse Petrolia, 411 Greenfield St., a 430-seat playhouse with summer theater and varied performers year-round; phone (519) 882-1221 or (800) 717-7694 for theater information and tickets.

Tea rooms and boutiques line the historic main travel routes where street names include Oil Street, Petrolia Line, Eureka, Tank, and Discovery Line, along with more unusual monikers such as Oozolofsky and Ignatiefna, named after a Russian who cared for a foreign driller's family while he worked the fields. Bridgeview Park, once a field of three-pole oil derricks, now is a scenic park setting, including a pond and covered bridge.

Tourism Sarnia-Lambton—Petrolia: 556 N. Christina St., Sarnia, ON, Canada N7T 5W6; phone (519) 336-3232 or (800) 265-0316.

Self-guiding tours: A brochure containing a map for a self-guiding walking tour of Petrolia's historic buildings is available at the Municipal Office, 411 Greenfield St.; phone (519) 882-2350.

SAVE **THE PETROLIA DISCOVERY,** on CR 4 1.3 km (.8 mi.) w. of jct. CR 21, is a 24-hectare (60-acre) living-history museum where visitors can see first-hand how crude oil was drawn from the ground in the late 19th century. The workshop and training grounds of Canadians who helped found the oil industry have been restored.

A small 1870s pioneer village includes a blacksmith shop, hardware store, woodworking mill and schoolhouse. Picnicking is permitted. Allow 1 hour, 30 minutes minimum. Daily 10-6, first Sat. in May-Labour Day; 10-4, day after Labour Day-Oct. 31. Admission $5, over 59 and students with ID $4, family rate $12. VI. Phone (519) 882-0897.

PICTON (G-10) pop. 4,563

Dedicated to the quaint resort life, the residents of Picton, on Quinte's Isle, indulge in craftwork, bicycling and maintaining a peaceful, scenic environment. Canada's first prime minister, Sir John A. Macdonald, grew up in town; he won his first case in the District Courthouse and Gaol, built in 1832. Nearby is Sandbanks Provincial Park *(see Recreation Chart)*. Other recreational activities include boating, scuba diving, cross-country skiing and snowmobiling.

Whattam's Memorial Walkway provides a walking tour linking Macaulay Heritage Park *(see attraction listing)* to Macaulay Mountain Conservation Area, with some 1,000 trees along the trail.

The Regent Theatre, 224 Main St., hosts a variety of events throughout the year, including a summer festival of live productions; phone (613) 476-7042 for information and tickets.

Prince Edward County Chamber of Tourism and Commerce: 116 Main St., P.O. Box 50, Picton, ON, Canada K0K 2T0; phone (613) 476-2421 or (800) 640-4717.

BERGERON'S EXOTIC ANIMAL SANCTUARY is 3.3 km (2 mi.) n. on Hwy. 49, 1 km (.6 mi.) w. on CR 6, then .3 km (.2 mi.) n. to 967 CR 5. A haven for unwanted animals, the sanctuary cares for more than 150 creatures. A group of big cats includes Siberian tigers, African lions, cougars and jaguars. Foxes, monkeys, wolves, deer, goats and coyotes are other residents. An aviary houses tropical parrots, and peacocks, geese, chickens and ducks roam the property. Visitors can see big cats being fed in summer.

Picnicking is permitted. Allow 30 minutes minimum. Daily 10-6, Mar. school break-Oct. 31; Sat.-Sun. 11-3, rest of year. Closed Dec. 25. Phone ahead to confirm schedule. Big cat feedings take place daily at 2, July-Aug. Admission $10; over 64 and ages 13-18, $8; ages 3-12, $5. Phone (613) 476-4212.

SAVE **MACAULAY HERITAGE PARK,** 1 blk. s. of Hwy. 33 at Union and Church sts., includes the restored St. Mary Magdalene Church and cemetery; the adjacent 1830 rectory; Macaulay House, restored to 1853; heritage gardens; and the early 19th-century carriage house. The church houses the Prince Edward County Museum, which has historical exhibits. Special events and craft demonstrations are held periodically.

Pets are permitted on the grounds, but not in the buildings; they must be leashed at all times. Tues.-Sun. 10-4:30, July 1-Labour Day; 1-4:30, Victoria Day weekend-June 30 and day after Labour Day-second Mon. in Oct. Admission to Macaulay House and museum $4; ages 5-14, $2; family rate $10. Phone (613) 476-3833.

POINT CLARK (G-6)

POINT CLARK LIGHTHOUSE NATIONAL HISTORIC SITE AND MUSEUM is 5 km (3 mi.) w. off Hwy. 21, following signs. Overlooking Lake Huron, the 27-metre (87-ft.) stone lighthouse was built 1855-59. A museum in the former lighthouse keeper's home contains artifacts about the history of the lighthouse and has several rooms furnished in period. A guided tour takes visitors up 8 flights of stairs to the top of the lighthouse.

Picnicking is permitted. Allow 30 minutes minimum. Daily 10-5, late June-Labour Day. Admission $3.50; under 12, $2.50; family rate (two adults and four children) $12. Phone (519) 395-2494, or (519) 395-3735 in the off-season.

POINT EDWARD (H-6)
pop. 2,101, elev. 182 m/597'

CASINOS

• **Point Edward Charity Casino** is at 2000 Venetian Blvd. Mon.-Wed. 9 a.m.-4 a.m., Thurs.-Sun. 24 hours. Phone (519) 383-7770 or (888) 394-6244.

POINT PELEE NATIONAL PARK (I-7)

Elevations in the park range from 174 metres (572 ft.) east of the group campground to 179 metres (588 ft.) at Northwest Beach. Refer to CAA/AAA maps for additional elevation information.

Fifty-six kilometres (35 mi.) southeast of Detroit and 10 kilometres (6 mi.) south of Leamington, Point Pelee (PEE-lee) National Park is the southernmost mainland point in Canada. The 15-square-kilometre (6-sq.-mi.) park is one of Canada's smallest national parks and one of its most popular summer resorts.

Only a third of the park is dry land; the rest is made up of marshland. The uplands consist of sand dunes surrounded by forests of hackberry, white ash, basswood, black walnut, shagbark hickory, sassafras, red oak, chestnut oak and sugar maple. The lowlands are composed of 1,000 hectares (2,470 acres) of marshland. On the west side is Pigeon Bay, known for its beautiful sunsets.

On both the Atlantic and Mississippi flyways and at the apex of the southern Ontario peninsula, the park is a natural sanctuary and critical stopover for migratory birds, butterflies and dragonflies. More than 375 bird species have been sighted. Monarch butterflies migrate to Mexico through Point Pelee from late August to mid-October. Such small water animals as minks and muskrats can be seen around the numerous ponds or from the Marsh Boardwalk.

General Information and Activities

The park is open daily 6 a.m.-9:30 p.m., Apr. 1-late Oct. (also 5 a.m.-6 a.m., in May); 7-6:30, rest of year. An observation tower at the beginning of the 1.4-kilometre (1-mi.) Marsh Boardwalk trail affords excellent views of the marsh. Canoes and bicycles can be rented from May to late October.

Interpretive programs by park staff are available, and special events are offered throughout the year. The park's nature trails are open all year. A free shuttle service is offered in the south end of the park from early April through late October. Phone (519) 322-2365 or (519) 322-2371. *See Recreation Chart.*

ADMISSION to the park Apr.-Oct. is $5; over 64, $4.25; ages 6-16, $2.50; family rate $12.50. Admission rest of year is $3.75; over 64, $3.25; ages 6-16, $2; family rate $9.50. An annual pass is $25; over 64, $20; ages 6-16, $12.50; family pass $63. Phone to verify prices.

PETS are permitted in the park only if they are leashed.

ADDRESS inquiries to the Superintendent's Office, Point Pelee National Park, 407 Monarch Ln., R.R. 1, Leamington, ON, Canada N8H 3V4; phone (519) 322-2365.

VISITOR CENTRE, 6 km (4 mi.) from the gate, has maps, interactive exhibits, interpretive programs and other displays explaining the major features of the park—forest, sand dunes and marsh. Slide shows and films are shown regularly in the theater. Daily 10-6, July 1-Labour Day; daily10-5, in Apr., June and day after Labour Day-Oct. 31; daily 8-5, in May; Sat.-Sun. 10-5, rest of year. Closed Jan. 1 and Dec. 25-26. Free. Phone (519) 322-2371.

PORT BURWELL (I-2)

PORT BURWELL HISTORIC LIGHTHOUSE AND MARINE MUSEUM is at 20 Pitt St. Built in 1840 overlooking Lake Erie, Port Burwell is one of the oldest wooden lighthouses in Canada. A climb to the top provides views of the harbor, lake and village. In a building opposite the lighthouse, the museum has both marine exhibits and artifacts depicting village life. A highlight is the collection of lighthouse lenses.

Guided tours are available. Allow 30 minutes minimum. Tues.-Sun. 10-5, mid-May through Labour Day. Admission $2 for each building, under 12 free, family rate $5. Phone (519) 874-4807.

PORT CARLING (F-8)

MUSKOKA LAKES MUSEUM, on CR 118 in Island Park, presents the area's history through changing and permanent exhibits. Highlights include the Hall Family Homestead, a two-story log cabin built in 1875; antique wooden rowboats, canoes and marine artifacts; and such various antiques as glassware, china, furniture, tools, postcards, photographs and toys.

Allow 30 minutes minimum. Tues.-Sat. 10-5, Sun. noon-4, July-Aug.; Fri.-Sat. 10-4; Sun. noon-4, Victoria Day weekend-June 30 and Sept. 1-second Mon. in Oct.; otherwise by appointment. Schedule may vary; phone ahead. Admission $3; over 64 and ages 5-18, $2; family rate $7. MC, VI. Phone (705) 765-5367.

Before you hit the open road, tear along the dotted line!

For reservations call
1-800-HOLIDAY

Valid at participating Holiday Inn® and Holiday Inn Express® hotels. One coupon per room per stay. Valid on each night of stay; no copies or facsimiles accepted. Not valid for groups or in conjunction with any other discount, promotion or special event as established by each independent operator. Not valid with employee or travel industry discounts. Blackout dates apply. Rooms limited and subject to availability. Void where taxed, restricted or otherwise prohibited by law. Coupon has no cash value. Offer valid March 1, 2005 to May 31, 2005. ®Trademarks of members of InterContinental Hotels Group. ©2004 InterContinental Hotels Group. All rights reserved. Most hotels are independently owned and/or operated. 2005CAA Ontario

Offer valid March 1 - May 31, 2005

$**10** OFF CAA/AAA room rate

See back for participating hotels.

For reservations call
1-800-HOLIDAY

Valid at participating Holiday Inn® and Holiday Inn Express® hotels. One coupon per room per stay. Valid on each night of stay; no copies or facsimiles accepted. Not valid for groups or in conjunction with any other discount, promotion or special event as established by each independent operator. Not valid with employee or travel industry discounts. Blackout dates apply. Rooms limited and subject to availability. Void where taxed, restricted or otherwise prohibited by law. Coupon has no cash value. Offer valid June 1, 2005 to August 31, 2005. ®Trademarks of members of InterContinental Hotels Group. ©2004 InterContinental Hotels Group. All rights reserved. Most hotels are independently owned and/or operated. 2005CAA Ontario

Offer valid June 1 - August 31, 2005

$**5** OFF CAA/AAA room rate

See back for participating hotels.

For reservations call
1-800-HOLIDAY

Valid at participating Holiday Inn® and Holiday Inn Express® hotels. One coupon per room per stay. Valid on each night of stay; no copies or facsimiles accepted. Not valid for groups or in conjunction with any other discount, promotion or special event as established by each independent operator. Not valid with employee or travel industry discounts. Blackout dates apply. Rooms limited and subject to availability. Void where taxed, restricted or otherwise prohibited by law. Coupon has no cash value. Offer valid September 1, 2005 to November 30, 2005. ®Trademarks of members of InterContinental Hotels Group. ©2004 InterContinental Hotels Group. All rights reserved. Most hotels are independently owned and/or operated. 2005CAA Ontario

Offer valid September 1 - November 30, 2005

$**10** OFF CAA/AAA room rate

See back for participating hotels.

For reservations call
1-800-HOLIDAY

Valid at participating Holiday Inn® and Holiday Inn Express® hotels. One coupon per room per stay. Valid on each night of stay; no copies or facsimiles accepted. Not valid for groups or in conjunction with any other discount, promotion or special event as established by each independent operator. Not valid with employee or travel industry discounts. Blackout dates apply. Rooms limited and subject to availability. Void where taxed, restricted or otherwise prohibited by law. Coupon has no cash value. Offer valid December 1, 2005 to February 28, 2006. ®Trademarks of members of InterContinental Hotels Group. ©2004 InterContinental Hotels Group. All rights reserved. Most hotels are independently owned and/or operated. 2005CAA Ontario

Offer valid December 1, 2005 - February 28, 2006

$**15** OFF CAA/AAA room rate

See back for participating hotels.

For reservations call 1-800-HOLIDAY

For reservations call 1-800-HOLIDAY
or your travel professional

ALBERTA
★ Calgary
  Dwtn-Conference Centre
● Calgary-University
▲ Edmonton
▼ Fort McMurray
★ Hinton
▲ Lethbridge
● Red Deer
● Rocky Mountain House
BRITISH COLUMBIA
★ International
  Vancouver Airport
● Kamloops
● Kelowna
▼ North Vancouver
◆ Osoyoos
▲ Salmon Arm
● Vancouver
● Vancouver-Airport
★ Vancouver-Centre (Broadway)
▼ Vancouver-Downtown

★ Victoria
★ Westbank
◆ Whistler Village Centre
MANITOBA
▼ Winnipeg - Downtown
★ Winnipeg Airport/West
★ Winnipeg-South
NEW BRUNSWICK
▲ Moncton
● Saint John - *Opening Soon*
NEWFOUNDLAND & LABRADOR
★ Stephenville
NOVA SCOTIA
● Halifax/Bedford
■ Halifax-Centre
★ Halifax-Harbourview
ONTARIO
▲ Barrie
★ Barrie-Hotel & Conference Centre
★ Brantford
★ Burlington-Hotel & Conference Center

★ Cambridge
● Cornwall
● Dryden
★ Fort Erie/Niagara Convention Centre
★ Guelph
▲ Guelph
● Hamilton-Stoney Creek
★ Kingston-Waterfront
● Kitchener-Waterloo
■ Mississauga
● Oakville-Centre
● Oshawa
▼ Ottawa-Downtown
▼ Ottawa-Kanata
★ Peterborough-Waterfront
★ Sarnia
★ Sault Ste. Marie-Waterfront
★ St. Catharines/Niagara
■ Toronto-Airport
● Toronto-Airport Area (Dixie Rd.)
★ Toronto-Airport East

■ Toronto-Brampton
● Toronto-East
▼ Toronto-Markham
★ Toronto-Mississauga
● Toronto-North York
★ Toronto-West
★ Toronto-Yorkdale
★ Trenton
■ Windsor (Ambassador Bridge)
PRINCE EDWARD ISLAND
▲ Charlottetown
QUEBEC
★ Gatineau-Ottawa Plz Chaudière
★ Montreal-Airport
■ Montreal-Centre Ville (Dwtn Conv Ctr)
★ Montreal-Longueuil
★ Montreal-Midtown
★ Pte Claire-Airport
■ Quebec City-Downtown
★ Saguenay Convention Centre

★denotes Holiday Inn® hotels. ■denotes Holiday Inn Select® hotels. ▼denotes Holiday Inn® Hotel & Suites. ◆denotes Holiday Inn SunSpree® Resort.
● denotes Holiday Inn Express® hotels. ▲denotes Holiday Inn Express® Hotel & Suites.

Holiday Inn
HOTELS · RESORTS

For reservations call 1-800-HOLIDAY

Holiday Inn
EXPRESS

ALBERTA
★ Calgary
  Dwtn-Conference Centre
● Calgary-University
▲ Edmonton
▼ Fort McMurray
★ Hinton
▲ Lethbridge
● Red Deer
● Rocky Mountain House
BRITISH COLUMBIA
★ International
  Vancouver Airport
● Kamloops
● Kelowna
▼ North Vancouver
◆ Osoyoos
▲ Salmon Arm
● Vancouver
● Vancouver-Airport
★ Vancouver-Centre (Broadway)
▼ Vancouver-Downtown

★ Victoria
★ Westbank
◆ Whistler Village Centre
MANITOBA
▼ Winnipeg - Downtown
★ Winnipeg Airport/West
★ Winnipeg-South
NEW BRUNSWICK
▲ Moncton
● Saint John - *Opening Soon*
NEWFOUNDLAND & LABRADOR
★ Stephenville
NOVA SCOTIA
● Halifax/Bedford
■ Halifax-Centre
★ Halifax-Harbourview
ONTARIO
▲ Barrie
★ Barrie-Hotel & Conference Centre
★ Brantford
★ Burlington-Hotel & Conference Center

★ Cambridge
● Cornwall
● Dryden
★ Fort Erie/Niagara Convention Centre
★ Guelph
▲ Guelph
● Hamilton-Stoney Creek
★ Kingston-Waterfront
● Kitchener-Waterloo
■ Mississauga
● Oakville-Centre
● Oshawa
▼ Ottawa-Downtown
▼ Ottawa-Kanata
★ Peterborough-Waterfront
★ Sarnia
★ Sault Ste. Marie-Waterfront
★ St. Catharines/Niagara
■ Toronto-Airport
● Toronto-Airport Area (Dixie Rd.)
★ Toronto-Airport East

■ Toronto-Brampton
● Toronto-East
▼ Toronto-Markham
★ Toronto-Mississauga
● Toronto-North York
★ Toronto-West
★ Toronto-Yorkdale
★ Trenton
■ Windsor (Ambassador Bridge)
PRINCE EDWARD ISLAND
▲ Charlottetown
QUEBEC
★ Gatineau-Ottawa Plz Chaudière
★ Montreal-Airport
■ Montreal-Centre Ville (Dwtn Conv Ctr)
★ Montreal-Longueuil
★ Montreal-Midtown
★ Pte Claire-Airport
■ Quebec City-Downtown
★ Saguenay Convention Centre

★denotes Holiday Inn® hotels. ■denotes Holiday Inn Select® hotels. ▼denotes Holiday Inn® Hotel & Suites. ◆denotes Holiday Inn SunSpree® Resort.
● denotes Holiday Inn Express® hotels. ▲denotes Holiday Inn Express® Hotel & Suites.

ALBERTA
★ Calgary
  Dwtn-Conference Centre
● Calgary-University
▲ Edmonton
▼ Fort McMurray
★ Hinton
▲ Lethbridge
● Red Deer
● Rocky Mountain House
BRITISH COLUMBIA
★ International
  Vancouver Airport
● Kamloops
● Kelowna
▼ North Vancouver
◆ Osoyoos
▲ Salmon Arm
● Vancouver
● Vancouver-Airport
★ Vancouver-Centre (Broadway)
▼ Vancouver-Downtown

★ Victoria
★ Westbank
◆ Whistler Village Centre
MANITOBA
▼ Winnipeg - Downtown
★ Winnipeg Airport/West
★ Winnipeg-South
NEW BRUNSWICK
▲ Moncton
● Saint John - *Opening Soon*
NEWFOUNDLAND & LABRADOR
★ Stephenville
NOVA SCOTIA
● Halifax/Bedford
■ Halifax-Centre
★ Halifax-Harbourview
ONTARIO
▲ Barrie
★ Barrie-Hotel & Conference Centre
★ Brantford
★ Burlington-Hotel & Conference Center

★ Cambridge
● Cornwall
● Dryden
★ Fort Erie/Niagara Convention Centre
★ Guelph
▲ Guelph
● Hamilton-Stoney Creek
★ Kingston-Waterfront
● Kitchener-Waterloo
■ Mississauga
● Oakville-Centre
● Oshawa
▼ Ottawa-Downtown
▼ Ottawa-Kanata
★ Peterborough-Waterfront
★ Sarnia
★ Sault Ste. Marie-Waterfront
★ St. Catharines/Niagara
■ Toronto-Airport
● Toronto Airport Area (Dixie Rd.)
★ Toronto-Airport East

■ Toronto-Brampton
● Toronto-East
▼ Toronto-Markham
★ Toronto-Mississauga
● Toronto-North York
★ Toronto-West
★ Toronto-Yorkdale
★ Trenton
■ Windsor (Ambassador Bridge)
PRINCE EDWARD ISLAND
▲ Charlottetown
QUEBEC
★ Gatineau-Ottawa Plz Chaudière
★ Montreal-Airport
■ Montreal-Centre Ville (Dwtn Conv Ctr)
★ Montreal-Longueuil
★ Montreal-Midtown
★ Pte Claire-Airport
■ Quebec City-Downtown
★ Saguenay Convention Centre

★denotes Holiday Inn® hotels. ■denotes Holiday Inn Select® hotels. ▼denotes Holiday Inn® Hotel & Suites. ◆denotes Holiday Inn SunSpree® Resort.
● denotes Holiday Inn Express® hotels. ▲denotes Holiday Inn Express® Hotel & Suites.

ALBERTA
★ Calgary
  Dwtn-Conference Centre
● Calgary-University
▲ Edmonton
▼ Fort McMurray
★ Hinton
▲ Lethbridge
● Red Deer
● Rocky Mountain House
BRITISH COLUMBIA
★ International
  Vancouver Airport
● Kamloops
● Kelowna
▼ North Vancouver
◆ Osoyoos
▲ Salmon Arm
● Vancouver
● Vancouver-Airport
★ Vancouver-Centre (Broadway)
▼ Vancouver-Downtown

★ Victoria
★ Westbank
◆ Whistler Village Centre
MANITOBA
▼ Winnipeg - Downtown
★ Winnipeg Airport/West
★ Winnipeg-South
NEW BRUNSWICK
▲ Moncton
● Saint John - *Opening Soon*
NEWFOUNDLAND & LABRADOR
★ Stephenville
NOVA SCOTIA
● Halifax/Bedford
■ Halifax-Centre
★ Halifax-Harbourview
ONTARIO
▲ Barrie
★ Barrie-Hotel & Conference Centre
★ Brantford
★ Burlington-Hotel & Conference Center

★ Cambridge
● Cornwall
● Dryden
★ Fort Erie/Niagara Convention Centre
★ Guelph
▲ Guelph
● Hamilton-Stoney Creek
★ Kingston-Waterfront
● Kitchener-Waterloo
■ Mississauga
● Oakville-Centre
● Oshawa
▼ Ottawa-Downtown
▼ Ottawa-Kanata
★ Peterborough-Waterfront
★ Sarnia
★ Sault Ste. Marie-Waterfront
★ St. Catharines/Niagara
■ Toronto-Airport
● Toronto-Airport Area (Dixie Rd.)
★ Toronto-Airport East

■ Toronto-Brampton
● Toronto-East
▼ Toronto-Markham
★ Toronto-Mississauga
● Toronto-North York
★ Toronto-West
★ Toronto-Yorkdale
★ Trenton
■ Windsor (Ambassador Bridge)
PRINCE EDWARD ISLAND
▲ Charlottetown
QUEBEC
★ Gatineau-Ottawa Plz Chaudière
★ Montreal-Airport
■ Montreal-Centre Ville (Dwtn Conv Ctr)
★ Montreal-Longueuil
★ Montreal-Midtown
★ Pte Claire-Airport
■ Quebec City-Downtown
★ Saguenay Convention Centre

★denotes Holiday Inn® hotels. ■denotes Holiday Inn Select® hotels. ▼denotes Holiday Inn® Hotel & Suites. ◆denotes Holiday Inn SunSpree® Resort.
● denotes Holiday Inn Express® hotels. ▲denotes Holiday Inn Express® Hotel & Suites.

PORT COLBORNE—*see Niagara Falls p. 128.*

PORT HOPE (G-9) pop. 11,718

Nestled in the Northumberland Hills along the Ganaraska River, Port Hope began in 1792 with the arrival of two United Empire Loyalists. By 1860 the enlarged harbor and the two railroads servicing the town had made it important in the lumbering and agricultural products trade. Because few changes occurred over the next 100 years, much of the town's original architecture remains intact.

Several of the town's large historic houses are open for tours during the October A.C.O. Historic House Tour; phone (905) 885-7929 for tickets and more information. Dorothy's Historic House Museum, at 3632 CR 9, is an 1800s historic working-man's cottage furnished with period artifacts; phone (905) 797-1170.

Said to be Canada's only remaining operational "atmospheric theater," The Capitol Theatre, at 14 Queen St., provides the illusion of being in a walled medieval courtyard. The theater is home to the Port Hope Festival Theatre, which presents professional theatrical productions in summer; phone (905) 885-1071, or (800) 434-5092 in Ontario for information. A variety of cultural events also are offered year-round.

Because fishing for rainbow trout on the Ganaraska River and for salmon on Lake Ontario is good, many fishing derbies are held throughout the year. Some 8,000 rainbow trout make their way upstream to spawn in the Ganaraska River each spring, attracting thousands of visitors; in September, the event is repeated by Lake Ontario salmon, with the same result. Additional recreational activities include bicycling, boating and hiking along the town's portion of the Waterfront Trail and the Ganaraska Hiking Trail.

Other events of interest include Float Your Fanny Down the Ganny River Race, the first Saturday in April, commemorating the 1980 severe flood that swept the downtown area. Crazy crafts (rafts made out of anything imaginable), canoes and kayaks participate in this race. September's Port Hope Fall Fair has been held since 1831 and includes a midway; arts and crafts; and livestock, horse and car shows. A farmers' market operates on Saturdays, May through October, behind the Town Hall.

Port Hope Tourism Information Centre: 14 Queen St., Port Hope, ON, Canada L1A 3Z4; phone (905) 885-5519, or (888) 767-8467 in Ontario.

CANADIAN FIRE FIGHTERS MUSEUM, Hwy. 28 to 95 Mill St. S., depicts the historical development of fire fighting in Canada 1750-1956. Exhibits, some offering hands-on experience, include fire-fighting equipment, breathing machines, photographs, alarms and antique extinguishers. Firetrucks are on the grounds. A 1912 horse- or 1890 hand-drawn water pumper and an 1881 hose wagon are displayed in the barn.

Daily 9-5, Victoria Day weekend-second Mon. in Oct.; otherwise by appointment. Hours may vary; phone ahead. Donations. Phone (905) 885-8985.

PORT PERRY (G-9) pop. 7,244

On the western shore of Lake Scugog, Port Perry offers many outdoor recreational pursuits, including fishing, boating, hiking, bicycling and bird-watching. Winter options include cross-country skiing, snowmobiling and ice fishing.

Scugog Tourist Information Centre: 269 Queen St., P.O. Box 1282, Port Perry, ON, Canada L9L 1B1; phone (905) 985-4971.

Shopping areas: Port Perry's Victorian heritage is evident in its downtown buildings, which provide the setting for antique, craft and gift shops.

SCUGOG SHORES HISTORICAL MUSEUM, VILLAGE & ARCHIVES is 1 km (.6 mi.) n. off Hwy. 7A at 16210 Island Rd. (CR 7). On Scugog Island, the village contains 11 19th-century buildings, many relocated from nearby areas. A print shop, Victorian house, log cabin, blacksmith shop, harness shop and a restored 1860 Methodist church are among the buildings featured. Extensive local archives also are available by appointment. Special events are offered throughout the year.

Guided tours are available. Picnicking is permitted. Daily 10-4, Victoria Day-Labour Day; Mon.-Fri. 10-4, rest of year. Closed major holidays. Admission by donation except during special events and for use of archives. Phone (905) 985-3589.

CASINOS

- **Great Blue Heron Charity Casino** is at 21777 Island Rd. Daily 24 hours. Phone (905) 985-4888 or (888) 294-3766.

WINERIES

- **Ocala Orchards Farm Winery Ltd.** is at 971 High Point Rd. Mon.-Sat. 10-5:30, Sun. noon-5, May-Dec.; Wed.-Sat. 10-5:30, Sun. noon-5, rest of year. Closed holidays. Phone (905) 985-9924 or (866) 985-9924.

PORT ROWAN (I-2)

BACKUS HERITAGE CONSERVATION AREA is at 1267 Backus Mill Rd. The scenic and historic park features the John Backhouse Mill; a pioneer village with log houses, a blacksmith shop, the Backus Homestead and an octagonal schoolhouse; camping; swimming; 12 kilometres (7.5 mi.) of nature trails; cross-country skiing; and fishing. A museum features storefronts and area history, and a nature center has displays about waterfowl, wildlife and area ecology.

Picnicking is permitted. Wed.-Sun. 11-4:30, July 1-Labour Day. Admission $5; over 64, $4; under 16, $1; maximum of $10 per private vehicle. AX,

DC, MC, VI. Phone (519) 586-2201 or (877) 990-9932. *See Recreation Chart.*

PRESCOTT (F-11) pop. 4,228

Maj. Edward Jessup founded Prescott in 1810 on land granted by England for his support during the American Revolution. The town name honors Gen. Robert Prescott, governor-in-chief of Canada 1797-1807.

Before the advent of the St. Lawrence Seaway, the town was the only deep-water port between Montréal and Toronto. Consequently, Prescott became a major embarkation point for travelers and goods destined for points west. Part of the town's 19th-century legacy survives in the stone houses built by army engineers after the War of 1812.

Tourism Prescott: 360 Dibble St., P.O. Box 160, Prescott, ON, Canada K0E 1T0; phone (613) 925-1861 or (800) 218-1131.

Self-guiding tours: A brochure for a self-guiding historic walking tour is available from the tourism office.

FORT WELLINGTON NATIONAL HISTORIC SITE, on Hwy. 2 along the St. Lawrence River, encompasses the 1812 fort, erected to defend the St. Lawrence River route during the War of 1812. Never besieged, the fort was abandoned shortly after the war. A second Fort Wellington was built in 1838 on the ruins of the first.

The fort consists of three original structures surrounded by earthworks, a palisade and a dry ditch. Costumed interpreters demonstrate drills and military tactics typical of an early 19th-century garrison. Open daily 10-5, Victoria Day weekend-Sept. 30; closed Good Friday and Easter. Admission $4; over 64, $3.50; ages 6-16, $2.50. Phone (613) 925-2896.

THE FORWARDERS' MUSEUM, Centre and Water sts., is in the 1810 Forwarders' Building, which once housed an 1829 post office and the American consulate. The museum commemorates the forwarding (shipping) industry on the St. Lawrence River during the first half of the 19th century. Displays are rotated monthly. Open Mon.-Sat. 10-5, Sun. noon-5, Victoria Day-Labour Day. Donations. Phone (613) 925-5788 to verify schedule.

PUKASKWA NATIONAL PARK (C-3)

Elevations in the park range from 184 metres (603 ft.) at Lake Superior to 640 metres (2,099 ft.) at Tip Top Mountain. Refer to CAA/AAA maps for additional elevation information.

On the north shore of Lake Superior, 320 kilometres (199 mi.) northeast of Thunder Bay, Pukaskwa (PUCK-a-saw) National Park encompasses 1,878 square kilometres (725 sq. mi.). The park is mostly wilderness that is accessible only by canoe, boat or trail. The entrance at Hattie Cove in the northwestern corner of the park can be reached via Hwy. 627, which extends from Hwy. 17 south and east of the town of Marathon.

Pukaskwa's rocky terrain is covered by forests of spruce, fir and cedar mixed with birch and aspen. Thick, fragrant moss blankets the thin layer of soil. The microclimate close to the lakeshore supports a variety of plants. The coves and weathered headlands along the rugged shore embrace cliffs, cobble beaches and pristine stretches of sand. Among wildlife are black bears, moose, wolves and woodland caribou.

General Information and Activities

The park is open all year. The visitor center at Hattie Cove offers interpretive programs, displays, information and a detailed park map; it is open daily, July through August. Campgrounds, beaches, picnic areas and hiking trails are nearby. A fee is charged for camping. In the back country, a hiking trail follows the coastline for 60 kilometres (44 mi.) and has several primitive campsites along the way. All visitors to the back country and winter campers must register, attend a safety orientation and pay fees before venturing out.

In winter, cross-country skiing, snowshoeing and back-country camping are permitted. In the spring the Pukaskwa and White rivers offer challenging white-water rapids. The adventurous can paddle or boat along the coast, but lake conditions can be unpredictable. Boats can be launched on the Pic River near the park entrance. *See Recreation Chart.*

ADMISSION is $4.50; over 64, $4; ages 6-16, $2.25; family rate $7.

PETS are permitted in the park only if they are leashed, crated or otherwise physically restricted at all times.

ADDRESS inquires to Pukaskwa National Park, P.O. Box 212, Heron Bay, ON, Canada P0T 1R0; phone (807) 229-0801, ext. 242.

QUEENSTON—*see Niagara Falls p. 128.*

RENFREW (E-10) pop. 7,942

Renfrew, in an area of lakes, rivers and forests, was named for the ancestral seat of the royal Stuarts by its Scottish founders in the 19th century. Local industry includes the manufacture of machinery, telecommunications equipment, electrical appliances, jet engine parts and grain products.

Renfrew and Area Chamber of Commerce: 161 Raglan St. S., Renfrew, ON, Canada K7V 1R2; phone (613) 432-7015.

McDOUGALL MILL MUSEUM is next to O'Brien Park off Stewart St. at Arthur St. A renovated flour mill built in 1855, the three-story stone building displays period clothing, wartime souvenirs, military uniforms, pioneer tools and a collection of local historical items. Daily 10-4, July 1-Labour Day.

Admission $2; ages 6-12, $1. Phone (613) 432-2129, or (613) 432-7015 rest of year.

STORYLAND, 13 km (8 mi.) n.w. on Storyland Rd., covers 16 hectares (40 acres) of heavily-treed park area. Included are the 122-metre-high (400-ft.) Champlain Lookout, offering a 56-kilometre (35-mi.) view; more than 200 animated storybook characters in 40 settings; a "dress-up cottage"; Frontierland; and playgrounds, jump 'n bounce, pedal boats; a water spray park and exercise and nature trails. A miniature golf course overlooks the Ottawa River valley.

Picnicking is permitted. Allow 3 hours minimum. Daily 9:30-6, second Sat. in June-Sun. after Labour Day. Admission $10.50; ages 5-15, $9.95; over 54 and ages 2-4, $8.95. MC, VI. Phone (613) 432-2222.

RICHMOND HILL—*see Toronto p. 208.*

RIDGETOWN (I-7) pop. 3,358

GREENVIEW AVIARIES PARK AND ZOO, off Hwy. 401 exit 101S (Kent Rd. 15) to CR 3 (Talbot Tr.), then 3 km (1.9 mi.) e., has 150 species of birds and exotic animals, some of which freely roam the park. Shakespeareland, a miniature village depicting Stratford County, England, and dedicated to the celebrated author, also is on the grounds. Picnicking is permitted. Food is available. Allow 2 hours minimum. Daily 9-8, May 1 to mid-Oct. Admission $8.50; over 64, $7.50; ages 4-15, $6.50. AX, MC, VI. Phone (519) 674-3025.

RIDGE HOUSE MUSEUM & GALLERY is 1 km (.6 mi.) s. off Main St. at 53 Erie St. S. The museum, in an 1874 home, features restored rooms filled with antiques, folk art and artifacts dating from the early 19th century. A gallery features changing exhibits. Guided tours are available. Allow 30 minutes minimum. Daily 10-4:30, June-Aug.; 1-4:30, rest of year. Closed major holidays. Phone to verify schedule. Donations. Phone (519) 674-2223.

ROCKPORT (F-11)

HERITAGE 1000 ISLANDS CRUISES, departs from the Boathouse Country Inn at 19 Front St. One-hour narrated cruises in circa 1928 tour boats provide information about both the Canadian and American sides of the 1000 Islands. An optional stopover at Boldt Castle is available *(see attraction listing in Gananoque p. 75)*; those visiting the castle return on a later boat.

Government-issued photo ID and proof of citizenship or a passport are required for Boldt Castle stopover. Non-residents of Canada or the U.S. may also need a U.S. visitor visa. One-hour non-stop cruise daily on the half-hour 10:30-4:30, July 1-Labour Day; on the half-hour 10:30-3:30, May-June and day after Labour Day to mid-Oct. Stopover cruise daily on the hour 10-5, July 1-Labour Day; 10:30-4:30, May-June and day after Labour Day to mid-Oct. Phone ahead to verify schedule.

Fare for 1-hour non-stop cruise $12; over 60 and students with ID $11; ages 4-12, $7. Fare for stopover cruise $15; over 60 and students with ID $13.50; ages 4-12, $10. There is an additional charge to tour Boldt Castle. AX, MC, VI. Phone (613) 659-3151 or (888) 229-9913.

ROCKPORT BOAT LINE, 3.2 km (2 mi.) e. of the Thousand Islands Bridge on the Thousand Islands Pkwy., offers 1-hour cruises aboard a triple-decker boat through the Thousand Islands area. A stopover cruise to Boldt Castle *(see attraction listing in Gananoque p. 75)* also is offered.

A photo ID and proof of citizenship or a passport are required for the Boldt Castle stopover cruise. One-hour nonstop cruise daily on the hour 9-5, July-Sept.; daily at 10, noon and 2, May-June and in Oct. Stopover cruise daily at 10:30, noon, 1:30 and 3, late June-Labour Day; Sat.-Sun. and Mon. holidays in late May and day after Labour Day-second Mon. in Oct. Phone to confirm schedule and availability.

Fare for non-stop cruise $14; over 64, $12; ages 4-11, $9. Fare for stopover cruise $16; over 64, $14; ages 4-11, $10. There is an additional charge to tour Boldt Castle. AX, MC, VI. Phone (613) 659-3402 or (800) 563-8687.

ROSEMONT (F-3)

DUFFERIN COUNTY MUSEUM & ARCHIVES, Hwy. 89 and CR 18 (Airport Rd.), is in a building resembling a barn. The museum has a collection of artifacts, photographs and farm implements depicting county history. Within the museum are three historic buildings: the 1914 two-story log McCutcheon House; an 1861 Orange Lodge, a building used as a meeting place by groups of Protestant Irish men; and Cromby Station, an original Canadian Pacific Railway flagging station.

Picnicking is permitted. Allow 1 hour minimum. Museum Mon.-Fri. 10-5, Sat. 10-4, Sun. noon-5, Victoria Day-second Mon. in Oct.; Tues.-Fri. 10-5, Sat. 10-4, Sun. noon-5, rest of year. Hours for archives vary; phone ahead. Closed Jan. 1 and Dec. 25-26. Admission $5; over 59, $4; ages 5-14, $2; family rate (two adults and up to four children) $12. MC, VI. Phone (705) 435-1881, or (877) 941-7787 in Canada.

ST. CATHARINES—*see Niagara Falls p. 129.*

ST. JACOBS (G-2) pop. 1,227

Originally called Jakobstettel, or "little town of many Jacobs," St. Jacobs is in an area that was settled by Mennonites from Pennsylvania after the American Revolution. Horse-drawn carriages are a familiar sight along village streets, which are lined with more than 100 shops of local retailers and artisans. Visitors can learn about the history of the world's favorite pancake topping at the Maple Syrup Museum, 8 Spring St.; phone (519) 664-1232.

Shopping areas: Three kilometres (1.8 mi.) south of town is St. Jacobs Factory Outlet Mall with name-brand stores carrying clothing, shoes, linens and china.

Thursday and Saturday (also Tuesday, June through August) just 2 kilometres (1.2 mi.) south of town shoppers can hunt for bargains at the St. Jacobs Farmers' Market and Flea Market where offerings include foodstuffs, handmade crafts items, clothing and housewares. A petting farm and picnic areas are on the market's grounds.

VISITOR CENTRE TELLING THE MENNONITE STORY, 1406 King St., presents the group's history, lifestyle and beliefs. Exhibits include replicas of a Swiss cave and a Mennonite meetinghouse; there also is a 13-minute DVD presentation about the Mennonites of Ontario. Guided tours are available by appointment. Allow 1 hour minimum. Mon.-Sat. 11-5, Sun. 1:30-5, Apr. 1-Dec. 24; Sat. 11-4:30, Sun. 2-4:30, rest of year. Closed Jan. 1 and Dec. 25-31. Donations. Phone (519) 664-3518.

ST. JOSEPH ISLAND (E-5) pop. 100

In the channel between Lake Huron and Lake Superior, St. Joseph Island, 30 kilometres (19 mi.) long and 24 kilometres (15 mi.) wide, is the westernmost island in the Manitoulin chain. The island offers full-service marinas, shops and eateries, campsites, scenic driving routes, bicycle tours and snowmobile trails, and is a favorite spot with anglers, hunters and swimmers. A wide assortment of wildlife as well as deposits of rare jasper conglomerate (pudding stone) can be found on St. Joseph. The island is reached via a toll-free bridge 3 kilometres (1.9 mi.) from Hwy. 17.

St. Joseph Island Chamber of Commerce: R.R. 2, Richards Landing, ON, Canada P0R 1J0; phone (705) 246-2581.

FORT ST. JOSEPH NATIONAL HISTORIC SITE is on the southern tip of the island via Hwy. 548. Within the 320-hectare (920-acre) site are the ruins of the fort, built in 1796 to protect the fur trade and consolidate British influence in the Upper Great Lakes area.

Film presentations about archeology and the fur trade are offered at the visitor center, which also houses historical and archeological exhibits. An animal sanctuary, a picnic area and nature trails are on the site.

Site and visitor center open daily 10-4:30, June 1-second Mon. in Oct. Admission $3.50; over 64, $3; ages 6-16, $1.75; family rate $8.75. Phone to verify prices. Phone (705) 246-2664, or (705) 941-6262 in the off-season.

ST. JOSEPH ISLAND MUSEUM is 10 km (6.5 mi.) s.e. of Hwy. 17 via Regional Rd. 548 and the bridge. The complex consists of a pioneer stone church; an 1880 log cabin; historic schoolhouses; a barn with farming relics; a 1912 general store; and the main display building.

Also featured are early 19th-century Fort St. Joseph artifacts and a 3,629-kilogram (8,000-lb.)

white pine log from one of the last trees in a virgin stand near the Bruce Mines. Archives are available. Wed.-Mon. 9:30-4:30, late June-Labour Day. Admission $4; over 60, $3; ages 5-12, $2; family rate $10. Phone (705) 246-2672.

ST. LAWRENCE ISLANDS NATIONAL PARK (F-10)

Elevations in the park range from 75 metres (245 ft.) at Stovin Island to 116 metres (380 ft.) at Hill Island. Refer to CAA/AAA maps for additional elevation information.

In the St. Lawrence River between Kingston and Brockville, the park consists of more than 20 widely scattered islands among the Thousand Islands (*see place listing p. 173*) and a 39-hectare (96-acre) area at Mallorytown Landing on the mainland. The park's headquarters, picnic areas and a children's play area are at the Mallorytown Landing location. A visitor center has displays about the natural and cultural history and settlement of the Thousand Islands region.

General Information and Activities

Access to the park by private vehicle is available only at the Mallorytown Landing entrance. Day use facilities are open Victoria Day weekend through the second Monday in October. Interpretive programs and hikes are conducted periodically on the mainland and on the islands. Transportation to the islands is not available from the park; visitors must hire or supply their own boats. Recreational activities include camping, boating, fishing, hiking, sea kayaking and scuba diving. See Recreation Chart.

ADMISSION is $6 per private vehicle; $15 per private vehicle and trailer. Rates apply Victoria Day weekend-second Mon. in Oct.

PETS are permitted in the park only if they are leashed; they are not permitted in the beach area.

ADDRESS inquiries to the Superintendent's Office, St. Lawrence Islands National Park, 2 CR 5, R.R. #3, Mallorytown, ON, Canada K0E 1R0; phone (613) 923-5261.

ST. MARYS (H-1) pop. 6,293

At the confluence of the Thames River and Trout Creek, St. Marys, known as The Stonetown, features a former limestone quarry that is now Canada's largest outdoor swimming pool. The limestone from the quarry was used to construct many of the town's fine 19th-century buildings. The Grand Trunk Trail Walkway is a conversion of part of the disused track of the railway into a picturesque public walkway spanning the Thames River.

St. Marys Tourism: 5 James St. N., P.O. Box 218, St. Marys, ON, Canada N4X 1B1; phone (519) 284-3500.

SAVE CANADIAN BASEBALL HALL OF FAME AND MUSEUM, 386 Church St. S., is in a turn-of-the-20th-century stone house and presents exhibits about Canadian involvement in baseball. Both regulation and youth-size baseball diamonds are on the 13-hectare (32-acre) grounds.

Picnicking is permitted. Allow 30 minutes minimum. Mon.-Sat. 10:30-4, Sun. noon-4, June 1 to mid-Oct.; Sat. 10:30-4, Sun. noon-4, in May. Admission $7.50; over 63, $6; students with ID and children $4; family rate $15. MC, VI. Phone (519) 284-1838 or (877) 250-2255.

THE ST. MARYS MUSEUM, 177 Church St. S., displays local memorabilia in an 1850s limestone house. The Resource Centre contains reference books and materials. Allow 30 minutes minimum. Mon.-Fri. 9:30-noon and 1-4:30, Sat.-Sun. 1-4:30, June 1-Labour Day; Mon.-Fri. 9:30-noon and 1-4:30, rest of year. Donations. Phone (519) 284-3556.

ST. THOMAS (I-1)
pop. 33,236, elev. 230 m/755'

St. Thomas is the home of the historic Talbot Settlement, where Col. Thomas Talbot began the settlement of Crown Lands around 1800. The city is known for its horticultural gardens. Noteworthy are the water gardens in 40-hectare (100-acre) Waterworks Park. Also worth a visit are the floral displays and wildlife sanctuary in 36-hectare (90-acre) Pinafore Park; the park is home to the Fantasy of Lights display in December.

Due to its location between Fort Erie and Windsor, trains also have been important in the development of St. Thomas. Railway artifacts and murals grace the downtown area.

A life-size statue of Jumbo the elephant was erected in 1985 across from the Elgin County Pioneer Museum. A phenomenal drawing card for the Barnum & Bailey Circus, the real Jumbo was billed as "the largest and heaviest elephant ever seen by mortal man, either wild or in captivity." Jumbo was killed in St. Thomas in 1885 by a locomotive while trying to protect a smaller elephant from an oncoming train; his mounted skin and skeleton nonetheless continued to tour with the circus for 2 years after his death.

City Hall, the Courthouse and the Old St. Thomas Church are some examples of the town's Victorian architecture. Recreational outlets include the historic Talbot Trail and the Trans Canada Hiking Trail.

St. Thomas-Elgin Tourist Association: 545 Talbot St., St. Thomas, ON, Canada N5R 6A1; phone (519) 631-8188 or (877) 463-5446.

ELGIN COUNTY PIONEER MUSEUM, w. off Hwy. 3 at 32 Talbot St., was the home of Dr. Elijah Duncombe. Pioneer relics and 19th-century medical equipment are displayed in an 1840s house. Period rooms are of the pioneer and Victorian eras, while galleries portray local history and display artifacts, including those of Col. Thomas Talbot. A church dating from 1824 is nearby.

Tues.-Sat. 9-5, Victoria Day-Labour Day; 1-5, rest of year. Closed holidays. Admission (includes Elgin Military Museum) $4; ages 4-18, $1. Phone (519) 631-6537.

ELGIN COUNTY RAILWAY MUSEUM is at 225 Wellington St., 1 blk s. of Talbot St. in the Michigan Central Railroad Shop. The historic 1913 railroad shop houses a collection of vintage locomotives and rolling stock, including steam and diesel locomotives, Pullman and baggage cars and several cabooses in addition to railway artifacts and memorabilia. Guided tours are available. Allow 1 hour minimum. Daily 10-4, late May-Labour Day. Donations. Phone (519) 637-6284.

ELGIN MILITARY MUSEUM, off Hwy. 3 at 30 Talbot St., has a collection of military artifacts and records illustrating the efforts and contributions of Elgin County residents to Canada's military history. Highlights include a World War I bunker, uniforms and weapons. Allow 30 minutes minimum. Tues.-Fri. 1-5, Sat. 9-noon and 1-5, Sun. 2-5; closed Dec. 25-Jan. 1. Admission (includes Elgin County Pioneer Museum) $4; ages 4-18, $1. Phone (519) 633-7641.

ST. THOMAS-ELGIN PUBLIC ART CENTRE, 301 Talbot St., displays works by Canadian artists through permanent and temporary exhibits. Tues.-Wed. 10-4, Thurs.-Fri. 10-9, Sat. noon-4, Sun. noon-3; closed holidays. Free. Phone (519) 631-4040.

WINERIES

- **Meadow Lane Winery** is at 44892 Talbot Line (Hwy. 3), across from the airport. Mon.-Sat. 10-5, Sun. noon-5; closed Dec. 25. Guided tours are available by appointment. Phone (519) 633-1933.

- **Quai du Vin Estate Winery** is 8 km (5 mi.) e. of Hwy. 4, following signs, at 45811 Fruit Ridge Line. Mon.-Sat. 10-5, Sun. noon-5; closed Dec. 25-26. Phone (519) 775-2216.

SARNIA (H-6) pop. 70,876, elev. 186 m/610'

Lake Huron's largest city, Sarnia is one of Ontario's busiest marina centers, with 1,400 berths for recreational boating and Great Lakes ship traffic exceeding 6,000 passes annually. Ship viewing is best below the Blue Water Bridge, at Point Edward Waterfront Park. The bridge, the fourth busiest crossing between Ontario and the United States, has been duplicated; one span now carries eastbound traffic, the other westbound.

Sarnia is the northern starting point for the St. Clair Parkway, one of three such recreational drives in Ontario. It hugs the meandering St. Clair River's park-lined shores, before heading inland to

Chatham and Dresden. Hiking trails are plentiful in the area.

The Sarnia Waterfront Festival offers more than 50 events from May to mid-September, including most days in July and August. Sarnia's Highland Games in mid-August include the North American Haggis Hurling Championships. Events are held in Centennial Park, a 1.6 kilometre- (1-mi.) long linear recreational area with historical and Great Lakes displays, ship viewing opportunities, a playground, fountain, marina and boat cruises.

Winter brings fun to the Sarnia and Port Huron areas with events such as the Celebration of Lights, when 60,000 twinkling bulbs and major displays brighten Centennial Park and downtown mid-November to early January, and the snow sculpting competition held in mid-January during SnowFest.

Hiawatha Horse Park, 1730 London Line, offers live harness racing May through November; phone (519) 542-5543.

Note: Policies concerning admittance of children to pari-mutuel betting facilities vary. Phone for information.

The Imperial Oil Centre for the Performing Arts, 168 N. Christina St., hosts a variety of theatrical performances and concerts and is home to Theatre Sarnia; phone (519) 332-6591 for information or (519) 344-7469 or (877) 344-7469 for tickets. Local farmers sell their produce year-round every Wednesday and Saturday at a farmers' market in the Mitton Village area, 110 Proctor St.

Tourism Sarnia-Lambton—Sarnia: 556 N. Christina St., Sarnia, ON, Canada N7T 5W6; phone (519) 336-3232 or (800) 265-0316.

Shopping areas: Lambton Mall, 1380 London Rd., offers more than 110 shops and services, including Sears.

BLUEWATER FUN PARK-ACTION ZONE, 1886 London Rd., features two waterslides, two speedslides, a leisure pool, bumper boats, a children's pool and beach volleyball as well as miniature golf. An indoor activities area includes laser and video games. An indoor/outdoor rock climbing facility is available.

Picnicking is permitted. Food is available. Outdoor park daily 10-7, mid-June through Labour Day; Sat.-Sun. and Mon. holidays 10-7, Victoria Day weekend to mid-June (weather permitting). Rock climbing Mon.-Sat. 11-9, Sun. noon-6, mid-June through Labour Day; Wed.-Fri. 5-10, Sat. 11-10, Sun. noon-6, rest of year. Laser and video games Mon.-Sat. 11-7 (also Fri.-Sat. 7-9 p.m.), Sun. noon-6, mid-June to mid-Sept.; Wed.-Fri. 4-9 (also Fri. 9 p.m.-midnight), Sat. 11 a.m.-midnight, Sun. noon-6, rest of year. Phone ahead to confirm activity hours.

Water park admission (includes leisure pool, beach volleyball and miniature golf) $4.25, under 3 free. Day pass (includes admission and rides) $15; under 6, $10. Indoor activities and rock climbing

on a pay-as-you-play basis. AX, MC, VI. Phone (519) 542-1083.

CANATARA PARK, on Lake Huron at 1200 Lake Chipican Dr., covers 105 hectares (259 acres) and has a beach with supervised swimming, a bathhouse, picnic area, playground and boat launch for centerboard sailboats. Other facilities include nature trails, a toboggan run, a bandshell, cross-country ski trails and a fitness circuit. A small farm introduces children to domestic animals and poultry. Various programs are conducted in the buildings near the farm.

Park open daily 8 a.m.-midnight. Children's farm open daily 8-7:30, Victoria Day-Labour Day; Mon.-Sat. 8-4, Sun. 9-4, rest of year. Park free. Animal farm by donations. Phone (519) 332-0330.

DISCOVERY HOUSE MUSEUM, 475 Christina St. N., is in a fully restored Victorian house, built about 1890. Among the displays are a working model of Sarnia's waterfront in the 1920s and a garden railway. Interactive displays as well as local-life and marine exhibits also are included. Allow 30 minutes minimum. Tues.-Fri. 9-5, Sat. 1-5; closed Jan. 1, Easter weekend and Dec. 25-26. Admission $3.50; over 64, $3; ages 5-12, $2; family rate (five persons) $8. Phone (519) 332-1556.

GALLERY LAMBTON, 150 N. Christina St. at the Bayside Mall, displays works from its permanent collection, which includes pieces by the Group of Seven as well as other Canadian artists. Changing exhibits also are presented. Allow 30 minutes minimum. Mon.-Sat. 10-5:30; closed holidays. Admission $2. Phone (519) 336-8127.

STONES 'N BONES MUSEUM is at 223 N. Christina St. Guided tours of the nature museum provide insights into the collections of fluorescent minerals, fossils, gemstones, seashells, insects, antlered and horned animals, butterflies and sharks, all displayed in a gallery-like setting. Allow 2 hours minimum. Daily 10-5, July-Aug.; Thurs.-Sun. and holiday Mon. 10-5, Mar.-June and Sept.-Dec. Closed Good Friday and Dec. 25 Admission $6; under 13, $3. MC, VI. Phone (519) 336-2100.

SAULT STE. MARIE (D-4) pop. 74,566

Facing each other across the St. Marys River are the Ontario and Michigan cities of Sault Ste. Marie. The river's rapids were discovered by Etienne Brulé in 1622, and the first permanent mission was founded by Père Marquette in 1669. Many eminent Jesuits were stationed at the mission until its abandonment in 1689. A French military post was established in 1750; it was garrisoned until the British took it over in 1762. The settlement was an important fur-trading post until 1842.

The Sault Locks connect Lake Superior with the St. Marys River and Lake Huron. The Canadian lock, now operated as a national historic site, was built in 1895 and is 77 metres (253 ft.) long, 15.4 metres (51 ft.) wide and 3 metres (10 ft.) deep. The lock provided the final link in an all-Canadian passageway between the St. Lawrence River and Lake Superior and eventually became a part of the St. Lawrence Seaway Authority. It is now used for recreational craft and integrates new and old technology. *See attraction listing.*

Other interesting local attractions include Bellevue Park, which has a playground, sailboat marina, greenhouses and attractive seasonal flower gardens. The marina serves as a Canadian customs checkpoint. Band concerts are held in the park in summer. Roberta Bondar Park and Pavilion presents outdoor festivals and special events throughout the year. Murals on the pavilion's fabric walls depict local scenes. A downtown boardwalk along the St. Marys River displays plaques about area history and serves as an observation point.

Recreational activities available in the area include bicycling, boating, golfing, hiking and fishing in summer, while winter offers skiing, snowshoeing, skating and snowmobiling.

The Bon Soo Winter Carnival is held from late January through early February. The 10-day affair features more than 125 activities, including curling, skating, skiing, snowmobiling, snow volleyball, sleigh rides, a "polar bear" swim, snow sculptures, entertainment and fireworks.

Sault Ste. Marie Chamber of Commerce: 334 Bay St., Sault Ste. Marie, ON, Canada P6A 1X1; phone (705) 949-7152.

Shopping areas: Station Mall, 293 Bay St. on the waterfront, has more than 120 stores including Sears and Zellers. Queenstown is a downtown shopping area on Queen Street E. between Pim and Dennis streets.

AGAWA CANYON TOUR TRAIN departs the Algoma Central Railway Inc. depot downtown at 129 Bay St. A 1-day excursion into the heart of the Canadian Shield wilderness, the 365-kilometre (228-mi.) round-trip includes a 2-hour stop at scenic Agawa Canyon Park and offers views of unspoiled forests, hills, lakes and streams in the rugged Algoma region.

Tour of the Line is an overnight trip over the entire Algoma Central Railway line, with an overnight stay in the French-Canadian town of Hearst *(see place listing p. 82).* Rates do not include hotel; reservations should be made in advance. The Snow Train is a 1-day winter tour through the Canadian winter countryside to Agawa Canyon.

Food is available on some routes. The Agawa Canyon train departs daily at 8 a.m. with return at 5:30 p.m., early June to mid-Oct. The Tour of the Line train operates year-round; phone for departure days and times. The Snow Train departs Sat. (and some Sun.) at 8 a.m. and returns at 4:45 p.m., Feb. 1 to mid-Mar. Phone ahead to confirm schedules.

Agawa Canyon fare early June to mid-Sept. $60; over 59, $51; ages 5-18, $21; under 5, $16. Fare rest of season $79; ages 5-18, $48; under 5, $23. Overnight fare $165; ages 5-18, $98; under 5, $57. Snow Train $63; ages 5-18, $33; under 5, $18. Phone to confirm prices. MC, VI. Phone (705) 946-7300 or (800) 242-9287. *See color ad & color ad p. 453.*

ART GALLERY OF ALGOMA, 10 East St. on the waterfront, is a community-oriented visual arts center offering monthly exhibitions of the works of local, national and international artists, in addition to the gallery's permanent collection. Cultural activities are designed to enrich and expand knowledge and appreciation of the visual arts. Programs include instruction, films and meet-the-artist receptions.

NOW! BOOK ON-LINE

The AGAWA CANYON · TOUR TRAIN ·

A one day rail adventure into the heart of the Canadian wilderness

All aboard for an incredible rail excursion as you wind your way towards a two hour stay in the pristine beauty of Agawa Canyon park. *Ask for a Holiday Package Accommodation guide.*

TOUR OPERATES DAILY: JUNE TO MID-OCTOBER
ALGOMA CENTRAL RAILWAY INC., P.O. BOX 130,
129 BAY ST., SAULT STE. MARIE 53 ON, P6A 6Y2
1-800-242-9287
www.agawacanyontourtrain.com

ONLY AN HOUR NORTH OF MACKINAW

Mon.-Sat. 9-8, June 1-Oct. 7; Mon.-Sat. 9-5, Sun. 1-4, Oct. 8-Dec. 31; Mon.-Sat. 9-5, rest of year. Closed holidays. Phone ahead to verify schedule. Donations. Phone (705) 949-9067.

CANADIAN BUSHPLANE HERITAGE CENTRE, 2.5 km. (1.6 mi.) e. of the International Bridge at 50 Pim St., commemorates Canada's history of bush flying and forest fire fighting. Interpretive exhibits include a fire tower, an operational engine test cell, a radio lab, fire station, bushplanes, float planes and water bombers and forest fire fighting artifacts. A film about the history of bushplane flying describes the plane's development and usage in fire fighting. The Children's Flight Centre offers hands-on flight exhibits.

Allow 30 minutes minimum. Daily 9-6, mid-May to mid-Oct.; 10-4, rest of year. Closed Jan. 1 and Dec. 25. Admission $10.50; over 54, $9.50; students with ID $5; grades K-8, $2. AX, MC, VI. Phone (705) 945-6242.

ERMATINGER/CLERGUE HERITAGE SITE, 831 Queen St. E., is typical of early Canadian architecture. The 1814 restored house of French fur trader and North West Co. officer Charles Ermatinger and his Ojibway wife contains period furnishings and household articles. The Clergue Blockhouse, on the remains of an early 19th-century North West Co. powder magazine, was the original house of Francis Clergue, who was involved in the city's early industrialization.

Daily 9:30-6, June 1-Oct. 9; Mon.-Fri. 9:30-4:30, mid-Apr. through May 31 and Oct. 10-Nov. 30; otherwise by appointment. Phone ahead to verify schedule. Blockhouse closed mid-Oct. to early Apr. Admission $5; over 59 and ages 3-12, $3; family rate (two adults and children under 12) $12. Phone (705) 759-5443, or (705) 759-5310 in the off-season.

LAKE SUPERIOR PROVINCIAL PARK— see Wawa p. 213.

LOCK TOURS CANADA departs the dock at Roberta Bondar Park and Pavilion at Foster Dr. for 2-hour cruises of the St. Marys River and the Sault Ste. Marie locks aboard the *Chief Shingwauk.* Dinner cruises also are offered. Sightseeing cruises depart daily, late May to mid-Oct. Fare $23.50; ages 13-18, $18.50; ages 5-12, $12. Rates may vary; phone ahead. Reservations required for dinner cruise. AX, MC, VI. Phone (705) 253-9850 or (877) 226-3665.

SAULT CANAL NATIONAL HISTORIC SITE, from the International Bridge, s. on Huron St. then just e. to 1 Canal Dr., interprets the many technological firsts and accomplishments related to the canal's 1887-95 construction and operation. The canal was converted to small craft use in 1998. The original buildings, a self-guiding nature trail and a visitor center are on the site.

Guided tours are available. Allow 1 hour minimum. Daily 9-9, mid-June through Labour Day; 10-8, mid-May to mid-June and day after Labour

Day to mid-Oct.; otherwise by appointment. Visitor center daily 10-8, mid-June through Labour Day; daily 8:30-4:30, mid-May to mid-June and day after Labour Day to mid-Oct.; Mon.-Fri. 8:30-4:30, rest of year. Closed Jan. 1, Good Friday, Easter Monday and Dec. 25-26. Hours and fees may vary; phone ahead. Free. Guided tours $2.25; over 64, $1.75; ages 6-16, $1.25. Phone (705) 941-6205.

SAULT STE. MARIE MUSEUM, downtown at 690 Queen St. E. in the historic Post Office, has three floors of exhibits depicting the heritage of Sault Ste. Marie. Included are marine and shipping artifacts, the Sports History Hall of Fame, a blacksmith shop and relics from prehistoric times to the recent past. The museum also features locally curated exhibits and special events.

Allow 30 minutes minimum. Mon.-Sat. 10-6, June 1 to mid-Oct.; Tues.-Sat. 9:30-4:30, rest of year. Closed holidays. Admission $5; over 54 and ages 13-19, $3; ages 7-12, $2; family rate (two adults and three students ages 13-19) $10. Rates may vary during special events. Phone (705) 759-7278.

SPRUCE HAVEN PETTING AND WILDLIFE ZOO is at 2016 Third Line W. With both a wildlife section and a petting area, the zoo features both exotic and farm animals. Cougars, lynx, ibex, deer, gray wolves, llamas and yaks are some of the more exotic residents, while the petting zoo has friendlier inhabitants such as rabbits, pot bellied pigs, donkeys, miniature horses, goats, ducks and sheep. The facility also serves as a rehabilitation center for injured and abandoned animals.

Picnicking is permitted. Allow 30 minutes minimum. Mon.-Sat. 10-5, Sun. 1-6, May-Dec. (weather permitting); closed holidays. Admission $5.50; ages 2-13, $3.50. VI. Phone (705) 779-2423.

CASINOS

• **Casino Sault Ste. Marie** is at 30 Bay St. W. Mon.-Wed. 9 a.m.-4 a.m., Thurs.-Sun. 24 hours. Phone (705) 759-0100 or (800) 826-8946.

SEAGRAVE (G-9)

NORTHWOOD BUFFALO & EXOTIC ANIMAL RANCH, 2192 Cookson Ln., is a 24-hectare (60-acre) walk-through park featuring exotic animals, including buffaloes, wolves, bears, monkeys, deer and many species of large cats as well as birds of prey. Allow 30 minutes minimum. Daily 10-5, Victoria Day weekend to mid-Oct. Admission $10; over 59, $9; ages 3-12, $8. Phone (905) 985-2738 to verify prices.

SEVERN BRIDGE (F-8)

MUSKOKA WILDLIFE CENTRE is at 1266 Hwy. 11N. The 20-hectare (50-acre) nature center features resident animals, many socialized and hand-raised, who cannot be returned to the wild. Among the rescued creatures, which can be seen in both indoor and outdoor exhibits, are birds of prey, bobcats, lynx, moose, foxes and wolves.

Picnicking is permitted. Daily 10-6, Victoria Day weekend-second Mon. in Oct.; daily noon-5, during Mar. school break and in late Dec.; Sat.-Sun. noon-5 (weather permitting), rest of year. Admission $8.75; over 64 and ages 13-17, $6.75; ages 2-12, $4.75; family rate (two adults and up to three children) $27. VI. Phone (705) 689-0222.

SHARON (F-4)

SAVE SHARON TEMPLE NATIONAL HISTORIC SITE AND MUSEUM, 18974 Leslie St., features an unusual three-story re-creation of Solomon's temple built by a pioneer Quaker sect, the Children of Peace. Now a national historic site, its grounds encompass several historic buildings in a park like setting. Guided 1-hour tours provide a history of the group's musical, artistic and political contributions to Canada. Special events are held throughout the season.

Tours are given Thurs.-Sun. 10-4:30, mid-May to mid-Oct.; closed holidays except July 1. Last tour leaves 1 hour before closing. Admission $5, under 16 free with an adult. MC, VI. Phone (905) 478-2389.

SHELBURNE (F-3) pop. 4,122

Incorporated in 1879, Shelburne was named after the Earl of Shelburne, a British statesman whose goal was to end the hostility between Canada and Great Britain as well as Canada and the United States. The Dufferin County community's recreational opportunities include fishing, horseback riding and nature trails for bicycling and walking, including access to the Bruce Trail just east of town. Winter brings opportunities for downhill and cross-country skiing, snowshoeing and snowmobiling.

Country music fans throng to this small rural town in early August for 4 days of traditional tunes, barbecue and a parade during the Canadian Open Old Time Fiddle Championship.

The Hills of Headwaters Tourism Association—Shelburne: P.O. Box 295, Orangeville, ON, Canada L9W 2L0; phone (519) 942-0314 or (800) 332-9744.

SIMCOE (I-3) pop. 14,175

Simcoe is in the center of an agricultural area known for tobacco, vegetables and small fruit. Bass and trout fishing can be enjoyed in nearby Long Point Bay. More than 65 Christmas scenes illuminate Simcoe's parks every evening throughout December during Christmas Panorama.

Simcoe Chamber of Commerce: 95 Queensway Dr., Simcoe, ON, Canada N3Y 2M8; phone (519) 426-5867.

CARILLON TOWER, jct. Wilson Ave. and Norfolk St. S. on the banks of the Lynn River, is a memorial to those who died in World Wars I and II. Daily 24 hours. Phone for concert schedule. Phone (519) 426-8600.

THE EVA BROOK DONLY MUSEUM AND NORFOLK COUNTY ARCHIVES, 109 Norfolk St. S., is in a building dating from the 1840s. The museum houses pioneer, Victorian and early 20th-century relics from the surrounding area. An archives library contains local history records and an extensive collection of family history resources for Ontario and early America.

A restored 1860s garden and a children's discovery room also are featured. Allow 30 minutes minimum. Tues.-Sat. 10-4:30. Museum admission $4, students $2. Archives $5. Phone (519) 426-1583.

NORFOLK ARTS CENTRE AT LYNNWOOD NATIONAL HISTORIC SITE is downtown at 21 Lynnwood Ave. The 1851 Greek Revival house is home to Lynnwood Arts Centre, featuring art exhibitions, children's programs, concerts and a film series, and the Norfolk County Sports Hall of Recognition, celebrating the area's sporting heritage and sports heroes. The site is surrounded by a park that includes a sculpture garden and rare Carolinian species. Tues.-Sat. 10-4; closed holidays. Donations. Phone (519) 428-0540.

SMITHS FALLS (E-11) pop. 9,140

Smiths Falls' location at the halfway point on the Rideau Canal, which runs from Ottawa to Kingston, made it an important trade center during the 19th century. The Rideau Canal and its environs are now a source of recreational activities, including boating, picnicking, jogging and biking. Approximately 60 lakes within a 64-kilometre (40-mi.) radius of Smiths Falls add to the leisure possibilities.

Smiths Falls and District Chamber of Commerce: 77 Beckwith St. N., Smiths Falls, ON, Canada K7A 2B8; phone (613) 283-1334 or (800) 257-1334.

HERITAGE HOUSE MUSEUM, Old Slys Rd., about 2 km (1.2 mi.) s.e. via Jasper Ave., is in a restored 1860 house. The restoration and furnishings reflect the lifestyle of the prominent mill owner whose family occupied the house 1867-93. Local history displays, traveling art shows and educational exhibits are among the museum's offerings.

Allow 30 minutes minimum. Daily 10:30-4:30, May 1-Dec. 24; Mon.-Fri. 10:30-4:30, rest of year. Closed Jan. 1 and Dec. 25. Admission $4; over 64, $3.50; ages 6-18, $3; family rate (two adults and two children) $12. Phone (613) 283-8560.

HERSHEY CANADA INC., 1 Hershey Dr. off Hwy. 43E, offers self-guiding tours with descriptions of the processes and machinery used in the production of chocolate. Production can be seen during weekdays only before 2:30. Three 5-minute videotapes are shown continuously. Mon.-Fri. 9-6, Sat. 9-5, Sun. 10-5; closed Jan. 1, Good Friday, Easter and Dec. 25-26. Free. Phone (613) 283-3300, ext. 245.

RIDEAU CANAL MUSEUM, 34 Beckwith St. S., is in a restored stone mill building in the town center. Built 1826-32 as a military supply route between Ottawa and Kingston, the canal joins the Rideau and Cataraqui rivers. Displays depict the history of the canal and include photographs, dioramas, watercolors and audiovisual presentations.

Allow 30 minutes minimum. Daily 10-4:30, mid-May to mid-Oct.; Sat.-Sun. 10-4:30, mid-Oct. to mid-Dec.; by appointment rest of year. Admission $3; over 60, $2.75; ages 6-18, $2; family rate (two adults and up to four school-age children) $10. Phone (613) 284-0505.

SMITHS FALLS RAILWAY MUSEUM, 90 William St. W., is housed in the 1914 Smiths Falls Canadian Northern railway station. This museum contains rolling stock, steam and diesel locomotives, restored cabooses, equipment and a 1947 Cadillac converted to railroad use.

Guided tours are available. Allow 30 minutes minimum. Daily 10-4:30, July 1-Labour Day; Sat.-Sun. 10-4:30, Victoria Day weekend-June 30 and day after Labour Day-second Mon. in Oct. Phone ahead to confirm hours. Museum admission $5; over 64 and ages 12-17, $3; ages 3-11, $2. MC, VI. Phone (613) 283-5696.

SOMBRA (I-6)

A small village on the banks of the St. Clair River, Sombra offers car ferry service to the United States (Marine City, Mich.) daily all year from 6:40 a.m. to 10:30 p.m. (weather permitting). The fare is $5 for cars, $3 for motorcycles and $2 for pedestrians; trucks are charged by weight.

Tourism Sarnia-Lambton—Sombra: 556 N. Christina St., Sarnia, ON, Canada N7T 5W6; phone (519) 336-3232 or (800) 265-0316.

Shopping areas: Boutiques housed in wooden Victorian houses and Tudor-style courtyard shops entice shoppers in this hamlet along the St. Clair Parkway.

SOMBRA MUSEUM, 3470 St. Clair Pkwy., is in a late 19th-century pioneer house. Displayed are marine, military, Indian and pioneer items. Daily 11-4:30, July-Aug.; 1-4 in June and Sept; Sat.-Sun. 1-4, Victoria Day weekend-May 31; by appointment rest of year. Admission $3; ages 6-17, $1; family rate $7. Phone (519) 892-3982.

SOUTHAMPTON (G-7) pop. 3,360

A resort town on Lake Huron at the mouth of the Saugeen River with 4 miles of sandy beaches, Southampton offers such recreational pursuits as salmon and trout fishing, boating, bicycling, hiking, tennis, snowmobiling, snowshoeing and cross-country skiing. A mile offshore is Chantry Island, a bird sanctuary and home to one of the area's many restored lighthouses.

Each year in October residents celebrate the autumn harvest with Pumpkinfest in nearby Port Elgin. The festival features more than 40 events as well as the world weigh-off competition.

Southampton Visitor Information Centre: 201 High St., P.O. Box 261, Southampton, ON, Canada N0H 2L0; phone (519) 797-2215 or (888) 757-2215.

Self-guiding tours: Brochures outlining a historic walking tour of the town can be obtained from the visitor information center.

BRUCE COUNTY MUSEUM & ARCHIVES, 33 Victoria St. N., 1 blk. n. and 1 blk. e. of Hwy. 21, is in a three-building complex. Galleries display antique farm and dentistry equipment, military memorabilia, 19th-century furniture, musical instruments, items from the Lake Huron shipping industry, Native artifacts, and photographs and models of ships. The main gallery has antique silver, china and crystal and quilts.

An 1870 log school, log cabin and re-created general store also are on the grounds. **Note:** The museum is closed for expansion and restoration. Reopening is planned for July 2005. Exhibits can be seen before that date in a temporary facility at 69 Victoria St. N. in the G.C. Huston Public School; phone ahead to confirm schedule. Picnic facilities are available. Allow 1 hour minimum. Mon.-Sat. 10-5, Sun. 1-5; closed Jan. 1 and Dec. 25-27. Phone to verify hours in late Dec.

Admission $6, over 59 and students with ID $5, family rate $15. Rates may vary during special events and exhibitions. VI. Phone (519) 797-2080, or (866) 318-8889 in Canada.

STIRLING (F-10) pop. 4,887

HASTINGS COUNTY MUSEUM OF AGRICULTURAL HERITAGE is at 437 Front St. W. at the Fair Grounds, following signs. The area's agricultural heritage is illustrated through displays of all aspects of farming and farm life. Restored buildings house collections of vintage steam engines and tractors, a 1940s restaurant and exhibits about harvesting and tilling. Visitors also can see an apple orchard, bees busy making honey and a furnished farmhouse.

Picnicking is permitted. Allow 1 hour, 30 minutes minimum. Daily 10-4, Victoria Day-Labour Day. Admission $2, under 12 free. Phone (613) 395-0015.

STRATFORD (G-1)
pop. 29,676, elev. 364 m/1,194'

The Stratford Festival of Canada began under a tent in 1953 when Shakespeare's plays were produced for the first time along the North American Stratford-upon-Avon River. Today it is ranked among the three great English-speaking theaters in the world. The season spans 30 weeks featuring Shakespeare, classical and contemporary productions in four indoor theaters.

Find Hotels As Easy As 1-2-3-4-5!

For reliable hotel stays matched to your needs, every time, use AAA's valuable two-part rating system:

- First, rest assured that *every* hotel designated **AAA Approved** upholds qualities like cleanliness, service, and value – important to members.

- Focus your selection using the descriptive **AAA Diamond Ratings** our professional evaluators give each Approved property, from basic to luxury – from one Diamond to five Diamonds.

For AAA members, finding the right hotel is that easy! Locate AAA Approved and Diamond rated properties in the TourBook® listings, in print and on aaa.com, and look for the bold red AAA logo on signage and billboards.

Read about **AAA Lodging Diamond Rating** requirements on page **16**.

Show Your Card
Approved Lodging

An expansive park system encompasses 1,000 acres throughout the city with areas for picnicking and walking. Several galleries display a wide range of art and exhibitions are regularly presented in the park. The downtown area offers distinctive shops and eateries.

Tourism Stratford: 47 Downie St., Stratford, ON, Canada N5A 1W7; phone (519) 271-5140 or (800) 561-7926.

GALLERY STRATFORD, 54 Romeo St., is in a heritage building surrounded by two parks. The gallery presents more than 14 exhibitions of traditional and contemporary works of art by local and international artists annually. Gardens accent the grounds of the gallery. Tues.-Sun. 9-5, May-Aug.; Tues.-Sun. 10-4, Sept.-Nov.; Tues.-Fri. and Sun. 1-4, Sat. 10-4, rest of year. Hours may vary; phone ahead to confirm schedule. Admission $5, over 64 and students with ID $4, under 13 free. MC, VI. Phone (519) 271-5271.

STRATFORD FESTIVAL OF CANADA productions are staged at the Festival Theatre, 55 Queen St.; the Tom Patterson Theatre, 111 Lakeside Dr.; the Avon Theatre, 99 Downie St.; and the Studio Theatre, jct. Waterloo and George sts. The internationally acclaimed Stratford Festival presents a 6-month repertory season in four distinctive venues, encompassing the works of William Shakespeare, other great playwrights of the past, contemporary drama and musical theater.

Among the works on the 2005 playbill are "The Tempest," "As You Like It," "The Lark," "Into the Woods," "Fallen Angels," "Cat on a Hot Tin Roof," "The Brothers Karamazov," "Orpheus Descending," "Measure for Measure," "Edward II" and "Hello, Dolly!"

Guided tours of the costume warehouse, the Festival Theatre and gardens are available; phone for schedule and prices. Visitors' Guides are available beginning February 1.

Ask about preview performances, fall discounts, senior and student discounted performances and family rates. Inquire about refund policies. Performances in all four theaters are Tues.-Sun. at 2 and 8,

Apr. 19-Nov. 6. Ticket prices range from $29.15 to $111.72. AX, MC, VI. For additional information phone (519) 273-1600 or (800) 567-1600.

STRATFORD-PERTH MUSEUM is at 270 Water St. This interactive museum in the former Stratford Normal School depicts the history of Perth County and Stratford. Displays feature the military history of the county, textiles and a children's area with an 1827 printing press. Changing exhibits also are featured. Allow 30 minutes minimum. Tues.-Sat. 10-5, Sun.-Mon. noon-5, May-Aug.; Tues.-Sat. 10-4, rest of year. Closed holidays. Donations. Phone (519) 271-5311.

STRATTON (C-8) pop. 447

SAVE **KAY-NAH-CHI-WAH-NUNG   HISTORICAL CENTRE** is e. on Hwy. 11 to Shaw Rd., then 5 km (3 mi.) s.e., following signs. "The place of the long rapids" preserves a village and ceremonial burial sites of the First Nations Peoples, in particular the Ojibway. Built into the banks of the Rainy River, a museum has exhibits, murals and dioramas tracing this trading center's history; an aquarium features the sturgeon found in area waters. Tribal members provide tours along a 3-kilometre (2 mi.) wooded trail to the burial mound complex.

Picnicking is permitted. Food is available. Allow 1 hour, 30 minutes minimum. Wed.-Fri. 11-8, Sat.-Sun. 8-8, May-Sept. Admission $10; over 55, $7.50; ages 3-14, $6. AX, MC, VI. Phone (807) 483-1163.

SUDBURY (D-7) pop. 103,879

See map page 171.

Although originally the offspring of the Canadian Pacific Railway, the Sudbury area developed as a lumbering community before becoming a world-known center for mining, smelting, refining and geological science. Geologists believe the mineral-rich Sudbury Basin was formed 2 billion years ago when a huge meteorite struck. The area's heritage is recounted in several area museums and attractions.

The City of Greater Sudbury is the result of an amalgamation in 2001 of Sudbury and seven neighboring towns—Capreol, Nickel Centre, Onaping

Dynamic Earth

A new family attraction for everyone on the third planet from the sun.

⑤ Sudbury Greater Grand

www.sudburytourism.ca   1-877-304-8222

Falls, Rayside-Balfour, Sudbury, Valley East and Walden—forming the largest center in northern Ontario.

The 3,627 square kilometres (1,417 sq. mi.) of the new city encompass more than 300 lakes which offer swimming, fishing and boating opportunities. Two provincial parks, Windy Lake and Fairbank, are within the region (see Recreation Chart); three others are within an hour's drive. The area has 10 golf courses, 10 beaches and numerous tennis courts open to the public. In the winter the Sudbury Trail Plan offers 1,300 kilometres (810 mi.) of marked and groomed snowmobile trails that wind and loop through the region.

South of Sudbury off Hwy. 69 near Alban is French River Country. Originating in Lake Nipissing and emptying in Lake Huron, the French River provides anglers with the opportunity to reel in walleye, muskellunge, northern pike and large and small mouth bass.

The Sudbury Theatre Centre, 170 Shaughnessy St., presents live professional theater from September to May; phone (705) 674-8381. In the summer live theater and concerts are performed at Bell Park, an open-air theater at Paris and York streets. The park is also the summer host of the Northern Lights Festival Boreal, a multicultural musical event. Other popular events are the Cinéfest international film festival; the Garlic Festival; and the Blueberry Festival.

Sudbury Downs, 12 kilometres (8 mi.) north on Hwy. 144, then east on Montée Principale, offers live harness racing on Wednesday and Saturday, March through December; phone (705) 855-9001.

Note: Policies concerning admittance of children to pari-mutuel betting facilities vary. Phone for information.

Rainbow Country Travel Association: Sudbury Welcome Centre, 2726 Whippoorwill Ave., Sudbury, ON, Canada P3G 1E9; phone (705) 522-0104 or (800) 465-6655.

Shopping areas: The New Sudbury Centre Mall, 1349 La Salle Blvd., offers Sears. Southridge Mall is at Paris and Regent streets and features Zellers.

ANDERSON FARM MUSEUM, 8 km (5 mi.) w. on Hwy. 17, 1.5 km (.9 mi.) w. on Hwy. 55, then 1.5 km (.9 mi.) n. on Hwy. 24, is a restored Finnish dairy farm. Walking tours of seven buildings portray the life of a dairy family. Picnicking is permitted. Allow 1 hour minimum. Daily 10-4, May-Sept.; by appointment rest of year. Last tour begins 1 hour before closing. Admission $4; students with ID and ages 4-12, $2; family rate $10. Phone (705) 692-4448.

COPPER CLIFF MUSEUM, Balsam and Power sts., displays early Canadian furnishings and utensils in a log cabin. Tues.-Sun. 11-4, June-Aug. Donations. Phone (705) 692-4448.

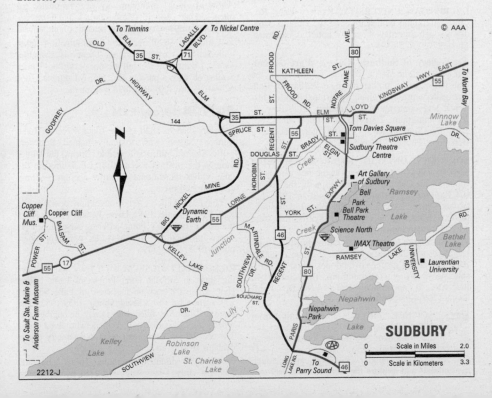

DYNAMIC EARTH is at 122 Big Nickel Rd., just n. of jct. Lorne St. Sudbury's mining heritage is explained through two exhibit galleries: One covers the geological forces that continually shape the Earth, and the other provides a three-level mine geared to children. A theater has a 20-minute audiovisual presentation tracing the 120-year mining history of the Sudbury area, with a hologram of miners explaining the difficulties their predecessors faced.

Then, as visitors descend seven stories in a glass-enclosed elevator, a multimedia show is projected onto rock walls and moving screens. During the following underground mine tour visitors meet miners from the past and present who relate mining stories. Outdoor trails with interpretive signage, a mining playground, scenic viewpoints and the Big Nickel monument, a local icon, also are part of the complex.

Picnicking is permitted. Food is available. Allow 2 hours minimum. Daily 9-6, late June-Labour Day; 9-5, late Apr.-late June; 10-4, early Mar.-late Apr. and day after Labour Day-late Oct. Last underground mine tour begins 1 hour before closing.

Admission $16; over 64 and ages 3-12, $13. Combination tickets are available with Science North, IMAX Theatre and Virtual Voyages Adventure Ride. Parking $4 mid-May through Labour Day; free rest of year. MC, VI. Phone (705) 523-4629, or (800) 461-4898 in Canada.

LAURENTIAN UNIVERSITY, Ramsey Lake Rd., offers 90-minute guided tours of the campus Monday through Saturday; 1 week's notice is requested. Phone (705) 673-6594.

Art Gallery of Sudbury (Galerie d'art de Sudbury), 251 John St. at Nelson, is housed in the mansion of early lumber magnate William J. Bell. The gallery presents changing art exhibits of historical and contemporary Canadian art. Allow 30 minutes minimum. Tues.-Fri. 1-5 (also Thurs.-Fri. 5-9), Sat.-Sun. noon-5; closed major holidays. Donations. Phone (705) 675-4871.

NORTHERN ONTARIO RAILROAD MUSEUM AND HERITAGE CENTRE is at the rail yard at 26 Bloor St. in Capreol. The museum, in the former CN Rail superintendant's home built in 1916, has artifacts, maps and photographs related to the railroading, lumbering and mining industries that were the city's main industries.

In addition to an HO gauge railroad display, a locomotive, a 19th-century wooden caboose and a 1912 railcar are displayed outdoors. Food is available. Allow 30 minutes minimum. Tues.-Sun. 11-4, June-Aug.; by appointment rest of year. Donations. Phone (705) 858-5050.

SCIENCE NORTH is 2 km (1.2 mi.) from Hwy. 69; take Paris St. to Ramsey Lake Rd. This hands-on facility looks at science as it occurs in everyday life. Visitors can see a 3-D film in an underground rock-walled cavern, touch live animals and explore the stars. A glass-enclosed butterfly gallery has about 400 free-flying butterflies as well as flowering plants.

Food is available. Allow 2 hours minimum. Daily 9-6, late June-Labour Day; 9-5, mid-May to late June; 10-4, early Mar. to mid-May and day after Labour Day-late Oct. Closed Jan. 1 and Dec. 24-26. Admission to science center $18; over 64 and ages 3-12, $15. A combination ticket that includes Virtual Voyages Adventure Ride, Dynamic Earth and the IMAX theater is available. An additional fee may be charged for special exhibits. AX, MC, VI. Phone (705) 523-4629, or (800) 461-4898 in Canada.

IMAX Theatre, 100 Ramsey Lake Rd., features a variety of films daily on a five-story screen backed by 7,600 watts of surround sound. Dinner packages and food are available. Allow 1 hour minimum. Showtimes vary with the season; phone ahead. Admission $8; over 64 and ages 3-12, $6.50. A combination ticket with Science North and Virtual Voyages Adventure Ride is available. AX, MC, VI. Phone (705) 523-4629, or (800) 461-4898 in Canada.

Virtual Voyages Adventure Ride, 100 Ramsey Lake Rd., features a motion simulator that moves with high-resolution animation on a big screen. The ride lasts 10-15 minutes. Note: The ride is not recommended for pregnant women or those with heart and back problems or other physical impairments. Allow 1 hour minimum to accommodate for queues. Daily noon-9; closed Jan. 1 and Dec. 24-26. Show times vary with the season; phone ahead.

Admission $6.50 per ride. A combination ticket with Science North and IMAX Theatre is available. Under 1 metre (39 in.) tall are not permitted. Under 5 must be with a parent. AX, MC, VI. Phone (705) 523-4629, or (800) 461-4898 in Canada.

SUTTON (F-9) pop. 6,324

Established in 1820 on the Black River of Lake Simcoe, Sutton was originally named Bouchers Mills. The old mill is still visible. During the winter months the town is a center for ice fishing on the lake. Other recreational activities include boating, canoeing and hiking.

The Lake Simcoe Arts Foundation operates the Red Barn Theatre, Lake Drive E. and Hedge Road in nearby Jackson's Point, offering several professional productions late May to mid-September; phone (905) 722-3249.

EILDON HALL MUSEUM is off Hwy. 48E following signs to Sibbald Point Provincial Park. Eildon Hall, within the park on the shore of Lake Simcoe, was owned by the Sibbald family 1839-1952. The renovated home is filled with family belongings and reflects the generations of farmers who lived there. The original log house, expanded to a country estate, contains artwork and interesting artifacts.

Allow 30 minutes minimum. Tues.-Thurs. and Sat. 1-4, July 1-late Aug. Museum by donations.

Park admission $9.50 per private vehicle Tues.-Thurs., $15 on Sat. Phone (905) 722-0277 or (905) 722-8061. *See Recreation Chart and the AAA/CAA Eastern Canada CampBook.*

ST. GEORGE'S CHURCH is 4 km (3 mi.) e. on Hedge Rd. beside Sibbald Point Provincial Park. The Anglican/Episcopal church was built in 1877 in memory of Susan Sibbald, a sponsor of the first church built on this site in 1839. Stephen Leacock, author and humorist, and Mazo de la Roche, novelist, are buried in the churchyard. Cemetery open daily 8 a.m.-dusk, May-Oct. Phone ahead for church hours. Phone (905) 722-3726.

THESSALON (E-5) pop. 1,386

The lumbering industry took hold in Thessalon in the latter part of the 19th century due to the availability of natural resources. The town, incorporated in 1892, at one time supported six lumber companies whose products included pulpwood, veneer and hardboards.

Recreational activities available in the area include fishing and boating on Lake Huron and area lakes, hiking and bird-watching. Winter activities include cross-country skiing and snowmobiling.

Municipality of Huron Shores Office: 7 Bridge St., P.O. Box 460, Iron Bridge, ON, Canada P0R 1H0; phone (705) 843-2033.

Self-guiding tours: A 45-kilometre (28-mi.) driving tour takes visitors through the Kirkwood Forest past various sites including a fish hatchery, the Thessalon Township Heritage Park Museum, a nature trail and tree nursery; phone the Ministry of Natural Resources at (800) 667-1940.

THESSALON TOWNSHIP HERITAGE PARK MUSEUM, 4 km (2.5 mi.) n. on Hwy. 129, has four log buildings, pioneer relics, early Indian tools and displays pertaining to the late 1800s logging, fishing and farming industries. Allow 30 minutes minimum. Mon.-Tues. 10:30-3, Wed.-Sun. 10-5, July-Aug.; by appointment in June and Sept. Donations. Phone (705) 843-2033.

THOUSAND ISLANDS

A French explorer called this region "Thousand Islands" and, although the islands number more than 1,800, the name has stuck. Some of these islands in the St. Lawrence River are mere rocks, others the size of a village, many are privately owned, but most can harbor only a house or summer camp. Stone mansions and Colonial houses dot the islands, and historical markers commemorate the French and Indian War and the War of 1812.

Separated by an international boundary, this region in eastern Ontario and northwestern New York shares the St. Lawrence River and Lake Ontario in common. The region became popular with vacationers in the 1870s, as expansive summer homes and hotels began to dot the landscape, and it has remained a favorite getaway over the years.

Connecting the two countries is the Thousand Islands International Bridge, providing a link between I-81 in New York and Hwy. 401 in Ontario. The bridge was opened in 1938 in a gesture of the ongoing friendship between the two countries by Prime Minister William Lyon Mackenzie King and President Franklin Delano Roosevelt.

In a scenic area surrounded by woods and water, recreation has always been a draw. Visitors to the Thousand Islands from both sides of the border take advantage of the abundance of waterways for sailing, fishing, canoeing, boating and shipwreck scuba diving. Those more prone to activities on land have plenty to choose from as well, as hiking, bicycling, picnicking, snowmobiling, cross-country skiing, camping and bird-watching provide plenty of opportunities to enjoy the outdoors.

The best way to see the islands is to take a boat tour offered by the boat lines described under Gananoque, Kingston, Lansdowne and Rockport. The islands embrace St. Lawrence Islands National Park *(see place listing p. 162).* Between the spans of the Thousand Islands International Bridge is an observation tower *(see Hill Island p. 83).*

The 1000 Islands Parkway, winding 37 kilometres (23 mi.) from Gananoque to Brockville, is an exceptionally scenic way to see the region by car. Another option is the St. Lawrence Recreational Trail, paralleling the river's shore for 50 kilometres (31 mi.) between Morrisburg and Cornwall. In addition to the cities mentioned above, other towns in the Thousands Islands listed individually are Ingleside and Prescott.

1000 Islands Gananoque Chamber of Commerce—Thousand Islands: 10 King St. E., Gananoque, ON, Canada K7G 1E6; phone (613) 382-3250 or (800) 561-1595.

DID YOU KNOW

The space shuttle arm was designed and built in Ontario.

A Truly Canadian Experience

Travelers have selected Thunder Bay, Ontario as one of the Top Ten Best Destinations around Lake Superior!

Call for your FREE Vacation Package and enter to win a Getaway in Thunder Bay.

CITY OF Thunder Bay
Superior by Nature

Ask for Operator 110
www.ThunderBay.ca 1-800-MOST-FUN

Live Canada's History

FORT WILLIAM HISTORICAL PARK NWC

Thunder Bay • Ontario • Canada
Step into the Past - to the Year 1815!

- Paddle a Voyageur Canoe
- Dine in the Historic Cantine
- Tour 42 Buidings
- Shop in the Trading Post

"Top Ten Attraction in Canada" - Toronto Star
Open Daily: Mid-May to mid-Oct.

Call: (807) 473-2344
www.fwhp.ca

ONTARIO

THUNDER BAY (C-12) pop. 109,016

In 1970 Fort William and adjacent Port Arthur combined to form Thunder Bay, one of Canada's newest cities and its third largest port. At the head of navigation on Lake Superior, Thunder Bay's fine harbor area has storage facilities for more than 100 million bushels of grain.

The International Friendship Gardens, at Victoria Avenue and Hyde Park Avenue in Chapples Park, is a network of individually landscaped gardens designed by and representing various ethnic groups. Striking scenery, on both the mainland and the island that protects the bay, surrounds the city. Mount McKay—on the Ojibway Reservation, south on Hwy. 61B—offers fine views of Thunder Bay.

Commemorating the city's rustic past, the Great Rendezvous Pageant at Fort William Historical Park in early July re-enacts a fur traders' rendezvous. The Thunder Bay Military Museum (*see attraction listing*) recounts the military history of northwestern Ontario.

A 2.7-metre-high (9-ft.) bronze statue of Terry Fox is east of Thunder Bay at a scenic overlook on Hwy. 11/17. Fox, who lost a leg to cancer at 18, attempted a cross-country marathon in 1980 to raise money for cancer research. A recurrence of the disease forced him to abandon the run after completing 5,373 kilometres (3,339 mi.). Despite his resolve to finish, he died the following year. The monument, about 12 kilometres (7 mi.) west of where Fox halted his run, faces westward in the direction of his goal.

Tourism Thunder Bay: Terry Fox Information Centre, Hwy. 11/17 E., Thunder Bay, ON, Canada; phone (807) 983-2041 or (800) 667-8386. *See color ad.*

Shopping areas: The widest shopping selection in Thunder Bay is at Intercity Mall, 1000 Fort William Rd. Its 110 stores include Sears.

BOULEVARD LAKE, the end of N. Algoma St. in Thunder Bay's northside, is surrounded by 74 hectares (182 acres) of natural forest and well-maintained parkland. Recreational facilities include a supervised beach area, tennis courts, picnic areas, playground equipment, canoe and paddleboat rentals and a miniature golf course. The Bluffs Scenic Lookout affords an excellent view of the city and of The Sleeping Giant (*see attraction listing*), a rock formation. Food is available. Daily 10-dusk. Free.

CENTENNIAL BOTANICAL CONSERVATORY, 1.5 km (.9 mi.) n. at 1601 Dease St., behind Chapples Park, contains identified foliage and flowering plants. Featured are tropical vegetation, cacti, succulents and seasonal displays. Daily 1-4; closed Good Friday and Dec. 25-26. Free. Phone (807) 622-7036 or (807) 625-2351.

CENTENNIAL PARK, n. on Boulevard Lake Park Rd. to Arundel St., then .7 km (.5 mi.) e. to Centennial Park Rd., is on the south side of the expressway. Embracing 57 hectares (141 acres), the park is part of the whole parkland which includes about 769 hectares (1,900 acres), including Trowbridge Campground and Kinsman Park on the north side of the expressway.

The park offers more than 20 kilometres (12 mi.) of skiing, bicycling and walking trails cutting through stands of pine trees and mature forests. Current River runs through the park, offering a scenic walk as well as trout fishing and swimming.

Exhibits include an animal farm, a reproduction of a typical early 20th-century northern Ontario logging camp and a museum displaying logging tools and equipment of the era. The Muskeg Express narrow-gauge train runs throughout the park in summer. In the winter sleigh rides and iced toboggan slides are offered.

Picnic facilities and food are available. Park open daily 7:30 a.m.-9 p.m. Barnyard open 8 a.m.-dusk. Museum and logging camp open daily 11-7, Victoria Day weekend-Labour Day. Train operates Wed.-Sun. noon-4, late May-Labour Day. Park free. Train rides $2.50; ages 6-12, $1. Sleigh rides $85 per hour; reservations are required. Phone (807) 683-5762 or (807) 625-2351.

CHIPPEWA PARK, on the shore of Lake Superior, 11 km (7 mi.) s. via Hwy. 61, is a 121-hectare (299-acre) woodland offering a campground, a wildlife park, amusement rides and picnic facilities.

Wildlife park daily 11-8, July 1-Labour Day; Mon.-Fri. 11-4, Sat.-Sun. 11-8, in June. Amusement rides daily 1-8, July 1-Labour Day; Sat.-Sun. 1-8, in June. Park free. Wildlife park $2; ages 6-11, $1. Adult rides $2.25. Book of 30 coupons for children's rides $13.50 (two or four coupons per ride). Phone (807) 625-2119. *See Recreation Chart and the AAA/CAA Eastern Canada CampBook.*

FORT WILLIAM HISTORICAL PARK is on Broadway Ave., 4 km (2.5 mi.) s.w. of jct. hwys. 11B, 17B and 61, via Hwy. 61. This massive reconstruction of the early 19th-century inland headquarters of the North West Company features 42 structures on 10 hectares (25 acres), including period craft areas, a working farm, a Native encampment and the Great Hall. Costumed staff portray historic characters and re-enact events from the fur trade era of 1815.

The living-history interpretive program features scripted dramatic vignettes, craft activities, building interpretations, daily activities and canoe arrivals with musket or cannon salutes. Themed weekend highlights and special events are presented throughout the summer, fall and winter. Daily canoe rides are offered July through August. Walking tours are offered during the early summer and fall.

Guided tours are available. Food is available. Daily 10-6, June 12-Labour Day; 10-5, May 15-June 11 and day after Labour Day-Oct. 13. Visitor center opens at 9:30.

Admission June 12-Labour Day $12; over 59 and students with ID $10; ages 6-12, $9; family rate (two adults and two children) $34 (each additional

youth $6.50, each additional student $9). Admission rest of year $10; over 59 and students with ID $9; ages 6-12, $8; family rate (two adults and two children) $31 (each additional youth $5.50, each additional student $7). VI. Phone (807) 577-8461 or (807) 473-2344. *See color ad p. 174.*

HILLCREST PARK, off hwys. 11B and 17B on N. High St. near Red River Rd., is on an escarpment overlooking the southern section of the city. The park affords a fine view of the Sleeping Giant and the general harbor area; there also are sunken gardens with more than 70 varieties of flowers, and a playground. Daily dawn-dusk. Free.

PAIPOONGE MUSEUM is 14 km (9 mi.) w. on Hwy. 11/17, then 2 km (1.2 mi.) s. on Hwy. 130 at jct. Rosslyn Rd. The museum's name means "winter" in Ojibway, but its exhibits depict the life of pioneers who settled the area in the late 19th century. Tues.-Sun. 1-5, May-Aug. Admission $2; ages 6-12, $1. Phone (807) 939-1262.

THE SLEEPING GIANT, on Lake Superior, is part of a peninsula extending into the lake from the vast forest area to the northeast of the city. Prominent in Ojibway Indian legends, the rock formation, 11.25 kilometres (7 mi.) long and 335 metres (1,099 ft.) high, resembles a giant sleeping figure. The area offers nature trails, back-country roads for walking, bicycling and driving and picnicking opportunities.

THUNDER BAY ART GALLERY, on the Confederation College campus at 1080 Keewatin St. at Red Lake Rd., features a permanent collection of works by First Nations artists as well as changing exhibitions and shows. Tues.-Thurs. noon-8, Fri.-Sun. noon-5. Admission $3, over 64 and students with ID $1.50, under 12 free; free to all on Wed. Phone (807) 577-6427.

THUNDER BAY MILITARY MUSEUM is in the northern section of town at 317 Park Ave. This museum is dedicated to preserving, displaying and interpreting northwestern Ontario's army, navy and air force heritage. Allow 1 hour minimum. Tues. 2-4 and 7-10 p.m., Thurs. and Sun. 2-4, Fri. 2-4 and 6-8 p.m.; by appointment otherwise. Closed major holidays. Donations. Phone (807) 343-5175.

THUNDER BAY MUSEUM, 425 Donald St. E., tells the 10,000-year-old story of northwestern Ontario through artifacts such as clothing and tools, technologies, photographs and documents. Exhibits change frequently. Daily 11-5, June 15-Labour Day; Tues.-Sun. 1-5, rest of year. Closed Jan. 1 and Dec. 25-26. Admission $3; ages 6-17, $1.50. Phone (807) 623-0801 to verify schedule and rates.

CASINOS

- **Thunder Bay Charity Casino** is at 50 S. Cumberland St. Mon.-Thurs. 9 a.m.-4 a.m., Fri.-Sun. 24 hours. Phone (807) 683-1935 or (877) 656-4263.

TILLSONBURG (H-2) pop. 14,052

ANNANDALE NATIONAL HISTORIC SITE is at 30 Tillson Ave. Built in the 1880s in the Aesthetic style by E.D. Tillson, the first mayor of Tillsonburg, and his wife Mary Ann, the restored house features three floors with period rooms as well as galleries with changing exhibits about local history. Highlights of the home are hand-painted ceilings, inlaid floors, wall coverings, ornate mantles and stained glass.

Mon.-Fri. 9-4, Sat. noon-4, Sun. 1-4, July-Aug.; Mon.-Fri. 9-4, Sun. 1-4, rest of year. Closed some holidays. Admission $4; students with ID $3; ages 6-12, $2; family rate (parents and school-age children) $10. Phone (519) 842-2294.

TIMMINS (B-6) pop. 43,686, elev. 314 m/1,030'

One of Canada's largest cities in area, Timmins also boasts one of the richest silver-zinc mines in the world and a reputation as a major gold producer. The Porcupine Gold Rush of 1909 transformed "The Porcupine Gold Fields," as Timmins was formerly known, from a fur-trading center into a mining town virtually overnight.

Named after Noah Timmins, who developed most of the region's mining potential, the city is at the center of the Porcupine mining area, which produces yields of copper, nickel, lead, tin, cadmium, gold, silver and zinc. Residents also work in forest-based industries.

Timmins Chamber of Commerce: 76 McIntyre Rd., P.O. Box 985, Schumacher, ON, Canada P4N 7H6; phone (705) 360-1900.

SHANIA TWAIN CENTRE is off Hwy. 101 (Algonquin Blvd.) Park Rd. exit, then .4 km (.2 mi.) e. to 1 Shania Twain Dr. The interpretive center, which honors Timmins' most famous native, has awards won by the recording artist and some of her costumes as well as footage from interviews and shows.

Food is available. Allow 30 minutes minimum. Daily 9-6, July-Aug.; 10-5, rest of year. Closed Jan. 1 and Dec. 25-26. Admission $9; over 55 and ages 7-18, $7; family rate (four people) $32. A combination ticket with the Timmins Gold Mine Tour is available. AX, MC, VI. Phone (705) 360-8500 or (800) 387-8466.

TIMMINS GOLD MINE TOUR, .5 km (.3 mi.) s. off Hwy. 101 (Algonquin Blvd.) Park Rd. exit, then e. on Shania Twain Dr. following signs, takes visitors through an authentic gold mine. Former miners act as guides, explaining the various rock types, escape routes and equipment. The tour lasts about 3 hours and includes a videotape presentation about mining. Gold panning and a gold pouring demonstration also are offered. The Hollinger Townsite Home, on the mine site, is typical of miners' houses of the 1920s.

Mining gear is provided. Warm attire and comfortable walking shoes are suggested. Tours daily at 9:30, 11:30, 1:30 and 3, July-Aug.; Wed.-Sun. at 10:30 and 1:30, mid-May through June 30 and Sept.-Oct. Arrive 15 minutes before the tour starts Admission $19; over 55 and ages 7-18, $17; family rate (two adults and two children) $60. A combination ticket is available with the Shania Twain Centre. AX, MC, VI. Phone (705) 360-8500 or (800) 387-8466.

TIMMINS MUSEUM: NATIONAL EXHIBITION CENTRE, off Hwy. 101 at 70 Legion Dr. in South Porcupine, contains local historic displays, changing arts and crafts exhibits, films and mining

Even More Ways to Travel With Someone You Trust®

AAA's exciting line of kid's travel products offer children the opportunity to have fun and learn with games, puzzles, coloring and activity books while they travel.

Purchase AAA travel publications at participating AAA club offices, on www.aaa.com/barnesandnoble and in fine book stores.

machinery pre-dating the 1940s. Picnicking is permitted. Allow 30 minutes minimum. Mon.-Fri. 9-5, Sat.-Sun. 1-5, Victoria Day-Labour Day; Tues.-Fri. 9-noon and 1-5, Sat.-Sun. 1-5, rest of year. Closed Jan. 1-2 and Dec. 25-26. Free. Phone (705) 235-5066.

TIVERTON (G-7) pop. 743

BRUCE POWER VISITORS' CENTRE is 5 km (3 mi.) n. on Hwy. 21, then w. on CR 4, following signs. At the center, which overlooks Bruce Power's nuclear generating stations and the province's first commercial wind farm, nuclear energy and the production of electricity are explained through films, exhibits and hands-on displays. Picnic facilities are available. Mon.-Fri. 9-4; closed holidays. Free. Phone (519) 361-7777.

TOBERMORY (F-6)

At the tip of the Bruce Peninsula, Tobermory and its two harbors, known as Little Tub and Big Tub, have been a haven for ships since Scottish immigrants arrived in the mid-19th century. The harbors offered sanctuary from the autumn gales that sank dozens of ships in the treacherous channel to the north. Georgian Bay's frigid waters preserve the shipwrecks in much the same condition as the day they foundered on the channel's shoals and reefs.

The water's exceptional clarity and the legacy of shipping scattered over the bay's bottom have made Tobermory a scuba diver's mecca and the headquarters for Fathom Five National Marine Park (see place listing p. 72). The park includes 19 nearby islands and protects 22 shipwrecks within its boundaries. Bruce Peninsula National Park (see place listing p. 63) also has its headquarters at Tobermory.

In addition to the national parks, the area offers excellent fishing in local lakes and streams; canoeing and kayaking also are popular activities. As the western terminus for the 782-kilometre (470-mi.) Bruce Trail (the eastern terminus is in Queenston), Tobermory also is popular with hikers. Catering to the needs of its visitors, the town offers a variety of outfitters ranging from dive shops to charter fishing boats. Other recreational activities include camping, bird-watching and bicycling. Winter activities include snowmobiling and cross-country skiing.

There are three lighthouses in the area: Cove Island Lighthouse was constructed in 1855; Big Tub Lighthouse was built in 1885; and Flowerpot Island Lighthouse was built in 1896.

Tobermory Chamber of Commerce: P.O. Box 250, Tobermory, ON, Canada N0H 2R0; phone (519) 596-2452.

Shopping areas: Tobermory is popular for its art galleries, craft and specialty shops.

BLUE HERON V, off Hwy. 6 at Little Tub Harbour, is a glass-bottom boat making 1.5-hour sightseeing cruises to Flowerpot Island, Big Tub Lighthouse and two visible shipwrecks; visitors can pre-arrange a drop off at Flowerpot Island for hiking and exploring.

The glass-bottom *Great Blue Heron* makes 2-hour cruises around Fathom Five National Marine Park (see place listing p. 72), visiting shipwrecks, Devil Island shoals, a lighthouse and Flowerpot Island.

Flowerpot Island tours depart daily at 11, 1 and 3:30, mid-May through June 30 and day after Labour Day-second Mon. in Oct.; Mon.-Sat. at 9, 10:30, 12:15, 1:50, 3:25 and 5, Sun. times vary depending upon scuba diving expeditions, July 1-Labour Day. National park cruises depart daily at 11, 1:15 and 3:30, late July-Labour Day; daily at 11 and 2:30, Victoria Day weekend and July 1-late July; daily at 1, late June-June 30 and Oct. 8-10; Sat.-Sun. at 1, mid-June to late June. Schedules may vary; phone ahead. All cruises are weather permitting.

Flowerpot Island tour fare $20; ages 4-12, $10. Additional fare for Flowerpot Island drop-off $4. National park tour fare $22; ages 4-12, $12. MC, VI. Phone (519) 596-2999.

MV *SEAVIEW III* CRUISES, next to the ferry terminal, offers 90-minute trips aboard a glass-bottom, double-deck boat to Flowerpot Island, where there are striking water-eroded rock formations. The Big Tub Harbour shipwrecks are visible just below the surface. Visitors may disembark to explore the island and return with another group. There also is a 2-hour sunset cruise along the shoreline of Georgian Bay.

Sightseeing cruises depart daily at 9, 10:45, 12:30, 2, 3:30 and 5, July 1-Labour Day; schedule varies mid-May through June 30 and day after Labour Day to mid-Oct. (weather permitting). Sunset cruise departs daily, July 1-Labour Day; schedule varies in spring and fall.

Fare for either cruise $18; over 64, $16; ages 6-12, $10. Fee for disembarking at Flowerpot Island $4. Phone to verify fares. Reservations are recommended. MC, VI. Phone (519) 596-2950, or (519) 343-3073 during the off-season.

PENINSULA AND ST. EDMUNDS TOWNSHIP MUSEUM, 3 km (1.9 mi.) s. on Hwy. 6, houses early 20th-century photographs, furniture and memorabilia in a restored 1898 schoolhouse and 1875 log cabin. An extensive maritime exhibit focuses on the history of the Bruce Peninsula and displays items retrieved from various shipwrecks. Allow 30 minutes minimum. Daily 11-4, July 1-Labour Day; Sat.-Sun. 11-4, Victoria Day-June 30 and day after Labour Day-second Mon. in Oct. Phone ahead to verify hours. Donations. Phone (519) 596-2452.

Toronto

City Population: 2,481,494
Elevation: 172 m/566 ft.

Popular Spots

© Angelo Cavali / SuperStock

Those who have had a hand in building Toronto, Canada's largest city and premier inland port, are credited with possessing a resplendent flair for blending old and new—tinkering ever so slightly with what precedes and what succeeds, bridging the gap between past and present with a keen and patient sense of the future.

In no uncertain terms, the city is strikingly cosmopolitan and has maintained this distinction by wisely, lovingly and consistently refurbishing itself, staving off the urban deterioration that has traditionally eroded the foundations of other North American cities.

When a young French explorer named Étienne Brûlé discovered the site in 1615, he saw thick forests and a nourishing body of water, two important components for establishing a thriving settlement. Five years later the French trading post Fort Toronto was established, attracting a legion of explorers, traders and others in search of profit and power to the fertile, pristine area.

Thus began the struggle for overseas dominance between France and Great Britain. The end of the Seven Years' War in 1763 and the Treaty of Paris determined Toronto's allegiance to Britain, a partnership that would last indefinitely and leave a formidable impression on the city's defining and ofttimes enviable character. As the British entered their new stronghold, so did Loyalists from the United States, escaping the rebellion of their countrymen against the king of England in 1776.

In 1787 the site of Toronto was established when a tract of land was purchased from the Mississauga Indians for £1,700, plus gifts and trinkets. Lieutenant Governor John Graves Simcoe decided in 1793 that the location would become the provincial capital, and the new town was named York.

During the War of 1812 the hamlet was attacked by American forces, who burned the governmental buildings. The Speaker's mace, seized during the assault, was not returned until 1934.

Intense loyalty to Great Britain culminated in the formation of the Family Compact, a group of pro-British government leaders and their supporters, many of whom have been immortalized on street signs throughout downtown Toronto. The organization's ideals of complete allegiance to Britain permeated politics and the social strata. However, a slow, steady influx of immigrants began to enter the country, and a band of reformers espousing home rule, led by Scotsman William Lyon Mackenzie, took matters into its own hands. Mackenzie's caustic remarks against the Family Compact in his newspaper, the *Colonial Advocate,* precipitated his rise in the political arena and to the Upper Canada (Ontario) Legislature in 1828.

Always a colorful character, Mackenzie had a knack for grandiloquence and was repeatedly kicked out of—then re-elected to—political office. It wasn't until 1835 that Toronto (the new name bestowed upon the town in 1834) was incorporated and Mackenzie was chosen as mayor. Further

Getting There — *starting on p. 184*

Getting Around — *starting on p. 185*

What To See — *starting on p. 188*

What To Do — *starting on p. 199*

Where To Stay — *starting on p. 474 & p. 518*

Where To Dine — *starting on p. 506 & p. 541*

Centreville Amusement Park, Toronto Islands Park
© Jim Schwabel / PictureQuest

angered by Britain's control over Canada and by his mayoral defeat in 1836, Mackenzie spearheaded an unsuccessful revolt against the government in 1837, in which he and his followers hoped to capture Toronto. The advent of the Rebellions of 1837 in Ontario and Québec motivated the British government to unite the two provinces and form a more responsible government.

Railroads carting goods and people from place to place were making the world much smaller. Their presence accelerated Toronto's economic growth and aided the city in becoming the regional trading center. A treaty with the United States offering Canada free market trade below its southern border further advanced the city as a leader in industry, distribution and trade.

By the late 1800s Toronto's citizenry of nearly 200,000 enjoyed a boom in building and business. Both Timothy Eaton and Robert Simpson rode this solidifying wave of supply and demand by opening two of the most successful retail outlets in Canada. Eaton's Department Store (now Sears) offered low prices and money-back guarantees; Simpson's (now The Bay) offered excellent service.

As Toronto fought its way through pockets of dissent against Great Britain and attempted to get its bearings as a new city, foreigners began to settle in the area. The first wave of immigrants was from Ireland, settlers fleeing an 1847 famine. During the early 1900s Toronto's population exploded to more than 500,000 as new immigrants of Italian and Eastern European Jewish descent entered the city and set up shop. Toronto's large ethnic neighborhoods enjoyed rapid growth, and the city's prominent English character, maintained for so many years, began to diminish.

A population boom of Chinese immigrants escalated protectionist feelings and gave birth to the Chinese Exclusion Act of 1923. When it was repealed 24 years later, the country experienced an influx of European, Southeast Asian and South American immigrants to its shores, pushing the percentage of foreign-born residents to more than 40 percent. Although the British influence in Toronto is still evident today, it was the gradual blending of diverse ethnic groups that some believe has prevented Toronto's urban demise, in contrast to the free-for-all effects of immigration experienced by New York City.

From outpost to growing city, Toronto survived its numerous adversities and a devastating 1904 fire that burned much of the city's business district. In all instances its citizens rebuilt, sticking to the original blueprint of patient, sensible growth. In response to the explosion in immigrant population after World War II, and to the city's difficulty in meeting its citizens' needs, the Ontario Municipal Board in 1953 recommended the formation of the

The Informed Traveler

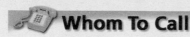 **Whom To Call**

Emergency: 911

Police (non-emergency): (416) 808-2222

Weather: (416) 661-0123

CAA Emergency Road Service: (416) 222-5222

Hospitals: Mount Sinai Hospital, (416) 596-4200; St. Joseph's Health Centre, (416) 530-6000; St. Michael's Hospital–Bond St. Site, (416) 360-4000; Sunnybrook & Women's College Health Sciences Centre–Sunnybrook Campus, (416) 480-6100; Toronto East General Hospital, (416) 461-8272.

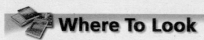 **Where To Look**

Newspapers

The Toronto area has five daily newspapers: the morning *Globe and Mail*, the *National Post*, the *Sun*, the *Star* and the *Corriere Canadese* (Italian). *Toronto Life* monthly magazine reports on restaurants and entertainment. *Where* has events, dining and shopping information. *Now* is a weekly magazine that provides information about city life, including movies, entertainment and events.

Radio

Toronto radio station 680 NEWS (680 AM) is an all-news station. Both CBC stations (94.1 FM and 99.1 FM) are members of National Public Radio.

Visitor Information

Tourism Toronto: 207 Queen's Quay W., P.O. Box 126, Toronto, ON, Canada M5J 1A7; phone (416) 203-2500 / (800) 499-2514 or (800) 363-1990.

Tourism Toronto is open Mon.-Fri. 9-5. The call center is open Mon.-Fri. 8:30-6, Sat. 9:30-6, Sun. 10-6 (also Mon.-Thurs. 6-8 p.m., July-Aug.).

The Ontario Travel Information Centre, in the Toronto Eaton Centre, Level 1, also dispenses travel material and handles tourist needs; the center is open Mon.-Fri. 10-9, Sat. 9:30-7 and Sun. noon-6.

 What To Pack

Most visitors are likely to be pleasantly surprised by Toronto's weather. The city's climate is not at all like the chilly stereotype of Canadian weather. Its geographical location on Lake Ontario is a moderating factor, and although heavy snowfalls can occur, such occasions are rare. Summer temperatures can reach the 90s in July and August, and mid-May to early June is considered by some travelers as the best time to visit. *For additional information see temperature chart p. 49.*

Even though snow is a possibility during a winter visit, it does not cause the city to come to a grinding stop; Toronto is well-equipped

© Gibson Stock Photography

for snow removal. Be sure to bring sturdy, waterproof boots, lots of warm clothes that can easily be layered, a heavy coat, gloves and a warm hat.

Warm summer temperatures can be accompanied by sticky humidity. Wear airy cotton clothing, comfortable walking shoes, sunglasses and a hat. Always bring along a windbreaker or lightweight sweater for cooler evenings.

Sales Tax: The federal Goods and Services Tax is 7 percent and applies to most goods, food/beverages and services, including hotel and motel accommodations. The Provincial Sales Tax is 8 percent on goods and restaurant food only, while the Room Tax is 5 percent on most hotel and motel accommodations. The Alcoholic Beverage Tax is 10 percent.

Metropolitan Council, a federated form of government. The council tackled such key issues as public services on a united front, while allowing local municipalities to retain some degree of independence.

During the 1940s and '50s wealth and prosperity enveloped the city. The first subway was opened, highways were built and suburbia went on a frenzied spending spree. Ethnic and intellectual diversity challenged the traditional puritanic beliefs and attitudes of Torontonians, and eventually forced the old guard to reconsider its rigid standards.

Much maligned at times, Toronto has been referred to as smug, prim and proper, and sanctimonious by outsiders and insiders alike. For decades on Sunday it was impossible to get an alcoholic drink or to while away your time shopping. Some stores were even forced to board up their windows so residents couldn't window shop on the Sabbath. Today, a more relaxed atmosphere prevails. If a store is closed on Sunday, it is by choice. Most shops, however, are open 7 days a week, and retail liquor stores are now permitted to do business on Sunday.

Toronto was the fastest growing North American city in the 1970s and was admired for its energy, synergism and innovative outlook. Self-imposed limits on building size and an awareness of the need to preserve its heritage changed the Toronto skyline. A 1971 proposal to build the Spadina Expressway failed miserably after residents and politicians alike voiced their opinion in favor of balanced and responsible development.

One would expect these tight reins to create a monotonous skyline—one filled with stodgy, brusque buildings void of personality and life. And indeed Toronto's architectural style initially tended toward sameness, but newer commercial buildings are bold and inviting and sport the distinctive signature of some of the world's most respected designers. Modern glass skyscrapers and the CN Tower now are downtown focal points, posing striking contrasts to the Victorian-era, Romanesque-style Ontario Legislative Buildings that sedately preside over the elegant lawns of nearby Queen's Park.

The look, feel and friendliness of this shining city attract millions of visitors each year to its shores, theaters, glowing nightlife and spirited ethnic neighborhoods. It is a city that has made deliberate changes to meet the growing needs of its citizens. An enviable gemstone, Toronto's accomplishments are proudly reflected on Lake Ontario.

© britishcolumbiaphotos / Alamy Images

Destination Toronto

Casa Loma, Toronto. The secret passages, tunnels and towers of this Scottish baronial castle may evoke memories of childhood fairy tales. (See listing page 190)

*T*o the Huron Indians, the site that became Toronto was a "meeting place." The French desired it for the fur trade. And British influence brought prosperity.

© 2004 Ontario Tourism

*D*iscover for yourself Toronto's perpetual allure. Landmarks old and new preserve the heritage of a cosmopolitan megacity bent on maintaining balance, in spite of progress.

© Paul A. Souders / Corbis

Ontario Science Centre, Toronto. Pretending to be an astronaut is just one of the many ways to have fun and learn about science at this very hands-on museum. (See listing page 195)

*P*laces included in this AAA Destination City:

Vaughan ●

400
407
427
427
403
QEW

Some municipalities in Ontario have combined or soon will combine with neighboring cities. These mergers will eliminate some existing cities and may affect street names, addresses and political boundaries referenced in this guide. For further information, please contact Ontario governing agencies or the local CAA club.

Black Creek Pioneer Village, Toronto.
This re-created 19th-century village
appears much the same today as it did
when it was settled by the early pioneers
of Upper Canada. (See listing page 189)

© 2004 Ontario Tourism

© 2004 Ontario Tourism

Royal Ontario Museum,
Toronto.
Canada's largest
museum features two
buildings filled with
more than 5 million art,
archeology and science
artifacts. (See listing
page 195)

Richmond Hill

1

Markham

ETR

Unionville

407

48

ETR

401

401

Toronto

See Vicinity map page 185

Centreville Amusement Park,
Toronto.
On an island in Toronto's harbor, this turn-of-the-20th-
century-style park offers more
than 30 rides and attractions.
(See listing page 198)

© 2004 Ontario Tourism

Getting There

By Car

The main approach routes from the south pass through either Buffalo or Detroit. When traveling from Buffalo, follow the Queen Elizabeth Way (QEW), which becomes the Gardiner Expressway near the city limits, to downtown Toronto.

The most direct route from Detroit is Hwy. 401 (the Macdonald-Cartier Freeway), which enters north Toronto. To reach the business district from Hwy. 401, exit at the Hwy. 427 interchange, then travel south to the Gardiner Expressway East.

The principal northern approaches to Toronto are Hwy. 400 from Barrie, Hwy. 404 from Newmarket and Hwy. 401 from Montréal and the Thousand Islands area. To gain access to the downtown area from Hwy. 401, take the exit onto the Don Valley Parkway and proceed south.

Air Travel

Lester B. Pearson International Airport is about 32 kilometres (20 mi.) northwest of downtown Toronto in nearby Mississauga. Named after a former Canadian prime minister and Nobel Peace Prize winner, Canada's busiest airport caters to airlines serving 300 destinations in 60 countries. To better serve the needs of its air travelers, the airport is undergoing a 10-year redevelopment program. Begun in 1999, the project entails combining two terminals into one, adding a new parking garage and two new runways and improving road accessibility.

To reach Toronto from the airport, use the Macdonald-Cartier Freeway (Hwy. 401), the Airport Expressway (Hwy. 409) or Hwy. 427. Hwy. 427 moves traffic south to the Gardiner Expressway; take the expressway east and you'll be in the center of the city. Although the airport is only a short distance away, be aware the trip into town could take more than an hour during weekday rush hours (7-9 a.m. and 4-7 p.m.).

Airport Express buses provide service to many downtown hotels and leave every 20 to 30 minutes; one-way fare is $15.50. Phone (905) 564-6333 for exact stops and additional information. An alternative bus to downtown Toronto is provided by the Toronto Transit Commission (TTC).

Taxis average $43 one way. Driving time is 45 to 90 minutes, more during rush hours. Cars with "TIA" on the license plates are the only ones authorized to shuttle passengers from Pearson. Limousine service also is available.

The Toronto City Centre Airport, on the Toronto Islands just south of downtown, handles commuter flights from Canada and the United States. A ferry at Bathurst Street shuttles visitors across the Western Channel; phone (416) 203-6942 for more information.

Several major rental car agencies serve the Toronto area. Be advised that in some cases you must be 25 or older to rent a car in Toronto. Car rental arrangements should be made before you depart. Your local AAA/CAA club can provide this assistance or additional information. Hertz, (416) 620-9620, (800) 263-0600 in Canada, or (800) 654-3131 out of Canada, offers discounts to CAA and AAA members.

Rail Service

Amtrak operates daily trains from Washington, D.C., New York and Chicago to Toronto. Passengers disembark at Union Station, near Front Street between Bay and York streets. Phone (800) 872-7245 for fare and schedule information.

Via Rail provides service to Canadian cities, including Windsor (opposite Detroit) and Sarnia (opposite Port Huron, Mich.) as well as to Buffalo, N.Y., from Union Station, 65 Front St. W.; phone (416) 366-8411 or (888) 842-7245.

Buses

Daily bus service connects Toronto with all sections of Canada and with many cities in the United States. Buses arrive and depart the Toronto Coach Terminal, 610 Bay St., north of City Hall; phone (416) 393-7911.

LESTER B. PEARSON INTERNATIONAL AIRPORT

To Brampton

Airport Rd

409

To Vaughan

427

Dixon Rd

Terminal 3

New Terminal (under long-term redevopment)

Terminal 1

Terminal 2

N

© 2004 maps.com

Getting Around

Street System

Expressways form an inner belt around the city. Traveling east and west are the Gardiner Expressway, skirting the southern edge of the city and downtown area, and the Macdonald-Cartier Freeway (Hwy. 401), in the north, as well as the 407 ETR, Ontario's first toll road, linking Burlington in the west with Pickering in the east. On the west, extending from the Macdonald-Cartier Freeway to the Gardiner Expressway, is Hwy. 427; on the east is the Don Valley Parkway.

Toll payments for those who use the 407 ETR are not collected in the usual way at a toll booth; as you travel the expressway, a photo of your license

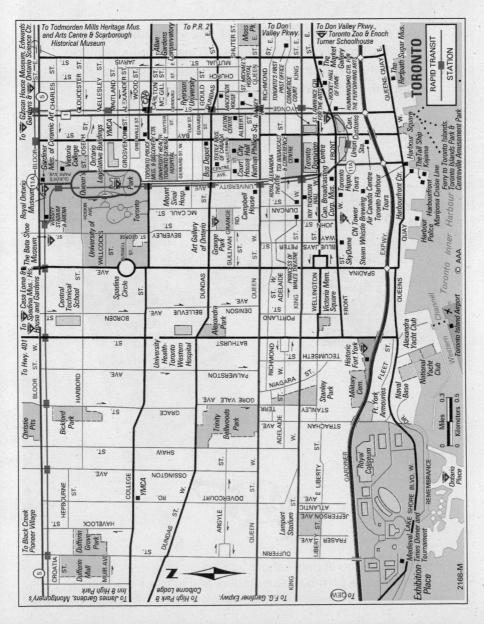

186

Even More Ways to Travel With Someone You Trust®

AAA publishes over 150 great titles including a full line of specialty travel guides. These books provide information ranging from how to pack a suitcase to where the best dog parks are located.

Purchase AAA travel publications at participating AAA club offices, on www.aaa.com/barnesandnoble and in fine book stores.

plate is taken and a bill for the amount due is mailed to your home address. The cost depends on the type of vehicle you were driving, the distance traveled and whether a transponder was · used; phone (888) 407-0407 for additional information.

Toronto proper is laid out somewhat like New York City, in an easy-to-follow grid pattern. Yonge Street (pronounced "Young"), the major north-south artery, determines which cross streets earn the distinction of east and which are considered west. The main east-west thoroughfare is Bloor Street. Northern numbering of streets begins at the lakefront. Successful maneuvering along the city's streets may be hampered by the lack of numbered routes, which let you follow their ascending or descending order. However, Toronto streets are easy to figure out as long as you have a good map.

Try to time your arrival for midmorning, midday or after the evening rush hour since it is easier to negotiate high-speed expressways and unfamiliar streets without excessive numbers of vehicles on the roads. Visitors may want to avoid driving in the business district during rush hour, 7-9 a.m. and 4-7 p.m.

, Unless otherwise posted, the downtown speed limit is 50 kilometres per hour (30 mph) and 25 kilometres per hour (15 mph) in all parks. Right turns on red are legal unless otherwise posted. Pedestrians using designated crosswalks **always** have the right-of-way. Pass all streetcars on the right, except on one-way streets or when the streetcars are stopped.

Parking

When visiting a large metropolitan city like Toronto, it's always wise not to do the driving yourself, as traffic usually and understandably moves slowly in busy downtown areas, particularly during rush hours. Finding a parking spot can be difficult, and parking in excess of 3 hours is prohibited on all roads, unless other parking prohibitions are posted. If you fail to obey these regulations, you may receive a parking ticket or have your vehicle towed.

Garage rates run $1.50-$5 an hour, with an average maximum of $12-$15 per day. Rates are sometimes lower on Sundays and after 6 p.m., when downtown workers head home leaving behind empty parking spaces.

Public parking lots are marked by a green sign bearing a large "P" and are scattered throughout the city. The most convenient are Nathan Phillips Square (City Hall) garage, University garage (at University Avenue and York Street) and the St. Lawrence Market garage (on Front Street). Be mindful of No Parking signs; the city adheres to a strict tow-away policy.

Taxis and Limousines

As in any large city, traveling by taxi can be costly. The initial or "flag drop" fare is $2.75, then 25c for each additional .19 kilometre (.12 mi.). You

CityPass

CityPass offers savings to those who plan visits to many Toronto attractions. The pass covers admission to six sites: Art Gallery of Ontario, Casa Loma, CN Tower, Ontario Science Centre, Royal Ontario Museum and the Toronto Zoo.

A CityPass ticket booklet, valid for 9 days once the first attraction is visited, is $49.50; ages 4-12, $31.75. CityPass can be purchased at participating attractions. For recorded information phone (707) 256-0490. *See color ad p. 189.*

also can expect to pay 25c for every 31 seconds you spend waiting in traffic. Tipping about 15 percent is customary, and there is a modest extra charge if the driver loads and unloads a passenger's baggage. Major cab companies are Arrow, (416) 233-1111; Diamond, (416) 366-6868; and Metro, (416) 504-8294.

Limousines often charge a flat rate for sightseeing excursions, more when you're just renting by the hour. The going rate depends on the size of the limo, but averages $50-$150 per hour.

Public Transportation

Public transportation in Toronto has come a long way since the first horse-drawn conveyance appeared in 1849. The city's subway system opened in 1954 with 7.25 kilometres (4.5 mi.) of track. Now covering almost 60 kilometres (40 mi.), the system combines attractive, clean facilities with fast service. It has been estimated that Toronto's rapid rail system can move 80,000 persons per hour in and out of the downtown area.

The north-south subway extends from Union Station on the south to as far north as Sheppard Avenue on the University-Spadina line, and to Finch on the Yonge line. On the Bloor-Danforth line, east-west cars travel from Kennedy Road on the east to Kipling Avenue on the west. The Sheppard line offers east-west travel from Yonge Street in the west to Don Mills Road in the east. Though additional lines operate during rush hours, these should not be counted upon for sightseeing excursions. Subway operation hours are Mon.-Sat. 6 a.m.-1:30 a.m. and Sun. 9 a.m.-1:30 a.m.

Harbourfront Centre / © Michele Burgess / SuperStock

Rapid Transit (RT) provides eastern connections from Kennedy Road to McCowan Station in the east end. For additional information and schedules phone the Toronto Transit Commission, (416) 393-4636; for lost and found phone (416) 393-4100.

Complementing the subway is a network of buses, trolley buses and streetcars. Bus routes connect with all subway stations and serve the entire area. Fares are $2.25 (10 tokens or tickets $19); over .64 and students with ID $1.50 (10 tickets $12.50); ages 2-12, 50c (10 tickets $4.25); day pass $7.75.

On Sundays and holidays a single 1-day pass may be used as a family pass to cover the fares of two adults and up to four children/youths under 19 or one adult and up to five children/youths under 19. Tokens can be used on subways, buses and streetcars; tickets also can be used on all vehicles, but some automatic subway entrances accept only tokens. Tokens may be purchased at stations; tickets are available at convenience store ticket agencies throughout the city. Buses and streetcars accept only exact change, tickets or tokens, so be prepared. Transfers between subways and buses are free; always grab one—whether you need it or not—on your way down to the train or from a streetcar or bus driver.

The provincial government operates Go Transit, a mass transit system linking Toronto to its outlying suburbs. This train and bus system covers more than 8,000 square kilometres (3,100 sq. mi.); fares vary according to the distance traveled. For fare and schedule information phone (416) 869-3200.

What To See

AIR CANADA CENTRE is at 40 Bay St., just s. of Union Station. The multi-purpose arena is the home of hockey's Maple Leafs and basketball's Raptors. One-hour guided tours visit the dressing rooms, an NBA regulation-size basketball court used for practices (based upon availability), an executive suite, a museum of Maple Leaf history and include a video demonstration of how the facility is converted from a hockey arena to a basketball court to a concert venue.

Allow 1 hour minimum. Tours are given daily on the hour 10-4, July 1-Labour Day; Wed.-Sat. on the hour 11-3, rest of year. Last tour begins at closing. Tours are not given when event scheduling conflicts. Fee $12; over 60 and students with ID $10; under 13, $8. AX, MC, VI. Phone (416) 815-5982.

ALLAN GARDENS CONSERVATORY, downtown between Gerrard, Jarvis, Sherbourne and Carlton sts. at 19 Horticultural Ave., has a large collection of tropical and exotic flowering plants from various regions of the world, including cacti and succulents as well as seasonal plants to supplement the permanent collection. The 1909 Palm House follows the tradition of the great Victorian glass greenhouses.

The Victorian Christmas Flower Show and the Spring Flower Display are highlights. Gardens open daily 10-5. The Christmas flower show runs the first Sun. in Dec.-first week in Jan.; the spring show runs mid-Jan. through Apr. 30. Free. Phone (416) 392-7288.

ART GALLERY OF ONTARIO, 317 Dundas St. W. in Grange Park 3 blks. w. of St. Patrick subway station, is one of North America's largest art museums. It comprises some 50 galleries that showcase more than 36,000 works of various media spanning 1,000 years.

The Henry Moore Sculpture Centre houses the largest public collection of works by that British sculptor. The Grange is one of the oldest brick houses in Toronto; it is a living museum of life in Upper Canada in the 1830s. Films, lectures and performances are offered at the gallery. A research library and archives are on the premises.

Guided tours and food are available. Allow 4 hours minimum. Tues.-Fri. 11-6 (also Wed. 6-8:30 p.m.), Sat.-Sun. and holidays 10-5:30; closed Jan. 1 and Dec. 25. Hours vary for the Grange; phone for schedule. Admission $12; over 64 and students with ID $9; ages 6-15, $6; family rate (up to seven persons) $25; free to all Wed. 6-8:30 p.m. Fees may vary during special events or exhibitions. AX, MC, VI. Phone (416) 979-6648.

THE BATA SHOE MUSEUM, 327 Bloor St. W. at the St. George subway station, explores footwear in the social and cultural life of mankind from ancient times to the present through an international collection. Among the permanent and rotating exhibits in the award-winning Raymond Moriyama building, designed to represent a lid resting on an open shoebox, are Egyptian sandals dating to 300 BC, smuggler's clogs and footwear worn by such personalities as Winston Churchill, Elton John, John Lennon, Marilyn Monroe and Pablo Picasso.

Four interactive displays take a look at footwear's many facets, including its evolution, its uses over time, its past and its place in our lives and imaginations. Highlights include "All about Shoes" and the "Starstruck" celebrity shoe display.

Allow 1 hour, 30 minutes minimum. Mon.-Sat. 10-5 (also Thurs. 5-8), Sun. noon-5, early June-Labour Day; Tues.-Sat. 10-5 (also Thurs. 5-8), Sun. noon-5, rest of year. Closed major holidays. Admission $8; over 65 and students with ID $6; ages 5-17, $4; family rate (one adult and up to four children under 18) $12 or (two adults and up to four children under 18) $20; free to all Thurs. 5-8. AX, MC, VI. Phone (416) 979-7799. *See ad p. 190.*

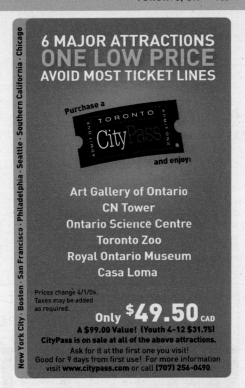

New York City · Boston · San Francisco · Philadelphia · Seattle · Southern California · Chicago

6 MAJOR ATTRACTIONS ONE LOW PRICE
AVOID MOST TICKET LINES

Purchase a

TORONTO
CityPass
ADMIT ONE

and enjoy:

Art Gallery of Ontario
CN Tower
Ontario Science Centre
Toronto Zoo
Royal Ontario Museum
Casa Loma

Prices change 4/1/06.
Taxes may be added
as required.

Only $49.50 CAD
A $99.00 Value! (Youth 4-12 $31.75)
CityPass is on sale at all of the above attractions.
Ask for it at the first one you visit!
Good for 9 days from first use! For more information
visit www.citypass.com or call (707) 256-0490.

BLACK CREEK PIONEER VILLAGE, 1.5 km (.9 mi.) s.e. of jct. Regional Rd. 7 (Hwy. 7) and Hwy. 400 at Jane St. and Steeles Ave. W., is an 1860s living-history village of more than 35 carefully restored buildings, including a school, church, doctor's house and mill with a water wheel. Craftsmen such as the tinsmith, blacksmith, miller, weaver and clock-maker ply their trades, and demonstrations of such domestic skills as spinning, quilting and hearth cooking are performed. Special events in the village are offered throughout the season.

Food is available. Allow 1 hour, 30 minutes minimum. Mon.-Fri. 9:30-4, Sat.-Sun. and holidays 11-5, May-June; Mon.-Fri. 10-5, Sat.-Sun. and holidays 11-5, July 1-Labour Day; Mon.-Fri. 9:30-4, Sat.-Sun. and holidays 11-4:30, day after Labour Day-Dec. 31. Closed Dec. 25-26. Admission $11; over 59 and students with ID $10; ages 5-14, $7. Parking $6. An additional fee may be charged for special events. AX, MC, VI. Phone (416) 736-1733.

CAMPBELL HOUSE, 160 Queen St. W. at University Ave. near Osgoode subway station, is an 1820s Georgian mansion built for Chief Justice of Upper Canada (1825-29) Sir William Campbell and his wife Hannah. Moved from its original location in 1972, the museum is beautifully restored and features a fine collection of period furnishings. Guided 30-minute tours conducted by costumed interpreters provide insight into Toronto's early history. Special events are offered throughout the year.

Mon.-Fri. 9:30-4:30, Sat.-Sun. and Mon. holidays noon-4:30, Victoria Day-second Mon. in Oct.; Mon.-Fri. 9:30-4:30 (also first three Sat. in Dec.), rest of year. Closed Jan. 1, Good Friday, Easter Mon., Labour Day, second Mon. in Oct. and Dec. 25-26. Last tour departs 30 minutes before closing. Admission $4.50; students with ID $3; over 64, $2.50; under 10, $2; family rate (two adults and two children) $10. Phone (416) 597-0227.

CANADIAN BROADCASTING CORPORATION MUSEUM, 250 Front St. W., relates the history of the CBC through a collection of more than 4,000 artifacts, interactive displays, a replica of a 1940 radio station and control room and a theater offering selections from television archives. Changing exhibits also are offered. Allow 30 minutes minimum. Mon.-Fri. 9-5, Sat. noon-4; closed holidays. Free. Phone (416) 205-5574.

CANADIAN MOTORSPORT HALL OF FAME is at the Hall of Fame Building at Exhibition Place, 160 Princess Blvd. The museum showcases an extensive collection of racing vehicles, including motorcycles, boats and cars, ranging from Formula One, Indy, dragsters, stock cars and go-carts. A hall of fame enshrines racing legends and other notable contributors to Canadian motorsports. Allow 30 minutes minimum. Tues.-Sat. 10-5; closed Jan. 1, Good Friday and Dec. 25-26. Donations. Phone (416) 263-3223.

CASA LOMA, 1 Austin Terr., at Spadina and Davenport rds., is a medieval-style castle 91 metres (300 ft.) high. Built by Canadian financier Sir Henry Pellatt 1911-14, its 98 rooms required $3.5 million and 300 men to build. Self-guiding audiotape tours are provided in eight languages, except during some special events. Decorated suites, secret passageways, a 244-metre (800-ft.) underground tunnel, towers and

Toronto's unique museum has stories and treasures from many lands

The Bata Shoe Museum

327 Bloor Street West, Toronto

Step in style to the heart of the city at the corner of Bloor and St. George Streets

www.batashoemuseum.ca   416.979.7799

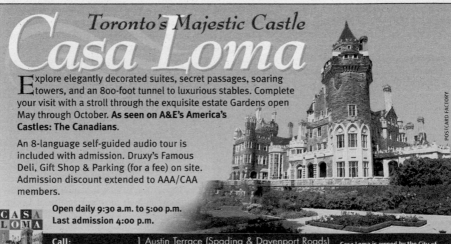

Toronto's Majestic Castle

Casa Loma

Explore elegantly decorated suites, secret passages, soaring towers, and an 800-foot tunnel to luxurious stables. Complete your visit with a stroll through the exquisite estate Gardens open May through October. **As seen on A&E's America's Castles: The Canadians.**

An 8-language self-guided audio tour is included with admission. Druxy's Famous Deli, Gift Shop & Parking (for a fee) on site. Admission discount extended to AAA/CAA members.

POSTCARD FACTORY

Open daily 9:30 a.m. to 5:00 p.m.
Last admission 4:00 p.m.

CASA LOMA TORONTO

Call:
(416) 923-1171

1 Austin Terrace (Spadina & Davenport Roads)
Toronto, Ontario M5R 1X8
www.casaloma.org Email: info@casaloma.org

Casa Loma is owned by the City of Toronto and has been operated by the Kiwanis Club of Casa Loma since 1937.

luxurious stables are some of the castle's many features. Two hectares (5 acres) of gardens surround the estate and are open May through October.

Food is available. Daily 9:30-5; closed Jan. 1, Dec. 24 at 1 p.m., and Dec. 25 and 31. Last admission 1 hour before closing. Admission $12; over 59 and ages 14-17, $7.50; ages 4-13, $6.75. Parking fee charged. AX, MC, VI. Phone (416) 923-1171. *See color ad p. 190.*

CITY HALL AND NATHAN PHILLIPS SQUARE, n.w. corner of Queen and Bay sts., is a striking complex created by Finnish architect Viljo Revell. The domed structure flanked by two curved office towers serves as council chambers.

The reflecting pool, in Nathan Phillips Square in front of City Hall, becomes a skating rink in winter. The square is a forum for festivals, concerts, art shows and civic ceremonies. Henry Moore's sculpture "The Archer" is among the complex's works of art. Self-guiding tours of City Hall are given Mon.-Fri. 8:30-4; closed holidays. Free. Phone (416) 338-0338.

CN TOWER, 301 Front St. W., at 553.33 metres (1,815 ft.), is considered the tallest building and free-standing structure in the world. The main observation decks afford panoramas of the entire Toronto area. On a clear day Niagara Falls and Buffalo are visible. Sky Pod, at 447 metres (1,465 ft.), is one of the world's highest public observatories. The 25-square-metre (265-sq.-ft.) Glass Floor Level at 342 metres (1,120 ft.) offers a view of the city through a different perspective; the floor is believed to be the highest glass floor in the world.

There is a revolving restaurant at the 350-metre (1,150-ft.) level and a café at the 346-metre (1,135-ft.) level. A variety of multimedia entertainment can be found at the base of the tower, including simulated motion rides, a theater and arcade games.

Food is available. Tower observation decks open daily 9 a.m.-11 p.m., May-Oct.; 10-10, rest of year. Hours may vary; phone ahead. Closed Dec. 25. Elevator to the observation decks (includes the glass floor) $18.99; over 64, $16.99; ages 4-12, $13.99. Additional $7.50 for Sky Pod. Theater and rides $8; arcade games are pay-as-you-play. AX, MC, VI. Phone (416) 360-8500 or (416) 868-6937.

EDWARDS GARDENS, 3.5 km (2.2 mi.) s. of Hwy. 401 exit 373 at Lawrence Ave. E. and Leslie St., has rock gardens, floral displays, a greenhouse and a flower-bordered path along the Don River on its 14 hectares (35 acres). The Toronto Botanical Garden provides horticultural information and houses a research library. Special events are held throughout the year.

Bicycles and dogs are not permitted. Food is available July-Aug. Daily dawn to dusk; closed Jan. 1 and Dec. 25. One-hour guided tours are given Tues. and Thurs. at 10, July-Aug. (weather permitting); phone ahead to confirm availability. Tours leave from the Toronto Botanical Garden at 777 Lawrence Ave. E. Information center open Mon.-Fri. 9:30-5, Sat.-Sun. and holidays noon-5, Apr.-Dec.; Mon.-Fri. 9:30-4, Sat.-Sun. and holidays

Edwards Gardens / © Gibson Stock Photography

noon-4, rest of year. Closed Good Friday and Dec. 24-31. Free. Phone (416) 392-8186 or (416) 397-1340.

ENOCH TURNER SCHOOLHOUSE, 1 blk. e. of Parliament St., just s. of King St. at 106 Trinity St., was Toronto's first free school. Built in 1848 by businessman Enoch Turner, the school was attended by working-class children from the mainly Irish neighborhod. The facility is currently visited by schoolchildren as part of a living-history program.

Allow 30 minutes minimum. Mon.-Fri. 10-4; closed holidays. The facility is sometimes rented out for private functions and therefore not open to visitors. Phone ahead to verify accessibility. Donations. Phone (416) 863-0010.

GARDINER MUSEUM OF CERAMIC ART, 111 Queen's Park Ave., houses a collection of 15th-through 18th-century ceramic pieces. Works include pre-Columbian, containing Olmec and Mayan figures and objects from cultures in Mexico, Ecuador, Colombia and Peru; Italian Renaissance Majolica (1400-1600); English Delftware (1600-1700); Continental and English porcelain (1700-1800); and Minton china (1800).

Note: The museum is closed for renovations; reopening is planned for November 2005. Phone ahead for schedule and rate information. Food is available. Mon.-Fri. 10-6 (also Tues. and Thurs. 6-8 p.m.), Sat.-Sun. 10-5; closed Jan. 1, 1 day in mid-Nov. and Dec. 25. Admission $10; over 64, students with ID and ages 5-12, $6; family rate (maximum four people) $24; free to all first Tues. of the month. Rates may vary during special events. AX, MC, VI. Phone (416) 586-8080.

GIBSON HOUSE MUSEUM, 5172 Yonge St. at Park Home Ave., is a Georgian-style brick house restored to the period of 1851. Furnishings and artifacts reflect the life of Scottish emigrant David Gibson, a surveyor and politician, and that of his wife and family. Many special events reflecting seasonal themes as well as workshops about hearth cooking and Scottish foods and customs are offered throughout the year. The Discovery Gallery features interactive displays. Guided 45-minute tours by costumed interpreters are available.

Tues.-Sun. and Mon. holidays noon-5, Jan.-Aug. and Oct. 1 to mid-Nov.; daily noon-5, mid-Nov. through Dec. 31. Closed Jan. 1, Good Friday and Dec. 24-26. Last tour begins 30 minutes before closing. Admission Jan. 1 to mid-Nov. $3.75; over 64 and ages 13-18, $2.25; ages 2-12, $1.75. Admission rest of year $4.25; over 64 and ages 13-18, $2.75; ages 2-12, $2.25. MC, VI. Phone (416) 395-7432.

HIGH PARK is at Bloor St. W. and Parkside Dr. A former estate, the park covers 161 hectares (400

Hockey Hall of Fame / © Gibson Stock Photography

acres). Features include the Hillside Gardens, Grenadier Pond, sunken gardens, flowers, hanging basket gardens, nature trails, an oak woodlands walking tour, ponds, rockeries and streams, animal paddocks, swimming and wading pools, catch and release fishing (valid license required), an open-air theater, playgrounds, picnic area, a scenic train tour and cross-country skiing.

Food is available. Daily dawn-dusk. Free. Phone (416) 392-1111, or (416) 368-3110 for the open-air theater.

Colborne Lodge, in High Park on Colborne Lodge Dr., was built in 1837. Once the home of park owner and architect John G. Howard and his wife Jemima, the lodge contains many of the couple's belongings, including furniture and water-colors. Colborne helped plan the city of Toronto. Two of Howard's carriages are displayed in the Coach House. The Howards' tomb and a restored 19th-century garden are on the grounds.

Allow 1 hour minimum. Tues.-Sun. noon-5, late Apr.-early Oct.; Tues.-Sun. noon-4, during Mar. school break and early Oct.-Dec. 31; Sat.-Sun. noon-4, rest of year. Closed Jan. 1, Good Friday and Dec. 25-26. Admission late Apr. to mid-Nov. $4; over 64 and ages 13-18, $2.75; ages 5-12, $2.50. Admission rest of year $5; over 64 and ages 13-18, $4; ages 5-12, $3.50. Admission may vary during special events. VI. Phone (416) 392-6916 to confirm hours.

HISTORIC FORT YORK, off Fleet St. be-tween Bathurst St. and Strachan Ave. at 100 Garrison Rd., is known as the birth-place of Toronto. Established in 1793, the fort is the site where the 1813 Battle of York took place during the War of 1812. Rebuilt 1813-16, eight original buildings have been restored to their 1812 appearance and depict early military life in Upper Canada.

Guides in period costumes conduct historical tours of the fort and barracks, providing visitors with an understanding of the lives of both officers and enlisted men. Seasonal demonstrations include cannon firing, music and cooking. Military drill and fife and drum demonstrations are pre-sented daily July through August.

Picnicking is permitted. Allow 2 hours minimum. Daily 10-5, Victo-ria Day weekend-Labour Day; Mon.-Fri. 10-4, Sat.-Sun. and Mon. holidays 10-5, Jan. 2-day before Victoria Day weekend and day after Labour Day to mid-Dec. Closed Good Friday. Schedule may vary Victoria Day weekend-June 30; phone ahead. Guided 1- to 2-hour tours are offered on the hour. Last tour departs 90 minutes before clos-ing. Admission $6; over 64 and ages 13-18, $3.25; ages 5-12, $3. MC, VI. Phone (416) 392-6907 to con-firm hours.

HOCKEY HALL OF FAME, at the corner of Yonge and Front sts. on the concourse level of BCE Place, showcases the sport of hockey. The Grand Ol' Houses of Hockey has a col-lection of goalie masks and pays tribute to great arenas and Stanley Cup playoff milestones. There also is a full-scale replica of the Montréal Canadiens' dressing room.

An actual game highlight can be announced at the TSN/RDS Broadcast Zone; and the NHLPA Be a Player Zone allows visitors to face hockey's best shooters and goaltenders. Another area is dedicated to various levels of the sport, including minor-league and women's hockey. The Royal Canadian Mint World of Hockey has international hockey artifacts and displays, with a feature on world and Olympic championships. NHL trophies and portraits and biographies of hall of fame members also are featured.

Food is available. Allow 2 hours minimum. Mon.-Sat. 9:30-6, Sun. 10-6, late June-Labour Day and during Mar. and Christmas school breaks; Mon.-Fri. 10-5, Sat. 9:30-6, Sun. 10:30-5, rest of year. Closed Jan. 1, induction day in Nov. and Dec. 25. Admission $12; over 64 and ages 4-13, $8. AX, MC, VI. Phone (416) 360-7765.

JAMES GARDENS, on Edenbridge Dr., is just e. of Royal York Rd. Four hectares (10 acres) of formal botanical gardens have spring-fed pools with rustic bridges, rare trees and colorful floral displays. Visitors can watch lawn bowling or follow wooded trails; cross-country skiing is available in the winter. Daily dawn-dusk. Free. Phone (416) 392-8186.

[SAVE] **MACKENZIE HOUSE,** 82 Bond St., was the home of Toronto's first mayor and leader of the Upper Canada Rebellion of 1837, an attempt to shift more civil authority to the populace and away from British-appointed officials. The dwelling, presented to William Lyon Mackenzie by grateful

citizens, is restored and furnished in mid-Victorian style. A functional, re-created 19th-century printing shop and the kitchen both offer demonstrations.

Allow 1 hour minimum. Tues.-Sun. noon-5, May 1-Labour Day; Tues.-Fri. noon-4, Sat.-Sun. noon-5, day after Labour Day-Dec. 31; Mon.-Fri. noon-4, Sat.-Sun. noon-5, during Mar. school break; Sat.-Sun. noon-5, rest of year. Closed Jan. 1, Good Friday and Dec. 25-26. Admission Jan. 1 to mid-Nov. $4; over 64 and ages 13-18, $2.75; ages 5-12, $2.50. Admission rest of year $5.50; over 64 and ages 13-18, $4; ages 5-12, $3.50. Phone (416) 392-6915 to confirm hours.

THE MARKET GALLERY, on the second floor of the South St. Lawrence Market at 95 Front St. E., offers changing exhibits about Toronto's history that include paintings, artifacts, photographs, maps and documents from the city's archival and fine art collections. Allow 30 minutes minimum. Wed.-Fri. 10-4, Sat. 9-4, Sun. noon-4; closed holidays. Free. Phone (416) 392-7604.

[SAVE] **MEDIEVAL TIMES DINNER AND TOURNA-MENT,** in Exhibition Place, offers a medieval four-course meal to be eaten without utensils, served by a costumed staff. A jousting tournament, battles and demonstrations of equestrian skill take place during dinner. Allow 3 hours minimum. Performances generally Wed.-Thurs. at 7, Fri.-Sat. at 7:30, Sun. at 3:30. Admission $59.95; under 13,

AAA/CAA DISCOUNT: MEMBERS ONLY!

Visit your local AAA/CAA office and receive a discount on an Ontario Place **PLAY ALL DAY PASS** that includes grounds admission plus unlimited use of most rides and attractions. This discount offer is available at participating AAA/CAA offices and is not available to the general public.
Park open May – September.

TORONTO STAR presents
Play All Day

🍁 **ontario place**

Toronto, Ontario, Canada

INFO: Group Sales 416-314-9933
1-866-ONE-4-FUN (Outside GTA)
www.ontarioplace.com

An Agency of the Government of Ontario

$41.95. Phone to verify schedule and prices. Reservations are required. AX, MC, VI. Phone (416) 260-1234 or (888) 935-6878.

[SAVE] MONTGOMERY'S INN, 3.5 km (2.2 mi.) e. of jct. Hwy. 427 and Regional Rd. 5 (Hwy. 5) at 4709 Dundas St. W., was built around 1830. The inn is restored to the 1847-50 period and depicts the lifestyle of country innkeeper Thomas Montgomery.

Guided 45-minute tours are available Tues.-Fri. 1-4:30, Sat.-Sun. and Victoria Day 1-5; closed Jan. 1, Good Friday, July 1, Nov. 11 and Dec. 24-26. Tea is served Tues.-Sun. 2-4:30. Admission $4; over 64 and students with ID $2; ages 5-12, $1; family rate $8. Tea $3. Phone (416) 394-8113.

 ONTARIO LEGISLATIVE BUILDINGS is in Queen's Park, 1 blk. n. of jct. University Ave. and College St.; all visitors must check in at the Main Information Desk in the front lobby. The building has served as the meeting place of Ontario's Provincial Parliament for more than a century. Within the sandstone structure, erected 1886-92, is the Legislative Chamber, exhibits about Ontario's history and a collection of early 19th- and 20th-century Canadian art.

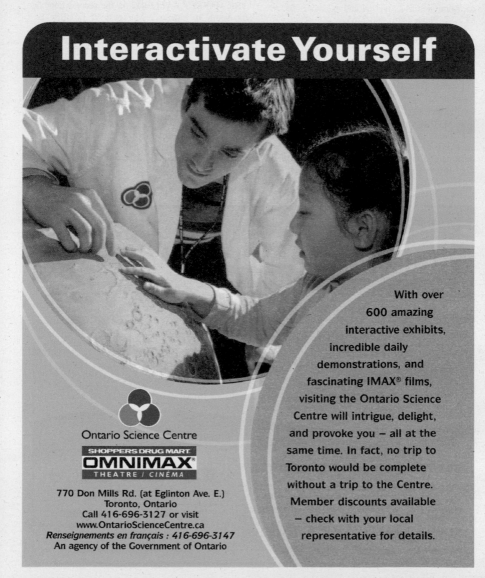

Interactivate Yourself

Ontario Science Centre

SHOPPERS DRUG MART
OMNIMAX®
THEATRE / CINÉMA

770 Don Mills Rd. (at Eglinton Ave. E.)
Toronto, Ontario
Call 416-696-3127 or visit
www.OntarioScienceCentre.ca
Renseignements en français : 416-696-3147
An agency of the Government of Ontario

With over 600 amazing interactive exhibits, incredible daily demonstrations, and fascinating IMAX® films, visiting the Ontario Science Centre will intrigue, delight, and provoke you – all at the same time. In fact, no trip to Toronto would be complete without a trip to the Centre. Member discounts available – check with your local representative for details.

Food is available. Allow 1 hour minimum. Guided half- and 1-hour tours Mon.-Fri. 10-4, Sat.-Sun. and holidays 9-4, Victoria Day weekend-Labour Day; Mon.-Fri. 10-4, rest of year. Closed Jan. 1, Good Friday, Easter Monday and Dec. 25-26. Last tour departs 1 hour before closing. Free. Phone (416) 325-7500 for daily tour schedule and reservations.

ONTARIO PLACE, 955 Lakeshore Blvd. W., on Lake Ontario across from Exhibition Place, was constructed as a showplace for the province and the nation. On 38 hectares (96 acres), the complex consists of five pods suspended over the lake on 32-metre (105-ft.) concrete columns. The grounds include winding canals, lakes, lagoons, a marina, parklands and a lakeside restaurant.

Other sites are miniature golf; virtual reality games; a motion simulator ride; children's entertainment; a water park; a flume ride; and bumper and pedal boats. Scenic helicopter rides are available. Cinesphere presents IMAX films year-round on an 18- by 24-metre (60- by 80-ft.) screen.

The Molson Amphitheatre is a 16,000-seat outdoor concert facility that presents musical events with national and international entertainers. Special events are offered throughout the season.

Pets are not permitted. Food is available. Complex open daily 10-8, late June-Labour Day; Sat.-Sun. 10-6, day after Labour Day-late Sept.; schedule varies Victoria Day weekend-late June. Phone ahead to confirm hours. Attractions generally close at dusk. Cinesphere open year-round.

Grounds admission $13, under 4 free. Play All Day Pass (includes gate admission) $29; over 64, $17; ages 4-5, $15. Season pass $50. Individual attraction tickets and Cinesphere rates vary. Fee for parking. Prices may increase during special events. Prices vary during the Canadian National Exhibition mid-Aug. through Labour Day. AX, MC, VI. Phone (416) 314-9900 or (866) 663-4386 for complex information, (416) 260-5600 for amphitheater information, or Ticketmaster at (416) 870-8000 for amphitheater tickets. *See color ad p. 193.*

ONTARIO SCIENCE CENTRE, 770 Don Mills Rd. at Eglinton Ave. E., allows visitors to explore the world of science and technology through more than 600 hands-on exhibits and demonstrations in 10 multi-themed exhibition halls.

Visitors can race an Olympic bobsled; ride a rocket chair in space; take a walk through a steamy tropical rain forest; touch a living tornado; or age 50 years with the Amazing Aging Machine. An OMNIMAX theater features a 24-metre (79-ft.) domed screen with wrap-around sound.

Demonstrations inform visitors about chemistry, papermaking and electricity, and a planetarium takes visitors on a trip through the night sky. KidSpark lets children under 9 learn as they play, while all ages can explore current science and technology issues in the Hot Zone. Touring exhibitions also are available.

Toronto Zoo / © Ralph Reinhold / PictureQuest

Food is available. Daily 10-5; closed Dec. 25. Hours may vary; phone ahead. Science center admission $14; over 64 and ages 13-17, $10; ages 4-12, $8. Theater $11; over 64 and ages 13-17, $8; ages 4-12, $7. Combination tickets are available. There are extra charges for special exhibits. Parking $8. AX, MC, VI. Phone (416) 696-3127, or (416) 696-1000 for theater reservations. *See color ad p. 194.*

PARAMOUNT CANADA'S WONDERLAND—*see Vaughan p. 210.*

THE REDPATH SUGAR MUSEUM, 95 Queens Quay E., provides information about sugar beet and cane growing areas; the history of sugar production, packaging, transportation and usage; and the Redpath family, which founded this company. Allow 1 hour minimum. Mon.-Fri. 10-noon and 1-3:30; closed holidays. Hours may vary due to on-site activities; phone to check availability. Free. Phone (416) 366-3561.

ROYAL ONTARIO MUSEUM, 100 Queen's Park at Bloor St. W. and Avenue Rd., is Canada's largest museum of natural history and human cultures with more than 5 million art, archeology and science objects.

Interactive exhibits include touchable specimens and armor to try on, and children will enjoy seeing an 80-million-year-old maiasaur and her baby and an active bee-hive. More than 1,000 Egyptian objects are displayed. Visitors can see Greek and Etruscan ceramics, sculpture and metalwork and a model of the Acropolis as it was during Athens' "Golden Age." The Islam Gallery depicts a town in a range of settings, including a Middle Eastern household, a Muslim shrine and a bazaar. European galleries boast a collection of arms and armor, with pieces dating from the Bronze Age to World War I.

Note: The museum is undergoing expansion and renovations through November 2006. Some galleries may not be available; phone to verify. Food is available. Allow 2 hours minimum. Daily 10-6 (also Fri. 6-9:30 p.m.). Guided 1-hour tours are offered Tues.-Fri. at 11, noon, 1, 2 and 3, Sat.-Mon.

at 1, 2 and 3 (also Sat. at 11 and Sun. at noon). "Come See the Mess" tours, exploring the history and current status of the museum's expansion and restoration project, are offered daily at 1:30. No tours on holidays. Closed Jan. 1, Dec. 24 and 31 at 4, and Dec. 25. Hours and tour schedule may vary; phone ahead.

Admission $15; over 64 and students with ID $12; ages 5-14, $10. Admission will increase during special exhibits. Admission by donations Fri. 4:30-9:30 (except during special exhibits). AX, MC, VI. Phone (416) 586-8000. See color ad.

ROYAL ONTARIO MUSEUM
NATURE • CIVILIZATION • DISCOVERY

Embark on a journey of discovery at Canada's leading international museum of human civilization and natural history. Explore our world-renowned collections of art, archaeology, science and nature, and don't miss the *Views of our Future: Work in Progress* & *The New Galleries* exhibits, depicting the bold architectural models of the Renaissance ROM renovation project.

SPECIAL EXHIBITION:
Feathered Dinosaurs
and the Origin of Flight
Until September 5, 2005

Organized by the Dinosaur Museum, Utah USA and The Liaoning Fossil Administration Office, China.

AAA/CAA members show your card and save!

RÖM

OPEN DAILY • FREE GUIDED TOURS • 416-586-8000 • WWW.ROM.ON.CA
BLOOR ST. W. AT AVENUE RD. • MUSEUM SUBWAY STOP • TORONTO, ON.

The ROM is an agency of the Government of Ontario.

SCARBOROUGH HISTORICAL MUSEUM, 1007 Brimley Rd., 1 blk. n. of Lawrence Ave. E., is part of Thomson Memorial Park. Comprised of four restored late 19th-century buildings, the museum brings the rural heritage of the Scarborough area of Toronto to life through displays, demonstrations and various year-round celebrations.

Picnicking is permitted. Allow 30 minutes minimum. Mon.-Fri. 10-4, mid-Mar. through day before Victoria Day and day after Labour Day to mid-Dec.; Wed.-Sun. and Mon. holidays noon-4, Victoria Day-Labour Day. Closed Good Friday, Victoria Day and Labour Day. Holiday hours may vary; phone to confirm. Admission $3; ages 5-12, $2; over 59 and students with ID $1.50. Phone (416) 338-8807.

SKYDOME is at Front and John sts., with tours departing from between Gates 1 and 2. Tours of the first fully retractable roofed stadium, home of baseball's Blue Jays and football's Argonauts, feature a film about the building's design and construction and a tour with visits to a skybox, the media center, club seats and a team dressing room or the field area (when available). A museum has artifacts unearthed during the dome's construction.

Allow 1 hour minimum. Tours depart daily on the hour 10-5, July-Aug. (event schedule permitting); opening and closing times and number of tours scheduled varies, rest of year. Phone for schedule. Fee for stadium tour $12.50; over 64 and ages 12-17, $8.50; ages 5-11, $7. A parking fee is charged. AX, MC, VI. Phone (416) 341-2770. See ad.

SPADINA MUSEUM: HISTORIC HOUSE AND GARDENS, next to Casa Loma at 285 Spadina Rd., was built in 1866 and is furnished with original pieces illustrating Victorian, Edwardian and Art Nouveau influences. A 15-minute video presentation precedes a guided tour of the house that was home to four generations of the prosperous Austin family. The tour provides insights into area history, the home's furnishings and those who lived there.

Self-guiding tours of the grounds include rose gardens, the English Flower Garden, Beehive Gateway and a grape arbor. Cooking demonstrations are featured in the Edwardian kitchen. Special events are offered throughout the year. Guided garden tours are available in summer; phone for schedule.

Allow 1 hour minimum. Tues.-Sun. noon-5, Apr.-Aug.; Tues.-Fri. noon-4, Sat.-Sun. noon-5, Sept.-Dec.; Sat.-Sun. noon-5, rest of year. Hours may vary; phone ahead. Closed Jan. 1, Good Friday and Dec. 25-26. Admission $6; over 64 and ages 13-18, $5; ages 6-12, $4. Gardens free when in season. Admission may increase during special events. MC, VI. Phone (416) 392-6910.

TEXTILE MUSEUM OF CANADA is at 55 Centre Ave., 1 blk. e. of University Ave. and 1 blk. s. of Dundas St. at the St. Patrick subway station. Internationally recognized for its collection

Go behind-the-scenes at SkyDome!

★ Enjoy a guided tour of the world's most innovative entertainment facility with a fully retractable roof.
★ Tours operate 7 days a week, event schedule permitting.

**Call
(416) 341-2770
or visit
skydome.com**

KONICA MINOLTA
PRESENTS

SKYDOME TOUR EXPERIENCE

of historic and ethnographic textiles and related artifacts, the museum is devoted exclusively to the collection, exhibition and documentation of traditional and contemporary textiles from around the world. The collection consists of more than 10,000 pieces. One-hour guided tours and a research library are available.

Allow 30 minutes minimum. Tues.-Fri. 11-5 (also Wed. 5-8), Sat.-Sun. noon-5; closed holidays. Guided tours are given Sun. at 2. Admission $8; over 64, students with ID and ages 5-14, $6; family rate (two adults and up to three children) $22; admission by donations Wed. 5-8. MC, VI. Phone (416) 599-5321.

TODMORDEN MILLS HERITAGE MUSEUM AND ARTS CENTRE, off Broadview Ave. at 67 Pottery Rd., was an important 19th-century millsite on the Don River. The five-building complex on 9 hectares (22 acres) consists of two restored pre-Confederation houses; the Brewery Gallery orientation building, in a former brewery; the Paper Mill Gallery and Theatre, offering visual and performing arts; and the Old Don Train Station. A wildflower preserve and scenic walkways also are on the grounds.

Picnicking is permitted. Grounds Tues.-Fri. 10-4:30, Sat.-Sun. and holidays noon-5, May-Sept.; Wed.-Fri. 10-4, Sat.-Sun. noon-4, Oct.-Dec. Grounds open noon-4 on special events days. Closed Victoria Day, Labour Day and Dec. 25-26.

Admission $3.50; over 59 and students with ID $2.25; ages 6-12, $1.50. Admission increases during some special events. Phone (416) 396-2819.

TORONTO AEROSPACE MUSEUM is in Downsview Park at 65 Carl Hall Rd. In a production hangar used by the de Havilland Aircraft Co. since the late 1930s, the museum has a collection of military and commercial aircraft, experimental planes and aviation artifacts. Visitors can see planes in various stages of restoration, aircraft engines, photographs and model displays.

Allow 1 hour minimum. Thurs.-Sat. 10-4, Sun. noon-4; closed major holidays. Admission $8; over 59, $6; students with ID $5; under 6 free; family rate (maximum four persons) $20. MC, VI. Phone (416) 638-6078.

TORONTO ISLANDS PARK occupies the harbor islands opposite the downtown area. The park is accessible only by ferry from the Bay Street Ferry Dock behind The Westin Harbour Castle hotel. If driving, park at the foot of Bay St.; if not, take the Bay Street bus. Transportation on and around the islands is by open-air trams, rental bicycles, quadracycles, canoes and rowboats.

The park has a boardwalk, beaches, bathhouses, boating lagoons, picnicking, gardens, play areas, sports facilities, fishing, rides, wading pools, tennis, bicycle rentals, tram rides, rowboats, canoes, disc golf, a pony ride and a children's farm. Of interest

Come Sail Away

This is your chance to sail on a real tall ship "Kajama". A 165 feet traditional square rigged Schooner.

For reservations, call

[416] 203-2322

Receive a 10% discount upon presentation of this ad.

www.tallshipcruisestoronto.com

are Avenue of the Islands; an illuminated promenade; a lagoon with waterfowl; and Gibraltar Point Lighthouse, one of Toronto's oldest landmarks.

Food is available. Pets on leash permitted. Ferries leave approximately every 30-45 minutes daily 6:35 a.m.-11:30 p.m. Round trip ferry $6; over 64 and students ages 15-18 with ID $3.50; under 15, $2.50. Tram $5; over 64 and students age 13-18 with ID $4; ages 2-12, $2. Separate admission for amusement park rides. Phone (416) 392-1111 for island information or (416) 392-8193 for ferry information.

Centreville Amusement Park is on Centre Island; take the Centre Island Ferry from Bay St. and Queens Quay at Harbourfront. This is a late 19th-early 20th-century style family-oriented amusement park. It has 30 rides, most geared toward younger children, and arcades, miniature golf and a petting zoo.

Food is available. Park open daily at 10:30, Victoria Day weekend-Labour Day; Sat.-Sun. at 10:30, May 1-day before Victoria Day weekend and day after Labour Day-late Sept. (weather permitting). Closing times vary; phone ahead. Admission free. Ride passes $24, under 49 inches $17, family rate (four persons) $72. Additional fee for ferry crossing. MC, VI. Phone (416) 203-0405.

TORONTO POLICE MUSEUM AND DISCOVERY CENTRE, in the atrium at Police Headquarters at 40 College St., between Bay and Yonge sts., features traditional and interactive exhibits about the history of the Police Service. Police vehicles, equipment and uniforms are on display.

Among the exhibits are Investigative Techniques, which showcases actual evidence from a variety of crimes; and Infamous Cases, which depicts nine of the more memorable criminal investigations in Police Service history. Food is available. Allow 30 minutes minimum. Mon.-Fri. 10-4:30, Sat.-Sun. noon-5, late May-Labour Day; Mon.-Fri. 10-4:30, rest of year. Phone ahead to verify schedule. Donations. Not recommended for under age 10. Phone (416) 808-7020.

TORONTO ZOO is 1.6 km (1 mi.) n. of Hwy. 401 off Meadowvale Rd. The zoo's 287 hectares (710 acres) contain more than 5,000 animals representing most of the world's geographic regions, underwater exhibits and seven themed pavilions—Indo-Malaya; Africa, featuring the Gorilla Rainforest; the Americas; Australasia; African Savanna; Eurasia; and the Canadian Domain—in natural habitat displays.

A popular way to see the zoo is aboard one of the seasonal Zoomobiles. Safari simulator, camel and pony rides are offered. Zellers Splash Island water play area is available seasonally.

Food, picnic facilities and stroller, wagon and wheelchair rentals are available. Allow 4 hours minimum. Daily 9-7:30, Victoria Day weekend-Labour Day; 9-6, mid-Mar. to day before Victoria Day weekend and day after Labour Day to mid-Oct.; 9:30-4:30, rest of year. Hours may vary; phone ahead. Closed Dec. 25. Camel rides daily, May 1-Labour Day; Sat.-Sun., mid-Mar. through Apr. 30 and day after Labour Day-Nov. 30 (weather permitting). Pony rides daily, late May-Labour Day; Sat.-Sun., day after Labour Day-Nov. 30 (weather permitting). Zoomobile daily May 1-Labour Day; Sat.-Sun. in Apr. and day after Labour Day-second Mon. in Oct. (weather permitting). Splash Island daily, late June-Labour Day; Sat.-Sun., early June-late June and day after Labour Day-Sept. 30 (weather permitting). Last admission 1 hour before closing.

© Gibson Stock Photography

Admission $18; over 64, $12; ages 4-12, $10. Zoomobile $5. Camel rides $5. Pony rides $4. Safari simulator ride $5. Parking $8 Mar.-Oct.; free rest of year. AX, MC, VI. Phone (416) 392-5900.

TORONTO'S FIRST POST OFFICE is 1.5 blks. e. of Jarvis and 1 blk. n. of King St. at 260 Adelaide St. E. Opened in 1833, the office is still in operation as a postal and philatelic outlet. A museum about the British North American postal system includes archives, exhibits and workshops, and offers special events. Of interest is a topographic model of Toronto in 1837.

Stationery, quill pens and sealing wax are provided for those who wish to write a letter as it was done in the 1830s. Allow 30 minutes minimum. Mon.-Fri. 9-4, Sat.-Sun. 10-4; closed major holidays and the Sun. preceding Mon. holidays when open. Free. Stationery supplies $1. Phone (416) 865-1833.

TSX BROADCAST & CONFERENCE CENTRE, 2 First Canadian Pl. in the Exchange Tower at 130 King St. W., with an entrance at the n.e. corner of King and York sts., is in Canada's premier market, the third largest stock exchange in North America. The center provides hands-on and interactive high-technology, entertaining displays about the stock market, trading and investing.

Allow 1 hour minimum. Open Mon.-Fri. 10-5, July-Aug.; Mon. and Fri. 10-5 (also some Tues.-Thurs.), rest of year. Closed holidays. The facility is sometimes rented out for private functions and may not be open to visitors; phone ahead. Free. Phone (416) 947-4676 or (800) 729-5556.

UNIVERSITY OF TORONTO is bounded by George St., College St., Bloor St. W., and University Ave. Guided 1-hour historical walking tours of the campus are offered. Tours depart from the Nona Mac-Donald Visitors Centre at 25 King's College Cir.

Mon.-Fri. at 10:30, 1 and 2:30, June-Aug. Free. Phone (416) 978-5000.

Justina M. Barnicke Art Gallery, at 7 Hart House Cir. at the University of Toronto, showcases art by Canadian artists of merit, including the Group of Seven and Emily Carr. Also featured are historical and contemporary Canadian art exhibits curated from the Hart House permanent collection or traveling exhibits from across Canada. Mon.-Fri. 11-7, Sat.-Sun. 1-4, Sept.-June; Mon.-Fri. 11-6, Sat. 1-4, rest of year. Closed holidays and the last 2 weeks of Dec. Free. Phone (416) 978-8398.

What To Do

Sightseeing

Toronto has an extensive network of underground walkways. The major walkway artery cuts an underground path between Dundas and Front streets, connecting the Toronto Coach Terminal, the Atrium on Bay, Toronto Eaton Centre, The Sheraton Centre Toronto Hotel, First Canadian Place, CBC Broadcast Centre, Toronto Dominion Centre, Royal Bank Plaza, Union Station, the Air Canada Centre and the south building of the Toronto Convention Centre.

Boat Tours

MARIPOSA CRUISE LINE, docked at the Queens Quay Terminal Building, at Queens Quay and York St., offers 1-hour narrated sightseeing tours of the harbor and Toronto Islands aboard the *Oriole,* a Victorian-style riverboat. Lunch, dinner and Sunday brunch cruises also are offered. Sightseeing cruises depart daily at 11, 12:15, 1:30, 2:45 and 4, mid-May through Sept. 30; otherwise varies Oct.-Dec. Sightseeing fare $17; over 64 and students with ID $15.50; ages 4-11, $12. AX, DC, MC, VI. Phone (416) 203-0178 or (866) 627-7672.

THE TALL SHIP *KAJAMA,* departing from Queens Quay W. at Lower Simcoe St., just w. of the Queens Quay Terminal building at the harborfront, is a 53-metre (175-ft.), three-masted schooner, originally launched in 1930 and used as a commercial sailing ship in Europe. Sailing trips along the harborfront and on Lake Ontario are offered; a cannon is fired on every sail.

Ninety-minute cruise departs daily at noon, 2 and 4, July 1-Labour Day; Mon.-Fri. at 3:30, Sat.-Sun at noon, 2 and 4, in June; Sat.-Sun. at noon, 2 and 4 in May and day after Labour Day-Sept. 30. Boarding is 30 minutes prior to departure. Fare $19.95; over 64, $17.95; under 13, $10.95. Reservations are recommended. AX, DC, MC, VI. Phone (416) 203-2322 or (800) 267-3866. *See color ad p. 198.*

TORONTO HARBOUR TOURS, departing from Pier 6, 145 Queens Quay W. at the foot of York St., features 1-hour cruises of Toronto's inner harbor and the Toronto Islands. An island stop is available. Departures every hour daily 10-7, June-Aug.; every hour daily 10-5 in May and Sept.; every hour daily 11-5, in Oct. Fare $20; ages 2-12, $10. AX, MC, VI. Phone (416) 869-1372.

[SAVE] **TORONTO HIPPO TOURS** departs from 151 Front St. W., at the s.e. corner of Simcoe and Front sts. Ninety-minute narrated tours in a 40-person amphibious bus give passengers an orientation of the city's main sights from a land perspective and then splash into Lake Ontario to view sights from the water.

Allow 1 hour, 30 minutes minimum. Departures daily on the hour 11-6, May-Oct. (weather permitting). Hours may vary in Oct.; phone ahead. Fare $35; over 65 and ages 13-17, $30; ages 3-12, $23; family rate (two adults and two children) $100. AX, MC, VI. Phone (416) 703-4476 or (877) 635-5510. *See color ad.*

Bus and Trolley Tours

[SAVE] Gray Line Sightseeing Tours offers a variety of Toronto city tours as well as daily excursions to Niagara Falls year-round. Tours leave from the Toronto Coach Terminal, 610 Bay St., and from most major downtown hotels; for information and

reservations phone (416) 594-3310 or (800) 353-3484.

Toronto City Tours offers a series of city excursions departing from most downtown hotels year-round. For information and reservations phone (416) 868-0400.

Niagara Tours has day trips to Niagara Falls that depart from most downtown hotels year-round. Departures are offered daily, including a night tour to view the light display and a seasonal winery tour; for information and reservations phone (416) 868-0400.

Swiftrans Niagara Tours, departing from most downtown Toronto hotels, offers daily narrated day trips to Niagara Falls. Reservations are required. Phone (416) 614-0999 or (888) 353-6111.

Industrial Tours

[SAVE] **STEAM WHISTLE BREWING,** adjacent to the Toronto Convention Centre and Air Canada Centre at 255 Bremner Blvd., is in the historic Canadian Pacific Railway John Street roundhouse. The brewery offers tours covering the history of the building, the origin of the company and the brewing process. A tasting of the company's Bavarian-style pilsner brew and a souvenir are included.

Allow 30 minutes minimum. Mon.-Sat. noon-6, Sun. and holidays noon-5, May 1-Labour Day; Mon.-Sat. and holidays noon-6, rest of year. Closed Jan. 1, Good Friday and Dec. 25. Tours are given on the hour beginning at 1. Last tour begins 1 hour before closing. Admission $4 (admission may be higher depending on the souvenir chosen). AX, MC, VI. Phone (416) 362-2337.

Walking Tours

Free guided walking tours exploring various neighborhoods are offered by Heritage Toronto. Some 35-69 walks, offered various Saturdays and Sundays mid-April to mid-October, explore Toronto's multi-faceted history; phone (416) 338-3886 or (416) 338-0684. The Royal Ontario Museum provides a series of guided walking tours Victoria Day weekend to late September; phone (416) 586-5797.

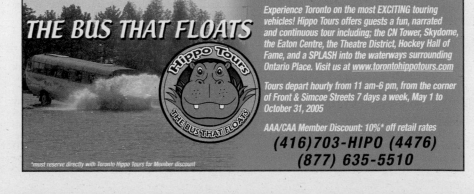

THE BUS THAT FLOATS

Hippo Tours

Experience Toronto on the most EXCITING touring vehicles! Hippo Tours offers guests a fun, narrated and continuous tour including; the CN Tower, Skydome, the Eaton Centre, the Theatre District, Hockey Hall of Fame, and a SPLASH into the waterways surrounding Ontario Place. Visit us at www.torontohippotours.com

Tours depart hourly from 11 am-6 pm, from the corner of Front & Simcoe Streets 7 days a week, May 1 to October 31, 2005

AAA/CAA Member Discount: 10%* off retail rates

(416)703-HIPO (4476)
(877) 635-5510

must reserve directly with Toronto Hippo Tours for Member discount

Guided walking tours of the Toronto Music Garden, 475 Queen's Quay W. between Bathurst Street and Spadina Avenue, are offered Wednesday at 11, June through September (also at 6, July through August), by the Toronto Botanical Garden; for information about the 1-hour tours phone (416) 397-1340. Information signs mark the trails of Discovery Walks, a series of self-guiding tours linking parks, gardens, beaches, neighborhoods and attractions; phone (416) 338-0338 or (416) 392-8186.

A brochure outlining a 1.5-hour self-guiding heritage walk of the Old Cabbagetown area is available. Many 19th-century homes and gardens are featured on the walk, which begins at the corner of Carlton and Parliament streets; phone (416) 921-0857 for information.

The Toronto Entertainment District, in the area bounded by Queen Street W. in the north and Queens Quay W. in the south, between Spadina Avenue and Yonge Street, is considered the city's top entertainment destination, offering a wealth of dining, nightlife, shopping, sports and theater options. Legends of the arts, entertainment and sports worlds, past and present, are honored on Canada's Walk of Fame, extending along King Street W. between John and Simcoe streets.

A self-guiding Art Walk brochure is available from the city. The walk highlights some 20 outdoor works of art and begins at the corner of Wellington and Windsor streets; phone (416) 338-0338. Guided 2-hour historical walking tours of the St. Lawrence Market neighborhood are offered Wednesday through Saturday at 10, beginning at the South Market foyer, 93 Front St. E.; phone (416) 392-0028 for information, reservations and tickets.

Spectator Sports

No matter the season, there is almost always a game to be enjoyed, whether it's baseball, football, hockey, lacrosse or soccer. Toronto sports fans feel there are no better places than the retractable-roofed **SkyDome** *(see attraction listing p. 197),* 1 Blue Jays Way, and the high-tech **Air Canada Centre** *(see attraction listing p. 188),* 40 Bay St.

Baseball

The **Toronto Blue Jays,** with consecutive World Series wins 1992-93, play at SkyDome from April through September. For information phone (416) 341-1111; for tickets phone (416) 341-1234.

Basketball

The NBA's **Toronto Raptors** have home-court advantage at the Air Canada Centre during their playing season, October to mid-April. For general information phone (416) 366-3865; for tickets phone Ticketmaster (416) 872-5000.

Football

There are some differences between U.S. and Canadian football—Canada has a slightly larger playing field with larger end zones and plays the game with three downs instead of four. Zealous fans

Toronto Harbour / Dick Loek; PhotoSensitive
Tourism Toronto

cheer the Canadian Football League's **Toronto Argonauts** to victory at SkyDome from June through October. For information phone (416) 341-2700; for tickets phone Ticketmaster at (416) 872-5000.

Hockey

Toronto fans love hockey so much that their **Toronto Maple Leafs** usually play home games before capacity crowds in the Air Canada Centre; the season runs from October to mid-April. You will notice many cars adorned with the blue Toronto Maple Leafs flag during the season, as fans proudly show their support. Although seats generally sell out every year, standing room tickets are sometimes available. Phone (416) 815-5700 for general information; for tickets phone Ticketmaster at (416) 872-5000.

Horse Racing

Horse racing is presented at **Woodbine Race Track,** 24 kilometres (15 mi.) northwest at 555 Rexdale Blvd. at Regional Rd. 27 (Hwy. 27). One of the largest tracks in North America, Woodbine has its live Thoroughbred season from mid-March to early December; Standardbreds generally run from late May through August and November through March. For information and schedule confirmation phone (416) 675-7223.

Note: Policies concerning admittance of children to pari-mutuel betting facilities vary. Phone for information.

Lacrosse

The NLL's four-time world champion Toronto Rock entertain fans at the Air Canada Centre from late December to mid-April. For information phone (416) 596-3075; for tickets phone Ticketmaster at (416) 872-5000.

Soccer

Fans of the game enjoy the local talent of the Toronto Lynx of the North American A-League. Games are played at Centennial Park Stadium from mid-May through mid-August; phone (416) 251-4625.

Recreation

Public recreational facilities in Toronto include beaches, a campground, golf courses, ice-skating rinks, ski and snowboard facilities, a skateboard park, swimming pools and tennis courts. City parks are ideal for a variety of activities, and the **Toronto Islands,** accessible by ferry, are favored for outdoor fun any time of year.

Bicycling

Courses used for jogging and walking double as great cycling tracks. Certainly the **Martin Goodman Trail,** extending 20 kilometres (14 mi.) along Toronto's waterfront, and numerous municipal parks are scenic and interesting. The **Humber River Trail** in the west end is a quiet, 16-kilometre (10 mi.) trail with some hills. The east end offers the **Don Valley Trail,** 18-kilometres (11 mi.) long and a bit more challenging.

High Park *(see attraction listing p. 192)* offers paved and natural courses with scenic views of the great outdoors. Cycling is popular, too, on the Toronto Islands; take the ferry across Toronto Harbour, then island hop at your leisure. You can rent a

Queen Street / © Gibson Stock Photography

bicycle on the mainland or at Toronto Island Bicycle Rental on **Centre Island;** phone (416) 203-0009.

Fishing

The weekend fisherman may be lucky enough to fill a creel on the Toronto Islands or on the shores of **Lake Ontario.** Wildlife management groups regularly stock these areas with perch, bass, salmon, trout and other species.

There are fishing boats that you can privately charter if you want to get serious about your salmon and trout fishing. The *Salmon Express,* the official guide boat of the Great Ontario Salmon Derby in July and August, offers barbecues on the Toronto Islands as part of their charter experience; phone (416) 931-7693. Phone the Ministry of Natural Resources Information Centre, (800) 667-1940, for information about fishing regulations and locations.

Golf

Toronto claims the highest ratio of golf courses per capita in North America, and its challenging golf courses are laid out against scenic backdrops of rolling hills, shade trees and rippling waters. The following offer at least 18 holes and are open to the public: Dentonia Park, (416) 392-2558, 781 Victoria Park Ave.; Don Valley, (416) 392-2465, 4200 Yonge St.; Humber Valley, (416) 392-2488, 40 Beattie Ave.; Scarlett Woods, (416) 392-2484, 1000 Jane St.; and Tam O'Shanter, (416) 392-2547, 2481 Birchmount Rd. Golf season lasts from mid-April to mid-November; phone Toronto Parks and Recreation, (416) 392-8186, or Access Toronto, (416) 338-0338, for more information.

Horseback Riding

An ideal setting for unfettered trail riding year-round is the **Rocking Horse Ranch** in Richmond Hill. Advance reservations are required; phone (905) 884-3292. Other stables, riding arenas and bridle trails can be found within the city and throughout the surrounding area. For a current list of establishments offering horses for rent phone the Ontario Equestrian Federation, (905) 709-6545.

Jogging and Walking

There's really no better way to see a city than by putting on a pair of sneakers and heading outdoors. For a planned workout, join the locals at some of the city's many trails. And don't forget it's always wise to run with a partner or group, even during daylight hours.

Any one of the series of parks hugging the Don Valley Parkway, running north from the Gardiner Expressway, then east, is a sure bet. Particularly popular with Torontonians is the 5-kilometre (3-mi.) trail at **E.T. Seton Park,** starting at Edwards Gardens on the park's northern end. **Taylor's Creek Park** has nearly 4 kilometres (2.5 mi.) of trails along the creek. Martin Goodman Trail, a favorite with the bicycling set, is equally appealing on foot. The west end offers its share of trails, including those in High Park and **Roundtree Mills Park,** and the Humber River Trail, also popular with bicyclists.

Tennis

Tennis buffs can take to any one of the dozens of multisurface municipal courts at 210 locations; generally they are open from April to October (weather permitting). Fees may vary, though many courts throughout the city are free; some have lights for night games. For an up-to-date schedule phone the Toronto Parks and Recreation Department, (416) 392-8186; Access Toronto, (416) 338-0338; or the Ontario Tennis Association, (416) 426-7135.

Water Sports

The city maintains approximately 60 outdoor swimming pools, all supervised by lifeguards from early June to early September. Those closest to downtown include **Alexandra Park**, at Bathurst Street and Dundas Street W.; **Alex Duff-Christie Pitts Park**, at Bloor Street W. and Christie Street; and **Riverdale Park**, west of Broadview Avenue and Riverdale W. near Danforth Avenue. For more information phone Toronto Parks and Recreation, (416) 392-8186, or the pool hot line at (416) 338-7665.

Canoeing and kayaking are favorite Canadian sports, and amateurs and professionals alike are challenged by the multitude of lakes and rivers in Ontario. The cost of renting a canoe or kayak ranges from $35 to $70 per day. Canoe rentals and complete outfitting are available in the Toronto area.

Winter Sports

As the temperature dips or snow begins to fall, many Torontonians venture out to enjoy winter in a variety of ways.

With 25 artificial rinks close to downtown and numerous others in the outlying areas, ice skating is one of the favorite leisure winter activities. The city maintains outdoor rinks that are open from November to March (weather permitting). **Harbourfront Centre** *(see attraction listing p. 205)* sports a supervised artificial rink open daily. The rink in downtown's **Nathan Phillips Square** *(see attraction listing p. 191)* becomes a reflecting pool when the ice melts. Admission is free and skate rentals are available at both sites. For more information about municipal rinks phone (416) 392-8186, or Access Toronto at (416) 338-0338.

Cross-country skiing remains a favorite for all ages. Trails are found on the Toronto Islands, at the Toronto Zoo, in High Park and along the ravines that stretch from downtown Toronto to the Ontario Science Centre.

Those in search of downhill skiing and snowboarding can find facilities for those sports at the North York Ski Centre in **Earl Bales Park** on Bathurst Street and at **Centennial Park Ski Hill.** Rentals and instruction are available at both locations; for more information phone (416) 338-6754. Downhill and cross-country skiing are available in several locations north of the city. **Penetang-Midland Coach Lines Ltd.** schedules daily ski trips by bus; phone the Toronto Coach Terminal at (416) 393-7911.

Shopping

For shoppers and browsers, Toronto beckons with street markets; sprawling malls, both above and below ground; and an abundance of ethnic neighborhoods and districts, many of which are attractions unto themselves.

The **Yonge-Dundas Square** entertainment venue, southeast corner of Yonge and Dundas streets, hosts a variety of celebrations, theatrical performances and concerts as well as an artisans market on Saturdays and Sundays from May through September.

Toronto has an impressive downtown shopping district extending from Yonge Street west to University Avenue and from King Street north to College Street. **Toronto Eaton Centre**, on Yonge Street between Dundas and Queen streets, is five levels of shopping spanning two blocks and offering more than 350 shops, services and eateries as well as the Ontario Travel Information Centre. Adjoining Toronto Eaton Centre is one of the city's largest department stores, **The Bay.**

The **Path Underground** is a system of walkways and levels featuring 27 kilometres (17 mi.) of shopping, services and entertainment from Union Station on Front Street to the Atrium on Bay, at Dundas Street. **First Canadian Place Shopping Centre**, King and Bay streets, is the largest in the Path and offers three levels of shopping with more than 120 stores and restaurants. Color-coded maps of the Path are available at the Toronto Convention and Visitors Association.

North of the downtown core, the **Yonge/Eglinton area**, at the junction of Yonge Street N. and Eglinton Avenue, is an upscale shopping district.

Antiques

Toronto has a number of good quality antique shops scattered around the city. Besides the immense **Toronto Antique Centre**, 276 King St. W., the **St. Lawrence North Market**, 92 Front St. E., has more than 80 dealers offering their wares on Sundays from dawn until 5 p.m.; there also are more than 20 other venues within a short distance.

Mirvish Village, on Markham Street near Bloor and Bathurst streets, is a group of Victorian-style buildings housing antiques, art stores, specialty gift shops and bookstores.

One Sunday each month, Toronto's longest running antique show, the **Heritage Antique Market**, opens it doors at the Bayview Village Shopping Centre with more than 70 selected dealers from Ontario and Québec in attendance.

Malls

From east to west, Toronto features mall emporiums that cater to everyone's taste in shopping. Most noteworthy are **Bayview Village Shopping Centre**, Bayview Avenue and Sheppard Avenue E.; **Dufferin Mall**, 900 Dufferin St., south of Bloor Street; **Fairview Mall**, Don Mills Road and Sheppard Avenue E.; **Promenade Mall**, Bathurst Street at Hwy.

7; **Scarborough Town Centre**, Hwy. 401 and Mc-Cowan Road; **Sherway Gardens**, Hwy. 427 and Queen Elizabeth Way; **Woodbine Centre**, Regional Rd. 27 (Hwy. 27) and Rexdale Boulevard, famous for its Fantasy Fair, an indoor amusement park and Victorian town; and **Yorkdale Shopping Centre**, on Dufferin Street at Hwy. 401.

Markets

To truly experience Toronto's multicultural diversity, visit one of the street markets. **Kensington Market**, west of Spadina Avenue between College and Dundas streets, on Baldwin Street, Augusta and Kensington avenues, represents people from more than 30 different backgrounds selling fresh fruits, vegetables and dry goods. It is one of the best areas to browse for vintage clothing. Take a moment to relax at one of the many outdoor cafes, then savour the meat shops of a bygone era.

St. Lawrence Market, 91-92 Front St. E., is a massive 19th-century brick building established in 1803. Farmers, fishermen and butchers bargain with customers amid an interesting array of gourmet or deli foods. Though open Tuesday through Friday during the week, the market is at its peak on Saturdays, when additional farmers are in attendance. Arrive early for the best selection of goods; the markets opens for brisk business at 5 a.m. on Saturdays.

Several other farmers' markets operate mid-June to late October—check out what's fresh at the market at the **East York Civic Centre**, 850 Coxwell Ave.; at the **Etobicoke Civic Centre**, 399 The West

Roy Thomson Hall / © Robert Harding World Imagery
Alamy Images

Mall; at the **Nathan Phillips Square Market**, at the corner of Bay and Queen streets at Toronto City Hall; at the **North York Farmers' Market**, at Mel Lastman Square, 5100 Yonge St.; at **Sherway Gardens Farmers' Market**, Hwy. 427 and Queen Elizabeth Way; and at the **York Civic Centre**, 2700 Eglinton Ave. W. Days and hours of operation vary.

Outlets

There are few true outlets to choose from in Toronto, but finding discount merchandise in a no-frills atmosphere still is possible.

Spadina Avenue, between Dundas and Front streets, is best known as a fashion district, with quite a collection of linen and clothing outlets. **Holt Renfrew Last Call**, 370 Steeles Ave. W., west of Yonge Street, is a popular place to shop for last season's hot items. **Honest Ed's**, 581 Bloor St. W. at Bathurst Street, is possibly Toronto's most famous shoestring shopping option, with four floors of bargain merchandise.

On the outskirts of Toronto's west end is one of Canada's premier factory retail outlets. **Dixie Value Outlet Mall**, Dixie Road and Queen Elizabeth Way at the Toronto/Mississauga border, has more than 100 retail outlets to satisfy anyone's craving for a bargain.

Specialty Districts

The **Bay-Bloor** area, centering on Bloor Street W. and the few blocks north and south between Yonge Street and Avenue Road, is one of Toronto's most prestigious shopping areas. A must-see part of the district is **Yorkville**. A quiet village in the 1800s and a hippie hangout in the 1960s, the area now offers a charming mix of old and new with restored Victorian houses, eclectic boutiques, outdoor cafes and flower-filled courtyards. It is a place to see and be seen; keep an eye out for Hollywood stars who happen to be in Toronto filming their latest flick. **Hazelton Lanes** is a charming street with exclusive shops.

The **Manulife Centre** is at Bloor and Bay streets. The **Holt Renfrew Centre**, 50 Bloor St. W., is Canada's answer to New York City's Saks Fifth Avenue.

The **Beach**, also known as The Beaches, is Toronto's best-known lakeside community. Stretching from Queen Street E. in the north to the lake in the south, between Coxwell and Victoria Park avenues, this older area of town exudes charm with large shaded trees and remarkable homes; a walking tour is a definite must-do. In the summer it is vibrant, as residents take to the streets to browse the bohemian shops and delis, either by foot or skateboard, usually with a dog tagging along.

Bloor West Village, along Bloor Street W. between Jane Street and Runnymeade Avenue, offers a wide variety of giftware boutiques, cafes and clothing stores with a a charming Old World flavor.

The **Distillery Historic District** is a Canadian heritage site and Toronto's newest arts, entertainment and cultural community. In the former Gooderham & Worts Distillery at 55 Mill St., it is one of the largest and best-preserved collections of Victorian industrial architecture in North America.

A visit to Toronto would be incomplete without experiencing one of the city's famous ethnic neighborhoods, whether seriously shopping for that unique item or just browsing and soaking in the sights and sounds. **Chinatown**, Spadina Avenue and Dundas Street W.; **Greektown**, Danforth Avenue between Chester and Jones avenues; **Little Italy**, College Street from Euclid Avenue to Shaw Street; and **Portuguese Village**, Dundas Street to Queen Street, Augusta Avenue to Shaw Street, all offer you a tantalizing taste of places far away.

HARBOURFRONT CENTRE at Queens Quay W. between York and Bathurst sts., is a center for urban arts, films, readings, concerts, festivals, lakeside dining and shopping. Queen's Quay Terminal, 207 Queens Quay W., has a variety of specialty shops, including an extensive collection of Canadian crafts and art objects.

An international marketplace is at 235 Queens Quay W., and a glass-roofed concert stage facing Lake Ontario hosts summer musical programs. Harbourfront Centre open daily year-round. International marketplace open Sat.-Sun., June 1-Labour Day. Phone (416) 973-4000.

Performing Arts

Home to more than 200 professional theater and dance companies, Toronto claims to be the third largest live theater center in the English-speaking world, after London and New York. More than 10,000 performances are offered each year at more than 90 venues, and productions average 75 a month.

Dance

Founded in 1951, the **National Ballet of Canada,** with more than 60 dancers, is one of the largest troupes in North America. Performances are held November through December and in February, late April and May at the **Hummingbird Centre for the Performing Arts**, 1 Front St. E.; phone (416) 345-9686 or (416) 393-7469 for information or Ticketmaster at (416) 872-2262 for tickets.

The **Toronto Dance Theatre,** with a modern repertoire, is best known for its bold and beautiful choreography. Performances are given at the 450-seat **Premiere Dance Theatre**, 207 Queens Quay W., in the Queen's Quay Terminal at Harbourfront Centre. The **Harbourfront Centre Theatre**, 231

Queens Quay W., has a three-story glass lobby and also offers an impressive dance program. For either venue, phone (416) 973-4000 for information and tickets.

Film

As the third-largest television and film production center in North America, Toronto plays host to a wealth of screenings each year. Retrospectives

Andrew Stawicki; PhotoSensitive / Tourism Toronto

and thematic showings can be seen at the following: **Bloor Cinema**, 506 Bloor St. W., (416) 516-2330; **Fox Theatre**, 2236 Queen St. E., (416) 691-7330; **Kingsway Theatre**, 3030 Bloor St. W., (416) 236-1411; **Music Hall**, 147 Danforth Ave., (416) 778-8272; and the **Paradise Cinema**, 1006 Bloor St. W., (416) 537-7040.

Music

One of Canada's foremost ensembles, the **Toronto Symphony Orchestra,** performs September through June in front of more than 400,000 patrons. The orchestra also performs frequent concerts on CBC radio. The **Toronto Mendelssohn Choir,** with 180 members, has been in existence since 1894. They performed much of the choral music for the movie "Schindler's List." Both groups perform at the 2,800-seat **Roy Thomson Hall**, 60 Simcoe St.; phone (416) 872-4255 for information and tickets.

Summer concerts are presented at the **Canadian National Exhibition Bandshell, Kingswood Music Theatre** at Paramount Canada's Wonderland in Vaughan *(see attraction listing p. 210)*, **Nathan Phillips Square** *(see attraction listing p. 191)*, **Molson Amphitheatre** at Ontario Place and in city parks. In the **Toronto Music Garden**, 475 Queen's Quay W. between Bathurst Street and Spadina Avenue, the compositions of Johann Sebastian Bach are interpreted through nature.

Special concerts are presented throughout the year at the **Air Canada Centre** and **SkyDome** as well as at **Massey Hall**, 178 Victoria St., and **Convocation Hall**, on the campus of the University of Toronto.

Opera

The **Canadian Opera Company** is the largest producer of opera in Canada, presenting seven fully-staged productions each season. Its performances of the classics, with occasionally more adventurous fare, take place from September to April. Home stage is the Hummingbird Centre for the Performing Arts, where opera enthusiasts have enjoyed performances by such visiting divas as Joan Sutherland, Marilyn Horne and Martina Arroyo. For information about performances phone (416) 363-6671; for tickets phone (416) 363-8231 or Ticketmaster at (416) 872-2262.

The **Toronto Operetta Theatre** specializes in lighter fare at the **St. Lawrence Centre for the Arts**, 27 Front St. E.; phone (416) 366-7723 for information and tickets.

Theater

"Broadway North," as Toronto sometimes is called, can be counted among the best cities in North America for live theater, ranking with New York City and Chicago. Venues are numerous and varied—some sleek and modern, others classically revived.

The **Main Stage Theatre** at the Toronto Centre for the Arts, 5040 Yonge St., has debuted Andrew Lloyd Webber's "Sunset Boulevard" and the revival of "Show Boat." For performance information phone (416) 733-9388; for tickets phone Ticketmaster at (416) 872-1111.

The restored **Royal Alexandra Theatre**, 260 King St. W., presents scintillating theater and treats the audience to the finest of amenities—plush carpeting and gilded embellishments amid cherry wood and marble surroundings. Just a few doors away at 300 King St. W. is the 2,000-seat **Princess of Wales Theatre**. One of the city's most beautiful buildings is the **Canon Theatre**, a once-spirited vaudeville showplace at 244 Victoria St. Phone (416) 593-0351 for information about all three theaters, or TicketKing at (416) 872-1212 or (800) 461-3333 for tickets.

Built in 1913, the elegant **Elgin and Winter Garden Theatre Centre**, 189-191 Yonge St., continues to impress patrons with top-notch theater; phone Ticketmaster at (416) 872-5555. Tours, offered on Thursday and Saturday, include both theaters, the lobbies, a backstage exhibit and a dressing room from the vaudeville era; phone (416) 314-2871 for tour information.

The St. Lawrence Centre for the Arts, at the corner of Front and Scott streets, contains the 875-seat Bluma Appel Theatre and the smaller Jane Mallet Theatre. Each presents a variety of contemporary and classical productions infused with the talents of the ingenious **Canadian Stage Company**. For more information phone (416) 366-1656; for tickets phone (416) 366-7723.

The **Factory Theatre**, 125 Bathurst St., is known for showing original Canadian works; phone (416) 504-9971. Wildly innovative plays are offered at the **Tarragon Theatre**, 30 Bridgman Ave.; phone (416) 531-1827.

More stage productions are offered at the **Hart House Theatre**, 7 Hart House Cir., (416) 978-8668; the **New Yorker Theatre**, 651 Yonge St., (416) 924-1249 for information or Ticketmaster at (416) 872-1111 for tickets; and **Theatre Passe Muraille**, 16 Ryerson Ave., (416) 504-7529.

The cast of the **Lorraine Kimsa Theatre for Young People**, 165 Front St. E., offers a variety of performances intended for children; phone (416) 363-5131 for more information or (416) 862-2222 for tickets.

Ticketmaster handles tickets for most of Toronto's major theaters; phone (416) 870-8000. Half-price tickets to professional performing arts events in the Toronto area are available on the day of the performance from the T.O. TIX booth in Yonge-Dundas Square at 1 Dundas St. E.; phone orders are not accepted. The booth is open Tuesday through Saturday noon-6; tickets for Sunday and Monday performances are sold on Saturday. Advance full-price tickets also can be obtained for many smaller non-profit theater companies or some out-of-town theaters; phone (416) 536-6468. The same phone number gives recorded information about available shows.

Toronto is a major center for radio and television production. For free tickets to Canadian Broadcasting Corporation shows phone (416) 205-3311.

Special Events

Enjoying the status of a vibrant world-class city, Toronto has something for everyone at any time of the year. The year begins with the **Toronto International Boat Show** and the **Metro Home Show** in January, followed by the **Chinese New Year** celebration. **Celebrate Toronto WinterCity Festival** and the **Canadian International Auto Show** follow in February. In March are the **St. Patrick's Day Parade**, **Canada Blooms**, the **Toronto Sportsmen's Show** and the **One of a Kind Spring Craft Show and Sale**. The **National Home Show** is held in April, along with the **Wine and Cheese Festival** on the outskirts of the city, followed by the **Toronto Jewish Film Festival** in early May and **Santé: The Bloor-Yorkville Wine Festival** in mid-May. Later in the month is the **Milk International Children's Festival of the Arts** at Harbourfront Centre and **Doors Open Toronto**, where the city's historic and architecturally significant sites open their doors to visitors for free.

Summer kicks off with the **Queen's Plate**, Canada's leading Thoroughbred race, and the prestigious **North America Cup**, both run in June at the Woodbine Race Track. The **International Dragon Boat Race Festival**, held at Centre Island in late June, is considered one of the largest in the world with more than 100 races as well as a cultural festival with crafts, international cuisine and entertainment.

Harbourfront Centre Summer Festivals begins in late June and runs through Labour Day. Films, food, dance, theater, crafts and music are featured. On the last Sunday in June, Toronto celebrates its diversity by hosting the world-famous **Gay Pride Parade**. The 10-day **Downtown Jazz Festival** beginning in late June presents performances, many free, by more than 2,000 musicians, while the **International CHIN Picnic** offers sports, international foods, music and dance by some 2,000 performers.

Early July offers the **Fringe: Toronto's Theatre Festival**, during which more than 100 national and international theater companies stage innovative productions. **Celebrate Toronto Street Festival** offers more than 1,200 performers and 700 attractions along Yonge Street. In mid-July top race car drivers compete in the 3-day **Molson Indy**, while the **Toronto Outdoor Art Exhibition** presents the works of some 500 artists. The **Beaches International Jazz Festival** features more than 70 bands and 1,000 musicians. Late July through early August brings **Caribana**, the city's popular Caribbean festival, and the **Rogers Cup** women's tennis championship.

August presents the **Fringe Festival of Independent Dance Artists**, featuring international artists staging works ranging from classical to very experimental, and the **Festival Bana y'Africa**, a celebration of African music, dance, food and culture. More than 900,000 residents and visitors alike flock to the **Taste of the Danforth** to celebrate Greek culture and food, while **Buskerfest** features the talents of street performers from around the globe. The end of summer is signaled with the **Canadian National Exhibition**, running from mid-August through Labour Day; one of the world's oldest and largest exhibitions, it is highlighted by displays, a horse show, live entertainment, a world-class air show and more than 500 attractions and 65 rides.

Autumn is ushered in by September's **Toronto International Film Festival**, in the downtown core. The **Toronto In-Water Boat Show** at Ontario Place also is held in September. October begins with the **Fall Home Show**. The **Toronto International Marathon** and the **Toronto Ski, Snowboard and Travel Show** are held in mid-October, followed by the **Creative Sewing and Needlework Festival**. The **International Festival of Authors** at Harbourfront Centre rounds out the month.

The **Royal Agricultural Winter Fair and Royal Horse Show** takes place in November, as does the long-running **Santa Claus Parade**, the **Canadian Aboriginal Festival** and the **One of a Kind Christmas Craft Show and Sale**, which runs through early December. The **Cavalcade of Lights** holiday celebration begins in late November and runs through New Year's Day. **A Historic Toronto Christmas** re-creates the days of Christmases past at the historical Colborne Lodge, Gibson House Museum, Mackenzie House and Spadina House from mid-November to early January.

A **New Year's Eve** celebration is held at Nathan Phillips Square at City Hall. **First Night Toronto Festival**, a family-oriented celebration popular with all ages, is held at various locations, including SkyDome.

Nightlife

A variety of entertainment possibilities abound throughout Toronto. Be aware that clubs cease serving alcohol at 2 a.m.; most dance clubs, though, stay open until 4 a.m.

Comedy Clubs

Canadian comedians Dan Aykroyd, John Candy, Eugene Levy, Andrea Martin, Mike Myers, Gilda Radner and Martin Short all honed their comedic skills on the stage at **The Second City**, 56 Blue Jays Way; phone (416) 343-0011 for reservations. The club also was the birthplace of SCTV.

Yuk Yuk's International is at 224 Richmond St. W. Howie Mandel started there, along with the man behind the mask, Jim Carrey. For more information phone (416) 967-6425.

Comedywood, with two locations available, 800 Steeles Ave. W. and 194 Bloor St. W., offers a variety of shows by top performers; phone (905) 761-0543 or (416) 966-9663 respectively for information and reservations. The **Laugh Resort**, 370 King St. W. in the concourse level of the Holiday Inn, attracts comedic icons such as Ellen Degeneres, Ray Romano, Adam Sandler and David Spade; phone (416) 364-5233.

Dance Clubs

Scattered across the city is a vast array of cabarets, outdoor bars and dance spots, whose names are constantly changing. For the most current information, consult either the *Where* or *Now* magazines, available free of charge in most major hotels, or pick up a copy of *Toronto Life* magazine at any newsstand or corner variety store.

If you want to go from club to club, explore Richmond Street between Peter and Simcoe streets for endless choices. One of the hotter spots for the 19- to 30-year-old crowd is **Lucid**, 126 John St., a multilevel complex with a 20-metre-high (66-ft.) atrium; phone (416) 345-8243. **Seven**, 224 Richmond St., boasts a year-round rooftop with a retractable glass enclosure and a barbecue pit; phone (416) 599-9797.

The **Courthouse Chamber Lounge**, 57 Adelaide St. E., offers dancing to today's popular music and hits from the past in a casual, relaxed atmosphere. In a historical 1853 building, the lounge has high ceilings and four fireplaces; phone (416) 214-9379. The **Lava Lounge**, 507 College St., is casually upscale and plays Latin, soul and funk; phone (416) 965-5282. For the mature clientele, try **Therapy Ultra Lounge**, 203 Richmond St., and please note that there is a dress code; phone (416) 977-3089.

The lively **Orbit Room** at 580 College St. plays jazz-inflected fusion and R&B. The club wins rave reviews from all age groups—no pretensions, just good music and great ambience. Be sure to get there early if you want a table; phone (416) 535-0613. A nice change of pace is offered at **Lula Lounge**, 1585 Dundas St. W., a Latin and Brazilian club with an eclectic mix of bohemian, salsa, and some flamenco and bellydancing tossed in for good measure; phone (416) 588-0307.

The **Phoenix Concert Theatre** presents exciting acts and live concerts; with three rooms and three decors to choose from, it suits everyone's taste. The theater is at 410 Sherbourne St.; phone (416) 323-1251.

Entertainment Complexes

The **Docks,** 11 Polson St., offers family fun during the day and beckons to the younger clubbing crowd at night. With 9 hectares (21 acres), it is probably Canada's largest patio party. The Docks boasts a lakeside pool, outdoor pool tables with one table right in the pool, beach volleyball courts, basketball courts, a mega swing ride, miniature golf, a drive-in theater, a sand beach and a driving range. And that's just outside. Inside there's mini putt, pool tables and darts. When you're ready to dance, there are three dance clubs, one with an open-style kitchen and fireplace; phone (416) 469-5655.

Jazz & Blues

Some music genres come and go, but jazz and blues have withstood the test of time. Toronto has a solid jazz following. The long-standing **Top O' The Senator,** 249-253 Victoria St., (416) 364-7517, is an institution in the city.

The **Montreal Bistro Restaurant and Jazz Club,** 65 Sherbourne St., features live jazz performances, from traditional to New Orleans style; phone (416)

363-0179. The **Rex Hotel & Jazz and Blues Bar,** 194 Queen St. W., presents top Canadian acts and up-and-coming performers in a casual atmosphere; phone (416) 598-2475.

Lisa's Café, 245 Carlaw Ave., offers a wonderful jazz brunch on Sundays; phone (416) 406-1101. At **The Reservoir Lounge,** 52 Wellington St., the musicians play right in your midst so you feel like you're part of the swing jazz and jump blues; phone (416) 955-0887. In the west end of the city you can enjoy Cajun-fusion food and great jazz at **Momo's Bistro,** 664 The Queensway; phone (416) 252-5560.

Rock

For local jammin' try **Cameron House,** 408 Queen St. W. It's close to the Ontario College of Art, so expect a younger crowd on weeknights and suburbanites on weekends; phone (416) 703-0811. Just down the road at the corner of Queen Street and Spadina Avenue, the **Horseshoe Tavern,** 370 Queen St. W., specializes in pop rock, blues and alternative bands, with an occasional visit by a country artist; phone (416) 598-4753.

"Give the crowd what it wants" is the motto at **The Rivoli,** 332-334 Queen St. W., where you can listen to good music, view the latest artwork and even catch some comedy acts and snippets of theater; phone (416) 596-1908. The **Velvet Underground,** 508 Queen St. W., offers alternative and new wave rock enthusiasts a small, intimate setting; phone (416) 504-6688.

The Toronto Vicinity

MARKHAM (F-5) pop. 208,165

Settled in 1794 by the United Empire Loyalists as well as by settlers from Germany, France and Great Britain, Markham began as an agricultural community. Over the years many corporations have flocked to the area, helping it become a center for high technology and innovative products and services.

Information Markham: 101 Town Centre Blvd., Markham, ON, Canada L3R 9W3; phone (905) 415-7500.

MARKHAM MUSEUM, 2.4 km (1.5 mi.) n. of Hwy. 7 to 9350 Hwy. 48, includes modern exhibit galleries and a 10-hectare (25-acre) historic village with restored houses, shops, rail stations and railway cars and an interactive "Hands-on House" log cabin. A land transportation building displays horse-drawn vehicles. Special events are offered throughout the year.

Allow 1 hour, 30 minutes minimum. Mon.-Sat. 10-5, Sun. 1-5 (also Mon. holidays), Victoria Day weekend-Labour Day; Mon.-Fri. 10-5, rest of year. Closed Jan. 1, Good Friday, July 1 and Dec. 25. Some buildings may not be available in the off-season. Admission Victoria Day weekend-Labour Day $5; over 64 and students with ID $4; ages 3-12, $3; family rate

(maximum two adults) $14. Admission by donation rest of year. VI. Phone (905) 294-4576.

RICHMOND HILL (F-4) pop. 132,030

In the late 19th century a rough trail was cut through the wilderness from York to Georgian Bay, serving as a military supply line for Lt. Gov. John Graves Simcoe. Farms were laid out along the route, a portion of which became Yonge Street, the main thoroughfare of Richmond Hill. The Duke of Richmond so impressed the residents of the community during a rest stop they named the village after him.

David Dunlap Observatory (University of Toronto) is 3 kilometres (1.9 mi.) north of Regional Road 107 (Hwy. 7), off Bayview Avenue at 123 Hillsview Dr. The observatory houses a 188-centimetre (74-in.) reflecting telescope, the largest in Canada. A guided dome tour and a talk about astronomy are included in programs offered by reservation Saturday evenings, May to early October (also Friday evenings, July through August); phone (416) 978-2016 or (416) 946-5719. *See color ad p. 209.*

York Region Tourism—Richmond Hill: 17250 Yonge St., 4th floor, P.O. Box 147, Newmarket, ON, Canada L3Y 6Z1; phone (905) 883-3442 or (888) 448-0000. *See color ad p. 209.*

EXPERIENCE
YORK REGION...

FOR CULTURE
Varley Gallery
Red Barn Theatre
McMichael Art Collection
Sharon Temple

FOR FUN
The Wave Pool
David Dunlap Observatory
Paramount Canada's Wonderland
Vaughan Mills

FOR OUTDOORS
Kortright Centre
Butterflies & Blooms
Stouffville Country Market
Sibbald Point Provincial Park

FOR MORE
Shopping
Golfing & Fishing
Wineries & Breweries
Festivals & Events

**For lots to see and do...
so close to Toronto!**

Ontario's Rising Star
York Region
Markham · Vaughan · Richmond Hill · Newmarket · Aurora
Georgina · Whitchurch-Stouffville · East Gwillimbury · King

**Visit our website or call
for Stay'n'Play packages
and more information**

1-888-448-0000   www.yorktourism.com

UNIONVILLE (F-4)

First settled by German pioneers in 1794, Unionville received its name only after the town post office opened in 1849. With more than 20 original period buildings, Unionville's Main Street section has retained much of its late 19th-century charm. Main Street also has antique and specialty shops.

On the first weekend in June, the community celebrates its heritage with the Unionville Village Festival. The holiday season is welcomed with Olde Tyme Christmas in December.

York Region Tourism—Unionville: 17250 Yonge St., 4th floor, P.O. Box 147, Newmarket, ON, Canada L3Y 6Z1; phone (905) 883-3442 or (888) 448-0000. *See color ad p. 209.*

SAVE **VARLEY ART GALLERY OF MARKHAM,** 216 Main St., features a permanent collection of works by portrait artist Frederick Varley, a founding member of the Group of Seven. Works by other regional and national artists, including contemporaries of Varley, as well as changing exhibitions also are shown.

Allow 1 hour minimum. Mon.-Sat. 10-5, Sun. noon-5, July-Aug.; Tues.-Sat. 10-5, Sun. noon-5, Apr.-June and Sept.-Oct.; Tues.-Sat. 10-4, Sun. noon-4, rest of year. Closed Jan. 1 and Dec. 25. Admission $4; over 64 and ages 12-17, $3; ages 6-11, $2; family rate (two adults and two children) $10. Rates may change during special events. AX, MC, VI. Phone (905) 477-9511. *See color ad p. 209.*

VAUGHAN (F-4)

 PARAMOUNT CANADA'S WONDERLAND is off Hwy. 400, Rutherford Rd. exit northbound or Major MacKenzie Dr. E. exit southbound at 9580 Jane St. This 121-hectare (330-acre) theme park has more than 200 attractions and 65 rides; one of North America's greatest variety of roller coasters; Splash Works, an 8-hectare (20-acre) water park; Hanna-Barbera Land, Scooby-Doo's Haunted Mansion and Kidzville participative play areas; and a climbing wall.

Entertainment includes live theater productions, dance shows, Hanna-Barbera and Nickelodeon walk-around characters and cliff divers.

Daily late May-Labour Day; open some weekends early May-late May and day after Labour Day-second Mon. in Oct. Gates open at 10; closing time varies. Phone to verify schedule and admission. Grounds only $25.99. Passport for grounds admission and most rides $49.99; over 59 and ages 3-6, $24.99. Parking $7.50. Concerts are available at an extra charge. AX, MC, VI. Phone (905) 832-7000 or (905) 832-8131. *See color ad p. 209.*

WINERIES

• **Magnotta Winery** is at 271 Chrislea Rd. Mon.-Fri. 9-9, Sat. 8:30-6, Sun. 11-5; closed Jan. 1, Easter and Dec. 25-26. Reservations are required for tours. Phone (905) 738-9463 or (800) 461-9463.

Ontario Legislative Buildings / © 2004 Ontario Tourism

This ends listings for the Toronto Vicinity.
The following page resumes the alphabetical listings of cities in Ontario.

TOTTENHAM (F-3) pop. 4,829

THE FALCONRY CENTRE, s. off CR 10 and n. of Hwy. 9 on 2nd Line, following signs, allows visitors a close-up look at more than 200 rare and endangered raptors, from chicks to full-grown. The centuries-old art of falconry is demonstrated during the Raptors in Flight show. Guests can feed the birds of prey and have their pictures taken with a hawk on their arm. Shows are given daily; phone for schedule.

Allow 2 hours minimum. Daily 10-4, mid-May to mid-Oct. Admission $9; over 64, $8; ages 3-12, $6; family rate (four people) $26. MC, VI. Phone (905) 936-1033 or (888) 782-5667.

SOUTH SIMCOE RAILWAY, 4 km (2.5 mi.) n. of Hwy. 9 on CR 10 to Mill St. W., offers narrated 55-minute tours through the scenic Beeton Creek Valley over 1870s railway lines in Ontario's only operating steam-powered trains. Passengers ride in 1920s open-window coaches pulled by coal-burning locomotives from 1883 and 1912. Special events include Easter bunny trains, fall color season and Santa trains.

Departures Sun.-Tues. at 10:30, noon, 1:30 and 3, July 1-Labour Day; Sun. and Mon. holidays at 10:30, noon, 1:30 and 3, Victoria Day weekend-June 30 and day after Labour Day-second Mon. in Oct. Phone for special event schedule. Schedule may vary; phone ahead. Passengers should arrive 30 minutes before departure. Fare $12; over 64, $10; ages 2-15, $7; under 2 seated on adult's lap free. Reservations required for special events only. MC, VI. Phone (905) 936-5815 (for reservations phone Mon.-Fri. noon-4).

TRENTON (G-10) pop. 17,200

ROYAL CANADIAN AIR FORCE MEMORIAL MUSEUM is at 8 Wing Trenton; from Hwy. 401 take exit 526 Sidney St. S. to CR 22E and follow signs to RCAF Rd. This museum features displays illustrating the social and historic facets of Air Force life and operations. Various aircraft are displayed in an outdoor lot. Visitors can observe the refurbishing of the only remaining Mark VII Halifax bomber, recovered from a Norwegian lake.

Allow 1 hour minimum. Daily 10-5, May-Sept.; Wed.-Sun. 10-5, rest of year. Closed Jan. 1, Good Friday, Easter Monday and Dec. 25. Free. Phone (613) 965-2140.

UNIONVILLE—see Toronto p. 210.

UXBRIDGE (G-8) pop. 17,377

UXBRIDGE HISTORICAL CENTRE, 2 km (1.2 mi.) n. of Hwy. 47 on Concession Rd. 6, depicts the history of the area settled by Quakers 1805-06. Ten buildings house exhibits including displays about author Lucy Maud Montgomery, pianist Glen Gould, artist David Milne, the Thomas Foster Memorial, the Oak Ridges Moraine and the Quaker settlers. The grounds offer a panorama of the region. An archives and research center is available. Special events are offered throughout the season.

Guided tours are available. Picnicking is permitted. Wed.-Fri. 1-4, Sat.-Sun. and holidays 10-4:45, Victoria Day weekend-Oct. 31. Admission $4; over 64 and students with ID $3; ages 6-12, $2; family rate $10. Phone (905) 852-5854.

VANDORF (F-4)

THE WHITCHURCH-STOUFFVILLE MUSEUM is 1 km (.6 mi.) e. off Hwy. 404 Bloomington Rd. exit, then 3 km (1.9 mi.) n. to 14732 Woodbine Ave. The area's rural 19th-century lifestyle is depicted through a restored log cabin, a one-room schoolhouse, a Victorian farmhouse and barn, and heritage gardens. Changing exhibits also are featured. Special events are offered year-round.

Guided tours are available. Allow 1 hour minimum. Wed.-Sun. 10-5, Victoria Day weekend-Labour Day; Mon.-Fri. 1-5, rest of year. Closed Good Friday, Easter Monday, the second Mon. in Oct. and Dec. 25-Jan. 1. Donations. A fee is charged during special events. Phone (905) 727-8954.

VAUGHAN—see Toronto p. 210.

VIENNA (I-2) pop. 566

THE EDISON MUSEUM OF VIENNA is off Hwy. 19, following signs, to 14 Snow St. The museum is in an 1853 house on land once owned by the Edison family. Thomas Edison's grandparents were village founders, and the future inventor spent many childhood summers in Vienna. The museum features Edison artifacts and furniture, some donated by Edison's cousin.

Guided tours are available. Allow 30 minutes minimum. Mon.-Fri. 10-5, Sat.-Sun. 10-5:30, mid-May through Labour Day; by appointment rest of year. Admission $2, under 12 free with an adult. Phone (519) 874-4999, or (519) 866-5521 in the off-season.

WALLACEBURG (I-6) pop. 11,114

[SAVE] **WALLACEBURG & DISTRICT MUSEUM,** 505 King St., depicts the industrial and cultural aspects of the area through displays of artifacts from the late 19th and early 20th centuries. The museum contains collections of Lee-Enfield rifles and hand-blown glass as well as rooms furnished in the period of the early 1900s and a room containing items manufactured in Wallaceburg. Allow 30 minutes minimum. Mon.-Sat. 10-4; closed major holidays. Admission $3; over 65 and ages 6-12, $2; family rate $7. Phone (519) 627-8962.

WASAGA BEACH (F-8) pop. 12,419

Wasaga Beach, 14 kilometres (9 mi.) of sandy coastline along Georgian Bay, is believed to be one of the world's longest freshwater beaches, but this matters little to those who come each summer to bask in the sun or swim, sail and fish in the bay. Hiking can be enjoyed in summer; winter activities include snowmobiling and cross-country skiing. Before it became a summer resort, Wasaga Beach was an important transportation route and the last part of the Nine Mile Portage canoe route, a vital supply route during the War of 1812.

Wasaga Chamber of Commerce: 550 River Rd. W., P.O. Box 394, Wasaga Beach, ON, Canada L0L 2P0; phone (705) 429-2247, or (866) 292-7242 in Ontario.

NANCY ISLAND HISTORIC SITE is on Nancy Island at Wasaga Beach Provincial Park, accessible by footbridge from the Mosley St. entrance. The HMS *Nancy* was sunk by an American flotilla at this site during the War of 1812. The charred hull has been recovered and now rests in an enclosure beside the museum. At the far side of the island is a replica of a late 19-century Great Lakes lighthouse.

A videotape presentation in the theater recounts the final naval encounters between Canada and the United States. With architecture inspired by the billowing sails of a Great Lakes schooner, the theater and museum complex offer information about the war, its participants and the history of the Wasaga Beach area.

Daily 10-6, mid-June through Labour Day; Sat.-Sun. 10-5, day after Labour Day-second Mon. in Oct.; Sat.-Sun. 10-6, late May to mid-June. Daily vehicle permit $12. Walk-in admission by donations. Phone (705) 429-2728, or (705) 429-2516 in the off-season.

WASAGA WATERWORLD, 1.5 km (.9 mi.) e. on Hwy. 92, has a wave pool, waterslides, paddle boats, an arcade, a whirlpool, bumper boats and a children's pool and play area.

Food and picnic facilities are available. Allow 1 hour minimum. Daily 10-6, late June-Labour Day (weather permitting). Day pass (includes both Waterworld parks and unlimited miniature golf) $22, under 42 inches tall free, family rate (four persons) $66 (additional family members $15). Sunset pass (after 3 p.m.) $15. MC, VI. Phone (705) 429-4400, or (800) 809-0896 in Canada.

WASAGA WATERWORLD BEACHFRONT PARK, on Beach Dr. between 1st and 2nd sts. (beach areas one and two), is a 107-metre (350-ft.) waterslide with four chutes. An 18-hole miniature golf course is on the grounds.

Food is available. Allow 30 minutes minimum. Waterslide daily 10-7, miniature golf daily 10-10, late June-Labour Day (weather permitting). Waterslide $2 for one ride, $10 for six rides. Miniature golf $5. Day pass (includes both Waterworld parks and unlimited miniature golf) $22, family rate (four persons) $66 (additional family members $15). Sunset pass (after 4 p.m.) $15. Under 42 inches tall not permitted on waterslide. MC, VI. Phone (705) 429-4400, or (800) 809-0896 in Canada.

WATERLOO (G-2) pop. 86,543

Settled in the early 1800s by an influx of Mennonite farmers and German immigrants, Ebytown was renamed Waterloo in honor of the British victory over France. Jacob C. Snider built a distillery in 1829; in 1870 Joseph E. Seagram bought a partnership in the business and eventually took over the operation, creating Seagram Distilleries.

Still largely rural along its outskirts and home to one of the largest Mennonite populations in Canada, the city is renowned as a center for industry and leading-edge technology. Two major insurance companies are headquartered in the city. Waterloo also is home to two university campuses—the University of Waterloo with 25,000 students, and Wilfrid Laurier University with a student body of 7,800.

Waterloo's 242-hectare (500-acre) RIM Park, in the city's northeast corner, is a recreational facility with 18 sports fields, trails, a golf course, parklands and outdoor sculpture. As one of the "twin cities" of Kitchener/Waterloo, the community celebrates Oktoberfest in early October with what is believed to be the largest such celebration in North America.

KW Tourism—Waterloo: 191 King St. W., Kitchener, ON, Canada N2G 1N1; phone (519) 570-3246 or (800) 265-6959.

BRUBACHER HOUSE MUSEUM, on the University of Waterloo campus at Columbia St. and N. Campus Dr., was built in the Pennsylvania-German Mennonite style. The restored 1850 structure is furnished in period, and its rural surroundings have been preserved. A 10-minute audiovisual presentation gives insight into early settlers' methods of barn raising and quilting.

Allow 1 hour minimum. Wed.-Sat. 2-5, May-Oct.; other times by appointment. Guided 1-hour tours are available upon request. Admission $2, under 12 free with adult. Phone (519) 886-3855.

CANADIAN CLAY & GLASS GALLERY, jct. Erb and Caroline sts., features changing exhibits of contemporary Canadian ceramics, glass, enamel art and stained-glass. Allow 30 minutes minimum. Tues.-Sat. 10-5, Sun. 1-5; closed Dec. 24-Jan. 1. Donations. Under 12 must be with an adult. Phone (519) 746-1882.

EARTH SCIENCES MUSEUM, on the University of Waterloo campus in the Centre for Environmental and Information Technology, displays natural history exhibits, including rocks, gems, minerals and fossils. Fossil exhibits include examples of Albertosaurus and Parasaurolophus, a T-rex head and dinosaur eggs. A rock garden has stones from across Canada. Hands-on exhibits also are featured. Mon.-Fri. 8:30-4:30; closed holidays and Dec. 25-Jan. 2. Free. Phone (519) 888-4567, ext. 2469.

RECREATIONAL ACTIVITIES
Horseback Riding
• **Horseback Adventures** departs from 535 Northfield Dr. E., Waterloo, ON, Canada N2J 4G8. Daily 9-dusk. Phone (519) 888-6503.

WAUPOOS (G-11)

ROSE HOUSE MUSEUM is at 3333 CR 8. Guides, sometimes dressed in period garb, lead visitors through this Loyalist pioneer home, built in 1804 using beams and lumber from the Lutheran Church that was formerly on the property. Lived in by five generations of the Rose family, the home offers a glimpse into early 19th-century life. Genealogical information is available.

Picnicking is permitted. Allow 30 minutes minimum. Thurs.-Mon. 10-4:30, July-Aug.; Sat.-Sun. 10-4:30, Victoria Day-June 30 and Sept. 1 to mid-Sept. Donations. Phone (613) 476-5439.

WAWA (C-4) pop. 3,279, elev. 366 m/1,201'

Wawa, meaning "wild goose" in Ojibway, was so named because of the geese that rested on Wawa Lake during migration. A giant statue of a Canada goose poised for flight guards the entrance to the town. Recreational activities available include boating, canoeing and kayaking, bird-watching, fishing, hiking, hunting and snowmobiling. In addition to Scenic High Falls *(see attraction listing)*, Silver Falls and Wawa Falls are nearby.

Regional Tourist Information Centre: Hwys. 17 and 101, P.O. Box 500, Wawa, ON, Canada P0S 1K0; phone (705) 856-2244, ext. 260 or (800) 367-9292, ext. 260.

LAKE SUPERIOR PROVINCIAL PARK, s. on Hwy. 17, is a rugged wilderness area on the northeastern shore of Lake Superior. Covering 1,565 square kilometres (600 sq. mi.), the park is traversed from north to south by Hwy. 17. Brook and lake trout fishing and hunting are permitted in season.

Nature programs, nature walks and interpretive talks are offered July through August. A trail leads to Agawa Rock, site of Agawa Indian pictographs. Daily May-Oct. Admission $9.50 per private vehicle. AX, MC, VI. Phone (705) 856-2284. *See Recreation Chart.*

SCENIC HIGH FALLS, 2.4 km (1.5 mi.) s. on Hwy. 17, then 3 km (1.9 mi.) w. on a gravel road, is a scenic waterfall on the Magpie River. The falls, 38 metres (125 ft.) across and 23 metres (75 ft.) high, are surrounded by a park area which includes a picnic shelter and an interpretive trail. Daily dawn-dusk, Victoria Day weekend-second Mon. in Oct. Free.

WELLAND—*see Niagara Falls p. 129.*

WELLINGTON (G-10) pop. 1,943

WELLINGTON COMMUNITY HISTORICAL MUSEUM, 290 Main St., is in an 1885 Quaker meetinghouse. The museum has exhibits about area history, the Society of Friends and the importance of Prince Edward County in the development of Canada's canning industry.

Allow 30 minutes minimum. Mon.-Sat. 10-4:30, July-Aug.; Fri.-Sat. 10-4:30, Victoria Day weekend-June 30 and Sept. 1-second Mon. in Oct.; by appointment rest of year. Admission $2; ages 13-17, $1. Phone (613) 399-5015.

WHITBY (F-5) pop. 87,413

Named after a town in Yorkshire, England, Whitby is a picturesque town on Lake Ontario and the oldest town in the Durham region. There are many examples of 19th-century architecture. Locals enjoy catching the temporary exhibits at The Station Gallery; phone (905) 668-4185.

Fishing and boating are enjoyed from the full-service Port Whitby Marina, while other recreational activities include hiking on the Waterfront Trail, bicycling and picnicking in one of the city's many parks. Cross-country skiing is a popular winter activity.

The Whitby Courthouse Theatre presents several productions each year at the Centennial Building, 416 Centre St. S.; phone (905) 668-1170 or the information center for information, or (905) 430-3774 for tickets.

Whitby Information Centre: 900 Brock St. S., Whitby, ON, Canada L1N 4L6; phone (905) 668-0552 or (800) 694-4829.

CULLEN GARDENS AND MINIATURE VILLAGE, 300 Taunton Rd. W., is 7 km (4 mi.) n. of Hwy. 401 and 1 km (.6 mi.) w. of Hwy. 12. The village has a collection of miniature reproductions, built to one-twelfth scale, of more than 160 historic and contemporary Ontario buildings. The miniatures, enhanced by tiny furniture, automobiles and accessories, are set in beautifully landscaped gardens.

The Cottage Country exhibit has more than 80 reproductions. A miniature lake has boats and outdoor scenes, and a carnival has rides and music. More than 170 types of plants and wildflowers can be found in the Ontario Wildflower Garden, and an outdoor theater provides summer entertainment. The gardens host a variety of seasonal displays.

The Petal Pet Valley Ride is a family-oriented wagon ride through the village valley. A miniature golf course, driving range and children's play area are available.

Food is available. Allow 2 hours minimum. Daily 9-8, late June-Labour Day; 10-10, mid-Nov. through the weekend after Jan. 1; 10-6, mid-Apr. to late June and day after Labour Day-second Mon. in Oct.; 10-5, second Tues. in Oct. to mid-Nov. Phone ahead to verify hours. Closed Dec. 25. Admission $12.50; over 59 and ages 13-18 with ID $9; ages 3-12, $5.50; family rate (up to five persons) $39.99. Additional fee for driving range. AX, MC, VI. Phone (905) 668-6606, (905) 686-1600, or (800) 461-1821 in Ontario and Québec.

Lynde House, just outside the tower gate to Cullen Gardens, is a restored 1812 dwelling furnished in mid-19th-century style. Costumed guides relate the history of the house and local area. Recordings and animated mannequins reflect family life in the 1850s. A 1930s period cellar has a photograph exhibit devoted to the history, development and growth of Whitby.

Allow 30 minutes minimum. Daily 9-8, late June-Labour Day; 10-10, mid-Nov. through the weekend after Jan. 1; 10-6, mid-Apr. to late June and day after Labour Day-second Mon. in Oct.; 10-5, second Tues. in Oct. to mid-Nov. Phone ahead to verify hours. Closed Dec. 25. Free with paid admission to Cullen Gardens and Miniature Village. Phone (905) 668-6606.

WILLIAMSTOWN (E-12)

THE NOR'WESTERS AND LOYALIST MUSEUM, 19651 John St., is in an 1862 Georgian-style building originally used as a school. The museum features exhibits about the exploration and fur trading conducted by the North West Co. and the story of the United Empire Loyalists who settled here in 1784 after the American Revolution. Replicas of a fur trading post and a trader's canoe, maps and photographs are featured.

Picnicking is permitted. Allow 1 hour minimum. Sun. and Tues.-Fri. 1-5, Sat. and holidays 9-5, Victoria Day-Labour Day; Sat. 10-5, Sun. 1-5, day after Labour Day-second Mon. in Oct. Admission $4; over 65, $2; students with ID $1; under 13 free. Phone (613) 347-3547.

WINDSOR (I-5) pop. 208,402, elev. 177 m/581'

Linked to Detroit by both tunnel and bridge, Windsor is one of the busiest points of entry along the U.S./Canadian border. The city also is one of Canada's major manufacturing centers, with an output exceeding that of some provinces. Despite its industrial image Windsor also is part of a rural region known for orchards and farmlands nurtured by the mildest climate in Ontario.

One symbol of the city's peaceful ties to the United States is the Charlie Brooks Memorial Peace Fountain, the centerpiece of Coventry Gardens, which honors Windsor's British sister city. In the Detroit River, this floating fountain is one of the largest in North America and presents a variety of water displays. The fountain is operational from late May to mid-October. Another of Windsor's riverfront parks is Dieppe Gardens, which has a promenade along the river and a variety of gardens.

The International Freedom Festival, held from late June to early July, jointly celebrates Canada Day (July 1) and U.S. Independence Day (July 4), and promotes peace, unity, freedom and friendship between the two countries. Tugboat races, sports events, concerts, dances, cultural events, craft exhibits, parades and fireworks are all included in the festivities. Other notable events include Bluesfest International in mid-July and the International Busker Festival in mid-August, featuring world-renowned street performers.

The farmers' market at Market Square, 2109 Ottawa St., offers fresh produce Tuesday through Sunday. Fort Malden National Historic Site *(see Amherstburg p. 51)* is about 29 kilometres (18 mi.) south. Windsor Raceway, 9.75 kilometres (6 mi.) southwest on CR 20 at 5555 Ojibway Pkwy., offers harness racing; phone (519) 969-8311.

Note: Policies concerning admittance of children to pari-mutuel betting facilities vary. Phone for information.

Convention & Visitors Bureau of Windsor, Essex County & Pelee Island—Windsor: 333 Riverside Dr. W., Suite 103, Windsor, ON, Canada N9A 5K4; phone (519) 255-6530 or (800) 265-3633.

Shopping areas: More than 175 stores, including The Bay and Sears, can be found at Windsor's Devonshire Mall, at 3100 Howard Ave. Tecumseh Mall, 7654 Tecumseh Rd. E., offers more than 60 shops and services, including Zellers.

For outlet shopping try Windsor Crossing Premium Outlets, 1555 Talbot Rd. (Hwy. 3) at Cousineau Road across from St. Clair College; shops include Adidas, Corningware Corelle Revere, Guess, Reebok and Tommy Hilfiger.

ART GALLERY OF WINDSOR is downtown at 401 Riverside Dr. W. Three floors of galleries and changing exhibits house more than 3,000 works of

Savings for all Seasons

No matter the season, Hertz offers CAA members exclusive discounts and benefits.

Operating in 150 countries at over 7,000 rental locations worldwide, Hertz makes traveling more convenient and efficient wherever and whenever you go. Hertz offers CAA members discounts up to 20% on car rentals worldwide.

To receive your exclusive CAA member discounts and benefits, mention your CAA membership card at time of reservation and present it at time of rental.

For reservations and program details, call your CAA Travel office or the Hertz/CAA Desk at **1-800-263-0600, Toronto 416-620-9620.**

Hertz rents Fords and other fine cars.
© REG. U.S. PAT. OFF. © HERTZ SYSTEM INC. 1999/2006/99

Hertz
exactly.

contemporary and historical art relevant to Canadian heritage. Allow 30 minutes minimum. Thurs.-Fri. noon-5 (also Fri. 5-8), Sat.-Sun. 11-5; closed major holidays. Admission $2. Phone (519) 977-0013.

CANADIAN CLUB BRAND CENTRE is at 2072 Riverside Dr. E. at jct. Walker Rd. A guided tour of the opulent 1894 office building where the founders of Hiram Walker worked provides information about the history of the Canadian Club brand of whiskey. Company memorabilia can be seen in an exhibit room, and a video presentation explains the production and aging of the whiskey. An art gallery has works by the Group of Seven. Drink samples are included.

Allow 2 hours minimum. Guided tours are given Wed.-Sat. on the hour noon-6, Sun. noon-4, early May-late Dec.; closed major holidays. Last tour begins 1 hour before closing. Admission $5; over 54, $4; under 19 free if accompanied by an adult. AX, MC, VI. Phone (519) 561-5499, or (800) 447-2609, ext. 499.

JACKSON PARK—QUEEN ELIZABETH II GARDEN, Tecumseh Rd. and Ouellette St., is a sunken garden composed of flowerbeds and shrubs. Rose gardens surround a Lancaster Bomber, a memorial to those in the Royal Canadian Air Force killed in World War II. Several memorials and monuments are in the park, including ones to Copernicus, the father of modern astronomy, and to poet Robert Burns. Daily dawn-11 p.m. Free. Phone (519) 253-2300 or (888) 519-3333.

ODETTE SCULPTURE PARK is in Assumption and Centennial parks, on the Detroit River along Riverside Dr. W., between the Ambassador Bridge and Cameron Ave. This outdoor art gallery features more than 25 pieces of contemporary sculpture along a waterfront promenade. Information boards along the walkway provide details about each piece of art. Allow 30 minutes minimum. Daily dawn-dusk. Free. Phone (519) 253-2300 or (888) 519-3333.

OJIBWAY PRAIRIE COMPLEX AND NATURE CENTRE is at 5200 Matchette Rd., just off Ojibway Pkwy. The 127-hectare (315-acre) natural area, which includes Tallgrass Prairie Heritage Park, Ojibway Park and the Black Oak Heritage Park, protects one of the few remaining portions of tallgrass prairie. The complex has wetlands, forest, savannah and prairie habitats, rare plants, insects, reptiles, birds and mammals.

Trail maps and exhibits about local wildlife and ecology are at the nature center. Picnicking is permitted. Allow 1 hour minimum. Complex open daily dawn-dusk. Nature center Thurs.-Tues. 10-5, Wed. 1-5. Nature center closed Dec. 25. Free. Phone (519) 966-5852.

PRIDE OF WINDSOR CRUISES departs from the dock at Riverside Dr. and Ouellette Ave. One-hour narrated sightseeing tours aboard the MV *Aurora*

Borealis cruise along the Detroit River and offer views of luxury homes, the Ambassador Bridge, the Canadian Club Distillery and Detroit's Renaissance Center. Lunch, brunch, dinner and sunset dinner dance cruises also are offered.

Food is available. Allow 1 hour minimum. Sightseeing cruises depart daily, late May-Sept. 30; phone for schedule. Fee for sightseeing cruise $10; under 5, $5. Reservations are required for meal cruises. AX, MC, VI ($25). Phone (519) 971-7797 or (800) 706-2607.

WINDSOR'S COMMUNITY MUSEUM, 254 Pitt St. W., is said to be one of the oldest surviving brick buildings along the Detroit River. It was headquarters for Gen. William Hull and Gen. Brock during the War of 1812. The 1812 structure contains exhibits about the history of Windsor and surrounding area. Of special interest is a hands-on history room for children. Tues.-Sat. 10-5, Sun. 2-5, May-Sept.; Tues.-Sat. 10-5, rest of year. Closed statutory holidays. Donations. Phone (519) 253-1812.

WINDSOR WOOD CARVING MUSEUM is at 850 Ouellette Ave., at the front of the Central Library. More than 150 hand-crafted carvings include cultural, historical and wildlife themes. Visitors may participate in hands-on woodcarving demonstrations and activities. Allow 30 minutes minimum. Tues.-Fri. 10-5, Sat. 10-4; closed major holidays, Easter weekend and Dec. 25-26. Donations. Phone (519) 977-0823.

CASINOS

- **Casino Windsor** is at 377 Riverside Dr. E. Daily 24 hours. Phone (519) 258-7878 or (800) 991-7777.

WINGHAM (F-1) pop. 2,885

NORTH HURON DISTRICT MUSEUM is at 273 Josephine St. The museum, in the former town post office building, features exhibits about Wingham's history. Included are displays about past businesses, old ovens, wood stoves, radios and televisions. Four changing exhibits are mounted each year. The Barn Dance Entertainment Museum preserves the heritage of Canadian country music.

Allow 30 minutes minimum. Daily 10-5, July-Aug.; Mon.-Fri. 10-4, rest of year. Closed Jan. 1, Good Friday, second Mon. in Oct. and Dec. 25-26. Admission $2, under 16 free. Phone (519) 357-1096.

WOODBRIDGE (F-4)

KORTRIGHT CENTRE FOR CONSERVATION, 2 km (1.2 mi.) w. of Hwy. 400 on Major Mackenzie Dr., then 1 km (.6 mi.) s. to 9550 Pine Valley Dr., is a 325-hectare (800-acre) complex in the scenic Humber River Valley. An interpretive center has exhibits about native fauna and flora and one of Canada's largest displays of renewable energy technologies. Seasonal conservation demonstrations are conducted at a bee house, maple syrup shack and wildlife pond. Nature and cross-country ski trails and a theater are available.

Food and picnicking are available. Daily 10-4; closed Dec. 25. Cross-country ski trails are available Nov.-Mar. (weather permitting). Admission $5; over 64 and ages 5-17, $3. Prices may increase during special events. Parking $2. MC, VI. Phone (905) 832-2289 or (416) 661-6600. *See color ad p. 209.*

WOODSTOCK (H-2)
pop. 33,061, elev. 289 m/948′

Woodstock, on the Thames River, is a manufacturing city settled in 1798. The Woodstock Museum (formerly the City Hall) in Museum Square was designed after the town hall in Woodstock, England. The belltower of Old St. Paul's Anglican Church, 723 Dundas St., served as a jail during the Mackenzie Rebellion of 1837. The 1834 church features original box pews and has a pioneer cemetery; phone (519) 537-3912 for information about tours.

A farmers' market is held Saturday mornings 7 to noon at the fairgrounds, and harness racing takes place there at Woodstock Raceway once a week from June to September; for racing information phone (519) 537-8212. The fairgrounds is the site of the Woodstock Wood Show usually held the first weekend of October. Reputed to be the largest of its kind in North America, this show features seminars, demonstrations and woodcrafts.

Note: Policies concerning admittance of children to pari-mutuel betting facilities vary. Phone for information.

Tourism Oxford: 419 Hunter St., P.O. Box 397, Woodstock, ON, Canada N4S 7Y3; phone (519) 539-9800, ext. 3355.

WOODSTOCK MUSEUM, 466 Dundas St., is housed in the 1853 town hall and features an 1879 council chamber and the restored 1889 Grand Hall, once used for concerts. Eight galleries interpret the story of Woodstock from 10,000 B.C. to the present. Allow 30 minutes minimum. Mon.-Sat. 10-5, May-Sept.; Tues.-Sat. 10-5, rest of year. Admission $3; ages 13-18, $1. Phone (519) 537-8411.

WOODVIEW (F-9)

PETROGLYPHS PROVINCIAL PARK is 6 km (4 mi.) e. on CR 6, following signs. Algonkian-speaking Indians carved images of turtles, snakes, birds and humans on limestone rock between 900 and 1400 A.D. Discovered in 1954, the petroglyphs are now enclosed in a protective building. The park also offers picnicking, hiking and interpretive trails. Evening programs are presented Tuesday and Wednesday during July and August; phone for schedule.

Allow 30 minutes minimum. Daily 10-5, mid-May through second Mon. in Oct. Admission $9.50 per private vehicle; over 65, $7.25 per private vehicle. AX, MC, VI. Phone (705) 877-2552.

Trust AAA/CAA for the Last Word on Quality ... Approved.

Choosing hotels that are AAA/CAA Approved means choosing with confidence. **AAA/CAA's professional evaluators** have been there and done the research, checking for qualities like cleanliness, service, and value — assigning a rating from one to five Diamonds.

Wherever you travel, take AAA/CAA's word for it: Approved! Choose your accommodations and Diamond ratings from the TourBook® listings, in print and on aaa.com, and look for the bright red AAA/CAA logo on billboards and signage.

For more information on AAA/CAA Lodging Diamond Ratings, turn to page 16.

Smithsonian
National Museum of American History
Behring Center

America on the Move is made possible by generous support from
General Motors Corporation, AAA, State Farm Companies Foundation, The History Channel,
United States Congress, U.S. Department of Transportation, ExxonMobil, American Public
Transportation Association, American Road & Transportation Builders Association,
Association of American Railroads, National Asphalt Pavement Association, The UPS Foundation.

See how we got here.

Immerse yourself in a new museum experience and explore how transportation has changed America. National Museum of American History, Washington, D.C. americanhistory.si.edu/onthemove.

AMERICA
ON THE MOVE

Because she believes that dreams really do come true.

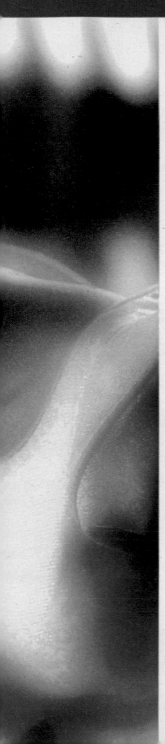

With enchanting Disney vacation rates at AAA/CAA Travel—they can.

We have a magical vacation for every Disney dream. And when you book your *AAA Vacations*® or *Disney Cruise Line*® package through your AAA/CAA Travel office, you'll enjoy special benefits and great values, too. Visit AAA/CAA Travel today and let the fairytale begin.

Travel
www.aaa.com

Disneyland® Resort
Walt Disney World® Resort
Disney Cruise Line®

As to Disney properties/artwork:
©Disney 4048020AMC0106

Ships' Registry: The Bahamas
CST#1022229-50

Howard Johnson®

We've gone from 28 flavors of ice cream to over 475 flavors of hotel.

We started as a modest chain of restaurant/ice cream stands sprinkled along the roadside. That was then. Today we have hotels everywhere from Charlottetown to Victoria. For every type of traveler. So whether you're on the road for pleasure or business we've got you covered. Also, be sure to check out our "Best Rate or it's Free" Guarantee*, as well as our loyalty program, TripRewards.®

howardjohnson.com
1-800-446-4656
Ask for SRP - SA3

triprewards*
It's fun to get more.

Go anywhere. Stay Here.℠

Howard Johnson
Go anywhere. Stay Here.℠

*Best Available Rate means the best non-qualified, publicly available rate on the Internet for the hotel, date and accommodations requested. Advance reservations are required on howardjohnson.com or 1-800-I-GO-HOJO. See howardjohnson.com for full details and requirments. ©2004 Howard Johnson International Inc. All rights reserved. Hotels are independently owned and operated.

Ontario

Black Creek
Pioneer Village, Toronto
© Bill Brooks
Alamy Images

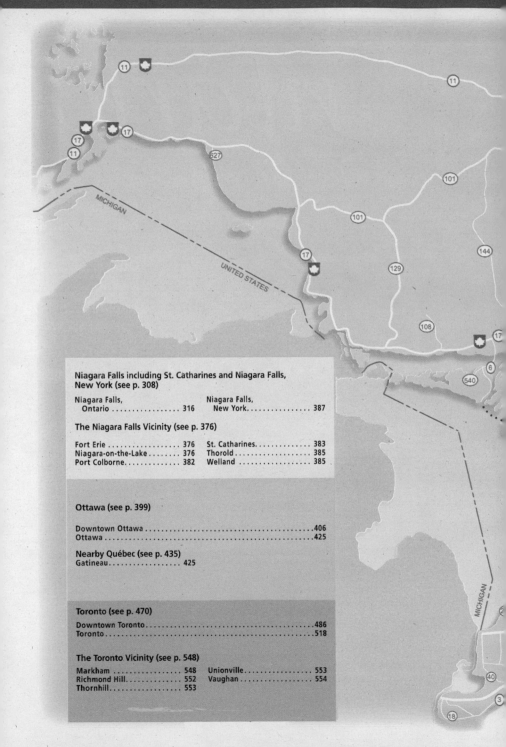

Ontario Orientation
Map to destinations

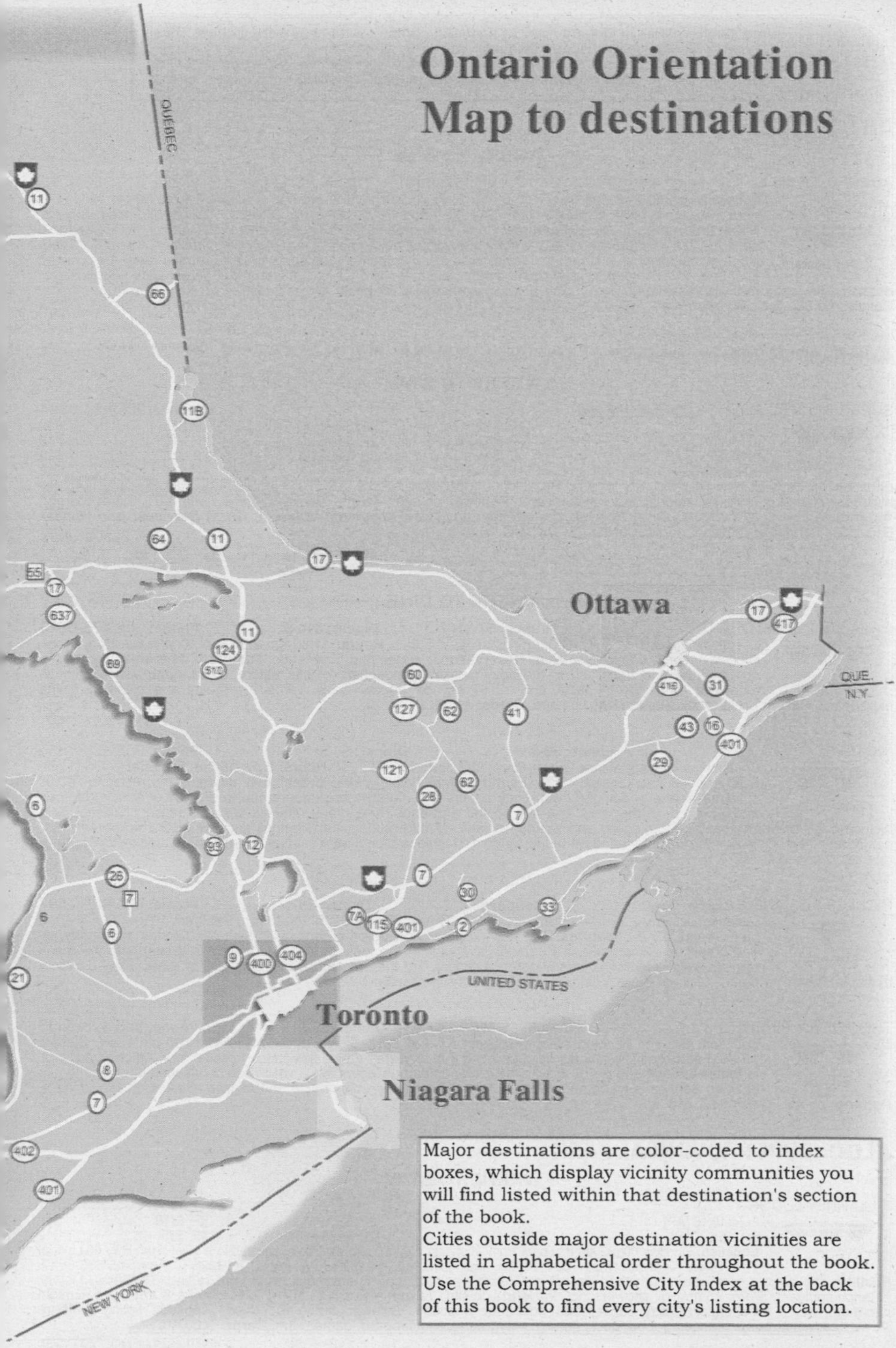

QUEBEC

11

66

11B

64   11

17

55
17   537

89

124
512

11

Ottawa

60

127   62   41

6

93   12

25
7

6

6

21

8

7

402

401

NEW YORK

QUE.
N.Y.

416   31

43   16
401

29

7

121

28   52

7

77   115   401   2

33

9   400   404

Toronto

UNITED STATES

30

Niagara Falls

Major destinations are color-coded to index
boxes, which display vicinity communities you
will find listed within that destination's section
of the book.
Cities outside major destination vicinities are
listed in alphabetical order throughout the book.
Use the Comprehensive City Index at the back
of this book to find every city's listing location.

Some municipalities in Ontario have or soon will combine with neighboring cities. These mergers will eliminate existing cities and may affect street names, addresses and political boundaries referenced in this guide. For further information, please contact Ontario governing agencies or the local CAA club.

ABERFOYLE

─── WHERE TO DINE ───

ABERFOYLE MILL *Menu on aaa.com* **Lunch:** $8-$18 **Dinner:** $16-$32 **Phone:** 519/763-1070
(CAA) **Location:** Hwy 401, exit 299, 3 km n on CR 46. 80 Brock Rd N1H 6H9. **Hours:** 11:30 am-2 & 5-9:30 pm, Mon-8:30 pm, Fri-10 pm, Sat 5 pm-10 pm, Sun 11 am-2 & 5-8:30 pm. Closed: 12/24-12/26; also 1/1-1/3. **Reservations:** suggested. **Features:** In a converted 1859 grist mill and furnished in early Canadian antiques, the restaurant provides a cozy country setting, complete with a glowing fireplace. Menu highlights include country pate, steamed mussels, fresh salad or homemade soup to start. Entrees range from mixed grill, beef and seafood to tasty pasta creations. Save room for ices, cake or fruit and cheese selections for dessert. The restaurant also features a fine choice of wine by the glass or bottle. Dressy casual; cocktails. **Parking:** on-site.
Continental
Cards: AX, DC, MC, VI. **Historic** ⊠

AJAX pop. 73,753

─── WHERE TO STAY ───

SUPER 8 MOTEL-AJAX *Book at aaa.com* **Phone:** (905)428-6884

	7/1-9/30	1P: $99-$124	2P: $99-$124	XP: $10	F12
	1/1-4/30	1P: $89-$114	2P: $94-$119	XP: $10	F12
Small-scale Hotel	5/1-6/30	1P: $94-$114	2P: $94-$114	XP: $10	F12
	10/1-12/31	1P: $94-$109	2P: $94-$109	XP: $10	F12

Location: Jct Bayly St from Hwy 401, exit Westney Rd, 1 km s. 210 Westney Rd S L1S 7P9. **Fax:** 905/428-7488. **Facility:** 64 one-bedroom standard units. 4 stories, interior corridors. **Parking:** on-site. **Terms:** package plans, pets ($10 extra charge). **Amenities:** hair dryers. *Some:* irons. **Pool(s):** heated indoor. **Leisure Activities:** whirlpool. **Guest Services:** coin laundry. **Business Services:** meeting rooms. **Cards:** AX, DC, MC, VI.

SOME UNITS
(ASK) (S/D) (🐾) (†††) (⊃⊂) (DATA PORT) (▣) / (⊠) /
FEE

─── WHERE TO DINE ───

CASA VERDE RISTORANTE **Lunch:** $7-$11 **Dinner:** $10-$25 **Phone:** 905/428-6243
Location: Pickering Village. 49 Old Kingston Rd L1T 3A5. **Hours:** 11:30 am-2:30 & 6-10 pm, Sat from 6 pm. Closed major holidays; also Sun. **Reservations:** suggested, weekends. **Features:** Dine on stuffed pasta, provimi veal and fresh fish in the cozy, relaxed atmosphere of this eatery. Good menu variety with an extensive selection of pasta and smart service makes Casa Verde a popular and pleasant dining experience. Casual dress; cocktails. **Parking:** on-site. **Cards:** AX, DC, MC, VI.
Italian
⊠

NICKELS **Lunch:** $6-$17 **Dinner:** $6-$17 **Phone:** 905/426-6860
Location: At Heritage Market Square Plaza. 95 Kingston Rd L1S 7J4. **Hours:** 8 am-10 pm, Fri & Sat 7 am-11 pm, Sun 7 am-10 pm. Closed: 12/25. **Features:** A nostalgic feeling passes over diners in the restaurant's 50s diner atmosphere, complete with cozy booths and old-style background music. Photos of Marilyn Monroe and Elvis adorn the walls and add to the ambience. The menu offers a good selection of casual fare, including lots of hearty sandwiches, soups and salads, as well as more substantial offerings such as BBQ chicken and ribs, pastas and beef. Desserts are decadent and it's fun to try an old fashioned ice cream sundae. Casual dress; cocktails. **Parking:** on-site. **Cards:** AX, MC, VI.
Canadian
⊠

PICKLES DELI AND EATERY **Lunch:** $6-$12 **Dinner:** $6-$12 **Phone:** 905/428-1597
Location: Jct Hwy 2. 5 Harwood Ave S L1S 2C1. **Hours:** 10 am-9 pm, Fri-10 pm, Sat 9 am-10 pm, Sun 9 am-9 pm. Closed: 12/25. **Features:** The true neighborhood delicatessen's piled-high sandwiches and hearty all-day breakfast items make it a popular favorite with the local crowd. The setting is casual, and the menu offers a wide selection of hearty home-style fare. Try the homemade cabbage rolls or roast turkey dinner, a treat that is sure to please. Casual dress; cocktails. **Parking:** on-site. **Cards:** MC, VI.
American
⊠

THE PORTLY PIPER **Lunch:** $5-$19 **Dinner:** $5-$19 **Phone:** 905/426-9535
Location: Between Harwood Ave and Westney Rd. 235 Bayly St W L1S 3K3. **Hours:** 11:30 am-1 am. Closed: 12/25. **Features:** The friendly neighborhood pub prepares a nice selection of casual fare. Among traditional favorites are fish and chips, shepherd's pie and hearty burgers, all of which can be washed down with a pint of beer. Service is warm and personable and the setting comfortable and relaxed. Casual dress; cocktails.
English
Parking: on-site. **Cards:** AX, MC, VI. (Ⓨ) (⊠)

ALGONQUIN PROVINCIAL PARK

─── WHERE TO STAY ───

KILLARNEY LODGE **Phone:** 705/633-5551

	6/24-10/16 [AP]	2P: $358-$558	XP: $119	D12
	5/13-6/23 [AP]	2P: $278-$368	XP: $99	D12

Cabin
Location: On Hwy 60; 32 km into park from west gate; 24 km from east gate. Located in a quiet area. Hwy 60-Lake of Two Rivers-Algonquin Park (Box 10005, Algonquin Park, ALGONQUIN PARK, P1H 2G9). **Fax:** 705/633-5667. **Facility:** The lodge's comfortably furnished log cabins are on a point of land in a tranquil, waterfront setting. 31 cabins. 1 story, exterior corridors. *Bath:* combo or shower only. **Parking:** on-site. **Terms:** open 5/13-10/16, office hours 8 am-8 pm, 2 night minimum stay - weekends, 3 day cancellation notice-fee imposed. **Dining:** dining room, see separate listing. **Leisure Activities:** rental boats, canoeing, boat-dock, fishing, playground, shuffleboard, game room. **Cards:** MC, VI.

(†††) (⊠) (🎿) (W) (Ⓩ)

------ **WHERE TO DINE** ------

KILLARNEY LODGE DINING ROOM   **Lunch:** $24   **Dinner:** $48   **Phone:** 705/633-5551
▼▼▼▼   **Location:** On Hwy 60; 32 km into park from west gate; 24 km from east gate; in Killarney Lodge. Hwy 60-Lake of Two
Rivers-Algonquin Park P1H 2G9. **Hours:** Open 5/14-10/20; noon-2 & 6-7:30 pm; noon-1 & 6-7 pm, Fri & Sat
Continental   noon-2 & 6-7:30 pm, Sun noon-2 & 6-7 pm 5/16-6/27. **Reservations:** required, for dinner. **Features:** Rustic
log cabin construction and a wonderful stone fireplace lend to the charming atmosphere. Full-course prix
fixe menus are presented for lunch and dinner. Guests may bring their own liquor, beer and wine. Casual dress. **Parking:** on-
site. **Cards:** MC, VI.   ⒶⒸ ☒

ALLISTON pop. 9,679

------ **WHERE TO STAY** ------

------ *The following lodging was either not evaluated or did not* ------
meet AAA rating requirements but is listed for your information only.

NOTTAWASAGA INN CONVENTION CENTRE &
   GOLF COURSE   **Phone:** 705/435-5501
   [fyi]   Not evaluated. **Location:** 3 km e; Hwy 400, 10 km w. 1110 Hwy 89 L9R 1A4. Facilities, services, and decor
characterize a mid-range property.

ALTON

------ **WHERE TO STAY** ------

THE MILLCROFT INN & SPA   **Phone:** (519)941-8111
Ⓒⓐⓐ Ⓢⓐⓥⓔ   All Year [ECP]   1P: $235-$350   2P: $235-$350   XP: $25   F12
▼▼▼▼ ▼▼▼▼   **Location:** 4 km n off Hwy 136 from Hwy 24, 1 km w on Queen St E, then just n. Located in a quiet area. 55 John St
L0N 1A0. Fax: 519/941-9192. **Facility:** This former knitting mill is on riverfront grounds in a peaceful, country
Country Inn   setting; a range of accommodations is offered. 52 one-bedroom standard units, some with whirlpools. 2-3
stories, interior/exterior corridors. **Parking:** on-site. **Terms:** check-in 4 pm, 2 night minimum stay -
weekends, 5 day cancellation notice-fee imposed, package plans, $4 service charge. **Amenities:** video
library, CD players, voice mail, irons, hair dryers. **Dining:** dining room, see separate listing. **Pool(s):** heated outdoor, heated
indoor. **Leisure Activities:** whirlpool, steamrooms, canoeing, paddleboats, hot tub, rowboats, 2 tennis courts, cross country
skiing, ice skating, bicycles, hiking trails, exercise room, spa, game room. **Guest Services:** valet laundry. **Business Services:**
meeting rooms. **Cards:** AX, DC, MC, VI. **Special Amenities: free expanded continental breakfast and free newspaper.**
SOME UNITS
ⓈⒹ 🍴 Ⓨ Ⓐ 🏊 ☒ Ⓦ ⒹⒶⓉⒶⓅⓄⓇⓉ 🛏 / ☒ ⓋⒸⓇ /

------ **WHERE TO DINE** ------

THE MILLCROFT INN DINING ROOM   **Lunch:** $18-$25   **Dinner:** $26-$46   **Phone:** 519/941-8111
Ⓒⓐⓐ   **Location:** 4 km n off Hwy 136 from Hwy 24, 1 km w on Queen St E, then just n; in The Millcroft Inn & Spa. 55 John St
L0N 1A0. **Hours:** 7:30 am-10, noon-2 & 6-9 pm, Sat & Sun 8 am-10:30, noon-2:30 & 6-9 pm.
▼▼▼▼ ▼▼▼▼   **Reservations:** suggested. **Features:** You'll enjoy the elegant and sophisticated atmosphere of this
distinctive country inn. The rich decor includes some tables overlooking the river and in-season patio dining
Continental   in a garden setting. An innovative menu features creative regional specialties. Semi-formal attire; cocktails.
Parking: on-site. **Cards:** AX, DC, MC, VI.   Ⓨ ☒

ARNPRIOR pop. 7,192

------ **WHERE TO STAY** ------

COUNTRY SQUIRE MOTEL   **Phone:** 613/623-6556
▼▼   All Year [CP]   1P: $52-$69   2P: $59-$89   XP: $12
Motel   **Location:** Hwy 17, exit White Lake Rd N. Located in a rural area. 111 Staye Court Dr K7S 3H6. Fax: 613/623-9337.
Facility: 15 one-bedroom standard units, some with whirlpools. 1 story, exterior corridors. **Parking:** on-site,
winter plug-ins. **Terms:** small pets only ($10 fee, no cats). **Leisure Activities:** playground, basketball,
horseshoes. **Business Services:** fax (fee). **Cards:** AX, DC, MC, VI.
SOME UNITS
Ⓐ Ⓢ Ⓚ ⓈⒹ ⊷ 🐾 🍴 ☒ ▤ 🖥 / ☒ ⓋⒸⓇ ⒹⒶⓉⒶⓅⓄⓇⓉ /
FEE

AURORA pop. 40,167

------ **WHERE TO STAY** ------

HOWARD JOHNSON HOTEL AURORA   *Book at aaa.com*   **Phone:** (905)727-1312
Ⓒⓐⓐ Ⓢⓐⓥⓔ   10/1-1/1   1P: $142-$152   2P: $152-$162   XP: $10   F17
5/1-9/30   1P: $132-$142   2P: $142-$152   XP: $10   F17
▼▼ ▼▼   1/2-4/30   1P: $124-$134   2P: $134-$144   XP: $10   F17
Location: 0.5 km n of Wellington St. 15520 Yonge St L4G 1P2. Fax: 905/727-4270. **Facility:** 97 units. 95 one-
Small-scale Hotel   bedroom standard units, some with whirlpools. 2 one-bedroom suites, some with whirlpools. 4 stories,
interior corridors. **Parking:** on-site. **Terms:** package plans, pets ($15 extra charge). **Amenities:** voice mail,
irons, hair dryers. *Some:* high-speed Internet (fee). **Dining:** 7 am-10 & 5-9 pm. **Leisure Activities:** racquetball court. **Guest
Services:** sundries, valet laundry. **Business Services:** meeting rooms. **Cards:** AX, DC, MC, VI. **Special Amenities: free
continental breakfast and free newspaper.**
SOME UNITS
ⓈⒹ 🐾 🍴 Ⓨ ⊕ 📷 ⒹⒶⓉⒶⓅⓄⓇⓉ 🛏 / ☒ ▤ 🖥 /
FEE

BALM BEACH

──── WHERE TO STAY ────

SUNPORT BEACH RESORT & MOTEL　　　　　　　　　　　　　　　　　**Phone: 705/361-1617**

♦♦♦ ♦♦♦　　6/27-9/6　　　　　　　　　1P: $180-$250
　　　　　　5/1-6/26　　　　　　　　1P: $85-$180
Motel　　　9/7-10/1　　　　　　　　1P: $85-$115
　　Location: 9 km w from Hwy 93, just s. Located on the waterfront. 24 Tiny Beaches Rd S L0L 2J0. Fax: 705/361-2575.
Facility: 8 units. 2 one- and 6 two-bedroom suites with kitchens. 1-2 stories (no elevator), exterior corridors. **Parking:** on-site.
Terms: open 5/1-10/1, office hours 7 am-11 pm, 30 day cancellation notice, package plans. **Leisure Activities:** rental boats,
canoeing, paddleboats, windsurfing, boat ramp, waterskiing. **Guest Services:** coin laundry. **Cards:** MC, VI.

　　　　　　　　　　　　　　　　　　　　🆂 🍴 ⊠ ⊠ 🎥 🅿 🗄 🖥 🖵

BANCROFT pop. 4,089

──── WHERE TO STAY ────

BEST WESTERN SWORD MOTOR INN　　***Book at aaa.com***　　　　　　**Phone: (613)332-2474**

🆒 🆂🅰🆅🅴　　All Year　　　　　　1P: $99-$114　　　2P: $99-$144　　　XP: $15　　　F12
♦♦♦ ♦♦♦　　**Location:** On Hwy 62 N; centre. Located in a commercial area. 146 Hastings St 1C0 (PO Box 28).
Motel　　　Fax: 613/332-5110. **Facility:** 48 units. 44 one-bedroom standard units. 4 one-bedroom suites ($160-$180),
　　some with whirlpools. 1-2 stories (no elevator), interior/exterior corridors. **Parking:** on-site, winter plug-ins.
　　Terms: small pets only ($5 extra charge). **Amenities:** irons, hair dryers. **Dining:** Sword Motor Inn
Restaurant, see separate listing. **Pool(s):** heated indoor. **Leisure Activities:** sauna, whirlpool, playground,
exercise room. **Guest Services:** gift shop, valet laundry. **Business Services:** meeting rooms. **Cards:** AX, CB, DC, DS, JC,
MC, VI. **Special Amenities:** free local telephone calls and early check-in/late check-out.　　SOME UNITS

　　　　　　　　　　　　　　　　　🆂 🛏 🍴 🛎 ⊠ 🄳🄰🅃🄰ᴾᴼᴿᵀ 🖥 / ⊠ 🗄 🖵 /
　　　　　　　　　　　　　　　　　　　　FEE

THE BRIDES' GATE INN & GRAIL SPRINGS SPA　　　　　　　　　　　**Phone: 613/332-0154**

♦♦♦ ♦♦♦　　Property failed to provide current rates
　　Location: 2 km s on Hwy 62, 2 km w. Located in a rural area, beside a small lake. 2004 Bay Lake Rd K0L 1C0.
Country Inn　　Fax: 613/332-4308. **Facility:** Cedar walls and Victorian decor accent the inn's attractive common areas; in
　　summer months, gardens enhance the well-maintained grounds. Smoke free premises. 16 one-bedroom
standard units, some with whirlpools. 3 stories (no elevator), interior corridors. **Parking:** on-site, winter plug-ins. **Terms:** check-
in 4 pm. **Amenities:** CD players, voice mail, hair dryers. **Dining:** The Brides' Gate Dining Room, see separate listing. **Leisure
Activities:** boating, canoeing, paddleboats, boat dock, fishing, cross country skiing, ice skating, hiking trails, spa. *Fee:*
horseback riding. **Business Services:** meeting rooms.　　　　　　　　　　　　　　　　SOME UNITS

　　　　　　　　　　　　　　　　🍴 ⊠ ⊠ 🎥 🄳🄰🅃🄰ᴾᴼᴿᵀ 🖥 / 🆅🅲🆁 /
　　　　　　　　　　　　　　　　　　　　　　　　　　　　FEE

──── WHERE TO DINE ────

THE BRIDES' GATE DINING ROOM　　　**Dinner:** $22-$35　　　　　**Phone: 613/332-0154**

♦♦♦ ♦♦♦　　**Location:** 2 km s on Hwy 62, 2 km w; in The Brides' Gate Inn & Grail Springs Spa. 2004 Bay Lake Rd K0L 1C0.
　　Hours: 6 pm-9 pm. **Reservations:** suggested. **Features:** Opt for a table in the cozy main dining room to
Continental　　enjoy the full effect of an intimate fireside ambience. The rural setting with a view of a small lake blends well
　　with the traditional fare served here. Dining on the screened porch is offered in season. Casual dress;
cocktails. **Parking:** on-site. **Cards:** AX, DC, MC, VI.　　　　　　　　　　　　　　　　⊠

SWORD MOTOR INN RESTAURANT　　**Lunch:** $8-$13　　**Dinner:** $11-$18　　**Phone: 613/332-2474**

♦♦♦ ♦♦♦　　**Location:** On Hwy 62 N; centre; in Best Western Sword Motor Inn. 146 Hastings St K0L 1C0. **Hours:** 7 am-8 pm,
　　Sat-Mon from 8 am; hours may vary off season. Closed: 12/25. **Features:** Prompt, friendly service,
Canadian　　generous portions and that touch of home in the cooking are hallmarks of this restaurant. Be sure to see the
　　sword collection. Casual dress; cocktails. **Parking:** on-site. **Cards:** AX, CB, DC, DS, JC, MC, VI.　　⊠

Delegate Travel Planning to Someone You Trust

Visit **aaa.com** and enjoy a whole new world of travel information.

AAA's Internet TripTik® provides interactive maps and search tools that make travel planning easy. Get hotel Diamond ratings, photos, and great room rates. Find countless places to eat and play.

Trust AAA to simplify travel planning.

**Travel with Confidence.
Travel with AAA.**

VITO'S PIZZERIA RESTAURANT   **Lunch:** $5-$21   **Dinner:** $5-$21   **Phone:** 613/332-4044

Italian
Location: On Hwy 62 N; centre. 143 Hastings St N K0L 1C0. **Hours:** 11 am-11 pm, Fri & Sat-midnight, Sun-9 pm. Closed: 1/1, 4/17, 12/25, 12/26. **Features:** Although pizza is popular, the restaurant is also about fettuccine, gnocchi, ravioli, veal dishes, salads and submarine sandwiches. Friendly servers present them all in a comfortable atmosphere. Casual dress; cocktails. **Parking:** on-site. **Cards:** AX, MC, VI.

BARRIE pop. 103,710

─── **WHERE TO STAY** ───

BEST WESTERN ROYAL OAK INN   *Book at aaa.com*   **Phone:** (705)721-4848

(CAA) (SAVE)

7/1-9/30	1P: $98-$115	2P: $105-$125	XP: $10	F12
5/1-6/30	1P: $88-$98	2P: $94-$104	XP: $10	F12
10/1-4/30	1P: $78-$98	2P: $82-$100	XP: $10	F12

Location: Hwy 400, exit 96A E (Dunlop St). Located in a commercial area. 35 Hart Dr L4N 5M3. Fax: 705/722-3688.
Small-scale Hotel **Facility:** 50 units. 48 one- and two-bedroom standard units, some with efficiencies. 2 stories (no elevator), interior corridors. **Parking:** on-site, winter plug-ins. **Amenities:** voice mail, irons, hair dryers. *Some:* high-speed Internet (fee). **Leisure Activities:** sauna, exercise room. **Guest Services:** valet laundry. **Cards:** AX, DC, DS, MC, VI. **Special Amenities:** free continental breakfast and free local telephone calls. *(See color ad p 230)*

SOME UNITS
[S D] [📶] [DATA PORT] [📶] [📶] [📶] / [✕] [VCR] /
FEE

COMFORT INN   *Book at aaa.com*   **Phone:** (705)722-3600

7/1-9/30 [CP]	1P: $95-$135	2P: $105-$145	XP: $10	F18
5/1-6/30 & 10/1-4/30 [CP]	1P: $90-$120	2P: $100-$130	XP: $10	F18

Location: Hwy 400, exit 96A E (Dunlop St). Located in a commercial area. 75 Hart Dr L4N 5M3. Fax: 705/722-4454.
Small-scale Hotel **Facility:** 60 one-bedroom standard units. 2 stories (no elevator), interior corridors. **Parking:** on-site, winter plug-ins. **Terms:** 12% service charge. **Amenities:** hair dryers. *Some:* irons. **Guest Services:** valet laundry. **Cards:** AX, DC, DS, JC, MC, VI.

SOME UNITS
[ASK] [S D] [🐾] [📶] [DATA PORT] [📶] / [✕] [📶] [📶] /

DAYS INN BARRIE   *Book at aaa.com*   **Phone:** (705)733-8989

7/1-9/30 [CP]	1P: $105-$140	2P: $105-$140	XP: $10	F18
5/1-6/30 & 10/1-4/30 [CP]	1P: $99-$135	2P: $99-$135	XP: $10	F18

Location: Hwy 400, exit 94 (Essa Rd), just s, then just e. Located in a commercial area. 60 Bryne Dr L4N 9Y4. Fax: 705/725-0982. **Facility:** 78 units. 70 one-bedroom standard units, some with whirlpools. 8 one-bedroom suites ($157-$225), some with whirlpools. 3 stories, interior corridors. **Parking:** on-site. **Terms:** small pets only ($10 extra charge, in designated units). **Amenities:** video games (fee), high-speed Internet, voice mail, irons, hair dryers. **Pool(s):** small heated indoor. **Leisure Activities:** whirlpool, exercise room. **Guest Services:** sundries, valet and coin laundry. **Business Services:** meeting rooms, business center. **Cards:** AX, DC, MC, VI. *(See color ad below)*

SOME UNITS
[ASK] [S D] [🐾] [🦢] [📶] [DATA PORT] [📶] [📶] [📶] / [✕] /
FEE

1-800-DAYS INN
www.daysinn.ca

Come On Inn...

DAYS INN
B A R R I E

- 78 Guestrooms with king or two queen size beds
- Suites with Jacuzzi, fireplace and kitchenette
- WorkZone™ rooms & suites
- 25" TV with cable and on-command movies
- Indoor pool, whirlpool and exercise room
- Complimentary European-style buffet breakfast
- Business centre and meeting rooms
- 24-hour gift and snack shop
- Guest laundry facility
- Wheelchair-accessble rooms and connecting rooms
- Complimentary local, calling card and toll-free calls
- Complimentary high speed Internet access in all rooms
- In-room fridge, microwave, coffee maker, hairdryer, iron and ironing board

triprewards
It's fun to get more.

Days Inn - Barrie   60 Bryne Drive   Barrie ON   L4N 9Y4   (Hwy. 400 exit Essa Road S.)
www.daysinnbarrie.com   Email: reservations@daysinnbarrie.com
Tel: 705.733.8989   Toll Free: 866.335.8989   Fax: 705.725.0982

HOLIDAY INN BARRIE-HOTEL & CONFERENCE CENTRE   *Book at aaa.com*

Phone: (705)728-6191

(CAA) (SAVE)

All Year   1P: $129-$179   2P: $139-$189   XP: $15   F18
Location: Hwy 400, exit 94 (Essa Rd), just e. Located in a commercial area. 20 Fairview Rd L4N 4P3.
Fax: 705/728-1718. **Facility:** 161 one-bedroom standard units. 3-5 stories, interior corridors. **Parking:** on-site. **Terms:** package plans. **Amenities:** high-speed Internet, voice mail, irons, hair dryers. *Some:* honor

Small-scale Hotel bars. **Dining:** 6:30 am-10 pm, cocktails. **Pool(s):** heated outdoor, heated indoor. **Leisure Activities:** sauna, whirlpool, playground, exercise room. **Guest Services:** valet and coin laundry. **Business Services:** conference facilities. **Cards:** AX, DC, DS, MC, VI. *(See color ad card insert)*

SOME UNITS

HOLIDAY INN EXPRESS HOTEL & SUITES BARRIE   *Book at aaa.com*

Phone: (705)725-1002

(CAA) (SAVE)

5/1-9/30 [ECP]   1P: $130-$170   2P: $130-$170   XP: $10   F19
10/1-4/30 [ECP]   1P: $127-$167   2P: $127-$167   XP: $10   F19
Location: Hwy 400, exit 90 (Molson Park Dr), just sw. Located in a commercial area. 506 Bryne Dr L4N 9P6.
Fax: 705/725-1003. **Facility:** 64 units. 64 one- and 3 two-bedroom standard units, some with efficiencies

Small-scale Hotel and/or whirlpools. 4 stories, interior corridors. **Parking:** on-site. **Terms:** pets ($15 extra charge). **Amenities:** high-speed Internet, dual phone lines, voice mail, irons, hair dryers. **Pool(s):** small heated indoor. **Leisure Activities:** whirlpool, exercise room. **Guest Services:** valet and coin laundry. **Business Services:** business center. **Cards:** AX, DC, DS, MC, VI. **Special Amenities:** free expanded continental breakfast and free local telephone calls. *(See color ad card insert & below)*

SOME UNITS

HORSESHOE RESORT

Phone: (705)835-2790

12/24-3/21   1P: $160-$220   2P: $160-$220   XP: $20   F12
5/1-9/30   1P: $160-$200   2P: $160-$200   XP: $20   F12
10/1-12/23 & 3/22-4/30   1P: $150-$190   2P: $150-$190   XP: $20   F12

Resort
Small-scale Hotel **Location:** Hwy 400, exit 117 (Horseshoe Valley Rd), 6 km e. Located in a rural area. 1101 Horseshoe Valley Rd W L4M 4Y8 (1101 Horseshoe Valley Rd-Comp 10, RR 1). Fax: 705/835-5232. **Facility:** Some guest rooms at this four-season hotel offer views of the valley, and several feature fireplaces. 102 one-bedroom standard units, some with whirlpools. 3 stories, interior corridors. **Parking:** on-site. **Terms:** check-in 4 pm, 2 night minimum stay - weekends, 7 day cancellation notice, [BP] & [MAP] meal plans available, package plans. **Amenities:** video games (fee), voice mail, irons, hair dryers. **Dining:** Silk's Fine Dining, see separate listing. **Pool(s):** small heated outdoor, small heated indoor. **Leisure Activities:** sauna, whirlpool, 2 lighted tennis courts, recreation programs, hiking trails, exercise room, spa. *Fee:* golf-36 holes, downhill & cross country skiing, bicycles, game room. **Guest Services:** gift shop. **Business Services:** conference facilities. **Cards:** AX, MC, VI.

SOME UNITS

TRAVELODGE BARRIE   *Book at aaa.com*

Phone: (705)734-9500

5/1-9/5   1P: $129-$179   2P: $129-$179   XP: $10   F17
9/6-4/30   1P: $109-$159   2P: $109-$159   XP: $10   F17
Location: Hwy 400, exit 96A E (Dunlop St). Located in a commercial area. 55 Hart Dr L4N 5M3. Fax: 705/734-0622.

Small-scale Hotel **Facility:** 96 one-bedroom standard units. 2 stories (no elevator), interior corridors. **Parking:** on-site. **Terms:** package plans. **Amenities:** video games (fee), voice mail, irons, hair dryers. **Pool(s):** heated indoor. **Leisure Activities:** whirlpool. **Guest Services:** valet laundry. **Business Services:** meeting rooms. **Cards:** AX, DC, DS, MC, VI.

SOME UNITS

Holiday Inn EXPRESS
HOTEL & SUITES
BARRIE

- Complimentary Deluxe Continental Breakfast
- Indoor pool/Whirlpool/Fitness Centre
- Free "High Speed" Internet Access
- Free Local Calls
- Walking Distance to Shopping & Restaurants

506 Bryne Drive, Barrie, ON L4N 9P6
Website: www.hiexpress.com/barrieon
For Reservations Call 1-866-725-1002

Best Western Royal Oak Inn
BARRIE

- Newly Renovated Rooms and Lobby
- Fridge/Microwave in all Rooms
- Efficiency Units • Fitness and Sauna Room
- Free "High Speed" Internet Access
- Free Continental Breakfast

35 Hart Drive, Barrie, ON L4N 5M3
Website: www.bestwestern.com
For Reservations Call 705-721-4848

——— WHERE TO DINE ———

CROCK & BLOCK   Lunch: $6-$9   Dinner: $7-$20   Phone: 705/728-7485

Steak & Seafood
Location: Hwy 400, exit Hwy 26 (Bayfield St), just w. 325 Bayfield St L4M 3C2. **Hours:** 11:30 am-10 pm, Fri & Sat-11 pm, Sun 10:30 am-9:30 pm. **Reservations:** suggested. **Features:** The atmosphere is informal and relaxed. Brick, exposed beams and dark wood walls add to the feeling of comfort. Prime rib is the house signature item. It is slow roasted with moist heat to maximize flavour. Choose between 8-, 12- or 16-ounce portions that are served with a choice of potato, au jus, a vegetable and traditional-style Yorkshire pudding. Casual dress; cocktails. **Parking:** on-site. **Cards:** AX, DC, MC, VI.

MOOSE WINOOSKI'S   Lunch: $5-$10   Dinner: $6-$20   Phone: 705/727-0077

Canadian
Location: Hwy 400, exit Hwy 26 (Bayfield St), 2 km w. 407 Bayfield St L4M 3C5. **Hours:** 11 am-1 am. Closed: 12/25. **Reservations:** accepted. **Features:** Follow the moose tracks in the entrance walkway into this restaurant which is designed like a northern Canadian log cabin. The warm wood finished interior has a large riverstone fireplace; booth and table seating is available. The atmosphere can be bustling. The varied menu offers chicken, pasta, burgers, ribs and salad. There is a logo shop on site. Casual dress; cocktails. **Parking:** on-site. **Cards:** AX, DC, MC, VI.

SILK'S FINE DINING   *Menu on aaa.com*   Lunch: $12-$18   Dinner: $23-$39   Phone: 705/835-2790

Canadian
Location: Hwy 400, exit 117 (Horseshoe Valley Rd), 6 km e; in Horseshoe Resort. 1101 Horseshoe Valley Rd L4M 4Y8. **Hours:** 7 am-11:30 & 5:30-10 pm. **Reservations:** required. **Features:** Diners are treated to polished, caring service and carefully prepared food. The menu changes in spring and fall, but the signature roasted rack of Washington State lamb is typically available throughout the year. Dressy casual; cocktails. **Parking:** on-site. **Cards:** AX, DC, MC, VI.

BARRY'S BAY pop. 1,259

——— WHERE TO STAY ———

MADAWASKA VALLEY INN   Phone: (613)756-9014

Country Inn
5/1-10/31 & 12/1-4/30 [BP]   1P: $85-$105   2P: $95-$115   XP: $10
Location: 1 km w. Located in a rural area. 19854 Hwy 60 K0J 1B0 (PO Box 611). **Facility:** Smoke free premises. 4 one-bedroom standard units. 2 stories (no elevator), interior/exterior corridors. *Bath:* combo or shower only. **Parking:** on-site, winter plug-ins. **Terms:** open 5/1-10/31 & 12/1-4/30, office hours 8 am-11 pm, 7 day cancellation notice-fee imposed, package plans. **Dining:** restaurant, see separate listing. **Leisure Activities:** whirlpool, snowmobiling, hiking trails. **Cards:** MC, VI.

SOME UNITS

MOUNTAIN VIEW MOTEL   Phone: (613)756-2757

Motel
5/1-10/31   1P: $69-$79   2P: $69-$94
11/1-4/30   1P: $55-$69   2P: $60-$79
Location: On Hwy 60, 4 km e. Located in a rural area. 18508 Hwy 60 E K0J 1B0 (RR 2, Box 101). Fax: 613/756-9488. **Facility:** 12 units. 11 one-bedroom standard units. 1 one-bedroom suite. 1 story, exterior corridors. **Parking:** on-site, winter plug-ins. **Terms:** office hours 7 am-11 pm, 7 day cancellation notice-fee imposed, [BP] meal plan available, small pets only. **Amenities:** *Some:* irons. **Leisure Activities:** playground. **Cards:** MC, VI.

SOME UNITS

——— WHERE TO DINE ———

MADAWASKA VALLEY INN   Dinner: $11-$29   Phone: 613/756-9014

Canadian
Location: 1 km w; in Madawaska Valley Inn. 19854 Hwy 60 K0J 1B0. **Hours:** Open 5/1-10/31 & 12/1-4/30; 5 pm-8 pm. Closed: 12/24, 12/25, 12/26. **Reservations:** accepted. **Features:** Buffalo steak, venison pie, schnitzels and lamb are among dishes served in hearty portions. Also on the menu are preparations of chicken, fish and pasta. A fireplace, wood-finished walls and a beamed ceiling help create a warm atmosphere. Casual dress; cocktails. **Parking:** on-site. **Cards:** MC, VI.

AAA CAA **Choose Well.**

Discover the secret to choosing well ... **AAA/CAA Approved**.

From simple motels to luxury resorts, rest assured. **AAA/CAA's professional evaluators** have tested the locks and peeked under the beds, checking for qualities like cleanliness, service, and value — assigning a rating from one to five Diamonds.

Choose your Diamond rated accommodations from theTourBook® listings, in print and on aaa.com, and look for the bold red AAA/CAA logo on signage and billboards.

For more information on **AAA/CAA Lodging Diamond Ratings**, turn to page 16.

BAYFIELD pop. 909

WHERE TO STAY

THE LITTLE INN OF BAYFIELD **Phone:** (519)565-2611

CAA SAVE

Historic Country Inn

All Year [BP] 2P: $175-$297 XP: $30 F

Location: Hwy 21, exit Main St, jct Catherine St. Located in a quiet area. 26 Main St N0M 1G0 (PO Box 100). Fax: 519/565-5474. **Facility:** This restored 1830s inn is in a village setting and offers an upscale, retreat-like ambience; wine and cooking events are available. Smoke free premises. 29 one-bedroom standard units, some with whirlpools. 2 stories (no elevator), interior corridors. *Bath:* combo or shower only. **Parking:** on-site. **Terms:** office hours 8 am-11 pm, 2 night minimum stay - seasonal and/or weekends, 3 day cancellation notice-fee imposed, [MAP] meal plan available, package plans, small pets only ($25 extra charge). **Amenities:** irons, hair dryers. *Some:* CD players. **Dining:** dining room, see separate listing. **Leisure Activities:** hiking trails, spa privileges. **Guest Services:** gift shop, valet laundry. **Business Services:** meeting rooms, fax (fee). **Cards:** AX, CB, DC, MC, VI. ***(See color ad below)***

SOME UNITS

FEE DATA PORT / VCR / FEE

THE MARTHA RITZ HOUSE **Phone:** 519/565-2325

Country Inn

5/1-11/1 1P: $120 2P: $120

Location: Hwy 21, exit Main St, jct Catherine St. 27 Main St N0M 1G0. **Facility:** 4 one-bedroom standard units. 2 stories (no elevator), interior corridors. **Parking:** street. **Terms:** open 5/1-11/1, office hours 10 am-9 pm, 4 day cancellation notice-fee imposed, small pets only ($25 extra charge, with prior approval). **Leisure Activities:** spa. **Cards:** AX, DC, MC, VI.

FEE

WHERE TO DINE

THE LITTLE INN DINING ROOM **Lunch:** $11-$18 **Dinner:** $25-$38 **Phone:** 519/565-2611

CAA

Continental

Location: Hwy 21, exit Main St, jct Catherine St; in The Little Inn of Bayfield. 26 Main St N0M 1G0. **Hours:** noon-2:30 & 5-9 pm, Sun from 11:30 am. **Reservations:** suggested. **Features:** Located on the main street of the quaint village, the Little Inn Dining Room is a lovely place for fine country dining. The chef features an innovative Continental menu, with a strong focus on local herbs and fresh produce, some grown in their own gardens. Rack of lamb, diver scallops and white fish are popular choices. An extensive wine list is also offered to complement the fine menu selections. Dressy casual; cocktails. **Parking:** on-site. **Cards:** AX, DC, MC, VI.

THE RED PUMP RESTAURANT **Lunch:** $9-$22 **Dinner:** $15-$30 **Phone:** 519/565-2576

CAA

Continental

Location: Hwy 21, exit Main St; between Charles and Catherine St. 21 Main St N0M 1G0. **Hours:** Open 5/1-12/31 & 4/1-4/30; noon-3 & 5-9 pm. Closed: 12/25, 12/26. **Reservations:** suggested. **Features:** Antiques, fresh flowers and fine artwork grace the warm, refined and relaxing dining room that overlooks lovely country gardens. Here you'll enjoy sophisticated and well-prepared cuisine. Outdoor patio dining and light lunch selections are also featured. Dressy casual; cocktails. **Parking:** street. **Cards:** AX, DC, MC, VI.

THE LITTLE INN OF BAYFIELD 1832
The Little Inn
INNKEEPING SINCE 1832
"Still...the perfect getaway."
Four Diamond Award
AAA
MAIN ST. BAYFIELD
1-800-565-1832
www.littleinn.com
innkeeper@littleinn.com

BELLEVILLE pop. 45,986

——— WHERE TO STAY ———

BEST WESTERN BELLEVILLE   *Book at aaa.com*   Phone: (613)969-1112

(CAA) [SAVE]

7/1-9/30 [CP]	1P: $135	2P: $135	XP: $10	F17
10/1-4/30 [CP]	1P: $115	2P: $115	XP: $10	F17
5/1-6/30 [CP]	1P: $112	2P: $112	XP: $10	F17

Small-scale Hotel **Location:** Hwy 401, exit 543A, 0.5 km s on Hwy 62 (N Front St). Located in a commerical area. 387 N Front St.K8P 3C8. Fax: 613/969-8461. **Facility:** 88 one-bedroom standard units. 3 stories, interior corridors. **Parking:** on-site, winter plug-ins. **Terms:** 3 day cancellation notice, small pets only (in smoking units). **Amenities:** high-speed Internet, voice mail, irons, hair dryers. **Pool(s):** heated indoor. **Leisure Activities:** whirlpool. **Guest Services:** valet laundry. **Business Services:** meeting rooms. **Cards:** AX, DC, DS, MC, VI. **Special Amenities:** free continental breakfast and free local telephone calls.

SOME UNITS

CLARION INN & SUITES   *Book at aaa.com*   Phone: (613)962-4531

(CAA) [SAVE]

6/1-9/30	1P: $110-$225	2P: $120-$245	XP: $10	F14
5/1-5/31 & 10/1-4/30	1P: $99-$199	2P: $99-$199	XP: $10	F14

Historic Small-scale Hotel **Location:** Hwy 401, exit 543A, 3 km s on Hwy 62 (N Front St); corner of Bridge St; downtown. Located in a commercial area. 211 Pinnacle St K8N 3A7. Fax: 613/966-5894. **Facility:** Built circa 1895, this property boasts an elaborate lobby and rooms with high ceilings. No two rooms are identical. 46 units. 14 one-bedroom standard units. 32 one-bedroom suites ($120-$299), some with efficiencies and/or whirlpools. 3 stories, interior corridors. *Bath:* combo or shower only. **Parking:** on-site. **Terms:** 7 day cancellation notice, package plans. **Amenities:** voice mail, irons, hair dryers. *Some:* dual phone lines, fax. **Dining:** 6:30 am-9:30 pm, cocktails, also, Cora's Breakfast & Lunch, see separate listing. **Leisure Activities:** exercise room. *Fee:* massage. **Guest Services:** complimentary and valet laundry. **Business Services:** business center. **Cards:** AX, CB, DC, DS, MC, VI. **Special Amenities:** free local telephone calls and free newspaper.

SOME UNITS

COMFORT INN   *Book at aaa.com*   Phone: (613)966-7703

7/1-9/30	1P: $98-$108	2P: $108-$118	XP: $10	F18
5/1-6/30	1P: $96-$106	2P: $106-$116	XP: $10	F18
10/1-4/30	1P: $95-$105	2P: $105-$115	XP: $10	F18

Small-scale Hotel **Location:** Hwy 401, exit 543A, 1 km s on Hwy 62 (N Front St). Located in a commercial area. 200 N Park St K8P 2Y9. Fax: 613/966-0274. **Facility:** 125 one-bedroom standard units. 2 stories (no elevator), interior corridors. **Parking:** on-site. **Terms:** pets (on ground floor, in smoking units). **Amenities:** *Some:* irons, hair dryers. **Guest Services:** valet laundry. **Business Services:** meeting rooms. **Cards:** AX, DC, DS, MC, VI.

SOME UNITS

QUALITY INN BELLEVILLE   Phone: 613/962-9211

[fyi]

All Year	1P: $99	2P: $99

Small-scale Hotel Under major renovation, scheduled to be completed October 2004. **Last rated:** ⬥⬥ **Location:** Hwy 401, exit 543A, just s on Hwy 62 (N Front St). Located in a commercial area. 407 N Front St K8P 3C8. Fax: 613/962-9300. **Facility:** 109 one-bedroom standard units, some with efficiencies, kitchens (no utensils) and/or whirlpools. 2 stories (no elevator), interior corridors. **Parking:** on-site. **Terms:** pets (in smoking units). **Amenities:** hair dryers. *Some:* irons. **Pool(s):** heated indoor. **Leisure Activities:** saunas, whirlpool. **Guest Services:** valet laundry. **Business Services:** meeting rooms. **Cards:** AX, DC, DS, JC, MC, VI.

SOME UNITS

RAMADA INN ON THE BAY   *Book at aaa.com*   Phone: (613)968-3411

7/1-9/30	1P: $170-$195	2P: $180-$205	XP: $10	F17
1/1-4/30	1P: $165-$190	2P: $175-$200	XP: $10	F17
5/1-6/30 & 10/1-12/31	1P: $160-$185	2P: $170-$195	XP: $10	F17

Small-scale Hotel **Location:** Hwy 2, 0.5 km s. Located adjacent to E Zwick Island Park. 11 Bay Bridge Rd K8N 4Z1. Fax: 613/968-5036. **Facility:** 124 units. 123 one-bedroom standard units. 1 one-bedroom suite. 4 stories, interior corridors. **Parking:** on-site. **Terms:** 3 day cancellation notice-fee imposed, small pets only (in smoking units). **Amenities:** video games (fee), voice mail, irons, hair dryers. *Some:* honor bars. **Pool(s):** heated outdoor, heated indoor. **Leisure Activities:** sauna, whirlpool, waterslide, lighted tennis court, tobogganing, playground, exercise room. **Guest Services:** valet laundry. **Business Services:** conference facilities. **Cards:** AX, DC, JC, MC, VI.

SOME UNITS

——— WHERE TO DINE ———

CORA'S BREAKFAST & LUNCH   Lunch: $6-$11   Phone: 613/962-9284

(CAA)

Canadian **Location:** Hwy 401, exit 543A, 3 km s on Hwy 62 (N Front St); corner of Bridge St; downtown; in Clarion Inn & Suites. 211 Pinnacle St K8N 3A7. **Hours:** 6 am-3 pm, Sun from 7 am. **Reservations:** accepted. **Features:** Breakfast items abound, with waffles, omelets, crepes and fresh fruit platters, plus the specialty, eggs Benedict. Also on the menu are salads, burgers, sandwiches and freshly squeezed juices. Booths are available, and the atmosphere can be bustling. Casual dress; cocktails. **Parking:** on-site. **Cards:** AX, CB, DC, DS, JC, MC, VI.

DINKEL'S RESTAURANT   Lunch: $7-$14   Dinner: $14-$29   Phone: 613/966-2556

(CAA)

Continental **Location:** Corner of Pinnacle St; centre. 44 Bridge St E K8N 1L6. **Hours:** 11:30 am-2:30 & 5-10 pm, Sat & Mon from 5 pm. **Closed:** 12/25; also Sun. **Reservations:** accepted. **Features:** A rich, dark wood decor adds to the comfortable atmosphere where featured selections include fresh fish, Angus beef, pasta, veal and lamb. Of note are the tasty stuffed chicken and crisp Caesar salad. Patio courtyard seating is available in season. Casual dress; cocktails. **Parking:** on-site. **Cards:** AX, DC, MC, VI.

PAULO'S ITALIAN TRATTORIA　　　**Lunch:** $7-$12　　　**Dinner:** $9-$18　　　**Phone:** 613/966-6542
▼▼▼
Location: Corner of Pinnacle St; centre. 38 Bridge St E K8N 1L6. **Hours:** 11:30 am-10 pm, Fri & Sat-11 pm, Sun-9:30 pm. **Closed:** 12/25. **Reservations:** accepted. **Features:** Wood-oven baked pizzas and preparations of
Italian　pasta, veal and steak are served in a casual atmosphere. The rich desserts also are worthy of praise. Casual dress; cocktails. **Parking:** street. **Cards:** AX, DC, MC, VI. ⊠

BLIND RIVER pop. 3,969

——— **WHERE TO STAY** ———

AUBERGE ELDO INN　　　　　　　　　　　　　　　　　　　　　　**Phone:** 705/356-2255
▼▼▼
All Year　　　　　1P: $74-$80　　　2P: $80-$89　　　XP: $10　　　　F12
Location: 1 km e. Located in a commercial area. Hwy 17 P0R 1B0 (PO Box 156). **Fax:** 705/356-9857.
Small-scale Hotel　**Facility:** Smoke free premises. 12 one-bedroom standard units. 1 story, interior corridors. **Parking:** on-site, winter plug-ins. **Terms:** office hours 7 am-11 pm. **Amenities:** voice mail. **Dining:** Christie's Restaurant, see separate listing. **Leisure Activities:** whirlpool, snowmobiling. **Guest Services:** area transportation. **Cards:** AX, DC, MC, VI.

🍽 ⊠ 🖧 ▯ 💻

LAKEVIEW INN　　　　　　　　　　　　　　　　　　　　　　　**Phone:** 705/356-0800
▼▼▼
5/1-9/30　　　　　1P: $66-$70　　　2P: $76-$80　　　XP: $5　　　　F10
10/1-4/30　　　　1P: $65-$69　　　2P: $74-$79　　　XP: $5　　　　F10
Motel　　**Location:** On Hwy 17, just e of Hwy 557. Located in a commercial area. 143 Causley St (Hwy 17) P0R 1B0 (PO Box 598). **Fax:** 705/356-0813. **Facility:** 15 one-bedroom standard units. 1 story, exterior corridors. **Parking:** on-site, winter plug-ins. **Terms:** office hours 7 am-11 pm, 3 day cancellation notice, package plans, small pets only (with prior approval). **Dining:** restaurant, see separate listing. **Leisure Activities:** snowmobiling. **Cards:** AX, MC, VI.

SOME UNITS
ASK S🄳 🐾 🍽 ▯ /⊠/

OLD MILL MOTEL　　　　　　　　　　　　　　　　　　　　　　**Phone:** 705/356-2274
▼▼
All Year　　　　　1P: $50-$60　　　2P: $62-$82　　　XP: $5　　　　F12
Location: Centre. Located in a commercial area. Hwy 17 & Woodward St P0R 1B0 (PO Box 251).
Motel　　**Fax:** 705/356-3521. **Facility:** 38 one-bedroom standard units. 2 stories (no elevator), exterior corridors. *Bath:* combo or shower only. **Parking:** on-site, winter plug-ins. **Terms:** office hours 7 am-11 pm, weekly rates available, package plans. **Leisure Activities:** snowmobiling, playground. **Cards:** AX, DC, MC, VI.

SOME UNITS
🍽 /⊠ ▯/

——— **WHERE TO DINE** ———

CHRISTIE'S RESTAURANT　　　**Lunch:** $5-$13　　　**Dinner:** $10-$30　　　**Phone:** 705/356-2255
▼▼ ▼▼
Location: 1 km e; in Auberge Eldo Inn. Hwy 17 P0R 1B0. **Hours:** 11 am-8 pm, Sat & Sun from 5 pm. Closed major holidays; also 12/20-1/4. **Reservations:** accepted. **Features:** Although the signature dish is local
Canadian　whitefish, such items as steak, chicken and pierogies also are prepared. A cappuccino or other specialty coffee paired with raspberry pie is a dessert not to be overlooked. The patio opens seasonally. The menu lists some low-carbohydrate choices. Casual dress; cocktails. **Parking:** on-site. **Cards:** AX, DC, MC, VI. ⊠

LAKEVIEW INN RESTAURANT　　　**Lunch:** $4-$8　　　**Dinner:** $9-$17　　　**Phone:** 705/356-1912
▼▼
Location: On Hwy 17, just e of Hwy 557; in Lakeview Inn. 143 Causley St P0R 1B0. **Hours:** 6:30 am-8 pm. Closed: 1/1, 12/24, 12/25, 12/26. **Reservations:** accepted. **Features:** Locals congregate here for a hearty breakfast,
Canadian　coffee and conversation or for the very popular fresh fish dinners. Casual dress; cocktails. **Parking:** on-site. **Cards:** AX, MC, VI. ⊠

BLOOMFIELD pop. 643

——— **WHERE TO DINE** ———

ANGELINE'S　　　　　　　**Lunch:** $8-$15　　　**Dinner:** $20-$27　　　**Phone:** 613/393-3301
▼▼ ▼▼
Location: Hwy 33, jct Rt 62. 433 Main St K0K 1G0. **Hours:** Open 5/1-1/1 & 2/1-4/30; 11:30 am-2 & 5:30-9:30 pm, Sun noon-2 pm; hours vary off season. **Closed:** Tues 9/1-1/14. **Reservations:** suggested.
Regional French　**Features:** The meticulously done dining room in this 1869 Loyalist house boasts classic French cooking with local spring lamb, organic chicken, pickerel and Viennese dessert with an emphasis on market-sensitive and local produce. Espresso/cappuccino is also offered. Casual dress; cocktails. **Parking:** on-site. **Cards:** AX, MC, VI. ⊠

BLOOMFIELD BRASSERIE RESTAURANT　　　**Lunch:** $6-$12　　　**Dinner:** $8-$17　　　**Phone:** 613/393-5111
▼▼ ▼▼
Location: Centre. 260 Main St K0K 1G0. **Hours:** 11 am-9 pm; to 4 pm 10/16-5/14. **Closed:** 1/1, 12/25.
Reservations: accepted. **Features:** The little brasserie is housed in a circa 1875 coach house. Exposed
Canadian　brick walls and a fireplace add to the cozy setting. Soups, salads, sandwiches, pasta dishes and other lighter fare are offered. The patio opens seasonally. Casual dress; beer & wine only. **Parking:** on-site.
Cards: MC, VI.
🅐🅒 ⊠

BRACEBRIDGE pop. 13,751

------ WHERE TO STAY ------

PATTERSON-KAYE LODGE   **Phone: 705/645-4169**
▼▼▼▼   Property failed to provide current rates
                         Location: 3.2 km nw on Hwy 118, 4.5 km w. 1360 Golden Beach Rd P1L 1W8 (RR 1). Fax: 705/645-5720.
Resort   **Facility:** Featured at this lakefront lodge are a cozy lounge with wood floors and cathedral ceilings, and a
Small-scale Hotel   seasonal dining room overlooking the water. 30 units. 16 one- and 1 two-bedroom standard units, some with
                         efficiencies and/or whirlpools. 4 one- and 5 two-bedroom suites, some with kitchens and/or whirlpools. 3
cabins and 1 cottage. 1-2 stories (no elevator), interior/exterior corridors. *Bath:* combo or shower only. **Parking:** on-site, winter
plug-ins. **Terms:** open 5/10-10/19 & 12/27-3/9, office hours 8 am-8 pm. **Pool(s):** heated outdoor. **Leisure Activities:** whirlpool,
rental boats, canoeing, paddleboats, sailboats, boat dock, waterskiing, fishing, 2 lighted tennis courts, cross country skiing,
snowmobiling, ice skating, recreation programs, rental bicycles, playground. **Guest Services:** gift shop, coin laundry.

SOME UNITS

[🍴 🏠 🏊 ⊠ 🎥 🐾 🌀 🔌 / 🖥 /]

TRAVELODGE BRACEBRIDGE   *Book at aaa.com*   **Phone: (705)645-2235**
ⓐ 🅂🅐🅥🅔   6/1-10/31 [CP]   1P: $119-$169   2P: $119-$169   XP: $10   F17
              5/1-5/31 & 11/1-4/30 [CP]   1P: $89-$159   2P: $89-$159   XP: $10   F17
▼▼▼ ▼▼▼   **Location:** Hwy 11, exit 189 (Hwy 42/Taylor Rd), 1 km w. Located in a residential area. 320 Taylor Rd P1L 1K1.
              Fax: 705/645-3266. **Facility:** 37 one-bedroom standard units, some with whirlpools. 1 story, exterior
Motel   corridors. **Parking:** on-site, winter plug-ins. **Terms:** office hours 7.30 am-11 pm. **Amenities:** hair dryers.
              Pool(s): heated outdoor. **Leisure Activities:** playground, horseshoes, volleyball. **Guest Services:** valet
laundry. **Business Services:** meeting rooms. **Cards:** AX, DC, JC, MC, VI. **Special Amenities:** free continental breakfast and
free local telephone calls.

SOME UNITS

[🅂🄳 🐾 🏊 ⊠ 🎥 🔌 🖥 / ⊠ 🎥 /]

------ WHERE TO DINE ------

THE OLD STATION RESTAURANT   **Lunch:** $6-$9   **Dinner:** $12-$20   **Phone:** 705/645-9776
ⓐ   **Location:** Corner of Dominion St. 88 Manitoba St P1L 1W3. **Hours:** 11 am-9 pm, Fri & Sat-10 pm; to 10 pm 7/1-
             8/31. Closed: 1/1, 12/25, 12/26; also Sun 11/1-4/30. **Reservations:** accepted. **Features:** On old main street
▼▼▼ ▼▼▼   near the town common, the little restaurant has a fireplace and a massive tree in the middle of the dining
Canadian   room. Guests can dine on the patio in season. The innovative menu lists fresh pasta, steak and seafood
             dishes. Casual dress; cocktails. **Parking:** street. **Cards:** AX, DC, MC, VI.   [🍽 ⊠]

BRAMPTON pop. 325,428

------ WHERE TO STAY ------

BEST WESTERN-BRAMPTON   *Book at aaa.com*   **Phone: (905)454-1300**
ⓐ 🅂🅐🅥🅔   5/1-9/30   1P: $109-$249   2P: $109-$249
              10/1-4/30   1P: $99-$229   2P: $99-$229
▼▼▼ ▼▼▼   **Location:** Hwy 410, exit Clark Blvd W, sw of Hwy 410 and 7. 30 Clark Blvd L6W 1X3. Fax: 905/454-0870.
              Facility: 136 units. 133 one-bedroom standard units. 3 one-bedroom suites ($199), some with whirlpools. 2
Small-scale Hotel stories (no elevator), interior/exterior corridors. **Parking:** on-site, winter plug-ins. **Terms:** cancellation fee
              imposed, [ECP] meal plan available, package plans. **Amenities:** video games (fee), voice mail, irons, hair
dryers. *Some:* dual phone lines. **Pool(s):** heated indoor. **Leisure Activities:** sauna, whirlpool. **Guest Services:** valet laundry.
Business Services: meeting rooms, business center. **Cards:** AX, DC, DS, MC, VI. **Special Amenities:** free expanded
continental breakfast and free room upgrade (subject to availability with advance reservations). *(See color ad p 519)*

SOME UNITS

[🅂🄳 🎮 🏊 🎥 DATA PORT 🖥 / ⊠ 🔌 🖥 /]

COMFORT INN   *Book at aaa.com*   **Phone: (905)452-0600**
▼▼▼ ▼▼▼   All Year [CP]   1P: $80-$119   2P: $90-$129   XP: $10   F18
             Location: Hwy 401, exit Hwy 410 N, 11 km to Hwy 7 E (Queen St), then 1 km w. 5 Rutherford Rd S L6W 3J3.
Small-scale Hotel Fax: 905/452-0781. **Facility:** 107 one-bedroom standard units. 2 stories (no elevator), interior corridors.
             Parking: on-site, winter plug-ins. **Terms:** pets (1st floor units). **Amenities:** hair dryers. *Some:* dual phone
lines, irons. **Guest Services:** valet laundry. **Cards:** AX, DC, DS, MC, VI.

SOME UNITS

[🄰🅂🄺 🅂🄳 🐾 🎮 🎥 DATA PORT 🖥 / ⊠ 🔌 🖥 /]

HOLIDAY INN SELECT TORONTO-BRAMPTON   *Book at aaa.com*   **Phone: (905)792-9900**
ⓐ 🅂🅐🅥🅔   All Year   1P: $140-$220   2P: $140-$220   XP: $20   F
             Location: Hwy 410 N, exit 7 (Queen St), 2 km e. 30 Peel Centre Dr L6T 4G3. Fax: 905/792-1740. **Facility:** 147
▼▼▼ ▼▼▼   units. 145 one-bedroom standard units. 2 one-bedroom suites. 6 stories, interior corridors. *Bath:* combo or
             shower only. **Parking:** on-site. **Terms:** package plans, small pets only ($50 extra charge). **Amenities:** video
Large-scale Hotel games (fee), high-speed Internet, dual phone lines, voice mail, irons, hair dryers. *Some:* fax. **Dining:** 6;30
             am-11 pm, cocktails. **Pool(s):** heated indoor. **Leisure Activities:** sauna, whirlpool, exercise room. **Guest**
Services: valet laundry. **Business Services:** conference facilities, business center. **Cards:** AX, CB, DC, DS, MC, VI.
Special Amenities: free local telephone calls and free newspaper. *(See color ad card insert)*

SOME UNITS

[🅂🄳 🐾 🍴 🍽 🏊 ⊠ 🎥 DATA PORT 🖥 / ⊠ 🔌 /]
FEE   FEE

MONTE CARLO INN-TORONTO-BRAMPTON SUITES   *Book at aaa.com*   **Phone: (905)453-5200**
ⓐ 🅂🅐🅥🅔   All Year   1P: $89-$109   2P: $99-$129   XP: $10   F12
             Location: 1 blk s of Hwy 7 on Airport Rd. 45 Coventry Rd L6T 4V7. Fax: 905/453-9500. **Facility:** 107 units. 103
▼▼▼ ▼▼▼   one-bedroom standard units, some with whirlpools. 4 one-bedroom suites ($119-$199) with whirlpools. 4
             stories, interior corridors. **Parking:** on-site. **Terms:** weekly rates available, [BP] meal plan available.
Small-scale Hotel **Amenities:** high-speed Internet, voice mail, irons, hair dryers. **Dining:** 6 am-11 pm. **Leisure**
             Activities: exercise room. **Guest Services:** valet laundry. **Business Services:** meeting rooms, business
center. **Cards:** AX, CB, DC, DS, JC, MC, VI. **Special Amenities:** free expanded continental breakfast and free newspaper.
(See color ad p 531)

SOME UNITS

[🅂🄳 🍴 🍽 🎥 DATA PORT 🔌 🖥 🖥 / ⊠ /]

MOTEL 6 #1902   **Book at aaa.com**   Phone: 905/451-3313
All Year   1P: $67-$79   2P: $73-$85   XP: $3   F17
Location: Hwy 410, exit Steeles Ave E, s on Tomken, then just w. 160 Steelwell Rd L6T 5T3. Fax: 905/451-7367.
Small-scale Hotel   **Facility:** 122 one-bedroom standard units. 3 stories, interior corridors. *Bath:* combo or shower only. **Parking:** on-site. **Terms:** small pets only. **Guest Services:** coin laundry. **Cards:** AX, CB, DC, DS, MC, VI.

──── WHERE TO DINE ────

BASSANO RESTAURANT   **Lunch:** $12-$16   **Dinner:** $15-$23   Phone: 905/451-2600
Location: 1.6 km s of Hwy 7. 485 Main St N (Hwy 10) L6X 1N8. **Hours:** 11 am-3 & 5-10 pm, Sat & Sun from 5
Northern   pm. Closed major holidays; also Mon & 1/1-1/15. **Reservations:** suggested. **Features:** Located in an
Italian   inviting, gracious old house, the dining rooms are on two floors in spacious, comfortable rooms. The menu
offers veal, seafood, red meat pasta and a tempting array of desserts. Casual dress; cocktails. **Parking:** on-site. **Cards:** AX, DC, MC, VI.

BRANTFORD pop. 86,417

──── WHERE TO STAY ────

BEST WESTERN BRANT PARK INN &
CONFERENCE CENTRE   **Book at aaa.com**   Phone: (519)753-8651
(CAA) (SAVE)   1/1-4/30   1P: $130-$220   2P: $140-$240   XP: $10   F12
5/1-12/31   1P: $125-$214   2P: $135-$224   XP: $10   F12
Location: Jct Hwy 403 and Wayne Gretzky Pkwy. 19 Holiday Dr N3T 5W5 (PO Box 1900). Fax: 519/753-2619.
Facility: 158 units. 142 one-bedroom standard units, some with whirlpools. 16 one-bedroom suites ($155-
Small-scale Hotel $215). 2-3 stories, interior corridors. **Parking:** on-site. **Terms:** cancellation fee imposed. **Amenities:** voice
mail, irons, hair dryers. *Some:* high-speed Internet, dual phone lines. **Dining:** 7 am-10 pm. **Pool(s):** heated
indoor, wading. **Leisure Activities:** sauna, whirlpool, playground, exercise room. **Guest Services:** valet and coin laundry.
Business Services: conference facilities. **Cards:** AX, DC, MC, VI. **Special Amenities: free local telephone calls and free
newspaper.**

COMFORT INN   **Book at aaa.com**   Phone: (519)753-3100
5/1-9/30   1P: $99-$129   2P: $109-$139   XP: $10   F18
1/1-4/30   1P: $94-$124   2P: $104-$134   XP: $10   F18
10/1-12/31   1P: $92-$122   2P: $102-$132   XP: $10   F18
Small-scale Hotel   **Location:** Just s of jct Hwy 403 and 24. 58 King George Rd N3R 5K4. Fax: 519/753-8138. **Facility:** 80 one-
bedroom standard units. 2 stories (no elevator), interior corridors. **Parking:** on-site, winter plug-ins. **Amenities:** irons, hair
dryers. *Some:* high-speed Internet. **Guest Services:** valet laundry. **Cards:** AX, DC, DS, JC, MC, VI.

DAYS INN   **Book at aaa.com**   Phone: (519)759-2700
(CAA) (SAVE)   All Year   1P: $91-$101   2P: $98-$112   XP: $10   F12
Location: Hwy 403, exit Wayne Gretzky Pkwy, 0.8 km n. 460 Fairview Dr N3R 7A9. Fax: 519/759-2089. **Facility:** 75
one-bedroom standard units, some with whirlpools. 2 stories (no elevator), interior corridors. **Parking:** on-
site, winter plug-ins. **Terms:** cancellation fee imposed, package plans, pets ($15 fee). **Amenities:** video
Small-scale Hotel   library, voice mail, irons, hair dryers. *Some:* dual phone lines. *Fee:* high-speed Internet. **Dining:** 11 am-11
pm, cocktails. **Guest Services:** valet laundry. **Business Services:** meeting rooms. **Cards:** AX, DC, MC, VI.
Special Amenities: free continental breakfast and free local telephone calls.

HOLIDAY INN BRANTFORD   **Book at aaa.com**   Phone: (519)758-9999
5/2-10/1   1P: $99-$229   2P: $99-$229
5/1-5/1 & 12/31-4/30   1P: $89-$209   2P: $89-$209
10/2-12/30   1P: $89-$200   2P: $89-$200
Small-scale Hotel   **Location:** Hwy 403, exit Wayne Gretzky Pkwy, 2 km s to Colborne St, then just w. 664 Colborne St N3S 3P8.
Fax: 519/758-1515. **Facility:** 98 one-bedroom standard units, some with whirlpools. 3 stories (no elevator), interior corridors.
Parking: on-site. **Amenities:** voice mail, irons, hair dryers. *Some:* high-speed Internet, dual phone lines. **Dining:** Spitfire Grill,
see separate listing. **Pool(s):** heated indoor. **Leisure Activities:** exercise room. **Guest Services:** valet and coin laundry.
Business Services: meeting rooms. **Cards:** AX, DC, DS, MC, VI. *(See color ad card insert)*

──── WHERE TO DINE ────

MOOSE WINOOSKI'S   **Lunch:** $6-$10   **Dinner:** $7-$16   Phone: 519/751-4042
Location: 0.5 km s of Hwy 403. 45 King George Rd N3R 5K2. **Hours:** 11 am-1 am, Thurs-Sat to 2 am. Closed:
12/25. **Features:** The casual restaurant features a fun atmosphere, Northern Canadian decor and a popular
American   seasonal patio. A children's play area makes this place great for families. Patrons can choose from tasty
appetizers, such as wings or skins, as well as hearty burgers, salads, pasta, pizza and the ever-favorite
chicken pot pie. Be prepared for huge portions. Casual dress; cocktails. **Parking:** on-site. **Cards:** AX, DC, MC, VI.

THE OLDE SCHOOL RESTAURANT AND PIANO BAR   **Lunch:** $10-$18   **Dinner:** $18-$30   **Phone:** 519/753-3131
▼▼▼▼   **Location:** Hwy 2, 0.8 km nw of Hwy 403. Hwy 2 W & 687 Powerline Rd N3T 5L8. **Hours:** 11:30 am-3 & 5-10 pm,
Canadian   Sat from 5 pm, Sun 11 am-3 & 5-10 pm. Closed: 12/25. **Reservations:** suggested. **Features:** Going to
school takes on a new meaning of being pampered at this restaurant. This 1911 rural school house has
been fully renovated to accommodate discerning diners. Natural wood finish and stained glass are
combined with interesting old school photos and memorabilia to create a comfortable atmosphere. The varied menu, good
selection of wine and unpretentious service are sure to please. Dressy casual; cocktails; entertainment. **Parking:** on-site.
Cards: AX, DC, MC, VI. Historic
                                                                                              🍸 ⊠

SPITFIRE GRILL   **Lunch:** $7-$18   **Dinner:** $7-$18   **Phone:** 519/758-9999
▼▼▼   **Location:** Hwy 403, exit Wayne Gretzky Pkwy, 2 km s to Colborne St, then just w; in Holiday Inn Brantford. 664
American   Colborne St N3S 3P8. **Hours:** 7 am-11 pm, Fri & Sat-midnight, Sun-10 pm. Closed: 12/25. **Features:** For a
loud, bustling atmosphere and a fun menu of casual fare, try the laid-back eatery. Diners can choose from a
variety of finger foods and appetizers, such as wings and chicken fingers, as well as burgers, pasta dishes
and full steak dinners. Casual dress; cocktails. **Parking:** on-site. **Cards:** AX, MC, VI.
                                                                                              ⊠

BRIGHTON pop. 9,449

——— WHERE TO STAY ———

BUTLER CREEK COUNTRY INN   **Phone:** (613)475-1248
▼▼▼ ▼▼   All Year [BP]   1P: $75-$105   2P: $85-$115   XP: $25
Bed & Breakfast   **Location:** Hwy 401, exit 509, 3.5 km s. Located adjacent to the Proctor Conservation area. 202 Hwy 30 K0K 1H0 (RR
7/Hwy 30-202). Fax: 613/475-5267. **Facility:** Smoke free premises. 6 units. 5 one-bedroom standard units. 1
one-bedroom suite. 2 stories (no elevator), interior/exterior corridors. *Bath:* some shared or private, combo
or shower only. **Parking:** on-site, winter plug-ins. **Terms:** office hours 8 am-10 pm, package plans. **Leisure Activities:** cross
country skiing, hiking trails. **Cards:** AX, MC, VI.
                                                                              SOME UNITS
                                          ⊠ 📺 ☎ 🖥 / 📶 📼 🛢 🖨 /

PRESQUILE BEACH MOTEL   **Phone:** (613)475-1010
▼▼   6/20-9/30   1P: $55-$85   2P: $65-$99   XP: $6
   6/1-6/19   1P: $55-$76   2P: $60-$85   XP: $6
Motel   10/1-4/30   1P: $50-$76   2P: $60-$85   XP: $6
   5/1-5/31   1P: $50-$73   2P: $55-$85   XP: $6
Location: Hwy 401, exit 509, 4 km s on Hwy 30, then 2 km w on Hwy 2. 243 Main St W K0K 1H0. Fax: 613/475-9430. **Facility:** 20 units.
16 one-bedroom standard units, some with efficiencies or kitchens. 4 one-bedroom suites ($73-$99) with kitchens. 1 story,
exterior corridors. *Bath:* combo or shower only. **Parking:** on-site, winter plug-ins. **Terms:** office hours 7 am-midnight, weekly
rates available. **Cards:** MC, VI.
                                                                              SOME UNITS
                                          🛏 📺 ☎ / ⊠ 🛢 🖨 /

BROCKVILLE pop. 21,357

——— WHERE TO STAY ———

BEST WESTERN WHITE HOUSE MOTEL   *Book at aaa.com*   **Phone:** (613)345-1622
(CAA) (SAVE)   7/1-9/30 [BP]   1P: $69-$109   2P: $79-$119   XP: $10   F12
▼▼ ▼▼   5/1-6/30 & 10/1-4/30 [BP]   1P: $59-$89   2P: $69-$99   XP: $10   F12
Motel   **Location:** Hwy 401, exit 698, 1.7 km s on N Augusta Rd, then 1.5 km e. Located in a residential area. 1843 Hwy 2 E
K6V 5T1. Fax: 613/345-4284. **Facility:** 56 one-bedroom standard units. 1 story, exterior corridors. **Parking:**
on-site, winter plug-ins. **Terms:** cancellation fee imposed, pets ($10 fee). **Amenities:** irons, hair dryers.
Dining: 7 am-2 & 5-8 pm. **Pool(s):** heated outdoor. **Guest Services:** valet laundry. **Business Services:**
meeting rooms. **Cards:** AX, DC, DS, JC, MC, VI. **Special Amenities:** free full breakfast and free local telephone calls.
                                                                              SOME UNITS
                             🅂 🛏 🍴 🍸 🏊 DATA/PORT 🖥 / ⊠ 🛢 🖨 /
                             FEE

COMFORT INN   *Book at aaa.com*   **Phone:** (613)345-0042
▼▼ ▼▼   7/1-8/31   1P: $99-$119   2P: $119-$129   XP: $5   F18
   5/1-6/30 & 9/1-12/31   1P: $89-$109   2P: $99-$119   XP: $5   F18
Small-scale Hotel   1/1-4/30   1P: $83-$103   2P: $93-$113   XP: $5   F18
Location: Hwy 401, exit 696, just w. Located in a commercial area. 7777 Kent Blvd K6V 6N7. Fax: 613/345-4868.
Facility: 75 one-bedroom standard units. 2 stories (no elevator), interior corridors. **Parking:** on-site, winter plug-ins.
Terms: pets ($8 extra charge). **Amenities:** video games (fee), voice mail. **Guest Services:** valet laundry. **Cards:** AX, DC, DS,
JC, MC, VI.
                                                                              SOME UNITS
                             A$K 🅂 🛏 ⊞ 📹 DATA/PORT 🖥 / ⊠ 🛢 🖨 /
                             FEE

DAYS INN BROCKVILLE 1000 ISLANDS   *Book at aaa.com*   **Phone:** (613)342-6613
(CAA) (SAVE)   5/1-10/31   1P: $69-$149   2P: $99-$199   XP: $10   F
▼▼ ▼▼   11/1-4/30   1P: $59-$139   2P: $89-$189   XP: $10   F
Small-scale Hotel   **Location:** Hwy 401, exit 696, just sw. Located in a commercial area. 160 Stewart Blvd K6V 4W6. Fax: 613/345-3811.
Facility: 84 one-bedroom standard units, some with whirlpools. 2 stories (no elevator), interior corridors.
Parking: on-site, winter plug-ins. **Terms:** cancellation fee imposed, package plans, 15% service charge.
Amenities: voice mail, irons, hair dryers. *Some:* dual phone lines. **Dining:** 7 am-2 & 5-9 pm, cocktails.
Pool(s): outdoor. **Leisure Activities:** exercise room. **Business Services:** meeting rooms. **Cards:** AX, DC, JC, MC, VI.
Special Amenities: free local telephone calls and free newspaper.
                                                                              SOME UNITS
                             🅂 🍴 🍸 🏊 DATA/PORT 🖥 / ⊠ 📼 🛢 🖨 /

QUALITY HOTEL ROYAL BROCK AND
CONVENTION CENTRE *Book at aaa.com*   Phone: (613)345-1400
(CAA) (SAVE)   6/30-9/30   1P: $89-$129   2P: $89-$149   XP: $10   F
              5/1-6/29   1P: $89-$109   2P: $109-$120   XP: $10   F
              10/1-4/30   1P: $89-$120   2P: $99-$120   XP: $10   F
              Location: Hwy 401, exit 696, just s. Located in a commercial/residential area. 100 Stewart Blvd K6V 4W3.
Small-scale Hotel **Fax:** 613/345-5402. **Facility:** 72 units. 70 one-bedroom standard units. 2 one-bedroom suites ($149-$249).
5 stories, interior corridors. **Parking:** on-site. **Terms:** weekly rates available, package plans, 15% service
charge. **Amenities:** voice mail, irons, hair dryers. **Dining:** 7 am-2 & 5-9 pm, cocktails. **Pool(s):** heated indoor. **Leisure
Activities:** saunas, whirlpool, steamrooms, 4 squash courts, spa. **Guest Services:** valet laundry. **Business Services:**
conference facilities, business center. **Cards:** AX, DC, JC, MC, VI. **Special Amenities:** free local telephone calls and free
newspaper.

SOME UNITS

TRAVELODGE   Phone: 613/345-3900
(CAA) (SAVE)   All Year   1P: $59-$99   2P: $69-$109   XP: $10   F16
              Location: Hwy 401, exit 696, just nw. Located in a commercial area. 7789 Kent Blvd K6V 6N7. **Fax:** 613/345-3953.
              Facility: 72 one-bedroom standard units, some with whirlpools. 2 stories (no elevator), interior corridors.
              Bath: shower only. **Parking:** on-site. **Terms:** cancellation fee imposed. **Amenities:** hair dryers. *Some* irons.
Small-scale Hotel **Leisure Activities:** exercise room. **Guest Services:** valet laundry. **Cards:** AX, CB, DC, JC, MC, VI.

SOME UNITS

——— **WHERE TO DINE** ———

BROCKBERRY CAFE   **Lunch:** $9-$11   **Dinner:** $14-$21   Phone: 613/498-2692
              Location: Corner of Bethune St; centre. 64 King St E K6V 1B3. **Hours:** 11 am-2 & 5-8 pm. Closed major holidays.
              Reservations: accepted. **Features:** The charming old stone townhouse is the setting for this cafe, which
Continental   presents a varied menu of pasta, seafood, steaks, salads and sandwiches. The patio overlooks the main
              street in summer. Casual dress; cocktails. **Parking:** on-site. **Cards:** AX, MC, VI.

NEW YORK RESTAURANT   **Lunch:** $7-$17   **Dinner:** $7-$17   Phone: 613/345-0015
              Location: On Hwy 2 (King St W); centre. 19 King St W K6V 3P7. **Hours:** 11 am-10 pm, Fri-11 pm, Sat noon-11
              pm, Sun noon-10 pm. Closed: 5/23, 10/10, 12/25. **Reservations:** accepted. **Features:** Examples of
Chinese   Szechuan, seafood and Canadian selections include General Tso's chicken and fresh jumbo shrimp with
              minced pork sauteed in black bean sauce. Another recent favorite is the delicious pork and broccoli dish
with steamed rice. Casual dress; cocktails. **Parking:** street. **Cards:** AX, MC, VI.

BURLINGTON pop. 150,836

——— **WHERE TO STAY** ———

ADMIRAL INN   *Book at aaa.com*   Phone: (905)639-4780
(CAA) (SAVE)   All Year   1P: $77-$87   2P: $87-$97   XP: $10   F12
              Location: QEW, exit Walker's Line Rd westbound, just s to Harvester Rd, then just w to S Service Rd; exit Guelph Line
              Rd eastbound, just s to Harvester Rd, then just e to S Service Rd. 3500 Billings Ct L7N 3N6. **Fax:** 905/639-1967.
              Facility: 67 one-bedroom standard units, some with whirlpools. 2 stories, interior corridors. **Parking:** on-
Small-scale Hotel site, winter plug-ins. **Amenities:** voice mail, irons, hair dryers. **Dining:** 7 am-10 pm, Fri & Sat-11 pm, Sun
from 8 am, cocktails. **Guest Services:** valet laundry. **Business Services:** meeting rooms, fax (fee).
Cards: AX, DC, MC, VI. **Special Amenities:** free local telephone calls and free newspaper. *(See color ad below)*

SOME UNITS

Admiral

HAMILTON

149 Dundurn Street N.
Hamilton, Ontario L8R 3E7
(905) 529-2311
1-866-236-4662

The Admiral Inns' two locations offer first class accommodations for the traveller with the most discriminating taste. At Admiral Inns you'll find clean, quality rooms, fully licensed dining lounges, modern meeting facilities and a friendly, efficient staff, all at affordable, competitive rates.

Our large, spacious rooms come equipped with either queen size or double beds. For that special evening try the "Admiral Suite", just perfect for a great weekend escape or a romantic honeymoon.

I-N-N-S

BURLINGTON

3500 Billings Court
Burlington, Ontario L7N 3N6
(905) 639-4780
1-866-236-4661

Breathtaking FALLS.
Brand New EXPERIENCE.

oday, there's a whole new energy. A whole new attitude.

Nowhere is this more evident than Niagara Fallsview Casino Resort. The Casino hums with non-stop excitement — while our restaurants create a stir with everything from steaks to seafood to sushi. The mood is relaxed and sophisticated, just like our luxurious accommodations.

And the entertainment? *Unforgettable.* Prepare to be dazzled at the Avalon Ballroom, where you can get up close and personal with legendary entertainers.

FALLSVIEW CASINO.

Niagara Falls, Canada • DiscoverNiagara.com

Call 1-888-FALLSVUE to book your Getaway today.

Know your limit, play within it! The Ontario Problem Gambling Helpline 1-888-230-3505.

CASINO • NIAGARA

Fun!
Friendly!
Exciting!

Casino Niagara
overflows with action!

- 100,000 square feet of gaming excitement
- Over 2,400 slot machines and 75 table games
- Over 8 restaurants
- FREE parking (park n' ride)

Book your overnight getaway today!
For special casino room rates call 1-888-918-2888 or visit DiscoverNiagara.com

CASINO • NIAGARA
More Prizes! More Winners! More Often!
1-888-WINFALL • DiscoverNiagara.com

Know your limit, play within it! The Ontario Problem Gambling Helpline 1-888-230-3505.
Must be at least 19 years of age.

BEST WESTERN BURLINGTON INN AND SUITES   *Book at aaa.com*   Phone: (905)639-2700

(CAA) (SAVE)

5/1-10/31	1P: $129-$189	2P: $129-$189	XP: $10 F12
11/1-4/30	1P: $99-$169	2P: $99-$169	XP: $10 F12

Location: QEW, exit Guelph Line Rd S, just s. 2412 Queensway Dr L7R 3T3. Fax: 905/639-0900. **Facility: 56** units. 52 one-bedroom standard units, some with whirlpools. 4 one-bedroom suites, some with whirlpools. 3
Small-scale Hotel stories, interior corridors. **Parking:** on-site. **Terms:** package plans. **Amenities:** high-speed Internet, voice mail, irons, hair dryers. **Pool(s):** heated indoor. **Leisure Activities:** whirlpool, exercise room. **Guest Services:** valet and coin laundry. **Business Services:** meeting rooms. **Cards:** AX, CB, DC, DS, JC, MC, VI.
Special Amenities: free expanded continental breakfast and free local telephone calls.

SOME UNITS

BURLINGTON ON THE LAKE TRAVELODGE HOTEL   *Book at aaa.com*   Phone: (905)681-0762

(CAA) (SAVE)

All Year [ECP]	1P: $139-$149	2P: $149-$159	XP: $10 F18

Location: Jct Brant. 2020 Lakeshore Rd L7R 4G8. Fax: 905/634-4398. **Facility:** 122 one-bedroom standard units, some with whirlpools. 7 stories, interior corridors. **Parking:** on-site, winter plug-ins. **Terms:** weekly rates available, small pets only ($5 extra charge). **Amenities:** high-speed
Small-scale Hotel Internet, voice mail, irons, hair dryers. *Fee:* dual phone lines. *Some:* dual phone lines. **Dining:** 6 am-10 pm, cocktails. **Pool(s):** heated indoor. **Leisure Activities:** saunas, whirlpool. **Guest Services:** valet laundry.
Business Services: meeting rooms. **Cards:** AX, DC, DS, JC, MC, VI. **Special Amenities: free expanded continental breakfast and free newspaper.** *(See color ad below)*

SOME UNITS

FEE

COMFORT INN   *Book at aaa.com*   Phone: (905)639-1700

(CAA) (SAVE)

6/1-9/30	1P: $90-$140	2P: $95-$145	XP: $5 F18
10/1-4/30	1P: $80-$130	2P: $85-$135	XP: $5 F18
5/1-5/31	1P: $80-$120	2P: $85-$125	XP: $5 F18

Location: QEW, exit Walker's Line Rd westbound, just s to Harvester Rd, then just w; exit Guelph Line Rd eastbound,
Small-scale Hotel just s to Harvester Rd, then just e. 3290 S Service Rd L7N 3M6. Fax: 905/639-8968. **Facility:** 99 one-bedroom standard units, some with whirlpools. 2 stories (no elevator), interior corridors. **Parking:** on-site, winter plug-ins. **Terms:** [CP] meal plan available, package plans, small pets only. **Amenities:** irons, hair dryers. **Guest Services:** valet laundry. **Business Services:** meeting rooms. **Cards:** AX, DC, DS, JC, MC, VI.

SOME UNITS

HOLIDAY INN BURLINGTON-HOTEL &
CONFERENCE CENTRE   *Book at aaa.com*   Phone: (905)639-4443

(CAA) (SAVE)

All Year	1P: $125-$169	2P: $125-$169	XP: $10 F18

Location: QEW, exit Guelph Line Rd, s to Service Rd. 3063 S Service Rd L7N 3E9. Fax: 905/333-4033.
Facility: 237 one-bedroom standard units. 6 stories, interior corridors. **Parking:** on-site, winter plug-ins.
Large-scale Hotel **Terms:** package plans. **Amenities:** voice mail, irons, hair dryers. *Some:* high-speed Internet, dual phone lines, honor bars. **Dining:** 6:30 am-10 pm, Sat & Sun from 7 am. **Pool(s):** heated indoor. **Leisure Activities:** sauna, whirlpool, lighted tennis court, holidome games area, exercise room, basketball. *Fee:* game room. **Guest Services:** gift shop, valet and coin laundry. **Business Services:** conference facilities, administrative services (fee). **Cards:** AX, DC, DS, MC, VI. *(See color ad card insert)*

SOME UNITS

Meet You Downtown...

Travelodge Hotel
BURLINGTON ON THE LAKE

...close to shops & restaurants.

- Minutes off the highway, right downtown.
- Indoor pool, whirlpool and saunas.
- Free continental breakfast buffet. Free Parking.
- Specialty rooms for couples or families.
- On-site restaurant and lounge with live music.
- Short drive from Toronto or Niagara Falls.
- Free high-speed Internet

2020 Lakeshore Road
Burlington, ON L7R 4G8
905-681-0762
1-800-578-7878
www.travelodge.com

MOTEL 6 CANADA #1900   *Book at aaa.com*   Phone: 905/331-1955

5/27-4/30	1P: $65-$75	2P: $71-$81	XP: $3 F17
5/1-5/26	1P: $59-$69	2P: $65-$75	XP: $3 F17

Small-scale Hotel   **Location:** QEW, exit Walker's Line Rd N to N Service Rd. 4345 N Service Rd L7L 4X7. **Fax:** 905/331-9427. **Facility:** 122 one-bedroom standard units. 3 stories, interior corridors. *Bath:* combo or shower only. **Parking:** on-site. **Guest Services:** coin laundry. **Cards:** AX, CB, DC, DS, MC, VI.

SOME UNITS

TOWN & COUNTRY MOTEL   Phone: 905/634-2383

5/1-9/30	1P: $58-$64	2P: $68-$76	XP: $10 F3
10/1-4/30	1P: $52-$60	2P: $65-$70	XP: $10 F3

Motel   **Location:** QEW, exit Plains Rd, on Hwy 2 W. 517 Plains Rd E L7T 2E2. **Fax:** 905/634-2384. **Facility:** 30 one-bedroom standard units, some with efficiencies and/or whirlpools. 1 story, interior corridors. **Parking:** on-site, winter plug-ins. **Terms:** 4 day cancellation notice. **Pool(s):** heated outdoor. **Cards:** AX, MC, VI.

reservations).   **Special Amenities:** free local telephone calls and preferred room (subject to availability with advance

SOME UNITS

TRAVELODGE BURLINGTON   Phone: (905)639-9290

All Year	1P: $89-$129	2P: $99-$139	XP: $10 F18

Location: QEW, exit Walker's Line Rd, just s. 950 Walker's Line Rd L7N 2G2. **Fax:** 905/639-6900. **Facility:** 116 one-bedroom standard units. 4 stories, interior corridors. **Parking:** on-site, winter plug-ins. **Terms:** package plans. **Amenities:** video games (fee), voice mail, irons, hair dryers. **Pool(s):** heated indoor. **Leisure** Small-scale Hotel **Activities:** whirlpool. **Guest Services:** valet laundry. **Cards:** AX, DC, DS, MC, VI.

(See color ad on TourBookMark)

SOME UNITS

FEE   FEE

--------- WHERE TO DINE ---------

THE KEG STEAKHOUSE AND BAR   **Dinner:** $17-$32   Phone: 905/681-1810

Location: Off QEW; between Walker's Line and Guelph Line rds. 3106 S Service Rd L7N 3E9. **Hours:** 4:30 pm-10:30 pm, Fri-11 pm, Sat 4 pm-11 pm, Sun 4 pm-9:30 pm. Closed: 12/25. **Features:** A longtime local Steak House   favorite for its mesquite-grilled steaks and relaxed atmosphere, the restaurant sustains a Western theme, with high, wood-beam ceilings, cozy booths and dim lighting. Among traditionally prepared dishes are escargot, French onion soup, bacon-wrapped scallops and prime rib. A slice of cheesecake and specialty coffee make the perfect ending. Casual dress; cocktails. **Parking:** on-site. **Cards:** AX, DC, MC, VI.

LA COSTA RESTAURANT   **Lunch:** $8-$34   **Dinner:** $8-$34   Phone: 905/634-7421

Location: Jct James St. 421 Brant St L7R 2G3. **Hours:** 11:30 am-midnight, Sat from noon, Sun 4:30 pm-10 pm. Closed: 1/1, 12/25, 12/26. **Reservations:** suggested. **Features:** In a quiet storefront, the restaurant exudes Mediterranean   contemporary Mediterranean bistro charm. With a wide range of regionally influenced dishes from osso buco to grilled shrimp aioli in full and half portions, diners are hard pressed to leave room for chocolate pate with creme anglaise. Dressy casual; cocktails. **Parking:** street. **Cards:** AX, DC, DS, MC, VI.

NAPOLEON'S   **Lunch:** $8-$18   **Dinner:** $18-$40   Phone: 905/637-7171

Location: 1.5 km e of Guelph Line Rd. 3455 Fairview L7N 2R4. **Hours:** 11:30 am-2:30 & 5-10 pm, Fri-11 pm, Sat 5 pm-11 pm. Closed major holidays; also Sun. **Reservations:** suggested. **Features:** The small, intimate Steak & Seafood   dining room provides a relaxed yet, elegant atmosphere. All entrees include hot, tasty garlic bread and a choice of soup or salad. Menu highlights include fine cuts of beef and extensive seafood options, and the chef serves generous portions. Flambe coffees prepared tableside are an excellent finish to a fine traditional dining experience. Dressy casual; cocktails. **Parking:** on-site. **Cards:** AX, DC, MC, VI.

PEPPERWOOD BISTRO   **Lunch:** $8-$18   **Dinner:** $12-$28   Phone: 905/333-6999

Location: Jct Brant St. 1455 Lakeshore Rd L7S 2J1. **Hours:** 11 am-11 pm, Thurs-Sat to 1 am; Sunday brunch. Closed: 12/25. **Reservations:** suggested. **Features:** Diners can choose from varied selections, including Continental   gourmet pizzas, pasta dishes and the popular steak and frites. A more casual setting is offered on the seasonal patio or in the lounge, which features home-brewed beers. The restaurant bustles during the Sunday jazz brunch and on Thursday through Saturday nights, when jazz entertainment keeps it hopping. Dressy casual; cocktails; entertainment. **Parking:** street. **Cards:** AX, CB, DC, MC.

RISTORANTE AMICI   **Lunch:** $14-$29   **Dinner:** $14-$29   Phone: 905/639-7555

Location: Jct Caroline. 515 John St L7R 2L1. **Hours:** 11:30 am-2 & 5-11 pm, Sat from 5 pm. Closed major holidays; also Sun. **Reservations:** suggested. **Features:** The restaurant exudes a warm, "you're Italian   family here" atmosphere, which is why locals return time and time again. Soft and relaxing music lends to an environment that caters to romantic dining, but anyone can feel at home. The menu lists an appealing variety of appetizers, entrees and desserts that use fresh ingredients and homemade sauces to ensure a great Italian meal from start to finish. Dressy casual; cocktails. **Parking:** on-site. **Cards:** AX, DC, MC, VI.

THE RUDE NATIVE BISTRO   **Lunch:** $7-$15   **Dinner:** $7-$15   Phone: 905/333-5233

Location: At Village Square. 420 Pearl St L7R 2N1. **Hours:** 11:30 am-2 am, Sun-1 am. Closed: 1/1, 12/25, 12/26. **Features:** An innovative menu featuring an exotic blend of Caribbean, Indian, and Asian cuisine and Caribbean   a fun, casual setting set the tone at the Rude Native. Diners here can start the meal with a tropical cocktail, to get the real island feel. The appetizer list is extensive including selections such as spring rolls, goat cheese, hummus and salads. Entrees include stir fry, wraps, pastas as well as jerk chicken and leg of lamb. Portions are hearty with varied degrees of spice to suit all taste buds. Casual dress; cocktails. **Parking:** street. **Cards:** AX, DC, MC, VI.

SONOMA COUNTY WINE BAR & GRILL   **Dinner:** $14-$30   **Phone:** 905/333-9463

Location: QEW, exit Walker's Line Rd S westbound to Harvestor Rd; exit Guelph Line Rd S eastbound to Harvestor Rd. 3135 Harvestor Rd L7N 3N8. **Hours:** 4 pm-1:30 am, Wed-11 pm, Thurs-11:30 pm. Closed: 1/1, 12/25, 12/26;
American   also Sun-Tues. **Reservations:** suggested. **Features:** The casual bistro has a distinct California theme in its decor and menu offerings. Diners can unwind in a large, open room with colorful wall murals and bright tablecloths. The wine garden terrace is popular in the summer months. An outstanding selection of wines by the glass complements such casual fare as pasta, stir-fry, gourmet pizza, burgers, entree salad and decadent desserts. Casual dress; cocktails. **Parking:** on-site. **Cards:** AX, DC, MC, VI.

CALABOGIE

──── WHERE TO STAY ────

CALABOGIE PEAKS RESORT   **Phone:** (613)752-2720
CAA SAVE   All Year   2P: $145-$185   XP: $10   F12
Location: Jct Hwy 511, 6 km w on Hwy 508. Located in a rural area. 30 Barrett Chute Rd K0J 1H0 (30 Bassett Chute Rd, Box 90). Fax: 613/752-2255. **Facility:** Nestled between Calabogie Lake and Dickson Mountain, this resort offers a lovely setting for four seasons of outdoor activities and indoor comfort. Smoke free premises.
Resort   25 units. 23 one-bedroom standard units, some with whirlpools. 2 one-bedroom suites with kitchens and
Small-scale Hotel whirlpools. 3 stories, interior corridors. **Parking:** on-site. **Terms:** check-in 4 pm, cancellation fee imposed, [AP], [BP] & [MAP] meal plans available, package plans. **Amenities:** video library (fee), DVD players, high-speed Internet, voice mail, irons, hair dryers. **Dining:** 8 am-9 pm, cocktails. **Pool(s):** heated indoor. **Leisure Activities:** whirlpool, rental boats, rental canoes, rental paddleboats, fishing, 4 lighted tennis courts, ice skating, tobogganing, rental bicycles, hiking trails, playground, exercise room, spa, basketball, horseshoes, volleyball. *Fee:* boat dock, golf-9 holes, downhill & cross country skiing, game room. **Guest Services:** sundries, airport transportation (fee)-Ottawa International Airport. **Business Services:** meeting rooms. **Cards:** AX, MC, VI. **Special Amenities:** free local telephone calls and early check-in/late check-out. *(See color ad p 426)*

SOME UNITS

CAMBRIDGE pop. 110,372

──── WHERE TO STAY ────

BEST WESTERN CAMBRIDGE HOTEL   *Book at aaa.com*   **Phone:** (519)623-4600
CAA SAVE   All Year   1P: $119-$169   2P: $119-$169   XP: $10   F16
Location: Hwy 401, exit 282, just s. 730 Hespeler Rd N3H 5L8. Fax: 519/623-2688. **Facility:** 106 units. 95 one-bedroom standard units. 11 one-bedroom suites. 7 stories, interior/exterior corridors. **Parking:** on-site.
Small-scale Hotel **Terms:** package plans. **Amenities:** video games (fee), voice mail, irons, hair dryers. **Pool(s):** heated indoor. **Leisure Activities:** sauna, whirlpool. **Guest Services:** valet and coin laundry. **Business Services:** meeting rooms. **Cards:** AX, CB, DC, DS, JC, MC, VI. **Special Amenities:** free expanded continental breakfast and free local telephone calls. *(See color ad below)*

SOME UNITS

Best Western Cambridge Hotel

730 Hespeler Rd.
Cambridge, ON N3H 5L8
TEl: (519) 623-4600
Fax: (519) 623-2688
Reservations 1-800-528-1234
www.bestwestern.com/ca/cambridgehotel

Indoor Pool, Sauna, Whirlpool
Complimentary Deluxe Continental Breakfast

Ask about our Great Family Packages!

COMFORT INN   *Book at aaa.com*

Phone: (519)658-1100

(CAA) (SAVE)

	1P: $105-$130	2P: $115-$140	XP: $10	F18
1/1-4/30 [ECP]	1P: $105-$130	2P: $115-$140	XP: $10	F18
5/1-5/31 [ECP]	1P: $103-$128	2P: $113-$138	XP: $10	F18
6/1-10/31 [ECP]	1P: $105-$125	2P: $115-$135	XP: $10	F18
11/1-12/31 [ECP]	1P: $102-$122	2P: $112-$132	XP: $10	F18

Small-scale Hotel **Location:** Hwy 401, exit 282, just n to Groh Ave. 220 Holiday Inn Dr N3C 1Z4. **Fax:** 519/658-6979. **Facility:** 83 one-bedroom standard units. 2 stories (no elevator), interior corridors. **Parking:** on-site, winter plug-ins. **Terms:** package plans. **Amenities:** voice mail, irons, hair dryers. *Some:* high-speed Internet. **Guest Services:** valet laundry. **Business Services:** meeting rooms. **Cards:** AX, CB, DC, DS, JC, MC, VI.

SOME UNITS

HILTON GARDEN INN   *Book at aaa.com*

Phone: (519)620-8936

(CAA) (SAVE)

All Year   1P: $129   2P: $129   XP: $10   F

Location: Hwy 401, exit 282, just s. 746 Old Hespeler Rd N3H 5L8. **Fax:** 519/620-8937. **Facility:** 123 units. 119 one-bedroom standard units, some with whirlpools. 4 one-bedroom suites ($199) with whirlpools. 5 stories, interior corridors. **Bath:** combo or shower only. **Parking:** on-site. **Terms:** cancellation fee imposed, package **Small-scale Hotel** plans. **Amenities:** video games (fee), high-speed Internet, voice mail, irons, hair dryers. *Some:* safes. **Dining:** 6:30 am-11 & 5-10 pm, Sat & Sun 7 am-noon & 5-10 pm. **Pool(s):** heated indoor. **Leisure Activities:** whirlpool, exercise room. **Guest Services:** sundries, valet and coin laundry, area transportation-within 8 km. **Business Services:** meeting rooms, business center. **Cards:** AX, DC, DS, JC, MC, VI. **Special Amenities:** free local telephone calls.

SOME UNITS

HOLIDAY INN CAMBRIDGE   *Book at aaa.com*

Phone: (519)658-4601

(CAA) (SAVE)

All Year   1P: $99-$124   2P: $99-$124

Location: Hwy 401, exit 282, just n to Groh Ave. 200 Holiday Inn Dr N3C 1Z4. **Fax:** 519/658-6860. **Facility:** 143 one-bedroom standard units. 2 stories (no elevator), interior corridors. **Parking:** on-site, winter plug-ins. **Amenities:** video games (fee), high-speed Internet, voice mail, irons, hair dryers. *Some:* dual phone lines. **Large-scale Hotel** **Dining:** 6:30 am-9:30 pm, cocktails. **Pool(s):** heated outdoor, heated indoor. **Leisure Activities:** sauna, whirlpool, tennis court, recreation programs, exercise room. **Guest Services:** valet and coin laundry. **Business Services:** conference facilities, business center. **Cards:** AX, DC, DS, MC, VI. **Special Amenities:** free newspaper and preferred room (subject to availability with advance reservations). *(See color ad card insert)*

SOME UNITS

FEE FEE

LANGDON HALL COUNTRY HOUSE HOTEL & SPA   *Book at aaa.com*

Phone: (519)740-2100

(CAA) (SAVE)

All Year   1P: $259-$329   2P: $259-$329

Location: Hwy 401, exit 275 to Homer Watson Blvd (Fountain St), 1 km s to Blair Rd, then follow signs 1 km to Langdon Dr. Located in a quiet rural area. RR 33 N3H 4R8 (1 Langdon Dr). **Fax:** 519/740-8161. **Facility:** With grounds encompassing some 200 acres, this converted 1898 mansion offers both woodland nature trails **Classic** and sunny country gardens. 53 units. 48 one-bedroom standard units, some with whirlpools. 2 one- and 3 **Country Inn** two-bedroom suites ($334-$659) with whirlpools. 3 stories, interior/exterior corridors. **Parking:** on-site and valet. **Terms:** check-in 4 pm, 7 day cancellation notice-fee imposed, [MAP] meal plan available, package plans, pets ($50 extra charge). **Amenities:** CD players, high-speed Internet, voice mail, irons, hair dryers. **Dining:** dining room, see separate listing. **Pool(s):** heated outdoor. **Leisure Activities:** saunas, whirlpools, steamrooms, tennis court, cross country skiing, recreation programs, billiards, croquet, bicycles, hiking trails, jogging, exercise room, spa, basketball, volleyball. **Guest Services:** gift shop, valet laundry. **Business Services:** meeting rooms, fax (fee). **Cards:** AX, DC, MC, VI. **Special Amenities:** free newspaper and preferred room (subject to availability with advance reservations).

SOME UNITS

FEE FEE

SUPER 8 MOTEL-CAMBRIDGE   *Book at aaa.com*

Phone: (519)622-1070

(CAA) (SAVE)

All Year   1P: $65-$98   2P: $65-$98   XP: $10   F12

Location: Hwy 401, exit 282, 1 km n. 650 Hespeler Rd N1R 6J8. **Fax:** 519/622-1512. **Facility:** 65 one-bedroom standard units, some with whirlpools. 2 stories (no elevator), interior corridors. **Parking:** on-site. **Terms:** cancellation fee imposed, small pets only. **Amenities:** video library, hair dryers. **Dining:** 5:30 am-8 **Small-scale Hotel** pm, Sun from 8 am; hours may vary in winter, wine/beer only. **Pool(s):** heated outdoor. **Guest Services:** coin laundry. **Business Services:** meeting rooms. **Cards:** AX, CB, DC, DS, JC, MC, VI. **Special Amenities: free continental breakfast and free local telephone calls.**

SOME UNITS

FEE

TRAVELODGE CAMBRIDGE   *Book at aaa.com*

Phone: (519)622-1180

	1P: $89-$99	2P: $89-$99	XP: $10	F15
5/1-10/31	1P: $89-$99	2P: $89-$99	XP: $10	F15
11/1-4/30	1P: $80-$93	2P: $80-$93	XP: $10	F15

Small-scale Hotel **Location:** Hwy 401, exit 282, 1 km s. 605 Hespeler Rd N1R 6J3. **Fax:** 519/740-0630. **Facility:** 60 one-bedroom standard units, some with whirlpools. 2 stories (no elevator), interior corridors. **Parking:** on-site. **Terms:** small pets only. **Amenities:** *Some:* irons, hair dryers. **Guest Services:** valet laundry. **Cards:** AX, DC, DS, MC, VI.

SOME UNITS

—————— WHERE TO DINE ——————

BLACKSHOP RESTAURANT

Lunch: $7-$16   Dinner: $12-$30   Phone: 519/621-4180

Location: Jct Parkhill Rd and George St; Hwy 401, exit Hwy 24, 5.5 km s to Parkhill Rd. 20 Hobson St N1S 2M6. **Hours:** 11:30 am-10 pm, Sat-11 pm, Sun 4:30 pm-9 pm. **Closed:** 12/24, 12/25, 12/26. **Continental** **Reservations:** accepted. **Features:** You'll discover casual bistro dining with an upscale, creative menu and professional service here with a distinct European flair. Featured fare from a variety of regional specialties are fresh fish and vegetarian dishes. Jazz is performed on Sunday evening. Dressy casual; cocktails. **Parking:** on-site. **Cards:** AX, DS, MC, VI.

CRABBY JOE'S TAPP AND GRILL　　　**Lunch:** $5-$20　　　**Dinner:** $5-$20　　　**Phone:** 519/622-8334

♦

American

Location: Hwy 401, exit 282, 2 km s. 440 Hespeler Rd N1R 6J7. **Hours:** 11 am-1 am, Fri & Sat-2 am. **Closed:** 12/25. **Features:** Remarks on the menu alluding to Crabby Joe's temper lend to a fun-filled atmosphere in which the staff provides warm, personable service. Casual fare is dished in hearty portions. Whether opting for a half-pound burger, tangy wings, pasta or sizzling fajitas, guests won't be disappointed with the food. Families are welcomed. Seating on the patio is popular during the summer. Casual dress; cocktails. **Parking:** on-site. **Cards:** AX, MC, VI.

GRAYSTONES RESTAURANT　　　**Dinner:** $15-$25　　　**Phone:** 519/653-7270

♦♦♦

Continental

Location: Hwy 401, exit Hwy 8 E, 1.3 km e. 210 King St E #8 N3H 3M6. **Hours:** 5 pm-9 pm. Closed major holidays; also Sun. **Reservations:** suggested, weekends. **Features:** An elegant atmosphere and flambe and tableside preparations make this a popular favorite with the local crowd. The daily table d'hote menu is an exceptional value. Among offerings are portobello mushrooms, pate or tossed greens followed by beef, poultry or seafood selections. It is hard to resist the elegant dessert trolley with tempting and decadent selections. Dressy casual; cocktails. **Parking:** on-site. **Cards:** AX, DC, MC, VI.

LANGDON HALL DINING ROOM &
　TERRACE　　　**Lunch:** $16-$22　　　**Dinner:** $26-$38　　　**Phone:** 519/740-2100

CAA ♦♦♦♦

Continental

Location: Hwy 401, exit 275 to Homer Watson Blvd (Fountain St), 1 km s to Blair Rd, then follow signs 1 km to Langdon Dr; in Langdon Hall Country House Hotel & Spa. RR 33 N3H 4R8. **Hours:** 7 am-10, noon-2 & 5-9:30 pm, Sat & Sun 7:30 am-10:30, noon-2 & 5-9:30 pm; also 6 pm-9 pm 10/1-5/31. **Reservations:** suggested. **Features:** The peacefully distinguished country manor's fine cuisine gives a nod toward regional specialties. Dishes are prepared with fresh ingredients harvested in the owner's organic gardens. Dressy casual; cocktails. **Parking:** on-site and valet. **Cards:** AX, DC, MC, VI.

THE RIVERBANK MILL　　　**Lunch:** $7-$12　　　**Dinner:** $15-$26　　　**Phone:** 519/740-2900

♦♦♦

Steak & Seafood

Location: Hwy 401, exit 282, 5.6 km s. 4 Park Hill Rd W N1R 1P1. **Hours:** 11:30 am-3 & 4:30-9 pm, Sat 4:30 pm-10 pm, Sun 10:30 am-2:30 & 5-9 pm. **Closed:** 12/25, 12/26. **Reservations:** suggested. **Features:** Overlooking the Grand River, the restored old mill is a lovely location for special occasion dining. Patrons enjoy good food and service in a peaceful, romantic setting. Menu highlights include fine cuts of aged beef cooked to order, as well as prime rib, poultry and seafood specials. Save room for one of the fabulous, decadent desserts. Dressy casual; cocktails. **Parking:** on-site. **Cards:** AX, MC, VI. **Historic**

CHAPLEAU pop. 2,832

——— **WHERE TO STAY** ———

RIVERSIDE MOTEL　　　　　　　　　　　　　　　　　　　　**Phone:** (705)864-0440

♦

Motel

All Year [CP]　　　　1P: $68-$88　　　　2P: $68-$98　　　　XP: $7　　　　F16
Location: Corner of Grey and Cherry sts. Located on the Chapleau River. 116 Cherry St P0M 1K0 (PO Box 699). **Fax:** 705/864-2318. **Facility:** 18 one-bedroom standard units. 2 stories (no elevator), exterior corridors. **Parking:** on-site, winter plug-ins. **Terms:** office hours 7:30 am-10 pm, package plans, small pets only (in smoking units). **Amenities:** voice mail, hair dryers. *Some:* DVD players, CD players. **Leisure Activities:** boat dock, fishing, snowmobiling. **Business Services:** fax (fee). **Cards:** AX, MC, VI.

SOME UNITS

Travel Planning Your Way

Visit **aaa.com** and enjoy a whole new world of travel information.

AAA/CAA's Internet TripTik® provides interactive maps and search tools that make travel planning easy. Get hotel Diamond ratings, photos, and great room rates. Find the best in restaurants and attractions.

Trust AAA/CAA to simplify travel planning.

Travel with Confidence.
Travel with AAA/CAA.

CHATHAM pop. 44,156

--------- WHERE TO STAY ---------

COMFORT INN   *Book at aaa.com*   **Phone:** (519)352-5500

	5/1-9/30	1P: $87-$94	2P: $97-$104	XP: $10	F18
	4/1-4/30	1P: $84-$91	2P: $94-$101	XP: $10	F18
Small-scale Hotel	10/1-3/31	1P: $82-$89	2P: $92-$99	XP: $10	F18

Location: Hwy 401, exit 81 (Bloomfield Rd), 5 km n. 1100 Richmond St N7M 5J5. Fax: 519/352-2520. **Facility:** 80 one-bedroom standard units. 2 stories (no elevator), interior corridors. **Parking:** on-site, winter plug-ins. **Terms:** package plans, small pets only. **Amenities:** irons, hair dryers. *Some:* dual phone lines. **Guest Services:** valet laundry. **Business Services:** meeting rooms. **Cards:** AX, CB, DC, DS, MC, VI.

SOME UNITS

TRAVELODGE CHATHAM   *Book at aaa.com*   **Phone:** 519/436-1200

| | 7/1-8/31 | 1P: $103-$110 | 2P: $110-$117 | XP: $7 | |
| Motel | 5/1-6/30 & 9/1-4/30 | 1P: $101-$108 | 2P: $108-$115 | XP: $7 | |

Location: Hwy 401, exit 81 (Bloomfield Rd), 5 km n. 555 Bloomfield Rd N7M 5J5. Fax: 519/436-0571. **Facility:** 103 one-bedroom standard units, some with whirlpools. 3 stories, interior corridors. **Parking:** on-site. **Terms:** package plans, pets ($25 deposit). **Amenities:** video games (fee), voice mail, irons, hair dryers. **Business Services:** meeting rooms. **Cards:** AX, DC, DS, MC, VI.

SOME UNITS

FEE

WHEELS INN RESORT   **Phone:** (519)351-1100

| CAA SAVE | All Year | 1P: $99-$149 | 2P: $99-$149 | XP: $10 | F18 |

Resort
Large-scale Hotel

Location: Hwy 401, exit 81 (Bloomfield Rd N) to jct Hwy 2, 1.5 km e, then 1.5 km w. 615 Richmond St at Keil Dr N7M 5K8. Fax: 519/436-5560. **Facility:** This family-oriented resort's indoor recreation areas include a pay-as-you-play amusement park, a video arcade and a fitness complex. 350 one-bedroom standard units, some with whirlpools. 2-10 stories, interior corridors. **Parking:** on-site. **Terms:** 2 night minimum stay - seasonal, cancellation fee imposed, package plans. **Amenities:** *Some:* irons, hair dryers. **Dining:** 2 restaurants, 7 am-11 pm, cocktails. **Pool(s):** heated indoor, heated indoor/outdoor. **Leisure Activities:** saunas, whirlpools, steamroom, waterslide, recreation programs, children's party room & maze, billiards, spa, shuffleboard. *Fee:* miniature golf, racquetball courts, 2 squash courts, aerobics, bowling, go-cart track, game room. **Guest Services:** gift shop, valet laundry. **Business Services:** conference facilities. **Cards:** AX, DC, DS, MC, VI. **Special Amenities:** free local telephone calls and free newspaper. *(See color ad below)*

SOME UNITS

FEE

--------- WHERE TO DINE ---------

ROSSINI'S RESTAURANT   **Lunch:** $6-$15   **Dinner:** $14-$20   **Phone:** 519/352-2920

Continental

Location: 5 km e on Hwy 2. 634 Grand Ave E N7L 1X6. **Hours:** 11:30 am-1:30 & 5-9:30 pm, Sat from 5 pm, Sun 4 pm-8:30 pm. Closed major holidays; also Mon. **Reservations:** suggested, weekends; also Mon. **Features:** In the same family and location for more than 50 years, the reputable, well-established restaurant provides a comfortable atmosphere and friendly service. Tasty dishes are served in generous portions. Dressy casual; cocktails. **Parking:** on-site. **Cards:** AX, MC, VI.

Southwestern Ontario's **WILD** Indoor/Outdoor Resort

Newly renovated rooms for a more relaxing stay!

High Speed Internet Connectability available within the complex

• Health Spa
• Waterslides
• Fitness Club
• Swimming pool
• Bowling Centre
• 350 guest rooms
• Miniature golf course
• Wild Zone Adventures indoor amusement park
• Go-karts, kiddie go-karts and kiddie bumper boats

AXLE ANNIE'S Casual FUN in the Wheels Inn newest Eatery, one of 4 within the 7 acre complex

Wheels! the inn place to be

PROVIDING GENERATIONS OF FUN FOR OVER 30 years

Wheelie's Tree House Crafts & Storytime for kids

WILD ZONE ADVENTURES

1-800-265-5257
www.wheelsinn.com • reservations@wheelsinn.com

CHATSWORTH pop. 6,280

------ WHERE TO STAY ------

KEY MOTEL
Phone: (519)794-2350
5/1-9/30   1P: $70-$80   2P: $70-$80   XP: $8   F11
10/1-4/30   1P: $60-$70   2P: $60-$70   XP: $8   F11
Motel   **Location:** On Hwy 6 and 10. 317051 Hwy 6/10 N0H 1G0 (RR 3). Fax: 519/794-3842. **Facility:** 14 one-bedroom standard units. 1-2 stories (no elevator), interior/exterior corridors. **Parking:** on-site, winter plug-ins. **Terms:** weekly rates available, pets (in smoking units). **Pool(s):** heated outdoor. **Leisure Activities:** cross country skiing, snowmobiling, hiking trails, jogging. **Cards:** AX, MC, VI.

SOME UNITS

CHESLEY pop. 1,880

------ WHERE TO STAY ------

SCONEVIEW BED & BREAKFAST
Phone: (519)363-6992
All Year [BP]   1P: $65-$85   2P: $85-$100   XP: $20   D15
Location: Jct Hwy 25 and County Line 10. 1645 Bruce Rd, RR 3 N0G 1L0. Fax: 519/363-5147. **Facility:** Smoke free premises. 5 one-bedroom standard units, some with whirlpools. 2 stories (no elevator), interior corridors. *Bath:* some shared or private, combo or shower only. **Parking:** on-site. **Terms:** 5 day cancellation
Bed & Breakfast   notice-fee imposed. **Amenities:** *Some:* irons, hair dryers. **Leisure Activities:** canoeing, hot tub, kayaks, cross country skiing, snowmobiling, picnic area, barbecue, hiking trails. **Special Amenities: free full breakfast and free newspaper.**

SOME UNITS

COBOURG pop. 17,172

------ WHERE TO STAY ------

BEST WESTERN COBOURG INN AND
CONVENTION CENTRE   *Book at aaa.com*   Phone: (905)372-2105
5/1-8/31   1P: $120-$140   2P: $130-$150   XP: $10   F16
9/1-4/30   1P: $115-$135   2P: $125-$150   XP: $10   F16
Location: Hwy 401, exit 472 (Burnham St S). Located in a commercial area. 930 Burnham St K9A 2X9. Fax: 905/372-5905. **Facility:** 87 one-bedroom standard units, some with whirlpools. 3 stories, interior
Small-scale Hotel   corridors. **Parking:** on-site, winter plug-ins. **Terms:** check-in 4 pm. **Amenities:** irons, hair dryers. **Dining:** 7 am-9 pm; Sunday brunch, cocktails. **Pool(s):** heated indoor. **Leisure Activities:** sauna, whirlpool. **Guest Services:** valet laundry. **Business Services:** conference facilities. **Cards:** AX, DC, DS, JC, MC, VI. **Special Amenities: free room upgrade and preferred room (each subject to availability with advance reservations).**

SOME UNITS

FEE FEE

COMFORT INN   *Book at aaa.com*   Phone: (905)372-7007
5/1-9/16   1P: $95-$125   2P: $110-$150   XP: $5   F17
9/17-12/31   1P: $90-$125   2P: $105-$150   XP: $5   F17
1/1-4/30   1P: $89-$125   2P: $99-$150   XP: $5   F17
Location: Hwy 401, exit 474, just se. Located in a commercial area. 121 Densmore Rd K9A 4J9. Fax: 905/372-9846.
Small-scale Hotel   **Facility:** 62 one-bedroom standard units. 2 stories (no elevator), interior corridors. **Parking:** on-site, winter plug-ins. **Terms:** [CP] meal plan available, package plans. **Amenities:** *Some:* irons, hair dryers. **Guest Services:** valet laundry. **Cards:** AX, CB, DC, DS, MC, VI. **Special Amenities: free local telephone calls and free room upgrade (subject to availability with advance reservations).**

SOME UNITS

FEE FEE

WOODLAWN TERRACE INN
Phone: 905/372-2235
All Year   1P: $129-$269   2P: $129-$269   XP: $30   D15
Location: Hwy 401, exit 474, 2.4 km s. 420 Division St K9A 4R3. Fax: 905/372-4673. **Facility:** This couples-oriented property, which dates from 1835, is close to a historic district and the waterfront. Smoke free
Historic   premises. 18 units. 16 one-bedroom standard units, some with whirlpools. 1 one- and 1 two-bedroom suites
Country Inn   ($199-$229). 2 stories (no elevator), interior corridors. *Bath:* combo or shower only. **Parking:** on-site. **Terms:** office hours 7 am-10 pm, [BP] meal plan available, package plans. **Amenities:** high-speed Internet, voice mail, irons, hair dryers. **Dining:** dining room, see separate listing. **Guest Services:** valet laundry. **Business Services:** meeting rooms. **Cards:** AX, DC, JC, MC, VI.

SOME UNITS

------ WHERE TO DINE ------

THE MATTERHORN RESTAURANT   *Menu on aaa.com*   **Lunch:** $6-$12   **Dinner:** $12-$20   **Phone:** 905/372-5231
Location: 0.4 km w of Division St. 95 King St W K9A 2M4. **Hours:** 11:30 am-2:30 & 5-9:30 pm. Closed major holidays; also Sun. **Reservations:** accepted. **Features:** A friendly greeting from "Werner," the chef/owner/operator, awaits diners as they pass the open kitchen of the cheery little restaurant. Meat is cut
Swiss   on site, and there are many creatively prepared schnitzels with unusual toppings. Desserts are made in-house and are great with an espresso, cappuccino or cafe latte. Casual dress; cocktails. **Parking:** street. **Cards:** AX, DC, MC, VI.

THE OASIS BAR & GRILL   **Lunch:** $8-$10   **Dinner:** $8-$25   **Phone:** 905/372-6634
Location: Just e of Division St. 31 King St E K9A 1K6. **Hours:** 11:30 am-11 pm, Wed-Fri to midnight, Sat noon-midnight, Sun noon-11 pm. Closed major holidays; also 12/24. **Reservations:** suggested. **Features:** A popular oasis from the usual, the small restaurant provides friendly service, a relaxed atmosphere and a
American   varied menu of creative dishes served in hearty portions. Daily chef's creations are a treat, as are fresh oysters. Entertainment is provided in the form of live music Wednesday night and Sunday jazz on the patio during summer months. Casual dress; cocktails. **Parking:** street. **Cards:** AX, DC, MC, VI.

WOODLAWN TERRACE INN DINING ROOM   **Lunch:** $9   **Dinner:** $18-$48   **Phone:** 905/372-2235
 Location: Hwy 401, exit 474, 2.4 km's; in Woodlawn Terrace Inn. 420 Division St K9A 3R9. **Hours:** 11:30 am-2 &
5:30-9 pm, Sat from 5:30 pm. **Closed:** 12/25, 12/26. **Reservations:** accepted. **Features:** Traditional dining
Continental   room decor creates a comfortable atmosphere. There is a popular luncheon buffet, and the dinner menu
centers on items such as Alberta beef, seafood and homemade pasta dishes. Dressy casual; cocktails.
Parking: on-site. **Cards:** AX, DC, MC, VI. **Historic**

🍷 ✕

COCHRANE pop. 5,690

———— **WHERE TO STAY** ————

BEST WESTERN SWAN CASTLE INN   **Book at aaa.com**   **Phone:** (705)272-5200
(AAA) (SAVE)   6/17-9/6   1P: $122-$200   2P: $132-$200   XP: $10   F12
5/1-6/16 & 9/7-4/30   1P: $112-$193   2P: $122-$193   XP: $10   F12
▼▼▼ ▼▼   **Location:** Centre. Located opposite the railway station. 189 Railway St P0L 1C0 (PO Box 1118). Fax: 705/272-4299.
Facility: 39 one-bedroom standard units, some with whirlpools. 3 stories, interior corridors. **Parking:** on-
Small-scale Hotel site, winter plug-ins. **Terms:** cancellation fee imposed, [ECP] meal plan available. **Amenities:** irons, hair
dryers. **Leisure Activities:** saunas, whirlpool, snowmobile compound, exercise room. *Fee:* billiards.
Business Services: meeting rooms. **Cards:** AX, DC, MC, VI.

SOME UNITS
S🅳 🍴➕ ✕ 🅳🅰🆃🅰 🖥 / ✕ 🆅🅲🆁 📧 /
FEE

COLLINGWOOD pop. 16,039

———— **WHERE TO STAY** ————

CRANBERRY RESORT   **Phone:** (705)445-6600
(AAA) (SAVE)   All Year   2P: $140-$375   XP: $10   F12
▼▼▼ ▼▼   **Location:** Jct Hwy 26. Located in a rural, residential area. 19 Keith Ave (RR 4) L9Y 4T9. Fax: 705/446-0270.
Facility: Situated close to skiing and within a short drive to town, the resort offers many opportunities for
family fun. Smoke free premises. 120 units. 90 one-bedroom standard units, some with kitchens. 14 one-
Resort   and 16 two-bedroom suites with kitchens and whirlpools. 3 stories, interior corridors. **Parking:** on-site.
Small-scale Hotel **Terms:** check-in 4 pm, 2 night minimum stay - weekends, 3 day cancellation notice-fee imposed, [BP] &
[MAP] meal plans available, package plans. **Amenities:** video games (fee), voice mail, hair dryers. *Some:*
irons. **Dining:** noon-11 pm, cocktails, restaurant, see separate listing. **Pool(s):** heated outdoor, small heated outdoor, heated
indoor, wading. **Leisure Activities:** whirlpool, rental boats, rental canoes, rental paddleboats, fishing, 8 tennis courts, recreation
programs, rental bicycles, hiking trails, playground, exercise room, spa, basketball, horseshoes, volleyball. *Fee:* marina, charter
fishing, golf-18 holes, indoor golf instruction, driving range, cross country skiing, snowmobiling, horseback riding, game room.
Guest Services: gift shop, coin laundry. **Business Services:** conference facilities. **Cards:** AX, MC, VI. **Special Amenities:**
free local telephone calls. *(See color ad below)*

SOME UNITS
S🅳 🍴 🍷 🏋 🏊 ✕ ✕ 🎥 🖥 / 🆅🅲🆁 🅳🅰🆃🅰 📧 🖨 /
FEE

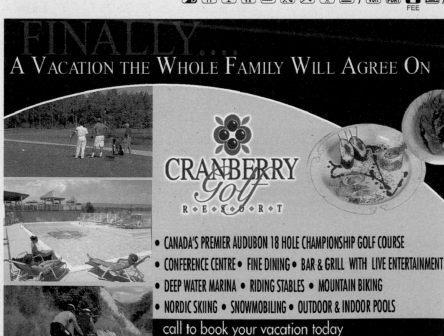

FINALLY...
A VACATION THE WHOLE FAMILY WILL AGREE ON

CRANBERRY
Golf
R · E · S · O · R · T

• CANADA'S PREMIER AUDUBON 18 HOLE CHAMPIONSHIP GOLF COURSE
• CONFERENCE CENTRE • FINE DINING • BAR & GRILL WITH LIVE ENTERTAINMENT
• DEEP WATER MARINA • RIDING STABLES • MOUNTAIN BIKING
• NORDIC SKIING • SNOWMOBILING • OUTDOOR & INDOOR POOLS

call to book your vacation today
705.445.6600 toll free 1.800.465.9077
COLLINGWOOD, ON www.cranberry-resort.on.ca

——— *The following lodgings were either not evaluated or did not* ———
meet AAA rating requirements but are listed for your information only.

BLUE MOUNTAIN RESORT   **Phone:** 705/445-0231
[fyi]   Not evaluated. **Location:** 11 km w on Hwy 26. 110 Jozo Weider Blvd L9Y 3Z2 (110 Jozo Weider Blvd, RR 3). Facilities, services, and decor characterize a mid-range property.

MOUNTAIN SPRINGS LODGE RESORT &
CONFERENCE CENTRE   **Phone:** 705/444-7776
[fyi]   Not evaluated. **Location:** 11 km w on Hwy 26 to Blue Mountain Rd. 796468 Grey CR 19, RR 3 L9Y 3Z2. Facilities, services, and decor characterize a mid-range property.

VACATION INN RESORT GEORGIAN MANOR   **Phone:** 705/445-9422
[fyi]   Not evaluated. **Location:** 3.5 km w on Hwy 26. 10 Vacation Inn Dr L9Y 5G4. Facilities, services, and decor characterize a mid-range property.

——— **WHERE TO DINE** ———

CRANBERRY CAFE   **Lunch:** $8-$13   **Dinner:** $12-$32   **Phone:** 705/445-6600
▼▼ ▼▼   **Location:** Jct Hwy 26; in Cranberry Resort. 19 Keith Ave (RR 4) L9Y 4T9. **Hours:** 7 am-9 pm; hours vary off season. **Reservations:** suggested. **Features:** The resort cafe offers generous portions, a varied menu and
Canadian   efficient, friendly service. Casual dress; cocktails. **Parking:** on-site. **Cards:** AX, DC, MC, VI.   ⊠

SIMCOE COUNTY RESTAURANT   **Lunch:** $7-$10   **Dinner:** $10-$18   **Phone:** 705/445-6957
▼▼ ▼▼   **Location:** Centre. 206 Hurontario St L9Y 2M2. **Hours:** 11:30 am-2 & 5-9 pm, Sat 11:30 am-9 pm. Closed: 12/25;
       also Sun & Mon. **Reservations:** accepted. **Features:** First-timers shouldn't be fooled by the unpretentious
Canadian   storefront facade. As the Swiss-trained owner-chefs attest, the little restaurant is "a bit different." An eclectic,
   international collection of food influences drives the menu, generating an interesting choice of dishes, many
of which can be shared. Casual dress; cocktails. **Parking:** street. **Cards:** MC, VI.   ⊠

CORNWALL pop. 45,640

——— **WHERE TO STAY** ———

BEST WESTERN PARKWAY INN & CONFERENCE
CENTRE   *Book at aaa.com*   **Phone:** (613)932-0451
(CAA) [SAVE]   All Year [ECP]   1P: $129-$159   2P: $129-$199   XP: $6   F12
▼▼ ▼▼   **Location:** Hwy 401, exit 789 (Brookdale Ave), 2.8 km s, then just w. Located in a commercial area. 1515 Vincent
   Massey Dr K6H 5R6. Fax: 613/938-5479. **Facility:** 94 units. 91 one-bedroom standard units, some with
   whirlpools. 3 one-bedroom suites with whirlpools. 2 stories (no elevator), interior corridors. **Parking:** on-site,
Small-scale Hotel   winter plug-ins. **Terms:** package plans. **Amenities:** high-speed Internet, voice mail, honor bars, irons, hair
   dryers. **Dining:** 2 restaurants, 6:30 am-11 pm, Sat & Sun from 7 am, cocktails. **Pool(s):** heated outdoor.
Leisure Activities: exercise room. **Guest Services:** valet laundry. **Business Services:** meeting rooms. **Cards:** AX, CB, DC,
DS, JC, MC, VI. **Special Amenities:** free expanded continental breakfast and free local telephone calls.
(See color ad below)

SOME UNITS

[S/D] [🐾] [🍽] [Ⓨ] [🏊] [🎦] [DATA PORT] [☕] / [⊠] [VCR] / FEE

Your home away from home.

★ Heated Outdoor Pool

★ Fitness Centre

★ Peppermills Grill & Bakery

★ Hops & Barley Lounge

★ Fireplace Rooms and Luxury Suites

★ Complimentary Continental Breakfast

★ Kids Stay Free

★ Special Packages Available

★ Free Wireless High Speed Internet

From Highway 401, Exit 789 Brookdale Ave.

1515 Vincent Massey Drive
Cornwall, Ontario K6H 5R6
For reservations call: **1-800-874-2595**
Tel: (613) 932-0451 Fax: (613) 938-5479

www.ParkwayInnCornwall.com

COMFORT INN-CORNWALL *Book at aaa.com* Phone: (613)937-0111

5/1-9/30	1P: $80-$217	2P: $88-$250	XP: $8	F19
10/1-4/30	1P: $72-$217	2P: $80-$225	XP: $8	F19

Location: Hwy 401, exit 789 (Brookdale Ave), 2.8 km s, then 0.7 km w. Located in a commercial area. 1625 Vincent Massey Dr K6H 5R6. Fax: 613/937-4051. **Facility:** 111 units. 107 one-bedroom standard units. 4 one-bedroom suites, some with whirlpools. 2 stories (no elevator), interior corridors. **Parking:** on-site, winter plug-ins. **Terms:** 7 day cancellation notice, package plans, pets ($15 fee, ground floor units). **Amenities:** irons, hair dryers. *Some:* high-speed Internet, dual phone lines. **Pool(s):** heated outdoor. **Leisure Activities:** exercise room. *Fee:* game room. **Guest Services:** valet and coin laundry. **Business Services:** meeting rooms. **Cards:** AX, DC, DS, MC, VI. **Special Amenities: free expanded continental breakfast and free local telephone calls.** *(See color ad below & card insert)*

SOME UNITS

DAYS INN-CORNWALL *Book at aaa.com* Phone: (613)937-3535

All Year	1P: $80-$195	2P: $80-$195	XP: $8	F17

Location: Hwy 401, exit 789 (Brookdale Ave), 2.8 km s, then 0.5 km w. Located in a commercial area. 1541 Vincent Massey Dr K6H 5R6. Fax: 613/937-0542. **Facility:** 60 one-bedroom standard units, some with whirlpools. 2 stories (no elevator), interior/exterior corridors. **Parking:** on-site, winter plug-ins. **Amenities:** irons, hair dryers. **Guest Services:** coin laundry. **Business Services:** meeting rooms. **Cards:** AX, CB, DC, DS, JC, MC, VI.

SOME UNITS

ECONO LODGE *Book at aaa.com* Phone: 613/936-1996

5/1-8/30	1P: $65-$75	2P: $78-$88	XP: $10
8/31-10/30	1P: $60-$70	2P: $72-$82	XP: $10
2/1-4/30	1P: $58-$70	2P: $72-$78	XP: $10
10/31-1/31	1P: $54-$64	2P: $65-$72	XP: $10

Small-scale Hotel Location: Hwy 401, exit 789 (Brookdale Ave), 3 km s. Located in a commercial area. 1142 Brookdale Ave K6J 4P4. Fax: 613/936-6884. **Facility:** 49 one-bedroom standard units. 1 story, interior/exterior corridors. **Parking:** on-site, winter plug-ins. **Terms:** 7 day cancellation notice-fee imposed, package plans, pets ($10 extra charge). **Guest Services:** valet laundry. **Business Services:** meeting rooms. **Cards:** AX, MC, VI. **Special Amenities: free continental breakfast and free local telephone calls.**

SOME UNITS

FIRST CANADA INNS Phone: 613/936-0400

5/1-10/15	1P: $84-$94	2P: $89-$99	XP: $6	F16
10/16-4/30	1P: $74-$84	2P: $79-$89	XP: $6	F16

Motel **Location:** Hwy 401, exit 789 (Brookdale Ave), 2.8 km s, then 0.6 km w. Located in a commercial area. 1618 Vincent Massey Dr K6H 5R6. Fax: 613/936-0413. **Facility:** 19 units. 17 one-bedroom standard units. 2 one-bedroom suites with efficiencies. 1 story, exterior corridors. **Parking:** on-site, winter plug-ins. **Terms:** office hours 7 am-midnight. **Amenities:** hair dryers. **Cards:** AX, DC, JC, MC, VI. **Special Amenities: free local telephone calls and preferred room (subject to availability with advance reservations).**

SOME UNITS

RAMADA INN & CONFERENCE CENTRE *Book at aaa.com* Phone: (613)933-8000

6/1-9/30	1P: $95-$149	2P: $95-$149	XP: $5	F18
5/1-5/31 & 10/1-4/30	1P: $89-$109	2P: $89-$109	XP: $5	F18

Small-scale Hotel Location: Hwy 401, exit 789 (Brookdale Ave), 4 km s. Located in a commercial area. 805 Brookdale Ave K6J 4P3. Fax: 613/933-3392. **Facility:** 118 units. 116 one-bedroom standard units. 2 one-bedroom suites with whirlpools, some with efficiencies. 2 stories (no elevator), interior corridors. **Parking:** on-site, winter plug-ins. **Terms:** [AP] meal plan available, package plans, small pets only. **Amenities:** high-speed Internet, voice mail, irons, hair dryers. *Some:* CD players. **Dining:** 6:30 am-2 & 4:30-10 pm, cocktails. **Pool(s):** heated indoor. **Leisure Activities:** sauna, whirlpool, playground, exercise room. **Guest Services:** gift shop, valet laundry. **Business Services:** conference facilities. **Cards:** AX, DC, DS, MC, VI. **Special Amenities: free local telephone calls and free newspaper.**

SOME UNITS

"The COMFORT you NEED at the PRICE you WANT!"

- Free Deluxe Continental Breakfast
- Free Hi Speed Internet
- In-room Movies & TV Games
- Guest Laundry Facilities
- Jacuzzi & Fireplace Suites
- Great Packages Available

Opening Summer 2005 - New Indoor Pool, Hot Tub, Steam Room & Fitness Centre

1625 Vincent Massey Drive, Cornwall, Ontario K6H 5R6
Phone: 613-937-0111 Fax: 613-937-4051
Call Toll Free: 1-800-228-5150
www.comfortinncornwall.com
comfort@comfortinncornwall.com

Comfort INN
BY CHOICE HOTELS
Cornwall

Hwy #401, Exit 789, then right at the 1st lights, then left on Vincent Massey Drive

SUPER 8 MOTEL   *Book at aaa.com*   Phone: (613)932-8888
(AAA) (SAVE)
| | 5/1-10/15 | 1P: $90-$99 | 2P: $99-$170 | XP: $10 | F12 |
| | 10/16-4/30 | 1P: $80-$90 | 2P: $90-$150 | XP: $10 | F12 |

Location: Hwy 401, exit 789 (Brookdale Ave), just sw. Located in a commercial area. 2694 Brookdale Ave K6J 5Y2. Fax: 613/932-9971. **Facility:** 50 units. 49 one-bedroom standard units, some with efficiencies and/or **Small-scale Hotel** whirlpools. 1 one-bedroom suite. 2 stories (no elevator), interior corridors. **Parking:** on-site, winter plug-ins. **Terms:** cancellation fee imposed, [CP] meal plan available, $1 service charge. **Amenities:** high-speed Internet, voice mail, hair dryers. *Some: Fee:* DVD players. **Pool(s):** small heated indoor. **Leisure Activities:** whirlpool, exercise room. **Guest Services:** coin laundry. **Business Services:** meeting rooms. **Cards:** AX, DC, MC, VI. **Special Amenities: free continental breakfast and free local telephone calls.**

SOME UNITS
(icons) VCR / FEE FEE

——— WHERE TO DINE ———

BRUYERE'S   **Lunch:** $4-$9   **Dinner:** $10-$17   Phone: 613/933-4800
Location: 0.7 km n of bridge to USA. 1225 Brookdale Ave K6J 4P7. **Hours:** 7 am-10 pm. Closed: 12/25.
Canadian   **Reservations:** accepted. **Features:** Prompt, friendly service, a relaxed atmosphere and tasty steak, chicken and ribs are restaurant hallmarks. Add to that list a good selection of wonderful pastries, prepared in-house and sure to tempt. Casual dress; cocktails. **Parking:** on-site. **Cards:** AX, DC, MC, VI.

CASA PAOLO   **Lunch:** $8-$13   **Dinner:** $15-$35   Phone: 613/938-3706
Location: Hwy 401, exit 789 (Brookdale Ave), 2.8 km s, then 0.5 km w. 1600 Vincent Massey Dr K6H 5R6. **Hours:** 11 am-10 pm, Sat-Mon from 4 pm. Closed: 12/25. **Reservations:** accepted. **Features:** The owner and chef Italian   specializes in homemade pasta as well as nicely prepared veal, chicken, steak and seafood dishes. Casual dress; cocktails. **Parking:** on-site. **Cards:** AX, MC, VI.

JAZZ MAGNOLIAS   **Lunch:** $7-$11   **Dinner:** $8-$17   Phone: 613/937-3535
Location: Hwy 401, exit 789 (Brookdale Ave), 2.8 km s, then 0.5 km w. 1539 Vincent Massey Dr K6H 5R6. **Hours:** 11 am-midnight. Closed: 12/25. **Reservations:** accepted. **Features:** Prepare for a casual and friendly American   atmosphere with Louisiana flair and for some dishes such as blackened catfish, chicken Creole and gumbo soup that will make you think of the Big Easy. Other varied fare such as pasta, wraps, fajitas, soups and sandwiches are also available. Casual dress; cocktails. **Parking:** on-site. **Cards:** AX, DC, JC, MC, VI.

CRYSTAL BEACH pop. 6,686

——— WHERE TO STAY ———

CRYSTAL BEACH MOTEL   Phone: 905/894-1750
| | 5/1-9/30 | 1P: $79 | 2P: $89 | |
| | 10/1-4/30 | 1P: $65 | 2P: $75 | |

Motel   **Location:** Hwy 3, 3.5 km s on RR 116 (Ridgeway Rd), follow signs. 122 Ridgeway Rd L0S 1B0 (PO Box 1261). Fax: 905/894-3691. **Facility:** Smoke free premises. 17 one-bedroom standard units. 1 story, exterior corridors. **Parking:** on-site. **Terms:** office hours 8 am-8 pm. **Pool(s):** outdoor. **Cards:** MC, VI.

SOME UNITS
(icons)

DRYDEN pop. 8,198

——— WHERE TO STAY ———

BEST WESTERN MOTOR INN   *Book at aaa.com*   Phone: (807)223-3201
(AAA) (SAVE)
| | All Year | 1P: $81-$90 | 2P: $85-$99 | XP: $4 | F12 |

Location: On Hwy 17. Located in a commercial area. 349 Government St P8N 2P4. Fax: 807/223-5647. **Facility:** 89 units. 88 one-bedroom standard units, some with whirlpools. 1 one-bedroom suite with whirlpool. 2 stories (no elevator), interior/exterior corridors. **Parking:** on-site, winter plug-ins. **Terms:** check-in 4 pm, pets in **Small-scale Hotel** smoking units. **Amenities:** high-speed Internet, voice mail, irons, hair dryers. *Some: Fee:* DVD players. **Dining:** Arroma Pizza & Family Restaurant, see separate listing. **Pool(s):** heated indoor. **Leisure Activities:** whirlpool, steamroom, exercise room. **Guest Services:** valet laundry. **Business Services:** meeting rooms. **Cards:** AX, CB, DC, DS, MC, VI. **Special Amenities: free local telephone calls and free newspaper.**

SOME UNITS
(icons) VCR / FEE FEE FEE

COMFORT INN   *Book at aaa.com*   Phone: (807)223-3893
	6/1-8/31	1P: $90-$100	2P: $95-$105	XP: $10	F18
	4/1-4/30	1P: $88-$97	2P: $92-$102	XP: $10	F18
Motel	5/1-5/31	1P: $85-$94	2P: $90-$99	XP: $10	F18
	9/1-3/31	1P: $81-$89	2P: $85-$94	XP: $10	F18

Location: On Hwy 17. Located in a commercial area. 522 Government St P8N 2P7. Fax: 807/223-5627. **Facility:** 62 one-bedroom standard units. 2 stories (no elevator), interior corridors. **Parking:** on-site, winter plug-ins. **Terms:** package plans, small pets only. **Amenities:** hair dryers. **Guest Services:** valet laundry. **Cards:** AX, DC, DS, MC, VI.

SOME UNITS
(icons)

HOLIDAY INN EXPRESS DRYDEN   *Book at aaa.com*   Phone: 807/223-3000
(AAA) (SAVE)
| | All Year | 1P: $98-$129 | | XP: $10 | F |

Location: On Hwy 17. Located in a commercial area. 585 Government St P8N 2P6 (PO Box 721, P8N 2Z4). Fax: 807/223-3017. **Facility:** 61 one-bedroom standard units. 2 stories (no elevator), interior corridors. *Bath:* combo or shower only. **Parking:** on-site, winter plug-ins. **Terms:** small pets only (in smoking units). **Small-scale Hotel Amenities:** high-speed Internet, dual phone lines, voice mail, irons, hair dryers. **Pool(s):** small heated indoor. **Leisure Activities:** steamroom, exercise room. **Guest Services:** valet laundry. **Business Services:** meeting rooms. **Cards:** AX, DC, DS, MC, VI. **Special Amenities: free expanded continental breakfast and free newspaper.** *(See color ad card insert)*

SOME UNITS
(icons)

------- **WHERE TO DINE** -------

ARROMA PIZZA & FAMILY RESTAURANT   **Lunch:** $5-$15   **Dinner:** $5-$15   **Phone:** 807/223-4688
Location: On Hwy 17; in Best Western Motor Inn. 349 Government St P8N 2P4. **Hours:** 7 am-10 pm. Closed: 12/25. **Reservations:** accepted. **Features:** If items such as Szechuan beef and noodles, Mandarin ribs, sweet and sour pork or lemon chicken don't tempt patrons, then they can opt instead for such Canadian fare as fresh walleye in season. Casual dress; cocktails. **Parking:** on-site. **Cards:** AX, MC, VI.

Pizza

RIVERVIEW LODGE   **Lunch:** $5-$10   **Dinner:** $13-$27   **Phone:** 807/223-4320
Location: Corner of Earl Ave and Victoria St. 148 Earl Ave P8N 1Y1. **Hours:** 11 am-2 & 5:30-9 pm. Closed major holidays; also Sun. **Reservations:** suggested. **Features:** Rustic elegance is defined at Riverview Lodge in a log cabin-style mansion dating from the early 20th-century. The menu features well-known European specialties such as snails, stuffed crepes, veal, poultry, and seafood as well as steak and prime rib. Casual dress; cocktails. **Parking:** on-site. **Cards:** AX, DC, MC, VI.

Continental

EAGLE LAKE

------- **WHERE TO STAY** -------

------- *The following lodging was either not evaluated or did not* -------
meet AAA rating requirements but is listed for your information only.

SIR SAM'S INN   **Phone:** 705/754-2188
[fyi]   Not evaluated. **Location:** Haliburton Village, follow Hwy 118 W, 5.5 km to CR 14 and Eagle Lake Rd #2, follow signs. Sir Sams Rd K0M 1M0 (General Delivery). Facilities, services, and decor characterize a mid-range property.

EGANVILLE pop. 1,230

------- **WHERE TO DINE** -------

THE GRANARY RESTAURANT/SCHNITZEL HAUS   **Lunch:** $5-$7   **Dinner:** $7-$17   **Phone:** 613/628-2723
Location: Hwy 60, just e of Hwy 41. 57 Bonnechere St K0J 1T0. **Hours:** 11 am-9 pm, Fri & Sat-10 pm. Closed: 12/25. **Reservations:** accepted. **Features:** The family restaurant prepares hearty food in ample portions. Characterized by an eclectic decor that incorporates a mix of wall murals, paintings, warm wood and fun additions such as a giant flying nymph, the dining room maintains a casual ambience. Deck dining is offered in season. Casual dress; cocktails. **Parking:** on-site. **Cards:** MC, VI.

German

ELLIOT LAKE pop. 11,956

------- **WHERE TO STAY** -------

DUNLOP LAKE LODGE   **Phone:** (705)848-8090
All Year   1P: $55-$65   2P: $65-$75   XP: $5   F12
Location: Hwy 17, 38.8 km n on Hwy 108, 0.8 km w, follow signs. Located in a remote area. 74 Dunlop Lake Rd P5A 2J7 (PO Box 277). Fax: 705/848-9469. **Facility:** 12 one-bedroom standard units. 1 story, interior corridors. **Parking:** on-site, winter plug-ins. **Terms:** office hours 7:30 am-1 am, cancellation fee imposed, weekly rates available, package plans, small pets only. **Amenities:** video library. **Leisure Activities:** rental boats, rental canoes, boat dock, fishing, cross country skiing, snowmobiling, hiking trails, playground. **Business Services:** meeting rooms. **Cards:** AX, MC, VI.

Small-scale Hotel

SOME UNITS

ELMIRA pop. 8,155

------- **WHERE TO DINE** -------

THE ELMIRA STONE CROCK   **Lunch:** $6-$11   **Dinner:** $8-$16   **Phone:** 519/669-1521
Location: Corner of Snyder. 59 Church St W N3B 1M8. **Hours:** 7 am-8:30 pm, Sun from 11 am. Closed: 12/25. **Features:** Traditional local cuisine in early Ontario atmosphere. Casual family dining with homemade soup and salad bar. Highlights include barbecue ribs, roasted chicken, mashed potatoes and gravy. Fresh baked pies featured for dessert. Casual dress; cocktails. **Parking:** on-site. **Cards:** AX, DC, MC, VI.

Canadian

ELORA

------- **WHERE TO STAY** -------

THE ELORA MILL INN   **Phone:** (519)846-9118
6/1-10/31 [BP]   1P: $130-$280   2P: $130-$280   XP: $50   D12
5/1-5/31 & 11/1-4/30 [BP]   1P: $125-$265   2P: $125-$265   XP: $50   D12
Location: At the foot of Mill St. 77 Mill St W N0B 1S0 (PO Box 218). Fax: 519/846-9911. **Facility:** Set in a quaint town, guests enjoy the peaceful country setting of this restored mill. Rooms are well-appointed. Smoke free premises. 32 units. 31 one-bedroom standard units, some with whirlpools. 1 one-bedroom suite. 2-4 stories, interior/exterior corridors. **Bath:** combo or shower only. **Parking:** on-site. **Terms:** check-in 4 pm, 2 night minimum stay - weekends, 7 day cancellation notice-fee imposed, package plans, 10% service charge. **Amenities:** voice mail, hair dryers. **Dining:** 8 am-10 pm, Fri & Sat-11 pm, dining room, see separate listing. **Guest Services:** sundries. **Business Services:** meeting rooms. **Cards:** AX, MC, VI.

Country Inn

SOME UNITS

——— **WHERE TO DINE** ———

THE ELORA MILL INN GORGE DINING
ROOM   Lunch: $14-$20   Dinner: $24-$39   Phone: 519/846-9118

Continental
Location: At the foot of Mill St; in The Elora Mill Inn. 77 Mill St W N0B 1S0. **Hours:** 8-10 am, 11-4 & 5-10 pm, Fri & Sat-11 pm; Sunday brunch. **Reservations:** suggested. **Features:** This dining room features a fine menu of Continental fare in an upscale yet comfortable atmosphere. Diners enjoy candlelit tables and lovely views of the gorge from some tables in the daylight hours. The chef offers a fine mix of fresh seasonal and regional ingredients, and the servers provide personable country hospitality. Dressy casual; cocktails. **Parking:** on-site. **Cards:** AX, MC, VI. ⊠

FENELON FALLS pop. 1,874

——— **WHERE TO DINE** ———

EGANRIDGE DINING ROOM   Lunch: $10-$15   Dinner: $15-$30   Phone: 705/738-5111
Continental
Location: Hwy 35, exit Hwy 121, 8 km n to Victoria County Rd 8, then 10 km e to E Beehive Rd, follow signs; in Eganridge Inn & Country Club. 26 Country Club Rd, RR 3 K0M 1N0. **Hours:** Open 5/1-12/31 & 2/1-4/30; 11:30 am-2:30 & 5:30-8 pm; hours may vary in winter. **Reservations:** suggested. **Features:** Located in a beautiful country setting, overlooking Sturgeon Lake, between the towns of Fenelon Falls and Bobcaygeon. The menu features fine Continental cuisine with highlights such as smoked salmon and rack of lamb. The dining room offers a stunning view of the lake and surrounding countryside from its large panoramic windows. The attractive interior design features high wood beam ceilings and candle lit tables providing diners with an elegant atmosphere. Casual dress; cocktails. **Parking:** on-site. **Cards:** AX, DC, MC, VI. ⊠

FENWICK

——— **WHERE TO STAY** ———

SCHAFERHOF B&B   Phone: (905)562-4929
Bed & Breakfast
All Year   1P: $65-$85   2P: $79-$99
Location: QEW, exit 57, 8 km s on Reg Rd 24, 3.5 km e on Reg Rd 669 (8th Ave) to 15th St, then just s. 2746 Moyer St, RR 3 L0S 1C0. Fax: 905/562-3028. **Facility:** Smoke free premises. 4 one-bedroom standard units. 1 story, interior/exterior corridors. *Bath:* some shared or private, combo or shower only. **Parking:** on-site. **Terms:** 3 day cancellation notice. **Amenities:** *Some:* hair dryers. **Leisure Activities:** playground, horseshoes. **Business Services:** fax (fee). **Cards:** AX, MC, VI.
SOME UNITS
(ASK) ⊠ ☎ / 🍴 📺 (VCR) 💻 /

FERGUS pop. 16,732

——— **WHERE TO STAY** ———

——— *The following lodging was either not evaluated or did not* ———
meet AAA rating requirements but is listed for your information only.

THE BREADALBANE INN   Phone: 519/843-4770
(fyi)   Not evaluated. **Location:** Jct Breadalbane, just w of Hwy 6. 487 St. Andrew St W N1M 1P2. Facilities, services, and decor characterize a mid-range property.

——— **WHERE TO DINE** ———

THE BREADALBANE INN   Lunch: $12-$16   Dinner: $21-$34   Phone: 519/843-4770
Continental
Location: Jct Breadalbane, just w of Hwy 6; in The Breadalbane Inn. 487 St. Andrew St W N1M 1P2. **Hours:** 11:30 am-3 & 5-8 pm, Fri & Sat-9 pm. **Reservations:** suggested. **Features:** In a historical country inn, the restaurant exudes a comfortable, upscale ambience. Indoor seating is available in the main dining room and garden conservatory; the outdoor patio is another seating option during nice weather. A local flair punctuates offerings of fine Continental cuisine. Dressy casual; cocktails. **Parking:** on-site. **Cards:** AX, DC, MC, VI. ⊠

FONTHILL

——— **WHERE TO STAY** ———

HIPWELL'S MOTEL   Phone: (905)892-3588
Motel
7/1-10/1   1P: $52-$65   2P: $75-$80
5/1-6/30   1P: $46-$56   2P: $65-$75
10/2-4/30   1P: $42-$56   2P: $52-$75
Location: 1.6 km w; centre. Located in a quiet area. 299 Regional Rd 20 L0S 1E0 (PO Box 253). Fax: 905/892-0068. **Facility:** 26 one-bedroom standard units, some with efficiencies. 1 story, exterior corridors. *Bath:* combo or shower only. **Parking:** on-site. **Terms:** pets ($5 extra charge). **Pool(s):** heated outdoor. **Cards:** DC, MC, VI.
SOME UNITS
(ASK) 🛏 🚲 / ⊠ 🛢 📠 /
FEE
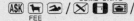

FORT ERIE —See Niagara Falls p. 376.

FORT FRANCES pop. 8,315

—— WHERE TO STAY ——

SUPER 8   *Book at aaa.com*   **Phone:** (807)274-4945
◆◆◆ ◆◆◆   All Year [ECP]   1P: $80-$129   2P: $89-$139   XP: $10   F16
                Location: On Hwy 11. Located in a commercial area. 810 Kings Hwy P9A 2X4. Fax: 807/274-4946. **Facility:** 59
Small-scale Hotel   units. 47 one-bedroom standard units, some with whirlpools. 12 one-bedroom suites. 3 stories, interior
                corridors. **Parking:** on-site, winter plug-ins. **Terms:** small pets only (in designated units). **Amenities:** hair
dryers. *Some:* DVD players, dual phone lines, irons. **Pool(s):** small heated indoor. **Leisure Activities:** whirlpool, steamroom,
exercise room. **Guest Services:** coin laundry. **Business Services:** fax. **Cards:** AX, DC, DS, MC, VI.

SOME UNITS

(ASK) (S/D) (🐕) (🛏) (🍳) (📷) (DATA PORT) (💻) / (❌) (VCR) (🔌) (📷) /

—— WHERE TO DINE ——

LA FLAMBEE   **Lunch:** $5-$12   **Dinner:** $12-$25   **Phone:** 807/274-1143
◆◆◆ ◆◆◆   **Location:** Centre. 232 Scott St P9A 1G7. **Hours:** 10 am-10 pm. Closed major holidays; also Sun.
             Reservations: accepted. **Features:** The menu provides excellent variety in well-prepared and nicely
International   presented dishes. Service is friendly and efficient, and there is a choice of booth or table seating. Casual
            dress; cocktails. **Parking:** street. **Cards:** AX, MC, VI.   (❌)

FRENCH RIVER

—— WHERE TO STAY ——

FRENCH RIVER TRADING POST MOTEL   **Phone:** 705/857-2115
(CAA) (SAVE)   4/15-4/30   1P: $67   2P: $72   XP: $10   F12
        5/1-10/31   1P: $65   2P: $70   XP: $10   F12
◆◆◆   **Location:** On Trans-Canada Hwy 69, 1 km n of French River Bridge. Located in a rural area. (RR 2, ALBAN).
            Fax: 705/857-3439. **Facility:** 10 one-bedroom standard units, some with efficiencies (utensils extra charge).
Motel   1 story, exterior corridors. **Parking:** on-site. **Terms:** open 5/1-10/31 & 4/15-4/30, office hours 8 am-9 pm,
            weekly rates available. **Guest Services:** gift shop. **Cards:** MC, VI.

SOME UNITS

(S/D) (🍴) (🏋) (📺) (🛜) (💻) / (❌) (🔌) (📷) /
FEE   FEE

—— WHERE TO DINE ——

HUNGRY BEAR RESTAURANT   **Lunch:** $7-$9   **Dinner:** $7-$12   **Phone:** 705/857-2115
(CAA)   **Location:** On Trans-Canada Hwy 69, 1 km n of French River Bridge. **Hours:** Open 5/1-10/30; 7 am-9 pm.
            Features: For more than 25 years, the family restaurant has been a traveler's oasis for flair and fun. There
◆◆◆.   is a soup and salad bar, an old-fashioned parlor with hard-scooped ice cream and such favorite menu items
            as fish and chips and Western and club sandwiches. Children enjoy meeting Hungry Bear and Blueberry
Canadian   Hound, who roam about during peak season. Primary meal periods may be busy. Casual dress. **Parking:**
            on-site. **Cards:** MC, VI.   (❌)

GANANOQUE pop. 5,167—See also LANSDOWNE.

—— WHERE TO STAY ——

BEST WESTERN COUNTRY SQUIRE RESORT   *Book at aaa.com*   **Phone:** (613)382-3511
(CAA) (SAVE)   6/24-9/3   1P: $99-$199   2P: $99-$199   XP: $10   F16
        5/1-6/23   1P: $99-$150   2P: $99-$150   XP: $5   F16
◆◆◆ ◆◆◆ ◆◆◆   9/4-10/31   1P: $99-$150   2P: $99-$150   XP: $10   F16
        11/1-4/30   1P: $80-$150   2P: $80-$150   XP: $5   F16
Small-scale Hotel   **Location:** Hwy 401, exit 647 eastbound; exit 648 westbound, 1 km w on Hwy 2 (King St). Located in a commercial,
            park-like setting. 715 King St E K7G 1H4. Fax: 613/382-4890. **Facility:** 68 units. 65 one-bedroom standard
units, some with whirlpools. 1 one-bedroom suite ($149-$229). 2 cabins ($89-$169). 2 stories (no elevator), interior/exterior
corridors. **Parking:** on-site, winter plug-ins. **Amenities:** voice mail, irons, hair dryers. **Dining:** Good Time Charly's, see separate
listing. **Pool(s):** outdoor, heated indoor. **Leisure Activities:** whirlpool, steamroom, lighted tennis court, trampoline, playground,
exercise room, basketball. *Fee:* squash courts, massage. **Guest Services:** gift shop. **Business Services:** meeting rooms.
Cards: AX, CB, DC, DS, MC, VI. **Special Amenities:** free local telephone calls and free newspaper. *(See color ad p 253)*

SOME UNITS

(S/D) (🍴) (🏋) (♿) (🛜) (❌) (🍳) (DATA PORT) (💻) / (❌) (VCR) (🔌) /
FEE   FEE

BLINKBONNIE HARBOR INN   **Phone:** (613)382-7272
(CAA) (SAVE)   7/1-9/5   1P: $116-$129   2P: $130-$150   XP: $10   F10
        5/1-6/30 & 9/6-10/30   1P: $80-$115   2P: $90-$124   XP: $10   F10
◆◆◆ ◆◆◆   **Location:** Corner of King St (Hwy 2); centre. Located in a historic, residential area. 50 Main St K7G 2L7.
            Fax: 613/382-4096. **Facility:** 47 one-bedroom standard units. 2 stories (no elevator), interior corridors.
Small-scale Hotel   **Parking:** on-site. **Terms:** open 5/1-10/30, cancellation fee imposed, package plans. **Dining:** 7 am-11 & 5-
            9:30 pm, cocktails. **Pool(s):** outdoor, heated indoor. **Leisure Activities:** sauna, whirlpools, exercise room.
Business Services: meeting rooms. **Cards:** AX, MC, VI. *(See color ad p 253)*   SOME UNITS

(S/D) (🍴) (🍷) (🏋) (🛜) (❌) (🍳) / (❌) (VCR) (🔌) /

Country Squire Resort

1000 Islands, Ont. Canada
715 King St. E. • Gananoque Ontario K7G 1H4
(613) 382-3511 • 1-800-267-9415
www.1000islandsbestwestern.com

- 68 Deluxe Rooms • King & Queen Beds
- Suites with Jacuzzi & Fireplace
- 100% Non-Smoking Rooms • Irons/Ironingboards
- Free Hot Breakfast Sunday to Thursday
- Freshly Brewed In-Room Coffee • Free High-speed wireless internet
- Good Time Charly's Bar & Grill • Poolside Garden Patio
- Spa • Indoor/Outdoor Pools • Squash, Basketball & Tennis Courts
- Trampoline • Hot Tub • Steam Room • Global Gym

 10% Discount Off Published Rates For AAA/CAA Members
24 Hr. Cancellation Policy

When you stay with us, You stay with Family

KIDS STAY FREE

The Blinkbonnie Harbor Inn

'In The Heart Of The 1000 Islands'

- 50 Rooms • Air Conditioned • Telephones and Cable TV
- Indoor and Outdoor Pools • 2 Whirlpools and Sauna
- English style Edwards Pub
- Fully licensed Rebecca's Dining Room

Call for our Great 2 and 3 night packages; including overnight accommodation, breakfast and dinner, and 2 of 3 attractions — 3 hour boat cruise ticket, live theatre play ticket or 18 holes of golf. All Bus Tour Group and Convention/ Meeting Room Packages also available upon request.

Call us now for reservations
1-800-265-7474 or (613) 382-7272.
50 Main Street, Gananoque, Ontario K7G 2L7
• Fax (613) 382-4096

Visit our website at: www.blinkbonnie.com

COMFORT INN 1000 ISLANDS *Book at aaa.com* **Phone:** (613)382-4728

(CAA) (SAVE)

7/1-9/4 [ECP]	1P: $89-$229	2P: $89-$229	XP: $10 F17
5/1-6/30 [ECP]	1P: $69-$139	2P: $69-$139	XP: $10 F17
9/5-4/30 [ECP]	1P: $59-$139	2P: $59-$139	XP: $10 F17

Motel

Location: Hwy 401, exit 647 eastbound; exit 648 westbound, 0.5 km w on Hwy 2 (King St). Located in a commercial area. 785 King St E K7G 1H4. **Fax:** 613/382-4387. **Facility:** 29 units. 26 one-bedroom standard units, some with whirlpools. 3 one-bedroom suites ($89-$299) with whirlpools. 2 stories (no elevator), interior/exterior corridors. **Parking:** on-site, winter plug-ins. **Amenities:** irons, hair dryers. **Pool(s):** small heated outdoor. **Cards:** AX, CB, DC, DS, JC, MC, VI. **Special Amenities:** free expanded continental breakfast and free local telephone calls. *(See color ad p 255)*

SOME UNITS

[S] [TI+] [⊜] [❄] [DATA PORT] [❚] [▣] / [✕] [▣] /

THE GANANOQUE INN **Phone:** (613)382-2165

All Year [CP]	1P: $179-$425	2P: $179-$425	XP: $20 F16

Historic
Small-scale Hotel

Location: Hwy 401, exit 645, 2.5 km s. 550 Stone St S K7G 2A8. **Fax:** 613/382-7912. **Facility:** Built in 1870, this riverfront property originally served as a carriage shop; some guest rooms offer river views. Smoke free premises. 59 units. 54 one-bedroom standard units, some with whirlpools. 5 one-bedroom suites, some with whirlpools. 3 stories (no elevator), interior/exterior corridors. *Bath:* combo or shower only. **Parking:** on-site. **Terms:** 5 day cancellation notice, package plans. **Amenities:** voice mail, irons, hair dryers. *Some:* CD players. **Dining:** dining room, see separate listing. **Leisure Activities:** boat dock. *Fee:* bicycles. **Guest Services:** valet laundry. **Business Services:** meeting rooms. **Cards:** AX, MC, VI.

SOME UNITS

(ASK) [TI] [Y] [✕] [VCR] [❄] [▣] / [DATA PORT] [❚] [▣] /

GRAY ROCK BED & BREAKFAST **Phone:** 613/382-1255

5/1-10/15 [BP]	1P: $99-$199	2P: $99-$199	XP: $35 D10
10/16-4/30 [BP]	1P: $85-$185	2P: $85-$185	XP: $35 D10

Bed & Breakfast

Location: Hwy 401, exit 647, 2 km e. Located in a residential area. 1000 Island Pkwy, RR 2 K7G 2V4 (13 Conner Dr, RR 2). **Facility:** Wooden case goods and fine bedcovers enhance the individually decorated rooms at this B&B bordered by farmlands and the 1000 Islands Parkway. Smoke free premises. 4 one-bedroom standard units, some with whirlpools. 2 stories (no elevator), interior corridors. *Bath:* some shared or private. **Parking:** on-site. **Terms:** office hours 8 am-9 pm, 2 night minimum stay - seasonal and/or weekends, age restrictions may apply, 7 day cancellation notice, package plans. **Amenities:** hair dryers. **Cards:** MC, VI.

(ASK) [✕] [❄] [☎]

HOLIDAY INN EXPRESS HOTEL & SUITES **Phone:** 613/382-8338

(fyi)

7/1-9/4 [ECP]	1P: $99-$249	2P: $99-$249	XP: $15
5/1-6/30 & 9/5-4/30 [ECP]	1P: $79-$149	2P: $79-$149	XP: $15

Small-scale Hotel Too new to rate, opening scheduled for May 2005. **Location:** Just w of jct Hwy 2, 401 and 1000 Islands Pkwy. 777 King St E K7G 1H4. **Fax:** 613/382-4387. **Amenities:** 60 units, coffeemakers, microwaves, refrigerators. **Cards:** AX, CB, DC, DS, JC, MC, VI. *(See color ad p 255)*

Premiere 1000 Island Resort

- 80 Modern Riverview Units
- Honeymoon Suites
- 2 Bedroom Cottages
- Whirlpools & Saunas
- Indoor & Outdoor Pools
- Tennis, Exercise Room
- Bike Rentals & Canoes
- Boat & Motor Rentals
- Fishing Packages
- Fully Licensed Dining Room Overlooking 1000 Islands
- 1000 Island Charity Casino
- Live Theatre (nearby)
- Smuggler's Glen - 18 Hole Golf Course on site
- Winter & Summer Packages Available

(see listing under Lansdowne)

GLEN HOUSE RESORT	Special Rates	(613) 659-2204	
6/24-9/05	1P: $105-$285 CND	2P/2B: $105-$285 CND	XP: $12 F12 CND
5/01-6/23 9/06-4/30	1P: $85-$165 CND	2P/2B: $85-$165 CND	XP: $12 F12 CND

P.O. Box 10 Gananoque, ON K7G 2T6

1 800 268-GLEN (4536)
www.glenhouseresort.com

LOCATION 409, 1000 Islands Parkway
Hwy 401 Eastbound, Exit 647 - 9km East 1000 Island Parkway
Westbound Exit 659 South to Parkway 5km West
Interstate 81 to 1000 Islands Parkway, 5km West.

GANANOQUE 🍁 1000 ISLANDS

Live Lobster

The Lobster TRAP
Steak Chicken Pasta

QUALITY
INN & SUITES
BY CHOICE HOTELS

Room Reservations
1·866·466·7912
650 King Street East • (613) 382-1453
Gananoque • 1000 Islands

1 & 2 Room Deluxe King
Whirlpool/Fireplace
Suites Available
★ ★ ★
FREE Hot Breakfast

RUMRUNNER

★ Dining Reservations
(613) 382-7317
★ Breakfast, Lunch & Dinner Specials
★ Kid's Menu

AAA Approved

WALKING DISTANCE TO
1000 Islands
CHARITY CASINO

doitintheislands.com

GANANOQUE 🍁 1000 ISLANDS

Comfort Inn
BY CHOICE HOTELS

1 & 2 Room Whirlpool Suites • Outdoor Heated Pool • Poolside Rooms Available • Free Deluxe Continental Breakfast
785 King St., E., Gananoque, (613) 382-4728 • Reservations: 1·866·466·6773

WALKING DISTANCE TO
1000 Islands
CASINO

www.doitintheislands.com

GANANOQUE 🍁 1000 ISLANDS

Gananoque's Newest Hotel 2005
Indoor Pool, Whirlpool / Fireplace Suites, Fitness Centre,
Express Start Breakfast Bar, Walk to 1000 Island's Casino

Holiday Inn
EXPRESS
HOTEL & SUITES

777 King Street East (613) 382-8338
Reservations: 1-866-301-2650
www.1000islandshotels.ca

MANSE LANE BED & BREAKFAST

	6/15-9/7	1P: $70-$155	2P: $75-$160	XP: $30
	9/8-10/18	1P: $70-$125	2P: $75-$130	XP: $30
Bed & Breakfast	5/1-6/14 & 10/19-4/30	1P: $65-$90	2P: $70-$98	XP: $30

Phone: 613/382-8642

Location: Hwy 401, exit 645, 2 km s. Located in a residential area. 465 Stone St S K7G 2A7. **Facility:** Smoke free premises. 4 one-bedroom standard units. 3 stories (no elevator), interior corridors. *Bath:* some shared or private, combo or shower only. **Parking:** on-site. **Terms:** office hours 7 am-10 pm, cancellation fee imposed. **Amenities:** hair dryers. **Pool(s):** outdoor. **Business Services:** fax. **Cards:** AX, CB, DC, MC, VI.

SOME UNITS

QUALITY INN & SUITES 1000 ISLANDS   *Book at aaa.com*

| | 7/1-9/4 [BP] | 1P: $89-$229 | 2P: $89-$229 | XP: $15 | F17 |
| | 5/1-6/30 & 9/5-4/30 [BP] | 1P: $69-$149 | 2P: $69-$149 | XP: $15 | F17 |

Phone: (613)382-1453

Location: Hwy 401, exit 647 eastbound; exit 648 westbound, 1 km w on Hwy 2 (King St). Located in a commercial area. 650 King St E K7G 1H3. Fax: 613/382-4387. **Facility:** 54 units. 46 one- and 4 two-bedroom standard units, some with whirlpools. 4 one-bedroom suites ($99-$349) with whirlpools. 2 stories (no elevator), interior corridors. **Parking:** on-site, winter plug-ins. **Amenities:** irons, hair dryers. **Dining:** Lobster Trap Seafood Restaurant, see separate listing. **Pool(s):** heated outdoor. **Business Services:** meeting rooms. **Cards:** AX, CB, DC, DS, JC, MC, VI. **Special Amenities:** free full breakfast and free local telephone calls. *(See color ad p 255)*

SOME UNITS

RAMADA PROVINCIAL INN   *Book at aaa.com*

	7/29-9/4	1P: $98-$199	2P: $98-$199	XP: $10	F16
	7/1-7/28	1P: $89-$159	2P: $89-$159	XP: $10	F16
Motel	9/5-10/31	1P: $79-$129	2P: $89-$149	XP: $10	F16
	5/1-6/30	1P: $79-$99	2P: $89-$129	XP: $10	F16

Phone: (613)382-2038

Location: Hwy 401, exit 647 eastbound; exit 648 westbound, 0.5 km w on Hwy 2 (King St). Located in a commercial area. 846 King St E K7G 1H3. Fax: 613/382-8663. **Facility:** Smoke free premises. 78 one-bedroom standard units, some with whirlpools. 1 story, exterior corridors. **Parking:** on-site. **Terms:** open 5/1-10/31. **Amenities:** voice mail, irons, hair dryers. **Dining:** Collectibles Restaurant, see separate listing. **Pool(s):** heated outdoor. **Leisure Activities:** lighted tennis court, basketball. **Guest Services:** gift shop. **Business Services:** meeting rooms. **Cards:** AX, DC, DS, MC, VI. *(See color ad below)*

SOME UNITS

RAMADA
Provincial
INN
1000 ISLANDS

- Olympic Sized Heated Outdoor Pool • Dining Rooms • Large Gift Shop
- Casino within Walking Distance • Coin Operated Laundry Facility
- All Rooms Ground Level • No-Smoking Rooms
- In-Room Irons • Complimentary Newspaper
- In-Room Hairdryer • In-Room Coffee
- Tennis Court • Basket Ball • Close to Area Attractions

DISCOUNT FOR CAA/AAA OR SENIORS

1-877-837-7768
www.provincialinn.com
846 King St. E., Gananoque
Ont. Canada K7G 1H3

Because the voyage of your dreams just happens to be theirs, too.

Trust AAA/CAA Travel to take you there.

On a *Disney Cruise Line* vacation, you'll find something enchanting for every member of the family–it's the kind of magic only Disney can create. And when you book through AAA/CAA Travel, you'll enjoy many special benefits! So call or stop by today.

Disney Cruise Line

Travel
www.aaa.com

CAA

Ships' Registry: The Bahamas

As to Disney properties/artwork: ©Disney

CST#1022229-50

TRAVELODGE 1000 ISLANDS   *Book at aaa.com*   Phone: (613)382-4282

7/1-9/4	1P: $79-$199	2P: $79-$199	XP: $10	F17
5/1-6/30 & 9/5-10/22	1P: $64-$129	2P: $64-$129	XP: $10	F17

Location: Hwy 401, exit 647 eastbound; exit 648 westbound, 1.5 km w on Hwy 2 (King St). Located in a commercial area. 555 King St E K7G 1H1. Fax: 613/382-4387. **Facility:** 27 units. 17 one-bedroom standard units. 1 one-

Motel   bedroom suite. 8 cabins and 1 cottage. 1 story, exterior corridors. **Parking:** on-site. **Terms:** open 5/1-10/22. **Dining:** 8 am-2 & 5-9 pm, cocktails. **Pool(s):** heated outdoor. **Cards:** AX, CB, DC, DS, JC, MC, VI.
Special Amenities: free local telephone calls and free newspaper. *(See color ad below)*

SOME UNITS

TRINITY HOUSE INN   Phone: (613)382-8383

| All Year | 1P: $90-$170 | 2P: $90-$170 |

Location: Corner of Pine St; centre. Located in a residential area. 90 Stone St S K7G 1Z8. Fax: 613/382-1599. **Facility:** A garden is featured on the grounds of this restored Victorian-style 1859 inn, which is close to

Historic   shops and within walking distance of the waterfront. Smoke free premises. 8 units. 6 one-bedroom standard
Country Inn   units. 2 one-bedroom suites ($160-$210), some with kitchens and/or whirlpools. 3 stories (no elevator),
interior corridors. *Bath:* combo or shower only. **Parking:** on-site, winter plug-ins. **Terms:** office hours 8 am-9 pm, age restrictions
may apply, 7 day cancellation notice-fee imposed, [BP] & [MAP] meal plans available, package plans, 10% service charge.
Amenities: hair dryers. *Some:* irons. **Dining:** dining room, see separate listing. **Cards:** MC, VI.

THE VICTORIA ROSE INN   Phone: 613/382-3368

6/17-10/14	2P: $135-$165	XP: $25
5/1-6/16	2P: $110-$140	XP: $25
10/15-4/30	2P: $90-$120	XP: $25

Location: Hwy 401, exit 645, 2 km s to Hwy 2 (King St), then 1 km w. Located in a residential area. 279 King St W K7G
2G7. Fax: 613/382-8803. **Facility:** Well-tended grounds and country gardens surround this 1872 inn offering
guest rooms appointed with fine wood furniture and many antiques. Smoke free premises. 9 units. 6 one-bedroom standard
units, some with whirlpools. 2 one- and 1 two-bedroom suites ($185-$210), some with whirlpools. 3 stories (no elevator), interior
corridors. **Parking:** on-site. **Terms:** office hours 7 am-10 pm, 7 day cancellation notice-fee imposed, package plans.
Amenities: hair dryers. *Some.* CD players. **Leisure Activities:** whirlpool. *Fee:* massage. **Business Services:** meeting rooms.
Cards: AX, DC, MC, VI.

SOME UNITS

★ ★ ★ ★ GANANOQUE • 1000 ISLANDS ★ ★ ★ ★

Travelodge

WELCOME NEWEST ROOMS and HEATED POOL
Pancake & Steak House

Pancake & Steak House • Outdoor Heated Pool

555 KING STREET EAST • GANANOQUE
1-800-578-7878 ★ (613)382-4282
www.travelodge1000islands.com

What Does a Perfect Vacation Sound Like?

The non-stop rhythm of a big city? The soft caress of waves on pure white sand?

No matter what vacation sounds best, visit aaa.com before you go.

Get an internet TripTik® and find TourBook® information:
- AAA/CAA Approved hotels and restaurants
- Destination descriptions and attraction information
- Interactive maps
- Complete driving directions

Make travel planning easy with aaa.com.

CLICK! Sounds like the start of a perfect vacation.

Travel with Confidence.
Travel with AAA/CAA.

--------- WHERE TO DINE ---------

ATHLONE INN DINING ROOM　　　　**Dinner:** $15-$30　　　　**Phone:** 613/382-3822
▼▼▼▼▼　　**Location:** 1 km w on Hwy 2 (King St W). 250 King St W K7G 2G6. **Hours:** 5 pm-9 pm; hours vary off season.
　　　　Closed: 1/1, 12/25. **Reservations:** accepted. **Features:** Built in 1874, this restaurant is housed in an old
French　　Victorian inn, surrounded by mature trees and attractive country gardens. The menu highlights Continental
　　　　and French cuisine, with an emphasis on fresh ingredients, including homemade bread and herbs grown in
their own garden. The friendly staff, provides personal and courteous service and go out of their way to ensure diners
satisfaction. In summer, a large outdoor patio is also featured for lunch and more casual dining. Casual dress; cocktails.
Parking: on-site. **Cards:** AX, DC, MC, VI.

COLLECTIBLES RESTAURANT　　　**Lunch:** $5-$9　　　**Dinner:** $13-$18　　　**Phone:** 613/382-2038
▼▼ ▼▼　　**Location:** Hwy 401, exit 647 eastbound; exit 648 westbound, 0.5 km w on Hwy 2 (King St); in Ramada Provincial Inn.
　　　　846 King St E K7G 1H3. **Hours:** Open 5/1-10/31; 8 am-8 pm; 7 am-9 pm 7/1-8/31. **Reservations:** accepted.
Canadian　**Features:** Close to the casino, the restaurant presents a varied menu in a dining room that displays
　　　　Thousand Islands memorabilia, including an antique St. Lawrence rowing skiff, model boats and trophy fish.
Casual dress; cocktails. **Parking:** on-site. **Cards:** AX, CB, DC, DS, MC, VI.

THE GANANOQUE INN DINING ROOM　　**Lunch:** $8-$12　　**Dinner:** $20-$30　　**Phone:** 613/382-2165
▼▼▼▼▼　　**Location:** Hwy 401, exit 645, 2.5 km s; at The Gananoque Inn. 550 Stone St K7G 2A8. **Hours:** Open 5/1-12/31 &
　　　　4/1-4/30; 7-10 am, 11:30-2 & 5:30-10 pm; from 5:30 pm 12/1-12/31 & 4/1-4/30. Closed: Mon-Thurs 12/1-
Continental　12/31 & 4/1-4/30. **Reservations:** suggested, for dinner. **Features:** The Gananoque Inn Dining Room,
　　　　features fine Continental cuisine and an excellent selection of wine by the glass and the bottle. It is situated
on the shores of the St. Lawrence River and offers diners the choice of sophisticated dining in the elegant dining room, or a
more relaxed ambience, on the large outdoor patio. Whatever their preference, diners will receive the same level of food and
service, and find themselves in a comfortable yet elegant atmosphere. Casual dress; cocktails. **Parking:** on-site. **Cards:** AX,
MC, VI.

GOOD TIME CHARLY'S　　*Menu on aaa.com*　　**Lunch:** $11-$18　　**Dinner:** $11-$18　　**Phone:** 613/382-5155
(AAA)　　**Location:** Hwy 401, exit 647 eastbound; exit 648 westbound, 1 km w on Hwy 2 (King St); in Best Western Country
▼▼ ▼▼　　Squire Resort. 715 King St E K7G 1H4. **Hours:** 7 am-11 pm. Closed: 12/25. **Reservations:** accepted.
　　　　Features: Well-placed TVs keep folks up-to-date with the latest sporting events, and the fireplace is inviting.
Canadian　Seating can be requested in booths or at tables. On the varied menu are chicken, steak, pasta, pizza,
　　　　salads and some Mexican dishes. Casual dress; cocktails. **Parking:** on-site. **Cards:** AX, MC, VI.

LOBSTER TRAP SEAFOOD RESTAURANT　　**Lunch:** $5-$11　　**Dinner:** $10-$35　　**Phone:** 613/382-7317
▼▼ ▼▼　　**Location:** Hwy 401, exit 647 eastbound; exit 648 westbound, 1 km w on Hwy 2 (King St); in Quality Inn & Suites 1000
　　　　Islands. 650 King St E K7G 1H3. **Hours:** 8 am-10 pm; hours may vary off season. Closed: 12/25.
Seafood　**Reservations:** accepted. **Features:** In addition to live lobsters and seafood, the restaurant prepares steak,
　　　　chicken and pasta. The dining room displays memorabilia from near and far. Casual dress; cocktails.
Parking: on-site. **Cards:** AX, CB, DC, DS, JC, MC, VI.

OSCAR'S MARINA GRILL　　　**Lunch:** $8-$24　　　**Dinner:** $9-$24　　　**Phone:** 613/382-6800
▼▼ ▼▼　　**Location:** Hwy 401, exit 647 eastbound; exit 648 westbound; in Thousand Islands Charity Casino. 380 Hwy 2 K7G 2V4.
　　　　Hours: 9 am-midnight. **Features:** With all-day breakfast items and such signature items as prime rib, ribs,
Canadian　Thousand Islands maple salmon and casino cheesecake, the varied menu is sure to please. The dining
　　　　room and lounge have an open concept with a pleasing and contemporary nautical theme. Due to Ontario
gaming laws, guests must be at least 19 years of age. Casual dress; cocktails. **Parking:** on-site. **Cards:** AX, MC, VI.

TRINITY HOUSE DINING ROOM　　　　**Dinner:** $12-$25　　　　**Phone:** 613/382-8383
▼▼▼▼▼　　**Location:** Corner of Pine St; centre; in Trinity House Inn. 90 Stone St S K7G 1Z8. **Hours:** 5:30 pm-8 pm; hours may
　　　　vary off season. Closed: 12/25; also Mon. **Reservations:** required, off season. **Features:** Patrons can enjoy
Continental　a relaxing respite on the patio beside the waterfall and gardens while dining at the lovely country inn.
　　　　Market-fresh entrees are artistically presented and include a selection of beef, chicken, fish and pasta. The
service is equally as pleasant. Casual dress; cocktails. **Parking:** on-site and street. **Cards:** MC, VI.

GEORGETOWN pop. 31,510

--------- WHERE TO STAY ---------

**BEST WESTERN INN ON THE
HILL-GEORGETOWN/HALTON HILLS**　　*Book at aaa.com*　　　　　**Phone:** (905)877-6986

(AAA) (SAVE)	5/1-12/31 [CP]	1P: $109-$139	2P: $119-$149	XP: $10　F12
	1/1-4/30 [CP]	1P: $99-$119	2P: $109-$129	XP: $10　F12

　　　　Location: On Hwy 7 at Delrex Blvd. Located in a commercial area. 365 Guelph St (Hwy 7) L7G 4B6.
▼▼ ▼▼　**Fax:** 905/873-2404. **Facility:** 63 units. 60 one-bedroom standard units. 3 one-bedroom suites ($169-$229)
Motel　with kitchens. 2 stories (no elevator), exterior corridors. **Parking:** on-site. **Amenities:** high-speed Internet,
　　　　irons, hair dryers. **Leisure Activities:** exercise room. **Cards:** AX, DC, DS, MC, VI. **Special Amenities:** free
continental breakfast and free local telephone calls.

SOME UNITS

GODERICH pop. 7,604

——— WHERE TO STAY ———

BENMILLER INN & SPA
Phone: (519)524-2191

(AAA) (SAVE)
5/31-10/31 [CP]   1P: $162-$296   2P: $180-$329   XP: $35   F12
▽▽▽▽ 5/1-5/30 & 11/1-4/30 [CP]   1P: $142-$210   2P: $158-$234   XP: $35   F12

Historic
Country Inn
Location: 8 km on Hwy 8 E to Huron Rd 1, left 3 km to Benmiller. Located in a quiet rural area. 81175 Benmiller Line N7A 3Y1 (RR 4). Fax: 519/524-5150. **Facility:** Fine wood furniture and an interior designed to reflect the building's history set the tone at this inn, a converted 1830s woolen mill. Smoke free premises. 57 units. 49 one-bedroom standard units, some with whirlpools. 8 one-bedroom suites. 2-4 stories, interior/exterior corridors. **Parking:** on-site, winter plug-ins. **Terms:** 2 night minimum stay - weekends, 7 day cancellation notice-fee imposed, [MAP] meal plan available, package plans, 12% service charge. **Amenities:** voice mail, irons, hair dryers. *Some:* DVD players, CD players. **Dining:** The Ivey Dining Room, see separate listing. **Pool(s):** heated indoor. **Leisure Activities:** sauna, whirlpool, fishing, bicycles, exercise room, spa. *Fee:* cross country skiing, snowshoes, game room. **Guest Services:** area transportation-harbour. **Business Services:** meeting rooms. **Cards:** AX, DC, DS, MC, VI.

SOME UNITS

[icons]

——— WHERE TO DINE ———

DRAGON KING BUFFET   **Lunch:** $8-$9   **Dinner:** $9-$20   **Phone:** 519/524-8088

▽▽▽
Chinese
Location: Jct Suncoast Dr. 411 Huron Rd N7A 3Y7. **Hours:** 11 am-9 pm. **Features:** A casual setting, good value and well-stocked buffet make this a popular choice for locals and tourists alike. The buffet lines up favourite Cantonese specialties, including wonton soup, egg rolls with homemade plum sauce, stir-fried vegetables, sweet and sour selections and varied preparations of pork, fish, beef and chicken. Desserts include tasty cakes, cookies and ice creams. Casual dress; cocktails. **Parking:** on-site. **Cards:** AX, MC, VI.

[icon]

THE IVEY DINING ROOM   **Lunch:** $10-$18   **Dinner:** $28-$38   **Phone:** 519/524-2191

▽▽▽
Continental
Location: 8 km on Hwy 8 E to Huron Rd 1, left 3 km to Benmiller; in Benmiller Inn & Spa. RR 4 N7A 3Y1. **Hours:** 7-10 am, Sat & Sun 8 am-10, noon-2 & 5:30-9 pm. **Reservations:** suggested. **Features:** Located in a restored old woolen mill surrounded by attractive country gardens, the Ivey Dining Room offers fine cuisine in a peaceful rural setting. The chef features a Continental menu with a focus on fresh, local and regional produce, herbs and meats. Select from starters such as seared scallops and shrimp, or fresh vegetable soup. Entrees include rack of lamb, sirloin steak and a daily salmon or pasta creation. All courses are colorfully and creatively presented. Dressy casual; cocktails. **Parking:** on-site. **Cards:** AX, DC, MC, VI.

[icons]

ROBINDALE'S FINE DINING   **Dinner:** $18-$25   **Phone:** 519/524-4171

▽▽▽
Canadian
Location: Corner of Hwy 21 and Hamilton St. 80 Hamilton St N7A 1P9. **Hours:** 5 pm-8 pm. Closed major holidays; also Mon 11/1-4/30. **Reservations:** suggested. **Features:** Warm and personable service provides a relaxed feeling in this elegantly restored Victorian home. The menu features hearty portions of creative cuisine with a focus on fresh ingredients and colorful presentation. Dessert is offered in the living room. Cocktails. **Parking:** on-site. **Cards:** MC, VI.

[icon]

GRAFTON

——— WHERE TO STAY ———

STE. ANNE'S, A HALDIMAND HILLS SPA   **Phone: (905)349-2493**

▽▽▽▽▽ All Year [AP]   1P: $480-$680   2P: $750-$950
Historic
Country Inn
Location: Hwy 401, exit 487, 3 km n. 1009 Massey Rd, RR 1 K0K 2G0. Fax: 905/349-3531. **Facility:** An on-site spa is the centrepiece of this property, which offers guest rooms in a stone house dating from 1857 and also in an annex. Smoke free premises. 30 one-bedroom standard units, some with whirlpools. 1-3 stories, interior corridors. **Parking:** on-site, winter plug-ins. **Terms:** check-in 4 pm, 2 night minimum stay - weekends, age restrictions may apply, 30 day cancellation notice-fee imposed, package plans. **Amenities:** CD players, safes, hair dryers. **Pool(s):** heated outdoor, heated indoor. **Leisure Activities:** saunas, whirlpools, steamrooms, 3 tennis courts, cross country skiing, recreation programs, bicycles, exercise room, spa. **Guest Services:** gift shop, valet laundry, area transportation (fee). **Business Services:** meeting rooms. **Cards:** AX, DC, MC, VI.

SOME UNITS

[icons]

GRAND BEND pop. 1,949

——— WHERE TO STAY ———

——— *The following lodging was either not evaluated or did not meet AAA rating requirements but is listed for your information only.* ———

OAKWOOD INN RESORT AND GOLF   **Phone:** 519/238-2324

[fyi]
Not evaluated. Location: Hwy 21 N N0M 1T0 (Hwy 21 N, Box 400). Facilities, services, and decor characterize a mid-range property.

——— WHERE TO DINE ———

LAKEVIEW CAFE   **Dinner:** $14-$34   **Phone:** 519/238-2622

▽▽▽
Continental
Location: At the foot of Main St; beachfront. 85 Main St N0M 1T0. **Hours:** 5 pm-10 pm. Closed: 12/25. **Reservations:** suggested. **Features:** The tastefully decorated restaurant presents a tantalizing menu of freshly prepared regional and Continental fare. The chef's changing seasonal dishes utilize the freshest of ingredients throughout the year. Highlights include steamed mussels, freshly made soups and creative salads to start, followed by mains such as rack of lamb with Stilton-infused polenta, seared scallops and shrimps over pasta and local fish selections. Homemade desserts are wonderfully decadent. Casual dress; cocktails. **Parking:** street. **Cards:** AX, MC, VI.

[icon]

THE OAK ROOM   **Lunch:** $10-$27   **Dinner:** $15-$35   **Phone:** 519/238-2324
Continental   **Location:** Hwy 21 N; in Oakwood Inn Resort and Golf. Hwy 21 N N0M 1T0. **Hours:** 7-10 am, 11:30-3 & 5-10 pm. **Reservations:** suggested. **Features:** Diners appreciate the lovely log cabin interior, large panoramic windows that overlook the putting green and the warm country hospitality offered from the staff. The chef has created a varied menu of fine Continental fare to suit all tastes. Highlights include snow crab cakes, smoked salmon and baked escargot to start, followed by such popular selections as rack of lamb, grilled seafood and daily pasta dishes. Casual dress; cocktails. **Parking:** on-site. **Cards:** AX, MC, VI.

GRAVENHURST pop. 10,899

———— WHERE TO STAY ————

PINE DALE INN MOTEL   **Phone:** 705/687-2822
Motel
6/19-9/12	1P: $90-$210	2P: $90-$210	XP: $10	F
5/1-6/18 & 9/13-4/30	1P: $80-$145	2P: $80-$145	XP: $10	F

Location: 1 km n of jct Hwy 11 and 169 via Hwy 169 to Pinedale Ln; 1 km n of business section exit. Located on a lake. 200 Pinedale Ln P1P 1B4. Fax: 705/687-9278. **Facility:** 23 units. 20 one-bedroom standard units with kitchens. 2 two- and 1 three-bedroom suites ($125-$210) with kitchens. 1-2 stories (no elevator), exterior corridors. **Parking:** on-site, winter plug-ins. **Terms:** office hours 7 am-11 pm, check-in 4 pm, cancellation fee imposed, package plans. **Pool(s):** heated outdoor. **Leisure Activities:** rental boats, rental canoes, rental paddleboats, boat dock, fishing, cross country skiing, snowmobiling, playground. **Guest Services:** coin laundry. **Cards:** AX, MC, VI.

GRIMSBY pop. 21,297

———— WHERE TO STAY ————

KITTLING RIDGE WINERY INN AND SUITES   *Book at aaa.com*   **Phone:** (905)309-7171
Small-scale Hotel
All Year	1P: $139	2P: $139

Location: Jct QEW and Casablanca. 4 Windward Dr L3M 4E8. Fax: 905/309-7172. **Facility:** 79 units. 63 one-bedroom standard units, some with whirlpools. 16 one-bedroom suites ($199-$429) with whirlpools. 7 stories, interior corridors. **Parking:** on-site. **Terms:** cancellation fee imposed. **Amenities:** dual phone lines, voice mail, safes, hair dryers. **Dining:** 6:30 am-9 pm, Fri & Sat-11 pm; to 7 pm, Thurs-8:30 pm, Fri & Sat-11 pm 12/1-4/30. **Pool(s):** heated indoor. **Leisure Activities:** whirlpool, exercise room. **Guest Services:** gift shop, valet laundry. **Business Services:** meeting rooms. **Cards:** AX, DC, MC, VI.

SOME UNITS

SUPER 8 MOTEL-GRIMSBY   *Book at aaa.com*   **Phone:** (905)309-8800
Small-scale Hotel
5/1-9/30 [ECP]	1P: $119-$139	2P: $119-$139	XP: $10	F
10/1-4/30 [ECP]	1P: $89-$109	2P: $89-$109	XP: $10	F

Location: QEW, exit 74 (Casablanca N). 11 Windward Dr L3M 4E9. Fax: 905/309-7834. **Facility:** 60 one-bedroom standard units. 4 stories, interior corridors. **Parking:** on-site. **Terms:** package plans. **Amenities:** high-speed Internet, voice mail, hair dryers. **Pool(s):** heated indoor. **Leisure Activities:** whirlpool, exercise room. **Guest Services:** coin laundry. **Business Services:** meeting rooms. **Cards:** AX, DC, DS, MC, VI. **Special Amenities:** free expanded continental breakfast and free local telephone calls.

SOME UNITS

GUELPH pop. 106,170

———— WHERE TO STAY ————

COMFORT INN GUELPH   *Book at aaa.com*   **Phone:** (519)763-1900
Small-scale Hotel
7/1-10/31	1P: $115-$135	2P: $125-$145	XP: $10	F17
1/1-4/30	1P: $108-$128	2P: $118-$138	XP: $10	F17
11/1-12/31	1P: $107-$127	2P: $117-$137	XP: $10	F17
5/1-6/30	1P: $105-$125	2P: $115-$135	XP: $10	F17

Location: Jct Hwy 6 and 7. 480 Silvercreek Pkwy N1H 7R5. Fax: 519/763-8330. **Facility:** 80 one-bedroom standard units. 2 stories (no elevator), interior corridors. **Parking:** on-site, winter plug-ins. **Terms:** pets (1st floor smoking units). **Amenities:** irons, hair dryers. *Some: Fee:* high-speed Internet. **Guest Services:** valet laundry. **Cards:** AX, CB, DC, DS, JC, MC, VI.

SOME UNITS
FEE   FEE

DAYS INN
G U E L P H

Come On Inn...

• Newly built and renovated in 2000
• Free Continental breakfast
• Children under 12 stay free
• Close to major shopping and business area
• 1 block south of the University of Guelph

1-800-DAYS INN
www.daysinn.ca

triprewards
It's fun to get more.

Days Inn - Guelph 785 Gordon Street
Guelph, ON N1G 1Y8

Tel   Fax
519-822-9112   519-822-5570

DAYS INN-GUELPH   *Book at aaa.com*
All Year [CP]   1P: $99-$109   2P: $109-$129   XP: $10   F17
Phone: (519)822-9112
Location: Hwy 401, exit 299 (Brock Rd), 11.5 km n. 785 Gordon St N1G 1Y8. Fax: 519/822-5570. **Facility:** 87 one-bedroom standard units. 2 stories, interior corridors. **Parking:** on-site, winter plug-ins. **Amenities:** voice mail, hair dryers. *Some:* dual phone lines, irons. **Guest Services:** valet laundry. **Business Services:** meeting rooms. **Cards:** AX, DC, DS, MC, VI. *(See color ad p 260)*

Small-scale Hotel

ASK SD DATA PORT / X VCR 🛏 🖨 💻 / FEE   SOME UNITS

HOLIDAY INN EXPRESS HOTEL & SUITES GUELPH   *Book at aaa.com*
CAA SAVE   All Year [ECP]   1P: $119-$199   2P: $129-$299   XP: $10   F18
Phone: (519)824-2400
Location: Jct Hwy 6 and 7. 540 Silvercreek Pkwy N N1H 6N3 (PO Box 1113). Fax: 519/824-2450. **Facility:** 53 units. 38 one-bedroom standard units, some with whirlpools. 15 one-bedroom suites ($159-$299). 3 stories, interior corridors. *Bath:* combo or shower only. **Parking:** on-site, winter plug-ins. **Terms:** package plans.

Small-scale Hotel   **Amenities:** high-speed Internet (fee), dual phone lines, voice mail, irons, hair dryers. **Pool(s):** heated indoor. **Leisure Activities:** whirlpool, exercise room. **Guest Services:** valet and coin laundry. **Business Services:** meeting rooms, business center. **Cards:** AX, CB, DC, DS, MC, VI. **Special Amenities:** free expanded continental breakfast and free local telephone calls. *(See color ad card insert & below)*

SD 🍴 ♿ 🏊 DATA PORT 🛏 🖨 💻 / X VCR / FEE   SOME UNITS

NEARBY ATTRACTIONS University of Guelph (5 km) • Grand River Raceway (10 km) • Elora Gorge Park (10 km) • Fergus (10 km) • St. Jacobs/Elmira (20 km) • African Lion Safari (30 km) • Wings of Paradise (10 km) **WE ARE CONVENIENTLY LOCATED AT THE JUNCTION OF HWY 6 & 7**

Free DELUXE BUFFET BREAKFAST
Featuring a variety of cereal, breads, fruit, & juices.
Also including: **HOT** Cinnamon Rolls,
Hard Boiled Eggs, and Smart Roast Coffee.
• Large suites: separate living room, bedroom, kitchenette
• Whirlpool suites: in-room fireplace, Jacuzzi
• Fridge, Microwave, High Speed Internet in ALL rooms
• Fitness Centre • Guest Laundry • Elevator
Large **INDOOR POOL & SPA**

Holiday Inn
EXPRESS
HOTEL & SUITES
540 Silvercreek Pkwy, North,
Guelph, ONTARIO–CANADA
TEL.: **(519) 824-2400**
TOLL FREE: 1-800-HOLIDAY

E-mail: freebreakfast@rogers.com • Web Site: **www.hiexpress.com/gelphon**   *Guelph's Newest Hotel*

SUPER 8 MOTEL

See you along the way.

Reservations:
800-800-8000
www.super8.com

A Great Value in Guelph
Completely Renovated!
• Clean, Comfortable Rooms
  with In-Room Coffee Maker,
  Fridge, Microwave, Hair Dryer,
  Iron & Ironing Board
• Whirlpool Suites
• Executive Suites
• Free Deluxe Continental Breakfast
• Free Weekday Newspaper
• Free TMN Movies • Kids Stay Free
• Restaurant on Premises
• Room Service Available
• Meeting Room Up To 35 People

Nearby: University of Guelph, Elora Gorge Park, St. Jacobs & Elmira & African Lion Safari, Cambridge, Kitchener/Waterloo - 10 Miles. Niagara Falls and Toronto - 50 Miles.

Call for Reservations: **519-836-5850**
On Junction of Highway 6 and Highway 7
281 Woodlawn Rd West at Silvercreek North • Guelph, ON N1H 7K7

HOLIDAY INN GUELPH   *Book at aaa.com*   Phone: (519)836-0231
(CAA) (SAVE)   All Year   1P: $125-$179   2P: $135-$189   XP: $15   F18
▼▼▼▼   **Location:** Jct Hwy 6 N and Stone Rd E, 8 km n of jct Hwy 401. 601 Scottsdale Dr N1G 3E7. Fax: 519/836-5329.
Facility: 136 one-bedroom standard units, some with whirlpools. 5 stories, interior corridors. **Parking:** on-
site. **Terms:** package plans. **Amenities:** high-speed Internet, voice mail, irons, hair dryers. **Dining:** 6:30
am-2:30 & 5-10 pm, cocktails. **Pool(s):** heated indoor. **Leisure Activities:** sauna, whirlpool, playground,
Large-scale Hotel   exercise room. *Fee:* game room. **Guest Services:** sundries, valet laundry. **Business Services:** conference
facilities. **Cards:** AX, DC, DS, MC, VI. *(See color ad card insert)*

SOME UNITS

🅂🄳 🐾 🍴 🍸 ⇆ 🗙 📶 (DATA PORT) 🖭 / 🗙 🔲 🖼 /
                                                      FEE FEE

RAMADA HOTEL & CONFERENCE CENTRE   *Book at aaa.com*   Phone: (519)836-1240
(CAA) (SAVE)   All Year   1P: $150-$195   2P: $160-$195   XP: $15   F18
▼▼▼▼   **Location:** Jct Gordon St and Stone Rd; 8 km n of Hwy 401 via Brock Rd. 716 Gordon St N1G 1Y6.
Fax: 519/763-5225. **Facility:** 104 one-bedroom standard units, some with whirlpools. 2-3 stories, interior
corridors. **Parking:** on-site. **Amenities:** voice mail, irons, hair dryers. **Dining:** 7 am-2 & 5-11 pm, cocktails.
Small-scale Hotel   **Pool(s):** heated outdoor. **Leisure Activities:** exercise room. **Guest Services:** valet laundry. **Business
Services:** conference facilities. **Cards:** AX, DC, DS, JC, MC, VI.

SOME UNITS

🅂🄳 🐾 🍴 🍸 ⇆ 📶 (DATA PORT) 🖭 / 🗙 🔲 🖼 /

SUPER 8 MOTEL-GUELPH   *Book at aaa.com*   Phone: (519)836-5850
(CAA) (SAVE)   All Year   1P: $100-$110   2P: $110-$120   XP: $10   F12
▼▼   **Location:** Jct Hwy 6 and 7. 281 Woodlawn Rd W N1H 7K7. Fax: 519/823-8873. **Facility:** 34 one-bedroom
standard units, some with whirlpools. 2 stories (no elevator), interior/exterior corridors. **Parking:** on-site,
winter plug-ins. **Terms:** [CP] meal plan available. **Amenities:** voice mail, irons, hair dryers. **Dining:** 11 am-
Motel   10 pm, cocktails. **Guest Services:** valet laundry. **Business Services:** meeting rooms. **Cards:** AX, CB, DC,
DS, JC, MC, VI. **Special Amenities:** free continental breakfast and free local telephone calls.
(See color ad p 261)

SOME UNITS

🅂🄳 🍴 📶 (DATA PORT) 🔲 🖭 / 🗙 🖼 /

TRAVELODGE INN AND SUITES   *Book at aaa.com*   Phone: (519)836-1331
▼▼▼   All Year   1P: $79-$179   2P: $89-$179   XP: $10   F14
Location: Just e of Wyndham. 106 Carden St N1H 3A3. Fax: 519/836-9627. **Facility:** 65 units. 57 one-bedroom
Small-scale Hotel   standard units, some with efficiencies. 4 one- and 4 two-bedroom suites with kitchens. 4 stories, interior
corridors. **Parking:** on-site. **Terms:** weekly rates available, package plans. **Amenities:** irons, hair dryers.
Leisure Activities: exercise room. **Guest Services:** valet and coin laundry. **Business Services:** meeting rooms. **Cards:** AX,
CB, DC, JC, MC, VI.

SOME UNITS

🅂🄳 🍴 🍸 (DATA PORT) 🖭 / 🗙 🔲 🖼 /

———— WHERE TO DINE ————

THE BOOKSHELF CAFE AND BISTRO   Lunch: $6-$9   Dinner: $9-$20   Phone: 519/821-3333
▼▼ ▼▼   **Location:** Between Baker and Wyndham sts. 41 Quebec St, 1st Floor N1H 2T1. **Hours:** 8:30 am-10 pm, Sun 10:30
am-9 pm. **Closed:** 1/1, 12/25, 12/26. **Reservations:** suggested. **Features:** This small cafe inside a
Continental   bookstore combines two of life's grandest leisure pursuits—reading and eating. The upbeat, modern
atmosphere features changing local artwork and a creative menu with market-fresh cuisine, large portions
and fresh dessert. Casual dress; cocktails. **Parking:** street. **Cards:** AX, MC, VI.   🗙

CAGNEY'S   Lunch: $7-$13   Dinner: $11-$30   Phone: 519/824-7740
▼▼ ▼▼   **Location:** 0.5 km e of Victoria. 648 York Rd N1E 6A4. **Hours:** 11:30 am-11 pm, Fri & Sat-11:30 pm, Sun 4 pm-10
pm. **Closed:** 12/25. **Reservations:** suggested. **Features:** Known among locals as the place to go for great
Steak & Seafood   Caesar salad, the restaurant also is popular for steaks, chicken, ribs, seafood and pasta. Lunch specials are
an excellent value, and children can order from their own menu. Casual dress; cocktails. **Parking:** on-site.
Cards: AX, MC, VI.   🗙

CARIBOU CREEK RESTAURANT & BAR   Lunch: $6-$10   Dinner: $9-$19   Phone: 519/836-4029
▼▼   **Location:** 1 km e of Hwy 6. 304 Stone Rd W N1G 3O4. **Hours:** 11:30 am-11 pm, Fri & Sat-midnight. **Closed:**
12/25. **Features:** This popular eatery offers a casual, fun atmosphere with a Northern Canadian theme. A
American   true substitute for cottage country dining, the eatery's menu features a fun selection of finger foods, burgers,
MC, VI.   pastas and grilled items with hearty portions offered. Casual dress; cocktails. **Parking:** on-site. **Cards:** AX,
                                                                                                    🗙

CHINA PARK RESTAURANT AND TAVERN   Lunch: $7-$15   Dinner: $10-$20   Phone: 519/836-3333
▼▼ ▼▼   **Location:** Corner of Speedvale. 230 Silvercreek Pkwy N N1H 7P8. **Hours:** 11 am-11 pm, Fri & Sat-midnight, Sun
11:30 am-10 pm. **Closed:** 12/25. **Features:** The casual restaurant offers a tasty Chinese buffet for both
Chinese   lunch and dinner, as well as an a la carte menu. An excellent value, the buffet lines up all the old-time
favorites, including a salad bar, wonton soup, egg rolls, ribs, chicken balls and many stir-fried specialties.
For those with a little room left after the main course, the sweet section includes cakes, cookies and ice cream. Casual dress;
cocktails. **Parking:** on-site. **Cards:** AX, MC, VI.   🗙

KALEIDOSCOPE CAFE AND WINE BAR   Lunch: $12-$15   Dinner: $15-$30   Phone: 519/763-9393
▼▼ ▼▼   **Location:** Jct MacDonell St. 9 Wyndham St N N1H 4E2. **Hours:** noon-9 pm, Fri & Sat-midnight. Closed major
holidays. **Reservations:** suggested. **Features:** In the centre of downtown, the trendy bistro attracts patrons
Continental   with its bright neon signs and modern, upbeat decor. Inside the bi-level restaurant, diners can order from a
fun, innovative menu that features choices ranging from gourmet wood-fire-baked pizzas and pasta to rack
of lamb and beef tenderloin. Decadent desserts are worth the splurge. Dressy casual; cocktails. **Parking:** street. **Cards:** AX,
DC, MC, VI.   🍸 🗙

THE OTHER BROTHER'S

Continental

Lunch: $7-$14   **Dinner:** $12-$28   **Phone:** 519/822-4465
Location: Between Quebec St and Woolwich. 37 Yarmouth St N1H 4G2. **Hours:** noon-2 & 5-close, Sat-Mon from 5 pm. **Features:** A distinctive, contemporary dining room with a menu to match makes this a favourite with locals and tourists alike. The menu offers a mix of innovative cuisine, and pizza on naan bread tops the score. Among other favorites are wraps on flat pastry, pastas, curries and grilled items. Check out the miniature cheeseburger appetizers or salmon pinwheels with mango dip. Dressy casual; cocktails. **Parking:** street. **Cards:** AX, DC, MC, VI.

HALIBURTON

─── **WHERE TO STAY** ───

LAKEVIEW MOTEL

Motel

			Phone: 705/457-1027	
6/1-9/5	1P: $85-$98	2P: $100-$113	XP: $15	D14
9/6-10/10	1P: $78-$90	2P: $93-$105	XP: $15	D14
10/11-4/30	1P: $70-$83	2P: $85-$98	XP: $15	D14
5/1-5/31	1P: $65	2P: $80	XP: $15	D14

Location: Jct Hwy 118, 2.5 km w on CR 121. Located in a rural area. (PO Box 485). Fax: 705/457-1144. **Facility:** 14 units. 13 one-bedroom standard units, some with kitchens. 1 two-bedroom suite ($90-$185) with kitchen. 2 stories (no elevator), exterior corridors. **Parking:** on-site, winter plug-ins. **Terms:** office hours 8 am-10:30 pm, 5 day cancellation notice, small pets only ($8 extra charge, in designated units). **Pool(s):** heated outdoor. **Leisure Activities:** whirlpool, cross country skiing. **Cards:** AX, DC, JC, MC, VI.

SOME UNITS
FEE

─── *The following lodgings were either not evaluated or did not* ───
meet AAA rating requirements but are listed for your information only.

DELTA PINESTONE GOLF & CONFERENCE RESORT

fyi

Phone: 705/457-1800
Not evaluated. Location: 6 km w on CR 121. (PO Box 809). Facilities, services, and decor characterize a mid-range property.

DOMAIN OF KILLIEN

fyi

Phone: 705/457-1100
Not evaluated. Location: Hwy 118, 2 km w, 10 km n on CR 19 to Carroll Rd, follow signs. Located in a wilderness/lakefront area. (PO Box 810). Facilities, services, and decor characterize a mid-range property.

HAMILTON pop. 490,268

─── **WHERE TO STAY** ───

ADMIRAL INN

Small-scale Hotel

Book at aaa.com
All Year   1P: $89-$99   2P: $99-$109   XP: $10   **Phone:** 905/529-2311
Location: Hwy 403, exit York Blvd. Located across from Dundurn Park. 149 Dundurn St N L8R 3E7. Fax: 905/529-9100. **Facility:** 58 one-bedroom standard units, some with whirlpools. 3 stories, interior corridors. **Parking:** on-site, winter plug-ins. **Terms:** [BP] & [CP] meal plans available. **Amenities:** voice mail, irons, hair dryers. *Some:* dual phone lines. **Dining:** 7 am-11 pm, cocktails. **Guest Services:** valet laundry. **Business Services:** meeting rooms, fax (fee). **Cards:** AX, CB, DC, JC, MC, VI.
Special Amenities: free local telephone calls and free newspaper. *(See color ad p 238)*

SOME UNITS

Stay Smart® In Hamilton-Stoney Creek.

- Free Breakfast Bar
- Free Wireless Internet
- Priority Club® Worldwide Rewards Program
- Executive & Whirlpool/Fireplace Rooms
- 45 Minutes From Niagara Falls & Toronto

Minutes Away From Downtown Hamilton
QEW, Exit 88 (Centennial Pkwy) South on Right
51 Keefer Court, Hamilton, ON L8E 4V4
905-578-1212 or 1-800 HOLIDAY
www.hiexpresshamilton.com

Holiday Inn **EXPRESS**

COMFORT INN *Book at aaa.com*
Phone: 905/560-4500

	6/1-9/30	1P: $112-$117	2P: $122-$127	XP: $10	F18
	5/1-5/31	1P: $109-$114	2P: $119-$124	XP: $10	F18
Small-scale Hotel	10/1-4/30	1P: $106-$111	2P: $116-$121	XP: $10	F18

Location: QEW, exit 88 (Hwy 20), 1 km s. 183 Centennial Pkwy N L8E 1H8. Fax: 905/560-6223. **Facility:** 60 one-bedroom standard units. 2 stories (no elevator), interior corridors. **Parking:** on-site. **Terms:** 10 day cancellation notice, 12% service charge. **Amenities:** irons, hair dryers. **Guest Services:** valet laundry. **Cards:** AX, DC, DS, JC, MC, VI.

SOME UNITS

HOLIDAY INN EXPRESS HAMILTON-STONEY CREEK *Book at aaa.com*
Phone: (905)578-1212

| | All Year | 1P: $129-$144 | 2P: $129-$144 | XP: $10 | F18 |

Location: QEW, exit 88 (Hwy 20). 51 Keefer Ct L8E 4V4. Fax: 905/578-6468. **Facility:** 136 one-bedroom standard units, some with whirlpools. 7 stories, interior corridors. **Parking:** on-site, winter plug-ins. **Terms:** cancellation fee imposed, package plans. **Amenities:** voice mail, irons, hair dryers. **Dining:** 6 am-11 pm, Fri & Sat 24 hours, cocktails. **Guest Services:** valet and coin laundry. **Business Services:** meeting rooms. **Cards:** AX, CB, DC, DS, JC, MC, VI. **Special Amenities:** free expanded continental breakfast and free newspaper. *(See color ad p 263 & card insert)*
Small-scale Hotel

SOME UNITS

KNIGHTS INN AT CLAPPISON CORNERS *Book at aaa.com*
Phone: (905)689-6615

| | 5/1-9/30 | 1P: $79-$109 | 2P: $89-$119 | XP: $10 | F17 |
| | 10/1-4/30 | 1P: $79-$99 | 2P: $89-$109 | XP: $10 | F17 |

Location: Jct Hwy 5 and 6. 15 Hwy 5 W L9H 7L5. Fax: 905/689-6615. **Facility:** 31 units. 28 one-bedroom standard units, some with efficiencies. 3 one-bedroom suites ($99-$149), some with kitchens and/or whirlpools. 1-2 stories, interior/exterior corridors. **Parking:** on-site, winter plug-ins. **Terms:** weekly rates available, package plans, small pets only ($15 fee). **Pool(s):** heated outdoor. **Leisure Activities:** whirlpool. **Cards:** AX, MC, VI. *(See color ad below)*
Motel

SOME UNITS

PINES MOTEL
Phone: 905/561-5652

| | All Year | 1P: $58-$76 | 2P: $70-$90 | XP: $5 | D7 |

Location: QEW, exit 88 (Hwy 20). 395 Centennial Pkwy N L8E 2X6. Fax: 905/561-8504. **Facility:** 18 one-bedroom standard units. 1 story, exterior corridors. **Parking:** on-site, winter plug-ins. **Cards:** AX, MC, VI.
Motel

SOME UNITS

RAMADA PLAZA HOTEL HAMILTON *Book at aaa.com*
Phone: (905)528-3451

| | All Year | 1P: $99-$149 | 2P: $99-$149 | XP: $10 | F18 |

Location: Between Walnut and Catherine sts. 150 King St E L8N 1B2. Fax: 905/528-8638. **Facility:** 218 units. 215 one-bedroom standard units, some with whirlpools. 3 one-bedroom suites ($149-$499) with whirlpools. 12 stories, interior corridors. **Parking:** on-site (fee). **Terms:** [BP] & [CP] meal plans available, package plans. **Amenities:** video games, high-speed Internet (fee), voice mail, safes, irons, hair dryers. *Some:* dual phone lines. **Dining:** 6 am-2 & 5-9 pm, Fri & Sat-10 pm, nightclub. **Pool(s):** heated indoor, wading. **Leisure Activities:** sauna, whirlpool, spa. **Guest Services:** gift shop, valet and coin laundry. **Business Services:** meeting rooms, administrative services (fee). **Cards:** AX, DC, DS, MC, VI. **Special Amenities:** free local telephone calls and free newspaper. *(See color ad p 265)*
Small-scale Hotel

SOME UNITS

Clean Rooms. Friendly Service.
Outstanding Value!

- Free Local Phone Calls
- Complimentary Newspapers
- Outdoor Pool & Spa
- Kitchen and Jacuzzi Suites
- In-room Coffee & Fridges   Available

15 Hwy. 5 West, Hamilton, Ontario L9H 7L5
For Reservations call (905) 689-6615 or 1-800-THE KNIGHTS
or visit us at *KnightsInn.com*

SHERATON HAMILTON *Book at aaa.com*

All Year   1P: $109-$199   2P: $109-$199   **Phone:** (905)529-5515   XP: $15   D12
Location: On Hwy 6 and 8 westbound; downtown. Located at Jackson Square Shopping Centre. 116 King St W L8P 4V3. Fax: 905/529-2609. **Facility:** 301 units. 298 one-bedroom standard units. 3 one-bedroom suites, some with whirlpools. 18 stories, interior corridors. **Parking:** on-site (fee) and valet. **Terms:** small pets only.
Large-scale Hotel **Amenities:** video games, high-speed Internet (fee), dual phone lines, voice mail, irons, hair dryers. *Some:* honor bars. **Dining:** 2 restaurants, 6:30 am-10:30 pm, Fri & Sat-midnight, cocktails. **Pool(s):** heated indoor.
Leisure Activities: whirlpool, exercise room. *Fee:* massage. **Guest Services:** gift shop, valet laundry. **Business Services:** conference facilities, business center. **Cards:** AX, MC, VI. *(See color ad p 5)*

SOME UNITS / FEE

STAYBRIDGE SUITES BY HOLIDAY INN   **Phone:** 905/577-9000
All Year [ECP]   1P: $143-$179   2P: $153-$189   XP: $19   F19
Too new to rate, opening scheduled for November 2004. **Location:** Hwy 403, exit King St, then e. 118 Market St
Small-scale Hotel   L8R 3P9. Fax: 905/577-4000. **Amenities:** 108 units, pets, coffeemakers, microwaves, refrigerators, pool. **Cards:** AX, CB, DC, DS, JC, MC, VI.

SUPER 8 MOTEL-HAMILTON AIRPORT/MOUNT
HOPE   *Book at aaa.com*   **Phone:** (905)679-3355
All Year   1P: $90-$110   2P: $95-$115   XP: $6   F12
Location: Jct Hwy 6 S and Homestead Dr. 2975 Homestead Dr L0R 1W0. Fax: 905/679-5109. **Facility:** 49 one-bedroom standard units. 2 stories (no elevator), interior corridors. **Parking:** on-site, winter plug-ins.
Small-scale Hotel   **Amenities:** video library. **Business Services:** meeting rooms. **Cards:** AX, CB, DC, DS, JC, MC, VI.

SOME UNITS / FEE

RAMADA PLAZA HOTEL

Hamilton's Community Hotel

- 218 spacious and comfortable guestrooms
- Luxurious Suites & Executive floors available
- Complimentary Wireless High Speed Internet
- $3 million Health & Wellness Center that includes an indoor pool, children's wading pool, giant sized jacuzzi, sauna and state of the art fitness centre
- Brand new "Anahita's Spa at the Ramada" offering a full line of esthetics, featuring Volcanic Mud imported from Costa Rica.
- Renovated Banquet and Meeting Facilities for groups of 10 to 1000
- Complimentary shuttle service to John C. Munro International Airport
- Home of Hamilton's Yuk Yuk's Comedy Club

30% AAA/CAA Discount
Off Published Rates

150 King Street East, Hamilton, Ontario 18N 1B2 ♦ 905-528-3451 or 1-800-2RAMADA
www.ramadahamilton.com

VISITORS INN

905-529-6979
1-800-387-4620

649 Main St.W. (at Hwy 403)
Hamilton, ON L8S 1A2

www.visitorsinn.com
reservations@visitorsinn.com

Luxurious & Affordable

Selected Best Choice in the Hamilton/Burlington Area
- by America's Best Choice Travel Guide

- ❖ 60 Modern Units & Jacuzzi Suites
- ❖ In Room High Speed Internet
- ❖ Cordless Phones, Coffee Makers
- ❖ In Room Irons & Safes
- ❖ All Queen & King Size Beds
- ❖ Efficiency Units & Mini-Bars
- ❖ Free Satellite, Cable TV & Radio
- ❖ Indoor Pool, Jacuzzi & Exercise Room
- ❖ Meeting Rooms & Dining Room
- ❖ Conveniently located minutes from downtown & McMaster University

VISITORS INN
Phone: 905/529-6979
(CAA) (SAVE) All Year   1P: $99-$124   2P: $109-$134   XP: $10   F12
▼▼▼ **Location:** Hwy 403, exit Main St W (Hwy 2 and 8). 649 Main St W L8S 1A2. Fax: 905/529-6979. **Facility:** 60 one-bedroom standard units, some with efficiencies and/or whirlpools. 4 stories, interior/exterior corridors. **Parking:** on-site, winter plug-ins. **Terms:** cancellation fee imposed. **Amenities:** high-speed Internet (fee),
Small-scale Hotel voice mail, safes, irons, hair dryers. *Some:* DVD players (fee), honor bars. **Dining:** 7 am-10 pm, cocktails. **Pool(s):** heated indoor. **Leisure Activities:** sauna, whirlpool, exercise room. **Guest Services:** valet and coin laundry. **Business Services:** meeting rooms. **Cards:** AX, DC, JC, MC, VI. **Special Amenities:** free local telephone calls and free newspaper. *(See color ad p 265)*

SOME UNITS

🛫 ⊪ 🏊 ⊠ (🎍) (DATA PORT) 🔒 💻 /⊠ (VCR) 🍽 /
FEE   FEE

———— WHERE TO DINE ————

ANCASTER OLD MILL INN   **Lunch:** $10-$16   **Dinner:** $18-$32   **Phone:** 905/648-1827
▼▼▼ **Location:** Hwy 403, 0.8 km w on Mohawk Rd, 0.8 km n, follow signs. 548 Old Dundas Rd L9G 3J4. **Hours:** 11:30 am-2 & 5-close, Sun 9:30 am-1:30 & 5-close; Sunday brunch. Closed: 12/26; also Tues-Fri 1/1-1/15 & Mon.
Canadian   **Reservations:** suggested. **Features:** Great views of the stream complement the pleasant country setting of this restored grain mill. Although the menu changes periodically, fresh vegetables, chicken, seafood, chops and steak prevail and are well presented. Dressy casual; cocktails. **Parking:** on-site. **Cards:** AX, DC, MC, VI.   🍽 ⊠

BLACK FOREST INN   **Lunch:** $7-$13   **Dinner:** $7-$13   **Phone:** 905/528-3538
(CAA) **Location:** 1.6 km e. 255 King St E L8N 1B9. **Hours:** 11:30 am-10:30 pm, Fri & Sat-11 pm, Sun noon-9:30 pm.
▼▼▼ Closed: 12/25, 12/26; also Mon. **Features:** The Bavarian atmosphere (complete with cuckoo clock) only adds to the memorable meal you'll have at the Black Forest Inn. Hearty portions of Austrian cuisine with emphasis on Wiener schnitzel, the house favorite, shines. A children's menu is available. Cocktails.
Austrian   **Parking:** on-site. **Cards:** AX, DC, MC, VI.   🍽 ⊠

IZZY'S RESTAURANT   **Dinner:** $12-$20   **Phone:** 905/521-1503
▼▼▼ **Location:** Hwy 403, exit Main St, 8 km e; corner of Main St W and Locke St S. 354 Main St W L8P 1K2. **Hours:** 4 pm-9 pm, Fri & Sat-10 pm. Closed major holidays; also Sun. **Reservations:** suggested. **Features:** This
Polish   European eatery presents hearty portions of Polish fare in a cozy, relaxed atmosphere. Pierogies (a pocket of pasta-like dough filled with potato, fruit, or meat) are quite popular and always on the menu. Continental dishes also are offered. Dressy casual; cocktails. **Parking:** no self-parking. **Cards:** AX, MC, VI.   ⊠

THE KEG STEAKHOUSE AND BAR   **Dinner:** $15-$30   **Phone:** 905/574-7880
▼▼ **Location:** 1.5 km s of Mohawk Rd; jct Lincoln Alexandria Pkwy. 1170 Upper James L9C 3B1. **Hours:** 4:30 pm-10:30 pm, Fri-11 pm, Sat 3 pm-11 pm, Sun 3 pm-9:30 pm. Closed: 12/25. **Features:** Well-known for its mesquite-
Steak House   grilled steaks and fun, laid-back atmosphere, the steak house is a longtime favorite with the local crowd. In addition to great beef, the traditional menu features seafood, grilled chicken, hickory ribs and pasta offerings. All meals come with a hot loaf of sourdough bread. Try a specialty coffee or tasty cheesecake for the perfect ending. Casual dress; cocktails. **Parking:** on-site. **Cards:** AX, DC, MC, VI.   🍽 ⊠

LA CANTINA RISTORANTE   **Lunch:** $9-$16   **Dinner:** $9-$34   **Phone:** 905/521-8989
▼▼ **Location:** Corner of Walnut and Jackson sts. 60 Walnut St S L8N 2L1. **Hours:** 11:30 am-2:30 & 4-10 pm, Fri-11 pm, Sat 4 pm-11 pm. Closed major holidays; also Sun & Mon. **Features:** The locals love La Cantina for its
Italian   home-style cooking and bustling atmosphere where a uniformed staff provides friendly service. There is a good selection of appetizers as well as pasta and veal. Casual dining in the La Spiga Pizzeria is also available. Casual dress; cocktails. **Parking:** street. **Cards:** AX, DC, MC, VI.   🍽 ⊠

LA PIAZZA ALLEGRA RISTORANTE ITALIANO   **Lunch:** $7-$17   **Dinner:** $13-$23   **Phone:** 905/777-8970
▼▼▼ **Location:** Jct Duke St. 180 James St S L8P 4V1. **Hours:** 11:30 am-10:30 pm, Sat & Sun from 4:30 pm. Closed major holidays. **Reservations:** suggested. **Features:** The popular restaurant has a strong local following for
Italian   its upscale yet relaxed ambience and fine menu of freshly prepared Italian fare. Menu highlights include such starters as calamari, portobello mushrooms and homemade soup, followed by a wide variety of pasta, veal and poultry offerings. Tempting desserts are worth a splurge. Dressy casual; cocktails. **Parking:** on-site. **Cards:** AX, MC, VI.   ⊠

LO PRESTI'S AT MAXWELL'S   **Lunch:** $10-$17   **Dinner:** $14-$50   **Phone:** 905/528-0205
▼▼▼ **Location:** Just e of Walnut St. 165 Jackson St E L8N 1L6. **Hours:** noon-2:30 & 5-10 pm, Sat from 5 pm. Closed major holidays; also Sun. **Reservations:** suggested. **Features:** Italian and Continental cuisines make a
Continental   grand entrance, in keeping with the elegant garden-like atmosphere of Lo Presti's. Well-appointed dining rooms are the setting for many a feast on house specialties such as steak au poivre (a classic flamed dish). Semi-formal attire; cocktails. **Parking:** on-site. **Cards:** AX, DC, MC, VI.   ⊠

THE OLD MAGILL HOUSE   **Dinner:** $22-$38   **Phone:** 905/540-9991
▼▼▼ **Location:** Jct Victoria. 309 Main St E L8N 1H8. **Hours:** 5 pm-10 pm. **Reservations:** suggested. **Features:** Roman pillars, archways and elegant artwork complement the candlelit tables at this
Steak & Seafood   sophisticated establishment. Diners will enjoy the intimate setting in several small dining rooms. The traditional steak and seafood menu features fine cooked-to-order beef in a variety of sauces, sided with lobster tail, shrimp or scallops. All meals include hot garlic bread and a tasty relish plate. Dressy casual; cocktails. **Parking:** on-site. **Cards:** AX, MC, VI.   ⊠

THE RUDE NATIVE BISTRO   **Lunch:** $8-$10   **Dinner:** $12-$21   **Phone:** 905/777-9504
▼▼ ▼▼   **Location:** Jct Hughson St N. 43 King William St L8R 1A2. **Hours:** 11:30 am-midnight, Thurs & Fri-2 am, Sat 3
pm-2 am, Sun 3 pm-11 pm. **Reservations:** suggested. **Features:** Diners enjoy the central downtown
Caribbean   location and the fun island menu, which takes them away for a few short moments as they gaze at bright,
Caribbean-style wall murals. The menu highlights an extensive selection of island specialties, including jerk
and Thai cuisine. Casual dress; cocktails. **Parking:** street. **Cards:** AX, DC, MC, VI.
     ✕

SHAKESPEARE STEAK AND
   SEAFOOD HOUSE   **Lunch:** $11-$26   **Dinner:** $16-$60   **Phone:** 905/528-0689
Ⓒ   **Location:** Hwy 8, 1 km e. 181 Main St E L8N 1H2. **Hours:** 11:30 am-2 & 5-10 pm, Sat 5 pm-11 pm. Closed
major holidays; also Sun. **Reservations:** suggested, weekends. **Features:** The Old World Tudor steak
▼▼ ▼▼   house has a long history of serving traditional steaks and seafood, as well as buffalo, wild boar and ostrich.
An extensive wine and spirit menu complements desserts such as hot apple beignet. Dressy casual;
Steak & Seafood   cocktails. **Parking:** on-site. **Cards:** AX, DC, MC, VI.
     ✕

THE SIRLOIN CELLAR   **Lunch:** $8-$17   **Dinner:** $16-$35   **Phone:** 905/525-8620
▼▼ ▼▼   **Location:** 1/2 blk n of King St; across from Jackson Square. 14 1/2 James St N L8R 2J9. **Hours:** 11:30 am-2:30 &
4:30-10 pm, Sat & Sun from 4:30 pm. Closed major holidays. **Reservations:** suggested. **Features:** The
Steak & Seafood   well-established restaurant offers a traditional setting and fine menu of old-time favorites, including escargot,
shrimp cocktail, prime rib, surf and turf and perfectly grilled steaks. The convenient downtown location is
near shopping, theatre, sports and entertainment venues. Casual dress; cocktails. **Parking:** street. **Cards:** AX, DC, MC, VI.
     ✕

HANOVER pop. 6,869

──────── WHERE TO STAY ────────

THE VICTORIAN MANOR BED & BREAKFAST   **Phone:** (519)364-1117
Ⓒ SAVE   All Year   1P: $70-$90   2P: $80-$100   XP: $20   F6
   Location: Just n of 10th St. 500 9th Ave N4N 2M3. **Facility:** Guests may gather in the charming common parlor
▼▼ ▼▼   or the inviting dining room, where breakfast is served on fine china. Smoke free premises. 5 one-bedroom
standard units. 3 stories, interior corridors. *Bath:* some shared or private, combo or shower only. **Parking:**
Bed & Breakfast   on-site. **Terms:** office hours 6 am-9 pm, age restrictions may apply, weekly rates available, package plans,
small pets only (with prior approval). **Amenities:** *Some:* hair dryers. **Leisure Activities:** sauna. **Guest**
Services: gift shop. **Cards:** VI. **Special Amenities: free local telephone calls and early check-in/late check-out.**
     SOME UNITS
     Ⓢ 🐾 ✕ ☎ / 📺 /

HAWKESBURY pop. 10,314

──────── WHERE TO STAY ────────

BEST WESTERN L'HERITAGE   *Book at aaa.com*   **Phone:** (613)632-5941
▼▼ ▼▼   All Year   1P: $90-$95   2P: $100-$105   XP: $10   F17
   Location: Jct Hwy 34, 3 km e. on Hwy 17. Located in a commercial area. 1575 Tupper St K6A 3T5.
Small-scale Hotel   Fax: 613/632-0233. **Facility:** 50 units. 46 one-bedroom standard units. 4 one-bedroom suites. 2 stories (no
elevator), interior corridors. **Parking:** on-site. **Terms:** small pets only. **Amenities:** voice mail, irons, hair
dryers. *Some:* high-speed Internet, dual phone lines. **Guest Services:** valet laundry. **Business Services:** meeting rooms.
Cards: AX, DC, DS, MC, VI.
     SOME UNITS
     ASK Ⓢ 🐾 🍴 🍸 DATA PORT 💻 / ✕ 📷 /

HUNTSVILLE pop. 17,338

──────── WHERE TO STAY ────────

COMFORT INN   *Book at aaa.com*   **Phone:** (705)789-1701
▼▼ ▼▼

	6/17-10/16	1P: $124-$147	2P: $144-$167
	1/1-4/30	1P: $98-$102	2P: $108-$112
	10/17-12/31	1P: $96-$101	2P: $106-$111
Small-scale Hotel	5/1-6/16	1P: $95-$100	2P: $105-$110

Location: Jct Hwy 60. Located in a commercial area. 86 King William St P1H 1E4. Fax: 705/789-8809. **Facility:** 73 one-bedroom
standard units. 2 stories (no elevator), interior corridors. **Parking:** on-site, winter plug-ins. **Terms:** cancellation fee imposed,
[CP] meal plan available, package plans, pets (on ground floor). **Amenities:** irons, hair dryers. **Guest Services:** valet laundry.
Cards: AX, CB, DC, DS, JC, MC, VI.
     SOME UNITS
     ASK Ⓢ 🐾 🍴 ⊛ DATA PORT 💻 / ✕ 📷 🍽 /

DEERHURST RESORT
Book at aaa.com
Phone: (705)789-6411

(CAA) (SAVE)

7/1-8/31	1P: $159-$319	2P: $159-$319	XP: $30	F18
9/1-10/16	1P: $139-$319	2P: $139-$319	XP: $30	F18
5/1-6/30	1P: $139-$279	2P: $139-$279	XP: $30	F18
10/17-4/30	1P: $119-$279	2P: $119-$279	XP: $30	F18

Resort
Large-scale Hotel
Location: Jct Hwy 11, 7 km e on Hwy 60 to Deerhurst Canal Rd (CR 23), then 2 km, follow signs. Located in a rural area. 1235 Deerhurst Dr P1H 2E8. Fax: 705/789-2431. **Facility:** This large complex in a scenic country setting has a private airstrip and offers a variety of accommodations. 445 units. 148 one-bedroom standard units, some with whirlpools. 180 one-, 103 two- and 14 three-bedroom suites, some with efficiencies, kitchens and/or whirlpools. 4 stories, interior/exterior corridors. **Parking:** on-site, winter plug-ins. **Terms:** check-in 4 pm, 2 night minimum stay - weekends, 7 day cancellation notice-fee imposed, $7 service charge. **Amenities:** video games, voice mail, hair dryers. *Some:* DVD players, CD players, high-speed Internet (fee), irons. **Dining:** 3 restaurants, 7 am-10 pm, cocktails, also, Eclipse, see separate listing. **Pool(s):** 3 heated outdoor, heated indoor, small heated indoor. **Leisure Activities:** saunas, whirlpools, steamrooms, rental boats, canoeing, paddleboats, 10 tennis courts (2 indoor, 8 lighted), racquetball court, 2 squash courts, cross country skiing, ice skating, recreation programs, hiking trails, jogging, playground, exercise room, spa, horseshoes. *Fee:* sailboats, windsurfing, boat dock, waterskiing, fishing, golf-36 holes, downhill skiing, snowmobiling, dog sledding, snow tubing, bicycles, horseback riding. **Guest Services:** gift shop, valet laundry, area transportation-ski slopes. **Business Services:** conference facilities, business center. **Cards:** AX, DC, DS, JC, MC, VI.

SOME UNITS

DELTA GRANDVIEW RESORT
Book at aaa.com
Phone: (705)789-4417

6/24-9/4	1P: $179-$249	2P: $179-$249	XP: $79	F17
5/1-6/23	1P: $99-$229	2P: $99-$229	XP: $79	F17
9/5-4/30	1P: $99-$219	2P: $99-$219	XP: $79	F17

Resort
Condominium
Location: Jct Hwy 11, 6 km e. Located in a quiet area. 939 Hwy 60 P1H 1Z4. Fax: 705/789-1674. **Facility:** An on-site observatory offers opportunities to study the night sky at this large, hillside property overlooking a valley and lake. 130 units. 50 one-bedroom standard units. 80 one-bedroom suites ($169-$489) with whirlpools, some with kitchens. 2-3 stories (no elevator), exterior corridors. **Parking:** on-site, winter plug-ins. **Terms:** check-in 4 pm, 14 day cancellation notice, [BP] & [MAP] meal plans available, package plans. **Amenities:** video library (fee), voice mail, irons, hair dryers. *Some:* DVD players, video games (fee), CD players. **Pool(s):** heated outdoor, heated indoor. **Leisure Activities:** sauna, whirlpool, canoeing, paddleboats, sailboats, boat dock, fishing, 2 tennis courts (1 indoor, 2 lighted), cross country skiing, ice skating, recreation programs, bicycles, hiking trails, jogging, exercise room, basketball, horseshoes, volleyball. *Fee:* waterskiing, charter fishing, golf-27 holes. **Guest Services:** gift shop, coin laundry. **Business Services:** conference facilities, administrative services (fee). **Cards:** AX, DC, MC, VI.

SOME UNITS

HOLIDAY INN HIDDEN VALLEY RESORT
Book at aaa.com
Phone: (705)789-2301

5/1-10/31	1P: $259	2P: $269	XP: $20	F12
11/1-4/30	1P: $109	2P: $119	XP: $20	F12

Resort
Small-scale Hotel
Location: Jct Hwy 11, 6.5 km e on Hwy 60 to Hidden Valley Rd, follow signs. Located in a rural area. 1755 Valley Rd P1H 1Z8. Fax: 705/789-6586. **Facility:** The property overlooks Pennsula Lake, while a ski area is adjacent to the property; units are comfortable with attractive pine furniture and country decor. 94 one-bedroom standard units, some with whirlpools. 3 stories (no elevator), interior corridors. **Parking:** on-site, winter plug-ins. **Terms:** check-in 4 pm, cancellation fee imposed, package plans. **Amenities:** video library (fee), voice mail, irons, hair dryers. **Pool(s):** heated outdoor, heated indoor, wading. **Leisure Activities:** sauna, boat dock, 3 lighted tennis courts, snowmobiling, recreation programs, playground, exercise room, basketball, horseshoes, volleyball. *Fee:* boats, canoes, paddleboats, fishing. **Business Services:** meeting rooms. **Cards:** AX, CB, DC, DS, MC, VI.

SOME UNITS

FEE

KING WILLIAM INN
Phone: 705/789-9661

(CAA) (SAVE)

6/3-10/16	1P: $99-$115	2P: $110-$125	XP: $10	F12
5/1-6/2 & 10/17-4/30	1P: $65-$85	2P: $75-$95	XP: $10	F12

Motel
Location: Hwy 60, 1 km s. Located in a commercial area. 23 King William St P1H 1G4. Fax: 705/789-7871. **Facility:** 32 units. 31 one- and 1 two-bedroom standard units, some with whirlpools. 2 stories (no elevator), exterior corridors. **Parking:** on-site, winter plug-ins. **Terms:** office hours 7:30 am-10:30 pm, 2 night minimum stay - seasonal and/or weekends, cancellation fee imposed. **Amenities:** hair dryers. *Some:* DVD players, dual phone lines, irons. **Business Services:** meeting rooms, fax (fee). **Cards:** AX, DC, DS, MC, VI. **Special Amenities: free local telephone calls and free newspaper.** *(See color ad below)*

SOME UNITS

FEE

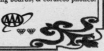

Be Our Guest

King William Inn

King William Inn

• Located in town, walking distance to shopping & fine restaurants.
• A short distance to Algonquin Park.
• Fine beaches, lakes, cycling, hiking, golfing, skiing.
• Spectacular fall colours all among breathtaking scenery.

• Jacuzzi/Fireplace/Sauna, Deluxe/ Fireplace& standard rooms available.
• All rooms have fridges, hair dryers & coffee makers.
• Business rooms have larger desks with power and data jacks.
• Irons & ironing boards, & cordless phones.

KING WILLIAM INN

Book Online @ www.kingwilliaminn.com
23 King William Street
Huntsville, ON P1H 1G4
Reservations: (705) 789-9661 • Toll Free 1-888-995-9169

RAINBOW INN
Phone: (705)789-5514

(CAA) (SAVE)

7/1-10/15	1P: $115	2P: $125	XP: $10	D15
10/16-4/30	1P: $59	2P: $69	XP: $10	D15
5/1-6/30	1P: $62	2P: $68	XP: $10	D15

Motel **Location:** Hwy 60, 0.7 km s; jct Cliffe St. Located in a commercial area. 32 King William St P1H 1G5. Fax: 705/789-0734. **Facility:** 17 one-bedroom standard units. 1 story, exterior corridors. **Parking:** on-site, winter plug-ins. **Terms:** office hours 7 am-11 pm. **Amenities:** hair dryers. *Some:* DVD players. **Business Services:** meeting rooms, fax (fee). **Cards:** AX, DC, MC, VI. **Special Amenities:** free local telephone calls and free newspaper.

SOME UNITS

TRAVELODGE *Book at aaa.com*
Phone: (705)789-5504

7/1-8/31	1P: $124-$174	2P: $134-$184	XP: $10	F
9/1-10/16	1P: $113-$164	2P: $123-$173	XP: $10	F
5/1-6/30 & 10/17-4/30	1P: $89-$129	2P: $99-$139	XP: $10	F

Small-scale Hotel **Location:** Hwy 11, exit 219 (Muskoka Rd 3), just e. Located in a commercial area. 225 Main St W P1H 1Y1. Fax: 705/789-2467. **Facility:** 37 units. 34 one- and 3 two-bedroom standard units, some with efficiencies or kitchens. 3 stories (no elevator), interior corridors. **Parking:** on-site, winter plug-ins. **Terms:** 30 day cancellation notice, [CP] meal plan available, 12% service charge. **Amenities:** hair dryers. **Leisure Activities:** sauna, whirlpool. **Cards:** AX, DC, MC, VI.

SOME UNITS

TULIP INN
Phone: 705/789-4001

6/1-10/20	1P: $95-$145	2P: $95-$145	XP: $10
3/1-4/30	1P: $80-$110	2P: $80-$110	XP: $10
10/21-2/28	1P: $70-$100	2P: $70-$100	XP: $10
5/1-5/31	1P: $70-$90	2P: $70-$90	XP: $10

Motel **Location:** Hwy 11, exit 226 (Muskoka Rd 3), follow signs for Arrowhead Park. Located in a rural area. 211 Arrowhead Park Rd P1H 2J4. Fax: 705/789-8443. **Facility:** 18 units. 17 one-bedroom standard units, some with efficiencies. 1 cottage ($180-$220). 1 story, exterior corridors. **Parking:** on-site, winter plug-ins. **Terms:** office hours 8 am-11 pm, 2 night minimum stay - weekends, 3 day cancellation notice-fee imposed, [CP] meal plan available. **Leisure Activities:** rental canoes. **Cards:** AX, DC, JC, MC, VI.

SOME UNITS

———— **WHERE TO DINE** ————

3 GUYS AND A STOVE **Lunch:** $6-$12 **Dinner:** $10-$30 Phone: 705/789-1815

American **Location:** Just e of Muskoka Rd 3. 143 Hwy 60 E P1H 2K6. **Hours:** 11 am-10 pm, Fri & Sat-11 pm; to 11 pm 7/1-9/5. Closed: 12/25; also 3 days in April. **Features:** Creative menu selections featuring Southern California and New Orleans-style cuisines prevail at this cleverly named and similarly decorated restaurant. Selections include fish, steak, pasta, ribs and a children's menu. Patio dining is offered in season. Casual dress; cocktails. **Parking:** on-site. **Cards:** AX, DC, MC, VI.

ECLIPSE **Dinner:** $15-$40 Phone: 705/789-6411

Canadian **Location:** Jct Hwy 11, 7 km e on Hwy 60 to Deerhurst Canal Rd (CR 23), then 2 km, follow signs; in Deerhurst Resort. 1235 Deerhurst Dr P1H 2E8. **Hours:** 7:30 am-11 & 5:30-10 pm. **Features:** Soaring ceilings, well-presented food, a highly developed wine list and friendly service await guests in the dining room. Casual dress; cocktails. **Parking:** on-site. **Cards:** AX, DC, DS, JC, MC, VI.

SANDPIPERS RESTAURANT **Dinner:** $16-$30 Phone: 705/789-6908

Continental **Location:** Hwy 60, 3.8 km e of jct Hwy 11. 365 Hwy 60 P1H 1B9. **Hours:** 5 pm-9 pm. Closed: 4/1-4/30 & 11/1-11/30; also Sun & Mon 1/1-3/31. **Reservations:** suggested. **Features:** Located directly off the main highway just outside of town, this pleasant country restaurant offers a fine blend of Continental cuisine with a Scandinavian flair. In the summer months take time to enjoy the attractive country gardens surrounding the restaurant. Inside you will enjoy the modern, upscale artwork with a local theme. Complement this with marinated herring, fresh seafood or meat selections and a basket of homemade breads and you will have a dining experience to remember. Dressy casual; cocktails. **Parking:** on-site. **Cards:** AX, MC, VI.

TALL TREES RESTAURANT **Lunch:** $8-$16 **Dinner:** $14-$30 Phone: 705/789-9769

(CAA)

Continental **Location:** Hwy 11, 2 km e on Muskoka Rd 3. 87 Main St W P1H 1X1. **Hours:** 11:30 am-9 pm; hours vary off season. Closed: Sun. **Reservations:** suggested. **Features:** Inviting, cozy, country decor and a casual ambience mark the setting in which to enjoy an eclectic menu that draws from, but is not restricted to, local produce. The chef-owner modifies the menu by season. There is a well-rounded wine list, and desserts are made in house. The patio opens during nice weather. All combined, this place is a nice find. Casual dress; cocktails. **Parking:** on-site. **Cards:** AX, DC, MC, VI.

INGERSOLL pop. 10,977

———— **WHERE TO STAY** ————

ELM HURST INN AND COUNTRY SPA
Phone: (519)485-5321

All Year [AP] 1P: $175-$225 2P: $185-$235 XP: $10

Country Inn **Location:** Jct Hwy 401 and 19 N. Located in a quiet rural area. 415 Harris St N5C 3J8 (PO Box 123, N5C 3K1). Fax: 519/485-6579. **Facility:** Aromatherapy, reflexology and Swedish massage are among the spa services offered at this country-setting inn. 49 units. 47 one-bedroom standard units, some with whirlpools. 2 one-bedroom suites with whirlpools. 3 stories, interior corridors. **Parking:** on-site. **Terms:** package plans. **Amenities:** video library (fee), high-speed Internet, voice mail, irons, hair dryers. *Some:* DVD players, CD players. **Dining:** restaurant, see separate listing. **Leisure Activities:** sauna, whirlpool, steamroom, hiking trails, exercise room, spa. *Fee:* game room. **Guest Services:** valet laundry. **Business Services:** meeting rooms. **Cards:** AX, DC, DS, JC, MC, VI.

SOME UNITS

TRAVELODGE INGERSOLL   *Book at aaa.com*   **Phone:** (519)425-1100

All Year   1P: $85-$99   2P: $95-$109   XP: $10   F18

Location: Hwy 401, exit 216 (Culloden Rd). 20 Samnah Crescent N5C 3J7. Fax: 519/425-1106. **Facility:** 98 units.

Small-scale Hotel   86 one-bedroom standard units. 12 one-bedroom suites. 3 stories, interior corridors. **Parking:** on-site.

Terms: package plans. **Amenities:** video games (fee), voice mail, irons, hair dryers. *Some:* dual phone lines. **Pool(s):** heated indoor. **Leisure Activities:** whirlpool. **Guest Services:** valet laundry. **Business Services:** meeting rooms. **Cards:** AX, DC, DS, MC, VI. *(See color ad on TourBookMark)*

SOME UNITS

──── WHERE TO DINE ────

ELM HURST INN   **Lunch:** $9-$16   **Dinner:** $20-$37   **Phone:** 519/485-5321

Location: Jct Hwy 401 and 19 N; in Elm Hurst Inn and Country Spa. Hwy 401 & Plank Rd N5C 3K1. **Hours:** 7-10:30 am, 11:30-2 & 5-9 pm, Sun 10:30 am-2 & 4-8 pm. Closed: for dinner 12/24. **Reservations:** suggested.

Features: Visitors enjoy elegant dining in a Victorian Gothic home with a picturesque country setting. The upscale yet relaxed atmosphere and good menu of fine Continental fare keep locals coming back.

Continental   Luncheon options include an upscale buffet offering specialty salads, soup, cheese and pate, as well as two daily hot selections and a full dessert array. Lighter options, such as sandwiches and burgers, are also available. Dressy casual; cocktails. **Parking:** on-site. **Cards:** AX, DC, MC, VI.

JACKSONS POINT

──── WHERE TO STAY ────

THE BRIARS INN & COUNTRY CLUB   **Phone:** (905)722-3271

5/1-10/23 [AP]   1P: $199-$295   2P: $298-$490   XP: $130   D11

10/24-4/30 [AP]   1P: $179-$245   2P: $278-$398   XP: $110   D11

Location: Hwy 48, through Sutton to Jacksons Point, 1 km e. 55 Hedge Rd, RR 1 L0E 1L0. Fax: 905/722-9698.

Facility: This estate on 200 acres of manicured grounds and gardens includes well-appointed traditional

Resort   rooms and rustic cottages. Smoke free premises. 90 units. 80 one-bedroom standard units, some with

Small-scale Hotel   whirlpools. 1 two-bedroom suite with whirlpool. 9 cottages. 1-2 stories (no elevator), interior/exterior corridors. **Parking:** on-site. **Terms:** check-in 4 pm, 2 night minimum stay - weekends, 21 day cancellation notice-fee imposed, weekly rates available, [MAP] meal plan available, package plans, 15% service charge. **Amenities:** high-speed Internet, voice mail, irons, hair dryers. **Dining:** 2 restaurants, 8 am-9:30, noon-1:30 & 6-8 pm, cocktails. **Pool(s):** 2 heated outdoor, heated indoor. **Leisure Activities:** sauna, whirlpool, canoeing, paddleboats, sailboats, fishing, boat cruises, kayaks, 4 tennis courts (2 lighted), cross country skiing, ice skating, tobogganing, sleigh rides, recreation programs, rental bicycles, playground, exercise room, spa. *Fee:* golf-18 holes. **Guest Services:** gift shop, valet laundry. **Business Services:** meeting rooms. **Cards:** AX, DC, MC, VI. **Special Amenities:** free local telephone calls and free newspaper.

(See color ad below)

SOME UNITS

The Briars is beautifully situated on sparkling Lake Simcoe just one hour from Toronto. Stay in the historic Manor House, Inn or Lakeside Cottages. Pamper yourself with a treatment in the Spa or play a round at the beautiful Briars Golf Club. Gracious dining, a variety of year-round activities and warm hospitality make The Briars perfect for any occasion.

1-800-465-2376 www.briars.ca/aaa

JORDAN

──── WHERE TO STAY ────

**BEST WESTERN BEACON HARBORSIDE RESORT
& CONFERENCE CENTRE**   *Book at aaa.com*   Phone: (905)562-4155

(CAA) (SAVE)	11/1-4/30	1P: $89-$229	2P: $89-$229	XP: $10	F12
	7/1-9/6	1P: $129-$189	2P: $129-$189	XP: $10	F12
▼▼▼	5/1-6/30	1P: $89-$169	2P: $89-$169	XP: $10	F12
	9/7-10/31	1P: $99-$149	2P: $99-$149	XP: $10	F12

Small-scale Hotel Location: QEW, exit 57. Located on Lake Ontario. 2793 Beacon Blvd L0R 1S0 (PO Box 70). **Fax:** 905/562-5524. **Facility:** 62 units. 49 one-bedroom standard units, some with whirlpools. 13 one-bedroom suites ($179-$329), some with whirlpools. 3 stories (no elevator), interior corridors. **Parking:** on-site. **Terms:** package plans, pets ($10 fee, with prior approval). **Amenities:** irons, hair dryers. **Dining:** 7 am-11 pm, cocktails. **Pool(s):** heated indoor. **Leisure Activities:** saunas, marina, fishing. *Fee:* charter fishing. **Business Services:** meeting rooms. **Cards:** AX, DC, DS, MC, VI. **Special Amenities: free local telephone calls and free room upgrade (subject to availability with advance reservations).**

SOME UNITS

[icons] SD 🛏 🍽 ⬇ 🐾 ✕ 📺 DATA PORT 💻 / ✕ /
FEE

INN ON THE TWENTY   Phone: (905)562-5336

▼▼ ▼▼	5/1-10/31	1P: $179-$352	2P: $179-$352	XP: $40	F12
	11/1-4/30	1P: $149-$325	2P: $149-$325	XP: $40	F12

Historic Country Inn **Location:** QEW, exit 57, 3 km s on Reg Rd 24, 3 km e on Reg Rd 81, then just n. Located in a quiet area. 3845 Main St L0R 1S0. **Fax:** 905/562-0009. **Facility:** A village-like setting within the Niagara wine region gives this upscale-country inn a retreat-like ambience. Smoke free premises. 29 one-bedroom standard units, some with whirlpools. 2 stories, interior/exterior corridors. **Parking:** on-site. **Terms:** 2 night minimum stay - weekends, 7 day cancellation notice-fee imposed, [AP] meal plan available, package plans. **Amenities:** video library, irons, hair dryers. *Some:* DVD players, CD players. **Dining:** On the Twenty, see separate listing. **Leisure Activities:** spa. **Business Services:** meeting rooms. **Cards:** AX, DC, MC, VI.

SOME UNITS

🍽 ✕ DATA PORT / VCR 💻 /

──── WHERE TO DINE ────

ON THE TWENTY   **Lunch:** $15-$26   **Dinner:** $22-$38   Phone: 905/562-7313

▼▼ ▼▼ **Location:** QEW, exit 57, 3 km s on Reg Rd 24, 3 km e on Reg Rd 81, then just n; in Inn on the Twenty. 3836 Main St L0R 1S0. **Hours:** 11 am-9:30 pm. **Closed:** 12/25. **Reservations:** suggested. **Features:** Located in a quaint **Regional Canadian** village, On the Twenty was created to provide a fine menu to complement the abundance of wines produced at the adjacent Cave Springs Winery. The chef focuses on using the freshest of local produce and home-grown herbs in the creative, ever-changing menu. Diners can take in a wonderful view of the attractive surrounding countryside from the large panoramic windows and will find themselves surrounded by an abundance of fresh flowers and plants. Dressy casual; cocktails. **Parking:** on-site. **Cards:** AX, DC, MC, VI. **Historic**

✕

KAPUSKASING pop. 9,238

──── WHERE TO STAY ────

COMFORT INN   *Book at aaa.com*   Phone: (705)335-8583

▼▼ ▼▼	5/1-9/30 & 1/1-4/30	1P: $95	2P: $104
	10/1-12/31	1P: $90	2P: $99

Small-scale Hotel Location: Hwy 11, corner of Brunelle Rd. Located in a commercial area. 172 Government Rd E P5N 2W9. **Fax:** 705/337-6535. **Facility:** 66 one-bedroom standard units. 2 stories (no elevator), interior corridors. **Parking:** on-site, winter plug-ins. **Terms:** 14 day cancellation notice, pets (in smoking units). **Amenities:** hair dryers. *Some:* irons. **Guest Services:** valet laundry. **Cards:** AX, CB, DC, DS, JC, MC, VI.

SOME UNITS

ASK SD 🛏 🍽 📷 DATA PORT / ✕ 💻 🖥 💻 /

KENORA pop. 15,838

──── WHERE TO STAY ────

**BEST WESTERN LAKESIDE INN & CONVENTION
CENTRE**   *Book at aaa.com*   Phone: (807)468-5521

▼▼ ▼▼	5/1-9/30	1P: $120-$299	2P: $130-$299	XP: $10	F
	10/1-4/30	1P: $110-$299	2P: $120-$299	XP: $10	F

Small-scale Hotel Location: Centre. Located at the lakeshore. 470 First Ave S P9N 1W5. **Fax:** 807/468-4734. **Facility:** 94 units. 93 one-bedroom standard units. 1 one-bedroom suite. 11 stories, interior corridors. **Parking:** on-site, winter plug-ins. **Terms:** 7 day cancellation notice, small pets only (with prior approval). **Amenities:** high-speed Internet (fee), voice mail, irons, hair dryers. **Dining:** The Waterside Restaurant, see separate listing. **Pool(s):** small heated indoor. **Leisure Activities:** sauna, boat dock. **Guest Services:** valet laundry. **Business Services:** conference facilities. **Cards:** AX, DC, MC, VI.

SOME UNITS

ASK SD 🛏 🍽 ⬇ 🐾 📷 DATA PORT 💻 / ✕ /

COMFORT INN   *Book at aaa.com*   Phone: (807)468-8845

▼▼ ▼▼	6/1-8/31	1P: $90-$115	2P: $100-$125	XP: $10	F16
	5/1-5/31 & 9/1-4/30	1P: $80-$101	2P: $90-$111	XP: $10	F16

Motel **Location:** 1.5 km e. Located in a commercial area. 1230 Hwy 17 E P9N 1L9. **Fax:** 807/468-1588. **Facility:** 75 one-bedroom standard units. 2 stories (no elevator), interior corridors. **Parking:** on-site, winter plug-ins. **Terms:** package plans, small pets only (in smoking units). **Amenities:** irons, hair dryers. **Leisure Activities:** *Fee:* game room. **Guest Services:** valet laundry. **Business Services:** meeting rooms. **Cards:** AX, CB, DC, DS, JC, MC, VI.

SOME UNITS

ASK SD 🛏 📷 DATA PORT / ✕ 💻 🖥 /

DAYS INN   *Book at aaa.com*   Phone: 807/468-2003

6/1-8/31   1P: $95   2P: $102

5/1-5/31 & 9/1-4/30   1P: $87   2P: $93

Small-scale Hotel **Location:** On Hwy 17, 1 km e. Located in a commercial area. 920 Hwy 17 E P9N 1L9 (PO Box 121). Fax: 807/468-8551. **Facility:** 51 one-bedroom standard units, some with whirlpools. 2 stories, interior/exterior corridors. **Parking:** on-site, winter plug-ins. **Terms:** small pets only (in designated units). **Amenities:** video library (fee), voice mail, hair dryers. **Pool(s):** small heated indoor. **Leisure Activities:** whirlpool, waterslide, exercise room. **Business Services:** meeting rooms. **Cards:** AX, DC, MC, VI.

SOME UNITS

(ASK) (S/D) 🐾 🍴 🍽 🏊 🍴 (DATA PORT) 🖥 💻 / 🗙 (VCR) / FEE

KENORA TRAVELODGE   *Book at aaa.com*   Phone: (807)468-3155

(CAA) (SAVE)   5/1-9/15   1P: $80-$120   2P: $105-$140

9/16-4/30   1P: $80-$105   2P: $90-$110

Location: 1 km e. Located in a commercial area. 800 Hwy 17 E P9N 1L9. Fax: 807/468-4780. **Facility:** 43 one-bedroom standard units, some with efficiencies and/or whirlpools. 2 stories (no elevator), interior corridors. Small-scale Hotel **Parking:** on-site, winter plug-ins. **Terms:** small pets only (in smoking units). **Amenities:** voice mail, hair dryers. *Some:* DVD players. **Dining:** 6 am-10 pm, cocktails. **Pool(s):** outdoor, heated indoor. **Leisure Activities:** sauna, whirlpool, playground, exercise room. **Business Services:** meeting rooms. **Cards:** AX, DC, MC, VI. **Special Amenities:** free local telephone calls and free newspaper.

SOME UNITS

(S/D) 🐾 🍴 🍽 🏊 🍴 📽 (DATA PORT) 🖥 💻 / 🗙 (VCR) 📷 /

──────── WHERE TO DINE ────────

THE WATERSIDE RESTAURANT   **Lunch:** $7-$15   **Dinner:** $12-$29   Phone: 807/467-8439

Location: Centre; in Best Western Lakeside Inn & Convention Centre. 470 First Ave S P9N 1W5. **Hours:** 6 am-3 & 5-10 pm; hours vary off season. Closed: 12/25, 12/26. **Reservations:** suggested. **Features:** Located on the Canadian top floor of a hotel with views of the Lake of the Woods, The Waterside offers both local and Continental specialties as well as a few delectable vegetarian and vegan creations. A hearty breakfast buffet is available until 3 pm. Casual dress; cocktails. **Parking:** on-site. **Cards:** AX, DC, MC, VI.

🍴 🗙

KILLALOE pop. 700

──────── WHERE TO STAY ────────

ANNIE'S INN   Phone: (613)757-0950

All Year [BP]   1P: $50   2P: $65-$95   XP: $15   F12

Location: Hwy 60, exit Maple St, 1 blk to Roche St, then w; driveway entrance is at the end of the street. Located in a Bed & Breakfast quiet area. 67 Roche St K0J 2A0 (Box 250). Fax: 613/757-0973. **Facility:** This large, newer home's grounds border a pond where guests may canoe or skate, depending on the season. 5 units. 4 one-bedroom standard units. 1 two-bedroom suite with kitchen and whirlpool. 2 stories (no elevator), interior corridors. **Parking:** on-site, winter plug-ins. **Terms:** office hours 8 am-9 pm, 7 day cancellation notice-fee imposed, weekly rates available, package plans. **Amenities:** *Some:* hair dryers. **Leisure Activities:** boating, canoeing, ice skating, hiking trails. **Cards:** AX, DC, MC, VI.

SOME UNITS

(ASK) 🗙 🗙 📽 🍴 / (VCR) 🖥 📷 /

KIMBERLEY

──────── WHERE TO STAY ────────

──────── *The following lodging was either not evaluated or did not* ────────
meet AAA rating requirements but is listed for your information only.

TALISMAN MOUNTAIN RESORT   Phone: 519/599-2520

[fyi]   Not evaluated. **Location:** 150 Talisman Mountain Dr N0C 1G0. Facilities, services, and decor characterize a mid-range property.

KINCARDINE pop. 11,029

──────── WHERE TO STAY ────────

──────── *The following lodging was either not evaluated or did not* ────────
meet AAA rating requirements but is listed for your information only.

BEST WESTERN GOVERNOR'S INN   Phone: 519/396-8242

[fyi]   Not evaluated. **Location:** Jct Hwy 21. 791 Durham St N2Z 1M4. Facilities, services, and decor characterize a mid-range property.

──────── WHERE TO DINE ────────

ERIE BELLE ENGLISH PUB   **Lunch:** $4-$10   **Dinner:** $4-$10   Phone: 519/396-4331

Location: 1/2 blk from Lake Huron; downtown. 259 Harbour St N2Z 2Y9. **Hours:** 11 am-9 pm; to 10 pm 6/1-8/31. Closed: 12/25. **Reservations:** suggested. **Features:** The rustic pub-style decor with stucco, weathered English wood walls and stained glass is the perfect setting for traditional English fare featuring fish and chips, steak and kidney pie and a good selection of imported beer. Patio dining is offered in season. Casual dress; cocktails. **Parking:** on-site. **Cards:** AX, DC, DS, MC, VI.

🍴 🗙

KINGSTON pop. 114,195

———— WHERE TO STAY ————

AMBASSADOR RESORT HOTEL   *Book at aaa.com*   **Phone:** (613)548-3605

	5/1-10/29	1P: $125-$219	2P: $125-$219	XP: $15 F18
	10/30-4/30	1P: $105-$175	2P: $105-$175	XP: $15 F18

Small-scale Hotel   **Location:** Hwy 401, exit 613 (Sydenham Rd), 3 km se. Located in a commercial area. 1550 Princess St K7M 9E3. Fax: 613/548-4673. **Facility:** 251 units. 249 one-bedroom standard units, some with whirlpools. 2 one-bedroom suites ($250-$350) with whirlpools. 6 stories, interior corridors. *Bath:* combo or shower only. **Parking:** on-site, winter plug-ins. **Terms:** check-in 4 pm. **Amenities:** video games (fee), voice mail, irons, hair dryers. *Some:* CD players, high-speed Internet. **Dining:** Mellow D's, see separate listing. **Pool(s):** heated indoor, wading. **Leisure Activities:** sauna, whirlpool, waterslide, putting green, exercise room, shuffleboard. *Fee:* racquetball court, game room. **Guest Services:** gift shop, valet and coin laundry, beauty salon. **Business Services:** conference facilities. **Cards:** AX, CB, DC, DS, JC, MC, VI.
(See color ad below)

SOME UNITS
ASK 〔❙❙〕 〔♟❙〕 🛶 ✗ 🐾 DATA PORT 💻 / ✗ VCR 🔒 🖨 /
                                                FEE   FEE   FEE

BEST WESTERN FIRESIDE INN   *Book at aaa.com*   **Phone:** (613)549-2211

(CAA) (SAVE)	1/1-4/30	1P: $164-$174	2P: $169-$199	XP: $20 F17
	5/1-10/31	1P: $164-$174	2P: $174-$194	XP: $20 F17
	11/1-12/31	1P: $159-$172	2P: $169-$192	XP: $20 F17

Small-scale Hotel   **Location:** Hwy 401, exit 615 (Sir John A MacDonald Blvd), 4 km sw. Located in a commercial area. 1217 Princess St K7M 3E1. Fax: 613/549-4523. **Facility:** 77 units. 69 one-bedroom standard units, some with whirlpools. 8 one-bedroom suites with whirlpools. 2 stories (no elevator), interior corridors. **Parking:** on-site, winter plug-ins. **Terms:** 3% service charge. **Amenities:** high-speed Internet, safes, irons, hair dryers. *Some:* DVD players, CD players. **Dining:** Bistro Stefan, see separate listing. **Pool(s):** heated outdoor. **Guest Services:** valet laundry. **Business Services:** meeting rooms. **Cards:** AX, CB, DC, DS, MC, VI. **Special Amenities:** free local telephone calls and free newspaper.

SOME UNITS
S/D ❄ 〔❙❙〕 〔♟❙〕 🛶 🐾 🔒 💻 / ✗ VCR DATA PORT /
                                            FEE

COMFORT INN   *Book at aaa.com*   **Phone:** (613)546-9500

(CAA) (SAVE)	7/1-9/30	1P: $99-$139	2P: $109-$169	XP: $10 F18
	5/1-6/30 & 1/1-4/30	1P: $90-$130	2P: $99-$139	XP: $10 F18
	10/1-12/31	1P: $95-$125	2P: $99-$139	XP: $10 F18

Small-scale Hotel   **Location:** Hwy 401, exit 617 (Division St), 0.3 km s to Dalton Ave. Located in a commerical area. 55 Warne Crescent K7K 6Z5. Fax: 613/546-9361. **Facility:** 103 one-bedroom standard units. 2 stories (no elevator), interior corridors. **Parking:** on-site, winter plug-ins. **Terms:** package plans, small pets only ($100 deposit, in designated units). **Amenities:** hair dryers. *Some:* irons. **Guest Services:** valet laundry. **Cards:** AX, CB, DC, DS, JC, MC, VI.

SOME UNITS
S/D 〔❙〕 〔♟❙〕 🐾 💻 / ✗ DATA PORT 🔒 🖨 /
                                  FEE   FEE   FEE

COMFORT INN   *Book at aaa.com*   **Phone:** (613)549-5550

	7/1-9/30	1P: $99-$139	2P: $109-$169	XP: $10 F18
	5/1-6/30 & 1/1-4/30	1P: $90-$130	2P: $99-$139	XP: $10 F18
	10/1-12/31	1P: $95-$125	2P: $99-$139	XP: $10 F18

Small-scale Hotel   **Location:** Hwy 401, exit 613 (Sydenham Rd), 4 km se. Located in a commercial/residential area. 1454 Princess St K7M 3E5. Fax: 613/549-1388. **Facility:** 59 one-bedroom standard units. 2 stories (no elevator), interior corridors. **Parking:** on-site, winter plug-ins. **Terms:** package plans, small pets only ($100 deposit, in designated units). **Amenities:** hair dryers. **Guest Services:** valet laundry. **Cards:** AX, CB, DC, DS, JC, MC, VI.

SOME UNITS
ASK S/D 〔❙〕 〔♟❙〕 🐾 💻 / ✗ DATA PORT 🔒 🖨 /
                                      FEE   FEE   FEE

REDEFINING HOSPITALITY

- 251 Deluxe Rooms, 24 with Whirlpool
- **Indoor Water Park** with New 100' Waterslide, Pool, Sauna, Whirlpool and Exercise Room
- Wireless High Speed Internet Access
- 19 Meeting Rooms - largest seats 600
- New JM's Restaurant & Lounge
- Kids Stay FREE!

AMBASSADOR
CONFERENCE RESORT
KINGSTON

1550 Princess Street • Kingston • 548-3605 • **1-800-267-7880** www.ambassadorhotel.com

DAYS INN KINGSTON HOTEL & CONVENTION
CENTRE *Book at aaa.com*

Phone: (613)546-3661

CAA SAVE

7/1-9/30	1P: $99-$122	2P: $109-$132	XP: $10 F18
10/1-4/30	1P: $88-$115	2P: $98-$125	XP: $10 F18
5/1-6/30	1P: $83-$110	2P: $93-$120	XP: $10 F18

Location: Hwy 401, exit 617 (Division St), south side. Located in a commercial area. 33 Benson St K7K 5W2. **Small-scale Hotel** Fax: 613/544-4126. **Facility:** 162 one-bedroom standard units. 2-3 stories (no elevator), interior corridors. **Parking:** on-site, winter plug-ins. **Terms:** package plans. **Amenities:** video games (fee), voice mail, hair dryers. *Some:* irons. **Dining:** 24 hours, wine/beer only. **Pool(s):** outdoor. **Leisure Activities:** exercise room. **Guest Services:** valet and coin laundry. **Business Services:** conference facilities, PC (fee). **Cards:** AX, CB, DC, DS, JC, MC, VI. **Special Amenities:** free local telephone calls and free newspaper. *(See color ad below)*

SOME UNITS

THE EXECUTIVE MOTEL INN & SUITES

Phone: 613/549-1620

CAA SAVE

5/1-10/15 [CP]	1P: $75-$99	2P: $89-$125	XP: $8 D10
10/16-4/30	1P: $59-$79	2P: $69-$109	XP: $8 D10

Location: Hwy 401, exit 623, 8 km s, then 2 km e. Located in a rural area. 794 Hwy 2 E K7L 4V1. Fax: 613/547-9698. **Facility:** 42 units. 22 one- and 4 two-bedroom standard units, some with efficiencies or kitchens. 16 one-bedroom suites ($99-$149). 2 stories (no elevator), exterior corridors. **Parking:** on-site, winter plug-ins.
Motel **Terms:** office hours 7 am-11 pm, 3 day cancellation notice-fee imposed, small pets only ($10 fee). **Amenities:** voice mail, hair dryers. *Some:* high-speed Internet, irons. **Pool(s):** outdoor. **Cards:** AX, DC, MC, VI. **Special Amenities:** free continental breakfast and free local telephone calls.

SOME UNITS

FOUR POINTS BY SHERATON HOTEL & SUITES
KINGSTON *Book at aaa.com*

Phone: (613)544-4434

5/1-10/29	1P: $189-$280	2P: $189-$280	XP: $15 F18
10/30-4/30	1P: $169-$199	2P: $169-$199	XP: $15 F18

Small-scale Hotel **Location:** Hwy 401, exit 615 (Sir John A MacDonald Blvd), left on King St, then right on Clarence St; downtown. Located in the historic business area. 285 King St E K7L 3B1. Fax: 613/548-1782. **Facility:** 171 units. 128 one-bedroom standard units. 43 one-bedroom suites ($229-$429), some with whirlpools. 9 stories, interior corridors. **Bath:** combo or shower only. **Parking:** on-site (fee). **Terms:** cancellation fee imposed, package plans. **Amenities:** video games (fee), high-speed Internet, voice mail, irons, hair dryers. **Dining:** Old Stones, see separate listing. **Pool(s):** heated indoor. **Leisure Activities:** sauna, whirlpool, exercise room. **Guest Services:** valet and coin laundry. **Business Services:** conference facilities, business center. **Cards:** AX, CB, DC, DS, JC, MC, VI. *(See color ad p 5 & p 275)*

SOME UNITS

GREEN ACRES INN

Phone: 613/546-1796

CAA SAVE

5/1-10/15	1P: $119-$149	2P: $129-$169	XP: $10 F12
10/16-4/30	1P: $89-$129	2P: $129-$139	XP: $10 F12

Location: Hwy 401, exit 611; Hwy 38, 3 km s, 0.5 km e on Princess St (Hwy 2). 2480 Princess St K7M 3G4. Fax: 613/542-5521. **Facility:** 31 units. 27 one-bedroom standard units, some with whirlpools. 3 one- and 1
Motel two-bedroom suites ($195-$275), some with efficiencies, kitchens and/or whirlpools. 1 story, exterior corridors. **Parking:** on-site, winter plug-ins. **Terms:** office hours 7 am-11 pm, cancellation fee imposed, package plans. **Amenities:** video library, irons, hair dryers. *Some:* DVD players, CD players, dual phone lines. **Pool(s):** heated outdoor. **Leisure Activities:** playground. *Fee:* massage. **Guest Services:** valet and coin laundry. **Business Services:** meeting rooms. **Cards:** AX, DC, MC, VI. **Special Amenities:** free local telephone calls and free newspaper. *(See color ad p 275)*

SOME UNITS

1-800-DAYS INN
www.daysinn.ca

DAYS INN
& CONFERENCE CENTRE
KINGSTON

Come On Inn...

- Free weekday newspaper and in-room coffee
- Free high-speed Internet
- Denny's restaurant open 24 hours
- Outdoor pool and patio; fitness room
- Pay per view movies, Nintendo
- Close to all major attractions
- Free membership at GoodLife Fitness while registered

trip**rewards**
It's fun to get more.

Days Inn - Kingston 33 Benson Street
Kingston, ON K7K 5W2

Tel	Toll Free	Fax
613-546-3661	800 267 7888	613 544 4126

www.daysinnkingston.com

Email: info@daysinnkingston.com

HOCHELAGA INN · *Book at aaa.com*   Phone: (613)549-5534

(CAA) (SAVE)

	7/1-10/31	1P: $145-$185	2P: $155-$195	XP: $20
	5/1-6/30	1P: $135-$160	2P: $145-$175	XP: $20
	11/1-4/30	1P: $115-$145	2P: $125-$155	XP: $20

Historic Bed & Breakfast

Location: Corner of Earl St; centre. Located in a historic neighborhood. 24 Sydenham St S K7L 3G9. Fax: 613/549-7870. **Facility:** A turret adds distinctive architectural detail to the exterior and interior of this elegant Victorian mansion built in the 1880s. Smoke free premises. 23 one-bedroom standard units, some with whirlpools. 3 stories (no elevator), interior corridors. *Bath:* combo or shower only. **Parking:** on-site, winter plug-ins. **Terms:** [ECP] meal plan available. **Amenities:** hair dryers. *Some:* DVD players, irons. **Guest Services:** valet laundry. **Business Services:** meeting rooms. **Cards:** AX, MC, VI. **Special Amenities: free expanded continental breakfast and free room upgrade (subject to availability with advance reservations).**

HOLIDAY INN KINGSTON-WATERFRONT   *Book at aaa.com*   Phone: (613)549-8400

(CAA) (SAVE)

| | 5/1-10/31 | 1P: $189-$249 | 2P: $199-$259 | XP: $15 | F18 |
| | 11/1-4/30 | 1P: $149-$199 | 2P: $169-$199 | XP: $15 | F18 |

Location: Corner of Ontario St; centre of downtown. 2 Princess St K7L 1A1. Fax: 613/549-3508. **Facility:** 197 units. 195 one-bedroom standard units. 2 two-bedroom suites. 6 stories, interior corridors. *Bath:* combo or **Small-scale Hotel** shower only. **Parking:** on-site (fee). **Terms:** package plans. **Amenities:** voice mail, irons, hair dryers. *Some:* high-speed Internet, dual phone lines. **Dining:** 7 am-10:30 & 5:30-9 pm, Sun 7 am-3 & 5:30-9 pm, cocktails. **Pool(s):** heated outdoor, heated indoor. **Leisure Activities:** sauna, whirlpool, indoor recreation area, basketball. *Fee:* game room. **Guest Services:** valet and coin laundry. **Business Services:** conference facilities. **Cards:** AX, DC, DS, MC, VI. *(See color ad card insert)*

SOME UNITS

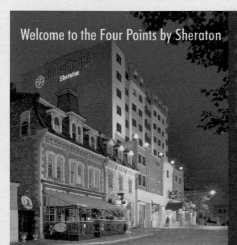

Welcome to the Four Points by Sheraton

- Picturesque views of Lake Ontario or Downtown Kingston
- 171 Deluxe Rooms - 47 Suites
- Wireless High Speed Internet Access
- Indoor Pool, Whirlpool, Sauna and Exercise Room
- Old Stones Restaurant and Lounge
- 12 meeting rooms seating up to 360 guests
- On-site underground parking

285 KING STREET EAST, KINGSTON • 544-4434 • 1-888-478-4333 • www.fourpointshotelkingston.com

GREEN ACRES INN
"...all the charm and attention to detail of a Country Inn..."

Our attractively decorated, well appointed rooms and suites are set amidst beautifully landscaped grounds and perennial gardens. We are ideally located 5 minutes from downtown Kingston with excellent shopping and dining nearby.

- Fridges
- Microwaves
- Coffee makers
- Outdoor Pool
- Laundry
- Fabulous Fireplace and Whirlpool Signature Suites
- Apartment Suites

2480 Princess Street
www.greenacresinn.com
613-546-1796 RESERVATIONS 1-800-267-7889

HOTEL BELVEDERE

Historic Bed & Breakfast

All Year [CP] 1P: $110-$250 2P: $110-$250 XP: $20 F13
Location: Between West and Lower Union sts; centre. Located in a historic neighborhood. 141 King St E K7L 2Z9. Fax: 613/546-4692. **Facility:** This red-brick Victorian's history as an inn dates to 1892; breakfast is served on the terrace in summer. 20 one-bedroom standard units. 3 stories (no elevator), interior corridors. *Bath:* combo or shower only. **Parking:** on-site. **Amenities:** high-speed Internet. *Some:* DVD players. **Guest Services:** valet laundry. **Business Services:** meeting rooms. **Cards:** AX, DC, JC, MC, VI.

Phone: (613)548-1565

SOME UNITS

(ASK) [📷] [DATA PORT] / (VCR) [🔌] /

HOWARD JOHNSON CONFEDERATION PLACE HOTEL   *Book at aaa.com*

Small-scale Hotel

(CAA) (SAVE)

6/1-9/5 1P: $159-$209 2P: $169-$239 XP: $10 F18
9/6-4/30 1P: $149-$179 2P: $159-$199 XP: $10 F18
5/1-5/31 1P: $119-$149 2P: $139-$179 XP: $10 F18
Location: Centre of downtown. Located in a commercial area. 237 Ontario St K7L 2Z4. Fax: 613/549-1508. **Facility:** 94 one-bedroom standard units, some with whirlpools. 6 stories, interior corridors. **Parking:** on-site (fee). **Terms:** small pets only ($15 fee, 1st floor units). **Amenities:** voice mail. *Some:* irons, hair dryers. **Dining:** 7 am-11 pm; hours vary off season, cocktails, nightclub. **Pool(s):** small heated outdoor. **Leisure Activities:** whirlpool, exercise room. **Guest Services:** valet laundry. **Business Services:** conference facilities. **Cards:** AX, CB, DC, DS, JC, MC, VI. **Special Amenities:** free local telephone calls and free newspaper.

Phone: (613)549-6300

SOME UNITS

[S/D] [🛏] [🍴] [🏊] [📷] [DATA PORT] [☕] / [✕] [🔌] /

FEE

PAINTED LADY INN

Historic Bed & Breakfast

All Year [BP] 1P: $89-$125 2P: $95-$165
Location: Between Sydenham and Clergy sts. Located in a historic residential area. 181 William St K7L 2E1. **Facility:** This aptly named grand Victorian mansion dates from 1870 and retains some furnishings original to the house. Smoke free premises. 9 one-bedroom standard units, some with efficiencies and/or whirlpools. 3 stories (no elevator), interior/exterior corridors. *Bath:* combo or shower only. **Parking:** on-site. **Terms:** office hours 9 am-10:30 pm, check-in 4 pm, 2 night minimum stay - weekends, 7 day cancellation notice. **Amenities:** hair dryers. *Some:* CD players. **Cards:** AX, MC, VI.

Phone: 613/545-0422

SOME UNITS

[✕] [📷] / [W] [DATA PORT] [🔒] [🔌] [📠] [☕] /

PEACHTREE INN   *Book at aaa.com*

Small-scale Hotel

(CAA) (SAVE)

7/1-4/30 [ECP] 1P: $90 2P: $100 XP: $10 F18
5/1-6/30 [ECP] 1P: $85 2P: $95 XP: $10 F18
Location: Hwy 401, exit 615 (Sir John A MacDonald Blvd), 4 km sw. Located above a shopping plaza. 1187 Princess St K7M 3E1. Fax: 613/546-9122. **Facility:** 76 one-bedroom standard units. 3 stories, interior corridors. **Parking:** on-site. **Terms:** cancellation fee imposed, small pets only (in smoking units). **Amenities:** hair dryers. *Some:* irons. **Guest Services:** valet laundry. **Business Services:** meeting rooms. **Cards:** AX, DC, DS, MC, VI.

Phone: 613/546-4411

SOME UNITS

[🛏] [🍴] [DATA PORT] [☕] / [✕] [VCR] [🔌] [📠] /

FEE FEE FEE

$2.50 DISCOUNT to AAA Cardholders

KINGSTON 1000 ISLANDS CRUISES
Food, Fun & Entertainment Ships!

★ 1½ or 3hr Sightseeing
★ Daily Lunch Cruise
★ Sunset Dinner Cruises
★ Live Entertainment

Reservations & Departures
1 Brock St., Kingston, ON K7L 1A2
1-800-848-0108

$2.50 DISCOUNT to AAA Cardholders

Triple Deck Island Queen   Reserve Online www.1000islandscruises.ca   Air Conditioned Island Star

RADISSON HOTEL KINGSTON HARBOURFRONT _Book at aaa.com_   Phone: (613)549-8100

(CAA) (SAVE)

7/1-10/31	1P: $189-$375	2P: $189-$375	XP: $15	F17
5/1-6/30	1P: $169-$350	2P: $169-$350	XP: $15	F17
11/1-4/30	1P: $129-$325	2P: $129-$325	XP: $15	F17

Location: On the harbour at the foot of Johnson St; downtown. 1 Johnson St K7L 5H7. Fax: 613/547-3241.
Small-scale Hotel **Facility:** 126 units. 125 one-bedroom standard units. 1 one-bedroom suite ($300-$450). 6 stories, interior corridors. **Parking:** on-site (fee). **Terms:** cancellation fee imposed. **Amenities:** voice mail, irons, hair dryers. *Fee:* video games, high-speed Internet. *Some:* CD players, honor bars. **Dining:** AquaTerra by Clark Restaubistro, see separate listing. **Pool(s):** heated indoor. **Leisure Activities:** whirlpool, steamroom, exercise room. **Guest Services:** valet laundry. **Business Services:** meeting rooms. **Cards:** AX, DC, DS, MC, VI. **Special Amenities: free local telephone calls and free newspaper.** *(See color ad below & p 521)*

SOME UNITS

(S D) (YI) (≈) (X) (▪) (DATA PORT) (▪) / (X) (▮) (▣) /
FEE

THE SECRET GARDEN BED & BREAKFAST INN   Phone: 613/531-9884

All Year   1P: $113-$139   2P: $139-$169
Location: Jct William St. 73 Sydenham St K7L 3H3. Fax: 613/531-9502. **Facility:** The living room, library and guest rooms of this centrally located 1888 home are furnished with antiques. Smoke free premises. 7 one-bedroom standard units. 3 stories (no elevator), interior corridors. *Bath:* combo or shower only. **Parking:** on-site. **Terms:** office hours 10 am-10 pm, check-in 4 pm, 2 night minimum stay - seasonal, 3 day cancellation notice-fee imposed, package plans, no pets allowed (owner's cat on premises). **Amenities:** hair dryers. **Cards:** AX, DC, MC, VI.

Historic Bed & Breakfast

SOME UNITS

(X) / (P) (DATA PORT) (Z) /

SUPER 8   _Book at aaa.com_   Phone: (613)542-7395

7/1-9/30	1P: $70-$189	2P: $80-$199	XP: $15	F12
5/1-6/30	1P: $59-$169	2P: $75-$179	XP: $10	F12
1/1-4/30	1P: $50-$155	2P: $65-$165	XP: $10	F12
10/1-12/31	1P: $50-$149	2P: $65-$155	XP: $10	F12

Small-scale Hotel

Location: Centre. Located in a commercial area. 720 Princess St K7L 1G2. Fax: 613/542-2675. **Facility:** 51 one-bedroom standard units, some with whirlpools. 2 stories (no elevator), interior corridors. **Parking:** on-site. **Cards:** AX, MC, VI.

SOME UNITS

(ASK) (S D) (YI+) / (X) (DATA PORT) (▮) (▣) /

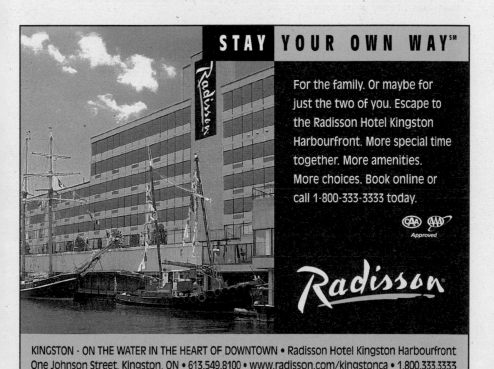

STAY YOUR OWN WAY℠

For the family. Or maybe for just the two of you. Escape to the Radisson Hotel Kingston Harbourfront. More special time together. More amenities. More choices. Book online or call 1-800-333-3333 today.

(CAA) (AAA) Approved

Radisson

KINGSTON - ON THE WATER IN THE HEART OF DOWNTOWN • Radisson Hotel Kingston Harbourfront
One Johnson Street, Kingston, ON • 613.549.8100 • www.radisson.com/kingstonca • 1.800.333.3333

—————— **WHERE TO DINE** ——————

AMADEUS CAFE RESTAURANT   Lunch: $4-$7   Dinner: $9-$15   Phone: 613/546-7468
Location: Between Montreal and Bagot sts; centre. 170 Princess St K7L 1B1. **Hours:** 11:30 am-10 pm. Closed: 12/25; also Sun. **Reservations:** suggested. **Features:** This small Austrian restaurant with a neat, unpretentious decor boasts selections of homemade noodles, goulash specials, schnitzel, sausage, pasta and steak. A secluded Bavarian beer garden patio is open in summer. Spiced wine is served in winter.
Austrian
Casual dress; cocktails. **Parking:** street. **Cards:** AX, MC, VI.

AQUATERRA BY CLARK RESTAUBISTRO   Lunch: $9-$11   Dinner: $15-$35   Phone: 613/549-8100
Location: On the harbour at the foot of Johnson St; downtown; in Radisson Hotel Kingston Harbourfront. 1 Johnson St K7L 5H7. **Hours:** 6:30 am-11 pm. **Reservations:** suggested. **Features:** Views of the yacht basin, Royal Military College and the ferry passing en route to Wolfe Island are hard to beat. Equally pleasing are the Certified Angus beef steaks and seafood. Dressy casual; cocktails. **Parking:** on-site. **Cards:** AX, DC, DS,
Steak & Seafood
JC, MC, VI.

ATOMICA PIZZERIA & BAR   Lunch: $8-$18   Dinner: $8-$18   Phone: 613/530-2118
Location: Centre. 71 Brock St K7L 1R8. **Hours:** 11:30 am-11 pm, Fri & Sat-midnight. Closed: 12/25. **Reservations:** accepted. **Features:** A wide assortment of gourmet toppings makes selecting an individual thin-crust pizza fun. The small dining room is interesting, and the wall behind the bar, which changes colors, is best viewed at night when its full effect can be experienced. Service is casual, friendly and efficient.
Pizza
Casual dress; cocktails. **Parking:** street. **Cards:** AX, DS, MC, VI.

AUNT LUCY'S DINNER HOUSE   Lunch: $7-$11   Dinner: $9-$25   Phone: 613/542-2729
Location: Jct Portsmouth Ave and Princess St (Hwy 2). 1399 Princess St K7M 3E9. **Hours:** 11:30 am-9:30 pm, Fri & Sat-10 pm, Sun 10 am-9:30 pm. **Reservations:** accepted. **Features:** For more than 55 years, the restaurant has nurtured a comfortable atmosphere. Efficient, friendly servers deliver high-quality steaks, fish and other items, such as pasta, salads and freshly baked desserts. Casual dress; cocktails. **Parking:** on-
Canadian
site. **Cards:** AX, MC, VI.

BISTRO STEFAN   Dinner: $19-$33   Phone: 613/549-2211
Location: Hwy 401, exit 615 (Sir John A MacDonald Blvd), 4 km sw; in Best Western Fireside Inn. 1217 Princess St K7M 3E1. **Hours:** 7 am-11 & 5-10 pm. Closed: 12/25. **Reservations:** suggested. **Features:** The comfortable bistro's warm, inviting atmosphere welcomes patrons to relax over carefully prepared and creatively presented dishes. Friendly, professional servers make some dishes tableside. Casual dress; cocktails.
Continental
Parking: on-site. **Cards:** AX, DC, MC, VI.

CASA DOMENICO   Lunch: $11-$17   Dinner: $14-$37   Phone: 613/542-0870
Location: Between King and Ontario sts; centre. 35 Brock St K7L 1R7. **Hours:** 11:30 am-10 pm, Fri & Sat-11 pm, Sun 5 pm-10 pm. Closed: 12/25. **Reservations:** suggested. **Features:** Casa Domenico, located across from historic City Hall and Market Square, offers a good selection of fresh pasta, chicken, seafood, steak and wine by the glass. House specialties include duck, rack of lamb and a wide array of homemade
Italian
desserts. Casual dress; cocktails. **Parking:** street. **Cards:** AX, DC, MC, VI.

CHEZ PIGGY   Lunch: $6-$12   Dinner: $13-$26   Phone: 613/549-7673
Location: Between King and Wellington sts; downtown. 68R Princess St K7L 4X8. **Hours:** 11:30 am-10 pm. Closed: 12/25, 12/26. **Reservations:** accepted. **Features:** Built as a livery stable in 1810 and now attractively restored, the old stable yard serves as an outdoor patio in summer. International home cooking with Thai, North African and Spanish influences showcases the eatery's delightful emphasis on the unusual. Casual
International
dress; cocktails. **Parking:** street. **Cards:** AX, DC, MC, VI.

CURRY ORIGINAL   Lunch: $6-$7   Dinner: $10-$15   Phone: 613/531-9376
Location: Centre. 253A Ontario St K7L 2Z4. **Hours:** 11:30 am-2 & 5-9:30 pm, Fri & Sat-10 pm, Sun 5 pm-9 pm. Closed: 1/1, 12/25, 12/26; also Mon. **Reservations:** accepted. **Features:** This restaurant, offering high quality, well-prepared Indian cuisine, has exposed limestone walls and a subtle Indian decor. A window on the kitchen allows the tandoor, a clay oven, to be seen in operation. Casual dress; cocktails. **Parking:**
Indian
street. **Cards:** AX, DC, MC, VI.

CURRY VILLAGE   Lunch: $6-$8   Dinner: $12-$15   Phone: 613/542-5010
Location: Between Montreal and Bagot sts; centre. 169A Princess St K7L 1A9. **Hours:** 11:30 am-2 & 5-9:30 pm, Fri & Sat-10 pm. Closed: 1/1, 12/24, 12/25; also Sun. **Reservations:** accepted. **Features:** Some Bangladeshi specials and vegetarian dishes. Butter chicken and Sag lamb are two popular and mild dishes. For those who prefer spicy hot, try the Vinda Loo. Friendly, efficient service and a high-quality product have kept this
Indian
restaurant a favourite. Casual dress; cocktails. **Parking:** street. **Cards:** AX, DC, MC, VI.

GOLDEN ROOSTER DELICATESSEN   Lunch: $6-$8   Phone: 613/542-5676
Location: Between Bagot and Wellington sts; centre. 111 Princess St K7L 1A8. **Hours:** 7:30 am-6 pm, Sat-5 pm. Closed major holidays; also Sun. **Features:** The popular, family-owned, European-style delicatessen and cafeteria offers a wide selection of in-house baked breads, pastries, cold cuts and cheese. Daily specials are good choices. Parking is validated for vehicles in the lot behind the eatery. Casual dress; beer & wine
Continental
only. **Parking:** on-site (fee) and street.

scountho

1-877-234-8408

On th

- 34 storey
- Spectacu
  beautiful
  two-room
- 'Experier
  Adventur
  only spira
- Rooftop
  restaurar
- Steps to
  most exc
- Closest h
  Niagara

sview *Rates*

Sele

Family Fun Packages

Reserv

Hilton
Niagara Falls
Fallsview

DAYS INN

Best
Western

otels.com

ct. Stay. Save.

Select the One Choice in Niagara Falls, Canada for Discount Rates on Branded Hotels that offer a variety of Fabulous Packages & Save you Money!

GRECOS GRILL & WINE BAR   **Lunch:** $7-$10   **Dinner:** $8-$15   **Phone:** 613/542-2229
Location: Princess St at Bagot St; centre. 167 Princess St K7L 1A9. **Hours:** 11 am-11 pm, Fri & Sat-midnight, Sun-10:30 pm. Closed: 12/25, 12/26. **Reservations:** suggested. **Features:** You'll dine on authentic Greek cuisine in an attractive and relaxed atmosphere peppered with pictures of Greece on the walls and some
Greek   seating by the windows. Generous portions prevail and are served by a professional and attentive service
staff. Casual dress; cocktails. **Parking:** street. **Cards:** AX, DC, MC, VI.

KINGSTON BREWING COMPANY   **Lunch:** $8-$13   **Dinner:** $8-$13   **Phone:** 613/542-4978
Location: Centre. 34 Clarence St K7L 1W9. **Hours:** 11 am-10 pm, Thurs-Sat to midnight. Closed: 12/25; also for dinner 12/24. **Features:** The brew pub produces its own varied selections of beer and wine. An on-site smokehouse is used in the preparation of ribs and soups. The decor is busy and the atmosphere friendly.
Canadian   The patio opens seasonally. Casual dress; cocktails. **Parking:** street. **Cards:** AX, DC, MC, VI.

LE CHIEN NOIR   **Lunch:** $8-$19   **Dinner:** $10-$28   **Phone:** 613/549-5635
Location: Centre. 69 Brock St K7L 1R8. **Hours:** 11 am-10 pm, Fri & Sat-11 pm. Closed: 12/25. **Reservations:** accepted. **Features:** Among the shops in the Old Kingston area, the bistro-style restaurant presents a mixed menu listing classic French offerings from soups and salads to full meals. Seating is close,
International   and some booths are available. The atmosphere is bustling. Casual dress; cocktails. **Parking:** street.
Cards: AX, DS, MC, VI.

LUKE'S   **Lunch:** $5-$8   **Dinner:** $9-$18   **Phone:** 613/531-7745
Location: Between Clergy and Sydenham sts. 264 Princess St K7L 1B5. **Hours:** 11:30 am-2:30 & 5-8:30 pm, Fri 11:30 am-3 & 5-9 pm, Sat 11 am-3 & 5-9 pm, Sun 11 am-3 pm. Closed major holidays; also Mon. **Reservations:** suggested, weekends. **Features:** Funky and fun, this casual little restaurant is a pleasant
American   respite from a busy world. Market fresh ingredients are used in the creative preparation of soups, salads
and sandwiches, and even the half-size portions are large. Casual dress; cocktails. **Parking:** street. **Cards:** AX, VI.

MCGINNIS LANDING   **Lunch:** $6-$13   **Dinner:** $8-$22   **Phone:** 613/384-2636
Location: Hwy 33 (Bath Rd), 0.5 km e of jct Gardiners Rd. 1530 Bath Rd W K7M 4X6. **Hours:** 11 am-11 pm, Sun noon-9 pm. Closed: 12/25. **Features:** Natural pine walls and memorabilia work to create an interesting decor at this family-oriented restaurant. Booth and table seating are available. The varied menu offers high
Canadian   quality and good value. Portions are generous. This restaurant is a long-time favorite. Located a short drive
from downtown and from the Cataraqui Shopping Centre. Casual dress; cocktails. **Parking:** on-site. **Cards:** AX, DC, MC, VI.

MELLOW D'S   **Lunch:** $8-$15   **Dinner:** $10-$18   **Phone:** 613/548-3605
Location: Hwy 401, exit 613 (Sydenham Rd), 3 km se; in Ambassador Resort Hotel. 1550 Princess St K7M 9E3. **Hours:** 7 am-2 & 5-10 pm. Closed: 12/25. **Reservations:** accepted. **Features:** Steak, pasta, chicken, fish, vegetable stir-fry and children's dishes are among offerings. Insiders know that the willing kitchen will
Canadian   produce breakfast items all day. Casual dress; cocktails. **Parking:** on-site. **Cards:** AX, CB, DC, DS, JC,
MC, VI.

THE MERCHANT MACLIAM   **Lunch:** $9-$14   **Dinner:** $8-$22   **Phone:** 613/547-1313
Location: Jct Ontario St, just s. 6A Princess St K7L 1A2. **Hours:** 11:30 am-9 pm, Fri & Sat 10 am-10 pm. Closed: 1/1, 12/25. **Reservations:** accepted. **Features:** Thick greystone walls, dartboards and heavy, timber beams contribute to the pub atmosphere. The seasonal patio affords a lake view. On the menu are such items as
English   fish and chips, shepherd's pie, steak and Guinness pie, pasta, wraps, liver, pork loin and lamb shank.
Casual dress; cocktails. **Parking:** street. **Cards:** AX, DC, MC, VI.

MINOS DOWNTOWN   **Lunch:** $8-$22   **Dinner:** $14-$30   **Phone:** 613/548-4654
Location: Just w of jct Princess St. 248 Ontario St K7L 5P7. **Hours:** 11 am-2:30 & 4:30-10 pm, Sun 4:30 pm-9:30 pm. Closed: 12/25. **Reservations:** accepted. **Features:** A longtime city favorite, this restaurant serves a good variety of classic Greek dishes such as mousaka (eggplant zucchini, potato and ground beef), souvlaki
Greek   (marinated pork), dolmadakia (ground beef and rice wrapped in grape leaves) and spanakopita (spinach
and feta cheese pie). The atmosphere is upbeat. Casual dress; cocktails. **Parking:** on-site (fee) and street. **Cards:** AX, DC, MC, VI.

MINOS VILLAGE   **Lunch:** $7-$14   **Dinner:** $11-$27   **Phone:** 613/384-2021
Location: Hwy 401, exit 611, 3 km s on Hwy 38, then 0.5 km w on Princess St (Hwy 2). 2762 Princess St K7P 2W6. **Hours:** 11:30 am-2:30 & 5-10 pm, Sat from 5 pm, Sun 4:30 pm-9:30 pm. Closed: 12/25. **Reservations:** accepted. **Features:** Minos offers a good selection of appetizers, steaks, chicken dishes and
Greek   salads, in addition to traditional Greek fare. Modern decor with an abundance of plants is inviting, as is the
friendly staff. Casual dress; cocktails. **Parking:** on-site. **Cards:** AX, DC, MC, VI.

OLD STONES   **Lunch:** $8-$12   **Dinner:** $13-$23   **Phone:** 613/544-4434
Location: Hwy 401, exit 615 (Sir John A MacDonald Blvd), left on King St, then right on Clarence St; downtown; in Four Points by Sheraton Hotel & Suites Kingston. 285 King St E K7L 3B1. **Hours:** 6:30 am-10:30 pm, Sat & Sun from 7 am. **Reservations:** accepted. **Features:** The pleasant second-floor restaurant nurtures a comfortable
Canadian   atmosphere, which includes a fireplace and a spacious lounge area. The menu mixes steak, chicken, beef
and pasta choices with a good selection of wines by the glass. A patio is open in season. Casual dress; cocktails. **Parking:** on-site (fee) and street. **Cards:** AX, CB, DC, DS, JC, MC, VI.

PHNOM-PENH RESTAURANT   **Lunch:** $5-$9   **Dinner:** $5-$9   **Phone:** 613/545-2607
Location: Centre. 335 King St E K7L 1B5. **Hours:** 11:30 am-10 pm. Closed: 1/1. **Reservations:** accepted. **Features:** Knowledgeable servers help guests to navigate the Thai and Cambodian dishes offered on the menu. The restaurant's soups are a full meal in themselves. Casual dress; beer & wine only. **Parking:**
Thai   street. **Cards:** MC, VI.

THE PILOT HOUSE OF KINGSTON
Lunch: $6-$12 **Dinner:** $6-$12 **Phone:** 613/542-0222
Location: Jct Johnson St. 265 King St E K7L 3B1. **Hours:** 11 am-11 pm. Closed: 1/1, 12/25. **Features:** This cozy little pub offers hearty meals and a good selection of beer. The seasonal, outdoor patio is popular.
English
Casual dress; cocktails. **Parking:** street. **Cards:** AX, MC, VI.

RISTORANTE LUIGINA
Dinner: $14-$28 **Phone:** 613/530-3474
Location: Jct Princess St (Hwy 2), just w. 354 King St K7L 3B6. **Hours:** 5:30 pm-10 pm. Closed: 12/25; also Sun & Mon. **Reservations:** accepted. **Features:** Fine cuisine is carefully prepared and presented at the comfortable restaurant. Servers are friendly and knowledgeable. Casual dress; cocktails. **Parking:** street.
Italian
Cards: AX, MC, VI.

RIVER MILL RESTAURANT
Lunch: $7-$16 **Dinner:** $13-$26 **Phone:** 613/549-5759
Location: On the waterfront. 2 Cataraqui St K7K 1Z7. **Hours:** 11:30 am-2:30 & 5-10 pm, Sat from 5 pm. Closed major holidays; also Sun. **Reservations:** suggested. **Features:** Located on the inner harbour in an old woolen mill, this restaurant has river views and tasteful surrounds. On Friday and Saturday night there is live piano music. Rack of lamb and three medallions of beef are signature menu items and there is a well-rounded wine list. Dressy casual; cocktails. **Parking:** on-site. **Cards:** AX, DC, MC, VI.
Continental

SLEEPLESS GOAT CAFE
Lunch: $5-$7 **Dinner:** $5-$9 **Phone:** 613/545-9646
Location: Jct Wellington St, just s. 91 Princess St K7L 1A6. **Hours:** 7 am-11 pm, Fri & Sat-midnight. Closed: 1/1, 12/25. **Features:** The atmosphere at the little cafe expresses a hint of bohemia. The original art on display and the hum of lively conversation add to the fun. Almost all vegetarian except for a few traditional breakfast items, the food is carefully made from high-quality ingredients. Desserts are prepared on site. Specialty coffees go well with such selections as falafel, samosa, salads, veggie burgers and pasta. This place is different and delightful. Casual dress; cocktails. **Parking:** street. **Cards:** VI.
Vegetarian

UPSTREAM RESTAURANT
Dinner: $17-$25 **Phone:** 613/547-2253
Location: Beside Confederation Basin. 6 Clarence St K7L 5H8. **Hours:** 5 pm-11 pm. Closed: 12/24-12/26; also Sun & Mon. **Reservations:** accepted. **Features:** Downtown yet tucked away, the cozy restaurant presents a varied menu of dishes that appeal to discriminating palates. Casual dress; cocktails. **Parking:** street.
International
Cards: AX, DC, JC, MC, VI.

WOODEN HEADS
Lunch: $10-$16 **Dinner:** $10-$16 **Phone:** 613/549-1812
Location: Centre. 192 Ontario St K7L 2Y8. **Hours:** 11:30 am-12:30 am. Closed: 12/25. **Reservations:** suggested. **Features:** The restaurant is popular for its gourmet pizza, which is prepared in an open kitchen and cooked in a wood-fired brick oven. Also offered are interesting dishes with a Mediterranean-Asian flair. Patio and back courtyard seating are available in season. Casual dress; cocktails.
Pizza
Parking: street. **Cards:** AX, DC, MC, VI.

KIRKLAND LAKE pop. 8,616

——— WHERE TO STAY ———

COMFORT INN
Book at aaa.com **Phone:** (705)567-4909
2/1-4/30	1P: $70-$135	2P: $70-$155	XP: $12
10/1-1/31	1P: $60-$125	2P: $60-$145	XP: $12
5/1-9/30	1P: $65-$130	2P: $65-$130	XP: $12

Small-scale Hotel **Location:** Rt 66, just w of centre. Located in a commercial area. 455 Government Rd W P0K 1A0 (PO Box 41, CHAPUT HUGHES). Fax: 705/567-5022. **Facility:** 65 one-bedroom standard units. 2 stories (no elevator), interior corridors. **Parking:** on-site, winter plug-ins. **Terms:** package plans, pets (in smoking units). **Amenities:** irons, hair dryers. **Guest Services:** valet laundry. **Cards:** AX, CB, DC, DS, JC, MC, VI.
SOME UNITS

KITCHENER pop. 190,399

——— WHERE TO STAY ———

COMFORT INN
Book at aaa.com **Phone:** (519)894-3500
| 6/1-10/19 [ECP] | 1P: $104-$120 | 2P: $114-$130 | XP: $5 | F18 |
| 5/1-5/31 & 10/20-4/30 [ECP] | 1P: $98-$114 | 2P: $108-$124 | XP: $5 | F18 |

Small-scale Hotel **Location:** Jct Weber St, Fairway Rd and Hwy 8; 5.6 km n of Hwy 401 via Hwy 8 and Weber St. 2899 King St E N2A 1A6. Fax: 519/894-1562. **Facility:** 100 one-bedroom standard units, some with whirlpools. 2 stories (no elevator), interior corridors. **Parking:** on-site, winter plug-ins. **Terms:** package plans. **Amenities:** video games, voice mail, irons, hair dryers. *Some:* high-speed Internet, dual phone lines. **Leisure Activities:** sauna, whirlpool, exercise room. **Guest Services:** valet laundry. **Cards:** AX, CB, DC, DS, JC, MC, VI. *(See color ad p 281)*
SOME UNITS

FOUR POINTS BY SHERATON KITCHENER
Book at aaa.com **Phone:** (519)744-4141
| All Year | 1P: $89-$169 | 2P: $89-$169 |

Large-scale Hotel **Location:** Corner of King and Benton sts; downtown. Located opposite Kitchener Farmer's Market. 105 King St E N2G 2K8. Fax: 519/578-6889. **Facility:** 202 units. 199 one-bedroom standard units. 3 one-bedroom suites. 4-9 stories, interior corridors. **Parking:** on-site. **Terms:** small pets only ($25 fee, in smoking units). **Amenities:** video games (fee), dual phone lines, voice mail, irons, hair dryers. **Pool(s):** heated indoor. **Leisure Activities:** sauna, whirlpool, exercise room. **Fee:** miniature golf. **Guest Services:** gift shop, valet laundry. **Business Services:** conference facilities, business center. **Cards:** AX, DC, DS, MC, VI. *(See color ad p 281 & p 5)*
SOME UNITS
FEE

HOLIDAY INN KITCHENER-WATERLOO *Book at aaa.com* Phone: (519)893-1211

(CAA) (SAVE)

	7/1-9/30	1P: $89-$154	2P: $89-$154
	1/1-4/30	1P: $89-$149	2P: $89-$149
	5/1-6/30	1P: $89-$144	2P: $89-$144
	10/1-12/31	1P: $89-$139	2P: $89-$139

Large-scale Hotel **Location:** Hwy 401, exit 278. 5.6 km w on Hwy 8, exit Weber St, then just e on King St. 30 Fairway Rd S N2A 2N2. Fax: 519/894-8518. **Facility:** 183 one-bedroom standard units. 2-6 stories, interior corridors. **Parking:** on-site. **Terms:** small pets only. **Amenities:** video games (fee), voice mail, irons, hair dryers. *Some:* high-speed Internet. **Dining:** 6:15 am-10:30 pm, cocktails. **Pool(s):** heated outdoor, heated indoor. **Leisure Activities:** sauna, whirlpool, exercise room. **Guest Services:** valet and coin laundry. **Business Services:** conference facilities. **Cards:** AX, DC, DS, JC, MC, VI. **Special Amenities:** free newspaper and preferred room (subject to availability with advance reservations). *(See color ad card insert)*

THE HOWARD JOHNSON HOTEL *Book at aaa.com* Phone: (519)893-1234

| | 5/1-8/31 | 1P: $89-$99 | 2P: $99-$109 | XP: $10 | F10 |
| | 9/1-4/30 | 1P: $79-$89 | 2P: $89-$99 | XP: $10 | F10 |

Small-scale Hotel **Location:** Hwy 401, exit 278, 6.4 km w on Hwy 8, exit Weber St W. 1333 Weber St E N2A 1C2. Fax: 519/893-2100. **Facility:** 102 one-bedroom standard units, some with whirlpools. 2-4 stories, interior/exterior corridors. **Parking:** on-site, winter plug-ins. **Terms:** cancellation fee imposed, package plans, pets ($50 deposit, $10 extra charge, in designated units). **Amenities:** video games (fee), voice mail, hair dryers. *Some:* irons. **Pool(s):** heated indoor. **Leisure Activities:** sauna, whirlpool. **Guest Services:** valet laundry. **Business Services:** conference facilities. **Cards:** AX, DC, DS, MC, VI.

The Comfort you Need at the Price you Want!

20% OFF Sun. -Thur. AAA Members

Comfort Inn
2899 King Street East
Kitchener, ON N2A 1A6
Phone: 519.894.3500 • Fax: 519.894.1562
www.choicehotels.ca/cn275

Choose from a wide selection of rooms including deluxe standard, business class, executive or the new "Uniquely Decorated Whirlpool Rooms" All guest rooms include:
• Complimentary Deluxe Continental Breakfast
• In-room coffee & pay per view movies
• In-room iron & ironing board
• Color cable TV w/remote & AM/FM clock radio
• Free local calls & voice mail
• **Fitness Room w/Whirlpool and Sauna**

800.228.1AAA
choicehotels.com

We'll see you there..

Comfort Inn
BY CHOICE HOTELS

© 2003 Choice Hotels International, Inc.

Toll-Free Reservations: 1-800-483-7812

Four Points
Sheraton

Tel: (519) 744-4141 Fax: (519) 578-6889
www.fourpoints.com/kitchener

Extensive Family Fun Centre!

• 201 guestrooms, including 15 suites
• Free parking
• Indoor pool, whirlpool, sauna
• Bowling lanes, mini-golf, video games

• Billiards, ping pong, squash courts
• Bistro 105 restaurant
• Easy driving distance from major area attractions
• Ask Us About Our Family Packages!

105 King Street East, Kitchener, ON N2G 2K8

MORNINGTON CRESCENT B&B
All Year [BP]
Bed & Breakfast
Phone: 519/743-4557
1P: $55-$100   2P: $75-$120   XP: $30   D16
Location: Hwy 86 N, exit University E, 1 km to Bridge St S, 0.5 km s to Bridal Tr, then just e. 11 Sunbridge Crescent N2K 1T4. Fax: 519/743-4557. **Facility:** Smoke free premises. 4 one-bedroom standard units, some with whirlpools. 1 story, interior corridors. *Bath:* some shared or private, combo or shower only. **Parking:** on-site.
Terms: office hours 7 am-10 pm. **Amenities:** video library, hair dryers. *Some:* high-speed Internet. **Pool(s):** heated outdoor. **Leisure Activities:** whirlpool, hiking trails. **Business Services:** meeting rooms. **Cards:** MC, VI.

SOME UNITS

RADISSON HOTEL KITCHENER *Book at aaa.com*
All Year
Phone: (519)894-9500
1P: $99-$149   2P: $99-$149   XP: $10   F18
Location: Hwy 401, exit 278, 6 km w on Hwy 8, exit Weber St. 2960 King St E N2A 1A9. Fax: 519/894-9144.
Small-scale Hotel
Facility: 172 units. 152 one-bedroom standard units. 20 one-bedroom suites. 12 stories, interior corridors. **Parking:** on-site. **Terms:** package plans. **Amenities:** video games, dual phone lines, voice mail, irons, hair dryers. *Some:* high-speed Internet. **Dining:** Del Dente's Casual Italian Dining, see separate listing. **Pool(s):** heated indoor. **Leisure Activities:** exercise room. **Guest Services:** valet laundry. **Business Services:** meeting rooms. **Cards:** AX, DC, DS, MC, VI. *(See color ad p 521, below & on TourBookMark)*

SOME UNITS

WALPER TERRACE HOTEL *Book at aaa.com*
All Year
Phone: (519)745-4321
1P: $115-$125   XP: $10   F18
Location: Corner of King and Queen sts; downtown. 1 King St W N2G 1A1. Fax: 519/745-3625. **Facility:** Built in
Historic
Small-scale Hotel
the 1890s, this Victorian-style hotel has high ceilings and a prime location; accommodations are comfortable and offer modern amenities. 79 units. 62 one-bedroom standard units. 17 one-bedroom suites ($119-$250). 5 stories, interior corridors. *Bath:* combo or shower only. **Parking:** on-site and valet. **Terms:** [AP], [BP], [CP], [ECP] & [MAP] meal plans available, package plans. **Amenities:** irons, hair dryers. *Some:* high-speed Internet. **Guest Services:** valet laundry. **Business Services:** meeting rooms. **Cards:** AX, DC, MC, VI.

SOME UNITS

FEE

STAY YOUR OWN WAY℠

$**89*** CDN

• Library Café for breakfast
• Adjoined to 3 great restaurants
• Indoor pool & fitness area
• Year round packages
• Convenient to areas largest shopping mall.

Radisson

KITCHENER - WATERLOO • Radisson Hotel Kitchener *Rate subject to availability, Sgl/Dbl occ.
2960 King Street East, Kitchener, ON N2A 1A9 • 519-894-9500
www.radisson.com/kitchenerca • 800-333-3333

The
WATERLOO INN
& Conference Centre

INDOOR POOL, SAUNA & WHIRLPOOL
155 GUESTROOMS • JACUZZI SUITES
5 MINUTES TO ST. JACOBS
AMPLE FREE PARKING

475 King St. N., Waterloo, ON   (519) 884-0220   1-800-361-4708
See our listing under "Waterloo"   www.waterlooinn.com   *Kitchener-Waterloo's Finest Hotel*

--------- **WHERE TO DINE** ---------

THE CHARCOAL STEAK HOUSE   **Lunch:** $6-$12   **Dinner:** $14-$34   **Phone:** 519/893-6570

Location: Hwy 401, exit 278, 6 km w on Hwy 8, exit Weber St; beside Radisson Hotel Kitchener. 2980 King St E N2A 1A9. **Hours:** 11:30 am-2 & 5-10 pm, Sat 4:30 pm-11 pm, Sun 10:30 am-2 & 5-10 pm. Closed: 12/25.
Steak House   **Reservations:** suggested. **Features:** The steak house is a longtime favorite with locals for its comfortable, relaxed setting and hearty portions of traditional fare. Favorites include fine beef offerings and the local specialty of pig tails and ribs prepared in barbecue or sweet sauce. Dressy casual; cocktails. **Parking:** on-site. **Cards:** AX, DC, MC, VI.

DEL DENTE'S CASUAL ITALIAN DINING   **Lunch:** $6-$14   **Dinner:** $6-$20   **Phone:** 519/893-2911
Location: Hwy 401, exit 278, 6 km w on Hwy 8, exit Weber St; in Radisson Hotel Kitchener. 2980 King St E (Lower Level) N2A 1A9. **Hours:** 11:30 am-11 pm, Fri-midnight, Sat 4:30 pm-midnight, Sun 4:30 pm-11 pm. Closed: 12/25. **Features:** Diners in both the bar and restaurant unwind in a loud, lively and bustling atmosphere.
Italian   Bright Mediterranean decor sets the tone, and interesting murals are painted on tabletops rather than traditional tablecloths. The restaurant is well-known for its freshly baked flowerpot bread and a good menu variety of creative pastas, gourmet pizzas and great sandwiches. Portions are hearty. Casual dress; cocktails. **Parking:** on-site. **Cards:** AX, DC, MC, VI.

LA COSTA   **Lunch:** $7-$24   **Dinner:** $10-$24   **Phone:** 519/744-7572
Location: Jct Ontario. 6 Charles St W N2G 1H2. **Hours:** 11:30 am-11 pm, Fri-midnight, Sat 4:30 pm-midnight, Sun 4:30 pm-10:30 pm. Closed: 1/1, 12/25, 12/26. **Reservations:** suggested. **Features:** Modern
Mediterranean   Mediterranean dining triumphs amid brick, stucco, European artwork and festive background music. The creative menu, which reflects inspirations from the coastal regions, lists varied antipasto, tapas, pasta and entrees in generous and well-presented full or half portions. Casual dress; cocktails. **Parking:** street. **Cards:** AX, DC, DS, MC, VI.

MOOSE WINOOSKI'S   **Lunch:** $7-$10   **Dinner:** $7-$14   **Phone:** 519/653-9660
Location: Hwy 8, 1.2 km n of Hwy 401; in Sports World. 100 Sports World Dr N2P 2J1. **Hours:** 11 am-1 am, Thurs-Sat to 2 am. Closed: 12/25. **Features:** Casual, fun atmosphere of a northern cabin. Features home-style meals. Hearty portions. Specialties include chicken pot pie, burgers and daily pizza. Many finger foods and
American   salad. Come hungry. Very family oriented. Casual dress; cocktails. **Parking:** on-site. **Cards:** AX, DC, MC, VI.

PETER MARTIN 20 KING   **Lunch:** $7-$15   **Dinner:** $7-$30   **Phone:** 519/745-8939
Location: Downtown. 41 King St W N2G 1A1. **Hours:** 11:30 am-11 pm, Sat 5:30 pm-10 pm. Closed major holidays; also Sun. **Reservations:** suggested. **Features:** With a pleasing dark cinnamon and clay color
Continental   scheme, the downtown eatery sports an upscale bistro atmosphere. Specialties include wood-oven pizza, fresh Atlantic salmon, grilled spicy shrimp, rack of lamb, calamari and steak. Desserts are worth saving room for. Dressy casual; cocktails. **Parking:** street. **Cards:** AX, DC, MC, VI.

KLEINBURG

--------- **WHERE TO DINE** ---------

CHARTREUSE RESTAURANT   **Lunch:** $8-$15   **Dinner:** $18-$33   **Phone:** 905/893-0475
Location: Directly s of Nashville Rd. 10512 Islington Ave L0J 1C0. **Hours:** 11:30 am-2:30 & 5-10 pm. Closed: 1/1, 12/25. **Reservations:** suggested. **Features:** On the main street of the charming village, the restaurant is set
Continental   among shops and art galleries. The dining room is relaxed and reflects an ambience and decor of yesteryear. The menu is varied. Pub dining is offered downstairs from 11:30 am-11 pm. Dressy casual; cocktails. **Parking:** on-site. **Cards:** AX, DC, MC, VI.

THE DOCTOR'S HOUSE RESTAURANT   **Lunch:** $14-$18   **Dinner:** $18-$68   **Phone:** 905/893-1615
Location: Just w at Islington Ave (CR 17). 21 Nashville Rd L0J 1C0. **Hours:** noon-3 & 5-11 pm, Sat noon-midnight, Sun 10:30 am-1:30 & 5-11 pm; Sunday brunch. **Reservations:** suggested. **Features:** The
Continental   atmosphere is bright, upscale, elegant and country—the perfect setting for afternoon tea served by a professional staff. And the brunch buffet is one of the best in the province, with a very extensive selection, including specialty seafood. Dressy casual; cocktails. **Parking:** on-site. **Cards:** AX, CB, DC, DS, MC, VI.

LAKEFIELD pop. 2,734

--------- **WHERE TO STAY** ---------

PINE VISTA RESORT   **Phone:** (705)877-2108

6/18-9/3 Wkly	2P: $1095-$1130
5/1-6/17 & 9/4-12/19 Dly	2P: $135-$200
12/20-3/19 Dly	2P: $150-$170

Resort Condominium   **Location:** 5 km n on Hwy 29, 19.2 km e on CR 6 (Stoney Lake Rd). Located in a rural/lakeside area. 932 Gilchrist Bay Rd, RR 2 K0L 2H0. Fax: 705/877-1320. **Facility:** These spacious, well-equipped one- to four-bedroom housekeeping cottages with kitchens are on Stony Lake in the Kawarthas. 24 units. 13 two- and 2 three-bedroom suites with kitchens and whirlpools. 9 cottages, some with whirlpools. 1-2 stories (no elevator), exterior corridors. **Parking:** on-site, winter plug-ins. **Terms:** open 5/1-3/19, office hours 9 am-8 pm, 2 night minimum stay - seasonal and/or weekends, 30 day cancellation notice-fee imposed, weekly rates available, package plans. **Amenities:** video library (fee), DVD players, hair dryers. **Pool(s):** heated outdoor. **Leisure Activities:** whirlpools, canoeing, paddleboats, fishing, cross country skiing, ice skating, tobogganing, hiking trails, playground, exercise room, sports court, basketball, horseshoes, shuffleboard, volleyball. **Fee:** boats, boat dock, bicycles, massage, game room. **Guest Services:** gift shop, coin laundry. **Business Services:** meeting rooms. **Cards:** DC, MC, VI.

SOME UNITS

SELWYN SHORES WATERFRONT BED & BREAKFAST

Phone: (705)652-0277

▼▼ ▼▼ All Year [BP]   1P: $79-$99   2P: $89-$109

Location: Hwy 23, 5.7 km n to CR 20 (Selwyn Shores Dr), just w, 2.3 km w on 12th line to Selwyn Shores Dr, then just s. Located in a residential, lakeside area. 2073 Selwyn Shores Dr, RR 3 K0L 2H0. Fax: 705/652-3389.

Bed & Breakfast   **Facility:** Smoke free premises. 5 one-bedroom standard units. 2 stories (no elevator), interior corridors. *Bath:* some shared or private, combo or shower only. **Parking:** on-site, winter plug-ins. **Terms:** office hours 7 am-11 pm, 2 night minimum stay - weekends, package plans. **Amenities:** *Some:* hair dryers. **Leisure Activities:** canoeing, paddleboats, boat dock, fishing. **Cards:** MC, VI.

SOME UNITS

🗶 🗶 🗶 💥 📠 🖉 / 🖵 📧 /

LANSDOWNE —See also GANANOQUE.

———— **WHERE TO STAY** ————

GLEN HOUSE RESORT

Phone: (613)659-2204

CAA SAVE   6/24-9/5   1P: $105-$285   2P: $105-$285   XP: $12   F12
  5/1-6/23 & 9/6-4/30   1P: $85-$165   2P: $85-$165   XP: $12   F12

▼▼ ▼▼   **Location:** 9.6 km e of Gananoque; 4.8 km w of 1000 Islands International Bridge. Located in a rural area, on the waterfront. 409-1000 Islands Pkwy K0E 1L0 (PO Box 10, GANANOQUE, K7G 2T6). Fax: 613/659-2232. **Facility:** A

Resort   variety of outdoor recreation opportunities is offered at this all-season resort dating from the early 1900s. 80
Small-scale Hotel   units. 76 one-bedroom standard units, some with whirlpools. 4 cottages ($1000-$2000). 2 stories, interior/exterior corridors. **Parking:** on-site, winter plug-ins. **Terms:** check-in 4 pm, 2 night minimum stay - weekends, 3 day cancellation notice, [MAP] meal plan available, package plans. **Amenities:** hair dryers. **Dining:** 8 am-10:30 & 5:30-8:30 pm; hours may vary off season, cocktails. **Pool(s):** heated outdoor, heated indoor. **Leisure Activities:** sauna, whirlpools, rental boats, rental canoes, rental paddleboats, fishing, tennis court, cross country skiing, ice skating, rental bicycles, playground, exercise room. *Fee:* boat dock, golf-18 holes, ski equipment. **Guest Services:** valet laundry. **Business Services:** conference facilities. **Cards:** AX, MC, VI. *(See color ad p 254)*

SOME UNITS

�⃣ 🍴 🍸 🏊 🗶 💥 💻 / 🗶 VCR 📠 🖵 📧 /
FEE

LEAMINGTON pop. 27,138

———— **WHERE TO STAY** ————

COMFORT INN   *Book at aaa.com*

Phone: (519)326-9071

▼▼ ▼▼   5/1-9/29 [CP]   1P: $80-$130   2P: $85-$140   XP: $5   F17
  9/30-4/30 [CP]   1P: $75-$120   2P: $75-$135   XP: $5   F17

Small-scale Hotel   **Location:** Just s of jct Talbot and Erie sts; on direct route to Point Pelee National Park. 279 Erie St S N8H 3C4. Fax: 519/326-3445. **Facility:** 62 one-bedroom standard units. 2 stories (no elevator), interior corridors. **Parking:** on-site, winter plug-ins. **Terms:** package plans, pets ($5 extra charge). **Amenities:** irons, hair dryers. **Guest Services:** valet laundry. **Cards:** AX, CB, DC, DS, JC, MC, VI.

SOME UNITS

ASK �⃣ 🐕 🍴 💦 📠 💻 / 🗶 🖵 /
  FEE   FEE   FEE

RAMADA LIMITED LEAMINGTON   *Book at aaa.com*

Phone: (519)325-0260

CAA SAVE   5/1-5/31 [ECP]   1P: $109-$169   2P: $119-$189   XP: $10   D20
  6/1-9/30 [ECP]   1P: $109-$149   2P: $119-$169   XP: $10   D20
▼▼ ▼▼ ▼▼   4/16-4/30 [ECP]   1P: $109-$129   2P: $119-$149   XP: $10   D20
  10/1-4/15 [ECP]   1P: $99-$129   2P: $109-$139   XP: $10   D20

Small-scale Hotel   **Location:** 1 km n of Talbot St. 201 Erie St N N8H 3A5. Fax: 519/325-0838. **Facility:** 70 one-bedroom standard units, some with efficiencies (no utensils) and/or whirlpools. 2 stories, interior corridors. *Bath:* combo or shower only. **Parking:** on-site. **Terms:** package plans, small pets only ($10 fee, with prior approval). **Amenities:** voice mail, irons, hair dryers. *Some:* high-speed Internet. **Pool(s):** heated indoor. **Leisure Activities:** sauna, whirlpool, exercise room. **Guest Services:** valet and coin laundry. **Business Services:** meeting rooms, business center. **Cards:** AX, DC, MC, VI. **Special Amenities:** free expanded continental breakfast and early check-in/late check-out.

SOME UNITS

�⃣ 🐕 🐾 🏊 🗶 📠 💻 / 🗶 🖵 📧 /
FEE

SUN PARLOR MOTEL

Phone: (519)326-6131

CAA SAVE   5/1-9/30   1P: $55-$68   2P: $65-$90   XP: $10   F9
  10/1-4/30   1P: $50-$60   2P: $58-$78   XP: $10   F9

▼▼   **Location:** On Hwy 3, 1 km w of Erie St. 135 Talbot St W N8H 1N2. Fax: 519/326-1801. **Facility:** 18 one-bedroom
Motel   standard units, some with kitchens and/or whirlpools. 1 story, exterior corridors. **Parking:** on-site. **Terms:** 7 day cancellation notice-fee imposed, pets ($10 extra charge). **Cards:** AX, MC, VI. **Special Amenities:** free local telephone calls and early check-in/late check-out.

SOME UNITS

�⃣ 🐕 🍴 💥 🖵 / 🗶 📧 /
FEE

TOWN N' COUNTRY MOTOR INN

Phone: 519/326-4425

▼▼ ▼▼   All Year   1P: $60-$80   2P: $69-$89   XP: $5   F12

Motel   **Location:** 1.1 km e of Erie St. 200 Talbot St E N8H 3X6. Fax: 519/326-4427. **Facility:** 16 one-bedroom standard units, some with whirlpools. 1 story, exterior corridors. **Parking:** on-site, winter plug-ins. **Pool(s):** outdoor. **Cards:** AX, DC, JC, MC, VI.

SOME UNITS

ASK �⃣ 🏊 💥 🖵 / 🗶 /

------ WHERE TO DINE ------

JORDANS FAVOURITE EATING PLACE   **Lunch:** $7-$12   **Dinner:** $9-$28   **Phone:** 519/322-1928
▼▼/▼ **Location:** Directly e of Erie St. 5 Nelson St N8H 1G6. **Hours:** 11:30 am-2 & 5-9 pm. Closed: Sun & Mon.
Reservations: suggested, weekends. **Features:** In a restored 1892 Victorian home, the charming
Continental downtown restaurant nurtures a cozy atmosphere. On the creative menu is a good variety of full entrees
and lighter fare. Lunchtime favorites include smoked sausage and pierogies, while dinners centre on pasta,
steak, seafood, chicken, ribs and veal. Among specialties are lobster and eight varieties of broiled fish filets. Cocktails. **Parking:**
on-site. **Cards:** AX, DC, MC, VI. ⊠

JOSE'S NOODLE FACTORY   **Lunch:** $5-$9   **Dinner:** $8-$22   **Phone:** 519/322-0182
▼▼ **Location:** On Hwy 3, 1.5 km w of Erie St. 221 Talbot St W N8H 4H8. **Hours:** 11 am-1 am. Closed: 12/25.
Features: The bustling eatery sustains a cantina feel in decor and menu offerings and features outdoor
American patio seating in season. The kitchen dishes hearty portions of Italian fare, including pasta, pizzas, sizzling
burgers, ribs, tasty wings and a great selection of finger foods. Watch for the changing daily specials, which
offer exceptional value and great taste. Casual dress; cocktails. **Parking:** on-site. **Cards:** AX, MC, VI. ⊡ ⊠

SEACLIFFE INN   **Dinner:** $7-$30   **Phone:** 519/324-9266
▼▼ **Location:** At the foot of Erie St. 388 Erie St S N8H 3E5. **Hours:** 2 pm-10 pm, Fri & Sat-11 pm; from 4 pm, Sat-11
pm 11/1-4/30. Closed: 12/25. **Reservations:** suggested. **Features:** An authentic nautical atmosphere, a
Steak & Seafood menu featuring steak, seafood and local fish and a friendly staff await you at the Seacliff Inn. In the summer
months, choose from indoor or outdoor patio dining with a lovely view of the waterfront. Arrive hungry as the
portions are hearty and the selections are all tempting. Casual dress; cocktails. **Parking:** on-site. **Cards:** AX, MC, VI. ⊠

SPAGO TRATTORIA AND PIZZERIA   **Lunch:** $7-$17   **Dinner:** $7-$17   **Phone:** 519/326-7080
▼▼ **Location:** Just w of Erie St. 22 Talbot St W N8H 1M4. **Hours:** 11:30 am-2:30 & 5-9:30 pm, Fri & Sat-10 pm, Sun
4 pm-9 pm, Mon 5 pm-9 pm. Closed: 12/25. **Features:** The cheerful trattoria presents a varied menu of
Italian casual fare, including made-to-order gourmet pizza; rich, tasty pasta dishes; and veal, chicken and seafood
specialties. Guests should save room for one of the tempting dessert choices in the glass display case near
the entrance. Casual dress; cocktails. **Parking:** street. **Cards:** AX, MC, VI. ⊠

TROPICANA THE LEAMINGTON DOCK   **Lunch:** $8-$10   **Dinner:** $10-$30   **Phone:** 519/326-2697
Ⓐ **Location:** At the end of Erie St S; on the dock. 500 Erie St S N8H 3W1. **Hours:** Open 5/1-1/1 & 3/15-4/30; 11 am-9
pm, Sat-10 pm, Sun 9 am-9 pm. Closed: 10/24, 12/25, 12/26. **Reservations:** accepted. **Features:** With a
▼▼ pleasant lake view, the eatery exudes a casual atmosphere and has a large foyer and plenty of windows
American throughout. Patrons who retreat to the open, airy and loft-like dining room can choose from a great selection
of sandwiches, pasta dishes and regional specialties, such as perch and pickerel. Casual dress; cocktails.
Parking: on-site. **Cards:** AX, DC, MC, VI. ⊡ ⊠

LION'S HEAD pop. 600

------ WHERE TO DINE ------

LION'S HEAD INN AND RESTAURANT   **Lunch:** $6-$10   **Dinner:** $8-$28   **Phone:** 519/793-4601
▼▼ **Location:** Jct Webster St. 8 Helen St N0H 1W0. **Hours:** 11 am-11 pm. Closed: 12/25. **Reservations:** suggested.
Features: The casual ambience of this historical 1879 inn complements a menu of traditional pub fare such
English as fish and chips, liver and onions, burgers and sandwiches. There's also a good selection of munchies. An
expanded menu includes steak, lobster and seafood. Casual dress; cocktails. **Parking:** on-site. **Cards:** AX,
MC, VI. **Historic** ⊠

LISTOWEL pop. 5,905

------ WHERE TO STAY ------

COUNTRY INN MOTEL   **Phone:** (519)291-1580
Ⓐ Ⓢ All Year   1P: $89-$139   2P: $99-$159   XP: $10   F12
Location: On Hwy 23 N, 3.5 km n of Main St. RR 1 Hwy 23 N-8500 Rd 164 N4W 3G6. Fax: 519/291-5868.
▼▼ **Facility:** 36 one-bedroom standard units, some with efficiencies and/or whirlpools. 2 stories, interior/exterior
Motel corridors. **Parking:** on-site. **Terms:** cancellation fee imposed, package plans, small pets only (in designated
units). **Amenities:** video library (fee), high-speed Internet, voice mail. *Some:* irons, hair dryers. **Leisure
Activities:** lighted tennis court, ice skating, basketball, game room. **Cards:** AX, MC, VI. **Special Amenities:**
free local telephone calls and free newspaper. SOME UNITS
Ⓢ 🐾 ⊠ Ⓥ Ⓡ 🖥 📠 / ⊠ 🖥 /

LONDON pop. 336,539

------ WHERE TO STAY ------

AIRPORT INN & SUITES   **Phone:** (519)457-1200
▼▼▼ All Year   1P: $94-$101   2P: $101-$108   XP: $5   F12
Location: Hwy 401, exit Airport Rd, 7.7 km n; corner of Airport Rd and Dundas St E. 2230 Dundas St E N5V 1R5.
Small-scale Hotel Fax: 519/659-1632. **Facility:** 103 one-bedroom standard units, some with efficiencies and/or whirlpools. 3
stories, interior corridors. **Parking:** on-site. **Terms:** small pets only ($10 extra charge). **Amenities:** irons,
hair dryers. **Guest Services:** valet laundry. **Business Services:** meeting rooms. **Cards:** AX, DC, DS, MC, VI.
SOME UNITS
ⒶⓈⓀ Ⓢ 🐾 📠 🖥 📠 / ⊠ /
FEE

BEST WESTERN LAMPLIGHTER INN & CONFERENCE CENTRE *Book at aaa.com*

Phone: (519)681-7151

(CAA) (SAVE)

1/1-4/30	1P: $139-$169	XP: $10 F12
5/1-12/31	1P: $129-$159	XP: $10 F12

Location: 3.7 km n off Hwy 401, exit 186 (Wellington Rd). 591 Wellington Rd S N6C 4R3. Fax: 519/681-3271. **Facility:** 172 units. 131 one-bedroom standard units, some with whirlpools. 41 one-bedroom suites, some **Small-scale Hotel** with whirlpools. 2-3 stories, interior corridors. **Parking:** on-site, winter plug-ins. **Terms:** package plans, small pets only ($5 extra charge). **Amenities:** video games (fee), high-speed Internet, voice mail, irons, hair dryers. **Dining:** 6:30 am-9 pm, cocktails. **Pool(s):** heated indoor. **Leisure Activities:** whirlpool, waterslide, exercise room. **Guest Services:** valet and coin laundry. **Business Services:** conference facilities. **Cards:** AX, DC, DS, MC, VI. **Special Amenities:** free local telephone calls and free newspaper. *(See color ad below)*

SOME UNITS

BEST WESTERN STONERIDGE INN & CONFERENCE CENTRE *Book at aaa.com*

Phone: (519)652-6022

(CAA) (SAVE)

All Year [CP]	1P: $79-$149	2P: $79-$149	XP: $10 F12

Location: Hwy 401, exit 177A, jct Hwy 4. 6675 Burtwistle Ln N6L 1H5. Fax: 519/652-1150. **Facility:** 71 one-bedroom standard units. 2 stories (no elevator), interior corridors. **Parking:** on-site, winter plug-ins. **Amenities:** video games (fee), voice mail, irons, hair dryers. **Dining:** Pasto's, see separate listing. **Leisure Small-scale Hotel Activities:** whirlpool. **Guest Services:** sundries, valet laundry. **Business Services:** conference facilities. **Cards:** AX, CB, DC, DS, JC, MC, VI. **Special Amenities:** free continental breakfast and free newspaper.

SOME UNITS

COMFORT HOTEL-DOWNTOWN *Book at aaa.com*

Phone: (519)661-0233

9/1-11/30	1P: $95-$169	2P: $95-$179	XP: $10 F18
5/1-8/31	1P: $95-$159	2P: $95-$169	XP: $10 F18
1/1-4/30	1P: $95-$160	2P: $95-$160	XP: $10 F18
12/1-12/31	1P: $80-$145	2P: $80-$150	XP: $10 F18

Small-scale Hotel

Location: Between Waterloo and Colborne sts. 374 Dundas St N6B 1V7. Fax: 519/661-0786. **Facility:** 124 units. 119 one-bedroom standard units. 5 one-bedroom suites ($90-$210). 10 stories, interior corridors. **Parking:** on-site. **Terms:** cancellation fee imposed, package plans. **Amenities:** high-speed Internet (fee), voice mail, hair dryers. *Some:* dual phone lines, irons. **Guest Services:** valet laundry. **Business Services:** meeting rooms. **Cards:** AX, DC, DS, MC, VI.

SOME UNITS

COMFORT INN *Book at aaa.com*

Phone: (519)685-9300

(CAA) (SAVE)

6/1-10/31	1P: $98-$123	2P: $108-$133	XP: $10 F18
5/1-5/31	1P: $95-$118	2P: $105-$128	XP: $10 F18
11/1-4/30	1P: $93-$110	2P: $103-$120	XP: $10 F18

Location: Hwy 401, exit 186B (Wellington Rd), just n. 1156 Wellington Rd N6E 1M3. Fax: 519/685-0081. **Small-scale Hotel Facility:** 79 one-bedroom standard units, some with whirlpools. 2 stories (no elevator), interior corridors. **Parking:** on-site. **Terms:** 30 day cancellation notice, pets (in smoking units). **Amenities:** voice mail, hair dryers. *Some:* dual phone lines, irons. **Guest Services:** valet laundry. **Cards:** AX, DC, DS, MC, VI. **Special Amenities:** free continental breakfast and free local telephone calls.

SOME UNITS

Best Western **Lamplighter Inn & Conference Centre**

In a word... **Spectacular**

- 172 Guest Rooms
- Jacuzzi Suites
- Year-round Tropical Paradise Under the Atrium
- Mountain Waterslide
- Indoor Pool
- Whirlpool
- Gazebo Bar

Reservations 1-888-232-6747
591 Wellington Rd. S. London ON N6C 4R5
(519) 681-7151 • www.lamplighterinn.ca

DAYS INN LONDON   *Book at aaa.com*   **Phone:** (519)681-1240
    All Year   1P: $79-$99   2P: $79-$99   XP: $10   F
    Location: Hwy 401, exit 186B (Wellington Rd), 1.5 km n. Located across from the White Oaks Mall. 1100 Wellington Rd
Small-scale Hotel S N6E 1M2. Fax: 519/681-0830. **Facility:** 143 one-bedroom standard units. 2 stories (no elevator), interior
    corridors. **Parking:** on-site. **Terms:** 12% service charge. **Amenities:** voice mail, hair dryers. *Some:* irons.
Pool(s): heated outdoor. **Leisure Activities:** exercise room. *Fee:* game room. **Guest Services:** valet laundry. **Cards:** AX, CB,
DC, DS, MC, VI. *(See color ad below)*

SOME UNITS

DELTA LONDON ARMOURIES   *Book at aaa.com*   **Phone:** (519)679-6111
   All Year   1P: $109-$169   2P: $109-$169   XP: $15   F18
    Location: On Hwy 2. 325 Dundas St N6B 1T9. Fax: 519/679-3957. **Facility:** 250 units. 247 one-bedroom
    standard units, some with whirlpools. 3 one-bedroom suites with whirlpools. 20 stories, interior corridors.
    Parking: on-site (fee) and valet. **Terms:** package plans, pets (in smoking units). **Amenities:** video games
Large-scale Hotel (fee), voice mail, irons, hair dryers. *Some:* high-speed Internet, dual phone lines, honor bars. **Dining:** 6:30
am-10 pm, cocktails. **Pool(s):** heated indoor, wading. **Leisure Activities:** saunas, whirlpool, putting green,
squash court, recreation programs, exercise room. **Guest Services:** valet laundry. **Business Services:** conference facilities.
Cards: AX, DC, DS, MC, VI. *(See ad below)*

SOME UNITS
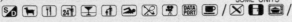

1-800-DAYS INN
www.daysinn.ca

trip rewards
It's fun to get more

Come On Inn... Stay Awhile.

- 143 Comfortable Rooms
- Complimentary parking & local calls
- Family restaurant
- Fitness centre with attached games room
- Outdoor heated pool & courtyard
- In-room coffee maker/hairdryer
- 5 minutes from highway 401
- Directly across from White Oaks mall

Days Inn - London
1100 Wellington Rd S., London, ON M6E 1M2
www.daysinnlondon.com   **Toll Free: 866.266.8266**

- London's premier hotel
- Located in the heart of downtown London
- Built in an original 1905 historic armoury
- Walking distance to theatres, parks, shopping and John Labatt Centre
- Only 45 minutes from the Stratford Festival
- One of London's best Sunday brunches

DELTA
LONDON ARMOURIES

Your room is ready

Weekend Getaway Rate	CANADA and U.S.	325 Dundas Street,
Cdn. Sgl./Dbl. U.S. Sgl./Dbl.	1-800-268-1133	London, ON N6B 1T9
$109.00 $99.00*	www.deltahotels.com	1-800-668-9999 Fax: 519-679-3957

Subject to availability *U.S. rate subject to exchange fluctuations

FOUR POINTS BY SHERATON HOTEL AND SUITES-LONDON *Book at aaa.com*

Phone: (519)681-0600

(CAA) (SAVE) All Year   1P: $109-$199   2P: $124-$214   XP: $15   F18
Location: Hwy 401, exit 186B (Wellington Rd), 1.5 km n. 1150 Wellington Rd S N6E 1M3. Fax: 519/681-8222. **Facility:** 181 units. 60 one-bedroom standard units. 121 one-bedroom suites ($119-$209), some with whirlpools. 2-5 stories, interior corridors. *Bath:* combo or shower only. **Parking:** on-site. **Terms:** [AP] & [BP]
Small-scale Hotel meal plans available, package plans. **Amenities:** video games (fee), dual phone lines, voice mail, irons, hair dryers. *Some:* high-speed Internet. **Dining:** 6:30 am-11 pm. **Pool(s):** heated indoor. **Leisure Activities:** saunas, exercise room. **Guest Services:** valet laundry. **Business Services:** conference facilities, business center. **Cards:** AX, CB, DC, DS, JC, MC, VI. **Special Amenities:** free newspaper and early check-in/late check-out.
(See color ad p 5)

SOME UNITS

(SD) (TI) (Y) (2) (X) (DATA PORT) (D) / (X) (B) (D) /

GOLDEN PHEASANT MOTEL LTD

Phone: 519/473-4551

Motel

Property failed to provide current rates
Location: Jct Wonderland Rd and Hwy 22 (Fanshawe Park Rd). 615 Fanshawe Park Rd W N6G 5B3. Fax: 519/471-2265. **Facility:** 40 one-bedroom standard units. 1 story, interior/exterior corridors. **Parking:** on-site. **Terms:** office hours 7 am-midnight. **Amenities:** hair dryers. **Pool(s):** heated outdoor.

SOME UNITS

(TI) (2) / (X) (B) /

HILTON LONDON ONTARIO *Book at aaa.com*

Phone: (519)439-1661

(CAA) (SAVE) All Year   1P: $99-$219   XP: $10   F18
Location: At King St and Wellington Rd. 300 King St N6B 1S2. Fax: 519/439-9672. **Facility:** This high-rise has ample meeting facilities, a well-equipped recreation area and nicely appointed, spacious guest rooms with oversize desks. 323 units. 311 one-bedroom standard units. 12 one-bedroom suites, some with whirlpools.
Large-scale Hotel 22 stories, interior corridors. **Parking:** on-site (fee) and valet. **Terms:** small pets only ($50 fee). **Amenities:** dual phone lines, voice mail, irons, hair dryers. *Fee:* video games, high-speed Internet. **Dining:** 6:30 am-11 pm, cocktails, also, London Grill, see separate listing. **Pool(s):** heated indoor, wading. **Leisure Activities:** sauna, whirlpool, exercise room. **Guest Services:** gift shop, valet laundry. **Business Services:** conference facilities, business center. **Cards:** AX, CB, DC, DS, JC, MC, VI. **Special Amenities:** free newspaper. *(See color ad below)*

SOME UNITS

(SD) (H) (TI) (24TI) (Y) (2) (X) (X) (DATA PORT) (D) / (X) (B) /
FEE

HOLIDAY INN HOTEL & SUITES-LONDON *Book at aaa.com*

Phone: (519)680-0077

(CAA) (SAVE) All Year   1P: $135-$155   2P: $135-$155   XP: $10   F18
Location: Hwy 401, exit 186 (Wellington Rd) westbound; exit 186B eastbound. 864 Exeter Rd N6E 1L5. Fax: 519/680-0087. **Facility:** 120 units. 90 one-bedroom standard units. 30 one-bedroom suites ($155-$175). 6 stories, interior corridors. *Bath:* combo or shower only. **Parking:** on-site. **Terms:** pets ($25 extra
Small-scale Hotel charge). **Amenities:** video games (fee), high-speed Internet, dual phone lines, voice mail, irons, hair dryers. **Dining:** 6:30 am-2 & 5-10 pm. **Pool(s):** heated indoor. **Leisure Activities:** whirlpool, exercise room. **Guest Services:** valet and coin laundry. **Business Services:** meeting rooms, business center. **Cards:** AX, DC, DS, MC, VI.
(See color ad p 289)

SOME UNITS

(H) (TI) (Y) (&) (2) (X) (DATA PORT) (D) / (X) (B) (D) /
FEE

TAKE ME TO A
GREAT GETAWAY.
TAKE ME TO THE HILTON.

$99-$219*
- Centrally located in the heart of downtown London
- 323 beautifully appointed guest rooms
- Large indoor pool, sauna whirlpool and fitness center

Just make advance reservations with a call to Hilton's dedicated AAA number, **1-800-916-2221**, or your local AAA travel office, and request "Plan Code AA."
Visit us online at **hilton.com**.

 Hilton HHonors

 Four Diamond Award

300 King St.
London, Ontario N6B1S2
519-439-1661

Hilton
London Ontario

Rates subject to availability, single/double occupancy for standard room, and are exclusive of tax and gratuities. Valid AAA membership card required for reservation and at check-in. *Offer valid from 5/1/05-4/30/06. ©2005 Hilton Hospitality, Inc.

IDLEWYLD INN *Book at aaa.com* Phone: (519)433-2891
(AA) (SAVE) All Year [ECP] 1P: $115-$250 2P: $115-$250 XP: $10 F10
◇◇◇ Location: Hwy 401, 5 km n via Wellington Rd, then just w. Located in a residential area. 36 Grand Ave N6C 1K8.
Fax: 519/433-2891. **Facility:** Whirlpools, fireplaces and upgraded amenities are offered in some
accommodations at this service-oriented 1878 Victorian mansion. Smoke free premises. 27 one-bedroom
Bed & Breakfast standard units, some with whirlpools. 3 stories, interior corridors. **Parking:** on-site. **Terms:** cancellation fee
imposed. **Amenities:** *Some:* hair dryers. **Guest Services:** valet laundry. **Business Services:** meeting
rooms. **Cards:** AX, MC, VI. **Special Amenities:** free expanded continental breakfast and free newspaper.

SOME UNITS
(S/D) (X) (📷) (DATA PORT) / (🖥) /
FEE

LONDON EXECUTIVE SUITES HOTEL *Book at aaa.com* Phone: (519)679-3932
(AA) (SAVE) 5/1-9/30 1P: $69-$109 2P: $69-$109 XP: $8 F14
10/1-4/30 1P: $65-$95 2P: $65-$95 XP: $8 F14
◇◇◇ Location: Between Waterloo and Colborne sts. 362 Dundas St N6B 1V8. Fax: 519/679-6526. **Facility:** 47 units. 12
one-bedroom standard units. 23 one- and 12 two-bedroom suites ($89-$169). 6 stories, interior corridors.
Small-scale Hotel **Parking:** on-site. **Terms:** weekly rates available, pets ($75 fee). **Amenities:** voice mail, irons. **Cards:** AX,
DC, MC, VI. **Special Amenities:** free local telephone calls and free newspaper.

SOME UNITS
(S/D) (🛏) (🍴) (📷) (DATA PORT) (🖥) (📠) (🖥) / (X) /
FEE

MARRIOTT RESIDENCE INN-LONDON *Book at aaa.com* Phone: (519)433-7222
◇◇◇ All Year [BP] 1P: $139-$199 2P: $139-$199 XP: $10 F18
Location: Jct King St. 383 Colborne St N6B 3P5. Fax: 519/433-7223. **Facility:** 116 units. 23 one-bedroom
. **Small-scale Hotel** standard units with kitchens. 81 one- and 12 two-bedroom suites with kitchens. 12 stories, interior corridors.
Parking: on-site. **Terms:** weekly rates available, package plans, pets ($150 fee). **Amenities:** high-speed
Internet, voice mail, irons, hair dryers. **Leisure Activities:** sauna, whirlpool, exercise room. **Guest Services:** valet and coin
laundry. **Business Services:** meeting rooms. **Cards:** AX, CB, DC, DS, JC, MC, VI.

SOME UNITS
(ASK) (S/D) (🛏) (🍴) (♿) (X) (DATA PORT) (🖥) (📠) (🖥) / (X) (VCR) /
FEE   FEE

QUALITY SUITES *Book at aaa.com* Phone: (519)680-1024
(AA) (SAVE) 5/1-10/1 [ECP] 1P: $109-$159 2P: $119-$179 XP: $10 F18
10/2-4/30 [ECP] 1P: $99-$139 2P: $109-$159 XP: $10 F18
◇◇◇ Location: Hwy 401, exit 186B (Wellington Rd), 1.6 km n. 1120 Dearness Dr N6E 1N9. Fax: 519/680-1036.
Facility: 118 units. 11 one-bedroom standard units. 107 one-bedroom suites. 3 stories, interior corridors.
Small-scale Hotel **Parking:** on-site, winter plug-ins. **Terms:** package plans. **Amenities:** irons, hair dryers. *Some:* honor bars.
Guest Services: sundries, valet and coin laundry. **Business Services:** meeting rooms. **Cards:** AX, DC,
DS, JC, MC, VI.

SOME UNITS
(S/D) (🛏) (🍴) (♿) (📷) (DATA PORT) (🖥) / (X) (🖥) (📠) /

BRAND NEW

LONDON, ONTARIO

- **Brand new hotel featuring 120
  luxurious guestrooms and suites**
- **Indoor pool, Whirlpool & Fitness Centre**
- **On site family restaurant**
- **Meeting and Banquet rooms**
- **Free High Speed Internet access**
- **Complimentary Business Centre**
- **Easy access off Hwy 401**
- **Shopping and entertainment nearby**

864 Exeter Road, London, ON N6E 1L5
Toll Free Reservations 1-800-HOLIDAY
Website: www.holiday-inn.com
Tel: 519-680-0077 • Fax: 519-680-0087

RADISSON HOTEL AND SUITES LONDON   *Book at aaa.com*   **Phone:** (519)668-7900
Ⓐ Ⓢ 8/1-9/30   1P: $109-$149   2P: $109-$149   XP: $15   F18
▼▼▼▼▼ 5/1-7/31 & 10/1-4/30   1P: $99-$139   2P: $99-$139   XP: $15   F18
Location: Jct Wellington and Southdale rds. 855 Wellington Rd S N6E 3N5. Fax: 519/668-7923. **Facility:** 144 units. 62 one-bedroom standard units. 82 one-bedroom suites, some with whirlpools. 10 stories, interior corridors. **Large-scale Hotel Parking:** on-site. **Terms:** package plans. **Amenities:** video games (fee), voice mail, irons, hair dryers. *Some:* high-speed Internet (fee), dual phone lines. **Dining:** Timbers Chop House, see separate listing. **Pool(s):** heated indoor. **Leisure Activities:** whirlpool, exercise room. *Fee:* game room. **Guest Services:** valet laundry. **Business Services:** meeting rooms. **Cards:** AX, DC, DS, MC, VI. *(See color ad p 521, below & on TourBookMark)*

SOME UNITS

🆘 🍴 🍸 🏊 ✖️ 📷 📠 🔌 🖥️ / ✖️ 🖨️ /

RAMADA INN   *Book at aaa.com*   **Phone:** (519)681-4900
Ⓐ Ⓢ All Year   1P: $90-$110   2P: $90-$110   XP: $10   F18
▼▼▼▼▼ **Location:** Jct Wellington Rd; Hwy 401, exit 186B (Wellington Rd N) westbound; exit 186 eastbound. 817 Exeter Rd N6E 1W1. Fax: 519/681-5065. **Facility:** 124 units. 122 one-bedroom standard units. 2 one-bedroom suites ($159-$199). 2 stories (no elevator), interior corridors. **Parking:** on-site. **Amenities:** voice mail, irons, hair dryers. **Small-scale Hotel Dining:** 6:30 am-10 pm, cocktails. **Pool(s):** heated indoor. **Leisure Activities:** sauna. *Fee:* game room. **Guest Services:** valet laundry. **Business Services:** meeting rooms, administrative services (fee). **Cards:** AX, DC, MC, VI. *(See color ad below)*

SOME UNITS

🆘 🍴 🍸 🏊 📷 📠 🔌 🖥️ / ✖️ 🖨️ /
FEE

STATIONPARK ALL SUITE HOTEL   *Book at aaa.com*   **Phone:** (519)642-4444
Ⓐ Ⓢ All Year   1P: $132-$172   2P: $132-$172   XP: $10   F12
▼▼▼▼▼ **Location:** Hwy 401, exit 186B (Wellington Rd), 9 km n to Pall Mall St. 242 Pall Mall St N6A 5P6. Fax: 519/642-2551. **Facility:** 126 one-bedroom suites ($169-$172). 12 stories, interior corridors. **Parking:** on-site. **Terms:** cancellation fee imposed, [CP] meal plan available, package plans, small pets only. **Large-scale Hotel Amenities:** video games (fee), high-speed Internet, voice mail, honor bars, irons, hair dryers. **Dining:** 7 am-11 pm, Fri & Sat-midnight, cocktails. **Leisure Activities:** sauna, whirlpool, exercise room. **Guest Services:** valet laundry. **Business Services:** meeting rooms. **Cards:** AX, DC, JC, MC, VI. **Special Amenities:** free local telephone calls and preferred room (subject to availability with advance reservations).

SOME UNITS

🆘 🐕 🍴 ✖️ 📷 📠 🖥️ / ✖️ /

STAY YOUR OWN WAY℠

FROM
$99*CDN
$75*US

• 5 mins. from Hwy.401
• Near attractions & White Oaks Mall
• Indoor pool, whirlpool & fitness centre
• Free high speed internet access
• Family restaurant, complimentary parking

Radisson

LONDON - WELLINGTON ROAD • Radisson Hotel & Suites London
855 Wellington Road South, London, ON N6E 3N5
519-668-7900 • www.radisson.com/londonca • 1-800-333-3333
Subject to availability and exchange rate at time of booking.

RAMADA®   London, Ontario
GOLD KEY RAMADA   *A very good place to be.*℠

Ramada Inn • 817 Exeter Road • London, Ontario N6E 1W1 • Phone: 519-681-4900

The Ramada Inn London is a well-appointed, full-service hotel, conveniently located at the corner of Exeter and Wellington Road directly off Highway 401.

• Newly Renovated 2003 • Indoor Pool
• Chelsea's Restaurant & Lounge
• In-Room Pay Movies • Electronic Key Card Locks
• In-Room Coffee Maker, Fridge, Hairdryer, Iron/Board
• Free High Speed Internet & Voicemail
• Meeting & Banquet Facilities for 3 to 300
• Ample Free Parking

©2003 Ramada Franchise Systems Inc. All rights reserved. All Ramada hotels are independently owned and operated.

Toll Free: 1-800-303-FREE
www.ramadainnlondon.com

TRAVELODGE LONDON SOUTH   *Book at aaa.com*   Phone: (519)681-1200

(CAA) (SAVE)   All Year   1P: $96-$126   2P: $96-$126   XP: $10   F18

Location: Hwy 401 W, exit 186B (Wellington Rd N); Hwy 401 E, exit 186A, corner of Wellington and Exeter rds. 800 Exeter Rd N6E 1L5. Fax: 519/681-6988. **Facility:** 126 units. 110 one-bedroom standard units, some with whirlpools. 16 one-bedroom suites with whirlpools, some with kitchens. 3 stories, interior corridors. **Parking:** Small-scale Hotel on-site. **Terms:** cancellation fee imposed. **Amenities:** video games (fee), voice mail. *Some:* irons, hair dryers. **Guest Services:** valet laundry. **Business Services:** meeting rooms. **Cards:** AX, DC, DS, MC, VI.

SOME UNITS

[icons]

THE WINDERMERE MANOR   *Book at aaa.com*   Phone: (519)858-1391

All Year   1P: $118   2P: $118   XP: $10   F18

Location: Jct Richmond and Pall Mall sts, 3 km n on Richmond St to Windermere Rd, 1 km w. 200 Collip Cir N6G 4X8. Small-scale Hotel Fax: 519/858-3394. **Facility:** 48 units. 18 one-bedroom standard units. 30 one-bedroom suites ($134). 4 stories, interior corridors. **Parking:** on-site. **Terms:** [BP] meal plan available. **Amenities:** high-speed Internet, voice mail, irons, hair dryers. **Leisure Activities:** exercise room. **Guest Services:** coin laundry. **Business Services:** meeting rooms. **Cards:** AX, DC, MC, VI.

SOME UNITS

[icons] FEE

------- **WHERE TO DINE** -------

BLUE GINGER LOUNGE AND GRILLE   Lunch: $8-$14   Dinner: $14-$34   Phone: 519/434-5777

(CAA)   **Location:** Jct Pall Mall St. 644 Richmond St N6A 3G6. **Hours:** 11:30 am-3 & 5-10 pm, Sat & Sun from 5 pm. Closed major holidays. **Reservations:** suggested. **Features:** Comprising the chef's exotic creations of Continental cuisine with Asian influences, the innovative menu keeps the locals coming back. Diners can select from such starters as "fire and ice," a mix of Asian vegetables rolled in sushi rice, wrapped in nori, Continental dipped in tempura and served with wasabi and sweet soya sauce. Among noteworthy entrees are rack of lamb, Chilean sea bass and Angus steak. The contemporary dining room has a sleek, modern look throughout. Dressy casual; cocktails. **Parking:** street. **Cards:** AX, DC, MC, VI.

[icons]

DAVID'S BISTRO   Lunch: $10-$12   Dinner: $16-$23   Phone: 519/667-0535

Location: Between Queens Ave and Dundas St. 432 Richmond St N6A 3C9. **Hours:** 5 pm-10 pm, Wed-Fri also 11:30 am-2:30 pm. Closed major holidays. **Reservations:** suggested. **Features:** Modern, upscale bistro Continental with bright, trendy interior highlighting changing local artwork. Friendly and knowledgable staff offer assistance with good selection of wine by the glass and the bottle, as well as describing daily 2- and 3-course blackboard specials. Innovative menu features starters such as crab cakes and Caesar salad with anchovies. Entrees include seafood stew, lamb shanks and creative pasta, poultry and beef selections. Dessert is worth saving room for. Dressy casual; cocktails. **Parking:** street. **Cards:** AX, DC, MC, VI.

[icon]

FELLINI KOOLINI'S ITALIAN CUISINI   Lunch: $5-$10   Dinner: $6-$20   Phone: 519/642-2300

Location: Between Richmond and Talbot sts. 155 Albert St N6A 1L9. **Hours:** 11 am-close, Sat from 11:30 am, Sun from 4 pm. **Features:** A fun, casual atmosphere prevails in the rustic restaurant's two floors of dining space. Italian The menu lets guests create their own pasta and pizza specials, which are served in hearty portions. Service is friendly. The patio is open seasonally. Casual dress; cocktails. **Parking:** on-site. **Cards:** AX, DC, MC, VI.

[icons]

GARLIC'S RESTAURANT   Lunch: $9-$16   Dinner: $13-$24   Phone: 519/432-4092

Location: Jct Dufferin. 481 Richmond St N6A 3E4. **Hours:** 11:30 am-11 pm, Fri & Sat-midnight. **Reservations:** suggested. **Features:** Modern, funky decor, a bustling atmosphere and friendly servers Continental make this place a nice setting for enjoying good food with good friends. The fun, creative menu lists scores of garlic lovers' favorites, including roasted garlic and brie bread, cream of garlic soup, pastas with roasted garlic and even garlic ice cream. Many dishes reflect an innovative mix of Asian influences. Cocktails. **Parking:** street. **Cards:** AX, DC, MC, VI.

[icon]

GREAT WEST STEAK HOUSE   Lunch: $7-$11   Dinner: $14-$20   Phone: 519/438-4149

Location: Jct Horton and Waterloo St, just e of Wellington Rd. 240 Waterloo St N6B 2N4. **Hours:** 11:30 am-10 pm, Fri & Sat-11 pm, Sun 10:30 am-9 pm. Closed: 12/25. **Features:** Steak and prime rib are the specialties of Steak House the house featured in the casual setting of a western railway roadhouse complete with train and railroad crossing accouterments. The menu also spotlights sandwiches and lighter entrees as well as a buffet and extensive salad bar. Casual dress; cocktails. **Parking:** on-site. **Cards:** AX, CB, DC, MC, VI.

[icons]

THE KEG STEAKHOUSE AND BAR   Dinner: $16-$32   Phone: 519/686-5811

Location: Hwy 401, exit 186B (Wellington Rd), 2 km n. 1059 Wellington Rd S N6E 1W4. **Hours:** 4 pm-midnight, Sat 3 pm-1 am, Sun 3 pm-11 pm. Closed: 12/25. **Features:** Mesquite-grilled steaks, a relaxed setting and Steak House personable service make the steak house a popular choice. Diners sample traditional favorites, such as escargot, French onion soup or bacon-wrapped scallops to start, followed by huge cuts of prime rib, steak, grilled seafood or chicken with a steaming baked potato. Top that off with a piece of cheesecake and a specialty coffee for the perfect ending. Casual dress; cocktails. **Parking:** on-site. **Cards:** AX, DC, MC, VI.

[icons]

LA CASA RISTORANTE   Lunch: $8-$18   Dinner: $14-$32   Phone: 519/434-2272

Location: Between Talbot and Richmond sts. 117 King St N6A 1C3. **Hours:** 11:30 am-11 pm. Closed major holidays; also Sun. **Reservations:** suggested, weekends. **Features:** The decor is modern and upbeat and Italian the atmosphere bustling in the relaxed restaurant. Freshly prepared cuisine—along the lines of steamed mussels and fresh salad starters and main courses of gourmet pizza, pasta, beef, veal, seafood and poultry—is served in good-size portions. Casual dress; cocktails. **Parking:** on-site (fee). **Cards:** AX, DC, MC, VI.

[icon]

LONDON GRILL   Lunch: $8-$20   Dinner: $19-$30   Phone: 519/430-6414
Location: At King St and Wellington Rd; in Hilton London Ontario. 300 King St N6B 1S2. **Hours:** 11:30 am-2:30 & 5-10:30 pm, Sat from 5:30 pm, Sun 11 am-2:30 & 5-10:30 pm. **Reservations:** suggested. **Features:** Fine table linens and a modern interior design contribute to the cozy, upscale mood of the dining room. The menu offers a choice of all-time favorites in ample portions, including shrimp cocktail, Caesar salad, rack of lamb and grilled steak as well as preparations of poultry, seafood and pasta. A tempting selection of desserts is offered tableside. Service is professional and friendly. Dressy casual; cocktails. **Parking:** on-site. **Cards:** AX, CB, DC, DS, JC, MC, VI.
Continental

LONDON STATION KEG RESTAURANT   Dinner: $17-$36   Phone: 519/438-0045
Location: Jct Pall Mall St; at old railway station. 664 Richmond St N6A 3G8. **Hours:** 3 pm-1 am, Fri & Sat-2 am. **Reservations:** accepted, except Sat. **Features:** In the heart of downtown, the restaurant presents diners its popular menu. While soaking up the history of London's rail, guests can sample classic favorites, such as slow-roasted prime rib, mesquite-grilled steaks and steaming baked potatoes. Casual dress. **Parking:** on-site (fee). **Cards:** AX, DC, MC, VI.
Steak House

MANCHURIA GARDE   Lunch: $8-$11   Dinner: $14-$16   Phone: 519/668-1234
Location: Hwy 401, exit 186B (Wellington Rd), 1.6 km n. 1130 Dearness Dr N6E 1N9. **Hours:** 11:30 am-10 pm, Fri & Sat-10:30 pm, Sun & holidays noon-10 pm. Closed: 12/25. **Reservations:** suggested. **Features:** The established restaurant has been pleasing diners for years with its extensive buffet of wide-ranging Chinese fare. Complements include an extensive salad and dessert bar. Casual dress; cocktails. **Parking:** on-site.
Chinese
Cards: AX, MC, VI.

MANDARIN   Lunch: $9-$13   Dinner: $16-$22   Phone: 519/680-5000
Location: Jct Commissioners Rd. 387 Wellington Rd S N6C 5Z6. **Hours:** 11:30 am-3 & 5-9:30 pm, Fri & Sat-10:30 pm, Sun & holidays 11:30 am-3 & 4:30-9:30 pm. Closed: 12/25, 12/26. **Reservations:** suggested, for dinner. **Features:** The popular chain's specialty is its extensive buffet, which includes not only hot and tasty Chinese items but also huge salad and dessert bars. The selection is varied enough to please all, especially those with hearty appetites. Casual dress; cocktails. **Parking:** on-site. **Cards:** AX, MC, VI.
Chinese

MARIENBAD RESTAURANT   Lunch: $8-$13   Dinner: $9-$23   Phone: 519/679-9940
Location: At Talbot St. 122 Carling St N6A 1H6. **Hours:** 11:30 am-10 pm, Thurs-Sat to 10:30 pm, Sun 4:30 pm-9 pm. Closed: 12/25. **Features:** In a delightful historical building dating back to 1854, the fine restaurant prepares a blend of European and Continental cuisine. Among choices are varied schnitzels, Hungarian goulash and beefsteak tartare, in addition to such traditional favorites as prime rib and preparations of pasta, chicken and vegetarian ingredients. European artwork and an interesting mural decorate the large dining room. Casual dress; cocktails. **Parking:** on-site (fee). **Cards:** AX, DC, MC, VI.
Continental

MICHAEL'S OFF BRADLEY   Lunch: $7-$12   Dinner: $14-$26   Phone: 519/680-3603
Location: Hwy 401, exit 186B (Wellington Rd), 2 km n. 1092 Dearness Dr N6E 1N9. **Hours:** 11:30 am-10 pm, Sat 4 pm-11 pm. Closed major holidays; also Sun. **Reservations:** suggested. **Features:** Diners peruse a fine Continental menu in a relaxed, upscale setting. Highlights include smoked salmon, shrimp cocktail or French onion soup to start, followed by traditional favorites such as grilled steak, prime rib and tasty seafood entrees. Pasta, veal and poultry selections are share menu space. Servers tempt patrons with a decadent dessert tray to end. Dressy casual; cocktails. **Parking:** on-site. **Cards:** AX, MC, VI.
Continental

MICHAEL'S ON THE THAMES   Lunch: $8-$15   Dinner: $14-$30   Phone: 519/672-0111
Location: 1 km w of Wellington Rd. 1 York St N0M 1A0. **Hours:** 11:30 am-2:30 & 5-9:30 pm, Fri-11 pm, Sat 5 pm-11 pm, Sun 5 pm-9:30 pm. **Reservations:** suggested. **Features:** Fine Continental cuisine, pianist entertainment and sophisticated service set the stage for a romantic dining experience. A local tradition, the restaurant provides a consistently high level of food and service. The staff is skilled at tableside and flambe presentations, and many guests finish their evening with flaming specialty coffees. Casual dress; cocktails; entertainment. **Parking:** on-site. **Cards:** AX, DC, MC, VI.
Continental

THE NEW HOOK'S RESTAURANT   Lunch: $9   Dinner: $13-$17   Phone: 519/686-7500
Location: Jct Wharncliffe and Southdale rds. 850 Wharncliffe Rd S N6J 2N4. **Hours:** 11:30 am-2:30 & 4:30-10 pm, Sun from 11 am. **Reservations:** accepted. **Features:** The casual restaurant is a longtime favorite with the local crowd, who enjoy the relaxed setting and extensive buffet. Diners can choose from a well-stocked salad bar, several soups, Chinese food favorites, several roasts, vegetables, potatoes and a wonderful dessert table with an array of tempting treats. Casual dress. **Parking:** on-site. **Cards:** AX, MC, VI.
American

OSCAR TAYLOR'S   Lunch: $8-$16   Dinner: $12-$30   Phone: 519/642-4882
Location: Jct Pall Mall St. 660 Richmond St N6A 5P6. **Hours:** 7 am-11 pm, Fri & Sat-midnight. Closed: 12/25. **Features:** The well-established steak house offers diners a choice of indoor or seasonal outdoor seating. The menu highlights fine cuts of Certified Angus beef and prime rib, grilled to order. Also offered is a variety of pasta and seafood options. The central location makes this place a popular choice with the local business crowd. On Sunday, brunch is a real treat. Casual dress; cocktails. **Parking:** on-site (fee). **Cards:** AX, DC, MC, VI.
Steak & Seafood

OUTBACK STEAKHOUSE   Dinner: $13-$22   Phone: 519/686-6025
Location: Corner of Wellington Rd; at Crossroads Centre. 765 Exeter Rd N6E 3T2. **Hours:** 4:30 pm-10:30 pm, Fri & Sat 4 pm-11 pm, Sun 4 pm-10 pm. Closed: 12/25. **Features:** Well-known for their "bloomin' onion" and casual Aussie atmosphere, the Outback Steakhouse offers diners a relaxed setting and a wide range of hearty casual fare. Steaks, chicken, ribs and chicken are popular choices; and now sizzling fajitas, pastas, and of course, the ever-popular burgers are also featured. A great choice for families and all-occasion dining. Casual dress; cocktails. **Parking:** on-site. **Cards:** AX, DC, MC, VI.
Steak House

PASTO'S   Lunch: $8-$15   Dinner: $12-$20   Phone: 519/652-7659
▼▼▼ ▼▼▼   **Location:** Hwy 401, exit 177A, jct Hwy 4; in Best Western Stoneridge Inn & Conference Centre. 6675 Burtwistle Ln N6L
Italian   1H5. **Hours:** 11 am-10 pm, Fri & Sat-11 pm. Closed major holidays; also Sun & 12/25-1/2.
Features: Directly off the major highway, the casual eatery builds its menu on freshly prepared Italian
cuisine. On the menu are gourmet pizzas, tasty pasta dishes and preparations of veal, chicken and beef.
Service is warm and personable. Casual dress; cocktails. **Parking:** on-site. **Cards:** AX, MC, VI.   🍽 ✕

TIMBERS CHOP HOUSE   Lunch: $7-$17   Dinner: $9-$31   Phone: 519/649-1103
▼▼▼ ▼▼▼   **Location:** Jct Wellington and Southdale rds; in Radisson Hotel and Suites London. 855 Wellington Rd S N6E 3N5.
Steak House   **Hours:** 6:30 am-11 pm, Sat from 8 am, Sun 8 am-9 pm, Mon & Tues 6:30 am-10:30 pm. Closed: 12/25,
12/26. **Features:** A relaxed setting with log cabins walls, and lots of wood accents complement the casual
menu of hearty fare. Steaks, ribs and seafood are popular menu items, but they also serve up great
burgers, pastas and entree size salads. The menu also features "early bird" specials and a popular Sunday brunch buffet,
making Timbers Chop House a popular favorite with locals and tourists alike. Casual dress; cocktails. **Parking:** on-site.
Cards: CB, DC, MC, VI.   🍽 ✕

VILLA CORNELIA   Dinner: $13-$23   Phone: 519/679-3444
▼▼▼ ▼▼▼   **Location:** Between Richmond and Talbot sts. 142 Kent St N6A 1L3. **Hours:** 5:30 pm-10 pm. Closed: 1/1, 12/25;
also Sun. **Reservations:** suggested. **Features:** The restored 1892 home invites guests to enjoy candlelight
Continental   dining in an elegant yet relaxed setting. The menu centers on fine Continental cuisine. Among appetizers
are homemade soup, salad, escargot and smoked salmon. Entrees include beef, pork, rack of lamb and
pasta selections, all of which are colorfully presented and generous in size. Available during the week, the prix fixe menu offers
exceptional value. Semi-formal attire; cocktails. **Parking:** on-site. **Cards:** AX, MC, VI. **Historic**   ✕

MACTIER

———— **WHERE TO STAY** ————

———— *The following lodging was either not evaluated or did not* ————
meet AAA rating requirements but is listed for your information only.

DELTA ROCKY CREST RESORT   Phone: 705/375-2240
[fyi]   Not evaluated. **Location:** Hwy 69, exit Hamer Bay Rd, follow signs. RR 1, Hamer Bay Rd P0C 1H0. Facilities,
services, and decor characterize a mid-range property.

MADOC pop. 2,044

———— **WHERE TO DINE** ————

TWO LOONS   Lunch: $5-$9   Dinner: $9-$26   Phone: 613/473-2744
▼▼▼ ▼▼▼   **Location:** On Hwy 62, 4 km s. 13200 Hwy 62 K0K 2K0. **Hours:** 9 am-10 pm; 8 am-11 pm 5/1-8/31. Closed:
Canadian   12/25. **Reservations:** required, weekends in summer. **Features:** Overlooking Moira Lake, Two Loons
makes buffet dining an art. Seafood, Chinese cuisine, and wings are just a few of the special offerings.
Entertainment is on tap Saturday night. Buffet dinner is highlighted Friday-Sunday. Saturday buffet is only
served 1/1-3/31. Casual dress; cocktails. **Parking:** on-site. **Cards:** AX, MC, VI.   🍽 ✕

MAGNETAWAN pop. 1,342

———— **WHERE TO STAY** ————

WOODLAND ECHOES COTTAGE RESORT   Phone: (705)387-3866
▼▼▼ ▼▼▼   6/12-9/17 [MAP]   2P: $120-$125
5/1-6/11 & 9/18-4/30 [MAP]   2P: $99-$108
Resort Cottage   **Location:** Hwy 11, exit Burks Falls Ontario St to Hwy 520 W, then 20 km. Located in a quiet area. 3 Victoria St P0A 1P0
(PO Box 59 AAA). Fax: 705/387-0216. **Facility:** This family resort is on picturesque grounds and offers
waterfront cottages. 10 cottages ($129-$190), some with whirlpools. 1 story, exterior corridors. **Parking:** on-site. **Terms:** office
hours 8 am-10 pm, check-out 9 am, 2 night minimum stay - weekends, 30 day cancellation notice-fee imposed, weekly rates
available, package plans. **Amenities:** *Some:* CD players, hair dryers. **Leisure Activities:** sauna, whirlpool, rental boats,
canoeing, paddleboats, sailboats, fishing, miniature golf, tennis court, cross country skiing, snowmobiling, ice skating, recreation
programs, bicycles, hiking trails, playground, basketball, horseshoes, volleyball. Fee: boat dock, massage. **Guest Services:** gift
shop, coin laundry. **Business Services:** meeting rooms. **Cards:** MC, VI.   SOME UNITS
🍴 🛗 ✕ 🏧 🎥 ☎ 🛏 📷 📺 / ✕ 📼 /
FEE

MANITOULIN ISLAND

———— **WHERE TO STAY** ————

HURON SANDS MOTEL   Phone: (705)377-4616
🅰🅰 SAVE   6/24-9/5   1P: $79   2P: $89
5/1-6/23 & 9/6-4/30   1P: $69   2P: $79
▼▼▼   **Location:** In Providence Bay; on Hwy 551, 27.2 km w of South Baymouth via 10th Side Rd, follow signs; centre. 5216
Motel   Hwy 551 P0P 1T0 (5216 Hwy 551, General Delivery Prov Bay, PROVIDENCE BAY). Fax: 705/377-5505.
Facility: 10 one-bedroom standard units. 1 story, exterior corridors. **Parking:** on-site, winter plug-ins.
Terms: office hours 6:30 am-11 pm, 3 day cancellation notice-fee imposed. **Amenities:** video library (fee).
Dining: 7 am-10 pm; 6:30 am-11 pm 6/21-9/02. **Leisure Activities:** snowmobiling. **Guest Services:** gift shop, coin laundry.
Cards: AX, MC, VI.   SOME UNITS
🛏 🍴 🎥 ☎ 🛏 / ✕ 📼 /
FEE

THE ISLAND LODGE Phone: (705)285-4343
CAA SAVE   6/1-9/15 [BP]   1P: $140   2P: $280

Location: In Whitefish Falls; parking and dock, just w of Hwy 6 (phone for boat at Espanola or Little Current). Located in a quiet secluded area. (PO Box 87, WHITEFISH FALLS). Fax: 705/285-0630. **Facility:** A scenic island setting gives the lodge a retreatlike ambience; the cottages offer privacy and good views. 16 cottages. 1 story, exterior corridors. **Parking:** on-site. **Terms:** open 6/1-9/15, office hours 8 am-8 pm, 30 day cancellation notice-fee imposed, weekly rates available, package plans, pets ($10 extra charge, with prior approval).
Cottage
Amenities: hair dryers. **Dining:** 8 am-10 & 6-8 pm, cocktails. **Leisure Activities:** rental boats, rental canoes, rental paddleboats, fishing, playground. *Fee:* sailboats, boat dock, fishing guides, kayaks. **Guest Services:** gift shop, coin laundry. **Business Services:** meeting rooms. **Cards:** AX, MC, VI. **Special Amenities: free full breakfast and early check-in/late check-out.**

SOME UNITS
FEE ⬚ ⬚ ⬚ ⬚ ⬚ ⬚ ⬚ ⬚ ⬚ / ⬚ ⬚ / FEE

MINDEMOYA MOTEL Phone: (705)377-4779
CAA SAVE   6/15-9/15   1P: $82-$92   2P: $82-$107   XP: $10   F12
              5/1-6/14 & 9/16-4/30   1P: $69-$79   2P: $79-$99   XP: $10   F12
Location: In Mindemoya; 1 km w of jct Hwy 551 and 542. Located in a rural area. 6375 Hwy 542 P0P 1S0 (RR 1, MINDEMOYA). **Facility:** 12 one-bedroom standard units, some with efficiencies or kitchens. 1 story, exterior corridors. **Parking:** on-site, winter plug-ins. **Terms:** office hours 7:30 am-11 pm, 3 day cancellation notice, small pets only (in designated units). **Cards:** MC, VI.
Motel

SOME UNITS
⬚ ⬚ ⬚ / ⬚ ⬚ ⬚ ⬚ /

------ **WHERE TO DINE** ------

GARDEN'S GATE   **Lunch:** $8-$21   **Dinner:** $8-$21   **Phone:** 705/859-2088
Location: In Tehkummah; jct Hwy 6, 1.7 km w. 316 Hwy 542 P0P 2C0. **Hours:** Open 5/1-10/24 & 4/1-4/30; 11 am-8 pm. Closed: Mon 5/1-6/30 & 9/1-10/31, also Tues & Wed 4/1-4/30. **Features:** The small, sweet restaurant offers casual, friendly service and a comfortable, country atmosphere. Fresh ingredients are used in carefully prepared dishes. Desserts are not to be ignored. Lovely gardens add a final touch of pleasure.
Canadian
Casual dress; cocktails. **Parking:** on-site. **Cards:** MC, VI.
⬚

GREEN ACRES RESTAURANT   **Lunch:** $5-$10   **Dinner:** $5-$10   **Phone:** 705/368-2428
Location: In Sheguiandah; 9.6 km s of Little Current. 10944 Hwy 6 P0P 1W0. **Hours:** 11:30 am-9 pm. Closed: 12/23-1/2. **Features:** The family-operated establishment takes pride in the in-house preparation of beef and turkey. The fish batter is made from the restaurant's own recipe. Pickerel dinners are available in season.
Canadian
Desserts include a good selection of fresh pies, butter tarts, date squares and hot apple dumplings. Casual dress. **Parking:** on-site. **Cards:** AX, MC, VI.
⬚

THE SCHOOL HOUSE RESTAURANT   **Dinner:** $13-$25   **Phone:** 705/377-4055
Location: In Providence Bay; centre. 46 McNevin St P0P 1T0. **Hours:** Open 5/22-10/15; 5 pm-9 pm. Closed: Mon. **Reservations:** suggested. **Features:** A small, historic schoolhouse houses the intimate dining room, where diners savor creatively prepared and artistically presented dishes of red meat, chicken and fish. This spot is a true treat in an off-the-beaten-path location. Casual dress; cocktails. **Parking:** street.
Continental
Cards: MC, VI. **Historic**
⬚ ⬚

MARATHON pop. 4,416

------ **WHERE TO STAY** ------

PENINSULA INN Phone: (807)229-0651
CAA SAVE   5/1-10/31   1P: $80-$85   2P: $90-$95   XP: $5   F10
              11/1-4/30   1P: $75-$80   2P: $85-$90   XP: $5   F10
Location: On Hwy 17, 2.4 km w of jct Hwy 626. Located in a commercial area. (PO Box 597). Fax: 807/229-2272. **Facility:** 21 one-bedroom standard units. 1 story, exterior corridors. **Parking:** on-site, winter plug-ins.
Motel
Terms: office hours 8 am-11 pm, 3 day cancellation notice-fee imposed, small pets only (in smoking units). **Dining:** 7 am-11 pm, cocktails. **Leisure Activities:** snowmobiling. **Cards:** AX, CB, DC, DS, MC, VI.
Special Amenities: free newspaper and early check-in/late check-out. *(See color ad below)*

SOME UNITS
⬚ ⬚ ⬚ ⬚ / ⬚ /

Peninsula Inn

• Excellent Accommodation • Open All Year
• Full Bath • Electric Heat • Colour TV
• Satellite Dishes • Phones • Air Conditioned
• Licensed Restaurant On Premises
Serving Fine Food and A Take-Out Service

 (807) 229-0510
Licensed Under L.L.B.O.

(807) 229-0651 • Fax (807) 229-2272
Hwy. 17, ½ mile West of Marathon, Ontario P0T 2E0

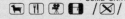

MARKHAM —See Toronto p. 548.

MASSEY

——— WHERE TO STAY ———

MOHAWK MOTEL CANADA   **Phone:** 705/865-2722
◇◇◇◇ All Year   2P: $67-$85   XP: $8   F12
      Location: Centre. Located in a commercial area. 335 Sable St ·P0P 1P0 (PO Box 429). **Fax:** 705/865-1015.
Motel **Facility:** 16 one-bedroom standard units, some with efficiencies. 1 story, interior/exterior corridors. **Parking:**
       on-site, winter plug-ins. **Terms:** office hours 7:30 am-11 pm, cancellation fee imposed, package plans, pets
($6 extra charge, with prior approval, in designated units). **Amenities:** hair dryers. *Some:* DVD players (fee). **Leisure**
Activities: snowmobiling. **Guest Services:** gift shop, coin laundry. **Cards:** MC, VI. *(See color ad below)*

SOME UNITS
(ASK) (🛏) (🍴) (📶) (📺) / (⊠) (VCR) (💻) /
     FEE   FEE

——— WHERE TO DINE ———

CROCK'S COUNTRY KITCHEN   **Lunch:** $4-$12   **Dinner:** $4-$12   **Phone:** 705/865-3041
◇ **Location:** On Hwy 17; centre. 370 Sable St P0P 1P0. **Hours:** 7 am-9 pm, Sun from 8 am. Closed: 1/1, 12/25,
      12/26. **Reservations:** accepted. **Features:** Hearty home-style cooking is served in generous portions. The
Canadian menu includes items such as hot sandwiches, pork chop dinner, veal parmigiana, oven-roasted chicken,
      liver and onions and fish and chips. Casual dress; cocktails. **Parking:** street. **Cards:** AX, MC, VI.   (⊠)

THE DRAGONFLY   **Lunch:** $5-$7   **Dinner:** $7-$17   **Phone:** 705/865-3456
◇◇ ◇◇ **Location:** Jct Hwy 17; centre. 205 Imperial St P0P 1P0. **Hours:** 11 am-10 pm, Sat & Sun from 7 am; from 7 am
      5/15-10/15; hours may vary off season. Closed: 12/25, 12/26; also Mon. **Reservations:** accepted.
Canadian **Features:** If a menu with some variety is of interest, then the offerings here will be welcomed. Panfried
      pickerel, Mexican fajitas and quesadillas, poached salmon, cobb salad, spanakopita and spicy Thai beef
skewers are only some of the interesting taste treats. Soups, salads, sandwiches and burgers, in addition to some vegetarian
dishes and a children's menu, also are offered. Casual dress. **Parking:** on-site. **Cards:** MC, VI.   (⊠)

MCKELLAR pop. 933

——— WHERE TO STAY ———

THE INN AT MANITOU   *Book at aaa.com*   **Phone:** (705)389-2171
(CAA) (SAVE) 6/23-9/8 [AP]   1P: $380-$550   2P: $560-$900   XP: $190   F
             5/13-6/22 & 9/9-10/16 [AP] 1P: $370-$485   2P: $540-$770   XP: $190   F
◇◇◇ ◇◇◇◇ **Location:** Hwy 124, exit McKellar Centre Rd, 8 km s, follow signs. Located on a lake in a rural area. 81 The Inn Rd P0G
Resort   1C0 (General Delivery). **Fax:** 705/389-3818. **Facility:** Manicured grounds, a lakeside setting and well-
Small-scale Hotel appointed common areas give this inn an elegant atmosphere. 34 units. 33 one-bedroom standard units,
             some with whirlpools. 1 cottage. 1 story, exterior corridors. **Parking:** on-site. **Terms:** open 5/13-10/16, office
hours 7 am-11 pm, check-in 4 pm, 2 night minimum stay - seasonal, 30 day cancellation notice-fee
imposed, package plans, 16% service charge, small pets only. **Amenities:** dual phone lines, voice mail, irons, hair dryers.
Some: CD players, safes, honor bars. **Dining:** dining room, see separate listing. **Pool(s):** heated outdoor. **Leisure**
Activities: saunas, whirlpool, boating, canoeing, boat dock, fishing, pontoon boat cruises, 13 tennis courts (1 indoor, 1 lighted),
recreation programs, bicycles, exercise room, spa. **Fee:** fishing guides, golf-18 holes, driving range. **Guest Services:** gift shop,
valet laundry, airport transportation (fee)-Parry Sound Airport. **Business Services:** meeting rooms. **Cards:** AX, DC, MC, VI.

SOME UNITS
(🔌) (🛏) (🍴) (🍷) (🛎) (🐚) (⊠) (🐾) (DATA PORT) / (⊠) (📺) (VCR) (📶) (📺) /
FEE

Mohawk Motel Canada
We Are Proud To Be Original
www.mohawkmotel.ca
Hwy 17, Massey Ontario

FREE - wireless internet
FREE - continental breakfast
FREE - movie channel
FREE - local calls & parking
(705) 865 2722
1866 865 2722

——— WHERE TO DINE ———

THE INN AT MANITOU DINING ROOM **Lunch:** $38   **Dinner:** $69   **Phone:** 705/389-2171
▼▼▼ ▼▼▼ **Location:** Hwy 124, exit McKellar Centre Rd, 8 km s, follow signs; in The Inn at Manitou. 81 The Inn Rd P0G 1C0.
Hours: Open 5/15-10/15; 7:45-10:30 am, 12:30-2 & 7-9 pm. **Reservations:** required. **Features:** A group of
French personable international staffers provides highly polished, friendly service. The wine list is well developed,
and expertise is available to assist with selections to pair with the carefully prepared and artistically
presented dishes. The lovely resort setting adds to the enjoyment of the dining experience. Dressy casual; cocktails. **Parking:**
on-site. **Cards:** AX, MC, VI. 🍽 ⊠

MEAFORD pop. 4,559

——— WHERE TO DINE ———

FISHERMAN'S WHARF **Lunch:** $6-$9   **Dinner:** $8-$19   **Phone:** 519/538-1390
▼▼ ▼▼ **Location:** Hwy 26, 0.6 km on Bayfield St to end; directly across from Meaford Harbour at Trowbridge and Bayfield sts.
12 Bayfield St N4L 1G1. **Hours:** 11:30 am-9 pm, Fri-10 pm, Sat 9 am-10 pm, Sun 9 am-9 pm; to 8 pm, Fri-9
Canadian pm, Sat 9 am-9 pm, Sun 9 am-8 pm 11/2-6/15. Closed: 12/25. **Reservations:** suggested, in summer.
Features: Located just outside of town overlooking the harbour, the outdoor patio and large panoramic
windows in the dining room offer wonderful views. Warm country hospitality shines through here with friendly and personal
service. Diners will find a good menu selection featuring casual Canadian fare with a regional focus on fresh local fish in season
with whitefish and splake a speciality. Creamy fish chowder and fish and chips are also popular favorites. Casual dress;
cocktails. **Parking:** on-site. **Cards:** AX, DC, MC, VI. 🍽 ⊠

MERRICKVILLE

——— WHERE TO STAY ———

SAM JAKES INN **Phone:** (613)269-3711
▼▼▼▼ All Year 1P: $163-$323   2P: $175-$335   XP: $32
Location: Corner of St. Lawrence St; centre. Located in a village setting. 118 Main St E K0G 1N0 (PO Box 580).
Country Inn Fax: 613/269-3713. **Facility:** Period decor and a garden patio area with a fountain and pergola enhance this
inn set in an 1861 limestone structure with contemporary additions. Smoke free premises. 33 units. 31 one-
bedroom standard units, some with whirlpools. 2 one-bedroom suites with whirlpools. 3 stories, interior corridors. **Parking:** on-
site. **Terms:** office hours 7 am-11 pm, check-in 4 pm, cancellation fee imposed, [AP] & [MAP] meal plans available, package
plans. **Amenities:** high-speed Internet (fee), voice mail, hair dryers. Some: irons. **Dining:** restaurant, see separate listing.
Leisure Activities: sauna, exercise room, spa. Fee: canoes. **Guest Services:** valet laundry. **Business Services:** meeting
rooms. **Cards:** AX, CB, DC, DS, MC, VI.
SOME UNITS
(A$K) (S/D) (¶) (🍽) (⊠) (⊠) (DATA PORT) (💻) / (VCR) (🛢) /
FEE   FEE

——— WHERE TO DINE ———

SAM JAKES INN DINING ROOM AND LOCK 21 **Lunch:** $7-$15   **Dinner:** $19-$35   **Phone:** 613/269-3711
▼▼▼▼ **Location:** Corner of St. Lawrence St; centre; in Sam Jakes Inn. 118 Main St E K0G 1N0. **Hours:** 7:30-10 am, 11-2 &
5-9:30 pm, Sat 8-11 am, 11:30-3 & 5-9:30 pm, Sun 8 am-3 & 5-8 pm. Closed: 12/25.
Canadian **Reservations:** suggested. **Features:** Attractive country-style décor. Outdoor patio dining in the summer.
Sunday brunch 10 am-2:30 pm. Featured menu items are prepared with local products and fresh seasonal
produce. The menu varies by season. Only VAQ wines are offered. Regional ales and a good selection of single malt whiskeys
are also available. Casual dress; cocktails. **Parking:** on-site. **Cards:** AX, CB, DC, DS, JC, MC, VI. 🍽 ⊠

MIDLAND pop. 16,214

——— WHERE TO STAY ———

COMFORT INN **Book at aaa.com** **Phone:** (705)526-2090
▼▼ ▼▼ 5/1-10/31 [CP] 1P: $109-$139   2P: $119-$149   XP: $10   F18
11/1-4/30 [CP] 1P: $99-$129   2P: $109-$139   XP: $10   F18
Small-scale Hotel **Location:** Jct King St and Hwy 12. Located in a commercial area. 980 King St L4R 4K5. Fax: 705/526-0419.
Facility: 60 one-bedroom standard units. 2 stories (no elevator), interior corridors. **Parking:** on-site, winter
plug-ins. **Terms:** cancellation fee imposed, package plans. **Amenities:** Some: irons, hair dryers. **Guest Services:** valet laundry.
Cards: AX, DC, MC, VI.
SOME UNITS
(A$K) (S/D) (🛏) (¶+) (🔌) (💻) / (⊠) (DATA PORT) (🛢) (📷) /

LITTLE LAKE INN BED & BREAKFAST **Phone:** 705/526-2750
(CAA) (SAVE) All Year [ECP] 1P: $115-$155   2P: $120-$160   XP: $25   D16
Location: Between Hwy 93 and King St. Located in a residential area. 669 Yonge St L4R 2E1. Fax: 705/526-9005.
▼▼ ▼▼ **Facility:** In-room fireplaces, period trim, an English garden and a parkside setting give this large cottage-
style home a town-and-country ambience. Smoke free premises. 4 units. 3 one-bedroom standard units with
Bed & Breakfast whirlpools. 1 one-bedroom suite with whirlpool. 1 story, interior corridors. **Parking:** on-site, winter plug-ins.
Terms: office hours 8 am-10 pm, 7 day cancellation notice-fee imposed, package plans. **Amenities:** video
library, DVD players, CD players, irons, hair dryers. **Guest Services:** area transportation-bus station. **Cards:** AX, DC, MC, VI.
Special Amenities: free expanded continental breakfast and free local telephone calls.
SOME UNITS
(⊠) (VCR) (DATA PORT) (🛢) / (☎) /

————— *The following lodging was either not evaluated or did not*
meet AAA rating requirements but is listed for your information only.

BEST WESTERN HIGHLAND INN AND
CONFERENCE CENTRE **Phone:** 705/526-9307
(fyi) Not evaluated. **Location:** Jct Hwy 12 and King St. 924 King St L4R 4L3 (PO Box 515). Facilities, services, and decor
characterize a mid-range property.

WHERE TO DINE

ANDREA'S RESTAURANT   **Lunch:** $10-$14   **Dinner:** $11-$18   **Phone:** 705/527-6528
▼▼ ▼▼   **Location:** Directly s of jct Hwy 12 and King St. 1004 King St L4R 4K5. **Hours:** 7 am-2 & 4:30-9 pm, Sat from 8 am,
Sun 8 am-2 pm. Closed major holidays; also Mon. **Reservations:** accepted. **Features:** This small dining
Continental   room is a bright and cheery choice for lunch and is cozy at dinner. Children are welcome; however, the
clientele is typically business folks. This is a family operation and Andrea has been a chef for 40 years. Fish,
red meat and creative menu selections are offered. Casual dress; cocktails. **Parking:** on-site. **Cards:** AX, MC, VI.   ⊠

MOM'S OF MIDLAND   **Lunch:** $5-$8   **Dinner:** $5-$17   **Phone:** 705/527-0700
▼▼ ▼▼   **Location:** Hwy 12, exit William St N, 0.3 km n. 200 Pillsbury Dr L4R 4K5. **Hours:** 7 am-9 pm, Sun & major holidays
from 9 am. **Reservations:** accepted. **Features:** Casual country atmosphere. Selection of pies made fresh
American   daily. Lunch and evening specials. The natural pine walls and glowing fireplace give this restaurant a
comfortable country atmosphere. A mixed menu featuring chicken, steak, sandwiches and salads is
complemented by lunch and evening specials served in hearty portions. A selection of pies are baked fresh daily. Casual dress;
cocktails. **Parking:** on-site. **Cards:** AX, MC, VI.   ⊠

MILTON pop. 31,471

WHERE TO STAY

HOLIDAY INN EXPRESS HOTEL & SUITES MILTON   **Phone:** 905/795-1011
[fyi]   All Year [ECP]   1P: $139-$289   2P: $139-$289   XP: $10   F16
Too new to rate, opening scheduled for February 2005. **Location:** Hwy 401 W, exit 320 (Hwy 25). 2750 High
Small-scale Hotel   Point Dr L9T 5G5. Fax: 905/876-4955. **Amenities:** 92 units, coffeemakers, microwaves, refrigerators, pool.
Cards: AX, DC, DS, MC, VI. *(See color ad below)*

MISSISSAUGA pop. 612,295   (See map and index starting on p. 479)

WHERE TO STAY

BEST WESTERN ADMIRAL HOTEL & SUITES
CONFERENCE CENTRE-MISSISSAUGA AIRPORT   *Book at aaa.com*   **Phone:** (905)795-1011   132
(CAA) (SAVE)   All Year [ECP]   1P: $139-$249   2P: $139-$249   XP: $10   F17
Location: Hwy 401, exit Hwy 10 (Hurontario St), 1.5 km n; just s of Derry Rd. 40 Admiral Blvd L5T 2W1.
▼▼▼▼   Fax: 905/795-1712. **Facility:** 90 units. 78 one-bedroom standard units. 12 one-bedroom suites ($159-$249),
some with whirlpools. 3 stories, interior corridors. *Bath:* combo or shower only. **Parking:** on-site.
Small-scale Hotel   **Terms:** package plans, pets ($25-$35 extra charge). **Amenities:** high-speed Internet, voice mail, irons, hair
dryers. **Pool(s):** heated indoor. **Leisure Activities:** sauna, whirlpool, exercise room. **Guest Services:**
sundries, valet and coin laundry. **Business Services:** meeting rooms. **Cards:** AX, DC, DS, MC, VI. **Special Amenities:** free
expanded continental breakfast and free local telephone calls. *(See color ad p 519)*
SOME UNITS
[icons] 🅢 🛏 🏊 ⊠ 🎥 [DATA PORT] 🍴 📺 📼 / ⊠ /
FEE

BEST WESTERN TORONTO AIRPORT WEST   *Book at aaa.com*   **Phone:** (905)670-8180   162
(CAA) (SAVE)   All Year   1P: $89-$199   2P: $89-$199   XP: $10   F18
Location: 0.4 km n from jct Hwy 401. 5825 Dixie Rd L4W 4V7. Fax: 905/670-8083. **Facility:** 164 units. 159 one-
▼▼▼▼   bedroom standard units, some with whirlpools. 5 one-bedroom suites ($139-$229) with whirlpools. 6 stories,
interior corridors. **Parking:** on-site. **Terms:** package plans. **Amenities:** video games (fee), voice mail, irons,
Small-scale Hotel   hair dryers. **Dining:** 7 am-2 & 5-10 pm, Sat & Sun from 8 am, cocktails. **Pool(s):** heated indoor. **Leisure
Activities:** sauna, whirlpool. **Guest Services:** sundries, valet laundry. **Business Services:** conference
facilities. **Cards:** AX, CB, DC, DS, MC, VI. **Special Amenities:** free local telephone calls and free room upgrade (subject to
availability with advance reservations). *(See color ad p 500)*
SOME UNITS
[icons] 🅢 🍴 🍸 🏊 🎥 [DATA PORT] 📺 / ⊠ 🍴 📺 /

Stay Smart® In
Milton, Ontario.

Meeting and Banquet Facility up to 250 people
Fitness Center • Fridges and Microwaves in all rooms
Indoor Swimming Pool and Whirlpool
High-speed Wireless Internet Access

Call (905) 795-1011 for reservations.
Fax: (905) 795-1712

Holiday Inn
EXPRESS®
HOTEL & SUITES
Stay Smart®

2750 High Point Dr.
Milton, ON

www.hiexpress.com

(See map and index starting on p. 479)

BEST WESTERN TRAVEL INN *Book at aaa.com* Phone: (416)620-1234 [122]
(CAA) (SAVE) All Year 1P: $109-$119 2P: $129-$149 XP: $10 F12
▼▼◆▼◆▼ Location: Jct Renforth Dr, 2.5 km w. 5503 Eglinton Ave W M9C 5K5. Fax: 416/620-1652. Facility: 80 one-
bedroom standard units, some with whirlpools. 3 stories, interior corridors. Parking: on-site.
Amenities: high-speed Internet, voice mail, irons, hair dryers. Dining: 6 am-11 pm. Leisure
Small-scale Hotel Activities: whirlpool, exercise room. Business Services: business center. Cards: AX, DC, MC, VI.
Special Amenities: free continental breakfast and free local telephone calls.

SOME UNITS
[S̄D̄] [✦] [🍴] [⬤] [🐾] [DATA PORT] [📶] [💻] / [✕] [📠] /

COMFORT INN AIRPORT WEST *Book at aaa.com* Phone: (905)624-6900 [129]
(CAA) (SAVE) 4/1-4/30 1P: $114-$134 2P: $124-$144 XP: $10 F18
5/1-10/31 1P: $109-$129 2P: $119-$139 XP: $10 F18
▼◆▼◆▼ 1/1-3/31 1P: $105-$125 2P: $115-$135 XP: $10 F18
11/1-12/31 1P: $99-$119 2P: $109-$129 XP: $10 F18
Small-scale Hotel Location: Hwy 401, exit Dixie Rd, then s. 1500 Matheson Blvd L4W 3Z4. Fax: 905/624-1114. Facility: 121 one-
bedroom standard units. 2 stories (no elevator), interior corridors. Parking: on-site. Terms: package plans.
Amenities: voice mail, hair dryers. Some: high-speed Internet, dual phone lines, irons. Dining: 6:30 am-10 pm, Sat & Sun from
7 am, cocktails. Guest Services: valet laundry. Cards: AX, DC, DS, MC, VI.

SOME UNITS
[S̄D̄] [✦] [🐾] [🍴] [🐾] [DATA PORT] [💻] / [✕] [📶] [📠] /

COMFORT INN & SUITES SHERIDAN PARK *Book at aaa.com* Phone: (905)823-8600 [138]
(CAA) (SAVE) All Year [ECP] 1P: $109-$179 2P: $109-$189 XP: $10 F18
▼◆▼◆▼ Location: QEW to Erin Mills Pkwy, n to N Sheridan Way, then w. 2085 N Sheridan Way L5K 2T2. Fax: 905/823-3800.
Facility: 90 units. 82 one-bedroom standard units, some with whirlpools. 8 one-bedroom suites ($129-
$249). 5 stories, interior corridors. Bath: combo or shower only. Parking: on-site. Terms: small pets only.
Small-scale Hotel Amenities: video games (fee), high-speed Internet, dual phone lines, voice mail, irons, hair dryers. Pool(s):
heated indoor. Leisure Activities: whirlpool, exercise room. Guest Services: valet and coin laundry.
Business Services: meeting rooms, fax (fee). Cards: AX, CB, DC, DS, JC, MC, VI. *(See color ad p 522)*

SOME UNITS
[S̄D̄] [🐾] [🍴] [🔆M] [🐾] [🌊] [🐾] [DATA PORT] [💻] / [✕] [📶] [📠] /

COMFORT INN MISSISSAUGA *Book at aaa.com* Phone: (905)858-8600 [124]
(CAA) (SAVE) All Year [ECP] 1P: $85-$89 2P: $92-$98 XP: $10 F16
▼◆▼ Location: Hwy 401, exit Erin Mills Pkwy, 2 km s. 2420 Surveyor Rd L5N 4E6. Fax: 905/858-8574. Facility: 115
one-bedroom standard units, some with whirlpools. 2 stories (no elevator), interior corridors. Parking: on-
site. Terms: cancellation fee imposed, pets ($10 extra charge). Amenities: voice mail, irons, hair dryers.
Small-scale Hotel Leisure Activities: exercise room. Fee: game room. Guest Services: valet and coin laundry. Cards: AX,
DC, DS, MC, VI. Special Amenities: free expanded continental breakfast and free newspaper.
(See color ad p 522)

SOME UNITS
[S̄D̄] [🐾] [🐾] [DATA PORT] [💻] / [✕] [📶] [📠] /
FEE

COURTYARD BY MARRIOTT *Book at aaa.com* Phone: (905)567-5566 [140]
▼◆▼◆▼ All Year 1P: $99-$199
Location: Hwy 401, exit Erin Mills Pkwy/Mississagua Rd, turn on Argentia Rd. 7015 Century Ave L5N 7K2.
Small-scale Hotel Fax: 905/567-1355. Facility: 144 units. 141 one-bedroom standard units, some with whirlpools. 3 one-
bedroom suites. 6 stories, interior corridors. Bath: combo or shower only. Parking: on-site.
Terms: cancellation fee imposed. Amenities: video games, high-speed Internet, dual phone lines, voice mail, irons, hair dryers.
Pool(s): heated indoor. Leisure Activities: whirlpool, exercise room. Guest Services: sundries, valet and coin laundry.
Business Services: meeting rooms, business center. Cards: AX, DS, MC, VI.

SOME UNITS
[ASK] [S̄D̄] [🍴] [🔆M] [🐾] [🌊] [🐾] [DATA PORT] [💻] / [✕] [📶] [📠] /

COURTYARD BY MARRIOTT
[fyi] Under construction, scheduled to open May 2005. Location: Hwy 401 W, exit Dixie Rd S to Eglinton Ave, then left.
5050 Creekbank Rd L4W 5R2 (7005 Century Ave, L5N 7K2). Planned Amenities: coffeemakers, pool.
Small-scale Hotel

DAYS INN-TORONTO MISSISSAUGA *Book at aaa.com* Phone: (905)238-5480 [155]
▼◆▼◆▼ All Year [ECP] 1P: $90-$120 2P: $90-$120 XP: $10 F12
Location: Hwy 401, exit Dixie Rd S, 1.5 km to Eglinton Ave, then 1 km w. Located in a commercial area. 4635 Tomken
Small-scale Hotel Rd L4W 1J9. Fax: 905/238-1031. Facility: 60 one-bedroom standard units, some with efficiencies and/or
whirlpools. 3 stories (no elevator), interior corridors. Parking: on-site. Amenities: voice mail, hair dryers.
Fee: video library, high-speed Internet. Some: irons. Guest Services: sundries, valet laundry. Business Services: PC (fee).
Cards: AX, DC, DS, MC, VI. *(See color ad p 524)*

SOME UNITS
[ASK] [S̄D̄] [🐾] [DATA PORT] [💻] / [✕] [VCR] [📶] [📠] /
FEE

DELTA MEADOWVALE RESORT AND
CONFERENCE CENTRE *Book at aaa.com* Phone: (905)821-1981 [149]
(CAA) (SAVE) All Year 1P: $99-$179 2P: $99-$179 XP: $20 F12
▼◆▼◆▼ Location: Hwy 401 W, exit 336 (Mississauga Rd), just s. Located in a commercial area. 6750 Mississauga Rd L5N 2L3.
Fax: 905/542-4036. Facility: 374 one-bedroom standard units. 15 stories, interior corridors. Parking: on-
site. Terms: cancellation fee imposed, weekly rates available, package plans, 3% service charge.
Large-scale Hotel Amenities: voice mail, irons, hair dryers. Fee: video games, high-speed Internet. Some: CD players.
Dining: 6:30 am-10:30 pm, cocktails. Pool(s): heated outdoor, heated indoor. Leisure Activities: saunas,
whirlpools, putting green, recreation programs. Fee: 4 lighted indoor tennis courts, 7 squash courts, massage. Guest Services:
gift shop, valet laundry. Business Services: conference facilities, business center. Cards: AX, DC, DS, MC, VI.
(See color ad p 525)

SOME UNITS
[S̄D̄] [🐾] [🍴] [⬤] [🌊] [🐾] [✕] [🐾] [DATA PORT] [💻] / [✕] [📶] /
FEE

(See map and index starting on p. 479)

DELTA TORONTO AIRPORT WEST *Book at aaa.com* Phone: (905)624-1144 **163**
(CAA) (SAVE) All Year 1P: $278 2P: $278 XP: $15 F18
▼▼▼ **Location:** 1 km s of jct Hwy 401 and Dixie Rd. 5444 Dixie Rd L4W 2L2. Fax: 905/624-9477. **Facility:** 297 one-bedroom standard units. 10 stories, interior corridors. **Parking:** on-site. **Terms:** cancellation fee imposed, [AP], [BP], [CP] & [ECP] meal plans available, package plans. **Amenities:** video games (fee), dual phone **Large-scale Hotel** lines, voice mail, irons, hair dryers. *Some:* high-speed Internet (fee). **Dining:** 6:30 am-10 pm, Sat & Sun from 7 am, cocktails. **Pool(s):** heated indoor. **Leisure Activities:** saunas, whirlpool, recreation programs, Children Creative Centre, exercise room. *Fee:* massage, game room. **Guest Services:** gift shop, valet laundry, beauty salon. **Business Services:** conference facilities, business center. **Cards:** AX, CB, DC, DS, JC, MC, VI. *(See color ad below)*

SOME UNITS
[icons] / ⊠ /

FAIRFIELD INN & SUITES BY MARRIOTT TORONTO
AIRPORT *Book at aaa.com* Phone: 905/673-9800 **156**
▼▼▼ 1/1-4/30 [ECP] 1P: $99-$153 2P: $99-$153
5/1-12/31 [ECP] 1P: $99-$135 2P: $99-$135
Small-scale Hotel **Location:** Jct Campus, just n of Airport Rd. 3299 Caroga Dr L4V 1A3. Fax: 905/673-8886. **Facility:** 170 units. 130 one-bedroom standard units, some with whirlpools. 40 one-bedroom suites ($99-$153), some with whirlpools. 11 stories, interior corridors. *Bath:* combo or shower only. **Parking:** on-site (fee). **Terms:** package plans, 3% service charge. **Amenities:** video games, high-speed Internet, dual phone lines, voice mail, irons, hair dryers. *Some:* CD players. **Pool(s):** heated indoor. **Leisure Activities:** whirlpool, exercise room. **Guest Services:** sundries, coin laundry. **Business Services:** meeting rooms, business center. **Cards:** AX, CB, DC, JC, MC, VI.

SOME UNITS
[icons] / ⊠ /

FOUR POINTS BY SHERATON MISSISSAUGA *Book at aaa.com* Phone: (905)670-0050 **158**
(CAA) (SAVE) All Year 1P: $95-$169 2P: $95-$169 XP: $10 F18
▼▼▼ **Location:** 1.3 km n of jct Hwy 401 and Dixie Rd. 6090 Dixie Rd L5T 1A6. Fax: 905/564-9555. **Facility:** 145 units. 143 one-bedroom standard units, some with whirlpools. 2 one-bedroom suites ($153-$189) with whirlpools. 8 stories, interior corridors. **Parking:** on-site. **Terms:** cancellation fee imposed, 3% service charge. **Small-scale Hotel** **Amenities:** video games (fee), high-speed Internet, dual phone lines, voice mail, irons, hair dryers. **Dining:** 6 am-11:30 pm, cocktails. **Pool(s):** heated indoor. **Leisure Activities:** sauna, whirlpool, exercise room. **Guest Services:** sundries, valet laundry. **Business Services:** meeting rooms, business center. **Cards:** AX, DC, MC, VI. **Special Amenities:** free newspaper and early check-in/late check-out. *(See color ad p 5 & p 526)*

SOME UNITS
[icons] / ⊠ /

FOUR POINTS TORONTO AIRPORT *Book at aaa.com* Phone: (905)678-1400 **130**
▼▼▼ All Year 1P: $99-$249 2P: $99-$249 XP: $15 F18
Location: 11.2 km n of jct QEW and Hwy 427 N, exit Hwy 401 via airport expressway. 6257 Airport Rd L4V 1E4. **Large-scale Hotel** Fax: 905/678-9130. **Facility:** 201 one-bedroom standard units, some with whirlpools. 7 stories, interior corridors. **Parking:** on-site (fee). **Terms:** cancellation fee imposed. **Amenities:** voice mail, irons, hair dryers. *Some:* high-speed Internet, dual phone lines, honor bars. **Pool(s):** heated indoor. **Leisure Activities:** sauna, whirlpool, exercise room. **Guest Services:** gift shop, valet and coin laundry. **Business Services:** conference facilities, administrative services (fee). **Cards:** AX, CB, DC, DS, JC, MC, VI.

SOME UNITS
(ASK) [icons] / ⊠ [icons] /
FEE

www.deltatorontoairportwest.com

DELTA
TORONTO AIRPORT WEST

- Ten minutes from Pearson International Airport
- Easy access to all major highways in Greater Toronto Area
- Ten minutes from Square One, Ontario's largest shopping centre
- Indoor pool, whirlpool, saunas, exercise room and games room
- Delta's friendly and helpful airport shuttle service and covered parking facilities are both complimentary
- Children's program

Your room is ready

905-624-1144
Fax: 905-624-9477
Toll Free: 1-800-737-3211

CANADA and U.S.
1-800-268-1133
www.deltahotels.com

5444 Dixie Road
Mississauga, ON
L4W 2L2

(See map and index starting on p. 479)

GLENERIN INN　　　　　　　　　　　　　　　　　　　　Phone: (905)828-6103　〔133〕

(CAA) (SAVE)

▼▼▽▼▽▼

Country Inn

All Year　　　　　　　　1P: $129-$149　　　2P: $129-$149
Location: QEW, exit Mississauga Rd, 4.5 km n cross Dundas St, then just w. Located in a residential area. 1695 The Collegeway L5L 3S7. Fax: 905/828-0891. **Facility:** Originally a summer retreat for a wealthy Toronto businessman, this 1927 inn was saved from demolition in 1984. Smoke free premises. 39 one-bedroom standard units, some with whirlpools. 2 stories (no elevator), interior corridors. *Bath:* combo or shower only. **Parking:** on-site. **Terms:** check-in 4 pm, 3 day cancellation notice-fee imposed, [ECP] meal plan available, 12% service charge. **Amenities:** high-speed Internet (fee), voice mail, hair dryers. **Dining:** 7 am-10 pm; Sunday brunch, cocktails. **Guest Services:** valet laundry. **Business Services:** conference facilities. **Cards:** AX, DC, MC, VI.

SOME UNITS
[S⊘] [¶] [♦↦] [✕] [≈] [DATA PORT] / [VCR] /
FEE

HAMPTON INN　　*Book at aaa.com*　　　　　　　Phone: (905)564-2122　〔131〕

(CAA) (SAVE)

▼▼▽▼▽▼

Small-scale Hotel

All Year　　　　　　　　1P: $139　　　2P: $149
Location: Hwy 401, exit Hwy 10 (Hurontario St), 2 km n to Derry Rd, then just e. Located in a commercial area. 7040 Edward Blvd L5S 1Z1. Fax: 905/564-5020. **Facility:** 69 one-bedroom standard units, some with whirlpools. 3 stories, interior corridors. *Bath:* combo or shower only. **Parking:** on-site. **Terms:** cancellation fee imposed, [ECP] meal plan available. **Amenities:** high-speed Internet, voice mail, irons, hair dryers. **Pool(s):** outdoor. **Leisure Activities:** limited exercise equipment. **Guest Services:** valet laundry. **Business Services:** business center. **Cards:** AX, DC, MC, VI. **Special Amenities:** free expanded continental breakfast and free local telephone calls. *(See color ad p 4 & p 527)*

SOME UNITS
[S⊘] [⅙M] [⅙] [≈] [≈] [DATA PORT] [◻] /[✕]/

HAMPTON INN & SUITES TORONTO AIRPORT　　*Book at aaa.com*　　Phone: (905)671-4730　〔157〕

(CAA) (SAVE)

▼▼▽▼▽▼

Small-scale Hotel

All Year [ECP]　　　　　　1P: $169-$189　　2P: $169-$189
Location: Hwy 401, exit Dixon Rd, 3.5 km w to Bresler Rd. 3279 Caroga Dr L4V 1A3. Fax: 905/671-4739. **Facility:** 149 one-bedroom standard units, some with whirlpools. 9 stories, interior corridors. *Bath:* combo or shower only. **Parking:** on-site. **Terms:** cancellation fee imposed, package plans, small pets only. **Amenities:** video games (fee), high-speed Internet, dual phone lines, voice mail, irons, hair dryers. **Pool(s):** heated indoor. **Leisure Activities:** exercise room. **Guest Services:** sundries. **Business Services:** meeting rooms, business center. **Cards:** AX, CB, DC, DS, MC, VI. **Special Amenities:** free expanded continental breakfast and free local telephone calls. *(See color ad p 4 & p 528)*

SOME UNITS
[S⊘] [✈] [🛏] [⅙M] [⅙] [≈] [≈] [DATA PORT] [◻] /[✕] [◻] [≈] /

HILTON GARDEN INN TORONTO/MISSISSAUGA　　*Book at aaa.com*　　Phone: (905)890-9110　〔141〕

(CAA) (SAVE)

▼▼▽▼▽▼

Small-scale Hotel

All Year　　　　　1P: $109-$229　　2P: $109-$229　　XP: $15　　F18
Location: Hwy 401, exit Hwy 10 (Hurontario St), 0.5 km s to Traders Blvd. 100 Traders Blvd L4Z 2H7. Fax: 905/890-9050. **Facility:** 154 units. 153 one-bedroom standard units. 1 one-bedroom suite with whirlpool. 6 stories, interior corridors. *Bath:* combo or shower only. **Parking:** on-site. **Terms:** cancellation fee imposed. **Amenities:** video games, high-speed Internet, dual phone lines, voice mail, irons, hair dryers. **Dining:** 6 am-2 & 5-10 pm, Sat & Sun 7 am-noon & 5-10 pm. **Pool(s):** heated indoor. **Leisure Activities:** whirlpool, exercise room. **Guest Services:** sundries, valet and coin laundry. **Business Services:** meeting rooms, business center. **Cards:** AX, CB, DC, DS, JC, MC, VI. **Special Amenities:** free local telephone calls and free newspaper.

SOME UNITS
[S⊘] [¶] [Y] [⅙M] [⅙] [≈] [≈] [DATA PORT] [◻] [≈] [◻] /[✕]/

HOLIDAY INN EXPRESS　　*Book at aaa.com*　　　　Phone: (905)238-3500　〔121〕

(CAA) (SAVE)

▼▼▽▼ ▽▼

Small-scale Hotel

All Year　　　　　　　　1P: $115
Location: Hwy 401, exit Dixie Rd S to Aerowood Dr W, then n. 5585 Ambler Dr L4W 3Z1. Fax: 905/238-8761. **Facility:** 127 one-bedroom standard units. 2 stories, interior corridors. **Parking:** on-site. **Amenities:** dual phone lines, voice mail, irons, hair dryers. **Guest Services:** valet and coin laundry. **Business Services:** meeting rooms. **Cards:** AX, CB, DC, DS, JC, MC, VI. *(See color ad card insert & p 527)*

SOME UNITS
[✈] [🛏] [≈] [DATA PORT] [◻] /[✕] [◻] /
FEE

HOLIDAY INN SELECT MISSISSAUGA　　*Book at aaa.com*　　Phone: (905)542-2121　〔137〕

▼▼▽▼▽▼

Large-scale Hotel

All Year　　　　　1P: $89-$139　　2P: $99-$149　　XP: $10　　F17
Location: Sw of Hwy 401 and Mississauga Rd; corner of Derry and Argentia rds. 2565 Argentia Rd L5N 5V4. Fax: 905/542-1916. **Facility:** 120 units. 86 one-bedroom standard units, some with whirlpools. 34 one-bedroom suites, some with whirlpools. 8 stories, interior corridors. *Bath:* combo or shower only. **Parking:** on-site. **Amenities:** video games (fee), high-speed Internet, dual phone lines, voice mail, irons, hair dryers. *Some:* safes. **Pool(s):** heated indoor. **Leisure Activities:** whirlpool, exercise room. **Guest Services:** sundries, valet laundry. **Business Services:** meeting rooms, business center. **Cards:** AX, DC, DS, MC, VI. *(See color ad card insert)*

SOME UNITS
[ASK] [S⊘] [✈] [¶] [≈] [≈] [DATA PORT] [◻] /[✕] [◻] [≈] /
FEE

HOLIDAY INN TORONTO-MISSISSAUGA　　*Book at aaa.com*　　Phone: (905)855-2000　〔135〕

(CAA) (SAVE)

▼▼▽▼▽▼

Large-scale Hotel

All Year　　　　　　1P: $109　　　2P: $129　　XP: $10　　F17
Location: QEW, exit Erin Mills Pkwy. Located in a commercial area. 2125 N Sheridan Way L5K 1A3. Fax: 905/855-1433. **Facility:** 151 one-bedroom standard units, some with whirlpools. 6 stories, interior corridors. **Parking:** on-site. **Terms:** [CP] meal plan available. **Amenities:** video games (fee), voice mail, irons, hair dryers. **Dining:** 6:30 am-midnight, cocktails. **Pool(s):** heated indoor. **Leisure Activities:** sauna, exercise room. **Guest Services:** gift shop, valet laundry, area transportation (fee)-within city limits. **Business Services:** meeting rooms. **Cards:** AX, CB, DC, DS, JC, MC, VI. **Special Amenities:** free newspaper. *(See color ad card insert)*

SOME UNITS
[S⊘] [¶] [Y] [≈] [≈] [DATA PORT] [◻] /[✕] [◻] [≈] /

(See map and index starting on p. 479)

HOLIDAY INN TORONTO-WEST   *Book at aaa.com*   Phone: (905)890-5700   160

(CAA) (SAVE)   All Year   1P: $119-$155   2P: $119-$155   XP: $15   F18
Location: Hwy 401, exit Hwy 10 S (Hurontario St); jct Hwy 401 and 10. 100 Britannia Rd E L4Z 2G1.
Fax: 905/568-0868. **Facility:** 138 one-bedroom standard units. 6 stories, interior corridors. **Parking:** on-site,
winter plug-ins. **Terms:** package plans, small pets only (1st floor units). **Amenities:** video games (fee), high-
Small-scale Hotel   speed Internet, voice mail, irons, hair dryers. **Dining:** 6:30 am-midnight, Wed-Fri to 1 am, Sat & Sun 7 am-
11 pm, cocktails. **Pool(s):** heated outdoor. **Leisure Activities:** sauna, whirlpool, exercise room. **Guest
Services:** valet laundry. **Business Services:** meeting rooms. **Cards:** AX, DC, DS, MC, VI. *(See color ad card insert)*

SOME UNITS
[icons] / [icons] /

HOMEWOOD SUITES BY HILTON
TORONTO-MISSISSAUGA   Phone: 905/564-5529

(fyi)   Under construction, scheduled to open May 2005. **Location:** Hwy 401, exit 342 (Hwy 10), then n, then right at
Annagem Blvd. 6430 Edwards Blvd L5T 2Y3. Fax: 905/564-5236. **Planned Amenities:** restaurant,
Small-scale Hotel   coffeemakers, microwaves, refrigerators, pool, tennis. *(See color ad p 305)*

MONTE CARLO INN AIRPORT SUITES   Phone: (905)564-8500   161

(CAA) (SAVE)   All Year [ECP]   1P: $79-$109   2P: $89-$129   XP: $10   F12
Location: Hwy 401, exit Hwy 10 (Hurontario St), 2 km n to Derry Rd, then just e. Located in a commercial area. 5 Derry
Rd E L5T 2H8 (7035 Edwards Blvd). Fax: 905/564-8400. **Facility:** 64 one-bedroom standard units, some with
whirlpools. 3 stories (no elevator), interior corridors. **Parking:** on-site, winter plug-ins. **Terms:** weekly rates
Small-scale Hotel   available, [BP] meal plan available, package plans. **Amenities:** voice mail, irons, hair dryers. **Dining:** 2:30
pm-midnight, cocktails. **Leisure Activities:** limited exercise equipment. **Guest Services:** valet laundry.
Business Services: meeting rooms, business center. **Cards:** AX, CB, DC, DS, JC, MC, VI. **Special Amenities:** free expanded
continental breakfast and free local telephone calls. *(See color ad p 531)*

SOME UNITS
[icons] / [icons] /

MONTE CARLO INN TORONTO WEST   *Book at aaa.com*   Phone: (905)273-9500   145

(CAA) (SAVE)   All Year [CP]   1P: $69-$109   2P: $79-$119   XP: $10   F12
Location: On Hwy 5, 1.5 km w of Hwy 427. 1886 Dundas St E L4X 1L9. Fax: 905/273-9775. **Facility:** 34 one-
bedroom standard units, some with whirlpools. 3 stories (no elevator), interior/exterior corridors. **Parking:**
on-site. **Terms:** weekly rates available, [BP] meal plan available, package plans. **Amenities:** hair dryers.
Small-scale Hotel   **Cards:** AX, CB, DC, DS, JC, MC, VI. **Special Amenities:** free continental breakfast and free local
telephone calls. *(See color ad p 531)*

SOME UNITS
[icons] / [icons] /

MOTEL 6 #1910   *Book at aaa.com*   Phone: 905/814-1664   125

All Year   1P: $65-$75   2P: $71-$81   XP: $3   F17
Location: Hwy 401, exit 333 (Winston Churchill Blvd), just s. 2935 Argentia Rd L5N 8G6. Fax: 905/814-9899.
Small-scale Hotel   **Facility:** 123 one-bedroom standard units. 3 stories, interior corridors. *Bath:* combo or shower only.
Parking: on-site. **Terms:** small pets only. **Guest Services:** coin laundry. **Cards:** AX, CB, DC, DS, MC, VI.

SOME UNITS
[icons] / [icons] /
FEE

NOVOTEL HOTEL MISSISSAUGA   *Book at aaa.com*   Phone: (905)896-1000   147

All Year   1P: $209-$239   2P: $209-$239   XP: $15   F16
Location: On Hwy 10 at Burnhamthorpe Rd; Hwy 401, exit Hwy 10 S (Hurontario St), 5 km. 3670 Hurontario St L5B
Large-scale Hotel   1P3. Fax: 905/896-2521. **Facility:** 325 units. 324 one-bedroom standard units. 1 one-bedroom suite with
whirlpool. 14 stories, interior corridors. **Parking:** on-site (fee). **Terms:** 2 night minimum stay - seasonal,
weekly rates available, package plans, 3% service charge, small pets only ($15 extra charge). **Amenities:** video games (fee),
voice mail, honor bars, irons, hair dryers. **Pool(s):** heated indoor. **Leisure Activities:** whirlpool, racquetball court, exercise
room. **Guest Services:** gift shop, valet laundry. **Business Services:** conference facilities. **Cards:** AX, DC, MC, VI.
(See color ad p 497)

SOME UNITS
[icons] / [icons] /
FEE

QUALITY HOTEL AIRPORT   *Book at aaa.com*   Phone: (905)624-9500   164

(CAA) (SAVE)   5/1-8/31   1P: $89-$99   2P: $94-$104   XP: $5   F12
9/1-4/30   1P: $79-$99   2P: $84-$104   XP: $5   F12
Location: Hwy 401, exit 346 (S Dixie Rd), w on Aerowood Dr, then just n. 5599 Ambler Dr L4W 3Z1.
Fax: 905/624-1382. **Facility:** 222 one-bedroom standard units. 6 stories, interior corridors. **Parking:** on-site.
Small-scale Hotel   **Amenities:** video games (fee), voice mail, irons, hair dryers. **Dining:** 7 am-midnight, Sat & Sun from 8 am,
cocktails. **Pool(s):** heated indoor. **Leisure Activities:** whirlpool. **Guest Services:** valet and coin laundry.
Business Services: meeting rooms. **Cards:** AX, DC, DS, MC, VI. *(See color ad p 535)*

SOME UNITS
[icons] / [icons] /
FEE

QUALITY INN AIRPORT WEST   *Book at aaa.com*   Phone: (905)890-1200   143

(CAA) (SAVE)   5/1-9/30   1P: $111-$132   2P: $118-$139   XP: $7   F18
1/1-4/30   1P: $109-$130   2P: $116-$137   XP: $7   F18
10/1-12/31   1P: $106-$127   2P: $113-$139   XP: $7   F18
Location: Hwy 401, exit Hwy 10 (Hurontario St); jct Hwy 401 and 10. 50 Britannia Rd E L4Z 2G2.
Small-scale Hotel   Fax: 905/890-5183. **Facility:** 108 one-bedroom standard units, some with whirlpools. 2 stories (no elevator),
interior corridors. *Bath:* combo or tub only. **Parking:** on-site, winter plug-ins. **Terms:** package plans.
Amenities: video games, dual phone lines, voice mail, irons, hair dryers. **Dining:** 7 am-2 & 5-10 pm, Sat & Sun 8 am-11:30 &
5-10 pm, cocktails. **Leisure Activities:** sauna, exercise room. **Guest Services:** valet laundry. **Business Services:** meeting
rooms. **Cards:** AX, DC, DS, MC, VI. **Special Amenities:** free newspaper and preferred room (subject to availability with
advance reservations). *(See color ad p 535)*

SOME UNITS
[icons] / [icons] /
FEE FEE

(See map and index starting on p. 479)

RADISSON HOTEL TORONTO-MISSISSAUGA *Book at aaa.com* Phone: (905)858-2424 127
CAA SAVE All Year 1P: $109-$159 2P: $109-$159 XP: $10 F18
Location: Sw of Hwy 401 and Mississauga Rd; corner of Derry and Argentia rds. Located in a commercial area. 2501 Argentia Rd L5N 4G8. Fax: 905/821-1592. **Facility:** 207 one-bedroom standard units, some with whirlpools. 8 stories, interior corridors. **Parking:** on-site, winter plug-ins. **Terms:** package plans, small pets only (in **Large-scale Hotel** smoking units). **Amenities:** video games (fee), voice mail, irons, hair dryers. *Some:* high-speed Internet, dual phone lines. **Dining:** 6 am-10:30 pm, cocktails. **Pool(s):** heated indoor. **Leisure Activities:** sauna, whirlpool, exercise room. **Guest Services:** gift shop, valet and coin laundry. **Business Services:** meeting rooms. **Cards:** AX, DC, DS, MC, VI. *(See color ad p 521 & on TourBookMark)*
SOME UNITS

RESIDENCE INN BY MARRIOTT *Book at aaa.com* Phone: (905)567-2577 142
All Year 1P: $159-$259
Location: Hwy 401, exit Erin Mills Pkwy/Mississauga Rd, s to Argentia Rd. 7005 Century Ave L5N 7K2. **Small-scale Hotel** Fax: 905/567-9965. **Facility:** 100 units. 58 one-bedroom standard units with efficiencies. 24 one- and 18 two-bedroom suites, some with efficiencies or kitchens. 5 stories, interior corridors. *Bath:* combo or shower only. **Parking:** on-site. **Terms:** cancellation fee imposed, 15% service charge, small pets only ($50-$100 fee). **Amenities:** video games (fee), high-speed Internet, dual phone lines, voice mail, irons, hair dryers. **Pool(s):** heated indoor. **Leisure Activities:** exercise room, sports court. **Guest Services:** valet and coin laundry. **Business Services:** meeting rooms. **Cards:** AX, DC, DS, MC, VI.
SOME UNITS

RESIDENCE INN BY MARRIOTT
fyi Under construction, scheduled to open May 2005. **Location:** Hwy 401 W, exit Dixie Rd S to Eglinton Ave, then left. 5070 Creekbank Rd L4W 5R2 (7005 Century Ave, L5N 7K2). **Planned Amenities:** pets, coffeemakers, **Small-scale Hotel** microwaves, refrigerators, pool, tennis.

SANDALWOOD SUITES HOTEL TORONTO AIRPORT *Book at aaa.com* Phone: (905)238-9600 153
CAA SAVE All Year [ECP] 1P: $99-$209 2P: $99-$209 XP: $15 F12
Location: Jct Eglinton Ave and Renforth Dr, 2.3 km w on Eglinton Ave. 5050 Orbitor Dr L4W 4X2. Fax: 905/238-8502. **Facility:** 186 units. 12 one-bedroom standard units with whirlpools. 170 one- and 4 two-bedroom suites with whirlpools. 3 stories, interior corridors. **Parking:** on-site. **Terms:** package plans, pets ($10 extra charge). **Small-scale Hotel Amenities:** video games (fee), CD players, dual phone lines, voice mail, irons, hair dryers. *Some:* high-speed Internet (fee). **Leisure Activities:** exercise room. **Guest Services:** sundries, coin laundry. **Business Services:** meeting rooms, PC. **Cards:** AX, DC, MC, VI. **Special Amenities:** free expanded continental breakfast and free newspaper. *(See color ad p 538)*
SOME UNITS

SHERATON GATEWAY HOTEL IN TORONTO INTERNATIONAL AIRPORT Phone: (905)672-7000 150
CAA SAVE All Year 1P: $99-$339 2P: $99-$339 XP: $15 F17
Location: In Lester B. Pearson International Airport. Box 3000, Toronto AMF L5P 1C4. Fax: 905/672-7100. **Facility:** This airport hotel offers elegant common areas, a 24-hour fitness center, meeting facilities and large guest rooms. 474 units. 469 one-bedroom standard units, some with whirlpools. 5 one-bedroom suites **Large-scale Hotel** ($375-$550). 8 stories, interior corridors. **Parking:** on-site (fee). **Terms:** package plans, small pets only. **Amenities:** dual phone lines, voice mail, safes, honor bars, irons, hair dryers. *Fee:* video games, high-speed Internet. *Some:* fax. **Dining:** 6 am-midnight, cocktails. **Pool(s):** heated indoor. **Leisure Activities:** saunas, whirlpool, steamrooms, exercise room. *Fee:* massage. **Guest Services:** gift shop, valet laundry. **Business Services:** conference facilities, business center. **Cards:** AX, CB, DC, DS, MC, VI. *(See color ad p 5 & p 538)*
SOME UNITS

STAGE WEST ALL SUITE HOTEL & THEATRE RESTAURANT *Book at aaa.com* Phone: (905)238-0159 123
CAA SAVE All Year [BP] 1P: $159-$179 2P: $159-$179 XP: $10 F16
Location: 1 km s of Hwy 401. 5400 Dixie Rd L4W 4T4. Fax: 905/238-9820. **Facility:** 224 units. 88 one-bedroom standard units. 136 one-bedroom suites, some with kitchens and/or whirlpools. 14 stories, interior corridors. **Parking:** on-site. **Terms:** package plans. **Amenities:** video games (fee), voice mail, safes, irons, hair **Large-scale Hotel** dryers. *Some:* high-speed Internet (fee). **Dining:** 2 restaurants, 6:30 am-11 pm, cocktails. **Pool(s):** heated indoor. **Leisure Activities:** whirlpool, waterslide, exercise room. *Fee:* pool tables, game room. **Guest Services:** gift shop, valet laundry. **Business Services:** meeting rooms, business center. **Cards:** AX, DC, DS, MC, VI. **Special Amenities:** free full breakfast.
SOME UNITS

STUDIO 6 MISSISSAUGA #1908 *Book at aaa.com* Phone: 905/502-8897 165
All Year 1P: $85-$95 2P: $91-$101 XP: $3 F17
Location: Hwy 401, exit Hwy 10 (Hurontario St). 60 Brittannia Rd E L4Z 2T2. Fax: 905/502-1855. **Facility:** 123 **Motel** one-bedroom standard units with efficiencies. 3 stories, interior corridors. *Bath:* combo or shower only. **Parking:** on-site. **Terms:** office hours 7 am-8 pm, pets ($25 fee). **Amenities:** voice mail. **Guest Services:** coin laundry. **Cards:** AX, CB, DC, DS, MC, VI.
SOME UNITS

(See map and index starting on p. 479)

SUPER 5 INN   Phone: (905)624-6424 **151**
5/1-9/30   1P: $65-$75   2P: $75-$85
10/1-4/30   1P: $60-$70   2P: $70-$80
Small-scale Hotel   **Location:** Just w of Hwy 427. Located in a commercial area. 2171 Dundas St E L4X 1M3. Fax: 905/624-2084.
Facility: 53 one-bedroom standard units, some with whirlpools. 2 stories (no elevator), interior/exterior
corridors. **Parking:** on-site, winter plug-ins. **Amenities:** hair dryers. **Cards:** AX, DC, VI.

SOME UNITS

TORONTO AIRPORT HILTON   *Book at aaa.com*   Phone: (905)677-9900   **146**
All Year   1P: $119-$249   2P: $119-$249   XP: $25   F18
Location: Hwy 401, exit Dixon Rd, 3.5 km w; 1 km from Lester B. Pearson International Airport. 5875 Airport Rd L4V
Large-scale Hotel   1N1. Fax: 905/677-7782. **Facility:** 413 units. 267 one-bedroom standard units, some with whirlpools. 146
one-bedroom suites. 9-11 stories, interior corridors. *Bath:* combo or shower only. **Parking:** on-site (fee).
Terms: small pets only. **Amenities:** dual phone lines, voice mail, irons, hair dryers. *Fee:* video games, high-speed Internet.
Some: honor bars. **Pool(s):** heated outdoor. **Leisure Activities:** saunas, exercise room. **Guest Services:** gift shop, valet
laundry. **Business Services:** conference facilities, business center. **Cards:** AX, DC, DS, JC, MC, VI.

SOME UNITS

TRAVELODGE TORONTO AIRPORT SOUTHWEST   *Book at aaa.com*   Phone: (905)238-3400   **159**
All Year [CP]   1P: $88-$125   2P: $95-$130   XP: $8   F17
Location: On Hwy 5, 2 km w of Hwy 427. Located in a commercial area. 1767 Dundas St E L4X 1L5.
Fax: 905/238-9457. **Facility:** 85 one-bedroom standard units, some with whirlpools. 2 stories (no elevator),
interior corridors. **Parking:** on-site, winter plug-ins. **Terms:** cancellation fee imposed. **Amenities:** voice mail.
Small-scale Hotel   *Some:* high-speed Internet, hair dryers. **Cards:** AX, CB, DC, DS, MC, VI. **Special Amenities: free
continental breakfast and free local telephone calls.** *(See color ad p 539)*

SOME UNITS

THE WATERSIDE INN   Phone: (905)891-7770   **136**
All Year   1P: $249-$659   2P: $289-$699   XP: $40   F12
Location: QEW, exit Hwy 10 S, just w on Lakeshore Blvd. 15 Stavebank Rd S L5G 2T2.
Fax: 905/891-5333. **Facility:** 86 units. 72 one- and 14 two-bedroom suites, some with kitchens. 14 stories,
Small-scale Hotel   interior corridors. **Parking:** on-site. **Terms:** check-in 4 pm, weekly rates available. **Amenities:** high-speed
Internet, dual phone lines, voice mail, honor bars, irons, hair dryers. *Some:* CD players. **Dining:** Breakwater Fine Dining, see
separate listing. **Guest Services:** valet laundry. **Business Services:** meeting rooms, business center. **Cards:** AX, DC, MC, VI.

SOME UNITS

———— **WHERE TO DINE** ————

AIELLI RISTORANTE   **Lunch:** $10-$20   **Dinner:** $14-$22   **Phone:** 905-278-2183   **212**
Location: Jct Mohawk. 286 Lakeshore Rd L5G 1H2. **Hours:** noon-11 pm, Sat & Sun from 5 pm. Closed: 4/17,
12/25. **Reservations:** suggested. **Features:** The restaurant offers diners a European flair and ambience in
Italian   both the decor and the menu choices. Highlights include such starters as tequila-marinated salmon and the
chef's mushroom creation of the day, followed by freshly made pastas, herbed veal chops, stuffed chicken
breast and rack of lamb. An excellent selection of wines is offered. Dressy casual; cocktails. **Parking:** on-site. **Cards:** AX, DC,
MC, VI.

ALIOLI RISTORANTE   **Lunch:** $10-$20   **Dinner:** $13-$30   **Phone:** 905/281-1122   **221**
Location: Just w of Hurontario St. 350 Burnhampthorpe Rd W L5B 3J1. **Hours:** 11:30 am-2 pm, Sat 5 pm-11 pm.
Closed major holidays; also Sun. **Reservations:** suggested. **Features:** Tucked in a busy commercial area,
Italian   the restaurant is a wonderful surprise. Colorful murals of Italy decorate the warm, comfortable dining room.
Representative of excellent, freshly prepared food is tempting antipasto, gourmet pizzas, pasta and risotto
dishes and yummy tiramisu. Servers are personable. Dressy casual; cocktails. **Parking:** on-site. **Cards:** AX, DC, MC, VI.

BIG DADDY'S CRAB SHACK & OYSTER BAR   **Lunch:** $9-$12   **Dinner:** $10-$15   **Phone:** 905/403-0331   **213**
Location: QEW, exit Erin Mills Pkwy, just s to Southdown Rd. D6-970 Southdown Rd L5J 2Y4. **Hours:** 11:30 am-1
am, Sat from noon, Sun noon-10 pm, Mon 11:30 am-10 pm. Closed: 12/25. **Reservations:** suggested.
Seafood   **Features:** A taste of New Orleans can be found in the small shopping plaza, where the bartenders shuck
oysters right in front of guests. The lively restaurant and bar features a wide variety of seafood, including
great blackened catfish, as well as jambalaya and pasta dishes. Casual dress; cocktails. **Parking:** on-site. **Cards:** AX, DC,
MC, VI.

BREAKWATER FINE DINING   **Lunch:** $10-$22   **Dinner:** $14-$35   **Phone:** 905/891-6225   **214**
Location: QEW, exit Hwy 10 S (Hurontario St S), just w on Lakeshore Blvd; in The Waterside Inn. 15 Stavebank Rd S
L5G 2T2. **Hours:** 7 am-11 pm, Sat from 8 am. Closed: 1/1, 12/26. **Reservations:** suggested. **Features:** The
Continental   elegant dining room presents a fine menu of innovative Continental fare that focuses strongly on fresh local
and regional ingredients. A sophisticated atmosphere makes the setting perfect for special-occasion or
business dining. Throughout the year, the chef plans creative theme events that make reserving a table worthwhile. The
waterfront locale lends itself to a nice stroll after a satisfying meal. Dressy casual; cocktails. **Parking:** on-site. **Cards:** AX, DC,
MC, VI.

(See map and index starting on p. 479)

BY THE WHARF SEAFOOD HOUSE   **Lunch:** $11-$24   **Dinner:** $22-$45   **Phone:** 905/625-5490   ⟨233⟩
▼▼▼▼   **Location:** Hwy 5, 1.5 km w of Hwy 427 N. 1855 Dundas St E L4X 1M1. **Hours:** 11:30 am-11 pm, Fri-midnight, Sat 5 pm-midnight, Sun 5 pm-10 pm. **Closed:** 1/1, 4/17, 12/25. **Reservations:** suggested. **Features:** Nautical
Steak & Seafood   decor with dim lighting and candlelit tables. Extensive menu selections featuring traditional favorites such as steamed mussels, clams or oysters Rockefeller to start. Mains include surf and turf, lobster tails, filet mignon or the popular Wharf's Platter for Two. Hearty portions. Casual dress; cocktails. **Parking:** on-site. **Cards:** AX, MC, VI.   ⊠

CANYON CREEK CHOP HOUSE   **Lunch:** $8-$22   **Dinner:** $11-$31   **Phone:** 905/279-3342   ⟨220⟩
▼▼ ▼▼   **Location:** Directly across from Square One Shopping Centre. 299 Rathburn Rd W L5B 4C1. **Hours:** 11:30 am-11 pm, Wed-Fri to midnight, Sat 2 pm-midnight, Sun 2 pm-10 pm. **Closed:** 12/25. **Features:** A relaxed,
Steak House   comfortable setting, a traditional steak house menu and an extensive wine list make this a popular favorite with locals and tourists alike. Diners enjoy great cuts of aged beef, ribs, chicken, huge pork chops or rack of lamb, all grilled to order. The wine list has an excellent selection of by-the-glass choices and bottles. Decadent desserts are worth the splurge. Casual dress; cocktails. **Parking:** on-site. **Cards:** AX, MC, VI.   ⊠

CHERRY HILL HOUSE   **Lunch:** $10-$25   **Dinner:** $10-$30   **Phone:** 905/275-9300   ⟨230⟩
▼▼▼▼   **Location:** Just w of Cawthra Rd; between Bloor and Dundas sts. 680 Silver Creek Blvd L5A 3Z1. **Hours:** noon-2:30 & 6-10 pm, Sat from 6 pm, Sun 5 pm-9 pm. **Closed:** 1/1, 12/26. **Reservations:** suggested. **Features:** Located
Continental   in a restored farmhouse, the dining rooms have the simple charm of a bygone era. The crackle of a natural log fireplace enhances the comfortable atmosphere. The menu offers creatively prepared chicken, veal, seafood, steak and pasta. A pub is on the lower level and there is a patio in season. Dressy casual; cocktails. **Parking:** on-site. **Cards:** AX, DC, MC, VI.   𝕐 ⊠

THE KEG STEAKHOUSE AND BAR   **Lunch:** $8-$22   **Dinner:** $16-$30   **Phone:** 905/567-9111   ⟨228⟩
▼▼ ▼▼   **Location:** Hwy 401, exit Mississauga Rd, 1 km s to Erin Mills Pkwy, then e. 6485 Mississauga Rd L5N 1A6. **Hours:** 11:30 am-2:30 & 5-11 pm, Sat & Sun-5 pm. **Closed:** 12/25. **Features:** Well-known for its mesquite-
Steak House   grilled steaks and fun, laid-back atmosphere, this steak house is a longtime favourite with the local crowd. In addition to great beef, the traditional menu features seafood, grilled chicken, hickory ribs and pasta offerings. All meals come with a hot loaf of sourdough bread. Try a specialty coffee or some tasty cheesecake for the perfect ending. Casual dress; cocktails. **Parking:** on-site. **Cards:** AX, DC, MC, VI.   ⊠

LA CASTILE MANOR   **Lunch:** $10-$22   **Dinner:** $15-$35   **Phone:** 905/625-1137   ⟨227⟩
▼▼ ▼▼   **Location:** Just w of Hwy 427. 2179 Dundas St E L4X 1M3. **Hours:** noon-2:30 & 5-11 pm, Wed-Fri to midnight, Sat 5 pm-midnight. **Closed:** 1/1, 12/25; also Sun. **Reservations:** suggested, required Fri & Sat.
Steak & Seafood   **Features:** La Castile's distinguished dining room offers traditional elegance—from its English Tudor construction to its inviting piano bar. Also discover an extensive selection of beef, seafood, chicken and prime rib dishes, as well as appetizers and dessert. Dressy casual; cocktails; entertainment. **Parking:** on-site. **Cards:** AX, DC, MC, VI.   ⊠

MILESTONE'S GRILL AND BAR   **Lunch:** $8-$25   **Dinner:** $8-$25   **Phone:** 905/828-9119   ⟨217⟩
▼▼ ▼▼   **Location:** Jct Dundas St and Winston Churchill Blvd. 3051 Vega Blvd L5L 5Y3. **Hours:** 10 am-11 pm, Sat & Sun 11 am-midnight. **Closed:** 12/25. **Features:** A bright, modern decor and a bustling atmosphere set the tone at
American   Milestone's Grill and Bar. The menu features an abundance of pastas, stone oven pizzas, sandwiches and burgers as well as an all day brunch menu with an innovative flair. Casual dress; cocktails. **Parking:** on-site. **Cards:** AX, DC, MC, VI.   𝕐 ⊠

MOOSKOKA WOODS GREAT CANADIAN EATERY   **Lunch:** $5-$10   **Dinner:** $5-$22   **Phone:** 905/567-7713   ⟨226⟩
▼▼   **Location:** Hwy 401, exit Mississauga Rd S, 1 km to Erin Mills Pkwy, then e. 6485 Mississauga Rd N L5N 1A2. **Hours:** 11 am-11 pm, Thurs & Fri-2 am, Sat noon-2 am, Sun noon-10 pm. **Closed:** 12/25.
American   **Features:** Themed after a northern cabin, the restaurant gives diners a taste of true country Canada in both the menu and decor. A rustic log theme with cartoon moose heads and chalkboard drawings sets the tone. The menu highlights hearty comfort foods such as burgers, wings, steaks and pasta. A children's menu also is featured. For those wanting a good old Canadian beer, the large, adjacent lounge beckons with its sports-loving crowd. Casual dress; cocktails. **Parking:** on-site. **Cards:** AX, MC, VI.   𝕐 ⊠

MUDDY DUCK   **Lunch:** $5-$16   **Dinner:** $8-$18   **Phone:** 905/275-9430   ⟨211⟩
▼▼ ▼▼   **Location:** Just w of Hwy 427. 2200 Dundas St E L4X 2V3. **Hours:** 11:30 am-11 pm, Sat & Sun from 9 am. **Closed:** 12/25. **Features:** A relaxed setting, friendly service and a mixed menu of casual fare keep locals
American   coming back. Popular favorites include hearty French onion soup, New England crab cakes, roaring ribs and burgers. Also offered is a good selection of entree salads, pasta dishes and seafood. The dessert display case shows off tempting treats. A tasty breakfast buffet is served to 2 pm on weekends. Casual dress; cocktails. **Parking:** on-site. **Cards:** AX, DC, MC, VI.   𝕐 ⊠

OLD BARBER HOUSE   **Lunch:** $8-$13   **Dinner:** $14-$42   **Phone:** 905/858-7570   ⟨218⟩
▼▼▼▼   **Location:** 0.5 km n of Eglinton Ave. 5155 Mississauga Rd L5N 2L9. **Hours:** 11:30 am-3 & 5-11 pm, Sat from 5 pm. Closed major holidays; also Sun. **Reservations:** suggested. **Features:** A converted older home, pleasant
Continental   background music and fireplaces accentuate fine dining on specialties of French, Mediterranean and North American cuisine. Several seafood, poultry and tender, cooked-to-order beef dishes are prepared in a variety of ways. Semi-formal attire; cocktails. **Parking:** on-site. **Cards:** AX, DC, MC, VI.   ⊠

(See map and index starting on p. 479)

PALMS COURT RESTAURANT　　　**Lunch:** $7-$15　　　**Dinner:** $10-$19　　　**Phone:** 905/896-0623　223

Canadian

Location: QEW W, exit Hwy 10 (Hurontario St), 1 km n; in Queentario Plaza. 2325 Hurontario St L5A 4C7. **Hours:** 11 am-10:30 pm, Sun-10 pm. Closed: 12/25. **Features:** The little restaurant has a bright, cheery dining room and a small, separate bar that is popular as an afternoon coffee and conversation stop. The varied menu offers light fare to full meals. Casual dress; cocktails. **Parking:** on-site. **Cards:** AX, MC, VI.

ROGUES　　　**Lunch:** $11-$16　　　**Dinner:** $14-$30　　　**Phone:** 905/822-2670　222

Northern Italian

Location: Just e of Erin Mills Pkwy; at Sherwood Forest Village. 1900 Dundas St W L5K 1P9. **Hours:** 11:30 am-2:30 & 5:30-10:30 pm, Sat from 5:30 pm. Closed major holidays; also Sun & 1/1-1/7. **Reservations:** required, weekends. **Features:** This restaurant is located in a small up-scale shopping complex. The atmosphere can be bustling and yet it is warm and intimate. An open kitchen allows guests to view a team of professional chefs in action. The menu is varied and demonstrates innovative preparation of fish, red meat and pasta, all of which are creatively presented. Worth a visit. Dressy casual; cocktails. **Parking:** on-site. **Cards:** AX, DC, MC, VI.

RUTH'S CHRIS STEAK HOUSE　　　**Lunch:** $17-$40　　　**Dinner:** $30-$60　　　**Phone:** 905/897-8555　216

Steak House

Location: Just w of Hurontario St. 77 City Centre Dr L5B 1M5. **Hours:** 11:30 am-2:30 & 5-10 pm, Fri & Sat-10:45 pm, Sun 5 pm-9 pm. Closed: 12/25, 12/26. **Reservations:** suggested. **Features:** Hot, tasty bread, generous sides suitable for sharing and huge portions of sizzling meats that melt in the mouth make the steak house a favourite of serious meat lovers. This location features a large lounge and upscale contemporary decor. Dressy casual; cocktails. **Parking:** on-site. **Cards:** AX, DC, MC, VI.

SCORPIO SEAFOOD　　　**Lunch:** $12-$23　　　**Dinner:** $18-$45　　　**Phone:** 905/564-3399　234

Steak & Seafood

Location: On Dixie Rd, 1.5 km n of Hwy 401. 1521 Trinity Dr L5T 1P6. **Hours:** 11 am-11 pm, Sat from 4 pm. Closed: Sun. **Reservations:** required. **Features:** Comfortable, upscale, candlelight dining is the setting; quality beef and seafood are the prize. A crisp garden salad, fresh steamed vegetables and baked potato accompany most selections. A tableside flambe presentation is just one notable feature. **Parking:** on-site. **Cards:** AX, DC, MC, VI.

TOPIARY'S　　　**Lunch:** $7-$20　　　**Dinner:** $20-$50　　　**Phone:** 905/677-3640　232

Steak & Seafood

Location: 0.5 km e of Airport Rd. 3215 Derry Rd E L4T 1A8. **Hours:** 11 am-11 pm, Sat 4 pm-midnight, Sun 4 pm-10 pm. Closed: 1/1, 12/25, 12/26. **Reservations:** suggested. **Features:** The distinguished, upscale dining room prepares traditional menu offerings with flair. Fabulous steak and fresh seafood are menu highlights. Try chateaubriand for two or Topiary's platter for two: a combination of steak and seafood delights. Desserts are delicious. After-dinner flaming coffees prepared at the table make for a perfect ending. Dressy casual; cocktails. **Parking:** on-site. **Cards:** AX, DC, MC, VI.

ZORRO'S STEAK & SEAFOOD HOUSE　　　**Lunch:** $8-$15　　　**Dinner:** $15-$32　　　**Phone:** 905/671-1149　229

Steak & Seafood

Location: Just n of Derry Rd. 7171 Torbram Rd L4T 3N4. **Hours:** 11:30 am-11 pm, Sat from 4:30 pm, Sun 4:30 pm-10 pm. Closed: 1/1, 12/25. **Reservations:** suggested. **Features:** The well-established steak and seafood restaurant sustains an upscale yet comfortable atmosphere. Guests are served hearty portions of traditional favourites, such as shrimp cocktail, broiled scallops, French onion soup and Caesar salad, as well as meat, seafood, pasta, ribs and chicken. All meals include hot garlic bread and a tasty relish tray. Regulars comment on how filling and satisfying the meals are. Dressy casual. **Parking:** on-site. **Cards:** AX, DC, MC, VI.

Homewood Suites by Hilton® Toronto Mississauga
6430 Edwards Blvd. • Mississauga, Ontario, Canada L5T 2Y3
Tel: (905) 564-5529 • Fax: (905) 564-5236

MAKE YOURSELF AT HOME.™

- Studio, one- and two-bedroom suites
- Fully equipped kitchens
- Indoor chlorine free pool
- Close to shopping, movies, restaurants, and entertainment

- Complimentary Suite Start™ hot breakfast daily and Welcome Home® reception† featuring a light meal and beverages Monday-Thursday evenings

The Hilton Family   Hilton HHonors®   Points & Miles

homewoodsuites.com
1-800-CALL-HOME®

Valid AAA membership card required for reservation and at check-in. Hilton HHonors® membership, earning of Points & Miles,® and redemption of points are subject to HHonors Terms and Conditions. †Subject to State and Local laws. ©2005 Hilton Hospitality, Inc.

MONETVILLE

―――― **WHERE TO STAY** ――――

MEMQUISIT LODGE

Phone: 705/898-2355

Property failed to provide current rates

Location: 20.8 km ne on west arm of Lake Nipissing, on Hwy 64 and Memquisit Lodge Rd; 36.8 km sw off Hwy 17, on Hwy 64. Located on lakeside. 506 Memquisit Rd P0M 2K0 (Box 1, Site 4, 506 Memquisit Rd). Fax: 705/898-2583. **Facility:** 16 cottages. 1 story, exterior corridors. *Bath:* combo or shower only. **Parking:** on-site. **Terms:** open 5/15-10/31, office hours 7 am-8 pm, pets (with prior approval). **Leisure Activities:** rental boats, rental canoes, paddleboats, fishing, playground, exercise room. *Fee:* boat dock. **Guest Services:** gift shop, coin laundry.

Cottage

SOME UNITS

MORRISBURG pop. 2,583

―――― **WHERE TO STAY** ――――

THE MCINTOSH COUNTRY INN & CONFERENCE CENTRE

Phone: (613)543-3788

| All Year | 1P: $79-$159 | 2P: $79-$159 | XP: $15 | F18 |

Location: Hwy 401, exit 750, 2 km s on Rt 31, then 1 km e. Located in a commercial area. 12495 Hwy 2 E K0C 1X0 (PO Box 1140). Fax: 613/543-3160. **Facility:** 59 units. 58 one-bedroom standard units, some with whirlpools. 1 one-bedroom suite ($169-$299). 2 stories (no elevator), interior corridors. **Parking:** on-site, winter plug-ins. **Terms:** package plans, small pets only ($20 fee, in smoking units). **Amenities:** high-speed Internet (fee), voice mail. *Some:* dual phone lines, irons, hair dryers. **Dining:** 7 am-9 pm, cocktails. **Pool(s):** heated outdoor. **Leisure Activities:** sauna, whirlpool, snowmobiling. *Fee:* massage. **Guest Services:** valet laundry. **Business Services:** meeting rooms. **Cards:** AX, CB, DC, DS, MC, VI. *(See color ad below)*

Small-scale Hotel

SOME UNITS

NEWBORO pop. 309

―――― **WHERE TO STAY** ――――

NEWBORO HOUSE BED & BREAKFAST

Phone: 613/272-3181

| 5/1-12/31 [BP] | 1P: $70 | 2P: $75 |

Location: On Hwy 42; centre. Located in the village. 31 Drummond St K0G 1P0 (PO Box 64). Fax: 613/272-3181. **Facility:** The B&B, a Second Empire-style brick house, is on a main village street and offers simple room decor. Smoke free premises. 3 one-bedroom standard units. 2 stories (no elevator), interior corridors. *Bath:* some shared or private, combo or shower only. **Parking:** on-site. **Terms:** open 5/1-12/31, office hours 8 am-9 pm, check-in 4 pm. **Cards:** VI.

Historic Bed & Breakfast

SOME UNITS

Great Packages with Area Attractions, Upper Canada Village & Golf Course

FREE high speed internet

Conferencing available

12495 Hwy. #2 East, Morrisburg, ON K0C 1X0

Tel: (613) 543-3788

Toll Free: 1-888-229-2850

www.mcintoshcountryinn.com

NEW HAMBURG pop. 7,003

——— WHERE TO DINE ———

THE WATERLOT INN — **Lunch:** $8-$12 — **Dinner:** $18-$28 — **Phone:** 519/662-2020
Location: Downtown; behind Royal Bank. 17 Huron St N3A 1K1. **Hours:** Open 5/1-3/1 & 4/1-4/30; 11:30 am-2 & 5-8:30 pm, Sun from 5 pm; Sunday brunch seatings 11:30 am & 1:30 pm. Closed: 12/25; also Mon.
Continental **Reservations:** suggested, weekends. **Features:** A quaint country atmosphere complements such French-influenced dining selections as Dover sole, rack of lamb and lobster. A three-course prix fixe meal is served on all days except Saturday. Dressy casual; cocktails. **Parking:** on-site. **Cards:** AX, DC, MC, VI.

NEWMARKET pop. 65,788

——— WHERE TO STAY ———

BEST WESTERN VOYAGEUR PLACE HOTEL — *Book at aaa.com* — **Phone:** (905)895-2131
All Year — 1P: $89-$179 — 2P: $89-$179 — XP: $10 — F17
Location: Jct Hwy 11 and 9. Located in a commercial area. 17565 Yonge St L3Y 5H6. Fax: 905/895-9651.
Facility: 97 one-bedroom standard units, some with efficiencies and/or whirlpools. 2-4 stories, interior/exterior corridors. **Parking:** on-site, winter plug-ins. **Terms:** package plans. **Amenities:** video games (fee), voice mail, irons, hair dryers. **Dining:** 7 am-10 pm, Sat 8 am-11 pm, Sun 8 am-2:30 pm, cocktails.
Small-scale Hotel **Guest Services:** valet laundry. **Business Services:** meeting rooms. **Cards:** AX, DC, DS, JC, MC, VI.
Special Amenities: free local telephone calls and free newspaper.

COMFORT INN — *Book at aaa.com* — **Phone:** (905)895-3355
7/1-9/30 — 1P: $103-$118 — 2P: $103-$128 — XP: $5 — F18
10/1-4/30 — 1P: $99-$109 — 2P: $109-$119 — XP: $5 — F18
5/1-6/30 — 1P: $97-$107 — 2P: $102-$117 — XP: $5 — F18
Small-scale Hotel **Location:** Hwy 404, exit 51 (Davis Dr). Located in a commercial area. 1230 Journey's End Cir L3Y 7V1.
Fax: 905/895-1176. **Facility:** 102 one-bedroom standard units. 2 stories (no elevator), interior corridors. **Parking:** on-site, winter plug-ins. **Amenities:** *Some:* irons, hair dryers. **Cards:** AX, DC, DS, MC, VI.

——— WHERE TO DINE ———

THE KEG STEAKHOUSE AND BAR — **Dinner:** $16-$30 — **Phone:** 905/830-0615
Location: 2 km n of Hwy 9. 18195 Yonge St L3Y 4V8. **Hours:** 4 pm-1 am. Closed: 12/25. **Features:** Well-known for its mesquite-grilled steaks and fun, laid-back atmosphere, this steak house is a longtime favorite with the Steak House local crowd. In addition to great beef, the traditional menu features seafood, grilled chicken, hickory ribs and pasta offerings. All meals come with a hot loaf of sourdough bread. Try a specialty coffee or some tasty cheesecake for the perfect ending. Casual dress; cocktails. **Parking:** on-site. **Cards:** AX, DC, MC, VI.

Roadtrip Perfected

Diamonds are the perfect work of nature. Make certain your next roadtrip is perfect by looking for the red hotel and restaurant Diamond ratings in AAA TourBooks® and online at aaa.com.

It's your assurance of high quality, great service and special savings for AAA Members.

  Travel with Confidence
Travel with AAA

Destination Niagara Falls
pop. 78,815

D ay or night, Niagara Falls captivates. Start with a look at the falls from one of several vantage points, then shop till closing time at duty-free stores and factory outlets.

I f you didn't see enough of the falls by day, return when the sun goes down and the lights go on. Now that's a show! Later in the evening, enjoy a theater performance. Or try your luck anytime at casino gambling.

© 2004 Ontario Tourism

Marching band.
It just wouldn't be a festival without a parade, and the thundering falls provides a scenic backdrop.

Wooden Indian statue.
Reminders of the area's native heritage are evident throughout Niagara Falls.

© Jon Davison Lonely Planet Images

City of St. Catharines

Bicycling, St. Catharines.
There are plenty of parks and trails in the Niagara Falls area where families can enjoy a bicycling outing.

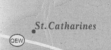

Niagara-on-the-Lake

St. Catharines

QEW

CAN USA

405

104

Thorold

Niagara Falls

Niagara Falls

20

See Vicinity map page 309

Welland

QEW

ON NY

190

290

Port Colborne •

Fort Erie •

See Vicinity map page 306

© 2004 Ontario Tourism

Shopping.
If you can tear yourself away from the spectacular views of the falls, a world of shopping awaits.

P laces included in this AAA Destination City:

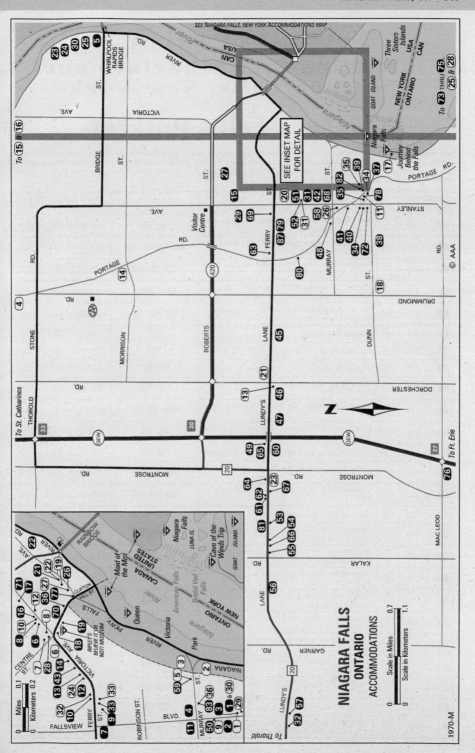

NIAGARA FALLS
ONTARIO
ACCOMMODATIONS

Scale in Miles
Scale in Kilometers

1970-M

© AAA

NIAGARA FALLS
including St. Catharines and Niagara Falls, New York

Niagara Falls, Ontario

This index helps you "spot" where approved accommodations and restaurants are located on the corresponding detailed maps. Lodging rate ranges are for comparison only and show the property's high season; rates are per night, unless only weekly (W) rates are available. Restaurant rate range is for dinner, unless only lunch (L) is served. Turn to the listing page for more detailed rate information and consult display ads for special promotions.

Spotter/Map Page Number	OA	NIAGARA FALLS, ONTARIO - Lodgings	Diamond Rating	Rate Range High Season	Listing Page
1 / p. 309	AAA	The Oakes Hotel Overlooking the Falls - see color ad starting on p 338	◇◇	$69-$999 SAVE	352
2 / p. 309	AAA	Renaissance Fallsview Hotel - see color ad p 359 & ad starting on p 118	◇◇◇◇	$179-$499 SAVE	358
3 / p. 309		Ramada Plaza Hotel Fallsview - see color ad p 357 & ad starting on p 118	◇◇◇	$179-$299	356
4 / p. 309	AAA	Holiday Inn by the Falls - see color ad p 344, p 371 & ad starting on p 118	◇◇◇	$110-$245 SAVE	343
5 / p. 309	AAA	Hampton Inn North of the Falls - see color ad p 324, p 4	◇◇◇	$89-$249 SAVE	342
6 / p. 309	AAA	Niagara Family Inn	◇	$55-$95 SAVE	352
7 / p. 309	AAA	Cadillac Motel	◇	$50-$130 SAVE	323
8 / p. 309	AAA	Chalet Inn and Suites - see color ad p 328	◇◇	$89-$229 SAVE	328
9 / p. 309	AAA	Travelodge near the Falls - see color ad p 368	◇◇	$89-$399 SAVE	368
10 / p. 309	AAA	Quality Hotel-Near the Falls - see color ad p 317	◇◇◇	$129-$309 SAVE	354
11 / p. 309	AAA	Best Western Fallsview - see color ad p 323 & ad starting on p 118	◇◇	$129-$299 SAVE	319
12 / p. 309	AAA	Days Inn Near the Falls - see color ad p 340	◇◇	$80-$299 SAVE	334
13 / p. 309	AAA	Howard Johnson by the Falls - see color ad card insert, p 350	◇◇	$99-$399 SAVE	345
14 / p. 309	AAA	Imperial Hotel and Suites - see color ad p 348	◇◇◇	$79-$359 SAVE	348
15 / p. 309	AAA	Camelot Inn - see color ad p 364	◇◇	$59-$229 SAVE	323
16 / p. 309		Days Inn Clifton Hill Casino - see color ad starting on p 338	◇◇	$49-$429	334
17 / p. 309	AAA	Hampton Inn at the Falls - see color ad p 341, starting on p 326, p 4	◇◇◇	$169-$429 SAVE	340
18 / p. 309	AAA	Comfort Inn Clifton Hill - see color ad starting on p 332	◇◇◇	$89-$289 SAVE	329
19 / p. 309	AAA	Quality Inn Clifton Hill - see color ad starting on p 332	◇◇	$79-$279 SAVE	355
21 / p. 309	AAA	Brock Plaza Hotel - see color ad starting on p 326, p 325	◇◇◇	$149-$799 SAVE	322
22 / p. 309	AAA	Aston Michael's Inn-By the Falls - see color ad p 318	◇◇◇	$88-$288 SAVE	316
23 / p. 309	AAA	Comfort Inn North of the Falls - see color ad p 324	◇◇	$79-$249 SAVE	331
24 / p. 309	AAA	Days Inn North of the Falls - see color ad p 324	◇◇	$78-$228 SAVE	336
25 / p. 309		Crystal Motel	◇◇	$79-$189	331
26 / p. 309	AAA	Sheraton on the Falls - see color ad starting on p 326, p 362, p 5, card insert	◇◇◇◇	$169-$999 SAVE	362

Spotter/Map Page Number	OA	**NIAGARA FALLS, ONTARIO - Lodgings (continued)**	Diamond Rating	Rate Range High Season	Listing Page
27 / p. 309	CAA	Red Carpet Inn and Suites, Fallsway - see color ad p 358	◆◆	$49-$199 SAVE	358
28 / p. 309	CAA	Days Inn & Suites by the Falls - see color ad p 335	◆◆◆	$89-$299 SAVE	331
29 / p. 309	CAA	Sunset Inn - see color ad p 364	◆◆	$79-$199 SAVE	364
30 / p. 309	CAA	Best Western Fireside Hotel - see color ad p 324	◆◆◆	$89-$249 SAVE	319
31 / p. 309	CAA	Fallsview Inn - see color ad p 337	◆◆	$46-$199 SAVE	337
32 / p. 309	CAA	Melody Motel	◆	$58-$98 SAVE	351
33 / p. 309	CAA	Courtyard by Marriott Niagara Falls - see color ad card insert, p 350	◆◆◆	$99-$399 SAVE	331
34 / p. 309	CAA	Vacation Inn - see color ad p 369	◆◆	$99-$275 SAVE	368
35 / p. 309	CAA	Horseshoe Falls Motor Inn - see color ad p 346 & ad starting on p 118	◆◆	$69-$269 SAVE	343
36 / p. 309	CAA	Travelodge Clifton Hill - see color ad p 367	◆◆◆	$89-$329 SAVE	366
37 / p. 309	CAA	Sheraton Fallsview Hotel & Conference Centre - see color ad p 361, p 5, card insert & ad starting on p 118	◆◆◆◆	$149-$429 SAVE	361
38 / p. 309		Aurora Motel	◆	$59-$179	316
39 / p. 309	CAA	Marriott Niagara Falls Fallsview and Spa - see color ad card insert, p 350	◆◆◆◆	$199-$599 SAVE	350
40 / p. 309	CAA	The President Motor Inn - see color ad p 353	◆	$69-$160 SAVE	354
41 / p. 309	CAA	Lincoln Motor Inn - see color ad p 349 & ad starting on p 118	◆◆	$89-$189 SAVE	349
42 / p. 309	CAA	Stanley Motor Inn - see color ad p 363 & ad starting on p 118	◆◆	$70-$150 SAVE	364
43 / p. 309	CAA	A Victoria Motor Inn	◆	$89-$199 SAVE	318
45 / p. 309	CAA	Best Western Cairn Croft Hotel - see color ad p 322	◆◆◆	$99-$199 SAVE	319
46 / p. 309	CAA	Knights Inn	◆◆	$79-$249 SAVE	348
47 / p. 309		Days Inn-Lundy's Lane - see color ad starting on p 338	◆◆	$45-$299	334
48 / p. 309	CAA	Knights Inn-By the Falls - see color ad starting on p 118	◆◆	$84-$254 SAVE	348
49 / p. 309	CAA	Ramada Suites Hotel - see color ad p 356	◆◆◆	$90-$230 SAVE	357
50 / p. 309	CAA	Hilton Niagara Falls Fallsview - see color ad inside front cover, p 343, p 375, card insert & ad starting on p 118	◆◆◆◆	$149-$499 SAVE	343
51 / p. 309		Econo Lodge near the Falls	◆◆	$85-$205	336
52 / p. 309		Doubletree Resort Lodge & Spa Fallsview - see color ad p 341	◆◆◆	$99-$299	336
53 / p. 309	CAA	Best Inn - see color ad p 319	◆◆	$69-$199 SAVE	319
54 / p. 309	CAA	Carriage House Motor Lodge - see color ad p 329	◆◆	$69-$130 SAVE	325
55 / p. 309	CAA	Howard Johnson Express Inn	◆◆	$65-$200 SAVE	347
56 / p. 309	CAA	Americana Resort & Spa - see color ad starting on p 320	◆◆◆	$139-$299 SAVE	316
57 / p. 309	CAA	A Gardens Inn	◆◆	$69-$129 SAVE	316
58 / p. 309	CAA	Clarion President Hotel & Suites by the Falls - see color ad p 330	◆◆◆	$99-$299 SAVE	328
59 / p. 309		Old Stone Inn - see color ad starting on p 118	◆◆◆	$135-$349	352
60 / p. 309	CAA	Comfort Inn Lundy's Lane - see color ad p 334	◆◆	$99-$269 SAVE	330
61 / p. 309	CAA	Advantage Inn	◆	$48-$118 SAVE	316

Spotter/Map Page Number	OA	NIAGARA FALLS, ONTARIO - Lodgings (continued)	Diamond Rating	Rate Range High Season	Listing Page
62 / p. 309	AA	Travelodge Bonaventure - see color ad p 366	▽▽▽	$79-$199 SAVE	366
63 / p. 309		Park Plaza	▽▽	$99-$189	353
64 / p. 309	AA	Flamingo Motor Inn - see color ad p 342 & ad starting on p 118	▽▽	$69-$179 SAVE	337
65 / p. 309	AA	Ramada Coral Resort Hotel - see color ad p 356	▽▽▽	$90-$200 SAVE	356
66 / p. 309	AA	Villager Lodge	▽▽	$69-$209 SAVE	368
67 / p. 309		Rodeway Inn & Suites	▽▽	$49-$189	358
68 / p. 309	AA	Days Inn Fallsview District - see color ad p 336 & ad starting on p 118	▽▽	$75-$275 SAVE	334
69 / p. 309		Kings Inn near the Falls	▽▽	$79-$199	348
70 / p. 309	AA	Thriftlodge Clifton Hill	▽	$89-$299 SAVE	365
71 / p. 309	AA	Skyline Inn - see color ad starting on p 326, p 363	▽▽	$99-$349 SAVE	363
72 / p. 309	AA	Rodeway Inn Fallsview - see color ad p 360 & ad starting on p 118	▽▽▽	$89-$259 SAVE	360
73 / p. 309	AA	Niagara Parkway Court Motel - see color ad p 352	▽	$49-$199 SAVE	352
74 / p. 309	AA	Surfside Inn - see color ad p 365	▽▽	$69-$229 SAVE	365
75 / p. 309	AA	Niagara Falls Motor Lodge - see color ad p 351	▽▽	$59-$138 SAVE	351
76 / p. 309	AA	Peninsula Inn & Resort	▽▽▽	$109-$249 SAVE	354
77 / p. 309		Hilltop Hotel	▽	$130-$200	342
78 / p. 309		Radisson Hotel & Suites Fallsview - see color ad p 521, p 355 & ad starting on p 118	▽▽▽	$179-$299	356
79 / p. 309	AA	Super 8 Hotel - see color ad p 364	▽▽▽	$59-$289 SAVE	365
80 / p. 309		Victorian Charm Bed and Breakfast	▽▽	$100-$185	368
81 / p. 309	AA	A-1 Motel	▽	$48-$118 SAVE	316
82 / p. 309	AA	Embassy Suites Niagara Falls Fallsview - see color ad card insert, p 350	▽▽▽	$189-$599 SAVE	337
83 / p. 309		Niagara Fallsview Casino Resort - see color ad inside front cover	▽▽▽▽	$319-$399	352
87 / p. 309	AA	Continental Inn	▽	$59-$119 SAVE	331
		NIAGARA FALLS, ONTARIO - Restaurants			
1 / p. 309		Konica Minolta Tower Centre/Pinnacle Restaurant	▽▽▽	$19-$48	372
2 / p. 309	AA	Edgewaters Tap & Grill	▽▽	$20-$40	371
3 / p. 309	AA	The Skylon Tower Dining Rooms - see color ad p 120, p 374	▽▽▽	$36-$84	374
4 / p. 309		Fine Kettle 'O' Fish	▽▽	$8-$30	371
5 / p. 309		The Millery Dining Room	▽▽▽	$21-$62	373
6 / p. 309		Hard Times	▽▽	$10-$23	372
7 / p. 309	AA	The Beef Baron	▽▽	$11-$35	370
8 / p. 309	AA	Mama Mia's	▽▽	$7-$22	373
9 / p. 309		The Watermark - see color ad inside front cover, p 375, card insert	▽▽▽	$25-$65	375
10 / p. 309	AA	Monticello Grille House & Wine Bar	▽▽▽	$15-$35	373
11 / p. 309		Outback Steakhouse	▽▽	$12-$25	373
12 / p. 309		Remington's of Montana Steak and Seafood	▽▽	$12-$39	373

Spotter/Map Page Number	OA	NIAGARA FALLS, ONTARIO - Restaurants (continued)	Diamond Rating	Rate Range High Season	Listing Page
⑬ / p. 309	ⒶⒶ	Carpaccio Restaurant and Wine Bar	◈◈◈	$9-$30	370
⑭ / p. 309		Delduca's	◈◈◈	$13-$22	371
⑮ / p. 309	ⒶⒶ	Whirlpool Restaurant	◈◈	$11-$22	376
⑯ / p. 309	ⒶⒶ	Queenston Heights Restaurant	◈◈◈	$21-$30	373
⑰ / p. 309	ⒶⒶ	Table Rock Restaurant	◈◈	$20-$35	374
⑱ / p. 309		The Love Boat II	◈◈	$8-$35	373
⑲ / p. 309		Twenty One Club	◈◈◈◈	$16-$61	375
⑳ / p. 309	ⒶⒶ	Capri Restaurant - see color ad p 370	◈◈◈	$10-$35	370
㉑ / p. 309		Frank's Tomato Pie	◈◈	$10-$28	371
㉒ / p. 309		The Rainbow Grille Fallsview Steakhouse	◈◈◈	$25-$50	373
㉓ / p. 309	ⒶⒶ	Mick and Angelo's Eatery and Bar	◈◈	$7-$20	373
㉔ / p. 309		Casa d'Oro Dining Lounge	◈◈◈	$19-$60	371
㉕ / p. 309		Betty's Restaurant	◈	$9-$15	370
㉖ / p. 309		Happy Wanderer	◈	$10-$40	372
㉗ / p. 309		Penthouse Restaurant	◈◈◈	$20-$40	373
㉘ / p. 309	ⒶⒶ	Legends on the Niagara	◈◈	$9-$23	372
㉙ / p. 309	ⒶⒶ	Terrapin Grille - see color ad card insert	◈◈◈	$26-$69	374
㉚ / p. 309		Rooftop Fallsview Dining Room	◈◈◈	$22-$55	374
㉛ / p. 309		Buchanans	◈◈	$19-$34	370
㉜ / p. 309		Brandino's Italian Ristorante and Cafe	◈◈◈	$16-$55	370
㉝ / p. 309	ⒶⒶ	The Keg Steakhouse and Bar - see color ad card insert	◈◈	$20-$55	372
㉞ / p. 309		Fallsview Dining Room	◈◈◈	$20-$45	371
㉟ / p. 309	ⒶⒶ	The Keg Steakhouse and Bar - see color ad card insert	◈◈	$17-$37	372
㊱ / p. 309		17 Noir	◈◈◈	$20-$50	370

Your key to Emergency Road Service...

Emergency Services

AAA is at your service. Your AAA membership card is the key to obtaining Emergency Road Service. AAA can help when your car stalls, you get a flat tire, you run out of gas and even when you're locked out. Anytime, anywhere, call **1-800-AAA-HELP** to get going again.

Speech/Hearing **Hearing Impaired: 1-800-955-4TDD.**

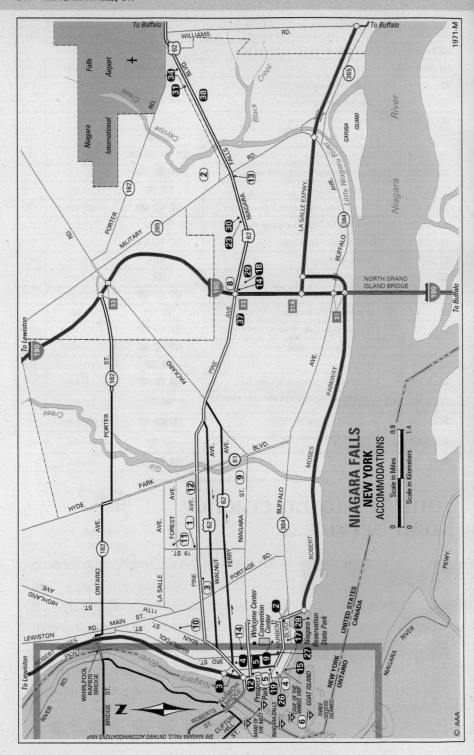

NIAGARA FALLS
NEW YORK
ACCOMMODATIONS

Scale in Miles
Scale in Kilometers

Nearby New York

This index helps you "spot" where approved accommodations and restaurants are located on the corresponding detailed maps. Lodging rate ranges are for comparison only and show the property's high season; rates are per night, unless only weekly (W) rates are available. Restaurant rate range is for dinner, unless only lunch (L) is served. Turn to the listing page for more detailed rate information and consult display ads for special promotions.

Spotter/Map Page Number	OA	NIAGARA FALLS, NEW YORK - Lodgings	Diamond Rating	Rate Range High Season	Listing Page
2 / p. 314	◈◈◈	Rodeway Inn at the Falls	◈◈	$69-$139 SAVE	389
3 / p. 314	◈◈◈	Howard Johnson Hotel (Closest to the Falls)	◈◈	$105-$215 SAVE	388
4 / p. 314	◈◈◈	Days Inn at the Falls	◈◈	$59-$199 SAVE	387
5 / p. 314	◈◈◈	Holiday Inn Select-Niagara Falls	◈◈◈	$125-$195 SAVE	388
9 / p. 314	◈◈◈	Ramada Inn by the Falls	◈◈	$99-$199 SAVE	389
12 / p. 314	◈◈◈	Comfort Inn The Pointe	◈◈	$119-$159 SAVE	387
14 / p. 314	◈◈◈	Howard Johnson Inn-Niagara	◈◈	$69-$139 SAVE	389
15 / p. 314	◈◈◈	Four Points by Sheraton	◈◈◈	$129 SAVE	388
17 / p. 314	◈◈◈	Hampton Inn-Niagara Falls	◈◈◈	$119-$199 SAVE	388
18 / p. 314	◈◈◈	Budget Host Inn	◈	$89-$239 SAVE	387
19 / p. 314		Quality Hotel and Suites "At the Falls"	◈◈	$99-$299	389
23 / p. 314	◈◈◈	Super 8 Motel	◈◈	$69-$179 SAVE	390
26 / p. 314	◈◈◈	The Red Coach Inn	◈◈◈	$139-$179 SAVE	389
27 / p. 314	◈◈◈	Holiday Inn at the Falls - see color ad p 345	◈◈◈	$99-$229 SAVE	388
28 / p. 314		Holley Rankine House	◈◈	$60-$120	388
29 / p. 314	◈◈◈	Swiss Cottage Inn	◈	$32-$169 SAVE	390
30 / p. 314		Quality Inn Niagara	◈◈	$39-$199	389
31 / p. 314	◈◈◈	Bel Aire Motel	◈	$58-$128 SAVE	387
34 / p. 314	◈◈◈	Best Western Summit Inn	◈◈	$79-$159 SAVE	387
37 / p. 314	◈◈◈	Econo Lodge at the Falls	◈◈	$50-$199 SAVE	387
38 / p. 314	◈◈◈	Thriftlodge	◈	$79-$99 SAVE	390
		NIAGARA FALLS, NEW YORK - Restaurants			
①/ p. 314	◈◈◈	Como Restaurant & Deli	◈◈	$7-$18	390
②/ p. 314		John's Flaming Hearth	◈◈	$12-$19	390
③/ p. 314		Pete's Market House Restaurant	◈	$4-$18	391
④/ p. 314	◈◈◈	The Red Coach Inn Restaurant	◈◈◈	$7-$20	391
⑥/ p. 314		Top of the Falls Restaurant	◈	$7-$25	391
⑧/ p. 314		Timber Lodge Steakhouse	◈◈	$9-$22	391
⑨/ p. 314		Koban's	◈	$8-$12	390
⑩/ p. 314	◈◈◈	Chu's Dining Lounge-Chinese Food	◈◈	$6-$11	390
⑪/ p. 314		Fortuna's	◈◈	$7-$17	390
⑫/ p. 314		Michael's	◈	$7-$9	390

NIAGARA FALLS pop. 78,815 (See map and index starting on p. 309)

Accommodations for the American side are listed under Niagara Falls, New York.

──────── WHERE TO STAY ────────

A-1 MOTEL
CAA SAVE   **Phone: (905)354-6038**   81

6/26-9/6	1P: $48-$98	2P: $68-$118	XP: $10	F12
5/1-6/25	1P: $38-$48	2P: $48-$78	XP: $10	F12
9/7-4/30	1P: $38-$58	2P: $48-$68	XP: $10	F12

Location: QEW, exit Hwy 20, 4.5 km w. 7895 Lundy's Ln L2H 1H3. Fax: 905/357-7854. **Facility:** 29 one-bedroom
Motel standard units, some with kitchens. 1 story, exterior corridors. *Bath:* combo or shower only. **Parking:** on-site.
Terms: 3 day cancellation notice-fee imposed, weekly rates available, package plans. **Pool(s):** heated
outdoor. **Leisure Activities:** playground. **Guest Services:** area transportation (fee)-casino. **Cards:** AX, DS, MC, VI.

SOME UNITS
(SD) 📶 🏊 🛗 / ✕ 🖼 /

ADVANTAGE INN   *Book at aaa.com*   **Phone: (905)374-4442**   61
CAA SAVE

6/26-9/6	1P: $48-$98	2P: $58-$118	XP: $10	F16
5/1-6/25	1P: $38-$78	2P: $48-$98	XP: $10	F16
9/7-4/30	1P: $38-$58	2P: $48-$78	XP: $10	F16

Location: QEW, exit Hwy 20, 4.6 km w. 7797 Lundy's Ln L2H 1H3. Fax: 905/357-1854. **Facility:** 35 one-bedroom
Motel standard units, some with efficiencies, kitchens (no utensils) and/or whirlpools. 1-2 stories (no elevator),
exterior corridors. *Bath:* combo or shower only. **Parking:** on-site, winter plug-ins. **Terms:** 3 day cancellation
notice-fee imposed, 12% service charge. **Pool(s):** heated outdoor. **Leisure Activities:** barbecue, playground. **Guest Services:**
area transportation (fee)-falls & casino. **Cards:** AX, DC, DS, MC, VI. **Special Amenities: free local telephone calls.**

SOME UNITS
📶 🏊 📺 🎥 🛗 / ✕ 🖼 /

A GARDENS INN   **Phone: (905)227-0891**   57
CAA SAVE

6/27-9/4	1P: $69-$119	2P: $79-$129	XP: $10	F12
5/1-6/26	1P: $59-$89	2P: $69-$99	XP: $10	F12
9/5-4/30	1P: $45-$79	2P: $55-$89	XP: $5	F12

Location: 9.2 km w on Hwy 20. 13055 Lundy's Ln L2E 6S4. Fax: 905/227-3720. **Facility:** 28 one-bedroom
Motel standard units, some with whirlpools. 1 story, exterior corridors. **Parking:** on-site. **Terms:** 3 day cancellation
notice-fee imposed, [BP] meal plan available, package plans. **Pool(s):** heated outdoor. **Leisure
Activities:** playground. **Cards:** AX, DC, DS, MC, VI. **Special Amenities: free local telephone calls and preferred room
(subject to availability with advance reservations).**

SOME UNITS
(SD) 🏊 📺 🎥 🛗 / ✕ /

AMERICANA RESORT & SPA   **Phone: (905)356-8444**   56
CAA SAVE

6/24-9/4	2P: $139-$299
9/5-10/20	2P: $99-$229
5/1-6/23 & 10/21-4/30	2P: $89-$199

Location: QEW, exit Hwy 20, 5.5 km w. 8444 Lundy's Ln L2H 1H4. Fax: 905/356-8576. **Facility:** 210 units. 191
Large-scale Hotel one-bedroom standard units, some with whirlpools. 19 one-bedroom suites ($139-$399), some with
whirlpools. 2-3 stories (no elevator), interior corridors. **Parking:** on-site. **Terms:** cancellation fee imposed,
package plans, 3% service charge. **Amenities:** voice mail, hair dryers. **Dining:** 7 am-11 pm, Fri & Sat-midnight, cocktails.
Pool(s): heated outdoor, 3 heated indoor, wading. **Leisure Activities:** sauna, whirlpools, steamrooms, indoor water park, wave
pool, lighted tennis court, squash court, playground, exercise room, basketball, shuffleboard, volleyball, game room. **Guest
Services:** gift shop, valet and coin laundry, area transportation (fee)-casino & falls. **Business Services:** conference facilities,
business center. **Cards:** AX, DC, DS, MC, VI. **Special Amenities: preferred room (subject to availability with advance
reservations).** *(See color ad starting on p 320)*

SOME UNITS
(SD) 🍽 🍸 🛗 🏋M 🏊 ✕ 🎥 DATA PORT 🛗 🖥 / ✕ /

ASTON MICHAEL'S INN-BY THE FALLS   *Book at aaa.com*   **Phone: (905)354-2727**   22
CAA SAVE

6/10-9/13 [CP]	1P: $88-$288	2P: $88-$288	
5/1-6/9 & 9/14-10/31 [CP]	1P: $58-$178	2P: $58-$178	
11/1-4/30 [CP]	1P: $48-$158	2P: $48-$158	

Location: Just n of Rainbow Bridge and QEW. 5599 River Rd L2E 3H3. Fax: 905/374-7706. **Facility:** 130 units.
Small-scale Hotel 129 one- and 1 two-bedroom standard units, some with whirlpools. 4 stories, interior corridors. **Parking:** on-
site. **Terms:** package plans. **Amenities:** video games (fee), voice mail, irons, hair dryers. **Dining:** 7 am-11
pm; 8 am-9 pm 11/1-4/30, cocktails. **Pool(s):** heated indoor, wading. **Leisure Activities:** sauna, whirlpool, exercise room. *Fee:*
game room. **Guest Services:** gift shop, valet laundry. **Business Services:** meeting rooms. **Cards:** AX, CB, DC, JC, MC, VI.
Special Amenities: free continental breakfast and free newspaper. *(See color ad p 318)*

SOME UNITS
(SD) 🍽 🍸 🏊 ✕ 🎥 DATA PORT 🖥 / ✕ 🛗 🖼 /

AURORA MOTEL   **Phone: 905/356-4490**   38

6/17-9/10	1P: $59-$169	2P: $69-$179	XP: $10	F10
5/1-6/16 & 9/11-4/30	1P: $39-$79	2P: $49-$89	XP: $5	F10

Location: Just w of Konica Minolta Tower. Located in a residential area. 5630 Dunn St L2G 2N7. Fax: 905/357-9631.
Motel **Facility:** 29 one-bedroom standard units. 2 stories (no elevator), exterior corridors. **Parking:** on-site.
Terms: 3 day cancellation notice, package plans, $10 service charge. **Pool(s):** heated outdoor. **Cards:** DC, MC, VI.

SOME UNITS
(ASK) (SD) 🏊 / ✕ /

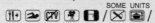

QUALITY HOTEL

Near The Falls

Quality Hotel
5257 Ferry Street
Niagara Falls, Ontario
Canada L2G 1R6
Tel. (905) 356-2842

AAA

Features

- 120 Spacious Rooms
- Breakfast Buffet Restaurant
- Heated Indoor Pool
- Whirlpool & Sauna
- Sundeck/Patio Children's Wading Pool
- In-room Pay Movies & Nintendo
- Gift Shop
- Family & Whirlpool Rooms
- Honeymoon Rooms with heartshaped tubs
- Hairdryers, Coffeemakers, Iron & Ironing board in all rooms
- Non-Smoking Rooms
- Free Parking

Only a short walk from The Falls, Victoria Park, the Casinos and many other attractions...

Special Packages
from October through May

RESERVATIONS 1 (800) 228-5151
ASK FOR PROPERTY CN152
www.qualityhotelniagara.com

(See map and index starting on p. 309)

A VICTORIA MOTOR INN   Phone: (905)374-6522   **43**

(CAA) (SAVE)	6/17-9/6	1P: $89-$129	2P: $99-$199	XP: $10	F16
	9/7-9/30	1P: $69-$99	2P: $79-$139	XP: $10	F16
♦♦♦♦	5/1-6/16 & 10/1-4/30	1P: $59-$79	2P: $79-$99	XP: $10	F16

Motel

Location: From Clifton Hill, just w. Located in a commercial area. 5869 Victoria Ave L2G 3L6. Fax: 905/374-3038. **Facility:** 33 one-bedroom standard units, some with whirlpools. 3 stories (no elevator), exterior corridors. **Parking:** on-site. **Terms:** 3 day cancellation notice-fee imposed, package plans, 3% service charge. **Dining:** 7 am-noon. **Pool(s):** heated outdoor. **Cards:** AX, DC, DS, MC, VI. **Special Amenities:** early check-in/late check-out and free room upgrade (subject to availability with advance reservations).

SOME UNITS

(S/D) (¶|) (🏊) (Z) /(X)/

Michael's Inn ASTON*
by the Falls on the River

10%
Discount on Standard Rooms to CAA/AAA Members
Extra persons in room stay FREE!

Closest Inn to the Falls on River Road, with on-site Free Parking.

★ Balcony Rooms with view of the Falls, the Niagara Gorge and the River
★ Family Rooms, Children Stay Free Package Deals All Year
★ Heart Shaped Tubs, Jacuzzis & Fireplaces
★ Tours of the Falls/Wineries

★ Cable TV, In-room Movies and Nintendo
★ New "Great Barrier Reef" Indoor Pool with Jacuzzi, Sauna, Fitness Centre and Games Room
★ Special Group Rates
★ Senior Citizen Rates Year-Round
★ Over 40 Golf Courses Nearby

Famous Theme Room Suites Include:
Jardin D'Amore, Midnight at the Oasis, Romance by the Falls, and more!

JUST A TWO-MINUTE WALK TO CASINO NIAGARA

EMBERS OPEN HEARTH –

Experience patio dining with a view of the Falls. World-class steaks, prime rib & other fine cuts of meat deliciously prepared by our Master Chef in the glass-enclosed open hearth kitchen.

FREE CONTINENTAL BREAKFAST TO CAA/AAA CARDHOLDERS

GREAT LOCATION!
Walking Distance to the Falls, Casino Niagara, Maid of the Mist & Skylon Tower

Michael's Inn

adjacent to the Rainbow Bridge & Highway 420
Visit us at www.michaelsinn.com

1-800-263-9390

5599 River Road
Niagara Falls, Canada L2E 3H3
905-354-2727

Even More Ways to Travel With Someone You Trust®

AAAs exciting line of kids travel products offer children the opportunity to have fun and learn with games, puzzles, coloring and activity books while they travel.

Purchase AAA travel publications at participating AAA club offices, on www.aaa.com/barnesandnoble and in fine book stores.

Sheraton on the Falls
HOTEL
NIAGARA FALLS

STAY IN THE CENTER OF IT ALL - THE FOUR-DIAMOND SHERATON ON THE FALLS NIAGARA'S PREMIER FAMILY RESORT

Only hotel directly in front of the Falls – surrounded by Niagara Parklands

Superb fallsviews – full panoramic views of both American and Horseshoe Falls – a breathtaking postcard view

Fallsview rooms and suites with fireplaces & private balconies – feel the magic of the mist from your room and watch fireworks over the Falls

Exciting family attractions – Marvel Superheroes Adventure City, MGM Studios Plaza, WWE Niagara Falls and The Hershey Store all directly connected to your hotel

Fantastic family dining – Rainforest Cafe, Hard Rock Cafe, Planet Hollywood all on-site

Why stay anywhere else? Your one-stop Niagara Falls Family Resort

5875 Falls Avenue, Niagara Falls, Ontario
1.888.229.9946
www.NiagaraFallsHotels.com

FALLSVIEW SPA

FALLSVIEW DINING

Special packages available to AAA/CAA Members:

Show Your Card
Approved Lodging

KIDS stay&eat **FREE**

- Kids stay & eat free when staying with their parents on AAA package.

- **Special Family Fun Packages** - including Marvel Adventure City Game tokens, meals and guest room

- **Special Romance Packages** - for AAA/CAA members – includes Hershey chocolate strawberries and wine in room

FALLSVIEW JACUZZI SUITE

TWO POOLS

(See map and index starting on p. 309)

BEST INN _Book at aaa.com_   Phone: (905)356-8280   **53**
CAA SAVE
5/1-9/30 [CP]   1P: $69-$199   2P: $69-$199   XP: $10   F12
10/1-4/30 [CP]   1P: $49-$79   2P: $49-$79   XP: $10   F12
Location: QEW, exit Hwy 20, 4.6 km w. 7800 Lundy's Ln L2H 1H1. Fax: 905/356-6948. **Facility:** 69 units. 68 one-bedroom standard units, some with whirlpools. 1 three-bedroom suite. 2 stories (no elevator), exterior
Motel corridors. **Parking:** on-site. **Dining:** 6 am-11 pm. **Pool(s):** heated outdoor. **Cards:** AX, DC, JC, MC, VI.
Special Amenities: free continental breakfast and free local telephone calls. _(See color ad below)_

SOME UNITS

BEST WESTERN CAIRN CROFT HOTEL _Book at aaa.com_   Phone: (905)356-1161   **45**
CAA SAVE
6/17-9/4   1P: $99-$199   2P: $99-$199   XP: $10   F17
9/5-10/29   1P: $79-$149   2P: $79-$149   XP: $10   F17
5/1-6/16 & 10/30-4/30   1P: $59-$129   2P: $59-$129   XP: $10   F17
Location: 2.4 km w. on Hwy 20. 6400 Lundy's Ln L2G 1T6. Fax: 905/356-8664. **Facility:** 165 one-bedroom
Small-scale Hotel standard units, some with whirlpools. 2-5 stories, interior/exterior corridors. **Parking:** on-site, winter plug-ins.
Terms: [AP] meal plan available, package plans. **Amenities:** video games (fee), irons, hair dryers.
Dining: 7 am-2 & 5-10 pm; to 9 pm weekdays off season, cocktails. **Pool(s):** heated indoor. **Leisure Activities:** whirlpools,
indoor children's play area. _Fee:_ game room. **Guest Services:** valet laundry, area transportation (fee)-casino & falls. **Business
Services:** meeting rooms. **Cards:** AX, DC, DS, MC, VI. _(See color ad p 322)_

SOME UNITS

FEE

BEST WESTERN FALLSVIEW _Book at aaa.com_   Phone: (905)356-0551   **11**
CAA SAVE
6/24-9/4   1P: $129-$299   2P: $129-$299   XP: $10   F12
9/5-10/9   1P: $99-$199   2P: $99-$199   XP: $10   F12
5/1-6/23 & 10/10-4/30   1P: $89-$199   2P: $89-$199   XP: $10   F12
Location: Jct Niagara River Pkwy, just n on Murray St. 6289 Fallsview Blvd L2G 3V7. Fax: 905/356-7773.
Small-scale Hotel **Facility:** Smoke free premises. 243 one-bedroom standard units, some with whirlpools. 4-6 stories,
interior/exterior corridors. **Parking:** on-site (fee). **Terms:** 3 day cancellation notice-fee imposed, package
plans, 3% service charge, small pets only. **Amenities:** video games, voice mail, irons, hair dryers. _Some:_ high-speed Internet.
Dining: 7 am-10 & 5-10 pm, Sat & Sun 8 am-9 pm, cocktails. **Pool(s):** heated outdoor, heated indoor. **Leisure
Activities:** sauna, whirlpools, playground. _Fee:_ game room. **Guest Services:** gift shop. **Business Services:** meeting rooms.
Cards: AX, CB, DC, DS, JC, MC, VI. _(See color ad p 323 & starting on p 118)_

BEST WESTERN FIRESIDE HOTEL _Book at aaa.com_   Phone: (905)374-2027   **30**
CAA SAVE
6/17-9/4   1P: $89-$249   2P: $89-$249   XP: $10   F12
5/1-6/16 & 9/5-4/30   1P: $69-$199   2P: $69-$199   XP: $10   F12
Location: 3 km n of Rainbow Bridge. 4067 River Rd L2E 3E5. Fax: 905/374-7746. **Facility:** 96 one-bedroom
standard units, some with whirlpools. 4 stories, interior corridors. **Parking:** on-site. **Terms:** 3 day
Small-scale Hotel cancellation notice, [MAP] meal plan available. **Amenities:** video library (fee), irons, hair dryers. **Dining:** 7
am-noon. **Pool(s):** heated indoor. **Leisure Activities:** sauna, whirlpool, exercise room. **Guest Services:**
area transportation-casino & falls. **Cards:** AX, DC, DS, MC, VI. **Special Amenities: early check-in/late check-out and free
room upgrade (subject to availability with advance reservations).** _(See color ad p 324)_

SOME UNITS

FEE

5 MINUTES TO SCENIC NIAGARA FALLS (3.5KM - 2 MILES)
A FAMILY PARADISE AT REASONABLE RATES

BEST INN

BEST INN

70 Self-Controlled Air Conditioned Units • Beautiful Heated Pool • Colour T.V.
• Children's Playground • Picnic area with B.B.Q's • Coffee Shop • Restaurant nearby
• Also 2 Air-Conditioned Cottages • 1 - 3 Bedroom Apartment

**Special Fall & Winter
Group, Senior & Corporate Rates.**
www.bestinn.ca
reservations@bestinnniagarafalls.com

BEST INN

**(905) 356-8280
1-800-391-5171**

7800 Lundy's Lane, Niagara Falls, Canada

The Ultimate

...with Ontario's only INDOOR WATERPARK!

WAVES
Indoor Waterpark

25,000 sq ft indoor waterpark enclosed in a stunning glass structure with retractable roof for tropical 84^0 weather all year round!

- Wave pool • Activity pool • Toddler pool
- 8 slides up to 3 storeys high • Hot spa
- Huge dumping bucket • Arcade

Senses
Spa & Boutique

Senses European luxury spa
• Signature services for women, men and couples
• Spa and accommodation romance packages available

1-800-263-3508 • americananiagara.com

Vacation Resort

- 210 beautiful guestrooms
- Family suites sleeping 8 - 10 people
- Kiddy bunk bed suites
- Jacuzzi & fireplace suites
- Passes for Waves Indoor Waterpark included with your room reservation!

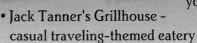

- Jack Tanner's Grillhouse - casual traveling-themed eatery
- Live standup entertainment at The House of Comedy
- Minutes to Falls, shopping, attractions and casinos

AMERICANA
RESORT AND SPA

8444 Lundy's Lane,
Niagara Falls, ON
905-356-8444

Call for details on our money-saving two to five night accommodation & meal packages.

1-800-263-3508 • americananiagara.com

BROCK PLAZA HOTEL   *Book at aaa.com*   **Phone:** (905)374-4444   ㉑

CAA SAVE	6/1-10/31	1P: $149-$799	2P: $149-$799	XP: $10	F17
	5/1-5/31	1P: $129-$699	2P: $129-$699	XP: $10	F17
◆◆◆	11/1-4/30	1P: $99-$599	2P: $99-$599	XP: $10	F17

Location: Entrance to Rainbow Bridge on Hwy 20; just n of the falls. Located next to a casino. 5685 Falls Ave L2E
6W7. Fax: 905/371-8347. **Facility:** This grand hotel, built in 1929, offers many rooms overlooking the falls;
Historic accommodations are cozy and well-appointed with modern amenities. 234 units. 221 one- and 6 two-
Large-scale Hotel bedroom standard units, some with whirlpools. 5 one- and 2 two-bedroom suites. 12 stories, interior
corridors. *Bath:* combo or shower only. **Parking:** on-site (fee). **Terms:** cancellation fee imposed, package plans.
Amenities: video games, voice mail, irons, hair dryers. **Dining:** The Rainbow Grille Fallsview Steakhouse, see separate listing.
Pool(s): heated indoor. **Leisure Activities:** sauna, whirlpool. **Guest Services:** gift shop, valet laundry. **Business Services:**
conference facilities. **Cards:** AX, DC, DS, MC, VI. *(See color ad starting on p 326 & p 325)*   SOME UNITS

Quality, Service and Hospitality with a fresh new face.

- **165 GUESTROOMS** – Jacuzzi and Family Suites
- Indoor Tropical Courtyard with two hot tubs and large heated pool
- **KIDZONE** features a 2 storey kids playpark, video games and large screen Disney Channel® TV
- **CROFT GARDEN GRILLE** serving breakfast, lunch and dinner daily
- **THE CROFT LOUNGE** ... dancing, entertainment & a new outdoor patio
- **BOURBON ST. BISTRO** for poolside snacks and drinks, featuring **PIZZA PIZZA®**
- Minutes from the Falls, Marineland and Niagara's Casinos
- Free parking and shuttle available (nominal fee/scheduled service)
- Family and Golf Packages
- **Ask for your CAA/AAA DISCOUNT**

Best Western Cairn Croft Hotel   www.cairncroft.com   1 800 263-2551

6400 LUNDY'S LANE • NIAGARA FALLS • CANADA • L2G 1T6 • 905-356-1161

CADILLAC MOTEL   Phone: (905)356-0830   **7**

 (CAA) (SAVE)   6/21-9/1   1P: $50-$100   2P: $80-$130   XP: $10   F12
            5/1-6/20   1P: $45-$65   2P: $55-$90   XP: $10   F12
▼▼▼   9/2-10/31 & 3/1-4/30   1P: $40-$60   2P: $50-$80   XP: $10   F12
Motel   **Location:** On Hwy 20, 0.6 km from the falls. Located in a commercial area. 5342 Ferry St L2G 1R7.
            Fax: 905/356-5624. **Facility:** 23 one-bedroom standard units. 1 story, exterior corridors. **Parking:** on-site.
            Terms: open 5/1-10/31 & 3/1-4/30, cancellation fee imposed. **Cards:** AX, DS, JC, MC, VI.

                                                                                            SOME UNITS

                                                    [SD] [ℍ] [Z] [🚭] [🖨] / [✕] /

CAMELOT INN   Phone: 905/354-3754   **15**

(CAA) (SAVE)   6/21-8/31   1P: $59-$179   2P: $59-$229   XP: $10   F12
            5/1-6/20 & 9/1-4/30   1P: $39-$129   2P: $39-$149   XP: $10   F12
▼▼▼ ▼▼▼   **Location:** Just n of Hwy 20; just s of Hwy 420. 5640 Stanley Ave L2G 3X5. Fax: 905/354-6683. **Facility:** 53 one-
Motel   bedroom standard units, some with whirlpools. 2 stories (no elevator), exterior corridors. **Parking:** on-site.
            Terms: office hours 8 am-2 am, package plans. **Amenities:** Some: hair dryers. **Pool(s):** outdoor.
            Cards: AX, MC, VI. **Special Amenities:** early check-in/late check-out and preferred room (subject to
availability with advance reservations). (See color ad p 364)

                                                                                            SOME UNITS

                                                    [ℍ] [🏊] [Z] / [✕] [🖨] /
                                                                                            FEE

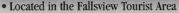

Located Within
Steps of
Beautiful
Niagara Falls,
Attractions and
New Casino!

Best Western Fallsview

- Located in the Fallsview Tourist Area
- A stroll away from Queen Victoria Park, Maid of the Mist, Marineland and adjacent to the Skylon Tower and IMAX Theatre
- Across the street from the "Newly Opened" Niagara Fallsview Casino Complex
- 100% non-smoking hotel & pet friendly
- *We now have a new lobby, new indoor pool and whirlpool and newly renovated restaurant and lounge*

... A Fun Hotel for the Whole Family!

6289 Fallsview Blvd.
Niagara Falls, ON
Canada L2G 3V7

905-356-0551

Great Family, Value & Romance Packages
Including Breakfasts & Dinner
Call Today for Details!

1-800-263-2580

EMAIL sales@bestwesternfallsview.com

www.bestwesternfallsview.com

The Long and Winding Road...

JUST MINUTES FROM THE FALLS & CASINO!

DAYS INN

NORTH OF THE FALLS
4029 River Road
1-877-263-2434 or (905) 356-6666
www.daysinnnorth.com

THE SCENIC NIAGARA PARKWAY

- Perfect for a serene, scenic getaway in picturesque Niagara

- Minutes to the attractions; miles from the hustle & bustle

- Choose from a line-up of brandname hotels

- Heated pools at each location

- Family-oriented style restaurants at each location

- Fantastic packages available; inquire to suit your needs!

- Free shuttle to Casino & Falls

Best Western

FIRESIDE HOTEL
4067 River Road
1-877-661-7035 or (905) 374-2027
www.bestwesternfiresidehotel.com

Hampton Inn

NORTH OF THE FALLS
4357 River Road
1-866-465-6077 or (905) 358-5555
www.hamptoninnniagarafalls.com

Comfort Inn
BY CHOICE HOTELS
NORTH OF THE FALLS
4009 River Road
1-866-565-0032 or (905) 356-0131
www.comfortinnniagarafalls.com

CARRIAGE HOUSE MOTOR LODGE

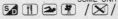

			Phone: (905)356-7799	**54**
6/24-9/4	1P: $69-$130	2P: $69-$130	XP: $10	F12
9/5-10/31	1P: $49-$99	2P: $49-$99	XP: $10	F12
5/1-6/23	1P: $45-$99	2P: $45-$99	XP: $10	F12
11/1-4/30	1P: $45-$89	2P: $45-$89	XP: $10	F12

Small-scale Hotel Location: QEW, exit Hwy 20, 4.9 km w. 8004 Lundy's Ln L2H 1H1. **Fax:** 905/358-6431. **Facility:** 120 one-bedroom standard units, some with whirlpools. 2 stories (no elevator), interior/exterior corridors. **Parking:** on-site. **Terms:** package plans. **Dining:** 7 am-noon; closed 11/1-4/30. **Pool(s):** heated outdoor, heated indoor. **Leisure Activities:** whirlpool. **Guest Services:** gift shop, area transportation (fee)-casino & falls. **Business Services:** meeting rooms. **Cards:** AX, DC, DS, MC, VI. **Special Amenities:** free local telephone calls and free newspaper. *(See color ad p 329)*

SOME UNITS

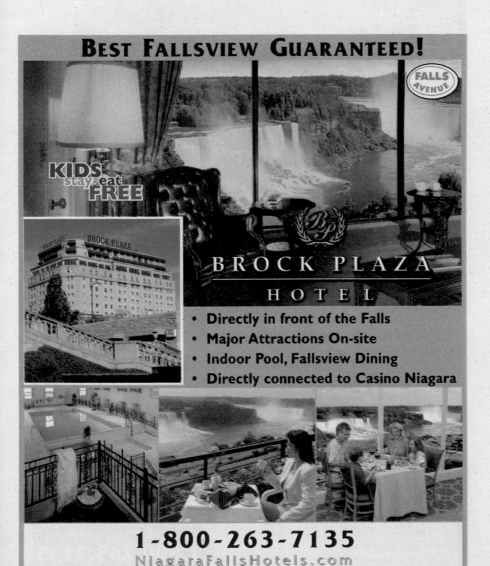

BEST FALLSVIEW GUARANTEED!

FALLS AVENUE

KIDS stay & eat FREE

BROCK PLAZA
HOTEL

• Directly in front of the Falls
• Major Attractions On-site
• Indoor Pool, Fallsview Dining
• Directly connected to Casino Niagara

1-800-263-7135
NiagaraFallsHotels.com

Falls Avenue-The Center of it All

Exciting family attractions, themed restaurants,

STAY IN THE ONLY HOTELS THAT ARE:
- Directly in front of the Falls
- Directly across from Maid of the Mist Boat Ride
- Surrounded by beautiful Niagara Parklands

DIRECTLY CONNECTED TO:
- Hard Rock Cafe and Club
- Rainforest Cafe
- Hershey Store
- Marvel Adventure City - Spider-Man The Ultimate Ride, Incredible Hulk Ride and tons of games
- Planet Hollywood
- MGM Studios Plaza
- WWE Niagara Falls Store & Drop Zone Ride
- Casino Niagara

Show Your Card
Approved Lodging

Book Your Package
1.800.263.7135
FallsAvenue.com

Directly in Front of The Falls
great fallsview hotels, Casino Niagara and more!

Sheraton on the Falls

Niagara's only 4-Diamond family resort. Best Fallsviews from spectacular fallsview rooms and suites, many with private balconies and fireplaces. Two pools, fallsview spa, and fallsview dining. Directly in front of the Falls.

1.888.229.9961

BROCK PLAZA

Directly in front of the Falls, fallsview suites with private terraces overlooking the Falls. Indoor pool, whirlpool and kids pool, Fallsview dining and direct connection to the Hershey Store and Casino Niagara.

1.800.263.7135

Skyline Inn

Family-sized suites, family fun waterslide and pool, plus a location that's unbeatable. One minute walk to Falls Avenue attractions and to Falls. Perkins Family Restaurant on-site.

1.888.229.9950

A family-fun hotel with indoor pool, whirlpool and more. Free parking, movies and hot breakfast. Super family themed suites. One minute walk to Falls Avenue, Clifton Hill and Falls.

1.800.688.3535

CHALET INN AND SUITES

Phone: (905)374-1921

(CAA) (SAVE)

	5/1-9/5	1P: $89-$149	2P: $99-$229	XP: $10	F12
	9/6-9/30	1P: $69-$109	2P: $99-$149	XP: $10	F12
	10/1-4/30	1P: $59-$109	2P: $69-$129	XP: $10	F12

Location: N on Clifton Hill, just e; 0.6 km from the falls. 5577 Ellen Ave L2G 3P5. Fax: 905/374-1868. **Facility:** 73
Small-scale Hotel units. 66 one- and 7 two-bedroom standard units, some with whirlpools. 3-5 stories, interior/exterior corridors. **Parking:** on-site. **Terms:** office hours 7 am-2 am, 3 day cancellation notice-fee imposed, package plans. **Pool(s):** heated outdoor, heated indoor. **Cards:** AX, CB, DC, DS, JC, MC, VI. *(See color ad below)*

SOME UNITS

CLARION PRESIDENT HOTEL & SUITES BY THE FALLS

Phone: (905)374-4142

(CAA) (SAVE)

| | 5/1-9/30 | 1P: $99-$199 | 2P: $99-$299 | XP: $10 | F18 |
| | 10/1-4/30 | 1P: $69-$199 | 2P: $99-$299 | XP: $10 | F18 |

Location: 1.2 km w on Hwy 20, then s. 6045 Stanley Ave L2G 3Y3. Fax: 905/358-3430. **Facility:** 192 one-bedroom standard units, some with whirlpools. 8 stories, interior corridors. **Parking:** on-site (fee).
Small-scale Hotel **Terms:** cancellation fee imposed, [BP] & [MAP] meal plans available, package plans. **Amenities:** video games (fee), voice mail, irons, hair dryers. *Some:* dual phone lines. **Dining:** 7 am-noon & 5-10 pm, cocktails. **Pool(s):** heated indoor. **Leisure Activities:** limited exercise equipment. **Guest Services:** valet laundry, area transportation (fee). **Business Services:** meeting rooms. **Cards:** AX, CB, DC, DS, MC, VI. **Special Amenities:** free newspaper and early check-in/late check-out. *(See color ad p 330)*

SOME UNITS

FEE   FEE

NEW 5 STOREY ADDITION WITH INDOOR POOL

~ INDOOR & OUTDOOR POOLS
~ FAMILY SUITES WITH
  ADJOINING ROOMS
~ JACUZZI ROOMS
  WITH FIREPLACES
~ SATELLITE TV
~ KING SIZE BEDS
~ FREE PARKING
~ GETAWAY PACKAGES
~ NON-SMOKING ROOMS

Chalet
Inn & Suites

NIAGARA FALLS CANADA
Ideally Located within easy walking distance
of Casino Niagara, Clifton Hill & the Falls!

5577 ELLEN AVENUE, NIAGARA FALLS, CANADA

toll free **1-866-287-1110** 905-374-1921 book on-line @ www.chalet-inn.net

GUARANTEED LOW HOTEL RATES

NiagaraFallsHotels.com

EVERY VISITOR WINS! GRAND PRIZE
Free Falls
Vacation

COMFORT INN CLIFTON HILL *Book at aaa.com* Phone: (905)358-3293 ⑱
5/1-10/31 [ECP] 1P: $89-$289 2P: $89-$289 XP: $12 F18
11/1-4/30 [ECP] 1P: $69-$199 2P: $69-$199 XP: $12 F18
Location: Jct Victoria Ave and Clifton Hill, just s. 4960 Clifton Hill L2E 6S8 (PO Box 60, NIAGARA FALLS).
Fax: 905/358-3818. **Facility:** 185 units. 173 one- and 12 two-bedroom standard units, some with whirlpools.
Small-scale Hotel 3 stories (no elevator), interior corridors. **Parking:** on-site. **Terms:** package plans. **Amenities:** irons, hair
dryers. **Dining:** 11 am-2 am, cocktails. **Pool(s):** heated indoor. **Leisure Activities:** whirlpool. *Fee:* miniature
golf. **Guest Services:** valet laundry. **Cards:** AX, CB, DC, DS, JC, MC, VI. **Special Amenities:** free expanded continental
breakfast and free local telephone calls. *(See color ad starting on p 332)* SOME UNITS

Affordable Hospitality

• Choose from 120 Attractive Motel Rooms
• Economical Drive-up Courtyard Rooms with
  2 Double Beds Surrounding the Outdoor Pool
• Manor House Rooms with 2 Queen Beds
• Romantic Suites with Heart-Shaped Whirlpools
• Satellite Colour TV • Free In-Room Movies
• Indoor Pool & Whirlpool overlooking Fireplace
• Minutes from the Falls, Casinos, Marineland,
  Golf and Major Attractions
• Walk to Factory
  Outlet Mall,
  Restaurants
  & Mini Golf
• Gift Shop
• Restaurant
• Sightseeing Tours
• Shuttle Bus to Falls and Casino in season
• Choose from our Romantic Getaways –
  Weekend Specials • Golf Packages • Group Rates
• Major Credit Cards Accepted • US Exchange

KIDS STAY FREE
From $59.50 Cdn/night
Courtyard Room with 2 double beds
for 2 adults & up to 2 kids under 12
May 31-June 29 & Aug 21- Sept 1, 2005
Sun-Thurs • Subject to availability

MANOR HOUSE

COURTYARD ROOMS

Carriage House Motor Lodge

8004 Lundy's Lane
Niagara Falls, Ontario, Canada L2H 1H1
Book on-line @ www.chfalls.com
Call for Reservations 905-356-7799
1-800-267-9887

COMFORT INN LUNDY'S LANE

CAA SAVE

				Phone: (905)354-1849	60
7/1-9/5 [CP]	1P: $99-$269	2P: $99-$269	XP: $5	F18
5/1-6/30 & 9/6-10/10 [CP]	1P: $69-$189	2P: $69-$189	XP: $5	F18
10/11-4/30 [CP]	1P: $64-$169	2P: $64-$169	XP: $5	F18

Location: QEW, exit Hwy 20; 5 km from downtown. 7514 Lundy's Ln L2H 1G8. Fax: 905/354-6619. **Facility:** 148 Small-scale Hotel one-bedroom standard units. 2-5 stories, interior/exterior corridors. **Parking:** on-site, winter plug-ins. **Terms:** 14 day cancellation notice. **Amenities:** video games, voice mail, hair dryers. **Pool(s):** heated indoor. **Leisure Activities:** sauna, whirlpool, exercise room. *Fee:* game room. **Business Services:** meeting rooms. **Cards:** AX, DC, DS, MC, VI. **Special Amenities:** free continental breakfast and free local telephone calls. *(See color ad p 334)*

SOME UNITS

5 MIN. WALK TO FALLS!

Clarion Hotel

BY CHOICE HOTELS

Clarion® President Hotel & Suites By-The-Falls

🕯 192 spacious guestrooms, including jacuzzi suites

🕯 All rooms feature colour cable TV (with remote), coffee makers, hairdryers and irons with full size iron boards.

🕯 Heated Indoor pool and fitness room open 24 hours

🕯 Special Honeymoon, Romance, Getaway and Seasonal Theme packages available throughout the year.

🕯 Close to all major attractions, including Marineland and Skylon Tower

🕯 Close to both Casino Niagara and the New Niagara Fallsview Casino

🕯 Visit our website at www.niagarafallshotelsinfo.com or email us at reservationsnfalls@cogeco.net

Clarion President Hotel & Suites By-The-Falls
6045 Stanley Ave., Niagara Falls, Ontario, Canada L2G 3Y3
Phone: 905-374-4142 • Fax: 905-358-3430

TOLL FREE RESERVATIONS 1-800-263-2566

COMFORT INN NORTH OF THE FALLS

Phone: (905)356-0131

(AA) (SAVE)

6/17-9/4	1P: $79-$249	2P: $79-$249	XP: $10	F12
5/1-6/16	1P: $59-$199	2P: $59-$199	XP: $10	F12
9/5-4/30	1P: $49-$169	2P: $49-$169	XP: $10	F12

Motel

Location: 3 km n of Rainbow Bridge. 4009 River Rd L2E 3E5. Fax: 905/356-3306. **Facility:** 66 one-bedroom standard units, some with whirlpools. 2 stories (no elevator), exterior corridors. **Parking:** on-site. **Terms:** 3 day cancellation notice, [MAP] meal plan available, package plans. **Amenities:** video library (fee). **Dining:** 7 am-10 pm 5/15-10/15. **Pool(s):** outdoor. **Guest Services:** area transportation-casino & falls. **Cards:** AX, DC, DS, MC, VI. **Special Amenities:** free local telephone calls and early check-in/late check-out. *(See color ad p 324)*

SOME UNITS

(SD) (†1) (⟲) (✦) (▣) / (✕) (VCR) / FEE

CONTINENTAL INN

Phone: (905)356-2449 **87**

(AA) (SAVE)

6/26-9/6	1P: $59-$99	2P: $69-$119	XP: $10	F12
5/1-6/25	1P: $49-$79	2P: $59-$99	XP: $10	1-F12
9/7-4/30	1P: $39-$69	2P: $49-$89	XP: $10	F12

Motel

Location: On Hwy 20, 1.5 km w from the falls. 5756 Ferry St L2G 1S7. Fax: 905/371-8202. **Facility:** 51 one-bedroom standard units, some with whirlpools. 2 stories (no elevator), exterior corridors. **Parking:** on-site. **Terms:** cancellation fee imposed. **Pool(s):** heated outdoor. **Cards:** AX, DC, DS, MC, VI.

SOME UNITS

(SD) (†1↑) (⟲) / (✕) (▤) (▣) /

COURTYARD BY MARRIOTT NIAGARA FALLS

Book at aaa.com

Phone: (905)358-3083 **33**

(AA) (SAVE)

6/16-9/2	1P: $99-$399	2P: $99-$399
5/1-6/15 & 9/3-4/30	1P: $79-$299	2P: $79-$299

Large-scale Hotel

Location: Jct Ferry St. 5950 Victoria Ave L2G 3L7. Fax: 905/358-8720. **Facility:** 258 one-bedroom standard units, some with whirlpools. 10 stories, interior corridors. *Bath:* combo or shower only. **Parking:** on-site (fee). **Terms:** 3 day cancellation notice-fee imposed, package plans. **Amenities:** video games, dual phone lines, voice mail, safes, irons, hair dryers. **Dining:** 6:30 am-11 pm, also, The Keg Steakhouse and Bar, see separate listing. **Pool(s):** outdoor, heated indoor. **Leisure Activities:** sauna, whirlpool, sun deck, exercise room. *Fee:* game room. **Guest Services:** gift shop, valet and coin laundry, area transportation (fee)-casino. **Business Services:** meeting rooms. **Cards:** AX, DC, DS, JC, MC, VI. *(See color ad card insert & p 350)*

SOME UNITS

(†1) (Y) (&) (⟲) (✕) (✦) (DATA PORT) (▣) / (✕) (▤) (▣) /

CRYSTAL MOTEL

Phone: (905)354-0460 **25**

6/26-9/6	1P: $79-$159	2P: $89-$189	XP: $10	F12
5/1-6/25 & 9/7-10/31	1P: $49-$99	2P: $59-$119	XP: $10	F12
11/1-4/30	1P: $49-$89	2P: $49-$109	XP: $10	F12

Motel

Location: 2.8 km n of falls on Niagara River Pkwy. 4267 River Rd L2E 3E7. Fax: 905/374-4972. **Facility:** 38 one-bedroom standard units, some with whirlpools. 2 stories (no elevator), exterior corridors. **Parking:** on-site. **Terms:** 3 day cancellation notice-fee imposed. **Pool(s):** heated outdoor. **Cards:** AX, DS, MC, VI.

SOME UNITS

(ASK) (SD) (†1↑) (⟲) (CTV) (✦) (▣) / (✕) /

DAYS INN & SUITES BY THE FALLS

Book at aaa.com

Phone: (905)357-2550 **28**

(AA) (SAVE)

7/1-9/4 [CP]	1P: $89-$299	2P: $89-$299	XP: $10	F16
5/1-6/30 & 9/5-4/30 [CP]	1P: $59-$199	2P: $59-$199	XP: $10	F16

Small-scale Hotel

Location: Jct Ellen Ave. 5068 Centre St L2G 3N9. Fax: 905/357-7771. **Facility:** 152 units. 142 one-bedroom standard units, some with whirlpools. 10 one-bedroom suites ($79-$429). 3-6 stories, interior corridors. *Bath:* combo or shower only. **Parking:** on-site. **Terms:** package plans. **Amenities:** voice mail, irons, hair dryers. **Pool(s):** heated indoor. **Leisure Activities:** whirlpool, exercise room. **Guest Services:** coin laundry. **Business Services:** meeting rooms. **Cards:** AX, DS, MC, VI. **Special Amenities:** free continental breakfast and free newspaper. *(See color ad p 335)*

SOME UNITS

(SD) (†1↑) (&) (⟲) (✦) (DATA PORT) (▣) (▣) / (✕) (▣) /

COMFORT INN WELLAND

NEWLY RENOVATED

- *20 km from Niagara Falls*
- *FREE Deluxe Continental Breakfast*
- *Ground Floor Rooms*
- *FREE Local Calls*
- *Jacuzzi Suite*
- *Business Centre*
- *FREE Wireless High Speed Internet*

BY CHOICE HOTELS

870 Niagara Street, Welland, Ontario L3C 1M3

Tel.: 905-732-1811

Toll Free: 1-800-228-5150

Clifton Hill

ATTRACTIONS · ENTERTAINMENT · DINING · SHOPPING

ONE BLOCK TO THE FALLS

Clifton Hill

Enjoy a spectacular location right next to the Falls! Plus:

- The Great Canadian Midway
- Movieland Wax Museum
- Ripleys Believe It or Not
- Maid of the Mist
- Ghost Blasters Dark Ride
- Retail Shopping Outlets
- Dinosaur Park Mini Golf
- Guiness World Records
- FX Thrill Ride Theatre
- Casino Niagara
- Niagara Parks
- Over 30 Restaurants

www.CliftonHillResorts.com

Comfort Inn

Clifton Hill
NIAGARA FALLS
CANADA

- AAA/CAA ♦♦♦ Special Value Rates
- Complimentary deluxe continental breakfast
- Tropical indoor pool and giant luxury whirlpool
- Ample free parking • KIDS UNDER 18 STAY FREE

1-800-263-2557

QUALITY INN

Clifton Hill
NIAGARA FALLS
CANADA

- Big outdoor pool with dragon slides & activity play center
- AAA/CAA special rates   • Large indoor pool/whirlpool
- Family and poolside suites • Golden Griddle restaurant
- Ample free parking   • KIDS UNDER 18 STAY FREE

1-800-263-7137

www.CliftonHillResorts.com

DAYS INN CLIFTON HILL CASINO   *Book at aaa.com*   Phone: (905)356-2461   16

11/1-12/31	1P: $49-$429	2P: $49-$429	XP: $10 F16
5/1-9/5	1P: $49-$399	2P: $49-$399	XP: $10 F16
9/6-10/31 & 1/1-4/30	1P: $49-$299	2P: $49-$299	XP: $10 F16

Small-scale Hotel   **Location:** Just e on Hwy 20. 5657 Victoria Ave L2G 3L5. Fax: 905/356-2467. **Facility:** 138 units. 136 one- and 2 two-bedroom standard units, some with whirlpools. 2-7 stories, interior/exterior corridors. **Parking:** on-site (fee). **Terms:** cancellation fee imposed, package plans, 3% service charge. **Amenities:** hair dryers. *Some:* voice mail, irons. **Dining:** Remington's of Montana Steak and Seafood, see separate listing. **Pool(s):** heated indoor. **Leisure Activities:** sauna, whirlpool. **Guest Services:** gift shop, area transportation (fee). **Cards:** AX, CB, DC, DS, JC, MC, VI.
(See color ad starting on p 338)

SOME UNITS

DAYS INN FALLSVIEW DISTRICT   *Book at aaa.com*   Phone: (905)356-5877   68

6/17-9/4	1P: $75-$275	2P: $75-$275	XP: $10 F12
9/5-4/30	1P: $65-$195	2P: $65-$195	XP: $10 F12
5/1-6/16	1P: $55-$195	2P: $55-$195	XP: $10 F12

Motel   **Location:** Just w of the falls via Murray St; between Konica Minolta and Skylon towers. 6408 Stanley Ave L2G 3Y5. Fax: 905/356-9452. **Facility:** 100 units. 98 one- and 2 two-bedroom standard units. 3 stories, interior/exterior corridors. **Parking:** on-site. **Terms:** 3 day cancellation notice, [MAP] meal plan available, package plans. **Amenities:** hair dryers. *Some:* irons. **Pool(s):** heated indoor. **Leisure Activities:** sauna. **Guest Services:** area transportation-casino. **Cards:** AX, DC, DS, MC, VI. **Special Amenities:** free local telephone calls and free room upgrade (subject to availability with advance reservations). *(See color ad p 336 & starting on p 118)*

SOME UNITS

DAYS INN-LUNDY'S LANE   *Book at aaa.com*   Phone: (905)358-3621   47

11/1-12/31	1P: $45-$299	2P: $45-$299	XP: $10 F16
5/1-9/5	1P: $45-$289	2P: $45-$289	XP: $10 F16
9/6-10/31	1P: $45-$199	2P: $45-$199	XP: $10 F16
1/1-4/30	1P: $45-$189	2P: $45-$189	XP: $10 F16

Small-scale Hotel   **Location:** QEW, exit Hwy 20, 3.8 km w. 7280 Lundy's Ln L2G 1W2. Fax: 905/356-7693. **Facility:** 136 one-bedroom standard units, some with whirlpools. 2-5 stories, interior/exterior corridors. **Parking:** on-site (fee). **Terms:** cancellation fee imposed, package plans, 3% service charge. **Amenities:** hair dryers. *Some:* irons. **Pool(s):** heated indoor. **Leisure Activities:** sauna, whirlpool, miniature golf, playground. **Guest Services:** area transportation (fee). **Cards:** AX, CB, DC, DS, JC, MC, VI.
(See color ad starting on p 338)

SOME UNITS

DAYS INN NEAR THE FALLS   *Book at aaa.com*   Phone: (905)374-3333   12

5/1-9/30	1P: $80-$299	2P: $80-$299	XP: $20 F12
10/1-4/30	1P: $70-$280	2P: $70-$280	XP: $20 F12

  Location: On Hwy 20, 0.6 km from the falls. 5943 Victoria Ave L2G 3L8. Fax: 905/374-0669. **Facility:** 117 one-bedroom standard units, some with whirlpools. 7 stories, interior corridors. **Parking:** on-site (fee). Small-scale Hotel   **Terms:** cancellation fee imposed. **Amenities:** hair dryers. *Some:* irons. **Pool(s):** heated indoor. **Leisure Activities:** sauna, whirlpool. *Fee:* game room. **Guest Services:** gift shop. **Cards:** AX, DS, MC, VI.
(See color ad p 340)

SOME UNITS

One of Niagara's Newest Hotels
Comfort Inn Lundy's Lane
7514 Lundy's Lane
Niagara Falls, ON L2H 1G8
905.354.1849

- Free Continental Breakfast
- Indoor Pool/Whirlpool/Fitness Room
- Free Local Calls
- 2.5 Miles to Casino Niagara/"The Falls"
- Adjacent to Canada One Factory Outlets
- Pay Per View Movies/Nintendo

800.228.1AAA
choicehotels.com   **We'll see you there**

© 2004 Choice Hotels International, Inc.

Comfort INN
BY CHOICE HOTELS

DAYS INN

& SUITES BY THE FALLS

Less then a 5 minute walk to the Falls, Casino and Dozens of Restaurants and Attractions

Phase 1 - Opened July 2001 **Phase 2** - Opened July 2003

ASK ABOUT OUR 2 NIGHT PACKAGES

FREE CONTINENTAL BREAKFAST & PARKING
IN ROOM COFFEE MAKER & REFRIGERATOR
HAIRDRYERS & IRON
INDOOR HEATED POOL • FITNESS ROOM • HOT TUB
EXTENDED STAY, JACUZZI & FAMILY SUITES AVAILABLE

5 OUT OF 5 RATING BY DAYS INN Triple A Rating

from $59 *off season**
* sun-thurs
from $79 *in season**

Direct-to-Hotel Toll Free Line: **1-866-706-ROOM(7666)**
Phone: **905-357-2550** Fax: **905-357-7771**
info@daysbythefalls.com   www.daysbythefalls.com

5068 Centre St (Near Clifton hill) Niagara Falls, Ontario, Canada, L2G 3N9

DAYS INN NORTH OF THE FALLS   *Book at aaa.com*   Phone: (905)356-6666   24
CAA SAVE   6/17-9/4   1P: $78-$228   2P: $78-$228   XP: $10   F12
            5/1-6/16 & 9/5-4/30   1P: $48-$168   2P: $48-$168   XP: $10   F12
            Location: 3 km n of Rainbow Bridge. 4029 River Rd L2E 3E5. Fax: 905/356-1800. **Facility:** 94 one-bedroom
            standard units, some with whirlpools. 4 stories (no elevator), interior/exterior corridors. **Parking:** on-site.
Small-scale Hotel **Terms:** 3 day cancellation notice, [MAP] meal plan available, package plans. **Amenities:** video library (fee).
            Some: irons, hair dryers. **Dining:** noon-10 pm; from 5 pm 10/15-5/14, cocktails. **Pool(s):** heated indoor.
Leisure Activities: sauna, whirlpool. **Guest Services:** area transportation-casino & falls. **Cards:** AX, DC, DS, MC, VI.
Special Amenities: free local telephone calls and early check-in/late check-out. *(See color ad p 324)*

SOME UNITS

FEE

DOUBLETREE RESORT LODGE & SPA FALLSVIEW   *Book at aaa.com*   Phone: (905)358-3817   52
            5/1-10/22   1P: $99-$299   2P: $99-$299   XP: $10   F18
            10/23-4/30   1P: $89-$189   2P: $89-$189   XP: $10   F18
Large-scale Hotel **Location:** Just w via Murray St, n on Fallsview Blvd; adjacent to Skylon Tower. 6039 Fallsview Blvd L2G 3V6.
            Fax: 905/358-3680. **Facility:** 224 units. 192 one-bedroom standard units, some with whirlpools. 32 one-
bedroom suites ($109-$339). 18 stories, interior corridors. **Parking:** on-site (fee). **Terms:** package plans. **Amenities:** video
games (fee), dual phone lines, voice mail, irons, hair dryers. **Dining:** Buchanans, see separate listing. **Pool(s):** 2 heated indoor.
Leisure Activities: sauna, whirlpool, exercise room, spa. *Fee:* game room. **Guest Services:** gift shop, valet and coin laundry.
Business Services: conference facilities, business center. **Cards:** AX, DC, DS, JC, MC, VI. *(See color ad p 341)*

SOME UNITS

ECONO LODGE NEAR THE FALLS   *Book at aaa.com*   Phone: (905)358-6243   51
            6/15-9/3   1P: $85-$205   2P: $85-$205   XP: $10   F16
            9/4-4/30   1P: $65-$105   2P: $65-$105   XP: $10   F16
Motel   5/1-6/14   1P: $65-$105   2P: $105   XP: $10   F16
            Location: 1.3 km w on Hwy 20, just s. 6000 Stanley Ave L2G 3Y1. Fax: 905/358-1864. **Facility:** 80 one-bedroom
standard units, some with whirlpools. 2 stories (no elevator), interior/exterior corridors. **Parking:** on-site. **Terms:** small pets only
($10 extra charge, limit 1). **Pool(s):** outdoor. **Business Services:** fax (fee). **Cards:** AX, CB, DC, DS, MC, VI.

SOME UNITS
FEE

Live the Excitement. Love the Location.

10% off Published Rates for AAA Members

ADJACENT to the NIAGARA FALLSVIEW CASINO RESORT & FALLS!

- Large Indoor Pool & Sauna
- Convenient Family Suites
- Free On-Site Parking for Guests
- Rooms with Private Balconies
- Kids 17 & under stay FREE
- Ask about our fabulous pkgs!

1-877-263-2526

DAYS INN ®
FALLSVIEW DISTRICT

6408 Stanley Ave., Niagara Falls, ON Canada
(905) 356-5877 www.daysinnfallsview.com

EMBASSY SUITES NIAGARA FALLS FALLSVIEW   *Book at aaa.com*   Phone: (905)356-3600   82

7/1-8/31 [BP]	1P: $189-$599	2P: $189-$599
5/1-6/30 [BP]	1P: $129-$599	2P: $129-$599
9/1-4/30 [BP]	1P: $119-$599	2P: $119-$599

Location: Adjacent to Konica Minolta Tower. 6700 Fallsview Blvd L2G 3W6. Fax: 905/356-0472. **Facility:** This large
Large-scale Hotel hotel, always bustling, features spacious, well-appointed suites and a central location close to the casino
and area attractions. 512 one-bedroom suites ($179-$799), some with whirlpools. 42 stories, interior
corridors. **Parking:** on-site (fee) and valet. **Terms:** 3 day cancellation notice-fee imposed, package plans. **Amenities:** video
games (fee), dual phone lines, voice mail, safes, honor bars, irons, hair dryers. **Dining:** 2 restaurants, 11 am-1 am, also, The
Keg Steakhouse and Bar, see separate listing. **Pool(s):** heated indoor. **Leisure Activities:** whirlpool, sun deck, exercise room,
game room. **Guest Services:** gift shop, complimentary evening beverages, valet and coin laundry, area transportation (fee)-
casino. **Business Services:** meeting rooms, business center. **Cards:** AX, CB, DC, DS, JC, MC, VI.
(See color ad card insert, p 350 & ad starting on p 118)

SOME UNITS

$\boxed{\text{↑}}$ $\boxed{\text{⊷}}$ $\boxed{\text{≈}}$ $\boxed{\text{✕}}$ $\boxed{\text{☀}}$ $\boxed{\text{DATA PORT}}$ $\boxed{\text{🛏}}$ $\boxed{\text{📠}}$ $\boxed{\text{▣}}$ / $\boxed{\text{✕}}$ /

FALLSVIEW INN   Phone: (905)374-4244   31

All Year	1P: $46-$199	2P: $46-$199	XP: $10
			F18

Location: 1.2 km w on Hwy 20, just s. 6170 Stanley Ave L2G 3Y4. Fax: 905/374-6142. **Facility:** 65 one-bedroom
standard units, some with whirlpools. 5 stories, interior corridors. **Parking:** on-site. **Terms:** 2 night minimum
stay - weekends, package plans. **Amenities:** hair dryers. **Dining:** 7 am-11 & 5-9 pm, cocktails. **Pool(s):**
Small-scale Hotel heated indoor. **Leisure Activities:** sauna, whirlpool. *Fee:* game room. **Cards:** AX, DC, MC, VI.
(See color ad below)

SOME UNITS

$\boxed{\text{S D}}$ $\boxed{\text{↑}}$ $\boxed{\text{⊷}}$ $\boxed{\text{≈}}$ $\boxed{\text{✕}}$ $\boxed{\text{☀}}$ / $\boxed{\text{✕}}$ $\boxed{\text{DATA PORT}}$ $\boxed{\text{🛏}}$ /

FEE

FLAMINGO MOTOR INN   Phone: (905)356-4646   64

6/24-8/27	1P: $69-$139	2P: $79-$179	XP: $10 F
5/1-6/23	1P: $49-$109	2P: $59-$129	XP: $10 F
8/28-11/30	1P: $49-$99	2P: $59-$129	XP: $10 F
2/1-4/30	1P: $49-$79	2P: $54-$99	XP: $10 F

Motel   **Location:** QEW, exit Hwy 20, 3.4 km w. 7701 Lundy's Ln L2H 1H3. Fax: 905/356-9373. **Facility:** 93 one-bedroom
standard units, some with whirlpools. 2 stories (no elevator), exterior corridors. **Parking:** on-site, winter
plug-ins. **Terms:** open 5/1-11/30 & 2/1-4/30, small pets only ($10 extra charge). **Amenities:** voice mail. **Pool(s):** heated
outdoor. **Cards:** AX, CB, DC, MC, VI. **Special Amenities:** free local telephone calls and free newspaper.
(See color ad p 342 & ad starting on p 118)

SOME UNITS

$\boxed{\text{S D}}$ $\boxed{\text{🛏}}$ $\boxed{\text{↑}}$ $\boxed{\text{≈}}$ $\boxed{\text{DATA PORT}}$ / $\boxed{\text{✕}}$ $\boxed{\text{🛏}}$ /

FEE   FEE

FALLSVIEW INN

JUST 3 BLOCKS FROM THE FALLS.
Walking distance to all major attractions.
Full service hotel offering well-appointed rooms.
All queen and king size beds.

ALL MAJOR CREDIT CARDS ACCEPTED

- Family & Single Rooms
- Restaurant-Lounge
- Games Room
- Direct Dial Phones
- Sauna/Hot Tub
- Free In-Room Movies
- Heated Indoor Pool
- Heart Shaped Jacuzzi Suites
- Just a few steps to Casino
- AAA-CAA Discounts

Toll Free U.S. and CANADA

(905) 374-4244
www.fallsviewhotels.com
6170 Stanley Ave., Niagara Falls, ON L2G 3Y4

2 NIGHT PACKAGE
$129.95 and up

Includes:
Dinner for two one evening.
Two breakfasts each morning.
Complimentary Bottle of Champagne.

Mid October to Mid May

Niagara Falls, Canada's
~ NEW BOUTIQUE-STYLE DAYS INN ~

DAYS INN Days Inn Clifton Hill/Casino

The All-New Unique Days Inn Clifton Hill/Casino is Quiet Comfort in the Heart of Major Niagara Attractions Featuring Beautifully Decorated Suites & Rooms!

ACROSS FROM CASINO NIAGARA, WALK TO CLIFTON HILL & THE FALLS!
NEW TOWER ROOMS, MANY WITH BAY WINDOWS & TERRACES, **COURTYARD ROOMS,**
JACUZZI SUITES AVAILABLE, NEW ELEGANT SKY-LIT POOL AND WHIRLPOOL, SAUNA,
2 DINING OPTIONS ON SITE: FAMILY FAVOURITE APPLEBEE'S GRILL & BAR
AND THE AWARD WINNING REMINGTON'S OF MONTANA'S • 5657 VICTORIA AVENUE

Try a Little Tenderness.
CASUAL YET ELEGANT FINE
DINING FEATURING NIAGARA'S
FINEST STEAK & SEAFOOD.

REMINGTONS
O F ~ M O N T A N A
STEAK & SEAFOOD

DAYS INN Days Inn Lundy's lane

Wonderful Family Resort Only Minutes to the Falls and Major Niagara Attractions!

YOUR DESTINATION FOR GREAT FAMILY RATES & FRIENDLY SERVICE ADJACENT
CANADA ONE OUTLET MALL, INDOOR POOL, WHIRLPOOL AND SAUNA, JACUZZI ROOMS,
DENNY'S RESTAURANT, DAIRY QUEEN & MINI-GOLF ON SITE • 7280 LUNDY'S LANE

Call Now for Unbeatable Getaway Packages

1-800-461-1251

Book On-line @ www.niagarahospitalityhotels.com

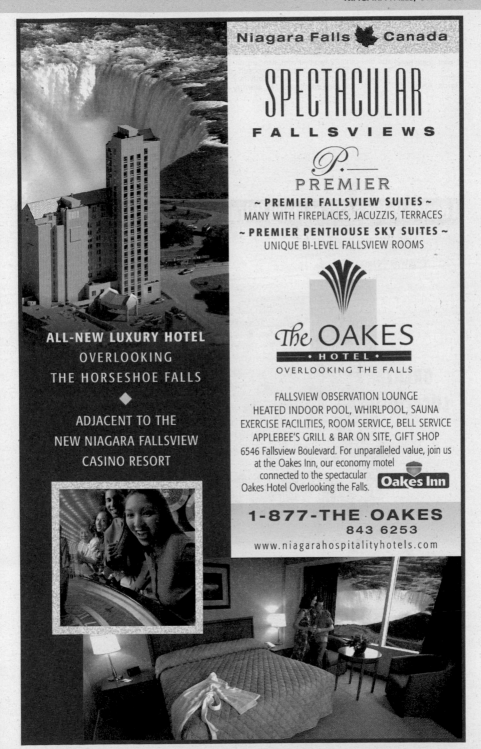

Niagara Falls Canada

SPECTACULAR
FALLSVIEWS

P.
PREMIER
~ PREMIER FALLSVIEW SUITES ~
MANY WITH FIREPLACES, JACUZZIS, TERRACES
~ PREMIER PENTHOUSE SKY SUITES ~
UNIQUE BI-LEVEL FALLSVIEW ROOMS

The OAKES
• HOTEL •
OVERLOOKING THE FALLS

FALLSVIEW OBSERVATION LOUNGE
HEATED INDOOR POOL, WHIRLPOOL, SAUNA
EXERCISE FACILITIES, ROOM SERVICE, BELL SERVICE
APPLEBEE'S GRILL & BAR ON SITE, GIFT SHOP
6546 Fallsview Boulevard. For unparalleled value, join us
at the Oakes Inn, our economy motel
connected to the spectacular
Oakes Hotel Overlooking the Falls.

Oakes Inn

1-877-THE OAKES
843 6253
www.niagarahospitalityhotels.com

ALL-NEW LUXURY HOTEL
OVERLOOKING
THE HORSESHOE FALLS

◆

ADJACENT TO THE
NEW NIAGARA FALLSVIEW
CASINO RESORT

HAMPTON INN AT THE FALLS   *Book at aaa.com*   Phone: (905)357-1626   ⓱

6/1-10/31	1P: $169-$429	XP: $10 F18
5/1-5/31	1P: $129-$389	XP: $10 F18
11/1-4/30	1P: $89-$299	XP: $10 F18

Location: At top of Clifton Hill; ne of the falls. 5591 Victoria Ave L2G 3L4. Fax: 905/357-5869. **Facility:** 127 units.
Small-scale Hotel 105 one- and 22 two-bedroom standard units, some with whirlpools. 6 stories, interior corridors. **Parking:** on-site. **Terms:** cancellation fee imposed, package plans. **Amenities:** video games, voice mail, irons. *Some:* hair dryers. **Pool(s):** heated indoor. **Leisure Activities:** sauna, whirlpool. **Guest Services:** gift shop, valet laundry. **Cards:** AX, CB, DC, DS, MC, VI. *(See color ad p 341, starting on p 326 & p 4)*

SOME UNITS

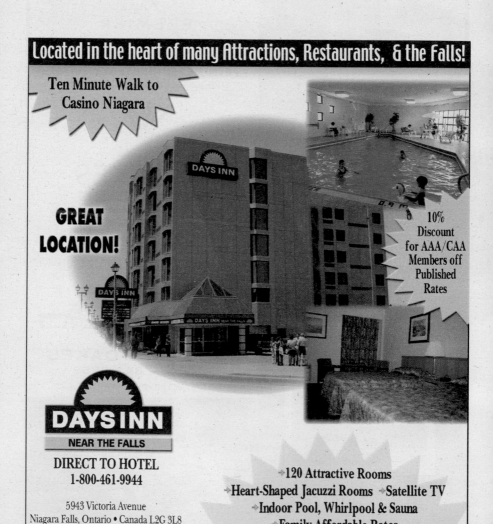

Located in the heart of many Attractions, Restaurants, & the Falls!

Ten Minute Walk to Casino Niagara

DAYS INN

GREAT LOCATION!

10% Discount for AAA/CAA Members off Published Rates

DAYS INN
NEAR THE FALLS

DIRECT TO HOTEL
1-800-461-9944

5943 Victoria Avenue
Niagara Falls, Ontario • Canada L2G 3L8
Tel. 905-374-3333 • Fax.905-374-0669

→120 Attractive Rooms
→Heart-Shaped Jacuzzi Rooms →Satellite TV
→Indoor Pool, Whirlpool & Sauna
→Family Affordable Rates
→Kids Stay Free

www.the.daysinn.com/niagarafalls06639

The Majestic Falls and Exciting Attractions at your Doorstep.

Ideally located two short blocks from the brink of the Falls, 400 yards to the Fallsview Casino complex. Grand Lodge architecture. 224 Riverview and Fallsview guestrooms, two-room family suites and whirlpool rooms with premium views. Buchanans Chophouse casual fine dining. Indoor amenities include a kids splash/family swimming pool, lap pool, sauna, fitness facility, outdoor hot tub. Rejuvenate body, mind and spirit at our Five Lakes Spa AVEDA. On-site self-parking. Just make advance reservations by calling *1-800-730-8609* or your local AAA travel office. Visit us online at *niagarafallsdoubletree.com*.

Hilton HHonors

DOUBLETREE®
RESORT LODGE & SPA
FALLSVIEW · NIAGARA FALLS

6039 Fallsview Blvd. • Niagara Falls, ON, Canada L2G 3V6 • 905-358-3817
800-730-8609 • Reservations: 800-222-TREE • www.niagarafallsdoubletree.com

Valid AAA membership card required for reservation and at check-in. ©2005 Hilton Hospitality, Inc.

ONE BLOCK TO FALLS

FALLS AVENUE

CAA AAA
Show Your Card
Approved Lodging

KIDS stay & eat FREE

Hampton Inn

• Themed Jacuzzi Suites
• Indoor Pool and Whirlpool
• Across from Casino Niagara & Major Attractions

Hampton Inn ®

AT THE FALLS

1-800-688-3535

NiagaraFallsHotels.com

FREE HOT BREAKFAST PARKING MOVIES

HAMPTON INN NORTH OF THE FALLS   *Book at aaa.com*   **Phone:** (905)358-5555   **5**
(CAA) (SAVE)   6/17-9/4 [ECP]   1P: $89-$249   2P: $89-$249   XP: $10   F12
              5/1-6/16 & 9/5-4/30 [ECP]   1P: $69-$199   2P: $69-$199   XP: $10   F12
🔷🔷🔷   **Location:** 2.8 km n of the falls. 4357 River Rd L2E 3E8. Fax: 905/358-0140. **Facility:** 105 one-bedroom standard
Small-scale Hotel units, some with whirlpools. 5 stories, interior corridors. **Parking:** on-site. **Terms:** 3 day cancellation notice,
package plans. **Amenities:** voice mail, irons, hair dryers. **Dining:** 6-10 am. **Pool(s):** heated indoor. **Leisure**
Activities: sauna, whirlpool, sun deck. **Guest Services:** area transportation-casino. **Cards:** AX, DC, DS,
MC, VI. **Special Amenities:** free expanded continental breakfast and free local telephone calls.
(See color ad p 324 & p 4)

SOME UNITS
(SD) (🍴) (&M) (📷) (🏊) (✕) (📹) (DATA PORT) (🖥) /(✕)/

HILLTOP HOTEL   **Phone:** 905/374-7777   **77**
🔷   6/30-9/5   1P: $130-$200   2P: $130-$200   XP: $10   F
    5/1-6/29 & 9/6-4/30   1P: $69-$130   2P: $69-$130   XP: $10   F
Motel   **Location:** Just s of jct Victoria Ave. 4955 Clifton Hill L2G 3N5. Fax: 905/354-8086. **Facility:** 40 one-bedroom
standard units, some with whirlpools. 3 stories (no elevator), interior corridors. *Bath:* combo or shower only.
Parking: on-site. **Terms:** package plans. **Cards:** AX, MC, VI.

(ASK) (SD) (🐕) (🍴+)

Enjoy the Clean, Comfort of the Flamingo Motor Inn

BEAUTIFUL HONEYMOON SUITES
featuring jacuzzi whirlpools in heart shaped tubs

OUR AMENITIES INCLUDE:
❦ Cable T.V. ❦ free local calls ❦ large heated pool with diving board ❦ walk to new outlet mall ❦ licensed restaurant adjacent ❦ sightseeing tours ❦ discount coupons ❦ free guest parking ❦ beautyrest mattresses ❦ waterbeds ❦ single and double adjoining rooms ❦ Seniors & bus tours welcome ❦ low off-season rates ❦ major credit cards accepted ❦ we speak French, German and Hungarian ❦ Shuttle service in season ❦ Easy access to Casino ❦ Wedding Chapel on-site ❦ Picnic area

LARGE CONNECTING FAMILY ROOMS
❦ Accommodate up to 12 people ❦
❦ Fair Exchange on U.S. Funds ❦

ASK ABOUT OUR SUMMER SUPER SAVER RATES
(excludes weekends & holidays)
(limited availability)

FLAMINGO MOTOR INN
7701 Lundy's Lane (Hwy. 20 west), Niagara Falls, Canada L2H 1H3
(905) 356-4646 • Fax (905) 356-9373
Toll Free Reservations: 1-800-738-7701

HILTON NIAGARA FALLS FALLSVIEW   *Book at aaa.com*   Phone: (905)354-7887   50
(CAA) (SAVE)   6/17-9/4   1P: $149-$499   2P: $149-$499   XP: $25   F12
   5/1-6/16 & 9/5-4/30   1P: $99-$299   2P: $99-$299   XP: $25   F12
Location: Hwy 20, just s. 6361 Fallsview Blvd L2G 3V9. Fax: 905/357-9300. **Facility:** Good views of the falls are offered from many of the hotel's rooms as well as from its rooftop restaurant; a waterslide is featured. 516 **Large-scale Hotel** one-bedroom standard units, some with whirlpools. 34 stories, interior corridors. **Parking:** on-site (fee) and valet. **Terms:** check-in 4 pm, 3 day cancellation notice, [AP] & [BP] meal plans available, package plans. **Amenities:** video games (fee), dual phone lines, voice mail, irons, hair dryers. **Dining:** 7 am-10:30 pm, cocktails, also, The Watermark, see separate listing. **Pool(s):** heated indoor. **Leisure Activities:** sauna, whirlpool, steamroom, waterslide. **Guest Services:** gift shop, valet laundry, area transportation (fee)-casino. **Business Services:** meeting rooms. *Fee:* administrative services, fax. **Cards:** AX, DC, DS, MC, VI. **Special Amenities:** free newspaper and free room upgrade (subject to availability with advance reservations). *(See color ad card insert, p 350 & ad starting on p 118)*

SOME UNITS

[icons]

HOLIDAY INN BY THE FALLS   Phone: (905)356-1333   4
(CAA) (SAVE)   6/17-9/4   1P: $110-$245   2P: $110-$245   XP: $10   F16
   9/5-10/9   1P: $89-$225   2P: $89-$225   XP: $10   F16
   5/1-6/16   1P: $75-$225   2P: $75-$225   XP: $10   F16
   10/10-4/30   1P: $69-$195   2P: $69-$195   XP: $10   F16
Small-scale Hotel **Location:** Just w from the falls; directly across from casino. Located adjacent to Skylon Tower. 5339 Murray St L2G 2J3. Fax: 905/356-7128. **Facility:** 122 one-bedroom standard units, some with whirlpools. 6 stories, interior corridors. **Terms:** package plans. **Amenities:** video games, dual phone lines, voice mail, irons, hair dryers. **Dining:** 8 am-10 pm; 7 am-11 pm 6/14-10/15, cocktails. **Pool(s):** heated outdoor, heated indoor. **Leisure Activities:** sauna, whirlpool. **Guest Services:** gift shop. **Cards:** AX, CB, DC, DS, JC, MC, VI. **Special Amenities:** free newspaper and preferred room (subject to availability with advance reservations). *(See color ad p 344, p 371 & ad starting on p 118)*

SOME UNITS

[icons]

HORSESHOE FALLS MOTOR INN   Phone: (905)358-9353   35
(CAA) (SAVE)   6/24-9/5   1P: $69-$269   2P: $69-$269   XP: $10   F12
   5/1-6/23 & 9/6-10/10   1P: $49-$179   2P: $49-$179   XP: $7   F12
   10/11-4/30   1P: $39-$139   2P: $39-$139   XP: $7   F12
Location: Opposite Konica Minolta Tower. 5481 Dunn St L2G 2N6. Fax: 905/356-7298. **Facility:** 64 one-bedroom **Small-scale Hotel** standard units, some with whirlpools. 2-4 stories, interior corridors. **Parking:** on-site. **Terms:** 2 night minimum stay - weekends, 4 day cancellation notice-fee imposed, [AP], [BP] & [MAP] meal plans available, package plans. **Amenities:** irons, hair dryers. **Dining:** 8 am-midnight; closed 11/30-3/15, cocktails. **Pool(s):** heated outdoor. **Leisure Activities:** whirlpool. **Cards:** AX, DS, MC, VI. **Special Amenities:** free local telephone calls and preferred room (subject to availability with advance reservations). *(See color ad p 346 & ad starting on p 118)*

SOME UNITS

[icons] FEE

Hilton
Niagara Falls
Fallsview

On the
Brink of it All!

- 34 storey luxury fallsview hotel
- Fallsview guest rooms, beautiful Jacuzzi® & convenient two-room family suites
- 'Experience the Falls™ Adventure Pool, with Niagara's only spiraling 3 storey waterslide
- Rooftop fallsview water-themed restaurant "The Watermark"
- Steps to the Falls & Niagara's most exciting attractions
- Closest hotel to the new Niagara Fallsview Casino Resort

(CAA) *Four Diamond Award* (AAA)

NIAGARA FALLSVIEW
CASINO RESORT

Indoor Glass Walkway to the New Casino!

6361 Fallsview Blvd., Niagara Falls, ON (905) 354-7887

Reservations 1-888-370-0324   www.hiltonniagarafalls.com

Holiday Inn By The Falls

In Niagara, why stay anywhere else?
Why indeed when one location offers it all... quality, comfort and convenience. Just 220 yds. from the Falls, next to the famous Skylon Tower, and right beside the magnificent new Casino. Plus free on-site parking.

★ Spacious well-appointed guest rooms with King or Queen-size bed and private balcony... or a luxury suite with whirl-pool bath for two.

★ **Coco's Terrace Steakhouse** offers superb dining by an open-hearth grill in a smart but casual indoor/outdoor setting... complete with a woodfire oven gourmet pizza bar.

★ Plus two celebrated restaurants right on site... the acclaimed **Wolfgang Puck Café** for the ultimate in casual dining... and the entertaining **Café TuTu Tango** with its multi-ethnic appetizer-style dishes.

★ Unwind at our luxury **Nordic Spa** with large sparkling pool, sauna and whirlpool.

★ Plus... **special value rates for AAA/CAA members**. Special package rates October thru May. So why stay anywhere else? Experience it all at Holiday Inn By The Falls!

5339 Murray St. (cor. Fallsview Blvd.), Niagara Falls, Ontario, Canada L2G 2J3

(905) 356-1333 • 1-800-263-9393   res@holidayinn.com   www.holidayinn.com

HOWARD JOHNSON BY THE FALLS   *Book at aaa.com*   Phone: 905/357-4040   **13**
  (CAA) (SAVE) 6/25-9/6   1P: $99-$399   2P: $99-$399   XP: $10   F16
            11/1-4/30   1P: $69-$399   2P: $69-$399   XP: $10   F16
  ▼▼▼▼▼ 5/1-6/24 & 9/7-10/31   1P: $69-$369   2P: $69-$369   XP: $10   F16
     — **Location:** On Hwy 20; 0.6 km from the falls. 5905 Victoria Ave L2G 3L8. Fax: 905/357-6202. **Facility:** 199 units.
Small-scale Hotel 186 one- and 13 two-bedroom standard units, some with whirlpools. 7 stories, interior corridors. **Parking:** on-site (fee). **Terms:** check-in 4 pm, package plans. **Amenities:** voice mail, hair dryers. *Some:* irons. **Pool(s):** heated indoor/outdoor. **Leisure Activities:** sauna, whirlpool. *Fee:* game room. **Guest Services:** valet and coin laundry, area transportation (fee)-casino. **Business Services:** meeting rooms. **Cards:** AX, DS, MC, VI.
(See color ad card insert & p 350)   SOME UNITS

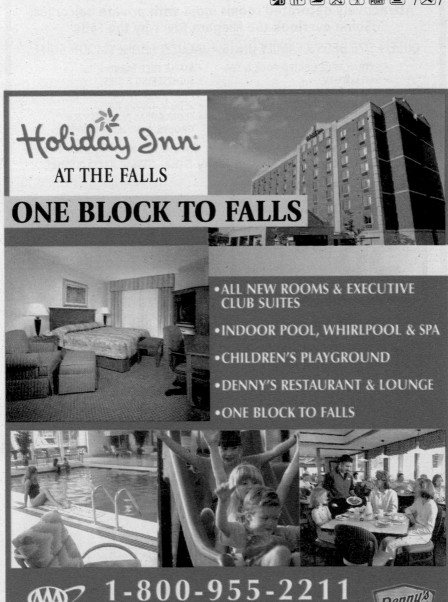

 HOLIDAY INN

AT THE FALLS

ONE BLOCK TO FALLS

• ALL NEW ROOMS & EXECUTIVE CLUB SUITES
• INDOOR POOL, WHIRLPOOL & SPA
• CHILDREN'S PLAYGROUND
• DENNY'S RESTAURANT & LOUNGE
• ONE BLOCK TO FALLS

1-800-955-2211
NiagaraFallsHotels.com

Denny's

HORSESHOE FALLS MOTOR INN

Within Walking Distance & Overlooking Horseshoe Falls!

**Attractively decorated rooms most with private balconies.
Some overlook the Niagara River by the Falls.**

QUEEN SIZE BEDS • FAMILY UNITS • JACUZZI / HONEYMOON SUITES

- EXTRA LARGE HEATED POOL & SPA
- SATELLITE TV
- FREE IN ROOM MOVIES
- REMOTE CONTROL TV RADIOS
- DIRECT DIAL PHONES, DATA PORTS
- ADJOINING ROOMS

- AMPLE FREE PARKING
- SIGHTSEEING TOURS
- FAVORABLE USA EXCHANGE
- SPECIAL GROUP RATES
- ECONOMICAL PACKAGES FOR
  GROUPS, FAMILIES & COUPLES

**Opposite The New Niagara Fallsview Casino Resort, Minolta Tower,
Incline to Horseshoe Falls, & Many Other Major Attractions!**

AAA MEMBER SPECIAL

$**38**.50 Dbl.   **FREE COFFEE**

Mar - June 16, Sept 6 - Nov (weekdays)

WE ♥ SENIORS
25% OFF weekdays Sept - June
10% OFF MEALS

KIDS STAY & EAT FREE*
*Food limit 1 per child with each
regularly priced adult meal purchased.
Member specials subject to availability.

MEMBER DISCOUNTS
(off published rates)
10% OFF year round
20% OFF weekdays year round
(except holidays & July 1 - Aug 24)

 5481 Dunn St., Niagara Falls, Canada L2G 2N6, 905-358-9353

www.horseshoefallsmotorinn.com

TOLL FREE 1-800-463-1938

HOWARD JOHNSON EXPRESS INN *Book at aaa.com* Phone: (905)358-9777 **55**

6/30-9/4 [CP] 1P: $65-$200 2P: $65-$200 XP: $10 F17
5/1-6/29 & 9/5-4/30 [CP] 1P: $45-$150 2P: $45-$150 XP: $10 F17

Motel

Location: QEW, exit Hwy 20, 5 km w. 8100 Lundy's Ln L2H 1H1. Fax: 905/358-0575. **Facility:** 84 one-bedroom standard units, some with whirlpools. 2 stories (no elevator), exterior corridors. **Parking:** on-site, winter plug-ins. **Terms:** cancellation fee imposed, [BP] meal plan available. **Pool(s):** heated outdoor. **Guest Services:** area transportation (fee)-casino. **Cards:** AX, DC, DS, MC, VI. **Special Amenities:** free continental breakfast and free local telephone calls.

SOME UNITS

Only 15 minutes from Niagara Falls & Casino Niagara

✳ **Holiday Inn**®
Fort Erie/Niagara - Convention Centre

"AWARD WINNING PROPERTY"

- Luxurious Rooms
- Whirlpool, Sauna & Indoor Pool
- Restaurant & Lounge
- Meeting and Banquet Facilities for up to 350 People

1-888-269-5550
1485 Garrison Road • Fort Erie, ON L2A 1P8

Excellent Quality Performer 2004

Getaway Packages
$99-$179
Gateway Gaming Package
Heart to Heart Romance Package
Golf Package • Theater Package
Cycling Package
Call Hotel for more information

Only 2 minutes from the Fort Erie Racetrack and Slots!

THE PRINCE OF WALES STAKES

IMPERIAL HOTEL AND SUITES
Phone: (905)356-2648 **14**

F12

5/1-9/30 [BP]   1P: $79-$359   2P: $79-$359   XP: $15   F12
10/1-4/30 [BP]   1P: $59-$299   2P: $59-$299   XP: $15   F12

Location: Hwy 20, 0.5 km from the falls. 5851 Victoria Ave L2G 3L6. Fax: 905/356-4068. **Facility:** 104 one-bedroom standard units, some with whirlpools. 10 stories, interior corridors. **Parking:** on-site (fee).

Small-scale Hotel **Terms:** check-in 4 pm, cancellation fee imposed, package plans. **Amenities:** voice mail. *Some:* irons, hair dryers. **Dining:** 7-11 am in season. **Pool(s):** heated indoor. **Leisure Activities:** whirlpool, exercise room. *Fee:* game room. **Guest Services:** gift shop, coin laundry. **Business Services:** meeting rooms, fax (fee). **Cards:** AX, DC, DS, JC, MC, VI. **Special Amenities:** free full breakfast and free local telephone calls. *(See color ad below)*

SOME UNITS

KINGS INN NEAR THE FALLS
Phone: (905)356-1233 **69**

6/18-9/4   1P: $79-$199   2P: $79-$199   XP: $15   F12
5/1-6/17 & 9/5-9/30   1P: $49-$149   2P: $49-$149   XP: $10   F12
Motel   10/1-4/30   1P: $44-$89   2P: $44-$89   XP: $10   F12

Location: On Hwy 20, 1 km from the falls. Located in a commercial area. 5525 Ferry St L2G 1S3. Fax: 905/374-6412. **Facility:** 44 one-bedroom standard units, some with whirlpools. 3 stories (no elevator), exterior corridors. **Parking:** on-site. **Terms:** office hours 8 am-2 am, 3 day cancellation notice-fee imposed, package plans. **Pool(s):** heated outdoor. **Leisure Activities:** *Fee:* game room. **Cards:** AX, DC, DS, JC, MC, VI.

SOME UNITS

KNIGHTS INN   *Book at aaa.com*
Phone: (905)354-6939 **46**

6/27-9/4   1P: $79-$249   2P: $79-$249   XP: $10   F16
5/1-6/26   1P: $55-$199   2P: $55-$199   XP: $10   F16
9/5-4/30   1P: $49-$199   2P: $49-$199   XP: $10   F16

Motel   **Location:** 3.4 km w on Hwy 20. Located in a commercial area. 7034 Lundy's Ln L2G 1V9. Fax: 905/354-3699. **Facility:** 64 one-bedroom standard units. 2 stories (no elevator), exterior corridors. **Parking:** on-site. **Pool(s):** heated outdoor. **Guest Services:** area transportation (fee)-casino. **Business Services:** fax (fee). **Cards:** AX, DC, DS, MC, VI. **Special Amenities:** free local telephone calls and free newspaper.

SOME UNITS

FEE   FEE

KNIGHTS INN-BY THE FALLS   *Book at aaa.com*
Phone: (905)358-8132 **48**

6/27-9/3   1P: $84-$254   2P: $84-$254   XP: $5   F16
5/1-6/26   1P: $59-$205   2P: $59-$205   XP: $5   F16
9/4-4/30   1P: $54-$205   2P: $54-$205   XP: $5   F16

Motel   **Location:** Jct Murray St. 6276 Main St L2G 6A4. Fax: 905/358-2777. **Facility:** 47 one-bedroom standard units, some with efficiencies and/or whirlpools. 1-2 stories (no elevator), exterior corridors. **Bath:** combo or shower only. **Parking:** on-site. **Terms:** package plans. **Pool(s):** heated outdoor, wading. **Leisure Activities:** whirlpool. **Cards:** AX, DC, MC, VI. **Special Amenities:** free local telephone calls and free room upgrade (subject to availability with advance reservations). *(See color ad starting on p 118)*

SOME UNITS

Stay & Play

1 block to Casino & the Falls.
Conveniently located right in the middle of all the excitement!

- 104 luxurious junior suites, studio jacuzzi suites with heart shaped tubs, spacious family suites that sleep up to 6 people • Refrigerators and coffee makers in all rooms
- **FREE** full breakfast • First class on-site restaurant • Shopping, attractions, dining and entertainment at your doorstep

IMPERIAL
Hotel & Suites

RESERVATIONS 1-800-263-2553 www.imperialniagara.com
5851 Victoria Avenue, Niagara Falls, Ontario, CANADA

LINCOLN MOTOR INN

Phone: (905)356-1748   **41**

(CAA) (SAVE)   ♦♦♦ ♦♦♦   Motel

6/30-8/27	1P: $89-$189	2P: $89-$189	XP: $10 F16
5/1-6/29 & 8/28-4/30	1P: $49-$149	2P: $40-$149	XP: $10 F16

Location: 0.3 mi w of the falls via Murray St; by Konica Minolta Tower. 6417 Main St L2G 5Y3. Fax: 905/356-7531. **Facility:** 60 units. 59 one- and 1 two-bedroom standard units, some with whirlpools. 2 stories (no elevator), exterior corridors. **Parking:** on-site. **Terms:** weekly rates available, [BP] & [MAP] meal plans available, package plans. **Amenities:** hair dryers. **Dining:** 7:30 am-noon. **Pool(s):** heated outdoor. **Leisure Activities:** whirlpool. **Cards:** AX, CB, DS, MC, VI. **Special Amenities:** free local telephone calls and free newspaper. *(See color ad below & ad starting on p 118)*

SOME UNITS

LOCATED IN THE HEART OF THE EXCITING FALLSVIEW TOURIST DISTRICT

ONE BLOCK TO THE "NEW" FALLSVIEW CASINO!

Lincoln Motor inn
fallsview district

NIAGARA'S WINNING COMBINATION!

- Extra AAA & Seniors discounts - midweek from September to June
- Heated outdoor pool & whirlpool
- Favourable US exchange rate
- Previous Innkeeper of the year winner
- Family & Jacuzzi suites

- Free full cooked to order breakfast
- Free parking
- Free in-room coffee
- Free in-room movies
- Kids stay Free

Ask about our Multi-Night packages!

6417 Main Street, Niagara Falls, Ontario
Canada L2G 5Y3   TEL 905-356-1748
www.LincolnMotorInn.com

Our Warm Hospitality Makes the Difference

... AND WALKING DISTANCE TO THE FALLS, RESTAURANTS, SHOPS, & ATTRACTIONS

TOLL FREE RESERVATIONS   1-800-263-2575

MARRIOTT NIAGARA FALLS FALLSVIEW AND SPA   *Book at aaa.com*   Phone: (905)357-7300   39

(CAA) (SAVE)   7/1-8/31   1P: $199-$599   2P: $199-$599
              5/1-6/30 & 9/1-4/30   1P: $129-$599   2P: $129-$599
▼▼▼ ▼▼▼ **Location:** Next to Konica Minolta Tower. 6740 Fallsview Blvd L2G 3W6. Fax: 905/357-0490. **Facility:** On a hilltop, the hotel offers good views of the falls from many of its guest rooms and common areas. 432 units. 395 **Large-scale Hotel** one-bedroom standard units, some with whirlpools. 37 one-bedroom suites ($189-$849), some with whirlpools. 23 stories, interior corridors. **Parking:** on-site (fee) and valet. **Terms:** 3 day cancellation notice-fee imposed, package plans. **Amenities:** video games (fee), high-speed Internet, dual phone lines, voice mail, safes, honor bars, irons, hair dryers. **Dining:** Terrapin Grille, see separate listing. **Pool(s):** heated indoor. **Leisure Activities:** saunas, whirlpools, steamroom, exercise room, spa. *Fee:* game room. **Guest Services:** gift shop, valet laundry, area transportation (fee)-casino. **Business Services:** meeting rooms, business center. **Cards:** AX, CB, DC, DS, JC, MC, VI.
(See color ad below, card insert & starting on p 118)

SOME UNITS

The only thing we overlook
   is **Niagara Falls**

SEE OUR AD IN THE FOLD-OUT CARD INSERT
OF THIS TOURBOOK

Marriott

NIAGARA FALLS FALLSVIEW & SPA

1-888-501-8916
www.marriotthotelniagarafalls.com
6740 Fallsview Blvd., Niagara Falls, Canada · Tel. (905) 357-7300

COURTYARD
Marriott

Just One Block
from the Falls &
Niagara Casinos

See our Ad in the Fold-out card
insert of this Tourbook

5950 Victoria Ave., Niagara Falls, ON L2G 3L7
905-358-3083   1-800-771-1123
www.niagarafallscourtyardhotel.com

Howard·Johnson

HOTEL BY THE FALLS

Located in the
Heart of the Tourist
District

See our Ad in the Fold-out card
insert of this Tourbook

5905 Victoria Avenue, Niagara Falls, Canada L2G 3L8
905-357-4040 **1-800-446-4656** (Ask for hotel 1210)
www.hojobythefalls.com

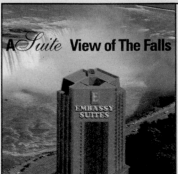

A *Suite* **View of The Falls**

EMBASSY
SUITES

CLOSEST HOTEL TO FALLS – BESIDE NIAGARA FALLSVIEW CASINO
Complimentary Cooked-to-Order Breakfast and Evening
Manager's Reception included with each Suite

See our Ad in the Fold-out card insert of this Tourbook

 **EMBASSY SUITES
HOTEL**

NIAGARA FALLS – FALLSVIEW

6700 Fallsview Blvd., Niagara Falls, ON L2G3W6
1-888-688-8288 embassysuitesfallsview.com

MELODY MOTEL　　　　　　　　　　　　　　　　　　　　　Phone: 905/227-1023 　**32**
(CAA) (SAVE) 　　6/26-9/9　　　　　1P: $58-$88　　　2P: $68-$98　　　XP: $10　　　F12
　　　　　5/1-6/25 & 9/10-4/30　　1P: $38-$48　　　2P: $48-$58　　　XP: $10　　　F12
◆◆◆　**Location:** 9.2 km w on Hwy 20. 13065 Lundy's Ln L2E 6S4. Fax: 905/227-3712. **Facility:** 20 one-bedroom
Motel　standard units, some with whirlpools. 1 story, exterior corridors. **Parking:** on-site, winter plug-ins.
　　Terms: office hours 9 am-midnight, 3 day cancellation notice-fee imposed, package plans. **Pool(s):** heated
　　outdoor. **Leisure Activities:** playground. **Cards:** AX, DC, DS, MC, VI. **Special Amenities: free local
telephone calls and preferred room (subject to availability with advance reservations).**
SOME UNITS

NIAGARA FALLS MOTOR LODGE　　　　　　　　　　　　Phone: (905)295-3569 　**75**
(CAA) (SAVE)　6/18-9/7　　　　　1P: $59-$138　　2P: $59-$138　　XP: $10　　　F12
　　　5/1-6/17　　　　　1P: $49-$99　　　2P: $49-$99　　　XP: $10　　　F12
◆◆ ◆◆　9/8-4/30　　　　　1P: $49-$79　　　2P: $49-$79　　　XP: $10　　　F12
Motel　**Location:** 2 km s of Horseshoe Falls on Niagara River Pkwy to Portage Rd S; 1.2 km s of Marineland. Located in a
　　residential area. 7950 Portage Rd S L2G 5Y8. Fax: 905/295-0022. **Facility:** 20 one-bedroom standard units. 2
　　stories (no elevator), exterior corridors. **Parking:** on-site. **Terms:** office hours 7 am-11 pm, 3 day
cancellation notice. **Pool(s):** heated outdoor. **Guest Services:** area transportation (fee)-local attractions. **Business Services:**
fax (fee). **Cards:** MC, VI. *(See color ad below)*
SOME UNITS

NIAGARA FALLS MOTOR LODGE

• Quiet Location • Spacious Family Rooms • Kids Stay Free • 2 KM from the Falls
• Senior Discount • Air Conditioned • Heated Swimming Pool • King & Queen Size Beds
• In Room Coffee Makers, Refrigerators, Microwaves • Adjacent to Marineland, People Movers & Several
Restaurants • Shuttle Bus to the Falls, Marineland & Casino • 2 KM from New 45 Hole Golf Course

Call Now For Reservations: 905-295-3569 or 1-800-667-7931 (US/Canada)
Fax (905)295-0022 • 7950 Portage Rd. S. Niagara Falls, Ontario, Canada L2G 5Y8

GUARANTEED LOW HOTEL RATES

NiagaraFallsHotels.com

EVERY VISITOR WINS!　GRAND PRIZE
Free Falls
Vacation

NIAGARA FALLSVIEW CASINO RESORT

Phone: 905/358-3255 83

7/1-9/6	1P: $319-$399	2P: $319-$399	XP: $50 F12
5/1-6/30 & 4/15-4/30	1P: $219-$289	2P: $219-$289	XP: $50 F12
9/7-4/14	1P: $189-$289	2P: $189-$289	XP: $50 F12

Large-scale Hotel **Location:** Jct Murray St. 6380 Fallsview Blvd L2G 7X5. Fax: 905/371-7931. **Facility:** This hotel features a large casino, a shopping gallery and an entertainment forum in addition to its elegantly appointed guest rooms. 374 units. 365 one-bedroom standard units, some with whirlpools. 9 one-bedroom suites with whirlpools. 35 stories, interior corridors. *Bath:* combo or shower only. **Parking:** on-site (fee) and valet. **Terms:** 3 day cancellation notice-fee imposed, package plans. **Amenities:** dual phone lines, voice mail, safes, irons, hair dryers. *Some:* CD players. **Dining:** 17 Noir, see separate listing. **Pool(s):** heated indoor. **Leisure Activities:** saunas, whirlpools, steamrooms, exercise room, spa. **Guest Services:** gift shop, valet laundry. **Business Services:** conference facilities, business center. **Cards:** AX, DC, MC, I. *(See color ad inside front cover)*

SOME UNITS

ASK SD ❌ 24 Y 🛋 🚲 ❌ ❌ DATA PORT 💻 / ❌ 🍳 💻 /

NIAGARA FAMILY INN

Phone: 905/354-9844 6

CAA SAVE

6/30-9/5	1P: $55-$95	2P: $69-$95	XP: $10 F12
5/1-6/29	1P: $39-$59	2P: $49-$79	XP: $10 F12
9/6-4/30	1P: $39-$59	2P: $49-$69	XP: $10 F12

Motel **Location:** Jct Clifton Hill, just e. 5612 Ellen Ave L2G 3P6. Fax: 905/354-6691. **Facility:** 36 one-bedroom standard units. 2 stories (no elevator), interior/exterior corridors. *Bath:* combo or shower only. **Parking:** on-site. **Terms:** 5 day cancellation notice-fee imposed. **Dining:** noon-midnight, cocktails. **Pool(s):** heated outdoor. **Business Services:** meeting rooms. **Cards:** AX, DS, MC, VI. **Special Amenities:** early check-in/late check-out and preferred room (subject to availability with advance reservations).

SOME UNITS

❌ 🚲 🛋 / ❌ /

NIAGARA PARKWAY COURT MOTEL

Phone: 905/295-3331 73

CAA SAVE

6/18-9/30	1P: $49-$129	2P: $49-$199	XP: $10 F12
5/1-6/17	1P: $49-$79	2P: $49-$129	XP: $10 F12
10/1-4/30	1P: $39-$69	2P: $39-$99	XP: $10 F12

Motel **Location:** 2.5 km s of the falls on Niagara River Pkwy. Located in a quiet area. 3708 Main St L2G 6B1. Fax: 905/295-3331. **Facility:** 19 one-bedroom standard units, some with efficiencies and/or whirlpools. 2 stories (no elevator), exterior corridors. **Parking:** on-site. **Terms:** weekly rates available, package plans, small pets only ($10 extra charge, in designated units). **Cards:** AX, DS, JC, MC, VI. *(See color ad below)*

SOME UNITS

SD 🛏 🛋 FEE ❌ 🍳 💻 / ❌ 🍳 /

THE OAKES HOTEL OVERLOOKING THE FALLS   *Book at aaa.com*

Phone: (905)356-4514 1

CAA SAVE

11/1-12/31	1P: $69-$999	2P: $69-$999	XP: $10 F16
5/1-9/5	1P: $69-$799	2P: $69-$799	XP: $10 F16
9/6-10/31	1P: $69-$499	2P: $69-$499	XP: $10 F16
1/1-4/30	1P: $69-$399	2P: $69-$399	XP: $10 F16

Large-scale Hotel **Location:** By Konica Minolta Tower; adjacent to casino. 6546 Fallsview Blvd L2G 3W2. Fax: 905/356-3651. **Facility:** 246 one-bedroom standard units, some with whirlpools. 2-21 stories, interior/exterior corridors. **Parking:** on-site (fee). **Terms:** cancellation fee imposed, package plans, 3% service charge. **Amenities:** voice mail, hair dryers. *Some:* high-speed Internet (fee), dual phone lines, irons. **Dining:** 7 am-midnight, cocktails. **Pool(s):** heated indoor. **Leisure Activities:** sauna, whirlpool, exercise room. **Guest Services:** gift shop, valet laundry, area transportation (fee)-casino. **Business Services:** meeting rooms, fax (fee). **Cards:** AX, CB, DC, DS, JC, MC, VI. *(See color ad starting on p 338)*

SOME UNITS

🛋 Y 🚲 ❌ 📷 🐾 DATA PORT 💻 / ❌ /

OLD STONE INN   *Book at aaa.com*

Phone: (905)357-1234 59

6/16-10/16	1P: $135-$289	2P: $145-$349	XP: $10 F12
10/17-4/30	1P: $105-$299	2P: $115-$349	XP: $10 F12
5/1-6/15	1P: $105-$249	2P: $115-$289	XP: $10 F12

Small-scale Hotel **Location:** Just w via Murray St, just n on Buchanan Ave. Located adjacent to Skylon Tower. 5425 Robinson St L2G 7L6. Fax: 905/357-9299. **Facility:** 114 one-bedroom standard units, some with whirlpools. 3 stories, interior/exterior corridors. **Parking:** on-site, winter plug-ins. **Terms:** check-in 4 pm, cancellation fee imposed, package plans. **Amenities:** video games, voice mail, hair dryers. **Dining:** The Millery Dining Room, see separate listing. **Pool(s):** heated outdoor, heated indoor. **Leisure Activities:** whirlpool. **Guest Services:** valet laundry, area transportation. **Business Services:** meeting rooms. **Cards:** AX, CB, DC, DS, JC, MC, VI. *(See color ad starting on p 118)*

SOME UNITS

ASK SD 🛋 Y 🚲 🐾 / ❌ DATA PORT 💻 /

— *Niagara Parkway Court Motel* —

Located on Scenic Niagara River. Just 1.5 miles from the Falls & 1/2 mile from Marineland. Exceptionally spacious comfortable rooms with Queen size beds, A/C, Cable T.V. All Rooms with kitchenette facilities, refrigerator, microwave oven, coffee maker, toaster, plus all necessary crockery and cutlery. Efficiency rooms with stove also available. Riverside walking/cycling trail, restaurants, coffee shops, banks, supermarkets, bars, shuttle bus to major attractions all at walking distance. Jaccuzi suites also available.

For reservations, call **1-888-786-7747** or (905) 295-3331

www.niagaraparkwaycourt.com

3708 Main Street (at Niagara Parkway South)
Ontario, Canada   L2G 6B1

PARK PLAZA

Phone: (905)353-1010   63
5/1-9/30   1P: $99-$189   2P: $99-$189   XP: $10   F18
10/1-4/30   1P: $85-$139   2P: $85-$139   XP: $10   F18
Large-scale Hotel **Location:** Jct Main and Ferry sts, just s. 5807 Ferry St L2G 1S8. Fax: 905/358-7131. **Facility:** 145 one-bedroom standard units, some with whirlpools. 2-11 stories, interior/exterior corridors. *Bath:* combo or shower only. **Parking:** on-site (fee). **Terms:** cancellation fee imposed, package plans. **Amenities:** voice mail, hair dryers. *Some:* honor bars. **Pool(s):** heated outdoor, heated indoor. **Leisure Activities:** sauna, whirlpool, exercise room. *Fee:* massage. **Guest Services:** area transportation. **Business Services:** meeting rooms. **Cards:** AX, DS, MC, VI.
SOME UNITS

Niagara Falls ✦ Canada

President Inn

600 Yards to
the Falls!
5 Minutes to
Marineland,
Outlet Malls
Fallsview Casino
Opposite Us

← President Motor Inn

NEW CASINO OPPOSITE US *Walk to the Falls!*

DATES	2 PERSONS - 1 BED 2 PERSONS - 2 BEDS	EXTRA PERSON
June 30 - Aug. 20 Sept 30 - Sept 04	$69 – $160	$10
June 11 - June 29 Aug. 21 - Sept 01	$59 – $150	$10
May 01 - June 10 Sept 05 - Oct. 31	$49 – $69	$10

Rates are higher during special events and holiday weekends

For Location & Value
✦ Economical Rates
✦ Pool ✦ Cable TV
✦ Air Conditioning
✦ Comfortable Rooms
✦ Family Suites
✦ Restaurants Adjacent
✦ Free Parking

GROUP TOUR RESERVATIONS: 1-800-263-2561

PRESIDENT MOTOR INN
6503 Stanley Avenue, Niagara Falls, Canada L2G 7L2
www.presidentmotorinn.com

Toll-Free Reservations 1 800 890 6295

PENINSULA INN & RESORT   Phone: (905)354-8812 ⑦⑥

ⒶⒶ ⓈⒶⓋⒺ   7/1-9/5   1P: $109-$249   2P: $109-$249   XP: $10   F12
           5/1-6/30 & 9/6-10/31   1P: $89-$189   2P: $89-$189   XP: $10   F12
▽▽▽▽   11/1-4/30   1P: $59-$159   2P: $59-$159   XP: $10   F12

Location: QEW, exit McLeod Rd, just w. Located in a quiet area. 7373 Niagara Square Dr L2E 6S5. **Small-scale Hotel** Fax: 905/354-7174. **Facility:** 95 units. 93 one-bedroom standard units, some with whirlpools. 2 one-bedroom suites ($129-$349). 5 stories, interior corridors. **Parking:** on-site. **Terms:** package plans, small pets only ($10 fee, with prior approval). **Amenities:** dual phone lines, voice mail, hair dryers. **Dining:** 7 am-11 & 5:30-9 pm, cocktails. **Pool(s):** heated indoor. **Leisure Activities:** sauna, whirlpool, exercise room, spa. **Guest Services:** gift shop, valet laundry, area transportation-casino & falls. **Business Services:** meeting rooms. **Cards:** AX, DC, JC, MC, VI.

SOME UNITS
🛏 🍴 🍸 🅱️Ⓜ 🏊 ✕ 🎦 [DATA PORT] 🖥 / ✕ 🛗 /
FEE   FEE

THE PRESIDENT MOTOR INN   Phone: 905/358-7272 ④⓪

ⒶⒶ ⓈⒶⓋⒺ   6/30-8/20   1P: $69-$160   2P: $69-$160   XP: $10   F10
           8/21-10/31   1P: $59-$79   2P: $59-$79   XP: $10   F10
▽▽   5/1-6/29   1P: $49-$79   2P: $49-$79   XP: $10   F10

Location: Corner of Stanley and Dixon aves; just w of Minolta Tower. 6503 Stanley Ave L2G 7L2. Fax: 905/356-0392. **Motel**   **Facility:** 42 one-bedroom standard units. 2 stories (no elevator), exterior corridors. **Parking:** on-site. **Terms:** open 5/1-10/31, cancellation fee imposed, package plans. **Pool(s):** outdoor. **Cards:** AX, MC, VI.

(See color ad p 353)

SOME UNITS
🅢Ⓓ 🍴➕ 🏊 ✇ / ✕ /

QUALITY HOTEL-NEAR THE FALLS   *Book at aaa.com*   Phone: (905)356-2842 ①⓪

ⒶⒶ ⓈⒶⓋⒺ   5/28-8/27   1P: $129-$309   2P: $129-$309   XP: $25   F16
           8/28-4/30   1P: $69-$289   2P: $69-$289   XP: $25   F16
▽▽▽▽   5/1-5/27   1P: $69-$249   2P: $69-$249   XP: $25   F16

Location: On Hwy 20, 0.7 km from the falls. 5257 Ferry St L2G 1R6. Fax: 905/356-6629. **Facility:** 120 one-**Small-scale Hotel** bedroom standard units, some with whirlpools. 11 stories, interior corridors. **Parking:** on-site. **Terms:** package plans. **Amenities:** video games, irons, hair dryers. **Dining:** 7 am-noon; hours may vary off season. **Pool(s):** heated indoor, wading. **Leisure Activities:** sauna, whirlpool, sun deck. **Guest Services:** gift shop. **Business Services:** meeting rooms. **Cards:** AX, CB, DC, DS, JC, MC, VI. *(See color ad p 317)*

SOME UNITS
🅢Ⓓ 🍴 🏊 ✕ 📺 🎦 🖥 / ✕ [DATA PORT] /

Enjoy the culture, enjoy the attractions, enjoy your stay in the heart of Niagara.

Holiday Inn
St.Catharines/ Niagara
2 North Service Road
St. Catharines

- Packages with local Niagara attractions
- Fun for the entire family in our state-of-the-art fitness centre and indoor/outdoor pool
- Family friendly hotel. KIDS STAY AND EAT FREE!
- Eight meeting rooms for weddings, banquets or any other occasion
- Exquisite Vecera Restaurant and Wine Bar

905-934-8000

QUALITY HOTEL
PARKWAY CONVENTION CENTRE
BY CHOICE HOTELS
327 Ontario St.
St. Catharines

- Winery and golf packages and many more!
- Family Entertainment Centre equipped with indoor pool and 40-lane bowling centre
- 17,000 square feet of meeting space
- JJ Kapps Backyard BBQ Grill famous for ribs!

905-688-2324

Howard Johnson
HOTEL
and Convention Centre
89 Meadowvale Drive
St. Catharines

- Howard Johnson Gold Medal winner 2003/2004
- Affordable recreational packages including fishing, cycling, hiking and more
- Indoor pool, 24-hour Perkins Family Restaurant
- Wrigley's Field Sports Bar

905-934-5400

Conveniently located directly off of the QEW highway.

www.heartofniagarahotels.com
Visit our website for links to all three hotels
PROPERTIES MANAGED BY HEART OF NIAGARA HOTELS

TOLL FREE RESERVATIONS 1-877-688-2324

QUALITY INN CLIFTON HILL   _Book at aaa.com_   Phone: (905)358-3601   **19**

(CAA) (SAVE)   5/1-10/31   1P: $79-$279   2P: $79-$279   XP: $12   F18
   11/1-4/30   1P: $59-$189   2P: $59-$189   XP: $12   F18

◇◇ ◇◇   **Location:** Jct Victoria Ave and Clifton Hill, just s. 4946 Clifton Hill L2E 6S8 (PO Box 60, NIAGARA FALLS).
   Fax: 905/358-3818. **Facility:** 263 units. 255 one- and 8 two-bedroom standard units, some with whirlpools.
Small-scale Hotel 2-3 stories (no elevator), interior/exterior corridors. **Parking:** on-site. **Terms:** package plans. **Dining:** 6:30
   am-11 pm; hours may vary off season, cocktails. **Pool(s):** heated outdoor, heated indoor, wading. **Leisure**
Activities: whirlpool, playground. **Guest Services:** gift shop, valet laundry. **Cards:** AX, CB, DC, DS, JC, MC, VI.
Special Amenities: free local telephone calls and free newspaper. _(See color ad starting on p 332)_

SOME UNITS

[⊕] [¶] [⊠] [▣] / [⊠] /

Niagara's Landmark Hotel Overlooking the Falls

NEW HOTEL

- 150 yards to Falls • 100 yards to new Casino • Walk to major attractions
- Deluxe rooms with mini-fridges, microwaves, coffee makers... • Packages
- Indoor pool, whirlpool... **OUTBACK** STEAKHOUSE® **Pizza Hut** Timothy's
- 4 dining options at hotel

RADISSON HOTEL & SUITES FALLSVIEW
6733 Fallsview Blvd., Niagara Falls, ON, Canada L2G 3W7 Fax: 905-374-2555

Telephone: 905-356-1944 or Toll Free:

1-877-FALLSVIEW _Radisson_®
www.niagarafallsview.com

RADISSON HOTEL & SUITES FALLSVIEW   *Book at aaa.com*   Phone: (905)356-1944   🔟
6/24-9/4   1P: $179-$299   2P: $179-$299   XP: $10   F18
5/1-6/23 & 3/2-4/30   1P: $149-$249   2P: $149-$249   XP: $10   F18
9/5-3/1   1P: $109-$249   2P: $109-$249   XP: $10   F18
Large-scale Hotel **Location:** Corner of Stanley Ave and Dunn St. Located across from Konica Minolta Tower. 6733 Fallsview Blvd L2G 3W7. Fax: 905/356-2858. **Facility:** 232 units. 218 one-bedroom standard units, some with whirlpools. 14 one-bedroom suites with whirlpools. 16 stories, interior corridors. **Parking:** on-site (fee) and valet. **Terms:** check-in 4 pm, 2 night minimum stay - seasonal and/or weekends, package plans. **Amenities:** video games, high-speed Internet (fee), dual phone lines, voice mail, irons, hair dryers. *Some:* safes. **Dining:** Outback Steakhouse, see separate listing. **Pool(s):** heated indoor. **Leisure Activities:** whirlpool, exercise room. *Fee:* massage. **Guest Services:** gift shop, valet laundry, area transportation (fee). **Business Services:** meeting rooms, business center. **Cards:** AX, DC, DS, MC, VI. *(See color ad , & ad starting on p 118)*

SOME UNITS

(A$K) (SD) [⏐⏐] (Y) (🛋) (🛟) (✕) (📷) (DATA PORT) (📺) / (✕) (🛏) (🖨) /

RAMADA CORAL RESORT HOTEL   *Book at aaa.com*   Phone: (905)356-6116   🔟
(CAA) (SAVE)   6/19-9/5   1P: $90-$200   2P: $90-$200   XP: $10   F16
5/1-6/18 & 9/6-4/30   1P: $70-$160   2P: $70-$160   XP: $10   F16
Location: QEW, exit Hwy 20 W; from downtown, 4 km w. 7429 Lundy's Ln L2H 1G9. Fax: 905/356-7121. **Facility:** 129 one-bedroom standard units, some with whirlpools. 4 stories, interior corridors. **Parking:** on-site, winter plug-ins. **Terms:** cancellation fee imposed, package plans. **Amenities:** video games (fee), voice mail, irons, hair dryers. **Dining:** 7 am-9 pm; to 2 pm 11/1-5/1, cocktails. **Pool(s):** heated outdoor, heated indoor. **Leisure Activities:** sauna, whirlpool, indoor children's play park. *Fee:* game room. **Guest Services:** gift shop, valet laundry, area transportation (fee)-attractions & casino. **Business Services:** meeting rooms, administrative services (fee). **Cards:** AX, DC, DS, JC, MC, VI. **Special Amenities:** free newspaper and early check-in/late check-out. *(See color ad below)*

Small-scale Hotel

SOME UNITS

(SD) [⏐⏐] (🛋) (🛟) (✕) (📷) (DATA PORT) (📺) / (✕) (🛏) /

RAMADA PLAZA HOTEL FALLSVIEW   Phone: 905/356-1501   🔟
6/24-9/4   1P: $179-$299   2P: $179-$299
5/1-6/23 & 9/5-10/29   1P: $99-$199   2P: $99-$199
10/30-4/30   1P: $79-$199   2P: $79-$199
Large-scale Hotel **Location:** In Konica Minolta Tower. 6732 Fallsview Blvd L2G 3W6. Fax: 905/356-8245. **Facility:** 42 one-bedroom standard units, some with whirlpools. 30 stories, interior corridors. *Bath:* combo or shower only. **Parking:** on-site (fee) and valet. **Terms:** check-in 4 pm, age restrictions may apply, package plans. **Amenities:** voice mail, safes, irons, hair dryers. **Dining:** Konica Minolta Tower Centre/Pinnacle Restaurant, see separate listing. **Leisure Activities:** exercise room privileges. **Guest Services:** gift shop, valet laundry, area transportation (fee). **Cards:** AX, DS, MC, VI. *(See color ad p 357 & ad starting on p 118)*

SOME UNITS

[⏐⏐] (DATA PORT) (🛏) (🖨) (📺) / (✕) /

RAMADA®
CORAL RESORT HOTEL

Just 2 miles west from Falls & Casino • 130 Spacious Guestrooms & Specialty Suites • In-room movies and Nintendo® • Indoor pools • Hot tub and sauna • Courtyard with outdoor pool, sundeck & gazebo • Kids indoor playpark, arcade • 2 restaurants, lounge • Canada One factory Outlet Mall adjacent • 10% AAA/CAA discount off published rates

TOLL FREE 1 800•663•6399
ramadaniagarafalls.com

7429 LUNDY'S LANE, NIAGARA FALLS, CANADA L2H 1G9 • 905-356-6116

RAMADA®
SUITES & CONFERENCE CENTRE

All luxurious two-room suites in a central location Falls/Casino Shuttle mid-May to mid Oct wkds balance of year Most livingroom with sleep sofa, second T.V. and fridge, separate bedroom with two queen or a king bed • Whirlpool suites and a 1,000 sq. ft. Roman themed Penthouse • Indoor pool, hot tub, Japanese spa and fitness room • Two dining options

TOLL FREE 1 866•307•8483
ramadasuitesniagarafalls.com

7389 LUNDY'S LANE, NIAGARA FALLS, CANADA L2H 2W9 • 905-356-6119

RAMADA SUITES HOTEL   *Book at aaa.com*   Phone: (905)356-6119
     6/19-9/5   1P: $90-$230   2P: $90-$230   XP: $10   F16
            5/1-6/18 & 9/6-4/30   1P: $90-$180   2P: $90-$180   XP: $10   F16
   **Location:** QEW, exit Hwy 20 W; from downtown, 4 km w. 7389 Lundy's Ln L2H 2W9. Fax: 905/356-7204.
            Facility: 73 units. 4 one-bedroom standard units with whirlpools. 69 one-bedroom suites, some with
Small-scale Hotel   whirlpools. 6 stories, interior corridors. **Parking:** on-site, winter plug-ins. **Terms:** cancellation fee imposed,
            package plans, 12% service charge. **Amenities:** video games (fee), voice mail, irons, hair dryers.
Dining: 11:30 am-11 pm; to 9 pm 11/1-5/1, cocktails. **Pool(s):** heated indoor. **Leisure Activities:** whirlpool, steamroom, indoor
squash court, exercise room. **Guest Services:** valet laundry, area transportation (fee)-attractions & casino. **Business Services:**
conference facilities, business center. **Cards:** AX, DC, DS, JC, MC, VI. **Special Amenities:** free newspaper and early check-
in/late check-out. *(See color ad p 356)*   SOME UNITS

Niagara's Most Unique Hotel
Breathtaking Views of the Falls

Located at the top of
KONICA
MINOLTA
TOWER CENTRE

The Pinnacle Restaurant

Fallsview Rooms

Fallsview Dining

RAMADA

Overlooking Falls
Canopy beds and
Jacuzzi whirlpools
Mini-fridges and
microwave ovens
Walk to Fallsview Casino,
Falls, parks, attractions...
Dining 500' above Falls
Ask about our packages

RAMADA
PLAZA HOTEL
Fallsview
1-866-FALLSVIEW

Ramada Plaza
Hotel Fallsview
6732 Fallsview Blvd.
Niagara Falls, ON
Canada L2G 3W6
www.niagaratower.com
Fax: 905-356-8245
Phone: 905-356-1501 or
Toll Free 1-866-325-5784

RED CARPET INN AND SUITES, FALLSWAY   *Book at aaa.com*   Phone: (905)374-7666   **27**
(CAA) (SAVE)   5/1-10/31 & 4/15-4/30   1P: $49-$199   2P: $49-$199   XP: $10   F10
▼▼▼ ▼▼▼   **Location:** Just s of Hwy 420 and Stanley Ave, just e. Located in a residential area. 5334 Kitchener St L2G 1B5.
Fax: 905/358-8221. **Facility:** 100 one-bedroom standard units, some with whirlpools. 2 stories (no elevator),
interior/exterior corridors. **Parking:** on-site. **Terms:** open 5/1-10/31 & 4/15-4/30, 7 day cancellation notice-
Motel   fee imposed. **Pool(s):** outdoor. **Leisure Activities:** saunas. **Guest Services:** coin laundry. **Business
Services:** fax (fee). **Cards:** AX, MC, VI. **Special Amenities:** free local telephone calls and early check-
in/late check-out. *(See color ad below)*   SOME UNITS

（SD）（☎）／（Ⓩ）（⊟）／
                                                                                                          FEE

RENAISSANCE FALLSVIEW HOTEL   *Book at aaa.com*   Phone: (905)357-5200   **2**
(CAA) (SAVE)   7/1-10/15   1P: $179-$499   2P: $179-$499   XP: $10   F18
▼▼▼ ▼▼▼ ▼▼▼ ▼▼▼   5/1-6/30   1P: $119-$299   2P: $119-$299   XP: $10   F18
                    10/16-12/31   1P: $109-$299   2P: $109-$299   XP: $10   F18
                    1/1-4/30   1P: $99-$259   2P: $99-$259   XP: $10   F18
Large-scale Hotel **Location:** Corner of Fallsview Blvd and Dixon Ave; just n of Konica Minolta Tower; directly across from Niagara
Fallsview Casino. 6455 Fallsview Blvd L2G 3V9. Fax: 905/357-3422. **Facility:** This centrally located hotel with
distinctive contemporary decor throughout guest rooms and public areas is convenient to the area's attractions. 262 one-
bedroom standard units, some with whirlpools. 18 stories, interior corridors. **Parking:** on-site (fee) and valet. **Terms:** check-in 4
pm, 3 day cancellation notice-fee imposed. **Amenities:** video games (fee), high-speed Internet, dual phone lines, voice mail,
irons, hair dryers. **Dining:** 6:30 am-midnight, cocktails, also, Rooftop Fallsview Dining Room, see separate listing. **Pool(s):**
heated indoor. **Leisure Activities:** saunas, whirlpool. **Fee:** racquetball court, squash court, massage. **Guest Services:** gift
shop, valet laundry. **Business Services:** conference facilities, business center. **Cards:** AX, CB, DC, DS, JC, MC, VI.
(See color ad p 359 & ad starting on p 118)   SOME UNITS

（⊩⊪）（▼）（ⓕ）（☎）（☒）（📹）（DATA PORT）（⊟）／（✕）（⊟）／
                                                                                                          FEE

RODEWAY INN & SUITES   Phone: (905)358-9833   **67**
▼▼▼ ▼▼▼   All Year [CP]   1P: $49-$189   2P: $49-$189   XP: $10   F16
Small-scale Hotel   **Location:** QEW, exit Hwy 20, 4 km w. 7720 Lundy's Ln L2H 1H1. Fax: 905/358-3090. **Facility:** 90 one-bedroom
standard units, some with whirlpools. 2-3 stories, interior/exterior corridors. **Parking:** on-site.
Terms: cancellation fee imposed, package plans. **Pool(s):** outdoor, heated indoor. **Leisure
Activities:** whirlpool. **Guest Services:** area transportation (fee). **Business Services:** fax (fee). **Cards:** AX, DC, DS, MC, VI.
                                                                                                     SOME UNITS

（ASK）（SD）（⊩⊪）（☎）（DATA PORT）（⊟）／（✕）／

RED CARPET INN.® & SUITES

5334 KITCHENER ST. NIAGARA FALLS, ONT. CANADA. L2G -1B5.

HOTEL DIRECT:(905) 374-7666 **FAX:**(905)358-8221

GROUP TOURS HOTLINE: (905) 374-8888

TOLL-FREE:(800)251-1962 OR (800)874-7798

ASK FOR PROPERTY CODE: "HRONNI"

www.RedCarpetInnandSuites.com   sales@RedCarpetInnandSuites.com

ON LINE RESERVATIONS: *www.RedCarpetInnandSuites.com*

EMBASSY SUITES HOTEL ®

NIAGARA FALLS – FALLSVIEW
6700 Fallsview Blvd., Niagara Falls, ON L2G 3W6
Phone: 905-356-3600

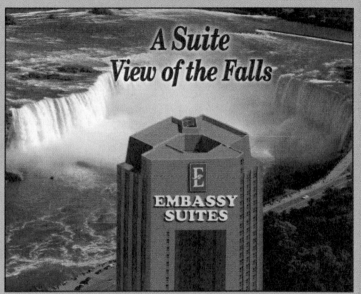

A Suite View of the Falls

EMBASSY SUITES

NIAGARA'S NEWEST ALL-SUITE FALLSVIEW HOTEL

- Closest Hotel to the Falls • View Falls from your Suite
- 42 Storeys – 512 Suites Overlooking Niagara Falls
- Complimentary Cooked-to-Order Breakfast
- Complimentary Evening Manager's Reception
- Located beside Niagara Fallsview Casino
- Indoor Pool, Whirlpool and Fitness Centre
- Fallsview Dining at The Keg® Steakhouse and Bar
- T.G.I. Friday's® Restaurant • Starbucks®
- Casinos and Attractions Shuttle • Games Room
- Awarded AAA Four Diamond Award
- See Falls Illuminations & Falls Fireworks from your Suite (Call for schedule)
- 2-Night Getaway Packages Available

RESERVATIONS: 1-888-688-8288
www.embassysuitesfallsview.com

See Niagara Falls from your Suite

EVERY ROOM INCLUDES:
- Each Room is a Spacious 2-Room Suite
- Complimentary Cooked-to-Order Breakfast
- Complimentary Evening Manager's Reception

WHIRLPOOL, FIREPLACE & PRESIDENTIAL SUITES AVAILABLE

2-Room Fallsview Suite
with spectacular
views

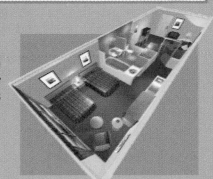

 EMBASSY SUITES HOTEL®

NIAGARA FALLS – FALLSVIEW

RESERVATIONS: **1-888-688-8288**
www.embassysuitesfallsview.com

UNIQUELY RENAISSANCE™

EARN **Marriott** REWARDS.

- Creating Experiences from $99
- Spectacular Fallsview Guestrooms and Dining
- 500 yards to Falls
- Jacuzzi Suites & Family Suites
- Whirlpool & Saunas
- Fitness Center
- Spa Services
- Niagara Fallsview Casino attached to Hotel

RENAISSANCE®
FALLSVIEW HOTEL
NIAGARA FALLS

6455 Fallsview Blvd., Niagara Falls, ON, Canada L2G 3V9 • 905-357-5200

1-800-363-3255 www.renaissancefallsview.com

RODEWAY INN FALLSVIEW *Book at aaa.com* Phone: (905)354-2322

CAA SAVE
▼▼▼▼

7/1-9/4	1P: $89-$259	2P: $89-$259	XP: $10 F17
5/1-6/30 & 9/5-4/30	1P: $59-$179	2P: $59-$179	XP: $10 F17

Location: Jct Dunn St. 6663 Stanley Ave L2G 3Y9. Fax: 905/354-4955. **Facility:** 61 one-bedroom standard units, some with whirlpools. 2-3 stories (no elevator), interior/exterior corridors. **Parking:** on-site. **Small-scale Hotel** **Terms:** cancellation fee imposed, package plans. **Amenities:** voice mail, irons, hair dryers. **Dining:** 2 restaurants, 7 am-midnight, cocktails. **Pool(s):** heated outdoor. **Leisure Activities:** playground. **Guest Services:** gift shop. **Business Services:** meeting rooms. **Cards:** AX, DC, DS, MC, VI. **Special Amenities:** free local telephone calls and free newspaper. *(See color ad below & ad starting on p 118)*

SOME UNITS

 / FEE

Rodeway Inn Fallsview

6663 Stanley Avenue, Niagara Falls, Canada L2G 3Y9
Formerly Quality Inn Fallsview

(905) 354-2322 * 1-866 633-4526

* Jacuzzi & Fireplace Suites * King & Queen Beds
* Coffee Makers * Hair Dryers * Irons/Ironing Boards
* Heated Outdoor Pool * Children's Playground
* Satellite T.V. * Air conditioned * Restaurant

www.rodewayinnfallsview.com

Park Free - Walk to the Falls,
Casino and Major Attractions

RODEWAY INN
BY CHOICE HOTELS
▼ ▼ ▼

A reliable technician
is around the corner!

Put your vehicle's care and maintenance in the capable hands of a certified CAA/AAA Approved Auto Repair technician. Whether you're at home or on a cross-country road trip, a CAA/AAA Approved Auto Repair facility is right around the corner. Look for the CAA/AAA sign or visit www.aaa.com to find convenient, dependable service and repair.

**Approved
Auto Repair
Services**

SHERATON FALLSVIEW HOTEL & CONFERENCE CENTRE *Book at aaa.com* (CAA) (SAVE)

Phone: (905)374-1077 **37**

7/1-9/4	1P: $149-$429	2P: $149-$429	XP: $20	F18
5/1-6/30 & 9/5-10/29	1P: $119-$389	2P: $119-$389	XP: $20	F18
10/30-4/30	1P: $99-$299	2P: $99-$299	XP: $20	F18

Location: Near Konica Minolta Tower. 6755 Fallsview Blvd L2G 3W7. Fax: 905/374-6224. **Facility:** Guest rooms in **Large-scale Hotel** this high-rise have modern, well-appointed decor; many offer very good views of the falls. 402 units. 376 one- and 8 two-bedroom standard units, some with whirlpools. 18 one-bedroom suites ($289-$999) with whirlpools. 32 stories, interior corridors. **Parking:** on-site (fee) and valet. **Terms:** cancellation fee imposed, [AP] & [BP] meal plans available, package plans, small pets only (with prior approval). **Amenities:** video games, high-speed Internet (fee), dual phone lines, voice mail, irons, hair dryers. *Some:* safes. **Dining:** 7 am-1 am, also, Fallsview Dining Room, see separate listing. **Pool(s):** heated indoor. **Leisure Activities:** sauna, whirlpool, exercise room. **Guest Services:** gift shop, valet laundry, area transportation-casino. **Business Services:** conference facilities, business center. **Cards:** AX, DC, DS, MC, VI. **Special Amenities:** free newspaper. *(See color ad below, p 5, ad starting on p 118 & card insert)*

SOME UNITS

(S) 🛏 🍽 🍸 🔥 &M 🏊 ✂ 📷 DATA PORT 💻 / ✕ VCR 🔲 📷 /

FEE

- 300 yards from the brink of the Falls
- 402 luxurious guestrooms & suites
- Award winning Fallsview Dining Room, Bistro & Cafe and Pub & Grill
- On-site Parking, indoor pool, whirlpool, sauna & fitness centre
- Minutes from Casinos, Marineland, Niagara Parks, IMAX Theatre, Aviary, Theatres, Wineries, Golf, Shopping & more!
- Awarded the the 2003 & 2004 CNN Ultimate Service Award for all of North America & CAA/AAA 4-Diamond rating for 13 consecutive years

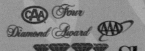

(CAA) *Four Diamond Award* (AAA)

Sheraton Fallsview
HOTEL & CONFERENCE CENTRE

Ask about our Kid's Eat Free Program*
*Some restrictions apply

6755 Fallsview Blvd., Niagara Falls, Ontario, Canada
1.877.353.2557   www.fallsview.com

SHERATON ON THE FALLS <u>*Book at aaa.com*</u>

(CAA) (SAVE)

6/1-10/31	1P: $169-$999	XP: $10	F18
5/1-5/31	1P: $129-$999	XP: $10	F18
11/1-4/30	1P: $99-$999	XP: $10	F18

Phone: (905)374-4445 26

Location: Entrance to Rainbow Bridge on Hwy 20. 5875 Falls Ave L2E 6W7. Fax: 905/371-0157. **Facility:** This **Large-scale Hotel** large hotel offers a hard-to-beat location; adjacent to a casino and directly across the street from the falls. Many units offer stunning views. 670 units. 659 one-bedroom standard units, some with whirlpools. 11 one-bedroom suites with whirlpools. 24 stories, interior corridors. **Parking:** on-site (fee) and valet. **Terms:** cancellation fee imposed, package plans, small pets only. **Amenities:** dual phone lines, voice mail, irons, hair dryers. *Fee:* video games, high-speed Internet. *Some:* CD players. **Dining:** 6 am-midnight, cocktails, also, Penthouse Restaurant, see separate listing. **Pool(s):** heated outdoor, heated indoor. **Leisure Activities:** spa. *Fee:* exercise room. **Guest Services:** gift shop, valet laundry. **Business Services:** conference facilities, business center. **Cards:** AX, CB, DC, DS, MC, VI.
(See color ad starting on p 326, below, p 5 & card insert)

SOME UNITS

(S D) (🐕) (🍴) (🍸) (🏊) (🎥) (DATA PORT) (🛏) / (🗙) (🔌) / FEE

Best Fallsview Guaranteed!

FALLS AVENUE

Sheraton

KIDS stay&eat **FREE**

(CAA) (AAA)
Show Your Card
Approved Lodging

- Directly in front of the Falls
- Penthouse Fallsview Restaurant
- Spa & Fitness Centre/Two Pools
- Fallsview Rooms - Fireplace/Balconies
- Marvel Comics Adventure City Rides & Games
- Connected to Casino Niagara

1-888-229-9962

NiagaraFallsHotels.com

(CAA) *Four Diamond Award* (AAA)

Sheraton on the Falls
H O T E L

SKYLINE INN **_Book at aaa.com_**

				Phone: (905)374-4444	**71**
6/1-10/31		1P: $99-$349	2P: $99-$349	XP: $10	F16
5/1-5/31		1P: $79-$329	2P: $79-$329	XP: $10	F16
11/1-4/30		1P: $59-$299	2P: $59-$299	XP: $10	F16

Location: At end of Rainbow Bridge. 4800 Bender Hill L2E 6W7. Fax: 905/374-0800. **Facility:** 206 one-bedroom
Small-scale Hotel standard units. 3 stories, interior/exterior corridors. **Parking:** on-site (fee). **Terms:** cancellation fee imposed,
package plans. **Amenities:** video games (fee), voice mail. **Dining:** 7 am-midnight; to 9 pm 12/1-3/31.
Leisure Activities: shared recreational facilities with Brock Plaza Hotel. **Guest Services:** gift shop, valet laundry. **Business
Services:** fax (fee). **Cards:** AX, DC, DS, MC, VI. *(See color ad starting on p 326 & below)*

SOME UNITS

One Block to Falls

The Falls' premier family hotel!

- Swimming pool and waterslide

- One block to Falls, family attractions, Hershey Store, Rainforest Cafe & more

- Large family suites & courtyard guest rooms available

- Perkins Family Restaurant & Bakery

KIDS stay & eat FREE

FALLS AVENUE

Perkins RESTAURANT & BAKERY

SKYLINE INN

Skyline Inn

1-800-263-7135

NiagaraFallsHotels.com

STANLEY MOTOR INN

2 blocks to the Falls, Skylon & Minolta Observation Towers.

Heart-Shaped Jacuzzi • Air-conditioned rooms • Color Cable TV • Outdoor Pool

• 1 Block to Casino • 1 Block from the Falls

(905) 358-9238 • Fax (905) 358-2840

6220 Stanley Avenue, Niagara Falls, Ontario, Canada

STANLEY MOTOR INN
Phone: (905)358-9238 ⓸⓶

CAA SAVE

▼▼▼ ▼▼▼

Motel

6/25-9/25	1P: $70-$120	2P: $90-$150	XP: $10	F12
5/1-6/24	1P: $60-$70	2P: $70-$85	XP: $10	F12
9/26-4/30	1P: $50-$60	2P: $60-$70	XP: $10	F12

Location: 2 blks from the falls; w of Skylon Tower. 6220 Stanley Ave L2G 3Y4. Fax: 905/358-2840. **Facility:** 49 one-bedroom standard units, some with whirlpools. 2 stories (no elevator), interior/exterior corridors. *Bath:* combo or shower only. **Parking:** on-site. **Terms:** office hours 7 am-midnight, pets ($10 extra charge). **Pool(s):** outdoor. **Guest Services:** coin laundry. **Cards:** AX, DC, DS, MC, VI. **Special Amenities:** free local telephone calls and preferred room (subject to availability with advance reservations). *(See color ad p 363 & ad starting on p 118)*

SOME UNITS

FEE   FEE

SUNSET INN
Phone: (905)354-7513 ⓶⓽

CAA SAVE

▼▼▼ ▼▼▼

Motel

6/23-9/1	1P: $79-$199	2P: $79-$199	XP: $10	F12
5/1-6/22 & 9/2-9/30	1P: $49-$149	2P: $49-$149	XP: $10	F12
10/1-4/30	1P: $49-$99	2P: $49-$99	XP: $10	F12

Location: 1.2 km w on Hwy 20, just n; s of Hwy 420. 5803 Stanley Ave L2G 3X8. Fax: 905/354-4766. **Facility:** 32 one-bedroom standard units, some with whirlpools. 2 stories (no elevator), exterior corridors. **Parking:** on-site, winter plug-ins. **Terms:** office hours 8 am-midnight, cancellation fee imposed. **Pool(s):** heated outdoor. **Cards:** AX, DC, DS, MC, VI. *(See color ad below)*

SOME UNITS

FEE

Comfortable, clean, affordable accommodations…minutes from the falls & Casinos

Sunset Inn 5803 Stanley Ave.
Toll Free: 1-877-354-7513 • Tel: (905) 354-7513
www.sunsetinnniagara.com
• Free Movies/Cable TV • Outdoor Heated Pool
• Phones • Jacuzzi

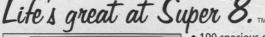

Camelot Inn 5640 Stanley Ave.
Toll Free: 1-888-354-3754 • Tel: (905) 354-3754
www.NiagaraCamelotInn.com
• Large Outdoor Pool with Jacuzzi • Remote CableTV
• 1 Block to Casino Shuttle • Picnic Patio with BBQs
• Free Internet Service

Kids stay free • Honeymoon Suites • Family Units • Scenic Tours

Life's great at Super 8. ™

KIDS STAY & EAT FREE Call for details

The Pride of Super 8

• 190 spacious guestrooms and suites
• Jacuzzi, fireplace and 2-room family suites
• Indoor and outdoor pools, sauna, whirlpool, fitness room, guest laundry • Free parking
• 10% discount at Pancakes Plus-House of Pancakes on site, serving breakfast and lunch
• Games room, gift shop, lounge
• Falls/Casino shuttle available
• AAA and Senior discount
• In-room movies and Playstation video game system
• In-room coffee maker, hair dryer, iron and ironing board

▼▼▼ ▼▼▼ ▼▼▼

5706 Ferry St.
Niagara Falls
Ontario
905-356-0052

SUPER 8 HOTEL ®

Enquire about our Attraction Packages

1-888-442-6095 • www.niagarafallssuper8.com

SUPER 8 HOTEL   *Book at aaa.com*   Phone: (905)356-0052   **79**

(CAA) (SAVE)   All Year   1P: $59-$289   2P: $59-$289   XP: $5   F12

Location: On Hwy 20, 1.5 km from the falls. 5706 Ferry St L2G 1S7. Fax: 905/356-7760. **Facility:** 190 units. 181 one-bedroom standard units, some with whirlpools. 9 one-bedroom suites ($99-$439). 7 stories, interior corridors. **Parking:** on-site, winter plug-ins. **Terms:** [BP] meal plan available, package plans. Small-scale Hotel **Amenities:** video games (fee), voice mail, hair dryers. *Some:* irons. **Dining:** 6 am-3 pm, cocktails. **Pool(s):** heated outdoor, heated indoor. **Leisure Activities:** sauna, whirlpool, exercise room. *Fee:* game room. **Guest Services:** gift shop, coin laundry, area transportation (fee)-casino. **Business Services:** meeting rooms. **Cards:** AX, CB, DC, DS, JC, MC, VI. **Special Amenities:** free local telephone calls. *(See color ad p 364)*

SOME UNITS

FEE

SURFSIDE INN   Phone: (905)295-4354   **74**

(CAA) (SAVE)   6/19-8/31   1P: $69-$229   2P: $69-$229   XP: $15   F

5/1-6/18   1P: $59-$189   2P: $59-$189   XP: $15   F

9/1-4/30   1P: $55-$139   2P: $55-$139   XP: $10   F

Location: 3.5 km s of Horseshoe Falls on Niagara River Pkwy. Located in a quiet area. 3665 Macklem St L2G 6C8. Motel   Fax: 905/295-4374. **Facility:** 31 one-bedroom standard units, some with efficiencies and/or whirlpools. 1 story, exterior corridors. **Parking:** on-site. **Terms:** office hours 7 am-11 pm, cancellation fee imposed, package plans. **Amenities:** hair dryers. **Pool(s):** heated outdoor. **Leisure Activities:** barbecue. **Cards:** AX, CB, DC, DS, JC, MC, VI. **Special Amenities:** free local telephone calls and early check-in/late check-out. *(See color ad below)*

SOME UNITS

THRIFTLODGE CLIFTON HILL   *Book at aaa.com*   Phone: (905)357-4330   **70**

(CAA) (SAVE)   6/16-9/5   1P: $89-$299   2P: $89-$299   XP: $10   F18

9/6-10/15   1P: $79-$299   2P: $79-$299   XP: $10   F18

5/1-6/15   1P: $69-$299   2P: $69-$299   XP: $10   F18

10/16-4/30   1P: $59-$299   2P: $59-$299   XP: $10   F18

Motel   **Location:** Just s on jct Victoria Ave. 4945 Clifton Hill L2G 3N5. Fax: 905/357-2223. **Facility:** 38 one-bedroom standard units. 2 stories (no elevator), exterior corridors. **Parking:** on-site. **Terms:** package plans. **Leisure Activities:** pool privileges. **Guest Services:** coin laundry. **Cards:** AX, MC, VI. **Special Amenities:** free local telephone calls and free newspaper.

SOME UNITS

Surfside Inn

RESERVATIONS
1-800-263-0713
Other **905-295-4354**

When you have only one holiday a year it should be the very best!

Award winning family operated one story 32 unit motel is located 1-1/2 miles south of the "Horseshoe Falls" on the Niagara River Parkway. The setting, acres of mature trees, flowers, sculptured lawns, and water. A 32 mile long recreation trail for hiking or biking passes our property. **Leave your car at motel & shuttle to the falls, casino & other attractions.** Close to Marineland and the "Falls" but far enough from the noise, crowds and commotion that at the end of the day you can retreat to the peace, quiet and beauty offered by the Surfside Inn. A relaxing dip in our **pool from sundeck** overlooking the river will make your day.

Internet Address: http://www.surfsideniagara.com
Email: surfsideniagara@falls.net

GUARANTEED LOW HOTEL RATES

NiagaraFallsHotels.com

EVERY VISITOR WINS!   GRAND PRIZE Free Falls Vacation

TRAVELODGE BONAVENTURE   *Book at aaa.com*   Phone: (905)374-7171   62
(CAA) (SAVE) 6/24-8/27   1P: $79-$189   2P: $89-$199   XP: $10   F17
◆◆◆   5/1-6/23 & 8/28-10/8   1P: $59-$129   2P: $64-$149   XP: $10   F17
◆◆◆◆   10/9-4/30   1P: $54-$99   2P: $59-$119   XP: $10   F17
Location: QEW, exit Hwy 20, 4.5 km w. 7737 Lundy's Ln L2H 1H3. Fax: 905/374-1151. **Facility:** 118 one-bedroom
Small-scale Hotel standard units, some with whirlpools. 3 stories, interior/exterior corridors. **Parking:** on-site, winter plug-ins.
Terms: package plans. **Amenities:** video games, voice mail, hair dryers. **Dining:** 7:30-11:30 am; closed
weekdays off season. **Pool(s):** heated outdoor, heated indoor. **Leisure Activities:** sauna, whirlpool, limited exercise equipment.
Guest Services: area transportation (fee)-casino & falls. **Business Services:** meeting rooms. **Cards:** AX, CB, DC, DS, MC, VI.
Special Amenities: free local telephone calls and free newspaper. *(See color ad below)*   SOME UNITS

[S/D] [☎] [🏊] [⊗] [🐕] [DATA PORT] [☕] / [⊗] [VCR] [🔒] /

TRAVELODGE CLIFTON HILL   *Book at aaa.com*   Phone: (905)357-4330   36
(CAA) (SAVE) 5/1-6/15 [CP]   1P: $89-$329   2P: $89-$329   XP: $10   F18
◆◆◆   10/16-4/30 [CP]   1P: $79-$329   2P: $79-$329   XP: $10   F18
◆◆◆◆   6/16-9/5 [CP]   1P: $129-$299   2P: $129-$299   XP: $10   F18
         9/6-10/15 [CP]   1P: $99-$299   2P: $99-$299   XP: $10   F18
Small-scale Hotel **Location:** Just s of jct Victoria Ave. 4943 Clifton Hill L2G 3N5. Fax: 905/357-2223. **Facility:** 68 units. 67 one- and
1 two-bedroom standard units, some with kitchens and/or whirlpools. 2 stories (no elevator), interior/exterior
corridors. **Parking:** on-site. **Terms:** package plans. **Amenities:** voice mail, irons, hair dryers. **Dining:** 11 am-1 am, cocktails.
Pool(s): heated outdoor. **Business Services:** meeting rooms. **Cards:** AX, MC, VI. **Special Amenities:** free continental
breakfast and free local telephone calls. *(See color ad p 367)*   SOME UNITS

[S/D] [☎] [🍴] [🏊] [DATA PORT] [☕] / [⊗] [VCR] [🔒] [🛒] /

Travelodge Bonaventure

Large, Heated Indoor & Outdoor Pools

- 118 spacious rooms • Cable TV
- In-room movies • Nintendo
- Whirlpool hot tub • Sauna
- Hair dryers • Free local calls
- In-room coffee • Restaurant
- Two-night packages available
- Walk to Outlet Mall • Sightseeing tours
- **Falls/Casino shuttle**

Honeymoon Suites with Heart Shaped Whirlpool Tubs

(CAA) ◆◆◆ (AAA)

10% AAA/CAA DISCOUNT *on standard rooms excl. holidays*

Web Site: www.niagaratravelodge.com
Tel.: (905) 374-7171 Fax: (905) 374-1151
Call Toll Free: **1-800-578-7878** and ask for
Travelodge Bonaventure Property #9780

7737 Lundy's Lane, Niagara Falls, Ontario, Canada L2H 1H3

At the Falls
beside Casino Niagara

- Closest motel to the Falls
- Beside Casino Niagara on Clifton Hill - *Fun by the Falls*
- KIDS STAY FREE • Free breakfasts
- Free in-room coffee & local calls
- Free parking • Currency exchange
- Restaurants & attractions on site
- Walk to the Casino, falls, parks & major attractions • Great packages

Travelodge Clifton Hill, 4943 Clifton Hill
Niagara Falls, Ontario, Canada L3G 3N5
travelodge@falls.com Fax 905-357-2223

RUBY TUESDAY
Awesome Food. Serious Salad Bar.

1-866-656-0307
www.falls.com

TRAVELODGE NEAR THE FALLS   *Book at aaa.com*   Phone: (905)374-7771   **9**

CAA SAVE

6/16-8/31	1P: $89-$399	2P: $89-$399
5/1-6/15	1P: $59-$269	2P: $59-$269
9/1-12/31	1P: $79-$249	2P: $79-$249
1/1-4/30	1P: $59-$229	2P: $59-$229

Small-scale Hotel Location: Jct Victoria Ave. 5234 Ferry St L2G 1R5. Fax: 905/374-1996. **Facility:** 87 one-bedroom standard units, some with whirlpools. 2-4 stories, interior/exterior corridors. *Bath:* combo or shower only. **Parking:** on-site (fee). **Terms:** [BP] meal plan available, package plans, 3% service charge. **Amenities:** hair dryers. **Dining:** 7 am-2 pm; 8 am-12:30 pm 10/1-6/30. **Pool(s):** heated indoor. **Leisure Activities:** sauna, whirlpool. **Cards:** AX, DC, MC, VI. **Special Amenities:** free local telephone calls and free newspaper. *(See color ad below)*

SOME UNITS

VACATION INN   Phone: (905)356-1722   **34**

CAA SAVE

6/30-8/20	1P: $99-$275	2P: $99-$275	XP: $10 F10
5/1-6/29, 8/21-12/29 & 4/1-4/30	1P: $79-$225	2P: $79-$225	XP: $10 F10

Location: Corner of Dixon Ave; 2 blks from Konica Minolta Tower. 6519 Stanley Ave L2G 7L2. Fax: 905/356-0392. **Facility:** 95 one-bedroom standard units, some with whirlpools. 3 stories (no elevator), interior corridors. **Small-scale Hotel** **Parking:** on-site. **Terms:** open 5/1-12/29 & 4/1-4/30, 2 night minimum stay - weekends, cancellation fee imposed, package plans. **Dining:** 7:30 am-11:30 & 4:30-8:30 pm, cocktails. **Pool(s):** heated outdoor. **Business Services:** fax (fee). **Cards:** AX, DS, MC, VI. *(See color ad p 369)*

SOME UNITS

VICTORIAN CHARM BED AND BREAKFAST   Phone: (905)357-4221   **80**

5/1-10/31 [BP]	1P: $100	2P: $150-$185	XP: $25 D10
11/1-4/30 [BP]	1P: $80	2P: $120-$140	XP: $25 D10

Bed & Breakfast Location: Between Main St and Drummond. 6028 Culp St L2G 2B7. Fax: 905/357-9115. **Facility:** Smoke free premises. 4 one-bedroom standard units, some with whirlpools. 2 stories (no elevator), interior corridors. **Parking:** on-site. **Terms:** office hours 7 am-11 pm, 2 night minimum stay - weekends, 7 day cancellation notice-fee imposed, weekly rates available, package plans. **Amenities:** video library, high-speed Internet, hair dryers. **Cards:** AX, DC, MC, VI.

SOME UNITS

VILLAGER LODGE   Phone: (905)354-3162   **66**

CAA SAVE

6/30-9/5	1P: $69-$209	2P: $69-$209	XP: $5 F12
5/1-6/29	1P: $49-$139	2P: $49-$139	XP: $5 F12
9/6-4/30	1P: $39-$129	2P: $39-$129	XP: $5 F12

Motel Location: QEW, exit Hwy 20, 5 km w. 8054 Lundy's Ln L2H 1H1. Fax: 905/354-8422. **Facility:** 32 one-bedroom standard units, some with efficiencies and/or whirlpools. 2 stories, exterior corridors. **Parking:** on-site, winter plug-ins. **Terms:** cancellation fee imposed, weekly rates available, package plans. **Amenities:** voice mail. **Pool(s):** heated outdoor. **Leisure Activities:** barbecue grills, playground. **Guest Services:** area transportation (fee)-casino. **Cards:** AX, CB, DC, DS, MC, VI. **Special Amenities:** free local telephone calls and free newspaper.

SOME UNITS

Travelodge.

NEAR THE FALLS

5234 FERRY STREET,
NIAGARA FALLS, ONTARIO L2G 1R5
(905) 374-7771

10% OFF
PUBLISHED RATES
FOR CAA MEMBERS
FOR ALL ROOM TYPES

HOTEL RESERVATIONS
1-800-440-9555

FEATURES OF THE TRAVELODGE
◆ Spacious Rooms ◆ Jacuzzi Suites ◆ Whirlpool
◆ Indoor Heated Pool ◆ Walking Distance to Casino
◆ Sauna ◆ In-Room Telephones
◆ Fax Service Available ◆ Satellite Movies
◆ Complimentary Coffee in Lobby ◆ Parking Fee

VACATION INN • NIAGARA FALLS • CANADA

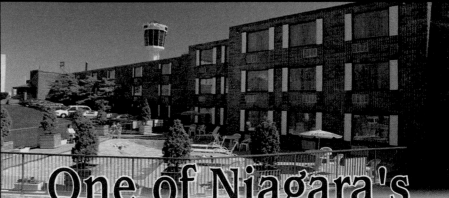

One of Niagara's Premier Locations
Just Walk to the Falls & New Casino Opposite Us

WALK TO:
FALLS • Maid of the Mist Boat Tours • MARINELAND
Scenic Tunnels (walk under the falls) • SKYLON TOWER
Niagara Parks Floral Displays • IMAX THEATER
Festival of Lights Displays • FALLSVIEW CASINO Opposite Us

WITHIN MINUTES OF:
- Shopping Malls
- Factory Outlet Malls
- Butterfly Conservatory
- Bird Aviary
- Winery Tours
- Golf Courses

UPGRADE TO A ROMANTIC JACUZZI SUITE

- 95 Attractive Rooms
- Air Conditioning
- Heated Outdoor Pool
- 25" Cable T.V. • Telephones
- 200 Seat Restaurant
- Daily Sightseeing Tours Available
- Free Parking

SPRING/FALL WEEKDAY PACKAGES
April 01 to June 29 and August 22 to December 29
INCLUDES: (for 2 persons)
- Room for 2 Nights
- American Breakfast 2 Mornings
- Lovely dinner one evening
- Free Parking

from $**149**.95*
U.S. per couple
* Price guaranteed when paid in
U.S. Currency or U.S. Traveller's Cheques

Vacation Inn
Toll-Free Reservations 1-800-263-2561
6519 Stanley Avenue, Niagara Falls Ontario, Canada L2G 7L2
Hotel Direct (905) 356-1722 • Fax (905) 356-0392

www.vacationniagara.com

——— WHERE TO DINE ———

17 NOIR

🔻🔻🔻

Continental

Dinner: $20-$50   **Phone:** 905/374-6928   ㊱
Location: Jct Murray St; in Niagara Fallsview Casino Resort. 6380 Fallsview Blvd L2G 7X5. **Hours:** 6 pm-midnight. **Reservations:** suggested. **Features:** This dining room features an upscale contemporary decor that is sure to please, in addition to a fine regional and Continental menu. The chef uses fresh seasonal ingredients in the traditional yet innovative menu and can be viewed creating each course in the open-concept kitchen. Large panoramic windows offer a great view, as does the seasonal outdoor patio. Dressy casual; cocktails. **Parking:** on-site (fee). **Cards:** AX, MC, VI.   🍸

THE BEEF BARON

Ⓒ🅰🅰

🔻🔻🔻

Steak House

Dinner: $11-$35   **Phone:** 905/356-6110   ⑦
Location: At top of Clifton Hill. 5019 Centre St L2G 3N5. **Hours:** 4 pm-11 pm, Sat & Sun from 3 pm; to 9 pm, Sat & Sun 3 pm-10 pm in winter. Closed: 12/24, 12/25. **Reservations:** suggested, in season. **Features:** Hungry? Really hungry? Order Baron's 26 oz. porterhouse. Prime rib and seafood are two more house favorites. Three dining rooms, trimmed in cherry wood, brass and Italian prints, mix well in the bustling summer atmosphere and quieter ambience of winter. Casual dress; cocktails. **Parking:** on-site (fee). **Cards:** AX, CB, DC, DS, JC, MC, VI.   ✕

BETTY'S RESTAURANT

🔻

Seafood

Lunch: $5-$10   **Dinner:** $9-$15   **Phone:** 905/295-4436   ㉕
Location: Niagara River Pkwy S to Main St, just w; in Chippawa District. 8921 Sodom Rd L2E 6S6. **Hours:** 8 am-9 pm. Closed: 12/25, 12/26. **Features:** Betty's pleasantly appointed, spacious dining room highlights the good-value home cooking served here. Seafood and fish are what they do best, but many other tasty dishes are offered. The fish and chips keeps regular patrons coming back for more. Casual dress; cocktails. **Parking:** on-site. **Cards:** AX, MC, VI.   ✕

BRANDINO'S ITALIAN RISTORANTE AND CAFE

🔻🔻🔻

Italian

     Lunch: $9-$15   **Dinner:** $16-$55   **Phone:** 905/354-8561   ㉜
Location: Just e of jct Ferry St. 5930 Victoria Ave L2G 3L7. **Hours:** noon-11 pm. Closed: 12/24, 12/25. **Reservations:** suggested. **Features:** Diners enjoy a comfortable yet upscale bistro atmosphere and a varied menu of fine Italian and Continental cuisine. Highlights include fresh, tasty pasta, steaks and seafood, as well as rib and chicken specialties. Service is warm and personable. Casual dress; cocktails. **Parking:** street. **Cards:** AX, DC, MC, VI.   ✕

BUCHANANS

🔻🔻

Continental

     Lunch: $12-$18   **Dinner:** $19-$34   **Phone:** 905/353-4111   ㉛
Location: Just w via Murray St, n on Fallsview Blvd; adjacent to Skylon Tower; in Doubletree Resort Lodge & Spa Fallsview. 6039 Fallsview Blvd L2G 3V6. **Hours:** 7 am-9:30 pm. **Features:** On the second level of the hotel, the dining room features a fine menu selection in a warm and cozy setting. Diners enjoy traditional favorites, such as fresh salads, homemade soups or baked brie to start, followed by a nice selection of grilled beef, chicken, seafood or pasta offerings. The service is warm and personable. Casual dress; cocktails. **Parking:** on-site. **Cards:** AX, DC, DS, JC, MC, VI.   🍸 ✕

CAPRI RESTAURANT

Ⓒ🅰🅰

🔻🔻🔻

Italian

     Lunch: $6-$14   **Dinner:** $10-$35   **Phone:** 905/354-7519   ⑳
Location: Hwy 20, 1 km from the falls. 5438 Ferry St L2G 1S1. **Hours:** 11 am-11 pm, Sat & Sun from 4 pm. Closed: 12/24-12/26; also Sun 1/1-3/31. **Reservations:** accepted. **Features:** The dining room offers an elegant, yet relaxed atmosphere for special occasion or family dining. The menu emphasizes Southern Italian cuisine and features a wide selection of homemade pasta as well as a full array of steak, seafood and poultry selections. Casual dress; cocktails. **Parking:** on-site. **Cards:** AX, CB, DC, JC, MC, VI.
(See color ad below)   🍸 ✕

CARPACCIO RESTAURANT AND WINE BAR

Ⓒ🅰🅰

🔻🔻🔻

Mediterranean

     Lunch: $7-$15   **Dinner:** $9-$30   **Phone:** 905/371-2063   ⑬
Location: Jct Dorchester Rd. 6840 Lundy's Ln L2G 1V6. **Hours:** 11:30 am-11 pm, Sat & Sun from 4 pm. Closed: 12/25. **Reservations:** suggested. **Features:** In the busy Lundy's Lane area, the popular eatery is a local favorite. Diners can enjoy patio seating in season or dine in the large, contemporary dining room. The chef prepares a fine mix of Mediterranean and Italian fare, which pairs with choices from the exceptional wine list. Offerings include gourmet pizzas, fresh pasta dishes, outstanding rack of lamb and preparations of veal, chicken and beef. Fresh, tasty desserts are well worth the calories. Casual dress; cocktails. **Parking:** on-site. **Cards:** AX, MC, VI.   🍸 ✕

the **CAPRI**
🔻🔻🔻
RESTAURANT
in Niagara Falls, Canada

Bring some joy to your life, dine in the Champagne Room or relax in the Living Room Lounge. Featuring Steaks, Seafood and Award Winning Italian Entrees.
• Children's Menu   • Ample Free Parking   • Major Credit Cards Accepted

5438 Ferry Street
905-354-7519

Winner of Readers Choice
Best Chef Award 1996

CASA D'ORO DINING LOUNGE **Lunch:** $10-$15 **Dinner:** $19-$60 **Phone:** 905/356-5646 ㉔

Italian
Location: Just e of jct Ferry St; jct w of Clifton Hill. 5875 Victoria Ave L2G 3L6. **Hours:** noon-10:30 pm, Sat 4 pm-11 pm. Closed: 12/25, 12/26. **Reservations:** suggested. **Features:** The restaurant, a popular choice with locals and tourists alike, offers a unique ambience created by elaborate wall murals of Italian and European themes as well as the pleasant outdoor patio area in season. The menu highlights include all the traditional favourites for that special occasion dining including shrimp cocktail, French onion soup, prime rib, steak, lobster and, of course, the excellent selection of fine Italian fare and pastas. Dressy casual; cocktails. **Parking:** street. **Cards:** AX, DS, MC, VI.

DELDUCA'S **Dinner:** $13-$22 **Phone:** 905/357-3638 ⑭

Italian
Location: Hwy 420, just n on Stanley Ave, just w on Morrison St. 4781 Portage Rd L2E 6B1. **Hours:** 5 pm-10 pm. Closed major holidays; also Sun. **Reservations:** suggested. **Features:** Enjoy the spacious, modern bistro-style atmosphere and featured fare of homemade pasta, ravioli, seafood, steak, veal and savory appetizers. Large portions are prepared fresh and presented attractively. Pleasant Mediterranean background music adds to the European ambience. Casual dress; cocktails. **Parking:** on-site. **Cards:** AX, MC, VI.

EDGEWATERS TAP & GRILL *Menu on aaa.com* **Lunch:** $10-$17 **Dinner:** $20-$40 **Phone:** 905/356-2217 ②
Ⓐ

Continental
Location: In Queen Victoria Park; on scenic route. 6345 Niagara River Pkwy L2E 6T2. **Hours:** Open 5/1-10/15; 11:30 am-10 pm; to 9 pm 5/1-6/18 & 9/5-10/15. **Features:** What better way to enjoy a breathtaking view of the falls than from an open air balcony while dining on an array of items, including some Canadian fare, prepared with fresh ingredients. A year-round cafeteria with more formal dining in season. Casual dress; cocktails. **Parking:** street. **Cards:** AX, MC, VI.

FALLSVIEW DINING ROOM **Lunch:** $8-$16 **Dinner:** $20-$45 **Phone:** 905/374-1077 ㉞

Continental
Location: Near Konica Minolta Tower; in Sheraton Fallsview Hotel & Conference Centre. 6755 Fallsview Blvd L2G 3W7. **Hours:** 7 am-10 pm. **Reservations:** suggested. **Features:** Diners are awed by the spectacular views overlooking the falls and upper river—that and the wonderful selection of salad, appetizer, entree and dessert on the daily buffet. A full a la carte menu is also offered with creative International items. Casual dress; cocktails. **Parking:** on-site. **Cards:** AX, DC, DS, JC, MC, VI.

FINE KETTLE 'O' FISH **Lunch:** $6-$9 **Dinner:** $8-$30 **Phone:** 905/357-3474 ④

Seafood
Location: Jct Huggins; in far back section of strip mall. 3641 Portage Rd L2J 2K8. **Hours:** 11:30 am-10 pm. Closed: 12/25, 12/26. **Features:** The casual, nautical setting at this popular eatery is enhanced by cozy corners and fish aquariums throughout. Good menu selections offer a wide range of fresh seafood—from fish and chips to lobster—as well as steak, chicken and stir-fry options. Casual dress; cocktails. **Parking:** on-site. **Cards:** AX, MC, VI.

FRANK'S TOMATO PIE **Lunch:** $7-$10 **Dinner:** $10-$28 **Phone:** 905/371-9111 ㉑

Italian
Location: Jct Dorchester Rd. 6889 Lundy's Ln L2G 1V7. **Hours:** 11 am-midnight, Fri & Sat-1 am. Closed: 1/1, 12/25. **Reservations:** suggested. **Features:** Located in a converted bank building, Frank's Tomato Pie is a favourite of locals and tourists alike. The atmosphere is casual but the food is certainly gourmet. You can experience the sounds and smells of the chefs at work through the open concept kitchen. Inside, you will find a funky decor of brick walls and mosaic tiles. In summer, the large outdoor patio is a main draw. Whatever the season, you will find fresh pasta, specialty pizzas, veal, seafood and poultry. Casual dress; cocktails. **Parking:** on-site. **Cards:** AX, DC, MC, VI.

STEAKHOUSE · PIZZA BAR · LOUNGE

SUPERB DINING BY THE OPEN-HEARTH GRILL

Enjoy our elegant indoor/outdoor setting on the hill... just above the Falls and right beside the new Casino. Choice-cut Steaks, Prime Rib, Chops and Chicken done to perfection for all to see on the flaming open-hearth grill. Plus succulent seafoods, delectable appetizers, crisp salads and decadent desserts. Daily specials.

Nightly entertainment on terrace in season. Free on-site parking. Open for breakfast, lunch and dinner year round. Children's menu. **Coco's Gourmet Pizza Bar** prepares its mouth-watering delights the traditional way in an authentic wood-fire oven. A unique restaurant and bar... where you can see the world pass by.

Holiday Inn By The Falls (next to Skylon Tower) 5339 Murray St., Niagara Falls, Canada (905) 356-1333

HAPPY WANDERER   **Lunch:** $5-$12   **Dinner:** $10-$40   **Phone:** 905/354-9825   26

Location: Near Konica Minolta Tower. 6405 Stanley Ave L2G 3Y6. **Hours:** 8 am-11 pm. **Closed:** 12/24. **Reservations:** accepted. **Features:** If you're looking for a fun, casual restaurant with a European atmosphere, this place is for you. Come hungry as you will be served heaping portions of homemade German cuisine. Choose from traditional favourites such as bratwurst, schnitzel, smoked pork or rolled beef rolls with homemade dumplings. The atmosphere is set by servers in traditional costumes and distinctive Bavarian decor. Saving room for dessert will be a challenge, but well worth it. Casual dress; cocktails. **Parking:** on-site. **Cards:** AX, MC, VI.

German

HARD TIMES   **Lunch:** $5-$8   **Dinner:** $10-$23   **Phone:** 905/374-3650   6

American

Location: At top of Clifton Hill. 5759 Victoria Ave L2G 3L6. **Hours:** noon-midnight; 4 pm-10 pm 11/1-12/31. **Closed:** 12/24, 12/25. **Reservations:** suggested, weekends in summer. **Features:** Large dining room featuring a mock ship as decorative centerpiece. Menu features huge portions with many fully inclusive meals featured. Select from prime rib, steak, ribs, chicken and seafood or the daily pasta special. Casual dress; cocktails. **Parking:** street. **Cards:** AX, DC, DS, JC, MC, VI.

THE KEG STEAKHOUSE AND BAR   **Dinner:** $17-$37   **Phone:** 905/374-5170   35

Steak House

Location: Adjacent to Konica Minolta Tower; in Embassy Suites Niagara Falls Fallsview. 6700 Fallsview Blvd L2G 3W6. **Hours:** 3 pm-midnight. **Features:** Diners at this eatery can enjoy the ever-popular mesquite-grilled steaks while taking in the stunning views of Niagara Falls from the restaurant's large panoramic windows. The ninth-floor location of this Keg makes it a very special dining experience. The menu features a tasty selection of appetizers such as shrimp cocktail or French onion soup, followed by grilled steaks, chicken or seafood. All entrees include fresh, hot sourdough bread. Casual dress; cocktails. **Parking:** valet. **Cards:** AX, CB, DC, DS, JC, MC, VI. *(See color ad card insert)*

THE KEG STEAKHOUSE AND BAR   **Lunch:** $10-$20   **Dinner:** $20-$55   **Phone:** 905/353-4022   33

Steak House

Location: Jct Ferry St; in Courtyard by Marriott Niagara Falls. 5950 Victoria Ave L2G 3L7. **Hours:** 11 am-1:30 am; to midnight 11/1-4/30. **Features:** Well-known for its mesquite-grilled steaks and fun, laid back atmosphere, this steak house is a longtime favourite with the local crowd. In addition to the great beef, the traditional menu features seafood, grilled chicken, hickory ribs and pasta offering. All meals come with a hot loaf of sourdough bread. Try the tasty cheesecake or the specialty coffees for the perfect ending. Casual dress; cocktails. **Parking:** on-site. **Cards:** AX, MC, VI. *(See color ad card insert)*

KONICA MINOLTA TOWER CENTRE/PINNACLE RESTAURANT   **Lunch:** $10-$27   **Dinner:** $19-$48   **Phone:** 905/356-1501   1

Continental

Location: In Konica Minolta Tower; in Ramada Plaza Hotel Fallsview. 6732 Fallsview Blvd L2G 3W6. **Hours:** 7 am-midnight. **Reservations:** suggested. **Features:** Diners can enjoy a bird's-eye view of the falls from atop the tower while relaxing in an upscale, yet relaxed, atmosphere. The menu lists traditional fare served in ample portions and with attractive plate presentations. Full a la carte and prix fixe specials are served. Casual dress; cocktails. **Parking:** on-site. **Cards:** AX, DC, DS, JC, MC, VI.

LEGENDS ON THE NIAGARA   **Lunch:** $7-$13   **Dinner:** $9-$23   **Phone:** 905/295-2241   28

American

Location: 5 km s of the falls. 9233 Niagara River Pkwy L2E 6T2. **Hours:** Open 5/1-11/15 & 4/1-4/30; dawn-1/2 hour after dusk. **Reservations:** accepted. **Features:** Diners enjoy a wonderful view of the golf course through the large panoramic windows or from the large patio. Casual fare—along the lines of wings, burgers and sandwiches—is available for breakfast, lunch and lighter meals, while larger entrees are served after 4 pm. Casual dress; cocktails. **Parking:** on-site. **Cards:** AX, DC, JC, MC, VI.

Lake House
Restaurant & Lounge

Mediterranean Cuisine

3100 North Service Road in Vineland

905-562-6777

www.lakehouserestaurant.com

Open for Lunch and Dinner 7 days a week
Children's menu available

THE LOVE BOAT II   Lunch: $8-$35   Dinner: $8-$35   Phone: 905/358-0660   (18)
Location: 1.1 km w of Konica Minolta Tower. 6130 Dunn St L2G 2P1. **Hours:** 11:30 am-9 pm, Sat from 3 pm, Sun 11:30 am-8 pm. Closed: 12/25. **Reservations:** accepted. **Features:** A collection of seafaring articles such as anchors, portholes and nets adds to this eatery's pleasant nautical ambience. Very extensive menu selection offering traditional favourites such as surf and turf or fish and chips as well as land lovers specials. Hearty portions. Friendly service. Casual dress; cocktails. **Parking:** on-site. **Cards:** AX, DC, MC, VI.
Seafood

MAMA MIA'S   Lunch: $5-$9   Dinner: $7-$22   Phone: 905/354-7471   (8)
Location: At top of Clifton Hill. 5719 Victoria Ave L2G 3L5. **Hours:** 11:30 am-11 pm; hours vary seasonally. Closed: 12/23-12/25. **Features:** What would an Italian eatery be without a good menu selection of lasagna, manicotti and cannelloni? You'll never find out because Mama Mia's serves all these house specialties and more in this quaint dining room. Steak and seafood also make an appearance. Casual dress; cocktails. **Parking:** on-site (fee). **Cards:** AX, DC, DS, JC, MC, VI.
Italian

MICK AND ANGELO'S EATERY AND
BAR   Lunch: $5-$10   Dinner: $7-$20   Phone: 905/357-6543   (23)
Location: QEW, exit Lundy's Ln; corner of Lundy's Ln and Montrose Rd. 7600 Lundy's Ln L2H 1H1. **Hours:** 11 am-12:30 am. Closed: 12/25. **Reservations:** accepted. **Features:** A diverse crowd patronizes this popular eatery and bar where an extensive menu, large portions and reasonable prices prevail. The specialty white pizza (sans tomato sauce) consists of oil, garlic and three cheeses. Entertainment is offered in season. Casual dress; cocktails. **Parking:** on-site. **Cards:** AX, MC, VI.
Italian

THE MILLERY DINING ROOM   Lunch: $10-$16   Dinner: $21-$62   Phone: 905/357-1234   (5)
Location: Just w via Murray St, just n on Buchanan Ave; in Old Stone Inn. 5425 Robinson St L2G 7L6. **Hours:** 7 am-3 & 4:30-10 pm. Closed: for dinner 12/24. **Reservations:** suggested. **Features:** Located in a wonderfully converted flour mill, the Millery Dining Room provides upscale dining in an elegant country setting. The dining room features high-beam cathedral ceilings and accent stone walls from the original structure of the early 1900s. The innovative menu features fine Continental cuisine with an emphasis on creativity in presentation and freshness of ingredients. It is the perfect choice for special occasion or business dining. Casual dress; cocktails. **Parking:** on-site. **Cards:** AX, DC, DS, JC, MC, VI.
Continental

MONTICELLO GRILLE HOUSE & WINE
BAR _Menu on aaa.com_   Lunch: $9-$35   Dinner: $15-$35   Phone: 905/357-4888   (10)
Location: Just e of jct Clifton Hill and Victoria Ave. 5645 Victoria Ave L2G 3L5. **Hours:** noon-10:30 pm. Closed: 12/24, 12/25. **Reservations:** accepted. **Features:** The brick and wood-beamed steak and seafood restaurant gives a nod to New Orleans with such menu items as spicy gumbo. Also offered are more traditional items. The wine list is extensive, and food portions are large. Specialty desserts such as bread pudding add to the theme. Casual dress; cocktails. **Parking:** on-site. **Cards:** AX, CB, DC, JC, MC, VI.
American

OUTBACK STEAKHOUSE   Dinner: $12-$25   Phone: 905/357-6284   (11)
Location: Corner of Stanley Ave and Dunn St; in Radisson Hotel & Suites Fallsview. 6733 Fallsview Blvd L2G 3W7. **Hours:** 4 pm-10 pm, Fri & Sat-11 pm. Closed: 12/25. **Features:** The restaurant sustains a fun, casual mood in a loud and bustling Aussie atmosphere. Huge portions of freshly grilled and barbecued foods—including well-spiced steaks, chicken and ribs dinners—are a challenge to finish but are too good to leave. Fresh bread, tasty salads and the ever-popular bloomin' onion starter bring back locals and tourists alike. Service is friendly. Casual dress; cocktails. **Parking:** on-site. **Cards:** AX, DC, DS, JC, MC, VI.
Steak House

PENTHOUSE RESTAURANT   Lunch: $10-$20   Dinner: $20-$40   Phone: 905/374-4444   (27)
Location: Entrance to Rainbow Bridge on Hwy 20; in Sheraton on the Falls. 5875 Falls Ave L2E 6W7. **Hours:** 7-11 am, 11:30-2 & 5-9:30 pm. **Reservations:** suggested. **Features:** There's always something to tempt all tastes on the all-you-can-eat breakfast, lunch and dinner buffet. Besides a spectacular view of the falls, the Penthouse offers daily entertainment in season; weekends off season. An a la carte menu is also available. Casual dress; cocktails. **Parking:** on-site (fee). **Cards:** AX, CB, DC, DS, JC, MC, VI.
American

QUEENSTON HEIGHTS
RESTAURANT _Menu on aaa.com_   Lunch: $13-$18   Dinner: $21-$30   Phone: 905/262-4274   (16)
Location: 10.4 km n of Rainbow Bridge, on scenic route. 14184 Niagara River Pkwy L2E 6T2. **Hours:** Open 5/1-1/9 & 4/15-4/30; 11:30 am-3 & 5-9 pm, Sat-10 pm, Sun 11 am-3 & 5-9 pm. Closed: 12/25, 12/26. **Reservations:** suggested. **Features:** Enjoy a panoramic view of the lower Niagara River and surrounding fruit lands from your table, while scanning a varied menu of such specialties as Atlantic salmon, Angus prime rib and seasonal fruit dessert. Patio lounge dining is offered in season. Casual dress; cocktails. **Parking:** on-site. **Cards:** AX, CB, DC, DS, MC, VI.
Continental

THE RAINBOW GRILLE FALLSVIEW STEAKHOUSE   Lunch: $8-$16   Dinner: $25-$50   Phone: 905/374-4444   (22)
Location: Entrance to Rainbow Bridge on Hwy 20, just n of the falls; in Brock Plaza Hotel. 5685 Falls Ave L2E 6W7. **Hours:** 7-10 am, 11-2 & 5-10 pm. **Reservations:** suggested. **Features:** Creative food presentation and good menu variety are hallmarks at the casually elegant restaurant. Poultry, beef, seafood, fresh vegetables and decadent desserts keep excellent company in the upscale dining room, which affords a fine view of the falls. Casual dress; cocktails. **Parking:** on-site (fee). **Cards:** AX, CB, DC, DS, JC, MC, VI.
American

REMINGTON'S OF MONTANA STEAK AND
SEAFOOD   Dinner: $12-$39   Phone: 905/356-4410   (12)
Location: Just e on Hwy 20; in Days Inn Clifton Hill Casino. 5657 Victoria Ave L2G 3L5. **Hours:** 4 pm-11 pm. **Reservations:** suggested. **Features:** A longtime favourite in the busy tourist area, the restaurant presents diners a traditional steak and seafood menu that is sure to please. Starters include French onion soup, shrimp cocktail and Caesar salad, followed by hearty portions of prime rib, steak or surf and turf offerings. Pasta, chicken and ribs also make menu appearances. Service is polished and professional, and the atmosphere is upscale yet comfortable. Dressy casual; cocktails. **Parking:** on-site. **Cards:** AX, CB, DC, DS, JC, MC, VI.
Steak & Seafood

ROOFTOP FALLSVIEW DINING ROOM   **Dinner:** $22-$55   **Phone:** 905/357-5200   ③⓪

Location: Corner of Fallsview Blvd and Dixon Ave; just n of Konica Minolta Tower; directly across from Niagara Fallsview Casino; in Renaissance Fallsview Hotel. 6455 Fallsview Blvd L2G 3V9. **Hours:** 5 pm-10 pm; to 11 pm 5/1-

Continental   10/31. **Reservations:** suggested. **Features:** Diners here enjoy a fine menu of traditional Continental fare with a Niagara touch, including a wine list featuring selections from the local wineries. Staff members offer warm, personable service to ensure a memorable dining experience. Views of Niagara Falls add to the atmosphere and are particularly enjoyed during the nightly illumination schedule. A perfect choice for a fine meal, personable service and a relaxed setting away from the hustle and bustle of the main tourist area. Dressy casual; cocktails. **Parking:** on-site. **Cards:** AX, DC, DS, JC, MC, VI.

THE SKYLON TOWER DINING ROOMS   **Lunch:** $24-$31   **Dinner:** $36-$84   **Phone:** 905/356-2651   ③

CAA

American

Location: In Skylon Tower. 5200 Robinson St L2G 2A3. **Hours:** 11:30 am-2:30 & 4:30-10 pm. **Reservations:** suggested. **Features:** Affording spectacular, panoramic views of Niagara Falls from its large windows, the revolving restaurant features a traditional menu of Continental fare. The cost to ascend the tower is $2, and diners are welcomed to visit the viewing area after dinner to capture some great photographs. More casual buffet dining is available at the Summit, one floor up. Casual dress; cocktails. **Parking:** on-site (fee). **Cards:** AX, DC, DS, JC, MC, VI. *(See color ad p 120 & below)*

TABLE ROCK RESTAURANT   *Menu on aaa.com*   **Lunch:** $10-$15   **Dinner:** $20-$35   **Phone:** 905/354-3631   ⑰

CAA

Continental

Location: At Horseshoe Falls. 6650 Niagara River Pkwy L2E 6T2. **Hours:** 11:30 am-9:30 pm, Sat-10 pm; 9 am-10 & 11:30-9:30 pm 7/1-8/31; hours may vary off season. Closed: 12/25. **Reservations:** accepted. **Features:** It's difficult to take your eyes off the outstanding view of the falls and the upper rapids long enough to make a choice from the menu featuring traditional fare and some Canadian dishes. Attentive and friendly service is the norm. Casual dress; cocktails. **Parking:** street. **Cards:** AX, DC, MC, VI.

TERRAPIN GRILLE   **Lunch:** $14-$45   **Dinner:** $26-$69   **Phone:** 905/357-7300   ㉙

CAA

Continental

Location: Next to Konica Minolta Tower; in Marriott Niagara Falls Fallsview and Spa. 6740 Fallsview Blvd L2G 3W6. **Hours:** 6 am-11 pm. **Reservations:** suggested. **Features:** The Terrapin Grille features a good selection of fine Continental cuisine. The dining room is dimly lit at dinner, providing a romantic atmosphere with a stunning backdrop of Niagara Falls seen through its panoramic windows. It is spectacular during the lighting up of the falls each evening. Staff members have good menu knowledge and provide professional, attentive service. Casual dress; cocktails. **Parking:** on-site. **Cards:** AX, CB, DC, DS, MC, VI.

(See color ad card insert)

SUPERB DINING ABOVE THE FALLS!

With two levels of fine dining to choose from, both overlooking the Falls.

Revolving Dining Room. At the height of dining excellence... featuring award-winning continental cuisine. One rotation hourly. Early dinner specials at 4:30 & 5:00 PM.

Summit Suite Dining Room. The ultimate in buffet-style dining... lunch and dinner. Famous Sunday brunch. Family affordable.

Observation Deck. Spectacular indoor/outdoor viewing.

5200 Robinson Street, Niagara Falls, Canada L2G 2A3
For Reservations Call: 905- 356-2651
Toll-Free: 1-888-686-1791   www.skylon.com

Skylon Tower

TWENTY ONE CLUB   **Lunch:** $10-$20   **Dinner:** $16-$61   **Phone:** 905/374-3598   ⑲

Location: Just n of Rainbow Bridge; in Casino Niagara, 2nd floor. 5705 Falls Ave L2G 7M9. **Hours:** 11:30 am-4 & 6-11 pm, Fri & Sat-midnight. **Reservations:** required, weekends. **Features:** Pianist entertainment, elaborate floral arrangements and cozy booths await diners at the sophisticated restaurant. The a la carte menu specializes in huge, tender cuts of beef and prime rib with accompaniments such as steaming baked potatoes, sizzling mushrooms and steamed asparagus. A wide selection of pasta dishes is also offered. Dressy casual; cocktails. **Parking:** valet. **Cards:** AX, CB, DS, MC, VI.

Steak House

THE WATERMARK   **Lunch:** $10-$25   **Dinner:** $25-$65   **Phone:** 905/354-7887   ⑨

Location: Hwy 20, just s; in Hilton Niagara Falls Fallsview. 6361 Fallsview Blvd L2G 3V9. **Hours:** 7 am-10:30 pm. **Reservations:** required, for dinner. **Features:** The contemporary dining room carries out a distinct water theme, thanks in part to its rooftop location. Large windows offer spectacular, panoramic views of the falls. The menu features a nice mix of traditional Continental fare prepared with market-fresh vegetables. At lunch, lighter options include burgers, sandwiches and pasta. Dressy casual; cocktails. **Parking:** on-site (fee). and valet. **Cards:** AX, CB, DC, DS, JC, MC, VI. **(See color ad inside front cover, below & card insert)**

Continental

THE WATERMARK

Fallsview

DINING ON LEVEL 33

Hilton
Niagara Falls
Fallsview

BREAKFAST LUNCH & DINNER

The Watermark Restaurant offers a multi-level panoramic fallsview dining experience, 555 feet above the famous Falls. Located on levels 33 and 34 of the luxurious Hilton Niagara Falls, this unique restaurant and lounge offers delectable dining for the discerning traveller. The view speaks for itself - come inspire both your awe and your appetite!

6361 Fallsview Blvd., Niagara Falls, ON (905) 354-7887

THE WATERMARK
905.353.7138 or 1.866.704.9302
www.watermarkrestaurant.com

* The Hilton name and logo are trademarks owned by Hilton. © 2001 Hilton Hotels.

WHIRLPOOL RESTAURANT   Lunch: $7-$10   Dinner: $11-$22   Phone: 905/356-7221   ⑮
(CAA)
▼▼ ▼▼
American
Location: 5.3 km n of Rainbow Bridge, on scenic route; in Public Whirlpool Golf Complex. 3351 Niagara River Pkwy L2E 6T2. **Hours:** Open 5/1-11/15 & 4/15-4/30; 11 am-dusk. **Reservations:** accepted. **Features:** Canadian dishes, snacks and daily seasonal featured fare are served in this casual, golf-course-view restaurant across from a whirlpool gorge. Try the very good chicken teriyaki atop angel hair pasta and an eye-appealing fruit plate for dessert. Casual dress; cocktails. **Parking:** on-site. **Cards:** AX, MC, VI. 🔲 ⊠

The Niagara Falls Vicinity

FORT ERIE pop. 28,143

——— **WHERE TO STAY** ———

COMFORT INN   *Book at aaa.com*   Phone: (905)871-8500
(CAA) (SAVE)
▼▼ ▼▼
Small-scale Hotel
All Year   1P: $85-$130   2P: $85-$130   XP: $8   F18
Location: QEW, exit 2 (Berti St) westbound; exit 1B (Concession Rd S) eastbound. 1 Hospitality Dr L2A 6G1. Fax: 905/871-9388. **Facility:** 71 one-bedroom standard units. 2 stories (no elevator), interior corridors. **Parking:** on-site. **Terms:** package plans, pets ($10 fee, 1st floor units). **Guest Services:** valet laundry. **Cards:** AX, DC, DS, MC, VI. **Special Amenities:** free continental breakfast and free newspaper.

SOME UNITS
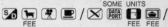
FEE   FEE   FEE

HOLIDAY INN FORT ERIE/NIAGARA-CONVENTION
CENTRE   *Book at aaa.com*   Phone: (905)871-8333
(CAA) (SAVE)
▼▼ ▼▼
Small-scale Hotel
6/27-9/7   1P: $79-$229   2P: $79-$229   XP: $10   F12
5/1-6/26 & 9/8-4/30   1P: $69-$199   2P: $69-$199   XP: $10   F12
Location: QEW, exit Gilmore Rd. 1485 Garrison Rd L2A 1P8. Fax: 905/871-5411. **Facility:** 107 units. 99 one- and 2 two-bedroom standard units. 6 one-bedroom suites ($229-$399) with whirlpools. 4 stories, interior corridors. **Parking:** on-site. **Terms:** cancellation fee imposed, weekly rates available, package plans. **Amenities:** voice mail, irons, hair dryers. *Some:* dual phone lines. **Dining:** 7 am-2 & 5-10 pm, cocktails. **Pool(s):** heated indoor. **Leisure Activities:** saunas, whirlpool, exercise room, spa. **Guest Services:** valet and coin laundry. **Business Services:** meeting rooms, business center. **Cards:** AX, CB, DC, MC, VI. **Special Amenities:** free local telephone calls and free newspaper. *(See color ad card insert & p 347)*

SOME UNITS
🔲
FEE

——— **WHERE TO DINE** ———

MING TEH   Lunch: $13-$20   Dinner: $13-$20   Phone: 905/871-7971
▼▼ ▼▼
Northern Chinese
Location: Peace Bridge in Canada, follow signs to Niagara Blvd. 126 Niagara Blvd L2A 3G6. **Hours:** Open 5/1-12/15 & 1/14-4/30; 11 am-10 pm. Closed: Mon. **Reservations:** suggested. **Features:** This very popular, classic restaurant serves innovative cuisine and remarkably seasoned dishes from a long and detailed list. Never fear—each dish is fully explained on the menu. Try favorites such as fresh made dumplings, escargot with chopped pork in garlic sauce or cubed chicken with tangerine peel and garlic. Dine while enjoying a peaceful view of the river in a relaxed casual setting. Casual dress; cocktails. **Parking:** on-site. **Cards:** VI. ⊠

NIAGARA-ON-THE-LAKE pop. 13,839

——— **WHERE TO STAY** ———

BLAIRPEN HOUSE COUNTRY INN   Phone: 905/468-3886
▼▼ ▼▼
Historic Bed
& Breakfast
6/1-11/1   2P: $145
5/1-5/31 & 11/2-4/30   2P: $95
Location: Downtown. Located in a historic residential area. 287 Davy St L0S 1J0 (PO Box 51). Fax: 905/468-3270. **Facility:** Renovated from an old school, the Blairpen House Country Inn is in the heart of town. Smoke free premises. 6 one-bedroom standard units, some with whirlpools. 2 stories (no elevator), interior/exterior corridors. **Parking:** on-site. **Terms:** office hours 9 am-9 pm, 2 night minimum stay - weekends, age restrictions may apply, 7 day cancellation notice, [BP] meal plan available. **Amenities:** *Some:* irons. **Business Services:** meeting rooms. **Cards:** MC, VI.

SOME UNITS
⊠ / Ⓦ 🔲 /

THE CHARLES INN   Phone: (905)468-4588
▼▼▼ ▼▼▼
Historic
Country Inn
All Year   2P: $170-$310   XP: $40   D12
Location: Jct Simcoe St. 209 Queen St L0S 1J0 (PO Box 642). Fax: 905/468-2194. **Facility:** The mansion has fine Georgian architecture and elegantly appointed guest rooms, which vary in size befitting its historic nature; a few are compact. Smoke free premises. 12 one-bedroom standard units, some with whirlpools. 3 stories (no elevator), interior corridors. *Bath:* combo or shower only. **Parking:** on-site. **Terms:** 2 night minimum stay - seasonal, age restrictions may apply, 10 day cancellation notice-fee imposed, [MAP] meal plan available, package plans. **Amenities:** irons, hair dryers. **Dining:** dining room, see separate listing. **Business Services:** meeting rooms. **Cards:** AX, DC, MC, VI. (ASK) 🔲

Experience the Difference Tradition Makes

NIAGARA-ON-THE-LAKE

Vintage Inns

For Reservations
1-888-669-5566

155 Byron Street
Niagara-on-the-Lake
ON L0S 1J0
CANADA

(905)468-2195
FAX (905)468-2227

www.vintageinns.com

*Committed to
personal service,
attention to detail
and gracious
hospitality.*

The Pillar and Post Inn, Spa and Conference Centre

"Step into a truly memorable experience"

Delight in the decor of 123 individually appointed guest rooms, a world class European Spa and fireside seating in the elegant dining rooms of the Pillar and Post Inn, Spa and Conference Centre.

The Prince of Wales Hotel

"A bygone era revisited"

Newly restored and renovated, discover 114 authentic Victorian guestrooms, world class dining and European Spa at The "New" Prince of Wales Hotel.

Queen's Landing Inn & Conference Resort

"Experience the renewed Georgian ambience"

While exploring the historic village of Niagara-on-the-Lake, stay at the Queen's Landing Inn. Awarded the CAA/AAA prize of excellence, our hotel promises luxuriously appointed guest rooms and exquisite dining overlooking the magnificent Niagara River.

The Oban Inn

"Since 1824 . . ."

The Oban Inn has been a Niagara landmark since 1824. Originally the home of Captain Duncan Milloy from Oban Scotland. This 26 room Inn is surrounded by beautiful English-style gardens overlooking Lake Ontario.

GATE HOUSE HOTEL
Phone: 905/468-3263

6/1-10/31 [CP]	1P: $195-$230	XP: $20	F11
5/1-5/31 [CP]	1P: $175-$210	XP: $20	F11
11/1-1/2 & 3/15-4/30 [CP]	1P: $145-$180	XP: $20	F11

Country Inn
Location: Jct Gate. 142 Queen St L0S 1J0. Fax: 905/468-7400. **Facility:** The contemporary inn has modern Italian decor, is walking distance from shops and theatres and features a fine dining room. 10 one-bedroom standard units. 2 stories (no elevator), interior corridors. **Parking:** on-site. **Terms:** open 5/1-1/2 & 3/15-4/30, 7 day cancellation notice-fee imposed, small pets only. **Amenities:** hair dryers. **Dining:** Ristorante Giardino, see separate listing. **Cards:** AX, DC, JC, MC, VI.

HARBOUR HOUSE HOTEL
Phone: (905)468-4683

All Year [ECP] 2P: $275-$325 F10

Small-scale Hotel
Location: Jct Ricardo St. 85 Melville St L0S 1J0 (PO Box 760). Fax: 905/468-0366. **Facility:** A delightful boutique hotel awaits guests offering upscale rooms with a unique contemporary flair; most with fireplaces and whirlpool tubs. Smoke free premises. 31 units. 29 one-bedroom standard units, some with whirlpools. 2 one-bedroom suites ($375-$415) with whirlpools. 3 stories, interior corridors. *Bath:* combo or shower only. **Parking:** on-site. **Terms:** office hours 8 am-11 pm, 2 night minimum stay - weekends, 10 day cancellation notice-fee imposed, package plans, pets ($25 fee). **Amenities:** video library, DVD players, CD players, dual phone lines, voice mail, irons, hair dryers. **Business Services:** meeting rooms. **Cards:** AX, MC, VI.

HOUSE ON THE RIVER
Phone: 905/262-4597

5/1-11/15 & 4/1-4/30	1P: $135-$145	2P: $135-$145	XP: $35

Bed & Breakfast
Location: Niagara River Pkwy, exit Service Rd 53. 14773 Niagara River Pkwy L0S 1J0. Fax: 905/262-0685. **Facility:** Smoke free premises. 4 one-bedroom standard units. 2 stories (no elevator), exterior corridors. *Bath:* shower only. **Parking:** on-site. **Terms:** open 5/1-11/15 & 4/1-4/30, 2 night minimum stay - weekends, 14 day cancellation notice-fee imposed. **Pool(s):** outdoor. **Leisure Activities:** bicycles. **Cards:** JC, MC.

MOFFAT INN
Phone: 905/468-4116

5/1-10/30 & 4/16-4/30	1P: $99-$179	2P: $99-$179	XP: $15
10/31-4/15	1P: $79-$169	2P: $79-$169	XP: $15

Historic Country Inn
Location: Downtown; where Queen St becomes Picton St. Located in the historic district. 60 Picton St L0S 1J0 (PO Box 578). Fax: 905/468-4747. **Facility:** Centrally located near shopping and the theatre, this 1835 inn offers a range of distinctive guest rooms. Smoke free premises. 23 units. 22 one-bedroom standard units. 1 two-bedroom suite ($325-$525) with kitchen. 2 stories (no elevator), interior/exterior corridors. **Parking:** on-site. **Terms:** 2 night minimum stay - seasonal, cancellation fee imposed. **Amenities:** hair dryers. *Some:* irons. **Business Services:** meeting rooms, fax (fee). **Cards:** AX, MC, VI.

SOME UNITS

THE OBAN INN
Book at aaa.com
Phone: (905)468-2165

5/1-10/31	1P: $225-$365	2P: $225-$365	XP: $50	F14
11/1-4/30	1P: $150-$275	2P: $150-$275	XP: $50	F14

Historic Country Inn
Location: Jct Gate. 160 Front St L0S 1J0. Fax: 905/468-4165. **Facility:** The inn overlooks Lake Ontario and features English-style gardens; guest rooms have a warm ambience. Smoke free premises. 26 units. 23 one-bedroom standard units. 3 one-bedroom suites, some with whirlpools. 3 stories, interior/exterior corridors. *Bath:* combo or shower only. **Parking:** on-site. **Terms:** office hours 7 am-11 pm, cancellation fee imposed, [AP] meal plan available. **Amenities:** hair dryers. *Some:* DVD players (fee), irons. **Dining:** dining room, see separate listing. **Leisure Activities:** shared facilities with Vintage Inn properties. *Fee:* spa services by arrangement, bicycles, massage. **Guest Services:** valet laundry, area transportation. **Business Services:** meeting rooms. **Cards:** AX, DC, DS, MC, VI. *(See color ad p 377)*

SOME UNITS

OLD BANK HOUSE
Phone: (905)468-7136

5/1-11/1 [BP]	1P: $145-$205	2P: $165-$225	XP: $40
11/2-4/30 [BP]	1P: $90-$165	2P: $125-$185	XP: $25

Historic Bed & Breakfast
Location: Corner of King and Front sts; centre. Located in a historic residential area. 10 Front St L0S 1J0 (PO Box 1708). Fax: 905/468-7136. **Facility:** This home across from Lake Ontario was built in the early 1800s and is in town close to the theatre and attractions. Smoke free premises. 9 one-bedroom standard units, some with whirlpools. 2 stories (no elevator), interior corridors. *Bath:* combo or shower only. **Parking:** on-site. **Terms:** office hours 8 am-8 pm, check-in 4 pm, 2 night minimum stay - weekends, age restrictions may apply, 14 day cancellation notice-fee imposed. **Amenities:** hair dryers. **Cards:** AX, MC, VI.

THE PILLAR & POST INN SPA & CONFERENCE
CENTRE
Book at aaa.com
Phone: (905)468-2123

5/1-11/29	1P: $225-$365	2P: $225-$365	XP: $50	F14
11/30-4/30	1P: $175-$305	2P: $175-$305	XP: $50	F14

Country Inn
Location: Just n on Hwy 55 (Mississauga St), just e; 13 mi from QEW. 48 John St L0S 1J0 (PO Box 1011). Fax: 905/468-3551. **Facility:** Fresh flowers are displayed in the inn's common areas; guest rooms have upscale country decor with Early American-style pine furniture. Smoke free premises. 123 units. 116 one-bedroom standard units, some with whirlpools. 7 one-bedroom suites with whirlpools. 2 stories, interior/exterior corridors. **Parking:** on-site and valet. **Terms:** cancellation fee imposed, [AP] meal plan available, pets ($35 extra charge). **Amenities:** video games (fee), voice mail, safes, honor bars, irons, hair dryers. **Dining:** Cannery & Carriages, see separate listing. **Pool(s):** heated outdoor, heated indoor. **Leisure Activities:** sauna, whirlpools, steamroom, spa. *Fee:* bicycles. **Guest Services:** gift shop, valet laundry, area transportation. **Business Services:** meeting rooms, business center. **Cards:** AX, DC, DS, MC, VI. *(See color ad p 377)*

SOME UNITS

THE PRINCE OF WALES HOTEL & SPA   *Book at aaa.com*   **Phone:** 905/468-3246

(CAA) (SAVE)   5/1-10/31   1P: $225-$365   2P: $225-$365   XP: $50   F14
                 11/1-4/30   1P: $175-$305   2P: $175-$305   XP: $50   F14

🔻🔻🔻 🔻🔻🔻   **Location:** Jct Picton and King sts; 14.4 km e of jct QEW and Hwy 55, via Hwy 55. 6 Picton St L0S 1J0 (PO Box 46).
                 Fax: 905/468-5521. **Facility:** A traditional afternoon tea is served in the drawing room at this landmark 1864
Historic   hotel, which is convenient to theatres and shopping districts. Smoke free premises. 110 units. 108 one-
Small-scale Hotel bedroom standard units, some with whirlpools. 2 one-bedroom suites with whirlpools. 2-3 stories,
                 interior/exterior corridors. **Parking:** valet. **Terms:** cancellation fee imposed, [AP] meal plan available, pets
($35 extra charge). **Amenities:** video games (fee), high-speed Internet, dual phone lines, voice mail, safes, irons, hair dryers.
Dining: 11 am-midnight, also, Escabeche, see separate listing. **Pool(s):** heated indoor. **Leisure Activities:** whirlpool, exercise
room, spa. **Guest Services:** valet laundry, area transportation-local attractions. **Business Services:** meeting rooms, business
center. **Cards:** AX, DC, DS, MC, VI. *(See color ad p 377)*

SOME UNITS

🛏️ 🍽️ 24️⃣ 🍸 📶 🐟 ✂️ ✖️ 🎥 📠 🔲 / VCR /
FEE

RIVERBEND
INN & VINEYARD

RIVERBEND; a secluded country inn nestled in its own vineyards along the Niagara River Parkway in the historic town of Niagara-on-the-Lake. Recently restored, all will enjoy the countryside from our bar and restaurant, vineyard patio or settle into one of our individually appointed rooms reflecting our commitment to the finer things in life.

16104 Niagara River Parkway · Niagara-on-the-Lake · Ontario
tel: 905-468-8866 · toll free: 1-888-955-5553 · www.riverbendinn.ca

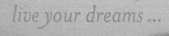

live your dreams ...

four-diamond dining
world-class spa
championship grade golf
state-of-the-art fitness & racquets

❈ WHITE OAKS RESORT & SPA
NIAGARA-on-the-LAKE

Four Diamond Award 🔶🔶🔶

1 800 263 5766 [North America] 1 905 688 2550 [International]

www.whiteoaksresort.com

QUEEN'S LANDING INN & CONFERENCE RESORT   *Book at aaa.com*   Phone: (905)468-2195

(AAA) [SAVE]
5/1-10/31	1P: $225-$365	2P: $225-$365	XP: $50	F14
11/1-4/30	1P: $175-$305	2P: $175-$305	XP: $50	F14

Location: Just n on King St, just e. 155 Byron St L0S 1J0 (PO Box 1180). Fax: 905/468-2227. **Facility:** Fresh roses are prominently displayed at this elegant resort; it features many rooms with fireplaces and whirlpools. **Small-scale Hotel** 142 units. 139 one-bedroom standard units, some with whirlpools. 3 one-bedroom suites with whirlpools. 3 stories, interior corridors. **Parking:** valet. **Terms:** cancellation fee imposed, [AP] meal plan available, small pets only ($100 deposit). **Amenities:** *Some:* DVD players (fee). **Dining:** Tiara Dining Room, see separate listing. **Pool(s):** heated indoor, saltwater. **Leisure Activities:** saunas, whirlpool, rental bicycles. **Guest Services:** valet laundry, area transportation. **Business Services:** conference facilities, business center. **Cards:** AX, DC, DS, MC, VI. *(See color ad p 377)*

SOME UNITS
[icons] FEE / [icons] FEE

RIVERBEND INN AND VINEYARD   Phone: (905)468-8866

(AAA) [SAVE]
5/1-10/31	1P: $215-$340	2P: $225-$350	XP: $25	F10
11/1-4/30	1P: $190-$315	2P: $200-$325	XP: $25	F10

Location: Jct John St. 16104 Niagara River Pkwy L0S 1J0. Fax: 905/468-8829. **Facility:** Set amongst acres of vineyards, this friendly, family-run inn offers elegantly appointed guest rooms, all with fireplaces. Smoke free **Country Inn** premises. 21 units. 20 one-bedroom standard units. 1 one-bedroom suite. 3 stories (no elevator), interior corridors. **Parking:** on-site. **Terms:** 7 day cancellation notice, [MAP] meal plan available, package plans, small pets only (with prior approval). **Amenities:** high-speed Internet, voice mail, hair dryers. **Dining:** dining room, see separate listing. **Guest Services:** valet laundry. **Business Services:** meeting rooms. **Cards:** AX, DC, DS, MC, VI. *(See color ad p 379)*

[icons]

THE RIVER BREEZE   Phone: 905/262-4046

All Year [BP]	1P: $120-$150	2P: $120-$150	XP: $35	D10

Location: Niagara River Pkwy, exit Service Rd 53. 14767 Niagara River Pkwy, RR 1 L0S 1J0. Fax: 905/262-0718. **Facility:** Handsome gardens and an open-air patio, where breakfast is served in summer, accent this **Bed & Breakfast** elegant home's riverfront grounds. Smoke free premises. 4 one-bedroom standard units. 2 stories (no elevator), interior corridors. *Bath:* combo or shower only. **Parking:** on-site. **Terms:** 2 night minimum stay - weekends, age restrictions may apply, 14 day cancellation notice-fee imposed. **Amenities:** hair dryers. **Pool(s):** outdoor. **Cards:** MC, VI.

[icons]

ROYAL PARK HOTEL   Phone: (905)468-5711

5/1-10/31	1P: $165-$250	2P: $165-$250	XP: $15	F10
11/1-4/30	1P: $155-$245	2P: $155-$245	XP: $15	F10

Location: Jct Wellington St. 92 Picton St L0S 1J0. Fax: 905/468-4988. **Facility:** Smoke free premises. 40 one-**Small-scale Hotel** bedroom standard units, some with whirlpools. 2 stories (no elevator), interior corridors. **Parking:** on-site. **Terms:** 3 day cancellation notice-fee imposed, package plans. **Amenities:** hair dryers. **Dining:** Restaurant and Patio at the Park, see separate listing. **Business Services:** meeting rooms. **Cards:** AX, MC, VI.

[icons]

VICTORIAN SUITES INN   Phone: (905)468-8777

(AAA) [SAVE]
All Year	1P: $269-$299	2P: $269-$299	XP: $40	D12

Location: From Queen St, 6 km w on Hwy 55 (Missassauga St). 1391 Niagara Stone Rd (Hwy 55) L0S 1J0. Fax: 905/468-4781. **Facility:** Smoke free premises. 6 one-bedroom standard units with whirlpools. 2 stories (no elevator), interior corridors. **Parking:** on-site. **Terms:** 2 night minimum stay - weekends, 7 day **Small-scale Hotel** cancellation notice-fee imposed, [ECP] meal plan available, $3 service charge. **Amenities:** video library, DVD players, CD players, irons, hair dryers. **Leisure Activities:** *Fee:* massage. **Cards:** AX, MC, VI. **Special Amenities: free local telephone calls and preferred room (subject to availability with advance reservations).**

[icons]

WHITE OAKS CONFERENCE RESORT AND SPA   *Book at aaa.com*   Phone: (905)688-2550

(AAA) [SAVE]
7/1-10/31	1P: $219-$289	2P: $229-$299	XP: $25	F12
5/1-6/30	1P: $159-$189	2P: $169-$199	XP: $25	F12
11/1-4/30	1P: $149-$169	2P: $159-$179	XP: $25	F12

Location: QEW, exit Glendale Ave, 8.5 km e. 253 Taylor Rd L0S 1J0. Fax: 905/688-2220. **Facility:** This all-**Resort** purpose resort offers luxurious rooms, an extensive recreation complex and modern convention facilities. **Large-scale Hotel** Smoke free premises. 220 units. 208 one-bedroom standard units, some with whirlpools. 12 one-bedroom suites ($189-$599) with whirlpools. 7 stories, interior corridors. **Parking:** on-site, winter plug-ins. **Terms:** check-in 4 pm, cancellation fee imposed, package plans, $5 service charge. **Amenities:** video games, high-speed Internet, dual phone lines, voice mail, safes, honor bars, irons, hair dryers. *Some:* DVD players, CD players. **Dining:** 6 am-11 pm, also, LIV, see separate listing. **Pool(s):** heated indoor. **Leisure Activities:** saunas, whirlpools, steamrooms, recreation programs, aerobic instruction, spa, basketball, volleyball. *Fee:* golf-27 holes, 8 indoor tennis courts, racquetball courts, game room. **Guest Services:** gift shop, valet laundry, area transportation (fee)-local attractions. **Business Services:** conference facilities, business center. **Cards:** AX, DC, MC, VI. **Special Amenities: free local telephone calls.** *(See color ad p 379)*

SOME UNITS
[icons] / [icons]

———— *The following lodging was either not evaluated or did not* ————
meet AAA rating requirements but is listed for your information only.

LAKEWINDS COUNTRY MANOR   Phone: 905/468-1888

[fyi]   Not evaluated. **Location:** Corner of Queen and Butler sts. 328 Queen St L0S 1J0 (PO Box 1483). Facilities, services, and decor characterize a mid-range property.

──────── WHERE TO DINE ────────

THE BUTTERY THEATRE RESTAURANT   **Lunch:** $9-$13   **Dinner:** $24-$29   **Phone:** 905/468-2564
Location: Centre; across from courthouse. 19 Queen St L0S 1J0. **Hours:** 11 am-11:30 pm. Closed: 12/25.
Reservations: accepted. **Features:** The British pub-type atmosphere inside as well as on the outdoor patio
American   is a welcome change of pace, with a varied menu of light lunches and full-course dinner selections. There
are also a medieval 4-course feast and entertainment on weekends. Dressy casual; cocktails. **Parking:**
street. **Cards:** AX, MC, VI.

CANNERY & CARRIAGES   *Menu on aaa.com*   **Lunch:** $10-$22   **Dinner:** $28-$45   **Phone:** 905/468-2123
Location: Just n on Hwy 55 (Mississauga St), just e; 13 mi from QEW; in The Pillar & Post Inn Spa & Conference
Centre. 48 John St L0S 1J0. **Hours:** 7 am-11, noon-2 & 5-9 pm, Fri & Sat-9:30 pm; 7 am-11, noon-2 & 6-9 pm
in winter; Sunday brunch 10:30 am-2 pm. **Reservations:** suggested. **Features:** Grapevines and fresh floral
Continental   arrangements create a delightful setting in this fine country inn. A good menu variety shows a strong
influence of regional produce and wines. Daily specialty breads are delicious complements. The focus is on
fine cuts of steak and seafood, with a full a la carte concept. The chef offers a showcase of sauces with
menu selections such as bearnaise with cabernet reduction, lemon butter or smoked-pepper cream. Dressy casual; cocktails.
Parking: on-site. **Cards:** AX, DC, DS, JC, MC, VI.

THE CHARLES INN DINING ROOM   **Lunch:** $10-$18   **Dinner:** $18-$28   **Phone:** 905/468-4588
Location: Jct Simcoe St; in The Charles Inn. 209 Queen St L0S 1J0. **Hours:** 11 am-3 & 5-9 pm.
Reservations: suggested. **Features:** The lovely dining room allows for seating in one of the elegant
Continental   Victorian rooms or on the wraparound verandah in the summer months. The chef prepares a wonderful
selection of fresh local and regional cuisine using herbs picked from the garden. Menu highlights include
cider-glazed pork tenderloin with glazed turnips, pot-roasted guinea hen and a variety of beef and fish options. Wines from local
wineries perfectly complement each meal. Dressy casual; cocktails. **Parking:** on-site. **Cards:** AX, MC, VI.

ESCABECHE   *Menu on aaa.com*   **Lunch:** $15-$25   **Dinner:** $35-$42   **Phone:** 905/468-3246
Location: Jct Picton and King sts; 14.4 km e of jct QEW and Hwy 55, via Hwy 55; in The Prince of Wales Hotel & Spa.
6 Picton St L0S 1J0. **Hours:** 7 am-10:30 pm. **Reservations:** suggested, for dinner. **Features:** Contemporary
French cuisine with emphasis on flavour and clean presentation makes a fine showing here in a most
elegant 19th-century Victorian dining room. Attentive service is what you'll experience. A very good selection
French   of Ontario wine is offered. Semi-formal attire; cocktails. **Parking:** on-site. **Cards:** AX, DC, JC, MC, VI.

FANS COURT   **Lunch:** $7-$10   **Dinner:** $13-$20   **Phone:** 905/468-4511
Location: Town centre. 135 Queen St L0S 1J0. **Hours:** Open 5/1-12/31 & 2/1-4/30; noon-9 pm. Closed: Mon.
Features: Centrally located in the main tourist area, the delightful restaurant presents a menu of traditional
Chinese   Chinese fare in the Hong Kong style. A lighter luncheon menu is also featured. During summer, patrons can
dine in the elegant, oriental-themed dining room or on the lovely casual patio, which boasts a relaxing
waterfall. Casual dress; cocktails. **Parking:** on-site. **Cards:** AX, MC, VI.

HILLEBRAND ESTATE WINERY RESTAURANT   **Lunch:** $13-$24   **Dinner:** $24-$42   **Phone:** 905/468-3201
Location: From Queen St, 6.5 km sw on Hwy 55 (Mississauga St). 1249 Niagara Stone Rd (Hwy 55) L0S 1J0.
Hours: noon-2:45 & 5:30-9 pm. Closed: 1/1, 12/25. **Reservations:** suggested. **Features:** Located at the
Continental   vineyards of the Hillebrand Estate Winery, this restaurant offers diners wonderful views from its large
panoramic windows, as well as outdoor patio dining in season. The chef has created a fine menu of regional
cuisine that perfectly complements the fine selection of wines Hillebrand has to offer. The staff are experts at pairing the food
and wines to give diners a true culinary adventure. Dressy casual; cocktails. **Parking:** on-site. **Cards:** AX, DC, MC, VI.

LIV   **Lunch:** $10-$25   **Dinner:** $25-$40   **Phone:** 905/688-2032
Location: QEW, exit Glendale Ave, 8.5 km e; in White Oaks Conference Resort and Spa. 235 Taylor Rd L0S 1J0.
Hours: 7 am-11 pm. Closed: 12/25. **Reservations:** suggested. **Features:** An innovative contemporary look
and equally distinctive menu welcome diners. The perfect beginning includes selections of Niagara's finest
Regional   wines, followed by fresh regional fare made with herbs from the hotel gardens. Fresh shrimp cocktail, tasty
Canadian   grilled fish, vegetarian pasta, hearty steaks and rack of lamb are a few dishes served with an artistic flair.
Desserts are tempting, as is the exceptionally wonderful cheese plate. Semi-formal attire; cocktails. **Parking:** on-site.
Cards: AX, DC, DS, MC, VI.

THE NEW ITALIAN PLACE (AT THE ANCHORAGE)   **Lunch:** $8-$21   **Dinner:** $8-$21   **Phone:** 905/468-2141
Location: Between Melville and King sts. 186 Ricardo St L0S 1J0. **Hours:** 11:30 am-11 pm, Fri & Sat-midnight.
Closed: 1/1, 12/25. **Reservations:** suggested. **Features:** Niagara's only seafood and Certified Angus beef
Seafood   restaurant. A relaxed, casual atmosphere, comfortable dining room with a nautical decor and a very good
fish and chips dish make it a local favourite. Waterfront outdoor dining is offered in season. Casual dress;
cocktails. **Parking:** on-site. **Cards:** AX, DC, MC, VI.

THE OBAN INN   **Lunch:** $12-$16   **Dinner:** $26-$36   **Phone:** 905/468-2165
Location: Jct Gate; in The Oban Inn. 160 Front St L0S 1J0. **Hours:** 7:30-10 am, 11:30-2 & 5-9 pm; fixed seating
5/1-11/30. Closed: for lunch 12/25. **Reservations:** suggested. **Features:** The Oban Inn dining room is
located in Niagara on the Lake and features large panoramic windows with peaceful views of the lake and
the lovely English gardens. An elegant atmosphere is created inside where diners will find crystal
Continental   chandeliers, fine tableware and fresh flowers. A fine Continental menu completes the picture, making this
the perfect choice for pre-theatre diners and those seeking an upscale meal in a relaxed historic inn. Dressy
casual; cocktails. **Parking:** on-site. **Cards:** AX, DC, JC, MC, VI.

THE OLDE ANGEL INN   **Lunch:** $8-$11   **Dinner:** $8-$35   **Phone:** 905/468-3411
◆◆◆ **Location:** Downtown. 224 Regent St L0S 1J0. **Hours:** 11:30 am-midnight. Closed: 12/25.
Reservations: suggested. **Features:** The history behind the inn is interesting, from its War of 1812
Canadian   structure to its resident ghost that lingers late at night. A good variety of sandwiches and pub fare is
served either in the pub area at front or in the main dining room. Diners in the latter also can select from a
full Continental menu and nightly set specials. Casual dress; cocktails. **Parking:** street. **Cards:** AX, DC, MC, VI. **Historic**

OLD TOWNE RESTAURANT   **Lunch:** $8-$11   **Dinner:** $16-$24   **Phone:** 905/468-2532
◆ **Location:** Centre. 61-63 Queen St L0S 1J0. **Hours:** 7 am-1 am; to 10 pm 11/1-12/31; to 5 pm 1/1-3/31. Closed:
12/25. **Features:** The cozy, modern diner provides bar, booth and table service. Lining the casual menu are
American   hearty breakfast dishes, homemade soups, gourmet burgers, sandwiches and light entrees. Casual dress;
cocktails. **Parking:** on-site. **Cards:** MC, VI.

PELLER ESTATES WINERY RESTAURANT   **Lunch:** $14-$19   **Dinner:** $24-$37   **Phone:** 905/468-4678
◆◆◆ ◆◆ **Location:** Jct Niagara River Pkwy. 290 John St L0S 1J0. **Hours:** noon-3 & 5-9 pm. Closed: 12/25.
Reservations: suggested. **Features:** Located at the Pellar Estates Winery, this restaurant features fine
Continental   regional and Continental fare paired with a selection of the finest wines the facility has to offer. Diners enjoy
a spectacular view of the surrounding vineyards from the large panoramic windows, or from the large
outdoor patio area in season. A changing chef's tasting menu is also featured. Dressy casual; cocktails. **Parking:** on-site.
Cards: AX, DC, MC, VI.

RESTAURANT AND PATIO AT THE PARK   **Lunch:** $9-$16   **Dinner:** $15-$28   **Phone:** 905/468-5711
◆◆◆ ◆◆◆ **Location:** Jct Wellington St; in Royal Park Hotel. 92 Picton St L0S 1J0. **Hours:** 8 am-9 pm, Mon-5 pm.
Reservations: suggested. **Features:** The patio is the main draw, attracting locals and theatregoers to its
Continental   pleasant setting. Indoors, diners enjoy a more upscale ambience, with cloth-covered tables and wood
accents. The menu's good mix of casual fare—ranging from entree salads and hearty sandwiches to pasta,
steak and seafood options—suits all taste buds. This place is across from the Festival Theatre. Casual dress; cocktails.
Parking: on-site. **Cards:** AX, MC, VI.

RISTORANTE GIARDINO   **Lunch:** $9-$14   **Dinner:** $26-$38   **Phone:** 905/468-3263
◆◆◆ ◆◆◆ **Location:** Jct Gate; in Gate House Hotel. 142 Queen St L0S 1J0. **Hours:** Open 5/1-1/5 & 3/15-4/30; 11:30 am-
2:30 & 5-9:30 pm. **Reservations:** required, weekends. **Features:** A sophisticated ambience permeates the
Northern   contemporary and elegant Italian dining room where a creative menu commands fine selections of
Italian   antipasto, fish, meat, classic osso buco, fresh pasta and dessert. An extensive wine list is also available.
Dressy casual; cocktails. **Parking:** on-site. **Cards:** AX, DC, MC, VI.

RIVERBEND INN DINING ROOM   **Lunch:** $9-$14   **Dinner:** $18-$29   **Phone:** 905/468-8866
Ⓐ **Location:** Jct John St; in Riverbend Inn and Vineyard. 16104 Niagara River Pkwy L0S 1J0. **Hours:** 7 am-11 pm.
Reservations: suggested. **Features:** The outstanding setting draws diners from around the region to gaze
◆◆◆ ◆◆◆ at the surrounding vineyards from the large covered patio or panoramic windows in the main dining room.
Perfectly complementing the setting is a menu that innovatively blends fresh Niagara region specialties with
Continental   fine local wines. Highlights include cider-braised lamb shank, seared red snapper and capon basted in
Serrano chili and white honey. Save room for the tasty Niagara apple cheesecake. Dressy casual; cocktails.
Parking: on-site. **Cards:** AX, DC, DS, MC, VI.

SHAW CAFE AND WINE BAR   **Lunch:** $7-$20   **Dinner:** $7-$20   **Phone:** 905/468-4772
Ⓐ **Location:** Across from Royal George Theatre. 92 Queen St L0S 1J0. **Hours:** 10 am-midnight, Mon-10 pm; 11 am-
6 pm, Fri-10 pm, Sat 10 am-10 pm, Sun 10 am-7 pm 11/1-4/30. Closed: 12/25. **Reservations:** not
accepted. **Features:** Theatregoers enjoy the casual, relaxed dining in Shaw's bi-level, circular layout
◆◆◆ overlooking the town centre. The menu includes a variety of salad, pizza, gourmet sandwiches and full
American   entrees. Decadent desserts and an extensive wine list are highlights. Casual dress. **Parking:** street.
Cards: AX, DC, DS, MC, VI.

TIARA DINING ROOM   *Menu on aaa.com*   **Lunch:** $11-$23   **Dinner:** $21-$43   **Phone:** 905/468-2195
Ⓐ **Location:** Just h on King St, just e; in Queen's Landing Inn & Conference Resort. 155 Byron St L0S 1J0. **Hours:** 7
am-11, noon-2 & 5-10 pm, Sun 7-10 am, 11-2 & 5-10 pm; 7:30 am-11, noon-2 & 6-9 pm off season.
◆◆◆ ◆◆◆ **Reservations:** suggested. **Features:** Distinctive dishes featuring Niagara-region produce, a seven-course
tasting menu and exotic presentation make Queen's Landing memorable. Candlelight and music
Continental   complement the upscale dining room where most tables offer a scenic view of the Niagara River. Dressy
casual; cocktails. **Parking:** on-site. **Cards:** AX, DC, JC, MC, VI.

PORT COLBORNE pop. 18,450

——— WHERE TO STAY ———

PORT MOTEL   **Phone:** 905/835-5202

	5/1-9/30	1P: $69-$89	2P: $79-$99	XP: $10	F18
Ⓐ SAVE	10/1-4/30	1P: $49-$69	2P: $59-$79	XP: $10	F18

◆◆◆ **Location:** 1 km w of jct Rt 58 and 3. 20134 Hwy 3 L3K 5V4 (RR 2, Box 11). **Fax:** 905/835-0789. **Facility:** 26 one-
Motel   bedroom standard units. 1 story, interior/exterior corridors. **Parking:** on-site, winter plug-ins. **Terms:** office
hours 8 am-8 pm, cancellation fee imposed, weekly rates available. **Pool(s):** heated outdoor. **Cards:** AX,
DC, MC, VI. **Special Amenities:** free local telephone calls and free newspaper.

SOME UNITS

------ **WHERE TO DINE** ------

M.T. BELLIES ON THE CANAL   **Lunch:** $7-$16   **Dinner:** $7-$16   **Phone:** 905/834-4224
▽▽▽ ▽▽▽   **Location:** Jct Victoria. 124 West St L3K 4C9. **Hours:** 11:30 am-9 pm, Fri-midnight, Sat 10 am-midnight, Sun 10
          am-9 pm. Closed: 12/25; also Mon & Tues 1/1-4/1. **Features:** Huge portions of tasty food are served in a
American   casual location overlooking the canal. Diners enjoy appetizer platters, wings and·rings, huge burgers and
          entree salads, as well as pasta, beef and poultry offerings. This place is great for families. Casual dress;
cocktails. **Parking:** street. **Cards:** AX, MC, VI.   ⊠

ST. CATHARINES pop. 129,170

------ **WHERE TO STAY** ------

CAPRI INN   **Phone:** 905/684-8515
(CAA) (SAVE)   6/27-10/1   1P: $79-$249   2P: $89-$259   XP: $10   F12
          5/1-6/26   1P: $79-$109   2P: $89-$119   XP: $10   F12
▽▽▽ ▽▽▽   10/2-4/30   1P: $65-$109   2P: $75-$119   XP: $10   F12
          Location: QEW, exit 47 (Ontario St). 391 Ontario St L2R 5L3. Fax: 905/684-8001. **Facility:** 30 one-bedroom
Motel   standard units. 2 stories (no elevator), exterior corridors. **Parking:** on-site. **Terms:** cancellation fee imposed,
          package plans. **Amenities:** voice mail. **Cards:** AX, DC, JC, MC, VI. **Special Amenities:** free local
telephone calls and free newspaper.

SOME UNITS
🔲 📶 📠 🔌 / ⊠ 🖼 /
FEE

COMFORT INN   *Book at aaa.com*   **Phone:** (905)687-8890
(CAA) (SAVE)   7/1-9/30   1P: $99-$139   2P: $109-$149   XP: $10   F18
          5/1-6/30   1P: $89-$99   2P: $99-$109   XP: $10   F18
▽▽▽ ▽▽▽   10/1-4/30   1P: $84-$99   2P: $94-$109   XP: $10   F18
          Location: QEW, exit 46 (Lake St); between Lake and Geneva sts. 2 Dunlop Dr L2R 1A2. Fax: 905/687-4033.
Small-scale Hotel **Facility:** 100 one-bedroom standard units. 2 stories (no elevator), interior corridors. **Parking:** on-site, winter
          plug-ins. **Terms:** package plans. **Amenities:** irons, hair dryers. **Dining:** 6:30 am-8 pm, cocktails. **Guest
Services:** valet laundry. **Cards:** AX, DC, DS, MC, VI.

SOME UNITS
🔲 📶 📠 🔌 / ⊠ 🖼 /
FEE FEE

HOLIDAY INN ST. CATHARINES/NIAGARA   *Book at aaa.com*   **Phone:** (905)934-8000
(CAA) (SAVE)   6/16-9/30   1P: $149-$299   2P: $149-$299   XP: $10   F18
          5/1-6/15 & 10/1-4/30   1P: $129-$209   2P: $129-$209   XP: $10   F18
▽▽▽ ▽▽▽   **Location:** QEW, exit 46 (Lake St), just e. 2 N Service Rd L2N 4G9. Fax: 905/934-9117. **Facility:** 139 one-bedroom
Small-scale Hotel   standard units. 2 stories (no elevator), interior corridors. **Parking:** on-site. **Terms:** pets ($15 fee).
          Amenities: video games (fee), voice mail, irons, hair dryers. **Dining:** 6:30 am-10 pm, cocktails. **Pool(s):**
          heated outdoor, heated indoor. **Leisure Activities:** whirlpool. *Fee:* massage. **Guest Services:** sundries,
valet and coin laundry. **Business Services:** meeting rooms, business center. **Cards:** AX, DC, DS, MC, VI. **Special Amenities:**
free local telephone calls and free newspaper. *(See color ad card insert & p 354)*

SOME UNITS
🔲 📶 📠 🔌 / ⊠ 🖼 /
FEE FEE

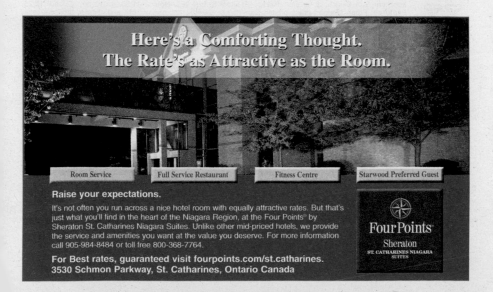

**Here's a Comforting Thought.
The Rate's as Attractive as the Room.**

Room Service   Full Service Restaurant   Fitness Centre   Starwood Preferred Guest

Raise your expectations.

It's not often you run across a nice hotel room with equally attractive rates. But that's
just what you'll find in the heart of the Niagara Region, at the Four Points® by
Sheraton St. Catharines Niagara Suites. Unlike other mid-priced hotels, we provide
the service and amenities you want at the value you deserve. For more information
call 905-984-8484 or toll free 800-368-7764.

For Best rates, guaranteed visit fourpoints.com/st.catharines.
3530 Schmon Parkway, St. Catharines, Ontario Canada

FourPoints
Sheraton
ST. CATHARINES NIAGARA
SUITES

HOWARD JOHNSON HOTEL & CONFERENCE
CENTRE   *Book at aaa.com*   Phone: (905)934-5400

(CAA) (SAVE)

| | 6/16-9/30 | 1P: $99-$289 | 2P: $99-$289 | XP: $10 | F18 |
| | 5/1-6/15 & 10/1-4/30 | 1P: $79-$189 | 2P: $79-$189 | XP: $10 | F18 |

Location: QEW, exit 46 (Lake St). 89 Meadowvale Dr L2N 3Z8. Fax: 905/646-8700. Facility: 97 one-bedroom standard units. 5 stories, interior corridors. Parking: on-site. Terms: pets ($5 extra charge).
Small-scale Hotel Amenities: voice mail, hair dryers. Some: irons. Dining: 24 hours, cocktails. Pool(s): heated indoor. Leisure Activities: sauna, exercise room, volleyball. Guest Services: valet laundry. Business Services: meeting rooms. Cards: AX, DC, DS, MC, VI. Special Amenities: free newspaper. (See color ad p 354)

SOME UNITS

QUALITY HOTEL PARKWAY CONVENTION
CENTRE   *Book at aaa.com*   Phone: (905)688-2324

(CAA) (SAVE)

| | 6/16-9/30 | 1P: $99-$299 | 2P: $99-$299 | XP: $10 | F18 |
| | 5/1-6/15 & 10/1-4/30 | 1P: $89-$199 | 2P: $89-$199 | XP: $10 | F18 |

Location: QEW, exit 47 (Ontario St), 0.8 km s. 327 Ontario St L2R 5L3. Fax: 905/684-6432. Facility: 125 one-bedroom standard units, some with whirlpools. 5 stories, interior corridors. Parking: on-site. Terms: check-
Large-scale Hotel in 4 pm. Amenities: video games (fee), voice mail, irons, hair dryers. Some: high-speed Internet. Dining: 6:30 am-1 am, cocktails. Pool(s): heated indoor. Leisure Activities: whirlpool, steamroom, billiards, video room, exercise room. Guest Services: sundries, valet laundry. Business Services: conference facilities, business center. Cards: AX, CB, DC, DS, JC, MC, VI. Special Amenities: free newspaper. (See color ad p 354)

SOME UNITS
FEE FEE

THE TRAVELODGE ST. CATHARINES   *Book at aaa.com*   Phone: (905)688-1646

(CAA) (SAVE)

| | 7/1-9/5 | 1P: $99 | 2P: $129 | XP: $10 | F16 |
| | 5/1-6/30 & 9/6-4/30 | 1P: $79 | 2P: $89 | XP: $10 | F16 |

Location: QEW, exit 47 (Ontario St). 420 Ontario St L2R 5M1. Fax: 905/688-1646. Facility: 50 one-bedroom standard units, some with whirlpools. 2 stories (no elevator), exterior corridors. Parking: on-site.
Motel Terms: pets ($10 extra charge). Amenities: hair dryers. Dining: 6:30 am-2 pm, cocktails. Pool(s): heated outdoor. Cards: AX, DC, MC, VI.

SOME UNITS
FEE

———— WHERE TO DINE ————

THE BLUE MERMAID SEAFOOD AND
STEAKHOUSE   Lunch: $15-$20   Dinner: $18-$45   Phone: 905/684-7465

(CAA)

Location: Opposite City Hall. 10 Market Street Square L2R 5C6. Hours: 11:30 am-2:30 & 5-10 pm, Sat 4:30 pm-midnight. Closed: Sun. Reservations: suggested. Features: Fresh seafood, shellfish and top-of-the-line Angus steak reigns supreme on this restaurant's well-thought-out menu. The formal wait staff is both professional and friendly; its skills evident at table-side presentations of salad, flambe and coffee. Semi-
Steak & Seafood formal attire; cocktails. Parking: on-site. Cards: AX, DC, MC, VI.

FINE KETTLE 'O' FISH   Lunch: $6-$9   Dinner: $8-$30   Phone: 905/938-3474

Location: S of Carlton, at far end of street. 20 Grote St L2N 2E7. Hours: 11:30 am-10 pm. Closed: 12/25. Features: Fresh seafood (fried, broiled, pan-fried or baked), ranging from fish and chips to broiled lobster,
Seafood show the diversity of menu items served in a casual, cozy setting. Additional selections such as burgers, pasta, steak and sandwiches are also offered. Casual dress; cocktails. Parking: on-site. Cards: AX,
MC, VI.

FRESCO'S EURO GRILL & BAR   Lunch: $5-$8   Dinner: $9-$22   Phone: 905/687-8088

Location: Rt 406 to Fourth Ave, just w; in Ridley Heights Plaza. 100 Fourth Ave L2S 3P3. Hours: 11 am-1 am, Sun-11 pm; Sunday brunch. Closed: 1/1, 12/25. Features: Bright wall murals enhance the casual, comfortable
American restaurant's Mediterranean theme. On the menu is a great variety of pastas, as well as lots of finger foods, burgers, sandwiches and grilled meats. Portions are huge, so come hungry. Locals frequent the all-you-can-eat Sunday brunch buffet and the Sunday night prime rib buffet. Casual dress; cocktails. Parking: on-site. Cards: AX, DC,
MC, VI.

LINA LINGUINI'S PASTA AND GRILLE   Lunch: $7-$11   Dinner: $7-$20   Phone: 905/984-5462

Location: Rt 406 to Fourth Ave, just w; in Ridley Square Plaza. 111 Fourth Ave L2S 3P3. Hours: 11 am-1 am, Sun-11 pm. Closed: 1/1, 12/25. Features: The popular eatery is great for family fun or a casual meal. The menu
Italian is filled with hearty Italian fare, including pastas, pizzas, hearty sandwiches, chicken and veal. On Wednesday night, a create-your-own pasta bar draws a crowd. Casual dress; cocktails. Parking: on-site.
Cards: AX, DC, MC, VI.

MARIE'S SEAFOOD DINING ROOM   Lunch: $8-$16   Dinner: $19-$27   Phone: 905/934-1677

Location: Jct Lakeport Rd; at Port Dalhousie Harbour. 1 Lock St L2N 5B4. Hours: 11 am-11 pm; 4:30 pm-10 pm 9/1-5/31. Closed: 12/24-12/26. Reservations: suggested. Features: A trip to the relaxed dining room is a
Seafood lovely outing for a special meal. In the tourist area of the harbour, the restaurant appeals to locals and tourists alike with a menu that features lobster by the pound, seafood platters for two, chowders, salads and some landlubbers' fare. Homemade desserts are yummy and well worth saving room for. Casual dress; cocktails. Parking: street. Cards: AX, MC, VI.

ST. CATHARINES KEG STEAKHOUSE AND BAR   **Dinner:** $15-$32   **Phone:** 905/680-4585
▼▼▼   **Location:** Directly e of Hwy 406. 344 Glendale Ave L2T 4E3. **Hours:** 3 pm-11 pm, Sat-1 am, Sun-10 pm.
          Reservations: suggested. **Features:** Known for its mesquite-grilled steaks and fun, laid-back atmosphere,
Steak & Seafood   the steak house is a longtime favorite with the local crowd. In addition to great beef, the traditional menu
          lists seafood, grilled chicken, hickory ribs and pasta dishes. Casual dress; cocktails. **Parking:** on-site.
Cards: AX, DC, MC, VI.
$\boxed{Y}$ $\boxed{X}$

SPAGUCCI'S MEDITERRANEAN GRILLE AND
  GRAPPA BAR   **Lunch:** $8-$11   **Dinner:** $10-$28   **Phone:** 905/938-5678
▼▼ ▼▼   **Location:** Jct QEW and Ontario St; in Henley Plaza. 395 Ontario St L2N 7N6. **Hours:** 11 am-midnight, Fri & Sat-1
          am. Closed: 12/25. **Features:** Diners here enjoy the garden-like setting complete with a large flowing water
Italian   fountain and an abundance of greenery. The menu offers a wide selection of casual Italian fare including
          fresh tasty pastas, made-to-order gourmet pizzas, as well as Mediterranean fare including grilled meats and
seafood specialties. Casual dress; cocktails. **Parking:** on-site. **Cards:** AX, MC, VI.
$\boxed{Y}$ $\boxed{X}$

WILDFIRE GRILLHOUSE AND LOUNGE   **Lunch:** $8-$16   **Dinner:** $16-$40   **Phone:** 905/988-9453
▼▼ ▼▼   **Location:** QEW, exit Ontario St N. 410 Ontario St L2R 5M1. **Hours:** 11:30 am-10 pm, Fri-11 pm, Sat 5 pm-11 pm,
          Sun 5 pm-10 pm. Closed major holidays. **Reservations:** suggested. **Features:** Quality steaks, chops and
Steak House   chicken—spiced, grilled to order and sided with steaming vegetables—are the featured fare. Among starters
          are exotic shrimp cocktail, mussels and specialty salads, and all choices come with a hot loaf of sourdough
bread. Contemporary decor adds to the experience, and large candles lend a cozy feel. Diners can choose from booth or table
seating. A specialty wine list is presented. Dressy casual; cocktails. **Parking:** on-site. **Cards:** AX, MC, VI.
$\boxed{Y}$ $\boxed{X}$

THOROLD pop. 18,048

——— **WHERE TO STAY** ———

FOUR POINTS BY SHERATON ST. CATHARINES   *Book at aaa.com*   **Phone:** (905)984-8484
▼▼▼▼▼   5/1-10/31   1P: $109-$199   2P: $109-$199   XP: $10   F17
          11/1-4/30   1P: $99-$154   2P: $99-$154   XP: $10   F17
Large-scale Hotel   **Location:** Hwy 406, exit St. David's Rd W. 3530 Schmon Pkwy L2V 4Y6 (3530 Schmon Pkwy, ST. CATHARINES).
          Fax: 905/984-6691. **Facility:** 129 units. 116 one- and 13 two-bedroom suites with efficiencies (no utensils),
some with whirlpools. 4 stories, interior corridors. *Bath:* combo or shower only. **Parking:** on-site. **Terms:** cancellation fee
imposed, pets ($15 extra charge). **Amenities:** video games (fee), dual phone lines, voice mail, irons, hair dryers. *Some:* high-
speed Internet. **Dining:** In Piazza Pasta and Wine Bar, see separate listing. **Pool(s):** heated indoor. **Leisure Activities:** sauna,
whirlpool, exercise room, basketball, volleyball. **Guest Services:** sundries, valet and coin laundry. **Business Services:**
conference facilities, business center. **Cards:** AX, DC, DS, MC, VI. *(See color ad p 383 & p 5)*
SOME UNITS
$\boxed{ASK}$ $\boxed{S_D}$ $\boxed{\text{†1}}$ $\boxed{Y}$ $\boxed{\text{占}}$ $\boxed{\approx}$ $\boxed{X}$ $\boxed{\text{賽}}$ $\boxed{\text{DATA PORT}}$ $\boxed{\text{🖥}}$ $\boxed{\text{🖨}}$ $\boxed{\text{🖭}}$ / $\boxed{X}$ $\boxed{VCR}$ /
FEE   FEE

——— **WHERE TO DINE** ———

DOM'S PASTA AND GRILL   **Lunch:** $5-$10   **Dinner:** $5-$19   **Phone:** 905/688-4202
▼▼▼   **Location:** Hwy 406, exit St. David's Rd W; at Merrittville Pkwy. 3250 Schmon Pkwy L2V 4Y6. **Hours:** 11 am-11 pm,
          Sun-9 pm. **Features:** The large dining room nurtures a relaxed setting for lunch, dinner and group dining.
Italian   Along with made-to-order pizzas and pasta dishes, the menu lists a great choice of finger foods and grilled
          items, including ribs, steaks and seafood. By the front door, a cabinet displaying decadent desserts is hard
to miss and resist. Casual dress; cocktails. **Parking:** on-site. **Cards:** AX, MC, VI.
$\boxed{X}$

IN PIAZZA PASTA AND WINE BAR   **Lunch:** $7-$11   **Dinner:** $15-$23   **Phone:** 905/984-8484
▼▼ ▼▼   **Location:** Hwy 406, exit St. David's Rd W; in Four Points by Sheraton St. Catharines. 3530 Schmon Pkwy L2V 4Y6.
          Hours: 6:30 am-11 pm. **Features:** This casual eatery offers a varied menu featuring lots of pastas and
Mediterranean   Italian fare as well as grilled steaks, seafood, burgers and sandwiches. To add to the menu variety, the
          restaurant features theme months highlighting different cuisines and decor accents. In the summer months,
the relaxing outdoor patio is a main draw for the locals and tourists alike. Casual dress; cocktails. **Parking:** on-site. **Cards:** AX,
CB, DC, DS, JC, MC, VI.
$\boxed{X}$

WELLAND pop. 48,402

——— **WHERE TO STAY** ———

BEST WESTERN ROSE CITY SUITES   *Book at aaa.com*   **Phone:** (905)732-0922
$\boxed{AAA}$ $\boxed{SAVE}$ 5/1-10/15   1P: $88-$125   2P: $88-$125   XP: $5   F12
          10/16-4/30   1P: $80-$100   2P: $80-$100   XP: $5   F12
▼▼▼▼   **Location:** 1 km w on E Main St, 1 km s. 300 Prince Charles Dr L3C 7B3. Fax: 905/732-0644. **Facility:** 69 one-
          bedroom suites, some with efficiencies or kitchens. 3 stories, interior corridors. **Parking:** on-site.
Small-scale Hotel **Terms:** package plans. **Amenities:** high-speed Internet, voice mail, irons, hair dryers. *Some:* honor bars.
          Dining: 6:30-10:30 am, Sat 7-11 am, Sun 7:30-11:30 am. **Leisure Activities:** saunas, exercise room.
Guest Services: valet laundry. **Business Services:** meeting rooms, business center. **Cards:** AX, DC, DS, MC, VI.
Special Amenities: free newspaper and early check-in/late check-out.
SOME UNITS
$\boxed{S_D}$ $\boxed{\text{†1}}$ $\boxed{\text{賽}}$ $\boxed{\text{DATA PORT}}$ $\boxed{\text{🖨}}$ $\boxed{\text{🖭}}$ / $\boxed{X}$ $\boxed{\text{🖥}}$ /

COMFORT INN   *Book at aaa.com*   **Phone:** 905/732-4811
▼▼ ▼▼   6/1-9/6   1P: $95-$102   2P: $100-$107   XP: $5   F17
          5/1-5/31 & 1/1-4/30   1P: $80-$85   2P: $85-$90   XP: $5   F17
          9/7-12/31   1P: $80-$85   2P: $85-$88   XP: $5   F17
Small-scale Hotel **Location:** 2.5 km n. 870 Niagara St L3C 1M3. Fax: 905/732-9654. **Facility:** 80 one-bedroom standard units,
some with whirlpools. 2 stories (no elevator), interior corridors. **Parking:** on-site, winter plug-ins. **Terms:** pets ($10 fee, in
smoking units on 1st floor). **Cards:** AX, DC, DS, MC, VI. *(See color ad p 331)*
SOME UNITS
$\boxed{ASK}$ $\boxed{\text{🛏}}$ $\boxed{\text{†1}}$ $\boxed{\text{🖭}}$ / $\boxed{X}$ $\boxed{\text{DATA PORT}}$ $\boxed{\text{🖥}}$ $\boxed{\text{🖨}}$ /
FEE

RAMADA INN-WELLAND
Phone: (905)735-6666

6/16-9/15 [ECP]	1P: $106-$140	2P: $106-$140	XP: $10 F12
5/1-6/15 & 9/16-4/30 [ECP]	1P: $90-$106	2P: $90-$106	XP: $10 F12

Small-scale Hotel **Location:** Hwy 20, 1.5 km se on Hwy 58. 1030 Niagara St N L3C 1M6. Fax: 905/735-6894. **Facility:** 76 one-bedroom standard units, some with whirlpools. 3 stories, interior corridors. **Parking:** on-site.
Amenities: voice mail, irons, hair dryers. **Pool(s):** heated indoor. **Leisure Activities:** sauna, whirlpool. **Guest Services:** sundries, valet laundry. **Business Services:** meeting rooms, fax (fee). **Cards:** AX, DS, JC, MC, VI.

SOME UNITS

(A$K) (S/D) (┤┤) (Y) (⌁) (CTV) (✦) (DATA PORT) (▣) / (✕) (VCR) (▤) /
                                                              FEE FEE

RED MILL INN
Phone: 905/732-2159

5/1-9/30	1P: $55-$65	2P: $65-$70	XP: $5 D14
10/1-2/28	1P: $50-$60	2P: $55-$65	XP: $5 D14
3/1-4/30	1P: $45-$50	2P: $55-$60	XP: $5 D14

Motel **Location:** 1 km se of Hwy 20. 1131 Niagara St N (Hwy 58) L3B 5N5. Fax: 905/732-4504. **Facility:** 22 units. 18 one-bedroom standard units. 4 one-bedroom suites with kitchens. 1 story, exterior corridors. **Parking:** on-site. **Terms:** weekly rates available. **Pool(s):** outdoor. **Cards:** AX, DC, MC, VI.

SOME UNITS

(A$K) (S/D) (⌁) (CTV) / (✕) (▤) (▣) /

─────── **WHERE TO DINE** ───────

M.T. BELLIES
Lunch: $5-$9   **Dinner:** $6-$18   **Phone:** 905/788-9474

Location: 0.5 km n on Niagara St; just n of jct Woodlawn. 871 Niagara St L3C 6Y1. **Hours:** 11 am-1 am, Sun-11 pm. Closed: 12/25. **Reservations:** suggested, weekends. **Features:** Big food and big fun are generously served up to any and all who are looking for a friendly, jovial atmosphere with heaping helpings of good food. Check out the amusing anecdotes throughout menu and decor. A children's menu is also available.
American

Casual dress; cocktails. **Parking:** on-site. **Cards:** AX, MC, VI.

(Y) (✕)

Your key to Emergency Road Service...

Emergency Services

AAA is at your service. Your AAA membership card is the key to obtaining Emergency Road Service. AAA can help when your car stalls, you get a flat tire, you run out of gas and even when you're locked out. Anytime, anywhere, call **1-800-AAA-HELP** to get going again. Speech/Hearing **Hearing Impaired: 1-800-955-4TDD.**

Nearby New York

NIAGARA FALLS, NEW YORK pop. 55,593   (See map and index starting on p. 314)

──── WHERE TO STAY ────

BEL AIRE MOTEL
Phone: (716)297-2250   **31**

AAA SAVE

6/19-9/6	1P: $58-$118	2P: $62-$128	XP: $8
5/1-6/18	1P: $38-$120	2P: $44-$120	XP: $5
9/7-10/13	1P: $38-$80	2P: $44-$80	XP: $6
10/14-4/30	1P: $36-$60	2P: $36-$70	XP: $5

Motel   **Location:** I-190, exit 22, 2 mi e. 9470 Niagara Falls Blvd 14304. Fax: 716/297-8712. **Facility:** 22 units. 19 one-bedroom standard units. 3 one-bedroom suites ($50-$149). 1 story, exterior corridors. *Bath:* combo or shower only. **Parking:** on-site. **Terms:** 3 day cancellation notice-fee imposed. **Pool(s):** heated outdoor. **Cards:** AX, MC, VI.

SOME UNITS

BEST WESTERN SUMMIT INN
Phone: (716)297-5050   **34**

AAA SAVE

5/17-9/5	1P: $79-$159	2P: $79-$159	XP: $10 F17
5/1-5/16 & 9/6-4/30	1P: $59-$139	2P: $59-$139	XP: $10 F17

Small-scale Hotel   **Location:** I-190, exit 22, 2.1 mi e on US 62 S. 9500 Niagara Falls Blvd 14304. Fax: 716/297-0802. **Facility:** 88 one-bedroom standard units, some with whirlpools. 2 stories (no elevator), interior corridors. **Parking:** on-site. **Terms:** weekly rates available, package plans, small pets only ($8 fee, with prior approval). **Amenities:** video library, irons, hair dryers. **Pool(s):** heated indoor. **Leisure Activities:** sauna. **Guest Services:** coin laundry. **Business Services:** meeting rooms, PC. **Cards:** AX, DC, DS, MC, VI. **Special Amenities:** free expanded continental breakfast.

SOME UNITS

FEE   FEE

BUDGET HOST INN   *Book at aaa.com*
Phone: (716)283-3839   **18**

AAA SAVE

7/1-8/31	1P: $89-$209	2P: $89-$239	XP: $8 F8
9/1-10/31	1P: $59-$169	2P: $69-$189	XP: $8 F8
5/1-6/30	1P: $59-$169	2P: $59-$189	XP: $8 F8
11/1-4/30	1P: $59-$129	2P: $59-$129	

Motel   **Location:** I-190, exit 22, just e on US 62 S. 6621 Niagara Falls Blvd 14304. Fax: 716/236-0586. **Facility:** 30 one-bedroom standard units, some with efficiencies. 1 story, exterior corridors. **Parking:** on-site. **Terms:** cancellation fee imposed, [CP] meal plan available, package plans, pets ($8 deposit). **Pool(s):** small outdoor. **Cards:** AX, DS, MC, VI. **Special Amenities: free continental breakfast and free local telephone calls.**

SOME UNITS

FEE

COMFORT INN THE POINTE   *Book at aaa.com*
Phone: (716)284-6835   **12**

AAA SAVE

6/17-9/4 [ECP]	1P: $119-$149	2P: $129-$159	XP: $10 F18
5/1-6/16 [ECP]	1P: $69-$149	2P: $79-$159	XP: $10 F18
9/5-10/22 [ECP]	1P: $69-$102	2P: $79-$112	XP: $10 F18
10/23-4/30 [ECP]	1P: $55-$92	2P: $65-$102	XP: $10 F18

Small-scale Hotel   **Location:** I-290 W to I-190, exit 21 (Robert Moses Pkwy) to State Reservation Park entrance. 1 Prospect Pointe 14303. Fax: 716/284-5177. **Facility:** 118 units. 117 one-bedroom standard units, some with whirlpools. 1 one-bedroom suite ($125-$400) with whirlpool. 6 stories, interior corridors. **Parking:** on-site. **Terms:** 2 night minimum stay - seasonal and/or weekends, package plans. **Amenities:** video games, voice mail, irons, hair dryers. **Dining:** 7 am-11 pm; hours vary off season, cocktails. **Leisure Activities:** exercise room. **Guest Services:** gift shop, valet laundry. **Business Services:** meeting rooms. **Cards:** AX, CB, DC, DS, JC, MC, VI. **Special Amenities: free expanded continental breakfast and free newspaper.**

SOME UNITS

DAYS INN AT THE FALLS   *Book at aaa.com*
Phone: (716)284-8801   **4**

AAA SAVE

5/1-9/30	1P: $59-$199	2P: $59-$199	XP: $10 F17
10/1-4/30	1P: $49-$159	2P: $49-$159	XP: $10 F17

Small-scale Hotel   **Location:** On SR 104; downtown; facing entrance to Rainbow Bridge to Canada. 443 Main St 14301. Fax: 716/284-8633. **Facility:** 168 one-bedroom standard units, some with whirlpools. 9 stories, interior corridors. **Parking:** on-site. **Terms:** package plans. **Amenities:** video games, hair dryers. *Some:* irons. **Dining:** 24 hours, cocktails. **Pool(s):** heated indoor. **Leisure Activities:** sauna, exercise room. **Guest Services:** valet and coin laundry. **Business Services:** meeting rooms. **Cards:** AX, DC, DS, MC, VI.

SOME UNITS

ECONO LODGE AT THE FALLS   *Book at aaa.com*
Phone: (716)283-1100   **37**

AAA SAVE

7/1-8/31	1P: $50-$199	2P: $55-$199	XP: $5 F16
5/1-6/30	1P: $39-$189	2P: $39-$189	XP: $5 F16
9/1-4/30	1P: $35-$100	2P: $35-$100	XP: $5 F16

Motel   **Location:** I-190, exit 22, 0.3 mi n on US 62. 5919 Niagara Falls Blvd 14304. Fax: 716/283-2150. **Facility:** 70 one-bedroom standard units, some with whirlpools. 2 stories (no elevator), exterior corridors. **Parking:** on-site. **Terms:** cancellation fee imposed. **Amenities:** voice mail, irons, hair dryers. **Pool(s):** heated outdoor. **Leisure Activities:** playground. *Fee:* game room. **Guest Services:** coin laundry. **Cards:** AX, DS, MC, VI. **Special Amenities: free local telephone calls and free newspaper.**

SOME UNITS

FEE FEE

(See map and index starting on p. 314)

FOUR POINTS BY SHERATON　*Book at aaa.com*　Phone: (716)285-2521　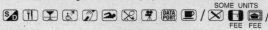　**15**

6/30-10/7	1P: $129	2P: $129	XP: $10　F
5/1-6/29	1P: $99	2P: $99	XP: $10　F
1/1-4/30	1P: $79	2P: $79	XP: $10　F
10/8-12/31	1P: $59	2P: $59	XP: $10　F

Large-scale Hotel Location: I-190, exit 21 (Robert Moses Pkwy) to City Traffic exit, just w on Rainbow Blvd. 114 Buffalo Ave 14303. Fax: 716/285-0963. **Facility:** 189 units. 183 one-bedroom standard units. 6 one-bedroom suites with efficiencies, some with whirlpools. 7 stories, interior corridors. *Bath:* combo or shower only. **Parking:** on-site. **Amenities:** video library (fee), dual phone lines, voice mail, irons, hair dryers. **Dining:** 6:30 am-11 pm; hours vary off season, cocktails. **Pool(s):** heated indoor. **Leisure Activities:** sauna, whirlpool, indoor children's playground, exercise room. *Fee:* game room. **Guest Services:** gift shop, valet and coin laundry. **Business Services:** meeting rooms, PC, fax (fee). **Cards:** AX, CB, MC, VI.

SOME UNITS

[icons] / FEE FEE

HAMPTON INN-NIAGARA FALLS　*Book at aaa.com*　Phone: (716)285-6666　**17**

7/1-8/21 [ECP]	1P: $119-$189	2P: $129-$199
8/22-10/31 [ECP]	1P: $89-$169	2P: $99-$179
5/1-6/30 [ECP]	1P: $89-$159	2P: $99-$169
11/1-4/30 [ECP]	1P: $64-$114	2P: $74-$124

Small-scale Hotel Location: I-190, exit 21 (Robert Moses Pkwy) to City Traffic exit, just w. 501 Rainbow Blvd 14303. Fax: 716/285-1423. **Facility:** 100 one-bedroom standard units, some with whirlpools. 5 stories, interior corridors. *Bath:* combo or shower only. **Parking:** on-site. **Terms:** check-in 4 pm, package plans. **Amenities:** video games, high-speed Internet, voice mail, safes, irons, hair dryers. **Pool(s):** small heated indoor. **Leisure Activities:** whirlpool, exercise room. **Guest Services:** valet and coin laundry. **Business Services:** meeting rooms. **Cards:** AX, DC, DS, MC, VI.

SOME UNITS

[icons] /

HOLIDAY INN AT THE FALLS　*Book at aaa.com*　Phone: (716)282-2211　**27**

6/24-9/5	1P: $99-$229	2P: $99-$229	XP: $10　F18
5/1-6/23	1P: $79-$139	2P: $79-$139	XP: $10　F18
9/6-4/30	1P: $69-$139	2P: $69-$139	XP: $10　F18

Location: Just s of Rainbow Mall; 2 blks from the falls; downtown. 231 Third St 14303. Fax: 716/282-2748. **Small-scale Hotel Facility:** 161 one-bedroom standard units, some with whirlpools. 8 stories, interior corridors. **Parking:** on-site. **Amenities:** video games, voice mail, irons, hair dryers. **Dining:** 24 hours, cocktails. **Pool(s):** heated indoor. **Leisure Activities:** sauna, whirlpool, playground, exercise room. *Fee:* game room. **Guest Services:** valet and coin laundry. **Business Services:** meeting rooms. **Cards:** AX, DC, DS, MC, VI. *(See color ad p 345)*

SOME UNITS

[icons] /

HOLIDAY INN SELECT-NIAGARA FALLS　*Book at aaa.com*　Phone: (716)285-3361　**5**

7/1-9/4	1P: $125-$195	2P: $125-$195	XP: $10　F18
5/1-6/30 & 9/5-10/29	1P: $95-$175	2P: $95-$175	XP: $10　F18
10/30-4/30	1P: $75-$125	2P: $75-$125	XP: $10　F18

Location: Third and Niagara sts; downtown. Located across from the Seneca Niagara Casino. 300 Third St 14303. **Small-scale Hotel** Fax: 716/285-3900. **Facility:** 397 units. 369 one-bedroom standard units. 28 one-bedroom suites ($199-$399), some with whirlpools. 6 stories, interior corridors. *Bath:* combo or shower only. **Parking:** on-site. **Terms:** package plans. **Amenities:** video library (fee), video games, dual phone lines, voice mail, irons, hair dryers. **Dining:** 6:30 am-10 pm; to 11 pm in summer; hours may vary in winter, cocktails. **Pool(s):** heated indoor. **Leisure Activities:** sauna, whirlpool, exercise room. *Fee:* game room. **Guest Services:** gift shop, valet and coin laundry. **Business Services:** conference facilities, fax (fee). **Cards:** AX, CB, DC, DS, JC, MC, VI.

SOME UNITS

[icons] / FEE FEE

HOLLEY RANKINE HOUSE　　Phone: (716)285-4790　**28**

All Year [BP]	1P: $60	2P: $120

Historic Bed & Breakfast

Location: I-190, exit 21 (Robert Moses Pkwy), just w on Buffalo Ave, then just s. Located in a residential area. 525 Riverside Dr 14303. **Facility:** This stately stone house was built in 1955. Smoke free premises. 5 one-bedroom standard units. 2 stories (no elevator), interior corridors. *Bath:* some shared or private, combo or shower only. **Parking:** on-site. **Terms:** 2 night minimum stay - weekends, age restrictions may apply, 7 day cancellation notice. **Amenities:** hair dryers. **Cards:** MC, VI.

SOME UNITS

[ASK] [icons] /

HOWARD JOHNSON HOTEL (CLOSEST TO THE FALLS)　*Book at aaa.com*　Phone: (716)285-5261　**3**

6/24-9/5 [ECP]	1P: $105-$215	2P: $105-$215	XP: $10　F18
9/6-10/21 [ECP]	1P: $95-$125	2P: $95-$125	XP: $10　F18
5/1-6/23 [ECP]	1P: $89-$120	2P: $89-$120	XP: $10　F18
10/22-4/30 [ECP]	1P: $79-$105	2P: $79-$105	XP: $10　F18

Small-scale Hotel Location: I-190, exit 21 (Robert Moses Pkwy), 2 mi e, just n to Rainbow Blvd, then just s. Located adjacent to Rainbow Bridge. 454 Main St 14301. Fax: 716/285-8536. **Facility:** 80 one-bedroom standard units, some with whirlpools. 5 stories, interior corridors. **Parking:** on-site. **Terms:** check-in 4 pm, 2 night minimum stay - seasonal and/or weekends, package plans, small pets only ($10 extra charge). **Amenities:** irons, hair dryers. **Pool(s):** heated indoor. **Leisure Activities:** sauna. *Fee:* game room. **Guest Services:** coin laundry. **Cards:** AX, CB, DC, DS, MC, VI. **Special Amenities:** free expanded continental breakfast and free newspaper.

SOME UNITS

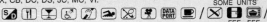

[icons] FEE / FEE FEE

(See map and index starting on p. 314)

HOWARD JOHNSON INN-NIAGARA   *Book at aaa.com*   Phone: (716)283-8791   **14**

AAA SAVE
WWW

6/21-9/14	1P: $69-$139	2P: $69-$139	XP: $10 F16
9/15-12/31	1P: $69-$89	2P: $69-$89	XP: $10 F16
5/1-6/20	1P: $59-$89	2P: $59-$89	XP: $10 F16
1/1-4/30	1P: $39-$69	2P: $39-$69	XP: $10 F16

Small-scale Hotel **Location:** I-190, exit 22, just e. 6505 Niagara Falls Blvd 14304. Fax: 716/283-9313. **Facility:** 88 one-bedroom standard units, some with whirlpools. 2 stories (no elevator), interior corridors. **Parking:** on-site. **Terms:** cancellation fee imposed, package plans. **Amenities:** irons, hair dryers. **Pool(s):** outdoor. **Guest Services:** coin laundry. **Business Services:** meeting rooms. **Cards:** AX, CB, DC, DS, JC, MC, VI. **Special Amenities:** free newspaper and early check-in/late check-out.

SOME UNITS

QUALITY HOTEL AND SUITES "AT THE FALLS"   *Book at aaa.com*   Phone: (716)282-1212   **19**

WWW WWW

6/17-9/15	1P: $99-$299	2P: $99-$299	XP: $15 F16
5/1-6/16	1P: $89-$299	2P: $89-$299	XP: $15 F16
9/16-4/30	1P: $79-$299	2P: $79-$299	XP: $15 F16

Small-scale Hotel **Location:** Downtown. 240 Rainbow Blvd 14303. Fax: 716/282-0051. **Facility:** 199 units. 185 one-bedroom standard units. 14 one-bedroom suites ($134-$309), some with whirlpools. 4 stories, interior corridors. **Parking:** on-site. **Terms:** cancellation fee imposed, pets ($20 extra charge). **Amenities:** voice mail, irons, hair dryers. **Pool(s):** small heated indoor. **Leisure Activities:** whirlpool. **Guest Services:** gift shop, valet laundry. **Business Services:** meeting rooms. **Cards:** AX, CB, DC, DS, JC, MC, VI.

SOME UNITS

QUALITY INN NIAGARA   *Book at aaa.com*   Phone: (716)283-0621   **30**

WWW WWW

All Year	1P: $39-$179	2P: $45-$199	XP: $10 F16

Small-scale Hotel **Location:** I-190, exit 22, 0.8 mi e. 7708 Niagara Falls Blvd 14304. Fax: 716/283-2121. **Facility:** 94 one-bedroom standard units, some with whirlpools. 2 stories (no elevator), interior corridors. **Parking:** on-site. **Terms:** cancellation fee imposed, [AP], [BP], [CP] & [ECP] meal plans available. **Amenities:** irons, hair dryers. **Pool(s):** indoor. **Guest Services:** valet laundry. **Business Services:** conference facilities. **Cards:** AX, CB, DC, DS, MC, VI.

SOME UNITS

RAMADA INN BY THE FALLS   *Book at aaa.com*   Phone: (716)282-1734   **9**

AAA SAVE
WWW WWW

7/1-9/5	1P: $99-$199	2P: $99-$199	XP: $13 F18
5/1-6/30	1P: $69-$199	2P: $69-$199	XP: $13 F18
11/1-4/30	1P: $49-$199	2P: $49-$199	XP: $13 F18
9/6-10/31	1P: $69-$179	2P: $69-$179	XP: $13 F18

Small-scale Hotel **Location:** I-190, exit 21 (Robert Moses Pkwy), 3.5 mi w; just s of Rainbow Mall. 219 Fourth St 14303. Fax: 716/282-1881. **Facility:** 112 one-bedroom standard units, some with whirlpools. 2 stories (no elevator), interior corridors. **Parking:** on-site. **Terms:** 2 night minimum stay - seasonal and/or weekends, [AP] & [BP] meal plans available, package plans. **Amenities:** voice mail, irons, hair dryers. **Dining:** 6:30 am-11 pm, cocktails. **Pool(s):** heated indoor. **Leisure Activities:** whirlpool. **Guest Services:** valet and coin laundry. **Business Services:** meeting rooms. **Cards:** AX, DS, MC, VI. **Special Amenities:** free newspaper.

SOME UNITS

THE RED COACH INN   Phone: (716)282-1459   **26**

AAA SAVE
WWW WWW

7/1-9/5 [ECP]	1P: $139-$179	2P: $139-$179	XP: $20
5/1-6/30 & 9/6-10/31 [ECP]	1P: $109-$139	2P: $109-$139	XP: $20
11/1-4/30 [ECP]	1P: $89-$129	2P: $89-$129	XP: $20

Historic Country Inn **Location:** Downtown. 2 Buffalo Ave 14303. Fax: 716/282-2650. **Facility:** Views of the rapids are a draw at this inn, which offers 18th-century furnishings and distinctively decorated suites, two with laundry machines. Smoke free premises. 15 units. 2 one-bedroom standard units with whirlpools. 8 one- and 5 two-bedroom suites ($129-$339) with whirlpools, some with kitchens. 3 stories (no elevator), interior/exterior corridors. **Parking:** on-site. **Terms:** 14 day cancellation notice-fee imposed, package plans. **Amenities:** CD players, voice mail, irons, hair dryers. **Dining:** restaurant, see separate listing. **Guest Services:** valet laundry. **Business Services:** meeting rooms. **Cards:** DS, MC, VI. **Special Amenities:** free expanded continental breakfast and free newspaper.

SOME UNITS

RODEWAY INN AT THE FALLS   *Book at aaa.com*   Phone: (716)284-9778   **2**

AAA SAVE
WWW WWW

6/15-9/10	1P: $69-$139	2P: $69-$139	XP: $10 F18
9/11-12/31	1P: $59-$89	2P: $59-$89	XP: $10 F18
5/1-6/14	1P: $49-$79	2P: $49-$79	XP: $10 F18
1/1-4/30	1P: $49-$69	2P: $49-$69	XP: $10 F18

Small-scale Hotel **Location:** I-190, exit 21 (Robert Moses Pkwy) to City Traffic exit, just n at Rainbow Blvd. Located near the falls. 795 Rainbow Blvd 14303. Fax: 716/284-5252. **Facility:** 39 one-bedroom standard units. 2 stories (no elevator), interior corridors. **Parking:** on-site. **Terms:** cancellation fee imposed, package plans. **Cards:** AX, CB, DC, DS, JC, MC, VI. **Special Amenities:** free local telephone calls and early check-in/late check-out.

SOME UNITS

(See map and index starting on p. 314)

SUPER 8 MOTEL   *Book at aaa.com*   Phone: (716)283-3151   **23**

(AAA) (SAVE)
7/1-8/31	1P: $69-$179	2P: $69-$179	XP: $10	F12
4/1-4/30	1P: $59-$69	2P: $59-$69	XP: $10	F12
5/1-6/30 & 9/1-3/31	1P: $49-$59	2P: $49-$59	XP: $10	F12

Location: I-190, exit 22, 0.6 mi e. 7680 Niagara Falls Blvd 14304. Fax: 716/215-0296. **Facility:** 73 one-bedroom
Small-scale Hotel standard units, some with whirlpools. 1-3 stories (no elevator), interior corridors. *Bath:* combo or shower
only. **Parking:** on-site. **Terms:** cancellation fee imposed, [CP] meal plan available, package plans.
Amenities: voice mail, hair dryers. **Pool(s):** heated outdoor. **Guest Services:** area transportation (fee)-Seneca Niagara Casino.
Business Services: PC (fee). **Cards:** AX, CB, DC, DS, MC, VI. **Special Amenities: free continental breakfast and free local
telephone calls.**

SOME UNITS

SWISS COTTAGE INN   Phone: (716)283-8142   **29**

(AAA) (SAVE)
| All Year | 1P: $32-$135 | 2P: $42-$169 | XP: $10 | F16 |

Location: I-190, exit 22, 0.5 mi e. 6831 Niagara Falls Blvd 14304. Fax: 716/283-2420. **Facility:** 31 one-bedroom
standard units. 1 story, exterior corridors. *Bath:* combo or shower only. **Parking:** on-site.
Motel   **Terms:** cancellation fee imposed, weekly rates available, package plans. **Pool(s):** small outdoor.
Cards: AX, DS, MC, VI. **Special Amenities: early check-in/late check-out and preferred room (subject
to availability with advance reservations).**

SOME UNITS

THRIFTLODGE   *Book at aaa.com*   Phone: (716)297-2660   **38**

(AAA) (SAVE)
| 6/1-9/30 | 1P: $79-$84 | 2P: $89-$99 |
| 5/1-5/31 & 10/1-4/30 | 1P: $45-$50 | 2P: $55-$60 |

Location: I-190, exit 22, 1.8 mi e. 9401 Niagara Falls Blvd 14304. Fax: 716/297-7675. **Facility:** 45 one-bedroom
standard units, some with whirlpools. 1 story, exterior corridors. **Parking:** on-site. **Terms:** small pets only
Motel   ($10 fee). **Pool(s):** outdoor. **Cards:** AX, DC, MC, VI. **Special Amenities: free continental
breakfast.**

SOME UNITS

──────── **WHERE TO DINE** ────────

**CHU'S DINING LOUNGE-CHINESE
FOOD**   Lunch: $6-$11   Dinner: $6-$11   Phone: 716/285-7278   **10**

(AAA)   **Location:** Jct US 62A and SR 104, 0.4 mi ne. 1019 Main St 14301. **Hours:** 11 am-11 pm. Closed: 12/25.
Features: Abundant servings of familiar Chinese choices are prepared individually and served piping hot.
Only the freshest and best ingredients are used to produce the most flavorful offerings. Friendly, fast service
is the norm in the family-owned and -operated restaurant. Casual dress; cocktails. **Parking:** street.
Chinese   **Cards:** AX, DS, MC, VI.

COMO RESTAURANT & DELI   Lunch: $4-$8   Dinner: $7-$18   Phone: 716/285-9341   **1**

(AAA)   **Location:** Jct SR 104, 1 mi s of US 62A. 2220 Pine Ave 14301. **Hours:** 11:30 am-10 pm, Fri & Sat-11 pm. Closed:
5/30, 7/4, 12/25. **Reservations:** suggested. **Features:** Family-owned since 1927, the restaurant consistently
delivers tasty homemade pasta and traditional American dishes. Generous portions and reasonable prices
make this a good choice for the value-conscious diner. Casual dress; cocktails. **Parking:** on-site.
Italian   **Cards:** AX, DS, MC, VI.

FORTUNA'S   Lunch: $5-$8   Dinner: $7-$17   Phone: 716/282-2252   **11**

Location: Jct 19th St and Forest. 827 19th St 14301. **Hours:** 4 pm-9:30 pm, Fri 11:30 am-10 pm, Sat 4 pm-10:30
pm, Sun noon-8:30 pm. Closed: 7/4, 11/24, 12/24, 12/25; also Mon & Tues. **Features:** Classic Italian fare
made from the freshest ingredients available and served by the friendly staff in a casual, subdued setting
Italian   distinguish this restaurant. Longtime favorites include handmade gnocchi and ravioli made from secret
family recipes. Casual dress; cocktails. **Parking:** on-site. **Cards:** AX, DS, MC, VI.

JOHN'S FLAMING HEARTH   Lunch: $5-$9   Dinner: $12-$19   Phone: 716/297-1414   **2**

Location: I-190, exit 22, 1.2 mi e on US 62, then 0.5 mi n on SR 265. 1965 Military Rd 14304. **Hours:** 11:30 am-3 &
4-10 pm, Fri & Sat-11 pm, Sun noon-9 pm. Closed: Mon. **Reservations:** suggested. **Features:** Chicken
Marsala, New York strip steak and Polynesian chicken are representative of tried-and-true menu selections.
American   The dining room is formally cozy. Desserts, such as the specialty pumpkin ice cream pie and homemade
apple pie, melt in the mouth. Casual dress; cocktails. **Parking:** on-site. **Cards:** AX, DC, DS, MC, VI.

KOBAN'S   Dinner: $8-$12   Phone: 716/282-5151   **9**

Location: 2 mi e from center. 3045 Niagara St 14301. **Hours:** 5 pm-10 pm, Sun 4 pm-9 pm. Closed major
holidays; also Mon & Tues. **Features:** Specialties at the tavern restaurant include steak, prime rib, seafood
American   and great French onion soup. Casual dress; cocktails. **Parking:** on-site.

MICHAEL'S   Lunch: $5-$7   Dinner: $7-$9   Phone: 716/282-4043   **12**

Location: Downtown. 3011 Pine Ave 14301. **Hours:** 11 am-11:30 pm, Fri & Sat-midnight. Closed: 4/16, 11/24,
12/25. **Features:** The small diner offers generous portions of Italian and American comfort foods at
Italian   reasonable prices. Servers are friendly and efficient. Casual dress; beer & wine only. **Parking:** on-site.
Cards: MC, VI.

(See map and index starting on p. 314)

PETE'S MARKET HOUSE RESTAURANT   **Lunch:** $3-$6   **Dinner:** $4-$18   **Phone:** 716/282-7225   ③
▼▼▼▼   **Location:** Jct SR 104, 0.8 mi s of US 62A. 1701 Pine Ave 14301. **Hours:** 11:15 am-2:15 & 4:30-9:30 pm, Fri 11:15
                 am-10:30 pm, Sat 11:15 am-3 & 3:30-10 pm, Sun 1 pm-10 pm. **Features:** The casual, popular dining spot
Traditional Steak occupies an 1800s-style building with original tin-type ceilings. The menu centers on all-American favorites,
& Seafood   such as thick sandwiches, homemade soups, juicy steaks, prime rib and lobster. Expect a friendly,
                 hometown atmosphere and service to match. Casual dress; cocktails. **Parking:** on-site.   🍽️ ✖️

THE RED COACH INN RESTAURANT   **Lunch:** $4-$9   **Dinner:** $7-$20   **Phone:** 716/282-1459   ④
ⓐⓐⓐ   **Location:** Downtown; in The Red Coach Inn. 2 Buffalo Ave 14303. **Hours:** 11:30 am-10 pm, Sun
                 noon-10 pm; 11:30 am-2:30 & 5-9 pm, Fri & Sat 11:30 am-10 pm, Sun 1 pm-9 pm 11/1-4/30. Closed: 12/25.
▼▼▼▼▼▼   **Reservations:** suggested. **Features:** The Tudor-style, tavern-like dining room has an Old World feel.
                 Selections on the varied menu display creative preparation and nice presentation. The house specialty is
American   succulent prime rib. Servers exhibit good menu knowledge and timely follow-up. Casual dress; cocktails.
                 Parking: on-site. **Cards:** DS, MC, VI.   🍽️ ✖️

TIMBER LODGE STEAKHOUSE   **Dinner:** $9-$22   **Phone:** 716/283-2548   ⑧
▼▼▼▼ ▼▼▼▼   **Location:** I-190, exit 22, just e. 6560 Niagara Falls Blvd 14304. **Hours:** 4 pm-10 pm, Fri-11 pm, Sat 3 pm-11 pm,
                 Sun noon-9 pm. Closed: 11/24, 12/25. **Features:** The casual steak house is decorated in a lodge-like motif
Steak House   of antler chandeliers and knotty pine furniture. The emphasis is on plentiful portions and value prices. In
                 addition to numerous selections of quality beef, the menu includes chicken, shrimp and fresh fish choices.
Come with a healthy appetite. Casual dress; cocktails. **Parking:** on-site. **Cards:** AX, DC, DS, MC, VI.   🍽️ ✖️

TOP OF THE FALLS RESTAURANT   **Lunch:** $5-$8   **Dinner:** $7-$25   **Phone:** 716/278-0337   ⑥
▼▼▼▼   **Location:** On Goat Island; at Terrapin Point. Goat Island-American Falls Park 14302. **Hours:** Open 5/28-10/1; 11
                 am-10 pm; Fri & Sat-7 pm, Thurs & Sun-5 pm 9/6-10/28. **Reservations:** accepted. **Features:** The stark
American   decor of the second floor dining room serves to accentuate all the more the excellent Horseshoe Falls
                 views, which are afforded from every table. Simple menu offerings include sandwiches, burgers, salad and
finger foods. Servers are pleasant. Casual dress; cocktails. **Parking:** on-site (fee). **Cards:** AX, DS, MC, VI.   🍽️ ✖️

This ends listings for the Niagara Falls Vicinity.
The following page resumes the alphabetical listings of
cities in Ontario.

NIAGARA-ON-THE-LAKE —*See Niagara Falls p. 376.*

NORTH BAY pop. 52,771

——— **WHERE TO STAY** ———

BEST WESTERN NORTH BAY   **Book at aaa.com**   Phone: (705)474-5800

(CAA) (SAVE)
♥♥♥ ♥♥♥

7/1-10/15	1P: $119-$189	2P: $129-$199	XP: $15	F18
5/1-6/30 & 10/16-4/30	1P: $89-$119	2P: $99-$129	XP: $15	F18

Location: Hwy 11, exit Lakeshore Dr, 4 km n on Hwy 11B. Located in a commercial area. 700 Lakeshore Dr P1A 2G4. Fax: 705/474-8699. **Facility:** 130 units. 128 one-bedroom standard units. 2 one-bedroom suites. 2 stories
Small-scale Hotel (no elevator), interior corridors. **Parking:** on-site, winter plug-ins. **Terms:** package plans. **Amenities:** video games (fee), voice mail, irons, hair dryers. *Some:* CD players. **Dining:** 7 am-10 pm, cocktails, also, Joso's, see separate listing. **Pool(s):** heated indoor. **Leisure Activities:** saunas, whirlpool, exercise room. **Guest Services:** valet laundry. **Business Services:** meeting rooms. **Cards:** AX, DC, DS, MC, VI. *(See color ad below)*

SOME UNITS
🆂🅳 🐾 🍽 🎣 ✕ 🎥 📠 💻 / ✕ 📶 🖼 /

CLARION RESORT PINEWOOD PARK   **Book at aaa.com**   Phone: (705)472-0810

(CAA) (SAVE)
♥♥♥ ♥♥♥ ♥♥♥

9/1-4/30	1P: $168-$185	2P: $168-$185	XP: $10	F18
5/1-8/31	1P: $158-$175	2P: $158-$175	XP: $10	F18

Location: Hwy 11, exit Lakeshore Dr, immediately turn s on Pinewood Park Dr, then 0.7 km. Located in a commercial
Resort area. 201 Pinewood Park Dr P1B 8J8 (PO Box 687). Fax: 705/472-4427. **Facility:** A round of golf or perhaps some cross country skiing in winter, it's all right at the back door of this hotel. 102 one-bedroom standard
Small-scale Hotel units, some with whirlpools. 3 stories (no elevator), interior corridors. **Parking:** on-site, winter plug-ins.
Terms: [AP], [BP], [CP], [ECP] & [MAP] meal plans available, package plans, small pets only (with prior approval). **Amenities:** voice mail, irons, hair dryers. *Some:* honor bars. **Dining:** 2 restaurants, 6 am-10 pm, cocktails. **Pool(s):** heated outdoor. **Leisure Activities:** saunas, whirlpool, snowmobiling, exercise room, volleyball. **Fee:** golf-18 holes, driving range, cross country skiing, ski equipment, massage, game room. **Guest Services:** valet and coin laundry. **Business Services:** conference facilities. **Cards:** AX, DC, DS, MC, VI. **Special Amenities:** free local telephone calls and free newspaper.

SOME UNITS
🆂🅳 🐾 🍽 🍷 📶 🎣 ✕ 📠 💻 / ✕ 📹 🖼 🖼 /
FEE   FEE   FEE

COMFORT INN   **Book at aaa.com**   Phone: (705)494-9444

(CAA) (SAVE)
♥♥♥ ♥♥♥

All Year	1P: $89-$109	2P: $99-$129	XP: $10	F18

Location: Hwy 11B, exit Lakeshore Dr, 4 km n of jct Hwy 11. Located in a commercial area. 676 Lakeshore Dr P1A 2G4. Fax: 705/494-8461. **Facility:** 81 one-bedroom standard units. 2 stories (no elevator), interior corridors. **Parking:** on-site, winter plug-ins. **Terms:** package plans. **Amenities:** irons, hair dryers. **Guest Services:**
Small-scale Hotel valet laundry. **Cards:** AX, CB, DC, DS, JC, MC, VI.

SOME UNITS
🆂🅳 🐾 🍽 🎥 💻 / ✕ 📠 🖼 /

COMFORT INN-AIRPORT   **Book at aaa.com**   Phone: (705)476-5400

♥♥♥ ♥♥♥

All Year	1P: $78-$160	2P: $87-$160	XP: $10	F18

Location: 3 km e on Hwy 11 and 17 Bypass at O'Brien St exit. Located in a commercial area. 1200 O'Brien St P1B
Small-scale Hotel 9B3. Fax: 705/476-1295. **Facility:** 60 one-bedroom standard units. 2 stories (no elevator), interior corridors. **Parking:** on-site, winter plug-ins. **Terms:** package plans. **Amenities:** irons, hair dryers. **Guest Services:**
valet laundry. **Cards:** AX, CB, DC, DS, JC, MC, VI.

SOME UNITS
🅰🆂🅺 🆂🅳 🐾 🍽 🎥 📠 💻 / ✕ 🖼 🖼 /
FEE

SUPER 8   **Book at aaa.com**   Phone: (705)495-4551

♥♥♥ ♥♥♥

All Year	1P: $76	2P: $87	XP: $10	F12

Location: Hwy 11, exit Lakeshore Dr, 4.5 km n on Hwy 11B. Located in a commercial area. 570 Lakeshore Dr P1A 2E6.
Small-scale Hotel Fax: 705/495-0794. **Facility:** 50 one-bedroom standard units, some with efficiencies. 3 stories (no elevator), interior corridors. **Bath:** combo or shower only. **Parking:** on-site, winter plug-ins. **Terms:** pets (with prior approval). **Amenities:** hair dryers. **Guest Services:** valet laundry. **Cards:** AX, DC, MC, VI.

SOME UNITS
🅰🆂🅺 🆂🅳 🐾 🍽 🔧 🎥 📠 / ✕ 📹 🖼 /
FEE

Best Western
Best Western North Bay
HOTEL AND CONFERENCE CENTRE
At Your Service.

AAA Specials

North Bay's Largest Conference Hotel.
www.bestwesternnorthbay.com

Free High Speed Internet
700 LAKESHORE DRIVE North Bay, ON P1A 2G4
(705) 474-5800 Toll Free 1-800-461-6199

TRAVELODGE-AIRPORT   **Book at aaa.com**   Phone: (705)495-1133
　　▽▽▽ ▽▽▽   All Year   .   1P: $99-$149   2P: $109-$149
Small-scale Hotel   **Location:** Jct Hwy 11, 17 and Seymour St. Located in a commercial area. 1525 Seymour St P1B 8G4. **Fax:** 705/495-1540. **Facility:** 100 one-bedroom standard units. 2 stories (no elevator), interior corridors. **Parking:** on-site, winter plug-ins. **Terms:** package plans. **Amenities:** video games (fee), voice mail, irons, hair dryers. **Pool(s):** heated indoor. **Leisure Activities:** whirlpool. **Guest Services:** valet laundry. **Cards:** AX, DC, DS, MC, VI.
(See color ad on TourBookMark)

SOME UNITS

（ASK）（S⃝）（🛏）（¶↑）（🏊）（🐕）（DATA PORT）（💻）／（✕）（🖬）（📷）／
　　　　　　　　　　　　　　　　　　　　　　　　　　　　FEE FEE

──── **WHERE TO DINE** ────

CHURCHILL'S PRIME RIB HOUSE   **Lunch:** $7-$17   **Dinner:** $20-$40   **Phone:** 705/476-7777
▽▽▽ ▽▽▽   **Location:** Hwy 11B, exit Lakeshore Dr, 4.3 km n of jct Hwy 11. 631 Lakeshore Dr P1A 2E7. **Hours:** 11 am-11 pm, Sat from 4 pm, Sun 4 pm-10 pm. Closed: 12/25, 12/26. **Reservations:** suggested. **Features:** Candles, a Steak House   grand piano, dark wood, stained glass and a glowing fireplace create an elegant yet relaxed atmosphere. The signature item, prime rib, is consistently lean and of top quality. Fresh pasta is also offered. In addition, there is a well-rounded wine list. Casual dress; cocktails. **Parking:** on-site. **Cards:** AX, DC, MC, VI.

（Ⅰ）（✕）

JACK TENNANT'S STEAK HOUSE   **Dinner:** $20-$45   **Phone:** 705/495-4114
▽▽▽ ▽▽▽   **Location:** Hwy 11B, exit Lakeshore Dr, 3.5 km n of jct Hwy 11. 786 Lakeshore Dr P1A 2G8. **Hours:** 5 pm-10 pm, Sun-9 pm. Closed: 12/25. **Reservations:** suggested. **Features:** Top-quality, never-frozen, custom-aged Steak & Seafood   Alberta beef is the signature dish, always cooked to order. Seafood also makes a menu appearance and can be ordered alone or in tandem with steak. Servers are professional and unpretentious. Casual dress; cocktails. **Parking:** on-site. **Cards:** AX, DC, JC, MC, VI.

（✕）

JAEGER MEISTERS   **Lunch:** $10-$15   **Dinner:** $10-$24   **Phone:** 705/476-3443
▽▽▽ ▽▽▽   **Location:** Centre. 130 Main St W P1B 2J5. **Hours:** 10 am-8 pm, Fri & Sat-9 pm, Sun-2 pm. Closed: 12/25, 12/26. **Reservations:** accepted. **Features:** The wonderful little bistro shows fun decor and includes booth Canadian   and table seating and an open grill. Weather permitting, the front of the restaurant is opened to the sidewalk. Among menu choices are prime rib, pork loin, chicken, salmon and an interesting, light crepe lasagna. Service is casual, efficient and friendly. Casual dress; beer & wine only. **Parking:** street. **Cards:** AX, MC, VI.

（✕）

JOSO'S   **Dinner:** $9-$22   **Phone:** 705/474-5800
▽▽ ▽▽   **Location:** Hwy 11, exit Lakeshore Dr, 4 km n on Hwy 11B; in Best Western North Bay. 700 Lakeshore Dr P1A 2G4. **Hours:** 4 pm-10 pm. Closed: 12/25. **Reservations:** accepted. **Features:** The menu offers a choice of beef, Canadian   chicken, fish or pasta. Service is friendly and efficient. Casual dress; cocktails. **Parking:** on-site. **Cards:** AX, DC, DS, MC, VI.

（✕）

PEACHY'S PUB & GRILL   **Lunch:** $6-$8   **Dinner:** $8-$17   **Phone:** 705/472-5672
▽▽▽ ▽▽   **Location:** Hwy 11B, exit Lakeshore Dr, 5 km n of jct Hwy 11. 540 Lakeshore Dr P1A 2E6. **Hours:** 11 am-11 pm. Closed major holidays. **Reservations:** accepted. **Features:** Hearty portions of pasta, salad, chicken, veal, Italian   pizza and finger foods are served in a casual, fun atmosphere by a wait staff that is both friendly and attentive. There are separate bar and lounge areas and seasonal outdoor patio dining. Casual dress; cocktails. **Parking:** on-site. **Cards:** AX, DC, MC, VI.

（Ⅰ）（✕）

THE WHITE OWL BISTRO   **Lunch:** $5-$11   **Dinner:** $16-$21   **Phone:** 705/472-2662
▽▽ ▽▽   **Location:** Hwy 11B, exit Lakeshore Dr, 4.3 km n of jct Hwy 11. 639 Lakeshore Dr P1A 2E9. **Hours:** 6:30 am-2:30 pm, Fri also 5 pm-9 pm, Sat 8 am-2:30 & 5-9 pm, Sun 8 am-2:30 pm. Closed major holidays; also 12/24. Canadian   **Reservations:** accepted. **Features:** Established in 1934, the sweet little bistro has an open kitchen and some tables that overlook the lawn and lake. The menu lists soups, salads, Montreal smoked meat, wraps and desserts prepared in-house. The more highly developed dinner menu is typically presented table d'hote. Casual dress; cocktails. **Parking:** on-site. **Cards:** AX, JC, MC, VI.

（✕）

OAKVILLE pop. 144,738

──── **WHERE TO STAY** ────

COUNTRY INN BY CARLSON   **Book at aaa.com**   Phone: (905)829-8020
（CAA）（SAVE）   7/1-9/30 [ECP]   1P: $125-$149   2P: $125-$149   XP: $10   F17
　　　　5/1-6/30 & 10/1-4/30 [ECP]   1P: $104-$149   2P: $104-$149   XP: $10   F17
▽▽▽ ▽▽▽   **Location:** QEW, exit 124 (Winston Churchill Blvd), directly s. 2930 S Sheridan Way L6J 7J8. **Fax:** 905/829-4168. **Facility:** 71 one-bedroom standard units, some with whirlpools. 2 stories, interior corridors. **Parking:** on-Small-scale Hotel   site, winter plug-ins. **Terms:** package plans. **Amenities:** voice mail, irons, hair dryers. **Leisure Activities:** exercise room. **Guest Services:** valet and coin laundry. **Business Services:** meeting rooms. **Cards:** AX, CB, DC, DS, JC, MC, VI. **Special Amenities:** free expanded continental breakfast and free local telephone calls. *(See color ad p 521)*

SOME UNITS

（S⃝）（¶）（DATA PORT）（💻）／（✕）（🖬）／

FAIRFIELD INN BY MARRIOTT   **Book at aaa.com**   Phone: 905/829-8444
▽▽ ▽▽   All Year   1P: $129   2P: $129
Small-scale Hotel   **Location:** QEW, exit 124 (Winston Churchill Blvd), 1 km s. 2937 Sherwood Heights Dr L6J 7L3. **Fax:** 905/829-4544. **Facility:** 65 one-bedroom standard units, some with whirlpools. 4 stories, interior corridors. *Bath:* combo or shower only. **Parking:** on-site. **Amenities:** high-speed Internet, dual phone lines, voice mail, irons, hair dryers. **Pool(s):** heated indoor. **Leisure Activities:** exercise room. **Guest Services:** valet laundry. **Business Services:** meeting rooms, business center. **Cards:** AX, DC, MC, VI.

SOME UNITS

（ASK）（S⃝）（&）（🏊）（¶）（DATA PORT）（🖬）（💻）／（✕）／

HILTON GARDEN INN TORONTO/OAKVILLE *Book at aaa.com* Phone: (905)829-1145

(CAA) (SAVE) All Year 1P: $109-$159 2P: $109-$159 XP: $20 F18
▼▼▼▼ Location: QEW, exit 124 (Winston Churchill Blvd), just s. 2774 S Sheridan Way L6J 7T4. Fax: 905/829-4690.
Facility: 97 one-bedroom standard units, some with whirlpools. 4 stories, interior corridors. *Bath:* combo or shower only. Parking: on-site. Amenities: video games, high-speed Internet, dual phone lines, voice mail,
Small-scale Hotel irons, hair dryers. Dining: 6:30 am-11, noon-2 & 5-10 pm. Pool(s): heated indoor. Leisure
rooms, business center. Cards: AX, DC, MC, VI. Special Amenities: free local telephone calls and free newspaper.
Activities: whirlpool, exercise room. Guest Services: sundries, coin laundry. Business Services: meeting

SOME UNITS

HOLIDAY INN OAKVILLE-CENTRE *Book at aaa.com* Phone: (905)842-5000

▼▼▼▼ All Year 1P: $135-$155 2P: $135-$155
Location: QEW, exit Trafalgar Rd, then s. 590 Argus Rd L6J 3J3. Fax: 905/842-5123. Facility: 145 units. 144
Small-scale Hotel one-bedroom standard units, some with whirlpools. 1 one-bedroom suite. 6 stories, interior corridors.
Parking: on-site. Terms: cancellation fee imposed, pets ($15 extra charge). Amenities: high-speed
Internet, voice mail, irons, hair dryers. Pool(s): heated indoor. Leisure Activities: sauna, whirlpool, exercise room. *Fee:* game
room. Guest Services: gift shop, valet laundry. Business Services: conference facilities. Cards: AX, CB, DC, DS, JC,
MC, VI. *(See color ad card insert)*

SOME UNITS

HOLIDAY INN SELECT HOTEL & SUITES OAKVILLE

@ BRONTE *Book at aaa.com* Phone: (905)847-1000
(CAA) (SAVE) All Year 1P: $139-$169 2P: $139-$169 XP: $15 F18
▼▼▼▼ Location: QEW, exit 111 (Bronte Rd/Hwy 25). 2525 Wyecroft Rd L6L 6P8. Fax: 905/847-0032. Facility: 144 units.
104 one-bedroom standard units, some with whirlpools. 40 one-bedroom suites ($159-$229). 7 stories,
interior corridors. Parking: on-site. Terms: cancellation fee imposed, package plans. Amenities: video
Small-scale Hotel games, high-speed Internet, dual phone lines, voice mail, honor bars, irons, hair dryers. *Some:* safes.
Dining: 6 am-11 pm. Pool(s): heated indoor. Leisure Activities: whirlpool, steamroom, exercise room.
Guest Services: sundries, valet and coin laundry. Business Services: meeting rooms, business center. Cards: AX, CB, DC,
DS, MC, VI. Special Amenities: free local telephone calls and free newspaper. *(See color ad p 530)*

SOME UNITS

MONTE CARLO INN-OAKVILLE SUITES *Book at aaa.com* Phone: (905)849-9500

(CAA) (SAVE) All Year [ECP] 1P: $79-$109 2P: $89-$119 XP: $10 F12
▼▼▼▼ Location: QEW, exit Trafalgar Rd S. 374 S Service Rd E L6J 2X6. Fax: 905/849-6405. Facility: 70 units. 68 one-
bedroom standard units, some with whirlpools. 2 one-bedroom suites ($109-$159) with whirlpools. 4 stories,
interior corridors. Parking: on-site, winter plug-ins. Terms: weekly rates available, package plans.
Small-scale Hotel Amenities: video games, high-speed Internet, voice mail, irons, hair dryers. Dining: 11 am-midnight,
cocktails. Leisure Activities: whirlpool, exercise room. Guest Services: valet and coin laundry. Business
Services: meeting rooms, business center. Cards: AX, CB, DC, DS, JC, MC, VI. Special Amenities: free expanded
continental breakfast and free local telephone calls. *(See color ad p 531)*

SOME UNITS

QUALITY HOTEL & SUITES-OAKVILLE *Book at aaa.com* Phone: (905)847-6667

▼▼▼▼ 5/1-10/31 1P: $109-$129 2P: $119-$139 XP: $10 F17
11/1-4/30 1P: $99-$119 2P: $109-$129 XP: $10 F17
Small-scale Hotel Location: QEW, exit 111 (Bronte Rd/Hwy 25), 0.4 km s. 754 Bronte Rd L6J 4Z3. Fax: 905/847-7447. Facility: 80
units. 78 one-bedroom standard units, some with whirlpools. 2 one-bedroom suites. 9 stories, interior
corridors. Parking: on-site. Terms: pets ($10 extra charge). Amenities: video games, dual phone lines, voice mail, irons, hair
dryers. Pool(s): heated indoor. Leisure Activities: sauna, whirlpool, exercise room. Guest Services: valet laundry. Business
Services: conference facilities, business center. Cards: AX, CB, DC, DS, MC, VI. *(See color ad p 534)*

SOME UNITS

The Last Word on Quality ... Approved.

Choose with confidence! **AAA/CAA Approved** and Diamond rated hotels promise quality, cleanliness, service, and value.

Wherever you travel, use the TourBook® listings, in print and on aaa.com, and look for the bright red AAA/CAA logo on billboards and signage.

For more information on **AAA/CAA** Lodging Diamond Ratings, turn to page 16.

Show Your Card

RAMADA INN AND CONVENTION CENTRE   **Book at aaa.com**   Phone: (905)845-7561

| | 7/1-10/31 | 1P: $109-$159 | 2P: $109-$159 | XP: $10 | F18 |
| | 5/1-6/30 & 11/1-4/30 | 1P: $99-$129 | 2P: $99-$129 | XP: $10 | F18 |

Small-scale Hotel **Location:** QEW, exit Trafalgar Rd, just n. 360 Oakville Place Dr L6H 6K8. Fax: 905/845-9450. **Facility:** 122 one-bedroom standard units, some with whirlpools. 2 stories (no elevator), interior corridors. **Parking:** on-site, winter plug-ins. **Terms:** pets ($25 fee). **Amenities:** video games, high-speed Internet, dual phone lines, voice mail, irons, hair dryers. **Pool(s):** heated outdoor. **Leisure Activities:** sauna, whirlpool, exercise room, volleyball. **Guest Services:** valet laundry. **Business Services:** meeting rooms, business center. **Cards:** AX, DC, DS, MC, VI.

SOME UNITS

(ASK) (S/D) (🛏) (📺) (📞) (🍴) (🔀) (📠) (DATA PORT) (💻) / (✕) (🔌) (🖥) /
FEE   FEE   FEE

──────── WHERE TO DINE ────────

IL FORNELLO   **Lunch:** $8-$15   **Dinner:** $12-$30   **Phone:** 905/338-5233

Italian   **Location:** QEW, exit 117 (Kerr St); directly n at Abbey Centre. 203 N Service Rd W L6M 3R2. **Hours:** 11:30 am-10 pm, Sun-9 pm. Closed major holidays. **Features:** Diners can sample tasty gourmet pizzas and freshly prepared pasta, as well as selections from the ever-popular luncheon buffet. Unusual choices are spelt pizza, a yeast- and dairy-free pizza, and gluten-free pasta for those on restricted diets. Casual dress; cocktails. **Parking:** on-site. **Cards:** AX, DC, MC, VI.

(✕)

JONATHANS OF OAKVILLE   **Dinner:** $20-$40   **Phone:** 905/842-4200

Continental   **Location:** Jct Church. 120 Thomas St L6J 3A8. **Hours:** 5:30 pm-9 pm, Fri & Sat-10 pm. Closed major holidays; also Sun. **Reservations:** suggested. **Features:** A prime downtown location and sophisticated atmosphere complement the fine Continental menu selections. Among starters are lobster bisque, wild mushroom soup with cognac, goat cheese salad and mushrooms in puffed pastry. Follow that with hearty rack of lamb, filet mignon, capon or fish and a fine bottle of wine from the extensive list. Lighter fare is served in the more relaxed lounge. Semi-formal attire; cocktails. **Parking:** street. **Cards:** AX, DC, MC, VI.

(📞) (✕)

THE KEG STEAKHOUSE AND BAR   **Dinner:** $18-$30   **Phone:** 905/842-7333

Steak House   **Location:** QEW, exit 117 (Kerr St), directly n; at Oakville Town Centre. 220 N Service Rd L6M 2Y3. **Hours:** 5 pm-10:30 pm, Fri 4:30 pm-11 pm, Sat 4 pm-11 pm, Sun 4 pm-9:30 pm. Closed: 12/25. **Features:** Well-known for its mesquite-grilled steaks and fun, laid-back atmosphere, the steak house is a longtime favorite with the local crowd. In addition to great beef, the traditional menu features seafood, grilled chicken, hickory ribs and pasta offerings. All meals come with a hot loaf of sourdough bread. Try a specialty coffee or tasty cheesecake for the perfect ending. Casual dress; cocktails. **Parking:** on-site. **Cards:** AX, DC, MC, VI.

(✕)

LA COSTA RESTAURANT   **Lunch:** $7-$24   **Dinner:** $7-$24   **Phone:** 905/339-0227

Mediterranean   **Location:** Jct Ford Dr. 2273 Royal Windsor Dr L6J 7X8. **Hours:** 11:30 am-11 pm, Fri-1 am, Sat 4:30 pm-1 am, Sun 4:30 pm-11 pm. Closed: 1/1, 12/25. **Reservations:** suggested. **Features:** Modern Mediterranean dining triumphs amid brick, stucco, European artwork and festive background music. The creative menu, which reflects inspirations from the coastal regions, lists varied antipasto, tapas, pasta and entrees in generous and well-presented full or half portions. Dressy casual; cocktails. **Parking:** on-site. **Cards:** AX, DC, DS, MC, VI.

(✕)

OLIVERS OF OAKVILLE   **Lunch:** $14-$30   **Dinner:** $19-$35   **Phone:** 905/845-9391

Continental   **Location:** Between Trafalgar Rd and Navy. 141 Lakeshore Rd E L6J 1H3. **Hours:** 5 pm-10 pm, Thurs & Fri also noon-2:30 pm, Sun 5 pm-9 pm. Closed major holidays; also 6/30-7/7. **Reservations:** suggested. **Features:** Impeccable service, elegant surroundings and fine Continental cuisine are what have made this establishment a longtime favourite with diners. The restaurant is a top choice for entertaining business clients or celebrating special occasions. The well-trained staff explains menu highlights and assists with wine selection. All menu items are prepared fresh to order and creatively presented with an artistic flair. The overall experience is truly memorable. Semi-formal attire; cocktails. **Parking:** on-site (fee). **Cards:** AX, DC, MC, VI.

(✕)

THE RUDE NATIVE BISTRO   **Dinner:** $9-$24   **Phone:** 905/465-0571

Caribbean   **Location:** Jct Lakeshore Rd; across from Bronte Village Mall. 119 Jones St L6L 3E7. **Hours:** 5 pm-10 pm. Closed: 1/1, 12/25, 12/26; also Sun & Mon. **Features:** An innovative menu featuring an exotic blend of Caribbean, Indian and Asian cuisine and a fun casual setting set the tone at the Rude Native. Diners here can start the meal with a tropical cocktail to get the real island feel. The appetizer list is extensive including selections such as hummus, goat cheese, spring rolls and salads. Main entrees include stir-fry, wraps and pastas, as well as jerk chicken and leg of lamb. Portions are hearty with varied degrees of spice to suit all taste buds. Casual dress; cocktails. **Parking:** on-site. **Cards:** AX, DC, MC, VI.

(✕)

THE RUDE NATIVE BISTRO   **Lunch:** $9-$22   **Dinner:** $9-$22   **Phone:** 905/844-3334

Caribbean   **Location:** Between Thomas and Navy. 142 Lakeshore Rd E L6J 1H3. **Hours:** 11:30 am-10 pm, Thurs-Sat to 11 pm, Sun-9 pm. Closed: 12/25, 12/26. **Features:** Although the restaurant is in Canada, the Caribbean seems just minutes away. The waterfall replica and tiki-style lounge, which offers a good variety of drinks, liquors and wine, evoke the feel of an island paradise. Bright colors and upbeat music lighten moods on the gloomiest of days. The menu lists a wide range of island and Thai fare that is made fresh and tailored to the diner's preferred level of spiciness. Casual dress; cocktails. **Parking:** street. **Cards:** AX, DC, MC, VI.

(✕)

STONEBOATS RESTAURANT   **Lunch:** $6-$13   **Dinner:** $15-$34   **Phone:** 905/825-2727

Continental   **Location:** Directly s of Lakeshore Rd at Bronte Harbour. 49 Bronte Rd L6L 3B7. **Hours:** noon-3 & 5-10 pm. Closed: 1/1. **Reservations:** suggested. **Features:** A lovely lakefront location and a prime outdoor patio in season are attractions at Stone Boats, but the fine Continental menu selection is what keep diners coming back. The wonderfully restored Stone House is a perfect setting to enjoy such delicacies as baked brie, oysters or tasty seafood chowder, followed by rack of lamb, New York steak or the fresh fish selection. Desserts are decadent and well worth the extra calories. Dressy casual; cocktails. **Parking:** on-site. **Cards:** AX, DC, MC, VI.

(📞) (✕)

TRATTORIA TIMONE **Lunch:** $7-$14 **Dinner:** $15-$22 **Phone:** 905/842-2906
▼▼▼ ▼▼ **Location:** Between Trafalgar Rd and Dunn St. 263 Lakeshore Rd E L6J 1H9. **Hours:** noon-2:30 & 5-10 pm, Mon &
Italian Tues from 5 pm. Closed: 1/1, 12/25, 12/26; also Sun. **Reservations:** suggested, required weekends.
Features: The downtown restaurant is perfect for a business luncheon or special occasion. The dining room
offers a relaxed setting with bright modern decor and an Italian theme. Appetizer favorites include baked
brie fritters, salmon tartar and salads. Among entrees are selected pasta, veal, risotto, duck and seafood selections. Casual
dress; cocktails. **Parking:** street. **Cards:** AX, DC, MC, VI. ⊠

ORANGEVILLE pop. 25,248

──────── WHERE TO STAY ────────

──────── *The following lodging was either not evaluated or did not* ────────
meet AAA rating requirements but is listed for your information only.

**HOCKLEY VALLEY RESORT AND CONFERENCE
CENTRE** **Phone:** 519/942-0754
[fyi] Not evaluated. **Location:** Hwy 10/24, 6.5 km on Hockley Valley Rd to 3rd line. RR 1 L9W 2Y8. Facilities, services, and
decor characterize a mid-range property.

ORILLIA pop. 29,121

──────── WHERE TO STAY ────────

BEST WESTERN COUCHICHING INN *Book at aaa.com* **Phone:** (705)325-6505

(CAA) (SAVE)	5/31-8/31 [ECP]	1P: $129-$189	2P: $129-$189	XP: $15 F18
▼▼▼ ▼▼	5/1-5/30 & 9/1-10/31 [ECP]	1P: $99-$119	2P: $99-$119	XP: $15 F18
	11/1-4/30 [ECP]	1P: $89-$109	2P: $89-$109	XP: $15 F18

Location: Jct Hwy 12 S and Couchiching Point Rd. Located in a commercial area. 440 Couchiching Point Rd L3V 6P8.
Small-scale Hotel Fax: 705/325-7662. **Facility:** 82 one-bedroom standard units, some with whirlpools. 2-4 stories, interior
corridors. **Parking:** on-site, winter plug-ins. **Terms:** check-in 4 pm, 30 day cancellation notice-fee imposed,
package plans. **Amenities:** dual phone lines, voice mail, irons, hair dryers. **Dining:** 4 pm-9 pm; hours may vary in winter,
cocktails. **Leisure Activities:** sauna, whirlpool, hiking trails, exercise room, spa. **Guest Services:** area transportation-bus
station, casino. **Business Services:** meeting rooms. **Cards:** AX, DC, DS, MC, VI. **Special Amenities:** free expanded
continental breakfast and free local telephone calls.

SOME UNITS
[S/D] [¶] [⊠] [▣] [DATA PORT] [▯] / [⊠] [▤] [▦] /

COMFORT INN *Book at aaa.com* **Phone:** (705)327-7744

▼▼▼ ▼▼	5/1-9/15	1P: $113-$123	2P: $123-$133	XP: $10 F
	9/16-10/31	1P: $105-$115	2P: $115-$125	XP: $10 F
Small-scale Hotel	11/1-4/30	1P: $95-$105	2P: $105-$110	XP: $10 F

Location: Hwy 11 N, exit Hwy 12, s on Memorial Ave; corner of Progress Dr and Memorial Ave. 75 Progress Dr (RR 1)
L3V 6H1. Fax: 705/327-1568. **Facility:** 80 one-bedroom standard units. 2 stories (no elevator), interior corridors. **Parking:** on-
site, winter plug-ins. **Terms:** package plans, pets ($10 extra charge, ground floor units). **Amenities:** hair dryers. *Some:* irons.
Guest Services: valet laundry. **Cards:** AX, DC, DS, MC, VI.

SOME UNITS
[A$K] [S/D] [🐾] [¶+] [▣] [DATA PORT] [▯] / [⊠] [▤] [▦] /
FEE

1-800-DAYS INN
www.daysinn.ca

DAYS INN
O R I L L I A

Come on Inn...

• Steps away from Casino Rama
• Complimentary newspaper and
  continental breakfast
• Comfortably furnished rooms with
  king or queen-size beds
• Jacuzzi and fireplace rooms available
• All rooms include fridge, microwave
  coffee maker, hairdryer and iron
• Indoor heated pool and whirlpool
• Fitness room, gift shop and 24 hr business centre
• Three meeting rooms

triprewards
It's fun to get more.

Days Inn - Orillia 5850 Rama Rd.
Orillia, Ontario L3V 6H6
www.daysinnorillia.com

Tel | Toll Free | Fax
705 326 8288 | 877 326 8288 | 705 323 9999

info@daysinnorillia.com

DAYS INN ORILLIA   *Book at aaa.com*

Phone: (705)326-8288

5/1-9/30	1P: $99-$169	2P: $109-$179	XP: $10	F18
1/1-4/30	1P: $89-$169	2P: $99-$179	XP: $10	F18
10/1-11/30	1P: $89-$159	2P: $99-$169	XP: $10	F18
12/1-12/31	1P: $79-$149	2P: $89-$159	XP: $10	F18

Small-scale Hotel

Location: Jct Hwy 12 and Rama Rd, 5 km n. Located in a rural area. 5850 Rama Rd L3V 6H6. **Fax:** 705/323-9999. **Facility:** 78 units. 71 one-bedroom standard units, some with whirlpools. 7 one-bedroom suites ($139-$209), some with whirlpools. 3 stories, interior corridors. **Parking:** on-site. **Amenities:** voice mail, irons, hair dryers. **Pool(s):** heated indoor. **Leisure Activities:** whirlpool, exercise room. **Guest Services:** sundries. **Business Services:** meeting rooms, business center. **Cards:** AX, CB, DC, DS, JC, MC, VI. *(See color ad p 396)*

SOME UNITS

ECONO LODGE   *Book at aaa.com*

Phone: (705)326-3554

5/1-12/31 [CP]	1P: $69-$89	2P: $79-$109	XP: $10	F18
1/1-4/30 [CP]	1P: $55-$79	2P: $79-$109	XP: $10	F18

Location: 0.5 km n of Hwy 12. Located in a commercial area. 265 Memorial Ave L3V 5X8. **Fax:** 705/326-5641. **Facility:** 52 one-bedroom standard units, some with whirlpools. 2 stories (no elevator), interior corridors.

Small-scale Hotel   **Parking:** on-site, winter plug-ins. **Terms:** small pets only. **Amenities:** *Some:* irons, hair dryers. **Cards:** AX, DC, MC, VI.

SOME UNITS

FEE   FEE

KEWADIN INN

Phone: (705)325-9511

5/1-9/1	1P: $72-$122	2P: $80-$130	XP: $8	F18
9/2-4/30	1P: $72-$100	2P: $80-$110	XP: $8	F18

Location: Jct Hwy 12 and Memorial Ave, just s. Located in a commercial area. 400 Memorial Ave L3V 6K8 (PO Box 970). **Fax:** 705/325-3682. **Facility:** 84 one-bedroom standard units. 2 stories (no elevator), interior corridors.

Small-scale Hotel   **Parking:** on-site. **Terms:** [BP] meal plan available, package plans. **Amenities:** irons, hair dryers. **Dining:** 7-9:30 am, Fri & Sat also 5-9 pm, Sun 8 am-2 pm, cocktails. **Pool(s):** heated indoor. **Leisure Activities:** sauna, whirlpool, tennis court. **Business Services:** meeting rooms. **Cards:** AX, DC, MC, VI. **Special Amenities:** free continental breakfast and free local telephone calls.

SOME UNITS

FEE

STONE GATE INN

Phone: (705)329-2535

All Year [BP]	1P: $109-$219	2P: $109-$219	XP: $10	F12

Location: Hwy 11, exit West St S northbound, 0.5 km s to Fittons Rd E, then just n; exit Laclie St southbound, 1 km s. Located in a commercial area. 437 Laclie St L3V 4P7. **Fax:** 705/329-3422. **Facility:** 48 units. 21 one-bedroom

Small-scale Hotel   standard units. 27 one-bedroom suites, some with kitchens and/or whirlpools. 4 stories, interior corridors. **Parking:** on-site. **Terms:** cancellation fee imposed, weekly rates available, package plans. **Amenities:** voice mail, irons, hair dryers. **Pool(s):** small heated indoor. **Leisure Activities:** whirlpool, exercise room. **Guest Services:** valet and coin laundry. **Business Services:** meeting rooms. **Cards:** AX, DC, MC, VI.

SOME UNITS

FEE

The following lodgings were either not evaluated or did not meet AAA rating requirements but are listed for your information only.

CASINO RAMA HOTEL

Phone: 705/329-3325

[fyi]   Not evaluated. **Location:** Jct Hwy 12 and Rama Rd, 5 km n. Located in a rural area. 5897 Rama Rd L0K 1T0 (PO Box 179, RR 6). Facilities, services, and decor characterize an upscale property.

FERN RESORT

Phone: 705/325-2256

[fyi]   Not evaluated. **Location:** 5 km s on Hwy 12, 2 km n on Rama Rd, then just w. RR 5, 4432 Fern Resort Rd L3V 6H5. Facilities, services, and decor characterize a mid-range property.

WHERE TO DINE

JOHN DORY SEAFOODS

Lunch: $6-$10   **Dinner:** $6-$25   Phone: 705/326-4800

Location: Hwy 11 N, exit Hwy 12, just s. 318 Memorial Ave L3V 5X6. **Hours:** 11:30 am-8:30 pm, Fri & Sat-9:30 pm. Closed: 12/25, 12/26. **Features:** Have your seafood cooked anyway you like: pan-fried, baked or steamed. But it's the halibut and chips that make a standout and ample meal. Those with larger appetites

Seafood   will enjoy the all-you-can-eat shrimp and crab. A children's menu is also available. Casual dress; cocktails. **Parking:** on-site. **Cards:** AX, MC, VI.

THE OSSAWIPPI EXPRESS

Lunch: $8-$15   **Dinner:** $15-$27   Phone: 705/329-0001

Location: Jct Centennial Dr and Missassaga St E. 210 Missassaga St E L3V 7L8. **Hours:** noon-9 pm, Fri & Sat-10 pm. Closed: 1/1, 12/25, 12/26; also Mon in winter. **Reservations:** suggested. **Features:** Go slow on this express, and enjoy the unique atmosphere of dining on restored railcars, dating back to 1896. There is a

Continental   terrace in season and a waterfront view to be savored. The varied menu is served up bistro style and after dining there is a gift shop to be explored. Casual dress; cocktails. **Parking:** on-site. **Cards:** AX, DC, MC, VI.

REMO'S RISTORANTE

Lunch: $7-$20   **Dinner:** $9-$29   Phone: 705/327-5326

Location: Jct Hwy 12. 480 West St L3V 5H4. **Hours:** noon-2 & 5-9 pm, Sat from 5 pm. Closed major holidays; also Sun. **Reservations:** suggested. **Features:** Pasta and an inviting atmosphere continue to draw guests

Italian   to this restaurant; patio dining is available in season. Casual dress; cocktails. **Parking:** on-site. **Cards:** AX, DC, MC, VI.

OSHAWA pop. 139,051

——— WHERE TO STAY ———

COMFORT INN **Book at aaa.com** Phone: (905)434-5000

5/1-8/31	1P: $79-$139	2P: $89-$149	XP: $10	F18
9/1-4/30	1P: $79-$129	2P: $89-$139	XP: $10	F18

Small-scale Hotel **Location:** Hwy 401, exit 416 (Park Rd), s to Bloor St, then 0.8 km w. 605 Bloor St W L1J 5Y6. Fax: 905/434-7678. **Facility:** 80 one-bedroom standard units. 2 stories (no elevator), interior corridors. **Parking:** on-site, winter plug-ins. **Amenities:** irons, hair dryers. *Some:* dual phone lines. **Guest Services:** valet laundry. **Cards:** AX, DC, DS, JC, MC, VI.

SOME UNITS

HOLIDAY INN OSHAWA **Book at aaa.com** Phone: (905)576-5101

6/1-9/30	1P: $129-$179	2P: $129-$179	XP: $15	F18
5/1-5/31 & 10/1-4/30	1P: $119-$149	2P: $119-$149	XP: $15	F18

Location: Hwy 401, exit 419 (Harmony Rd). 1011 Bloor St E L1H 7K6. Fax: 905/576-3296. **Facility:** 194 units. 192 one-bedroom standard units. 2 one-bedroom suites. 7 stories, interior corridors. *Bath:* combo or shower only. **Small-scale Hotel Parking:** on-site. **Terms:** package plans, pets ($10 extra charge). **Amenities:** voice mail, irons, hair dryers. *Some:* high-speed Internet, dual phone lines. **Dining:** 6:30 am-1 am. **Pool(s):** heated outdoor, heated indoor. **Leisure Activities:** sauna, whirlpool, exercise room. *Fee:* game room. **Guest Services:** valet laundry. **Business Services:** conference facilities. **Cards:** AX, DC, DS, MC, VI. *(See color ad card insert)*

SOME UNITS

OSHAWA TRAVELODGE **Book at aaa.com** Phone: (905)436-9500

All Year	1P: $89-$119	2P: $99-$129	XP: $10	F18

Location: Hwy 401, exit 412 (Thickson Rd N). 940 Champlain Ave L1J 7A6. Fax: 905/436-9544. **Facility:** 120 units. 114 one-bedroom standard units. 6 one-bedroom suites. 3 stories, interior corridors. **Parking:** on-site. Small-scale Hotel **Terms:** package plans, pets ($25 extra charge). **Amenities:** video games, voice mail, irons, hair dryers. **Pool(s):** heated indoor. **Leisure Activities:** whirlpool. **Guest Services:** valet laundry. **Business Services:** meeting rooms. **Cards:** AX, DC, DS, MC, VI. *(See color ad on TourBookMark)*

SOME UNITS

——— WHERE TO DINE ———

THE KEG STEAKHOUSE **Dinner:** $16-$30 Phone: 905/571-3212

Steak House **Location:** Jct Gibb; at far corner of Oshawa Centre. 255 Stevenson Rd L1J 6Y4. **Hours:** 5 pm-10:30 pm, Fri 4:30 pm-11 pm, Sat 4 pm-11 pm, Sun 4 pm-10 pm. **Closed:** 12/25. **Features:** Well-known for their mesquite-grilled steaks and a fun, laid-back atmosphere, The Keg is a longtime favorite with the local crowd. Diners come back for the traditional menu which, in addition to great beef, features seafood, grilled chicken, hickory ribs and pasta offerings, all served with a hot loaf of sourdough bread. Try one of the specialty coffees or cheesecake for the perfect ending. Casual dress; cocktails. **Parking:** on-site. **Cards:** AX, DC, MC, VI.

Delegate Travel Planning to Someone You Trust

Visit **aaa.com** and enjoy a whole new world of travel information.

AAA's Internet TripTik® provides interactive maps and search tools that make travel planning easy. Get hotel Diamond ratings, photos, and great room rates. Find countless places to eat and play.

Trust AAA to simplify travel planning.

Travel with Confidence.
Travel with AAA.

Destination Ottawa
pop. 774,072

*B*ound by rivers, bisected by a canal and bordered by parks, picturesque Ottawa has a playful side, and a colorful one as well.

A profusion of tulips bursts forth in spring, signaling the beginning of the Tulip Festival and a summer of outdoor recreational pursuits. Ottawa's hottest playgrounds are the coolest places to be in winter, too.

© 2004 Ontario Tourism

Alfresco dining.
A beautiful summer day is even more enjoyable when taking time for a meal at one of Ottawa's outdoor cafes.

Byward Market, Ottawa.
Farmers, merchants and shoppers have gathered in this district since the 1830s; it's still an ideal place to buy food, or perhaps something frivolous. (See mention page 148)

Pierre St. Jacques
Ottawa Tourism

© J. Nettis / Robertstock

A young Ottawa Indian.
The heritage and culture of Ottawa's early residents are remembered at festivals and powwows.

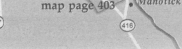

*P*laces included in this AAA Destination City:

Nearby Québec
Gastineau..................435

Some municipalities in Ontario have combined or soon will combine with neighboring cities. These mergers will eliminate some existing cities and may affect street names, addresses and political boundaries referenced in this guide. For further information, please contact Ontario governing agencies or the local CAA club.

© 2004 Ontario Tourism

Ice skating.
When Ottawa's waterways freeze over in winter, skaters take to the ice to practice their racing form.

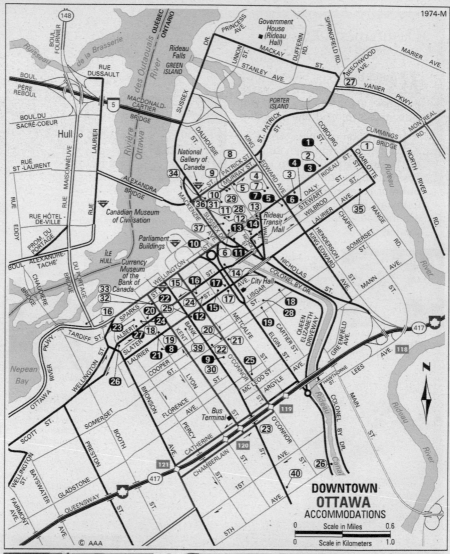

1974-M

DOWNTOWN
OTTAWA
ACCOMMODATIONS

© AAA

AAA CAA **Choose Well.**

Discover the secret to choosing well … **AAA/CAA Approved.**

From simple motels to luxury resorts, rest assured. **AAA/CAA's professional evaluators** have tested the locks and peeked under the beds, checking for qualities like cleanliness, service, and value — assigning a rating from one to five Diamonds.

Choose your Diamond rated accommodations from the TourBook® listings, in print and on aaa.com, and look for the bold red AAA/CAA logo on signage and billboards.

For more information on **AAA/CAA Lodging Diamond Ratings,** turn to page 16.

Downtown Ottawa

This index helps you "spot" where approved accommodations and restaurants are located on the corresponding detailed maps. Lodging rate ranges are for comparison only and show the property's high season; rates are per night, unless only weekly (W) rates are available. Restaurant rate range is for dinner, unless only lunch (L) is served. Turn to the listing page for more detailed rate information and consult display ads for special promotions.

Spotter/Map Page Number	OA	DOWNTOWN OTTAWA - Lodgings	Diamond Rating	Rate Range High Season	Listing Page
1 / p. 400	CAA	Econo Lodge Downtown - see color ad p 412	◈	$90-$150 SAVE	412
3 / p. 400	CAA	Days Inn-Downtown (Ottawa) - see color ad p 412	◈◈	$129-$139 SAVE	411
4 / p. 400		Auberge McGEE'S Inn	◈◈◈	$98-$168	408
5 / p. 400	CAA	Quality Hotel Ottawa, Downtown	◈◈	$134-$144 SAVE	419
6 / p. 400	CAA	Gasthaus Switzerland Inn	◈◈◈	$108-$188 SAVE	413
7 / p. 400		Courtyard by Marriott Ottawa	◈◈◈	$155-$209	411
8 / p. 400	CAA	A Mid-Towne Heritage B & B	◈◈◈	$99-$144 SAVE	407
9 / p. 400		Bostonian Executive Suites	◈◈◈	$159-$189	409
10 / p. 400	CAA	Fairmont Chateau Laurier - see color ad p 414	◈◈◈◈	$199-$419 SAVE	412
11 / p. 400		The Westin Ottawa - see color ad p 5, p 420	◈◈◈◈	$159-$235	421
12 / p. 400	CAA	ARC the.hotel - see color ad p 408	◈◈◈	$159-$199 SAVE	407
13 / p. 400	CAA	Les Suites Hotel Ottawa - see color ad p 415	◈◈◈	$179-$209 SAVE	415
14 / p. 400		Novotel Ottawa Hotel - see color ad p 416	◈◈◈	$145	416
15 / p. 400		Residence Inn by Marriott	◈◈◈	$145-$250	420
16 / p. 400	CAA	Sheraton Ottawa Hotel - see color ad p 5	◈◈◈	$129-$260 SAVE	420
17 / p. 400		Lord Elgin Hotel - see color ad p 416	◈◈◈	$125-$175	416
18 / p. 400	CAA	Holiday Inn Hotel & Suites - see color ad p 414, card insert	◈◈◈	$125-$135 SAVE	414
19 / p. 400	CAA	Cartier Place Suite Hotel - see color ad p 410	◈◈◈	$109-$229 SAVE	410
20 / p. 400	CAA	Crowne Plaza Ottawa - see color ad p 411	◈◈◈	$95-$239 SAVE	411
21 / p. 400	CAA	Minto Place Suite Hotel - see color ad p 417	◈◈◈◈	$125-$262 SAVE	416
22 / p. 400	CAA	Ottawa Marriott - see color ad p 418	◈◈◈	$159-$199 SAVE	418
23 / p. 400	CAA	Delta Ottawa Hotel and Suites - see color ad p 413	◈◈◈	$139-$199 SAVE	412
24 / p. 400	CAA	Albert at Bay Suite Hotel - see color ad p 406	◈◈◈	$132-$199 SAVE	406
25 / p. 400	CAA	Best Western Victoria Park Suites - see color ad p 409	◈◈◈	$120-$170 SAVE	408
26 / p. 400	CAA	Albert House Inn - see color ad p 407	◈◈◈	$98-$168 SAVE	407
27 / p. 400	CAA	Radisson Hotel Ottawa Parliament Hill - see color ad p 521, on TourBookMark	◈◈◈	$129-$189 SAVE	420
28 / p. 400	CAA	Aristocrat Suite Hotel - see color ad p 407	◈◈	$119-$179 SAVE	408
		DOWNTOWN OTTAWA - Restaurants			
1 / p. 400		Mukut Indian Restaurant	◈◈	$6-$14	424
2 / p. 400		Sitar Restaurant	◈◈	$9-$15	424
3 / p. 400		Nate's Deli	◈	$5-$14	424

Spotter/Map Page Number	OA	DOWNTOWN OTTAWA - Restaurants (continued)	Diamond Rating	Rate Range High Season	Listing Page
④ / p. 400		Le Caveau de Szechwan	◆◆	$8-$20	423
⑤ / p. 400		Cafe Spiga Trattoria	◆◆◆	$11-$24	421
⑥ / p. 400	CAA	**Sante Restaurant**	◆◆◆	$15-$20	424
⑦ / p. 400		Le Jardin	◆◆◆◆	$8-$33	423
⑧ / p. 400		Clair de Lune	◆◆◆	$18-$26	421
⑨ / p. 400	CAA	**Meditheo Restaurant & Bar**	◆◆◆	$13-$27	423
⑩ / p. 400		Blue Cactus Bar & Grill	◆◆	$10-$25	421
⑪ / p. 400	CAA	**Zak's Diner**	◆◆	$7-$13	424
⑫ / p. 400	CAA	**Courtyard Restaurant**	◆◆	$15-$28	422
⑬ / p. 400		The Marble Works Steak House	◆◆	$16-$30	423
⑭ / p. 400	CAA	**Le Cafe**	◆◆	$16-$29	423
⑮ / p. 400		The Carleton Restaurant & Lounge	◆◆◆	$22-$30	421
⑯ / p. 400		The Mill Restaurant	◆◆	$15-$25	424
⑰ / p. 400		Friday's Roast Beef House & Piano Parlour	◆◆	$17-$35	422
⑱ / p. 400		Bay Street Bistro	◆◆	$10-$17	421
⑲ / p. 400		Noah's	◆◆◆	$14-$24	424
⑳ / p. 400		Le Metro Cafe Restaurant	◆◆◆	$15-$20	423
㉑ / p. 400	CAA	**Mamma Teresa Ristorante**	◆◆◆	$12-$30	423
㉒ / p. 400		Fairouz	◆◆◆	$15-$20	422
㉓ / p. 400		New Delhi Indian Cuisine	◆◆	$10-$14	424
㉔ / p. 400		ARC Lounge	◆◆◆	$22-$32	421
㉕ / p. 400		Egg Spectation	◆◆	$8-$12(L)	422
㉖ / p. 400		Canal Ritz	◆◆	$8-$15	421
㉗ / p. 400		El Meson Restaurant	◆◆◆	$15-$25	422
㉘ / p. 400		The Fish Market Restaurant	◆◆	$13-$32	422
㉙ / p. 400		Empire Grill	◆◆◆	$14-$30	422
㉚ / p. 400		Savana Cafe	◆◆	$13-$19	424
㉛ / p. 400		Haveli Indian Restaurant	◆◆	$8-$23	423
㉜ / p. 400		Cafe Toulouse	◆◆	$11-$20	421
㉝ / p. 400		Merlot	◆◆◆	$26-$45	423
㉞ / p. 400		The Earl of Sussex Pub	◆◆	$9-$15	422
㉟ / p. 400	CAA	**Signatures @ Le Cordon Bleu Paris**	◆◆◆◆	$29-$40	424
㊱ / p. 400		Kinki Asian Fusion	◆◆	$14-$22	423
㊲ / p. 400		Eighteen	◆◆◆	$14-$34	422
㊴ / p. 400		Beckta Dining & Wine	◆◆◆◆	$26-$35	421
㊵ / p. 400		Flipper's	◆◆	$10-$25	422

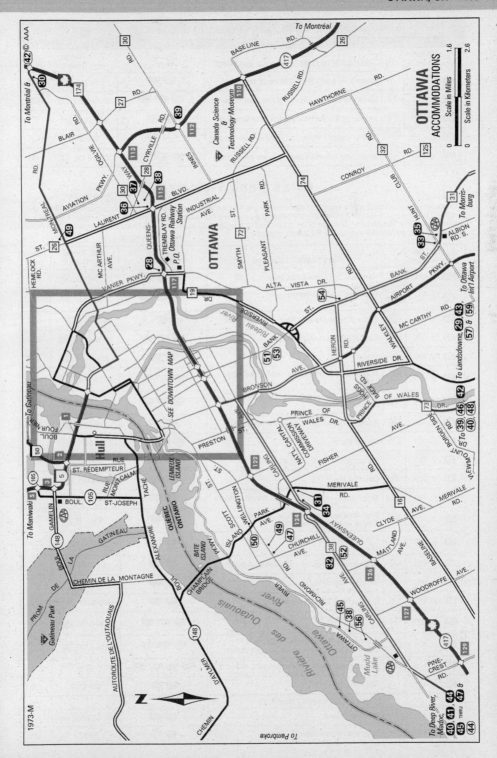

OTTAWA
ACCOMMODATIONS

Scale in Miles
Scale in Kilometers

✈ Airport Accommodations

Spotter/Map Page Number	OA	OTTAWA INTERNATIONAL AIRPORT	Diamond Rating	Rate Range High Season	Listing Page
35 / p. 403	CAA	Adam's Airport Inn, 6.1 km e of terminal	◆◆	$84-$99 SAVE	425
29 / p. 403	CAA	Days Inn Ottawa Airport, 5 km w of terminal	◆◆◆	$139-$149 SAVE	428
42 / p. 403	CAA	Monterey Inn Resort, 7.5 km w of terminal	◆◆	$99-$139 SAVE	431
43 / p. 403		Rideau Heights Motor Inn, 7.2 km w of terminal	◆◆	$99-$109	431
33 / p. 403	CAA	Southway Inn of Ottawa, 5 km e of terminal	◆◆◆	$110-$138 SAVE	431

Ottawa and Vicinity

This index helps you "spot" where approved accommodations and restaurants are located on the corresponding detailed maps. Lodging rate ranges are for comparison only and show the property's high season; rates are per night, unless only weekly (W) rates are available. Restaurant rate range is for dinner, unless only lunch (L) is served. Turn to the listing page for more detailed rate information and consult display ads for special promotions.

Spotter/Map Page Number	OA	OTTAWA - Lodgings	Diamond Rating	Rate Range High Season	Listing Page
28 / p. 403	CAA	Hampton Inn - see color ad p 4, p 430	◆◆◆	$135-$145 SAVE	430
29 / p. 403	CAA	Days Inn Ottawa Airport - see color ad p 429	◆◆◆	$139-$149 SAVE	428
30 / p. 403	CAA	Econo Lodge-Ottawa East - see ad p 430	◆	$80-$99 SAVE	430
31 / p. 403	CAA	Best Western Macies Hotel	◆◆◆	$109-$139 SAVE	426
32 / p. 403	CAA	Webb's Motel	◆◆	$85-$100 SAVE	433
33 / p. 403	CAA	Southway Inn of Ottawa - see color ad p 419	◆◆◆	$110-$138 SAVE	431
34 / p. 403	CAA	Travelodge Hotel & Convention Centre - see color ad p 432	◆◆◆	$169-$189 SAVE	432
35 / p. 403	CAA	Adam's Airport Inn - see color ad p 425	◆◆	$84-$99 SAVE	425
36 / p. 403	CAA	Chimo Hotel	◆◆◆	$165-$195 SAVE	427
37 / p. 403		WelcomINNS - see color ad p 432	◆◆	$95-$105	433
38 / p. 403	CAA	Comfort Inn	◆◆	$95-$125 SAVE	428
39 / p. 403	CAA	Travelodge - see color ad on TourBookMark	◆◆	$99-$149 SAVE	432
40 / p. 403	CAA	Best Western Barons Hotel & Conference Centre - see color ad p 425	◆◆	$117 SAVE	426
41 / p. 403		The Days Inn Ottawa West - see color ad p 429	◆◆	$106-$129	429
42 / p. 403	CAA	Monterey Inn Resort - see color ad p 431	◆◆	$99-$139 SAVE	431
43 / p. 403		Rideau Heights Motor Inn	◆◆	$99-$109	431
44 / p. 403	CAA	Comfort Inn Ottawa West	◆◆	$99-$151 SAVE	428
45 / p. 403	CAA	Country Inn & Suites By Carlson - see color ad p 521, p 428	◆◆	$125-$155 SAVE	428
46 / p. 403	CAA	Holiday Inn Select Hotel & Suites Ottawa-Kanata - see color ad card insert	◆◆◆	$119-$199 SAVE	431
47 / p. 403	CAA	Brookstreet Hotel - see color ad p 427	◆◆◆◆	$139-$299 SAVE	426
49 / p. 403		The Mirada Inn	◆◆	$89-$110	431
		OTTAWA - Restaurants			
38 / p. 403		The Keg Manor	◆◆	$15-$32	434
39 / p. 403		Grillman's Fresh Eatery	◆◆	$7-$18	434

Spotter/Map Page Number	OA	**OTTAWA** - Restaurants (continued)	Diamond Rating	Rate Range High Season	Listing Page
(40) / p. 403		Oggi Ristorante	◆◆◆	$10-$21	434
(42) / p. 403		Pearl of India	◆◆	$6-$14	434
(44) / p. 403	CAA	**Perspectives Restaurant**	◆◆◆◆	$20-$35	434
(45) / p. 403		D'arcy McGee's	◆◆	$7-$19	433
(46) / p. 403		The Miller's Oven	◆◆	$4-$7(L)	434
(47) / p. 403		Newport Restaurant	◆◆	$8-$11	434
(48) / p. 403		The Pines at the Monterey	◆◆	$12-$24	434
(49) / p. 403		Juniper	◆◆◆	$33-$44	434
(50) / p. 403		The Amber Garden Restaurant	◆◆	$13-$19	433
(51) / p. 403		Siam Kitchen	◆◆	$9-$13	434
(52) / p. 403		Bellardita's	◆◆◆	$14-$37	433
(53) / p. 403		Barley Mow Pub	◆◆	$8-$16	433
(54) / p. 403		Flying Piggy's Bistro Italiano	◆◆	$10-$24	433
(56) / p. 403		The Lindenhof Restaurant	◆◆	$12-$17	434
(57) / p. 403		Barley Mow Pub	◆◆	$8-$16	433
(59) / p. 403		Graffiti's	◆◆	$9-$30	433

Travel Planning Your Way

Visit **aaa.com** and enjoy a whole new world of travel information.

AAA/CAA's Internet TripTik® provides interactive maps and search tools that make travel planning easy. Get hotel Diamond ratings, photos, and great room rates. Find the best in restaurants and attractions.

Trust AAA/CAA to simplify travel planning.

Travel with Confidence.
Travel with AAA/CAA.

DOWNTOWN OTTAWA   (See map and index starting on p. 400)

─────── **WHERE TO STAY** ───────

ALBERT AT BAY SUITE HOTEL   *Book at aaa.com*   Phone: (613)238-8858   24
(CAA) (SAVE)   All Year   1P: $132-$199   2P: $132-$199   XP: $10   F17
◆◆◆◆   **Location:** Corner of Bay St. Located in a high-rise residential/commercial area. 435 Albert St K1R 7X4.
Fax: 613/238-1433. **Facility:** 197 units. 177 one- and 20 two-bedroom suites with kitchens. 12 stories,
interior corridors. **Parking:** on-site. **Terms:** check-in 4 pm, package plans. **Amenities:** video games (fee),
Small-scale Hotel high-speed Internet, voice mail, irons, hair dryers. *Some:* fax. **Dining:** Bay Street Bistro, see separate
listing. **Leisure Activities:** saunas, whirlpool, kids club 7/1-8/31, exercise room. **Guest Services:** valet and
coin laundry. **Business Services:** meeting rooms. **Cards:** AX, DC, DS, JC, MC, VI. **Special Amenities:** free local telephone
calls and free newspaper. *(See color ad below)*   SOME UNITS

(S/D) (◻) (⊠) (☆) (DATA PORT) (◻) (▭) (▱)   / (⊠) /

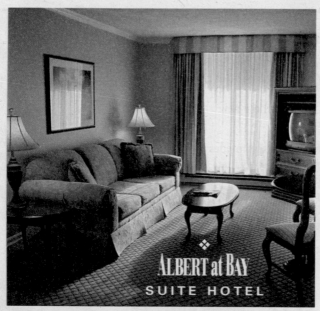

absolutely AAA

Free Wireless High Speed Internet

The **a**lbert at **b**ay Suite Hotel offers abundant space and a host of comforting amenities:

- **Newly Renovated Suites!**

- Remarkably spacious—one or two bedroom suites with full kitchens

- Fitness centre, sauna, whirlpool

- Bay Street Bistro and Black Bear Pub

- Free Kids' Club (July and August)

- **Special CAA/AAA rate $119** (single or double occupancy, subject to availability)

- Parking included

❖ **ALBERT at BAY**
SUITE HOTEL

absolutely **a**lbert at **b**ay   435 Albert Street, Ottawa, Ontario
613.238.8858   800.267.6644   albertatbay.com

Downtown Ottawa

(See map and index starting on p. 400)

ALBERT HOUSE INN

 (AAA) (SAVE)

Historic Bed & Breakfast

All Year [BP]   1P: $98-$148   2P: $108-$168   **Phone:** (613)236-4479   26
XP: $15
Location: Between Bay St and Bronson Ave. Located at the west end of downtown. 478 Albert St K1R 5B5. **Fax:** 613/237-9079. **Facility:** Individually decorated accommodations of various sizes are offered at this circa 1875 house. 17 units. 16 one-bedroom standard units, some with whirlpools. 1 one-bedroom suite. 3 stories (no elevator), interior corridors. *Bath:* combo or shower only. **Parking:** on-site (fee), winter plug-ins. **Terms:** office hours 8 am-midnight, 2 night minimum stay - seasonal and/or weekends, age restrictions may apply, 3 day cancellation notice. **Amenities:** high-speed Internet, hair dryers. **Leisure Activities:** bike storage. **Business Services:** fax (fee). **Cards:** AX, DC, MC, VI. **Special Amenities:** free full breakfast and free local telephone calls. *(See color ad below)*

SOME UNITS
(DATA PORT) / (X) (VCR) /
FEE

A MID-TOWNE HERITAGE B & B

(AAA) (SAVE)

Historic Bed & Breakfast

All Year [BP]   1P: $99-$129   2P: $114-$144   **Phone:** (613)236-1169   8
XP: $15
Location: 1 blk s of Laurier Ave. Located in a commercial/residential area. 220 Lyon St N K1R 5V7. **Fax:** 613/234-4706. **Facility:** This restored circa 1891 family home offers easy access to Parliament Hill. Many attractions, festivals and the business core are nearby. Smoke free premises. 4 units. 3 one-bedroom standard units. 1 one-bedroom suite ($144-$159). 2 stories (no elevator), interior corridors. **Parking:** on-site, winter plug-ins. **Terms:** office hours 10 am-10 pm, 2 night minimum stay - weekends, age restrictions may apply, 7 day cancellation notice-fee imposed, package plans. **Amenities:** video library, hair dryers. **Leisure Activities:** bike & ski storage. **Guest Services:** valet laundry. **Business Services:** business center. **Cards:** AX, MC, VI. **Special Amenities:** free full breakfast and free local telephone calls.

SOME UNITS
(†↑) (†↑↑) (X) (🖥) (✆) / (VCR) (DATA PORT) /
FEE

ARC THE.HOTEL   *Book at aaa.com*

(AAA) (SAVE)

Small-scale Hotel

5/1-10/10   1P: $159-$199   2P: $159-$199   **Phone:** (613)238-2888   12
XP: $20   F18
10/11-4/30   1P: $159-$189   2P: $159-$189   XP: $20   F18
Location: Between Metcalfe and O'Connor St. Located in the business district. 140 Slater St K1P 5H6. **Fax:** 613/238-0053. **Facility:** 112 units. 110 one-bedroom standard units. 2 one-bedroom suites. 8 stories, interior corridors. **Parking:** valet. **Terms:** package plans. **Amenities:** CD players, high-speed Internet (fee), dual phone lines, voice mail, safes, honor bars, hair dryers. *Some:* irons. **Dining:** ARC Lounge, see separate listing. **Leisure Activities:** exercise room. *Fee:* massage. **Guest Services:** valet laundry. **Business Services:** meeting rooms, business center. **Cards:** AX, DC, DS, MC, VI. *(See color ad p 408)*

SOME UNITS
(S🅿) (†↑) (Y) (↟) (✆) (DATA PORT) (🖥) / (X) (VCR) /
FEE

Come and experience our heritage ambiance, modern comforts and exceptional service.

• Convenient downtown location
• Fabulous, full hot breakfasts
• Free high speed internet guest desk and wireless (WiFi)

478 Albert Street Ottawa
1-800-267-1982 • www.albertinn.com

A ARISTOCRAT SUITE HOTEL
Downtown Ottawa
141 Cooper Street
Ottawa · ON · Canada
1.800.563.5634
aristocratsuites.com
info@aristocratsuites.com

Enjoy Apartment Size Suites
Studios
1 or 2 Bedrooms
Spectacular Penthouse Suites

Carmello's Restaurant
Room Service
Business Centre
HSIA
Fitness Facilities
Meeting Rooms

The luxury of space
the comforts of home

(See map and index starting on p. 400)

ARISTOCRAT SUITE HOTEL *Book at aaa.com* Phone: (613)236-7500 28
(CAA) (SAVE) All Year 1P: $119-$179 2P: $119-$179 XP: $15 F18
◈◈ ◈◈ Location: Between Elgin and Cartier sts. 141 Cooper St K2P 0E8. Fax: 613/563-2836. Facility: 216 units. 36 one-
bedroom standard units with kitchens. 170 one- and 10 two-bedroom suites, some with kitchens. 9 stories,
interior corridors. Parking: on-site (fee). Terms: cancellation fee imposed, weekly rates available, pets ($10
Small-scale Hotel extra charge, in designated units). Amenities: video games (fee), voice mail, irons, hair dryers. Some: high-
speed Internet. Dining: 7:30 am-11 pm, cocktails. Leisure Activities: sauna, whirlpool, exercise room.
Guest Services: valet and coin laundry. Business Services: meeting rooms, business center. Cards: AX, CB, DC, DS, JC,
MC, VI. *(See color ad p 407)*

SOME UNITS
(S/D) [≒] [¶¶] [⊠] [⊼] [🖬] [🖴] [🖵] / [⊠] /
FEE

AUBERGE MCGEE'S INN Phone: (613)237-6089 4
◈◈◈◈ All Year [ECP] 1P: $98-$158 2P: $108-$168 XP: $20 F12
Location: Corner of Nelson St. Located in a residential area. 185 Daly Ave K1N 6E8. Fax: 613/237-6201. Facility: A
market, government offices and the university are walking distance from this red brick Victorian dating from
Historic Bed 1886. Smoke free premises. 14 one-bedroom standard units, some with whirlpools. 3 stories (no elevator),
& Breakfast interior corridors. Bath: combo or shower only. Parking: on-site, winter plug-ins. Terms: office hours 8 am-9
pm, cancellation fee imposed, weekly rates available. Amenities: voice mail, hair dryers. Some: CD players. Guest Services:
complimentary laundry. Business Services: fax (fee). Cards: AX, MC, VI.

SOME UNITS
(ASK) (S/D) [⊠] [DATA PORT] [🖵] / [VCR] [🖴] /

BEST WESTERN VICTORIA PARK SUITES *Book at aaa.com* Phone: (613)567-7275 25
(CAA) (SAVE) 5/1-6/30 & 9/1-10/31 [CP] 1P: $120-$170 2P: $120-$170 XP: $10 F16
◈◈◈◈ 7/1-8/31 & 11/1-4/30 [CP] 1P: $110-$170 2P: $110-$170 XP: $10 F16
Location: Between Gladstone Ave and McLeod St. Located in a residential area. 377 O'Connor St K2P 2M2.
Fax: 613/567-1161. Facility: 123 units. 74 one-bedroom standard units. 49 one-bedroom suites. 8 stories,
Small-scale Hotel interior corridors. Parking: on-site. Terms: package plans, 3% service charge. Amenities: video games
(fee), voice mail, irons, hair dryers. Some: high-speed Internet. Leisure Activities: saunas, exercise room.
Guest Services: valet and coin laundry. Business Services: meeting rooms. Cards: AX, CB, DC, DS, JC, MC, VI.
Special Amenities: free continental breakfast and free newspaper. *(See color ad p 409)*

SOME UNITS
(S/D) [⊼] [DATA PORT] [🖴] [🖵] [🖵] / [⊠] /

Chic Affordable Luxury

In The Heart of Downtown Ottawa

ARC
THE. HOTEL

140 Slater Street, Ottawa 613.238.2888 1.800.699.2516
www.arcthehotel.com

(See map and index starting on p. 400)

BOSTONIAN EXECUTIVE SUITES *Book at aaa.com*   **Phone:** (613)594-5757   **9**
　　　　　　　　　　All Year　　　　　1P: $159-$189　　　2P: $159-$189　　　XP: $10　　　F17
▽▽▽▽   **Location:** Between Bank and O'Connor sts. Located in a high-rise residential area. 341 MacLaren St K2P 2E2.
Small-scale Hotel   Fax: 613/594-5774. **Facility:** 117 units. 63 one-bedroom standard units with efficiencies. 54 one-bedroom suites with efficiencies. 9 stories, interior corridors. **Parking:** on-site (fee), winter plug-ins. **Terms:** check-in 4 pm, cancellation fee imposed, 3% service charge, small pets only (with prior approval). **Amenities:** video games (fee), high-speed Internet, dual phone lines, voice mail, irons, hair dryers. **Guest Services:** valet and coin laundry. **Business Services:** meeting rooms. **Cards:** AX, MC, VI.

SOME UNITS

(A$K) (S/D) (🐾) (🛗) (🛎) (DATA PORT) (🛏) (📺) (📼) / (⊠) (VCR) /

i enjoy COMPLETE COMFORT—AND EXCEPTIONAL VALUE.

- SPACIOUS STANDARD AND ONE-BEDROOM SUITES WITH KITCHENETTES
- EXECUTIVE SUITES WITH WHIRLPOOL BATHTUBS
- COMPLIMENTARY DELUXE CONTINENTAL BREAKFAST
- FREE PARKING WITH CAA/AAA RATE
- PENTHOUSE FITNESS CENTRE AND SAUNAS
- FREE LOCAL CALLS AND IN-ROOM COFFEE
- FROM $109-$170 PER NIGHT
  (SGL/DBL PER NIGHT AFTER DISCOUNT)

377 O'Connor Street, at the corner of Gladstone,
Ottawa, Ontario 613 567 7275

Reservations: 800 465 7275 victoriapark.com

BEST WESTERN
VICTORIA PARK
SUITES

Downtown Ottawa

(See map and index starting on p. 400)

CARTIER PLACE SUITE HOTEL   *Book at aaa.com*   **Phone:** (613)236-5000   **19**

(CAA) (SAVE)   All Year   1P: $109-$229   2P: $109-$229   XP: $10   F16

Location: Between Elgin and Cartier sts. Located in a high-rise residential area. 180 Cooper St K2P 2L5. **Fax:** 613/238-4105. **Facility:** 253 units. 24 one-bedroom standard units with kitchens. 200 one- and 29 two-bedroom suites ($109-$229) with kitchens, some with whirlpools. 12 stories, interior corridors. **Parking:** on-site (fee). **Terms:** check-in 4 pm, cancellation fee imposed, [CP] meal plan available, package plans, small pets only ($8 extra charge). **Amenities:** video games (fee), voice mail, irons, hair dryers. *Some:* safes. **Dining:** 6:30 am-11 pm; Sunday brunch, cocktails. **Pool(s):** heated indoor. **Leisure Activities:** sauna, whirlpool, children's playroom, bike storage, playground, exercise room, shuffleboard. **Guest Services:** valet and coin laundry. **Business Services:** meeting rooms. **Cards:** AX, DC, MC, VI. **Special Amenities:** free local telephone calls and free newspaper.
(See color ad below)

Small-scale Hotel

SOME UNITS

[icons] FEE ... / FEE

www.suitedreams.com

Located between the Rideau Canal and trendy Elgin Street.

250 Luxurious Studio, One and Two Bedroom Suites, 4 V.I.P. Suites with Ensuite Jacuzzi, Deluxe Banquet Facilities, Indoor Pool, Whirlpool, Sauna, Exercise and Games Room. Garden Patio and Playground with Shuffleboard.

BEST Independent Hotel AWARD WINNER Traveller's Choice Awards Toronto's Tourist Magazine

Cartier Place
SUITE HOTEL

"One of the Best Buys in Town"
— The Sunday New York Times

Downtown Ottawa
180 Cooper Street
phone: (613) 236-5000
fax: (613) 238-3842
For Reservations
1-800-236-8399

2 MINUTES FROM DOWNTOWN OTTAWA

Fabulous View of Parliament Hill
139 bedrooms, indoor pool, restaurant and bar

COMPLIMENTARY:
• Free local telephone calls
• Free wireless internet (WIFI) available
• Irons & ironing boards in every room
• Children under the age of 18 stay free in the same room as their parents

Best Western

1-800-265-8550 or (819) 770-8550
www.bestwestern.com/ca/cartierhotel
Email:bwcartier@videotron.ca

131 Laurier Street
Gatineau (Hull-Ottawa), Quebec

**Special Rate for CAA/AAA Members-$99 per night

(See map and index starting on p. 400)

COURTYARD BY MARRIOTT OTTAWA   *Book at aaa.com*   Phone: (613)241-1000   **7**
▼▼▼▼   1/1-4/30   1P: $155-$209   2P: $155-$209   XP: $15   F18
    5/1-12/31   1P: $149-$199   2P: $149-$199   XP: $15   F18
Small-scale Hotel   **Location:** Between George and York sts; in Byward Market area. Located in a commercial area. 350 Dalhousie St K1N 7E9. Fax: 613/241-4804. **Facility:** 183 one-bedroom standard units. 4 stories, interior corridors. **Parking:** on-site (fee). **Terms:** cancellation fee imposed, 3% service charge. **Amenities:** video games (fee), high-speed Internet, voice mail, irons, hair dryers. **Pool(s):** heated indoor, wading. **Leisure Activities:** whirlpool, exercise room. **Guest Services:** valet and coin laundry. **Business Services:** conference facilities. **Cards:** AX, DC, DS, MC, VI.

SOME UNITS

ASK 🅢🄳 🍴 ⛱ 🔧 📷 🕷 💾 📠 💻 / ⊗ 🛢 🖵 /

CROWNE PLAZA OTTAWA   *Book at aaa.com*   Phone: (613)237-3600   **20**
CAA SAVE   All Year   1P: $95-$239   2P: $95-$239   XP: $15   F18
▼▼▼▼   **Location:** Entrance corner of Albert St. Located in a commercial area. 101 Lyon St K1R 5T9. Fax: 613/237-2351.
    Facility: 411 one-bedroom standard units. 26 stories, interior corridors. **Parking:** on-site (fee).
Large-scale Hotel   **Terms:** package plans, 3% service charge. **Amenities:** video games (fee), CD players, dual phone lines, voice mail, irons, hair dryers. *Some:* high-speed Internet (fee). **Dining:** 6:30 am-11 pm, cocktails. **Pool(s):** heated indoor. **Leisure Activities:** saunas, children's playroom, exercise room, basketball. **Guest Services:** gift shop, valet laundry. **Business Services:** conference facilities, business center. **Cards:** AX, CB, DC, JC, MC, VI. **Special Amenities:** free local telephone calls and free newspaper. *(See color ad below)*

SOME UNITS

🅢🄳 🍴 ⛱ 🔧 ✕ 🕷 📠 💻 / ⊗ VCR 🛢 /
FEE

DAYS INN-DOWNTOWN (OTTAWA)   *Book at aaa.com*   Phone: (613)789-5555   **3**
CAA SAVE   5/1-10/31   1P: $129-$139   2P: $129-$139   XP: $10   F17
    11/1-4/30   1P: $109-$119   2P: $109-$119   XP: $10   F17
▼▼▼▼   **Location:** Between Nelson St and King Edward Ave. Located in a commercial area. 319 Rideau St K1N 5Y4.
    Fax: 613/789-6196. **Facility:** 74 units. 72 one-bedroom standard units, some with whirlpools. 2 one-
Small-scale Hotel   bedroom suites ($149-$259), some with whirlpools. 4 stories, interior/exterior corridors. **Parking:** on-site, winter plug-ins. **Terms:** cancellation fee imposed, small pets only. **Amenities:** high-speed Internet, voice mail, irons, hair dryers. **Dining:** 7 am-3 pm, cocktails. **Leisure Activities:** exercise room. **Guest Services:** valet and coin laundry. **Business Services:** meeting rooms. **Cards:** AX, CB, DC, DS, MC, VI. **Special Amenities:** free newspaper and early check-in/late check-out. *(See color ad p 412)*

SOME UNITS

🅢🄳 🛏 🍴 🕷 📠 🛢 💻 / ⊗ /

www.crowneottawa.ca

CROWNE PLAZA®

OTTAWA

THE PLACE TO MEET.

• Full service restaurant & lounge

• Health club • Indoor pool

• Kids activity centre • Basketball court

• Priority Club points with every stay

• In the heart of entertainment and shopping

• Steps to Parliament Hill and major attractions

TOLL FREE: **1-800-2CROWNE**
TEL: **613-237-3600** • FAX: **613-237-2351**
101 LYON STREET, OTTAWA, ONTARIO K1R 5T9

email: crowneottawa@chiphospitality.com

(See map and index starting on p. 400)

DELTA OTTAWA HOTEL AND SUITES   *Book at aaa.com*   Phone: (613)238-6000   23
(CAA) (SAVE)   5/1-7/4 & 9/6-12/8   1P: $139-$199   2P: $139-$199   XP: $20   F18
7/5-9/5 & 12/9-4/30   1P: $129-$189   2P: $129-$189   XP: $20   F18
Location: Corner of Lyon St. Located in a commercial area. 361 Queen St K1R 7S9. Fax: 613/238-2290.
Facility: 328 units. 269 one-bedroom standard units. 46 one- and 13 two-bedroom suites ($139-$199). 10-
Large-scale Hotel 18 stories, interior corridors. **Parking:** on-site (fee). **Terms:** cancellation fee imposed, 3% service charge,
pets ($50 fee). **Amenities:** video games (fee), voice mail, irons, hair dryers. *Some:* CD players, high-speed
Internet. **Dining:** 2 restaurants, 6:30 am-10 pm, cocktails. **Pool(s):** heated indoor. **Leisure Activities:** saunas, whirlpool,
waterslide, children's creative centre, exercise room. *Fee:* game room. **Guest Services:** gift shop, complimentary laundry.
Business Services: meeting rooms, business center. **Cards:** AX, DC, DS, JC, MC, VI. *(See color ad p 413)*

SOME UNITS

FEE   FEE

ECONO LODGE DOWNTOWN   *Book at aaa.com*   Phone: (613)789-3781   1
(CAA) (SAVE)   5/1-10/31 [CP]   1P: $90-$125   2P: $110-$150   XP: $10   F16
11/1-4/30 [CP]   1P: $80-$110   2P: $99-$125   XP: $10   F16
Location: Between Chapel and Augusta sts. Located in a commercial area. 475 Rideau St K1N 5Z3.
Fax: 613/789-0207. **Facility:** 60 one-bedroom standard units, some with whirlpools. 2 stories (no elevator),
Motel   exterior corridors. **Parking:** on-site, winter plug-ins. **Terms:** cancellation fee imposed. **Amenities:** hair
dryers. **Cards:** AX, CB, DC, DS, JC, MC, VI. **Special Amenities:** free continental breakfast and free
local telephone calls. *(See color ad below)*

SOME UNITS

FAIRMONT CHATEAU LAURIER   *Book at aaa.com*   Phone: (613)241-1414   10
(CAA) (SAVE)   9/3-10/28   1P: $199-$419   XP: $40
5/1-9/2 & 10/29-4/30   1P: $189-$329   XP: $40
Location: Just e of Parliament buildings. 1 Rideau St K1N 8S7. Fax: 613/562-7030. **Facility:** A permanent
photography exhibit is featured in the lobby and other common areas of this hotel, which overlooks a canal.
Classic Historic   426 units. 413 one-bedroom standard units. 13 one-bedroom suites, some with whirlpools. 6 stories, interior
Large-scale Hotel corridors. **Parking:** on-site (fee) and valet. **Terms:** cancellation fee imposed, package plans, small pets only
($25 extra charge). **Amenities:** voice mail, honor bars, irons, hair dryers. *Fee:* video games, high-speed
Internet. *Some:* CD players, safes. **Dining:** 2 restaurants, 6:30 am-10 pm, cocktails. **Pool(s):** heated indoor. **Leisure
Activities:** saunas, rental bicycles, exercise room. *Fee:* in-line skates, massage. **Guest Services:** gift shop, valet laundry.
Business Services: conference facilities, business center. **Cards:** AX, DC, MC, VI. *(See color ad p 414)*

SOME UNITS

FEE

Come on Inn...

OTTAWA
• Free high speed Internet
• Preferred AAA/CAA rates
• 4 blocks to the Parliament buildings
• Free parking
• Tour bus pick-up
• Minutes away from Casino du Hull
• Steps away from Byward Market

It's fun to get more.

1-800-DAYS INN
www.daysinn.ca

Days Inn - Ottawa Downtown   Tel   Toll Free   Fax
319 Rideau Street, Ottawa ON K1N 5Y4   613 789-5555   800 329-7466   613 789-6196
www.thedaysinn.com/ottawa12423   email: daysinnottawa@ohrhma.biz

Econo Lodge

Downtown Ottawa

BY CHOICE HOTELS

475 Rideau Street • Ottawa, ON K1N 5Z3
**Rooms with fridge and microwave and rooms with
whirlpool bath available.**

Recently renovated rooms from $95 to $150 Cdn. (Sgl./Dbl. Occ.)
Free High Speed Internet, Free Continental Breakfast & Free Parking. Short walk to
Parliament, the Congress Centre & most tourist attractions.

Parking at your door and local telephone calls free.
www.choicehotels.ca/cn630
For reservations call 613-789-3781 or toll-free **800-263-0649**

(See map and index starting on p. 400)

GASTHAUS SWITZERLAND INN

Historic Bed & Breakfast

All Year [BP]   1P: $108-$168   2P: $118-$188

Phone: 613/237-0335 6

XP: $20

Location: Corner of Cumberland St. Located in a residential area. 89 Daly Ave K1N 6E6. Fax: 613/594-3327. **Facility:** This 1872 heritage house has varied-size, brightly decorated rooms, some with gas fireplaces and duvet-covered beds. Smoke free premises. 22 one-bedroom standard units, some with whirlpools. 3 stories (no elevator), interior corridors. *Bath:* combo or shower only. **Parking:** on-site, winter plug-ins. **Terms:** office hours 7 am-11 pm, 2 night minimum stay - weekends, age restrictions may apply, 7 day cancellation notice-fee imposed. **Amenities:** hair dryers. *Some:* CD players. **Guest Services:** valet laundry. **Cards:** AX, CB, DC, JC, MC, VI. **Special Amenities: free full breakfast and free local telephone calls.**

- Wide variety of accommodations, from standard rooms to studios and suites with kitchenettes and balconies
- Giant indoor waterslide and indoor swimming pool
- Health club
- Children's Creative Centre
- Close to Parliament Buildings, Museum of Civilization, Museum of Nature, Sparks Street pedestrian mall and the Rideau Canal
- Easy access to the National Arts Centre, National Gallery and Byward Market
- Gallery Café, Jester's Lounge, Capital Dining Room
- Children 6 and under eat free and children 7-12 eat for half price when accompanied by a paying adult

361 Queen Street,
Ottawa, ON K1R 7S9
613-238-6000
Fax: 613-238-2290

*Offer valid between May 1, 2005, and April 30, 2006. Rate will fluctuate with the seasons and is subject to availability. Rate is based on single/double occupancy, per room, per night. U.S. rate subject to exchange fluctuation.

DELTA
OTTAWA
HOTEL AND SUITES

Your room is ready

Special CAA/AAA Getaway Rate
$119CDN*
for a standard room, or ask about our studio kitchenettes for only $20 more!

CANADA and U.S.
1-800-268-1133
www.deltahotels.com

Special CAA/AAA Getaway Rate
$92US*
for a standard room, or ask about our studio kitchenettes for only $20 more!

(See map and index starting on p. 400)

HOLIDAY INN HOTEL & SUITES   *Book at aaa.com*   **Phone:** (613)238-1331   🔞

(CAA) (SAVE)   All Year   1P: $125   2P: $135   XP: $10   F18
Location: Corner of Cartier St. 111 Cooper St K2P 2E3. Fax: 613/230-2179. **Facility:** 229 units. 198 one-
🔷🔷🔷🔷 bedroom standard units, some with kitchens and/or whirlpools. 31 one-bedroom suites ($144-$154) with
kitchens. 16 stories, interior corridors. *Bath:* combo or shower only. **Parking:** on-site (fee). **Terms:** check-in
Large-scale Hotel 4 pm, 15% service charge. **Amenities:** dual phone lines, voice mail, irons, hair dryers. *Some:* high-speed
Internet. **Dining:** 7 am-10 pm, cocktails. **Leisure Activities:** exercise room. **Guest Services:** valet and coin
laundry. **Business Services:** meeting rooms. **Cards:** AX, DC, DS, MC, VI. **Special Amenities:** free newspaper and free
room upgrade (subject to availability with advance reservations). *(See color ad below & card insert)*

SOME UNITS

🛏 🍴 🍸 🛗 👤 📹 [DATA PORT] 💻 / ✖ [VCR] 🔲 📼 /
FEE

YOUR CASTLE AWAITS

Old world charm and elegant surroundings
centrally located in the heart of Canada's
vibrant capital city. Let us welcome you!

Fairmont
CHÂTEAU LAURIER
OTTAWA

Reservations 1-800-441-1414   www.fairmont.com

Fairmont Château Laurier, 1, Rideau Street, Ottawa ON K1N 8S7   613-241-1414

NEW in downtown Ottawa!

Holiday Inn®
HOTEL & SUITES
Ottawa - DOWNTOWN

Your familiar place to stay
Choice Canal-side location,
with 229 guestrooms and suites

• One- or two-bedroom
  suites/kitchenettes
• Jacuzzi/whirlpool suites
• High-speed wireless
  internet
• Casual dining at Lane's
• Fitness facility
• Business centre
• Complimentary
  newspaper
• A Priority Club
  Rewards hotel

1800 267-8378

T: 613 238-1331   F: 613 230-2179   www.hiottawa.ca   reservations@hiottawa.ca

111 Cooper Street
Ottawa ON K2P 2E3

(See map and index starting on p. 400)

LES SUITES HOTEL OTTAWA   *Book at aaa.com*

CAA SAVE

♦♦♦♦♦

			Phone: (613)232-2000	**13**
5/1-10/31	1P: $179-$209	2P: $179-$209	XP: $20	F18
11/1-4/30	1P: $169-$199	2P: $169-$199	XP: $20	F18

Location: Between Nicholas and Waller sts. 130 Besserer St K1N 9M9. Fax: 613/232-1242. **Facility:** 243 units. 6 one-bedroom standard units. 136 one- and 101 two-bedroom suites with kitchens. 22 stories, interior **Large-scale Hotel** corridors. **Parking:** on-site (fee). **Terms:** package plans, pets ($25 fee). **Amenities:** video games (fee), voice mail, irons, hair dryers. *Some:* high-speed Internet (fee), fax, safes. **Dining:** 6:30 am-10:30 pm, Sun 7 am-9 pm. **Pool(s):** heated indoor. **Leisure Activities:** saunas, whirlpool, steamrooms, exercise room. **Guest Services:** complimentary and valet laundry. **Business Services:** meeting rooms. **Cards:** AX, DC, DS, MC, VI. *(See color ad below)*

SOME UNITS

(icons) FEE

Give yourself the Suite Advantage

Treat your family to a Two-Bedroom Suite!

Great downtown location • Steps from shopping, restaurants, attractions
Spacious one- and two-bedroom suites with full kitchens, ensuite laundry
Free local calls • Indoor pool • High-speed Internet available

Exceptional value, great service — experience it at
Les Suites Hotel, Ottawa.

KIDS stay for FREE!

LES SUITES
HOTEL   OTTAWA

Child & Youth Friendly Ottawa   Ottawa: L'Amie de la Jeunesse

Reservations 1-800-267-1989 • www.les-suites.com
130 Besserer St., Ottawa, ON K1N 9M9 • (613) 232-2000 • Fax (613) 232-1242

(See map and index starting on p. 400)

LORD ELGIN HOTEL   *Book at aaa.com*   Phone: (613)235-3333   **17**
All Year   1P: $125-$165   2P: $135-$175   XP: $10   F18
Location: Between Laurier Ave and Slater St. Located opposite National Arts Centre and Confederation Park. 100 Elgin
Large-scale Hotel   St K1P 5K8. Fax: 613/235-3223. **Facility:** 355 units. 350 one-bedroom standard units. 3 one- and 2 two-
bedroom suites, some with efficiencies and/or whirlpools. 11 stories, interior corridors. *Bath:* combo or
shower only. **Parking:** valet. **Terms:** package plans, 3% service charge, small pets only (with prior approval). **Amenities:** voice
mail, irons, hair dryers. *Some:* high-speed Internet, safes. **Pool(s):** heated indoor. **Leisure Activities:** sauna, whirlpool, exercise
room. **Guest Services:** gift shop, valet laundry. **Business Services:** meeting rooms, business center. **Cards:** AX, CB, DC, DS,
JC, MC, VI. *(See color ad below)*

SOME UNITS

MINTO PLACE SUITE HOTEL   *Book at aaa.com*   Phone: (613)232-2200   **21**
All Year   1P: $125-$262   2P: $125-$262   XP: $15   F18
Location: Corner of Lyon St; in Minto Place. Located in a high-rise office/shopping complex. 433 Laurier Ave W K1R
7Y1. Fax: 613/232-6962. **Facility:** In the business district, the hotel has an attractively landscaped sun deck;
some guest rooms feature full kitchens. 417 units. 72 one-bedroom standard units, some with efficiencies.
Large-scale Hotel   270 one- and 75 two-bedroom suites, some with efficiencies or kitchens. 31 stories, interior corridors.
Parking: on-site (fee). **Terms:** package plans, 3% service charge. **Amenities:** voice mail, irons, hair dryers.
Fee: video games, high-speed Internet. *Some:* dual phone lines. **Dining:** Noah's, see separate listing. **Pool(s):** heated indoor.
Leisure Activities: sauna, whirlpool. **Guest Services:** valet laundry. **Business Services:** meeting rooms. **Cards:** AX, CB, DC,
DS, JC, MC, VI. **Special Amenities:** free local telephone calls and free newspaper. *(See color ad p 417)*

SOME UNITS

NOVOTEL OTTAWA HOTEL   *Book at aaa.com*   Phone: (613)230-3033   **14**
5/1-6/30 & 9/1-10/31   1P: $145   2P: $145   XP: $15   F16
7/1-8/31 & 11/1-4/30   1P: $130   2P: $130   XP: $15   F16
Location: Corner of Daly Ave. Located across from shopping centre. 33 Nicholas St K1N 9M7. Fax: 613/760-4765.
Large-scale Hotel   **Facility:** 281 units. 280 one-bedroom standard units. 1 one-bedroom suite. 9 stories, interior corridors.
Parking: on-site (fee). **Terms:** small pets only. **Amenities:** voice mail, irons, hair dryers. *Fee:* video games, high-speed Internet.
Some: honor bars. **Pool(s):** heated indoor. **Leisure Activities:** saunas, whirlpool, steamrooms, exercise room. **Guest
Services:** valet laundry. **Business Services:** meeting rooms. **Cards:** AX, CB, DC, DS, JC, MC, VI. *(See color ad below)*

SOME UNITS

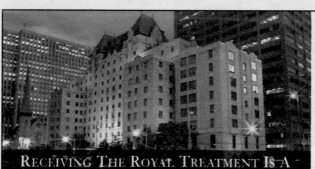

LORD ELGIN
Since 1941

RESERVATIONS
1-800-267-4298
WWW.LORDELGIN.CA

RECEIVING THE ROYAL TREATMENT IS A
GIVEN WHEN YOU STAY WITH LORD ELGIN.

NOVOTEL
Accor hotels

Relax With Us. Whether holding a meeting
or relaxing in the tranquility of your room, we'll
make sure your stay at Novotel exceeds all
expectations. Relax and enjoy yourself at
Novotel.

Novotel Ottawa
33 Nicholas St.
Ottawa, Ontario, K1N 9M7
(613) 230-3033 • 800-NOVOTEL

www.novotel.com   www.accorhotels.com

ACCOR   **A new perspective on our Hotels and Services**

MINTO PLACE
SUITE HOTEL

A HOTEL FOR ALL SEASONS

- Spacious studio, 1 and 2 bedroom suites
- Fully equipped kitchens
- Restaurants and room service
- Indoor pool, whirlpool and sauna
- Children 18 years and under stay free in parents' suite
- Ask about our Kids' Club
- High speed Internet access in all suites and meeting rooms

Whether you visit Ottawa in the spring, summer, fall or winter, you'll always find an array of attractions, festivals and events. Minto Place Suite Hotel is ideally located just steps from Parliament Hill and all major sites and shopping areas.

RESERVATIONS:
Ottawa: (613) 782-2350 • Canada & U.S.A.: 1-800-267-3377
Fax: (613) 232-6962

433 Laurier Avenue West, Ottawa, Ontario K1R 7Y1
Web Site: www.mintohotel.com • email: mpshotel@minto.com

Four Diamond Award

(See map and index starting on p. 400)

OTTAWA MARRIOTT   *Book at aaa.com*

Phone: (613)238-1122   **22**

9/1-12/31	1P: $159-$199	2P: $159-$199	XP: $20	F17
5/1-6/30	1P: $159-$199	2P: $199	XP: $20	F17
1/1-4/30	1P: $129-$149	2P: $129-$149	XP: $20	F17
7/1-8/31	1P: $119-$139	2P: $119-$139	XP: $20	F17

Large-scale Hotel **Location:** Corner of Queen St. Located in the business district. 100 Kent St K1P 5R7. Fax: 613/783-4229. **Facility:** 480 units. 474 one-bedroom standard units. 6 one-bedroom suites, some with whirlpools. 28 stories, interior corridors. **Parking:** on-site (fee) and valet. **Terms:** 2 night minimum stay - seasonal, 7 day cancellation notice-fee imposed, package plans, small pets only. **Amenities:** dual phone lines, voice mail, irons, hair dryers. *Fee:* video games, high-speed Internet. **Dining:** 6:30 am-6 pm, also, Merlot, Cafe Toulouse, see separate listings. **Pool(s):** heated indoor. **Leisure Activities:** saunas, whirlpool, miniature golf, recreation programs. *Fee:* pool table, massage, game room. **Guest Services:** gift shop, valet and coin laundry. *Fee:* tanning facility. **Business Services:** conference facilities, business center. **Cards:** AX, CB, DC, DS, JC, MC, VI. **Special Amenities:** free newspaper. *(See color ad below)*

SOME UNITS

TREAT YOURSELF TO MARRIOTT IN THE HEART OF DOWNTOWN OTTAWA.

Exceptional location in the heart of the entertainment and shopping district, convenient to Parliament, dining, museums, theatres and attractions.

Comfortable, elegantly furnished guest rooms; fine dining and great views in *Merlot*, Ottawa's only revolving rooftop restaurant; free meals for kids under the age of 6.

Indoor pool, whirlpool and health club; games room with pool table, air hockey, foosball and 4 Nintendo stations; activity and arts centre with tree house and daily movie viewing; 9-hole miniature golf, ball hockey court and basketball half court.

Earn Marriott Rewards® points or miles for your stay. Going above and beyond. IT'S THE MARRIOTT WAY.℠

$119-$189 CDN   CAA/AAA rates for 1-4 persons, subject to availability.

Marriott.
OTTAWA

100 Kent Street
(Kent and Queen)
Ottawa, Ontario
Canada, K1P 5R7
613-238-1122

information@
ottawamarriott.com

Call your travel agent or
1-800-853-8463 or visit
Ottawamarriott.com

(See map and index starting on p. 400)

QUALITY HOTEL OTTAWA, DOWNTOWN — *Book at aaa.com* — Phone: (613)789-7511 — **5**

5/1-10/31	1P: $134	2P: $144	XP: $10 F18
11/1-4/30	1P: $122	2P: $134	XP: $10 F18

Location: Corner of King Edward Ave. Located in a commercial area. 290 Rideau St K1N 5Y3. Fax: 613/789-2434. **Facility:** 212 one-bedroom standard units. 19 stories, interior corridors. **Parking:** on-site (fee). **Small-scale Hotel** **Terms:** check-in 4 pm, weekly rates available, 3% service charge, pets (in smoking units). **Amenities:** video games (fee), high-speed Internet, voice mail, hair dryers. *Some:* irons. **Dining:** 7 am-11 pm, cocktails. **Guest Services:** valet laundry. **Business Services:** meeting rooms. **Cards:** AX, CB, DC, DS, JC, MC, VI.

Visiting OTTAWA

stay Inn...

Southway Inn OTTAWA

Consumers' Choice Award 2004 For Business Excellence

the heart of Ottawa South

corner of Bank & Hunt Club

Inn ...style style

Inn ...sync aménitiés

Inn ...comfort confort

• 170 spacious guest rooms & suites
• Indoor pool, fitness, whirlpool & sauna
• *the Shallows* Restaurant • FREE Parking
• FREE high-speed internet access
• Meeting Rooms • *5 minutes from the airport* • CLOSE to major attractions

Reservations. Toll Free.
1.877.688.4929
2431 rue Bank Street (at Hunt Club), Ottawa, Ontario K1V 8R9
www.southway.com

(See map and index starting on p. 400)

RADISSON HOTEL OTTAWA PARLIAMENT HILL *Book at aaa.com* **Phone:** (613)236-1133 27

CAA SAVE

5/1-10/15	1P: $129-$169	2P: $139-$189	XP: $20	F18
10/16-4/30	1P: $119-$159	2P: $129-$169	XP: $20	F18

Location: Corner of Bay and Queen sts. Located in a commercial, residential area. 402 Queen St K1R 5A7. Fax: 613/236-2317. **Facility:** 176 units. 170 one-bedroom standard units. 6 one-bedroom suites with

Small-scale Hotel efficiencies. 11 stories, interior corridors. **Parking:** on-site (fee). **Terms:** package plans, small pets only ($25 fee). **Amenities:** video games (fee), dual phone lines, voice mail, irons, hair dryers. *Some:* high-speed Internet. **Dining:** 7 am-11 pm, cocktails. **Leisure Activities:** whirlpool, exercise room. **Guest Services:** valet and coin laundry. **Business Services:** meeting rooms. **Cards:** AX, DC, DS, MC, VI. *(See color ad p 521 & on TourBookMark)*

SOME UNITS

(S/D) (icons) FEE /

RESIDENCE INN BY MARRIOTT *Book at aaa.com* **Phone:** (613)231-2020 15

5/1-10/31 & 1/1-4/30 [BP]	1P: $145-$250	2P: $145-$250	XP: $15	F18
11/1-12/31 [BP]	1P: $139-$245	2P: $139-$245	XP: $15	F18

Small-scale Hotel **Location:** Corner of Elgin St. Located in a commercial area. 161 Laurier Ave W K1P 5J2. Fax: 613/231-2090. **Facility:** 162 units. 28 one-bedroom standard units with efficiencies. 116 one- and 18 two-bedroom suites with kitchens, some with whirlpools. 14 stories, interior corridors. **Parking:** on-site (fee). **Terms:** cancellation fee imposed, 3% service charge, pets ($150 fee). **Amenities:** video games (fee), voice mail, irons, hair dryers. **Pool(s):** heated indoor. **Leisure Activities:** saunas, whirlpool, exercise room. *Fee:* massage. **Guest Services:** valet and coin laundry. **Business Services:** conference facilities. **Cards:** AX, DC, DS, MC, VI.

SOME UNITS

(ASK) (S/D) (icons) FEE / X /

SHERATON OTTAWA HOTEL *Book at aaa.com* **Phone:** (613)238-1500 16

CAA SAVE

All Year	1P: $129-$260	2P: $129-$260	XP: $20	F18

Location: Corner of O'Connor St. Located in the business district. 150 Albert St K1P 5G2. Fax: 613/235-2723. **Facility:** 236 one-bedroom standard units. 18 stories, interior corridors. **Parking:** valet. **Terms:** small pets only. **Amenities:** video games (fee), high-speed Internet, voice mail, irons, hair dryers. *Some:* fax.

Large-scale Hotel **Dining:** The Carleton Restaurant & Lounge, see separate listing. **Pool(s):** heated indoor. **Leisure Activities:** saunas, exercise room. **Guest Services:** gift shop, valet laundry. **Business Services:** conference facilities, business center. **Cards:** AX, CB, DC, DS, JC, MC, VI. **Special Amenities:** free newspaper. *(See color ad p 5)*

SOME UNITS

(S/D) (icons) / X /

MEMBER OF STARWOOD PREFERRED GUEST

• Each room features the Heavenly Bed® and Heavenly Bath®
• Along the banks of the Rideau Canal
• Spectacular views of Parliament Hill
• Walking distance to Byward Market and to most attractions
• Westin Kids Club® (Kids 10 and under eat free with adult meal)
• SPG points for every stay
• 24-hour full-service WestinWORKOUT℠ powered by Reebok including indoor pool

THE WESTIN
OTTAWA

Let us reserve your stay. Call 1-800-937-8461 or visit us at www.westin.com/ottawa

(See map and index starting on p. 400)

THE WESTIN OTTAWA   *Book at aaa.com*   Phone: 613/560-7000   ⑪
▼▼▼▼ ▼▼▼▼ All Year   1P: $159-$235   2P: $159-$235   XP: $20   F19
Large-scale Hotel **Location:** Corner of Rideau St. Located adjacent to the Rideau Centre Complex. 11 Colonel By Dr K1N 9H4.
Fax: 613/234-5396. **Facility:** Large guest rooms, many with views of the city, are featured at the hotel,
which has underground access to a shopping complex and government offices. 487 units. 457 one-bedroom
standard units. 30 one-bedroom suites ($299-$1600). 24 stories, interior corridors. **Parking:** on-site (fee) and valet.
Terms: cancellation fee imposed, package plans, small pets only (with prior approval). **Amenities:** dual phone lines, voice mail,
honor bars, irons, hair dryers. *Fee:* video games, high-speed Internet. **Pool(s):** heated indoor. **Leisure Activities:** saunas,
whirlpool, exercise room. *Fee:* massage. **Guest Services:** gift shop, valet laundry. **Business Services:** conference facilities,
business center. **Cards:** AX, DC, DS, JC, MC, VI. *(See color ad p 5 & p 420)*   SOME UNITS

🛏 🍴 24🕐 🍽 📶 ⚙ ⚙ ⚙ ☂ 🏋 DATA PORT 🖥 / ☒ VCR 📷 /
                                                              FEE   FEE

─────── **WHERE TO DINE** ───────

ARC LOUNGE   **Lunch:** $11-$16   **Dinner:** $22-$32   **Phone:** 613/238-2888   ㉔
▼▼▼ ▼▼▼ **Location:** Between Metcalfe and O'Connor St; in ARC the.hotel. 140 Slater St K1P 5H6. **Hours:** 7-10 am, 11:30-1:30
& 5:30-10 pm, Sat 7 am-noon & 5:30-10 pm, Sun 7 am-noon. Closed major holidays.
Continental **Reservations:** suggested. **Features:** The restaurant marches to the beat of a different drummer. A
professional, creative twist is applied to the seasonally changing menu. The dining room is small, and tables
are closely spaced. Guests can savor the difference. Dressy casual; cocktails. **Parking:** valet and street. **Cards:** AX, DS,
MC, VI.   🍽 ☒

BAY STREET BISTRO   **Lunch:** $7-$10   **Dinner:** $10-$17   **Phone:** 613/234-1111   ⑱
▼▼▼ ▼▼▼ **Location:** Corner of Bay St; in Albert at Bay Suite Hotel. 160 Bay St K1R 7X4. **Hours:** 11 am-11 pm, Sat & Sun-10
Italian pm. Closed: 12/25-12/27. **Reservations:** accepted. **Features:** A busy bistro-style atmosphere spotlights the
well-prepared Italian-American cuisine served at this eatery. There is also an all-you-can-eat lunch buffet.
Validated evening parking is available. Sidewalk terrace dining is offered in summer. Casual dress;
cocktails. **Parking:** street. **Cards:** AX, DC, MC, VI.   🍽 ☒

BECKTA DINING & WINE   **Dinner:** $26-$35   **Phone:** 613/238-7063   ㊴
▼▼▼▼ ▼▼▼▼ **Location:** Between Kent and Bank sts. 226 Nepear St K2P 0B8. **Hours:** 5:30 pm-10 pm. Closed major holidays.
International **Reservations:** suggested. **Features:** Once patrons step through the door of the old house, the caring staff
begins to work toward creating an exceptional dining experience. Artistically presented dishes line the
eclectic menu, but more adventuresome diners can trust in the chef to create a memorable surprise dish for
each course. The wine list, which lists some by-the-glass choices, is worth a look. Dressy casual; cocktails. **Parking:** street.
Cards: AX, DC, MC, VI.   🍽 ☒

BLUE CACTUS BAR & GRILL   **Lunch:** $8-$12   **Dinner:** $10-$25   **Phone:** 613/241-7061   ⑩
▼▼▼ ▼▼▼ **Location:** Corner of Clarence St; in Byward Market area. 2 Byward Market K1N 7A1. **Hours:** 11:30 am-10 pm, Fri &
Southwest Sat-11 pm. Closed: 12/25. **Features:** The upbeat Southwest decor and a casual friendly atmosphere, which
American can be boisterous at times, combine to make this a favorite meeting spot. High stools at tall tables in the bar
area and large bar windows create the perfect perch for people watching. Steak, ribs and chicken as well as
some Tex-Mex standards are all served up in generous portions. Casual dress; cocktails. **Parking:** street.
Cards: AX, DC, MC, VI.   🍽 ☒

CAFE SPIGA TRATTORIA   **Lunch:** $9-$18   **Dinner:** $11-$24   **Phone:** 613/241-4381   ⑤
▼▼▼ ▼▼▼ **Location:** Corner of Murray St; in Byward Market area. 271 Dalhousie St K1N 7E5. **Hours:** 11:30 am-2:30 & 5-11
Italian pm, Sat from 5 pm, Sun 5 pm-10 pm. Closed: 12/25, 12/26. **Reservations:** suggested. **Features:** The
stylish corner trattoria serves modern and traditional Italian dishes, such as linguine with mushrooms and
light broth, veal parmigiana, osso buco with risotto and an excellent assortment of desserts, including
delicious praline ice cream cake. Portuguese dishes also make a menu appearance. Casual dress; cocktails. **Parking:** street.
Cards: AX, DC, MC, VI.   ☒

CAFE TOULOUSE   **Lunch:** $10-$19   **Dinner:** $11-$20   **Phone:** 613/783-4202   ㉜
▼▼▼ ▼▼▼ **Location:** Corner of Queen St; in Ottawa Marriott. 100 Kent St K1P 5R7. **Hours:** 6:30 am-11 pm, Sat & Sun from 7
Continental am. **Reservations:** suggested. **Features:** The mixed fare of pasta, gourmet pizza, sandwiches, burgers and
stir-fry combined with the fun of a bustling atmosphere keep this bistro on the popular list. Casual dress;
cocktails. **Parking:** on-site (fee) and valet. **Cards:** AX, DC, DS, MC, VI.   🍽 ☒

CANAL RITZ   **Lunch:** $8-$15   **Dinner:** $8-$15   **Phone:** 613/238-8998   ㉖
▼▼▼ ▼▼▼ **Location:** Jct 5th Ave and Queen Elizabeth Dr. 375 Queen Elizabeth Dr K1S 5M5. **Hours:** 11:30 am-11 pm. Closed:
Italian 12/25. **Reservations:** suggested. **Features:** Located on the canal in a pleasant residential, park-like setting,
Canal Ritz features pasta, pizza, veal and chicken and a Saturday and Sunday brunch. Try the notable
chocolate pecan pie for dessert. The terrace has lovely views. The parking lot is on 5th Ave. Casual dress;
cocktails. **Parking:** on-site. **Cards:** AX, DC, MC, VI.   ☒

THE CARLETON RESTAURANT & LOUNGE   **Lunch:** $10-$18   **Dinner:** $22-$30   **Phone:** 613/238-1500   ⑮
▼▼▼ ▼▼▼ **Location:** Corner of O'Connor St; in Sheraton Ottawa Hotel. 150 Albert St K1P 5G2. **Hours:** 6:30 am-10:30, noon-
Continental 2:30 & 5:30-10:30 pm. **Reservations:** suggested. **Features:** Casual dining in elegant surroundings; smart
casual dress suggested. An a la carte menu is offered; however, the primary focus is a self-service buffet
featuring prime roast beef. The lounge area is a popular meeting spot for the local office crowd. Dressy
casual; cocktails. **Parking:** valet. **Cards:** AX, DC, DS, JC, MC, VI.   🍽 ☒

CLAIR DE LUNE   **Lunch:** $12-$18   **Dinner:** $18-$26   **Phone:** 613/241-2200   ⑧
▼▼▼ ▼▼▼ **Location:** Between Parent Ave and Dalhousie St; in Byward Market area. 81B Clarence St K1N 5P5. **Hours:** 11:30
French am-11 pm, Sun-10 pm. Closed: 1/1, 10/24, 12/25. **Reservations:** suggested. **Features:** Braised veal with
lentils and butternut squash is just one excellent recommendation from the modern French menu at this
casually chic restaurant. Both rooftop and terrace dining are popular in summer. Casual dress; cocktails.
Parking: street. **Cards:** AX, DC, MC, VI.   🍽 ☒

(See map and index starting on p. 400)

COURTYARD RESTAURANT   Lunch: $7-$12   Dinner: $15-$28   Phone: 613/241-1516   ⑫
Location: Just e of Sussex Dr; in Byward Market area. 21 George St K1N 8W5. Hours: 11:30 am-2 & 5:30-10 pm; 11:30 am-10 pm 5/15-9/5. Closed: 12/24-12/26. Reservations: suggested. Features: Contemporary menu choices of chicken, fish, steak and a favorite maple sugar pie are served in the restaurant's historic stone building. Courtyard seating is offered in summer and parking is available in the adjacent pay lot. Casual
Continental   dress; cocktails. Parking: on-site (fee). Cards: AX, DC, MC, VI.

THE EARL OF SUSSEX PUB   Lunch: $5-$11   Dinner: $9-$15   Phone: 613/562-5544   ㉞
Location: Jct Murray St. 431 Sussex Dr K1N 9M6. Hours: 11 am-11 pm. Reservations: suggested.
Features: This friendly pub is located opposite the National Gallery of Canada, close to the mint and within
British   sight of the Parliament buildings. In addition to traditional fare such as fish and chips, bangers and mash and steak and kidney pie, the menu also includes sandwiches, wings, pasta and salads. There is a patio in season. Casual dress; cocktails; entertainment. Parking: street. Cards: AX, DC, MC, VI.

EGG SPECTATION   Lunch: $8-$12   Phone: 613/569-6505   ㉕
Location: Corner of Laurier Ave. 171 Bank St K2P 1W5. Hours: 6 am-5 pm. Closed: 1/1, 12/25.
Reservations: required. Features: Breakfast at noon here is no problem. Many egg dishes are served in a
American   bustling atmosphere wrapped in funky decor. Other menu items include soup, salads, sandwiches, pasta and a selection of freshly squeezed juices. Casual dress; cocktails. Parking: street. Cards: AX, DC,
MC, VI.

EIGHTEEN   Lunch: $13-$15   Dinner: $14-$34   Phone: 613/244-1188   ㊲
Location: Just e of Sussex Dr; in Byward Market area. 18 York St K1N 5T5. Hours: 11:30 am-11 pm. Closed: 1/1, 12/25, 12/26; also Sun. Reservations: accepted. Features: The 18th-century heritage building, with
French   exposed gray stone walls and contemporary art, creates an inviting atmosphere. Service is polished and caring. Seasonal menus take advantage of fresh, high-quality ingredients. Creatively prepared and presented dishes pair with selections from a superior wine list. Casual dress; cocktails. Parking: street. Cards: AX, MC, VI.
Historic

EL MESON RESTAURANT   Lunch: $10-$18   Dinner: $15-$25   Phone: 613/744-8484   ㉗
Location: Just e of Vanier Pkwy. 94 Beechwood Ave K1L 8B2. Hours: 11:30 am-2:30 & 5-10 pm, Sat & Sun from 5 pm. Closed: 1/1, 4/17, 12/25, 12/26; also 3 weeks in Aug. Reservations: suggested. Features: In an old Victorian mansion, the restaurant serves a variety of chicken, red meat and splendid seafood dishes that
Mediterranean   are artfully prepared and presented. Fine Iberian cuisine is served in a professional and friendly manner. Dressy casual; cocktails. Parking: on-site. Cards: AX, DC, MC, VI.

EMPIRE GRILL   Lunch: $11-$16   Dinner: $14-$30   Phone: 613/241-1343   ㉙
Location: Jct Parent Ave; in Byward Market area. 47 Clarence St K1N 9K1. Hours: 11:30 am-11 pm, Sun from 11 am. Closed: 12/25. Reservations: suggested. Features: The bustling restaurant is popular with the
Continental   business crowd and visitors to the capital. A varied menu, efficient, friendly service and a comfortable, contemporary decor should please the discerning diner. Casual dress; cocktails. Parking: street.
Cards: AX, DC, MC, VI.

FAIROUZ   Lunch: $10-$15   Dinner: $15-$20   Phone: 613/233-1536   ㉒
Location: Between Bank and O'Connor sts. 343 Somerset St W K2P 0J8. Hours: 11:30 am-2:30 & 5-10 pm, Sat & Sun from 5 pm. Closed: for dinner 12/24 & 12/25. Reservations: suggested. Features: Kebabs, hummus,
Lebanese   tabbouleh, marinated chicken and lamb dishes await the diner at Fairouz. This restaurant was named after a popular Lebanese singer. Located in an old house in Somerset Village, a popular dining destination, the atmosphere is casual and the surroundings are comfortable and candlelit at night. The food, although simply presented, is delightfully different. There is parking for a fee at a lot a few doors away at the east end of the block. Casual dress; cocktails. Parking: street. Cards: AX, DC, MC, VI.

THE FISH MARKET RESTAURANT   Lunch: $9-$23   Dinner: $13-$32   Phone: 613/241-3474   ㉘
Location: Corner of William St. 54 York St K1N 5T1. Hours: 11:30 am-2 & 5-10 pm, Fri & Sat-11 pm, Sun 11:30 am-3 & 5-10 pm. Closed: 1/1, 12/25. Reservations: accepted. Features: In the heart of the historic Byward
Seafood   Market area, the popular restaurant serves generous portions of fresh fish and some alternative dishes. The atmosphere can be bustling, and the decor carries out a fun, nautical theme. Casual dress; cocktails.
Parking: street. Cards: AX, DC, DS, JC, MC, VI.

FLIPPER'S   Lunch: $7-$12   Dinner: $10-$25   Phone: 613/232-2703   ㊵
Location: Between 4th and 5th aves; in 5th Ave Court, 2nd floor. 819 Bank St K1S 3V9. Hours: 11:30 am-2 & 5-10 pm, Sun 5 pm-9 pm. Closed: 12/24, 12/25, 12/26. Features: For more than 20 years, the restaurant has
Seafood   been serving high-quality seafood. The second-floor spot shows funky decor, as well as exposed brick walls, bare wood floors and ocean-related collectibles perched and hung about the dining room. Service is casual and friendly. Gluten-free dishes are available. Casual dress; cocktails. Parking: street. Cards: MC, VI.

FRIDAY'S ROAST BEEF HOUSE & PIANO PARLOUR   Lunch: $10-$18   Dinner: $17-$35   Phone: 613/237-5353   ⑰
Location: Between Laurier Ave and Gloucester St. 150 Elgin St K2P 1L4. Hours: 11:30 am-2:30 & 5-9 pm.
Reservations: accepted. Features: Located at the Grant House built in 1875. Noted for prime rib of beef
Steak & Seafood but also features steak and Atlantic salmon. Casual dress; cocktails; entertainment. Parking: on-site (fee).
Cards: AX, CB, DC, MC, VI. Historic

(See map and index starting on p. 400)

HAVELI INDIAN RESTAURANT   Lunch: $10-$13   Dinner: $8-$23   Phone: 613/241-1700   ③①
Indian
Location: Just w of Byward Market. 39 Clarence St K1N 5P4. **Hours:** 11:30 am-2 & 5-9:30 pm, Thurs-10 pm, Fri-10:30 pm, Sat 5 pm-10:30 pm, Sun 11:30 am-2 & 5-9 pm. Closed major holidays. **Reservations:** suggested. **Features:** Traditional fare is spiced hot, or not, depending on how guests order it. At lunch and on Sunday, only the buffet is available. Casual dress; cocktails. **Parking:** street. **Cards:** AX, MC, VI.

KINKI ASIAN FUSION   Lunch: $14-$22   Dinner: $14-$22   Phone: 613/789-7559   ③⑥
Asian
Location: Just w of Byward Market. 41 York St K1N 5S7. **Hours:** 11:45 am-12:30 am, Fri & Sat-1 am. Closed: 12/25. **Reservations:** suggested. **Features:** With exposed stone walls, natural wood floors and potted bamboo growing tall, this restaurant feels far removed from the bustle of the historic market area outside. Asian fusion dishes take creative advantage of carefully selected specialty ingredients. Presentations are artful. Dressy casual; cocktails. **Parking:** street. **Cards:** AX, DC, MC, VI.

LE CAFE   Lunch: $10-$15   Dinner: $16-$29   Phone: 613/594-5127   ①④
Canadian
Location: In National Arts Centre. 53 Elgin St K1P 5W1. **Hours:** noon-2 & 5:30-11 pm, Sat from 5:30 pm; Mon-Fri noon-11 pm 6/1-8/31. Closed: 12/25; also Sun. **Reservations:** suggested. **Features:** Art centre goers and lunchtime business crowds enjoy haute Canadian cuisine on the popular canal-side terrace which allows for more casual dining. Beef filet with peppercorn sauce and shrimp is perfectly prepared. Smoking is only permitted on the terrace. Dressy casual; cocktails. **Parking:** on-site (fee). **Cards:** AX, DC, MC, VI.

LE CAVEAU DE SZECHWAN   Lunch: $8-$12   Dinner: $8-$20   Phone: 613/562-2882   ④
Nouvelle Chinese
Location: Between Dalhousie and Cumberland sts; in Byward Market area. 129 York St K1N 5T4. **Hours:** 11:30 am-3 & 5-11 pm, Sat & Sun from noon. Closed: 12/25. **Reservations:** suggested. **Features:** This restaurant's modern decor is pleasantly subtle with neutral colors and soft lighting. But the all-you-can-eat menu is anything but tame. Hunan and Szechuan cuisine rules with house favorites of tea-smoked duck and spicy spinach chicken. Casual dress; cocktails. **Parking:** street. **Cards:** AX, DC, MC, VI.

LE JARDIN   Dinner: $8-$33   Phone: 613/241-1424   ⑦
French
Location: Between Dalhousie and Cumberland sts; in Byward Market area. 127 York St K1N 5T4. **Hours:** 5:30 pm-11 pm. Closed: 12/24. **Reservations:** suggested. **Features:** Located in an old house at the edge of the historic market area, this restaurant has long been a favorite of leading politicians and dignitaries. The atmosphere is relaxed and elegant. Classic French cuisine is offered a la carte or table d'hote. Gourmet carry-out is available. Fee parking is directly across the road. Dressy casual; cocktails. **Parking:** street. **Cards:** AX, DC, MC, VI.

LE METRO CAFE RESTAURANT   Lunch: $15-$20   Dinner: $15-$20   Phone: 613/230-8123   ②⓪
French
Location: Between Bank and O'Connor sts. 327 Somerset St W K2P 0J8. **Hours:** 11:30 am-2:30 & 5:30-10:30 pm, Sat from 5:30 pm; extended hours in summer. Closed: 12/25; also Sun. **Reservations:** suggested. **Features:** This sophisticated, upscale bistro boasts a dramatic decor and definite flair for the Gothic and theatrical. The ambience is conservative yet maintains a level of warmth. Summer offers a casual streetside terrace. The eatery is open at 5:30 on holidays. Dressy casual; cocktails. **Parking:** on-site. **Cards:** AX, DC, MC, VI.

MAMMA TERESA RISTORANTE   Lunch: $9-$12   Dinner: $12-$30   Phone: 613/236-3023   ②①
Italian
Location: Corner of O'Connor St. 300 Somerset St W K2P 0J6. **Hours:** 11 am-11 pm, Sat 5 pm-11:30 pm, Sun 5 pm-10 pm. Closed: 12/25. **Reservations:** suggested. **Features:** Comfortable dining room in a red brick house. Veal, pasta and a wide range of classic Italian dishes are offered. This restaurant has long been a popular dining spot. A separate bar area maintains a bustling atmosphere in the evenings. Limited free parking is accessible via O'Connor St. Casual dress; cocktails. **Parking:** on-site. **Cards:** AX, DC, MC, VI.

THE MARBLE WORKS STEAK HOUSE   Dinner: $16-$30   Phone: 613/241-6764   ①③
Canadian
Location: Corner of Rideau St. 14 Waller St K1N 9C4. **Hours:** 5 pm-10 pm, Thurs-Sat to 10:30 pm; Sunday brunch 10 am-2 pm. Closed: 12/25, 12/26. **Reservations:** suggested. **Features:** Built in 1866 as a marble factory, the historic building has exposed beams and limestone walls. A longtime favorite lunch destination for the business crowd, the casual restaurant features steak, pasta, seafood and chicken dishes. An English-style pub also is on site. Among offerings are a Thursday and Friday roast beef lunch buffet and Saturday night murder mystery dinner theatre. The parking lot is directly across the road. Casual dress; cocktails. **Parking:** on-site (fee). **Cards:** AX, DC, MC, VI.

MEDITHEO RESTAURANT & BAR   *Menu on aaa.com*   Lunch: $7-$14   Dinner: $13-$27   Phone: 613/562-2500   ⑨
Mediterranean
Location: Corner of William St; in Byward Market area. 77 Clarence St K1N 5P5. **Hours:** 11 am-11 pm, Sat & Sun from 9 am. Closed: 12/25. **Reservations:** suggested. **Features:** Mediterranean cuisine featuring fresh fish, seafood, Middle Eastern dishes and fresh pasta dominates the menu here. Flavorful bread and dessert, including an excellent tiramisu, are made on the premises. Many wines by the glass are also available. Casual dress; cocktails. **Parking:** street. **Cards:** AX, DC, MC, VI.

MERLOT   Lunch: $26   Dinner: $26-$45   Phone: 613/783-4212   ③③
Continental
Location: Corner of Queen St; in Ottawa Marriott. 100 Kent St K1P 5R7. **Hours:** 5:30 pm-10:30 pm, Sun 10:30 am-2:30 pm. **Reservations:** suggested. **Features:** Occupying a revolving rooftop space, the urban oasis combines delightful fare and caring service with fabulous changing views of Canada's capital city. Dressy casual; cocktails. **Parking:** on-site (fee) and valet. **Cards:** AX, DC, DS, MC, VI.

(See map and index starting on p. 400)

THE MILL RESTAURANT
Lunch: $8-$12   **Dinner:** $15-$25   **Phone:** 613/237-1311   [16]
Location: Just w of du Portage Bridge. 555 Ottawa River Pkwy K1P 5R4. **Hours:** 11:30 am-2:30 & 5-10 pm, Fri & Sat 5 pm-11 pm. Closed: 7/1; also for dinner 12/24. **Reservations:** accepted. **Features:** This renovated 1840 sawmill overlooks the Ottawa River and prides itself on its roast beef house specialty, but generous portions of fish, seafood, chicken and pasta are also available along with daily specials and a good selection of homemade desserts. Casual dress; cocktails. **Parking:** on-site. **Cards:** AX, DC, MC, VI. **Historic**

Canadian

MUKUT INDIAN RESTAURANT
Lunch: $6-$8   **Dinner:** $6-$14   **Phone:** 613/789-2220   [1]
Location: Between Charlotte and Wurtemberg sts. 610 Rideau St K1N 6A2. **Hours:** 11:30 am-2 & 5-10 pm, Sun from 5 pm. Closed: 12/25, 12/26. **Reservations:** suggested. **Features:** Mukut is pronounced "mookoot" and means crown. The restaurant has simple, pleasant surroundings and plays traditional Indian background music. The specialty is cooking using a tandoor, an oven made of clay. The result is interesting flavors for vegetables and meat. Spiced tea is served with milk and sugar on the side, perhaps a concession to North American taste. Borfi, a coconut-flavored sweet, proves an interesting finish to the meal. Casual dress; cocktails. **Parking:** on-site. **Cards:** AX, DC, MC, VI.

Indian

NATE'S DELI
Lunch: $5-$12   **Dinner:** $5-$14   **Phone:** 613/789-9191   [3]
Location: Just e of King Edward Ave. 316 Rideau St K1N 5Y5. **Hours:** 7 am-11 pm, Fri & Sat-midnight. Closed: 12/25. **Features:** For good reason, the long-established delicatessen is one of the city's favorite eating spots. The atmosphere is one of organized hustle and bustle as guests are served large, lean smoked-meat sandwiches, matzo ball soup and super desserts. Casual dress; cocktails. **Parking:** street. **Cards:** AX, CB, DC, MC, VI.

Deli/Subs
Sandwiches

NEW DELHI INDIAN CUISINE
Lunch: $10-$14   **Dinner:** $10-$14   **Phone:** 613/237-4041   [23]
Location: 0.3 km s of Hwy 417; 0.3 km n of 1st Ave. 683 Bank St K1S 3T8. **Hours:** 11:45 am-2 & 5-10:30 pm, Sun from 5 pm. Closed: 12/25. **Reservations:** suggested. **Features:** Located in the Glebe, this bright yet cozy restaurant offers a good variety of classic Indian cuisine. Vegetarian specialties are available and a luncheon buffet is featured Monday-Friday. Help is offered if there is uncertainty regarding the degree of spiciness of certain dishes. A good representation of food from the Asian sub-continent. Casual dress; cocktails. **Parking:** on-site. **Cards:** AX, DC, MC, VI.

Indian

NOAH'S
Lunch: $7-$19   **Dinner:** $14-$24   **Phone:** 613/782-2422   [19]
Location: Corner of Lyon St; in Minto Place; in Minto Place Suite Hotel. 407 Laurier Ave W K1R 7Y1. **Hours:** 7 am-11 pm, Sat & Sun from 8 am. **Reservations:** suggested. **Features:** At the shopping concourse level of Minto Place, the casually sophisticated restaurant offers seating at booths and tables, as well as on the terrace, weather permitting. This is a popular meeting spot for professionals and shoppers. The menu lists full dinners, as well as lighter fare. Parking is underground. Casual dress; cocktails. **Parking:** on-site (fee). **Cards:** AX, DC, JC, MC, VI.

Continental

SANTE RESTAURANT
Lunch: $10-$13   **Dinner:** $15-$20   **Phone:** 613/241-7113   [6]
Location: Northeast corner of Rideau St and Sussex Dr; on 2nd floor above CIBC. 45 Rideau St K1N 5W8. **Hours:** 11:30 am-10 pm. Closed major holidays; also Sun. **Reservations:** suggested. **Features:** The large windows and second floor location afford diners an interesting cityscape view. The menu has an excellent range of items including beef, chicken, seafood and vegetarian dishes, all carefully prepared and artfully presented. Casual dress; cocktails. **Parking:** no self-parking. **Cards:** AX, DC, MC, VI.

Continental

SAVANA CAFE
Lunch: $9-$10   **Dinner:** $13-$19   **Phone:** 613/233-9159   [30]
Location: Between Bank and Kent sts. 431 Gilmour St K2P 0R5. **Hours:** 11:30 am-3 & 5-10 pm, Sat from 5 pm. Closed: 12/25; also Sun. **Reservations:** accepted. **Features:** Fusion works well in a mix of Caribbean and Southeast Asian cuisine. The result is delightful dishes that keep guests returning for more. The atmosphere is relaxed, particularly on the seasonal patio. Casual dress; cocktails. **Parking:** street. **Cards:** AX, DC, MC, VI.

Caribbean

SIGNATURES LE CORDON BLEU
PARIS   *Menu on aaa.com*   **Lunch:** $29-$40   **Dinner:** $29-$40   **Phone:** 613/236-2433   [35]
Location: Jct Range Rd. 453 Laurier Ave E K1N 6R4. **Hours:** 11:30 am-2 & 5:30-10 pm. Closed: 12/25; also Sun & Mon. **Reservations:** required. **Features:** From the fine stemware and specialty china to the impeccable service, the restaurant, which is close to Embassy Row in a circa 1875 mansion, exudes refinement. Delightful to peruse, the menu lists dishes that have been creatively crafted and beautifully presented. For a special occasion or memorable dining experience, this establishment ranks among the finest. Semi-formal attire; cocktails. **Parking:** on-site. **Cards:** AX, CB, DC, DS, JC, MC, VI.

French

SITAR RESTAURANT
Lunch: $9   **Dinner:** $9-$15   **Phone:** 613/789-7979   [2]
Location: Corner of Chapel St. 417 Rideau St K1N 5Y9. **Hours:** 11:45 am-2 & 5-10:30 pm, Sun from 5 pm. Closed: 12/25. **Reservations:** suggested, weekends. **Features:** A varied menu of excellent Indian cuisine features selections from all parts of India including flavourful fish and spiced coconut. A good selection of vegetarian dishes, a refined decor and comfortable furnishings round out your dining experience. Casual dress; cocktails. **Parking:** street. **Cards:** AX, DC, MC, VI.

Indian

ZAK'S DINER
Lunch: $7-$13   **Dinner:** $7-$13   **Phone:** 613/241-2401   [11]
Location: Corner of Clarence St; in Byward Market area. 16 Byward Market K1N 7A1. **Hours:** 8 am-10 pm, Fri & Sat 24 hours. Closed: 12/25. **Features:** Enjoy a meal at this authentic 1950s family-style diner, complete with a soda fountain, table-side jukeboxes and various period memorabilia. Flavourful hamburgers, deli sandwiches, salad and all-day breakfast top the nice selection of menu offerings. Casual dress; cocktails. **Parking:** street. **Cards:** AX, DC, MC, VI.

American

OTTAWA pop. 774,072   (See map and index starting on p. 403)

———— **WHERE TO STAY** ————

ADAM'S AIRPORT INN

CAA SAVE
♦♦♦ ♦♦♦

Small-scale Hotel

All Year   1P: $84-$94   2P: $94-$99

Phone: (613)738-3838 **35**
XP: $10   F18

Location: Jct Hunt Club Rd and Bank St, 1 km s. Located in a commercial area. 2721 Bank St K1T 1M8. **Fax:** 613/736-8211. **Facility:** 62 one-bedroom standard units, some with whirlpools. 2 stories (no elevator), interior corridors. **Parking:** on-site, winter plug-ins. **Terms:** pets ($10 extra charge). **Amenities:** high-speed Internet, hair dryers. **Leisure Activities:** exercise room. **Guest Services:** coin laundry. **Business Services:** meeting rooms. **Cards:** AX, DC, MC, VI. **Special Amenities:** free continental breakfast and free newspaper. *(See color ad below)*

SOME UNITS

FEE DATA PORT   FEE

ADAM'S AIRPORT INN

Your Best Choice!

RESERVATIONS:
1 800 261-5835

2721 BANK ST.
OTTAWA K1T 1M8
(613) 738-3838

*M*inutes from the international airport, Rideau Carleton Raceway - Casino and down town Ottawa, Adam's Inn offers exceptional service, superb accommodations and very affordable rates.

• 62 Large elegant rooms • Suites with jacuzzi • Conference Room
• Fitness room & laundry facilities • Complimentary breakfast

Visit us @ www.adamsairportinn.com

THE WORLD'S LARGEST HOTEL CHAIN®

• 15% AAA Discount Off Published Rates
• Fireplace Suites & Whirlpools
• Family Packages & Group Rates
• Restaurant & Patio
• Heated Indoor Pool, Whirlpool, Sauna & Fitness Room
• In-room Movies & Games
• King & Queen Beds
• Minutes From Corel Centre
• Free Parking

Best Western

Best Western Baron's Hotel
Each Best Western hotel is independently owned and operated.

3700 Richmond Road • Nepean, ON 613.828.2741
www.bestwestern.com/ca/baronshotel
For Toll Free Reservations Call: 866.214.1239

(See map and index starting on p. 403)

BEST WESTERN BARONS HOTEL & CONFERENCE CENTRE *Book at aaa.com*

CAA SAVE — All Year   1P: $117   2P: $117   XP: $5   Phone: (613)828-2741   **40**   F17

Location: Hwy 417, exit 130, 2 km s. Located in a commercial area. 3700 Richmond Rd K2H 5B8. Fax: 613/596-4742. **Facility:** 83 units. 75 one-bedroom standard units, some with efficiencies and/or whirlpools. 8 one-bedroom suites ($138). 2 stories (no elevator), interior corridors. *Bath:* combo or shower only. **Small-scale Hotel** **Parking:** on-site, winter plug-ins. **Terms:** package plans, pets ($10 extra charge). **Amenities:** video games (fee), voice mail, irons, hair dryers. *Some: Fee:* high-speed Internet. **Dining:** 7 am-11 pm, Sat from 8 am, Sun 8 am-9 pm, cocktails. **Pool(s):** heated indoor. **Leisure Activities:** sauna, whirlpool, exercise room. **Guest Services:** valet and coin laundry. **Business Services:** conference facilities. **Cards:** AX, DC, DS, JC, MC, VI. **Special Amenities: free local telephone calls and free newspaper.** *(See color ad p 425)*

SOME UNITS

BEST WESTERN MACIES HOTEL *Book at aaa.com*

CAA SAVE — All Year   1P: $109-$129   2P: $114-$139   XP: $5   Phone: (613)728-1951   **31**   F14

Location: Hwy 417, exit 124, 0.5 km e. Located in a commercial area. 1274 Carling Ave K1Z 7K8. Fax: 613/728-1955. **Facility:** 123 one-bedroom standard units. 2-4 stories, interior corridors. *Bath:* combo or shower only. **Small-scale Hotel** **Amenities:** video games (fee), high-speed Internet, voice mail, safes, irons, hair dryers. *Some:* dual phone lines. **Dining:** 7 am-10 pm, Sun 8 am-9 pm, cocktails. **Pool(s):** heated outdoor. **Leisure Activities:** saunas, whirlpool, exercise room. **Guest Services:** valet laundry. **Business Services:** meeting rooms. **Cards:** AX, CB, DC, DS, JC, MC, VI. **Special Amenities: free local telephone calls and early check-in/late check-out.**

SOME UNITS

BROOKSTREET HOTEL *Book at aaa.com*

CAA SAVE — All Year   1P: $139-$299   XP: $25   Phone: (613)271-1800   **47**   F17

Location: Hwy 417, exit 138 (March Rd), 3.7 km n, just e on Solandt Dr to Legget Dr, then just n. 525 Legget Dr K2K 2W2. Fax: 613/271-1850. **Facility:** The property features boutique touches throughout and old fashioned, caring service. 276 units. 241 one-bedroom standard units. 35 one-bedroom suites ($199-$329), some with whirlpools. 18 stories, interior corridors. **Parking:** on-site (fee) and valet. **Terms:** check-in 4 pm, cancellation **Resort** **Large-scale Hotel** fee imposed, package plans, 3% service charge, small pets only ($20 fee, with prior approval). **Amenities:** high-speed Internet, dual phone lines, voice mail, safes, honor bars, irons, hair dryers. *Some:* CD players. **Dining:** Perspectives Restaurant, see separate listing. **Pool(s):** heated outdoor, heated indoor, 2 wading. **Leisure Activities:** whirlpools, steamrooms, ice skating, snowshoeing, sleigh rides, exercise room, spa. *Fee:* golf-18 holes. **Guest Services:** valet laundry. **Business Services:** conference facilities. **Cards:** AX, DC, DS, MC, VI. **Special Amenities: free newspaper.** *(See color ad p 427)*

SOME UNITS

CALABOGIE PEAKS RESORT
...closer than you think!

Eastern Ontario's
Real Resort Experience!

Ask for CAA rates. See our listing under Calabogie.

1.800.669.4861
getaway • ski • board • spa
golf • tennis • hiking
touring • waterfront

www.calabogie.com/CAA

(See map and index starting on p. 403)

CHIMO HOTEL   *Book at aaa.com*   **Phone:** (613)744-1060 

CAA SAVE   1/1-4/30   1P: $165   2P: $195   XP: $10   F18

           5/1-12/31   1P: $160   2P: $190   XP: $10   F18

Location: Hwy 417, exit 115 (St. Laurent Blvd), just n to Lemieux St, then just e. Located in a commercial area. 1199 Joseph Cyr St K1J 7T4. Fax: 613/744-7845. **Facility:** 256 units. 231 one-bedroom standard units. 25 one-

Large-scale Hotel bedroom suites, some with whirlpools. 10 stories, interior corridors. **Parking:** on-site. **Terms:** package plans, 3% service charge. **Amenities:** dual phone lines, voice mail, irons, hair dryers. *Some:* high-speed Internet. **Dining:** 7 am-10:30 pm, cocktails. **Pool(s):** heated indoor. **Leisure Activities:** sauna, whirlpool, lifeguard on duty, exercise room. **Guest Services:** valet laundry. **Business Services:** meeting rooms. **Cards:** AX, CB, DC, DS, MC, VI.

Special Amenities: free newspaper.

SOME UNITS

B] impressed!

An un4gettable 4-diamond experience for as little as $139*.

Brookstreet Hotel is a destination beyond compare! Ottawa's pre-eminent boutique resort hotel offers you a wealth of leisure opportunities.

Some of what we offer on-site:
- Perspectives Restaurant, four-diamond dining
- The Marshes Golf Club
- Au Naturel Wellness & Medical Spa
- Flex Fitness Studio
- Outdoor, indoor and children's pools
- Winter Wonderland including skating, sleigh rides and cross-country skiing

...and nearby:
- Shopping centres
- Galleries and museums
- Saunders Farm
- Corel Centre
- Bell Sensplex

...and so much more!

A sensational resort experience just minutes from downtown Ottawa.

*Price per night, double occupancy. Subject to availability.

brookstreet
HOTEL

work·play·getaway

www.brookstreethotel.com
525 Legget Drive Ottawa ON K2K 2W2
1 888 826-2220

CAA Four Diamond Award AAA

(See map and index starting on p. 403)

COMFORT INN *Book at aaa.com* Phone: (613)744-2900   38

CAA SAVE

5/1-9/30   1P: $95-$115   2P: $105-$125   XP: $10   F18
10/1-4/30   1P: $90-$100   2P: $100-$120   XP: $10   F18

Location: Hwy 417, exit 115 (St. Laurent Blvd), then ne. Located in a commercial area. 1252 Michael St K1J 7T1. Fax: 613/746-0836. **Facility:** 69 one-bedroom standard units. 2 stories (no elevator), interior corridors.

Small-scale Hotel **Parking:** on-site, winter plug-ins. **Terms:** 3% service charge, pets (in ground floor units). **Amenities:** voice mail, irons, hair dryers. **Guest Services:** valet laundry. **Cards:** AX, DC, DS, MC, VI.

SOME UNITS

FEE FEE

COMFORT INN OTTAWA WEST *Book at aaa.com* Phone: (613)592-2200 44

CAA SAVE

All Year   1P: $99-$109   2P: $141-$151   XP: $10   F19

Location: Hwy 417, exit 138 (Eagleson Rd), 0.6 km s, then 0.3 km w on Katimavik Rd. Located in a residential area. 222 Hearst Way K2L 3A2. Fax: 613/591-9600. **Facility:** 146 units. 145 one-bedroom standard units. 1 one-bedroom suite with efficiency and whirlpool. 2 stories (no elevator), interior corridors. **Parking:** on-site,

Small-scale Hotel winter plug-ins. **Terms:** small pets only (in smoking units). **Amenities:** voice mail, irons, hair dryers. *Some:* high-speed Internet, dual phone lines. **Dining:** 6:30 am-10 pm, Sun 7 am-noon, cocktails. **Leisure Activities:** exercise room. **Guest Services:** valet and coin laundry. **Business Services:** meeting rooms. **Cards:** AX, CB, DC, DS, JC, MC, VI.

SOME UNITS

COUNTRY INN & SUITES BY CARLSON *Book at aaa.com* Phone: (613)599-7767 45

CAA SAVE

11/1-4/30 [ECP]   1P: $125-$155   2P: $125-$155   XP: $10   F18
5/1-10/31 [ECP]   1P: $119-$149   2P: $119-$149   XP: $10   F18

Location: Hwy 417, exit 140 (Terry Fox Dr), 0.5 km s. Located in a commercial area. 578 Terry Fox Dr K2L 4G8. Fax: 613/599-9971. **Facility:** 98 units. 60 one-bedroom standard units, some with whirlpools. 38 one-

Small-scale Hotel bedroom suites ($149-$169), some with whirlpools. 4 stories, interior corridors. **Parking:** on-site. **Amenities:** dual phone lines, voice mail, irons, hair dryers. *Fee:* video games, high-speed Internet. **Pool(s):** small heated indoor. **Leisure Activities:** sauna, exercise room. **Guest Services:** valet and coin laundry. **Business Services:** meeting rooms, business center. **Cards:** AX, CB, DC, DS, JC, MC, VI. *(See color ad p 521 & below)*

SOME UNITS

DAYS INN OTTAWA AIRPORT *Book at aaa.com* Phone: (613)739-7555 29

CAA SAVE

All Year [CP]   1P: $139-$149   2P: $139-$149

Location: Between Bank St and Riverside Dr. Located in a commercial area. 366 Hunt Club Rd K1V 1C1. Fax: 613/739-7005. **Facility:** 81 units. 74 one-bedroom standard units, some with whirlpools. 7 one-bedroom suites ($249-$299), some with whirlpools. 3 stories, interior corridors. **Parking:** on-site.

Small-scale Hotel **Terms:** cancellation fee imposed. **Amenities:** video games (fee), high-speed Internet, voice mail, irons, hair dryers. **Pool(s):** small heated indoor. **Leisure Activities:** whirlpool, limited exercise equipment. **Guest Services:** valet and coin laundry. **Business Services:** meeting rooms, business center. **Cards:** AX, CB, DC, DS, JC, MC, VI. **Special Amenities:** free continental breakfast and free newspaper. *(See color ad p 429)*

SOME UNITS

FEE

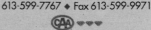

Country Hospitality.

COUNTRY INN & SUITES
BY CARLSON

800-456-4000
www.countryinns.com/ottawaon_west

Country Inn & Suites By Carlson
Ottawa-West

578 Terry Fox Drive
Kanata, ON K2V 1A1
613-599-7767 ◆ Fax 613-599-9971

CAA ▼▼▼

Located next to Corel Centre ◆ Whirlpool suites ◆ Indoor pool & exercise room
Complimentary light & healthy breakfast ◆ Executive business centre
High speed Internet access ◆ In-room movies
Iron & ironing boards in all rooms ◆ Meeting rooms available

Please refer to the property location listing for more information.

10% MEMBER DISCOUNT OFF PUBLISHED RATES.

(See map and index starting on p. 403)

THE DAYS INN OTTAWA WEST   **Book at aaa.com**   **Phone:** 613/726-1717   **41**
▼▼▼ ▼▼▼ All Year [ECP]   1P: $106-$129   2P: $109-$129   XP: $10   F17
          Location: Hwy 417, exit 134, 1.5 km s. Located in a commercial area. 350 Moodie Dr K2H 8G3. Fax: 613/726-1462.
Small-scale Hotel **Facility:** 128 units. 124 one-bedroom standard units. 3 one- and 1 two-bedroom suites ($160-$200) with
voice mail, irons, hair dryers. *Some:* CD players. **Dining:** D'arcy McGee's, see separate listing. **Leisure Activities:** exercise
room. **Guest Services:** valet laundry. **Business Services:** meeting rooms. **Cards:** AX, DC, DS, JC, MC, VI.
(See color ad below)

SOME UNITS

🛏 🍴 📷 DATA PORT 🖥 / ⊠ 🛗 🍽 /

Come On Inn...

. Free high speed Internet

. Free continental breakfast

. Minutes to the Ottawa airport

. Heated indoor pool & hot tub

. Business centre

. Meeting rooms

1-800-DAYS INN
www.daysinn.ca

triprewards
It's fun to get more.

Days Inn - Ottawa Airport 366 Hunt Club Road
Ottawa, ON K1V 1C1
www.daysinnottawa.com

Tel   Toll Free   Fax
613 739 7555   866 468 4442   613 739 7005
reservations@daysinnottawa.com

OTTAWA WEST

Come On Inn...

• Continental
  breakfast

• Free parking

• D'Arcy McGees
  Irish pub onsite

• Free high speed
  Internet

• Fitness centre onsite

• Jacuzzi suites
  available

• 15 minutes to
  Parliament Hill

• 5 minutes from
  the Corel Centre

• Ask about our great
  AAA/CAA rates

1-800-DAYS INN
www.daysinn.ca

triprewards
It's fun to get more.

Days Inn - Ottawa West 350 Moodie Drive
Ottawa, ON K2H 8G3
www.daysinnottawawest.com

Tel   Toll Free   Fax
613-726-1717   800-616-7719   613-726-1462
reservations@daysinnottawawest.com

(See map and index starting on p. 403)

ECONO LODGE-OTTAWA EAST   *Book at aaa.com*   Phone: (613)745-1531   ⑳
(AAA) (SAVE)   5/1-9/30 [CP]   1P: $80-$95   2P: $90-$99   XP: $10   F17.
    10/1-4/30 [CP]   1P: $75-$85   2P: $85-$95   XP: $10   F17
    Location: Hwy 417, exit 113, 2.5 km e on Hwy 174 to Montreal Rd W exit. Located in a commercial area. 2098 Montreal
    Rd K1J 6M8. Fax: 613/748-3743. **Facility:** 46 one-bedroom standard units, some with efficiencies, kitchens
Motel   and/or whirlpools. 2 stories (no elevator), exterior corridors. **Parking:** on-site, winter plug-ins. **Terms:** office
    hours 7 am-2 am, package plans, small pets only ($10 extra charge, with prior approval). **Amenities:** voice
mail, hair dryers. **Some:** CD players. **Guest Services:** valet laundry. **Cards:** AX, DC, MC, VI. **Special Amenities:** free
continental breakfast and free local telephone calls. *(See ad below)*

SOME UNITS
(SD) (🛏) (🍴) (DATA PORT) (💻) / (✕) (VCR) (📠) (🖥) /
        FEE   FEE   FEE

HAMPTON INN   *Book at aaa.com*   Phone: (613)741-2300   ㉘
(AAA) (SAVE)   All Year [ECP]   1P: $135   2P: $145
(♦♦♦)   **Location:** Hwy 417, exit 117, jct Riverside Dr and Vanier Pkwy. Located in a commercial/residential area. 100 Coventry
    Rd K1K 4S3. Fax: 613/741-8689. **Facility:** 179 units. 170 one-bedroom standard units. 9 one-bedroom suites
Small-scale Hotel   **Amenities:** high-speed Internet, voice mail, irons, hair dryers. **Pool(s):** heated indoor. **Leisure**
    ($170-$180). 5 stories, interior corridors. **Parking:** on-site. **Terms:** 3 day cancellation notice.
    Activities: whirlpool, exercise room. **Guest Services:** valet and coin laundry. **Business Services:** meeting
rooms. **Cards:** AX, DC, MC, VI. **Special Amenities:** free expanded continental breakfast. *(See color ad p 4 & below)*

SOME UNITS
(SD) (🍸) (🏊) (📹) (DATA PORT) (📠) (🖥) (💻) / (✕) /

Econo Lodge-East

$75-$99*

- Free Parking
- Free Continental Breakfast
- Pet Friendly
- Close to Downtown & Attractions
- In-Room Coffee & Refrigerators
- Deluxe Room with Fireplace &
  Jacuzzi Available

*Excludes specialty/deluxe rooms. Single/double. Based on availability.

$5.00 Off with this ad
(some restrictions apply)

2098 Montreal Rd.
Ottawa, ON K1J 6M8
613-745-1531
Toll Free: 800-665-0306

Econo Lodge
BY CHOICE HOTELS

"Where nice is just a way of life"
100% Satisfaction Guarantee

● 179 Rooms ● Complimentary Deluxe Continental Breakfast ● Indoor
Pool, Whirlpool & Fitness Room ● Complimentary Indoor Parking and
Morning Newspaper ● Complimentary Local Calls ● Complimentary
Long Distance Calling Card Calls ● Complimentary Movie Channel
● Evening Cocktail Lounge ● Valet and Guest Laundry Available
● 24 Hour Coffee/Tea Service Available in Lobby ● In-Room Iron/Board,
Coffee Maker, Hair Dryer, Voice Mail, Data Ports & Internet Access

Hampton Inn Ottawa
100 Coventry Road, Ottawa Ontario K1K-4S3
(Located off 417 at Vanier Parkway/Riverside Drive Exit 117)
613-741-2300 • Toll Free: 1-800-426-7866
www.hampton-inns.com ● e-mail address: yowcn_hampton@hilton.com

(See map and index starting on p. 403)

HOLIDAY INN SELECT HOTEL & SUITES
OTTAWA-KANATA _Book at aaa.com_   Phone: (613)271-3057   46
(AA) (SAVE)   All Year   1P: $119-$199   2P: $129-$199   XP: $15   F18
              Location: Hwy 417, exit 140 (Terry Fox Dr) eastbound, just ne; exit 139 (Castlefrank Rd/Kanata Ave), just nw. Located
              in a commercial area. 101 Kanata Ave K2T 1E6. Fax: 613/271-3060. **Facility:** 152 units. 46 one-bedroom
              standard units, some with whirlpools. 106 one-bedroom suites. 9 stories, interior corridors. _Bath:_ combo or
Small-scale Hotel shower only. **Parking:** on-site. **Terms:** package plans. **Amenities:** high-speed Internet, dual phone lines,
              voice mail, irons, hair dryers. _Some:_ safes. **Dining:** Graffiti's, see separate listing. **Pool(s):** small heated
indoor. **Leisure Activities:** whirlpool, exercise room. **Guest Services:** valet laundry. **Business Services:** conference facilities,
business center. **Cards:** AX, DC, DS, MC, VI. _(See color ad card insert)_

SOME UNITS
🛢️ 🍴 🏋️ ⚙️ 🚭 🏊 📹 📠 ☕ / ✕ 📺 📶 📷 /
FEE

THE MIRADA INN   Phone: (613)741-1102   49
              All Year   1P: $89-$95   2P: $99-$110   XP: $10   F12
              Location: Jct St. Laurent Blvd, just e. Located in a commercial area. 545 Montreal Rd K1K 0V1. Fax: 613/741-3409.
Motel   **Facility:** 75 one-bedroom standard units, some with efficiencies or kitchens. 2 stories (no elevator),
              interior/exterior corridors. _Bath:_ combo or shower only. **Parking:** on-site, winter plug-ins. **Terms:** pets (with
prior approval). **Pool(s):** outdoor. **Business Services:** meeting rooms. **Cards:** AX, DC, MC, VI.

SOME UNITS
(ASK) 🛢️ 🐾 🍴 🍸 📹 📠 / ✕ 📺 📶 📷 /
FEE

MONTEREY INN RESORT _Book at aaa.com_   Phone: (613)288-3500   42
(AA) (SAVE)   All Year [ECP]   1P: $99-$129   2P: $109-$139   XP: $10   F12
              Location: 0.8 km s of Hunt Club Rd. 2259 Prince of Wales Dr K2E 6Z8. Fax: 613/226-5900. **Facility:** 86 units. 79
              one-bedroom standard units, some with whirlpools. 7 one-bedroom suites ($179-$229) with efficiencies and
              whirlpools. 2-4 stories, exterior corridors. **Parking:** on-site, winter plug-ins. **Terms:** cancellation fee
Small-scale Hotel imposed, 3% service charge. **Amenities:** high-speed Internet, voice mail, irons, hair dryers. **Dining:** The
              Pines at the Monterey, see separate listing. **Pool(s):** heated outdoor. **Leisure Activities:** sauna, whirlpool,
playground, exercise room. **Guest Services:** valet and coin laundry, airport transportation-Ottawa International Airport, area
transportation (fee). **Business Services:** meeting rooms. **Cards:** AX, DC, DS, JC, MC, VI. _(See color ad below)_

SOME UNITS
🛢️ ✈️ 🍴 📹 ✕ 🚭 📠 📶 ☕ / ✕ 📷 /

RIDEAU HEIGHTS MOTOR INN   Phone: 613/226-4152   43
              5/1-10/10   1P: $99-$109   2P: $99-$109   XP: $10   F16
              10/11-4/30   1P: $89-$99   2P: $89-$99   XP: $10   F16
Motel   **Location:** Hwy 16 (Prince of Wales Dr), 0.5 km n of Hunt Club Rd. Located in a residential area. 72 Rideau Heights Dr
              K2E 7A6. Fax: 613/226-8655. **Facility:** 36 one-bedroom standard units. 1-2 stories (no elevator), exterior
corridors. **Parking:** on-site, winter plug-ins (fee). **Terms:** small pets only ($20 extra charge, in smoking units). **Amenities:** hair
dryers. _Some:_ high-speed Internet. **Business Services:** fax (fee). **Cards:** AX, DC, MC, VI.

SOME UNITS
(ASK) 🛢️ 🐾 / ✕ 📶 ☕ /
FEE   FEE

SOUTHWAY INN OF OTTAWA   _Book at aaa.com_   Phone: (613)737-0811   33
(AA) (SAVE)   All Year   1P: $110-$118   2P: $118-$138   XP: $20   F12
              Location: On Hwy 31, corner of Hunt Club Rd. Located in a commercial area. 2431 Bank St K1V 8R9.
              Fax: 613/737-3207. **Facility:** 170 units. 160 one-bedroom standard units, some with efficiencies and/or
              whirlpools. 10 one-bedroom suites, some with kitchens and/or whirlpools. 3-6 stories, interior corridors.
Small-scale Hotel **Parking:** on-site, winter plug-ins. **Terms:** 3 day cancellation notice, pets ($30 extra charge).
              Amenities: high-speed Internet, voice mail, safes, irons, hair dryers. _Some:_ CD players, fax. **Dining:** 6:30
am-11 pm, cocktails. **Pool(s):** heated indoor. **Leisure Activities:** sauna, whirlpool, exercise room. **Guest Services:** valet and
coin laundry. **Business Services:** conference facilities, business center. **Cards:** AX, DC, JC, MC, VI. **Special Amenities:** free
newspaper. _(See color ad p 419)_

SOME UNITS
🛢️ 🐾 🍴 🍸 📹 ✕ 🚭 📠 📶 ☕ / ✕ 📺 📷 /
FEE

Monterey Inn
RESORT
& CONFERENCE CENTRE

2259 Prince of Wales Dr., Ottawa, ON, Fax: 613-226-5900

Free Parking • AAA members 10% discount on meals
Free deluxe continental buffet breakfast with room
• Free local telephone calls • Free high speed internet
access • Special family, student and senior rates • Most
rooms overlook the water • Free coffee and refrigerator in
each room • Pool, exercise room, hot tub and sauna

Reservations call 1-800-565-1311   www.montereyinn.com

(See map and index starting on p. 403)

TRAVELODGE *Book at aaa.com* Phone: (613)745-1133 ③⑨
(CAA) (SAVE) 11/1-4/30 1P: $99-$149 2P: $109-$149 XP: $10 F18
◆◆◆◆ 5/1-10/31 1P: $95-$135 2P: $99-$139 XP: $10 F18
Location: Hwy 417, exit 112 (Innes Rd), just e. Located in a commercial area. 1486 Innes Rd K1B 3V5.
Fax: 613/745-7380. **Facility:** 129 one-bedroom standard units. 3 stories, interior corridors. **Parking:** on-site,
Small-scale Hotel winter plug-ins. **Terms:** package plans. **Amenities:** video games (fee), voice mail, irons, hair dryers.
Pool(s): small heated indoor. **Leisure Activities:** whirlpool. **Guest Services:** valet laundry. **Business
Services:** meeting rooms. **Cards:** AX, DC, DS, MC, VI. *(See color ad on TourBookMark)*

SOME UNITS
     / /

TRAVELODGE HOTEL & CONVENTION CENTRE *Book at aaa.com* Phone: (613)722-7600 ③④
(CAA) (SAVE) All Year [CP] 1P: $169-$189 2P: $169-$189 XP: $10 F12
◆◆◆◆ **Location:** Just e of jct Kirkwood Ave. Located in a commercial area. 1376 Carling Ave K1Z 7L5. Fax: 613/722-2226.
Facility: 196 one-bedroom standard units. 3 stories, interior corridors. **Parking:** on-site. **Terms:** 15%
service charge. **Amenities:** voice mail, irons, hair dryers. **Dining:** 6:30 am-9:30 pm, cocktails. **Pool(s):**
Small-scale Hotel wading. **Leisure Activities:** waterslide, lifeguard on duty, wave pool, exercise room. **Guest Services:** gift
shop, valet laundry. **Business Services:** meeting rooms. **Cards:** AX, DC, DS, MC, VI. **Special Amenities:**
free newspaper and free room upgrade (subject to availability with advance reservations). *(See color ad below)*

SOME UNITS

FEE

Ottawa Ontario
Work Rest or Play

- Complimentary Breakfast
- Complimentary Parking
- Executive Floor & Lounge
- Wireless Internet
- Restaurant & lounge
- Indoor Waterpark & Fitness facility
- Conference Rooms

* Single/double occupancy. Based on availability.

Travelodge Hotel
OTTAWA WEST

$119* S/D

Call for Reservations
800-578-7878

1376 Carling Ave. • Ottawa, ON K1Z 7L5 • Tel: 800-267-4166 • www.travelodgeottawa.com

OTTAWA

Welcom*INNS*

- Complimentary Continental Breakfast
- Free Parking and Local Calls • Sauna,
Whirlpool and Fitness Facilities • In-Room
Coffee and Fridges • Minutes to Downtown
and Shopping

Welcoming You While You Stay!

1220 Michael Street, Ottawa
Tel.: 748-7800 www.welcominns.com e-mail: inns@storm.ca

1-800-387-4381

(See map and index starting on p. 403)

WEBB'S MOTEL   Phone: (613)728-1881   32

(CAA) (SAVE)   All Year   1P: $85-$95   2P: $95-$100   XP: $5   D16
           Location: Hwy 417, exit 126, 0.5 km n on Maitland Ave, then 0.5 km e. Located in a commercial area. 1705 Carling Ave
◆◆◆ ◆◆◆ K2A 1C8. Fax: 613/728-4516. **Facility:** 79 units. 72 one-bedroom standard units. 7 one-bedroom suites
           ($115-$125) with kitchens. 1-2 stories (no elevator), interior/exterior corridors. **Parking:** on-site, winter plug-
Motel   ins. **Terms:** small pets only. **Amenities:** voice mail. *Some:* irons. **Guest Services:** coin laundry. **Business**
           Services: fax (fee). **Cards:** AX, DC, MC, VI. **Special Amenities:** free local telephone calls and early
check-in/late check-out.

SOME UNITS

🛏 🕪 / ⊠ 🖭 🔌 🖳 /

WELCOMINNS   ***Book at aaa.com***   Phone: (613)748-7800   37

◆◆◆ ◆◆◆ 5/1-10/31 [CP]   1P: $95   2P: $105   XP: $10   F18
           11/1-12/31 [CP]   1P: $90   2P: $98   XP: $10   F18
Small-scale Hotel 1/1-4/30 [CP]   1P: $90   2P: $95   XP: $10   F18
           Location: Hwy 417, exit 115 (St. Laurent Blvd N) to Lemieux St, just e. Located in a commercial area. 1220 Michael St
K1J 7T1. Fax: 613/748-0499. **Facility:** 109 one-bedroom standard units. 7 stories, interior corridors. **Parking:** on-site, winter
plug-ins. **Terms:** cancellation fee imposed, package plans. **Amenities:** voice mail, irons, hair dryers. **Leisure Activities:** sauna,
whirlpool, exercise room. **Guest Services:** valet and coin laundry. **Cards:** AX, DC, MC, VI. *(See color ad p 432)*

SOME UNITS

(ASK) (SD) 🕪 ⊠ / ⊠ 🖭 🔌 🖳 /

─────── **WHERE TO DINE** ───────

THE AMBER GARDEN RESTAURANT   **Lunch:** $7-$13   **Dinner:** $13-$19   **Phone:** 613/725-2757   50
◆◆◆ ◆◆◆ **Location:** Just e of Island Park. 1 Richmond Rd K1Y 2X1. **Hours:** noon-2:30 & 5:30-9:30 pm, Sat from 5:30 pm.
           Closed major holidays; also Sun, Mon, 1/1-1/15 & 7/1-7/21. **Reservations:** suggested. **Features:** The
International unusual restaurant prepares Hungarian, Polish, Czech, Slovak, Russian and Ukrainian fare according to
           traditional recipes drawn from the various regions of central Europe. No additives are used. Dishes vary
from cabbage rolls and paprikash to more complex preparations such as Russian kulebiaka, a pastry stuffed with beef, wild
mushrooms, vegetables and boneless stuffed quail. Homemade hand-sealed pierogies are also a favorite. Casual dress;
cocktails. **Parking:** on-site. **Cards:** AX, DC, MC, VI.   ⊠

BARLEY MOW PUB   **Lunch:** $8-$16   **Dinner:** $8-$16   **Phone:** 613/730-1279   57
◆◆◆ ◆◆◆ **Location:** At Euclid Ave. 1060 Bank St K1S 3X2. **Hours:** 11 am-midnight, Sat from 10 am, Sun 10 am-10 pm.
           Closed: 12/25. **Reservations:** accepted. **Features:** Located a short walk from the canal, this small pub
Canadian   offers a warm atmosphere, super fish and chips and an outdoor patio in season. Casual dress; cocktails.
           Parking: on-site. **Cards:** AX, DC, MC, VI.   🍸 ⊠

BARLEY MOW PUB   **Lunch:** $8-$16   **Dinner:** $8-$16   **Phone:** 613/599-6098   53
◆◆◆ ◆◆◆ **Location:** Hwy 417, exit 138 (March Rd), 15 km n. 700 March Rd K2K 2V9. **Hours:** 11 am-midnight, Sat from 10
           am, Sun 10 am-10 pm. Closed: 12/25. **Reservations:** accepted. **Features:** An inviting meeting spot, this
Canadian   pub has an impressive selection of draft beer and a menu which offers traditional pub fare, such as fish and
           chips and bangers and mash. There are some interesting, internationally inspired dishes also. Casual dress;
cocktails. **Parking:** on-site. **Cards:** AX, DC, MC, VI.   🍸 ⊠

BELLARDITA'S   **Lunch:** $8-$14   **Dinner:** $14-$37   **Phone:** 613/728-5757   52
◆◆◆◆◆◆   **Location:** Hwy 417, exit 126, 0.5 km n on Maitland Ave, then 0.5 km e. 1696 Carling Ave K2A 1C6. **Hours:** 11 am-9
           pm, Wed-Fri to 10 pm, Sat 5 pm-10 pm, Sun 4 pm-9 pm. Closed: 12/25. **Reservations:** suggested,
Italian   weekends. **Features:** Guests are treated to a warm, comfortable and inviting atmosphere and a good
MC, VI.   selection of pasta. The wine list is well-rounded. Casual dress; cocktails. **Parking:** on-site. **Cards:** AX,
                                                                                                    ⊠

D'ARCY MCGEE'S   **Lunch:** $7-$19   **Dinner:** $7-$19   **Phone:** 613/596-4226   45
◆◆◆ ◆◆◆ **Location:** Hwy 417, exit 134, 1.5 km s; in The Days Inn Ottawa West. 360 Moodie Dr K2H 8G3. **Hours:** 11 am-
           midnight, Wed-Sat to 1 am. Closed: 12/25. **Reservations:** accepted. **Features:** The comfortable pub offers
Irish   favourites such as brides, chicken pie, shepherd's pie and Irish stew, as well as wings, mussels and wraps.
DC, MC, VI. In addition, there is a good selection of beer on tap. Casual dress; cocktails. **Parking:** on-site. **Cards:** AX,
                                                                                                    🍸 ⊠

FLYING PIGGY'S BISTRO ITALIANO   **Lunch:** $8-$12   **Dinner:** $10-$24   **Phone:** 613/526-4900   54
◆◆◆ ◆◆◆ **Location:** Just s of Heron Rd. 1665 Bank St K1V 7Z2. **Hours:** 11:30 am-2 & 5-9 pm, Fri-10 pm, Sat 5 pm-10 pm,
           Sun 5 pm-9 pm. Closed major holidays. **Reservations:** suggested. **Features:** The popular neighborhood
Italian   restaurant serves fabulous homemade pasta, bread and desserts in pleasant surroundings. A small terrace
           is open seasonally. Casual dress; cocktails. **Parking:** on-site. **Cards:** AX, DC, MC, VI.
                                                                                                    ⊠

GRAFFITI'S   **Lunch:** $8-$11   **Dinner:** $9-$30   **Phone:** 613/271-2381   59
◆◆◆ ◆◆◆ **Location:** Hwy 417, exit 140 (Terry Fox Dr) eastbound, just ne; exit 139 (Castlefrank Rd/Kanata Ave), just nw; in
           Holiday Inn Select Hotel & Suites Ottawa/Kanata. 101 Kanata Ave K2T 1E6. **Hours:** 6:30 am-11 pm, Sat & Sun
Italian   from 7 am. Closed: for dinner 12/24. **Reservations:** accepted. **Features:** Bread baked in-house, pasta,
           pizza, steak, fish, soups and salads are served in a casual atmosphere by friendly, efficient servers. Casual
dress; cocktails. **Parking:** on-site. **Cards:** AX, DC, DS, JC, MC, VI.   ⊠

(See map and index starting on p. 403)

GRILLMAN'S FRESH EATERY   **Lunch:** $7-$18   **Dinner:** $7-$18   **Phone:** 613/226-2881   ③⑨
Location: Jct Prince of Wales Dr. 111 Colonnade Rd K2E 7M3. **Hours:** 7 am-11 pm. Closed: 12/25, 12/26.
Reservations: accepted. **Features:** There is lots of choice on the menu including stir-fry, seafood,
sandwiches and burgers; however, these folks are known for their baby back ribs. There is also a soup and
American   salad bar. Casual dress; cocktails. **Parking:** on-site. **Cards:** AX, MC, VI.

JUNIPER   **Lunch:** $11-$15   **Dinner:** $33-$44   **Phone:** 613/728-0220   ④⑨
Location: Jct Smirle Ave. 1293 Wellington St K1Y 3B1. **Hours:** 11:30 am-2 & 5:30-9 pm, Fri & Sat-10 pm. Closed
major holidays; also Mon. **Reservations:** accepted. **Features:** The neighborhood bistro offers a varied
International   menu and an inspired approach to cooking. Add to these a wine list that is well rounded, and Juniper offers
a recipe for fine dining. The urban sophistication of the decor is pleasing, and fun folk art adds a humorous
touch. Casual dress; cocktails. **Parking:** street. **Cards:** AX, DC, MC, VI.

THE KEG MANOR   **Dinner:** $15-$32   **Phone:** 613/724-1242   ③⑧
Location: 1.7 km e of Woodroffe Ave. 529 Richmond Rd K2A 0G3. **Hours:** 5 pm-10 pm, Fri-11 pm, Sat 4:30 pm-
11 pm, Sun 4:30 pm-10 pm. Closed: 12/25. **Reservations:** accepted. **Features:** The restaurant prepares
Steak House   succulent, mesquite-grilled steaks in the distinctive setting of a converted old mansion. Ambience exudes
from the various rooms of the house's two floors of dining space. Casual dress; cocktails. **Parking:** on-site.
Cards: AX, MC, VI.

THE LINDENHOF RESTAURANT   **Lunch:** $7-$11   **Dinner:** $12-$17   **Phone:** 613/725-3481   ⑤⑥
Location: Just w of Woodroffe Ave. 965 Richmond Rd K2B 6R1. **Hours:** 11:30 am-2:30 & 5-10 pm, Sat from 5
pm, Sun 11 am-2 & 5-10 pm. Closed: 12/24-12/26. **Reservations:** suggested, weekends. **Features:** Long
German   an Ottawa favorite for traditional German cuisine. This restaurant offers seniors portions for those with a
more modest appetite. Special events such as Oktoberfest, a special menu featuring a wild game festival,
and a German Christmas market in the lower level starting mid-November are some activities to watch for. Casual dress;
cocktails. **Parking:** on-site. **Cards:** AX, DC, MC, VI.

THE MILLER'S OVEN   **Lunch:** $4-$7   **Phone:** 613/692-4304   ④⑥
Location: In Manotick; centre. 1137 Mill St K4M 1A9. **Hours:** 9 am-3 pm. Closed major holidays.
Features: Located in a charming old area of Manotick, this unusual restaurant is popular with locals for its
high quality, house-prepared fare. Seniors and students volunteer as servers to help offset costs, and profits
Canadian   go to benefit seniors in the township. The lemon meringue pies, with their "mile high" meringue, are
legendary. Casual dress. **Parking:** street.

NEWPORT RESTAURANT   **Lunch:** $8-$11   **Dinner:** $8-$11   **Phone:** 613/722-9322   ④⑦
Location: Jct Churchill Ave. 334 Richmond Rd K1Z 6X6. **Hours:** 6 am-10 pm, Fri & Sat-11 pm, Sun-9 pm.
Closed: 1/1, 12/25. **Reservations:** accepted. **Features:** This neighbourhood deli is popular with locals for its
crispy crust pizzas, but the menu also offers sandwiches (including smoked meat), burgers, pastas, salads,
Canadian   fish and a variety of appetizers and side dishes such as fried smelts, poutine and chicken wings. Casual
dress; cocktails. **Parking:** on-site. **Cards:** AX, DC, MC, VI.

OGGI RISTORANTE   **Lunch:** $6-$13   **Dinner:** $10-$21   **Phone:** 613/692-5027   ④⓪
Location: In Manotick; centre. 5536 Main St K4M 1A5. **Hours:** 11 am-10 pm, Sat & Sun from 5 pm. Closed: 1/1,
12/25, 12/26. **Reservations:** accepted. **Features:** In the lovely old village of Manotick, the restaurant
Italian   prepares a good selection of salads, pasta and veal dishes. The atmosphere is romantic. Casual dress;
cocktails. **Parking:** on-site. **Cards:** AX, DC, MC, VI.

PEARL OF INDIA   **Lunch:** $5-$9   **Dinner:** $6-$14   **Phone:** 613/834-6554   ④②
Location: In Orleans; between Orleans Blvd and Jeanne d'Arc St. 2181 St. Joseph Blvd K1C 1E7. **Hours:** 11:30 am-
2 & 5-10 pm, Sun from 5 pm. Closed: 12/25, 12/26. **Reservations:** suggested. **Features:** Classic Indian
Indian   cuisine is served and food cooked in a tandoor oven is featured. Some popular dishes are "Butler chicken,"
a mild curry preparation, and for those who favour spicy hot, "lamb Vindaloo" should fill the bill. Some
English beer is on tap. Casual dress; cocktails. **Parking:** on-site. **Cards:** AX, MC, VI.

PERSPECTIVES RESTAURANT   *Menu on aaa.com* **Lunch:** $11-$15 **Dinner:** $20-$35 **Phone:** 613/271-3555   ④④
(CAA)   **Location:** Hwy 417, exit 138 (March Rd), 3.7 km n, just e on Solandt Dr to Legget Dr, then just n; in Brookstreet Hotel.
525 Legget Dr K2K 2W2. **Hours:** 6:30 am-3 & 6-11 pm. **Reservations:** accepted. **Features:** Overlooking
fairways seven and eight of the Marshes Golf Club, the restaurant offers polished, friendly service and
varied dishes that have a hint of Asian touches applied to them. When time allows, the executive chef can
Continental   be found roaming the dining room checking on his guests. Casual dress; cocktails. **Parking:** on-site (fee)
and valet. **Cards:** AX, DC, DS, JC, MC, VI.

THE PINES AT THE MONTEREY   **Lunch:** $8-$14   **Dinner:** $12-$24   **Phone:** 613/288-3501   ④⑧
Location: 0.8 km s of Hunt Club Rd; in Monterey Inn Resort. 2259 Prince of Wales Dr K2E 6Z8. **Hours:** 7 am-10 pm.
Closed major holidays. **Reservations:** accepted. **Features:** Fish, steak, chicken and pasta dishes are nicely
Canadian   served in generous portions. Casual dress; cocktails. **Parking:** on-site. **Cards:** AX, CB, DC, DS, JC,
MC, VI.

SIAM KITCHEN   **Lunch:** $7-$9   **Dinner:** $9-$13   **Phone:** 613/730-3954   ⑤①
Location: Corner of Aylmer Ave. 1050 Bank St K1S 3X2. **Hours:** 11:30 am-2 & 5-10 pm, Sat from 5 pm, Sun 5
pm-9:30 pm. Closed: 1/1, 10/10, 12/25, 12/26; also 7/1. **Reservations:** accepted. **Features:** Casual service,
unpretentious presentation and affordable prices make Siam Kitchen a popular restaurant. The spiced
Thai   ginger squid salad is unusual and very good; the curry chicken and rice is flavorful. Daily luncheon and
dinner specials are available. Casual dress; cocktails. **Parking:** on-site. **Cards:** AX, DC, MC, VI.

Nearby Québec

GATINEAU pop. 102,898

——— WHERE TO STAY ———

BEST WESTERN CARTIER HOTEL & CONFERENCE
CENTRE   *Book at aaa.com*   **Phone:** (819)770-8550
(CAA) (SAVE) All Year   1P: $99-$189   2P: $99-$189
▼▼▼ ▼▼▼ **Location:** Between rue St-Laurent and St-Etienne, just e of Alexandria Bridge; in Hull sector. 131 rue Laurier J8X 3W3.
Fax: 819/770-9705. **Facility:** 142 units. 125 one-bedroom standard units, some with kitchens. 17 one-
bedroom suites ($139-$189), some with kitchens and/or whirlpools. 9 stories, interior corridors. **Parking:** on-
Small-scale Hotel site (fee). **Terms:** check-in 4 pm. **Amenities:** voice mail, irons, hair dryers. **Dining:** 7 am-1 & 5-10 pm.
Pool(s): heated indoor. **Leisure Activities:** exercise room. **Guest Services:** valet laundry. **Business
Services:** meeting rooms. **Cards:** AX, CB, DC, DS, MC, VI. **Special Amenities:** free newspaper. *(See color ad p 410)*
SOME UNITS
(🅢🅓) (❤️) (🏊) (📠) (📺) / (❌) (📶) (🍽️) /

CHATEAU CARTIER RELAIS-RESORT   *Book at aaa.com*   **Phone:** (819)778-0000
▼▼▼ ▼▼▼ All Year   1P: $139-$299   2P: $139-$299   XP: $20   F18
Location: On Hwy 148, 1 km w of Champlain Bridge; in Aylmer sector. 1170 chemin Aylmer J9H 5E1.
Resort **Fax:** 819/777-2518. **Facility:** The resort features a spa and extensive recreational facilities. 129 units. 39
Large-scale Hotel one-bedroom standard units, some with whirlpools. 90 one-bedroom suites. 6 stories, interior corridors.
Parking: on-site. **Terms:** check-in 4 pm, package plans, small pets only ($25 fee). **Amenities:** video games
(fee), voice mail, honor bars, irons, hair dryers. **Pool(s):** heated indoor. **Leisure Activities:** saunas, whirlpool, steamrooms,
cross country skiing, ice skating, tobogganing, hiking trails, exercise room, spa, volleyball. *Fee:* golf-18 holes, 2 lighted tennis
courts, racquetball courts, bicycles. **Guest Services:** sundries, valet laundry. **Business Services:** conference facilities,
business center. **Cards:** AX, CB, DC, DS, MC, VI.
SOME UNITS
(ASK) (🅢🅓) (🛏️) (🍽️) (🍴) (🏊) (❌) (🎬) (📶) (📺) / (❌) (📶) /
FEE

COMFORT INN GATINEAU   *Book at aaa.com*   **Phone:** (819)243-6010
(CAA) (SAVE) 5/1-10/15   1P: $110-$125   2P: $120-$140   XP: $10   F17
           10/16-4/30   1P: $90-$110   2P: $100-$120   XP: $10   F17
▼▼▼ ▼▼▼ **Location:** Hwy 50, exit 140, 2 km e. 630 boul La Gappe J8T 9Z6. Fax: 819/243-4668. **Facility:** 81 one-bedroom
standard units. 2 stories (no elevator), interior corridors. **Parking:** on-site, winter plug-ins. **Terms:** [CP] meal
Small-scale Hotel plan available, pets (on ground floor). **Amenities:** irons, hair dryers. **Guest Services:** valet laundry.
Cards: AX, CB, DC, DS, MC, VI.
SOME UNITS
(🅢🅓) (🛏️) (📶) (🎬) (📶) (📺) / (❌) /

FOUR POINTS BY SHERATON & CONFERENCE
CENTRE GATINEAU-OTTAWA   *Book at aaa.com*   **Phone:** (819)778-6111
(CAA) (SAVE) All Year   1P: $99   2P: $99   XP: $20   F18
▼▼▼ ▼▼▼ **Location:** Corner rue Victoria, across from Canadian Museum of Civilization; in Hull sector. 35 rue Laurier J8X 3X4.
Fax: 819/778-3647. **Facility:** 201 units. 194 one-bedroom standard units. 7 one-bedroom suites ($150-
$250). 9 stories, interior corridors. **Parking:** on-site (fee). **Terms:** small pets only. **Amenities:** video games
Large-scale Hotel (fee), high-speed Internet, dual phone lines, voice mail, irons, hair dryers. **Dining:** 6:30 am-10 pm, cocktails.
Pool(s): heated indoor. **Leisure Activities:** whirlpool, exercise room. **Guest Services:** gift shop, valet
laundry. **Business Services:** conference facilities, business center. **Cards:** AX, CB, DC, DS, JC, MC, VI. **Special Amenities:**
free newspaper.
SOME UNITS
(🅢🅓) (🛏️) (🍽️) (🍴) (🏊) (🎬) (📶) (📺) / (❌) (📶) /

HILTON LAC LEAMY   *Book at aaa.com*   **Phone:** (819)790-6444
(CAA) (SAVE) All Year   1P: $159-$319   2P: $159-$319   XP: $20   F18
Location: Adjacent to Casino du Lac Leamy; in Hull sector. 3 boul du Casino J8Y 6X4. Fax: 819/790-6408.
▼▼▼ ▼▼▼ **Facility:** In addition to impressive banquet rooms, this upscale casino hotel built in 2001 has elegant guest
rooms with marble baths and one or two beds. 349 units. 314 one-bedroom standard units. 35 one-bedroom
Large-scale Hotel suites, some with whirlpools. 20 stories, interior corridors. **Parking:** on-site and valet. **Terms:** package
plans, $2 service charge. **Amenities:** CD players, dual phone lines, voice mail, safes, honor bars, irons, hair
dryers. *Fee:* video games, high-speed Internet. **Dining:** 2 restaurants, 6 am-11 pm, cocktails, entertainment. **Pool(s):** heated
outdoor, heated indoor, 2 wading. **Leisure Activities:** sauna, whirlpools, steamrooms, boat dock, 2 lighted tennis courts, cross
country skiing, theatre, bicycles, playground, exercise room, spa, game room. *Fee:* ice skating. **Guest Services:** gift shop, valet
laundry. **Business Services:** conference facilities, business center. **Cards:** AX, CB, DC, DS, JC, MC, VI.
(See color ad p 436)
SOME UNITS
(🎲) (🍽️) (24T) (🍴) (🏋️) (🄼) (❌) (🏊) (❌) (🎬) (📶) (📺) / (❌) (VCR) (📶) (🍽️) /
FEE

HOLIDAY INN PLAZA LA CHAUDIERE
GATINEAU-OTTAWA   *Book at aaa.com*   **Phone:** (819)778-3880
(CAA) (SAVE) 5/1-10/31   1P: $112   2P: $112   XP: $15   F17
           11/1-4/30   1P: $90   2P: $90   XP: $15   F17
▼▼▼ ▼▼▼ **Location:** 0.8 km w of Portage Bridge at Rt 148 and rue Montcalm; in Hull sector. 2 rue Montcalm J8X 4B4.
Fax: 819/778-7324. **Facility:** 232 units. 221 one-bedroom standard units. 11 one-bedroom suites ($150-
Large-scale Hotel $200), some with kitchens. 14 stories, interior corridors. **Parking:** on-site (fee) and street. **Terms:** [AP] meal
plan available, package plans, pets (must be supervised). **Amenities:** video games (fee), voice mail, irons,
hair dryers. **Dining:** 6:30 am-10 pm, cocktails. **Pool(s):** heated indoor. **Leisure Activities:** saunas, whirlpool, exercise room.
Fee: bicycles. **Guest Services:** gift shop, valet laundry. **Business Services:** conference facilities, business center. **Cards:** AX,
DC, DS, MC, VI. **Special Amenities:** free newspaper and early check-in/late check-out. *(See color ad p 437)*
SOME UNITS
(🅢🅓) (🛏️) (🍽️) (🍴) (🏊) (❌) (🎬) (📶) (📺) / (❌) (VCR) (📶) (🍽️) /
FEE

The Lac-Leamy experience

CASINO • HOTEL • THEATRE • RESTAURANTS • CONFERENCE CENTRE • SPA

Unforgettable Getaway Packages!

The Casino du Lac-Leamy and Hilton Lac-Leamy, located in Gatineau (Hull), Québec, provide the perfect escape for a memorable experience. Chose from a variety of options including gourmet dining, sightseeing tours or a day at the spa.

For reservations:
1-888-278-7777

Casino Package:

from $98* CDN

One-night at the Hilton Lac-Leamy.

Buffet-style breakfast.

Casino Privilèges Club card.

One casino cash certificate per stay worth up to $20 CDN.

Special Casino souvenir.

Just five minutes from downtown Ottawa.

*Rates per person, per day, double occupancy. Taxes not included and subject to availability.
Hilton Lac-Leamy and the Casino du Lac-Leamy are owned and operated independently from Hilton Hotels Corporation and Hilton International Co.

HOTEL CLARION GATINEAU-OTTAWA   *Book at aaa.com*   **Phone:** (819)568-5252

(CAA) (SAVE)   All Year   1P: $105-$150   2P: $105-$150   XP: $10   F18
Location: Hwy 50, exit 139, 1.6 km se on boul Maloney ouest (Hwy 148), then just sw. 111 rue Bellehumeur J8T 6K5.
Fax: 819/568-0753. **Facility:** 116 units. 115 one-bedroom standard units, some with whirlpools. 1 one-bedroom suite ($175-$225) with whirlpool. 2 stories (no elevator), interior corridors. **Parking:** on-site, winter
Small-scale Hotel plug-ins. **Terms:** package plans. **Amenities:** voice mail, irons, hair dryers. *Some:* high-speed Internet (fee), dual phone lines, safes, honor bars. **Dining:** 6:30 am-11 pm, Sat & Sun from 7:30 pm, cocktails. **Pool(s):** heated outdoor. **Leisure Activities:** spa. *Fee:* saunas, exercise room. **Guest Services:** sundries, valet laundry. *Fee:* tanning facility. **Business Services:** conference facilities, business center. **Cards:** AX, CB, DC, DS, MC, VI. **Special Amenities:** free local telephone calls and free newspaper. *(See color ad below)*

SOME UNITS

HOTEL LES SUITES VICTORIA   **Phone:** (819)777-8899

5/1-12/31   1P: $90-$95   2P: $90-$95   XP: $10   F
1/1-4/30   1P: $95   2P: $95   XP: $10   F
Location: 0.5 km e on rue Laurier from Portage Bridge, 0.3 km n; in Hull sector. 1 rue Victoria J8X 1Z6.
Small-scale Hotel **Fax:** 819/777-2211. **Facility:** 39 units. 16 one-bedroom standard units with efficiencies. 23 one-bedroom suites ($109-$125) with kitchens, some with whirlpools. 3 stories, interior corridors. **Parking:** on-site. **Terms:** check-in 4 pm.
Amenities: voice mail, irons, hair dryers. *Some:* dual phone lines. **Guest Services:** valet and coin laundry. **Business Services:** meeting rooms. **Cards:** AX, DC, DS, MC, VI.

SOME UNITS
FEE

MOTEL CASINO   **Phone:** 819/776-8888

(CAA) (SAVE)   All Year   1P: $69-$79   2P: $79-$89   XP: $10   F11
Location: Hwy 50, exit 134, 0.3 km n on rue Montcalm; in Hull sector. 275 boul St-Joseph J8Y 3Y2.
Fax: 819/776-5843. **Facility:** 25 one-bedroom standard units, some with whirlpools. 2 stories, interior
Motel corridors. **Parking:** on-site, winter plug-ins. **Amenities:** hair dryers. **Guest Services:** area transportation-casino. **Cards:** AX, DC, MC, VI.

SOME UNITS

Holiday Inn
Plaza la Chaudiere
GATINEAU/OTTAWA
2 Montcalm Street, Gatineau, (Quebec) ON
(819) 778-3880 Toll Free (800) 567-1962
reservationchaudiere@rosdevhotels.com

$112.00 PER NIGHT Dbl. Occ.
A Great value at the best rate

UPON PRESENTATION OF THIS AD, ENJOY 2 FREE FULL AMERICAN BREAKFASTS EVERY MORNING
Ideal setting for leisure and the Hotel and the Parks are pet friendly.

Contemporary elegance describes the decor at the Holiday Inn Plaza la Chaudière. 232 beautifully appointed rooms (460 sq. ft.) and suites, with commanding views through our floor to ceiling bay windows (70 sq. ft.), of the Gatineau Hills, the Chaudiere falls or the Casino du Lac Leamy.

Relax after a long day, rent a bicycle with safety equipment and venture into the Outaouais along the "Route Verte" (extensive bicycle paths 4,000km completed) direct access from the hotel or lounge at our large swimming pool or saunas.

CONFERENCE CENTER
GATINEAU • OTTAWA

Come and discover the region's many activities, while experiencing the comfort and the services of *Clarion Hotel* - Gatineau.

Only 8 minutes from Ottawa!

SPECIAL PACKAGES AVAILABLE
CONTACT US!

• 3 suites - 116 rooms
• Restaurant, bar
• Free parking
• Free coffee in every room
• Outdoor pool with terrace & landscaped gardens

Clarion Hotel
BY CHOICE HOTELS

(819) 568-5252
1 877 568-5252
www.hotelclariongatineauottawa.com

RAMADA PLAZA MANOIR DU CASINO   *Book at aaa.com*   Phone: (819)777-7538
ⒸⒶ (SAVE)   All Year [BP]   1P: $135-$169   2P: $145-$179   XP: $15   F18

Location: Hwy 5, exit 3, follow signs; in Hull sector. 75 rue Edmonton J8Y 6W9. Fax: 819/777-0277. **Facility:** 174 one-bedroom standard units with whirlpools. 3 stories, interior corridors. **Parking:** on-site, winter plug-ins. **Terms:** check-in 4 pm. **Amenities:** high-speed Internet (fee), voice mail, irons, hair dryers. *Some:* dual
Small-scale Hotel phone lines, safes. **Dining:** 7 am-10:30 pm, cocktails. **Pool(s):** heated indoor. **Leisure Activities:** saunas, whirlpool. **Guest Services:** gift shop, valet laundry, beauty salon. **Business Services:** meeting rooms, PC.
Cards: AX, DC, MC, VI. **Special Amenities:** free full breakfast and free local telephone calls.

SOME UNITS

(S/D) (ⓘⓘ) (Ⓨ) (≈) (ⓦ)FEE (Ⓢ) (DATA PORT) (Ⓓ) / (Ⓧ)FEE (VCR) (Ⓗ) (Ⓔ) /

——— **WHERE TO DINE** ———

CAFE HENRY BURGER   **Lunch:** $10-$22   **Dinner:** $20-$36   Phone: 819/777-5646
Location: Across from Canadian Museum of Civilization; in Hull sector. 69 rue Laurier J8X 3V7. **Hours:** noon-3 & 6-11 pm, Sat & Sun from 6 pm; noon-11 pm, Sat & Sun from 6 pm 5/15-9/15. Closed: 12/24-12/26; also 1/1-1/14. **Reservations:** suggested. **Features:** Small dining rooms in the large, 19th-century home are
French   charming spots in which to enjoy creative, market-sensitive cuisine. The owner/chef prepares such wonderful dishes as roasted salmon, rack of lamb and wild game. Lighter fare is served on the terrace. Dressy casual; cocktails. **Parking:** on-site. **Cards:** AX, DC, JC, MC, VI.
(Ⓧ)

LE BACCARA   **Dinner:** $29-$49   Phone: 819/772-6210
ⒸⒶ   **Location:** Hwy 5 N, exit 3 (boul du Casino); in Casino du Lac Leamy; in Hull sector. 1 boul du Casino J8Y 6W3. **Hours:** 5:30 pm-11 pm. **Reservations:** suggested. **Features:** Atop Casino du Lac Leamy, the dining room has a bank of oversized windows that afford a view of the distant Ottawa skyline. Custom table settings, fine crystal stemware and arguably the most attentive and intuitive service in all of Quebec make this a favorite
Continental   place for special occasions. Also adding to the experience are wonderful contemporary French cuisine and given to food preparation. the soothing sounds of the harpist. As guests pass the open kitchen, they can watch the detailed attention given to food preparation. Semi-formal attire; cocktails; entertainment. **Parking:** on-site and valet. **Cards:** AX, DC, MC, VI.
(Ⓧ)

MAISON SAMORN   **Lunch:** $8-$15   **Dinner:** $12-$20   Phone: 819/595-0232

Location: Corner rue Victoria; in Hull sector. 53 rue Kent J8X 3J9. **Hours:** 11:30 am-2 & 5-10 pm, Mon-2 pm, Sat & Sun from 5 pm. Closed: 1/1, 12/25. **Reservations:** accepted. **Features:** Thai cuisine is served in a cozy, informal dining room. Among specialties are jumbo shrimp, Pad Thai, fried rice with seafood, salmon in red
Thai   curry and a choice of soups. Casual dress; cocktails. **Parking:** on-site. **Cards:** MC, VI.
(Ⓧ)

RESTAURANT LE TARTUFFE   **Lunch:** $14-$18   **Dinner:** $28-$38   Phone: 819/776-6424
Location: Corner rue Papineau. 133 Notre-Dame-de-Lile Gatineau J8X 3T2. **Hours:** 11:30 am-2 & 5:30-10 pm, Sat from 5:30 pm. Closed major holidays; also Sun, 12/23-1/2. **Reservations:** suggested. **Features:** The vintage Victorian home serves fine regional cuisine, including creative preparations of grilled salmon,
Regional French   braised corn-fed chicken, roasted Barbarie duck breast, stuffed rabbit, roasted red deer, grilled veal chops, Alberta beef and rack of lamb. Casual dress. **Parking:** street. **Cards:** AX, CB, DC, DS, JC, MC, VI.
(Ⓧ)

RISTORANTE FIORENTINA   **Lunch:** $10-$15   **Dinner:** $11-$25   Phone: 819/770-7273
Location: Just ne of rue Montcalm. 189 boul St-Joseph J8Y 3X2. **Hours:** 11 am-11 pm, Fri-midnight, Sat 5 pm-11 pm, Sun 5 pm-10 pm. Closed: 12/24, 12/25. **Reservations:** accepted. **Features:** The cozy 1896 Victorian-style home houses several comfortable dining rooms where guests can relax and enjoy a wide variety of
Italian   home-style dishes. Casual dress; cocktails. **Parking:** on-site and street. **Cards:** AX, DC, DS, MC, VI.
(Ⓧ)

STERLING   **Lunch:** $16-$43   **Dinner:** $15-$43   Phone: 819/568-8788

Location: Hwy 50, exit 139, 1 km se on boul Maloney ouest (Rt 148), then 2.1 km sw on Greber. 835 rue Jacques-Cartier J8T 2W3. **Hours:** 11 am-10 pm, Fri-11 pm, Sat 5 pm-11 pm, Sun 5 pm-10 pm. Closed: 12/25. **Reservations:** accepted. **Features:** This vintage waterfront home houses a stylish and contemporary steak
Steak & Seafood   and seafood restaurant. Start with a serving of beef tartare, oysters on the half shell, caviar, smoked salmon or duck foie gras terrine. Main courses include clams, snow crab, grilled lobster, fresh fish, veal rib chops, filet mignon, porterhouse or rib steak. Casual dress; cocktails. **Parking:** on-site. **Cards:** AX, DC, MC, VI.
(Ⓨ) (Ⓧ)

This ends listings for Ottawa.
The following page resumes the alphabetical listings
of cities in Ontario.

Sheraton Fallsview

HOTEL & CONFERENCE CENTRE

6755 Fallsview Boulevard
Niagara Falls, Ontario L2G 3W7

1-877-35-FALLS (32557)

e. sheraton@fallsview.com www.fallsview.com

Fallsview Dining & more!

- Enjoy upscale dining in our Fallsview Dining Room with delectable breakfast, lunch & dinner buffets as well as a full tantalizing a la carte menu.

- For a more leisurely meal enjoy La Piazza Bistro & Cafe or Stanley's Pub & Grill. Ask about our live entertainment schedule during your stay.

- Room Service offers a romantic Candlelight Dinner Service that can be enjoyed in the comforts of your room or suite.

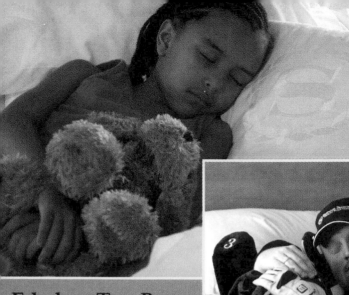

Fabulous Two-Room Family Suites Help Everyone Sleep Sweetly!

- Located just 300 yards from the edge of the breathtaking and legendary Niagara Falls with unrivaled and completely unobstructed views from all our Fallsview guestrooms & suites.

- 402 oversized and well-appointed guestrooms & specialty suites. Choose from a traditional Greenview Guestroom to a luxurious two-storey Loft Suite with floor to ceiling windows and fireplace, every room furnished with warm and contemporary décor & upscale amenities.

- Our fitness facilities and indoor swimming pool, whirlpool and sauna will refresh and rejuvenate you. All FREE of charge to our guests.

- Within walking distance of the Falls and all major attractions including the Fallsview Casino Resort, Maid of the Mist Boat Ride, Marineland and the Niagara Parks. World class golfing including the new Thundering Waters Golf Club opening 2005, award winning wineries, theatres and outlet shopping are all nearby.

The Original & Still the Best Fallsview Hotel!

OWEN SOUND pop. 21,431

—————— WHERE TO STAY ——————

BEST WESTERN INN ON THE BAY AND
CONFERENCE CENTRE *Book at aaa.com*   Phone: (519)371-9200
(CAA) (SAVE)   5/1-10/10   1P: $130-$250   2P: $130-$250   XP: $10   F18
        10/11-4/30   1P: $95-$220   2P: $95-$220   XP: $10   F18
▼▼▼▼   **Location:** 1.5 km n of 10th St E. 1800 2nd Ave E N4K 5R1 (PO Box 516). **Fax:** 519/371-6740. **Facility:** 100 units.
        85 one-bedroom standard units, some with whirlpools. 15 one-bedroom suites ($160-$250). 2-4 stories,
Small-scale Hotel interior corridors. **Parking:** on-site. **Terms:** 2 night minimum stay - seasonal and/or weekends, package
        plans. **Amenities:** irons, hair dryers. *Some:* high-speed Internet, dual phone lines. **Dining:** 7 am-10 pm,
cocktails. **Leisure Activities:** sauna, whirlpools, exercise room. **Guest Services:** valet laundry. **Business Services:** meeting
rooms. **Cards:** AX, CB, DC, DS, MC, VI. **Special Amenities: free local telephone calls and early check-in/late check-out.**

SOME UNITS

[SD] [TV] [X] [camera] [DATA PORT] [microwave] / [X] [fridge] [tray] /
FEE

COMFORT INN   *Book at aaa.com*   Phone: (519)371-5500
(CAA) (SAVE)   All Year   1P: $85-$125   2P: $95-$145   XP: $10   F18
▼▼▼▼   **Location:** Jct Hwy 6, 10, 21 and 26. 955 9th Ave E N4K 6N4. **Fax:** 519/371-6438. **Facility:** 60 one-bedroom
        standard units. 2 stories (no elevator), interior corridors. **Parking:** on-site, winter plug-ins. **Terms:** package
        plans, small pets only. **Amenities:** voice mail, hair dryers. *Some:* irons. **Guest Services:** valet laundry.
Small-scale Hotel **Cards:** AX, CB, DC, DS, JC, MC, VI. **Special Amenities: free continental breakfast and free**
        newspaper.

SOME UNITS

[SD] [paw] [camera] [DATA PORT] [microwave] / [X] [fridge] /

DAYS INN HOTEL AND CONVENTION CENTRE   *Book at aaa.com*   Phone: (519)376-1551
▼▼▼▼   All Year   1P: $79-$159   2P: $89-$169   XP: $10   F12
        Location: Jct Hwy 6 and 10. 950 6th St E N4K 1H1. **Fax:** 519/376-4288. **Facility:** 79 one-bedroom standard
Small-scale Hotel units. 3 stories (no elevator), interior corridors. **Parking:** on-site. **Terms:** package plans, pets ($20 extra
indoor. charge). **Amenities:** high-speed Internet, voice mail, safes (fee), hair dryers. *Some:* irons. **Pool(s):** heated
Leisure Activities: saunas, whirlpool, exercise room, game room. **Guest Services:** valet laundry. **Business Services:**
meeting rooms. **Cards:** AX, DC, DS, MC, VI. *(See color ad below)*

SOME UNITS

(ASK) [SD] [paw] [TV] [Y] [pool] [X] [DATA PORT] [microwave] / [X] [fridge] /
FEE

DIAMOND MOTOR INN   Phone: (519)371-2011
▼▼▼▼   6/28-10/2   1P: $69-$89   2P: $69-$89   XP: $10   F
        5/1-6/27   1P: $59-$79   2P: $59-$79   XP: $10   F
Motel   10/3-4/30   1P: $49-$69   2P: $49-$69   XP: $10   F
        Location: On Hwy 6 and 10; 0.5 km s of jct Hwy 21 and 26. 713 9th Ave E (Hwy 6/10) N4K 3E6. **Fax:** 519/371-9460.
Facility: 22 one-bedroom standard units. 1-2 stories (no elevator), interior/exterior corridors. **Parking:** on-site, winter plug-ins.
Terms: office hours 8 am-11 pm, cancellation fee imposed. **Pool(s):** heated outdoor. **Cards:** AX, MC, VI.

SOME UNITS

(ASK) [SD] [TV+] [remote] [camera] [DATA PORT] [fridge] [tray] [microwave] / [X] /

DAYS INN
& CONFERENCE CENTRE
OWEN SOUND

Come On Inn...

• Full service hotel

• Indoor pool with
  sauna and whirlpool

• Licensed restaurant
  and lounge

• WorkZone™ rooms available

1-800-DAYS INN
www.daysinn.ca

triprewards
It's fun to get more.

Days Inn - Owen Sound 950-6th Street East   Tel   Toll Free   Fax
Owen Sound, ON N4K 1H1   519-376-1551 877-775-2614 519-376-4288

Email:daysinn@bmts.com

OWEN SOUND INN

▼▼▼

Phone: (519)371-3011

5/1-11/30	1P: $49-$145	2P: $55-$150	XP: $5
12/1-4/30	1P: $40-$85	2P: $45-$90	XP: $5

Small-scale Hotel **Location:** Jct Hwy 6, 10, 26 and 21; follow Hwy 6 and 10 1 km s. 485 9th Ave E N4K 3E2. Fax: 519/376-6892. **Facility:** 27 one-bedroom standard units. 2 stories (no elevator), interior corridors. **Parking:** on-site, winter plug-ins. **Terms:** small pets only ($10 extra charge). **Amenities:** voice mail. *Some:* hair dryers. **Cards:** AX, MC, VI.

SOME UNITS
(ASK) (SD) (🛏) (🐾) (DATA PORT) (🎛) (📺) / (✕) (VCR) /
FEE

TRAVELODGE

▼▼▼

Book at aaa.com

Phone: (519)371-9297

6/30-9/30	1P: $100-$120	2P: $110-$130	XP: $10	F18
5/1-6/29 & 10/1-4/30	1P: $89-$109	2P: $99-$119	XP: $10	F18

Small-scale Hotel **Location:** Jct Hwy 6, 10, 21 and 26. 880 10th St E N4K 1T4. Fax: 519/376-1567. **Facility:** 63 one-bedroom standard units, some with efficiencies (no utensils) and/or whirlpools. 3 stories (no elevator), interior corridors. **Parking:** on-site, winter plug-ins. **Terms:** 15 day cancellation notice, [CP] meal plan available, small pets only ($10 extra charge). **Guest Services:** valet laundry. **Business Services:** meeting rooms. **Cards:** AX, CB, DC, DS, JC, MC, VI.

SOME UNITS
(ASK) (SD) (🛏) (DATA PORT) (📺) / (✕) (🎛) (📺) /
FEE

――――――― WHERE TO DINE ―――――――

TEIN BO RESTAURANT

▼▼ ▼▼▼

Chinese

cocktails. **Parking:** on-site. **Cards:** AX, MC, VI.

Lunch: $4-$8   **Dinner:** $7-$15   **Phone:** 519/371-9733

Location: 1.6 km se on Hwy 6 and 10. 775 9th Ave E N4K 3E6. **Hours:** 11 am-10 pm, Fri & Sat-11 pm, Sun-9 pm. Closed: 12/25. **Reservations:** suggested. **Features:** A wide variety of Chinese and North American dishes are specialties and served in a casual, relaxed atmosphere. Hearty portions and simple yet colorful presentation of tasty cooked-to-order cuisine is the norm. A full takeout menu is also offered. Casual dress;

(✕)

PARIS pop. 9,881

――――――― WHERE TO DINE ―――――――

TRADING POST RESTAURANT & TAVERN

◈▼

Chinese

Cards: AX, MC, VI.

Lunch: $5-$8   **Dinner:** $6-$12   **Phone:** 519/442-4332

Location: Hwy 5, 1 km e on Hwy 2. 118 Dundas St E N3L 3H6. **Hours:** 11:30 am-9 pm. Closed: 12/25. **Reservations:** suggested, weekends. **Features:** The casual restaurant offers country dining in a relaxed, no-frills diner atmosphere. On the menu are simple Canadian fare and a full selection of Chinese dishes. Hearty portions make this spot popular with the locals. Casual dress; cocktails. **Parking:** on-site.

(✕)

THE WHITE HORSE RESTAURANT

▼▼ ▼▼▼

American

Lunch: $10   **Dinner:** $15   **Phone:** 519/442-7887

Location: 1 km e of jct Hwy 2 and 5. 115 Dundas St E N3L 3H2. **Hours:** 11:30 am-2 & 5-close, Sat from 5 pm. Closed: 12/25; also Mon. **Reservations:** suggested, weekends. **Features:** A pleasant country setting complements the equally charming country decor and old-fashioned hospitality. Diners enjoy an extensive hot and cold buffet for lunch, dinner and Sunday brunch. In addition to the well-stocked salad bar, patrons can choose from such hot items as roast beef, Yorkshire pudding, fish, chicken, sausages and hot vegetables. Tasty homemade treats in the dessert section top off the meal perfectly. Casual dress; cocktails. **Parking:** on-site. **Cards:** AX, MC, VI.

(✕)

PARRY SOUND pop. 6,124

――――――― WHERE TO STAY ―――――――

COMFORT INN

▼▼ ▼▼▼

Book at aaa.com

Phone: (705)746-6221

6/1-10/15	1P: $128-$154	2P: $138-$164	XP: $10	F18
5/1-5/31	1P: $94-$120	2P: $104-$130	XP: $10	F18
1/1-4/30	1P: $92-$118	2P: $102-$128	XP: $10	F18
10/16-12/31	1P: $91-$117	2P: $101-$127	XP: $10	F18

Small-scale Hotel **Location:** Hwy 69, exit 224 (Bowes St), just w. 120 Bowes St P2A 2L7. Fax: 705/746-1544. **Facility:** 61 one-bedroom standard units. 2 stories (no elevator), interior corridors. **Parking:** on-site, winter plug-ins. **Terms:** pets (in smoking units). **Amenities:** irons, hair dryers. **Guest Services:** valet laundry. **Cards:** AX, DC, DS, JC, MC, VI.

SOME UNITS
(ASK) (SD) (🛏) (🍴) (🐾) (DATA PORT) (📺) / (✕) /

GEORGIAN INN & SUITES

▼▼ ▼▼

Phone: (705)746-5837

5/1-5/19	2P: $116-$179
5/20-6/30	2P: $100-$170
7/1-10/31 & 11/1-4/30	2P: $90-$149

Small-scale Hotel **Location:** Hwy 69, exit Parry Sound Dr, 2 km w. Located in a commercial area. 48 Joseph St P2A 2G5. Fax: 705/746-9051. **Facility:** 54 units. 53 one-bedroom standard units, some with whirlpools. 1 one-bedroom suite ($160-$180). 1-2 stories (no elevator), interior/exterior corridors. **Parking:** on-site, winter plug-ins. **Terms:** package plans. **Amenities:** irons, hair dryers. **Dining:** Georgian Breezes Cafe, see separate listing. **Pool(s):** heated indoor. **Leisure Activities:** sauna, whirlpool, exercise room. **Business Services:** meeting rooms. **Cards:** AX, MC, VI.

SOME UNITS
(ASK) (SD) (🛏) (🍴) (🏊) (✕) (DATA PORT) (📺) / (✕) (VCR) (🎛) (📺) /

LOG CABIN INN

▼▼ ▼▼▼

Motel

Phone: 705/746-7122

All Year [ECP]	1P: $89-$150	2P: $89-$150	XP: $8	F3

Location: Hwy 69, exit 220 (Hunter Dr), 1.9 km w on Oastler Park Dr, then 1.2 km s. Located in a rural area. RR 2 (Little Beaver Rd) P2A 2W8. Fax: 705/746-8060. **Facility:** 6 one-bedroom standard units with whirlpools. 1 story, exterior corridors. **Parking:** on-site, winter plug-ins. **Terms:** office hours 9:30 am-11:30 pm, 3 day cancellation notice, weekly rates available, [MAP] meal plan available, package plans, pets ($20 fee). **Dining:** dining room, see separate listing. **Leisure Activities:** canoeing, horseshoes, volleyball. **Business Services:** meeting rooms. **Cards:** AX, MC, VI.

SOME UNITS
(🛏) (🍴) (✕) (✕) (🎛) (📺) / (VCR) /
FEE

RESORT TAPATOO

Phone: (705)378-2208

Resort
Small-scale Hotel

All Year [MAP] 1P: $58-$215 2P: $77-$312 XP: $15 D12
Location: Hwy 69, exit 217, 6.2 km sw. Located in a rural, lakeside area. Otter Lake Rd P2A 2X5 (PO Box 384). Fax: 705/378-2379. **Facility:** This well-established resort is located in a beautiful, quiet area. Rooms vary from traditional and cozy to very well-appointed contemporary units. 60 units. 44 one-bedroom standard units, some with whirlpools. 8 one-bedroom suites ($95-$152), some with whirlpools. 8 cottages ($157-$204). 3 stories (no elevator), interior/exterior corridors. *Bath:* combo or shower only. **Parking:** on-site, winter plug-ins. **Terms:** office hours 8 am-10 pm, 8 day cancellation notice-fee imposed, package plans, 5% service charge. **Amenities:** *Some:* irons, hair dryers. **Dining:** dining room, see separate listing. **Pool(s):** heated pool. **Leisure Activities:** sauna, whirlpool, canoeing, paddleboats, fishing, cross country skiing, snowmobiling, ice skating, recreation programs, exercise room, spa. *Fee:* boats, boat dock, waterskiing. **Guest Services:** *Fee:* tanning facility. **Business Services:** meeting rooms. **Cards:** AX, DC, MC, VI.

SOME UNITS
(ASK) [=] [=] [=] [=] [=] [=] [=] / (AC) (VCR) /

WINNETOU RESORTS

Phone: (705)342-9967

(CAA) (SAVE)

Cottage

All Year 2P: $113-$1440 XP: $25
Location: 14 km n on Hwy 69, 10 km w on Hwy 559 to Dillon Rd, follow signs. Located on the shore of Lake Huron's Georgian Bay. 234 Dillon Rd P0G 1G0 (RR 1, NOBEL). Fax: 705/342-1291. **Facility:** 10 cottages. 1 story, exterior corridors. *Bath:* combo or shower only. **Parking:** on-site, winter plug-ins. **Terms:** office hours 9 am-7 pm, check-out 9 am, 2 night minimum stay, 30 day cancellation notice-fee imposed. **Leisure Activities:** sauna, whirlpool, rental boats, canoeing, paddleboats, sailboats, fishing, kayaks, playground, exercise room. *Fee:* boat dock. **Guest Services:** coin laundry. **Cards:** MC, VI.

SOME UNITS
[=] [=] (AC) [=] [=] [=] [=] / (VCR) /
FEE

--------- WHERE TO DINE ---------

GEORGIAN BREEZES CAFE

Phone: 705-746-5368

Canadian

Dinner: $7-$22
Location: Hwy 69, exit Parry Sound Dr, 2 km w; in Best Western Georgian Inn. 48 Joseph St P2A 2G5. **Hours:** 4 pm-9 pm. **Closed:** 12/23-12/30. **Reservations:** accepted. **Features:** This little dining room has a menu that offers good variety including Certified Angus steak, pasta, fish, chicken, pizza and finger foods. Casual dress; cocktails. **Parking:** on-site. **Cards:** MC, VI.

[=]

LOG CABIN INN DINING

Phone: 705-746-7122

Continental

Lunch: $7-$11 Dinner: $15-$38
Location: Hwy 69, exit 220 (Hunter Dr), 1.9 km w on Oastler Park Dr, then 1.2 km s; in Log Cabin Inn. RR 2 (Little Beaver Rd) P2A 2W8. **Hours:** 11 am-2:30 & 5-10 pm; 5 pm-9 pm 10/15-5/15. **Closed:** 12/24-12/26. **Reservations:** accepted. **Features:** Dine in the comfort of an original log cabin. Comfortable new additions have been added to the building. Bask in the warmth of a natural fireplace and enjoy the art of local artists that is on display. Specialties include market fresh fish, lamb and steak. Sunday brunch 5/24-10/5. Casual dress; cocktails. **Parking:** on-site. **Cards:** AX, MC, VI.

(AC) [=]

RESORT TAPATOO DINING ROOM

Phone: 705-378-2208

Continental

Lunch: $8-$19 Dinner: $14-$28
Location: Hwy 69, exit 217, 6.2 km sw; in Resort Tapatoo. Otter Lake Rd P2A 2X5. **Hours:** 8 am-10 pm; 8 am-noon & 5-9 pm 10/16-6/14. **Reservations:** accepted. **Features:** The short drive on a gravel road is worth it for the lovely lake views afforded from most tables in the dining room. The menu offers a variety of schnitzels and a favorite, Ontario pickerel. Casual dress; cocktails. **Parking:** on-site. **Cards:** AX, DC, MC, VI.

[=] [=]

TRAPPER'S CHOICE RESTAURANT

Phone: 705-746-9491

American

Lunch: $5-$13 Dinner: $8-$18
Location: Hwy 69, exit Parry Sound Downtown, north entrance; in front of Parry Sound Mall. 50 Joseph St P2A 2G5. **Hours:** 7 am-11 pm; 8 am-10 pm 11/1-6/1. **Closed:** 1/1, 4/17, 12/25. **Features:** This small restaurant, favoured by locals, has a relaxed atmosphere and offers a screened-in porch in season. Two favoured dishes are fresh panfried pickerel (may not be available February and March) and liver with onions, bacon or both. Portions are hearty. Casual dress; cocktails. **Parking:** on-site. **Cards:** AX, MC, VI.

[=]

PEMBROKE pop. 13,490

--------- WHERE TO STAY ---------

BEST WESTERN PEMBROKE INN & CONFERENCE CENTRE   *Book at aaa.com*

Phone: (613)735-0131

Small-scale Hotel

All Year 1P: $124-$199 2P: $124-$199 XP: $10 F
Location: Jct Hwy 17 and 41. Located in a commercial area. One International Dr K8A 6W5. Fax: 613/735-0078. **Facility:** 70 units. 69 one-bedroom standard units, some with efficiencies. 1 one-bedroom suite. 2 stories, interior corridors. **Parking:** on-site, winter plug-ins. **Terms:** package plans, small pets only ($10 extra charge, in designated units). **Amenities:** video games (fee), voice mail, irons, hair dryers. **Pool(s):** heated indoor. **Leisure Activities:** saunas, whirlpool, snowmobiling, playground, basketball. **Guest Services:** gift shop, valet laundry. **Business Services:** conference facilities. **Cards:** AX, CB, DC, MC, VI.

SOME UNITS
(ASK) (SD) [=] [=] [=] [=] [=] [=] (DATA PORT) [=] / [=] [=] [=] /
FEE

COLONIAL FIRESIDE INN

Phone: (613)732-3623

Motel

All Year 1P: $53-$68 2P: $63-$88 XP: $5 F12
Location: Jct Hwy 17, 5 km n on Forest Lea Rd, just e. Located in a commercial area. 1350 Pembroke St W K8A 7A3. Fax: 613/732-4232. **Facility:** 25 one-bedroom standard units, some with efficiencies and/or whirlpools. 1-2 stories (no elevator), exterior corridors. *Bath:* combo or shower only. **Parking:** on-site, winter plug-ins. **Terms:** office hours 7:30 am-11 pm, small pets only ($10 extra charge, in designated units). **Amenities:** *Some:* hair dryers. **Pool(s):** small outdoor. **Leisure Activities:** playground. **Guest Services:** valet laundry. **Cards:** AX, MC, VI.

SOME UNITS
(ASK) (SD) [=] [=] [=] [=] (DATA PORT) / [=] (VCR) [=] [=] [=] /
FEE   FEE

COMFORT INN *Book at aaa.com*   Phone: (613)735-1057

7/1-8/31	1P: $99-$169	2P: $99-$169	XP: $10	F18
5/1-6/30	1P: $99-$159	2P: $99-$159	XP: $10	F18
9/1-12/31	1P: $99-$139	2P: $99-$139	XP: $10	F18
1/1-4/30	1P: $99-$129	2P: $99-$129	XP: $10	F18

Small-scale Hotel

Location: 1.6 km e on Old Hwy 17. Located in a commercial area. 959 Pembroke St E K8A 3M3. Fax: 613/735-7685. **Facility:** 61 one-bedroom standard units, some with whirlpools. 2 stories (no elevator), interior corridors. **Parking:** on-site, winter plug-ins. **Amenities:** voice mail, irons, hair dryers. **Guest Services:** valet laundry. **Cards:** AX, CB, DC, DS, JC, MC, VI.

SOME UNITS

(ASK) (S☐) (🛏) (📶) (📷) (DATA PORT) (💻) / (✕) (🔒) (📠) /

PERTH pop. 6,003

──────── WHERE TO STAY ────────

TAY INN-PERTH   Phone: (613)267-3300

(CAA) (SAVE)

5/1-10/31	1P: $59-$79	2P: $69-$89	XP: $7	F18
11/1-4/30	1P: $49-$59	2P: $59-$69	XP: $7	F18

Motel

Location: Hwy 7, jct Hwy 511. Located in a commercial area. 125 Dufferin St K7H 3A5. Fax: 613/267-3305. **Facility:** 18 one-bedroom standard units. 1 story, exterior corridors. *Bath:* combo or shower only. **Parking:** on-site, winter plug-ins. **Terms:** office hours 7 am-11 pm. **Pool(s):** outdoor. **Cards:** AX, DC, MC, VI. **Special Amenities:** free local telephone calls.

SOME UNITS

(📶) (🛏) (📷) / (✕) (🔒) /

──────── *The following lodging was either not evaluated or did not* ────────
meet AAA rating requirements but is listed for your information only.

MCCREARY'S BEACH RESORT   Phone: 613/267-4450

(fyi)   Not evaluated. **Location:** 12.8 km e on Hwy 7, 1.6 km s on Mississippi W Shore Dr. Waterfront, rural location beside campground. 155 McCreary's Beach Rd K7H 3N8 (PO Box 1401, RR 6). Facilities, services, and decor characterize a mid-range property.

──────── WHERE TO DINE ────────

FIDDLEHEADS   **Lunch:** $7-$13   **Dinner:** $13-$23   **Phone:** 613/267-1304

Location: Centre; opposite Stewart Park. 53 Herriott St K7H 1T5. **Hours:** 11:30 am-9 pm, Sun-8 pm. Closed major holidays; also Sun & Mon 10/8-5/31. **Reservations:** suggested. **Features:** Exposed wood beams and grey stone walls combine with original art to create a pleasing decor, and the bustle of the open kitchen adds to the fun. Seafood, red meat, pasta, pizza and finger foods are all offered. Casual dress; cocktails.

American

Parking: on-site. **Cards:** MC, VI.

(🍴) (✕)

PETERBOROUGH pop. 71,446

──────── WHERE TO STAY ────────

BEST WESTERN OTONABEE INN *Book at aaa.com*   Phone: (705)742-3454

(CAA) (SAVE)

7/1-10/9	1P: $119-$135	2P: $119-$135	XP: $5	F16
5/1-6/30 & 10/10-4/30	1P: $109-$129	2P: $109-$129	XP: $5	F16

Location: 2.5 km e of The Parkway. Located in a riverside area. 84 Lansdowne St E K9J 6Z3 (PO Box 366). Fax: 705/742-3454. **Facility:** 75 units. 72 one-bedroom standard units, some with efficiencies. 3 one-

Small-scale Hotel bedroom suites ($159-$199). 2 stories, interior corridors. **Parking:** on-site, winter plug-ins. **Amenities:** voice mail, irons, hair dryers. **Dining:** 7-10 am, Sat & Sun 7:30-11 am. **Pool(s):** heated indoor. **Leisure Activities:** whirlpool, playground. *Fee:* boat dock. **Guest Services:** valet laundry. **Business Services:** conference facilities. **Cards:** AX, DC, DS, MC, VI. **Special Amenities:** free local telephone calls and free newspaper.

SOME UNITS

(S☐) (🍴) (📶) (✕) (📷) (DATA PORT) (🔒) (💻) / (✕) (📠) /

COMFORT INN & SUITES *Book at aaa.com*   Phone: (705)740-7000

(CAA) (SAVE)

5/1-9/30	1P: $109-$189	2P: $119-$199	XP: $10	F16
10/1-4/30	1P: $105-$185	2P: $115-$195	XP: $10	F16

Location: 0.6 km w of jct Hwy 28. Located in a commercial area. 1209 Lansdowne St W K9J 7M2. Fax: 705/745-0506. **Facility:** 104 one-bedroom standard units, some with whirlpools. 3 stories, interior

Small-scale Hotel corridors. **Parking:** on-site, winter plug-ins. **Terms:** 2 night minimum stay - seasonal and/or weekends. **Amenities:** voice mail, irons, hair dryers. *Fee:* video games, high-speed Internet. **Dining:** 11 am-10 pm, cocktails. **Pool(s):** small heated indoor. **Leisure Activities:** whirlpool. **Guest Services:** valet laundry. **Business Services:** meeting rooms. **Cards:** AX, DC, DS, MC, VI. **Special Amenities:** free local telephone calls.

SOME UNITS

(S☐) (🍴) (📶) (📷) (DATA PORT) (💻) / (✕) (🔒) (📠) /

HOLIDAY INN PETERBOROUGH-WATERFRONT   Phone: (705)743-1144

(CAA) (SAVE)

7/1-8/31	1P: $105-$135	2P: $105-$135	
5/1-6/30 & 9/1-4/30	1P: $100-$120	2P: $100-$120	

Location: Jct Lansdowne and George sts, 0.5 km n. 150 George St N K9J 3G5. Fax: 705/740-6557. **Facility:** 153 one-bedroom standard units, some with whirlpools. 4 stories, interior corridors. **Parking:** on-site, winter

Small-scale Hotel plug-ins. **Terms:** 2 night minimum stay - seasonal and/or weekends, package plans. **Amenities:** video games (fee), voice mail, irons, hair dryers. **Dining:** 6:30 am-10 pm, cocktails. **Pool(s):** small heated indoor/outdoor. **Leisure Activities:** sauna, whirlpool, boat dock, fishing, indoor recreation area, indoor childrens activity center, exercise room. **Guest Services:** valet and coin laundry. **Business Services:** conference facilities. **Cards:** AX, CB, DC, DS, JC, MC, VI. **Special Amenities:** free newspaper. *(See color ad card insert)*

SOME UNITS

(🍴) (🍴) (📶) (✕) (📷) (DATA PORT) (💻) / (✕) (🔒) (📠) /

FEE

KING BETHUNE GUEST HOUSE & SPA   *Book at aaa.com*   **Phone:** (705)743-4101
▼▼▼ ▼▼▼
All Year [BP]   1P: $84-$225   2P: $115-$275   XP: $25   F3
Location: From Charlotte and George St (clock tower), 1 blk s on George St to King St, then just w. Located in a
Bed & Breakfast   residential area. 270 King St K9J 2S2. **Facility:** Smoke free premises. 3 one-bedroom standard units. 2 stories
(no elevator), interior corridors. *Bath:* combo or shower only. **Parking:** on-site, winter plug-ins. **Terms:** office
hours 6 am-10 pm, 14 day cancellation notice-fee imposed, pets ($10 extra charge). **Amenities:** CD players, dual phone lines,
hair dryers. **Leisure Activities:** bicycles. *Fee:* massage. **Guest Services:** valet laundry. **Cards:** AX, VI.

SOME UNITS
🛏 ✕ VCR 🐾 DATA/PORT 🍽 / 🖥 /
FEE

QUALITY INN   *Book at aaa.com*   **Phone:** (705)748-6801
CAA SAVE
5/1-9/30   1P: $115-$125   2P: $125-$135   XP: $5   F18
▼▼▼ ▼▼▼
10/1-4/30   1P: $105-$115   2P: $115-$125   XP: $5   F18
Location: 3 km from jct Hwy 115 and Bypass. Located in a commercial area. 1074 Lansdowne St W K9J 1Z9.
Fax: 705/748-6254. **Facility:** 117 one-bedroom standard units, some with whirlpools. 2 stories (no elevator),
Small-scale Hotel   interior corridors. **Parking:** on-site, winter plug-ins. **Terms:** cancellation fee imposed, [BP] meal plan
available, pets (1st floor units). **Amenities:** video games (fee), hair dryers. *Some:* irons. **Guest Services:**
valet laundry. **Business Services:** meeting rooms. **Cards:** AX, DC, MC, VI. **Special Amenities: free full breakfast and free
local telephone calls.**

SOME UNITS
SD 🛏 🐾 🍽 / ✕ DATA/PORT 🖥 📷 /

ROBYN'S MOTEL   **Phone:** 705-745-3225
▼
Property failed to provide current rates
Location: On Hwy 7, 2.5 km e of Television Rd. Located in a commercial area. 1136 Hwy 7 E K9J 6X8 (RR 7, Station
Motel   Main). Fax: 705/745-3225. **Facility:** 11 one-bedroom standard units. 1 story, exterior corridors. *Bath:* shower
only. **Parking:** on-site, winter plug-ins. **Terms:** office hours 9:30 am-11 pm, pets (no cats).

SOME UNITS
🐾 🐾 🖥 / ✕ /

------- **WHERE TO DINE** -------

CAROUSEL RESTAURANT & TAVERN   **Lunch:** $5-$9   **Dinner:** $7-$14   **Phone:** 705-745-0060
▼▼▼ ▼▼▼
Location: 2.5 km e on Hwy 7B. 116 Lansdowne St E K9J 7N9. **Hours:** 7 am-10 pm, Thurs-Sat to midnight, Sun 8
am-10 pm. **Reservations:** suggested, weekends. **Features:** Varied menu choices and lunch and dinner
American   buffets make the Carousel Restaurant a nice, long-standing, family-oriented eatery. Beef, ham and roast
beef make good showings as well as generous portions and consistently prompt and friendly service.
Casual dress; cocktails. **Parking:** on-site. **Cards:** AX, MC, VI.   ✕

THE SPAGHETTI HOUSE FAMILY RESTAURANT   **Lunch:** $6-$8   **Dinner:** $9-$16   **Phone:** 705-748-6666
▼▼▼ ▼▼▼
Location: On Hwy 28, 1 km n of jct Hwy 28 and Lansdowne St. 1090 Clonsilla Ave K9J 5Y5. **Hours:** 11 am-10 pm,
Thurs-Sat to 11 pm. Closed: 12/25. **Features:** This family-oriented restaurant offers a simple decor and a
Italian   comfortable atmosphere. A popular choice is the "house special spaghetti" which has pepperoni,
mushrooms, onions, green peppers and meatballs with meat sauce. Vegetarian dishes are available. Casual
dress; cocktails. **Parking:** on-site. **Cards:** AX, MC, VI.   ✕

PICKERING pop. 87,139

------- **WHERE TO STAY** -------

COMFORT INN   *Book at aaa.com*   **Phone:** (905)831-6200
CAA SAVE
7/1-9/30   1P: $90-$155   2P: $95-$160   XP: $10   F18
5/1-6/30 & 10/1-12/31   1P: $85-$135   2P: $90-$145   XP: $10   F18
▼▼▼ ▼▼▼
1/1-4/30   1P: $80-$125   2P: $85-$130   XP: $10   F18
Location: Hwy 401, exit 394 N (White's Rd) to Hwy 2, 0.5 km w. 533 Kingston Rd L1V 3N7. Fax: 905/831-6025.
Small-scale Hotel   **Facility:** 146 one-bedroom standard units. 2 stories (no elevator), interior corridors. **Parking:** on-site, winter
plug-ins. **Terms:** [ECP] meal plan available, package plans, small pets only. **Amenities:** voice mail, irons,
hair dryers. *Some:* dual phone lines. **Leisure Activities:** exercise room. **Guest Services:** valet and coin laundry. **Business
Services:** meeting rooms. **Cards:** AX, CB, DC, DS, JC, MC, VI.

SOME UNITS
SD 🛏 🍽 🐾 DATA/PORT 🖥 / ✕ 🖥 /

------- **WHERE TO DINE** -------

BOB CAYGEON'S RESTAURANT   **Lunch:** $5-$15   **Dinner:** $7-$15   **Phone:** 905-831-9258
▼▼▼
Location: Directly n of Hwy 401. 1790 Liverpool Rd L1V 1V9. **Hours:** 11:30 am-midnight. Closed: 12/25.
Features: Relaxed cottage country decor and a fun menu of casual favorites, such as wings, burgers, pasta
and fajitas, make the restaurant a popular choice. Families and locals frequent this place for filling, tasty
American   meals. Casual dress; cocktails. **Parking:** on-site. **Cards:** AX, MC, VI.   🍸 ✕

MANDARIN   **Lunch:** $9-$13   **Dinner:** $16-$22   **Phone:** 905/619-1000
▼▼ ▼▼
Location: Directly e of Brock Rd. 1725 Kingston Rd L1V 1C5. **Hours:** noon-3 & 5-9:30 pm, Fri & Sat-10:30 pm.
Closed: 12/25, 12/26. **Reservations:** suggested. **Features:** The popular chain's specialty is its extensive
Chinese   buffet, which includes not only hot and tasty Chinese items but also huge salad and dessert bars. The
selection is varied enough to please all, especially those with hearty appetites. Casual dress; cocktails.
Parking: on-site. **Cards:** AX, MC, VI.   ✕

MELANIE PRINGLES RESTAURANTS   **Lunch:** $6-$8   **Dinner:** $8-$13   **Phone:** 905/420-1956
▼▼▼ **Location:** Hwy 401, exit 394 N (White's Rd); corner of Kingston and White's rds. 705 Kingston Rd L1V 1A8. **Hours:** 11 am-1 am, Sun-11 pm. Closed: 12/25. **Features:** The nostalgic diner, complete with jukeboxes and
Canadian photographs of old-time movie stars, is a perfect spot for family dining. The menu features a wide range of
casual fare, including finger foods, such as wings and nachos, main-course salads, hot dogs, burgers, fish
and chips and pastas. At lunch, many diners enjoy the fast and healthy all-you-can-eat soup, salad and sandwich bar. Casual
dress; cocktails. **Parking:** on-site. **Cards:** AX, MC, VI.   ⊠

PICTON pop. 4,563

———— WHERE TO STAY ————

MERRILL INN   **Phone:** (613)476-7451
▼▼▼▼ 5/1-10/31 [ECP]   1P: $159-$229   2P: $159-$229   XP: $15   F10
11/1-4/30 [ECP]   1P: $125-$199   2P: $125-$199   XP: $15   F10
Historic **Location:** Corner of Johnston St; centre. Located in a residential area. 343 Main St E K0K 2T0 (PO Box 1318).
Country Inn Fax: 613/476-8283. **Facility:** Set amid neighboring mansions on a tree-lined street, this 1870 inn is walking
distance from downtown. Smoke free premises. 13 units. 12 one-bedroom standard units, some with
whirlpools. 1 one-bedroom suite. 3 stories (no elevator), interior corridors. *Bath:* combo or shower only. **Parking:** on-site.
Terms: office hours 8 am-10 pm, 2 night minimum stay - seasonal and/or weekends, 3 day cancellation notice-fee imposed,
[MAP] meal plan available, package plans. **Amenities:** video library, hair dryers. *Some:* CD players. **Dining:** Sir Edward's
Restaurant & Wine Bar, see separate listing. **Guest Services:** valet laundry. **Business Services:** meeting rooms. **Cards:** AX,
DC, MC, VI.   (A$K) (S⊡) (†↑) (⊠) (VCR) (DATA PORT)

THE WARING HOUSE RESTAURANT, INN &
COOKERY SCHOOL   **Phone:** (613)476-7492
(CAA) (SAVE) All Year   1P: $125-$220   2P: $125-$220   XP: $110
▼▼▼▼ **Location:** 2 km w at Hwy 33 and CR 1. Located in a rural area. 395 Sandy Hook Rd K0K 2T0 (PO Box 20024, K0K
3V0). Fax: 613/476-6648. **Facility:** This inn dating from 1860, which is furnished with antiques, is close to
Historic town but in a country setting. Smoke free premises. 17 one-bedroom standard units, some with whirlpools. 2
Country Inn stories (no elevator), interior corridors. *Bath:* combo or tub only. **Parking:** on-site. **Terms:** office hours 8 am-
9 pm, 2 night minimum stay - seasonal and/or weekends, age restrictions may apply, 3 day cancellation
notice-fee imposed, [MAP] meal plan available, package plans. **Amenities:** hair dryers. **Dining:** restaurant,
see separate listing. **Leisure Activities:** croquet, hiking trails, horseshoes. **Guest Services:** gift shop. **Business Services:**
meeting rooms. **Cards:** AX, DC, MC, VI.
SOME UNITS
(†↑) (⊻) (⊠) (⊠) / (VCR) (▱) /

———— WHERE TO DINE ————

SIR EDWARD'S RESTAURANT & WINE BAR   **Lunch:** $9-$13   **Dinner:** $17-$26   **Phone:** 613/476-7451
▼▼▼ **Location:** Corner of Johnston St; centre; in Merrill Inn. 343 Main St E K0K 2T0. **Hours:** 11:30 am-2 & 5-9 pm; hours
may vary in winter. Closed: 12/25, 12/26; also Sun. **Reservations:** suggested. **Features:** Good things come
Canadian in small packages and this little restaurant offers an excellent selection of local, Canadian and import wines,
many by the glass. The food is carefully prepared from market-fresh ingredients and creative variations of
fish, chicken and red meat dishes are offered, as well as pasta that is made in-house. There is a patio available in season.
Casual dress; cocktails. **Parking:** on-site. **Cards:** AX, DC, MC, VI.   ⊠

THE WARING HOUSE RESTAURANT &
INN   **Lunch:** $6-$11   **Dinner:** $14-$40   **Phone:** 613/476-7492
(CAA) **Location:** 2 km w at Hwy 33 and CR 1; in The Waring House Restaurant, Inn & Cookery School. 395 Sandy Hook Rd
K0K 2T0. **Hours:** 8 am-2 & 5-9 pm; hours may vary in winter. **Reservations:** suggested. **Features:** The
▼▼▼ circa-1860 stone house is a distinctive dining setting. A good selection of fish, lamb, pork and beef dishes is
Regional offered; house specialties include such dishes as prime rib and Atlantic salmon. Homemade desserts are
Canadian delicious. Casual dress; cocktails. **Parking:** on-site. **Cards:** AX, DC, MC, VI. **Country Inn**   (⊻) ⊠

PLANTAGENET pop. 1,103

———— WHERE TO STAY ————

MOTEL DE CHAMPLAIN 2004   **Phone:** (613)673-5220
▼▼ All Year   1P: $80-$90   2P: $80-$90   XP: $12   F12
Location: Jct CR 9. Located in a rural area. 5999 Hwy 17 K0B 1L0 (PO Box 179). **Facility:** 20 one-bedroom
Motel standard units, some with whirlpools. 1 story, interior/exterior corridors. **Parking:** on-site, winter plug-ins.
Terms: office hours 7 am-11 pm, 5 day cancellation notice, package plans, small pets only (with prior
approval). **Amenities:** hair dryers. **Dining:** restaurant, see separate listing. **Business Services:** meeting rooms, fax (fee).
Cards: AX, MC, VI.
SOME UNITS
(A$K) (🛏) (†↑) (DATA PORT) (🖥) / (⊠) (VCR) /

———— WHERE TO DINE ————

MOTEL DE CHAMPLAIN RESTAURANT   **Lunch:** $8-$17   **Dinner:** $8-$17   **Phone:** 613/673-5220
▼▼ **Location:** Jct CR 9; adjacent to Motel de Champlain 2004. 5999 Hwy 17 K0B 1L0. **Hours:** 6 am-midnight, Sun-11
pm. Closed: 1/1, 12/25. **Reservations:** accepted. **Features:** This little restaurant is the hot spot in this rural
Canadian area and it may be busy at peak meal periods. Save some room for the in-house prepared desserts. Casual
dress; cocktails. **Parking:** on-site. **Cards:** AX, MC, VI.   ⊠

PORT CARLING

———— WHERE TO STAY ————

DELTA SHERWOOD INN   *Book at aaa.com*   **Phone:** (705)765-3131

(CAA) (SAVE)
	5/27-9/4 [MAP]	1P: $281-$447	2P: $348-$514	XP: $20	F12
	9/5-10/22 [MAP]	1P: $261-$427	2P: $328-$494	XP: $20	F12
▽▽▽▽▽	10/23-4/30 [MAP]	1P: $171-$337	2P: $238-$404	XP: $20	F12
	5/1-5/26 [MAP]	1P: $226-$309	2P: $293-$369	XP: $20	F12

Resort   **Location:** Hwy 169, n of jct Hwy 118; on Lake Joseph. 1090 Sherwood Rd P0B 1J0 (PO Box 400).
Small-scale Hotel Fax: 705/765-6668. **Facility:** Tall pines and a sandy lake beach set the scene at this established resort offering a diverse range of room types. 49 units. 39 one-bedroom standard units, some with whirlpools. 10 cottages ($282-$783), some with whirlpools. 2-3 stories (no elevator), interior/exterior corridors. *Bath:* combo or shower only. **Parking:** on-site, winter plug-ins. **Terms:** check-in 4 pm, 2 night minimum stay - weekends, 14 day cancellation notice-fee imposed, weekly rates available, package plans, 15% service charge. **Amenities:** voice mail, irons, hair dryers. **Dining:** dining room, see separate listing. **Leisure Activities:** whirlpool, canoeing, paddleboats, sailboats, boat dock, fishing, kayaks, tennis court, cross country skiing, ice skating, bicycles, hiking trails, exercise room, spa, horseshoes. **Business Services:** meeting rooms. **Cards:** AX, DC, JC, MC, VI. **Special Amenities:** free local telephone calls and free newspaper.

SOME UNITS
  ⓢ (🍴) ✕ (DATA PORT) (▯) / ✕ (AC) (VCR) 🖥 🖥 /

———— WHERE TO DINE ————

DELTA SHERWOOD INN DINING
ROOM   **Lunch:** $8-$17   **Dinner:** $20-$35   **Phone:** 705/765-3131
(CAA)   **Location:** Hwy 169, just n of jct Hwy 118; on Lake Joseph; in Delta Sherwood Inn. 1090 Sherwood Rd P0B 1J0.
Hours: 8 am-4 & 6-9 pm. **Reservations:** required. **Features:** In a charming country setting with panoramic
▽▽▽   windows, the restaurant excels at creating a mood for romantic dining. Personable servers will explain
selections from the sophisticated menu, which offers a choice of changing regional and Continental
Continental   specialties. Dressy casual; cocktails. **Parking:** on-site. **Cards:** AX, DC, MC, VI.   ✕

ENRICO'S   **Dinner:** $16-$29   **Phone:** 705/762-5501
▽▽▽   **Location:** Jct Hwy 118 and 169, 5 km s on Hwy 169; in Cranberry Marsh Cove Resort. 3571 Muskoka Rd Hwy 169 P0B
1J0. **Hours:** 5:30 pm-9:30 pm. **Reservations:** suggested. **Features:** Well-prepared and creatively presented
Italian   fish, lamb, veal, steak and homemade pasta dishes are served in a comfortable atmosphere by friendly
servers. Dressy casual; cocktails. **Parking:** on-site. **Cards:** AX, DC, MC, VI.   ✕

PORT COLBORNE —See Niagara Falls p. 382.

PORT ELGIN pop. 6,766

———— WHERE TO STAY ————

PORT ELGIN SUPER 8 MOTEL   *Book at aaa.com*   **Phone:** 519/832-2058
▽▽▽▽	7/1-9/4	1P: $135-$180	2P: $135-$180	XP: $10	D18
	9/5-4/30	1P: $110-$150	2P: $110-$150	XP: $5	D18
Small-scale Hotel	6/1-6/30	1P: $110-$145	2P: $110-$145	XP: $5	D18
	5/1-5/31	1P: $94-$125	2P: $94-$125	XP: $5	D18

Location: South end of town. Hwy 21 S N0H 2C0 (Box 614). Fax: 519/389-4547. **Facility:** 55 units. 53 one-bedroom standard units, some with whirlpools. 2 one-bedroom suites ($150-$240), some with whirlpools. 2 stories (no elevator), interior corridors. **Parking:** on-site, winter plug-ins. **Terms:** 2 night minimum stay - seasonal, package plans. **Amenities:** high-speed Internet, voice mail, hair dryers. *Some:* irons. **Pool(s):** outdoor, heated indoor. **Leisure Activities:** sauna, whirlpool, exercise room. **Guest Services:** coin laundry. **Business Services:** meeting rooms. **Cards:** AX, DC, MC, VI.

SOME UNITS
(🍴) ➟ ✕ (DATA PORT) 🖥 / ✕ (VCR) 🖥 (▯) /

———— *The following lodging was either not evaluated or did not* ————
meet AAA rating requirements but is listed for your information only.

COLONIAL MOTEL   **Phone:** 519/832-2021
(fyi)   Not evaluated. **Location:** 1.5 km s of jct Hwy 21 (Goderich St) and Market St; centre. 235 Goderich St (Hwy 21) N0H
2C1. Facilities, services, and decor characterize a mid-range property.

———— WHERE TO DINE ————

ANDRE'S SWISS COUNTRY DINING   **Dinner:** $15-$20   **Phone:** 519/832-2461
▽▽▽   **Location:** On Hwy 21 (Goderich St); just s of Bruce County 17. 442 Goderich St N0H 2C4. **Hours:** Open 5/1-2/28 &
4/1-4/30; 5 pm-10 pm. **Closed:** 12/24-12/26; also Sun & Mon. **Reservations:** suggested. **Features:** Among
Swiss   offerings of creative European cuisine are such tasty and filling specialties as various homemade schnitzels.
For dessert, diners are privy to such temptations as apple strudel and homemade banana ice cream. The
atmosphere is relaxed in the cozy dining room. Casual dress. **Parking:** on-site. **Cards:** AX, MC, VI.   ✕

PORT HOPE pop. 11,718

——— WHERE TO STAY ———

BUTTERNUT INN BED & BREAKFAST
Phone: (905)885-4318

All Year [BP] 1P: $110-$140 2P: $125-$160 XP: $40 F10
Location: Hwy 401, exit 461, 2.4 km s on Hwy 2, 0.8 km e on Ridout St, just n on Pine St, then just e. Located in a residential area. 36 North St L1A 1T8. Fax: 905/885-5464. **Facility:** A solarium and secret garden are featured at this restored 1847 Neo-Classic-style home, the onetime residence of the Great Farini. Smoke free premises. 4 one-bedroom standard units, some with whirlpools. 2 stories (no elevator), interior corridors. *Bath:* combo or shower only. **Parking:** on-site, winter plug-ins. **Terms:** office hours 7 am-10 pm, check-in 4 pm, age restrictions may apply, 3 day cancellation notice-fee imposed, package plans. **Cards:** AX, MC, VI.

Historic Bed & Breakfast

SOME UNITS

COMFORT INN
Phone: (905)885-7000

7/1-9/5	1P: $99-$175	2P: $109-$195	XP: $5 F18
9/6-4/30	1P: $95-$175	2P: $105-$195	XP: $5 F18
5/1-6/30	1P: $95-$175	2P: $105-$175	XP: $5 F18

Location: Hwy 401, exit 464, just n. Located in a commercial area. Hwy 401 & 28 L1A 3Z3 (PO Box 397). *Small-scale Hotel* Fax: 905/885-7070. **Facility:** 91 one-bedroom standard units, some with whirlpools. 3 stories, interior corridors. **Parking:** on-site, winter plug-ins. **Terms:** package plans, small pets only (in smoking units). **Amenities:** video games (fee), irons, hair dryers. *Some:* honor bars. **Business Services:** meeting rooms. **Cards:** AX, CB, DC, DS, JC, MC, VI. **Special Amenities:** free continental breakfast and free local telephone calls.

SOME UNITS

DR. CORBETT'S INN
Phone: 905/885-8686

All Year [BP] 1P: $110-$125 2P: $120-$170 XP: $20 F3
Location: Jct Augusta, just s of Hwy 2. Located in a commercial/residential area. 86 John St L1A 2Z2. Fax: 905/885-6467. **Facility:** Built in 1857. 10 one-bedroom standard units, some with whirlpools. 3 stories *Historic Small-scale Hotel* (no elevator), interior corridors. *Bath:* combo or tub only. **Parking:** on-site. **Terms:** office hours 6 am-11 pm, package plans. **Amenities:** voice mail, irons, hair dryers. **Dining:** The Palm, see separate listing. **Guest Services:** complimentary laundry, area transportation. **Cards:** AX, DC, MC,VI. *(See color ad below)*

SOME UNITS

THE HILL & DALE MANOR
Phone: 905/885-5992

All Year [BP] 1P: $110-$125 2P: $125-$175 XP: $20 D10
Location: Just s of Hwy 2. Located in a quiet area. 47 Pine St S L1A 3E6. Fax: 905/885-6467. **Facility:** A short walk from the historic downtown area, this restored mansion dating from 1800 is on four private acres and offers well-appointed rooms. Smoke free premises. 6 one-bedroom standard units. 2 stories (no elevator), interior corridors. *Historic Bed & Breakfast* **Parking:** on-site. **Terms:** office hours 6 am-11 pm, package plans. **Amenities:** hair dryers. **Leisure Activities:** *Fee:* massage. **Guest Services:** complimentary laundry, area transportation-train and bus station. **Cards:** AX, DC, MC, VI. **Special Amenities:** free full breakfast and free local telephone calls.

SOME UNITS

DR. CORBETT'S INN
FINE LODGING IN HISTORIC PORT HOPE

86 John Street, Port Hope, ON L1A 2Z2

Experience the Difference

Featuring

The Palm Restaurant for fine dining and

The Blue Parrot Lounge for the casual meal

Toll Free: 1-800-383-3316 Take Out
Telephone: 905-885-8686 www.drcorbettsinn.com

THE HILLCREST, A HALDIMAND HILLS SPA   **Phone:** (905)349-2493
All Year [AP]   1P: $480-$680   2P: $750-$950
Location: Hwy 401, exit Hwy 2, 2.5 km s to Bramley Rd, then s. 175 Dorset St W L1A 1G4. Fax: 905/349-3156.
Historic   **Facility:** Built in the Beaux Arts style, this 1874 mansion is on handsome manicured grounds and offers
Country Inn   some rooms with views of Lake Ontario. Smoke free premises. 7 units. 6 one-bedroom standard units,
                  some with whirlpools. 1 one-bedroom suite with whirlpool. 3 stories (no elevator), interior corridors. *Bath:*
combo or tub only. **Parking:** on-site, winter plug-ins. **Terms:** check-in 4 pm, 2 night minimum stay - weekends, age restrictions
may apply, 30 day cancellation notice-fee imposed, package plans. **Amenities:** CD players, safes, hair dryers. **Pool(s):** heated
outdoor. **Leisure Activities:** sauna, whirlpools, exercise room, spa. **Guest Services:** area transportation (fee). **Business
Services:** meeting rooms. **Cards:** AX, DC, MC, VI.

SOME UNITS

LANTERN INN & SUITES   **Phone:** 905/885-2449
All Year   1P: $125-$165   2P: $125-$165   XP: $20   F14
Location: Jct Walton St; downtown. 2 Mill St L1A 2S5. Fax: 905/885-5355. **Facility:** Located close to the theatre
Historic   and antique shops, this little hotel is a part of, yet removed from, the hustle and bustle of this quaint little
Small-scale Hotel town. Smoke free premises. 16 units. 12 one- and two-bedroom standard units, some with kitchens. 1
                  one-bedroom suite with kitchen. 3 stories, interior corridors. **Parking:** on-site. **Terms:** office hours 5 am-1
am. **Amenities:** high-speed Internet, voice mail, hair dryers. **Dining:** The Left Bank Bistro & Bar, see separate listing.
Cards: AX, MC, VI.

SOME UNITS

————— WHERE TO DINE —————

THE LEFT BANK BISTRO & BAR   **Lunch:** $8-$12   **Dinner:** $10-$30   **Phone:** 905/885-0995
Location: Jct Walton St; downtown; in Lantern Inn & Suites. 1 Walton St L1A 1M8. **Hours:** 11 am-10 pm, Sun-2:30
pm. Closed: 1/1, 12/25; also Mon. **Reservations:** accepted. **Features:** Located riverside, with a patio in
French   season, this comfortable bistro has a warm and casual atmosphere. Whether dining in the main dining room
                  with its exposed brick wall and fireplace or in the more lively bar area, the menu offers options for varied
tastes. Casual dress; cocktails. **Parking:** street. **Cards:** AX, MC, VI.

THE PALM   **Lunch:** $9-$13   **Dinner:** $15-$29   **Phone:** 905/885-8686
Location: Jct Augusta, just s of Hwy 2; in Dr. Corbett's Inn. 86 John St L1A 2Z2. **Hours:** 11:30 am-11 pm, Fri & Sat-
midnight, Sun-9 pm. Closed: 12/25. **Reservations:** accepted. **Features:** At this great place to eat, guests
Continental   can sip martinis at the bar or relax with a juicy steak while enjoying piped-in big band music. Daily offerings
                  include lobster, filet mignon and carpaccio, as well as varied Italian dishes. Skillet-roasted imported mussels
are a popular item. Desserts should not be missed. Casual dress; cocktails. **Parking:** on-site. **Cards:** AX, DC, MC, VI.
Historic

PORT PERRY pop. 7,244

————— WHERE TO DINE —————

WATERS EDGE RESTAURANT   **Lunch:** $6-$12   **Dinner:** $6-$12   **Phone:** 905/985-4888
Location: Jct Hwy 7A and Island Rd, 8 km n. 21777 Island Rd L9L 1B6. **Hours:** 6-10:30 am, 11-4:30 & 5-10:30
pm. **Reservations:** not accepted. **Features:** Located in the Great Blue Heron Charitable Casino & Bingo,
Canadian   this restaurant sports large, open spaces similar to its rural setting. Salad, sandwiches, fish and chips, ribs,
                  burgers and pasta dominate the menu as well as a selection of dessert. Lunch and dinner buffet. Casual
dress. **Parking:** on-site. **Cards:** MC, VI.

PORT SEVERN

————— WHERE TO STAY —————

THE INN AT CHRISTIE'S MILL   **Phone:** (705)538-2354
6/1-8/31   1P: $80-$95   2P: $85-$110   XP: $10   F5
5/1-5/31 & 9/1-4/30   1P: $45-$55   2P: $54-$65   XP: $5   F5
Small-scale Hotel **Location:** Hwy 400, exit 156, follow signs 1 km s. Located on waterside. 263 Port Severn Rd N L0K 1S0 (Box 125).
                  Fax: 705/538-1836. **Facility:** Smoke free premises. 45 units. 44 one-bedroom standard units. 1 three-
bedroom suite with kitchen. 2 stories, interior/exterior corridors. **Parking:** on-site. **Terms:** check-in 4 pm, weekly rates available.
Amenities: voice mail, hair dryers. *Some:* DVD players, high-speed Internet. **Dining:** Twigs, see separate listing. **Pool(s):** small
heated indoor. **Leisure Activities:** sauna, whirlpools, canoeing, paddleboats, boat dock, tennis court, exercise room, spa.
Guest Services: valet laundry. **Business Services:** meeting rooms. **Cards:** AX, DC, MC, VI.

SOME UNITS

————— WHERE TO DINE —————

TWIGS   **Lunch:** $8-$20   **Dinner:** $16-$30   **Phone:** 705/538-2354

Location: Hwy 400, exit 156, follow signs 1 km s; in The Inn at Christie's Mill. 263 Port Severn Rd N L0K 1S0.
Hours: 8 am-10, noon-3 & 5-9 pm. Closed: 12/25. **Reservations:** suggested. **Features:** Fine Continental
cuisine is served in a relaxed country setting marked by wood-beam ceilings and a panoramic view of the
surrounding waterfront. On sunny summer days, guests often favour the attractive outdoor patio, where they
Continental   can order from the same menu and receive the same warm service. Casual dress; cocktails. **Parking:** on-
site. **Cards:** AX, DC, MC, VI.

PORT STANLEY pop. 2,521

──────── WHERE TO STAY ────────

INN ON THE HARBOUR **Phone:** 519/782-7623

▼▼▼▼
6/1-9/30 [CP]	1P: $115-$185	2P: $125-$195	XP: $25	F9
5/1-5/31 & 10/1-10/31 [CP]	1P: $110-$170	2P: $115-$180	XP: $25	F9
11/1-4/30 [CP]	1P: $100-$150	2P: $100-$160	XP: $25	F9

Small-scale Hotel   **Location:** At the foot of Main St. Located on the harbourfront. 202 Main St N5L 1H6. **Fax:** 519/782-7728. **Facility:** Smoke free premises. 12 one-bedroom standard units, some with kitchens and/or whirlpools. 3 stories (no elevator), interior corridors. *Bath:* combo or shower only. **Parking:** on-site. **Terms:** office hours 9 am-7 pm, 5 day cancellation notice-fee imposed, package plans. **Amenities:** hair dryers. **Business Services:** meeting rooms. **Cards:** MC, VI.

SOME UNITS
(ASK) (¶↑✦) (⟨⟩⁺) (✕) (DATA PORT) (🖃) (⌨) / (VCR) (📷) /

KETTLE CREEK INN **Phone:** (519)782-3388

▼▼▼▼
All Year	1P: $115-$185	2P: $145-$215	XP: $15

Country Inn   **Location:** Corner of Main St and Hwy 4; downtown. 216 Joseph St N5L 1C4. **Fax:** 519/782-4747. **Facility:** Country-style decor accents the resort's varied accommodations, and some rooms feature gas fireplaces. Smoke free premises. 15 units. 10 one-bedroom standard units. 5 one-bedroom suites with whirlpools. 2 stories (no elevator), interior/exterior corridors. **Parking:** on-site. **Terms:** office hours 9 am-10 pm, 2 night minimum stay - weekends, 7 day cancellation notice-fee imposed, [MAP] meal plan available, package plans. **Amenities:** irons, hair dryers. **Dining:** dining room, see separate listing. **Leisure Activities:** *Fee:* massage. **Business Services:** meeting rooms. **Cards:** AX, CB, DC, MC, VI.

SOME UNITS
(ASK) (¶↑) (✕) (🖃) (⌨) / (VCR) /

──────── WHERE TO DINE ────────

KETTLE CREEK INN **Lunch:** $7-$12 **Dinner:** $19-$34 **Phone:** 519/782-3388

▼▼▼▼
Canadian   **Location:** Corner of Main St and Hwy 4; downtown; in Kettle Creek Inn. 216 Joseph St N5L 1C4. **Hours:** 11 am-9 pm. Closed: 12/25, 12/26. **Reservations:** suggested, weekends. **Features:** Specialties include perch, venison, steak, chicken and pasta, with emphasis on local produce. The 1930s-style interior features local artwork and many windows, while outside the focus is on the English garden and gazebo. Parking is offered behind the inn. Casual dress; cocktails. **Parking:** on-site. **Cards:** AX, DC, DS, MC, VI.

(¶↑) (✕)

PORT SYDNEY

──────── WHERE TO STAY ────────

THE TRILLIUM RESORT & SPA **Phone:** 705/385-1212

▼▼▼▼
7/1-10/15 [MAP]	2P: $140-$170
5/1-6/30 & 10/16-4/30 [MAP]	2P: $120-$150

Resort Cottage   **Location:** Hwy 11, exit S Mary Lake Rd, 9 km e, follow signs. Located in a quiet rural area. 848 Clearwater Lake Rd (RR 1) P0B 1L0. **Fax:** 705/385-1283. **Facility:** Set in a wooded area on Lake Devine, this resort offers cozy, pine-furnished guest rooms and bi-level chalets with a retreat-like ambience. 18 cottages. 1-2 stories (no elevator), exterior corridors. **Parking:** on-site. **Terms:** office hours 8 am-5 pm, 2 night minimum stay - seasonal and/or weekends, age restrictions may apply, 14 day cancellation notice-fee imposed, package plans, 15% service charge. **Amenities:** video library, hair dryers. **Pool(s):** heated outdoor. **Leisure Activities:** saunas, whirlpools, canoeing, paddleboats, boat dock, fishing, tennis court, cross country skiing, ice skating, bicycles, hiking trails, exercise room, spa. **Business Services:** meeting rooms. **Cards:** AX, MC, VI.

(¶↑) (⌁) (⟲) (✕) (✕) (A/C) (CTV) (VCR) (🖃) (⌨) (⌨)

PRESCOTT pop. 4,228

──────── WHERE TO STAY ────────

DEWAR'S INN ON THE RIVER **Phone:** 613/925-3228

▼▼ ▼▼
6/15-9/15 [ECP]	1P: $66-$90	2P: $66-$90	XP: $8
9/16-4/30 [ECP]	1P: $58-$81	2P: $58-$81	XP: $8
5/1-6/14 [ECP]	1P: $56-$79	2P: $56-$79	XP: $8

Motel   **Location:** Hwy 401, exit 716, 1.5 km s, then 2.7 km w on King St W (Hwy 2). Located by a river. 1649 Hwy 2 K0E 1T0 (RR 1). **Fax:** 613/925-1152. **Facility:** 18 units. 12 one-bedroom standard units, some with efficiencies. 6 cottages. 1 story, exterior corridors. **Parking:** on-site. **Terms:** office hours 7:30 am-10 pm, age restrictions may apply, 30 day cancellation notice-fee imposed. **Amenities:** *Some:* irons. **Leisure Activities:** boat dock. **Cards:** AX, JC, MC, VI.

SOME UNITS
(A/C) (DATA PORT) (🖃) (⌨) / (✕) (VCR) (📷) /

RENFREW pop. 7,942

──────── WHERE TO STAY ────────

THE RENFREW INN *Book at aaa.com* **Phone:** (613)432-8109

(CAA) (SAVE)
5/1-10/15 [ECP]	1P: $109-$124	2P: $114-$129	XP: $5	F12
10/16-4/30 [ECP]	1P: $99-$114	2P: $104-$119	XP: $5	F12

▼▼▼ ▼▼
Small-scale Hotel   **Location:** Hwy 17, exit O'Brien Rd. Located in a quiet rural area. 760 Gibbons Rd K7V 4A2 (PO Box 99). **Fax:** 613/432-9720. **Facility:** 65 one-bedroom standard units. 5 stories, interior corridors. **Parking:** on-site, winter plug-ins. **Terms:** weekly rates available, package plans, pets ($10 extra charge). **Amenities:** *Some:* hair dryers. **Dining:** 7 am-10 pm; hours vary in winter, cocktails. **Pool(s):** heated outdoor. **Leisure Activities:** small playground, exercise room, basketball, volleyball. **Guest Services:** valet laundry. **Business Services:** meeting rooms. **Cards:** AX, MC, VI. **Special Amenities:** free expanded continental breakfast and free newspaper.

SOME UNITS
(S/D) FEE (🛒) (¶↑) (¶) (⌁) (✕) (🐾) (⌨) / (✕) (VCR) FEE (DATA PORT) (🖃) FEE /

THE ROCKY MOUNTAIN HOUSE**Phone: 613/432-5801**
▼▼ All Year 1P: $69-$79 2P: $69-$89
Location: Jct Bruce St. Located in a commercial area. 409 Stewart St N K7V 1Y4. Fax: 613/432-9865. **Facility:** 31
Motel one-bedroom standard units, some with whirlpools. 2 stories (no elevator), exterior corridors. **Parking:** on-
site. **Terms:** office hours 9 am-9 pm, package plans, small pets only (in smoking units). **Amenities:** hair
dryers. **Dining:** restaurant, see separate listing. **Business Services:** meeting rooms. **Cards:** AX, MC, VI.

SOME UNITS

(ASK) (S/D) (🛏) (🍴) (📠) / (✕) (💻) /

────── WHERE TO DINE ──────

THE ROCKY MOUNTAIN HOUSE **Lunch:** $6-$15 **Dinner:** $6-$15 **Phone:** 613/432-5801
▼▼ ▼▼ **Location:** Jct Bruce St. 409 Stewart St N K7V 1Y4. **Hours:** 8 am-9 pm. Closed: 12/25. **Reservations:** accepted.
Features: With tongue in cheek, the restaurant is referred to as Renfrew's only "pine-dining" experience, a
Canadian nod to the warm pine walls and beams that give this place its rustic feel. The varied menu lists sandwiches,
salads, fish, steaks and interesting schnitzels. Service is casual, efficient and friendly. Casual dress;
cocktails. **Parking:** on-site. **Cards:** AX, MC, VI. (✕)

RICHMOND HILL —See Toronto p. 552.

RIVER VALLEY

────── WHERE TO STAY ──────

LAKE OBABIKA LODGE **Phone: 705/561-8409**
Property failed to provide current rates
▼▼▼ ▼▼▼ **Location:** River Valley, follow Hwy 805 (gravel road), then 55 km, follow signs. Located in a quiet secluded area. (PO
Box 1). **Facility:** The lodge has gardens, grand lawns and luxury accommodations in a wilderness setting;
Resort Cottage each cabin has a screened porch and a fireplace or wood stove. 7 cottages. 1-2 stories (no elevator);
exterior corridors. **Parking:** on-site. **Terms:** open 5/21-10/1, office hours 7 am-10 pm. **Amenities:** hair dryers. **Leisure
Activities:** sauna, whirlpool, boating, canoeing, boat dock, waterskiing, fishing, recreation programs, exercise room, basketball,
horseshoes. **Guest Services:** gift shop, tanning facility. **Business Services:** meeting rooms.

SOME UNITS

(🍴) (🍸) (✕) (🅰️) (🐾) (🅯) (📠) (💻) / (VCR) /

ROSEMONT

────── WHERE TO DINE ──────

THE GLOBE RESTAURANT **Lunch:** $11-$18 **Dinner:** $18-$27 **Phone:** 705/435-6981
▼▼▼ **Location:** Centre. Hwy 89 L0N 1R0. **Hours:** noon-2, 2:15-4:30 & 5-9 pm, Fri & Sat-9:30 pm. Closed: Tues.
Reservations: suggested. **Features:** A rural setting complements this former coachstop inn restored to
Canadian 1860 period. Candlelight enhances the experience where contemporary dining and fresh, hearty food is The
Globe's forte. Homemade pie and cobbler are highlights. Afternoon tea is also served. Casual dress;
cocktails. **Parking:** on-site. **Cards:** AX, DC, MC, VI. **Historic** (✕)

ROSSPORT pop. 112

────── WHERE TO STAY ──────

THE WILLOWS INN BED & BREAKFAST **Phone: 807/824-3389**
▼▼ ▼▼ 5/1-11/30 1P: $65-$110 2P: $85-$130 XP: $20 F
Location: Centre. 1 Main St P0T 2R0 (PO Box 21). Fax: 807/824-3492. **Facility:** Smoke free premises. 4 one-
Bed & Breakfast bedroom standard units, some with whirlpools. 2 stories (no elevator), interior corridors. *Bath:* combo or
shower only. **Parking:** on-site, winter plug-ins. **Terms:** open 5/1-11/30, office hours 7:30 am-11 pm, 7 day
cancellation notice-fee imposed, package plans. **Amenities:** video library, hair dryers. *Some:* DVD players. **Guest Services:**
area transportation. **Cards:** AX, MC, VI.

SOME UNITS

(🛏) (✕) (🅰️) (VCR) / (DATA PORT) (🅯) /

ST. AGATHA

────── WHERE TO DINE ──────

ANGIE'S KITCHEN **Lunch:** $5-$14 **Dinner:** $5-$25 **Phone:** 519/747-1700
(CAA) **Location:** Jct Hwy 12 and 19. 1761 Erb's Rd W N0B 2L0. **Hours:** 10 am-8 pm, Sat from 9 am, Sun 9 am-7 pm.
▼▼ ▼▼ Closed major holidays; also Mon. **Features:** There are plenty of hearty and light entrees available in Angie's
large, country dining room. Home-style cooking such as homemade bread, rolled ribs, schnitzel, and fish
Canadian and chips complement lighter lunch items of mix-and-match soup, salad and sandwiches. Dressy casual;
beer & wine only. **Parking:** on-site. **Cards:** MC, VI. (✕)

ST. CATHARINES —See Niagara Falls p. 383.

ST. JACOBS pop. 1,227

──────── WHERE TO STAY ────────

BEST WESTERN ST. JACOBS COUNTRY INN *Book at aaa.com*   Phone: (519)884-9295

(CAA) (SAVE)   All Year [ECP]   1P: $149-$239   2P: $149-$239   XP: $10   F17

▼▼◆▼▼   **Location:** 3 km s on King St to Farmers Market Rd, follow signs. Located next to St. Jacobs Farmers Market and Outlet Mall. 50 Benjamin Rd E N2V 2J9 (50 Benjamin Rd E, WATERLOO). Fax: 519/884-2532. **Facility:** 119 units. 116 one-bedroom standard units, some with whirlpools. 3 one-bedroom suites. 3 stories, interior corridors. *Bath:* **Small-scale Hotel** combo or shower only. **Parking:** on-site. **Amenities:** high-speed Internet, voice mail, irons, hair dryers. **Leisure Activities:** whirlpool, steamroom, exercise room. **Guest Services:** area transportation-local businesses. **Business Services:** meeting rooms. **Cards:** AX, DC, DS, MC, VI. **Special Amenities:** free expanded continental breakfast and free local telephone calls. *(See color ad p 557)*

SOME UNITS

[icons]

──────── *The following lodgings were either not evaluated or did not meet AAA rating requirements but are listed for your information only.* ────────

BENJAMIN'S RESTAURANT & INN   Phone: 519/664-3731

(fyi)   Not evaluated. **Location:** Jct Front St. 17 King St N0B 2N0 (Box 389). Facilities, services, and decor characterize a mid-range property.

JAKOBSTETTEL GUEST HOUSE   Phone: 519/664-2208

(fyi)   Not evaluated. **Location:** Just w of Main St. 16 Isabella St N0B 2N0. Facilities, services, and decor characterize a mid-range property.

──────── WHERE TO DINE ────────

BENJAMIN'S RESTAURANT & INN   **Lunch:** $8-$14   **Dinner:** $17-$30   Phone: 519/664-3731

▼▼◆▼▼   **Location:** Jct Front St. 1431 King St N N0B 2N0. **Hours:** 11:30 am-9 pm. Closed: 1/1, 12/25, 12/26. **Reservations:** suggested. **Features:** Located in a quaint village in the heart of Mennonite country, **Continental** Benjamin's Restaurant and Inn offers diners Continental and regional cuisine with an emphasis on fresh local ingredients. Popular choices include smoked farmers sausage and homemade dutch apple pie. The dining room offers an upscale country charm with its solid wood beams and heavy stucco walls. Outdoor patio dining is also featured in the summer months. Dressy casual; cocktails. **Parking:** on-site. **Cards:** AX, DC, MC, VI.

[icon]

THE STONE CROCK   **Lunch:** $6-$11   **Dinner:** $8-$16   Phone: 519/664-2286

▼▼▼   **Location:** Between Albert and Cedar sts. 1396 King St N N0B 2N0. **Hours:** 7 am-8:30 pm, Sun from 11 am. Closed: 12/25. **Features:** Traditional fare is served in a charming early-Ontario atmosphere. Choose either **Canadian** the well-stocked buffet or a la carte menu, both of which offer hearty portions of home-style cooking. Homemade pie is a specialty. A breakfast buffet is open Saturday 8 am-11 am. Casual dress; cocktails. **Parking:** on-site. **Cards:** AX, DS, MC, VI.

[icon]

ST. MARYS pop. 6,293

──────── WHERE TO STAY ────────

STONE WILLOW INN   Phone: 519/284-4140

(CAA) (SAVE)   5/1-10/31   1P: $99-$189   2P: $99-$189   XP: $15   F12

▼▼◆▼▼   11/1-4/30   1P: $89-$169   2P: $89-$169   XP: $15   F12

Location: Hwy 7, follow CR 9, 3.5 km n; opposite the golf course. 940 Queen St E N4X 1B3 (PO Box 457). Fax: 519/284-4126. **Facility:** The inn, conveniently located for golf excursions, offers spacious guest rooms **Country Inn** warmed by homey, country decor. Smoke free premises. 25 units. 24 one-bedroom standard units, some with whirlpools. 1 one-bedroom suite with whirlpool. 2 stories (no elevator), interior corridors. *Bath:* combo or shower only. **Parking:** on-site. **Terms:** 7 day cancellation notice-fee imposed, package plans. **Amenities:** hair dryers. **Dining:** 7 am-9 pm, cocktails. **Guest Services:** gift shop, valet laundry. **Cards:** AX, DC, MC, VI.

SOME UNITS

[icons]

WESTOVER INN   Phone: (519)284-2977

▼▼◆▼▼   7/1-8/31   1P: $135-$270   2P: $145-$285   XP: $25   F12

   5/1-6/30 & 9/1-10/31   1P: $115-$250   2P: $135-$275   XP: $25   F12

Historic   11/1-4/30   1P: $110-$210   2P: $120-$220   XP: $25   F12

Country Inn **Location:** Jct Queen and Thomas sts. 0.5 km s. 300 Thomas St N4X 1B1 (PO Box 280). Fax: 519/284-4043. **Facility:** Set on 19 acres of manicured grounds and country gardens, this 1867 Victorian mansion offers a variety of accommodations. Smoke free premises. 22 units. 19 one-bedroom standard units, some with whirlpools. 3 one-bedroom suites. 2 stories (no elevator), interior/exterior corridors. **Parking:** on-site, winter plug-ins. **Terms:** office hours 7:30 am-8 pm, cancellation fee imposed, package plans. **Amenities:** video library, hair dryers. *Some:* DVD players. **Dining:** dining room, see separate listing. **Pool(s):** outdoor. **Leisure Activities:** bicycles, hiking trails. **Business Services:** meeting rooms. **Cards:** AX, DC, MC, VI.

SOME UNITS

[icons]

──────── WHERE TO DINE ────────

DAMEN'S   **Lunch:** $7-$11   **Dinner:** $10-$15   Phone: 519/284-3424

▼▼▼   **Location:** Just s of Queen St W. 17 Water St S N4X 1A6. **Hours:** 11 am-9 pm, Sun-7:30 pm. Closed: 12/25, 12/26; also Mon. **Reservations:** suggested. **Features:** Centrally located in the picturesque town, Damen's **Canadian** offers casual country dining at its best. Diners can select from the a la carte menu or a daily lunch and supper buffet. The food is wholesome, with home-style cooking featured. Cocktails. **Parking:** on-site. **Cards:** AX, MC, VI.

[icon]

WESTOVER INN   Lunch: $7-$14   Dinner: $19-$39   Phone: 519/284-2977
Location: Jct Queen and Thomas sts, 0.5 km s; in Westover Inn. 300 Thomas St N4X 1B1. Hours: 7:30-10:30 am,
11:30-2 & 5-10 pm; last seating 8:30 pm. Closed: 12/24, 12/25, 12/26; also for dinner 1/1.
Continental   Reservations: suggested. Features: Located in a quaint town, the dining room is at the main house of the
historical inn. Built in 1867 as a Victorian mansion, it has since been converted into a first class inn, offering
accommodations and fine dining. The menu offers a fine choice of Continental cuisine with a focus on fresh ingredients. Diners
can choose from a prix fixe or a la carte menu with specialties such as rack of lamb in a rich Gorgonzola sauce, and homemade
chocolate truffles. Dressy casual; cocktails. Parking: on-site. Cards: AX, DC, MC, VI.

ST. THOMAS pop. 33,236

——— WHERE TO STAY ———

CARDINAL COURT MOTEL   Phone: 519/633-0740
(CAA) (SAVE)   All Year   1P: $60-$69   2P: $70-$79   XP: $6
Location: On Hwy 4, 6.5 km s of jct Hwy 4 and 401, exit 177A. 10401 Sunset Rd, RR 7 N5P 3T2. Fax: 519/633-9616.
Facility: 14 one-bedroom standard units. 1 story, exterior corridors. Bath: combo or shower only. Parking:
Motel   on-site, winter plug-ins. Terms: office hours 8 am-11 pm, 3 day cancellation notice, [CP] meal plan
available. Cards: MC, VI. Special Amenities: free continental breakfast.

COMFORT INN   *Book at aaa.com*   Phone: (519)633-4082
(CAA) (SAVE)   5/1-10/31   1P: $85-$100   2P: $85-$105   XP: $10   F3
11/1-4/30   1P: $80-$95   2P: $80-$100   XP: $10   F3
Location: 6.5 km e on Hwy 3. 100 Centennial Ave N5R 5B2. Fax: 519/633-8294. Facility: 79 one-bedroom
standard units, some with whirlpools. 2 stories (no elevator), interior corridors. Parking: on-site, winter plug-
Small-scale Hotel   ins. Terms: cancellation fee imposed, weekly rates available, small pets only ($10 extra charge). Leisure
Activities: exercise room. Guest Services: valet laundry. Business Services: meeting rooms. Cards: AX,
DC, DS, MC, VI.

SARNIA pop. 70,876

——— WHERE TO STAY ———

BEST WESTERN GUILDWOOD INN   *Book at aaa.com*   Phone: (519)337-7577
(CAA) (SAVE)   All Year   1P: $125-$141   2P: $125-$141
Location: 1 km e of Bluewater Bridge. 1400 Venetian Blvd N7T 7W6. Fax: 519/332-3925. Facility: 95 units. 86
one-bedroom standard units, some with whirlpools. 9 one-bedroom suites ($189-$219), some with
whirlpools. 2 stories (no elevator), interior/exterior corridors. Parking: on-site, winter plug-ins.
Small-scale Hotel   Terms: package plans. Amenities: video games (fee), irons, hair dryers. Dining: 6:30 am-9 pm, Sat & Sun
from 7 am, cocktails. Pool(s): outdoor. Guest Services: valet laundry, area transportation-Hiawatha
Racetrack/Slots & Point Edward Charity Casino. Business Services: conference facilities. Cards: AX, DC, DS, MC, VI.
Special Amenities: free newspaper and free room upgrade (subject to availability with advance reservations).

BLUEWATER MOTEL   Phone: 519/542-5535
(CAA) (SAVE)   All Year   1P: $56-$60   2P: $68-$76   XP: $8   D12
Location: Hwy 402, exit Airport Rd S, 2 km w on CR 22. 1626 London Rd N7T 7H2. Fax: 519/542-2756. Facility: 26
units. 25 one- and 1 two-bedroom standard units, some with efficiencies or kitchens. 1 story, exterior
corridors. Bath: combo or shower only. Parking: on-site, winter plug-ins. Terms: cancellation fee imposed,
Motel   weekly rates available, package plans. Amenities: hair dryers. Pool(s): outdoor. Cards: AX, MC, VI.
Special Amenities: free local telephone calls.

COMFORT INN   *Book at aaa.com*   Phone: 519/383-6767
All Year   1P: $112-$122
Location: Jct Church St. 815 Mara St N7V 1X4 (751 N Christina St, N7V 1X5). Fax: 519/383-8710. Facility: 100
one-bedroom standard units, some with whirlpools. 3 stories, interior corridors. Parking: on-site, winter
Small-scale Hotel   plug-ins. Terms: check-in 4 pm, package plans. Amenities: irons, hair dryers. Leisure Activities: exercise
room. Guest Services: valet laundry. Business Services: meeting rooms. Cards: AX, DC, DS, MC, VI.

HOLIDAY INN SARNIA   *Book at aaa.com*   Phone: 519/336-4130
7/1-9/30   1P: $110-$195   2P: $110-$195
10/1-4/30   1P: $110-$150   2P: $110-$150
5/1-6/30   1P: $105-$145   2P: $105-$145
Small-scale Hotel   Location: E of Bluewater Bridge. 1498 Venetian Blvd N7T 7W6. Fax: 519/332-3326. Facility: 151 one-bedroom
standard units. 2 stories (no elevator), interior corridors. Parking: on-site, winter plug-ins. Terms: package plans, small pets
only ($25 fee). Amenities: video games, high-speed Internet, voice mail, irons, hair dryers. Pool(s): heated outdoor, heated
indoor. Leisure Activities: sauna, whirlpool, playground, exercise room. Fee: golf-9 holes. Guest Services: valet and coin
laundry, area transportation. Business Services: conference facilities. Cards: AX, DC, DS, MC, VI.
(See color ad card insert)

VILLAGE INN **Book at aaa.com** Phone: (519)344-1157
▼▼▼ All Year 1P: $150-$170
Location: Jct Hwy 402. 751 N Christina St N7V 1X5. Fax: 519/344-5561. **Facility:** 48 units. 46 one-bedroom
Small-scale Hotel standard units, some with whirlpools. 2 one-bedroom suites ($300-$325) with whirlpools. 2 stories (no
elevator), interior corridors. **Parking:** on-site. **Terms:** package plans. **Amenities:** voice mail, irons, hair
dryers. **Leisure Activities:** exercise room. **Guest Services:** valet laundry. **Business Services:** meeting rooms. **Cards:** AX, DC,
DS, MC, VI.

SOME UNITS

(ASK) (S.D) (🍴) (Y) (🐾) (DATA PORT) (💻) / (X) (📠) /
FEE

──────── WHERE TO DINE ────────

BOATHOUSE RESTAURANT **Lunch:** $7-$14 **Dinner:** $10-$25 Phone: 519/383-7770
▼▼▼ ▼▼ Location: In Port Edward Charity Casino. 2000 Venetian Blvd N7T 8G4. **Hours:** 11 am-midnight, Thurs-Sat 24
hours. **Features:** The popular spot offers diners a peaceful break from the active gaming area. Scenic
American panoramas of the lovely waterfront are offered from large windows. The menu has items to suit all taste
buds, from burgers and salads to fajitas, sizzling steaks and pasta entrees. Daily specials provide great
value. Casual dress; cocktails. **Parking:** on-site. **Cards:** AX, MC, VI.
(X)

THE BRIGANTINE RESTAURANT **Lunch:** $7-$12 **Dinner:** $15-$19 Phone: 519/542-5553
▼▼▼ ▼▼ Location: Hwy 402, exit Airport Rd S, 1.5 km w on Hwy 7. 1717 London Rd N7T 7H2. **Hours:** 11 am-2 & 5-10 pm,
Sat from 4 pm, Sun 4 pm-9 pm. Closed major holidays. **Reservations:** suggested. **Features:** Brick and
Steak & Seafood textured stucco walls, wood-beam ceilings, cozy fireplace and nautical accents give diners a relaxed,
comfortable feeling. Good menu variety with light luncheon features and extensive dinner selections with a
focus on seafood are also a plus. Dressy casual; cocktails. **Parking:** on-site. **Cards:** AX, DC, MC, VI.
(X)

ON THE FRONT RESTAURANT AND LOUNGE **Lunch:** $7-$11 **Dinner:** $18-$30 Phone: 519/332-4455
▼▼▼ Location: Jct Exmouth St; top of Nova Building. 201 N Front St (14th Floor) N7T 7T9. **Hours:** 11:30 am-3 & 5-close,
Sat & Sun from 5 pm. Closed major holidays. **Reservations:** suggested. **Features:** This restaurant offers
spectacular views of the waterfront area from its large panoramic windows. Dim lighting and modern decor
Continental set the tone for the cozy lounge or upscale dining room featuring an open concept kitchen where diners can
watch the chefs at work. The menu is innovative featuring selections such as leg of lamb, pork loin, a variety of steaks and
seafood options. A good wine list is also offered. Casual dress; cocktails. **Parking:** on-site and street. **Cards:** AX, DC, DS,
MC, VI.
(Y) (X)

RIZZO'S RESTAURANT **Lunch:** $5-$10 **Dinner:** $7-$18 Phone: 519/337-7944
▼▼ Location: Jct Exmouth. 563 N Front St N7T 7N8. **Hours:** 11 am-9 pm, Fri & Sat-10 pm, Sun 10 am-9 pm.
Closed: 12/25. **Features:** The locals frequent this simple, large dining room, in which a menu of finger
American foods, casual fare and full meals is served, along with changing daily specials. Wholesome dishes are
presented in hearty portions. Casual dress; cocktails. **Parking:** on-site. **Cards:** AX, MC, VI.
(X)

SHELDRAKES RESTAURANT **Lunch:** $7-$13 **Dinner:** $15-$29 Phone: 519/344-1640
▼▼▼ Location: Between Lochiel St and George. 216 N Front St N7T 6A4. **Hours:** 11:30 am-10 pm. Closed: 1/1, 12/24,
12/25, 12/26; also Sun. **Reservations:** suggested. **Features:** Enhancing the cozy restaurant's
Continental Mediterranean theme are heavy stucco walls, candlelit tables and European artwork. The menu
incorporates an innovative selection of fare, including rack of lamb, fresh fish, pork loin and grilled chicken.
Rich, creamy and decadent bacon soup is a tasty starter, making it hard to save room for dessert. Dressy casual; cocktails.
Parking: on-site. **Cards:** AX, MC, VI.
(X)

SICILY RESTAURANT & PIZZERIA **Dinner:** $11-$20 Phone: 519/542-7782
▼▼▼ ▼▼ Location: Hwy 402, exit 6, 0.5 km s to Hwy 7, 1.8 km e. 1754 London Rd (Golden Mile) N7W 1A1. **Hours:** 4 pm-11
pm. Closed major holidays; also Sun. **Reservations:** suggested. **Features:** Modern, tastefully appointed
Italian dining room with relaxed atmosphere. Festive Italian background music sets the tone. Good menu selection
featuring generous portions. Highlights include an extensive pasta selection, pizza, beef, veal and poultry.
Wholesome home-style cooking. Cocktails. **Parking:** on-site. **Cards:** AX, DC, MC, VI.
(X)

WAGGS STEAK AND SEAFOOD **Lunch:** $7-$9 **Dinner:** $13-$27 Phone: 519/344-4422
▼▼▼ ▼▼ Location: Between Exmouth and London Rd. 420 Christina St N N7T 5W1. **Hours:** 11 am-9:30 pm, Sat 4 pm-10
pm, Sun 4 pm-9 pm. Closed major holidays. **Reservations:** suggested. **Features:** The attractive dining
Steak & Seafood room is a cozy spot in which friendly servers deliver selections from a menu that includes hearty portions of
steak, seafood, prime rib and stir-fry. Save room for the elegantly presented desserts. A senior menu is
offered only from 4 pm to 6 pm. Casual dress; cocktails. **Parking:** on-site. **Cards:** AX, DC, MC, VI.
(Y) (X)

SAUBLE BEACH

──────── WHERE TO STAY ────────

LAKEVIEW MOTEL Phone: 519-422-1501
▼▼ ▼▼ 7/1-8/31 2P: $130-$150 XP: $20 F12
5/1-6/30 & 9/1-10/31 2P: $65-$95 XP: $10 F12
Motel Location: Just e of jct Hwy 21. 625 Main St N0H 2G0. **Facility:** 15 units. 11 one-bedroom standard units. 4 two-
bedroom suites with kitchens. 1 story, exterior corridors. **Parking:** on-site. **Terms:** open 5/1-10/31, 2 night
minimum stay - weekends, 3 day cancellation notice-fee imposed, weekly rates available. **Pool(s):** heated outdoor. **Leisure
Activities:** playground, horseshoes. **Cards:** MC, VI.

SOME UNITS

(🍴) (🏊) (X) (🎦) (🐾) (🚲) (📠) / (🖥) (💻) /

SAULT STE. MARIE pop. 74,566

------ WHERE TO STAY ------

ADAMS MOTEL   **Phone:** 705/254-4345

All Year   1P: $59-$99   2P: $59-$99

Location: 4.4 km n on Hwy 17B. Located adjacent to a miniature golf centre. 647 Great Northern Rd P6B 5A1.

Motel   **Fax:** 705/942-4116. **Facility:** 29 units. 27 one- and 1 two-bedroom standard units, some with efficiencies or kitchens. 1 two-bedroom suite ($69-$149). 1 story, exterior corridors. **Parking:** on-site, winter plug-ins.

Terms: office hours 8 am-midnight, cancellation fee imposed, weekly rates available, package plans. **Leisure Activities:** snowmobiling. **Cards:** AX, MC, VI.

SOME UNITS

    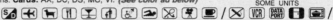

ALGOMA'S WATER TOWER INN   *Book at aaa.com*   **Phone:** (705)949-8111

	9/16-10/16	1P: $149-$179	2P: $149-$179	XP: $10	F18
	5/1-9/15	1P: $129-$169	2P: $129-$169	XP: $10	F18
	10/17-4/30	1P: $119-$169	2P: $119-$169	XP: $10	F18

Small-scale Hotel
Location: Jct Hwy 17 and Second Line. Located in a commercial area. 360 Great Northern Rd P6B 4Z7 (PO Box 787, P6A 5N3). **Fax:** 705/949-1912. **Facility:** 180 units. 177 one-bedroom standard units, some with whirlpools. 3 one-bedroom suites with whirlpools. 5 stories, interior corridors. *Bath:* combo or shower only. **Parking:** on-site, winter plug-ins. **Terms:** package plans. **Amenities:** video games (fee), hair dryers. *Some:* irons. *Fee:* high-speed Internet. **Dining:** Lone Star Texas Grill and Bar, see separate listing. **Pool(s):** heated indoor, wading. **Leisure Activities:** sauna, whirlpools, exercise room, spa. *Fee:* game room. **Guest Services:** gift shop, valet laundry, area transportation-downtown. **Business Services:** meeting rooms. **Cards:** AX, DC, DS, MC, VI. *(See color ad below)*

SOME UNITS

FEE   FEE   FEE

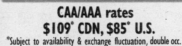

Algoma's
WATER TOWER
~ INN ~

CAA/AAA rates
$109* CDN, $85* U.S.
*Subject to availability & exchange fluctuation, double occ.

ADVENTURES FROM THE INN AND AROUND ALGOMA

We are your **Trailhead** for your multi-day adventures as you explore the Algoma Region of the Great Lakes Heritage Coast. Our Great Lakes Explorer's Club includes services of our Adventure Host and Partners and loads of Algoma travel information. Get our **Inn-Credible Gift Bag** worth over $75 when you check in for a package.

www.watertowerinn.biz   1-800-461-0800   (705) 949-8111

TOUR
•OF THE LINE•

Travel to the end of steel on a unique rail excursion to Hearst, Ontario. For more info contact the Algoma Central Railway.

1-800-242-9287
www.algomacentralrailway.com

Catalina Motel
TRAIN PACKAGE

For year-round Tour of the Line and winter snowmobile accommodation packages contact:

Catalina Motel
1-800-561-9810
www.touroftheline.com

AMBASSADOR MOTEL Phone: 705/759-6199

7/1-10/16	1P: $69-$79	2P: $79-$99	XP: $5 F10
5/1-6/30	1P: $59-$69	2P: $69-$79	XP: $5 F10
Motel 10/17-4/30	1P: $49-$59	2P: $64-$79	XP: $5 F10

Location: 6.4 km n on Hwy 17. Located in a commercial area. 1275 Great Northern Rd P6A 5K7. Fax: 705/759-8178. **Facility:** 16 one-bedroom standard units. 1 story, exterior corridors. **Parking:** on-site, winter plug-ins. **Terms:** office hours 7 am-midnight, cancellation fee imposed, package plans, pets ($10 fee). **Pool(s):** heated indoor. **Leisure Activities:** sauna, whirlpools, snowmobiling, ice skating, playground, basketball, horseshoes. **Cards:** AX, MC, VI.

SOME UNITS
FEE

BEL-AIR MOTEL Phone: (705)945-7950

(AA) (SAVE) All Year 1P: $48-$89 2P: $59-$99 XP: $5 F5

Motel **Location:** 2 km n on Hwy 17B. Located in a commercial area. 398 Pim St P6B 2V1. Fax: 705/942-9919. **Facility:** 30 one-bedroom standard units, some with kitchens. 2 stories (no elevator), exterior corridors. **Bath:** combo or shower only. **Parking:** on-site, winter plug-ins. **Terms:** office hours 9 am-3 am, cancellation fee imposed, package plans, small pets only ($5 extra charge). **Amenities:** video library. **Guest Services:** coin laundry. **Cards:** AX, CB, DC, JC, MC, VI. **Special Amenities:** early check-in/late check-out.

SOME UNITS
FEE

CATALINA MOTEL Phone: (705)945-9260

9/9-10/10	1P: $108	2P: $108	XP: $11 F12
5/1-9/8 & 10/11-4/30	1P: $88	2P: $88	XP: $9 F12

Motel **Location:** 3.2 km n on Hwy 17B. Located in a commercial area. 259 Great Northern Rd P6B 4Z2. Fax: 705/254-5422. **Facility:** 17 one-bedroom standard units. 1 story, exterior corridors. **Parking:** on-site. **Terms:** office hours 7 am-midnight, cancellation fee imposed, package plans, small pets only ($10 fee). **Amenities:** hair dryers. **Cards:** AX, DS, MC, VI. **Special Amenities:** free local telephone calls and early check-in/late check-out. *(See color ad p 453)*

SOME UNITS
FEE

COMFORT INN *Book at aaa.com* Phone: (705)759-8000

9/8-10/15	1P: $114-$129	2P: $124-$139
6/21-9/7	1P: $99-$119	2P: $109-$129
Small-scale Hotel 10/16-4/30	1P: $86-$101	2P: $96-$111
5/1-6/20	1P: $85-$100	2P: $95-$110

Location: 3.6 km n on Hwy 17B. Located in a commercial area. 333 Great Northern Rd P6B 4Z8. Fax: 705/759-8538. **Facility:** 81 one-bedroom standard units. 2 stories (no elevator), interior/exterior corridors. **Parking:** on-site, winter plug-ins. **Terms:** package plans, 3% service charge. **Amenities:** voice mail, irons, hair dryers. **Leisure Activities:** snowmobiling. **Guest Services:** valet laundry. **Cards:** AX, CB, DC, DS, JC, MC, VI.

SOME UNITS
FEE

1-800-DAYS INN
www.daysinn.ca

triprewards
It's fun to get more.

DAYS INN
SAULT STE. MARIE

Come On Inn... Stay Awhile.

In-room coffee • Free weekday newspaper
Indoor pool, sauna & fitness room • Cellar Tap pub & restaurant
Across the street from the 130-store Station Mall
Ten minute walk to the Charity Casino
Five minute walk to the Agawa Canyon Tour Train

Days Inn - Sault Ste Marie 320 Bay Street
Sault Ste Marie, ON P6A 1X1
www.daysinnsault.com

Tel Toll Free Fax
705 759 8200 888 329 7776 705 942 9500

Email: info@daysinnsault.com

DAYS INN SAULT STE. MARIE *Book at aaa.com* **Phone:** (705)759-8200
(CAA) (SAVE) All Year 1P: $120-$147 2P: $130-$157 XP: $10 F18
Location: Corner of Bruce St. Located opposite Station Shopping Mall. 320 Bay St P6A 1X1. **Fax:** 705/942-9500.
Facility: 115 units. 112 one- and 3 two-bedroom standard units, some with efficiencies. 3 stories, interior corridors. **Parking:** on-site, winter plug-ins. **Terms:** package plans. **Amenities:** video library, hair dryers.
Small-scale Hotel *Some:* irons. *Fee:* video games. **Dining:** 7 am-midnight, cocktails. **Pool(s):** heated indoor. **Leisure Activities:** sauna, exercise room. *Fee:* game room. **Business Services:** meeting rooms. **Cards:** AX, CB, DC, DS, JC, MC, VI. *(See color ad p 454)*

SOME UNITS

GLENVIEW COTTAGES **Phone:** 705/759-3436
All Year 1P: $79-$109 2P: $99-$140 XP: $10 F5
Location: 9.6 km n on Hwy 17. Located in a rural area. 2611 Great Northern Rd P6A 5V4. **Fax:** 705/759-9060.
Cottage **Facility:** 30 cottages. 1 story, exterior corridors. **Parking:** on-site, winter plug-ins. **Terms:** office hours 8 am-11 pm, 5 day cancellation notice, weekly rates available, package plans, small pets only ($5 extra charge, in designated units). **Pool(s):** heated outdoor. **Leisure Activities:** sauna, whirlpool, fishing, cross country skiing, snowmobiling, hiking trails, playground, basketball, horseshoes, volleyball. **Guest Services:** coin laundry. **Business Services:** meeting rooms. **Cards:** AX, DC, DS, MC, VI.

SOME UNITS

HOLIDAY INN SAULT STE. MARIE-WATERFRONT *Book at aaa.com* **Phone:** (705)949-0611
(CAA) (SAVE) 9/16-10/15 1P: $125-$189 2P: $125-$189 XP: $15 F18
5/1-9/15 1P: $119-$169 2P: $119-$169 XP: $15 F18
10/16-4/30 1P: $115-$155 2P: $115-$155 XP: $15 F18
Location: On the waterfront. Located behind Station Mall. 208 St. Marys River Dr P6A 5V4. **Fax:** 705/945-6972.
Small-scale Hotel **Facility:** 195 units. 189 one-bedroom standard units. 6 one-bedroom suites, some with whirlpools. 9 stories, interior corridors. **Parking:** on-site, winter plug-ins. **Terms:** check-in 4 pm, package plans, small pets only (1st floor smoking units). **Amenities:** voice mail, irons, hair dryers. *Some:* high-speed Internet, honor bars. **Dining:** 7 am-10 pm, cocktails. **Pool(s):** heated indoor. **Leisure Activities:** sauna, whirlpool, exercise room. **Guest Services:** gift shop, valet laundry. **Business Services:** conference facilities. **Cards:** AX, DC, DS, MC, VI. *(See color ad card insert)*

SOME UNITS

HOLIDAY MOTEL **Phone:** 705/759-8608
All Year 1P: $49-$64 2P: $49-$74 XP: $4 F12
Location: Jct Hwy 17 and 17B, just e. Located in a commercial area. 435 Trunk Rd P6A 3T1. **Fax:** 705/759-0857.
Motel **Facility:** 29 one-bedroom standard units. 1 story, exterior corridors. *Bath:* combo or shower only. **Parking:** on-site, winter plug-ins. **Terms:** office hours 8 am-midnight, package plans, small pets only. **Cards:** AX, MC, VI.

SOME UNITS

NORTHLANDER MOTEL **Phone:** 705/254-6452
(CAA) (SAVE) 7/1-10/9 1P: $55-$80 2P: $55-$85 XP: $5 F12
5/1-6/30 & 10/10-4/30 1P: $49-$65 2P: $49-$70 XP: $5 F12
Location: 3 km n on Hwy 17B. Located in a commercial area. 243 Great Northern Rd P6B 4Z2. **Fax:** 705/254-4427.
Motel **Facility:** Smoke free premises. 22 units. 20 one- and 2 two-bedroom standard units. 1 story, exterior corridors. **Parking:** on-site, winter plug-ins. **Terms:** office hours 8 am-midnight, package plans. **Cards:** AX, MC, VI. **Special Amenities:** free local telephone calls and early check-in/late check-out.

SOME UNITS

QUALITY INN-BAY FRONT *Book at aaa.com* **Phone:** (705)945-9264
(CAA) (SAVE) 9/9-10/16 1P: $132-$147 2P: $142-$157 XP: $10 F19
6/17-9/8 1P: $126-$141 2P: $136-$151 XP: $10 F19
10/17-4/30 1P: $109-$124 2P: $119-$134 XP: $10 F19
5/1-6/16 1P: $106-$121 2P: $116-$131 XP: $10 F19
Small-scale Hotel **Location:** Opposite Station Mall. Located in a commercial area. 180 Bay St P6A 6S2. **Fax:** 705/945-9766.
Facility: 110 units. 102 one-bedroom standard units, some with whirlpools. 8 one-bedroom suites ($166-$252), some with whirlpools. 7 stories, interior corridors. **Parking:** on-site, winter plug-ins. **Terms:** package plans. **Amenities:** video games (fee), high-speed Internet, voice mail, irons, hair dryers. *Some:* dual phone lines. **Dining:** Gran Festa Ristorante, see separate listing. **Pool(s):** heated indoor. **Leisure Activities:** sauna, whirlpool, exercise room. **Guest Services:** valet laundry. **Business Services:** meeting rooms. **Cards:** AX, CB, DC, DS, MC, VI. **Special Amenities:** free local telephone calls and free newspaper.

SOME UNITS

SATELITE MOTEL **Phone:** 705/759-2897
All Year 1P: $50-$95 2P: $50-$95
Location: 3 km n on Hwy 17B. Located in a commercial/residential area. 248 Great Northern Rd P6B 4Z6.
Motel **Fax:** 705/253-9698. **Facility:** 25 one-bedroom standard units. 1 story, exterior corridors. **Parking:** on-site, winter plug-ins. **Terms:** office hours 9 am-11 pm, cancellation fee imposed, package plans. **Cards:** AX, JC, MC, VI.

SOME UNITS

SLEEP INN   *Book at aaa.com*   **Phone:** (705)253-7533

9/8-10/14	1P: $112	2P: $121	XP: $10 F18
6/15-9/7	1P: $102	2P: $112	XP: $10 F18
5/1-6/14 & 10/15-4/30	1P: $77	2P: $87	XP: $10 F18

Small-scale Hotel   **Location:** Between East and Church sts; downtown. Located in a quiet area. 727 Bay St P6A 6Y3. **Fax:** 705/253-7667. **Facility:** 58 one-bedroom standard units. 2 stories (no elevator), interior corridors. *Bath:* combo or shower only. **Parking:** on-site, winter plug-ins. **Terms:** small pets only (in designated units). **Amenities:** *Some:* high-speed Internet. **Leisure Activities:** sauna, whirlpool, limited exercise equipment. **Guest Services:** valet laundry. **Cards:** AX, DC, DS, MC, VI.

SOME UNITS

SUPER 8   *Book at aaa.com*   **Phone:** (705)254-6441

7/1-10/9	1P: $80-$110	2P: $80-$110	XP: $10 F18
5/1-6/30 & 10/10-4/30	1P: $70-$90	2P: $70-$90	XP: $10 F18

Location: 2 km n on Hwy 17B. Located in a commercial, residential area. 184 Great Northern Rd P6B 4Z3. **Fax:** 705/254-4388. **Facility:** 68 one-bedroom standard units, some with whirlpools. 2 stories (no elevator), Small-scale Hotel interior corridors. **Parking:** on-site, winter plug-ins. **Terms:** package plans. **Amenities:** high-speed Internet, voice mail, hair dryers. *Some:* irons. **Leisure Activities:** exercise room. **Business Services:** meeting rooms. **Cards:** AX, DS, MC, VI.

SOME UNITS

TRAVELODGE   *Book at aaa.com*   **Phone:** (705)759-1400

9/7-10/18 [CP]	1P: $120	2P: $130	XP: $10 F18
6/16-9/6 [CP]	1P: $111	2P: $121	XP: $10 F18
5/1-6/15 & 10/19-4/30 [CP]	1P: $99	2P: $109	XP: $10 F18

Location: Opposite Station Mall. Located in a commercial area. 332 Bay St P6A 1X1. **Fax:** 705/759-1266. Small-scale Hotel **Facility:** 65 one-bedroom standard units, some with whirlpools. 3 stories, interior corridors. **Parking:** on-site, winter plug-ins. **Terms:** check-in 4 pm, package plans, pets (in smoking units). **Amenities:** video library (fee), high-speed Internet, voice mail, irons, hair dryers. *Some:* fax. **Dining:** 6 am-1 am, cocktails. **Leisure Activities:** sauna, exercise room. **Guest Services:** valet laundry. **Business Services:** meeting rooms. **Cards:** AX, CB, MC, VI. **Special Amenities:** free continental breakfast and free local telephone calls.

SOME UNITS

Know *Before* You Go

Travel plans become crystal clear in the pages of AAA TourBooks® or online at **aaa.com**.

Each of the advertisers makes your travel choices easier by featuring photographs, detailed descriptions, toll-free numbers and Web addresses for their hotels, restaurants or attractions.

**Travel with Confidence.
Travel with AAA.**

-------- **WHERE TO DINE** --------

A THYMELY MANNER   **Dinner:** $25-$40   **Phone:** 705/759-3262
▼▼▼▼ **Location:** Between Spring St and Brock. 531 Albert St E P6A 2K3. **Hours:** 5:30 pm-11 pm. Closed major holidays;
also Sun & Mon. **Reservations:** suggested. **Features:** Emphasis is placed on a creative menu of fresh
Continental   ingredients and imaginative presentation of steak, pasta and fish. Some special wines and coffee are also
offered. The same attention to detail is paid to the cozy, intimate, older, home atmosphere. Casual dress;
cocktails. **Parking:** on-site. **Cards:** AX, DC, MC, VI.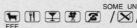

CESIRA'S ITALIAN CUISINE   **Lunch:** $5-$12   **Dinner:** $10-$25   **Phone:** 705/949-0600
▼▼ ▼▼ **Location:** Between Queen and Albert sts. 133 Spring St P6A 3A2. **Hours:** 11 am-2:30 & 5-10 pm, Sat from 5 pm.
Closed major holidays; also Sun. **Reservations:** accepted. **Features:** Homemade, traditional Italian cuisine
Italian   reflects a distinctive blend of tastes whose foundations are based on fresh veal, chicken, beef, seafood and
hand-made pasta. Sauce and pasta recipes were handed down from the owner's grandmother. Casual
dress; cocktails. **Parking:** on-site. **Cards:** AX, DC, MC, VI.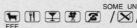

GIOVANNI'S FAMILY RESTAURANT   **Lunch:** $4-$8   **Dinner:** $10-$20   **Phone:** 705/942-3050
▼▼ ▼▼ **Location:** Hwy 17 N, 0.4 km n of jct Hwy 17, 17B and 550. 516 Great Northern Rd P6B 4Z9. **Hours:** 11:30 am-11
pm. Closed: 1/1, 12/25. **Reservations:** suggested. **Features:** One tasty recommendation is the veal
Italian   Marsala with mushrooms, peppers and onions over fresh angel hair pasta. For dessert, an excellent choice
is a slice of cheesecake with strawberries and whipped cream. The ambience is warm, cozy and subdued.
Casual dress; cocktails. **Parking:** on-site. **Cards:** AX, MC, VI.

GRAN FESTA RISTORANTE   **Lunch:** $6-$9   **Dinner:** $11-$20   **Phone:** 705/945-9322
▼▼▼▼ **Location:** Opposite Station Mall; in Quality Inn-Bay Front. 180 Bay St P6A 6S2. **Hours:** 6:30 am-11 pm. Closed:
12/24, 12/25. **Reservations:** accepted. **Features:** Restaurant hallmarks include a comfortable atmosphere
Italian   and a varied menu of pasta, pizza, chicken, veal, fish and steak. Prime rib is a popular choice. Service is
attentive. Casual dress; cocktails. **Parking:** on-site. **Cards:** AX, DC, MC, VI.

LONE STAR TEXAS GRILL AND BAR   **Lunch:** $6-$10   **Dinner:** $10-$25   **Phone:** 705/945-7610
▼▼ ▼▼ **Location:** Jct Hwy 17 and Second Line; in Algoma's Water Tower Inn. 360 Great Northern Rd P6B 4Z7. **Hours:** 6:30
am-10 pm. **Features:** For a fun, casual atmosphere and some Tex-Mex menu options, diners need look no
American   further. Quesadillas, fajitas, tacos, catfish, chicken, ribs, pasta and steak all are available. Casual dress;
cocktails. **Parking:** on-site. **Cards:** AX, DC, DS, MC, VI.

NEW GOLDEN DRAGON RESTAURANT   **Lunch:** $5-$7   **Dinner:** $8-$18   **Phone:** 705/949-3276
▼▼ **Location:** Jct Hwy 17 N and Northern Ave E; northwest corner of strip mall. 264 Great Northern Rd E P6B 4H6.
Hours: 9 am-11 pm, Fri & Sat-midnight, Sun noon-10 pm. Closed: 12/25, 12/26. **Reservations:** accepted.
Chinese   **Features:** Chinese fare takes centre stage with not only the standards but also combination platters such as
chow mein with chicken, shrimp, beef and vegetables. A menu of Canadian dishes is also offered. A popular
buffet is served 4:30 pm-8:30 pm daily. Casual dress; cocktails. **Parking:** on-site. **Cards:** MC, VI.

PANNA   **Lunch:** $9-$13   **Dinner:** $15-$35   **Phone:** 705/949-8484
▼▼▼▼ **Location:** Jct March St. 472 Queen St E P6A 1Z8. **Hours:** 10 am-10 pm. Closed major holidays; also Sun.
Reservations: accepted. **Features:** The restaurant's young chefs are skilled, creative and ever-capable of
Mediterranean   pleasing even the most discerning palate. Casual dress; cocktails. **Parking:** street. **Cards:** AX, MC, VI.

SEVERN BRIDGE

-------- **WHERE TO DINE** --------

SEVERN RIVER INN   **Lunch:** $6-$11   **Dinner:** $15-$30   **Phone:** 705/689-6333
▼▼ ▼▼ **Location:** Hwy 11, exit Cowbell Ln northbound; exit Southwood Rd southbound, just se. 1002 Cowbell Ln P0E 1N0.
Hours: 11 am-9 pm; hours vary off season. Closed: 12/25, 12/26; also Sun-Thurs in winter.
Canadian   **Reservations:** suggested. **Features:** Located in a 1907 building, the dining room has offerings such as
salads, seafood, chicken, pork, beef, lamb and pasta. Some tables overlook the river; the seasonal patio is
popular. Casual dress; cocktails. **Parking:** on-site and street. **Cards:** MC, VI.

SHARBOT LAKE

-------- **WHERE TO STAY** --------

SHARBOT LAKE COUNTRY INN   **Phone:** 613/279-2198
Property failed to provide current rates
▼▼ ▼▼ **Location:** 3.5 km s of jct Hwy 7. Located on the lake. 14152 Hwy 38 K0H 2P0 (PO Box 255). **Fax:** 613/279-2589.
Facility: 10 one-bedroom standard units. 1 story, exterior corridors. **Parking:** on-site, winter plug-ins.
Motel   **Terms:** office hours 8 am-8 pm, pets ($10 extra charge, with prior approval). **Leisure Activities:** boat dock.
Business Services: meeting rooms, fax (fee).

SOME UNITS
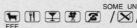
FEE

SIMCOE pop. 14,175

———— WHERE TO STAY ————

COMFORT INN
Book at aaa.com　　　　　　　　　　　　　　　　　　　　**Phone:** (519)426-2611
All Year　　　　　　　　1P: $76-$140　　　2P: $86-$150　　　XP: $4　　　　F18
Location: 0.5 km e on Hwy 3. 85 Queensway E N3Y 4M5. **Fax:** 519/426-0053. **Facility:** 61 one-bedroom
Small-scale Hotel　standard units. 2 stories (no elevator), interior corridors. **Parking:** on-site, winter plug-ins. **Terms:** [ECP]
meal plan available, package plans, small pets only (on ground floor). **Amenities:** hair dryers. *Some:* irons.
Guest Services: valet laundry. **Cards:** AX, CB, DC, DS, JC, MC, VI.

TRAVELODGE SIMCOE　*Book at aaa.com*　　　　　　　　　　　**Phone:** (519)426-4751
All Year　　　　　　　　1P: $105　　　　　2P: $110　　　　　XP: $5　　　　F9
Location: 1 km w. 385 Queensway W (Hwy 3) N3Y 2M9. **Fax:** 519/426-2222. **Facility:** 60 one-bedroom standard
Small-scale Hotel　units, some with efficiencies and/or whirlpools. 2 stories (no elevator), interior/exterior corridors. **Parking:**
on-site. **Terms:** [ECP] meal plan available, package plans, pets ($10 extra charge). **Amenities:** voice mail.
Some: hair dryers. **Pool(s):** heated indoor. **Leisure Activities:** sauna, whirlpool, steamroom, 2 tennis courts, racquetball courts,
playground. **Guest Services:** valet and coin laundry. **Business Services:** meeting rooms. **Cards:** AX, DC, JC, MC, VI.

———— WHERE TO DINE ————

THE BLUE ELEPHANT PUB AND RESTAURANT　　**Dinner:** $10-$25　　　　**Phone:** 519/428-2886
Location: Between Victoria and Water sts. 96 Norfolk St S N3Y 2W2. **Hours:** 5 pm-9 pm. Closed major holidays;
Thai　also Sun. **Reservations:** suggested. **Features:** Patrons of the upscale restaurant dine in the rooms of a fine
old home. Among eclectic dishes are traditional Thai preparations and entrees influenced by the southern
United States. Dishes range from fish and pasta to red meat and poultry. Casual dress; cocktails. **Parking:**
on-site. **Cards:** AX, MC, VI.

CHRISTIEN'S　　　　　　**Lunch:** $5-$11　　　　**Dinner:** $8-$20　　　　**Phone:** 519/426-1769
Location: Corner of West and Talbot sts; in Simcoe Town Centre Mall. 150 West St N3Y 5C1. **Hours:** 11:30 am-9
American　pm, Fri-10 pm. Closed: 7/1, 9/5, 12/25. **Features:** Families will enjoy this casual dining facility that
specializes in chicken and ribs. A central fireplace and rough-cut pine walls create a pleasant atmosphere.
Casual dress; cocktails. **Parking:** on-site. **Cards:** AX, MC, VI.

DALLAS STEAKHOUSE　　　**Lunch:** $5-$8　　　　**Dinner:** $9-$22　　　　**Phone:** 519/426-2696
Location: Just w of Hwy 24. 50 Queensway W (Hwy 3) N3Y 4K8. **Hours:** 11 am-11 pm, Sat from 4 pm, Sun 11
Steak House　am-10 pm. **Reservations:** suggested. **Features:** The Texan saloon-style decor with wood floors, polished
wood tables, booths and Western-style bar is the perfect setting for hearty portions of Tex-Mex. The menu
includes steak, chicken, ribs and munchies, as well as Southwestern choices such as fajitas. Casual dress;
cocktails. **Parking:** on-site. **Cards:** AX, MC, VI.

SIOUX LOOKOUT pop. 5,336

———— WHERE TO STAY ————

BEST WESTERN SIOUX LOOKOUT INN　　　　　　　　　　　**Phone:** 807/737-4444
[fyi]　3/1-4/30　　　　　　　1P: $120-$140　　2P: $120-$140　　XP: $10　　　F12
5/1-2/28　　　　　　　1P: $100-$120　　2P: $100-$120　　XP: $10　　　F12
Small-scale Hotel　Too new to rate. **Location:** N on Hwy 72. 2 Sturgeon River Rd P8T 1C5 (PO Box 5000). **Fax:** 807/737-4498.
Amenities: 59 units, coffeemakers, refrigerators, pool. **Cards:** AX, CB, DC, MC, VI.

SMITHS FALLS pop. 9,140

———— WHERE TO STAY ————

BEST WESTERN COLONEL BY INN　*Book at aaa.com*　　　　　　**Phone:** 613/284-0001
5/1-10/31 & 4/1-4/30　　1P: $79-$99　　　2P: $87-$115　　XP: $8　　　　F12
11/1-3/31　　　　　　　1P: $69-$89　　　2P: $77-$105　　XP: $8　　　　F12
Small-scale Hotel　**Location:** 1.2 km s on Hwy 15. Located in a commercial area. 88 Lombard St K7A 4G5. **Fax:** 613/284-0694.
Facility: 40 one-bedroom standard units, some with whirlpools. 2 stories (no elevator), interior/exterior
corridors. **Parking:** on-site. **Terms:** cancellation fee imposed, pets ($10 extra charge, in designated areas). **Amenities:** irons,
hair dryers. **Pool(s):** heated outdoor. **Guest Services:** valet laundry. **Business Services:** meeting rooms. **Cards:** AX, CB, DC,
DS, JC, MC, VI.

COMFORT INN　　　*Book at aaa.com*　　　　　　　　　　　**Phone:** (613)283-5150
5/1-10/31　　　　　　　1P: $89-$129　　　2P: $99-$139　　XP: $10　　　F13
11/1-4/30　　　　　　　1P: $69-$109　　　2P: $79-$119　　XP: $10　　　F13
Location: Jct Hwy 15 and 29, just ne. Located adjacent to downtown and opposite Rideau Canal Lock. 33 Centre St
K7A 3B8. **Fax:** 613/283-5000. **Facility:** 64 units. 62 one- and 2 two-bedroom standard units. 5 stories, interior
Small-scale Hotel　corridors. **Parking:** on-site. **Terms:** cancellation fee imposed. **Amenities:** voice mail. **Business Services:**
newspaper.　meeting rooms. **Cards:** AX, CB, DC, DS, MC, VI. **Special Amenities:** free local telephone calls and free

ROGER'S MOTEL   Phone: 613/283-5200

All Year   1P: $50-$75   2P: $55-$85   XP: $8   F

Location: 1.6 km s on Hwy 15. Located in a commercial area. 178 Lombard St K7A 5B8. Fax: 613/283-5200.

Motel   **Facility:** 16 one-bedroom standard units, some with whirlpools. 1 story, exterior corridors. **Parking:** on-site, winter plug-ins. **Terms:** office hours 7 am-11 pm, cancellation fee imposed, small pets only ($10 extra charge). **Amenities:** hair dryers. **Cards:** AX, MC, VI.

SOME UNITS

ASK SD 🛏 🐕 DATA PORT 🖥 / ✕ VCR /
FEE

──────── **WHERE TO DINE** ────────

ROB ROY'S PUB   **Lunch:** $8-$10   **Dinner:** $8-$10   Phone: 613/283-9093

Location: Jct Chambers St; centre. 32 Beckwith St S K7A 2A8. **Hours:** 11 am-11 pm, Sun noon-9 pm. Closed: 1/1, 12/25. **Features:** Small and friendly, this pub is a local favourite. Known for their fish and chips, they

British   also serve shepherd's pie, steak and kidney pie, bangers and mash, soups and salads. There is a fireplace in the rear dining area and a patio in season. Casual dress; cocktails. **Parking:** street. **Cards:** AX, CB, DC, MC, VI.

🍽

SOUTHAMPTON pop. 3,360

──────── **WHERE TO STAY** ────────

SOLOMON KNECHTEL HOUSE BED & BREAKFAST   Phone: 519/797-2585

All Year [BP]   1P: $95-$130   2P: $95-$130   XP: $20   F3

Location: Hwy 21, exit Morpeth, 1 blk e. 106 Victoria St S N0H 2L0. **Facility:** On a quiet street just three blocks

Historic Bed   from the beach and many unique attractions, this 1897 home is the perfect choice for exploring the area.
& Breakfast   Smoke free premises. 4 one-bedroom standard units. 2 stories (no elevator), interior corridors. *Bath:* combo or shower only. **Parking:** on-site. **Terms:** office hours 9 am-9 pm, check-in 4 pm, 7 day cancellation notice-fee imposed, package plans. **Amenities:** hair dryers. **Cards:** MC, VI.

SOME UNITS

✕ AC ☎ 🖥 / 📺 VCR /

──────── **WHERE TO DINE** ────────

DUFFY'S FAMOUS FISH AND CHIPS   **Lunch:** $6-$10   **Dinner:** $6-$10   Phone: 519/797-5972

Location: Just e of Hwy 21. 151 High St N0H 2L0. **Hours:** Open 5/1-12/31 & 3/1-4/30; 11:30 am-9 pm, Fri & Sat-10 pm; Thurs-Sat to 8 pm, Sun 4 pm-8 pm 3/1-5/31 & 11/1-12/31. **Features:** This place fits the bill for

Seafood   those in the mood for fish and chips. Cod, halibut and Alaskan pollock all are freshly battered to the diner's liking. Fresh whitefish is featured in season. Other tasty favourites are the homemade pies, such as chicken, lamb, steak and kidney and shepherd's. The atmosphere is country cozy, and servers are friendly. Casual dress; cocktails. **Parking:** street. **Cards:** AX, MC, VI.

🍽 ✕

STONEY CREEK

──────── **WHERE TO DINE** ────────

EDGEWATER MANOR   **Lunch:** $15-$20   **Dinner:** $25-$35   Phone: 905/643-9332

Location: QEW, exit Fruitland Rd; 1 blk at lakefront. 518 Fruitland Rd L8E 5A6. **Hours:** noon-2:30 & 5-9 pm, Sat 5 pm-9:30 pm. Closed major holidays; also Sun. **Reservations:** required. **Features:** On the shores of Lake

Continental   Ontario, the hidden gem is set in the midst of a new housing development. The restored mansion has an interesting history and offers a grand setting for a fine Continental meal. Lunch diners enjoy a panoramic view of the lake, and at dinner the elegant mansion features candlelit tables to offset the high ceilings, stone walls and fine floral arrangements. Dressy casual. **Parking:** on-site. **Cards:** AX, DC, MC, VI.

✕

What Does a Perfect Vacation Sound Like?

The non-stop rhythm of a big city? The soft caress of waves on pure white sand?

No matter what vacation sounds best, visit aaa.com before you go.

Get an internet TripTik® and find TourBook® information:

- AAA/CAA Approved hotels and restaurants
- Destination descriptions and attraction information
- Interactive maps
- Complete driving directions

Make travel planning easy with aaa.com.

CLICK! Sounds like the start of a perfect vacation.

**Travel with Confidence.
Travel with AAA/CAA.**

STRATFORD pop. 29,676

———— WHERE TO STAY ————

ARDEN PARK HOTEL Phone: 519/275-2936

	5/30-10/8	1P: $157-$225	2P: $157-$225	XP: $10	F12
	5/1-5/29 & 10/9-11/6	1P: $129-$165	2P: $129-$165	XP: $10	F12
Small-scale Hotel	11/7-4/30	1P: $94-$165	2P: $94-$165	XP: $10	F12

Location: Jct Romeo St. 552 Ontario St N5A 6W4 (PO Box 1040). Fax: 519/275-2938. **Facility:** 138 units. 115 one-bedroom standard units. 23 one-bedroom suites with whirlpools. 4-5 stories, interior corridors. **Parking:** on-site. **Terms:** cancellation fee imposed, small pets only (in smoking units). **Amenities:** Some: high-speed Internet. **Pool(s):** heated indoor. **Leisure Activities:** whirlpool, exercise room. **Guest Services:** valet laundry. **Business Services:** meeting rooms. **Cards:** AX, DC, MC, VI. *(See color ad below)*

SOME UNITS

MAJER'S MOTEL Phone: 519/271-2010

| | 5/1-11/15 [CP] | 1P: $70-$75 | 2P: $84-$98 | XP: $16 | F6 |
| | 11/16-4/30 | 1P: $40-$48 | 2P: $52-$60 | XP: $16 | F6 |

Location: 4 km e on Hwy 7 and 8. 2970 Ontario St E N5A 6S5 (RR 4). Fax: 519/273-7951. **Facility:** Smoke free premises. 31 one-bedroom standard units. 1 story, exterior corridors. **Parking:** on-site, winter plug-ins. **Motel** **Terms:** 2 night minimum stay - weekends, 10 day cancellation notice-fee imposed. **Pool(s):** heated outdoor. **Business Services:** fax (fee). **Cards:** AX, MC, VI. **Special Amenities: free continental breakfast and free local telephone calls.**

STEWART HOUSE INN Phone: (519)271-4576

	7/1-9/5 [BP]	1P: $200-$350	2P: $200-$350	
	5/1-6/30 & 9/6-10/9 [BP]	1P: $175-$300	2P: $175-$300	
Historic Bed	10/10-4/30 [BP]	1P: $125-$225	2P: $125-$225	
& Breakfast				

Location: Just s of Huron. Located in a residential area. 62 John St N N5A 6K7. **Facility:** Silver-tray coffee service, fine china and a living room with an antique player piano set the tone at this elegant 1870s Victorian mansion. Smoke free premises. 5 one-bedroom standard units. 2 stories (no elevator), interior corridors. **Bath:** combo or shower only. **Parking:** on-site. **Terms:** 2 night minimum stay - seasonal and/or weekends, age restrictions may apply, 15 day cancellation notice-fee imposed, package plans. **Amenities:** hair dryers. **Pool(s):** heated outdoor. **Cards:** AX, MC, VI.

STONE MAIDEN INN Phone: 519/271-7129

| | 7/1-9/30 [BP] | 1P: $155-$270 | 2P: $155-$270 | XP: $25 | F3 |
| | 5/1-6/30, 10/1-12/20 & 4/1-4/30 [BP] | 1P: $135-$250 | 2P: $135-$250 | XP: $25 | F3 |

Location: Just s of Ontario St. 123 Church St N5A 2R3. Fax: 519/271-4615. **Facility:** Turndown service, homemade cookies and afternoon tea are some of the extras offered at this restored 1872 Victorian-style mansion. Smoke free premises. 15 one-bedroom standard units, some with whirlpools. 3 stories (no elevator), interior corridors. **Bath:** combo or shower only. **Parking:** on-site. **Terms:** open 5/1-12/20 & 4/1-4/30, office hours 7:30 am-10:30 pm, 2 night minimum stay - seasonal and/or weekends, 15 day cancellation notice-fee imposed. **Amenities:** hair dryers. Some: CD players, irons. **Leisure Activities:** bicycles. **Business Services:** fax. **Cards:** AX, JC, MC, VI.

SOME UNITS

STRATFORD SUBURBAN MOTEL Phone: 519/271-9650

| | 5/1-11/10 | 1P: $79-$99 | 2P: $89-$109 | XP: $15 | |

Location: 4.8 km e on Hwy 7 and 8. 2808 Ontario St E N5A 6S5. Fax: 519/271-0193. **Facility:** Smoke free premises. 25 one-bedroom standard units. 1 story, exterior corridors. **Parking:** on-site. **Terms:** open 5/1-**Motel** 11/10, 5 day cancellation notice-fee imposed, [CP] meal plan available. **Amenities:** voice mail, irons, hair dryers. **Pool(s):** heated outdoor. **Leisure Activities:** tennis court. **Cards:** MC, VI.

SWAN MOTEL Phone: 519/271-6376

| | 5/24-11/13 | 1P: $94-$115 | 2P: $94-$115 | XP: $15 | F5 |
| | 5/1-5/23 | 1P: $85-$105 | 2P: $85-$105 | XP: $15 | F5 |

Location: 2.5 km s of Ontario St; from downtown core. Located in a quiet area. Downie St S N5A 6S3 (RR 2, 3765 **Motel** Perth Rd 112). Fax: 519/271-0682. **Facility:** Smoke free premises. 24 one-bedroom standard units. 1 story, exterior corridors. **Parking:** on-site. **Terms:** open 5/1-11/13, office hours 8 am-10 pm, 10 day cancellation notice-fee imposed. **Amenities:** irons, hair dryers. **Pool(s):** outdoor. **Cards:** MC, VI.

STRATFORD THEATRE ESCAPES

Complete Theatre Packages

1 night *Arden Park Hotel*, dinner, breakfast, theatre ticket, all taxes & tips.
Early Savings pricing from **$239**
(**$169 US**) per person, double occupancy.

Call Theatre Vacations
1-877-356-6385
www.theatrevacations.com

THEATRE
VACATIONS

TOUCHSTONE MANOR   Phone: 519/273-5820

(AAA) (SAVE)   6/1-9/30 [BP]   1P: $255-$330   2P: $255-$330   XP: $50
               5/1-5/31, 10/1-12/20 &
◆◆◆ ◆◆◆   1/20-4/30 [BP]   1P: $155-$205   2P: $155-$205   XP: $50
               Location: 0.5 km w of Erie St. 325 St. David St N5A 1E1. Fax: 519/273-2817. **Facility:** A lovely inn featuring
Bed & Breakfast elegantly appointed public areas and guest rooms; breakfast is served in a formal setting with fine china and
               silverware. Smoke free premises. 4 one-bedroom standard units. 3 stories, interior corridors. *Bath:* combo or
shower only. **Parking:** on-site. **Terms:** open 5/1-12/20 & 1/20-4/30, office hours 8 am-8 pm, age restrictions may apply, 7 day
cancellation notice-fee imposed. **Amenities:** CD players, high-speed Internet, irons, hair dryers. **Cards:** AX, JC, MC, VI.

(X) (W) (Z) (D)

──────── *The following lodging was either not evaluated or did not* ────────
meet AAA rating requirements but is listed for your information only.

FESTIVAL INN   Phone: 519/273-1150
(fyi)   Not evaluated. **Location:** 3 km e on Hwy 7 and 8. 1144 Ontario St N5A 6W1 (PO Box 811). Facilities, services, and
               decor characterize a mid-range property.

──────── **WHERE TO DINE** ────────

BENTLEY'S   **Lunch:** $5-$12   **Dinner:** $8-$18   Phone: 519/271-1121
◆◆ ◆◆   **Location:** Between Downie and Waterloo sts S. 99 Ontario St N5A 3H1. **Hours:** 11:30 am-midnight, Sun & Mon-10
               pm. Closed: 12/25. **Features:** Centrally located downtown, Bentley's features hearty portions of casual fare.
Canadian   Burgers, fish and chips, nachos, wings and pasta are popular favorites. The decor is casual pub style,
               featuring wood floors, cozy booths and a long bar for dining or a beer. Take time to look at the interesting
wall murals on your way out. Casual dress; cocktails. **Parking:** on-site. **Cards:** AX, DC, MC, VI.

(Y) (X)

BIJOU   **Lunch:** $15-$25   **Dinner:** $36-$45   Phone: 519/273-5000
◆◆◆   **Location:** Directly beside Allens Alley. 105 Erie St N5A 2M5. **Hours:** Open 5/1-12/31 & 3/1-4/30; 5 pm-9 pm; also
               Fri-Sun also 11:30 am-1 pm 5/1-10/31. Closed: 12/25; also Mon. **Reservations:** required. **Features:** A
French   bright bistro decor, cozy ambience and abundant market-fresh specials are highlights of the restaurant. The
               daily changing blackboard menu lists fresh local and regional fare. This spot is perfect for a fine meal in a
relaxed, bustling setting. Cocktails. **Parking:** street. **Cards:** AX, MC, VI.

(X)

CARTER'S ON DOWNIE RESTAURANT   **Lunch:** $9-$17   **Dinner:** $27-$38   Phone: 519/271-9200
◆◆◆   **Location:** Directly across from Avon Theatre. 116 Downie St N5A 1X1. **Hours:** Open 5/1-12/31; 11:30 am-1:30 &
               5-close, Sun from 5 pm. Closed: 12/25; also Mon. **Reservations:** suggested. **Features:** The restaurant is a
Continental   popular choice for pre-theatre dining. The cozy dining room sustains an upscale country ambience, with
               wood tables and chairs, fresh flowers and wood accents throughout. In addition to the popular chef's tasting
menu, highlights include mixed greens and chilled and hot soups to start; entrees of pork tenderloin, pan-roasted, grain-fed
chicken and braised halibut; and tempting desserts. Dressy casual; cocktails. **Parking:** street. **Cards:** AX, DC, MC, VI.

(X)

THE CHURCH RESTAURANT   **Lunch:** $13-$25   **Dinner:** $29-$46   Phone: 519/273-3424
◆◆◆ ◆◆◆   **Location:** Corner of Waterloo St. 70 Brunswick St N5A 6V6. **Hours:** Open 5/1-12/31; 11:30 am-1:30 & 5-8:30 pm.
               Closed major holidays; also Mon. **Reservations:** suggested. **Features:** The Church Restaurant is centrally
Continental   located downtown, close to the theatres. The dining room is housed in an elegantly restored church and
               features high cathedral ceilings and stained-glass windows. The menu features prix fixe and a la carte
selections and an extensive wine list to complement the fine Continental cuisine. Staff provides professional, attentive service
and are experts in timing meals for theatre patrons. Dressy casual; cocktails. **Parking:** on-site. **Cards:** AX, DC, MC, VI.

(Y) (X)

FELLINI'S ITALIAN CAFFE' AND GRILL   **Lunch:** $7-$10   **Dinner:** $9-$18   Phone: 519/271-3333
◆◆◆   **Location:** Between Downie and Waterloo sts. 107 Ontario St N5A 3H1. **Hours:** 11 am-8 pm, Fri & Sat-9 pm, Sun
               11:30 am-8 pm. Closed: 12/25. **Features:** The popular, bistro-style eatery sports a bustling atmosphere and
Italian   casual decor. Pasta in thick sauce, soup and a crisp salad make a great meal. Also on the menu are
               gourmet oven-baked pizzas and sandwiches. Although reservations are not accepted, there is a call-ahead
wait list. Casual dress; cocktails. **Parking:** street. **Cards:** MC, VI.

(X)

KEYSTONE ALLEY CAFE   **Lunch:** $7-$11   **Dinner:** $19-$29   Phone: 519/271-5645
◆◆◆   **Location:** Between Downie and Waterloo sts. 34 Brunswick St N5A 3L8. **Hours:** 11:30 am-2 & 5-9 pm, Closed
               major holidays; also Sun & Mon. **Reservations:** suggested. **Features:** The local theatre crowd appreciates
Continental   the casual, relaxed atmosphere and innovative menu featuring a good variety of hot and cold appetizers,
               seafood, beef, lamb and pasta entrees and fabulous desserts. Outdoor patio dining is available in season.
Dressy casual; cocktails. **Parking:** street. **Cards:** AX, DC, MC, VI.

(X)

THE OLD PRUNE   **Lunch:** $8-$20   **Dinner:** $58-$78   Phone: 519/271-5052
◆◆◆   **Location:** Corner of Albert and Nile sts. 151 Albert St N5A 3K5. **Hours:** Open 5/20-10/31; seatings 11:30 am-
               12:30 & 5-8:15 pm, Sun 5 pm-7 pm, Tues 5 pm-8:15 pm. Closed: Mon. **Reservations:** suggested.
Continental   **Features:** Set in a restored Edwardian home close to the theatres, The Old Prune features three
               comfortable rooms for dining. The menu is prix fixe, focusing on fresh ingredients and regional specialties.
Select from starters such as sweet potato ravioli or chicken liver mousse, followed by grain-fed chicken or Ontario squab. The
portions are comfortable so you can enjoy their decadent desserts. Fresh flowers, fine artwork and a lovely garden all add to
the peaceful setting. Dressy casual; cocktails. **Parking:** on-site. **Cards:** AX, MC, VI.

(X)

PAZZO RISTORANTE **Lunch:** $7-$15 **Dinner:** $15-$26 **Phone:** 519/273-6666

▼▼▼▼ **Location:** Jct Downie St. 70 Ontario St N5A 3H2. **Hours:** Open 5/1-11/30; 11:30 am-10 pm. Closed: Mon.
Reservations: suggested. **Features:** Theatregoers and locals alike enjoy the bright, artistic decor and
innovative menu. The chef uses fresh regional ingredients to create starters such as chilled asparagus
Italian soup, warmed goat cheese bruschetta and Caesar salad. Among entree selections are several fresh pasta
dishes, including decadent mushroom gnocchi, as well as fish, chicken and beef options. Blackberry shortcake with sour cream
ice cream is a delightful finish. Cocktails. **Parking:** street. **Cards:** AX, DC, MC, VI.

PAZZO RISTORANTE BAR AND PIZZA **Lunch:** $10-$17 **Dinner:** $13-$29 **Phone:** 519/273-6666

▼▼▼ **Location:** Jct Downie St; basement level below Pazzo Ristorante. 70 Ontario St N5A 3H2. **Hours:** 11:30 am-3 & 5-
midnight, Sun-10 pm. Closed: 1/1, 12/25, 12/26; also Mon. **Reservations:** suggested. **Features:** The casual
Italian pizzeria offers a nice change of pace for theatregoers and locals who prefer a departure from the fine-dining
experience of the upstairs restaurant but still want gourmet fare. Made-to-order pizzas and pastas, which
top the score here, are complemented by a good wine list and some tempting dessert choices. Casual dress; cocktails.
Parking: street. **Cards:** AX, DC, MC, VI.

RUNDLES RESTAURANT **Lunch:** $30 **Dinner:** $68-$80 **Phone:** 519/271-6442

▼▼▼▼▼ **Location:** Just s from jct Hwy 7 and 8. 9 Cobourg St N5A 5Z9. **Hours:** Open 6/1-10/31; 5 pm-8:30 pm, Sat & Sun
also 11:30 am-1:15 pm. Closed: Mon. **Reservations:** required. **Features:** Conveniently located in the
Continental theatre district, Rundles offers diners the perfect blend of tastes and flavors. The menu features a creative
blend of Continental and regional cuisine with its prix fixe and special gourmet selections. The atmosphere
is modern with a high-tech interior design featuring unique, feather-cushioned chairs and individually designed plate covers.
With its innovative menu and interior design, Rundles offers a truly memorable dining experience. Dressy casual. **Parking:**
street. **Cards:** AX, DC, MC, VI.

STRATHROY pop. 12,805

——— WHERE TO STAY ———

STRATHROY MOTOR INN **Phone:** (519)245-4480

(CAA) (SAVE) All Year 1P: $66 2P: $79 XP: $11 F11
▼▼ ▼▼ **Location:** Hwy 402, exit 65 (Hwy 81), 1 km s. 28540 Centre Rd, RR 5 N7G 3H6. **Fax:** 519/245-4487. **Facility:** 31
one-bedroom standard units. 2 stories (no elevator), exterior corridors. **Parking:** on-site, winter plug-ins.
Motel **Terms:** office hours 7 am-11 pm. **Business Services:** meeting rooms. **Cards:** AX, MC, VI.
Special Amenities: free local telephone calls and early check-in/late check-out.

SOME UNITS

SUDBURY pop. 103,879

——— WHERE TO STAY ———

BEST WESTERN DOWNTOWN SUDBURY
CENTRE-VILLE *Book at aaa.com* **Phone:** (705)673-7801

(CAA) (SAVE) All Year 1P: $105 2P: $105 XP: $11 F12
▼▼ ▼▼ **Location:** Centre. Located in a commercial area. 151 Larch St P3E 1C3. **Fax:** 705/673-5296. **Facility:** 45 one-
bedroom standard units, some with whirlpools. 4 stories, interior corridors. **Parking:** on-site. **Terms:** pets
($15 extra charge). **Amenities:** irons, hair dryers. **Guest Services:** valet laundry. **Business Services:**
Small-scale Hotel meeting rooms. **Cards:** AX, DC, MC, VI. **Special Amenities:** free local telephone calls.

SOME UNITS
FEE   FEE

COMFORT INN *Book at aaa.com* **Phone:** (705)522-1101

▼▼▼ ▼ 5/1-10/31 1P: $89-$133 2P: $89-$156 XP: $10 F18
11/1-4/30 1P: $79-$127 2P: $79-$137 XP: $10 F18
Small-scale Hotel **Location:** 5 km s on Hwy 46. Located in a commercial area. 2171 Regent St S P3E 5V3. **Fax:** 705/522-2687.
Facility: 80 one-bedroom standard units. 2 stories (no elevator), interior corridors. **Parking:** on-site, winter
plug-ins. **Terms:** cancellation fee imposed, package plans, pets (ground floor units). **Amenities:** irons, hair dryers. **Guest**
Services: valet laundry. **Cards:** AX, DC, DS, MC, VI.

SOME UNITS
FEE

COMFORT INN *Book at aaa.com* **Phone:** (705)560-4502

▼▼▼ ▼ 5/1-9/30 1P: $85-$155 2P: $95-$175 XP: $15 F18
1/1-4/30 1P: $85-$150 2P: $95-$160 XP: $10 F18
10/1-12/31 1P: $80-$150 2P: $90-$160 XP: $10 F18
Small-scale Hotel **Location:** Kingsway at Second Ave. Located in a commercial area. 440 Second Ave N P3B 4A4. **Fax:** 705/560-0107.
Facility: 81 one-bedroom standard units. 2 stories (no elevator), interior corridors. **Parking:** on-site, winter plug-ins.
Terms: pets (in smoking units). **Amenities:** irons, hair dryers. **Guest Services:** valet laundry. **Cards:** AX, CB, DC, DS, JC,
MC, VI.

SOME UNITS

DAYS INN SUDBURY *Book at aaa.com* **Phone:** (705)674-7517

▼▼▼ ▼ 1/1-4/30 1P: $120-$130 2P: $130-$150 F16
5/1-12/31 1P: $110-$118 2P: $120-$135 XP: $10
Small-scale Hotel **Location:** Centre of downtown. Located in a commercial area. 117 Elm St P3C 1T3. **Fax:** 705/688-0369. **Facility:** 64
one-bedroom standard units. 3 stories, interior corridors. **Parking:** on-site. **Amenities:** voice mail, irons, hair
dryers. **Pool(s):** small heated indoor. **Leisure Activities:** sauna, limited exercise equipment. **Guest Services:** valet laundry.
Business Services: meeting rooms. **Cards:** AX, CB, DC, MC, VI.

SOME UNITS
FEE

HOLIDAY INN HOTEL SUDBURY

CAA SAVE ◆◆ ◆◆

Small-scale Hotel

All Year   1P: $99   2P: $99   Phone: (705)522-3000

Location: Hwy 69 (Regent St), just n of Paris St. Located in a commercial area. 1696 Regent St S P3E 3Z8. **Fax:** 705/522-8067. **Facility:** 188 units. 184 one-bedroom standard units, some with whirlpools. 4 one-bedroom suites. 3-6 stories, interior/exterior corridors. **Parking:** on-site, winter plug-ins. **Terms:** check-in 4 pm. **Amenities:** video games (fee), voice mail, irons, hair dryers. **Dining:** 2 restaurants, 6:30 am-10 pm, cocktails. **Pool(s):** heated indoor. **Leisure Activities:** sauna, whirlpool, exercise room. **Guest Services:** gift shop, valet laundry. **Business Services:** conference facilities. **Cards:** AX, DC, MC, VI. *(See color ad below)*

SOME UNITS

BRAND NEW

Holiday Inn HOTEL

Sudbury... At Your Service

- **197 Brand New Rooms & Suites**
- **Restaurant & Cocktail Lounge**
- **Kids Stay & Eat Free**
- **Indoor Heated Pool & Fitness Centre**
- **Executive Suites with Microwaves & Refrigerators**
- **King Whirlpool Suites**
- **Free Cable TV**
- **Free Local Calls**
- **Free High Speed Wireless Internet Access**
- **Free Parking**

Holiday Inn Hotel
**1696 Regent Street
Sudbury, ON
705.522.3000 or 1.800.461.4822**

PRIORITY CLUB   AIR MILES   CAA   AAA   aeroplan
Approved

144   17 E
To North Bay
Big Nickel Mine   Paris St.   Hwy. 69-17 By-pass
17 W   Regent St.   Science Centre
To Sault Ste. Marie
Holiday Inn HOTEL   To Toronto
South-West By-pass   69 S

®Aeroplan is a Registered Trademark of Air Canada.

®Trademarks of AIR MILES® International Trading B.V. used under license by Loyalty Management Group Canada Inc. and Holiday Inn.

HOWARD JOHNSON PLAZA HOTEL *Book at aaa.com* **Phone:** (705)675-5602

▼▼▼ ▼▼▼

1/1-4/30	1P: $107-$139	2P: $107-$139
5/1-12/31	1P: $105-$139	2P: $105-$139

Small-scale Hotel **Location:** Just w of Paris St; centre. Located in a commercial area. 50 Brady St P3E 1C8. **Fax:** 705/675-5024. **Facility:** 76 one-bedroom standard units. 2 stories (no elevator), interior corridors. **Parking:** on-site, winter plug-ins. **Terms:** package plans. **Amenities:** voice mail, irons, hair dryers. **Leisure Activities:** exercise room. **Guest Services:** valet laundry. **Business Services:** meeting rooms. **Cards:** AX, CB, DC, DS, JC, MC, VI.

SOME UNITS
ASK S🄳 ▮¶ 🖢 🖭 📡 ▣ / ✕ VCR 🔒 / FEE

QUALITY INN & CONFERENCE CENTRE *Book at aaa.com* **Phone:** (705)675-1273

(AAA) (SAVE)
▼▼▼ ▼▼▼

9/1-4/30	1P: $85-$175	2P: $89-$200	XP: $5 F18
5/1-8/31	1P: $80-$175	2P: $85-$200	XP: $5 F18

Location: Jct Hwy 55 and 80 (Paris St), 0.5 km s, just e. Located in a commercial area. 390 Elgin St S P3B 1B1. **Fax:** 705/671-1766. **Facility:** 100 units. 93 one-bedroom standard units. 7 one-bedroom suites ($135-$175), Small-scale Hotel some with kitchens. 4 stories, interior corridors. **Parking:** on-site, winter plug-ins. **Terms:** weekly rates available, package plans, small pets only (1st floor units). **Amenities:** voice mail. *Some:* irons, hair dryers. **Dining:** 7 am-2 & 5-10 pm, cocktails. **Pool(s):** heated indoor. **Leisure Activities:** whirlpool. *Fee:* game room. **Guest Services:** valet laundry. **Business Services:** conference facilities. **Cards:** AX, DC, DS, MC, VI. **Special Amenities:** free local telephone calls and free newspaper.

SOME UNITS
S🄳 🛏 ▮¶ 🖭 🏊 📡 ▣ / ✕ 🔒 🖨 /

RAMADA INN & CONVENTION CENTRE *Book at aaa.com* **Phone:** (705)675-1123

▼▼▼ ▼▼▼

All Year	1P: $89-$139	2P: $99-$149 XP: $10 F12

Location: Jct St. Anne Rd and Notre Dame Ave; downtown. Located adjacent to a shopping mall. 85 St. Anne Rd P3E 4S4. **Fax:** 705/675-7727. **Facility:** 147 units. 144 one-bedroom standard units. 3 one-bedroom suites ($175-Small-scale Hotel $299), some with whirlpools. 4 stories, interior corridors. **Parking:** on-site. **Terms:** cancellation fee imposed, package plans, pets ($20 fee, in ground floor smoking units). **Amenities:** voice mail, irons, hair dryers. *Some:* high-speed Internet. **Pool(s):** heated indoor. **Leisure Activities:** whirlpool. **Guest Services:** valet and coin laundry. **Business Services:** conference facilities, business center. **Cards:** AX, DC, DS, MC, VI.

SOME UNITS
ASK S🄳 🛏 ▮¶ 🕸 🏊 ⊞ 📡 ▣ / ✕ VCR 📡 🔒 🖨 /
FEE   FEE   FEE FEE

TRAVELODGE HOTEL SUDBURY *Book at aaa.com* **Phone:** 705/522-1100

(AAA) (SAVE)
▼▼▼ ▼▼▼

7/1-9/30	1P: $119-$149	2P: $129-$159	XP: $10 F18
5/1-6/30 & 10/1-4/30	1P: $99-$139	2P: $109-$149	XP: $10 F18

Location: 1.5 km n of jct Hwy 69 (Regent St). Located in a commercial area. 1401 Paris St P3E 3B6. **Fax:** 705/522-1668. **Facility:** 140 units. 105 one-bedroom standard units. 35 one-bedroom suites. 4 stories, Small-scale Hotel interior corridors. **Parking:** on-site, winter plug-ins. **Terms:** package plans, pets (in designated units). **Amenities:** video games (fee), voice mail, irons, hair dryers. **Dining:** 7 am-10 pm, cocktails. **Pool(s):** heated indoor. **Leisure Activities:** whirlpool, exercise room. **Guest Services:** coin laundry. **Business Services:** meeting rooms. **Cards:** AX, DC, DS, MC, VI. *(See color ad on TourBookMark)*

SOME UNITS
🛏 ▮¶ 🏊 🖭 📡 ▣ / ✕ VCR 🔒 🖨 /
FEE

TRAVELWAY INN **Phone:** (705)522-1122

(AAA) (SAVE)
▼▼▼ ▼▼▼

All Year	1P: $105	2P: $111 XP: $6 F18

Location: Jct Ramsey Lake Rd. Located next to the Science North Science Centre. 1200 Paris St P3E 5V4. **Fax:** 705/522-3877. **Facility:** 84 one-bedroom standard units. 2 stories (no elevator), interior corridors. **Parking:** on-site, winter plug-ins. **Amenities:** irons, hair dryers. **Dining:** Simon's Cafe & Deli, see separate Small-scale Hotel listing. **Guest Services:** sundries, valet and coin laundry. **Business Services:** meeting rooms. **Cards:** AX, MC, VI. **Special Amenities:** free local telephone calls and free newspaper. *(See color ad below)*

SOME UNITS
S🄳 ▮¶ 🖭 📡 🔒 ▣ / ✕ /

Travelway Inn
SUDBURY

Travelway Inn - Sudbury
1200 Paris Street
Sudbury, ON P3E5V4

- 85 guestrooms with extra vanity & double or queen beds
- In-room coffee makers, fridge, iron & ironing boards & hairdryer
- Guest laundry (coin operated)
- Simon's Café restaurant (full service)
- ACROSS from Science North/IMAX Theatre

Tel: 705-522-1122 • 800-461-4883
www.travelwayinnsudbury.com

-------- **WHERE TO DINE** --------

CULPEPPERS RESTAURANT Lunch: $6-$12 Dinner: $10-$25 Phone: 705/522-2422

Canadian
Location: 4.8 km s on Hwy 69 (Regent St); corner of Paris St. 1835 Regent St P3E 3Z7. **Hours:** 11 am-11 pm, Fri & Sat-midnight, Sun 10 am-10 pm. **Reservations:** accepted. **Features:** Dark wood, brass and plants create a warm atmosphere and there is an atrium that is bright and cheery during the day. A comfortable raised bar area overlooks part of the dining room. The menu is varied offering something for most tastes and a hot buffet is also featured at lunch. Casual dress; cocktails. **Parking:** on-site. **Cards:** AX, DC, MC, VI.

MR PRIME RIB Lunch: $7-$15 Dinner: $15-$35 Phone: 705/566-5353
Steak & Seafood
Location: Between LaSalle Blvd and Kingsway Hwy. 777 Barrydowne Rd P3A 3T6. **Hours:** 11 am-10:30 pm, Sat from 4 pm, Sun 4 pm-9:30 pm. **Closed:** 12/25, 12/26. **Reservations:** suggested. **Features:** This dining room has a relaxed and cozy atmosphere with subdued lighting in the evening. US Certified Angus beef is featured, as well as chicken, seafood and some Greek dishes. Portions are generous. The restaurant is wheelchair accessible. Casual dress; cocktails. **Parking:** on-site. **Cards:** AX, DC, MC, VI.

PASTA E VINO RISTORANTE Dinner: $10-$25 Phone: 705/674-3050
Italian
Location: On Paris St at Cherry. 118 Paris St P3E 3E1. **Hours:** 5 pm-10 pm. Closed major holidays; also Sun. **Reservations:** suggested. **Features:** Italian cuisine is the hallmark at this cozy, somewhat romantic former 1920s home with pictures of Italy decorating the walls. Generous portions of pasta are freshly prepared, including a very good cannelloni dish and mussels in a tomato-based sauce. Casual dress; cocktails. **Parking:** on-site. **Cards:** AX, DC, MC, VI.

RISTORANTE VERDICCHIO Lunch: $5-$13 Dinner: $13-$28 Phone: 705/523-2794
Italian
Location: Just off Kelly Lake Rd; at West End Business Park. 1351 D Kelly Lake Rd P3E 5P5. **Hours:** 11:30 am-2:30 & 5-10 pm, Mon & Sat from 5 pm. Closed major holidays; also Sun. **Reservations:** suggested. **Features:** Contributing to the eatery's elegant ambience is a garden-like setting accented by a goldfish pond. Creative Italian fare is made-to-order, and a prix fixe menu is featured on Monday. The wine list is exclusively Italian. Dressy casual; cocktails. **Parking:** on-site. **Cards:** AX, DC, MC, VI.

SEAFOOD NORTH Lunch: $6-$17 Dinner: $6-$17 Phone: 705/522-4133
Seafood
Location: 2 km n of Hwy 46. 1543 Paris St P3E 3B7. **Hours:** 11:30 am-8:30 pm, Fri-9 pm, Sun 4 pm-8:30 pm. **Closed:** 12/25. **Reservations:** accepted. **Features:** This small unpretentious restaurant is simply furnished in a nautical theme. The display cooler of fish at the entrance and the open kitchen create the air of a fishmongers shop, which it also is. A modest wine list complements the menu. Large portions of halibut and chips are a favourite. Casual dress; cocktails. **Parking:** on-site. **Cards:** AX, MC, VI.

SIMON'S CAFE & DELI Lunch: $10-$15 Dinner: $15-$25 Phone: 705/522-5649
Canadian
Location: Jct Ramsey Lake Rd; in Travelway Inn. 1200 Paris St P3E 5V4. **Hours:** 7 am-9:30 pm, Sun-9 pm. **Closed:** 1/1, 12/25, 12/26. **Reservations:** accepted. **Features:** Busy at peak times, the restaurant buzzes with all the hustle and bustle of an open kitchen cafe. Friendly servers are on the go. A good selection of dishes reflects influences from around the world. Food is well-prepared and generously presented. Patrons should save room for one of the tempting desserts, prepared at the cafe. Casual dress; cocktails. **Parking:** on-site. **Cards:** VI.

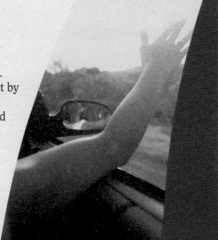

Roadtrip
Perfected

Diamonds are the perfect work of nature. Make certain your next roadtrip is perfect by looking for the red hotel and restaurant Diamond ratings in AAA TourBooks® and online at aaa.com.

It's your assurance of high quality, great service and special savings for AAA Members.

   **Travel with Confidence
Travel with AAA**

THESSALON pop. 1,386

------ WHERE TO STAY ------

CAROLYN BEACH MOTOR INN
Phone: (705)842-3330

(CAA) (SAVE)

Motel

6/18-10/9	1P: $77-$85	2P: $85-$105	XP: $5		F11
5/1-6/17	1P: $72-$80	2P: $77-$90	XP: $5		F11
10/10-4/30	1P: $72-$75	2P: $77-$82	XP: $5		F11

Location: Just w on Hwy 17; jct Hwy 17B. Located on Lake Huron. 1 Lakeside Dr P0R 1L0 (PO Box 10). Fax: 705/842-2031. **Facility:** 50 one-bedroom standard units. 1 story, exterior corridors. **Parking:** on-site, winter plug-ins. **Terms:** office hours 7 am-11 pm, small pets only ($10 extra charge). **Dining:** restaurant, see separate listing. **Leisure Activities:** fishing, snowmobiling. *Fee:* canoes, kayaks. **Business Services:** meeting rooms. **Cards:** AX, MC, VI. *(See color ad below)*

SOME UNITS

FEE   FEE

------ WHERE TO DINE ------

CAROLYN BEACH RESTAURANT   *Menu on aaa.com*   **Lunch:** $7-$10   **Dinner:** $14-$22   **Phone:** 705/842-3330

(CAA)

Canadian

Location: Just w on Hwy 17; jct Hwy 17B; in Carolyn Beach Motor Inn. 1 Lakeside Dr P0R 1L0. **Hours:** Open 5/1-11/5 & 1/15-4/30; 7:30 am-8 pm; hours vary off season. Closed: 4/1-4/14. **Reservations:** accepted. **Features:** Lending to a feel of cozy comfort are pine-clad walls, interesting photography and many tables that afford scenic views of Lake Huron. A screened deck area is pleasant in season. Yellow perch and pickerel (walleye) are popular local favorites, as are the many homemade desserts. This place may be busy at peak meal times. Casual dress; cocktails. **Parking:** on-site. **Cards:** AX, MC, VI.

THORNHILL —See Toronto p. 553.

THOROLD —See Niagara Falls p. 385.

We're beautiful...by nature

Carolyn Beach
M O T O R   I N N

www.carolynbeach.algoma.on.ca
carolynbeach@bellnet.ca

Lake Front Accommodations & Cuisine
Located on the Trans-Canada Highway on the corner of Hwy 17 and 17b, west exit. 80 kilometers east of Sault Ste. Marie, 220 kilometers west of Sudbury.

Call us: 705.842.3330 | Reservations only: 1.800.461.2217

AAA CAA **Rest Assured.**

Enjoy the quality assurance of **AAA/CAA Approved** and Diamond rated hotels. **AAA/CAA's professional evaluators** have peeked under the beds, checked the bathroom and tested the locks – everything you'd do, and then some.

Turn to the TourBook® lodging listings, in print and on aaa.com.

For more information on AAA/CAA Lodging Diamond Ratings, turn to page 16.

Show Your Card

THUNDER BAY pop. 109,016

✈ Airport Accommodations

OA	THUNDER BAY	Diamond Rating	Rate Range High Season	Listing Page
ⒶⒶ	Best Western Crossroads Motor Inn, 2 km ne of airport	▽▽ ▽▽	$99-$150 SAVE	467
	Comfort Inn, 2 km ne of airport	▽▽ ▽▽	$89-$129	467

──────── WHERE TO STAY ────────

BEST WESTERN CROSSROADS MOTOR INN *Book at aaa.com* **Phone: (807)577-4241**
ⒶⒶ SAVE All Year [CP] 1P: $99-$130 2P: $105-$150 XP: $10 F12
▽▽ ▽▽ **Location:** Jct Hwy 61, 17 and 11, just e. Located in a commercial area. 655 W Arthur St P7E 5R6.
Small-scale Hotel Fax: 807/475-7059. **Facility:** 85 units. 83 one-bedroom standard units. 2 one-bedroom suites. 3 stories, interior corridors. **Parking:** on-site, winter plug-ins. **Terms:** small pets only. **Amenities:** voice mail, irons, hair dryers. *Some:* high-speed Internet. **Leisure Activities:** exercise room. **Guest Services:** valet laundry. **Cards:** AX, CB, DC, DS, MC, VI. **Special Amenities:** free continental breakfast and early check-in/late check-out.

SOME UNITS

BEST WESTERN NOR'WESTER RESORT HOTEL *Book at aaa.com* **Phone: (807)473-9123**
ⒶⒶ SAVE All Year 1P: $122-$249 2P: $132-$249 XP: $5 F12
▽▽ ▽▽ **Location:** 9.2 km sw of jct Hwy 11, 17 and 61, exit Loch Lomond Rd. Located in a quiet rural area. 2080 Hwy 61 P7J 1B8. Fax: 807/473-9600. **Facility:** 91 units. 87 one-bedroom standard units, some with whirlpools. 4 one-bedroom suites ($139-$249), some with whirlpools. 2 stories (no elevator), interior corridors. **Parking:** on-site, winter plug-ins. **Terms:** 30 day cancellation notice, pets (with prior approval). **Amenities:** video library (fee), voice mail, irons, hair dryers. *Some:* high-speed Internet. **Dining:** 7 am-midnight, cocktails. **Pool(s):** heated indoor. **Leisure Activities:** sauna, whirlpool, Thunder Bay Tournament Centre, hiking trails. *Fee:* private saunas & steam rooms. **Guest Services:** valet laundry. **Business Services:** meeting rooms. **Cards:** AX, DC, DS, MC, VI. **Special Amenities:** free local telephone calls.

SOME UNITS

FEE

COMFORT INN *Book at aaa.com* **Phone: (807)475-3155**
▽▽ ▽▽ 6/1-9/15 1P: $89-$119 2P: $99-$129 XP: $10 F18
9/16-4/30 1P: $85-$115 2P: $85-$115 XP: $10 F18
Motel 5/1-5/31 1P: $82-$98 2P: $82-$98 XP: $10 F18
Location: Jct Hwy 11, 17 and 61, just e. Located in a commercial area. 660 W Arthur St P7E 5R8. Fax: 807/475-3816. **Facility:** 80 one-bedroom standard units. 2 stories (no elevator), interior corridors. **Parking:** on-site, winter plug-ins. **Terms:** package plans. **Amenities:** irons, hair dryers. **Guest Services:** valet laundry. **Cards:** AX, CB, DC, DS, JC, MC, VI.

SOME UNITS

ECONO LODGE *Book at aaa.com* **Phone: (807)344-6688**
ⒶⒶ SAVE 5/1-9/30 1P: $80-$120 2P: $85-$140 XP: $10 F12
10/1-4/30 1P: $75-$95 2P: $80-$120 XP: $10 F12
▽▽ ▽▽ **Location:** Jct Harbour Expwy, 1 km e. Located in a commercial area. 686 Memorial Ave P7B 3Z5.
Small-scale Hotel Fax: 807/345-6833. **Facility:** 49 one-bedroom standard units. 2 stories (no elevator), interior corridors. **Parking:** on-site, winter plug-ins. **Dining:** 5 pm-11 pm; closed Sun, cocktails. **Guest Services:** valet and coin laundry. **Cards:** AX, DC, DS, MC, VI.

SOME UNITS

FEE

SUPER 8 MOTEL *Book at aaa.com* **Phone: 807/344-2612**
ⒶⒶ SAVE 5/1-9/30 1P: $75-$105 2P: $85-$115 XP: $10 F12
10/1-4/30 1P: $68-$98 2P: $78-$108 XP: $10 F12
▽▽ ▽▽ **Location:** Jct Hwy 11, 17 and Harbour Expwy, 3 km e on Harbour Expwy, 2 km n. Located in a commercial area. 439 Memorial Ave P7B 3Y6. Fax: 807/344-4801. **Facility:** 50 units. 49 one-bedroom standard units. 1 one-bedroom suite with kitchen. 2 stories (no elevator), interior corridors. **Parking:** on-site, winter plug-ins. **Terms:** pets (in designated units). **Amenities:** *Some: Fee:* high-speed Internet. **Guest Services:** coin laundry. **Cards:** AX, DC, DS, MC, VI. **Special Amenities:** free continental breakfast and free local telephone calls.

SOME UNITS

FEE

VICTORIA INN *Book at aaa.com* **Phone: 807/577-8481**
▽▽ ▽▽ All Year 2P: $90
Small-scale Hotel **Location:** 0.8 km e of jct Hwy 11B, 17B and 61 (western access to town). Located in a commercial area. 555 W Arthur St P7E 5R5. Fax: 807/475-8961. **Facility:** 182 units. 180 one- and 2 two-bedroom standard units. 3 stories, interior corridors. **Parking:** on-site, winter plug-ins. **Terms:** 14 day cancellation notice, pets (in smoking units). **Amenities:** video games (fee), voice mail, irons, hair dryers. **Pool(s):** heated indoor, wading. **Leisure Activities:** sauna, whirlpool, waterslide, exercise room. **Guest Services:** valet and coin laundry. **Business Services:** conference facilities. **Cards:** AX, DC, MC, VI.

SOME UNITS

THE WHITE FOX INN   **Phone:** 807/577-3699
▼▼▼▼   All Year [BP]   1P: $110-$219
    Location: Hwy 61, 1.8 km se on 15th Side Rd, 1.8 km ne. Located opposite a golf course. 1345 Mountain Rd (RR 4)
Country Inn   P7J 1C3. Fax: 807/577-8080. **Facility:** This elegant mansion on a wooded estate just outside the city offers
    tastefully decorated accommodations, some with hand-carved mahogany furniture. Smoke free premises. 9
one-bedroom standard units with whirlpools. 2 stories (no elevator), interior corridors. **Parking:** on-site, winter plug-ins.
Terms: office hours 8 am-11 pm, check-in 4 pm, 7 day cancellation notice, package plans. **Amenities:** video library, CD players,
high-speed Internet, irons, hair dryers. **Dining:** Mount View Dining Room in White Fox Inn, see separate listing. **Leisure
Activities:** bicycles, hiking trails. **Guest Services:** valet laundry. **Business Services:** meeting rooms. **Cards:** AX, DC, MC, VI.

(A$K) (✈) (¶¶) (✕) (VCR) (DATA PORT) (▯)

———— **WHERE TO DINE** ————

AURORA GRILLE   **Lunch:** $8-$24   **Dinner:** $14-$30   **Phone:** 807/346-4477
▼▼▼▼   **Location:** Jct Pearl St. 45 Court St S P7B 2W7. **Hours:** 11:30 am-midnight, Thurs-1 am, Fri 11 am-1 am, Sat
    noon-1 am, Sun 11:30 am-9 pm. Closed: 12/25. **Reservations:** accepted. **Features:** A pleasant bistro
Canadian   atmosphere and friendly, capable service are combined with well-presented and creatively prepared dishes
    at the downtown restaurant. Casual dress; cocktails. **Parking:** on-site. **Cards:** AX, DC, MC, VI.   (Y) (✕)

BISTRO ONE   **Dinner:** $15-$30   **Phone:** 807/622-2478
▼▼▼▼   **Location:** 0.6 km n of Marina Park Overpass; corner of McIntyre St. 555 Dunlop St P7B 6S1. **Hours:** 5 pm-10 pm.
    Closed major holidays; also Sun & Mon. **Reservations:** suggested. **Features:** Unpretentious,
Continental   knowledgeable servers guide you through a dynamic menu including Atlantic salmon, New Zealand rack of
    lamb and Alberta tenderloin, just to name a few of the specialties offered in this progressive, unassuming
bistro with a cozy atmosphere. Dressy casual; cocktails. **Parking:** on-site. **Cards:** AX, DC, MC, VI.   (✕)

GIORG RISTORANTE   _Menu on aaa.com_   **Lunch:** $7-$24   **Dinner:** $10-$32   **Phone:** 807/623-8052
(CAA)   **Location:** At E Miles St; north entrance to Victoriaville Centre. 114 N Syndicate Ave T7C 3V7. **Hours:** 5:30 pm-10
▼▼▼▼   pm, Fri noon-2 & 5:30-11 pm, Sat 5:30 pm-11 pm. Closed: 1/1; also Sun, Mon & 12/24-12/27.
    Reservations: suggested. **Features:** This upbeat and trendy Italian restaurant features a blackboard menu
Northern   brought to your table by the wait staff; an open kitchen and a wide selection of fresh pasta, with emphasis
Italian   on seafood preparations. Of note are the creatively plated and tasty desserts. Private dining room available
    for up to 24 people. If you're in town on a Monday, try a cooking class; not offered during the summer.
    Casual dress; cocktails. **Parking:** street. **Cards:** AX, DC, MC, VI.   (✕)

HOITO RESTAURANT   **Lunch:** $4-$8   **Dinner:** $7-$13   **Phone:** 807/345-6323
▼▼▼ ▼▼▼   **Location:** At Algoma St. 314 Bay St P7B 1S1. **Hours:** 7 am-8 pm, Sat & Sun from 8 am. Closed: 12/25.
    Features: Established in 1918, Hoito serves ample portions of traditional Finnish dishes such as viili
Ethnic   (clabbered milk), Karjalan piirakka (meat and potato soup) and great pancakes. Some Canadian dishes are
    also offered. The eatery may be very busy at peak times. Casual dress. **Parking:** on-site (fee) and street.
Cards: MC, VI.   (✕)

MOUNT VIEW DINING ROOM IN WHITE FOX INN   **Lunch:** $10-$15   **Dinner:** $18-$30   **Phone:** 807/577-3699
▼▼▼▼   **Location:** Hwy 61, 1.8 km se on 15th Side Rd, 1.8 km ne; in The White Fox Inn. 1345 Mountain Rd (RR 4) P7J 1C3.
    Hours: 8 am-10 & 5-9 pm, Fri also 11:30 am-2 pm. Closed: 12/24. **Reservations:** suggested.
    Features: Dine on a menu of New World cuisine while surrounded by pleasant wooded acreage, an elegant
American   decor and quiet, relaxing ambience. Mount View's culinary creations harmonize the influences of both
American continents and preserves their European accents. Casual dress; cocktails. **Parking:** on-site. **Cards:** AX, DC, MC, VI.
    (✕)

NEEBING ROAD HOUSE   **Dinner:** $16-$28   **Phone:** 807/475-0792
(CAA)   **Location:** 9.2 km sw of jct Hwy 11, 17 and 61 at Loch Lomond Rd. 2121 Hwy 61 P7C 4V2. **Hours:** 5 pm-10 pm.
    Closed: 12/24-12/26. **Reservations:** suggested. **Features:** This spot popular with locals features a number
▼▼ ▼▼   of International house specialties including prime rib, steak, seafood, pasta and chicken. The casual, rustic
    atmosphere complements the performance of an unassuming and attentive wait staff. Casual dress;
Continental   cocktails. **Parking:** on-site. **Cards:** AX, DC, DS, MC, VI.   (Y) (✕)

THE NORDIC DINING ROOM   **Dinner:** $18-$29   **Phone:** 807/577-1121
▼▼▼ ▼▼▼   **Location:** 0.4 km w of jct Hwy 11, 17 and 61; in Valhalla Inn-Thunder Bay. 1 Valhalla Rd P7E 6J1. **Hours:** 5:30
    pm-9:30 pm, Sun 10:30 am-2:30 pm. Closed: 12/24, 12/25. **Reservations:** suggested. **Features:** An
Canadian   attractive Scandinavian decor with vaulted ceilings and teak appointments creates a spacious, warm and
    intimate atmosphere. The cuisine offers creations inspired from Northern as well as Southern Europe. Some
Canadian seafood is also featured. Casual dress; cocktails. **Parking:** on-site. **Cards:** AX, DC, DS, MC, VI.   (Y) (✕)

UP IN SMOKE BBQ & GRILL   **Lunch:** $5-$12   **Dinner:** $8-$26   **Phone:** 807/577-7444
▼▼▼ ▼▼   **Location:** Just e of jct Arthur St W. 230 Leland Ave S P7E 2N5. **Hours:** 11 am-9 pm, Sat from 4 pm. Closed major
    holidays; also Sun & Mon. **Reservations:** accepted. **Features:** Cozy, eclectic and casual, the restaurant
Barbecue   lets guests experience some Southern flavor in the North. The menu comprises Cajun po' boys, shrimp
    etouffee, corn-fried catfish, blackened pickerel and jambalaya, as well as salads, wings and, of course,
barbecue ribs. When available, the smoked, slow-roasted prime rib is a treat. Casual dress; cocktails. **Parking:** on-site.
Cards: AX, MC, VI.   (✕)

TILLSONBURG pop. 14,052

——— WHERE TO STAY ———

SUPER 8 MOTEL-TILLSONBURG
Book at aaa.com
(CAA) (SAVE)
Small-scale Hotel

All Year 1P: $88-$98 2P: $98-$108 XP: $5 F12 **Phone:** (519)842-7366
Location: Hwy 19, just e. 92 Simcoe St N4G 2J1. **Fax:** 519/842-6176. **Facility:** 61 one-bedroom standard units. 2 stories (no elevator), interior corridors. **Parking:** on-site, winter plug-ins. **Terms:** weekly rates available. **Amenities:** voice mail. *Some:* irons. **Dining:** 6 am-2 pm, Fri-Sun to 8 pm, cocktails. **Leisure Activities:** sauna, whirlpool. **Guest Services:** valet laundry. **Business Services:** meeting rooms. **Cards:** AX, DC, DS, MC, VI. **Special Amenities:** free local telephone calls and free newspaper.

SOME UNITS
(S/D) (🛏) (⫿⫿) (DATA PORT) (▣) / (✕) (🖨) /

TIMMINS pop. 43,686

——— WHERE TO STAY ———

COMFORT INN
Book at aaa.com
Small-scale Hotel

All Year 1P: $95 2P: $105 XP: $10 F18 **Phone:** (705)264-9474
Location: Hwy 101, 0.5 km e of Hwy 655. Located in a commercial area. 939 Algonquin Blvd E P4N 7J5 (PO Box 1190). **Fax:** 705/360-1969. **Facility:** 91 one-bedroom standard units. 2 stories (no elevator), interior corridors. **Parking:** on-site, winter plug-ins. **Terms:** 30 day cancellation notice, package plans, small pets only (in smoking units). **Amenities:** irons, hair dryers. **Guest Services:** valet laundry. **Cards:** AX, DC, JC, MC, VI.

SOME UNITS
(ASK) (S/D) (🛏) (⫿⫿) (🐾) (▣) / (✕) (DATA PORT) (🖨) (🖼) /
FEE

——— WHERE TO DINE ———

THE FISHBOWL RESTAURANT
Canadian

Lunch: $7-$15 **Dinner:** $9-$25 **Phone:** 705/267-3940
Location: Hwy 101, 3.8 km w on Hwy 655. 942 Riverside Dr P4N 3W2. **Hours:** 11 am-10 pm, Thurs-Sat to 11 pm, Sun 4 pm-9 pm. Closed major holidays. **Reservations:** accepted. **Features:** This casual eatery offers pleasant contemporary decor and furnishings in a friendly atmosphere. Menu features chicken, gourmet burgers, sandwiches, pasta and a wide selection of fish and seafood. In summer, guests may enjoy the seasonal outdoor patio. Casual dress; cocktails. **Parking:** on-site. **Cards:** AX, DC, MC, VI.

(🍽) (✕)

TOBERMORY

——— WHERE TO STAY ———

COACH HOUSE INN
Motel

6/26-9/4 2P: $98-$102 XP: $7 F15 **Phone:** (519)596-2361
5/7-6/25 & 9/5-10/11 2P: $59-$85 XP: $7 F15
Location: Hwy 6, 2 km s of ferry docks. 7189 Hwy 6 N0H 2R0 (PO Box 178). **Fax:** 519/596-2361. **Facility:** Smoke free premises. 38 one-bedroom standard units. 1-2 stories (no elevator), exterior corridors. *Bath:* combo or shower only. **Parking:** on-site. **Terms:** open 5/7-10/11, office hours 8 am-midnight. **Pool(s):** outdoor. **Leisure Activities:** horseshoes, shuffleboard, volleyball. **Cards:** MC, VI.

SOME UNITS
(🔥) (✕) (✕) (☎) / (🎬) (🖨) /

GRANDVIEW MOTEL AND DINING ROOM
Motel

7/1-9/5 2P: $110-$130 XP: $10 F **Phone:** 519/596-2220
5/1-6/30 & 9/6-10/16 2P: $65-$110 XP: $10 F
Location: On Earl St at Bay; at the mouth of Little Tub Harbour. 8 Earl St N0H 2R0 (PO Box 35). **Fax:** 519/596-8045. **Facility:** Smoke free premises. 18 one-bedroom standard units. 2 stories (no elevator), exterior corridors. *Bath:* combo or shower only. **Parking:** on-site. **Terms:** open 5/1-10/16, office hours 9 am-10 pm, 3 day cancellation notice, [ECP] meal plan available. **Dining:** dining room, see separate listing. **Cards:** MC, VI. *(See color ad below)*

(⫿⫿) (✕) (🎬) (☎)

——— WHERE TO DINE ———

GRANDVIEW DINING ROOM
Continental

Dinner: $20-$28 **Phone:** 519/596-2220
Location: On Earl St at Bay; at the mouth of Little Tub Harbour; in Grandview Motel and Dining Room. 8 Earl St N0H 2R0. **Hours:** Open 5/1-10/21; 5 pm-8 pm; to 9 pm 7/1-8/31. **Reservations:** not accepted. **Features:** Diners enjoy outstanding views of the harbor from the large panoramic windows or the large outdoor patio as they feast on local specialties. Highlights include fresh local whitefish served in a variety of ways, as well as tasty pork, beef, chicken and pasta, all freshly created with an innovative local touch. Warm, personable service is full of honest country hospitality. Casual dress; cocktails. **Parking:** on-site. **Cards:** MC, VI. *(See color ad below)*

(🎬) (✕)

DINING & ACCOMMODATIONS

- 18 spotless units with a view of Tobermory's harbours.
- Fully licensed dining room and patios serving fresh Georgian Bay Whitefish, steak, pork tenderloin, chicken, pasta and more!

The Only Thing We Overlook Is Georgian Bay

GRANDVIEW

For information and reservations
P.O. Box 35
Tobermory, ON, N0H 2R0
Tel: (519) 596-2220 Fax: (519) 596-8045
Email: grandview@log.on.ca
www.grandview-tobermory.com

Visa, Mastercard, American Express, Interac

Destination Toronto
pop. 2,481,494

*T*orontonians are as passionate about their personal recreation as they are about supporting the city's professional sports teams. Catch the fever and head for the rink or dome of choice.

*S*hopping, too, is a pastime worthy of enthusiasm. Notable options include the upscale Bloor-Yorkville area, downtown's Toronto Eaton Centre and Harbourfront Centre.

© Reuters/Andrew Wallace Corbis

Toronto Maple Leafs.
The city is passionate about its NHL team, which plays in the high-tech Air Canada Centre. (See mention page 0)

See Vicinity map page 479

© 2004 Ontario Tourism

Festivals, Toronto.
Of the many music festivals in Toronto, those featuring jazz as their theme always draw a crowd.

Vaughan

*P*laces included in this AAA Destination City:

Some municipalities in Ontario have combined or soon will combine with neighboring cities. These mergers will eliminate some existing cities and may affect street names, addresses and political boundaries referenced in this guide. For further information, please contact Ontario governing agencies or the local CAA club.

© 2004 Ontario Tourism

Dining, Toronto.
Hospitable restaurateurs make dining in Toronto's multicultural bistros a memorable experience.

Richmond Hill

Markham

Unionville

Thornhill

See Downtown map page 479

Toronto

© 2004 Ontario Tourism

Golfing, Toronto.
Challenging holes draw golfers to the many links in Toronto and the surrounding area; some courses even come with local landmarks as a backdrop.

Toronto Eaton Centre.
A shopping spree can take you to quaint enclaves, specialty districts, underground concourses or such expansive venues as Toronto Eaton Centre. (See mention page 0)

© 2004 Ontario Tourism

- In the heart of Toronto, close to major attractions, theatres and shopping
- On-site Ticketing Hotline with access to the best seats for Toronto's hottest shows
- Six restaurants/lounges, including our self-serve market-style food emporium
- High-speed Internet access available in a selection of rooms
- Adult-only pool and fitness centre
- Family recreation area with pool, whirlpool, saunas and the 4-storey "Corkscrew"- downtown Toronto's only indoor waterslide
- Children's Creative Centre with supervised childcare and teen Starcade
- Full- and half-day supervised activities for kids aged 5-12 through Camp Chelsea
- Children under 18 stay free in parent's room; children 6 and under eat free and children 7-12 eat for half price when accompanied by a paying adult

33 Gerrard Street West,
Toronto, ON
M5G 1Z4
1-800-CHELSEA (243-5732)
416-595-1975
Fax 416-585-4302
www.deltachelsea.com

DELTA
CHELSEA
DOWNTOWN TORONTO

Your room is ready

Special CAA/AAA Rate	CANADA and U.S.	Special CAA/AAA Rate
$140–$165 CDN*	1-800-268-1133 www.deltahotels.com	**$100–$125** US*

* Subject to availability. Some conditions, restrictions apply. Taxes, gratuities extra. U.S. price subject to exchange rate fluctuations. Single/Double occ.

Find Hotels As Easy As 1-2-3-4-5!

AAA's valuable rating system makes hotel selection easy for members:

- *Every* **AAA Approved** property offers quality, cleanliness, service, and value.
- The one to five **AAA Diamond Ratings** guide your selection, from basic to luxury.

Find AAA Approved and Diamond rated properties in the TourBook® listings, in print and on aaa.com, and look for the bold red AAA logo on signage and billboards.

Read about **AAA Lodging Diamond Rating** requirements on page **16**.

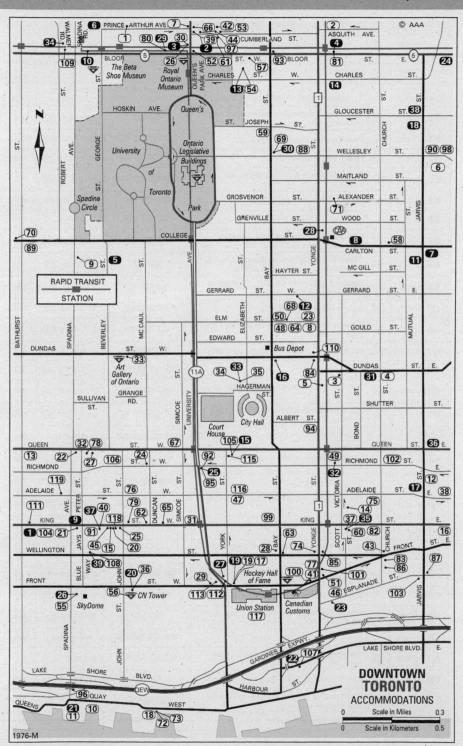

© AAA

RAPID TRANSIT
■ STATION

DOWNTOWN
TORONTO
ACCOMMODATIONS

Scale in Miles
0   0.3

Scale in Kilometers
0   0.5

1976-M

Downtown Toronto

This index helps you "spot" where approved accommodations and restaurants are located on the corresponding detailed maps. Lodging rate ranges are for comparison only and show the property's high season; rates are per night, unless only weekly (W) rates are available. Restaurant rate range is for dinner, unless only lunch (L) is served. Turn to the listing page for more detailed rate information and consult display ads for special promotions.

Spotter/Map Page Number	OA	DOWNTOWN TORONTO - Lodgings	Diamond Rating	Rate Range High Season	Listing Page
1 / p. 473	CAA	Travelodge Toronto Downtown West - see color ad p 486	◆◆	$149-$169 SAVE	505
2 / p. 473	CAA	Four Seasons Hotel	◆◆◆◆	$335-$580 SAVE	494
3 / p. 473	CAA	Park Hyatt Toronto	◆◆◆◆	$199-$399 SAVE	498
4 / p. 473	CAA	Toronto Marriott Bloor Yorkville - see color ad p 504	◆◆◆◆	$259-$279 SAVE	503
5 / p. 473		Beverley Place Bed & Breakfast	◆◆◆	$65-$120	487
6 / p. 473		Annex House Bed & Breakfast	◆◆◆	$80-$95	486
7 / p. 473	CAA	Best Western Primrose Hotel, Toronto Downtown - see color ad p 487	◆◆◆	$129-$299 SAVE	487
8 / p. 473	CAA	Days Hotel & Conference Centre-Toronto Downtown - see color ad p 490	◆◆	$119-$169 SAVE	490
9 / p. 473	CAA	Holiday Inn Toronto On King (Downtown) - see color ad p 492	◆◆◆	$229-$289 SAVE	494
10 / p. 473	CAA	Quality Hotel Midtown	◆◆◆	$109-$199 SAVE	498
11 / p. 473	CAA	Ramada Hotel and Suites Downtown - see color ad p 500	◆◆◆	$119-$199 SAVE	500
12 / p. 473	CAA	Delta Chelsea Hotel - see color ad p 472	◆◆◆	$165 SAVE	492
13 / p. 473	CAA	Windsor Arms	◆◆◆◆	$295-$2000 SAVE	505
14 / p. 473	CAA	Comfort Hotel-Downtown - see color ad p 489	◆◆	$139-$189 SAVE	490
15 / p. 473	CAA	The Sheraton Centre Toronto Hotel - see color ad p 5, p 502	◆◆◆◆	$379-$439 SAVE	501
16 / p. 473		Toronto Marriott Downtown Eaton Centre - see color ad p 504	◆◆◆	$169-$299	503
17 / p. 473	CAA	Quality Hotel Downtown - see color ad p 498	◆◆◆	$149-$167 SAVE	498
18 / p. 473		Cawthra Square Inn	◆◆◆	$139-$319	489
19 / p. 473	CAA	The Fairmont Royal York - see color ad p 491	◆◆◆◆	$179-$329 SAVE	494
20 / p. 473	CAA	InterContinental Toronto Centre - see color ad p 496	◆◆◆◆	$269 SAVE	496
21 / p. 473	CAA	Radisson Plaza Hotel Admiral Toronto - see color ad p 521, p 499	◆◆◆	$189 SAVE	498
22 / p. 473	CAA	The Westin Harbour Castle - see color ad p 5, p 505	◆◆◆◆	$239-$389 SAVE	505
23 / p. 473	CAA	Novotel Toronto Centre - see color ad p 497	◆◆◆	$174-$229 SAVE	497
24 / p. 473	CAA	Clarion Hotel and Suites Selby - see color ad p 489	◆◆	$119-$209 SAVE	489
25 / p. 473		Hilton Toronto	◆◆◆◆	$313-$394	494
26 / p. 473	CAA	Renaissance Toronto Hotel at SkyDome - see color ad p 501	◆◆◆	$189-$279 SAVE	501
27 / p. 473	CAA	The Strathcona Hotel - see color ad p 503	◆◆	$129-$149 SAVE	502
28 / p. 473	CAA	Courtyard by Marriott Downtown Toronto - see color ad p 504	◆◆◆	$159-$245 SAVE	490
29 / p. 473	CAA	InterContinental Toronto	◆◆◆◆	$200-$2000 SAVE	495

Spotter/Map Page Number	OA	DOWNTOWN TORONTO - Lodgings (continued)	Diamond Rating	Rate Range High Season	Listing Page
30 / p. 473	CAA	**The Sutton Place Hotel**	◆◆◆◆	$199-$500 SAVE	503
31 / p. 473		Bond Place Hotel	◆◆	$109-$129	487
32 / p. 473	CAA	**Cambridge Suites Hotel - see color ad p 488**	◆◆◆	$199 SAVE	487
33 / p. 473		Metropolitan Hotel	◆◆◆◆	$229-$279	496
34 / p. 473		Casa Loma Inn - see color ad p 488	◆◆	$95-$165	488
35 / p. 473		Le Royal Meridien King Edward Hotel	◆◆◆◆	Failed to provide	496
36 / p. 473	CAA	**Comfort Suites City Centre**	◆◆◆	$109-$509 SAVE	490
37 / p. 473		Hotel Le Germain	◆◆◆◆	$225-$395	494
38 / p. 473		Gloucester Square Inns of Toronto	◆◆◆	$139-$319	494
39 / p. 473		SoHo Metropolitan Hotel	◆◆◆◆	$280-$460	501
		DOWNTOWN TORONTO - Restaurants			
1 / p. 473		Opus Restaurant on Prince Arthur	◆◆◆◆	$29-$39	514
2 / p. 473		Indochine Noodle Cafe & Restaurant	◆◆	$9-$20	511
3 / p. 473		Torch Bistro	◆◆◆	$24-$36	516
4 / p. 473		Amalfi Italian Ristorante	◆◆	$20-$29	506
5 / p. 473		The Superior Restaurant	◆◆	$15-$30	516
6 / p. 473		Provence Delices	◆◆◆	$15-$24	515
7 / p. 473		Boba	◆◆◆	$24-$35	508
8 / p. 473		Barberian's Steak House	◆◆◆	$25-$70	507
9 / p. 473		Lee Garden	◆◆	$15-$25	512
10 / p. 473		Pier 4 Storehouse Restaurant	◆◆	$17-$33	515
11 / p. 473		Commodore's	◆◆◆◆	$23-$37	509
12 / p. 473		Bombay Palace	◆◆	$10-$15	508
13 / p. 473		Left Bank	◆◆	$12-$23	512
14 / p. 473		Rosewater Supper Club	◆◆◆	$22-$40	515
15 / p. 473		Rain	◆◆◆◆	$29-$33	515
16 / p. 473		Hiro Sushi Restaurant	◆◆	$20-$30	510
17 / p. 473	CAA	**Benihana Restaurant**	◆◆◆	$30-$42	507
18 / p. 473		Boat House Bar and Grill	◆	$8-$26	508
19 / p. 473	CAA	**Epic**	◆◆◆◆	$23-$39	509
20 / p. 473		Fred's Not Here Smokehouse and Grill	◆◆◆	$16-$21	510
21 / p. 473		Wayne Gretzky's Restaurant	◆◆	$7-$26	517
22 / p. 473		Babur	◆◆	$9-$20	506
23 / p. 473	CAA	**Bangkok Garden**	◆◆◆	$25-$40	506
24 / p. 473		The Fifth	◆◆◆	$85-$90	510
25 / p. 473		Urban	◆◆◆	$15-$48	517
26 / p. 473		Morton's of Chicago	◆◆◆	$35-$55	514

Spotter/Map Page Number	OA	DOWNTOWN TORONTO - Restaurants (continued)	Diamond Rating	Rate Range High Season	Listing Page
27 / p. 473		Tortilla Flats Texas Bar & Grill	◈	$7-$12	517
28 / p. 473		Canoe Restaurant and Bar	◈◈◈◈	$24-$42	508
29 / p. 473		Joe Badali's Ristorante Italiano	◈◈	$9-$25	511
30 / p. 473		Annona	◈◈◈◈	$18-$32	506
31 / p. 473		Il Fornello	◈◈	$14-$17	511
32 / p. 473		Le Select Bistro	◈◈◈	$18-$30	513
33 / p. 473		Bodega Restaurant	◈◈◈	$16-$30	508
34 / p. 473	CAA	**Hemispheres Restaurant Bistro**	◈◈◈	$13-$23(L)	510
35 / p. 473		Lai Wah Heen	◈◈◈	$30-$40	512
36 / p. 473		Azure	◈◈◈◈	$35-$50	506
37 / p. 473		Cafe Victoria	◈◈	$17-$35	508
38 / p. 473		Montreal Bistro/Jazz Club	◈◈◈	$12-$23	513
39 / p. 473	CAA	**Truffles**	◈◈◈◈◈	$27-$37	517
40 / p. 473		Luce	◈◈◈◈	$29-$38	513
41 / p. 473		Shopsy's Delicatessen Restaurant	◈◈	$8-$13	516
42 / p. 473		Yamato Japanese Restaurant	◈◈	$15-$33	517
43 / p. 473		Hothouse Cafe Inc	◈◈	$8-$20	510
44 / p. 473		Bellini's	◈◈◈	$14-$29	507
45 / p. 473		La Fenice	◈◈◈	$15-$30	512
46 / p. 473		The Old Spaghetti Factory	◈◈	$9-$15	514
47 / p. 473		Duke of Westminster	◈	$7-$15	509
48 / p. 473		Oro	◈◈◈	$20-$42	514
49 / p. 473	CAA	**Resto Portico**	◈◈◈	$15-$38	515
50 / p. 473	CAA	**Le Commensal Fine Vegetarian Cuisine**	◈◈	$10-$15	512
51 / p. 473		Penelope Restaurant	◈◈	$10-$14	514
52 / p. 473		Prego Della Piazza	◈◈◈	$16-$33	515
53 / p. 473		Le Trou Normand	◈◈	$6-$39	513
54 / p. 473		The Courtyard Cafe	◈◈◈◈	$29-$42	509
55 / p. 473		The Bistro	◈◈◈	$18-$25	507
56 / p. 473		360 The Restaurant at the CN Tower	◈◈◈	$31-$75	506
57 / p. 473		Dynasty Chinese Cuisine	◈◈◈	$15-$30	509
58 / p. 473		George Bigliardi's Dining Lounge	◈◈◈	$18-$30	510
59 / p. 473		Bistro 990	◈◈◈	$14-$43	508
60 / p. 473		Cyrano's	◈◈	$13-$29	509
61 / p. 473		Sassafraz	◈◈◈	$20-$40	516
62 / p. 473		Filet of Sole	◈◈	$14-$35	510
63 / p. 473		Far Niente	◈◈◈	$16-$36	509

Spotter/Map Page Number	OA	DOWNTOWN TORONTO - Restaurants (continued)	Diamond Rating	Rate Range High Season	Listing Page
64 / p. 473		Il Fornello	♦♦	$10-$25	511
65 / p. 473		Barootes Casual Dining	♦♦♦	$15-$32	507
66 / p. 473		Il Posto	♦♦♦	$16-$35	511
67 / p. 473		Japanese Restaurant Ematei	♦♦	$15-$24	511
68 / p. 473		Adega Restaurante	♦♦♦	$14-$30	506
69 / p. 473	ⒶⒶ	**Accents Restaurant and Bar**	♦♦♦	$28-$38	506
70 / p. 473		Chiado	♦♦♦	$25-$50	509
71 / p. 473		Carman's	♦♦♦	$40-$48	509
72 / p. 473		Il Fornello	♦♦	$12-$25	511
73 / p. 473		Pearl Harbourfront Restaurant	♦♦♦	$20-$35	514
74 / p. 473		Bymark Restaurant & Bar	♦♦♦♦	$30-$45	508
75 / p. 473		Nami	♦♦♦	$25-$27	514
76 / p. 473		Avalon	♦♦♦	$30-$45	506
77 / p. 473		Marche (BCE Place) Restaurant	♦	$5-$15	513
78 / p. 473		Peter Pan Bistro	♦♦♦	$9-$17	514
79 / p. 473		Dunn's Famous Delicatessen	♦♦	$7-$18	509
80 / p. 473		Signatures	♦♦♦♦	$20-$25	516
81 / p. 473		Matisse	♦♦♦	$16-$33	513
82 / p. 473	ⒶⒶ	**Tom Jones Steakhouse & Seafood**	♦♦♦	$25-$60	516
83 / p. 473	ⒶⒶ	**Le Papillon Restaurant Francais**	♦♦♦	$10-$25	513
84 / p. 473		Mr. Greenjeans Restaurant	♦	$6-$22	513
85 / p. 473		Jump Cafe & Bar	♦♦♦	$18-$28	512
86 / p. 473		The Keg Steakhouse and Bar	♦♦	$15-$30	512
87 / p. 473		Ristorante Romagna Mia	♦♦♦	$19-$30	515
88 / p. 473		Segovia Restaurant	♦♦♦	$14-$19	516
89 / p. 473		Plaza Flamingo Restaurant	♦♦	$11-$17	515
90 / p. 473		The Keg Mansion	♦♦	$18-$30	512
91 / p. 473		YYZ Restaurant & Wine Bar	♦♦♦	$22-$30	517
92 / p. 473		Tundra	♦♦♦♦	$22-$45	517
93 / p. 473		Pangaea	♦♦♦	$25-$39	514
94 / p. 473		Baton Rouge Restaurant	♦♦	$10-$32	507
95 / p. 473		Ruth's Chris Steak House	♦♦♦	$28-$52	515
96 / p. 473		Ichiban Sushi House	♦♦	$8-$22	511
97 / p. 473		Jacques' Bistro du Parc	♦♦♦	$16-$29	511
98 / p. 473		Rashnaa Restaurant	♦♦	$7-$14	515
99 / p. 473		Ho Shim Japanese and Korean Restaurant	♦♦	$8-$20	510
100 / p. 473		acqua	♦♦♦	$18-$35	506

Spotter/Map Page Number	OA	DOWNTOWN TORONTO - Restaurants (continued)	Diamond Rating	Rate Range High Season	Listing Page
101 / p. 473		Biff's	◆◆◆	$25-$34	507
102 / p. 473		Golden Thai	◆◆◆	$8-$20	510
103 / p. 473		Biagio Ristorante	◆◆◆	$20-$40	507
104 / p. 473		Susur	◆◆◆◆	$35-$45	516
105 / p. 473		Michael Seltzer's Le Biftheque Steakhouse	◆◆	$9-$39	513
106 / p. 473		Milestone's Grill and Bar	◆◆	$8-$25	513
107 / p. 473		Toula	◆◆◆	$14-$45	517
108 / p. 473		Senses	◆◆◆◆	$29-$46	516
109 / p. 473		Splendido Bar and Grill	◆◆◆◆	$20-$40	516
110 / p. 473		The Pickle Barrel	◆◆	$7-$19	514
111 / p. 473		Blowfish Restaurant & Sake Bar	◆◆◆	$12-$24	508
112 / p. 473	CAA	**Bardi's Steak House**	◆◆◆	$24-$50	507
113 / p. 473		Canyon Creek Chop House	◆◆	$11-$31	508
115 / p. 473		The Keg Steakhouse and Bar	◆◆	$16-$30	512
116 / p. 473		Hy's Steak House	◆◆◆	$30-$49	511
117 / p. 473		Harbour Sixty Steakhouse	◆◆◆	$25-$45	510
118 / p. 473		Kit Kat Bar and Grill	◆◆	$13-$34	512
119 / p. 473		Tutti Matti	◆◆◆	$7-$30	517

THE WESTIN PRINCE
TORONTO

Rates from $119.00 to $159.00

Whether you're here for business or pleasure, we have anticipated your every need. Critically acclaimed restaurants to suit every taste. Knowledgeable and friendly staff. Even complimentary parking. No detail has been overlooked to assure your complete comfort and convenience. Winner of the prestigious CAA four diamond award for 28 consecutive years. Your room at The Westin Prince has everything you need for work or sheer relaxation.

900 York Mills Road, Toronto, Ontario   M3B 3H2
416-444-2511   1-800-WESTIN-1   www.westin.com/prince

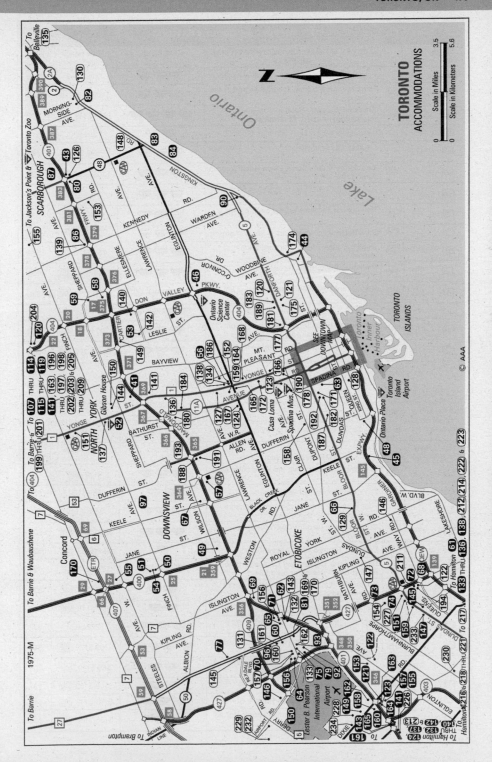

TORONTO
ACCOMMODATIONS

Scale in Miles
Scale in Kilometers

© AAA

✈ Airport Accommodations

Spotter/Map Page Number	OA	LESTER B PEARSON INTERNATIONAL AIRPORT	Diamond Rating	Rate Range High Season	Listing Page
130 / p. 479		Four Points Toronto Airport, 1.6 km w of airport	◆◆◆	$99-$249	299
157 / p. 479	CAA	Hampton Inn & Suites Toronto Airport, 1 km of airport	◆◆◆	$169-$189 SAVE	300
150 / p. 479	CAA	Sheraton Gateway Hotel In Toronto International Airport, in terminal 3	◆◆◆◆	$99-$339 SAVE	302
92 / p. 479		Carlingview Airport Inn, 2 km e of airport	◆◆	$89-$99	519
79 / p. 479		Courtyard by Marriott Toronto Airport, 2 km e of airport	◆◆◆	$99-$175	523
62 / p. 479	CAA	Doubletree International Plaza Hotel Toronto Airport, 3.2 km e of airport	◆◆◆	$109-$258 SAVE	526
64 / p. 479		Holiday Inn Select Toronto-Airport, 1.5 km e of airport	◆◆◆	$119-$199	529
65 / p. 479	CAA	Holiday Inn Toronto-Airport East, 3.2 km e of airport	◆◆◆	$109-$179 SAVE	530
60 / p. 479	CAA	Park Plaza Toronto Airport, 3 km e of airport	◆◆◆	$99-$249 SAVE	533
70 / p. 479	CAA	Quality Suites Toronto Airport, 2 km e of airport	◆◆◆	$156-$176 SAVE	534
71 / p. 479	CAA	Radisson Suite Hotel Toronto Airport, 4 km e of airport	◆◆◆	$119-$189 SAVE	535
81 / p. 479	CAA	Renaissance Toronto Airport Hotel, 3 km e of airport	◆◆◆◆	$239-$269 SAVE	536
93 / p. 479		Toronto Airport Marriott Hotel, 2 km e of aiport	◆◆◆◆	$109-$249	537
75 / p. 479	CAA	Travelodge Hotel Toronto Airport (Dixon Road), 2 km w of airport	◆◆◆	$99-$160 SAVE	539
96 / p. 479	CAA	Wyndham Bristol Place-Toronto Airport, 1 km w of airport	◆◆◆	$119-$205 SAVE	540

Toronto and Vicinity

This index helps you "spot" where approved accommodations and restaurants are located on the corresponding detailed maps. Lodging rate ranges are for comparison only and show the property's high season; rates are per night, unless only weekly (W) rates are available. Restaurant rate range is for dinner, unless only lunch (L) is served. Turn to the listing page for more detailed rate information and consult display ads for special promotions.

Spotter/Map Page Number	OA	TORONTO - Lodgings	Diamond Rating	Rate Range High Season	Listing Page
43 / p. 479	CAA	Best Western Executive Inn - see color ad p 518	◆◆◆	$129 SAVE	518
44 / p. 479		Days Inn-Toronto East Beaches	◆◆	$89-$199	523
45 / p. 479		Four Points by Sheraton Toronto Lakeshore - see color ad p 5	◆◆◆	$135-$145	526
46 / p. 479	CAA	Crowne Plaza Toronto Don Valley - see color ad p 523	◆◆◆	$149-$219 SAVE	523
48 / p. 479	CAA	Days Inn Toronto West Lakeshore	◆	$99-$159 SAVE	524
49 / p. 479	CAA	Days Hotel & Conference Centre-Toronto Airport East - see color ad p 524	◆◆◆	$99-$249 SAVE	523
50 / p. 479	CAA	Holiday Inn Express Toronto-North York - see color ad p 529, card insert	◆◆	$99-$159 SAVE	529
51 / p. 479	CAA	Comfort Inn - see color ad p 529	◆◆	$69-$149 SAVE	520
52 / p. 479	CAA	Novotel Toronto North York - see color ad p 497	◆◆◆	$259-$279	532
53 / p. 479	CAA	The Westin Prince Toronto - see color ad p 478, p 5	◆◆◆◆	$139-$179 SAVE	540
54 / p. 479	CAA	Travelodge Toronto North (North York) - see color ad p 529, on TourBookMark	◆◆	$89-$149 SAVE	539
55 / p. 479		Super 8 Toronto North	◆◆	$100-$160 SAVE	537
56 / p. 479	CAA	Best Western Roehampton Hotel & Suites	◆◆◆	$119-$149 SAVE	518
57 / p. 479	CAA	Holiday Inn Toronto-Yorkdale - see color ad card insert	◆◆◆	$135-$189 SAVE	530

Spotter/Map Page Number	OA	TORONTO - Lodgings (continued)	Diamond Rating	Rate Range High Season	Listing Page
58 / p. 479	CAA	Radisson Hotel Toronto East - see color ad p 521, on TourBookMark	◆◆◆	$119-$169 (SAVE)	534
59 / p. 479	CAA	Ramada Hotel & Conference Centre	◆◆◆	$99-$129 (SAVE)	535
60 / p. 479	CAA	Park Plaza Toronto Airport	◆◆◆	$99-$249 (SAVE)	533
61 / p. 479	CAA	Motel 27	◆◆	$70-$105 (SAVE)	532
62 / p. 479	CAA	Doubletree International Plaza Hotel Toronto Airport - see color ad p 526	◆◆◆	$109-$258 (SAVE)	526
63 / p. 479		Palmerston Inn Bed & Breakfast	◆◆◆	$100-$225	532
64 / p. 479		Holiday Inn Select Toronto-Airport - see color ad card insert	◆◆◆	$119-$199	529
65 / p. 479	CAA	Holiday Inn Toronto-Airport East - see color ad p 530, card insert	◆◆◆	$109-$179 (SAVE)	530
66 / p. 479	CAA	The Old Mill Inn & Spa - see color ad p 532	◆◆◆◆	$290-$630 (SAVE)	532
67 / p. 479	CAA	Travelodge Hotel and Conference Centre Toronto - see color ad p 538	◆◆◆	$109-$169 (SAVE)	539
68 / p. 479	CAA	Stay Inn - see color ad p 537	◆◆	$89-$105 (SAVE)	536
69 / p. 479	CAA	Quality Hotel & Suites Toronto Airport East - see color ad p 533, p 486	◆◆	$69-$159 (SAVE)	533
70 / p. 479	CAA	Quality Suites Toronto Airport - see color ad p 534	◆◆◆	$156-$176 (SAVE)	534
71 / p. 479	CAA	Radisson Suite Hotel Toronto Airport - see color ad p 521, on TourBookMark	◆◆◆	$119-$189 (SAVE)	535
72 / p. 479		Deluxe Inn - see color ad p 525	◆◆	$65-$85	526
73 / p. 479	CAA	Valhalla Inn-Toronto - see color ad p 540	◆◆◆	$109-$155 (SAVE)	540
74 / p. 479	CAA	Ramada Hotel Toronto Airport	◆◆◆	$119-$129 (SAVE)	536
75 / p. 479	CAA	Travelodge Hotel Toronto Airport (Dixon Road)	◆◆◆	$99-$160 (SAVE)	539
77 / p. 479	CAA	Comfort Hotel Airport North - see color ad p 520	◆◆	$119-$209 (SAVE)	520
79 / p. 479		Courtyard by Marriott Toronto Airport - see color ad p 522	◆◆◆	$99-$175	523
80 / p. 479	CAA	Holiday Inn Express Toronto-East - see color ad card insert, p 518	◆◆◆	$95-$159 (SAVE)	528
81 / p. 479	CAA	Renaissance Toronto Airport Hotel - see color ad p 536	◆◆◆◆	$239-$269 (SAVE)	536
82 / p. 479	CAA	Grand Motel	◆◆	$65-$90 (SAVE)	528
83 / p. 479		Comfort Inn	◆◆	$69-$129	522
84 / p. 479	CAA	Park Motel	◆	$60-$78 (SAVE)	533
86 / p. 479		Delta Toronto East	◆◆◆	$149-$199	525
87 / p. 479	CAA	Travelodge Toronto East - see color ad on TourBookMark	◆◆◆	$119-$149 (SAVE)	539
90 / p. 479		Days Inn Toronto East Lakeview	◆◆◆	$65-$110	524
92 / p. 479		Carlingview Airport Inn - see color ad p 520	◆◆	$89-$99	519
93 / p. 479		Toronto Airport Marriott Hotel - see color ad p 504	◆◆◆◆	$109-$249	537
96 / p. 479	CAA	Wyndham Bristol Place-Toronto Airport	◆◆◆	$119-$205 (SAVE)	540
97 / p. 479		Montecassino Hotel & Suites	◆◆◆	$99-$399	530
		TORONTO - Restaurants			
120 / p. 479		Pan on the Danforth	◆◆	$13-$22	546
121 / p. 479		Avra Traditional Greek Cuisine & Seafood House	◆◆	$11-$40	541
122 / p. 479		Via Allegro Ristorante	◆◆◆◆	$15-$44	547
123 / p. 479		Scaramouche Restaurant	◆◆◆	$26-$44	547
124 / p. 479	CAA	EDO	◆◆◆	$14-$20	542

Spotter/Map Page Number	OA	TORONTO - Restaurants (continued)	Diamond Rating	Rate Range High Season	Listing Page
126 / p. 479		The Keg Steakhouse and Bar	◆◆	$15-$30	543
127 / p. 479		Centro Grill & Wine Bar	◆◆◆◆	$27-$43	542
128 / p. 479		Cities	◆◆◆	$13-$21	542
129 / p. 479	CAA	**The Old Mill**	◆◆◆◆	$29-$45	545
130 / p. 479		Sisters Eatery	◆◆	$15-$17	547
131 / p. 479		Lone Star Texas Grill	◆	$9-$28	544
132 / p. 479		Sushi-ya Japan	◆◆◆	$11-$23	547
133 / p. 479		The Keg Steakhouse and Bar	◆◆	$15-$30	543
134 / p. 479		North 44	◆◆◆◆	$30-$50	545
135 / p. 479		Black Dog Pub	◆◆	$7-$19	541
136 / p. 479		Trapper's Restaurant	◆◆◆	$15-$33	547
137 / p. 479		Cuisine of India	◆◆◆	$7-$15	542
138 / p. 479		Grazie Ristorante	◆◆	$8-$17	542
139 / p. 479		Sagano	◆◆◆	$24-$38	546
140 / p. 479		The David Duncan House	◆◆◆	$25-$40	542
141 / p. 479		Auberge Du Pommier	◆◆◆◆	$33-$39	541
142 / p. 479		Katsura	◆◆◆	$18-$50	543
143 / p. 479		Alfredo's	◆◆◆	$13-$25	541
144 / p. 479		Milestone's Grill and Bar	◆◆	$8-$25	545
145 / p. 479		J.J. Muggs Gourmet Grille	◆◆	$5-$19	543
146 / p. 479		Latina's Restaurant	◆◆	$10-$25	544
147 / p. 479		Millers Country Fare	◆◆	$7-$18	545
148 / p. 479		Bombay Palace	◆◆	$11-$15	541
149 / p. 479		The Keg Steakhouse and Bar	◆◆	$15-$30	544
150 / p. 479		The Keg Steakhouse and Bar	◆◆	$16-$30	543
151 / p. 479		Pickle Barrel Centrepoint	◆◆	$8-$19	546
152 / p. 479		The Pickle Barrel	◆◆	$7-$19	546
153 / p. 479		The Old Scott House	◆◆◆	$20-$50	545
154 / p. 479		The Keg Steakhouse and Bar	◆◆	$16-$35	543
155 / p. 479		Dragon Dynasty Chinese Cuisine	◆◆◆	$15-$30	542
156 / p. 479		Milestone's Grill and Bar	◆◆	$8-$25	545
157 / p. 479		Graffiti's Italian Eatery	◆◆	$8-$25	542
158 / p. 479		Indian Rice Factory	◆◆	$8-$16	543
159 / p. 479		Square Restaurant	◆◆◆	$29-$40	547
160 / p. 479	CAA	**Zachary's**	◆◆◆◆	$25-$36	548
161 / p. 479		Le Biftheque Steakhouse	◆◆	$14-$40	544
162 / p. 479		Mikado	◆◆◆	$22-$42	545
163 / p. 479		Pickle Barrel	◆◆	$7-$19	546
164 / p. 479		Across The Road	◆◆◆	$20-$37	541
165 / p. 479		Zucca Trattoria	◆◆◆	$12-$26	548
166 / p. 479		Brownes Bistro	◆◆◆	$14-$37	541
167 / p. 479		Lichee Garden	◆◆	$15-$40	544
168 / p. 479		Grano	◆◆	$13-$25	542

Spotter/Map Page Number	OA	TORONTO - Restaurants (continued)	Diamond Rating	Rate Range High Season	Listing Page
169 / p. 479		Olio-A Mediterranean Grille	▽▽▽	$18-$33	546
170 / p. 479		Outback Steakhouse	▽▽	$12-$25	546
171 / p. 479		Kensington Kitchen	▽▽	$8-$16	544
172 / p. 479		Il Fornello	▽▽	$10-$30	543
174 / p. 479		Il Fornello	▽▽	$12-$30	543
175 / p. 479		Il Fornello	▽▽	$12-$30	543
177 / p. 479		Lakes	▽▽▽	$15-$29	544
178 / p. 479		Le Paradis Brasserie Bistro	▽▽▽	$12-$18	544
180 / p. 479		The Lobster Trap	▽▽	$18-$50	544
181 / p. 479		Mariko Japanese Restaurant	▽▽	$9-$19	545
182 / p. 479		La Forchetta	▽▽▽	$12-$28	544
183 / p. 479		Pappas Grill	▽▽	$11-$16	546
184 / p. 479		Richlee's	▽▽▽	$18-$38	546
186 / p. 479		Summit House Grill	▽▽	$9-$25	547
187 / p. 479		Southern Accent Cajun, Creole & Soul Restaurant	▽▽	$12-$25	547
188 / p. 479		Milestone's Grill and Bar	▽▽	$8-$25	545
189 / p. 479		Astoria Shish Kebob House	▽▽	$10-$19	541
190 / p. 479		Thai Magic Restaurant	▽▽▽	$10-$13	547
191 / p. 479		Pickle Barrel Grand	▽▽	$8-$12	546
192 / p. 479		Trattoria Giancarlo	▽▽▽	$19-$33	547
193 / p. 479		Marky's Delicatessen & Restaurant	▽	$8-$20	545
194 / p. 479		Canyon Creek Chophouse	▽▽	$16-$29	542
		RICHMOND HILL - Lodgings			
107 / p. 479	CAA	**Best Western Parkway Hotel Toronto North - see color ad p 537**	▽▽▽	$105-$139 SAVE	552
108 / p. 479	CAA	**Sheraton Parkway Toronto North Hotel, Suites & Conference Centre - see color ad p 537, p 5**	▽▽▽▽	$132-$152 SAVE	552
		RICHMOND HILL - Restaurants			
196 / p. 479		Spezzo	▽▽▽	$12-$33	553
197 / p. 479		Saigon Star	▽▽	$10-$20	553
198 / p. 479		The Keg Steakhouse and Bar	▽▽	$16-$30	553
199 / p. 479		Ming's Malaysian Chinese Cuisine	▽▽	$7-$23	553
200 / p. 479		Galaxie Diner	▽	$6-$13	552
201 / p. 479		Il Piatto Vecchio	▽▽▽	$12-$32	552
		MARKHAM - Lodgings			
110 / p. 479		Courtyard by Marriott	▽▽▽	$149-$169	548
111 / p. 479		Hilton Garden Inn Toronto/Markham	▽▽▽	$132	548
112 / p. 479		Residence Inn by Marriott	▽▽▽	$169-$229	551
114 / p. 479		Staybridge Suites Toronto-Markham	▽▽▽	$139-$209	551
115 / p. 479	CAA	**Comfort Inn - see color ad p 548**	▽▽▽	$108-$128 SAVE	548
116 / p. 479	CAA	**Hilton Suites Toronto/Markham Conference Centre & Spa - see color ad p 549**	▽▽▽▽	$115-$180 SAVE	549
117 / p. 479	CAA	**Monte Carlo Inn Toronto-Markham - see color ad p 531**	▽▽▽	$89-$129 SAVE	550

Spotter/Map Page Number	OA	MARKHAM - Lodgings (continued)	Diamond Rating	Rate Range High Season	Listing Page
118 / p. 479		Howard Johnson Hotel Toronto-Markham - see color ad p 549	◈◈◈	$89-$159	550
119 / p. 479	CAA	Radisson Hotel Toronto-Markham - see color ad p 521	◈◈◈	$119-$149 SAVE	551
120 / p. 479	CAA	Holiday Inn Hotel & Suites Toronto-Markham - see color ad p 530, card insert	◈◈	$119-$169 SAVE	550
		MARKHAM - Restaurants			
202 / p. 479		Mino's Japanese Restaurant	◈◈◈	$10-$25	552
203 / p. 479		Frankie Tomatto's All You Can Eat Italian Feast	◈◈	$13-$17	551
204 / p. 479		Le Biftheque	◈◈	$10-$30	551
205 / p. 479		Peter's Fine Dining	◈◈◈	$22-$60	552
206 / p. 479		Fire and Ice	◈◈	$8-$17	551
207 / p. 479	CAA	Essence of Unionville Restaurant	◈◈◈	$12-$33	551
208 / p. 479		Tivoli Garden Restaurant	◈◈	$13-$25	552
209 / p. 479		Al Dente Ristorante Italiano	◈◈◈	$14-$25	551
		MISSISSAUGA - Lodgings			
121 / p. 479	CAA	Holiday Inn Express - see color ad card insert, p 527	◈◈	$115 SAVE	300
122 / p. 479	CAA	Best Western Travel Inn	◈◈◈	$109-$149 SAVE	298
123 / p. 479	CAA	Stage West All Suite Hotel & Theatre Restaurant	◈◈◈	$159-$179 SAVE	302
124 / p. 479	CAA	Comfort Inn Mississauga - see color ad p 522	◈◈	$85-$98 SAVE	298
125 / p. 479		Motel 6 #1910	◈◈	$65-$81	301
127 / p. 479	CAA	Radisson Hotel Toronto-Mississauga - see color ad p 521, on TourBookMark	◈◈◈	$109-$159 SAVE	302
129 / p. 479	CAA	Comfort Inn Airport West	◈◈	$114-$144 SAVE	298
130 / p. 479		Four Points Toronto Airport	◈◈◈	$99-$249	299
131 / p. 479	CAA	Hampton Inn - see color ad p 4, p 527	◈◈◈	$139-$149 SAVE	300
132 / p. 479	CAA	Best Western Admiral Hotel & Suites @ Conference Centre-Mississauga Airport - see color ad p 519	◈◈◈	$139-$249 SAVE	297
133 / p. 479	CAA	Glenerin Inn	◈◈◈	$129-$149 SAVE	300
135 / p. 479	CAA	Holiday Inn Toronto-Mississauga - see color ad card insert	◈◈◈	$109-$129 SAVE	300
136 / p. 479		The Waterside Inn	◈◈◈	$249-$699	303
137 / p. 479		Holiday Inn Select Mississauga - see color ad card insert	◈◈◈	$89-$149	300
138 / p. 479	CAA	Comfort Inn & Suites Sheridan Park - see color ad p 522	◈◈◈	$109-$189 SAVE	298
140 / p. 479		Courtyard by Marriott	◈◈◈	$99-$199	298
141 / p. 479	CAA	Hilton Garden Inn Toronto/Mississauga	◈◈◈	$109-$229 SAVE	300
142 / p. 479		Residence Inn by Marriott	◈◈◈	$159-$259	302
143 / p. 479	CAA	Quality Inn Airport West - see color ad p 535	◈◈◈	$111-$139 SAVE	301
145 / p. 479	CAA	Monte Carlo Inn Toronto West - see color ad p 531	◈◈	$69-$119 SAVE	301
146 / p. 479		Toronto Airport Hilton	◈◈◈	$119-$249	303
147 / p. 479		Novotel Hotel Mississauga - see color ad p 497	◈◈◈	$209-$239	301

Spotter/Map Page Number	OA	MISSISSAUGA - Lodgings (continued)	Diamond Rating	Rate Range High Season	Listing Page
149 / p. 479	ⒸAA	Delta Meadowvale Resort and Conference Centre - see color ad p 525	◇◇◇	$99-$179 SAVE	298
150 / p. 479	ⒸAA	Sheraton Gateway Hotel In Toronto International Airport - see color ad p 5, p 538	◇◇◇◇	$99-$339 SAVE	302
151 / p. 479		Super 5 Inn	◇◇	$65-$85	303
153 / p. 479	ⒸAA	Sandalwood Suites Hotel Toronto Airport	◇◇◇	$99-$209 SAVE	302
155 / p. 479		Days Inn-Toronto Mississauga - see color ad p 524	◇◇	$90-$120	298
156 / p. 479		Fairfield Inn & Suites by Marriott Toronto Airport	◇◇◇	$99-$153	299
157 / p. 479	ⒸAA	Hampton Inn & Suites Toronto Airport - see color ad p 4, p 528	◇◇◇	$169-$189 SAVE	300
158 / p. 479	ⒸAA	Four Points by Sheraton Mississauga - see color ad p 5, p 526	◇◇◇	$95-$169 SAVE	299
159 / p. 479	ⒸAA	Travelodge Toronto Airport Southwest - see color ad p 539	◇◇	$88-$130 SAVE	303
160 / p. 479	ⒸAA	Holiday Inn Toronto-West - see color ad card insert	◇◇◇	$119-$155 SAVE	301
161 / p. 479	ⒸAA	Monte Carlo Inn Airport Suites - see color ad p 531	◇◇	$79-$129 SAVE	301
162 / p. 479	ⒸAA	Best Western Toronto Airport West - see color ad p 500	◇◇◇	$89-$199 SAVE	297
163 / p. 479	ⒸAA	Delta Toronto Airport West - see color ad p 299	◇◇◇	$278 SAVE	299
164 / p. 479	ⒸAA	Quality Hotel Airport - see color ad p 535	◇◇	$89-$104 SAVE	301
165 / p. 479		Studio 6 Mississauga #1908	◇◇	$85-$101	302
		MISSISSAUGA - Restaurants			
211 / p. 479		Muddy Duck	◇◇	$8-$18	304
212 / p. 479		Aielli Ristorante	◇◇◇	$14-$22	303
213 / p. 479		Big Daddy's Crab Shack & Oyster Bar	◇◇	$10-$15	303
214 / p. 479		Breakwater Fine Dining	◇◇◇◇	$14-$35	303
216 / p. 479		Ruth's Chris Steak House	◇◇◇	$30-$60	305
217 / p. 479		Milestone's Grill and Bar	◇◇	$8-$25	304
218 / p. 479		Old Barber House	◇◇◇	$14-$42	304
220 / p. 479		Canyon Creek Chop House	◇◇	$11-$31	304
221 / p. 479		Alioli Ristorante	◇◇	$13-$30	303
222 / p. 479		Rogues	◇◇◇	$14-$30	305
223 / p. 479		Palms Court Restaurant	◇◇	$10-$19	305
226 / p. 479		Mooskoka Woods Great Canadian Eatery	◇	$5-$22	304
227 / p. 479		La Castile Manor	◇◇	$15-$35	304
228 / p. 479		The Keg Steakhouse and Bar	◇◇	$16-$30	304
229 / p. 479		Zorro's Steak & Seafood House	◇◇◇	$15-$32	305
230 / p. 479		Cherry Hill House	◇◇◇	$10-$30	304
232 / p. 479		Topiary's	◇◇◇	$20-$50	305
233 / p. 479		By the Wharf Seafood House	◇◇◇	$22-$45	304
234 / p. 479		Scorpio Seafood	◇◇◇	$18-$45	305
		VAUGHAN - Lodgings			
170 / p. 479		Courtyard by Marriott Vaughan	◇◇◇	$119-$165	554

DOWNTOWN TORONTO   (See map and index starting on p. 473)

──────── WHERE TO STAY ────────

ANNEX HOUSE BED & BREAKFAST   **Phone:** 416/920-3922   **6**

| All Year | 1P: $80-$85 | 2P: $90-$95 | XP: $20 | D12 |

Location: Jct Bloor St and St. George, 0.5 km n on St. George to Bernard, just w to Madison Ave, then just n. Located
Bed & Breakfast in a residential area. 147 Madison Ave M5R 2S6. Fax: 416/920-3922. **Facility:** Set in a pedestrian-friendly area
close to the university, this B&B offers four simple but pleasant guest rooms on its second level. Smoke free
premises. 4 one-bedroom standard units. 3 stories (no elevator), interior corridors. **Bath:** combo or shower only. **Parking:** on-
site. **Terms:** office hours 7 am-10:30 pm, 2 night minimum stay - seasonal and/or weekends.

SOME UNITS

Downtown Toronto
Downtown Toronto's Best Kept Secret

Travelodge

Ask For Discounted AAA/CAA Rates

- Excellent Location
- Newly Renovated
- Free Parking
- Free Continental Breakfast

- Walk to Entertainment and Theatre District, CN Tower, Convention Center and Business Area

For Reservations Call
800-578-7878

621 King Street West • Toronto, Ontario M5V 1M5
Tel: 416-504-7441 • www.TravelodgeTorontoDowntown.com

"Experience the Difference"

TORONTO

QUALITY
HOTEL & SUITES
BY CHOICE HOTELS

Deluxe Guestrooms & Suites • Restaurant & Lounge • Fitness Room
FREE SHUTTLE TO/FROM THE AIRPORT FOR GUESTS STAYING WITH US
Complimentary parking, local calls, In-room coffee and newspaper

Only minutes away from your next experience whatever you choose,
be it shopping, Harness racing, Canada's Wonderland, Metro Zoo,
Golfing or the fascinating world of Toronto Downtown!

Property Direct 416-240-9090 or **Toll Free 1-800-228-5151** ask for property CN310.
2180 Islington Avenue, Toronto, Ontario M9P 3P1. www.choicehotels.ca/cn310
*Located between Hwys 400, 427 & 409 at the centre of the hub of Toronto. Located just south of the 401
at exit 365 Islington Ave. Conveniently located in the quiet community of Etobicoke.*

(See map and index starting on p. 473)

BEST WESTERN PRIMROSE HOTEL, TORONTO
DOWNTOWN   *Book at aaa.com*   Phone: (416)977-8000   **7**

5/1-10/31	1P: $129-$299	2P: $139-$299	XP: $10 F16
3/31-4/30	1P: $95-$199	2P: $95-$199	XP: $10 F16
11/1-12/31	1P: $85-$199	2P: $85-$199	XP: $10 F16
1/1-3/30	1P: $80-$199	2P: $80-$199	XP: $10 F16

Large-scale Hotel **Location:** Jct Carlton and Jarvis sts. 111 Carlton St M5B 2G3. Fax: 416/977-6323. **Facility:** 341 units. 337 one-bedroom standard units. 4 one-bedroom suites. 23 stories, interior corridors. **Parking:** on-site (fee). **Amenities:** irons, hair dryers. *Some:* high-speed Internet. **Dining:** 7 am-10 pm, cocktails. **Pool(s):** outdoor. **Leisure Activities:** saunas, exercise room. **Guest Services:** gift shop, valet laundry. **Business Services:** conference facilities, fax (fee). **Cards:** AX, DC, DS, MC, VI. **Special Amenities:** free local telephone calls and free newspaper.
(See color ad below)

SOME UNITS

[🛎️] [♿] [📶] [🍴] [🍸] [🏋️] [🐾] [🚭] [DATA PORT] [💻] / [✕] [📞] /
FEE   FEE

BEVERLEY PLACE BED & BREAKFAST   Phone: 416/977-0077   **5**

All Year [BP]	1P: $65-$85	2P: $80-$120	XP: $20

Historic Bed & Breakfast **Location:** Just s of College St. Located in a residential area. 226 Beverley St M5T 1Z3. Fax: 416/599-2242. **Facility:** Near the university, in a neighborhood shared with students, this well-kept B&B offers three guest rooms in a main house and three across the street. Smoke free premises. 6 one-bedroom standard units. 3 stories (no elevator), interior corridors. *Bath:* some shared or private, combo or shower only. **Parking:** on-site (fee). **Terms:** office hours 8 am-10 pm, age restrictions may apply, 3 day cancellation notice-fee imposed. **Cards:** AX, MC, VI.

[✕] [📞]

BOND PLACE HOTEL   *Book at aaa.com*   Phone: (416)362-6061   **31**

5/1-10/31	1P: $109-$129	2P: $109-$129	XP: $15 F14
11/1-4/30	1P: $79-$99	2P: $79-$99	XP: $15 F14

Small-scale Hotel **Location:** Just e off corner of Yonge and Dundas sts. Located adjacent to Eaton Centre. 65 Dundas St E M5B 2G8. Fax: 416/360-6406. **Facility:** 287 one-bedroom standard units. 19 stories, interior corridors. **Parking:** on-site (fee). **Terms:** cancellation fee imposed, package plans. **Amenities:** hair dryers. *Some:* irons. **Guest Services:** valet laundry. **Business Services:** meeting rooms. **Cards:** AX, DC, DS, MC, VI.

SOME UNITS

[ASK] [🛎️] [🍴] [🍸] [🚭] [💻] / [✕] [DATA PORT]

CAMBRIDGE SUITES HOTEL   *Book at aaa.com*   Phone: (416)368-1990   **32**

5/1-10/31	1P: $199		XP: $25 F12
11/1-4/30	1P: $179		XP: $25 F12

Large-scale Hotel **Location:** Just e of Yonge St. Located in the financial district. 15 Richmond St E M5C 1N2. Fax: 416/601-3750. **Facility:** 229 units. 227 one- and 2 two-bedroom suites, some with whirlpools. 22 stories, interior corridors. **Parking:** on-site (fee). **Terms:** cancellation fee imposed, package plans, 3% service charge, pets ($300 fee). **Amenities:** video games (fee), dual phone lines, voice mail, fax, honor bars, irons, hair dryers. *Some:* CD players, high-speed Internet (fee), safes. **Dining:** Resto Portico, see separate listing. **Leisure Activities:** sauna, whirlpool, exercise room. **Guest Services:** valet and coin laundry. **Business Services:** meeting rooms, business center. **Cards:** AX, DC, DS, MC, VI. **Special Amenities:** free expanded continental breakfast and free local telephone calls.
(See color ad p 488)

SOME UNITS

[🐾] [🍴] [🍸] [♿] [✕] [📹] [DATA PORT] [🔌] [🍽️] [💻] / [✕] [VCR] /
FEE

THE ONLY BEST WESTERN HOTEL LOCATED IN THE HEART OF DOWNTOWN TORONTO

BEST WESTERN PRIMROSE HOTEL
111 Carlton Street, Toronto, M5B 2G3
416-977-8000   1-800-268-8082
www.torontoprimrosehotel.com
reservations@torontoprimrosehotel.com

Best Western

Offering the ultimate in luxury and affordability. Modern spacious rooms, outdoor pool, saunas, exercise room, elegant lobby restaurant and bar, gift shop, business centre, Tim Horton's cafe.

Prime location, just minutes away from financial district, major sports facilities, world-class shopping, theatre, art galleries and restaurants.

Rates from **$109.⁰⁰** *sgl/dbl*

Subject to availabilty and taxes

(2 Children under 12 share parents room FREE)

• Senior Discounts
• Theatre Packages available

Additional packages and savings available at your local AAA office.

MENTION THIS ADVERTISEMENT WHEN BOOKING & RECEIVE GIFT ON CHECK-IN

(See map and index starting on p. 473)

CASA LOMA INN

Phone: (416)924-4540

5/1-10/31	1P: $95-$150	2P: $100-$165	XP: $15
11/1-4/30	1P: $80-$130	2P: $90-$150	XP: $10

Historic
Small-scale Hotel

Location: Jct Bloor St and Spadina Ave, just w on Bloor St to Walmer Rd, just n. Located in a busy, residential area. 21 Walmer Rd M5R 2W7. Fax: 416/975-5485. **Facility:** The inn offers small, tastefully appointed guest rooms and modern amenities. Smoke free premises. 28 one-bedroom standard units, some with kitchens and/or whirlpools. 3 stories (no elevator), interior corridors. **Parking:** on-site (fee). **Terms:** office hours 9 am-10 pm, 7 day cancellation notice. **Amenities:** voice mail. **Guest Services:** coin laundry. **Business Services:** meeting rooms. **Cards:** AX, MC, VI. *(See color ad below)*

CAMBRIDGE
·SUITES·
HOTEL

Toronto

• Spacious Suites with Separate Living & Bedroom Areas • Deluxe Complimentary Continental Breakfast Buffet • Hi-Speed Internet Access • Award-winning cuisine in Resto Portico • Fully Equipped Business Centre • Convenient Downtown Location • On-site Parking

15 Richmond Street East
Toronto, Ontario, Canada M5C 1N2

800.463.1990 416.368.1990
www.cambridgesuitestoronto.com

real suite

Casa Loma Inn
Neighborhood Comfort - Private Elegance

Downtown Toronto - Prime Location
• Subway a minute from the Inn • Walking distance to the Casa Loma Castle, Yorkville, ROM, University, Restaurants & Shopping • 26 only non-smoking newly renovated rooms (3 with jacuzzi), all with opening windows • Meeting room • One suite with full kitchen

casalomainn@sympatico.ca

21 Walmer Road, Toronto, On M5R 2W7
Tel. (416) 924-4540 Fax. (416) 975-5485

(See map and index starting on p. 473)

CAWTHRA SQUARE INN   Phone: (416)966-0013   18
          5/1-10/31   1P: $139-$319   2P: $139-$319   XP: $20   F12
          4/1-4/30   1P: $129-$309   2P: $129-$309   XP: $20   F12
          11/1-3/31   1P: $119-$299   2P: $119-$299   XP: $20   F12
Bed & Breakfast **Location:** Directly w of Jarvis St. 10 Cawthra Square M4Y 2H6. Fax: 416/966-4494. **Facility:** This inn features elegantly appointed public areas and a peaceful back garden in the summer months. Guests enjoy the outdoor terraces. Smoke free premises. 4 units. 1 one- and 1 two-bedroom standard units. 1 one- and 1 two-bedroom suites with whirlpools. 3 stories (no elevator), interior corridors. *Bath:* combo or shower only. **Parking:** on-site (fee). **Terms:** 14 day cancellation notice-fee imposed, package plans. **Amenities:** video library, CD players, voice mail, hair dryers. **Leisure Activities:** spa. **Cards:** AX, DC, MC, VI.

(ASK) (S) (🐾) (✕) (VCR) (DATA PORT)

CLARION HOTEL AND SUITES SELBY   *Book at aaa.com*   Phone: (416)921-3142   24
          5/1-10/31 [CP]   1P: $119-$209   2P: $119-$209   XP: $10   F18
          11/1-4/30 [CP]   1P: $109-$199   2P: $109-$199   XP: $10   F18
          Location: Just s of Bloor St. Located in a commercial, residential area. 592 Sherbourne St M4X 1L4.
          Fax: 416/923-3177. **Facility:** 82 units. 79 one-bedroom standard units, some with whirlpools. 3 one-
Small-scale Hotel bedroom suites. 4 stories, interior corridors. *Bath:* combo or shower only. **Parking:** on-site (fee). **Amenities:** high-speed Internet, voice mail, irons, hair dryers. **Guest Services:** coin laundry. **Business Services:** meeting rooms. **Cards:** AX, DS, MC, VI. **Special Amenities:** free continental breakfast and free newspaper.
(See color ad below)

SOME UNITS

(S) (🍴) (▣) / (✕) (DATA PORT) (🛗) /

Historic Selby Hotel
Located in Downtown Toronto
• Complimentary Continental Breakfast
• Free High-Speed Internet & Local Calls
• In-Room Coffee Maker, Hair Dryer, Iron & Board
• Fitness Center
• Historic Mansion Suites with wood-burning
  fireplaces available
• Walking Distance to Yorkville Shopping District
• Conveniently located across from Subway Station and
  Area Attractions

800.228.1AAA
choicehotels.com

© 2004 Choice Hotels International, Inc.

**Clarion Hotel
& Suites Selby**
592 Sherbourne
Street
Toronto, ON M4X 1L4
Tel: 416.921.3142

We'll see you there..

Clarion
Hotel & Suites

WHEN YOU'RE LIVING OUT OF A SUITCASE...

Comfort Hotel
BY CHOICE HOTELS

In Toronto...
Comfort Hotel Downtown
15 Charles Street East
Toronto, Ontario, Canada M4Y 1S1

www.choicehotels.ca/cn228
Email: sales@comfort.nhgi.com

• Heart of downtown, Bloor & Yonge • Yorkville shopping district
• Restaurant • Cable TV • Newly renovated in 2001

For reservations call 416-924-1222 or toll-free 1-800-228-5150

(See map and index starting on p. 473)

COMFORT HOTEL-DOWNTOWN *Book at aaa.com* Phone: (416)924-1222 🔞
(CAA) (SAVE)

7/1-10/31	1P: $139-$179	2P: $149-$189	XP: $10	F18
5/1-6/30	1P: $129-$169	2P: $139-$179	XP: $10	F18
11/1-4/30	1P: $119-$159	2P: $129-$169	XP: $10	F18

Location: On Charles St, e of Yonge St. 15 Charles St E M4Y 1S1. Fax: 416/927-1369. **Facility:** 113 units. 104
Small-scale Hotel one-bedroom standard units. 9 one-bedroom suites. 10 stories, interior corridors. **Parking:** on-site (fee).
Terms: 2 night minimum stay - seasonal, 3% service charge. **Amenities:** voice mail, irons, hair dryers.
Some: dual phone lines. **Dining:** 7 am-10:30, noon-2:30 & 5-9:30 pm, cocktails. **Guest Services:** valet laundry. **Business Services:** meeting rooms. **Cards:** AX, DC, DS, MC, VI. *(See color ad p 489)*

SOME UNITS

COMFORT SUITES CITY CENTRE *Book at aaa.com* Phone: (416)362-7700 🔞
(CAA) (SAVE)

| 5/1-10/15 | 1P: $109-$509 | 2P: $109-$509 | XP: $10 | F17 |
| 10/16-4/30 | 1P: $89-$449 | 2P: $89-$449 | XP: $10 | F17 |

Location: Jct Jarvis St. 200 Dundas St E M5A 4R6. Fax: 416/362-7706. **Facility:** 151 units. 125 one-bedroom
standard units, some with whirlpools. 24 one- and 2 two-bedroom suites ($169-$509) with whirlpools. 7
Small-scale Hotel stories, interior corridors. *Bath:* combo or shower only. **Parking:** on-site (fee). **Terms:** [AP] & [CP] meal
plans available, package plans. **Amenities:** dual phone lines, voice mail, irons, hair dryers. *Fee:* video
games, high-speed Internet. **Dining:** 11:30 am-midnight. **Pool(s):** heated indoor. **Leisure Activities:** whirlpool, exercise room,
game room. **Guest Services:** gift shop, valet and coin laundry. **Business Services:** meeting rooms, business center.
Cards: AX, DC, DS, MC, VI. **Special Amenities:** free local telephone calls and free newspaper.

SOME UNITS

**COURTYARD BY MARRIOTT DOWNTOWN
TORONTO** *Book at aaa.com* Phone: (416)924-0611 🔞
(CAA) (SAVE)

4/1-4/30	1P: $159-$245	2P: $159-$245	XP: $15	F16
5/1-10/31	1P: $149-$225	2P: $149-$225	XP: $15	F16
11/1-3/31	1P: $129-$185	2P: $129-$185	XP: $15	F16

Location: Just n of jct College St. Located in a commercial, residential area. 475 Yonge St M4Y 1X7.
Large-scale Hotel Fax: 416/924-8692. **Facility:** 575 units. 550 one-bedroom standard units. 25 one-bedroom suites ($179-
$455). 17 stories, interior corridors. **Parking:** valet. **Amenities:** video games (fee), high-speed Internet, dual
phone lines, voice mail, irons, hair dryers. **Dining:** 6:30 am-10 pm, Fri-1 am, cocktails. **Pool(s):** small heated indoor, wading.
Leisure Activities: whirlpool, exercise room. **Guest Services:** gift shop, complimentary and valet laundry. **Business Services:**
conference facilities. **Cards:** AX, CB, DC, DS, JC, MC, VI. **Special Amenities:** free full breakfast and free newspaper.
(See color ad p 504)

SOME UNITS

**DAYS HOTEL & CONFERENCE CENTRE-TORONTO
DOWNTOWN** *Book at aaa.com* Phone: (416)977-6655 🔞
(CAA) (SAVE)

| 5/1-10/31 | 1P: $119-$169 | 2P: $119-$169 | XP: $15 | F17 |
| 11/1-4/30 | 1P: $89-$119 | 2P: $89-$119 | XP: $15 | F17 |

Location: Adjacent to Maple Leaf Gardens. 30 Carlton St M5B 2E9. Fax: 416/977-0502. **Facility:** 538 one-
bedroom standard units. 23 stories, interior corridors. **Parking:** on-site (fee). **Terms:** check-in 4 pm,
Large-scale Hotel cancellation fee imposed, [AP], [BP], [CP] & [ECP] meal plans available, package plans, 3% service charge.
Amenities: voice mail, hair dryers. *Some:* irons. **Dining:** 7 am-10:30 pm, cocktails. **Pool(s):** heated indoor.
Leisure Activities: saunas, exercise room. **Guest Services:** gift shop, valet and coin laundry. **Business Services:** meeting
rooms. **Cards:** AX, CB, DC, DS, JC, MC, VI. **Special Amenities:** free newspaper and preferred room (subject to availability
with advance reservations). *(See color ad below)*

SOME UNITS

It's fun to get more.

1-800-DAYS INN
www.daysinn.ca

DAYS HOTEL
& CONFERENCE CENTRE
TORONTO DOWNTOWN

You are always welcome...

- Affordable peace of mind - central to everything
- 538 well-appointed guestrooms with fridge,
  coffee maker and hairdryer
- Windows Restaurant - family friendly dining
- The Beer Cellar - Toronto's newest gathering place
- Indoor pool, saunas and fitness facilities
- Other on-site amenities include: Coffee Zone - coffee and
  Internet cafe, Budget car rental, gift shop and barber shop

Independently owned and
operated by Interras Hotel Management

Days Hotel & Conference Centre – Toronto Downtown	**Tel**	**Fax**
30 Carlton St. Toronto ON M5B 2E9	416 977 6655	416 977 0502
www.dayshoteltoronto.ca	Email: reservations@dayshoteltoronto.ca	

WHY STAY IN A HOTEL WHEN YOU CAN STAY IN A LANDMARK.

Experience the excitement of Toronto from the luxury of The Fairmont Royal York. Let us welcome you to the heart of the city.

THE FAIRMONT
ROYAL YORK

Minimum
10% to 25% off selected packages
Special Offer for CAA/AAA members

Places in the heart.

Call your travel agent or 1 800 441 1414   www.fairmont.com

This offer is valid until April 30, 2006. Discount applies to room rate portion of package only.
Subject to availability of rooms allocated to this program.

(See map and index starting on p. 473)

DELTA CHELSEA HOTEL   *Book at aaa.com*   Phone: 416/595-1975   **12**

5/1-10/31	1P: $165	2P: $165	XP: $20	F18
2/28-4/30	1P: $155	2P: $155	XP: $20	F18
11/1-2/27	1P: $140	2P: $140	XP: $20	F18

Location: W of Yonge St; just s of College St. 33 Gerrard St W M5G 1Z4. Fax: 416/585-4362. **Facility:** 1590 one-bedroom standard units. 27 stories, interior corridors. **Parking:** on-site (fee) and valet. **Terms:** [BP], [CP] & [ECP] meal plans available, small pets only. **Amenities:** video games (fee), voice mail, irons, hair dryers. *Some:* CD players, high-speed Internet (fee), fax. **Dining:** 3 restaurants, 6:30 am-midnight, Fri & Sat-1 am, cocktails. **Pool(s):** 2 heated indoor. **Leisure Activities:** saunas, whirlpools, waterslide, exercise room. *Fee:* children's activity centre, game room. **Guest Services:** gift shop, valet and coin laundry. **Business Services:** conference facilities, business center. **Cards:** AX, DC, DS, JC, MC, VI. *(See color ad p 472)*

Large-scale Hotel

SOME UNITS / FEE

Not that we're bragging,

about our location, smack dab in the spotlight of Toronto's Entertainment District. Heck, you can even walk to theatres, sporting events, shopping and over 150 restaurants, bars and clubs.

Ok.

We're bragging.

Call for our Viva Toronto brochure with all-inclusive entertainment packages starting at $209. CDN, $161*. US.

370 King Street West
TORONTO
Ontario M5V 1J9
CANADA

Tel: 416-599-4000
Fax: 416-599-7394
TTY: 416-595-2521
E-mail: info@hiok.com
www.hiok.com

Holiday Inn
ON KING
TORONTO
The Unexpected.

Owned and operated by Showmart Management Limited. Showmart Management Limited is a Swiss owned company. * U.S. price based on current exchange rate.

Value Seekers

Discover Canada. Save with us.

Canada is waiting to amaze and delight you and The Hilton Family of Hotels can help you discover it for less. As a CAA/AAA member simply call our dedicated number to take advantage of special rates. So wherever you go across Canada, stay and save with the Hilton Family of Hotels.

1-800-916-2221
www.hiltonfamilycanada.com

FOR WHATEVER YOU SEEK

The Hilton Family ®

 Hilton   CONRAD   DOUBLETREE   E EMBASSY SUITES HOTELS   Hampton Inn   Hampton Inn & Suites   Hilton Garden Inn   HOMEWOOD SUITES Hilton

 Hilton HHonors Points & Miles   Rates subject to availability, single/double occupancy for standard accommodations, and are exclusive of tax and gratuities. Valid CAA/AAA membership card required for reservation and at check-in. Hilton HHonors membership, earning of Points & Miles® and redemption of points are subject to HHonors Terms and Conditions. ©2004 Hilton HHonors Worldwide.

VANCOUVER & AREA • KAMLOOPS • CALGARY • EDMONTON • WINNIPEG • WINDSOR • LONDON • CAMBRIDGE
NIAGARA FALLS • TORONTO & AREA • OTTAWA • GATINEAU • MONTRÉAL & AREA • QUÉBEC CITY • SAINT JOHN

(See map and index starting on p. 473)

THE FAIRMONT ROYAL YORK   *Book at aaa.com*   Phone: (416)368-2511   **19**

(CAA) (SAVE)   All Year   1P: $179-$329   2P: $179-$329   XP: $20
▽▽▽▽ ▽▽▽▽   **Location:** QEW/Gardiner Expwy, exit n on York or Bay sts; entrance on Wellington St. Located opposite Union Station.
100 Front St W M5J 1E3. Fax: 416/368-9040. **Facility:** Wall murals and elaborate ceiling treatments
distinguish this landmark hotel which is across the street from the transit system. 1365 units. 1306 one-
Classic   bedroom standard units. 59 one-bedroom suites. 25 stories, interior corridors. **Parking:** on-site (fee) and
Large-scale Hotel   valet. **Terms:** package plans, pets ($25 extra charge). **Amenities:** video games (fee), voice mail, honor
bars, irons, hair dryers. *Some:* CD players, dual phone lines. *Fee:* high-speed Internet. **Dining:** 5
restaurants, 6:30 am-midnight, cocktails, also, Epic, Benihana Restaurant, see separate listings, entertainment. **Pool(s):** heated
indoor. **Leisure Activities:** saunas, whirlpool, steamrooms, exercise room, spa. **Guest Services:** gift shop, valet laundry.
Business Services: conference facilities, business center. Cards: AX, CB, DC, DS, JC, MC, VI. *(See color ad p 491)*

SOME UNITS
[SD] [🐾] [🛏] [24⁀] [Y] [🛋] [⬆M] [⬇] [✕] [🎬] [DATA PORT] [🖥] / [✕] [📶] /
FEE   FEE

FOUR SEASONS HOTEL   *Book at aaa.com*   Phone: (416)964-0411   **2**

(CAA) (SAVE)   4/1-4/30   1P: $335-$540   2P: $365-$580   XP: $30   F13
▽▽▽ ▽▽▽   5/1-3/31   1P: $325-$530   2P: $355-$570   XP: $30   F13
Location: Corner of Avenue Rd and Cumberland Ave. Located in a shopping district. 21 Avenue Rd M5R 2G1.
Fax: 416/964-2301. **Facility:** Known for its afternoon tea service, this service-oriented hotel features
Large-scale Hotel   upscale accommodations. 380 units. 229 one-bedroom standard units. 151 one-bedroom suites ($485-
$570), some with kitchens. 32 stories, interior corridors. **Parking:** on-site (fee) and valet. **Terms:** package
plans. **Amenities:** video games, high-speed Internet, dual phone lines, voice mail, safes, honor bars, irons, hair dryers. *Some:*
CD players, fax. **Dining:** 2 restaurants, 6:30 am-11 pm, cocktails, also, Truffles, see separate listing. **Pool(s):** heated
indoor/outdoor. **Leisure Activities:** saunas, whirlpool, exercise room. *Fee:* spa services in room, massage. **Guest Services:**
gift shop, valet laundry, area transportation-financial district. **Business Services:** conference facilities, business center.
Cards: AX, DC, DS, JC, MC, VI. **Special Amenities:** free newspaper.

SOME UNITS
[🐾] [🍴] [24⁀] [Y] [🛋] [⬇] [✕] [🎬] [DATA PORT] / [✕] [VCR] [🖥] [📷] /

GLOUCESTER SQUARE INNS OF TORONTO   Phone: (416)966-0013   **38**

▽▽▽ ▽▽▽   5/1-9/30   1P: $139-$319   2P: $139-$319   XP: $20   F12
10/1-10/31 & 4/1-4/30   1P: $129-$309   2P: $129-$309   XP: $20   F12
11/1-3/31   1P: $119-$299   2P: $119-$299   XP: $20   F12
Bed & Breakfast   **Location:** Jct Gloucester. 512-514 Jarvis St M4Y 2H6. Fax: 416/966-4494. **Facility:** The rooms here are in two
adjacent mansions that have been beautifully restored to their original grandeur. The elegant public areas are a highlight.
Smoke free premises. 26 one-bedroom standard units, some with whirlpools. 3 stories (no elevator), interior corridors. *Bath:*
some shared or private, combo or shower only. **Parking:** on-site (fee). **Terms:** 14 day cancellation notice-fee imposed, [BP]
meal plan available, package plans. **Amenities:** video library, CD players, high-speed Internet, voice mail, hair dryers. **Leisure
Activities:** *Fee:* massage. **Business Services:** meeting rooms. Cards: AX, DC, JC, MC, VI.

[ASK] [SD] [🛏] [✕] [VCR] [DATA PORT]

HILTON TORONTO   Phone: (416)869-3456   **25**

▽▽▽ ▽▽▽   1/1-4/30   1P: $313-$394   2P: $313-$394   XP: $20   F18
5/1-11/3   1P: $299-$359   2P: $299-$359   XP: $20   F18
Large-scale Hotel   11/4-12/31   1P: $239-$279   2P: $239-$279   XP: $20   F18
Location: Jct University Ave. Located in a commercial area. 145 Richmond St W M5H 2L2. Fax: 416/869-3187.
Facility: Meeting facilities and a fitness center are featured at this art deco-style high-rise; rooms have a distinctive
contemporary design. 601 one-bedroom standard units. 32 stories, interior corridors. *Bath:* combo or shower only. **Parking:** on-
site (fee). **Terms:** 3 day cancellation notice-fee imposed, small pets only ($50 fee). **Amenities:** dual phone lines, voice mail,
honor bars, irons, hair dryers. *Fee:* video games, high-speed Internet. *Some:* CD players. **Dining:** Tundra, Ruth's Chris Steak
House, see separate listings. **Pool(s):** heated indoor/outdoor. **Leisure Activities:** saunas, whirlpool, exercise room. *Fee:*
massage. **Guest Services:** gift shop, valet laundry. **Business Services:** conference facilities, business center. Cards: AX, CB,
DC, DS, JC, MC, VI.

SOME UNITS
[ASK] [🐾] [🍴] [24⁀] [Y] [🛋] [⬇] [✕] [🎬] [DATA PORT] [🖥] / [✕] [📶] /
FEE

HOLIDAY INN TORONTO ON KING (DOWNTOWN)   *Book at aaa.com*   Phone: (416)599-4000   **9**

(CAA) (SAVE)   7/1-10/31   1P: $229-$289   2P: $229-$289   XP: $25   F19
5/1-6/30   1P: $219-$279   2P: $219-$279   XP: $25   F19
▽▽▽ ▽▽▽   11/1-4/30   1P: $199-$259   2P: $199-$259   XP: $25   F19
Location: Between Spadina Ave and Peter St. 370 King St W M5V 1J9. Fax: 416/599-7394. **Facility:** 425 units.
Large-scale Hotel   417 one-bedroom standard units. 8 one-bedroom suites. 20 stories, interior corridors. *Bath:* combo or
shower only. **Parking:** on-site (fee). **Terms:** check-in 4 pm, package plans, 3% service charge.
Amenities: video games (fee), high-speed Internet, dual phone lines, voice mail, irons, hair dryers. **Dining:** 6:30 am-2 & 5-10
pm, cocktails. **Pool(s):** heated outdoor. **Leisure Activities:** saunas, sun deck, exercise room. *Fee:* massage. **Guest Services:**
gift shop, valet laundry. **Business Services:** conference facilities, business center. Cards: AX, CB, DC, DS, JC, MC, VI.
Special Amenities: free newspaper. *(See color ad p 492)*

SOME UNITS
[SD] [🛏] [🍴] [Y] [🛋] [⬇] [✕] [🎬] [DATA PORT] [🖥] / [✕] [📶] /

HOTEL LE GERMAIN   *Book at aaa.com*   Phone: (416)345-9500   **37**

▽▽▽ ▽▽▽   All Year [ECP]   1P: $225-$395   2P: $225-$395   XP: $30   F12
Location: Between John St and Blue Jays Way. 30 Mercer St M5V 1H3. Fax: 416/345-9501. **Facility:** A boutique
Small-scale Hotel   hotel, the property offers luxurious accommodations with a contemporary flair; guest rooms have custom
furniture and stylish baths. 122 units. 118 one-bedroom standard units. 4 one-bedroom suites ($400-$2200).
11 stories, interior corridors. *Bath:* combo or shower only. **Parking:** valet. **Terms:** package plans, pets ($30 extra charge).
Amenities: CD players, high-speed Internet, dual phone lines, voice mail, safes, honor bars, irons, hair dryers. **Dining:** Luce,
see separate listing. **Leisure Activities:** exercise room. *Fee:* massage. **Guest Services:** valet laundry. **Business Services:**
meeting rooms, administrative services (fee). Cards: AX, DC, MC, VI.

SOME UNITS
[🛏] [🍴] [🎬] [DATA PORT] / [✕] /
FEE

(See map and index starting on p. 473)

INTERCONTINENTAL TORONTO   *Book at aaa.com*   Phone: (416)960-5200
   All Year   1P: $200-$2000   2P: $225-$2000   XP: $25   F12
Location: Just w of Avenue Rd. Located in a commercial area. 220 Bloor St W M5S 1T8. Fax: 416/960-8269.
Facility: Marble floors and fresh floral arrangements give this hotel's lobby an upscale, sophisticated ambience. 210 units. 199 one-bedroom standard units. 11 one-bedroom suites, some with whirlpools. 8
Large-scale Hotel stories, interior corridors. **Parking:** on-site (fee) and valet. **Terms:** 7 day cancellation notice-fee imposed, package plans, 15% service charge, small pets only ($50 deposit, with prior approval). **Amenities:** CD players, high-speed Internet, dual phone lines, voice mail, safes, honor bars, irons, hair dryers. *Fee:* video library, video games. *Some:* fax. **Dining:** Signatures, see separate listing. **Pool(s):** heated indoor. **Leisure Activities:** saunas, steamroom, exercise room. *Fee:* massage. **Guest Services:** gift shop, valet laundry. **Business Services:** conference facilities, business center. **Cards:** AX, DC, MC, VI. **Special Amenities:** free newspaper.

SOME UNITS

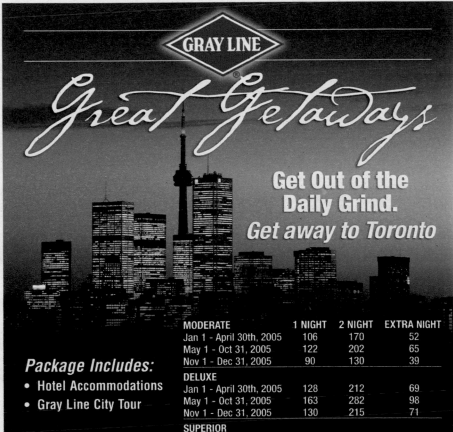

GRAY LINE

Great Getaways

Get Out of the Daily Grind.
Get away to Toronto

Package Includes:

• Hotel Accommodations

• Gray Line City Tour

For information or to book please call

1-800-594-3310

or e-mail to:
toronto@grayline.com

Great Getaways. Great Prices.

MODERATE	1 NIGHT	2 NIGHT	EXTRA NIGHT
Jan 1 - April 30th, 2005	106	170	52
May 1 - Oct 31, 2005	122	202	65
Nov 1 - Dec 31, 2005	90	130	39
DELUXE			
Jan 1 - April 30th, 2005	128	212	69
May 1 - Oct 31, 2005	163	282	98
Nov 1 - Dec 31, 2005	130	215	71
SUPERIOR			
Jan 1 - April 30th, 2005	135	228	76
May 1 - Oct 31, 2005	164	285	99
Nov 1 - Dec 31, 2005	140	238	80

Prices are per person in Canadian Dollars and are based on double occupancy. 7% Goods and Services Tax is additional.

(See map and index starting on p. 473)

INTERCONTINENTAL TORONTO CENTRE   *Book at aaa.com*   Phone: (416)597-1400   ⑳
CAA SAVE   5/1-10/31   1P: $269   XP: $20   F18
11/1-4/30   1P: $249   XP: $20   F18
▼▼▼▼ ▼▼▼▼ **Location:** Between Spadina and University aves. Located attached to the convention centre. 225 Front St W M5V 2X3.
Fax: 416/597-8128. **Facility:** Accommodations are well-appointed, and many offer views of the lake and
Large-scale Hotel SkyDome; common areas are spacious and luxurious. 586 units. 564 one-bedroom standard units. 22 one-
bedroom suites, some with whirlpools. 25 stories, interior corridors. **Parking:** on-site (fee) and valet.
Terms: package plans. **Amenities:** high-speed Internet, dual phone lines, voice mail, honor bars, irons, hair dryers. *Some:* DVD
players, CD players. **Dining:** 6 am-1 am, cocktails, also, Azure, see separate listing. **Pool(s):** heated indoor, wading. **Leisure
Activities:** saunas, whirlpool, exercise room, spa. **Guest Services:** gift shop, valet laundry. **Business Services:** conference
facilities, business center. **Cards:** AX, DC, DS, JC, MC, VI. **Special Amenities: free newspaper.** *(See color ad below)*

SOME UNITS
[S⊘] [¶¶] [24↑] [▼] [⇌] [⊠] [✦] [DATA PORT] [⬛] / [⊠] [⬛] /
FEE

LE ROYAL MERIDIEN KING EDWARD HOTEL   *Book at aaa.com*   Phone: 416-863-3131   ㉟
Property failed to provide current rates
▼▼▼▼ ▼▼▼▼ **Location:** Just e of Yonge St. Located in the financial district. 37 King St E M5C 1E9. Fax: 416/367-5515.
Classic   **Facility:** Afternoon tea is available at this historic hotel; a decorative ceiling treatment is of interest in the
Large-scale Hotel cafe. 294 units. 262 one-bedroom standard units. 32 one-bedroom suites. 18 stories, interior corridors.
Parking: on-site (fee) and valet. **Terms:** small pets only ($50 extra charge). **Amenities:** video games (fee),
dual phone lines, voice mail, honor bars, irons, hair dryers. *Some:* DVD players (fee), CD players. **Dining:** Cafe Victoria, see
separate listing. **Leisure Activities:** exercise room, spa. **Guest Services:** gift shop, valet laundry. **Business Services:** meeting
rooms, business center.

SOME UNITS
[⛺] [¶¶] [24↑] [▼] [✦] [DATA PORT] / [⊠] [VCR] /
FEE   FEE

METROPOLITAN HOTEL   *Book at aaa.com*   Phone: (416)977-5000   ㉝
▼▼▼▼ ▼▼▼▼ All Year   1P: $229-$279   2P: $229-$279
Location: Just s of Dundas St. Located in a commercial area. 108 Chestnut St M5G 1R3. Fax: 416/977-9513.
Large-scale Hotel **Facility:** This European-style hotel offers recreational facilities, two restaurants, luxurious common areas
and well-appointed rooms. 422 units. 364 one-bedroom standard units. 52 one- and 6 two-bedroom suites.
26 stories, interior corridors. **Parking:** on-site (fee) and valet. **Terms:** cancellation fee imposed, package plans, small pets only.
Amenities: video games (fee), CD players, voice mail, safes, honor bars, irons, hair dryers. *Some:* DVD players, high-speed
Internet (fee), dual phone lines, fax. **Dining:** Hemispheres Restaurant Bistro, Lai Wah Heen, see separate listings. **Pool(s):**
heated indoor. **Leisure Activities:** saunas, whirlpool, exercise room. *Fee:* massage. **Guest Services:** gift shop, valet laundry,
area transportation. **Business Services:** conference facilities, business center. **Cards:** AX, CB, DC, DS, JC, MC, VI.

SOME UNITS
[ASK] [✦] [⛺] [¶¶] [▼] [♿] [⇌] [⊠] [✦] [DATA PORT] [⬛] / [⊠] [VCR] [⬛] [▣] /
FEE

In the centre of Toronto you can find the best Canada has to offer.

In downtown Toronto you'll find the best theatre, dining, shopping and world-
famous attractions. Now you can stay at a luxury hotel, located right on Front
Street, with easy access to all of it. Our expert Clef d'Or Concierges will help
you plan a memorable visit. And after a day of exploring our city, you can
indulge in Victoria Spa, dine in the exquisite Azure Restaurant or simply relax
in your comfortable guest room. One hotel understands you.

Rates From $249 CAD per night

INTERCONTINENTAL.
TORONTO CENTRE

225 Front Street West Toronto, Ontario M5V 2X3
www.torontocentre.intercontinental.com
416-597-1400

©2005 InterContinental Hotels Group. All rights reserved.

(See map and index starting on p. 473)

NOVOTEL TORONTO CENTRE *Book at aaa.com*   Phone: (416)367-8900 🗺23

4/15-4/30	1P: $174-$229	2P: $174-$229	XP: $25	F16
5/1-11/30	1P: $169-$225	2P: $169-$225	XP: $25	F16
12/1-4/14	1P: $139-$219	2P: $139-$219	XP: $25	F16

Location: Just ne of Gardiner Expwy via Yonge St. 45 The Esplanade M5E 1W2. Fax: 416/360-8285. **Facility:** 262 **Large-scale Hotel** one-bedroom standard units. 9 stories, interior corridors. **Parking:** on-site (fee). **Terms:** 2 night minimum stay - seasonal, cancellation fee imposed, pets ($20 extra charge). **Amenities:** video games, voice mail, honor bars, irons, hair dryers. *Some:* high-speed Internet. **Dining:** 6:30 am-midnight. **Pool(s):** heated indoor. **Leisure Activities:** saunas, whirlpool, exercise room. **Guest Services:** gift shop, valet laundry. **Business Services:** meeting rooms. **Cards:** AX, DS, MC, VI. *(See color ad below)*   SOME UNITS

Novation Room

Relax with us.

Nobody welcomes visitors like Novotel. We offer convenient locations close to major highways, theaters, shopping and local landmarks. All of our Toronto properties feature pools, fitness centers, saunas and indoor parking. When you're ready to unwind, stop by Café Nicole and enjoy cocktails and great international cuisine. Room service from Café Nicole is also available. Whatever your needs, we will help make the most of your stay. Discover what makes Novotel a leading hospitality brand, with over 370 locations worldwide.

Novotel Toronto Centre
45 The Esplanade
Toronto,
Ontario M5E 1W2
(416) 367-8900

Novotel Mississauga
3670 Hurontario St.
Missisauga,
Ontario L5B 1P3
(905) 896-1000

Novotel North York
3 Park Home Ave.
North York
Ontario M2N 6L3
(416) 733-2929

1-800 NOVOTEL   *www.novotel.com*   *www.accorhotels.com*

Additional Canadian Locations: Montréal Centre, Ottawa
Mexico: Monterrey Valle and Mexico Santa Fé **United States:** New York City -Times Square

 ▶ **A new perspective on our Hotels and Services**

(See map and index starting on p. 473)

PARK HYATT TORONTO *Book at aaa.com*   Phone: (416)925-1234   **3**
Ⓐ SAVE   All Year   1P: $199-$399   2P: $199-$399
Location: Corner of Bloor St W. Located in Yorkville shopping area. 4 Avenue Rd M5R 2E8. Fax: 416/924-4933.
▼▼▼ ▼▼▼▼   **Facility:** A lounge on this hotel's roof offers good views of the city skyline; rooms and common areas are elegantly furnished. 346 units. 320 one-bedroom standard units. 26 one-bedroom suites, some with
Large-scale Hotel   whirlpools. 15-18 stories, interior corridors. *Bath:* combo or shower only. **Parking:** on-site (fee) and valet.
Terms: 14 day cancellation notice-fee imposed. **Amenities:** CD players, high-speed Internet, dual phone lines, voice mail, safes, honor bars, irons, hair dryers. *Some:* DVD players. **Dining:** 6:30 am-11 pm, cocktails, also, Annona, see separate listing. **Leisure Activities:** steamrooms, exercise room, spa. *Fee:* saunas, whirlpools. **Guest Services:** gift shop, valet laundry, area transportation-downtown. **Business Services:** conference facilities, business center. **Cards:** AX, CB, DC, DS, JC, MC, VI.

SOME UNITS
〔🍴〕〔24↑〕〔🍽〕〔👤〕〔✂〕〔📷〕〔DATA PORT〕/〔✕〕〔🛏〕〔📠〕〔🖥〕/

QUALITY HOTEL DOWNTOWN   *Book at aaa.com*   Phone: (416)367-5555   **17**
Ⓐ SAVE   6/1-10/31 [ECP]   1P: $149-$167   2P: $149-$167   XP: $10   F18
5/1-5/31 [ECP]   1P: $136-$156   2P: $136-$156   XP: $10   F18
▼▼▼▼   1/1-4/30 [ECP]   1P: $110-$156   2P: $110-$156   XP: $10   F18
11/1-12/31 [ECP]   1P: $122-$138   2P: $122-$138   XP: $10   F18
Small-scale Hotel   **Location:** West side of Jarvis St; between Adelaide and Richmond sts; 1 km n off Gardiner Expwy at Jarvis St exit. 111 Lombard St M5C 2T9. Fax: 416/367-3470. **Facility:** 196 one-bedroom standard units. 15 stories, interior corridors. **Parking:** on-site (fee). **Terms:** small pets only. **Amenities:** video games (fee), voice mail, irons, hair dryers. *Some:* high-speed Internet. **Leisure Activities:** limited exercise equipment. **Guest Services:** gift shop, valet laundry. **Business Services:** meeting rooms. **Cards:** AX, CB, DC, DS, MC, VI. *(See color ad below)*

SOME UNITS
〔S D〕〔🛏〕〔🍴〕〔📷〕〔DATA PORT〕〔🖥〕/〔✕〕〔🛏〕/
FEE FEE

QUALITY HOTEL MIDTOWN   *Book at aaa.com*   Phone: (416)968-0010   **10**
Ⓐ SAVE   5/1-9/30   1P: $109-$199   2P: $109-$199   XP: $10   F18
10/1-4/30   1P: $99-$179   2P: $99-$179   XP: $10   F18
▼▼▼▼   **Location:** Just w of St. George. 280 Bloor St W M5S 1V8. Fax: 416/968-7765. **Facility:** 209 one-bedroom standard units. 14 stories, interior corridors. **Parking:** on-site (fee). **Terms:** [AP] & [CP] meal plans
Small-scale Hotel   available, package plans. **Amenities:** voice mail, irons, hair dryers. *Some:* dual phone lines. **Dining:** 2 restaurants, 7 am-11 pm. **Guest Services:** valet laundry. **Business Services:** meeting rooms, fax (fee).
Cards: AX, DC, DS, JC, MC, VI.

SOME UNITS
〔S D〕〔🛏〕〔🍴〕〔🍽〕〔👥〕〔📷〕〔DATA PORT〕〔🖥〕/〔✕〕〔🛏〕/

RADISSON PLAZA HOTEL ADMIRAL TORONTO   *Book at aaa.com*   Phone: (416)203-3333   **21**
Ⓐ SAVE   4/1-4/30   1P: $189   2P: $189   XP: $20   F16
5/1-11/30   1P: $179   2P: $179   XP: $20   F16
▼▼▼▼   12/31-3/31   1P: $145   2P: $145   XP: $20   F16
12/1-12/30   1P: $139   2P: $139   XP: $20   F16
Small-scale Hotel   **Location:** QEW E to Gardiner Expwy, exit Bay St S. Located on Lake Ontario. 249 Queen's Quay W M5J 2N5. Fax: 416/203-3100. **Facility:** 157 one-bedroom standard units. 8 stories, interior corridors. **Parking:** on-site (fee). **Amenities:** voice mail, irons, hair dryers. *Some:* high-speed Internet (fee). **Dining:** Commodore's, see separate listing. **Pool(s):** small heated outdoor. **Leisure Activities:** whirlpool, exercise room. **Guest Services:** gift shop, valet laundry. **Business Services:** conference facilities, business center. **Cards:** AX, DC, MC, VI. **Special Amenities:** free newspaper. *(See color ad p 521 & p 499)*

SOME UNITS
〔🍴〕〔🍽〕〔🏊〕〔📷〕〔🖥〕/〔✕〕〔🛏〕/

Toronto's Choices

Quality Hotel Midtown
Fashionably located... affordably priced!

QUALITY HOTEL
BY CHOICE HOTELS

Quality Hotel Downtown
Downtown Sophistication, country hospitality!!

$99 - $169
single or double
280 Bloor Street West
(in Yorkville)
Reservations: 416-968-0010

$89 - $169 single or double
including deluxe continental
breakfast!!
111 Lombard Street
(in Distillery District)
Reservations: 416-367-5555

Visit us online at www.selectcanadianhotels.com

We welcome AAA Cardholders and we LOVE pets!!!

STAY DOWNTOWN   STAY RELAXED

A boutique-style hotel at Toronto's Harbourfront. The best of both worlds; a downtown location, on the lake, in a vacation setting. 157 renovated guestrooms with a great view of the city, marina or harbour. AAA Four Diamond-Award winning Restaurant for 10 consecutive years. Outdoor swimming pool overlooking Toronto Harbour, fitness facility, indoor whirlpool.
THE ONLY THING WE OVERLOOK IS THE LAKE!

Radisson

TORONTO - HARBOURFRONT
Radisson Admiral Hotel • 249 Queens Quay West
Toronto, ON M5J 2N5 • 416-203-3333
www.radissonadmiral.com • 1-800-333-3333

STAY YOUR OWN WAY℠

Savings for all Seasons

No matter the season, Hertz offers CAA members exclusive discounts and benefits.

Operating in 150 countries at over 7,000 rental locations worldwide, Hertz makes traveling more convenient and efficient wherever and whenever you go. Hertz offers CAA members discounts up to 20% on car rentals worldwide.

To receive your exclusive CAA member discounts and benefits, mention your CAA membership card at time of reservation and present it at time of rental.

For reservations and program details, call your CAA Travel office or the Hertz/CAA Desk at **1-800-263-0600**, Toronto **416-620-9620**.

Hertz rents Fords and other fine cars.
® REG. U.S. PAT. OFF. © HERTZ SYSTEM INC., 1999/2006-99

Hertz
exactly.

(See map and index starting on p. 473)

RAMADA HOTEL AND SUITES DOWNTOWN   *Book at aaa.com*   Phone: (416)977-4823   **11**

(CAA) (SAVE)   5/1-10/31   1P: $119-$199   2P: $119-$199   XP: $15   F
            11/1-4/30   1P: $89-$149   2P: $89-$149   XP: $15   F

▼▼▼▼   **Location:** S of jct Carlton and Jarvis sts. 300 Jarvis St M5B 2C5. Fax: 416/977-4830. **Facility:** 102 units. 57 one-bedroom standard units. 38 one- and 7 two-bedroom suites ($159-$309). 10 stories, interior corridors.

Small-scale Hotel   **Parking:** on-site (fee). **Terms:** package plans. **Amenities:** voice mail, irons, hair dryers. *Some:* high-speed Internet. **Dining:** 7 am-2 & 5-9 pm; dinner hours may vary seasonally, cocktails. **Pool(s):** heated indoor. **Leisure Activities:** sauna, whirlpool, steamroom, squash court, ping pong, exercise room. **Guest Services:** valet laundry. **Business Services:** meeting rooms. **Cards:** AX, DC, MC, VI. **Special Amenities:** free newspaper and free room upgrade (subject to availability with advance reservations). *(See color ad below)*

SOME UNITS

🆂 🛏 🍽 🏊 🕼 🎥 📠 💻 / 🗙 🔌 📺 /

RAMADA® Hotel & Suites
DOWNTOWN TORONTO

A BOUTIQUE STYLE HOTEL WITH FACILITIES FOUND IN LARGER HOTELS

• Convenient Location   • Restaurant
• Spacious Guestrooms   • Indoor Pool
• Conference Facilities

TEL: (416) 977-4823   FAX: (416) 977-4830
Toll free: 1-800-567-2233
www.ramadahotelandsuites.com

300 JARVIS ST., TORONTO, ONTARIO, CANADA M5B 2C5

Best Western

Toronto Airport West
Hotel & Conference Centre

TEL
(905) 670-8180

FAX
(905) 670-8083

Toll-free
1-800-260-3333

• Newly Renovated Guest Rooms & Suites
• Free Parking
• Free Local Calls
• Restaurant & Lounge
• Minutes From Downtown Toronto
• Shuttle Service Available

The World's Largest Hotel Chain®
www.bestwesterntorontoairportwest.com

5825 DIXIE ROAD (NORTH OF 401), MISSISSAUGA, ONTARIO L4W 4V7

Delegate Travel Planning to Someone You Trust

Visit aaa.com and enjoy a whole new world of travel information.

AAA's Internet TripTik® provides interactive maps and search tools that make travel planning easy. Get hotel Diamond ratings, photos, and great room rates. Find countless places to eat and play.

Trust AAA to simplify travel planning.

Travel with Confidence.
Travel with AAA.

(See map and index starting on p. 473)

RENAISSANCE TORONTO HOTEL AT SKYDOME   *Book at aaa.com*   Phone: (416)341-7100   **26**

CAA SAVE

| | 5/1-10/31 | 1P: $189-$279 | 2P: $189-$279 | XP: $25 | F18 |
| | 11/1-4/30 | 1P: $169-$259 | 2P: $169-$259 | XP: $25 | F18 |

Location: Jct Front St. Located adjacent to SkyDome. 1 Blue Jays Way M5V 1J4. Fax: 416/341-5091.
Facility: Some units with view of stadium. 348 units. 301 one-bedroom standard units. 47 one-bedroom
Large-scale Hotel suites, some with whirlpools. 11 stories, interior corridors. **Parking:** on-site (fee) and valet.
Terms: cancellation fee imposed, package plans. **Amenities:** dual phone lines, voice mail, irons, hair
dryers. *Fee:* video games, high-speed Internet. **Dining:** The Bistro, see separate listing. **Pool(s):** heated indoor. **Leisure
Activities:** saunas, whirlpool, squash courts. *Fee:* massage. **Guest Services:** gift shop, valet laundry. **Business Services:**
conference facilities, business center. **Cards:** AX, CB, DC, DS, MC, VI. **Special Amenities: free full breakfast and free
newspaper.** *(See color ad below)*

SOME UNITS

THE SHERATON CENTRE TORONTO HOTEL   *Book at aaa.com*   Phone: (416)361-1000   **15**

CAA SAVE

| | 5/1-11/19 | 1P: $379-$439 | 2P: $379-$439 | XP: $30 | F18 |
| | 11/20-4/30 | 1P: $320-$380 | 2P: $320-$380 | XP: $30 | F18 |

Location: Opposite Toronto Civic Centre and City Hall. 123 Queen St W M5H 2M9. Fax: 416/947-4854.
Facility: Waterfalls and a garden are featured in the hotel's centre court; many rooms offer good views of
Large-scale Hotel the city. 1377 units. 1307 one-bedroom standard units. 70 one-bedroom suites, some with whirlpools. 11-43
stories, interior corridors. **Parking:** on-site (fee) and valet. **Terms:** cancellation fee imposed, package plans,
small pets only. **Amenities:** video games, dual phone lines, voice mail, irons, hair dryers. *Some:* high-speed Internet (fee),
safes, honor bars. **Dining:** 3 restaurants, 6 am-11 pm, cocktails, also, Michael Seltzer's Le Biftheque Steakhouse, see separate
listing. **Pool(s):** heated indoor/outdoor. **Leisure Activities:** saunas, whirlpool, spa. *Fee:* exercise room. **Guest Services:** gift
shop, valet and coin laundry. **Business Services:** conference facilities, business center. **Cards:** AX, JC, MC, VI.
(See color ad p 5, p 502)

SOME UNITS

SOHO METROPOLITAN HOTEL   *Book at aaa.com*   Phone: (416)599-8800   **39**

| | All Year | 1P: $280-$460 | 2P: $280-$460 | XP: $40 | F18 |

Location: Jct Blue Jays Way. 318 Wellington St W M5V 3T4. Fax: 416/599-8801. **Facility:** This distinctive hotel
offers guests contemporary style and luxury in the entertainment district. 88 one-bedroom standard units. 20
Small-scale Hotel stories, interior corridors. **Parking:** on-site (fee) and valet. **Terms:** cancellation fee imposed.
Amenities: DVD players, CD players, high-speed Internet, dual phone lines, voice mail, safes, honor bars, irons, hair dryers.
Dining: Senses, see separate listing. **Pool(s):** heated indoor. **Leisure Activities:** whirlpool, steamrooms. *Fee:* massage. **Guest
Services:** valet laundry, area transportation. **Business Services:** meeting rooms, business center. **Cards:** AX, DC, MC, VI.

SOME UNITS

UNIQUELY RENAISSANCE

A SPECIAL rAAAte.

AAA/CAA members receive 15% discount.

The Renaissance Toronto Hotel at SkyDome is
the hottest urban resort located in the heart of
the entertainment and financial districts. 70 of
the 348 guestrooms, as well as the Diamonds bar
and the Bistro restaurant, overlook the stadium.
Don't forget to check out our fully equipped fitness club with indoor pool, whirlpool, sauna and
5 international squash courts.

**15% discount off published rates, complimentary
buffet breakfast for two, and a complimentary
newspaper. Call 1-800-237-1512 today to reserve
your AAA/CAA rate.**

RENAISSANCE
TORONTO HOTEL
AT SKYDOME

One Blue Jays Way, Toronto, Ontario
p: 416.341.7100 | f: 416.341.5091 | tf: 800.237.1512
renaissancetorontoskydome.com
e: reservations@renaissancetoronto.com

(See map and index starting on p. 473)

THE STRATHCONA HOTEL   *Book at aaa.com*   **Phone:** 416/363-3321 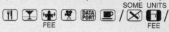

    5/1-10/31   1P: $129-$149   2P: $129-$149   XP: $10   F12
             11/1-4/30   1P: $109-$119   2P: $109-$119   XP: $10   F12

Location: Just n of Front St. 60 York St M5J 1S8. Fax: 416/363-4679. **Facility:** 194 units. 193 one-bedroom standard units. 1 one-bedroom suite ($399). 12 stories, interior corridors. *Bath:* combo or shower only. **Small-scale Hotel** **Parking:** no self-parking. **Terms:** cancellation fee imposed. **Amenities:** video games (fee), voice mail, irons, hair dryers. *Some:* dual phone lines. *Fee:* high-speed Internet. **Dining:** 2 restaurants, 6:30 am-10 pm, Sun-2 pm. **Guest Services:** valet laundry. **Business Services:** meeting rooms. **Cards:** AX, DC, DS, MC, VI. *(See color ad p 503)*

SOME UNITS

FEE   FEE

Stay
and Play

Ask for your special membership rate

Just steps from the Eaton Centre shopping mall, the best in live theatre, dining and renowned attractions...we're in the heart of it all! Don't forget your bathing suits - enjoy the largest indoor/outdoor hotel pool in the city! Stroll among the 2.5 acre waterfall gardens, enjoy superb meals in our three restaurants and lounges including the convenience of in-room dining. Pamper yourself in the plush comfort of our Sheraton Sweet Sleeper℠ Bed.

Call 1-800-325-3535 or your travel planner.
Visit www.sheraton.com/centretoronto. Best rates, guaranteed.

Sheraton Centre
Toronto
H O T E L

sheraton.com/centretoronto

  Preferred Lodging Partner

MEMBER OF STARWOOD PREFERRED GUEST

* Subject to availability. Rate valid until May 2006.

(See map and index starting on p. 473)

THE SUTTON PLACE HOTEL   *Book at aaa.com*   Phone: (416)924-9221   ③⓪
    ⓒⒶⒶ ⓈⒶⓋⒺ   5/1-10/31   1P: $199-$500   2P: $199-$500   XP: $20   F18
                  11/1-4/30   1P: $189-$500   2P: $189-$500   XP: $20   F18
▼▼▼▼ ▼▼▼▼ **Location:** Jct Wellesley St. 955 Bay St M5S 2A2. Fax: 416/924-1778. **Facility:** Traditional-style interiors are
        featured at this luxury high-rise in a central location. 375 units. 316 one-bedroom standard units, some with
Large-scale Hotel kitchens. 42 one- and 17 two-bedroom suites ($500-$3000) with kitchens, some with whirlpools. 33 stories,
        interior corridors. **Parking:** on-site (fee) and valet. **Terms:** cancellation fee imposed, small pets only ($150
deposit). **Amenities:** video games (fee), dual phone lines, voice mail, irons, hair dryers. *Some:* CD players, fax, safes, honor
bars. *Fee:* high-speed Internet. **Dining:** Accents Restaurant and Bar, see separate listing. **Pool(s):** heated indoor. **Leisure
Activities:** saunas, exercise room. *Fee:* massage. **Guest Services:** gift shop, valet laundry. **Business Services:** conference
facilities, business center. **Cards:** AX, DC, JC, MC, VI. **Special Amenities:** free newspaper.   SOME UNITS

🐑 🍽 24⁷ ⚊ ⛨ ⤢ ⊠ 🏈 🔌 ▣ / ⊠ VCR 🛁 🖥 /
FEE   FEE

TORONTO MARRIOTT BLOOR YORKVILLE   *Book at aaa.com*   Phone: (416)961-8000   ④
    ⓒⒶⒶ ⓈⒶⓋⒺ   12/1-4/30   1P: $259-$279   2P: $259-$279   XP: $20   F18
                  5/1-11/30   1P: $249-$269   2P: $249-$269   XP: $20   F18
▼▼▼▼ ▼▼▼▼ **Location:** Just e of Yonge St. Located in part of a retail arcade. 90 Bloor St E M4W 1A7. Fax: 416/961-4635.
        Facility: The hotel is linked to shopping and the subway system and offers well-appointed rooms with
Large-scale Hotel modern amenities. 258 units. 243 one-bedroom standard units. 15 one-bedroom suites. 11 stories, interior
        corridors. *Bath:* combo or shower only. **Parking:** on-site (fee) and valet. **Terms:** 3% service charge.
Amenities: dual phone lines, voice mail, irons, hair dryers. *Fee:* video games, high-speed Internet. **Dining:** Matisse, see
separate listing. **Leisure Activities:** saunas, exercise room. *Fee:* massage. **Guest Services:** valet and coin laundry, area
transportation-downtown. **Business Services:** meeting rooms, business center. **Cards:** AX, CB, DC, DS, JC, MC, VI.
(See color ad p 504)   SOME UNITS

Ⓢⓓ 🍽 ⚊ ⚙M ⊠ 🏈 🔌 ▣ / ⊠ 🛁 🖥 /

**TORONTO MARRIOTT DOWNTOWN EATON
CENTRE**   *Book at aaa.com*   Phone: (416)597-9200   ⑯
▼▼▼▼ ▼▼▼▼ All Year   1P: $169-$299   2P: $169-$299
        Location: Just s of Dundas St. Located adjacent to Eaton Centre. 525 Bay St M5G 2L2. Fax: 416/597-9211.
Large-scale Hotel **Facility:** An attractive plaza with a Gothic-style church and several fountains forms the backdrop for this
        service-oriented hotel. 459 units. 444 one-bedroom standard units. 15 one-bedroom suites ($450-$699),
some with whirlpools. 18 stories, interior corridors. **Parking:** on-site (fee) and valet. **Terms:** package plans, small pets only.
Amenities: video games, high-speed Internet (fee), voice mail, irons, hair dryers. **Pool(s):** heated indoor. **Leisure
Activities:** saunas, whirlpool, exercise room. *Fee:* massage. **Guest Services:** gift shop, valet laundry. **Business Services:**
conference facilities, business center. **Cards:** AX, DC, DS, JC, MC, VI. *(See color ad p 504)*   SOME UNITS

ⒶⓈⓀ 🐑 🍽 ⚊ ⛨ ⚙M ⤢ ⊠ 🏈 🔌 ▣ / ⊠ 🛁 🖥 /

THE STRATHCONA HOTEL
Downtown Toronto

Location,   A downtown boutique hotel nestled in the heart of
         the entertainment, dining, sports and financial district.

           • Steps to Air Canada Centre, CN tower, Metro
Location,   Convention Centre, Queens Quay, Harbourfront,
              SkyDome and Union Station

           • Wellington Racquet & Fitness Club next door

Location. • York Street Cafe and Pub in hotel

           • Ask about our AAA special for the month

           • *NEW* highspeed wireless internet

                        Approved

              60 York Street, Toronto, ON M5J 1S8
          Tel: (416) 363-3321 • Fax: (416) 363-4679
                   Toll Free: 1-800-268-8304
              email: info@thestrathconahotel.com
                   www.thestrathconahotel.com

475 Yonge Street
Toronto • Ontario
M4Y 1X7 • Canada
Phone: 1 416-924-0611
Fax: 1 416-924-8692
Toll Free: 1-800-847-5075
sales@courtyardtoronto.com
www.courtyard.com/yyzcy

*Great location at great value!
Located in the heart of downtown Toronto,
walking distance to fashionable shopping,
restaurants, museums, galleries, theatre
and attractions, the Courtyard by Marriott
Downtown Toronto is popular with all our
guests. When finished a remarkable day
of activities, relax in our pool, whirlpool
or work out in our fitness club.
Afterwards you can continue to set the tone
for your visit by enjoying great cuisine and
service at the hotel's Yonge Street Grille.*

Marriott.
TORONTO BLOOR
YORKVILLE

90 Bloor Street East
Toronto • Ontario
M4W 1A7 • Canada
Phone: 1 416-961-8000
Fax: 1 416-961-4635
Toll Free: 1-800-859-7180
www.marriott.com/yyzmc

*A hotel should be a reflection of its city
and its neighbourhood. Located in
fashionable Bloor-Yorkville, at the bustling
crossroads of Yonge and Bloor streets,
the Toronto Marriott Bloor Yorkville does
just that. At our doorstep, enjoy
Toronto's top restaurants, shopping at
the biggest brands flagship stores,
quaint boutiques, historic museums and
more than 30 private galleries.
This newly renovated hotel along with
our unique Matisse Restaurant & Bar
and personable, attentive service truly enhances
your visit to our dynamic city.*

Marriott.
TORONTO
EATON CENTRE

525 Bay Street
Toronto • Ontario
M5G 2L2 • Canada
Phone: 1 416-597-9200
Fax: 1 416-597-9211
Toll Free: 1-800-905-0667
www.marriotteatoncentre.com

*In the heart of downtown, the Toronto Marriott
Eaton Centre is within walking distance of all the
main attractions, including theatres, galleries and
restaurants. A shopaholic's dream, the hotel is
connected to the famous Eaton Centre shopping
complex via an indoor walkway. With a fitness
centre, pool and fully-equipped "Rooms That Work,"
Toronto Marriott Eaton Centre appeals to
business and leisure travellers alike.
This luxury hotel boasts three fabulous
restaurants including the popular JW's
Steakhouse - home of the 16 oz bone-in filet.*

Marriott.
TORONTO AIRPORT

901 Dixon Road
Toronto • Ontario
M9W 1J5 • Canada
Phone: 1 416-674-9400
Fax: 1 416-674-8292
Toll Free: 1-800-905-2811
www.marriott.com/yyzot

*Whether you're travelling for business, pleasure,
or planning a meeting, the Toronto Airport
Marriott focuses on what it takes to make
your trip successful. Your business objectives will
stay on course with the convenient workstations
in "The Room that Works", the services of our
full-service Business Centre, and the amenities
of our Concierge Level. Conveniently located
close to all major highways connecting the
Greater Toronto Area you will find it easy
to access any of the great attractions in
and around the city. Count on Marriott
dependability to make your stay a memorable one.*

(See map and index starting on p. 473)

TRAVELODGE TORONTO DOWNTOWN WEST   *Book at aaa.com*   Phone: (416)504-7441
(CAA) (SAVE)   6/1-9/30   1P: $149-$169   2P: $149-$169   XP: $10   F17
    5/1-5/31 & 10/1-4/30   1P: $139-$159   2P: $139-$159   XP: $10   F17
▼▼▼ ▼▼▼   **Location:** QEW, Gardiner Expwy to Spadina Ave N to King St W; between Bathurst St and Spadina Ave. Located in a
    commercial area. 621 King St W M5V 1M5. Fax: 416/504-4722. **Facility:** 85 one-bedroom standard units. 3
Small-scale Hotel   stories, interior corridors. **Parking:** on-site. **Terms:** [CP] meal plan available. **Amenities:** voice mail, irons,
    hair dryers. **Guest Services:** coin laundry. **Business Services:** meeting rooms. **Cards:** AX, CB, DC, DS,
MC, VI. **Special Amenities: free continental breakfast and free local telephone calls.** *(See color ad p 486)*

SOME UNITS
(S D) (DATA PORT) (□) / (X) /

THE WESTIN HARBOUR CASTLE   *Book at aaa.com*   Phone: (416)869-1600   22
(CAA) (SAVE)   3/26-4/30   1P: $239-$389   XP: $30   F17
    5/1-11/27   1P: $239-$369   XP: $30   F17
▼▼▼ ▼▼▼ ▼▼▼   11/28-3/25   1P: $139-$299   XP: $30   F17
    Location: At the foot of Bay St; on shore of Lake Ontario. One Harbour Sq M5J 1A6. Fax: 416/869-0573.
Large-scale Hotel   **Facility:** Just minutes from the waterfront, this hotel overlooks Toronto Bay and Lake Ontario and features a
    rooftop restaurant. 977 units. 931 one-bedroom standard units. 40 one- and 6 two-bedroom suites. 35
stories, interior corridors. **Parking:** on-site (fee) and valet. **Amenities:** dual phone lines, voice mail, honor bars, irons, hair
dryers. *Some:* high-speed Internet (fee), fax. **Dining:** 2 restaurants, 6:30 am-1 am, cocktails, also, Toula, see separate listing.
Pool(s): heated indoor. **Leisure Activities:** saunas, whirlpool, lighted tennis court, childrens activity centre, exercise room, spa.
Fee: squash. **Guest Services:** gift shop, valet laundry, area transportation-Eaton Centre. *Fee:* tanning facility. **Business
Services:** conference facilities, business center. **Cards:** AX, DC, JC, MC, VI. *(See color ad p 5, & below)*

SOME UNITS
(S D) (11) (24) (↑) (≈) (X) (♥) (DATA PORT) (□) / (X) /

WINDSOR ARMS   *Book at aaa.com*   Phone: (416)971-9666   13
(CAA) (SAVE)   All Year [CP]   1P: $295-$2000   XP: $30   F12
▼▼▼ ▼▼▼   **Location:** Jct Bloor St. Located in a residential area. 18 St. Thomas St M5S 3E7. Fax: 416/921-9121. **Facility:** Said
    to be frequented by visiting celebrities, the property has an ambience reminiscent of hotels in Europe. 28
Small-scale Hotel   units. 7 one-bedroom standard units with whirlpools. 21 one-bedroom suites ($425-$2000) with whirlpools. 5
    stories, interior corridors. **Parking:** on-site (fee) and valet. **Terms:** package plans, $4 service charge, small
pets only. **Amenities:** DVD players, CD players, high-speed Internet, dual phone lines, voice mail, safes,
honor bars, irons, hair dryers. **Dining:** 7 am-2 am, also, The Courtyard Cafe, see separate listing. **Pool(s):** heated indoor.
Leisure Activities: saunas, steamrooms, exercise room, spa. **Guest Services:** valet laundry, area transportation-downtown
commercial district, beauty salon. **Business Services:** meeting rooms, PC (fee). **Cards:** AX, DC, MC, VI. **Special Amenities:
free continental breakfast and free newspaper.**

SOME UNITS
(S D) (🍴) (11) (24) (Y) (↑) (≈) (X) (VCR) (♥) (DATA PORT) / (X) /

CAA/AAA
rates
from $139* CDN
to $229* CDN

m o d e r n
l u x u r y

sometimes, no reason is the
perfect reason to get away
The food tastes even sweeter. The beds feel even softer.
The bath seems even more relaxing. When you can
experience Westin at rates like these, the world suddenly
seems like a much better place.

For reservations call us at 416-869-1600 or 1-800-WESTIN-1.
Visit westin.com/harbourcastle to get the best rates online.
Guaranteed.

MEMBER OF (○) STARWOOD PREFERRED GUEST®

THE WESTIN
HARBOUR CASTLE
TORONTO

(AAA)
Four Diamond
Award

*Basic room rates do not include taxes. Rates are per room, per night, based on single/double occupancy and availability. A limited number of rooms may be available
at these rates and additional restrictions and black-out dates may apply. Please mention promotional code CAA/AAA when making your reservation. Not responsible
for omissions or typographical errors. Not to be combined with other offers or promotions. ©2004 Starwood Hotels & Resorts Worldwide, Inc.

(See map and index starting on p. 473)

———— **WHERE TO DINE** ————

360 THE RESTAURANT AT THE CN TOWER   **Lunch:** $31-$37   **Dinner:** $31-$75   **Phone:** 416/362-5411   56
▼▼▼▼▼   **Location:** At the top of the CN Tower. 301 Front St W M5V 2T6. **Hours:** 11 am-2 & 4:30-10 pm, Sat-10:30 pm;
Continental   Sunday brunch 10:30 am-2 pm. Closed: 1/1, 12/25; also for lunch 1/2-5/10. **Reservations:** suggested.
Features: Enjoy freshly prepared fare in the comfortable setting of this revolving restaurant. House
specialties include chicken, prime rib, pasta and rack of lamb, plus cheesecake and chocolate mousse.
Views are spectacular. Dressy casual. **Parking:** on-site. **Cards:** AX, CB, DC, DS, MC, VI.   ✗

ACCENTS RESTAURANT AND BAR   **Lunch:** $12-$16   **Dinner:** $28-$38   **Phone:** 416/324-5633   69
(AAA)   **Location:** Jct Wellesley St; in The Sutton Place Hotel. 955 Bay St M5S 2A2. **Hours:** 7 am-10:30 pm.
▼▼▼▼   **Reservations:** suggested. **Features:** The sophisticated restaurant offers an elegant dining experience. A
Continental   seasonal Continental menu features such appetizers as grilled quail satay and house-smoked Atlantic
salmon. Outstanding dishes include lobster ravioli, beef ravioli with glazed goat cheese and roast lamb loin.
Dressy casual; cocktails. **Parking:** on-site (fee) and valet. **Cards:** AX, DC, JC, MC, VI.   ▼ ✗

ACQUA   **Lunch:** $12-$17   **Dinner:** $18-$35   **Phone:** 416/368-7171   100
▼▼▼▼   **Location:** Jct Yonge and Front sts; at northwest corner; entrance through BCE Place. 10 Front St W M5J 2P3.
Continental   **Hours:** 11:30 am-11:30 pm, Sat from 5 pm. Closed major holidays; also Sun. **Reservations:** required.
Features: The restaurant bustles thanks to its modern, striking decor, an innovative, Mediterranean-
influenced menu and a central location near the theatre and sports stadiums. This is a popular choice for
business luncheons. The staff is used to a full house. Lining the menu is a good choice of seafood, pasta and game dishes, as
well as lighter luncheon fare. The long bar is a favorite stop for an after-work martini or glass of wine from the extensive wine
list. Cocktails. **Parking:** on-site. **Cards:** AX, DC, MC, VI.   ✗

ADEGA RESTAURANTE   **Lunch:** $8-$17   **Dinner:** $14-$30   **Phone:** 416/977-4338   68
▼▼▼▼   **Location:** Between Yonge and Bay sts. 33 Elm St M5G 1H1. **Hours:** 11:30 am-2:30 & 5-11 pm, Sat from 5 pm.
Mediterranean   Closed major holidays; also Sun. **Reservations:** suggested. **Features:** Mediterranean decor complements
Portuguese preparations of tiger shrimp, fresh fish, lobster and rack of lamb. Dressy casual; cocktails.
Parking: street. **Cards:** AX, DC, MC, VI.   ✗

AMALFI ITALIAN RISTORANTE   **Lunch:** $12-$14   **Dinner:** $20-$29   **Phone:** 416/861-0643   4
▼▼▼ ▼▼   **Location:** Corner of Dundas St; e of Canon Theatre. 227 Church St M5B 1Y7. **Hours:** 5:30 pm-9:30 pm, Wed &
Italian   Thurs also noon-2 pm. Closed major holidays; also Sun & Mon; call for closing dates.
Reservations: suggested. **Features:** A fine selection of freshly prepared Italian cuisine is served in the
intimate, Mediterranean-style atmosphere of this eatery in the theatre district. House favorites include veal,
pasta, steak, seafood and risotto, as well as a good selection of desserts. Semi-formal attire; cocktails. **Parking:** street.
Cards: AX, DC, MC, VI.   ✗

ANNONA   **Lunch:** $12-$21   **Dinner:** $18-$32   **Phone:** 416/925-1234   30
▼▼▼▼   **Location:** Corner of Bloor St W; in Park Hyatt Toronto. 4 Avenue Rd M5R 2E8. **Hours:** 6:30 am-11 pm.
Continental   **Reservations:** suggested. **Features:** Annona offers elegant dining in a distinguished setting and a fine
selection of traditional Continental cuisine with an innovative flair. Exceptional presentation, skilled
professional service with a personal touch and an outstanding menu are the keys to this restaurant's
success. Let the dessert menu tempt you; it's well worth the calories! Dressy casual; cocktails. **Parking:** on-site (fee) and valet.
Cards: AX, DC, DS, JC, MC, VI.   ✗

AVALON   **Lunch:** $14-$25   **Dinner:** $30-$45   **Phone:** 416/979-9918   76
▼▼▼▼   **Location:** Between Duncan and Dundas sts; just w of Unversity Ave. 270 Adelaide St W M5H 1X6. **Hours:** 5:30 pm-10
Continental   pm, Thurs also noon-2 pm. Closed major holidays; also Sun & Mon. **Reservations:** required. **Features:** The
MC, VI.   restaurant presents a chef's sampling and wine-pairing menu, as well as a la carte Continental selections
that reflect a Mediterranean influence. Dressy casual; cocktails. **Parking:** street. **Cards:** AX, DC, JC,
✗

AZURE   **Lunch:** $14-$26   **Dinner:** $35-$50   **Phone:** 416/597-8142   36
▼▼▼ ▼▼   **Location:** Between Spadina and University aves; in InterContinental Toronto Centre. 225 Front St W M5V 2X3.
Continental   **Hours:** 6:30 am-11 pm. **Reservations:** suggested. **Features:** The contemporary dining room is a distinctive
setting in which patrons can browse an equally distinctive menu. A Canadian flair punctuates the chef's
offerings of fine Continental cuisine. Many fresh local and regional ingredients factor into the food. The
dining room is marked by high ceilings and panoramic windows overlooking the busy city streets. This place is near the city's
theatre and entertainment district. Dressy casual; cocktails. **Parking:** on-site (fee). **Cards:** AX, CB, DC, JC, MC, VI.   ▼ ✗

BABUR   **Lunch:** $11   **Dinner:** $9-$20   **Phone:** 416/599-7720   22
▼▼ ▼   **Location:** Just w of Peter St. 273 Queen St W M5V 1Z9. **Hours:** 11:45 am-2:30 & 5-10:30 pm, Sun-9:30 pm.
Indian   **Reservations:** suggested. **Features:** The restaurant features Northern Indian cuisine, including tandoori
dishes, Indian lentils and vegetarian choices. At lunchtime, the buffet is popular. The casual dining room
employs a semi-open-kitchen concept in which diners can watch chefs at work. Casual dress; cocktails.
Parking: street. **Cards:** AX, DC, MC, VI.

BANGKOK GARDEN   *Menu on aaa.com*   **Lunch:** $20-$30   **Dinner:** $25-$40   **Phone:** 416/977-6748   23
(AAA)   **Location:** Between Yonge and Bay sts. 18 Elm St M5G 1G7. **Hours:** 11:30 am-2:30 & 5-10 pm, Sat & Sun from 5
▼▼▼▼   pm. Closed major holidays. **Reservations:** suggested. **Features:** Thai cuisine is served in lush
Thai   surroundings. Buffets stocked with such items as curry puffs, glass noodles, lemon shrimp soup, curries and
stir-fry foods are set up for lunch on weekdays and for dinner from Sunday through Tuesday. An extensive a
la carte menu is also available. Casual dress; cocktails. **Parking:** street. **Cards:** AX, DC, MC, VI.   ✗

(See map and index starting on p. 473)

BARBERIAN'S STEAK HOUSE   Lunch: $16-$50   Dinner: $25-$70   Phone: 416/597-0335   (8)
Steak House
Location: S of Gerrard St; just w of Yonge St. 7 Elm St M5G 1H1. **Hours:** noon-2:30 & 5-midnight, Sat & Sun from 5 pm. Closed: 12/25. **Reservations:** suggested. **Features:** Traditional steak house offering cozy ambience in several small rooms. Sophisticated, yet comfortable atmosphere. Entrees are all served with hot garlic bread and cold relish plate. Appetizers include old-time favourites such as shrimp cocktail, escargot and French onion soup, as well as a tasty pate selection. Steaks are the specialty here all cooked fresh to order and served sizzling. Very popular locally and with tourists. Dressy casual; cocktails. **Parking:** street. **Cards:** AX, DC, MC, VI.

BARDI'S STEAK HOUSE   Lunch: $20-$45   Dinner: $24-$50   Phone: 416/366-9211   (112)
CAA
Steak & Seafood
Location: At Front St. 56 York St M5J 1S8. **Hours:** 11:30 am-10:30 pm, Sat from 5 pm. Closed major holidays; also Sun. **Reservations:** suggested. **Features:** Around since 1966, the well-established steak house still pleases diners with its hearty cuts of fine beef. Traditional starters include jumbo shrimp cocktail, tomato and onion salad and French onion soup. Steaks are sure to please, but seafood, tangy ribs and chicken entrees provide a change of pace. Save room for cheesecake, the perfect ending to a fine meal. Dressy casual; cocktails. **Parking:** no self-parking. **Cards:** AX, MC, VI.

BAROOTES CASUAL DINING   Lunch: $11-$23   Dinner: $15-$32   Phone: 416/979-7717   (65)
Continental
Location: Between Simcoe and Duncan sts. 220 King St W M5H 1K4. **Hours:** 11:30 am-2:30 & 4:30-9:30 pm, Sat from 4:30 pm. Closed major holidays; also Sun. **Reservations:** accepted. **Features:** The house specialties at this popular restaurant, located in the heart of the theatre district, are numerous and notable. Regular diners are partial to the Louisiana shrimp stir-fry, the Singapore vermicelli and the intimacy created by huge oak arches. Dressy casual; cocktails. **Parking:** no self-parking. **Cards:** AX, DC, MC, VI.

BATON ROUGE RESTAURANT   Lunch: $10-$32   Dinner: $10-$32   Phone: 416/593-9667   (94)
American
Location: Just n of Queen St. 216 Yonge St M5B 1N5. **Hours:** 11 am-11 pm, Sat 11:30 am-midnight, Sun noon-10 pm. Closed major holidays. **Reservations:** suggested. **Features:** Polished, dark-wood tables and brick walls surround the dining room, which offers a view of Yonge Street. Near Eaton Centre and many stage venues, the restaurant caters to shoppers and theatregoers. Menu specialties include hearty portions of ribs, beef and burgers, all grilled over hickory and hardwoods, as well as chicken, pasta and fish selections. For dessert, it's hard to beat the Southern-style apple cobbler. Dressy casual; cocktails. **Parking:** on-site. **Cards:** AX, CB, DC, MC, VI.

BELLINI'S   Dinner: $14-$29   Phone: 416/929-9111   (44)
Italian
Location: Between Bay St and Avenue Rd. 101 Yorkville Ave M5R 1C1. **Hours:** 5 pm-10 pm, Fri-10:30 pm, Sat-11 pm. Closed: 12/24-12/26. **Reservations:** suggested. **Features:** The prime Yorkville location provides a cozy, romantic atmosphere, a sophisticated menu and attentive service. Diners can savor a good selection of wine by the glass and bottle, as well as preparations of veal, beef, rack of lamb, poultry, seafood and freshly made pasta. The chef dishes up large portions and pays attention to presentation. It is worth saving room for dessert. Dressy casual; cocktails. **Parking:** street. **Cards:** AX, DC, MC, VI.

BENIHANA RESTAURANT   *Menu on aaa.com*   Lunch: $12-$23   Dinner: $30-$42   Phone: 416/860-5002   (17)
CAA
Japanese
Location: QEW/Gardiner Expwy, exit n on York or Bay sts; entrance on Wellington St; in The Fairmont Royal York. 100 Front St W M5J 1E3. **Hours:** noon-2 & 5:30-9:30 pm, Fri-10 pm, Sat 5:30 pm-11 pm, Sun 5:30 pm-9:30 pm. Closed major holidays. **Reservations:** suggested. **Features:** A longtime favourite with patrons of the hotel, the restaurant treats diners to a wide variety of freshly prepared Japanese cuisine. Chefs dazzle guests at the cooking tables as they flip salt and pepper shakers and flambe menu items. An extensive sushi menu is also featured. Dressy casual; cocktails. **Parking:** on-site (fee). **Cards:** AX, DC, DS, JC, MC, VI.

BIAGIO RISTORANTE   Lunch: $15-$25   Dinner: $20-$40   Phone: 416/366-4040   (103)
Italian
Location: Jct Jarvis St. 155 King St E M5C 1G9. **Hours:** noon-2:30 & 5:30-10 pm, Sat from 5:30 pm. Closed major holidays; also Sun. **Reservations:** suggested. **Features:** Diners enjoy the elegant yet comfortable atmosphere, complete with elaborate crown moldings and upscale table settings. A wonderful selection of fine Italian cuisine is the highlight. Among offerings are homemade specialty pasta, seafood and veal selections. The extensive wine list complements the menu. During popular special event nights, locals visit to try the chef's full tasting menu paired with wines. Dressy casual; cocktails. **Parking:** street. **Cards:** AX, DC, MC, VI.

BIFF'S   Lunch: $14-$22   Dinner: $25-$34   Phone: 416/860-0086   (101)
Continental
Location: At Yonge St. 4 Front St E M5E 1G4. **Hours:** noon-2:30 & 5-10 pm, Thurs & Fri-10:30 pm, Sat 5 pm-10 pm, Sun 5 pm-9:30 pm. Closed: 1/1, 12/25. **Reservations:** suggested. **Features:** Located in the heart of the business and entertainment district, Biff's caters to the both the "power lunch" crowd and the theatregoers. The large, bustling dining room offers a modern, upscale feel and the menu offers a nice selection of innovative fare. At lunch the daily quiche specials are popular. Other day and evening selections include fresh fish, roasted chicken and beef. Be sure to save room for the decadent desserts, such as apple crisp in a fresh pastry or the cheeses. Dressy casual; cocktails. **Parking:** on-site (fee). **Cards:** AX, DC, MC, VI.

THE BISTRO   Lunch: $9-$18   Dinner: $18-$25   Phone: 416/341-5045   (55)
American
Location: Jct Front St; in Renaissance Toronto Hotel at SkyDome. 1 Blue Jays Way M5V 1J4. **Hours:** 6:30 am-2 & 5:30-10 pm, Sat & Sun from 7 am. **Reservations:** suggested. **Features:** The funky, bi-level restaurant offers super views of the field from many tables. Baseball umpires' calls are broadcast in the dining room. Casual dress; cocktails. **Parking:** on-site. **Cards:** AX, DC, DS, JC, MC, VI.

(See map and index starting on p. 473)

BISTRO 990 Lunch: $12-$25 Dinner: $14-$43 Phone: 416/921-9990 (59)
♦♦♦ French
Location: 0.5 km s of Bloor St. 990 Bay St M5S 2A5. **Hours:** noon-3 & 5:30-11 pm, Sat & Sun from 5:30 pm. Closed: for lunch holidays. **Reservations:** suggested. **Features:** The upscale bistro is a longtime favourite with locals and visiting celebrities. Large murals, candlelit tables and an open-concept kitchen contribute to the bustling atmosphere. A good meal might begin with chicken pate accompanied by onion-blend chutney and wafers; feature a creative, colorful entree built around beef, veal, lamb or seafood; then wrap up with a dessert that's equally fabulous in taste and presentation. Dressy casual; cocktails. **Parking:** on-site (fee). **Cards:** AX, DC, MC, VI.

BLOWFISH RESTAURANT & SAKE BAR Lunch: $12-$20 Dinner: $12-$24 Phone: 416/860-0606 (111)
♦♦♦ Japanese
Location: Corner of King and Bathurst sts. 668 King St W M5V 1M7. **Hours:** 11:30 am-2:30 & 5-2 am. Closed major holidays; also Sun. **Reservations:** suggested. **Features:** Evoking the feel of a nightclub, the posh sushi bar is a must stop for sushi lovers. In an old barn building, the chic setting incorporates high vaulted ceilings, upscale decor and a funky atmosphere. The menu doesn't list average choices but instead focuses on distinctive, imaginative creations that tantalize the taste buds. Casual dress; cocktails. **Parking:** street. **Cards:** AX, DC, MC, VI.

BOAT HOUSE BAR AND GRILL Lunch: $8-$20 Dinner: $8-$26 Phone: 416/203-6300 (18)
♦ American
Location: At Queens Quay Terminal. 207 Queens Quay W M5J 1A7. **Hours:** 11 am-midnight; to 9 pm, Fri & Sat-10 pm 11/1-4/30. Closed: 1/1, 12/25. **Reservations:** suggested. **Features:** The Boat House Bar and Grill is a great spot for a casual meal harbour side. Tasty entrees range from fish and chips and pasta to sandwiches and burgers. Outdoor patio dining is available in season. Casual dress; cocktails. **Parking:** on-site (fee). **Cards:** AX, DC, MC, VI.

BOBA Dinner: $24-$35 Phone: 416/961-2622 (7)
♦♦ Continental
Location: N of Bloor St. 90 Avenue Rd M5R 2H2. **Hours:** 5:30 pm-10 pm, Fri & Sat-10:30 pm. Closed major holidays; also Sun & 12/25-1/6. **Reservations:** suggested. **Features:** Generous portions of creatively presented Continental cuisine are served in a relaxed setting. Favorites include seafood cakes, rack of lamb and Atlantic salmon. A sampler plate is one of many fabulous dessert selections. The interior design gives a nod to modern styling. Dressy casual; cocktails. **Parking:** street. **Cards:** AX, DC, MC, VI.

BODEGA RESTAURANT Lunch: $9-$14 Dinner: $16-$30 Phone: 416/977-1287 (33)
♦♦♦ French
Location: Between McCaul and Beverley St. 30 Baldwin St M5T 1L3. **Hours:** 11:30 am-10:30 pm. **Reservations:** suggested. **Features:** The converted old house's cozy, comfortable atmosphere and lovely seasonal patio make the restaurant a favorite with the locals. The staff details the freshly prepared and creative menu selections and highlights the daily blackboard specials and changing offerings of wine by the glass. Choose from pate, escargot or goat cheese salad to start, then savor a main course of rack of lamb, beef or seafood with rich sauces. The desserts are excellent. Dressy casual; cocktails. **Parking:** on-site. **Cards:** AX, DC, MC, VI.

BOMBAY PALACE Lunch: $11 Dinner: $10-$15 Phone: 416/368-8048 (12)
♦♦ Indian
Location: Just n of King St. 71 Jarvis St M5C 2H2. **Hours:** noon-3 & 5:30-10:30 pm, Fri & Sat-11 pm. **Reservations:** suggested, weekends. **Features:** The well-established Indian restaurant features a fine menu selection, with an extensive luncheon buffet and a full a la carte dinner menu. Enhancing the dining room atmosphere are interesting artwork and artifacts and soft, ethnic music. Among traditional and exotic favorites are clay-oven-baked breads, tandoori chicken, curried specialties and a full vegetarian selection. Cocktails. **Parking:** street. **Cards:** AX, DC, JC, MC, VI.

BYMARK RESTAURANT & BAR Lunch: $20-$35 Dinner: $30-$45 Phone: 416/777-1144 (74)
♦♦ ♦♦ Continental
Location: Just w of jct Yonge St; in TD Canada Trust, concourse level. 66 Wellington St W M5K 1J3. **Hours:** 11:30 am-2:30 & 5-10 pm, Sat from 5 pm. Closed major holidays; also Sun. **Reservations:** suggested. **Features:** The restaurant oozes sophistication via its architectural design elements, glass walk-though wine vault and the four subtly textured columns that define the dining room. While what is reputed to be the world's most expensive hamburger is on the menu, the restaurant has become known for both its use of fresh local and regional ingredients and its creative interpretations of classic cuisine. Dressy casual; cocktails. **Parking:** valet and street. **Cards:** AX, DC, DS, MC, VI.

CAFE VICTORIA Lunch: $9-$23 Dinner: $17-$35 Phone: 416/863-3131 (37)
♦♦♦ Continental
Location: Just e of Yonge St; in Le Royal Meridien King Edward Hotel. 37 King St E M5C 1E9. **Hours:** 6:30 am-10 pm, Sat from 7:30 am, Sun 7:30 am-5 pm. **Reservations:** suggested. **Features:** Elaborate Victorian architecture and an abundance of lush greenery make a wonderful setting for Cafe Victoria's creative menu of fine food. Of note is a popular and elaborate Sunday brunch served in an elegant decor. A pre-theatre menu is offered 5 pm-7 pm. Casual dress; cocktails. **Parking:** on-site (fee) and valet. **Cards:** AX, DC, JC, MC, VI.

CANOE RESTAURANT AND BAR Lunch: $17-$25 Dinner: $24-$42 Phone: 416/364-0054 (28)
♦♦ ♦♦ Continental
Location: In TD Canada Trust Building, 54th floor. 66 Wellington St W M5K 1H6. **Hours:** noon-2:30 & 5-10 pm, Fri-10:30 pm. Closed major holidays; also Sat & Sun. **Reservations:** required. **Features:** Patrons enjoy spectacular views from this restaurant. Innovative dishes, including preparations of caribou and salmon, show a strong Canadian influence. The seven-course tasting menu is a treat, as are the sushi offerings. The modern dining room bustles with the noise of sizzling food from the open-concept kitchen and the buzz of diners' conversations. Dressy casual; cocktails. **Parking:** on-site (fee). **Cards:** AX, DC, MC, VI.

CANYON CREEK CHOP HOUSE Lunch: $8-$22 Dinner: $11-$31 Phone: 416/596-2240 (113)
♦♦ Steak House
Location: Jct York St; across from convention centre. 156 Front St W M5J 2L6. **Hours:** 11:30 am-11 pm, Tues & Wed-midnight, Thurs & Fri-1 am, Sat 4 pm-1 am, Sun 4 pm-11 pm. Closed: 12/25. **Features:** A relaxed, comfortable setting, a traditional steak house menu and an extensive wine list make this a popular favourite with locals and tourists alike. Diners enjoy great cuts of aged beef, ribs, chicken, huge pork chops or rack of lamb, all grilled to order. The wine list has an excellent selection of by-the-glass choices and bottles. Decadent desserts are worth the splurge. Casual dress; cocktails. **Parking:** on-site (fee). **Cards:** AX, MC, VI.

(See map and index starting on p. 473)

CARMAN'S
Steak & Seafood

Dinner: $40-$48   **Phone:** 416/924-8697   71

Location: Just e of Yonge St. 26 Alexander St M4Y 1B4. **Hours:** 5 pm-11 pm. Closed major holidays; also Sun. **Features:** The elegant, traditional steak house is interestingly appointed with a collection of ornaments. Although the menu focuses on large portions of steak, lobster and seafood, it also offers diversity in veal, lamb and rib preparations. Satisfying entrees include all kinds of extras, including hot garlic bread, a piping-hot baked potato and a relish plate of pickles, peppers, marinated olives and cottage cheese. Sweet pastries and coffee are a nice way to end the meal. Casual dress; cocktails. **Parking:** street. **Cards:** AX, MC, VI.

CHIADO
Mediterranean

Dinner: $25-$50   **Phone:** 416/538-1910   70

Location: Just w of Ossington. 864 College St M6H 1A3. **Hours:** 5 pm-10 pm, Fri & Sat-11 pm. Closed: 1/1, 12/24, 12/25. **Reservations:** suggested. **Features:** Fine European artwork adorns the walls of this fast-paced restaurant. The focus is on fine Mediterranean and Portuguese cuisine with an endless selection of fresh seafood specialties. Decisions are hard, with starters such as grilled goat cheese, calamari and steamed clams. Seafood stew is a hearty entree that seafood lovers will be hard-pressed to match. The spicy seafood shrimp also is notable. Skilled staffers will debone fish tableside. Decadent desserts are a fitting way to end a meal. Dressy casual; cocktails. **Parking:** street. **Cards:** AX, DC, MC, VI.

COMMODORE'S
Continental

Lunch: $14-$21   **Dinner:** $23-$37   **Phone:** 416/203-3333   11

Location: QEW E to Gardiner Expwy, exit Bay St S; in Radisson Plaza Hotel Admiral Toronto. 249 Queen's Quay W M5J 2N5. **Hours:** noon-2:30 & 5:30-10 pm, Sat from 5:30 pm. Closed major holidays; also Sun. **Reservations:** suggested. **Features:** Exceptional service and exquisite dining in the heart of downtown is precisely what Commodore's is known for. The quality of its professional, well-timed service is just as memorable. It's worth the wait for a window seat: The views are fantastic. Dressy casual; cocktails. **Parking:** on-site (fee). **Cards:** AX, CB, DC, DS, JC, MC, VI.

THE COURTYARD CAFE
Continental

Lunch: $16-$20   **Dinner:** $29-$42   **Phone:** 416/971-9666   54

Location: Jct Bloor St; in Windsor Arms. 18 St. Thomas St M5S 3E7. **Hours:** 7-10:30 am, 11-2 & 5-11 pm, Mon-2 pm, Sun 10:30 am-3:30 pm. **Reservations:** suggested. **Features:** A garden courtyard setting lends elegant ambience to the large, open-concept dining room. The menu features spa, bistro and gourmet cuisine to satisfy every appetite. Evening guests will experience pleasant music from a pianist on the overhead balcony. The wine list is extensive. Dressy casual; cocktails. **Parking:** on-site (fee) and valet. **Cards:** AX, DC, MC, VI.

CYRANO'S
Steak & Seafood

Lunch: $6-$14   **Dinner:** $13-$29   **Phone:** 416/362-4342   60

Location: Between Yonge and Church sts. 73 King St E M5C 1G3. **Hours:** noon-11 pm. Closed major holidays; also Sun. **Features:** Steak, seafood and the house-specialty back ribs are served in an elegant atmosphere. Other menu offerings include rack of lamb, chicken, scallops, shrimp and lobster tail. At lunchtime, selections are casual. The established restaurant has been under operation of the same owners and in the same location since 1959. Casual dress; cocktails. **Parking:** street. **Cards:** AX, DC, MC, VI.

DUKE OF WESTMINSTER
English

Lunch: $7-$15   **Dinner:** $7-$15   **Phone:** 416/368-2761   47

Location: Between Bay and York sts; at First Canadian Place. 77 Adelaide St W M5X 1A6. **Hours:** 11 am-10 pm, Thurs & Fri-11 pm. Closed major holidays; also Sat & Sun. **Reservations:** suggested. **Features:** Eat your fish and chips the way they were meant to be eaten, wrapped in newspaper, at this charming English pub-like eatery. There's also traditional fare of steak and kidney pie and shepherd's, pie as well as burgers, sandwiches and finger foods. Casual dress; cocktails. **Parking:** on-site (fee). **Cards:** AX, DC, MC, VI.

DUNN'S FAMOUS DELICATESSEN
American

Lunch: $7-$18   **Dinner:** $7-$18   **Phone:** 416/599-5464   79

Location: Between Duncan and John sts. 284A King St W M5V 1J2. **Hours:** 7:30 am-8 pm, Wed-Sat to 11 pm. **Features:** Located in the theatre district, busy and bustling Shopsy's sports an extensive delicatessen menu the likes of corned beef sandwiches, soups, salads and pasta. Try the chicken noodle with matzo balls soup for a satisfying and tasty meal treat. Cocktails. **Parking:** street. **Cards:** AX, MC, VI.

DYNASTY CHINESE CUISINE
Chinese

Lunch: $15-$20   **Dinner:** $15-$30   **Phone:** 416/923-3323   57

Location: Between Bay St and Avenue Rd. 131 Bloor St W, Suite 211 M5S 1T8. **Hours:** 11 am-3:45 & 5:30-10:30 pm, Sat & Sun from 10 am. **Reservations:** suggested. **Features:** Cantonese and Szechuan specialties, including fresh seafood and Peking duck, are served in the modern, upscale restaurant. A la carte options include such distinctive dishes as stir-fried squid or eel skewers. Dim sum is featured daily for lunch. Casual dress; cocktails. **Parking:** on-site (fee). **Cards:** AX, MC, VI.

EPIC   *Menu on aaa.com*

Continental

Lunch: $14-$19   **Dinner:** $23-$39   **Phone:** 416/860-6949   19

Location: QEW/Gardiner Expwy, exit n on York or Bay sts; entrance on Wellington St; in The Fairmont Royal York. 100 Front St M5J 1E3. **Hours:** 7 am-10, noon-2 & 5:30-10 pm, Fri-11 pm, Sat 7 am-11 & 5:30-11 pm, Sun 7 am-2 & 5:30-10 pm. **Reservations:** suggested. **Features:** Located on the lobby level of the hotel, this elegant dining room features innovative Continental cuisine in a modern upscale setting. Diners may select from the chef's tasting menu in addition to the a la carte specialties. Dressy casual; cocktails. **Parking:** on-site (fee) and valet. **Cards:** AX, DC, DS, JC, MC, VI.

FAR NIENTE
American

Lunch: $16-$27   **Dinner:** $16-$36   **Phone:** 416/214-9922   63

Location: Jct Wellington St. 187 Bay St M5L 1G5. **Hours:** 11:30 am-11 pm, Sat from 5 pm. Closed major holidays; also Sun. **Reservations:** suggested. **Features:** California-style cuisine is served in the upbeat dining room, which is decorated with plants and greenery. Menu selections vary from hearty portions of grilled steak and salmon to a variety of pasta and vegetarian dishes. Parking is validated after 5:30 pm on weekdays and all day on weekends. Semi-formal attire; cocktails. **Parking:** on-site (fee). **Cards:** AX, DC, MC, VI.

(See map and index starting on p. 473)

THE FIFTH
Dinner: $85-$90   Phone: 416/979-3005   (24)
Location: Jct Duncan St. 225 Richmond St W M5V 1W3. Hours: 6 pm-11:30 pm. Closed major holidays; also Sun-Wed. Reservations: required. Features: A freight-elevator ride to the second-floor dining room starts the evening's adventure. Guests exit into a modern, upscale room complete with a sit-down bar and cozy
Continental   sofas by the glowing fireplace. Pleasant, light music enhances the five-course meal, which changes frequently throughout the season. The fabulous cheese selection deliciously completes the meal. Reservations are a must, so plan ahead for this memorable experience. Formal attire; cocktails. Parking: street. Cards: AX, DC, MC, VI.

FILET OF SOLE
Lunch: $8-$25   Dinner: $14-$35   Phone: 416/598-3256   (62)
Location: Just n of King St. 11 Duncan St M5H 3G6. Hours: 11:45 am-2:30 & 5-10 pm, Fri-11 pm, Sat 5 pm-11:30 pm, Sun 4 pm-10 pm; to 6 pm 12/24. Closed: 1/1, 12/25. Reservations: suggested. Features: On the menu are such tempting morsels as lobster, crab, steak and a signature dish of chicken and shrimp, in
Seafood   addition to daily and extensive fresh fish specials. The atmosphere at the eatery in the theatre district is bustling. Casual dress; cocktails. Parking: street. Cards: AX, DC, MC, VI.

FRED'S NOT HERE SMOKEHOUSE AND GRILL
Lunch: $9-$16   Dinner: $16-$21   Phone: 416/971-9155   (20)
Location: Between Peter and John sts. 321 King St W M5V 1J5. Hours: 11:30 am-2:30 & 5-10 pm, Sat 5 pm-11:30 pm, Sun 4 pm-10 pm. Closed: 1/1, 12/25. Reservations: suggested. Features: In the heart of the entertainment district, the popular restaurant offers diners an innovative menu of Continental cuisine
Continental   prepared with an Asian flair. Take time to study the interesting wall mural that explores the world and local sights. Service is warm, personable and professional. Dressy casual; cocktails. Parking: on-site (fee). Cards: AX, MC, VI.

GEORGE BIGLIARDI'S DINING LOUNGE
Lunch: $12-$20   Dinner: $18-$30   Phone: 416/922-9594   (58)
Location: Just n of Carlton St. 463 Church St M4Y 2C5. Hours: noon-3 & 5-11 pm, Sat from 5 pm, Sun 5 pm-10 pm. Closed: 12/25. Reservations: accepted. Features: The preferred choice for celebrities when it opened more than 25 years ago, the restaurant now is serving its third generation of patrons. The dining room
Steak & Seafood   features rich, wood accents, high, beamed ceilings and fine artwork. Smoking is permitted only in the more casual lounge, which is open for lunch and dinner. Among menu choices are sirloin and rib steak, filet mignon, Dover sole and Atlantic salmon. Casual dress; cocktails. Parking: on-site (fee) and street. Cards: AX, DC, MC, VI.

GOLDEN THAI
Lunch: $8-$10   Dinner: $8-$20   Phone: 416/868-6668   (102)
Location: At Richmond St. 105 Church St M5C 2G3. Hours: 11:30 am-10 pm, Sat & Sun 5 pm-11 pm. Closed major holidays; also 12/24. Reservations: suggested. Features: It's easy to forget this restaurant is downtown, as its dining room is enveloped in lush greenery, authentic Thai ornaments and wall murals of
Thai   the exotic Orient. The descriptive menu lists a la carte selections and inclusive meals, all of which are freshly prepared and spiced to taste. Casual dress; cocktails. Parking: street. Cards: AX, DC, MC, VI.

HARBOUR SIXTY STEAKHOUSE
Lunch: $18-$25   Dinner: $25-$45   Phone: 416/777-2111   (117)
Location: Between York and Bay sts. 60 Harbour St M5J 1B7. Hours: 11:30 am-midnight. Closed: 12/24, 12/25; also Sat & Sun. Reservations: suggested. Features: The upscale steak house is in the Historic Harbour Commission Building, dating back to 1917. Huge portions of perfectly prepared steak and seafood, with
Steak House   equally large sides, are perfect for sharing. Seating options range from casual in the lounge to more elegant in the main dining room to bustling directly in front of the cooking station. The extensive wine list lines up perfect complements to the fine cuts of beef. Dressy casual; cocktails. Parking: on-site (fee). Cards: AX, DC, MC, VI.

HEMISPHERES RESTAURANT BISTRO
Lunch: $13-$23   Phone: 416/599-8000   (34)
(AAA)
Location: Just s of Dundas St; in Metropolitan Hotel. 110 Chestnut St M5G 1R3. Hours: 7 am-2:30 pm, Sat & Sun from 7:30 am. Reservations: suggested. Features: Creative menu items, a notable wine list, artistic presentation and top-notch service make the distinctive bistro popular. The innovative menu features a
Continental   blend of Continental cuisine with an Asian influence. Patrons can select from the following short list of specialties: scallop of foie gras and soya-glazed ahi tuna. Dressy casual; cocktails. Parking: on-site. Cards: AX, DC, DS, JC, MC, VI.

HIRO SUSHI RESTAURANT
Lunch: $12-$15   Dinner: $20-$30   Phone: 416/304-0550   (16)
Location: Between Jarvis and George sts. 171 King St E M5A 1J4. Hours: noon-2:30 & 5:30-10 pm, Sat from 5:30 pm. Closed major holidays; also Sun & Mon. Reservations: required. Features: Due to limited
Japanese   seating, reservations are a must at the intimate restaurant, where the chef/owner makes fresh sushi, sashimi and maki sushi. Casual dress; beer & wine only. Parking: street. Cards: AX, MC, VI.

HO SHIM JAPANESE AND KOREAN RESTAURANT
Lunch: $8-$20   Dinner: $8-$20   Phone: 416/368-6852   (99)
Location: First Canadian Place, concourse level. 100 King St W M5X 1A6. Hours: 7 am-8:30 pm. Closed major holidays; also Sat & Sun. Features: Popular with the business crowd, the bustling diner serves a full range
Japanese   of Japanese and Korean specialties, such as sushi and tempura, in charming bento boxes. Casual dress; cocktails. Parking: on-site (fee). Cards: AX, DC, MC, VI.

HOTHOUSE CAFE INC
Lunch: $8-$20   Dinner: $8-$20   Phone: 416/366-7800   (43)
Location: Jct Front St. 35 Church St M5E 1T3. Hours: 11 am-11:30 pm, Wed & Thurs-midnight, Fri & Sat-1 am, Sun 9:30 am-11 pm. Closed: 12/25. Reservations: suggested. Features: Fresh ingredients make all of
American   Hothouse's specialties notable. Pasta, thin-crust gourmet pizza, steak, seafood, burgers and a variety of desserts top the list of taste-tempting treats. The atmosphere is bustling; the service is casual and friendly. Cocktails. Parking: on-site (fee). Cards: AX, DC, MC, VI.

(See map and index starting on p. 473)

HY'S STEAK HOUSE   **Lunch:** $15-$30   **Dinner:** $30-$49   **Phone:** 416/364-6600 ⑯

Location: Between York and Bay sts; on north side. 120 Adelaide St W M5H 1T1. **Hours:** 11:30 am-2 & 5:30-10 pm, Sat & Sun from 5:30 pm. Closed major holidays. **Reservations:** suggested. **Features:** A rich decor with dim lighting and fine artwork complements a traditional menu of hearty cuts of fine beef and an extensive wine list. Highlights include prawn cocktails, made-to-order Caesar salad, prime rib and a steak-and-lobster-combination. The large piano lounge is a nice place in which to start or finish a successful business meal or romantic dining experience. Dressy casual; cocktails. **Parking:** on-site (fee). **Cards:** AX, MC, VI.

Steak House

ICHIBAN SUSHI HOUSE   **Lunch:** $8-$22   **Dinner:** $8-$22   **Phone:** 416/204-1799 ⑯

Location: Between Bay St and Spadina Ave. 262 Queen's Quay W, Unit 5 M5J 1B5. **Hours:** 11:30 am-11 pm. **Reservations:** accepted. **Features:** Varied dining spots such as at a sushi bar, in a booth, at a table or in a small, private, curtained room are offered, though all settings are Asian influenced and contemporary. The many sushi and sashimi offerings are of high quality and are creatively presented. Casual dress. **Parking:** street. **Cards:** MC, VI.

Japanese

IL FORNELLO   **Lunch:** $10-$15   **Dinner:** $14-$17   **Phone:** 416/977-2855 ㉛

Location: Just w of University Ave. 214 King St W M5H 3S6. **Hours:** 11:30 am-10 pm, Thurs & Fri-11 pm, Sat 4:30 pm-11 pm. Closed: 12/25; also Sun. **Reservations:** suggested. **Features:** Large windows facing King Street attract passersby to the bustling eatery in the heart of the theatre district. Inside, diners enjoy a tempting menu of gourmet pizzas baked in a wood-fire oven, freshly made pastas or grilled meat and seafood selections. A European feel is created with shiny tile floors and brick walls, and the atmosphere is always lively. Cocktails. **Parking:** on-site (fee). **Cards:** AX, DC, MC, VI.

Italian

IL FORNELLO   **Lunch:** $8-$12   **Dinner:** $10-$25   **Phone:** 416/598-1766 ㉔

Location: Between Yonge and Bay sts. 35 Elm St M5G 1M1. **Hours:** 11:30 am-2 & 5-10 pm, Sat from 5 pm, Sun 5 pm-9 pm. Closed major holidays. **Reservations:** suggested. **Features:** On Elm Street in the city's "restaurant row," the popular eatery sustains a charming ambience in a restored bi-level house. Diners can nosh on gourmet pizzas baked in a wood-fire oven, freshly prepared pasta dishes and grilled meat, poultry and seafood selections. Casual dress; cocktails. **Parking:** street. **Cards:** AX, DC, MC, VI.

Italian

IL FORNELLO   **Lunch:** $10-$20   **Dinner:** $12-$25   **Phone:** 416/861-1028 ㉒

Location: At Queens Quay Terminal, main floor. 207 Queens Quay W M5J 1A7. **Hours:** 8:30 am-11 pm, Sat & Sun from 10:30 am. Closed: 1/1, 12/25. **Features:** In addition to the popular menu, featuring gourmet pizzas baked in a wood-fire oven and tasty pasta dishes, diners at this location of Il Fornello enjoy wonderful views of the harbourfront from large, panoramic windows. The outdoor patio is a main draw in the summer months. Casual dress; cocktails. **Parking:** on-site (fee). **Cards:** AX, DC, MC, VI.

Italian

IL POSTO   **Lunch:** $10-$22   **Dinner:** $16-$35   **Phone:** 416/968-0469 ⑯

Location: Just e of Avenue Rd; in York Square. 148 Yorkville Ave M5R 1C2. **Hours:** noon-3 & 5:30-11 pm. Closed major holidays; also Sun. **Reservations:** suggested. **Features:** Seafood and pasta are what Il Posto does best. All menu selections are creatively and freshly prepared including the flavourful lobster ravioli served in a truffle broth with rice. Dessert, too, is notable with many fresh, well-presented choices. Dressy casual; cocktails. **Parking:** no self-parking. **Cards:** AX, DC, MC, VI.

Northern
Italian

INDOCHINE NOODLE CAFE & RESTAURANT   **Lunch:** $7-$10   **Dinner:** $9-$20   **Phone:** 416/922-5840 ②

Location: Just n of Bloor St; just e of Yonge St. 4 Collier St M4W 1L7. **Hours:** 11:30 am-3 & 5-10 pm, Fri & Sat-11 pm, Sun 5 pm-10 pm. Closed major holidays. **Reservations:** suggested. **Features:** Convenient to the main library and the trendy Yorkville area, the popular restaurant prepares an interesting blend of Asian cuisine, including Vietnamese, Thai and Malaysian specialties in full-course or a la carte selections. Highlights include hot and sour soup, homemade spring rolls, satay, brochettes and stir-fries served with either noodles or rice. Diners unwind in a small, simple dining room with a bustling, modern atmosphere. Cocktails. **Parking:** street. **Cards:** AX, MC, VI.

Asian

JACQUES' BISTRO DU PARC   **Lunch:** $14-$19   **Dinner:** $16-$29   **Phone:** 416/961-1893 ㉙

Location: Between Bay St and Avenue Rd. 126A Cumberland St, 2nd Floor M5R 1A6. **Hours:** 11:30 am-3 & 5-10:30 pm, Sun-10:30 pm. **Reservations:** suggested. **Features:** Fresh baguettes, market salad, decadent desserts and a vast variety of omelets prepared to order are highlights of the menu. Casual dress. **Parking:** street. **Cards:** AX, MC, VI.

French

JAPANESE RESTAURANT EMATEI   **Lunch:** $8-$16   **Dinner:** $15-$24   **Phone:** 416/340-0472 ㉖

Location: Just n of Queen St. 30 St. Patrick St, 1st Floor M5T 3A3. **Hours:** 11:45 am-2:30 & 5:30-10:30 pm, Sat from 5:30 pm, Sun 5:30 pm-10 pm. Closed major holidays. **Reservations:** suggested. **Features:** Japanese cuisine is prepared in a relaxed, comfortable atmosphere. The tempura is well presented with shrimp, vegetables and steamed rice, and accompanied by a chilled salad and hot miso soup. A sushi bar is also open with colorful and tasty concoctions. Cocktails. **Parking:** street. **Cards:** AX, DC, JC, MC, VI.

Japanese

JOE BADALI'S RISTORANTE ITALIANO   **Lunch:** $8-$15   **Dinner:** $9-$25   **Phone:** 416/977-3064 ㉙

Location: Just w of University Ave. 156 Front St W M5J 2L6. **Hours:** 11:30 am-10 pm, Fri-11 pm, Sat noon-11 pm, Sun noon-9 pm. Closed: 1/1, 12/25, 12/26. **Features:** In a restored warehouse, the huge dining room presents an extensive menu of casual Italian fare and benefits from a great location in the heart of the city's theatre and sports complex district. Locals and tourists alike frequent this place. Casual dress; cocktails. **Parking:** on-site (fee). **Cards:** AX, DC, MC, VI.

Italian

(See map and index starting on p. 473)

JUMP CAFE & BAR   **Lunch:** $15-$20   **Dinner:** $18-$28   **Phone:** 416/363-3400   85

Continental

Location: Jct Yonge and Wellington sts; in Commerce Court East, court level. 18 Wellington St W M5L 1G4. **Hours:** 11:45 am-11 pm, Sat from 5 pm. Closed major holidays; also Sun. **Reservations:** suggested. **Features:** Power lunches, after-work martinis and successful business dinners are the norm at the upbeat restaurant, near theatres and sporting complexes in the heart of the city's business district. Diners enjoy fresh, spicy, innovative cuisine prepared with Continental and Mediterranean influences. Dressy casual; cocktails. **Parking:** on-site (fee). **Cards:** AX, DC, MC, VI.

THE KEG MANSION   **Dinner:** $18-$30   **Phone:** 416/964-6609   90

Steak House

Location: Directly n of Wellesley St. 515 Jarvis St M4Y 2H7. **Hours:** 5 pm-11 pm, Fri-midnight, Sat 4 pm-midnight, Sun 4 pm-11 pm. Closed: 12/25. **Features:** The restaurant prepares succulent, mesquite-grilled steaks in the distinctive historical setting of a converted mansion. Diners can unwind amid the old-fashioned ambience that fills the various rooms of the house's two floors of dining space. Casual dress; cocktails. **Parking:** on-site. **Cards:** AX, DC, MC, VI.

THE KEG STEAKHOUSE AND BAR   **Lunch:** $8-$22   **Dinner:** $16-$30   **Phone:** 416/703-1773   115

Steak House

Location: Just s of Queen St. 165 York St M5H 3RS. **Hours:** 11:30 am-11 pm, Fri-midnight, Sat 4 pm-midnight, Sun 4 pm-10 pm. Closed: 12/25. **Features:** Sizzling mesquite-grilled steaks, hot sourdough bread and such tasty starters as French onion soup and bacon-wrapped scallops are among old-time favourites that keep diners coming back. This location is convenient to city hall and the large Eaton Centre shopping complex. Casual dress; cocktails. **Parking:** street. **Cards:** AX, DC, MC, VI.

THE KEG STEAKHOUSE AND BAR   **Dinner:** $15-$30   **Phone:** 416/367-0685   86

Steak House

Location: Directly s on Front St. 12 Church St M5E 1M1. **Hours:** 5 pm-10:30 pm, Fri & Sat-midnight. Closed: 12/25. **Features:** Well-known for its great mesquite-grilled steaks, this Keg is centrally located close to the entertainment and sports district and is the perfect place for a pre- or after-event meal. In the summer months, an outdoor patio is also featured. Casual dress; cocktails. **Parking:** street. **Cards:** AX, DC, MC, VI.

KIT KAT BAR AND GRILL   **Lunch:** $9-$14   **Dinner:** $13-$34   **Phone:** 416/977-4461   118

Italian

Location: Just w of John St. 297 King St W M5V 1J5. **Hours:** 11:30 am-11:30 pm, Sat 4:30 pm-12:30 am, Sun 4:30 pm-11:30 pm. Closed: 1/1, 4/17, 12/25. **Reservations:** suggested. **Features:** An eclectic mix of decor, a loud, bustling atmosphere and a fun menu are distinct features of the popular eatery. In the heart of the entertainment district, the restaurant is a longtime favorite of the theatre crowd before or after the show. Ask for a booth in the rear, and take time to look at all the interesting ornaments scattered throughout the dining room. This is not the spot for a quiet meal, but the menu and funky atmosphere are rewarding. Casual dress; cocktails. **Parking:** on-site (fee). **Cards:** AX, DC, MC, VI.

LA FENICE   **Lunch:** $11-$21   **Dinner:** $15-$30   **Phone:** 416/585-2377   45

Italian

Location: Between Peter and John sts. 319 King St W M5V 1J5. **Hours:** 11:30 am-2:30 & 5:30-10:30 pm, Sat 5:30 pm-11 pm. Closed major holidays; also Sun. **Reservations:** suggested. **Features:** The modern, upscale restaurant features a colorful interior and bustling atmosphere. A Mediterranean influence punctuates preparations of freshly prepared seafood and pasta, as well as daily selections showcased tableside. Guests can choose from a good list of wines by the glass or bottle. Dressy casual; cocktails. **Parking:** street. **Cards:** AX, DC, JC, MC, VI.

LAI WAH HEEN   **Lunch:** $16-$25   **Dinner:** $30-$40   **Phone:** 416/977-9899   35

Chinese

Location: Just s of Dundas St; in Metropolitan Hotel. 108 Chestnut St M5G 1R3. **Hours:** 11:30 am-3 & 5:30-10:30 pm. **Reservations:** suggested. **Features:** Discover an extensive and sometimes exotic selection of fine cuisine in the modern, upscale atmosphere that is Lai Wah Heen. Some of the many excellently prepared entrees employ such delicacies as sea cucumber and jellyfish. Dim sum is featured at lunch. Dressy casual; cocktails. **Parking:** on-site. **Cards:** AX, DC, DS, JC, MC, VI.

LE COMMENSAL FINE VEGETARIAN CUISINE   *Menu on aaa.com*   **Lunch:** $8-$12   **Dinner:** $10-$15   **Phone:** 416/596-9364   50

Vegetarian

Location: Jct Bay and Dundas sts; entrance on Elm St. 655 Bay St M5G 2K4. **Hours:** 11:30 am-10 pm, Sat & Sun from noon. Closed: 1/1, 12/25, 12/26. **Features:** An upscale self-service buffet features an extensive and creative selection of hot and cold items such as leek pot pie, sweet potato kasha and lasagna, plus a variety of desserts. Your meal cost is determined by weight. Parking is complimentary after 6 pm. Casual dress; beer & wine only. **Parking:** on-site (fee). **Cards:** AX, DC, MC, VI.

LEE GARDEN   **Dinner:** $15-$25   **Phone:** 416/593-9524   9

Cantonese

Location: S of College St; between Cecil and Darcy sts. 331 Spadina Ave M5T 2E9. **Hours:** 4 pm-midnight, Fri & Sat-1 am. **Features:** The modestly decorated restaurant serves Cantonese food in a bustling atmosphere. Casual dress; cocktails. **Parking:** street. **Cards:** AX, MC, VI.

LEFT BANK   **Dinner:** $12-$23   **Phone:** 416/504-1626   13

Continental

Location: Just e of Bathurst St; between Portland St and Denison Ave. 567 Queen St W M5V 2B6. **Hours:** 6 pm-10:30 pm. Closed: Sun-Wed. **Reservations:** suggested. **Features:** In the trendy Queen Street area, the restaurant has two halves: a restaurant and a full bar that takes over when the kitchen closes at 10:30 pm. Casual dress; cocktails. **Parking:** street. **Cards:** AX, DC, MC, VI.

(See map and index starting on p. 473)

LE PAPILLON RESTAURANT
FRANCAIS   *Menu on aaa.com*   **Lunch:** $8-$15   **Dinner:** $10-$25   **Phone:** 416/363-3773   83
Ⓐ   **Location:** Just s of Front St. 16 Church St M5E 1M1. **Hours:** noon-2:30 & 5-11 pm, Sat 11 am-midnight, Sun 11 am-10 pm. Closed: 1/1, 12/25, 12/26; also 12/31. **Reservations:** suggested. **Features:** The spotlight shines brightly on French Canadian specialties and a wide selection of savory and sweet crepes. Piping-hot French onion soup and tasty meat pie with wholesome vegetables are popular favorites. The mood is cozy and French   relaxed. Casual dress; cocktails. **Parking:** on-site. **Cards:** AX, DC, MC, VI.   ☒

LE SELECT BISTRO   **Lunch:** $11-$14   **Dinner:** $18-$30   **Phone:** 416/596-6405   32
Location: Just e of Spadina Ave. 328 Queen St W M5V 2A2. **Hours:** 11:30 am-midnight, Sat-1 am, Sun-11 pm. Closed: 12/25. **Reservations:** suggested. **Features:** This authentic Paris bistro provides a bustling atmosphere and good menu selection including fresh frites. Leave your calorie counter at home; all the fare French   is rich and flavourful. Quiche, omelets, pasta, seafood, cheese and pastries are favourites. Dressy casual. **Parking:** street. **Cards:** AX, CB, DC, MC, VI.   ☒

LE TROU NORMAND   **Lunch:** $5-$20   **Dinner:** $6-$39   **Phone:** 416/967-5956   53
Location: Just w of Bellair St. 90 Yorkville Ave M5R 1B9. **Hours:** noon-3 & 6-10 pm, Sat-11 pm. Closed: Sun. **Reservations:** suggested. **Features:** Le Trou Normand's authentic French country atmosphere blends well French   with its fine selection of filet mignon, rack of lamb, sweet breads and other fare. Of note is the fresh lobster out of the shell. Outdoor patio dining is available in season. Dressy casual; cocktails. **Parking:** street. **Cards:** AX, DC, MC, VI.   ☒

LUCE   **Dinner:** $29-$38   **Phone:** 416/599-5823   40
Location: Between John St and Blue Jays Way; in Hotel Le Germain. 30 Mercer St M5V 1H3. **Hours:** 5:30 pm-10:30 pm, Thurs-Sat to 11 pm, Sun-10 pm. Closed: 1/1, 12/25. **Reservations:** suggested. **Features:** In the heart Italian   of the entertainment district at a stylish hotel, the restaurant is appointed in contemporary decor. The fine menu focuses on innovative Italian cuisine. In addition to changing a la carte offerings, the chef prepares a selection of a la minute dishes for a nightly changing menu. This is a great place to explore great taste sensations. Dressy casual; cocktails. **Parking:** on-site (fee). **Cards:** AX, DC, MC, VI.   Ⓨ ☒

MARCHE (BCE PLACE) RESTAURANT   **Lunch:** $5-$10   **Dinner:** $5-$15   **Phone:** 416/366-8986   77
Location: Just n of Front St at BCE Place. 42 Yonge St M5E 1T1. **Hours:** 7:30 am-2 am. **Reservations:** not accepted. **Features:** The marketplace-style eatery offers fast, freshly prepared food of various types, including Asian, American, French and Italian. This popular place is formatted as an indoor, open-air market International   where patrons can either stay to eat or take food to go. Heavy foot traffic comes from the business district crowd. Casual dress; cocktails. **Parking:** on-site (fee). **Cards:** AX, DC, MC, VI.   ☒

MATISSE   **Lunch:** $15-$25   **Dinner:** $16-$33   **Phone:** 416/920-6500   81
Location: Just e of Yonge St; in Toronto Marriott Bloor Yorkville. 90 Bloor St E M4W 1A7. **Hours:** 6:30 am-11 pm. **Reservations:** suggested. **Features:** Upscale, trendy dining room with innovative decor featuring wall murals and artwork throughout. Bustling atmosphere. Classy bar area perfect for that after-work martini. Canadian   Creative menu featuring Canadian regional cuisine. Light- or full-entree selections available. Choose from Bay of Fundy salmon, crab cakes, sea bass, gourmet pizza or beef and poultry selections. Homemade apple calvados or tiramisu is an excellent choice to finish. Casual dress; cocktails. **Parking:** on-site (fee). **Cards:** AX, DC, DS, JC, MC, VI.   Ⓨ ☒

MICHAEL SELTZER'S LE BIFTHEQUE STEAKHOUSE   **Lunch:** $6-$14   **Dinner:** $9-$39   **Phone:** 416/366-4333   105
Location: Opposite Toronto Civic Centre and City Hall; in The Sheraton Centre Toronto Hotel. 96 Richmond St W M5H 2A3. **Hours:** 11:30 am-10 pm, Fri & Sat-11 pm. Closed: 12/25. **Reservations:** suggested. **Features:** The reputable restaurant treats diners to huge cuts of well-aged and perfectly seasoned steak and prime rib. A Steak House   tasty meal might include a good starter—such as shrimp cocktail or French onion soup—and an entree of beef, seafood, lamb or ribs. Casual dress; cocktails. **Parking:** on-site (fee). **Cards:** AX, DC, MC, VI.   ☒

MILESTONE'S GRILL AND BAR   **Lunch:** $8-$25   **Dinner:** $8-$25   **Phone:** 416/595-1990   106
Location: At Richmond St. 132 John St M5V 2E3. **Hours:** 11 am-1 am, Fri-2 am, Sat 10 am-2 am, Sun 10 am-midnight. Closed: 12/25. **Features:** A bright, modern decor and a bustling atmosphere set the tone at the Milestone's Bar and Grill. The menu features an abundance of pastas, stone-oven pizzas, sandwiches and American   burgers, as well as an all-day brunch menu with an innovative flair. The large dining room features a contemporary lounge and an open-concept kitchen. Casual dress; cocktails. **Parking:** no self-parking. **Cards:** AX, DC, MC, VI.   Ⓨ ☒

MR. GREENJEANS RESTAURANT   **Lunch:** $6-$15   **Dinner:** $6-$22   **Phone:** 416/979-1212   84
Location: In Eaton Centre, 4th floor. 220 Yonge St M5B 2H1. **Hours:** 11 am-11 pm, Fri & Sat-1 am, Sun-10 pm. Closed: 12/25. **Reservations:** suggested. **Features:** Two floors of dining and a large bar all project a bustling, fun mood at the casual restaurant. The menu features huge portions of both food and drinks. Try American   finger-food appetizers—such as nachos, wings and spring rolls—or tasty soups or salads before digging into main courses of burgers, sandwiches, fish and chips, pasta, stir-fry, chicken or ribs. Desserts are decadent. An enclosed smoking room is available. Casual dress; cocktails. **Parking:** on-site (fee). **Cards:** AX, DC, DS, MC, VI.   ☒

MONTREAL BISTRO/JAZZ CLUB   **Lunch:** $8-$14   **Dinner:** $12-$23   **Phone:** 416/363-0179   38
Location: Jct Adelaide St E. 65 Sherbourne St M5A 2P9. **Hours:** 11:30 am-11 pm, Fri-midnight, Sat 5:30 pm-midnight. Closed major holidays; also Sun. **Reservations:** suggested. **Features:** Elegant yet relaxed atmosphere in authentic French manor. Cozy country decor. Good menu selection highlighting items such French   as French Canadian pea soup, specialty omelettes and steak and frites. Live jazz entertainment rounds out the club. Great choice for good food and a fun evening out. Casual dress; cocktails. **Parking:** street. **Cards:** AX, DC, MC, VI.

(See map and index starting on p. 473)

MORTON'S OF CHICAGO   **Dinner:** $35-$55   **Phone:** 416/925-0648   26
▼▼▼   **Location:** Jct Prince Arthur Ave. 4 Avenue Rd M5R 2E8. **Hours:** 5:30 pm-11 pm, Sat from 5 pm, Sun 5 pm-10 pm. Closed major holidays. **Reservations:** suggested. **Features:** Patrons should make sure to reserve
Steak House   ahead for the popular, well-known steak house. Large portions, including huge cuts of fine beef and plentiful seafood, are the norm. Even the vegetables are oversized, with baked potatoes big enough for sharing. Servers will showcase menu items tableside and tempt diners with a decadent dessert selection. Cocktails. **Parking:** on-site (fee) and valet. **Cards:** AX, DC, MC, VI.   ✕

NAMI   **Lunch:** $8-$20   **Dinner:** $25-$27   **Phone:** 416/362-7373   75
▼▼▼   **Location:** Just w of Church St. 55 Adelaide St E M5C 1K6. **Hours:** noon-2:30 & 5:30-10:30 pm, Sat from 5:30 pm. Closed major holidays; also Sun. **Reservations:** suggested. **Features:** Sushi pizza and a wealth of
Japanese   more traditional Japanese fare make Nami a special treat for diners. Hot pot cooking and full teriyaki and tempura options are on the menu. There is an extensive sushi bar, plus table and booth seating are available. Dressy casual; cocktails. **Parking:** street. **Cards:** AX, DC, MC, VI.   ✕

THE OLD SPAGHETTI FACTORY   **Lunch:** $9-$15   **Dinner:** $9-$15   **Phone:** 416/864-9761   46
▼▼   **Location:** Between Yonge and Church sts; directly s of Front St. 54 The Esplanade M5E 1A6. **Hours:** 11:30 am-10 pm, Fri & Sat-midnight. Closed: 12/24, 12/25. **Features:** Tiffany lamps, old-fashioned carousels and a
Italian   restored old streetcar are a few distinctive decor elements in the restored warehouse dining room. Tasty meals of pasta with hot bread, soup or salad and ice cream are a good value. Casual dress; cocktails. **Parking:** on-site (fee). **Cards:** AX, DC, MC, VI.   ✕

OPUS RESTAURANT ON PRINCE ARTHUR   **Dinner:** $29-$39   **Phone:** 416/921-3105   1
▼▼ ▼▼   **Location:** Between Avenue Rd and Bedford. 37 Prince Arthur Ave M5R 1B2. **Hours:** 5:30 pm-11:30 pm. Closed: 12/25. **Reservations:** suggested. **Features:** The small, upscale dining room shows a European flair in
Continental   design and artwork. Tables are draped in fine linens and set with fresh flowers and candles. Regional influences are evident in some selections of fine Continental cuisine. Presentations are excellent. The extensive wine selection is a perfect complement. Casual dress; cocktails. **Parking:** street. **Cards:** AX, DC, MC, VI.   ✕

ORO   **Lunch:** $18-$38   **Dinner:** $20-$42   **Phone:** 416/597-0155   48
▼▼▼   **Location:** Just e of Bay St. 45 Elm St M5G 1H1. **Hours:** Open 5/1-12/23 & 1/13-4/30; noon-2:30 & 5:30-10 pm, Sat from 5:30 pm. Closed major holidays; also Sun. **Reservations:** suggested. **Features:** Upscale, modern
Continental   atmosphere featuring fine tableware and art pieces throughout. Innovative menu with a strong focus on Italian, Asian and Mediterranean influences. Exotic presentation featuring starters such as seared scallops, mussels or shrimp bisque. Entrees include veal, beef, seafood and pasta creations. Outstanding desserts. Dressy casual; cocktails. **Parking:** on-site. **Cards:** AX, DC, MC, VI.   ✕

PANGAEA   **Lunch:** $15-$28   **Dinner:** $25-$39   **Phone:** 416/920-2323   93
▼▼▼   **Location:** Directly n of Bloor St; on east side. 1221 Bay St M5R 3P5. **Hours:** 11:30 am-11 pm. Closed major holidays; also Sun. **Reservations:** suggested. **Features:** Contemporary decor is fitting of the city's modern
Continental   Bay/Bloor area and is a hit with the business crowd. Modern art, high ceilings, a large bar and linen table settings set the tone. Coupled with an innovative Continental menu and an extensive wine list, the combination is a winner. A relaxing afternoon tea is served daily. Dressy casual; cocktails. **Parking:** no self-parking. **Cards:** AX, DC, MC, VI.   ✕

PEARL HARBOURFRONT RESTAURANT   **Lunch:** $10-$20   **Dinner:** $20-$35   **Phone:** 416/203-1233   73
▼▼▼   **Location:** Queens Quay Terminal, 2nd floor. 207 Queens Quay W, 2nd Floor M5J 1A7. **Hours:** 11 am-3 & 5-11 pm, Sun from 10:30 am. **Reservations:** suggested. **Features:** After spending the day shopping and touring
Chinese   around the harbourfront, diners find this restaurant a great place to unwind. Professional staffers provide pampering service and offer thoughtful suggestions from the extensive menu. Representative of traditional and exotic Chinese cuisine are such highlights as shark's fin soup, Peking duck and dim sum platters. Simple decor characterizes the comfortable dining room, which has many tables overlooking the harbour. Dressy casual; cocktails. **Parking:** on-site (fee). **Cards:** AX, MC, VI.   ✕

PENELOPE RESTAURANT   **Lunch:** $7-$12   **Dinner:** $10-$14   **Phone:** 416/947-1159   51
▼▼   **Location:** Just e of Yonge St. 6 Front St E M5E 1G4. **Hours:** 11:30 am-10 pm, Thurs & Fri-11:30 pm, Sat 4:30 pm-11:30 pm. Closed major holidays; also Sun. **Reservations:** suggested. **Features:** A fun atmosphere
Greek   awaits you in this bustling, Mediterranean-themed restaurant with white-washed walls and lots of greenery. Featured is traditional Greek fare with wholesome ingredients and simple, colorful presentation. Patio dining is offered in season. Casual dress; cocktails. **Parking:** on-site (fee). **Cards:** AX, DC, MC, VI.   ✕

PETER PAN BISTRO   **Lunch:** $8-$13   **Dinner:** $9-$17   **Phone:** 416/593-0917   78
▼▼▼   **Location:** Jct Peter St. 373 Queen St W M5V 2A4. **Hours:** noon-midnight, Sat-1 am, Sun-close. Closed: 12/25. **Reservations:** suggested. **Features:** A prime location in the city's popular Queen Street district makes the
Continental   restaurant a popular stop for a meal or a decadent dessert with coffee. The small, cozy dining room has old-fashioned wood booths, an old wood bar and several tables facing Queen Street for interesting people-watching. The innovative menu lists changing specials and a fabulous dessert selection. Dressy casual; cocktails. **Parking:** street. **Cards:** AX, CB, DC, DS, MC, VI.   ☕ ✕

THE PICKLE BARREL   **Lunch:** $7-$19   **Dinner:** $7-$19   **Phone:** 416/977-6677   110
▼▼▼   **Location:** At Dundas St; in Atrium on the Bay. 312 Yonge St M5G 2B2. **Hours:** 8 am-11 pm, Tues-Thurs to midnight, Fri & Sat-1 am. Closed: 12/25. **Features:** At a busy intersection, this location of the popular
American   delicatessen is the perfect spot for a break from the office or shopping or for pre-event dining. The menu lists a wide selection of traditional deli fare, as well as pasta dishes and grilled meats, chicken and ribs. Desserts are an event. In the summer months, the patio is the perfect spot for a cool drink and a tasty meal. Casual dress; cocktails. **Parking:** on-site (fee). **Cards:** AX, DC, DS, MC, VI.   ✕

(See map and index starting on p. 473)

PIER 4 STOREHOUSE RESTAURANT   **Lunch:** $13-$20   **Dinner:** $17-$33   **Phone:** 416/203-1440   ⑩
Location: At the harbourfront. 245 Queens Quay W M5J 2K9. **Hours:** 11:30 am-2:30 & 4:30-11 pm; from 4:30 pm 11/1-3/31. Closed: 1/1, 12/25; also Mon 11/1-3/31. **Reservations:** suggested. **Features:** In a prime waterfront location that affords views of the harbour, the restaurant sports a pleasant, nautical theme. On the varied menu are steak, pasta and such seafood items as live lobster. In the summer, patio dining and a lighter menu are available at Wally Magoo's Marine Bar. Dressy casual; cocktails. **Parking:** street. **Cards:** AX, DC, DS, MC, VI.

Seafood

PLAZA FLAMINGO RESTAURANT   **Lunch:** $7-$13   **Dinner:** $11-$17   **Phone:** 416/603-8884   ⑧⑨
Location: Just e of Bathurst St. 423 College St M5T 1T1. **Hours:** 11 am-11 pm, Fri & Sat-midnight. **Reservations:** suggested. **Features:** The established restaurant sets out a reasonably priced daily buffet and presents a show of flamenco dance Thursday through Saturday night. Dressy casual; cocktails. **Parking:** on-site (fee) and street. **Cards:** AX, MC, VI.

Spanish

PREGO DELLA PIAZZA   **Lunch:** $14-$20   **Dinner:** $16-$33   **Phone:** 416/920-9900   ⑤②
Location: Jct Avenue Rd. 150 Bloor St W M4S 2X9. **Hours:** noon-midnight, Sun 5 pm-10 pm. Closed major holidays; also Sun 1/1-4/30. **Reservations:** suggested. **Features:** One excellent choice is fresh gnocchi—flavorful and served in a thick pesto sauce. Some head straight for dessert and with good reason; fresh pastries, cakes, cheeses and sorbet are available. Seasonal patio dining and validated 2-hour parking are offered. Dressy casual; cocktails. **Parking:** on-site. **Cards:** AX, DC, MC, VI.

Italian

PROVENCE DELICES   **Lunch:** $15-$24   **Dinner:** $15-$24   **Phone:** 416/924-9901   ⑥
Location: Cross section of Wellesley St and Parliament. 12 Amelia St M4X 1E1. **Hours:** noon-2 & 6-10 pm. **Reservations:** required. **Features:** This charming country French bistro provides a casual atmosphere for a most leisurely dining experience where you'll enjoy both the atmosphere and the exceptional finely prepared dishes. All meal courses are quite good and prepared fresh each day. Dressy casual; cocktails. **Parking:** street. **Cards:** AX, DC, MC, VI.

French

RAIN   **Dinner:** $29-$33   **Phone:** 416/599-7246   ⑮
Location: Just w of John St. 19 Mercer St M5V 1H2. **Hours:** 5:30 pm-10:30 pm, Thurs-Sat to 11 pm. Closed major holidays; also Sun. **Reservations:** required. **Features:** An innovative, Asian-influenced menu and a unique contemporary setting put Rain in a class of its own. Diners are greeted by a tranquil waterfall, dim lighting and trendy upscale setting. The menu concept features a wonderful array of "sharing platters," that the waiters term as group or family-style dining, and a sampling of several courses is recommended. Highlights include sugarcane prawns, fire-roasted Japanese sirloin and Rain sashimi. It is a dining adventure. Dressy casual; cocktails. **Parking:** street. **Cards:** AX, DC, MC, VI.

Asian

RASHNAA RESTAURANT   **Lunch:** $6-$8   **Dinner:** $7-$14   **Phone:** 416/929-2099   ⑨⑧
Location: Just e of Parliament. 307 Wellesley St E M4X 1H2. **Hours:** 11:30 am-11:30 pm. **Reservations:** accepted. **Features:** Sri Lankan and south Indian entrees are specialties at the modest neighborhood restaurant. Casual dress; cocktails. **Parking:** street. **Cards:** AX, MC, VI.

South Indian

RESTO PORTICO   **Lunch:** $15-$24   **Dinner:** $15-$38   **Phone:** 416/601-3774   ㊼
Location: Just e of Yonge St; in Cambridge Suites Hotel. 15 Richmond St E M5C 1N2. **Hours:** 7 am-10:30 & 11:30-10:30 pm, Sat & Sun-11 pm. Closed: 12/25, 12/26. **Reservations:** suggested. **Features:** Fresh market cuisine with Northern Italian and French influences grace a menu that changes according to availability of seasonal ingredients. Each menu item is created with unique artistry and creativeness. Enjoy the cozy appeal of this elegant atmosphere. Close to theatre district and downtown attractions. Casual dress; cocktails. **Parking:** on-site (fee). **Cards:** AX, DC, DS, MC, VI.

Continental

RISTORANTE ROMAGNA MIA   **Lunch:** $14-$22   **Dinner:** $19-$30   **Phone:** 416/363-8370   ⑧⑦
Location: Jct Jarvis St. 106 Front St E M5A 1E1. **Hours:** noon-3 & 5-10 pm, Thurs-Sat to 11 pm. Closed major holidays; also Sun. **Reservations:** suggested. **Features:** Known for its hand-made pastas and award-winning risotto, the bustling restaurant is a local favorite. The menu lists a wide range of antipasti, as well as fresh soups and salads. Other features include fresh seafood, beef and poultry. Diners enjoy pleasant music and watching tableside preparation of the risotto in large clay bowls. Casual dress; cocktails. **Parking:** street. **Cards:** AX, DC, MC, VI.

Italian

ROSEWATER SUPPER CLUB   **Lunch:** $9-$21   **Dinner:** $22-$40   **Phone:** 416/214-5888   ⑭
Location: Just e of Yonge St; between King and Adelaide sts. 19 Toronto St M5C 2R1. **Hours:** 11:30 am-2:30 & 5:30-10:30 pm, Thurs & Fri-11:30 pm, Sat 5:30 pm-11 pm. Closed major holidays; also Sun. **Reservations:** suggested. **Features:** Live jazz music contributes to the sophisticated restaurant's relaxing atmosphere. Chefs prepare meals in a glass-enclosed viewing kitchen. A splash of contemporary design elements creates an aura of elegance, and attentive servers are aptly skilled. Imagination is evident in creative dish presentations. Save room for dessert, which is always a special treat. Dressy casual; cocktails. **Parking:** street. **Cards:** AX, CB, DC, DS, MC, VI.

Continental

RUTH'S CHRIS STEAK HOUSE   **Dinner:** $28-$52   **Phone:** 416/955-1455   ⑨⑤
Location: Jct University Ave; in Hilton Toronto. 145 Richmond St W M5H 4B3. **Hours:** 5 pm-10 pm, Sat-10:30 pm. Closed: 12/25, 12/26. **Reservations:** suggested. **Features:** Near many hotels and several shopping and entertainment areas, the restaurant presents a menu that stands on its own with the fine reputation from its many North American locations. Huge, sizzling steaks are expected and delivered. All menu items are a la carte and served up in sharing-size portions. It's a challenge to save room for dessert, but the effort is worthwhile. Dressy casual; cocktails. **Parking:** on-site (fee). **Cards:** AX, DC, MC, VI.

Steak House

(See map and index starting on p. 473)

SASSAFRAZ Lunch: $14-$23 Dinner: $20-$40 Phone: 416/964-2222 (61)

Continental

Location: Corner of Bellair St. 100 Cumberland St M5R 1A6. **Hours:** 11:30 am-2 am. Closed: 12/25. **Reservations:** suggested. **Features:** French and Californian influences populate the menu, which offers vegetable tarts, grilled rack of Ontario pork and snow crab and potato pancakes. Art deco stylings lend a distinctive, upbeat feel to the dining room. The wine selection is excellent. Dressy casual; cocktails. **Parking:** street. **Cards:** AX, DC, DS, MC, VI.

SEGOVIA RESTAURANT Lunch: $12 Dinner: $14-$19 Phone: 416/960-1010 (88)

Spanish

Location: Yonge and Wellesley sts. 5 St. Nicholos St M4Y 1W5. **Hours:** 11:30 am-2 & 5-10 pm, Fri & Sat-11 pm. Closed major holidays; also Sun. **Reservations:** suggested, weekends. **Features:** The wildly decorated restaurant serves wonderful foods from Spain, as well as reasonably priced wines from the country. Casual dress; cocktails. **Parking:** no self-parking. **Cards:** AX, MC, VI.

SENSES Dinner: $29-$46 Phone: 416/979-2622 (108)

Continental

Location: Jct Blue Jays Way; in SoHo Metropolitan Hotel. 318 Wellington St W M5V 3T4. **Hours:** 6 pm-10 pm. Closed: Mon & Tues. **Reservations:** suggested. **Features:** In the heart of the entertainment district, the restaurant has slick contemporary decor and an innovative menu. Dining here is an event on its own. Menu highlights include seviche of prawns, hot foie gras and warm mushroom rolls to start; entrees of braised beef ribs and tea-smoked squab breasts; and equally creative and splurge-worthy desserts. Dressy casual; cocktails. **Parking:** on-site. **Cards:** AX, DS, JC, MC, VI.

SHOPSY'S DELICATESSEN RESTAURANT Lunch: $7-$10 Dinner: $8-$13 Phone: 416/365-3333 (41)

American

Location: Corner of Front St; across from O'Keefe Centre. 33 Yonge St M5E 1G4. **Hours:** 7 am-11 pm, Thurs & Fri-midnight, Sat 8 am-midnight, Sun 8 am-9 pm. Closed: 12/25. **Features:** The well-established delicatessen is in the heart of the city's theatre and sporting event area and directly across the street from the Hockey Hall of Fame, making it the perfect choice for pre-theatre or pre-event dining. Representative of the hearty fare are smoked meat deli sandwiches and Shopsy's famous hot dogs. Other favourites include matzo ball soup, cabbage rolls and the decadent cheesecake. Casual dress; cocktails. **Parking:** on-site. **Cards:** AX, DC, MC, VI.

SIGNATURES Lunch: $10-$16 Dinner: $20-$25 Phone: 416/324-5885 (80)

Continental

Location: Just w of Avenue Rd; in InterContinental Toronto. 220 Bloor St W M5S 1T8. **Hours:** 7 am-3 & 6-11 pm, Sun-3 pm. **Reservations:** suggested. **Features:** Fresh flowers and fine china and silverware contribute to an elegant, sophisticated setting. Creative dishes, including lighter lunch items, employ fresh ingredients and artistic presentation. In the warmer months, the lovely courtyard terrace is a nice spot for outdoor dining. Dressy casual; cocktails. **Parking:** on-site (fee) and valet. **Cards:** AX, CB, DC, JC, MC, VI.

SPLENDIDO BAR AND GRILL Dinner: $20-$40 Phone: 416/929-7788 (109)

Continental

Location: Jct Bloor St and Spadina Ave, just s on Spadina Ave to Harbord St, then w. 88 Harbord St M5S 1G5. **Hours:** 5 pm-11 pm. Closed major holidays; also Mon. **Reservations:** suggested. **Features:** Innovative flair punctuates the Continental menu, and the dining room perpetuates a contemporary feel. Diners can select from a changing chef's tasting menu or from fine a la carte selections. A meal might incorporate Mediterranean seafood soup or seared scallops as a starter and rack of lamb, a fine New York cut or the seafood special as the entree. It's worth saving room for one of the special desserts. Dressy casual; cocktails. **Parking:** valet. **Cards:** AX, DC, MC, VI.

THE SUPERIOR RESTAURANT Lunch: $8-$24 Dinner: $15-$30 Phone: 416/214-0416 (5)

Continental

Location: Just s of Dundas St. 253 Yonge St M5B 1N8. **Hours:** 11:30 am-11 pm. Closed major holidays; also Sun. **Reservations:** suggested. **Features:** Contemporary styling of eclectic cuisine runs the gamut from choice steak and fresh Atlantic salmon to osso buco with saffron orzo. Vaulted ceilings and a modern decor set the pace for the bustling atmosphere and smartly attired, friendly wait staff. Casual dress; cocktails. **Parking:** street. **Cards:** AX, DC, MC, VI.

SUSUR Dinner: $35-$45 Phone: 416/603-2205 (104)

Continental

Location: Just e of Bathurst St. 601 King St W M5V 1M5. **Hours:** 6 pm-10:30 pm. Closed major holidays; also Sun. **Reservations:** required. **Features:** The chef's ever-changing tasting menu is a showcase for innovative cuisine. Diners are surprised and tantalized each evening with a five-course menu based on fresh specialty ingredients and the creator's mood. This is the perfect opportunity to sit back, relax and prepare to be pampered. Trendy modern decor with interesting changing artwork and design highlights also contribute to the unforgettable experience. Dressy casual; cocktails. **Parking:** street. **Cards:** AX, DC, MC, VI.

TOM JONES STEAKHOUSE & SEAFOOD Lunch: $10-$29 Dinner: $25-$60 Phone: 416/366-6583 (82)

CAA

Steak & Seafood

Location: Jct King and Church sts, just w on King St, then s. 17 Leader Ln M5E 1L8. **Hours:** 11:30 am-midnight, Sat from 5 pm, Sun 5 pm-10 pm. Closed: 12/24-12/26. **Reservations:** suggested. **Features:** Convenient to the theatre, hotel and financial districts, Tom Jones spotlights well-prepared traditional steak house fare in an elegant setting. The upstairs piano bar features nightly entertainment. Dressy casual; cocktails. **Parking:** on-site (fee). **Cards:** AX, CB, DC, DS, JC, MC, VI.

TORCH BISTRO Dinner: $24-$36 Phone: 416/364-7517 (3)

Steak House

Location: Between Dundas and Shuter sts. 253 Victoria St M5B 1T8. **Hours:** 5 pm-11 pm. Closed: 1/1, 12/25; also Sun & Mon. **Reservations:** suggested. **Features:** Opt for fine dining in the restaurant or more casual fare in the 1929 historical diner, open from 7:30 am. Dry-aged beef, home-smoked fresh Atlantic salmon and homemade desserts are the stars. Live jazz is performed Tuesday-Sunday; a cover charge may apply. Dressy casual; cocktails; entertainment. **Parking:** street. **Cards:** AX, DC, JC, MC, VI.

(See map and index starting on p. 473)

TORTILLA FLATS TEXAS BAR & GRILL   **Lunch:** $7-$12   **Dinner:** $7-$12   **Phone:** 416/593-9870   27
American   **Location:** Between University and Spadina aves. 429 Queen St W M5V 2A5. **Hours:** 11:30 am-1 am, Sun & Mon-midnight. Closed: 12/25, 12/26. **Features:** A fun-filled atmosphere in both the interior and menu designs makes the eatery a hit with the locals. Adding to the Tex-Mex feel are wood booths and floors and neon signs throughout. The menu features old-time favorites, such as sizzling fajitas, quesadillas, nachos, tacos and burgers, all served in heaping portions. A frozen margarita or cold beer makes a great addition. The patio offers seating in the summer months. Casual dress; cocktails. **Parking:** street. **Cards:** AX, DC, MC, VI.

TOULA   **Lunch:** $14-$40   **Dinner:** $14-$45   **Phone:** 416/777-2002   107
Italian   **Location:** At the foot of Bay St; on shore of Lake Ontario; in The Westin Harbour Castle. One Harbour Sq, 38th Floor M5J 1A6. **Hours:** noon-2:30 & 5-10:30 pm. **Reservations:** suggested. **Features:** Modern, trendy and innovative are a few words to describe the dining room design. Atop the hotel, the restaurant affords wonderful views of city and lake from its large windows. Fine Italian cuisine is prepared with fresh market ingredients. Service is polished and sophisticated. Dressy casual; cocktails; entertainment. **Parking:** on-site (fee). **Cards:** AX, DC, DS, MC, VI.

TRUFFLES   *Menu on aaa.com*   **Dinner:** $27-$37   **Phone:** 416/964-0411   39
Continental   **Location:** Corner of Avenue Rd and Cumberland Ave; in Four Seasons Hotel. 21 Avenue Rd M5R 2G1. **Hours:** 6 pm-11 pm. Closed: Sun. **Reservations:** suggested. **Features:** Enjoy a superb dining experience in simple yet elegant surroundings. Pass through the wrought iron gates and be greeted by funky art and wood-carved pigs, which add to the theme of this restaurant. Prepare your tastebuds for a fantastic selection of daring and creative cuisine, ranging from specialty seafood and meat selections to vegetarian options. Or consider trying the chef's daily tasting menu, coupled with wine pairing for a flavour sensation you won't soon forget! Semi-formal attire; cocktails. **Parking:** on-site. **Cards:** AX, CB, DC, DS, JC, MC, VI.

TUNDRA   **Lunch:** $13-$20   **Dinner:** $22-$45   **Phone:** 416/860-6800   92
Canadian   **Location:** Jct University Ave; in Hilton Toronto. 145 Richmond St W M5H 2L2. **Hours:** 6:30 am-11, 11:30-2 & 5:30-10 pm, Sat & Sun 6:30 am-noon & 5:30-10 pm. **Reservations:** suggested. **Features:** Reflecting elements of the Canadian tundra, the stark and minimalist restaurant also has surprise pockets of warmth and beauty. Mimicking the decor, Canadian cuisine is highlighted in a creative and globally influenced manner. Dressy casual; cocktails. **Parking:** on-site (fee). **Cards:** AX, CB, DC, DS, JC, MC, VI.

TUTTI MATTI   **Lunch:** $8-$11   **Dinner:** $7-$30   **Phone:** 416/597-8839   119
Italian   **Location:** Just s of King St. 364 Adelaide St W M5V 1R7. **Hours:** noon-3 & 6-10 pm, Sat 6 pm-10:30 pm. Closed: 12/24, 12/25, 12/26; also 1/2 & Sun. **Features:** Patrons peruse a fine Italian menu in a cozy, modern setting. The open kitchen enables diners to watch the chef create each course fresh to order, and skill and detail are evident in the preparation and presentation. Menu highlights include hand-rolled pastas, fresh seafood, veal and roast suckling pig. It's well worth saving room for one of the desserts made in house. Dressy casual. **Parking:** street. **Cards:** AX, DC, MC, VI.

URBAN   **Lunch:** $9-$28   **Dinner:** $15-$48   **Phone:** 416/598-5656   25
Continental   **Location:** Just w of John St. 303 King St W M5V 1J5. **Hours:** 11:30 am-midnight, Thurs-Sat to 1 am. Closed: 1/1, 12/25. **Reservations:** suggested, weekends. **Features:** Windows that open into the busy city streets, brick walls and an open-concept kitchen create an inviting and bustling bistro feel. In the summer months, diners can choose from indoor or patio seating. The menu lists a good selection of Continental fare with a focus on market-fresh ingredients. On the more casual lunch menu are pizzas, burgers, salads and sandwiches, while dinner offers a wider selection, including many grilled meats and seafood selections. Casual dress; cocktails. **Parking:** street. **Cards:** AX, DC, MC, VI.

WAYNE GRETZKY'S RESTAURANT   **Lunch:** $7-$26   **Dinner:** $7-$26   **Phone:** 416/979-7825   21
Canadian   **Location:** Jct King St. 99 Blue Jays Way M5V 9G9. **Hours:** 11:30 am-1 am, Thurs-Sat to 2 am, Sun-11 pm. Closed: 12/25, 12/26. **Reservations:** suggested. **Features:** The casual, sports-oriented atmosphere here leads the way to a variety of festive and hearty fare such as burgers, pork ribs, pizza, pasta, chicken stir-fry and sandwiches. Located near the SkyDome, this eatery also offers outdoor patio dining in season. Casual dress; cocktails. **Parking:** on-site (fee). **Cards:** AX, DC, MC, VI.

YAMATO JAPANESE RESTAURANT   **Lunch:** $7-$19   **Dinner:** $15-$33   **Phone:** 416/927-0077   42
Japanese   **Location:** Between Yorkville and Cumberland aves. 18-24 Bellair St M5R 2C7. **Hours:** 11:30 am-3 & 5-11 pm, Fri-midnight, Sat noon-midnight, Sun noon-10 pm. Closed: 12/25. **Reservations:** suggested. **Features:** The restaurant features two styles of traditional Japanese dining: a full sushi bar with expanded menu offerings or a teppanyaki grill where chefs entertain diners with flaming grills and spinning salt shakers as they prepare meals to order. The menu comprises full-course meals. Casual dress; cocktails. **Parking:** street. **Cards:** AX, DC, MC, VI.

YYZ RESTAURANT & WINE BAR   **Dinner:** $22-$30   **Phone:** 416/599-3399   91
Continental   **Location:** Just s of King St. 345 Adelaide St M5H 1H9. **Hours:** 5 pm-10 pm, Thurs-Sat to 11 pm. Closed major holidays. **Reservations:** suggested. **Features:** Designed to look like an airport terminal, the contemporary dining room is the perfect setting for the chef's innovative menu. Featuring market-fresh ingredients, Continental dishes reflect an Asian flair. Among starters are such exotic selections as sauteed wild mushrooms with Japanese eggplant and seared beef carpaccio. Entrees include a seafood steamer and broiled scallops with lobster mashed potatoes. Dressy casual; cocktails. **Parking:** street. **Cards:** AX, DC, MC, VI.

TORONTO pop. 2,481,494   (See map and index starting on p. 479)

──────── WHERE TO STAY ────────

BEST WESTERN EXECUTIVE INN   *Book at aaa.com*   **Phone:** 416/430-0444   **43**
(CAA) (SAVE)   All Year   1P: $129   2P: $129   XP: $10   F17
▼▼▼▼   **Location:** Hwy 401, exit 383 (Markham Rd), then s. 38 Estate Dr M1H 2Z1. Fax: 416/430-0555. **Facility:** 95 one-bedroom standard units, some with whirlpools. 4 stories, interior corridors. **Parking:** on-site. **Terms:** package plans, 3% service charge. **Amenities:** high-speed Internet, dual phone lines, voice mail, Small-scale Hotel irons, hair dryers. **Pool(s):** heated indoor. **Leisure Activities:** sauna, whirlpool, exercise room. **Business Services:** meeting rooms, business center. **Cards:** AX, DC, DS, MC, VI. **Special Amenities:** free expanded continental breakfast and free local telephone calls. *(See color ad below)*   SOME UNITS

[icons] SOME UNITS

BEST WESTERN ROEHAMPTON HOTEL & SUITES   *Book at aaa.com*   **Phone:** (416)487-5101   **56**
(CAA) (SAVE)   All Year   1P: $119-$149   XP: $10   F17
▼▼▼▼   **Location:** Just n of Eglinton Ave. 808 Mt. Pleasant Rd M4P 2L2. Fax: 416/487-5390. **Facility:** 109 one-bedroom standard units. 10 stories, interior corridors. **Parking:** valet. **Terms:** 30 day cancellation notice. **Amenities:** video games (fee), dual phone lines, voice mail, irons, hair dryers. **Dining:** 7 am-10 & 5-10 pm, Small-scale Hotel cocktails. **Pool(s):** heated outdoor. **Leisure Activities:** exercise room. **Guest Services:** valet and coin laundry. **Business Services:** meeting rooms. **Cards:** AX, DC, DS, JC, MC, VI. **Special Amenities:** free room upgrade and preferred room (each subject to availability with advance reservations).   SOME UNITS

[icons] SOME UNITS

Wake Up and Smell the Cinnamon Rolls.

- Free Express Start™ Breakfast Bar
- Free Local and 1-800 Phone Calls
- Priority Club® Rewards Benefits
- Newly Renovated
- Free High-Speed Internet Connection

Holiday Inn
EXPRESS
Stay Smart®

$89*-**$159**
per night

From the Airport: Take 409E/401E ramp. to 401 E Express, Exit 383 Markham S. Turn Rt.on Progress Ave.and Rt. on Estate Dr. Call for further assistance.

For Reservations Call 1-888-897-0107

© 2004-2005 InterContinental Hotels Group. All rights reserved. Most hotels are independently owned and/or operated.*Single/Double Occ.

50 Estate Drive
Scarborough, ON M1H-2Z1
www.hiexpress.com/yyz-east
Tel(416)439-9666
Fax(416)439-4295

- Indoor Pool, Whirlpool, Sauna & Exercise Room
- Complimentary Continental Breakfast
- Elevator access to guest rooms
- All rooms include: fridge, microwave, iron, hair dryer & coffee maker
- Children under 17 stay free with parents

Best Western Executive Inn

Newly built at Markham Road & Hwy 401 only minutes away from Toronto's best shopping, restaurants & attractions

38 Estate Drive, Toronto East (Scarborough)
ON, Canada M1H 2Z1
(416) 430-0444   Fax (416) 430-0555
www.bestwestern.com/executiveinnontario
66088@hotel.bestwestern.com
For Reservations Call   **1-800-528-1234**

THE WORLD'S LARGEST HOTEL CHAIN®

STAY YOUR OWN WAY™

Show this bookmark at check-in and you will get an additional $10 off the already discounted CAA/AAA rate at participating Radisson properties in Ontario and Quebec.

1-800-333-3333 • www.radisson.com

KITCHENER-WATERLOO
Radisson Hotel Kitchener • 519-894-9500

LONDON
Radisson Hotel & Suites London
519-668-7900

TORONTO - MISSISSAUGA
Radisson Hotel Mississauga • 905-858-2424

OTTAWA
Radisson Hotel Ottawa Parliament Hill
613-236-1133

TORONTO - AIRPORT
Radisson Suite Hotel Toronto Airport
416-242-7400

TORONTO EAST
Radisson Hotel Toronto East • 416-493-7000

WINDSOR
Radisson Hotel Windsor • 519-977-9777

LAVAL, QC
Radisson Hotel Laval • 450-682-9000

* Offer subject to availability. Some restrictions apply.
Not applicable to Groups. One coupon per room, per day.
Offer valid March 1, 2005 to Feb. 28, 2006.

TourBookMark

Lodging Listing Symbols

Member Values
(see pg. 14)

- AAA Official Appointment
- SAVE Offers minimum 10% discount or lowest public rate
- ASK May offer discount
- S Offers senior discount
- fyi Informational listing only

Member Services

- Airport transportation
- Pets allowed
- Restaurant on premises
- Restaurant off premises (walking distance)
- 24-hour room service
- Cocktail lounge
- Child care

Accessibility Features
(see pg. 18)

- Accessibility features
- Roll-in showers
- Hearing impaired

Leisure Activities

- Full Service Casino
- Pool
- Health Club on premises
- Health Club off premises
- Recreational activities

In-Room Amenities

- Designated non-smoking rooms
- No air conditioning
- No TV
- No Cable TV
- VCR
- Movies
- Data port/modem line
- No telephones
- Refrigerator
- Microwave
- Coffee maker

Call property for detailed information about fees & restrictions relating to the lodging listing symbols.

Lodging Reservation and Deposit Definitions

Reservation:

A temporary hold on lodgings, usually until 4 or 6 p.m. on the arrival date.

Reservation Confirmation:

Once the reservation process is complete, a "confirmation number" is assigned to the guest for future reference. When ample notice is given, a copy of the reservation details and confirmation number is mailed to the guest.

Credit Card Guaranteed Reservation:

When reserved lodgings have been secured with a credit card number, the room will be held for the first night regardless of arrival time, but will be billed to the credit card if the guest fails to arrive at all (is a "no show"). Credit card guarantees usually pertain to the first night only.

Reservation Deposit:

These funds are collected from the guest in advance of arrival to secure reserved lodgings. A reservation deposit can be in the form of cash, check, money order, credit card transaction or other means to transfer funds. One or more days' payment may be required depending on the length of the stay.

Prepaid Reservation:

Reserved lodgings that are fully paid in advance of arrival.

Cancellation Policy:

Published terms/conditions set by lodging by which the guest can cancel a reservation and recover all, or a portion of, the deposit/full payment. Sometimes a "service charge" or "cancellation fee" is levied regardless of how far in advance the reservation was cancelled.

Cancellation Number:

Upon receipt of a cancellation, it is customary for lodgings to assign a "cancellation number" that is given to the caller

SAVINGS & REWARDS GALORE!

Take **5%** off the already discounted CAA/AAA rate, earn Guest Rewards and Hbc Rewards bonus points at participating Travelodge properties.

Travelodge
Inns ~ Hotels ~ Suites

Ask for the Bookmark Savings Galore Rate!
Travelodge Reservations:
1-800-578-7878

Participating Properties:

Travelodge Burlington QEW	905-639-9290
Travelodge Ingersoll	519-425-1100
Travelodge Airport North Bay	705-495-1133
Travelodge Oshawa	905-436-9500
Travelodge Ottawa East	613-745-1133
Travelodge Toronto East	416-299-9500
Travelodge Sudbury	705-522-1100
Travelodge Toronto North	416-663-9500
Travelodge Hotel Downtown Windsor	519-258-7774

Hbc Rewards is a trademark of Hudson's Bay Company, used under license. Earn Hbc Rewards bonus points on published rates only. Based upon availability. To qualify for Travelodge Guest Rewards, guests must pay a published rate or higher. Ten Guest Rewards points are awarded for each lodging dollar spent, not valid for dollars spent on incidentals or taxes. The Travelodge Guest Rewards Program rules, rewards and point levels are subject to change at any time without notice. See the Official Rules for complete details. © 2004 Travelodge Hotels, Inc. Offer valid March 1, 2005 to February 28, 2006. Not applicable for groups. Some restrictions may apply.

(See map and index starting on p. 479)

CARLINGVIEW AIRPORT INN   *Book at aaa.com*   **Phone:** (416)675-3303   92

All Year   1P: $89-$99   2P: $89-$99

Small-scale Hotel   **Location:** QEW, exit Hwy 427 N to Dixon Rd E, 1 km to Carlingview Dr, then just s. 221 Carlingview Dr M9W 5E8.
Fax: 416/675-6524. **Facility:** 112 one-bedroom standard units. 3 stories, interior/exterior corridors. **Parking:** on-site. **Terms:** 30 day cancellation notice-fee imposed, small pets only ($15 fee). **Amenities:** voice mail, hair dryers. **Guest Services:** valet laundry. **Cards:** AX, DC, JC, MC, VI. *(See color ad p 520)*   SOME UNITS

ASK SD FEE ... / SOME UNITS

Best Western

A Destination of Distinction...

- Near Hwy 410 just 11 miles from Toronto's International Airport
- Deluxe continental breakfast
- Guest laundry, amenities...

Best Western Brampton, 30 Clark Blvd. Brampton, Ontario L6W 1X3
www.bestwestern.com/ca/brampton 905-454-1300 1-800-WESTERN

THE WORLD'S LARGEST HOTEL CHAIN®

- Conveniently located 1km from Hwy 401, 407 & 410
- Close to downtown Toronto
- 90 spacious Guest Rooms & Suites
- Banquet & Meeting Facility up to 200 People
- Each Room & Suite Features: Coffee Maker, Iron/Board, Hairdryer, High Speed Internet, Fridge & Microwave
- FREE Deluxe Continental Breakfast
- Indoor Swimming Pool, Whirlpool, Sauna & Exercise Room

Best Western

Best Western Admiral Hotel & Suites & Conference Center
Each Best Western hotel is independently owned and operated.

40 Admiral Blvd. • Missassauga, Ontario • 905.795.1011
www.bwadmiral.com • Fax: 905.795.1712
Call Toll Free: 800.528.1234

(See map and index starting on p. 479)

COMFORT HOTEL AIRPORT NORTH *Book at aaa.com* Phone: (416)740-9500

5/1-10/31 1P: $119-$199 2P: $129-$209 XP: $10 F17
11/1-4/30 1P: $109-$199 2P: $119-$199 XP: $10 F17
Location: Jct Hwy 27 and Rexdale Blvd. Located in a commercial area. 445 Rexdale Blvd M9W 6P8. Fax: 416/740-1256. **Facility:** 175 one-bedroom standard units. 13 stories, interior corridors. **Parking:** on-site. **Terms:** package plans. **Amenities:** video games (fee), voice mail, hair dryers. **Dining:** 7 am-10 pm, cocktails. **Pool(s):** heated indoor. **Leisure Activities:** whirlpool. **Guest Services:** valet laundry. **Business Services:** meeting rooms. **Cards:** AX, DC, DS, MC, VI. **Special Amenities:** free local telephone calls and free newspaper.
(See color ad below)

Small-scale Hotel

SOME UNITS

COMFORT INN *Book at aaa.com* Phone: (416)736-4700
All Year [CP] 1P: $69-$149 2P: $69-$149 XP: $10
Location: Hwy 400, exit Finch Ave E, just n. 66 Norfinch Dr M3N 1X1. Fax: 416/736-4842. **Facility:** 144 one-bedroom standard units. 2 stories (no elevator), interior corridors. **Parking:** on-site. **Terms:** package plans, 3% service charge, pets (ground floor units). **Amenities:** irons, hair dryers. **Dining:** 4 pm-11 pm, cocktails. **Guest Services:** valet and coin laundry. **Business Services:** meeting rooms, fax (fee). **Cards:** AX, CB, DC, DS, JC, MC, VI. *(See color ad p 529)*

Small-scale Hotel

SOME UNITS
FEE FEE

A Whole New Carlingview Awaits

- Close to Toronto's International Airport, Hwys 427, 401, 409, and 407.

- Complimentary 24 hour direct airport shuttle, light continental breakfast and coffee service.

- On-site restaurant/lounge.

- Fully renovated guest-rooms and lobby with complimentary parking.

- Enjoy an indoor pool, whirlpool and fitness centre adjacent to the hotel.

Call 1-877-675-3303

 **Carlingview** AIRPORT INN

221 Carlingview Drive, Toronto, Ontario M9W 5E8
Tel: (416) 675-3303 www.carlingview.ca

Managed by Atlific Hotels & Resorts **atlific**

SERVICES
- In-room Coffee Makers
- Complimentary local calls
- RoomService
- Free parking
- Non smoking rooms available
- Irons & Ironing Boards available
- 25" Colour Television and remote
- Wheelchair accessible
- Restaurant & Lounge on premises

RECREATION
- Indoor heated swimming pool
- Indoor whirlpool

LOCATION
- Conveniently Located at the intersection of Highway 27 and Rexdale Blvd.
- 172 newly renovated guest rooms and suites

DISTANCE TO AIRPORT
- 8 Km from Lester B. Pearson International Airport
- Airport shuttle service available

ATTRACTIONS
- Walking distance to Woodbine Shopping Centre (over 100 stores, 6 movie theatres)
- Walking distance to Woodbine Racetrack & Casino
- Downtown Toronto (25 Kms South)
- Skydome and CN Tower (25 Kms South)
- Paramount Canada's Wonderland (15 Kms Northeast)
- Wild Water Kingdom (8 Kms West).

 Comfort Hotel
BY CHOICE HOTELS
Airport North
445 Rexdale Boulevard
Etobicoke, Ontario
M9W 6K5
Tel: 416-740-9500
Fax: 416-740-1256
e-mail:
gm@comfortairport.nhgi.com

STAY YOUR OWN WAY™

Kingston

Kitchener

London

Niagara Falls

Ottawa

Toronto

Airport

East

Harbourfront

Markham

Mississauga

Windsor

GREAT AAA RATES

Discover. Explore. Experience more at Radisson. More hospitality. More choices to make it easy to Stay Your Own Way. Book online at www.radisson.com or call 800-333-3333.

Radisson
HOTELS & RESORTS

Ask for the AAA member discount.

STAY YOUR OWN WAY™

The welcome is warmer in the Country.

◇ Complimentary breakfast

◇ Easy access to major interstate highways

◇ Warm, friendly service

COUNTRY INNS & SUITES BY CARLSON
A cozy stay at a comfortable price

800-456-4000
www.countryinns.com

ONTARIO Oakville *(Toronto)* • Ottawa-West *(Kanata)*

10% MEMBER DISCOUNT OFF PUBLISHED RATES. NO RESTRICTIONS.

(See map and index starting on p. 479)

COMFORT INN   **Book at aaa.com**   Phone: (416)269-7400   **83**
All Year   1P: $69-$129   2P: $69-$129   XP: $10   F18
Location: Hwy 401, exit 383 (Markham Rd), 5 km s to Hwy 2 (Kingston Rd), then 1 km w. 3306 Kingston Rd M1M 1P8.
Small-scale Hotel   Fax: 416/269-7579. **Facility:** 81 one-bedroom standard units, some with whirlpools. 2 stories (no elevator), interior corridors. **Parking:** on-site. **Terms:** [CP] meal plan available, package plans, 3% service charge.
Amenities: video games (fee), voice mail. *Some:* irons, hair dryers. **Guest Services:** valet laundry. **Cards:** AX, CB, DC, DS, JC, MC, VI.

SOME UNITS

Comfort Inn & Suites
Sheridan Park

- 22 km from Downtown Toronto
- FREE Deluxe Continental Breakfast
- Indoor Heated Pool & Spa and Fitness Centre
- Onsite Business Centre
- Free High Speed Internet in Every Room
- Meeting Rooms Available
- Onsite Guest Laundry

Tel.: (905) 823-8600
Toll Free: 1-800-228-5150

2085 North Sheridan Way,
Mississauga, ON L5K 2T2

BY CHOICE HOTELS

"We're More Than a Place to Stay!"
We at the Comfort Inn Meadowvale are offering:

- Whirlpool Suites
- Deluxe Complimentary Continental Breakfast
- Complimentary Newspaper
- Free Local Calls • Free Parking
- In-Room Coffee & Coffee Makers
- Fitness Room
- Business services
- Wireless High Speed Internet in all rooms.

Tel: 905-858-8600 • 1-800-228-5150
Comfort Inn Meadowvale, 2420 Surveyor Rd,
Mississauga, Ontario, Canada L5N 4E6

BY CHOICE HOTELS

AAA Discounts *and* Marriott Rewards®

Impeccable service and close to
Paramount Canada's Wonderland,
and Toronto's largest shopping malls.

Call 1-800-791-9442

- Complimentary 24 hour direct Airport Shuttle Service to Pearson International Airport
- *Courtyard Café* for breakfast
- Indoor pool and jacuzzi
- Complimentary high-speed Internet

COURTYARD Marriott
TORONTO AIRPORT

231 Carlingview Drive, Toronto, Ontario M9W 5E8 Tel: (416) 675-0411 Marriott.com/YYZAP

(See map and index starting on p. 479)

COURTYARD BY MARRIOTT TORONTO AIRPORT   *Book at aaa.com*   **Phone:** (416)675-0411   **79**
All Year   1P: $99-$175   2P: $99-$175
Location: Directly s of jct Dixon Rd. 231 Carlingview Dr M9W 5E8. Fax: 416/675-0433. **Facility:** 168 units. 167
Small-scale Hotel   one-bedroom standard units. 1 one-bedroom suite. 8 stories, interior corridors. **Parking:** on-site (fee).
Terms: 30 day cancellation notice-fee imposed, package plans. **Amenities:** high-speed Internet, dual phone
lines, voice mail, irons, hair dryers. **Pool(s):** heated indoor. **Leisure Activities:** whirlpool, exercise room. **Guest Services:** coin
laundry. **Business Services:** meeting rooms. **Cards:** AX, DC, JC, MC, VI. *(See color ad p 522)*

SOME UNITS
ASK SD ⊞ ▼ ➹ ☎ 🎥 PORT 💻 / ✕ 🔲 🖥 /

CROWNE PLAZA TORONTO DON VALLEY   *Book at aaa.com*   **Phone:** (416)449-4111   **46**
CAA SAVE   All Year   1P: $149-$219   2P: $149-$219   XP: $20   F18
Location: Don Valley Pkwy, exit 375 (Wynford Dr); jct Don Valley Pkwy and Eglinton Ave E. 1250 Eglinton Ave E M3C
1J3. Fax: 416/385-6700. **Facility:** 353 units. 350 one-bedroom standard units. 3 one-bedroom suites. 6
stories, interior corridors. *Bath:* combo or shower only. **Parking:** on-site (fee). **Terms:** package plans, 3%
Large-scale Hotel   service charge, small pets only ($20 extra charge). **Amenities:** CD players, high-speed Internet, dual phone
lines, voice mail, irons, hair dryers. **Dining:** 6:30 am-10 pm, Sat & Sun from 7 am, cocktails. **Pool(s):**
heated outdoor, heated indoor. **Leisure Activities:** sauna, whirlpool, steamroom, children's play centre. *Fee:* game room.
Guest Services: gift shop, valet and coin laundry. **Business Services:** conference facilities, business center. **Cards:** AX, CB,
DC, DS, JC, MC, VI. **Special Amenities:** free newspaper. *(See color ad below)*

SOME UNITS
SD 🐾 ¶¶ ▼ ♿ ➹ ✦ ✕ 🎥 PORT 💻 / ✕ 🔲 /
FEE   FEE

DAYS HOTEL & CONFERENCE CENTRE-TORONTO
AIRPORT EAST   **Phone:** (416)249-8171   **49**
CAA SAVE   All Year   1P: $99-$249   2P: $99-$249   XP: $10   F
Location: 0.5 km w of Jane St. Located in a commercial, residential area. 1677 Wilson Ave M3L 1A5.
Fax: 416/243-7342. **Facility:** 199 units. 195 one-bedroom standard units. 4 one-bedroom suites with
whirlpools. 4-7 stories, interior corridors. **Parking:** on-site. **Terms:** [BP] meal plan available, package plans.
Large-scale Hotel   **Amenities:** voice mail, irons, hair dryers. *Fee:* video games, high-speed Internet. *Some:* dual phone lines.
Dining: 6:30 am-2 & 5-10 pm, cocktails. **Pool(s):** heated indoor. **Leisure Activities:** sauna, whirlpool,
limited exercise equipment. **Guest Services:** gift shop, valet laundry. **Business Services:** conference facilities. **Cards:** AX, DC,
DS, MC, VI. **Special Amenities:** free newspaper and early check-in/late check-out. *(See color ad p 524)*

SOME UNITS
SD ⊞ ¶¶ ▼ ➹ ✕ 🎥 PORT 💻 / ✕ 🔲 /

DAYS INN-TORONTO EAST BEACHES   *Book at aaa.com*   **Phone:** (416)694-1177   **44**
     10/1-12/31   1P: $89-$199   2P: $89-$199   XP: $10   F16
     7/1-9/30   1P: $89-$199   2P: $89-$199   XP: $15   F16
     1/1-4/30   1P: $89-$165   2P: $89-$165   XP: $10   F16
Small-scale Hotel   5/1-6/30   1P: $89-$159   2P: $89-$159   XP: $10   F16
Location: Just e of Coxwell Ave. Located across from Greenwood Park. 1684 Queen St E M4L 1G6. Fax: 416/694-1146. **Facility:** 50 one-
bedroom standard units, some with efficiencies (no utensils) and/or whirlpools. 2 stories (no elevator), interior corridors.
Parking: on-site. **Terms:** cancellation fee imposed. **Amenities:** irons, hair dryers. **Cards:** AX, CB, DC, DS, MC, VI.

SOME UNITS
ASK SD 🎥 PORT / ✕ 🔲 💻 /

Located among Toronto's most popular attractions, the
Crowne Plaza Toronto Don Valley offers both convenience
and a better night sleep with **Sleep Advantage™** program
We feature indoor and outdoor pools, **Spa Wellness
Centre**, restaurant and lobby bar to add to a perfect stay.
We proudly brew **Starbucks** coffee. Please call today for
our current packages. **Mention this ad at check-in and
receive a $5.00 rebate on your daily rate.**

CROWNE PLAZA
TORONTO DON VALLEY
Ideal for Business. Perfect for Pleasure.

1250 Eglinton Avenue East, Toronto, Ontario 1-416-449-4111 Email: reservations@cptdv.com   www.crowneplazadv.com

(See map and index starting on p. 479)

DAYS INN TORONTO EAST LAKEVIEW   *Book at aaa.com*   Phone: (416)261-8100

All Year [CP]   1P: $65-$110   2P: $65-$110   XP: $10   F
Small-scale Hotel   **Location:** Hwy 401, exit 378S, 6 km on Warden Ave to Kingston Rd, then just e. 2151 Kingston Rd M1N 1T5.
Fax: 416/261-0102. **Facility:** 60 one-bedroom standard units, some with whirlpools. 3 stories, interior corridors. **Parking:** on-site. **Amenities:** voice mail, irons, hair dryers. *Some:* high-speed Internet.
Cards: AX, MC, VI.

SOME UNITS

DAYS INN TORONTO WEST LAKESHORE   *Book at aaa.com*   Phone: (416)532-9900

5/1-9/30   1P: $99-$149   2P: $109-$159   XP: $15   F12
10/1-4/30   1P: $69-$99   2P: $79-$109   XP: $15   F12
Location: Jct King and Queen sts W and The Queensway. Located in a commercial area. 14 Roncesvalles Ave M6R
Small-scale Hotel   2K3. **Fax:** 416/532-9440. **Facility:** 43 one-bedroom standard units. 3 stories (no elevator), interior corridors.
Parking: no self-parking. **Terms:** pets ($10 extra charge). **Amenities:** video library (fee), hair dryers. *Some:*
cocktails. **Business Services:** fax (fee). **Cards:** AX, DC, DS, MC, VI. **Special Amenities:** free full breakfast and free local
telephone calls.

SOME UNITS

DAYS HOTEL
& CONFERENCE CENTRE
TORONTO AIRPORT EAST

1-800-DAYS INN
www.daysinn.ca

- The closest full service hotel to Paramount Canada's Wonderland. Packages available
- Close to downtown and most attractions in the Greater Toronto area
- Easily accessible from both Hwys. 400 and 401
- 197 rooms with coffee maker, iron and iron boards
- Free airport shuttle and parking
- Onsite restaurant and patio lounge
- Indoor pool, sauna, whirlpool, fitness centre

CAA Approved

trip rewards
It's fun to get more

Days Hotel & Conference Centre - Toronto Airport East
1677 Wilson Avenue, Toronto, Ontario M3L 1A5
www.daysto.com

Tel: 416.249.8171
Fax: 416.243.7342
email: info@daysto.com

1-800-DAYS INN
www.daysinn.ca

DAYS INN
MISSISSAUGA

Come on Inn...

- **Newly renovated hotel**
- **Complimentary newspaper and continental breakfast**
- **Free local calls**
- **Free parking**
- **Extended cable package**
- **Free high speed Internet available**

trip rewards
It's fun to get more

Days Inn - Toronto Missisauga
4635 Tomken Road, Mississauga ON L4W 1J9
www.daysinnmississauga.com

Tel
905 238 5480

Fax
905 238 1031

Daysinnmississauga@rogers.com

(See map and index starting on p. 479)

DELTA TORONTO EAST   *Book at aaa.com*   Phone: 416/299-1500 [86]
All Year   1P: $149-$199   2P: $149-$199   XP: $25   F18
Location: Just ne of jct Hwy 401 and Kennedy Rd, exit 379. 2035 Kennedy Rd M1T 3G2. Fax: 416/299-8959.
Large-scale Hotel   **Facility:** 368 units. 361 one-bedroom standard units, some with whirlpools. 7 one-bedroom suites. 3-14
stories, interior corridors. **Parking:** on-site (fee) and valet. **Terms:** cancellation fee imposed, pets ($30 extra
charge). **Amenities:** video games, voice mail, irons, hair dryers. *Some:* CD players, high-speed Internet, honor bars.
Dining: Sagano, see separate listing. **Pool(s):** heated indoor. **Leisure Activities:** saunas, whirlpool, waterslide, putting green,
recreation programs, exercise room, spa, game room. **Guest Services:** gift shop, valet laundry. **Business Services:**
conference facilities, business center. **Cards:** AX, DC, DS, JC, MC, VI.

SOME UNITS

FEE   FEE

6750 Mississauga Road,
Mississauga, ON L5N 2L3
Tel. 905-821-1981
Fax. 905-542-4038
www.deltameadowvale.com

CANADA and U.S.A.
1-800-422-8238

DELTA
MEADOWVALE
RESORT AND CONFERENCE CENTRE

- Deluxe guest rooms with walkout balconies
- Outdoor and indoor pools, whirlpool, steam rooms
- State-of-the-art fitness centre with tennis and squash courts*
- Close to major shopping centres
- Golf packages featuring Lionhead Golf and Country Club*
- Kids 6 and under eat FREE
- Close to Paramount Canada's Wonderland and other Toronto attractions
- Children's Creative Centre
- Seasonal outdoor patio, Splashes, with five-hole putting green
  *Some charges may apply.

Your room is ready

Cdn. Sgl/Dbl
$109
subject to availability

Canada and U.S.
1-800-268-1133
www.deltahotels.com

U.S. Sgl/Dbl
$80**
**U.S. exchange rate subject to change.

GREAT VALUE

Comfortable & Affordable Rooms
- Fridge • Hair Dryer • Free Movies • Local Calls
- Fax Services • Morning Coffee • Minutes From
  Downtown, Airport, Subway & City Bus
- Corporate & Business Travellers
JACUZZI SUITES WITH SAUNA
1554 The Queensway, Toronto, ON M8Z 1T5

DELUXE INN

Tel: 416-252-5205 • 1-888-206-4820

(See map and index starting on p. 479)

DELUXE INN

Phone: (416)252-5205 — 72

Small-scale Hotel

5/1-9/30	1P: $65-$75	2P: $75-$85	XP: $5	D18
10/1-4/30	1P: $60-$70	2P: $70-$80	XP: $5	D18

Location: Hwy 427, exit The Queensway, 1 km e. 1554 The Queensway M8Z 1T5. Fax: 416/252-9763. **Facility:** 48 one-bedroom standard units, some with whirlpools. 2 stories (no elevator), interior/exterior corridors. **Parking:** on-site. **Amenities:** hair dryers. **Cards:** AX, CB, DC, MC, VI. ***(See color ad p 525)***

SOME UNITS

A$K

DOUBLETREE INTERNATIONAL PLAZA HOTEL TORONTO AIRPORT Book at aaa.com

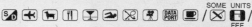

Phone: (416)244-1711 — 62

CAA SAVE

Large-scale Hotel

1/1-4/30	1P: $109-$258	2P: $109-$258	XP: $25	F18
5/1-12/31	1P: $99-$238	2P: $99-$238	XP: $20	F18

Location: Jct Hwy 27 N, just w of jct Hwy 401. 655 Dixon Rd M9W 1J3. Fax: 416/244-8031. **Facility:** 433 units. 416 one-bedroom standard units, some with whirlpools. 17 one-bedroom suites ($149-$2500), some with whirlpools. 12 stories, interior corridors. *Bath:* combo or shower only. **Parking:** on-site (fee). **Terms:** package plans. **Amenities:** video games (fee), dual phone lines, voice mail, irons, hair dryers. *Some:* safes, honor bars. **Dining:** 2 restaurants, 6 am-11 pm, also, Alfredo's, see separate listing, nightclub. **Pool(s):** heated indoor, wading. **Leisure Activities:** sauna, whirlpool, waterslide, recreation programs in summer, exercise room, game room. *Fee:* massage. **Guest Services:** gift shop, valet laundry. **Business Services:** conference facilities, business center. **Cards:** AX, DC, DS, MC, VI. **Special Amenities: preferred room (subject to availability with advance reservations).** ***(See color ad below)***

SOME UNITS

DATA PORT

FEE

FOUR POINTS BY SHERATON TORONTO LAKESHORE Book at aaa.com

Phone: (416)766-4392 — 45

Small-scale Hotel

5/1-10/31	1P: $135-$145	2P: $135-$145	XP: $10	F17
1/1-4/30	1P: $129-$139	2P: $129-$139	XP: $10	F17
11/1-12/31	1P: $125-$135	2P: $125-$135	XP: $10	F17

Location: Between Ellis and Windermere. Located opposite Lakeshore Park. 1926 Lakeshore Blvd W M6S 1A1. Fax: 416/766-1278. **Facility:** 152 one-bedroom standard units. 4 stories, interior corridors. *Bath:* combo or shower only. **Parking:** on-site. **Terms:** cancellation fee imposed. **Amenities:** dual phone lines, voice mail, irons, hair dryers. **Leisure Activities:** sauna, whirlpool, steamroom, exercise room. **Guest Services:** valet laundry. **Business Services:** meeting rooms, fax (fee). **Cards:** AX, CB, DC, JC, MC, VI. ***(See color ad p 5)***

SOME UNITS

A$K DATA PORT

You're always welcomed at Doubletree.

The Doubletree International Plaza Hotel Toronto Airport is perfect for business or family getaways, ideally located close to highway 401, 407, QEW and 400. Our hotel features full-service restaurants, bar night club, complimentary airport shuttle, an indoor water park and available high-speed Internet access in all guestrooms. Just call Doubletree's dedicated AAA number, *1-877-655-5697* or your local AAA travel office. Visit us online at *doubletree.com.*

Hilton HHonors

DOUBLETREE INTERNATIONAL PLAZA HOTEL TORONTO AIRPORT

655 Dixon Road • Toronto, ON M9W 1J3 • 416-244-1711

Valid AAA membership card required for reservation and at check-in. ©2005 Hilton Hospitality, Inc.

- 145 Spacious Guestrooms
- Indoor Pool, Whirlpool
- Sauna & Fitness Centre
- Complimentary Parking
- Complimentary shuttle from Toronto Airport
- Meeting facilities for 10 - 250
- Many In-Room Facilities

Local attractions include: Paramount Canada's Wonderland, Woodbine Racktrack & Slots, Playdium, Hershey Centre, Square One Shopping Centre, Royal Woodbine Golf Club, Wild Water Kingdom, Downtown Toronto

6090 Dixie Road, Mississauga, Ontario L5T 1A6
Phone: (905) 670-0050 Fax: (905) 564-9555
Reservations (800) 387-0287
www.fourpoints.com/mississuaga

Four Points Sheraton MISSISSAUGA

Always Right Where You Need Us...

Conveniently located near Hwy. 401, 410 & 407. Minutes away from a range of restaurants, recreation facilities and shops. This 69 room Inn features an outdoor heated pool, Jacuzzi and standard king and double rooms. We also feature a *Complimentary Hot Breakfast, Indoor Gym, High Speed Internet Access, 24 hr. Business Centre, Free Movie Channel and Free Local Calls.*

TORONTO-MISSISSAUGA
7040 Edwards Blvd.,
Mississauga, ON L5S 1Z1
www.hamptoninn.com

A PROUD MEMBER OF HILTON FAMILY OF BRANDS.

Reservations: 1-800-HAMPTON
Tel.: (905) 564-2122
Fax: (905) 564-5020

Stay Smart® In Mississauga.

• Free Express Start™ Breakfast Bar
• Free Local Phone Calls • Priority Club® Rewards Benefits
• Complimentary Parking • Close to Major Attractions
• Free High-Speed Wireless Internet

Conveniently located off of HWY 401.
For Reservations Call 1-888-897-0107

© 2004-2005 InterContinental Hotels Group. All rights reserved. Most hotels are independently owned and/or operated.

Holiday Inn
EXPRESS®
Stay Smart®

5585 Ambler Drive
Mississauga, ON L4W 3Z1

(905) 238-3500
www.hiexpress.com/aaa

Holiday Inn
EXPRESS®
WHITBY/TORONTO

905.665.8400
1.800.HOLIDAY
180 Consumers Drive
Hwy 401 & Brock St. Whitby

• Complimentary Deluxe Continental Breakfast
• Free Parking and Free Local Calling
• On-site Fitness Facilities
• In-room Coffee Maker and Hair Dryer
• Iron & Ironing Board
• 2 Line Speaker Phone with Data ports and Voice Mail
• In-room Movies
• Executive Rooms
• Whirlpool Suites
• 5 Minutes to Cullen Gardens
• 30 Minutes to Toronto

www.hiexpress.com/whitbyontario
email: hiexwhitby@nhgi.com

STAY SMART™ options for the leisure traveller.

GRAND MOTEL

Motel

Phone: 416/281-8393   82

6/21-9/10	1P: $65-$75	2P: $70-$90	XP: $5	F12
5/1-6/20 & 9/11-4/30	1P: $54-$65	2P: $59-$80	XP: $5	F12

Location: Hwy 401, exit 387S via Morningside Ave, then e. 4626 Kingston Rd M1E 2P6. Fax: 416/281-0460. **Facility:** 22 one-bedroom standard units with whirlpools. 2 stories (no elevator), exterior corridors. **Parking:** on-site, winter plug-ins. **Terms:** office hours 9 am-11 pm, weekly rates available. **Pool(s):** outdoor. **Cards:** AX, JC, MC, VI. **Special Amenities:** free local telephone calls and early check-in/late check-out.

SOME UNITS

HOLIDAY INN EXPRESS TORONTO-EAST   *Book at aaa.com*

Small-scale Hotel

Phone: (416)439-9666   80

5/1-9/30	1P: $95-$149	2P: $99-$159	XP: $10	F18
10/1-4/30	1P: $89-$139	2P: $95-$149	XP: $10	F18

Location: Just sw of jct Hwy 401 and Markham Rd. 50 Estate Dr M1H 2Z1. Fax: 416/439-4295. **Facility:** 138 one-bedroom standard units. 2-3 stories (no elevator), interior corridors. *Bath:* combo or shower only. **Parking:** on-site. **Terms:** package plans. **Amenities:** video games, high-speed Internet, voice mail, irons, hair dryers. **Leisure Activities:** exercise room. **Guest Services:** valet laundry. **Business Services:** meeting rooms. **Cards:** AX, DC, DS, MC, VI. *(See color ad card insert & p 518)*

SOME UNITS

Stay Here.
Save Here.

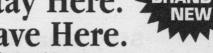
BRAND NEW

- 149 Brand New Rooms & Suites
- Complimentary Hot Breakfast
- Indoor Heated Pool & Fitness Centre
- Studio Suites with Microwaves & Refrigerators
- King Whirlpool Suites
- Free Movie Channel
- Free 24 hours Airport Shuttle
- Free Local Calls
- Free High Speed Internet Access
- Free Parking
- Convenient access to Hwys 427, 401, 409, & 407

TORONTO-AIRPORT
3279 Caroga Drive, Mississauga, ON
Canada L4V 1A3
Tel: (905) 671-4730 • 1-800-HAMPTON
Fax: (905) 671-4739
www.hamptoninn.com
www.torontoairportontario.hamptoninn.com

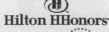
Hilton HHonors
Points & Miles

HOLIDAY INN EXPRESS TORONTO-NORTH YORK   *Book at aaa.com*   Phone: (416)665-3500 **50**
Ⓐ SAVE   All Year   1P: $99-$149   2P: $109-$159   XP: $10   F18
Location: Hwy 400, exit Finch Ave E. 30 Norfinch Dr M3N 1X1. Fax: 416/665-0807. Facility: 163 one-bedroom
standard units. 7 stories, interior corridors. Parking: on-site, winter plug-ins. Terms: package plans.
Amenities: video games (fee), voice mail, irons, hair dryers. Guest Services: valet and coin laundry.
Small-scale Hotel Business Services: meeting rooms. Cards: AX, DC, DS, MC, VI. *(See color ad below & card insert)*

SOME UNITS

FEE

HOLIDAY INN SELECT TORONTO-AIRPORT   *Book at aaa.com*   Phone: (416)675-7611 **64**
1/1-4/30   1P: $119-$199   2P: $119-$199   XP: $15   F18
5/1-12/31   1P: $119-$189   2P: $119-$189   XP: $15   F18
Large-scale Hotel Location: 3.2 km w of jct Hwy 401. 970 Dixon Rd M9W 1J9. Fax: 416/675-9162. Facility: 445 one-bedroom
standard units. 12 stories, interior corridors. Bath: combo or shower only. Parking: on-site (fee) and valet.
Amenities: video games (fee), voice mail, irons, hair dryers. Pool(s): heated outdoor, heated indoor. Leisure
Activities: sauna, whirlpool, playground, exercise room. Fee: massage. Guest Services: gift shop, valet and coin laundry.
Business Services: conference facilities, business center. Cards: AX, DC, MC, VI. *(See color ad and card insert)*

SOME UNITS
FEE

Toronto's Gateway to the North presents

3great hotels
IN ONE GREAT LOCATION!

Toronto's <u>closest</u> hotels to Canada's Wonderland and the new Vaughan Mills Mall

20 min. to downtown Toronto and 15 min. to Pearson International Airport

Holiday Inn Express North York   30 Norfinch Drive
Email: whg4106agm@whg.com   www.hiexpress.com/yyz-northyork
Phone: 416-665-3500 or 1-800-HOLIDAY
- **FREE** Express Start Deluxe Continental Breakfast
- **FREE** Parking
- **FREE** High-Speed Internet Access Available
- New Simply Smart Guest Bathroom Experience

Holiday Inn EXPRESS

Comfort Inn North York   66 Norfinch Drive
Email: cn283@whg.com   www.choicehotels.ca/cn283
Phone: 416-736-4700 or 1-800-228-5150
- **FREE** Continental Breakfast
- **FREE** Parking
- **FREE** High-Speed Internet Access Available
- Drive-up Rooms Available

Comfort Inn
by Choice Hotels

Travelodge Toronto North   50 Norfinch Drive
Email: whg7118gs@whg.com   www.the.travelodge.com/northyork09777
Phone: 416-633-9500 or 1-800-578-7878
- **FREE** Continental Breakfast
- **FREE** Parking
- **FREE** High-Speed Internet Access Available
- Pool and Whirlpool on Site

Travelodge

HOLIDAY INN TORONTO-AIRPORT EAST *Book at aaa.com* Phone: (416)240-7511 65
CAA SAVE
5/1-9/30   1P: $109-$179   2P: $109-$179   XP: $15   F18
10/1-4/30   1P: $99-$169   2P: $99-$169   XP: $15   F18
Location: E of jct Hwy 27 N and Dixon Rd; w of jct Hwy 401 and Dixon Rd. 600 Dixon Rd M9W 1J1.
Fax: 416/240-7519. **Facility:** 191 one-bedroom standard units, some with whirlpools. 5 stories, interior
Small-scale Hotel corridors. *Bath:* combo or shower only. **Parking:** on-site (fee). **Terms:** package plans. **Amenities:** video
games, voice mail, irons, hair dryers. **Dining:** 24 hours, wine/beer only. **Pool(s):** heated indoor. **Leisure**
Activities: exercise room. *Fee:* game room. **Guest Services:** valet laundry. **Business Services:** conference facilities, business
center. **Cards:** AX, DC, DS, MC, VI. *(See color ad card insert)*

SOME UNITS

HOLIDAY INN TORONTO-YORKDALE *Book at aaa.com* Phone: (416)789-5161 57
CAA SAVE
5/1-10/31 & 1/1-4/30   1P: $135-$189   2P: $135-$189
11/1-12/31   1P: $129-$189   2P: $129-$189
Location: Just s of jct Hwy 401 and Dufferin St; Hwy 401 W, exit 365 (Allen Rd S and Yorkdale Rd) to Dufferin St.
Located in a commercial area. 3450 Dufferin St M6A 2V1. Fax: 416/785-6845. **Facility:** 370 one-bedroom
Large-scale Hotel standard units. 12 stories, interior corridors. **Parking:** on-site (fee), winter plug-ins. **Terms:** cancellation fee
imposed, [BP] meal plan available, package plans. **Amenities:** video games (fee), voice mail, irons, hair
dryers. *Some:* safes. **Dining:** 6 am-11 pm, Sat & Sun from 7 am; Sunday brunch, cocktails. **Pool(s):** heated indoor. **Leisure**
Activities: sauna, whirlpool, children's program on weekends, daily in summer; pool table, exercise room. **Guest Services:** gift
shop, valet laundry. **Business Services:** conference facilities, business center. **Cards:** AX, CB, DC, DS, MC, VI.
Special Amenities: free newspaper and preferred room (subject to availability with advance reservations).
(See color ad card insert)

SOME UNITS

FEE

MONTECASSINO HOTEL & SUITES *Book at aaa.com* Phone: (416)630-8100 97
All Year [CP]   1P: $99-$399   2P: $99-$399   XP: $10
Location: On Chesswood Dr at Sheppard Ave. Located in a commercial area. 3710 Chesswood Dr M3J 2W4.
Fax: 416/630-1929. **Facility:** 104 units. 52 one-bedroom standard units. 52 one-bedroom suites, some with
Small-scale Hotel efficiencies. 5 stories, interior corridors. **Parking:** on-site. **Terms:** small pets only. **Amenities:** voice mail,
hair dryers. *Some:* irons. **Guest Services:** valet laundry. **Business Services:** conference facilities. **Cards:** AX, CB, DC, DS,
MC, VI.

SOME UNITS

FEE

Stay happy together.

10% Off Best Flex Corp. Rate

- Easy access to Hwy's #401, #404, and #407
- Beautifuly renovated guestrooms and public areas
- Quincy's Market Fresh Restaurant & Lobby Bar
- Close to Toronto's major attractions, Canada's Wonderland, Science Centre and the new Vaughan Mills Shopping Centre.

Kids Eat and Stay Free
Call the hotel for details.

Holiday Inn

For Reservations Call 905-474-0444 or 1-800-HOLIDAY
www.holiday-inn.com/aaa

Toronto-Marham
7095 Woodbine Avenue
Markham, Ontario, Canada

Holiday Inn
SELECT
HOTEL & SUITES

- 144 Luxurious Guest Rooms
- 2-Room Suites with Kitchenette
- Free High-Speed Internet Access
- Indoor Pool & Fitness Facility
- 24-Hour Business Centre
- New Upscale Restaurant
- 14 Conference & Banquet Rooms
- Elegant Wedding Packages

www.oakvillehotel.com • sales@oakvillehotel.com

Ph: 905.847.1000 • Direct Reserve: 800.880.3188 • 2525 Wyecroft Rd., Oakville, ON (QEW & Bronte Rd.)

Visiting the Toronto Area? Enjoy the Luxury & Comforts of

 **Monte Carlo Inns**

"Your home away from home"

Central Reservations US/CAN 1-800-363-6400
www.montecarloinns.com

- Complimentary Breakfast
- Free High Speed Internet
- Digital Movie System
- Restaurant / Lounge / Patio
- Close To Major Attractions
- In Room: Microwave, Coffee Maker, Fridge, Iron & Board

- Fitness Facility
- Complimentary Business Centre
- Executive / Theme Suites
- Conference & Board Rm Facilities
- Affordable Rates

5 Locations To Meet All Your Hotel Needs

Airport Suites
Mississauga
(905) 564-8500

Oakville Suites
Oakville
(905) 849-9500

Brampton Suites
Brampton
(905) 453-5200

Toronto - Markham
Markham
(905) 513-8100

Toronto - West
Mississauga
(905) 273-9500

Toronto
Vaughan Suites
Coming Soon

"Watch for our new Airport Suites Expansion"

Luxury, Comfort and Value

MOTEL 27

Motel

CAA SAVE

Phone: 416/255-5500 **61** F

5/1-10/31	1P: $70-$99	2P: $75-$105	XP: $5 F
11/1-4/30	1P: $65-$95	2P: $70-$100	XP: $5 F

Location: W of jct Hwy 427 and Evans Ave. Located across from Sherway Gardens Mall. 650 Evans Ave M8W 2W6. **Fax:** 416/255-5500. **Facility:** 47 one-bedroom standard units, some with whirlpools. 2 stories (no elevator), interior/exterior corridors. **Parking:** on-site. **Amenities:** *Some:* hair dryers. **Guest Services:** sundries. **Cards:** AX, DC, MC, VI. **Special Amenities:** free local telephone calls and early check-in/late check-out.

SOME UNITS

NOVOTEL TORONTO NORTH YORK   *Book at aaa.com*

Large-scale Hotel

Phone: (416)733-2929 **52**

All Year   1P: $259-$279

Location: Hwy 401, exit Yonge St, 1 km n, then just w. Located next to a shopping complex and transit line. 3 Park Home Ave M2N 6L3. **Fax:** 416/733-3403. **Facility:** 260 units. 258 one-bedroom standard units. 2 one-bedroom suites. 19 stories, interior corridors. *Bath:* combo or shower only. **Parking:** on-site (fee). **Terms:** 2 night minimum stay - seasonal, cancellation fee imposed, package plans, 3% service charge, small pets only. **Amenities:** video games (fee), high-speed Internet, voice mail, honor bars, irons, hair dryers. *Some:* safes. **Pool(s):** heated indoor. **Leisure Activities:** saunas, exercise room. **Guest Services:** gift shop, valet laundry. **Business Services:** meeting rooms. **Cards:** AX, DC, DS, MC, VI. *(See color ad p 497)*

SOME UNITS

THE OLD MILL INN & SPA   *Book at aaa.com*

Country Inn

CAA SAVE

Phone: (416)236-2641 **66**

9/1-12/31	1P: $290-$630	2P: $290-$630	XP: $25 F11
5/1-8/31 & 4/1-4/30	1P: $280-$599	2P: $280-$599	XP: $25 F11
1/1-3/31	1P: $255-$530	2P: $255-$530	XP: $25 F11

Location: Jct Jane and Bloor sts, just w on Bloor St to Humber Blvd, follow signs. 21 Old Mill Rd M8X 1G5. **Fax:** 416/232-3709. **Facility:** Luxurious guest rooms with fine wood furniture and equally appealing public areas are well-suited to both business and leisure travelers. Designated smoking area. 59 units. 46 one-bedroom standard units with whirlpools. 13 one-bedroom suites with whirlpools. 6 stories, interior corridors. **Parking:** on-site and valet. **Terms:** check-in 4 pm, 8 day cancellation notice-fee imposed, package plans, 3% service charge. **Amenities:** CD players, high-speed Internet (fee), dual phone lines, voice mail, safes, honor bars, irons, hair dryers. **Dining:** dining room, see separate listing. **Leisure Activities:** steamrooms, tennis court privileges, hiking trails, jogging, exercise room, spa. *Fee:* bicycles. **Business Services:** conference facilities, administrative services (fee). **Cards:** AX, DC, MC, VI. **Special Amenities:** free expanded continental breakfast and free newspaper. *(See color ad below)*

PALMERSTON INN BED & BREAKFAST

Bed & Breakfast

Phone: 416/920-7842 **63**

All Year   1P: $100-$195   2P: $130-$225

Location: Directly n of college. 322 Palmerston Blvd M6G 2N6. **Fax:** 416/960-9529. **Facility:** The B&B is on a peaceful residential street close to the center of town; rooms are tastefully decorated. Smoke free premises. 6 one-bedroom standard units. 3 stories (no elevator), interior corridors. *Bath:* some shared or private, combo or shower only. **Parking:** on-site. **Terms:** office hours 9 am-6 pm, 2 night minimum stay - weekends, age restrictions may apply, 30 day cancellation notice. **Amenities:** video library, hair dryers. **Cards:** MC, VI.

SOME UNITS

Escape **Reality for a While**

Your Toronto Getaway Retreat

CAA Four Diamond Award AAA

CAA/AAA Members Enjoy 15% OFF*

Premium Continental Breakfast and Free Parking included.

OLD MILL INN & SPA   Getaway Packages and Rates www.oldmilltoronto.com/caa

1.866.653.6455

PARK MOTEL

Motel

	1P:	2P:	Phone: 416/261-7241	84
7/1-8/31	1P: $60-$70	2P: $60-$78	XP: $10	F12
9/1-4/30	1P: $53-$60	2P: $53-$68	XP: $5	F12
5/1-6/30	1P: $53-$60	2P: $53-$68	XP: $10	F12

Location: Directly e of McCowan Rd. 3126 Kingston Rd M1M 1P2. Fax: 416/261-7243. **Facility:** 17 one-bedroom standard units. 1 story, exterior corridors. **Parking:** on-site. **Terms:** 7 day cancellation notice-fee imposed. **Cards:** AX, MC, VI.

SOME UNITS

PARK PLAZA TORONTO AIRPORT *Book at aaa.com*

Large-scale Hotel

	1P:	2P:	Phone: (416)675-1234	60
All Year	1P: $99-$249	2P: $99-$249	XP: $20	F18

Location: Just w of jct Hwy 27 and Dixon Rd W. Located in a commercial area. 33 Carlson Ct M9W 6H5. Fax: 416/675-3436. **Facility:** 505 units. 496 one-bedroom standard units. 9 one-bedroom suites. 12 stories, interior corridors. *Bath:* combo or shower only. **Parking:** on-site (fee). **Amenities:** voice mail, irons, hair dryers. *Some:* high-speed Internet, honor bars. **Dining:** 6:30 am-11 pm, cocktails. **Pool(s):** heated indoor. **Leisure Activities:** sauna, whirlpool, exercise room. **Guest Services:** gift shop, valet and coin laundry. **Business Services:** conference facilities, administrative services (fee). **Cards:** AX, CB, DC, DS, JC, MC, VI. **Special Amenities:** free continental breakfast and free newspaper.

SOME UNITS

QUALITY HOTEL & SUITES TORONTO AIRPORT EAST *Book at aaa.com*

Small-scale Hotel

	1P:	2P:	Phone: (416)240-9090	69
All Year	1P: $69-$139	2P: $69-$159	XP: $10	F18

Location: Hwy 401, exit 356. 2180 Islington Ave M9P 3P1. Fax: 416/240-9944. **Facility:** 192 units. 176 one-bedroom standard units. 16 one-bedroom suites ($139-$199). 14 stories, interior corridors. **Parking:** on-site. **Terms:** weekly rates available, [AP], [BP], [CP], [ECP] & [MAP] meal plans available, package plans, 3% service charge, pets ($10 extra charge). **Amenities:** voice mail, irons, hair dryers. **Dining:** 7 am-10 pm, cocktails. **Leisure Activities:** limited exercise equipment. **Guest Services:** valet laundry. **Business Services:** meeting rooms. **Cards:** AX, CB, DC, DS, JC, MC, VI. **Special Amenities:** free local telephone calls and free room upgrade (subject to availability with advance reservations). *(See color ad below & p 486)*

SOME UNITS

"Experience the Difference"

TORONTO

QUALITY HOTEL & SUITES

BY CHOICE HOTELS

Deluxe Guestrooms & Suites • Restaurant & Lounge • Fitness Room

FREE SHUTTLE TO/FROM THE AIRPORT FOR GUESTS STAYING WITH US

Complimentary parking, local calls, In-room coffee and Newspaper
Only minutes away from your next experience
whatever you choose, be it shopping, Harness racing,
Canada's Wonderland, Metro Zoo, Golfing or the
fascinating world of Toronto Downtown!

30% Off Published Rates*

* Subject to availability

Property Direct 416-240-9090 or **Toll Free 1-800-228-5151** ask for property CN310.
2180 Islington Avenue, Toronto, Ontario M9P 3P1. www.choicehotels.ca/cn310

*Located between Hwys 400, 427 & 409 at the centre of the hub of Toronto. Located just south of the
401 at exit 365 Islington Ave. Conveniently located in the quiet community of Etobicoke.*

QUALITY SUITES TORONTO AIRPORT   *Book at aaa.com*   Phone: (416)674-8442   [70]
CAA SAVE   All Year   1P: $156-$167   2P: $166-$176   XP: $10   F18
Location: 1 km w of jct Hwy 27 N and Dixon Rd. 262 Carlingview Dr M9W 5G1. Fax: 416/674-3088. **Facility:** 254 one-bedroom suites. 12 stories, interior corridors. **Parking:** on-site (fee). **Terms:** cancellation fee imposed, [BP] meal plan available. **Amenities:** high-speed Internet, voice mail, irons, hair dryers. *Some:* honor bars.
Large-scale Hotel **Dining:** Graffiti's Italian Eatery, see separate listing. **Leisure Activities:** exercise room. **Guest Services:** gift shop, valet laundry. **Business Services:** meeting rooms. **Cards:** AX, DC, MC, VI.
(See color ad below)

SOME UNITS
[icons] FEE

RADISSON HOTEL TORONTO EAST   *Book at aaa.com*   Phone: (416)493-7000   [58]
CAA SAVE   All Year   1P: $119-$159   2P: $129-$169   XP: $20   F18
Location: Hwy 401, exit for Victoria Park N to Consumer's Rd, then w. 55 Hallcrown Pl M2J-4R1. Fax: 416/493-0681.
Facility: 240 one-bedroom standard units. 9 stories, interior corridors. *Bath:* combo or shower only.
Parking: on-site. **Terms:** package plans, small pets only. **Amenities:** dual phone lines, voice mail, irons,
Large-scale Hotel hair dryers. *Some:* high-speed Internet. **Dining:** 6:30 am-10 pm, Sat & Sun from 7:30 am, cocktails.
Pool(s): heated indoor. **Leisure Activities:** whirlpool, exercise room. **Guest Services:** gift shop, valet
laundry. **Business Services:** conference facilities. **Cards:** AX, DC, DS, MC, VI. *(See color ad p 521 & on TourBookMark)*

SOME UNITS
[icons]

Incredible Quality and Value at the Toronto Airport

Minutes from the airport, convenient to highways, ideal for business and leisure travellers. 100% Satisfaction Guarantee.

- all suite hotel • extended stay suites available • covered parking
- shuttle service • Graffiti's Italian Eatery & Saloon
- complimentary coffee & weekday newspaper
- Fitness Centre, Gift Shop

Quality Suites Toronto Airport
262 Carlingview Drive,
Toronto, ON M9W 5G1
416-674-8442 Fax: 416-674-3088

1-877-755-4900
www.choicehotels.ca/cn309

QUALITY SUITES
BY CHOICE HOTELS

QUALITY HOTEL & SUITES

**754 Bronte Road
Oakville, ON L6J 4Z3
Tel: 905.847.6667
Fax: 905.847.7447
Reservations:1.800.228.5151**
www.choicehotels.ca/cn135

Indoor Pool, Whirlpool & Sauna
Special AAA Rates Available

Affordable Luxury!

RADISSON SUITE HOTEL TORONTO AIRPORT *Book at aaa.com*   Phone: (416)242-7400   **71**

All Year   1P: $119-$179   2P: $129-$189   XP: $15   F18
Location: Just e of jct Hwy 27; 0.3 km w of jct Hwy 401. 640 Dixon Rd M9W 1J1. Fax: 416/242-9888. **Facility:** 216 one-bedroom suites. 15 stories, interior corridors. **Parking:** on-site (fee). **Terms:** package plans, small pets only. **Amenities:** video games, dual phone lines, voice mail, honor bars, irons, hair dryers. *Some:* high-
Large-scale Hotel speed Internet. **Dining:** 6:30 am-11 pm, Sat & Sun from 7:30 am. **Leisure Activities:** exercise room. **Guest Services:** sundries, valet laundry. **Business Services:** meeting rooms. **Cards:** AX, DC, DS, MC, VI.
(See color ad p 521 & on TourBookMark)

SOME UNITS

RAMADA HOTEL & CONFERENCE CENTRE *Book at aaa.com*   Phone: (416)493-9000   **59**

All Year   1P: $99-$109   2P: $119-$129
Location: Just s of Sheppard Ave. 185 Yorkland Blvd M2J 4R2. Fax: 416/493-5729. **Facility:** 285 one-bedroom standard units, some with whirlpools. 10 stories, interior corridors. **Parking:** on-site (fee). **Terms:** cancellation fee imposed, 3% service charge. **Amenities:** video games (fee), high-speed Internet, **Large-scale Hotel** voice mail, irons, hair dryers. **Dining:** 6:30 am-10 pm, Sat & Sun from 7 am, cocktails. **Pool(s):** heated indoor. **Leisure Activities:** sauna, exercise room. **Guest Services:** gift shop, valet laundry. **Business Services:** conference facilities, business center. **Cards:** AX, DC, DS, MC, VI. **Special Amenities:** free local telephone calls and free newspaper.

SOME UNITS

TORONTO/MISSISSAUGA

Quality Inn Airport West

**50 Britannia Road East
Mississauga, Ontario L4Z 2G2**

- 108 Guest Rooms • Jacuzzi Suites
- Free Parking •Restaurant & Lounge
- Exercise Room & Sauna
- Free Wireless High-Speed Internet Connections
- Easy Access to All Major Highways & Downtown Toronto
- Special Rates for CAA/AAA Members
- 100% GUEST SATISFACTION

Visit our Website or Send us an Email
www.choicehotels.ca/cn070
sales@qualityinnairportwest.com

• **RESERVATIONS 905.890.1200** • **TOLL-FREE 1.800.228.5151**

From

$79 to $110. CDN
Sgl/Dbl/per Night

BY CHOICE HOTELS

- 222 well appointed rooms
- All rooms feature voicemail, iron, ironing board, coffee maker, remote control cable television with on demand movie system and Nintendo
- Airport Shuttle Available
- Complimentary Parking
- Complimentary Local Calls
- Indoor Pool and Whirlpool
- TJ's Grillhouse Restaurant serving breakfast, lunch and dinner

905-624-9500 • **www.qualityhotelairport.com** • fax: **905-624-1382**
Toronto Airport • 5599 Amber Drive • Mississauga Ontario • L4W3Z1

RAMADA HOTEL TORONTO AIRPORT *Book at aaa.com* Phone: (416)621-2121 **74**

CAA SAVE
5/1-10/31   1P: $119-$129   2P: $119-$129   XP: $10   F16
11/1-4/30   1P: $109-$119   2P: $109-$119   XP: $10   F16

Location: Hwy 427, exit Holiday Dr southbound; exit Burnhamthorpe Rd northbound. Located in a commercial area. 2 Holiday Dr M9C 2Z7. Fax: 416/621-9840. **Facility:** 178 units. 176 one-bedroom standard units. 2 one-
Large-scale Hotel bedroom suites ($199-$299). 2-6 stories, interior corridors. **Parking:** on-site. **Terms:** package plans, 3% service charge, pets ($50 deposit, $20 extra charge). **Amenities:** video games, dual phone lines, voice mail, hair dryers. *Some:* high-speed Internet, safes, irons. **Dining:** 6:30 am-11:30 pm. **Pool(s):** outdoor, heated indoor. **Leisure Activities:** sauna, whirlpool, exercise room. **Guest Services:** valet laundry. **Business Services:** meeting rooms, fax (fee). **Cards:** AX, DC, MC, VI.

SOME UNITS

RENAISSANCE TORONTO AIRPORT HOTEL *Book at aaa.com* Phone: (416)675-6100 **81**

CAA SAVE
12/1-4/30   1P: $239-$269   2P: $239-$269   XP: $20   F18
5/1-11/30   1P: $229-$259   2P: $229-$259   XP: $20   F18

Location: Jct Hwy 27 N and Dixon Rd. 801 Dixon Rd M9W 1J5. Fax: 416/675-4022. **Facility:** The hotel has upscale, contemporary decor in both the guest rooms and public areas, and features a lovely waterfall in the
Large-scale Hotel centre courtyard. 249 units. 243 one-bedroom standard units. 6 one-bedroom suites. 8 stories, interior corridors. *Bath:* combo or shower only. **Parking:** on-site (fee). **Terms:** 3% service charge, pets ($50 deposit). **Amenities:** video games (fee), high-speed Internet, dual phone lines, voice mail, irons, hair dryers. *Some:* CD players. **Dining:** Olio-A Mediterranean Grille, see separate listing. **Pool(s):** heated indoor. **Leisure Activities:** whirlpool, exercise room. **Guest Services:** gift shop, valet laundry. **Business Services:** conference facilities, business center. **Cards:** AX, CB, DC, DS, JC, MC, VI. *(See color ad below)*

SOME UNITS

STAY INN *Book at aaa.com* Phone: (416)259-7899 **68**

CAA SAVE
All Year   1P: $89-$99   2P: $95-$105   XP: $10   F16

Location: QEW E, exit Evans Ave; Hwy 427 S, exit Evans Ave; jct East Mall. 560 Evans Ave M8W 2W1. Fax: 416/259-3369. **Facility:** 65 one-bedroom standard units, some with whirlpools. 2 stories (no elevator), interior corridors. *Bath:* combo or shower only. **Parking:** on-site. **Amenities:** high-speed Internet, voice mail,
Small-scale Hotel hair dryers. *Some:* irons. **Guest Services:** valet and coin laundry. **Business Services:** meeting rooms. **Cards:** AX, DC, MC, VI. **Special Amenities:** free continental breakfast and free newspaper.
(See color ad p 537)

SOME UNITS

UNIQUELY RENAISSANCE

A SPECIAL RAAATE.

AAA/CAA members receive 15% discount.*

Close to Paramount Canada's Wonderland, Square One Shopping Mall, and Royal Woodbine Golf and Country Club, the Renaissance Toronto Airport Hotel is a perfect location for stopping over on business or pleasure. The family will enjoy our skylit glass-domed swimming pool and be tantalized by our new restaurant, Olio: A Mediterranean Grill. For more information, or to book your guaranteed rates, phone us today!

Call 1.800.668.1444 today to reserve your AAA/CAA rate.
*Off published rates

RENAISSANCE.
TORONTO HOTEL
AIRPORT

801 Dixon Road, Toronto, Ontario
p:416.675.6100 | f:416.675.4022 | tf: 800.668.1444
renaissancehotels.com/yyzta
e: reservations@renaissancetorontoairport.com

SUPER 8 TORONTO NORTH *Book at aaa.com*   Phone: 905/760-2120   **55**
5/1-9/30 [CP]   1P: $100-$160   2P: $100-$160   XP: $10   F17
10/1-4/30 [CP]   1P: $89-$110   2P: $89-$120   XP: $10   F17
Location: Hwy 400 S, exit Finch Ave, e on Norfinch Dr; jct Hwy 400 and Steeles Ave. 3400 Steeles Ave W L4K 1A2.
Fax: 905/760-2116. **Facility:** 85 units. 55 one-bedroom standard units. 30 one-bedroom suites. 4 stories,
Small-scale Hotel interior corridors. **Parking:** on-site. **Terms:** weekly rates available. **Amenities:** hair dryers. *Some:* irons.
Pool(s): heated indoor. **Leisure Activities:** whirlpool, waterslide. **Guest Services:** coin laundry. **Cards:** AX,
DC, DS, MC, VI. **Special Amenities: free continental breakfast and free local telephone calls.**

SOME UNITS

TORONTO AIRPORT MARRIOTT HOTEL *Book at aaa.com*   Phone: (416)674-9400   **93**
All Year   1P: $109-$249   2P: $109-$249
Location: Corner of Dixon Rd and Carlingview Dr. 901 Dixon Rd M9W 1J5. Fax: 416/674-8292. **Facility:** The
Large-scale Hotel hotel's modern, well-appointed guest rooms are complemented by the luxury of its comfortable common
areas. 424 units. 419 one-bedroom standard units. 5 one-bedroom suites. 9 stories, interior corridors.
Parking: on-site (fee) and valet. **Terms:** check-in 4 pm, package plans, pets ($20 fee). **Amenities:** voice mail, irons, hair
dryers. *Fee:* video games, high-speed Internet. *Some:* dual phone lines. **Dining:** Mikado, see separate listing. **Pool(s):** heated
indoor. **Leisure Activities:** saunas, whirlpool, exercise room. **Guest Services:** gift shop, valet and coin laundry. **Business
Services:** conference facilities, business center. **Cards:** AX, DC, DS, MC, VI. *(See color ad p 504)*

SOME UNITS

Comfort & Convenience in Toronto's West End

- Affordable rates
- 65 large spacious guest rooms
- Close to major attractions
- FREE PARKING
- Meeting room facilities
- Airport Shuttle

- COMPLIMENTARY Continental Breakfast
- COMPLIMENTARY high speed internet access & data port
- Westend location allows easy access to QEW, 427, 401, 407 and is also close to malls, airport, transit routes, Casino and more...

Stay Inn

OPEN MARCH 2003

Highway 401 / The Queensway / The West Mall / Queen Elizabeth Way / To Downtown Toronto / 427 North / The East Mall / Kipling Ave. / Evans Ave. / To Niagara Falls

560 Evans Ave., Toronto • 1-888-445-4473 or 416-259-7899 • www.stayinn.ca

PARKWAY HOTELS – One Ideal Location in North Toronto

- Closest Full Service Hotel to Paramount Canada's Wonderland
- Near Hwy 7, Hwy 404, Hwy 401, Hwy 407 & Hwy 400
- 311 Sheraton Guestrooms - Coffee maker, Mini Fridge, Hairdryer, Voicemail, In-Room Movies, Sony PlayStation, Internet
- 129 Best Western Guestrooms - Coffee maker, Fridge/microwave, Hairdryer, Voicemail, In-Room Movies, Sony PlayStation, Internet
- Casual / Fine Dining & Lounge with Live Entertainment
- Pizza Hut Express On-Site
- Free Indoor / Outdoor Parking
- Health Club – Indoor / Outdoor Pool, Whirlpool, Steam rooms, Racquet / Tennis Courts, Basketball / Volleyball Courts
- Wonderland Packages, Romance Escape Rates, Weekend Specials

 Sheraton Parkway Toronto North Hotel, Suites & Conference Centre

600 Hwy 7 East (at Leslie), Richmond Hill, Ontario L4B 1B2 • (905) 881-2121 • Fax (905) 881-7841 • For Reservations Call 1-800-668-0101

5050 Orbitor Drive
Mississaugua, ON L4W 4x2
Visit us online at www.sandalwoodhotel.com

SANDALWOOD
SUITES
HOTEL

- Close to Paramount Canada's Wonderland
- Near Hwy 401, Hwy 427, Hwy 400 & QEW
- One- Bedroom Suite with separate bedroom, living room, kitchen & Jacuzzi tub.
- Complimentary buffet breakfast
- Complimentary parking and airport shuttle service
- Wonderland packages & Weekend specials
- Complimentary High-Speed Internet access

Suite
CAD $99.00
sgl/dbl occupancy
Subject to Availability.
For Reservations Call
905.238.9600
or
1.800.387.3355

See *for yourself.*

- Connected to Terminal 3 at Pearson International Airport
- 24 hour access to dining, fitness and shuttle transportation
- AAA Four Diamond Award Recipient

Call 866-782-7737 or visit sheraton.com/gatewaytoronto

MEMBER OF ⓈTARWOOD PREFERRED GUEST

Ⓢ
**Sheraton
Gateway Hotel**
IN TORONTO INTERNATIONAL AIRPORT
Toronto, Ontario

© 2005 Starwood Hotels & Resorts Worldwide, Inc.

TORONTO, ONTARIO
Great Rates and a Great Deal More

- Full service hotel
- Free parking (RV parking)
- Restaurant & Lounge
- Indoor Pool
- Easy access to all highways & local attractions
- In room coffee maker

**Travelodge
Hotel** ®

$79-$99 *

Call for Reservations
800-578-7878
www.travelodgehoteltoronto.com

*Single/Double occupancy, based on availability. Not available on Holiday Weekends

2737 Keele St • Toronto, Ont. M3M2E9 • Phone (416) 636-4656

TRAVELODGE HOTEL AND CONFERENCE CENTRE
TORONTO *Book at aaa.com*   Phone: (416)636-4656 [67]

(CAA) (SAVE)   5/1-9/5   1P: $109-$149   2P: $109-$169   XP: $15   F18
             9/6-4/30   1P: $99-$149   2P: $99-$169   XP: $15   F18
▼▼▼▼▼ **Location:** Jct Hwy 401 and Keele St N. 2737 Keele St M3M 2E9. Fax: 416/633-5637. **Facility:** 361 units. 355 one-
             bedroom standard units. 6 one-bedroom suites. 9-10 stories, interior corridors. **Parking:** on-site.
Large-scale Hotel **Terms:** cancellation fee imposed, package plans, pets ($25 extra charge). **Amenities:** voice mail, irons, hair
             dryers. *Some:* dual phone lines. **Dining:** 2 restaurants, 7 am-11 pm. **Pool(s):** heated indoor. **Leisure**
Activities: saunas, whirlpool, exercise room. **Guest Services:** gift shop, valet laundry. **Business Services:** conference
facilities. **Cards:** AX, DC, DS, MC, VI. *(See color ad p 538)*

SOME UNITS

TRAVELODGE HOTEL TORONTO AIRPORT (DIXON
ROAD) *Book at aaa.com*   Phone: (416)674-2222 [75]

(CAA) (SAVE)   All Year   1P: $99-$160   XP: $10   F18
▼▼▼ **Location:** Corner of Carlingview Dr and Dixon Rd. 925 Dixon Rd M9W 1J8. Fax: 416/674-5757. **Facility:** 283 one-
             bedroom standard units, some with whirlpools. 17 stories, interior corridors. **Parking:** on-site (fee).
             Terms: cancellation fee imposed, package plans, small pets only. **Amenities:** high-speed Internet, voice
Small-scale Hotel mail, irons, hair dryers. *Some:* dual phone lines, safes. *Some:* dual phone lines. **Dining:** 6:30 am-1 am, cocktails.
             Pool(s): heated indoor. **Leisure Activities:** saunas, whirlpool, exercise room. **Guest Services:** gift shop,
valet laundry. **Business Services:** meeting rooms. **Cards:** AX, CB, DC, DS, MC, VI. **Special Amenities:** free newspaper and
preferred room (subject to availability with advance reservations).

SOME UNITS

TRAVELODGE TORONTO EAST *Book at aaa.com*   Phone: (416)299-9500 [87]

(CAA) (SAVE)   7/1-8/31   1P: $119-$139   2P: $119-$149   XP: $10   F18
             5/1-6/30 & 9/1-4/30 1P: $99-$119   2P: $109-$129   XP: $10   F18
▼▼▼ **Location:** Jct Hwy 401 and Markham Rd, just n on Markham Rd. 20 Milner Business Ct M1B 3C6.
             Fax: 416/299-6172. **Facility:** 155 one-bedroom standard units. 6 stories, interior corridors. **Parking:** on-site.
Small-scale Hotel **Terms:** package plans, small pets only. **Amenities:** video games, voice mail, irons, hair dryers. *Some:* dual
             phone lines. **Dining:** 11 am-11 pm, cocktails. **Pool(s):** heated indoor. **Leisure Activities:** whirlpool. **Guest**
Services: valet laundry. **Cards:** AX, DC, DS, MC, VI. *(See color ad on TourBookMark)*

SOME UNITS

FEE FEE

TRAVELODGE TORONTO NORTH (NORTH YORK) *Book at aaa.com*   Phone: 416/663-9500 [54]

(CAA) (SAVE)   All Year   1P: $89-$139   2P: $99-$149   XP: $10   F18
             Location: Hwy 400, exit Finch Ave E. 50 Norfinch Dr M3N 1X1. Fax: 416/663-8480. **Facility:** 182 one-bedroom
▼▼ ▼▼ standard units. 6 stories, interior corridors. **Parking:** on-site. **Terms:** package plans, small pets only.
             Amenities: video games (fee), voice mail, irons, hair dryers. *Some:* high-speed Internet. **Pool(s):** heated
Small-scale Hotel indoor. **Leisure Activities:** whirlpool. **Guest Services:** valet and coin laundry. **Business Services:** meeting
             rooms. **Cards:** AX, DC, DS, MC, VI. *(See color ad p 529 & on TourBookMark)*

SOME UNITS

FEE

Travelodge.

STAY SATISFIED

TORONTO SOUTHWEST

Carriage Inn

We are conveniently located to all major attractions:

- 15 min to downtown Toronto
- 15 min to CN Tower
- 15 min to Sky Dome
- 10 min to Ontario Place
- 1 hour to Niagara Falls
- 25 min to Canada's Wonderland
- 25 min to Ontario Science Centre
- 20 min to Casa Loma

- 10 min. to Pearson Int'l Airport
- 5 min to Subway (Kipling)
- 5 min to major shopping malls
- Complimentary continental breakfast

Also for your convenience
French and Spanish are spoken
when available.

1767 Dundas St. East
Mississauga, Ontario • L4X 1L5 CANADA
Hotel: (905) 238-3400
Fax: (905) 238-9457

For Reservations Call:
1-800-578-7878

VALHALLA INN-TORONTO   *Book at aaa.com*   Phone: (416)239-2391   **73**
(CAA) (SAVE)   All Year   1P: $109-$155   2P: $109-$155   XP: $10   F18
▼▼▼▼▼   **Location:** 17.6 km w on east side of Hwy 427; 3.2 km s of Hwy 427, exit Burnhamthorpe Rd, just e, then s
on East Mall. Located in a residential area. 1 Valhalla Inn Rd M9B 1S9. Fax: 416/239-8764. **Facility:** 240 one-
bedroom standard units. 2-12 stories, interior corridors. **Parking:** on-site (fee). **Terms:** cancellation fee
Large-scale Hotel imposed, package plans. **Amenities:** voice mail, hair dryers. *Some:* high-speed Internet (fee), irons.
Dining: 2 restaurants, 6:30 am-11:30 pm, cocktails, entertainment. **Pool(s):** heated indoor. **Leisure**
Activities: sauna. **Guest Services:** gift shop, valet laundry. **Business Services:** conference facilities, business center.
Cards: AX, DC, DS, MC, VI. *(See color ad below)*

SOME UNITS

THE WESTIN PRINCE TORONTO   *Book at aaa.com*   Phone: (416)444-2511   **53**
(CAA) (SAVE)   5/1-10/31 & 4/1-4/30   1P: $139-$179   2P: $139-$179   XP: $20   F17
▼▼▼▼ ▼▼▼▼   11/1-3/31   1P: $125-$175   2P: $125-$175   XP: $20   F17
Location: 1 km s of Hwy 401 via Leslie St exit to York Mills Rd E. Located in a commercial area. 900 York Mills Rd M3B
3H2. Fax: 416/444-9597. **Facility:** On 15 acres of park-like grounds, the hotel's rooms and public areas
Large-scale Hotel feature a contemporary environment designed for comfort. 384 units. 372 one-bedroom standard units. 12
one-bedroom suites ($395-$2000). 22 stories, interior corridors. **Parking:** on-site and valet. **Terms:** package
plans. **Amenities:** video games (fee), dual phone lines, voice mail, safes, irons, hair dryers. *Some:* high-speed Internet (fee).
Dining: 3 restaurants, 6:30 am-10 pm, cocktails, also, Katsura, see separate listing. **Pool(s):** heated outdoor. **Leisure**
Activities: sauna, whirlpool, putting green, lighted tennis court, playground, exercise room. *Fee:* massage. **Guest Services:** gift
shop, valet laundry. **Business Services:** conference facilities, business center. **Cards:** AX, DC, JC, MC, VI.
(See color ad p 478 & p 5)

SOME UNITS

WILLOWDALE INN   Phone: (416)850-6666
▼▼▼▼▼   5/16-8/31   1P: $119   2P: $155   XP: $15   F18
5/1-5/15   1P: $115   2P: $145   XP: $15   F18
Small-scale Hotel   9/1-4/30   1P: $100   2P: $134   XP: $15   F18
Location: Jct Yonge St and Sheppard Ave, 0.5 km to Willowdale Ave, directly n. 170 Willowdale Ave M2N 4Y6.
Fax: 416/221-0810. **Facility:** Smoke free premises. 12 units. 1 one-bedroom standard unit. 11 one-bedroom suites ($160-$189).
2 stories (no elevator), interior corridors. **Parking:** on-site (fee). **Terms:** cancellation fee imposed, weekly rates available.
Amenities: high-speed Internet, voice mail, hair dryers. **Guest Services:** complimentary laundry. **Cards:** MC, VI.

WYNDHAM BRISTOL PLACE-TORONTO AIRPORT   *Book at aaa.com*   Phone: (416)675-9444   **96**
(CAA) (SAVE)   All Year   1P: $119-$205   2P: $119-$205   XP: $20   F18
▼▼▼▼▼   **Location:** 3 km w of jct Hwy 401. Located across from the airport. 950 Dixon Rd M9W 5N4. Fax: 416/675-4426.
Facility: 287 units. 284 one-bedroom standard units. 3 one-bedroom suites. 15 stories, interior corridors.
Parking: on-site (fee) and valet. **Terms:** cancellation fee imposed, pets (with prior approval).
Large-scale Hotel **Amenities:** CD players, dual phone lines, voice mail, honor bars, irons, hair dryers. *Fee:* video games, high-
speed Internet. **Dining:** 6:30 am-10 pm, also, Zachary's, see separate listing. **Pool(s):** heated indoor.
Leisure Activities: saunas, exercise room. **Guest Services:** gift shop, valet laundry. **Business Services:** conference facilities,
business center. **Cards:** AX, CB, DC, DS, JC, MC, VI.

SOME UNITS

AAA/CAA TORONTO ADVENTURE

$109* CDN.

Single/Double Occupancy, Kids Stay Free
*Some restrictions apply. Other Packages available.

A City Hotel In A Country Setting only minutes from Toronto's
major sites and attractions such as Canada's Wonderland,
Ontario Place, CN Tower, Skydome and major shopping.

• 240 Spacious Rooms with 31" Colour Cable TV/Video on Demand
• Skylit Indoor Pool/Sauna and Sundeck
• 2 Restaurants, 2 Lounges, Seasonal Patio
• Fitness, Squash, Golf & Tennis nearby
• Ample parking (nominal fee)

Toll Free in USA & Canada

1-800-268-2500 or call your travel agent

Valhalla Inn
TORONTO

1 Valhalla Inn Road, Toronto, Ontario, Canada M9B 1S9
Highway 427 & Burnhamthorpe Rd.

Phone: (416) 239-2391 Fax: (416) 239-8764 Internet: www.valhalla-inn.com E-mail: reservations@valhalla-inn.com

──────── *The following lodging was either not evaluated or did not* ────────
meet AAA rating requirements but is listed for your information only.

THE GRAND HOTEL AND SUITES TORONTO   **Phone:** 416/863-9000
(fyi)   Not evaluated. **Location:** Jct Dundas St. 225 Jarvis St M5B 2C1. Facilities, services, and decor characterize a mid-
             range property.

──────── **WHERE TO DINE** ────────

ACROSS THE ROAD   **Dinner:** $20-$37   **Phone:** 416/486-1111   (164)
▼▼▼   **Location:** Just s of Eglinton Ave. 679 Mt. Pleasant Rd M4S 2N2. **Hours:** 6 pm-10:30 pm. Closed major holidays.
             Reservations: suggested. **Features:** Located in a bright, modern dining room, the delightful bistro-type
Continental restaurant offers diners a wonderful selection of fine fare to suit all taste buds. Select from starter salads
             and soups, appetizer or full-portion pastas, seafood, beef, rack of lamb or game. The chef offers a
wonderful array of daily specials featuring market-fresh ingredients and an innovative flair. Dressy casual; cocktails. **Parking:**
street. **Cards:** AX, DC, MC, VI.   ☒

ALFREDO'S   **Lunch:** $12-$16   **Dinner:** $13-$25   **Phone:** 416/246-7904   (143)
▼▼▼   **Location:** Jct Hwy 27 N, just w of jct Hwy 401; in Doubletree International Plaza Hotel Toronto Airport. 655 Dixon Rd
             M9W 1J3. **Hours:** 11:30 am-2:30 & 5-10:30 pm, Sat from 5 pm. Closed major holidays; also for lunch Sun
Italian   7/1-8/31. **Reservations:** suggested. **Features:** Fine Italian and Continental cuisine awaits at the cozy
             restaurant in the International Plaza Hotel and Convention Centre, near Toronto International Airport. The
elegant dining room showcases fine Italian artwork and candlelit tables. Sophisticated cuisine—including lobster bisque, fresh
pastas and preparations of veal and lamb—is perfectly complemented by a sweet ending from the elaborate dessert trolley.
Service is formal. Dressy casual; cocktails. **Parking:** on-site. **Cards:** AX, DC, DS, MC, VI.   ☒

ASTORIA SHISH KEBOB HOUSE   **Lunch:** $5-$9   **Dinner:** $10-$19   **Phone:** 416/463-2838   (189)
▼▼   **Location:** Jct Chester Ave. 390 Danforth Ave M4K 1P3. **Hours:** 11 am-midnight, Fri & Sat-1 am. Closed: 12/25;
             also Greek Easter. **Features:** In the heart of the city's Greek community, the restaurant opens its wonderful
Greek   patio in the summer months. The staff serves a good variety of hearty Greek cuisine, including freshly grilled
             kebabs, moussaka and tasty appetizers. Casual dress; cocktails. **Parking:** street. **Cards:** AX, DC, MC, VI.
                                                                                              ☒

AUBERGE DU POMMIER   **Lunch:** $17-$21   **Dinner:** $33-$39   **Phone:** 416/222-2220   (141)
▼▼▼ ▼▼▼   **Location:** Hwy 401, exit Yonge St, 1 km s. 4150 Yonge St M2P 6C6. **Hours:** 11:30 am-2:30 & 5-10:30 pm, Sat
             from 5 pm. Closed major holidays; also Sun. **Reservations:** suggested. **Features:** In a cozy French manor
French   with stone walls and glowing fireplaces, the restaurant exudes a distinct European ambience. Tables are
             gracefully set in fine linen covers with candles and fresh flowers, creating an elegant, upscale tone. The
often-changing Continental menu lists a wide selection of traditional favorites with innovative flairs. Professional staffers pride
themselves in attention to detail and assist in finding the perfect wine to complement menu selections. Dressy casual; cocktails.
Parking: on-site (fee). **Cards:** AX, DC, MC, VI.   ⊕ ☒

AVRA TRADITIONAL GREEK CUISINE & SEAFOOD
HOUSE   **Lunch:** $7-$14   **Dinner:** $11-$40   **Phone:** 416/463-0334   (121)
▼▼   **Location:** Jct Pape and Danforth aves. 702 Pape Ave M4K 3S7. **Hours:** 11 am-10 pm, Fri & Sat-3 am, Sun-11
             pm. **Features:** The well-established restaurant is in the heart of Danforth, the city's well-known Greek
Greek   community. The ornate dining room reflects a classical Greek atmosphere, with pillars and gold-leaf-
             accented ceilings. Diners can sample hearty portions of traditional fare, including all-time favorites such as
roast lamb, souvlaki, moussaka and spinach pie, as well as the chef's daily creations. Casual dress; cocktails. **Parking:** on-site
(fee). **Cards:** AX, DC, MC, VI.   ☒

BLACK DOG PUB   **Lunch:** $7-$19   **Dinner:** $7-$19   **Phone:** 416/286-4544   (135)
▼▼   **Location:** Hwy 401, exit Whites Rd, directly s. 87 Island Rd (West Rouge) M1C 2P6. **Hours:** 11:30 am-11 pm.
             Closed: 12/25. **Features:** The true neighborhood pub lets diners choose from finger foods by the glowing
Continental fireplace or full meals in the main dining room or on the popular patio. Among favourites are fish and chips,
             shepherd's pie, burgers, wings and pasta dishes. A great beer, wine and single-malt menu is presented.
Casual dress; cocktails. **Parking:** on-site. **Cards:** AX, MC, VI.   ⊕ ☒

BOMBAY PALACE   **Lunch:** $9-$11   **Dinner:** $11-$15   **Phone:** 416/431-5577   (148)
▼▼   **Location:** Hwy 401, exit 383 (Markham Rd), 2 km s; in Painted Post Plaza. 795 Markham Rd M1H 2Y1. **Hours:** 11:45
             am-3 & 5:15-10:30 pm. **Reservations:** suggested. **Features:** In a busy commercial and residential area of
Indian   the suburbs, the popular Indian restaurant lets diners sample varied dishes from the extensive luncheon
             buffet or from the exotic a la carte dinner menu. Soft, ethnic background music and distinct Indian artwork
lend to the relaxed, comfortable atmosphere. Casual dress; cocktails. **Parking:** on-site. **Cards:** AX, DC, MC, VI.   ☒

BROWNES BISTRO   **Lunch:** $10-$15   **Dinner:** $14-$37   **Phone:** 416/924-8132   (166)
▼▼▼   **Location:** Jct Yonge St and Woodlawn Ave, 1.5 km n of Bloor St. 4 Woodlawn Ave M4T 1C1. **Hours:** noon-2 & 5:30-
             10:30 pm, Sat & Sun from 5:30 pm. Closed major holidays. **Reservations:** suggested. **Features:** Just
Continental outside of the city's core, the small, cozy restaurant features an open-concept kitchen and a relaxed
             ambience. A good choice is the colourfully presented and amply portioned grilled chicken in a tangy sesame
sauce. Other specialties include gourmet pizza, lamb shanks with seasonal vegetables, pasta and New York strip steak, all
nicely prepared and served by an attentive staff. Casual dress; cocktails. **Parking:** street. **Cards:** AX, DC, MC, VI.   ☒

CANYON CREEK CHOPHOUSE   **Lunch:** $8-$24   **Dinner:** $16-$29   **Phone:** 416/621-6255 (194)
Location: Jct Hwy 427; directly across from Sherway Gardens. 1900 The Queensway M9C 5H5. **Hours:** 11:30 am-midnight; hours may vary holidays. Closed: 12/25. **Reservations:** accepted. **Features:** A relaxed, comfortable setting, a traditional steak house menu and an extensive wine list make this a popular favourite with locals and tourists alike. Diners here enjoy great cuts of aged beef, ribs, chicken, huge pork chops or rack of lamb all grilled to order. The wine list has an excellent selection by the glass and the bottle to enhance the overall dining experience. The decadent desserts are the perfect ending especially when sided with a glass of ice wine or a specialty coffee. Dressy casual; cocktails. **Parking:** on-site. **Cards:** AX, DC, MC, VI.
Steak House

CENTRO GRILL & WINE BAR   **Dinner:** $27-$43   **Phone:** 416/483-2211 (127)
Location: 1 km n of Eglinton Ave. 2472 Yonge St M4P 2H5. **Hours:** 5 pm-11:30 pm. Closed major holidays; also Sun. **Reservations:** suggested. **Features:** The restaurant's atmosphere bustles in an upscale, contemporary setting. High ceilings, a semi-open-concept kitchen and a large, unobstructed dining room allow all to be seen. Diners delight in the highly innovative menu, which reflects a strong focus on fresh, regional ingredients prepared with a California flair. Creative, artistic presentations are a highlight of most meals. Dressy casual; cocktails; entertainment. **Parking:** valet. **Cards:** AX, DC, MC, VI.
Continental

CITIES   **Dinner:** $13-$21   **Phone:** 416/504-3762 (128)
Location: 1 km w of Bathurst St. 859 Queen St W M6J 1G4. **Hours:** 5:30 pm-9 pm, Thurs-10 pm, Fri & Sat-11 pm. Closed: 1/1, 12/24, 12/25. **Reservations:** suggested. **Features:** Streetcars stop out front of the restaurant, which serves reasonably priced entrees and wines. Dressy casual; cocktails. **Parking:** street. **Cards:** AX, MC, VI.
Continental

CUISINE OF INDIA   **Lunch:** $10   **Dinner:** $7-$15   **Phone:** 416/229-0377 (137)
Location: Hwy 401, exit Yonge St, 2 km n; 1 km s of Finch Ave. 5222 Yonge St M2N 5P6. **Hours:** 11:30 am-2:30 & 5:30-10 pm, Fri & Sat-10:30 pm. Closed: 1/1, 12/25. **Reservations:** suggested. **Features:** The bustling restaurant is known for freshly prepared and perfectly spiced Indian cuisine. Diners gaze through the glass window surrounding the chef to catch a glimpse of fresh bread being prepared and daily specials being created. The lunch buffet enables guests to sample some of the chef's highlights, while at dinner there is an extensive a la carte menu with more exotic items. All are freshly prepared and flavorful. Casual dress; cocktails. **Parking:** on-site. **Cards:** AX, DC, MC, VI.
Indian

THE DAVID DUNCAN HOUSE   **Lunch:** $8-$16   **Dinner:** $25-$40   **Phone:** 416/391-1424 (140)
Location: Don Valley Pkwy, exit York Mills Rd, 1 km w to Don Mills, then just n. 125 Moatfield Dr M3B 3L9. **Hours:** 11:30 am-3 & 5-11 pm, Sat & Sun from 5 pm. **Reservations:** suggested. **Features:** An elegant, art nouveau atmosphere prevails in the restored 1865 mansion. The extensive menu centers on generous portions of steak, seafood, pasta, appetizers, salads and desserts. Service is professional and knowledgeable. Semi-formal attire; cocktails. **Parking:** on-site. **Cards:** AX, DC, MC, VI.
Steak & Seafood

DRAGON DYNASTY CHINESE CUISINE   **Lunch:** $10-$15   **Dinner:** $15-$30   **Phone:** 416/321-9000 (155)
Location: Jct Brimley Rd and Huntingwood; at Chartwell Shopping Center. 2301 Brimley Rd M1S 5B8. **Hours:** 10:30 am-4 & 5:30-11 pm, Sat & Sun from 9:30 am. **Reservations:** suggested. **Features:** In a busy, residential area in the heart of a Chinese community, the large restaurant prepares a wonderful selection of fine cuisine. Food is freshly made in a variety of styles and comes in hearty portions for sharing. The two-course Peking duck option is popular. Large tables lend to a banquet-style atmosphere in the brightly lit dining room. Service is highly professional and personable. Dressy casual; cocktails. **Parking:** on-site. **Cards:** MC, VI.
Chinese

EDO   **Dinner:** $14-$20   **Phone:** 416/322-3033 (124)
Location: Just w of Avenue Rd. 484 Eglinton Ave W M5N 1A5. **Hours:** 5 pm-10:30 pm. **Reservations:** suggested. **Features:** In the Eglinton district, the local favourite boasts a simplistic, yet detailed, decor of sleek, modern appointments. The fusion of hot popular jazz tunes with fine Japanese cuisine is a surprisingly winning combination. Chefs are skilled at creating intricate sushi and sashimi, and the helpful staff ably explains unfamiliar menu items. Dressy casual; cocktails. **Parking:** street. **Cards:** AX, DC, MC, VI.
Japanese

GRAFFITI'S ITALIAN EATERY   **Lunch:** $8-$25   **Dinner:** $8-$25   **Phone:** 416/213-1300 (157)
Location: 1 km w of jct Hwy 27 N and Dixon Rd; in Quality Suites Toronto Airport. 262 Carlingview Dr M9W 5G1. **Hours:** 6:30 am-10 pm, Sat & Sun from 7 am. **Features:** The casual eatery serves a wide selection of tasty pasta dishes and made-to-order gourmet pizzas in a relaxed, comfortable setting. Portions are hearty and feature fresh, wholesome ingredients. It's worth saving room for one of the decadent desserts. Casual dress; cocktails. **Parking:** on-site (fee). **Cards:** AX, MC, VI.
Italian

GRANO   **Lunch:** $11-$14   **Dinner:** $13-$25   **Phone:** 416/440-1986 (168)
Location: 0.5 km s of Eglinton Ave. 2035 Yonge St M4S 2A2. **Hours:** 10 am-11 pm. Closed major holidays; also Sun. **Features:** All regions of Italian cuisine are well-represented here, including traditional and contemporary fare. Calamari, homemade ravioli and a large selection of antipasto are served in a bustling atmosphere of frescos, ceramics, painted floors and courtyards. Casual dress; cocktails. **Parking:** street. **Cards:** AX, DC, MC, VI.
Italian

GRAZIE RISTORANTE   **Lunch:** $8-$17   **Dinner:** $8-$17   **Phone:** 416/488-0822 (138)
Location: Just n of Eglinton Ave. 2373 Yonge St M4P 2C8. **Hours:** noon-11 pm, Fri & Sat-midnight. Closed: 1/1, 4/17, 12/25. **Features:** Intimate table seating and a bustling atmosphere make this eatery casual and fun. A wide selection of hearty Italian fare is offered, from pasta and pizza to bruscetta and homemade tiramisu. Undecided? Try the pasta with olive oil, feta cheese and red peppers. Casual dress; cocktails. **Parking:** street. **Cards:** AX, DC, MC, VI.
Italian

IL FORNELLO   Lunch: $8-$15   Dinner: $12-$30   Phone: 416/691-8377   (174)
Location: Just e of Woodbine. 1968 Queen St E M4E 1C9. **Hours:** 11:30 am-10 pm, Fri & Sat-11 pm. Closed:
1/1, 12/25. **Features:** Gourmet pizza cooked in a wood-fired oven is an Il Fornello specialty; the bustling
atmosphere comes complements of the diners, the busy wait staff and the open kitchen where you can see
Italian   your meal prepared. A daily luncheon buffet is also featured. Cocktails. **Parking:** street. **Cards:** AX, DC,
MC, VI.

IL FORNELLO   Lunch: $8-$15   Dinner: $12-$30   Phone: 416/466-2931   (175)
Location: Directly w of Pape Ave. 576 Danforth Ave M4K 1R1. **Hours:** 11:30 am-10 pm, Fri-11 pm, Sat 11 am-11
pm, Sun 10:30 am-10 pm. Closed: 12/25. **Features:** Set in a casual atmosphere with European flair is a
varied menu of wood-fire baked gourmet pizza and an array of specialty pasta. There's a good selection of
Italian   tasty starters and appetizers such as steamed mussels, bruscetta and a variety of soup and salad. Casual
dress; cocktails. **Parking:** street. **Cards:** AX, DC, MC, VI.

IL FORNELLO   Lunch: $8-$15   Dinner: $10-$30   Phone: 416/920-8291   (172)
Location: Just n of St. Clair Ave; jct Delisle Ave. 1560 Yonge St M4T 2S9. **Hours:** 11:30 am-9:30 pm, Tues-Thurs
to 11 pm, Fri-10:30 pm, Sat 4:30 am-10:30 pm. Closed: 12/25. **Features:** Gourmet pizza cooked in a
wood-fired oven is an Il Fornello specialty; the bustling atmosphere comes complements of the diners, the
Italian   busy service staff and the open kitchen where you can see your meal prepared. A daily luncheon buffet is
also featured. Casual dress; cocktails. **Parking:** street. **Cards:** AX, DC, MC, VI.

INDIAN RICE FACTORY   Lunch: $8-$16   Dinner: $8-$16   Phone: 416/961-3472   (158)
Location: Just e of Bathurst St. 414 Dupont St M5R 1V9. **Hours:** noon-2:30 & 5-10:30 pm. Closed major
holidays. **Reservations:** suggested. **Features:** The small dining room features modern, yet traditional,
decor, including interesting Indian artwork and wall displays accented by suspended lighting. The ambience
Indian   is relaxed. The menu lists a wide selection of freshly prepared Indian cuisine with a wonderful choice of
complementary sauces. Servers are helpful in explaining unfamiliar menu items, and chefs ensure the spice level is adjusted to
suit individual tastes. Casual dress; cocktails. **Parking:** street. **Cards:** DC, MC, VI.

J.J. MUGGS GOURMET GRILLE   Lunch: $5-$19   Dinner: $5-$19   Phone: 416/674-5450   (145)
Location: Jct Rexdale Blvd and Hwy 27; in Woodbine Centre, Hwy 27 entrance. 500 Rexdale Blvd M9W 6K5.
Hours: 8 am-1 am, Thurs-Sat to 2 am, Sun-midnight. Closed: 12/25. **Reservations:** suggested, weekends.
Features: Dine in an attractive, airy dining room where stained glass, Tiffany lamps and plants give off a
American   garden-like ambience. As formal as it may sound, the setting is really casual and fun with hearty portions of
varied fare served by an equally friendly staff. Casual dress; cocktails. **Parking:** on-site. **Cards:** AX, DC, MC, VI.

KATSURA   Lunch: $15-$25   Dinner: $18-$50   Phone: 416/444-2511   (142)
Location: 1 km s of Hwy 401 via Leslie St exit to York Mills Rd E; in The Westin Prince Toronto. 900 York Mills Rd M3B
3H2. **Hours:** noon-2:30 & 6-10 pm, Sat from 6 pm, Sun 6 pm-9:30 pm. **Reservations:** suggested.
Features: The Japanese restaurant entertains patrons with good teppanyaki cooking in a lively atmosphere.
Japanese   Skillful chefs cook to order at table grills, and traditionally attired servers cater to guests. A tatami sushi bar
is also showcased. Casual dress; cocktails. **Parking:** on-site. **Cards:** AX, DC, JC, MC, VI.

THE KEG STEAKHOUSE AND BAR   Lunch: $8-$15   Dinner: $16-$30   Phone: 416/225-2841   (150)
Location: At Sheppard Centre. 4841 Yonge St M2N 5X3. **Hours:** 11:30 am-10:30 pm, Fri-11 pm, Sat 4:30 pm-11
pm, Sun 4 pm-10:30 pm. **Features:** Well-known for its mesquite-grilled steaks and fun, laid-back
atmosphere, this steak house is a longtime favourite with the local crowd. In addition to great beef, the
Steak House   traditional menu features seafood, grilled chicken, hickory ribs and pasta offerings. All meals come with a
hot loaf of sourdough bread. Try a specialty coffee or some tasty cheesecake for the perfect ending. Casual dress; cocktails.
Parking: on-site (fee). **Cards:** AX, DC, MC, VI.

THE KEG STEAKHOUSE AND BAR   Lunch: $8-$20   Dinner: $15-$30   Phone: 416/438-1452   (126)
Location: Just sw of jct Hwy 401 and Markham Rd. 60 Estate Dr M1H 2Z1. **Hours:** 11:30 am-1 am, Sat from 4:30
pm, Sun 4 pm-11 pm. Closed: 12/25. **Features:** Well-known for its mesquite-grilled steaks and fun, laid-
back atmosphere, the steak house is a longtime favourite with the local crowd. In addition to great beef, the
Steak House   traditional menu features seafood, grilled chicken, hickory ribs and pasta offerings. All meals come with a
hot loaf of sourdough bread. Try a specialty coffee or tasty cheesecake for the perfect ending. Casual dress; cocktails. **Parking:**
on-site. **Cards:** AX, DC, MC, VI.

THE KEG STEAKHOUSE AND BAR   Lunch: $8-$22   Dinner: $16-$35   Phone: 416/626-3707   (154)
Location: Jct Bloor St. 291 The West Mall M9C 4Z6. **Hours:** 11:30 am-2:30 & 5-10:30 pm, Sat 4:30 pm-11 pm,
Sun 4 pm-10 pm. Closed: 12/25. **Features:** Well-known for its mesquite-grilled steaks and fun, laid-back
atmosphere, this steak house is a longtime favourite with the local crowd. In addition to great beef, the
Steak House   traditional menu features seafood, grilled chicken, hickory ribs and pasta offerings. All meals come with a
hot loaf of sourdough bread. Try a specialty coffee or some tasty cheesecake for the perfect ending. Casual dress; cocktails.
Parking: on-site. **Cards:** AX, DC, MC, VI.

THE KEG STEAKHOUSE AND BAR   Lunch: $8-$22   Dinner: $15-$30   Phone: 416/675-2311   (133)
Location: Jct Carlingview Dr. 927 Dixon Rd M9W 1J8. **Hours:** 11:30 am-1 am, Sat from 4 pm, Sun 4 pm-11 pm.
Closed: 12/25. **Features:** Well-known for its mesquite-grilled steaks and fun, laid-back atmosphere, the
steak house is a longtime favourite with the local crowd. In addition to great beef, the traditional menu
Steak House   features seafood, grilled chicken, hickory ribs and pasta offerings. All meals come with a hot loaf of
sourdough bread. Try a specialty coffee or tasty cheesecake for the perfect ending. Casual dress; cocktails. **Parking:** on-site.
Cards: AX, MC, VI.

THE KEG STEAKHOUSE AND BAR   **Lunch:** $8-$20   **Dinner:** $15-$30   **Phone:** 416/446-1045   (149)
Location: 0.5 km s of Hwy 401. 1977 Leslie St M3B 2N3. **Hours:** 11:30 am-2:30 & 5-10:30 pm, Fri-11 pm, Sat 4:30 pm-11 pm, Sun 4 pm-10 pm. Closed: 12/25. **Features:** This bustling eatery is popular with the business crowd at lunch for a quick bite or the mesquite-grilled entrees for which the chain is famous.
Steak & Seafood
Dinner patrons continue to enjoy the relaxed setting and the tender cuts of beef, chicken, seafood and ribs, served up with steaming baked potatoes and hot sourdough bread. An outdoor patio is also featured in season. Casual dress; cocktails. **Parking:** on-site. **Cards:** AX, DC, MC, VI.

KENSINGTON KITCHEN   **Lunch:** $6-$13   **Dinner:** $8-$16   **Phone:** 416/961-3404   (171)
Location: W of Spadina Ave. 124 Harbord St M5S 1G8. **Hours:** 11:30 am-10 pm. Closed: 1/1, 12/25. **Reservations:** suggested. **Features:** The casual restaurant serves freshly prepared Middle Eastern and Moroccan cuisine, such as couscous, lamb and vegetarian options. The dining room is marked
Middle Eastern
by brightly coloured tables and chairs and interesting wall ornaments. Friendly, personable servers will help in explaining any unfamiliar menu items. Casual dress; cocktails. **Parking:** street. **Cards:** AX, DC, MC, VI.

LA FORCHETTA   **Dinner:** $12-$28   **Phone:** 416/534-3100   (182)
Location: Just w of jct Clinton St; in Little Italy. 613 College St M6G 1B5. **Hours:** 5 pm-10:30 pm. Closed major holidays. **Features:** Squashed between a number of other Italian restaurants, the quiet, upscale spot
Italian
nurtures a warm ambience that draws many people to peek through the windows. Unexpected flavours and influences permeate such dishes as Sicilian spring rolls and gnocchi with sun-dried tomato and ricotta. Dressy casual; cocktails. **Parking:** street. **Cards:** AX, DC, DS, MC, VI.

LAKES   **Lunch:** $11-$16   **Dinner:** $15-$29   **Phone:** 416/966-0185   (177)
Location: 1 km n of Bloor St. 1112 Yonge St M4W 2L6. **Hours:** noon-3 & 6-10 pm, Sat & Sun from 6 pm. Closed major holidays. **Reservations:** suggested. **Features:** Diners are treated to a relaxed, comfortable
Continental
atmosphere in a modern setting. The menu centers on innovative Continental cuisine prepared with market-fresh ingredients. Highlights include starters such as wild mushroom soup and calamari and goat cheese appetizers, as well as entrees built around seafood, pasta and beef. Decadent, homemade desserts make the perfect finish. Dressy casual; cocktails. **Parking:** street. **Cards:** AX, DC, MC, VI.

LATINA'S RESTAURANT   **Lunch:** $8-$12   **Dinner:** $10-$25   **Phone:** 416/259-9273   (146)
Location: Just n of jct QEW and Islington Ave, west end exit, 1.6 km e; just e of Royal York Rd. 690 The Queensway M8Y 1K9. **Hours:** 11:30 am-10 pm, Fri-10:30 pm, Sat 5 pm-11 pm, Sun 5 pm-9:30 pm. Closed: 1/1, 12/25,
Italian
12/26. **Reservations:** suggested, weekends. **Features:** For over 35 years this restaurant has been serving generous portions of quality fare in a casual setting that is enjoyed by families, couples and business folks alike. Casual dress; cocktails. **Parking:** street. **Cards:** AX, DC, MC, VI.

LE BIFTHEQUE STEAKHOUSE   **Lunch:** $6-$13   **Dinner:** $14-$40   **Phone:** 416/798-4333   (161)
Location: Just w of jct Hwy 27 and Dixon Rd. 25 Carlson Ct M9W 6A2. **Hours:** 11:30 am-10 pm, Sat noon-11 pm, Sun noon-10 pm. Closed: 12/25. **Reservations:** suggested, weekends. **Features:** Near Toronto
Steak House
International Airport, the huge restaurant is separated into several smaller rooms. As the name suggests, steak—fine cuts of beef fresh from the grill—is the main focus. For hearty appetites, a 24-ounce cut of prime rib is offered. All entrees include fresh bread and a tasty garden salad. Accustomed to a bustling atmosphere, the staff provides fast, efficient service. Casual dress; cocktails. **Parking:** on-site. **Cards:** AX, DC, MC, VI.

LE PARADIS BRASSERIE BISTRO   **Lunch:** $8-$15   **Dinner:** $12-$18   **Phone:** 416/921-0995   (178)
Location: Just n of Dupont St. 166 Bedford Rd M5R 2K9. **Hours:** noon-2:30 & 6-11 pm, Sat from 5:30 pm, Sun & Mon 5:30 pm-10 pm. **Reservations:** accepted. **Features:** Reminiscent of a French bistro, the "Designers
Continental
Walk" eatery prides itself on an innovative menu of North African specialties. Seasonal variations include a selection of seafood, beef and lamb dishes, as well as a "tarte" of the day. Casual dress; cocktails. **Parking:** on-site (fee). **Cards:** AX, DC, MC, VI.

LICHEE GARDEN   **Lunch:** $7-$19   **Dinner:** $15-$40   **Phone:** 416/322-8898   (167)
Location: Jct Dundas St. 480 University Ave M5G 1V2. **Hours:** 11:30 am-11:30 pm, Fri & Sat-12:30 am, Sun-10:30 pm. Closed: 12/25. **Reservations:** suggested, weekends. **Features:** Extensive selection of freshly
Chinese
prepared dishes in a casual, relaxed dining room. Great for family dining. Choose from traditional favourites such as garlic spare ribs, wonton soup with pork and a variety of stir-fried items. Mild or spicy sauces available. Casual dress; cocktails. **Parking:** on-site (fee). **Cards:** AX, DC, MC, VI.

THE LOBSTER TRAP   **Lunch:** $7-$22   **Dinner:** $18-$50   **Phone:** 416/787-3211   (180)
Location: Hwy 401, exit Avenue Rd, 1 km s. 1962 Avenue Rd M5M 4A1. **Hours:** noon-2 & 5-10 pm, Sat & Sun from 5 pm. Closed: 12/25. **Features:** Couples and families continue to enjoy this long-established restaurant
Seafood
where casual service and market fresh seafood are the order of the day. The signature menu item is a one-to four-pound lobster. Casual dress; cocktails. **Parking:** street. **Cards:** AX, DC, MC, VI.

LONE STAR TEXAS GRILL   **Lunch:** $8-$12   **Dinner:** $9-$28   **Phone:** 416/674-7777   (131)
Location: 3 km w of jct Hwy 401. 930 Dixon Rd M9W 1J9. **Hours:** 11:30 am-11 pm, Thurs-Sat to 2 am, Sun noon-11 pm. Closed: 12/25. **Features:** Huge Texas steaks, sizzling fajitas, juicy burgers and a variety of Tex-Mex fare make this a popular favorite with the locals. Diners who meet the 72-ounce steak challenge
American
will get their meal for free. Casual decor and friendly service suit the menu options. Casual dress; cocktails. **Parking:** on-site. **Cards:** AX, MC, VI.

MARIKO JAPANESE RESTAURANT Lunch: $7-$14 Dinner: $9-$19 Phone: 416/463-8231 181
Japanese
professional.
Location: Just w of Chester Ave; in Carrot Common. 348 Danforth Ave M4K 1N8. Hours: noon-2:30 & 5:30-10 pm, Sun 5:30 pm-9 pm. Closed: 1/1, 12/25. Reservations: suggested. Features: Tasty, authentic Japanese cuisine is cooked fresh at your table and features sushi, tempura and teriyaki, along with an array of hot and cold appetizers and grilled items. Full-course meals are also available. The service is both polite and professional. Casual dress; cocktails. Parking: street. Cards: AX, MC, VI.

MARKY'S DELICATESSEN & RESTAURANT Lunch: $8-$20 Dinner: $8-$20 Phone: 416/638-1081 193
Jewish
Congress.
Location: Jct Bathurst St and Wilson Ave. 280 Wilson Ave M3H 1S8. Hours: 9 am-1 am, Fri-3 pm, Sat 1/2 hour after sunset-1:30 am, Sun 9 am-midnight. Closed: Jewish holidays. Features: This Glatt kosher delicatessen serves a variety of house specials including great deli, finger food, beef, chicken, pasta, soup, salad, stir-fry and more than 100 additional tasty treats, all under the supervision of the Canadian Jewish Congress. Casual dress; cocktails. Parking: on-site. Cards: AX, MC, VI.

MIKADO Dinner: $22-$42 Phone: 416/674-1954 162
Japanese
Service
Location: Corner of Dixon Rd and Carlingview Dr; in Toronto Airport Marriott Hotel. 901 Dixon Rd M9W 1J5. Hours: 5:30 pm-10 pm. Closed major holidays. Reservations: suggested. Features: Fresh Atlantic salmon, tuna steak, and filets are the house specialties at this popular and fun Japanese steak house. Enjoy sushi and sashimi platters as well. Skilled and entertaining chefs prepare your cooked-to-order meal at your table. Service is prompt and efficient. Dressy casual; cocktails. Parking: on-site. Cards: AX, CB, DC, DS, JC, MC, VI.

MILESTONE'S GRILL AND BAR Lunch: $8-$25 Dinner: $8-$25 Phone: 416/225-2552 144
American
Location: Hwy 401, exit Yonge St, 2.8 km n; opposite North York City Hall. Unit A13-5095 Yonge St M2N 6Z4. Hours: 11 am-10 pm, Fri & Sat-midnight. Closed: 12/25. Features: A bright, modern decor and a bustling atmosphere set the tone at Milestone's Grill and Bar. The menu features an abundance of pastas, stone-oven pizzas, sandwiches and burgers, as well as an all-day brunch menu with an innovative flair. Diners at this location will enjoy the large street-level lounge or the 2nd-level dining room which features large windows overlooking the interesting uptown sights. The decor features an open-concept kitchen and a wood-burning stove. Casual dress; cocktails. Parking: on-site (fee). Cards: AX, DC, MC, VI.

MILESTONE'S GRILL AND BAR Lunch: $8-$25 Dinner: $8-$25 Phone: 416/789-9940 188
American
pastas,
exotic
Location: Jct Hwy 401 and Dufferin St, exit Allen Rd; at Yorkdale Shopping Centre. 17-3401 Dufferin St M2A 6T9. Hours: 11 am-midnight, Fri-1 am, Sat 10 am-1 am, Sun 10 am-11 pm. Closed: 12/25. Features: Milestone's Grill and Bar is the perfect spot to rest after a day of shopping or for a post- or pre-movie meal. The modern decor offers a relaxing ambience, and the menu features a perfect blend of tasty comfort foods including pastas, huge sandwiches, burgers and a variety of all-day brunch selections. Tasty desserts will boost your energy level or an exotic cocktail will delight in the cozy bar area. Casual dress; cocktails. Parking: on-site. Cards: AX, DC, MC, VI.

MILESTONE'S GRILL AND BAR Lunch: $8-$25 Dinner: $8-$25 Phone: 416/245-6262 156
American
complements
Location: Directly e of jct Hwy 27. 646 Dixon Rd M9W 1J1. Hours: 11 am-midnight, Fri-1 am, Sat 10 am-1 am, Sun 10 am-11 pm. Closed: 12/25. Features: Popular with the local business crowd, the bustling eatery is close to the International Centre and the city's airport hotels. Diners enjoy the relaxed setting and casual menu featuring pasta, pizza, roasted chicken and a tasty choice of egg and brunch options. A nice wine list complements the menu. Casual dress; cocktails. Parking: on-site. Cards: AX, DC, MC, VI.

MILLERS COUNTRY FARE Lunch: $7-$11 Dinner: $7-$18 Phone: 416/234-5050 147
Canadian
Location: 3 km e of jct Hwy 427, just e of Kipling. 5140 Dundas St W M9A 1C2. Hours: 11 am-9:30 pm, Sat & Sun from 10 am. Closed: 12/25. Features: The casual, country atmosphere defines the fare at Millers; wholesome, generously portioned, home-style cooking. Flavourful chicken, ribs, homemade apple pie and brown Betty are the house specialties. The wait staff is friendly and efficient. Casual dress; cocktails. Parking: on-site. Cards: AX, DC, MC, VI.

NORTH 44 Dinner: $30-$50 Phone: 416/487-4897 134
Continental
Location: 1 km n of Eglinton Ave. 2537 Yonge St M4P 2H9. Hours: 5 pm-10 pm, Thurs-Sat to 11 pm. Closed major holidays; also Sun. Reservations: suggested. Features: A second-floor piano lounge, an elegant dining room and a highly innovative menu lure diners to the upscale restaurant. The menu is ever-changing, with a focus on fresh regional ingredients and creativity in presentation and preparation. High ceilings contribute to the dining room's modern appeal. Service is detailed and attentive. Semi-formal attire; cocktails; entertainment. Parking: valet. Cards: AX, DC, MC, VI.

THE OLD MILL *Menu on aaa.com* Lunch: $9-$22 Dinner: $29-$45 Phone: 416/236-2641 129
Continental
longtime
site.
Location: Jct Jane and Bloor sts, just w on Bloor St to Humber Blvd, follow signs; in The Old Mill Inn and Spa. 21 Old Mill Rd M8X 1G5. Hours: noon-2:30, 3-5 & 6-10 pm, Thurs-Sat to 10:30 pm, Sun 10:30 am-2:30, 3:30-5 & 5:30-9 pm. Closed: 12/24. Reservations: suggested. Features: Striking, 19th-century English architecture sets an elegant stage. Old English charm exudes from the gracious Tudor building in an upscale residential area across from attractive parklands. In addition to a la carte selections, the restaurant features an extensive daily luncheon buffet, traditional afternoon tea and a spectacular Sunday brunch. This spot is a longtime tradition for fine dining. Jackets required Friday and Saturday. Dressy casual; cocktails; entertainment. Parking: on-site. Cards: AX, DC, MC, VI.

THE OLD SCOTT HOUSE Lunch: $9-$18 Dinner: $20-$50 Phone: 416/296-2222 153
Continental
A
Location: Hwy 401, exit McCowan Rd, just s. 520 Progress Ave M1P 2K2. Hours: 11:30 am-10 pm, Sat-11 pm, Sun 4 pm-10 pm. Closed: 12/26; also for lunch holidays. Reservations: suggested. Features: Continental cuisine complements the elegant ambience you'll find in this restored 1841 farmhouse. The menu spotlights flavourful fare of beef, fish and poultry. The downstairs lounge offers live entertainment Friday and Saturday. A dinner theatre is featured Saturday. Dressy casual; cocktails. Parking: on-site. Cards: AX, DC, MC, VI. Historic

OLIO-A MEDITERRANEAN GRILLE   **Lunch:** $15-$26   **Dinner:** $18-$33   **Phone:** 416/675-6100

Mediterranean

Location: Jct Hwy 27 N and Dixon Rd; in Renaissance Toronto Airport Hotel. 801 Dixon Rd M9W 1J5. **Hours:** 6 am-10 pm. **Reservations:** suggested. **Features:** At the hotel, the dining room offers contemporary decor and a menu of innovative fine Mediterranean cuisine. The lounge's fun tapas menu tempts the taste buds, while the main dining room is where diners can sample such treats as Italian brick chicken, fresh fish, lamb chops and varied tasty pizzas and pasta dishes. Dressy casual; cocktails. **Parking:** on-site. **Cards:** AX, CB, DC, JC, MC, VI.

OUTBACK STEAKHOUSE   **Dinner:** $12-$25   **Phone:** 416/679-2925   (170)

Steak House

Location: Jct Hwy 27 N and Dixon Rd. 801 Dixon Rd M9w 1J5. **Hours:** 4:30 pm-10:30 pm, Fri 11:30 am-11:30 pm, Sat 3 pm-11:30 pm, Sun 4 pm-10 pm. Closed: 12/25. **Features:** Diners enjoy the steak house's consistent menu and fun, casual atmosphere. The location is convenient to the airport and offers the same tasty appetizers, hearty steaks and barbecue entrees for which this chain is well-known. For a change of pace, try sizzling fajitas or a tasty pasta selection. Casual dress; cocktails. **Parking:** on-site. **Cards:** AX, DC, MC, VI.

PAN ON THE DANFORTH   **Dinner:** $13-$22   **Phone:** 416/466-8158   (120)

Greek

Location: Between Carlan and Logan sts; just w of Pape Ave. 516 Danforth Ave M4K 1P6. **Hours:** 5 pm-11 pm, Fri & Sat-midnight. Closed: 12/24, 12/25. **Reservations:** suggested, weekends. **Features:** Choices include mezedakia—a choice of three dips: feta, olive and bulga pilaf—as well as moussaka, braised lamb shank and smoked double pork chops. Casual dress; cocktails. **Parking:** on-site (fee). **Cards:** AX, MC, VI.

PAPPAS GRILL   **Lunch:** $7-$9   **Dinner:** $11-$16   **Phone:** 416/469-9595   (183)

Greek

Location: Between Logan St and Chester Ave; jct Arundel Ave. 440 Danforth Ave M4K 1P4. **Hours:** 11:30 am-11 pm, Fri-1 am, Sat 11 am-1 am, Sun 11 am-11 pm. Closed: 1/1, 12/25. **Reservations:** suggested, weekends. **Features:** In the popular Danforth area, the restaurant presents a fun, expansive menu of mostly Greek fare, such as calamari, salads, kebabs and lamb entrees. Also listed are gourmet pizzas baked over a wood fire and lighter fare, such as pasta and burgers. During summer, patrons can sit on the patio, which recalls a wonderful European ambience. Casual dress; cocktails. **Parking:** street. **Cards:** AX, MC, VI.

THE PICKLE BARREL   **Lunch:** $7-$19   **Dinner:** $7-$19   **Phone:** 416/485-1244   (152)

American

Location: At Eglinton Ave; in Yonge/Eglinton Centre, 2nd floor. 2300 Yonge St M4P 1E4. **Hours:** 9 am-11 pm. Closed: 12/25. **Features:** In a busy shopping mall, the casual eatery serves a wide selection of classic delicatessen fare, such as matzo ball soup, corned beef, pastrami and roast beef sandwiches, as well as tasty pickles. However, the menu doesn't stop there, as it also lists hearty entree salads, delectable finger foods, pasta dishes, steaks and tasty barbecue ribs and chicken. The glass dessert display is sure to tempt patrons to indulge in a decadent finish. Casual dress; cocktails. **Parking:** on-site (fee). **Cards:** AX, DC, MC, VI.

PICKLE BARREL   **Lunch:** $7-$19   **Dinner:** $7-$19   **Phone:** 416/493-4444   (163)

American

Location: Between Finch and Steeles aves. 5941 Leslie St M2H 1J8. **Hours:** 9 am-11 pm, Fri & Sat-midnight. Closed: 12/25. **Features:** The established local favourite prepares consistently good delicatessen fare in a bustling atmosphere accented by bright, modern decor. Sandwiches, shish kebab and barbecue chicken are house favourites. Desserts, especially the cheesecake, are a highlight. Casual dress; cocktails. **Parking:** on-site. **Cards:** AX, DC, JC, MC, VI.

PICKLE BARREL CENTREPOINT   **Lunch:** $7-$11   **Dinner:** $8-$19   **Phone:** 416/226-4444   (151)

American

Location: Corner of Yonge St and Steeles Ave; in Centrepoint Mall. 6508 Yonge St M2M 3X4. **Hours:** 9 am-10 pm. Closed: 12/25. **Reservations:** not accepted. **Features:** In a popular shopping mall, the casual eatery serves a wide selection of classic delicatessen fare, such as matzo ball soup, corned beef, pastrami and roast beef sandwiches, as well as tasty pickles. However, the menu doesn't stop there, as it also lists hearty entree salads, delectable finger foods, pasta dishes, steaks and tasty barbecue ribs and chicken. Save room for a huge ice cream sundae or creamy cheesecake. Casual dress; beer & wine only. **Parking:** on-site. **Cards:** AX, DC, MC, VI.

PICKLE BARREL GRAND   **Lunch:** $8-$12   **Dinner:** $8-$12   **Phone:** 416/785-8881   (191)

American

Location: Jct Hwy 401 and Dufferin St; in Yorkdale Shopping Centre. 1 Yorkdale Rd, Unit 12F M6A 3A1. **Hours:** 9 am-midnight. Closed: 12/25. **Features:** Patrons appreciate the convenient mall location and the modern, bustling atmosphere. On the menu are all the traditional delicatessen favorites, such as steaming matzo ball soup, cabbage rolls and heaping smoked-meat sandwiches. Displays in the dessert case are sure to tempt. Those looking for lighter alternatives might mull over the wonderful salad selection or try a heart-smart offering. Casual dress; cocktails. **Parking:** on-site. **Cards:** AX, DC, MC, VI.

RICHLEE'S   **Lunch:** $12-$17   **Dinner:** $18-$38   **Phone:** 416/483-9818   (184)

Mediterranean

Location: 1 km s of Hwy 401. 1959 Avenue Rd M5M 4A3. **Hours:** 11:30 am-3 & 5-10:30 pm, Sat & Sun from 5 pm. Closed major holidays. **Reservations:** suggested. **Features:** The elegant, upscale dining room is infused with Old World charm. The menu focuses on fine Mediterranean cuisine with a Portuguese influence. Among freshly prepared and beautifully presented seafood dishes are preparations of calamari, mussels and shrimp. The wine list is outstanding. Service is detailed and professional. Dressy casual; cocktails. **Parking:** street. **Cards:** AX, DC, MC, VI.

SAGANO   **Lunch:** $16-$26   **Dinner:** $24-$38   **Phone:** 416/299-0562   (139)

Japanese

Location: Just ne of jct Hwy 401 and Kennedy Rd, exit 379; in Delta Toronto East. 2035 Kennedy Rd M1T 3G2. **Hours:** 11:30 am-2:30 & 5:30-10:30 pm, Sat & Sun from 5:30 pm. Closed: 12/25. **Reservations:** suggested. **Features:** The rooftop restaurant offers a relaxed, yet upscale, atmosphere that borrows heavily from Japanese tradition in both its decor and menu. Full-course meals and a la carte specialties include tempura dishes, kebobs and an extensive selection of sushi varieties. Dressy casual; cocktails. **Parking:** on-site. **Cards:** AX, DC, DS, MC, VI.

SCARAMOUCHE RESTAURANT   Dinner: $26-$44   Phone: 416/961-8011   123
Continental
Location: Jct St. Clair Ave W and Avenue Rd, 0.5 km s on Avenue Rd to Edmund, then just w. 1 Benvenuto Pl M4V 2L1. **Hours:** 5:45 pm-10 pm. Closed major holidays; also Sun. **Reservations:** suggested. **Features:** You'll enjoy creative and upscale dining in a bustling atmosphere with fine views of the city skyline. Lobster bisque is rich and served with thick cream; entrees of beef, veal, seafood and pasta are well-prepared and presented with flair. Dressy casual; cocktails. **Parking:** on-site and valet. **Cards:** AX, DC, MC, VI.

SISTERS EATERY   Lunch: $9-$14   Dinner: $15-$17   Phone: 416/282-8243   130
American
Location: Hwy 401, exit Morningside Dr, 5 km s to Kingston Rd, then directly e. 4 Old Kingston Rd M1E 2P3. **Hours:** noon-2:30 & 5-9 pm, Sat 11 am-2:30 & 4-9 pm, Sun 11 am-2:30 & 4-8 pm. Closed: 12/24, 12/25, 12/26. **Reservations:** suggested. **Features:** The well-established eatery has been attracting hungry diners since 1957 with its extensive buffet and tasty a la carte menu. The cozy country atmosphere and friendly service complement the delicious home-style cooking. Palate-pleasing buffet choices range from soups and many salad fixings to an array of hot items, including beef, pastas, chicken and vegetables. Homemade desserts are good meal-enders. Guests should arrive hungry, as the temptations are endless. Casual dress; cocktails. **Parking:** on-site. **Cards:** AX, DC, MC, VI. ✕

SOUTHERN ACCENT CAJUN, CREOLE & SOUL
RESTAURANT   Dinner: $12-$25   Phone: 416/536-3211   187
Cajun
Location: Jct Bloor and Bathurst sts, just w on Bloor St to Markham St, just s. 595 Markham St M6G 2L7. **Hours:** 5:30 pm-10:30 pm, Fri & Sat-11 pm. Closed major holidays; also Mon. **Reservations:** suggested. **Features:** Exposed brick walls and background blues add to the funky feel of this fun eatery located in a busy shopping district. The menu offers Cajun and Creole cuisine, creatively presented and served by a friendly staff. A street-side patio is open in season. Casual dress; cocktails. **Parking:** street. **Cards:** AX, DC, DS, MC, VI. ✕

SQUARE RESTAURANT   Dinner: $29-$40   Phone: 416/486-0090   159
Continental
Location: Just s of Eglinton Ave. 692 Mt. Pleasant Rd M4S 2N3. **Hours:** 5:30 pm-9:30 pm, Thurs-Sat to 10 pm. Closed major holidays. **Reservations:** suggested. **Features:** Don't forget to phone ahead for reservations or you might be disappointed as Square Restaurant is a popular choice with the local crowd. Guests delight in the loud, bustling atmosphere and enjoy the tight table spacing which suits the style of operation. In addition to the ever-popular steak and frites, the menu also features an innovative selection of fish, poultry and game selections, as well as some tasty and decadent desserts. A gourmet Sunday brunch is also featured. Dressy casual. **Parking:** on-site (fee). **Cards:** AX, DC, MC, VI. ✕

SUMMIT HOUSE GRILL   Lunch: $8-$15   Dinner: $9-$25   Phone: 416/440-0030   186
Continental
Location: E of Yonge St. 40 Eglinton Ave E M4P 3A2. **Hours:** 11:30 am-10 pm, Wed-11 pm, Thurs-Sat to midnight, Sun 10 am-10 pm. Closed: 12/25. **Reservations:** suggested. **Features:** In the uptown area, the restaurant is popular with the business crowd. The setting is casual in the bar/lounge area and more upscale and modern in the main dining room, which has deep leather booths and contemporary lighting. The chef uses fresh regional ingredients to prepare a good mix of innovative fare in addition to some home-style cooking. In the summer months, the streetfront patio is a draw. Casual dress; cocktails. **Parking:** street. **Cards:** AX, DC, MC, VI. ✕

SUSHI-YA JAPAN   Lunch: $9-$15   Dinner: $11-$23   Phone: 416/249-9666   132
Japanese
Location: Between Hwy 27 and Martin Grove Rd. 621 Dixon Rd M9W 1H7. **Hours:** 11:30 am-10:30 pm, Sun from 5 pm. **Features:** On the airport strip and near many hotels, the restaurant offers a wonderful change of pace for both travelers and locals. The small dining room exudes a Japanese ambience, with a peaceful waterfall and interesting decor accents. The skilled chef prepares excellent sushi, sashimi, teriyaki and tempura offerings, including several full-course meals. Casual dress; cocktails. **Parking:** on-site. **Cards:** AX, DC, MC, VI. ✕

THAI MAGIC RESTAURANT   Dinner: $10-$13   Phone: 416/968-7366   190
Thai
Location: Jct MacPherson Ave, 1 km n of Bloor St. 1118 Yonge St M4W 2L6. **Hours:** 5:30 pm-11 pm, Sat from 5 pm. Closed major holidays; also Sun. **Reservations:** suggested, weekends. **Features:** Authentic Thai decor and cuisine complement the bright, bustling dining room. A la carte or full-course meals for the more adventuresome who like to sample are provided with varied levels of spiciness and exotic sauces to suit individual tastes. Cocktails. **Parking:** street. **Cards:** AX, MC, VI. ✕

TRAPPER'S RESTAURANT   Lunch: $10-$15   Dinner: $15-$33   Phone: 416/482-6211   136
Continental
Location: Hwy 401, exit Yonge St, 2.5 km s. 3479 Yonge St M4N 2N3. **Hours:** 11:30 am-2:30 & 5-10 pm, Sat & Sun from 5 pm. Closed: 12/25. **Reservations:** suggested. **Features:** The modern setting nurtures a relaxed yet upscale atmosphere. Innovative North American cuisine reflects a strong Canadian influence. Menu starters include a fabulous carrot and cheddar soup, several creative salads and mussels, any of which can be followed up with a tempting entree of rack of lamb, glazed pork, salmon/trout, seafood or pasta. Guests can choose from an extensive selection of by-the-glass wines, and the dessert array is wonderful. Dressy casual; cocktails. **Parking:** street. **Cards:** AX, DC, MC, VI. ✕

TRATTORIA GIANCARLO   Dinner: $19-$33   Phone: 416/533-9619   192
Italian
Location: Jct College and Clinton sts, just w of Bathurst St; in Little Italy. 41-43 Clinton St M6J 2N9. **Hours:** 6 pm-10:30 pm. Closed major holidays; also Sun. **Reservations:** required. **Features:** Enjoy the relaxed feeling you'll get from this small, cozy dining room with an upscale, modern decor. The menu offers freshly prepared and creatively presented appetizers, pasta, beef, veal and seafood, plus a large wine list. Dine on the patio in season. Dressy casual; cocktails. **Parking:** no self-parking. **Cards:** AX, DC, MC, VI. ✕

VIA ALLEGRO RISTORANTE   Lunch: $15-$44   Dinner: $15-$44   Phone: 416/622-6677   122
Italian
Location: Jct Hwy 427; across from Sherway Gardens. 1750 The Queensway M9C 5H5. **Hours:** 11:30 am-10:30 pm, Fri & Sat-11:30 pm. Closed: 1/1, 4/17, 12/25. **Reservations:** suggested. **Features:** A mix of contemporary Italian and Continental dishes are served in a loud, bustling atmosphere. Take time to look around and spot the oversized wooden pepper shakers, all in working order, and the hand-painted wood-fired pizza ovens. Menu selections—including freshly made pizza, pasta dishes, veal, farm-raised beef and items from the full-course chef's tasting menu—suit every taste. Dessert creations are freshly made. The wine list is outstanding. Casual dress; cocktails. **Parking:** on-site. **Cards:** AX, DC, MC, VI. ✕

ZACHARY'S
Continental

Lunch: $13-$20 **Dinner:** $25-$36 **Phone:** 416/675-9444 〔160〕
Location: 3 km w of jct Hwy 401; in Wyndham Bristol Place-Toronto Airport. 950 Dixon Rd M9W 5N4. **Hours:** noon-2 & 6-10 pm, Sat from 6 pm, Sun 11 am-2 pm. Closed major holidays. **Reservations:** required. **Features:** The popular fine-dining restaurant exudes a European style. Memorable menu items are prepared in an imaginative way that's visually unforgettable. Although guests are encouraged to leave the calorie counter at home, there are lighter, healthier choices for those who can resist the urge to splurge. The staff is attentive. Semi-formal attire; cocktails. **Parking:** on-site. **Cards:** AX, DC, DS, JC, MC, VI. 🗙

ZUCCA TRATTORIA
Italian

Dinner: $12-$26 **Phone:** 416/488-5774 〔165〕
Location: Just s of Eglinton Ave. 2150 Yonge St M5S 2A8. **Hours:** 5:30 pm-10 pm. Closed major holidays. **Reservations:** suggested. **Features:** A bustling, modern dining room with a comfortable ambience and an innovative northern Italian menu keep locals coming back to this nice spot in the popular Yonge/Eglinton area of the city. Diners enjoy starters such as seared scallops, followed by a selection of freshly made pasta, veal, poultry and seafood dishes. The focus is on regional ingredients, and plate presentations are artistic and detailed. Dressy casual; cocktails. **Parking:** street. **Cards:** AX, DC, MC, VI. 🗙

The Toronto Vicinity

MARKHAM pop. 208,165 (See map and index starting on p. 479)

———— WHERE TO STAY ————

COMFORT INN
Small-scale Hotel

Book at aaa.com **Phone:** (905)477-6077 〔115〕
All Year 1P: $108-$118 2P: $118-$128 XP: $5 F18
Location: Hwy 401, exit 375, 9 km n; Hwy 404, exit Hwy 7, just e, then s. 8330 Woodbine Ave L3R 2N8. Fax: 905/477-9664. **Facility:** 140 one-bedroom standard units, some with whirlpools. 2 stories (no elevator), interior corridors. **Parking:** on-site, winter plug-ins. **Terms:** cancellation fee imposed, weekly rates available, package plans, 3% service charge, pets ($15 extra charge). **Amenities:** video games (fee), voice mail, irons, hair dryers. Some: high-speed Internet (fee), dual phone lines. **Pool(s):** heated indoor, wading. **Leisure Activities:** steamroom, exercise room. **Guest Services:** valet and coin laundry. **Business Services:** meeting rooms. **Cards:** AX, CB, DC, DS, JC, MC, VI. **Special Amenities:** free local telephone calls and early check-in/late check-out. *(See color ad below)*

SOME UNITS

🆂 🐾 ▯➜ 🐟 📺 DATA PORT 💻 / 🗙 🔌 📠 /
FEE

COURTYARD BY MARRIOTT
Small-scale Hotel

Book at aaa.com **Phone:** (905)707-6533 〔110〕
5/1-9/30 1P: $149-$169 2P: $149-$169
10/1-4/30 1P: $139-$169 2P: $139-$169
Location: Hwy 7 and Leslie St. 65 Minthorn Blvd L3T 7N5. Fax: 905/707-6955. **Facility:** 144 units. 141 one-bedroom standard units, some with whirlpools. 3 one-bedroom suites ($169). 6 stories, interior corridors. **Bath:** combo or shower only. **Parking:** on-site. **Terms:** 15% service charge. **Amenities:** video games (fee), high-speed Internet, dual phone lines, voice mail, irons, hair dryers. **Pool(s):** heated indoor. **Leisure Activities:** whirlpool, exercise room. **Guest Services:** sundries, valet and coin laundry. **Business Services:** meeting rooms, business center. **Cards:** AX, DC, DS, MC, VI.

SOME UNITS

ASK 🆂 ▯▯ 🍽 🆖 🖾 🐟 📺 DATA PORT 💻 / 🗙 🔌 📠 /

HILTON GARDEN INN TORONTO/MARKHAM
Small-scale Hotel

Book at aaa.com **Phone:** (905)709-8008 〔111〕
All Year 1P: $132 2P: $132 XP: $20 F16
Location: Hwy 404, exit Hwy 7, 0.5 km w. 300 Commerce Valley Dr E L3T 7X3. Fax: 905/709-6008. **Facility:** 145 units. 140 one-bedroom standard units. 5 one-bedroom suites ($231). 6 stories, interior corridors. **Bath:** combo or shower only. **Parking:** on-site. **Amenities:** video games, high-speed Internet, dual phone lines, voice mail, safes, irons, hair dryers. **Pool(s):** heated indoor. **Leisure Activities:** whirlpool, exercise room. **Guest Services:** sundries. **Business Services:** meeting rooms, business center. **Cards:** AX, DC, JC, MC, VI.

SOME UNITS

ASK 🆂 ▯▯ 🍽 🆖 🖾 🐟 📺 DATA PORT 🔌 📠 💻 / 🗙 /

"The COMFORT you NEED at the PRICE you WANT!"

• Continental Breakfast Available • Complimentary In-room Coffee/Tea
• In-room Movies & Nintendo • Guest Laundry Facilities
• Free Hi Speed Internet • Free Parking & Local Calls

Indoor Pool • Hot Tub • Steam Room • Fitness Centre

8330 Woodbine Ave., Markham, Ontario, L3R 2N8
Phone: 905-477-6077 Fax: 905-477-9664
Call Toll Free 1-800-228-5150
Website: www.comfortinnmarkham.com
Email: comfort@comfortinnmarkham.com

Comfort INN
BY CHOICE HOTELS
(See Listing under Markham)

MARKHAM
Greater Toronto

20 Minutes to Central Toronto, Metro Toronto Zoo
or Canada's Wonderland

GOLD AWARD
CHOICE HOTELS
HOSPITALITY

(See map and index starting on p. 479)

HILTON SUITES TORONTO/MARKHAM
CONFERENCE CENTRE & SPA   *Book at aaa.com*   **Phone:** (905)470-8500   116

 All Year   1P: $115-$180   2P: $115-$180   XP: $20   F17

Location: Hwy 404, exit Hwy 7, 2.4 km e. 8500 Warden Ave L6G 1A5. Fax: 905/477-8611. **Facility:** Distinctive architecture, fully equipped conference facilities, an on-site health club and a full spa enhance these well-appointed suites. 500 one-bedroom suites, some with whirlpools. 4-10 stories, interior corridors. **Parking:** Large-scale Hotel on-site. **Terms:** check-in 4 pm, cancellation fee imposed, package plans. **Amenities:** voice mail, irons, hair dryers. *Fee:* video games, high-speed Internet. *Some:* dual phone lines, honor bars. **Dining:** 3 restaurants, 6:30 am-11 pm, cocktails, also, Essence of Unionville Restaurant, Mino's Japanese Restaurant, see separate listings, entertainment. **Pool(s):** heated indoor. **Leisure Activities:** saunas, whirlpool, steamrooms, spa. *Fee:* squash, aerobic instruction. **Guest Services:** gift shop, valet and coin laundry, area transportation-within 5 km. **Business Services:** conference facilities, business center. **Cards:** AX, CB, DC, JC, MC, VI. *(See color ad below)*

SOME UNITS

TAKE ME TO A

GREAT GETAWAY.

TAKE ME TO THE HILTON.

An all-suite hotel with the luxury and service that Hilton is famous for. Located in Northeast Toronto, close to Canada's Wonderland, The Zoo, Science Center and historic Unionville. Facilities include Holtz the Spa—a world class facility; Club Markham—a state of the art health club, an indoor pool and award-winning cuisine. Just make advance reservations with a call to Hilton's dedicated AAA number, at **1-800-916-2221**, or your local AAA travel office. Visit us online at **www.torontomarkham.hilton.com**.

8500 Warden Avenue
Markham, ON CA L6G1A5
905-470-8500 • 1-800-668-8800

Hilton HHonors

Hilton Suites
Toronto/Markham
Conference Centre & Spa

Valid AAA membership card required for reservation and at check-in. Hilton HHonors® membership, earning of Points & Miles® and redemption of points are subject to HHonors Terms and Conditions. ©2005 Hilton Hospitality, Inc.

555 Cochrane Drive,
Markham, Ontario L3R 8E3
www.hojomarkham.com

 *Howard Johnson*
HOTEL
TORONTO-MARKHAM

Tel: 905-479-5000
Fax: 905-479-1186
Hotel Direct Reservations
Toll-Free: 1-877-703-4656

GOLD MEDAL

triprewards

• **Large** Indoor Pool, Sauna,
Whirlpool & Fitness Centre

• **20 minutes** from downtown
Toronto, Toronto Zoo, Science
Centre & Canada's Wonderland

• **Free Parking** & Local phone
calls • Kids stay FREE program**

• In-room coffee, hairdryer,
iron & board

• On-site family restaurant &
lounge • Business Centre

FROM
$89⁰⁰
TO
$109⁰⁰* CAD

*Rates are per night + applicable taxes, for 2 Double Beds, Double Occupancy.
Subject to room availability.
**Kids under 17 stay free in parents room with existing bedding.

(See map and index starting on p. 479)

HOLIDAY INN HOTEL & SUITES TORONTO-MARKHAM
Book at aaa.com

Phone: (905)474-0444 **120**

CAA SAVE

5/1-8/31	1P: $119-$159	2P: $129-$169	XP: $15	F18
9/1-4/30	1P: $109-$149	2P: $119-$159	XP: $15	F18

Location: Just n of Steeles Ave. 7095 Woodbine Ave L3R 1A3. Fax: 905/474-1877. **Facility:** 299 units. 264 one-bedroom standard units. 35 one-bedroom suites, some with whirlpools. 13 stories, interior corridors. **Large-scale Hotel Parking:** on-site (fee). **Terms:** package plans, pets ($20 fee). **Amenities:** video games (fee), high-speed Internet, dual phone lines, voice mail, irons, hair dryers. **Dining:** 6:30 am-10 pm, Sat & Sun from 7 am, cocktails. **Pool(s):** heated indoor. **Leisure Activities:** sauna, whirlpool, exercise room. **Guest Services:** gift shop, valet and coin laundry, area transportation-within 5 km. **Business Services:** conference facilities, fax. **Cards:** AX, DC, DS, MC, VI. *(See color ad p 530 & card insert)*

SOME UNITS

HOWARD JOHNSON HOTEL TORONTO-MARKHAM
Book at aaa.com

Phone: (905)479-5000 **118**

5/1-9/30	1P: $89-$149	2P: $99-$159	XP: $10	F17
10/1-4/30	1P: $79-$149	2P: $89-$159	XP: $10	F17

Small-scale Hotel Location: Hwy 404 N, exit Hwy 7E to E Valhalla Dr. 555 Cochrane Dr L3R 8E3. Fax: 905/479-1186. **Facility:** 172 one-bedroom standard units. 3 stories, interior corridors. **Parking:** on-site, winter plug-ins. **Terms:** weekly rates available, [BP] meal plan available, package plans, small pets only ($20 deposit). **Amenities:** video games (fee), voice mail, irons, hair dryers. *Some:* high-speed Internet. **Pool(s):** heated indoor. **Leisure Activities:** sauna, whirlpool, exercise room. **Guest Services:** valet and coin laundry. **Business Services:** meeting rooms, business center. **Cards:** AX, DC, DS, MC, VI. *(See color ad p 549)*

SOME UNITS

MONTE CARLO INN TORONTO-MARKHAM
Book at aaa.com

Phone: (905)513-8100 **117**

CAA SAVE

All Year [ECP]	1P: $89-$119	2P: $99-$129	XP: $10	F12

Location: 0.5 km n of Hwy 7. 8900 Woodbine Ave L3R 5K6. Fax: 905/513-9100. **Facility:** 83 units. 80 one-bedroom standard units, some with whirlpools. 3 one-bedroom suites ($129-$199) with whirlpools. 4 stories, interior corridors. **Parking:** on-site. **Terms:** weekly rates available, package plans. **Small-scale Hotel Amenities:** high-speed Internet, dual phone lines, voice mail, irons, hair dryers. **Dining:** 6 am-11 pm. **Leisure Activities:** exercise room. **Guest Services:** valet laundry. **Business Services:** meeting rooms, business center. **Cards:** AX, CB, DC, DS, JC, MC, VI. **Special Amenities:** free expanded continental breakfast and free local telephone calls. *(See color ad p 531)*

SOME UNITS

Everything
Travel

Dreams Become Reality With AAA/CAA Travel

EXPLORE THE MOUNTAINS, THE DESERTS, AND THE CITIES - ANYWHERE, ANYTIME -
WITH AAA/CAA, A TRUSTED NAME IN TRAVEL FOR 100 YEARS.
LET AAA/CAA TRAVEL TAKE CARE OF ALL YOUR TRAVEL NEEDS.
TO RECEIVE EXCLUSIVE AAA/CAA MEMBER BENEFITS, CALL OR VISIT YOUR
NEAREST AAA/CAA TRAVEL OFFICE, OR CLICK ON www.aaa.com TODAY.

AAA Travel CAA

Travel With Someone You Trust.
www.aaa.com

(See map and index starting on p. 479)

RADISSON HOTEL TORONTO-MARKHAM — *Book at aaa.com* — Phone: (905)477-2010 ◆119
(CAA) (SAVE)   All Year [BP]   1P: $119-$149   2P: $119-$149   XP: $15   F17
▼▼▼▼   **Location:** Hwy 404, exit Hwy 7, then e. Located in a commercial area. 50 E Valhalla Dr L3R 0A3. Fax: 905/477-2026.
Facility: 204 units. 178 one-bedroom standard units. 26 one-bedroom suites ($144-$174), some with
whirlpools. 15 stories, interior corridors. **Parking:** on-site. **Terms:** 3% service charge, small pets only ($25
Large-scale Hotel fee). **Amenities:** video games (fee), high-speed Internet, dual phone lines, voice mail, irons, hair dryers.
Some: CD players, honor bars. **Dining:** Tivoli Garden Restaurant, see separate listing. **Pool(s):** heated
indoor. **Leisure Activities:** sauna, whirlpool, exercise room. **Guest Services:** gift shop, valet laundry, area transportation-within
5 km. **Business Services:** conference facilities. **Cards:** AX, CB, DC, DS, JC, MC, VI. **Special Amenities:** free local telephone
calls and free newspaper. *(See color ad p 521)*
SOME UNITS
🅂🄳 🛏 🍴 🍽 🛋 🏊 ⊠ 📷 DATA🔌 🔌 💻 /⊠ 📠/
FEE

RESIDENCE INN BY MARRIOTT — *Book at aaa.com* — Phone: (905)707-7933 ◆112
▼▼▼▼   5/1-9/30   1P: $169-$229   2P: $169-$229
10/1-4/30   1P: $149-$209   2P: $149-$209
Small-scale Hotel **Location:** Directly s of jct Hwy 7 and Leslie St. 55 Minthorn Blvd L3T 7N5. Fax: 905/707-8044. **Facility:** 100 units.
58 one-bedroom standard units, some with efficiencies or kitchens. 24 one- and 18 two-bedroom suites,
some with efficiencies or kitchens. 5 stories, interior corridors. *Bath:* combo or shower only. **Parking:** on-site. **Terms:** 15%
service charge, pets ($8 extra charge). **Amenities:** video games (fee), high-speed Internet, dual phone lines, voice mail, irons,
hair dryers. **Pool(s):** heated indoor. **Leisure Activities:** exercise room, sports court. **Guest Services:** valet and coin laundry.
Business Services: meeting rooms. **Cards:** AX, DC, DS, MC, VI.
SOME UNITS
(ASK) 🅂🄳 🛏 🛋 🏊 📷 DATA🔌 🔌 💻 /⊠/
FEE

STAYBRIDGE SUITES TORONTO-MARKHAM — *Book at aaa.com* — Phone: (905)771-9333 ◆114
▼▼▼▼   All Year [ECP]   1P: $139-$209   2P: $139-$209
Small-scale Hotel **Location:** Jct Hwy 404 and 7, w on Hwy 7, then e. 355 S Park Rd L3T 7W2. Fax: 905/771-9336. **Facility:** 120
units. 59 one-bedroom standard units. 38 one- and 23 two-bedroom suites. 4 stories, interior corridors.
Bath: combo or shower only. **Parking:** on-site. **Terms:** 6 day cancellation notice, pets ($75 fee).
Amenities: dual phone lines, voice mail, irons, hair dryers. *Fee:* video games, high-speed Internet. **Pool(s):** heated indoor.
Leisure Activities: exercise room. **Guest Services:** sundries, valet and coin laundry. **Business Services:** meeting rooms,
business center. **Cards:** AX, CB, DC, DS, MC, VI.
SOME UNITS
(ASK) 🅂🄳 🛏 🛋 🏊 📷 DATA🔌 🔌 💻 /⊠/
FEE

——— **WHERE TO DINE** ———

AL DENTE RISTORANTE ITALIANO — Lunch: $9-$15   Dinner: $14-$25   Phone: 905/471-5670 ◆209
▼▼▼   **Location:** Just n of Hwy 7. 39 Main St L3P 1X3. **Hours:** 11:30 am-2:30 & 5:30-10 pm, Sat & Sun from 5:30 pm.
Closed major holidays. **Reservations:** suggested, weekends. **Features:** A perfect spot for special occasion
Italian   dining, the modern, upscale dining room is built around a semi-open-kitchen concept. In the summer
months, diners can take advantage of the outdoor patio. The highlight here is the good menu selection,
featuring starters such as steamed mussels, bruschetta and escargot, and main courses prepared with made-to-order pasta, as
well as veal, poultry and seafood. Dressy casual; cocktails. **Parking:** on-site. **Cards:** AX, DC, MC, VI.
⊠

**ESSENCE OF UNIONVILLE
RESTAURANT** — Lunch: $10-$29   Dinner: $12-$33   Phone: 905/470-8500 ◆207
(CAA)   **Location:** Hwy 404, exit Hwy 7, 2.4 km e; in Hilton Suites Toronto/Markham Conference Centre & Spa. 8500 Warden
▼▼▼   Ave L6G 1A5. **Hours:** 6:30 am-11 pm, Sat & Sun from 7 am. **Reservations:** suggested. **Features:** The
restaurant provides an ideal setting for informal dining, a business meeting or a special occasion repast.
Canadian   Among offerings are finger foods, full meals and an upscale weekday lunch buffet. The cuisine eclectically
blends International influences, which is why diners find items such as a Montreal smoked meat sandwich,
pasta jambalaya, tandoori chicken, tuna nicoise and smoked baby ribs. There is also a wonderful
assortment of fresh bakery items. Casual dress; cocktails. **Parking:** on-site. **Cards:** AX, CB, DC, MC, VI.
🅂Ⓜ 🍽 ⊠

FIRE AND ICE — Lunch: $8-$17   Dinner: $8-$17   Phone: 905/947-1900 ◆206
▼▼ ▼▼   **Location:** Directly w of Woodbine Ave on Hwy 7 and Cochrane Dr. 25 Cochrane Dr L3R 9S1. **Hours:** 11:30 am-10
pm, Fri-11 pm, Sat noon-11 pm, Sun noon-9:30 pm. Closed: 12/25. **Reservations:** suggested.
Asian   **Features:** Diners enjoy a memorable experience as they select a made-to-order stir-fry meal. After choosing
from such proteins as steak, chicken and shrimp, guests visit the self-service vegetable bar to select
veggies and sauce. The chef then cooks the healthy meal to order. Entrees include the salad bar and ice cream for dessert.
This place is a great choice for wholesome food in a bustling atmosphere. Casual dress; cocktails. **Parking:** on-site. **Cards:** AX,
MC, VI.
🍽 ⊠

**FRANKIE TOMATTO'S ALL YOU CAN EAT ITALIAN
FEAST** — Lunch: $9-$13   Dinner: $13-$17   Phone: 905/940-1900 ◆203
▼▼ ▼▼   **Location:** Just n of Steeles Ave. 7225 Woodbine Ave L3R 1A3. **Hours:** 11:30 am-2:30 & 5-10 pm, Sat noon-2:30
& 4-11 pm, Sun 11:30 am-2:30 & 4-9:30 pm. Closed: for lunch holidays. **Reservations:** accepted.
Italian   **Features:** An extensive 14-station buffet awaits diners at the fun, casual spot, which is suited to family and
group dining. Food is sure to please all taste buds. Choices include antipasto, fresh fruit, barbecue items,
baked goods, pizza, pasta, soups, salads, seafood, rotisserie meats and carved selections. For the perfect ending, browse the
spumoni and gelato bar, as well as the pastry table. Casual dress. **Parking:** on-site. **Cards:** AX, MC, VI.
⊠

LE BIFTHEQUE — Lunch: $8-$30   Dinner: $10-$30   Phone: 905/305-1808 ◆204
▼▼ ▼▼   **Location:** Just w of Steeles Ave. 7501 Woodbine Ave L3R 2W1. **Hours:** 11:30 am-10 pm, Fri-11 pm, Sat noon-11
pm, Sun noon-10 pm. Closed: 12/25. **Features:** The restaurant satisfies the cravings of folks in the mood
Steak House   for a sizzling steak. Huge portions of traditional steak house fare—including fine steaks, prime rib and
seafood selections—keep locals coming back. Among starters are shrimp cocktail, French onion soup and
escargot. Meals come with a tasty house salad and the ever-popular Biftheque croutons. Diners should arrive with a hearty
appetite. Casual dress; cocktails. **Parking:** on-site. **Cards:** AX, MC, VI.
🍽 ⊠

(See map and index starting on p. 479)

MINO'S JAPANESE RESTAURANT   **Lunch:** $8-$19   **Dinner:** $10-$25   **Phone:** 905/470-8800   (202)
Location: Hwy 404, exit Hwy 7, 2.4 km e; in Hilton Suites Toronto/Markham Conference Centre &. 8500 Warden Ave
LG6 1A5. **Hours:** 11 am-2 & 5:30-11 pm, Sun from 5:30 pm. **Reservations:** suggested. **Features:** The
delightful restaurant features an authentic Japanese decor and menu. The skilled chef prepares a wide
Japanese   range of sushi, sashimi, teriyaki and tempura offerings, as well as hot pot specialties. Green tea ice cream is
the perfect finish. Dressy casual; cocktails. **Parking:** on-site. **Cards:** AX, CB, DC, MC, VI.   X

PETER'S FINE DINING   **Dinner:** $22-$60   **Phone:** 905/294-9039   (205)
Location: Hwy 7, 1 km w of Hwy 48 (Markham Rd). 5701 Hwy 7 L3P 1B1. **Hours:** 5 pm-11 pm. Closed major
holidays; also Sun. **Reservations:** suggested. **Features:** You'll discover good food in a relaxed yet elegant
Steak & Seafood atmosphere where generous portions of steak and seafood are served by a professional wait staff.
Appetizers include shrimp cocktail, French onion soup, fresh Caesar salad and a complimentary relish tray.
Dressy casual; cocktails. **Parking:** on-site. **Cards:** AX, DC, MC, VI.   X

TIVOLI GARDEN RESTAURANT   **Lunch:** $8-$17   **Dinner:** $13-$25   **Phone:** 905/305-5493   (208)
Location: Hwy 404, exit Hwy 7, just e; in Radisson Hotel Toronto-Markham. 50 E Valhalla Dr L3R 0A3. **Hours:** 6:30
am-2 & 5-10 pm, Sat & Sun from 7 am. **Reservations:** suggested. **Features:** A Scandinavian design lends
Continental   character to the cozy, relaxed restaurant. Large windows draw in natural light and offer great views into the
attractive centre courtyard garden. The menu, which centres on fine Continental cuisine, also includes such
lighter selections as burgers, sandwiches and salads. The carving buffet and made-to-order pasta nights draw crowds from
Thursday through Saturday. Casual dress; cocktails. **Parking:** on-site. **Cards:** AX, MC, VI.   Y X

RICHMOND HILL pop. 132,030   (See map and index starting on p. 479)

------- **WHERE TO STAY** -------

BEST WESTERN PARKWAY HOTEL TORONTO
NORTH *Book at aaa.com*   **Phone:** (905)881-2600   (107)
(CAA) (SAVE)   11/1-12/31   1P: $105-$139   2P: $105-$139   XP: $15   F17
5/1-8/31   1P: $105-$109   2P: $105-$109   XP: $15   F17
9/1-10/31 & 1/1-4/30   1P: $109   2P: $109   XP: $15   F17
Location: Jct Hwy 401 and Don Valley Pkwy, exit 375 via Don Valley Pkwy (Hwy 404), 8 km n to jct Hwy 7, then 1 km
Small-scale Hotel w. Located in a commercial area. 600 Hwy 7 E L4B 1B2. Fax: 905/882-7841. **Facility:** 129 one-bedroom standard
units. 3 stories (no elevator), interior corridors. **Parking:** on-site. **Terms:** cancellation fee imposed, [BP] &
[CP] meal plans available, package plans, 3% service charge, small pets only. **Amenities:** video games (fee), high-speed
Internet, voice mail, irons, hair dryers. **Pool(s):** heated outdoor, 2 heated indoor. **Leisure Activities:** sauna, whirlpools,
steamrooms, lighted tennis court, basketball. **Fee:** 5 squash courts, game room. **Guest Services:** gift shop, valet laundry.
Business Services: conference facilities. **Cards:** AX, DC, MC, VI. *(See color ad p 537)*   SOME UNITS

SHERATON PARKWAY TORONTO NORTH HOTEL,
SUITES & CONFERENCE CENTRE *Book at aaa.com*   **Phone:** (905)881-2121   (108)
(CAA) (SAVE)   5/1-10/31   1P: $132-$152   2P: $132-$152   XP: $15   F17
11/1-12/31   1P: $129-$149   2P: $129-$149   XP: $15   F17
1/1-4/30   1P: $135   2P: $135   XP: $15   F17
Location: Jct Hwy 401 and Don Valley Pkwy, exit 375 via Don Valley Pkwy (Hwy 404), 8 km n to jct Hwy 7, then 1 km
Large-scale Hotel w. Adjoins a shopping mall. 600 Hwy 7 E L4B 1B2. Fax: 905/882-3100. **Facility:** The upscale hotel features
comfortable meeting facilities and an extensive fitness area among its luxuries. 311 units. 226 one-bedroom
standard units, some with whirlpools. 85 one-bedroom suites. 7-10 stories, interior corridors. **Parking:** on-site.
Terms: cancellation fee imposed, [BP] & [CP] meal plans available, package plans. **Amenities:** video games (fee), high-speed
Internet, dual phone lines, voice mail, irons, hair dryers. *Some:* fax. **Dining:** 2 restaurants, 6 am-11 pm, cocktails. **Pool(s):**
heated outdoor, 2 heated indoor. **Leisure Activities:** sauna, whirlpools, steamrooms, lighted tennis court, basketball. **Fee:** 5
squash courts, game room. **Guest Services:** gift shop, valet laundry, area transportation-within 5 km. **Business Services:**
conference facilities, business center. **Cards:** AX, DC, MC, VI. **Special Amenities:** free newspaper.
(See color ad p 537 & p 5)   SOME UNITS

------- **WHERE TO DINE** -------

GALAXIE DINER   **Lunch:** $6-$13   **Dinner:** $6-$13   **Phone:** 905/884-5577   (200)
Location: Jct Elgin Mills. 10737 Yonge St L4C 9M9. **Hours:** 7 am-10 pm, Sun from 8 am. Closed: 12/25.
Reservations: accepted. **Features:** Guests can drift back to the nifty 50s in the diner with old-style booths
and nostalgic memorabilia. Home-style food includes all-day breakfast items, tasty burgers, hot dogs, pot
American   roast and meatloaf. This true flash from the past offers good-value meals. Casual dress. **Parking:** on-site.
Cards: AX, MC, VI.   X

IL PIATTO VECCHIO   **Lunch:** $12-$18   **Dinner:** $12-$32   **Phone:** 905/884-8091   (201)
Location: Jct Rutherford Rd. 9301 Bathurst St L4C 9S2. **Hours:** noon-3 & 5:30-10 pm, Sat from 5:30 pm, Mon-3
pm. Closed: 1/1, 12/25; also Sun. **Reservations:** suggested. **Features:** In a small strip plaza in a residential
Italian   area, the restaurant employs a warm, hospitable staff in an upscale yet relaxed setting. Menu highlights
include a wide selection of homemade pasta, veal, seafood and poultry offerings. Save room for a decadent
dessert. Casual dress; cocktails. **Parking:** on-site. **Cards:** AX, DC, MC, VI.   X

(See map and index starting on p. 479)

THE KEG STEAKHOUSE AND BAR   Lunch: $8-$16   Dinner: $16-$30   Phone: 905/882-0500   (198)
▽▽ ▽▽   **Location:** Jct Hwy 7. 135 York Blvd L4B 3B4. **Hours:** 11:30 am-2:30 & 5-11 pm, Fri & Sat from 4 pm, Sun 4 pm-
                    10 pm. **Closed:** 12/25. **Features:** Well-known for its mesquite-grilled steaks and fun, laid-back atmosphere,
Steak House   this steak house is a longtime favourite with the local crowd. In addition to great beef, the traditional menu
                    features seafood, grilled chicken, hickory ribs and pasta offerings. All meals come with a hot loaf of
sourdough bread. Try a specialty coffee or some tasty cheesecake for the perfect ending. Casual dress; cocktails. **Parking:** on-
site. **Cards:** AX, DC, MC, VI.

MING'S MALAYSIAN CHINESE CUISINE   Lunch: $7-$23   Dinner: $7-$23   Phone: 905/883-3123   (199)
▽▽ ▽▽   **Location:** Just n of Elgin Mills; at Upper Yonge Place Plaza. 10909 Yonge St, Unit 16, Upper Yonge Pl L4C 3E3.
                    Hours: noon-10 pm, Fri & Sat-11 pm. **Closed:** Mon. **Reservations:** suggested. **Features:** Diners enjoy the
Chinese   relaxed setting and warm, personable service, as well as the wide variety of freshly prepared Malaysian
                    cuisine. Among offerings are a good choice of tasty appetizers, such as satay, spicy soups, and rice, noodle
and curry specialties. The menu is perfect for sampling new dishes and sharing with friends and family. This place is known for
its exotic bubble tea menu—something distinctive to enhance the dining experience. Casual dress; beer only. **Parking:** on-site.
Cards: MC, VI.

SAIGON STAR   Lunch: $5-$10   Dinner: $10-$20   Phone: 905/731-7221   (197)
▽▽ ▽▽   **Location:** 0.5 km e of Bayview. 330 Hwy 7 E, Unit 113 L4B 3P8. **Hours:** 11 am-11 pm. **Features:** Freshly
                    prepared noodles, rice, lots of steamed vegetables and Vietnamese combination platters with soup and
Vietnamese   spring rolls are great menu finds at Saigon Star. The atmosphere is relaxed with intimate seating, and the
                    service is prompt and attentive. Casual dress; cocktails. **Parking:** on-site. **Cards:** AX, MC, VI.

SPEZZO   Lunch: $10-$33   Dinner: $12-$33   Phone: 905/886-9703   (196)
▽▽▽▽▽   **Location:** Jct E Beaver Creek and Hwy 7. 140 York Blvd L4B 1J8. **Hours:** 11 am-10 pm, Fri-11 pm, Sat 5 pm-11
                    pm. **Closed** major holidays; also Sun. **Reservations:** suggested. **Features:** Tucked in a busy commercial
Italian   area, the bustling restaurant appeals to professionals and locals. Representative of the upscale menu are
                    such choices as smoked salmon appetizers, freshly prepared pasta dishes, grilled meat and fish. The chef
also prepares a selection of innovative daily specials. The dessert menu lists a sweet-tooth version of spaghetti and meatballs
that shouldn't be missed. Dressy casual; cocktails. **Parking:** on-site. **Cards:** AX, DC, MC, VI.

THORNHILL

—— **WHERE TO DINE** ——

BATON ROUGE RESTAURANT   Lunch: $9-$18   Dinner: $9-$29   Phone: 905/764-6959
▽▽▽ ▽▽▽   **Location:** Just s of Hwy 7. 230 Commerce Court Valley Dr E L3T 7Y3. **Hours:** 11 am-10 pm, Tues-Thurs to 11 pm,
                    Fri & Sat-midnight. **Closed:** 12/25. **Reservations:** suggested. **Features:** The local favorite spices up tasty
Steak House   ribs, chicken and steaks with homemade sauces. Among lighter options are entree salads, sandwiches and
                    burgers. The cozy decor incorporates leather booths and polished wood tables that lend to a warm,
comfortable atmosphere. In a busy commercial area, this place is convenient to many office and hotel complexes. Casual dress;
cocktails. **Parking:** on-site. **Cards:** AX, MC, VI.

TERRA RESTAURANT   Lunch: $16-$30   Dinner: $18-$50   Phone: 905/731-6161
▽▽▽ ▽▽▽   **Location:** Directly s of Hwy 407 at Kirk. 8199 Yonge St L3T 2C6. **Hours:** 11:30 am-2:30 & 6-10 pm, Thurs & Fri-11
                    pm, Sat 6 pm-11 pm, Sun 11 am-2:30 & 6-10 pm. **Closed** major holidays. **Reservations:** suggested.
International   **Features:** A modern sleek decor, a sophisticated and bustling atmosphere, professional wait staff and a
                    highly innovative menu satisfy diners at Terra. The chef dazzles guests with a daily changing menu
emphasizing fresh specialty ingredients and complemented by an extensive selection of wines by the full and half bottle. For the
adventuresome diner, the chef's tasting menu with an optional wine pariing is sure to please. Semi-formal attire; cocktails.
Parking: on-site. **Cards:** AX, DC, DS, MC, VI.

UNIONVILLE

—— **WHERE TO DINE** ——

LIVINGWATER RESTAURANT & CAKE GALLERY   Lunch: $8-$12   Dinner: $13-$20   Phone: 905/479-8310
▽▽▽ ▽▽▽   **Location:** 0.5 km n of Hwy 7; in Unionville Planning Mill. 139 Main St L3R 2G6. **Hours:** 11 am-9 pm, Fri-10 pm, Sat
                    & Sun 10 am-10 pm. **Closed:** 12/25. **Reservations:** suggested. **Features:** Choose from an array of house
Continental   specialties including beef Wellington, chicken Marsala, salmon and Key West pasta and a large selection of
                    homemade desserts. Creativity is quite evident in the colourful presentation of all of Livingwater's tasty
dishes. Casual dress; beer & wine only. **Parking:** on-site. **Cards:** AX, MC, VI.

OLD COUNTRY INN   Lunch: $10-$11   Dinner: $14-$20   Phone: 905/477-2715
▽▽▽ ▽▽▽   **Location:** 198 Main St L3R 2G9. **Hours:** noon-10 pm, Sun-9 pm. **Closed:** 12/25. **Reservations:** suggested,
                    weekends. **Features:** This Viennese restaurant is located in a century-old country home in a quaint village.
Austrian   Menu highlights include specialties such as goulash soup, herring or smoked trout to start, with an extensive
                    main course schnitzel selection. The Black Forest cake is a popular favorite for dessert. Casual dress;
cocktails. **Parking:** on-site. **Cards:** AX, DC, MC, VI. **Historic**

VAUGHAN (See map and index starting on p. 479)

──── WHERE TO STAY ────

COURTYARD BY MARRIOTT VAUGHAN *Book at aaa.com* **Phone:** (905)660-9938 [170]

▼▼▼▼▼ All Year 1P: $119-$165

Small-scale Hotel **Location:** Hwy 7 at Jane; Hwy 400, exit Hwy 7, then e. 150 Interchange Way L4K 5P7. Fax: 905/660-3988. **Facility:** 144 units. 141 one-bedroom standard units, some with whirlpools. 3 one-bedroom suites ($175-$195). 6 stories, interior corridors. *Bath:* combo or shower only. **Parking:** on-site. **Terms:** weekly rates available, [BP] & [CP] meal plans available, package plans. **Amenities:** video games (fee), high-speed Internet, dual phone lines, voice mail, irons, hair dryers. **Pool(s):** heated indoor. **Leisure Activities:** whirlpool, exercise room. **Guest Services:** sundries, valet and coin laundry. **Business Services:** meeting rooms, business center. **Cards:** AX, DC, MC, VI.

SOME UNITS

(ASK) (S⊘) (†1) (Y) (&M) (&) (≈) (⚙) (DATA PORT) (▣) / (✕) (🔒) (🖼) /

Ontario Legislative Buildings / © 2004 Ontario Tourism

This ends listings for the Toronto Vicinity.
The following page resumes the alphabetical listings of cities in Ontario.

TRENTON pop. 17,200

WHERE TO STAY

COMFORT INN **Book at aaa.com**   Phone: (613)965-6660

(CAA) (SAVE)

7/1-9/30	1P: $109-$129	2P: $119-$139	XP: $10 F16
5/1-6/30	1P: $99-$119	2P: $109-$129	XP: $10 F16
10/1-4/30	1P: $89-$109	2P: $99-$119	XP: $10 F16

Location: Hwy 401, exit 526 (Glen Miller Rd S). Located in a commercial area. 68 Monogram Pl K8V 6S3 (PO Box 22067). Fax: 613/965-1385. **Facility:** 75 one-bedroom standard units. 2 stories (no elevator), interior corridors. **Parking:** on-site, winter plug-ins. **Terms:** [ECP] meal plan available, package plans, pets (in designated units, on ground floor). **Amenities:** *Some:* irons, hair dryers. **Guest Services:** valet laundry. **Business Services:** meeting rooms. **Cards:** AX, CB, DC, DS, JC, MC, VI. **Special Amenities:** free local telephone calls and free newspaper.

Small-scale Hotel

SOME UNITS
(S̲D̲) (🛏) (ⅈ→) (&M) (🍽) (▥) / (✕) (DATA PORT) (🔒) (🖥) /
FEE

HOLIDAY INN TRENTON **Book at aaa.com**   Phone: (613)394-4855

6/5-9/3	1P: $133-$150	2P: $133-$160
9/4-4/30	1P: $114-$120	2P: $114-$120
5/1-6/4	1P: $111	2P: $111

Small-scale Hotel

Location: Hwy 401, exit 526 (Glen Miller Rd S). Located in a commercial area. 99 Glen Miller Rd K8V 5P8. Fax: 613/392-0635. **Facility:** 108 one-bedroom standard units. 3 stories, interior corridors. **Parking:** on-site, winter plug-ins. **Terms:** [AP] meal plan available, small pets only ($5 extra charge, in smoking units). **Amenities:** video games (fee), voice mail, irons, hair dryers. **Pool(s):** heated indoor. **Leisure Activities:** sauna, whirlpools, racquetball court, exercise room. **Guest Services:** valet laundry. **Business Services:** conference facilities. **Cards:** AX, DC, MC, VI. *(See color ad card insert)*

SOME UNITS
(ASK) (S̲D̲) (🛏) (ⅈ) (▽) (🔌) (✕) (🍽) (DATA PORT) (▥) / (✕) (🔒) /
FEE   FEE

PARK MOTEL   Phone: 613-392-1251

(CAA) (SAVE)

All Year	1P: $88-$98	2P: $110-$128	XP: $8 F10

Motel

Location: Hwy 2 (Dundas St), just e of jct Flindall St. Located in a commercial area. 276 Dundas St E K8V 1M2. Fax: 613/392-2184. **Facility:** 25 units. 17 one-bedroom standard units, some with efficiencies. 8 two-bedroom suites ($156-$170) with kitchens. 1 story, exterior corridors. **Parking:** on-site, winter plug-ins. **Amenities:** irons, hair dryers. **Leisure Activities:** basketball. **Cards:** AX, MC, VI.

(S̲D̲) (ⅈ→) (VCR) (DATA PORT) (🔒) (🖥) (▥)

WHERE TO DINE

TOMASSO'S CASUAL DINING   Lunch: $8-$18   Dinner: $8-$18   Phone: 613/392-4333

Italian

Location: Centre. 39 Front St K8V 5R5. **Hours:** 11 am-10 pm, Sun from 4 pm. Closed: 1/1, 10/10, 12/25, 12/26. **Reservations:** accepted. **Features:** Generous portions of pasta, ribs, chicken and veal specialties are served in a comfortable atmosphere. Booth and table seating are available, as are seats on the covered deck in season. The riverside setting is pleasant. Casual dress; cocktails. **Parking:** street. **Cards:** AX, DC, MC, VI.

(✕)

TWEED pop. 5,612

WHERE TO STAY

PARK PLACE MOTEL   Phone: 613/478-3134

All Year	1P: $59-$98	2P: $64-$98

Motel

Location: Hwy 37, 0.5 km s of centre. Located adjacent to a park with a playground. 43 Victoria St K0K 3J0 (Box 257). Fax: 613/478-3134. **Facility:** 12 units. 10 one-bedroom standard units. 2 one-bedroom suites ($98) with efficiencies. 1 story, exterior corridors. **Parking:** on-site, winter plug-ins. **Terms:** office hours 7 am-11 pm, weekly rates available, package plans, pets (with prior approval). **Cards:** MC, VI.

SOME UNITS
(ASK) (🛏) (🔒) / (✕) (🖥) /

WHERE TO DINE

THE GATEWAY RESTAURANT   Lunch: $4-$9   Dinner: $8-$15   Phone: 613/478-2530

Canadian

Location: Centre. 327 Victoria St K0K 3J0. **Hours:** 6 am-8 pm, Wed-Fri to 9 pm, Sat 7 am-9 pm, Sun 7 am-8 pm. Closed: 12/25, 12/26. **Features:** This is the restaurant where locals and travelers alike stop for coffee and conversation or a full meal. Casual dress; cocktails. **Parking:** street. **Cards:** AX, MC, VI.

(✕)

UNIONVILLE —See Toronto p. 553.

VAUGHAN —See Toronto p. 554.

VERMILION BAY

WHERE TO DINE

VILLAGE CORNER   Lunch: $4-$10   Dinner: $8-$15   Phone: 807/227-2183

American

Location: Jct Trans-Canada Hwy 17 and Hwy 105; beside Esso Service Station. **Hours:** 6 am-9 pm. Closed: 12/22-1/2. **Features:** Village Corner's salad, burgers, sandwiches and steak are delivered to your table in large portions by busy servers in pleasant and casual surroundings. There's also a coffee shop area for travellers stopping in for a quick respite from the road. Casual dress; cocktails. **Parking:** on-site. **Cards:** MC, VI.

(✕)

VINELAND pop. 2,443

——— WHERE TO DINE ———

**MARK PICONE AT VINELAND
ESTATES WINERY RESTAURANT** *Menu on aaa.com* **Lunch:** $22-$25 **Dinner:** $34-$38 **Phone:** 905/562-7088
CAA **Location:** QEW, exit Victoria Ave (Hwy 24), 4.5 km s to Moyer Rd, then e, follow signs. 3620 Moyer Rd L0R 2C0.
Hours: 11:30 am-2:30 & 5-9 pm. Closed: 12/24, 12/25; also Good Friday, Mon & Tues 1/1-3/31.
Reservations: suggested. **Features:** In the middle of Niagara's wine district at the Vineland Estate Winery,
the dining room offers the perfect opportunity to sample some of the region's fine wines with innovative
Continental preparations of local fare. The chef's creative lunch and dinner menus highlight top-quality regional
ingredients. Sublime food and wine and a stunning location make for a memorable dining experience.
Dressy casual; cocktails. **Parking:** on-site. **Cards:** AX, DC, MC, VI.

VINELAND STATION

——— WHERE TO STAY ———

DAYS INN-NIAGARA REGION *Book at aaa.com* **Phone:** (905)562-4101

6/28-9/2	1P: $99-$199	2P: $99-$199	XP: $10	F18
5/1-6/27	1P: $59-$199	2P: $69-$199	XP: $10	F18
9/3-10/13	1P: $59-$199	2P: $59-$199	XP: $10	F18
10/14-4/30	1P: $49-$149	2P: $49-$149	XP: $10	F18

Small-scale Hotel
Location: QEW, exit 57. 3305 N Service Rd L0R 2E0. Fax: 905/562-7781. **Facility:** 64 units. 60 one-bedroom standard units, some
with whirlpools. 4 one-bedroom suites with whirlpools. 2 stories (no elevator); interior corridors. **Parking:** on-site.
Terms: cancellation fee imposed, [AP], [BP] & [CP] meal plans available, package plans. **Amenities:** voice mail, hair dryers.
Some: irons. **Pool(s):** heated indoor. **Leisure Activities:** whirlpool, limited exercise equipment. *Fee:* game room. **Business
Services:** meeting rooms. **Cards:** AX, DC, DS, MC, VI.

——— WHERE TO DINE ———

**LAKE HOUSE RESTAURANT AND
LOUNGE** **Lunch:** $13-$19 **Dinner:** $21-$30 **Phone:** 905/562-6777
CAA **Location:** QEW, exit 57. 3100 N Service Rd L0R 2E0. **Hours:** 10:30 am-3:30 & 4-10 pm. Closed: 1/1, 12/25.
Reservations: suggested. **Features:** Locals and tourists alike frequent the restaurant for its quaint, house-
like structure, fabulous views of Lake Ontario and a fine menu of varied Continental fare. Service is warm
and personable, and portions are hearty. Casual dress; cocktails. **Parking:** on-site. **Cards:** AX, MC, VI.
Mediterranean *(See color ad p 372)*

VIOLET HILL

——— WHERE TO DINE ———

MRS. MITCHELL'S **Lunch:** $7-$11 **Dinner:** $23-$28 **Phone:** 519/925-3627
Location: Hwy 89, 4.3 km w of jct Dufferin Rd 18 (Airport Rd). RR 4 L0N 1S8. **Hours:** noon-2 & 5-9 pm, Sat & Sun
from 11 am. **Reservations:** suggested. **Features:** In a peaceful rural setting, the restaurant is a favorite
Canadian stop for travellers taking a lovely country drive. Diners can indulge in lunch, dinner or a traditional afternoon
tea. The menu features fresh country fare, with baked scones and breads as highlights. Dinner entrees
include hot pan bread made from a 17th-century recipe, a perfect complement to the distinctive decor of the restored 18th-
century schoolhouse. Casual dress; cocktails. **Parking:** on-site. **Cards:** AX, MC, VI. **Historic**

WALLACEBURG pop. 11,114

——— WHERE TO STAY ———

SUPER 8 MOTEL *Book at aaa.com* **Phone:** 519/627-0781
All Year 1P: $59-$99 2P: $69-$99 XP: $10
Location: On Hwy 40 (McNaughton Ave), south side of town. 76 McNaughton Ave N8A 1R9. Fax: 519/627-0781.
Small-scale Hotel **Facility:** 47 one-bedroom standard units. 2 stories (no elevator), interior corridors. **Parking:** on-site, winter
plug-ins. **Terms:** pets ($10 fee). **Cards:** AX, DS, MC, VI.

WASAGA BEACH pop. 12,419

——— WHERE TO STAY ———

KINGSBRIDGE INN **Phone:** (705)429-6364
5/1-11/5 1P: $45-$150 2P: $45-$150
Location: Hwy 92, just n. Located in a commercial area. 268 Main St L0L 2P0. Fax: 705/429-3837. **Facility:** 29
Motel units. 20 one-bedroom standard units, some with efficiencies, kitchens and/or whirlpools. 5 one- and 3 two-
bedroom suites ($80-$275) with efficiencies. 1 cottage ($150-$350). 1 story, exterior corridors. *Bath:* combo
or shower only. **Parking:** on-site. **Terms:** open 5/1-11/5, 2 night minimum stay - weekends, cancellation fee imposed, weekly
rates available, small pets only ($20 extra charge, with prior approval). **Pool(s):** heated outdoor. **Leisure Activities:** sauna,
whirlpool, playground, volleyball. **Cards:** DC, MC, VI.

LUAU MOTEL, COTTAGES & SUITES **Phone:** 705/429-2252

6/2-9/14	1P: $155-$265	2P: $185-$265	XP: $20
9/15-4/30	1P: $95-$225	2P: $95-$245	XP: $20
5/1-6/1	1P: $95-$195	2P: $95-$195	XP: $20

Motel
Location: 1 km w. Located on the waterfront. 231 Mosley St L0L 2P0 (PO Box 280). **Fax:** 705/429-6141. **Facility:** 25 units. 15 one-bedroom standard units, some with whirlpools. 2 one- and 8 two-bedroom suites ($165-$275) with efficiencies, some with whirlpools. 2 stories (no elevator), exterior corridors. **Parking:** on-site, winter plug-ins. **Terms:** office hours 8 am-10 pm, 21 day cancellation notice-fee imposed, weekly rates available. **Amenities:** *Some:* DVD players, voice mail, hair dryers. **Pool(s):** heated outdoor. **Leisure Activities:** playground. **Guest Services:** gift shop. **Cards:** MC, VI.

SOME UNITS

SAGA RESORT **Phone:** 705/429-2543

6/15-9/14	–	1P: $145-$195	2P: $145-$195	XP: $20 F16
5/1-6/14		1P: $89-$179	2P: $89-$179	XP: $20 F16
9/15-4/30		1P: $79-$169	2P: $79-$169	XP: $20 F16

Motel
Location: Hwy 92, 1 km n at bridge. 88 Main St L9Z 2K9. **Fax:** 705/429-7569. **Facility:** 14 units. 8 one-bedroom standard units with kitchens, some with whirlpools. 6 two-bedroom suites with kitchens and whirlpools. 2 stories (no elevator), exterior corridors. **Parking:** on-site. **Terms:** office hours 8 am-10 pm, check-in 4 pm, 15 day cancellation notice-fee imposed, [CP] meal plan available. **Amenities:** voice mail, hair dryers. **Pool(s):** heated outdoor. **Leisure Activities:** whirlpools, horseback riding, playground, basketball, shuffleboard, volleyball. **Cards:** AX, DC, DS, MC, VI.

SOME UNITS

FEE

WATERDOWN

──────── **WHERE TO DINE** ────────

LORD BYRON STEAK & SEAFOOD HOUSE **Dinner:** $20-$40 **Phone:** 905/689-6648

Location: Just s of jct Hwy 5 and Main St. 10 Main St S L0R 2H0. **Hours:** 4 pm-10 pm, Fri & Sat-11 pm. Closed major holidays; also Mon. **Reservations:** suggested, weekends. **Features:** Freshly prepared, traditional steak house fare is served in a relaxed yet elegant atmosphere at Lord Byron. Wooden room dividers afford
Steak House
privacy when dining, and the fine artwork and fireplace create a discernible ambience. Service is professional. Dressy casual; cocktails. **Parking:** on-site. **Cards:** AX, DC, MC, VI.

WATERLOO pop. 86,543

──────── **WHERE TO STAY** ────────

COMFORT INN **Book at aaa.com** **Phone:** (519)747-9400

5/1-10/31	1P: $99-$149	2P: $109-$159	XP: $10 F18
11/1-4/30	1P: $89-$149	2P: $99-$159	XP: $10 F18

Small-scale Hotel
Location: East side off Weber St, 0.3 km s of Hwy 86. 190 Weber St N N2J 3H4. **Fax:** 519/747-2134. **Facility:** 85 one-bedroom standard units. 2 stories (no elevator), interior corridors. **Parking:** on-site, winter plug-ins. **Terms:** cancellation fee imposed, package plans. **Amenities:** voice mail, irons, hair dryers. **Guest Services:** valet laundry. **Cards:** AX, DC, DS, JC, MC, VI.

SOME UNITS

The Premier Hotel Of St. Jacobs Country

- *Charming guest rooms & luxury suites*
- *Complimentary deluxe continental breakfast*
- *Jumbo spa*
- *Theatre & shopping packages*
- *Convenient to two farmers' markets, outlet mall, Village of St. Jacobs!*

1-800-972-5371

See listing under "St. Jacobs"

THE WORLD'S LARGEST HOTEL CHAIN

Best Western
St. Jacobs Country Inn
www.stjacobscountryinn.com

Benjamin Rd. E., Waterloo ON, Canada • Tel. (519) 884-9295 • Fax (519) 884-2532

DESTINATION INN *Book at aaa.com* Phone: 519/884-0100

(CAA) (SAVE)
Small-scale Hotel

All Year 1P: $107 2P: $107 XP: $10
Location: Just n of jct Hwy 85 and King St N. Located opposite a shopping mall. 547 King St N N2L 5Z7. Fax: 519/746-8638. **Facility:** 52 one-bedroom standard units. 2 stories (no elevator), interior corridors. **Parking:** on-site, winter plug-ins. **Terms:** [CP] meal plan available. **Amenities:** high-speed Internet, voice mail, irons, hair dryers. **Business Services:** business center. **Cards:** AX, DC, JC, MC, VI.

SOME UNITS

LES DIPLOMATES B&B (EXECUTIVE GUEST HOUSE) Phone: (519)725-3184

Bed & Breakfast

All Year [BP] 1P: $98-$134 2P: $98-$156 XP: $28 F10
Location: Hwy 85 N, exit King St, s to Columbia, w to Hazel St, then e. 100 Blythwood Rd N2L 4A2. Fax: 519/746-2613. **Facility:** Set in a quiet residential area with a wooded back lot, this peaceful property features elegant decor throughout. Smoke free premises. 4 one-bedroom standard units, some with whirlpools. 2 stories (no elevator), interior/exterior corridors. **Parking:** on-site. **Terms:** office hours 7 am-11 pm, check-in 3:30 pm, cancellation fee imposed, weekly rates available, package plans, small pets only ($10 extra charge, in designated units). **Amenities:** high-speed Internet, hair dryers. *Some:* DVD players, irons. **Leisure Activities:** exercise room. **Guest Services:** coin laundry. **Cards:** AX, DC, MC, VI.

SOME UNITS

FEE

THE WATERLOO HOTEL Phone: 519/885-2626

Historic
Small-scale Hotel

5/1-12/23 & 12/27-4/30 [ECP] 1P: $140-$170 2P: $140-$170
Location: Jct Erb and King sts. 2 King St N N2J 2W7. Fax: 519/885-4774. **Facility:** Rooms at this restored 1890 hotel are individually decorated with fine wood furniture and antiques. Smoke free premises. 14 one-bedroom standard units. 3 stories (no elevator), interior corridors. *Bath:* combo or shower only. **Parking:** on-site. **Terms:** open 5/1-12/23 & 12/27-4/30, office hours 7 am-11 pm, cancellation fee imposed. **Amenities:** high-speed Internet, hair dryers. *Some:* irons. **Guest Services:** valet laundry. **Business Services:** fax (fee). **Cards:** AX, DC, MC, VI.

THE WATERLOO INN & CONFERENCE CENTRE *Book at aaa.com* Phone: (519)884-0220

(CAA) (SAVE)

Small-scale Hotel

All Year 1P: $135 2P: $135 XP: $15 F16
Location: 3 km n on King St, jct Hwy 85. 475 King St N N2J 2Z5. Fax: 519/884-0321. **Facility:** 155 units. 153 one-bedroom standard units, some with whirlpools. 2 one-bedroom suites with whirlpools. 2-4 stories, interior corridors. **Parking:** on-site, winter plug-ins. **Terms:** package plans, small pets only ($15 extra charge, in designated units). **Amenities:** video games, high-speed Internet (fee), dual phone lines, voice mail, honor bars, irons, hair dryers. **Dining:** Rushes Restaurant, see separate listing. **Pool(s):** heated indoor. **Leisure Activities:** sauna, whirlpool, exercise room. **Guest Services:** gift shop, valet laundry. **Business Services:** conference facilities, business center. **Cards:** AX, CB, DC, DS, JC, MC, VI. **Special Amenities:** free newspaper and free room upgrade (subject to availability with advance reservations). *(See color ad p 282)*

SOME UNITS

FEE FEE FEE

—— WHERE TO DINE ——

ALI-BABA STEAK HOUSE Lunch: $6-$16 Dinner: $14-$34 Phone: 519/886-2550

Continental

Location: Centre; opposite Waterloo Square. 130 King St S N2J 1P5. **Hours:** 11:30 am-2:30 & 4:30-10 pm, Sat 4:30 am-11 pm, Sun 4:30 pm-8:30 pm, Mon & Tues 4:30 pm-10 pm. **Reservations:** suggested. **Features:** Dine in a spacious and attractive dining room with a distinctive decor of wooden walls and silk flowers throughout. Specialties spotlight prime rib, stir-fry, schnitzel, salmon and steak along with chicken and pasta. The service is friendly and efficient. Casual dress; cocktails. **Parking:** street. **Cards:** MC, VI.

ANGIE'S KITCHEN Lunch: $4-$12 Dinner: $4-$12 Phone: 519/886-2540

Canadian

Location: Between King St and Bridgeport. 47 Erb St W N2L 1S8. **Hours:** 7 am-7 pm, Thurs & Fri-8 pm, Sat & Sun 7:30 am-3 pm. Closed major holidays. **Features:** Good value and casual diner surroundings complement just what you'd expect to find: hearty portions of home-style meals with specialties such as fish and chips, schnitzel, rolled ribs, roast beef and country breakfast fare. The service is friendly. Casual dress; cocktails. **Parking:** on-site. **Cards:** MC, VI.

CARIBOU CREEK RESTAURANT & BAR Lunch: $6-$12 Dinner: $7-$19 Phone: 519/880-1189

American

Location: 0.5 km n of jct Hwy 85; corner of Northfield Dr. 5883 King St N N2V 2E5. **Hours:** 11:30 am-11 pm, Fri & Sat-midnight, Sun-10 pm. Closed: 12/25. **Features:** Designed like a Northern cabin, the casual eatery enables diners to experience a country cottage feel. Examples of hearty fare include piping hot soups, tasty salads, heaping sandwiches and burgers, as well as pasta selections and grilled ribs and steaks. Patrons can relax and dig in to a tasty meal. Casual dress; cocktails. **Parking:** on-site. **Cards:** AX, DC, MC, VI.

JANET LYNN'S BISTRO Lunch: $10-$12 Dinner: $16-$24 Phone: 519/725-3440

Continental

Location: Hwy 86, exit King St, 4 km s. 92 King St S N2J 1P5. **Hours:** 11:30 am-2 & 5:30-10 pm, Fri-11 pm, Sat 5:30 pm-11 pm. Closed major holidays; also Sun & Mon. **Reservations:** suggested. **Features:** You'll be impressed by the look and the food: an upscale, bustling, bistro-style eatery with murals and a French decor, with a fine selection of dishes using fresh ingredients and taking their cue from distinctive French and Italian influences. Dressy casual; cocktails. **Parking:** street. **Cards:** AX, DC, DS, MC, VI.

THE RUDE NATIVE BISTRO Lunch: $6-$13 Dinner: $9-$20 Phone: 519/886-3600

Caribbean

Location: Adjacent to Waterloo Centre Shopping Complex. 15 King St S N2J 2W7. **Hours:** 11:30 am-10 pm, Fri-11 pm, Sat noon-11 pm, Sun noon-2 & 4-9 pm. Closed: 1/1, 12/25, 12/26. **Features:** A fun and distinctive style characterizes the restaurant, which is appointed in decor that fits an island native theme—such as wooden statues and wall murals. Lining the menu is an extensive selection of island specials, including jerk, Thai cuisine and casual fare. This place is popular locally. Casual dress; cocktails. **Parking:** street. **Cards:** AX, MC, VI.

RUSHES RESTAURANT   **Lunch:** $9-$17   **Dinner:** $16-$28   **Phone:** 519/884-0220
Location: 3 km n on King St, jct Hwy 85; in The Waterloo Inn & Conference Centre. 475 King St N N2J 2Z5. **Hours:** 7 am-3 & 5-11 pm. **Reservations:** suggested. **Features:** An upscale, contemporary dining room, excellent wine list
Continental and fine menu of innovative Continental cuisine make the restaurant a hit with locals and visitors alike. The chef focuses on fresh local and regional ingredients and shows creativity in preparation technique and presentation. Service is professional and personable. Dressy casual; cocktails. **Parking:** on-site. **Cards:** AX, CB, DC, DS, MC, VI.

SOLE RESTAURANT & WINE BAR   **Lunch:** $8-$19   **Dinner:** $13-$27   **Phone:** 519/747-5622
Location: Centre. 83 Erb St W, Bldg 2 N2L 6C2. **Hours:** 11:30 am-10 pm, Fri & Sat-11 pm, Sun 4:30 pm-9 pm.
Reservations: accepted. **Features:** Located at the centre of town in a historic building, with original yellow
Continental brick and large wooden beams, this restaurant offers a mix of Continental and Mediterranean fare complimented by a well-rounded wine list offering many varieties by the glass or half bottle. Service is friendly and casual, yet professional. Dressy casual; cocktails. **Parking:** on-site. **Cards:** AX, DC, MC, VI. **Historic**

WAWA pop. 3,279

——— WHERE TO STAY ———

KINNIWABI PINES MOTEL/COTTAGES   **Phone:** (705)856-7302
All Year [CP]   1P: $65-$75   2P: $75-$89   XP: $10   F10
Location: Hwy 17, 5.3 km s of jct Hwy 101. Located in a quiet area. 52 Hwy 17 P0S 1K0 (PO Box 1429).
Motel   Fax: 705/856-2772. **Facility:** 15 units. 12 one-bedroom standard units, some with efficiencies. 3 cottages ($110-$140). 1 story, exterior corridors. *Bath:* combo or shower only. **Parking:** on-site, winter plug-ins.
Terms: office hours 9 am-midnight, package plans, small pets only ($10 extra charge, in smoking units). **Amenities:** *Some:* hair dryers. **Leisure Activities:** sauna, whirlpool, fishing, cross country skiing, snowmobiling, hiking trails, game room. *Fee:* canoes, bicycles. **Cards:** AX, MC, VI.

SOME UNITS

THE MYSTIC ISLE MOTEL   **Phone:** (705)856-1737
(CAA) (SAVE)   All Year   1P: $56-$62   2P: $62-$68   XP: $10
Location: On Hwy 17, 5.2 km s of jct Hwy 101. Located in a quiet area. 109 Hwy 17 S P0S 1K0 (PO Box 557).
Fax: 705/856-1738. **Facility:** 14 one-bedroom standard units. 1 story, exterior corridors. **Parking:** on-site,
Motel   winter plug-ins. **Terms:** office hours 7:30 am-midnight, cancellation fee imposed. **Amenities:** hair dryers.
Leisure Activities: cross country skiing, snowmobiling, hiking trails. **Guest Services:** area transportation-restaurants in winter. **Business Services:** fax (fee). **Cards:** AX, DC, DS, JC, MC, VI. **Special Amenities:** free local telephone calls and preferred room (subject to availability with advance reservations).

SOME UNITS

PARKWAY MOTEL   **Phone:** 705/856-7020
All Year   1P: $59-$65   2P: $65-$75   XP: $8   F8
Location: Hwy 17, 4 km s of jct Hwy 101. 938 Hwy 17 P0S 1K0 (PO Box 784). Fax: 705/856-4953. **Facility:** 13
Motel   one-bedroom standard units. 1 story, exterior corridors. **Parking:** on-site, winter plug-ins. **Terms:** office hours 7 am-11 pm, small pets only. **Amenities:** video library (fee). *Some:* DVD players (fee). **Leisure Activities:** whirlpool, snowmobiling. **Cards:** MC, VI.

SOME UNITS

SPORTSMAN'S MOTEL   **Phone:** 705/856-2272
All Year   1P: $62   2P: $75   XP: $10   F6
Location: Hwy 101, 2.4 km e of jct Hwy 17. Located in a commercial area. 45 Mission Rd P0S 1K0.
Motel   Fax: 705/856-1318. **Facility:** 36 one-bedroom standard units, some with efficiencies. 2 stories (no elevator), exterior corridors. **Parking:** on-site, winter plug-ins. **Terms:** office hours 6 am-midnight, small pets only ($10 extra charge, in smoking units). **Cards:** AX, CB, DC, MC, VI.

SOME UNITS

WAWA NORTHERN LIGHTS MOTEL & CHALETS   **Phone:** 705/856-1900
(CAA) (SAVE)   All Year [ECP]   1P: $69-$99   2P: $79-$109   XP: $10   D12
Location: 8 km n of jct Hwy 101. Located in a rural/commercial area. 237 Hwy 17 P0S 1K0 (PO Box 1150, O0S 1K0).
Fax: 705/856-0594. **Facility:** 16 one-bedroom standard units. 1 story, exterior corridors. **Parking:** on-site,
Motel   winter plug-ins. **Terms:** office hours 8 am-midnight. **Dining:** 5 pm-10 pm; hours vary off season, cocktails. **Leisure Activities:** snowmobiling, hot tub. **Cards:** AX, DS, MC, VI. **Special Amenities:** free expanded continental breakfast and free local telephone calls. *(See ad below)*

SOME UNITS

Wawa Northern Lights Motel, Restaurant & Chalets

237 Highway 17 North, Wawa, Ontario

In Room Coffee/Tea, Free Local Calls, Free Expanded

Continental Breakfast / Licensed Restaurant / Room

Service / Triple Rooms (3double beds) available

10% Discount off published rates for CAA/AAA members

3 Bedroom Chalets & 2 Bedroom House

nlmotel.com
Toll Free 1-800-937-2414

────── WHERE TO DINE ──────

CEDARHOF
German

Lunch: $6-$8   **Dinner:** $13-$20   **Phone:** 705/856-1136
Location: 5.4 km s of jct Hwy 101. Hwy 17 S P0S 1K0. **Hours:** Open 5/1-11/30; 7 am-9 pm; hours vary in season. **Features:** This casual dining room has a cozy country atmosphere with cedar walls and bright sunflower colors. The menu features European and Canadian specialties, including fresh Lake Superior trout, charbroiled steak, chicken Kiev, cabbage rolls and perogies, bratwurst and sauerkraut, Wiener schnitzel and Hungarian goulash. Casual dress; cocktails. **Parking:** on-site. **Cards:** MC, VI.

KINNIWABI PINES RESTAURANT
Canadian

Lunch: $7-$15   **Dinner:** $15-$30   **Phone:** 705/856-7226
Location: 5.3 km s of jct Hwy 101. 56 Hwy 17 S P0S 1K0. **Hours:** Open 5/1-11/30 & 4/10-4/30; 7 am-10 pm. **Reservations:** suggested. **Features:** Hearty meals, home-style preparation; fresh baked pies. Casual dress; cocktails. **Parking:** on-site. **Cards:** AX, MC, VI.

WELLAND —See Niagara Falls p. 385.

WHITBY pop. 87,413

────── WHERE TO STAY ──────

CANADIANA INN
Motel

Phone: (905)668-3686
All Year   1P: $70-$90   2P: $75-$120
Location: Hwy 401, exit 410 (Brock St/Hwy 12), 1.6 km n to Dundas St, then 1 km e. 732 Dundas St E (Hwy 2) L1N 2J7. Fax: 905/666-3350. **Facility:** 26 one-bedroom standard units. 1 story, exterior corridors. *Bath:* combo or shower only. **Parking:** on-site, winter plug-ins. **Terms:** office hours 9 am-3 am, cancellation fee imposed. **Amenities:** hair dryers. **Pool(s):** heated outdoor. **Cards:** AX, DC, DS, MC, VI. **Special Amenities:** free local telephone calls and free newspaper.

SOME UNITS

HOLIDAY INN EXPRESS WHITBY
Small-scale Hotel

Book at aaa.com
All Year [CP]   1P: $129-$139

Phone: (905)665-8400
XP: $10   F18
Location: Hwy 401, exit 410 (Brock St/Hwy 12). 180 Consumers Dr L1N 9S3. Fax: 905/665-8402. **Facility:** 93 units. 86 one-bedroom standard units, some with whirlpools. 7 one-bedroom suites ($179-$259), some with whirlpools. 4 stories, interior corridors. **Parking:** on-site. **Terms:** package plans. **Amenities:** dual phone lines, voice mail, irons, hair dryers. *Fee:* video games, high-speed Internet. **Leisure Activities:** exercise room. **Guest Services:** valet laundry. **Business Services:** meeting rooms. **Cards:** AX, DC, DS, MC, VI. **Special Amenities:** free continental breakfast and free room upgrade (subject to availability with advance reservations). *(See color ad p 527)*

SOME UNITS

MOTEL 6 #1907
Small-scale Hotel

Book at aaa.com
5/27-10/8   1P: $75-$85   2P: $81-$91   XP: $3   F17
5/1-5/26 & 10/9-4/30   1P: $67-$77   2P: $73-$83   XP: $3   F17

Phone: 905/665-8883
Location: Hwy 401, exit 410 (Brock St/Hwy 12), just ne. 165 Consumers Dr L1N 1C4. Fax: 905/665-8373. **Facility:** 124 one-bedroom standard units. 3 stories, interior corridors. *Bath:* combo or shower only. **Parking:** on-site. **Guest Services:** coin laundry. **Cards:** AX, CB, DC, DS, MC, VI.

SOME UNITS

Residence Inn Marriott

Residence Inn by Marriott Whitby

Service so Memorable
NOW OPEN!

160 Consumers Drive
Whitby, ON, Canada L1N 9S3
(905) 444-9756 • Fax: (905) 444-9758
Reservations: 1-800-331-3131
www.marriott.com/yyzwy

"Where people away from home feel they are among friends"

Our hotel amenities include:
- Complimentary hot breakfast buffet
- Indoor swimming pool
- Exercise room
- Rooms with fireplaces available
- High speed internet in all rooms
- Same-day dry cleaning
- Complimentary grocery shopping service
- Meeting room
- Complimentary weeknight BBQ
- Faxing/copying/printing
- In-room modem line
- Studio, one & two bedroom suites available

QUALITY SUITES *Book at aaa.com* **Phone:** (905)432-8800

(CAA) (SAVE)

7/1-8/31 [ECP]	1P: $145-$189	2P: $155-$199	XP: $10	F18
9/1-4/30 [ECP]	1P: $135-$175	2P: $145-$185	XP: $10	F18
5/1-6/30 [ECP]	1P: $134-$164	2P: $144-$174	XP: $10	F18

Location: Hwy 401, exit 412 (Thickson Rd), 0.5 km n to Champlain Ave, then 1 km e. 1700 Champlain Ave L1N 6A7.
Small-scale Hotel **Fax:** 905/432-2937. **Facility:** 104 units. 12 one-bedroom standard units. 92 one-bedroom suites. 3 stories, interior corridors. **Parking:** on-site. **Terms:** small pets only. **Amenities:** voice mail, hair dryers. *Some:* irons.
Leisure Activities: limited exercise equipment. **Guest Services:** valet and coin laundry. **Business Services:** meeting rooms.
Cards: AX, CB, DC, DS, JC, MC, VI.

SOME UNITS

RESIDENCE INN BY MARRIOTT, WHITBY **Phone:** 905/444-9756

(fyi)

All Year [BP] 1P: $119-$159 2P: $119-$159
Too new to rate, opening scheduled for January 2005. **Location:** Hwy 401, exit 410 (Brock St/Hwy 12). 160
Small-scale Hotel Consumers Dr L1N 9S3. **Fax:** 905/444-9758. **Amenities:** 83 units, pets, coffeemakers, microwaves, refrigerators, pool. **Terms:** 7 day cancellation notice. **Cards:** AX, MC, VI. *(See color ad p 560)*

——— **WHERE TO DINE** ———

KREBS RESTAURANTS **Lunch:** $7-$10 **Dinner:** $12-$30 **Phone:** 905/668-9369

Location: 1.6 km n on Brock St (Hwy 12), 3 km n of Hwy 401 via Brock St/Hwy 12, exit 410B. 918 Brock St N L1N 4J6.
Hours: 11:30 am-9 pm, Fri-10 pm, Sat 5 pm-10 pm, Sun 11 am-2:30 & 4-9 pm. Closed: 12/25, 12/26.
Steak House **Reservations:** suggested, weekends. **Features:** As evidenced by its loyal local following, Krebs offers a variety of well-prepared selections, including lighter entrees like quiche and sandwiches and full meals of steak, seafood, meatloaf and stir-fry. The greenhouse decor boasts lots of plants. Cocktails. **Parking:** on-site. **Cards:** AX, DC, MC, VI.

MELANIE PRINGLES **Lunch:** $5-$12 **Dinner:** $6-$19 **Phone:** 905/430-1959

Location: Hwy 401, exit 412 (Thickson Rd), 1.4 km n. 80 Thickson Rd S L1N 7T2. **Hours:** 11 am-1 am, Sun-11 pm.
Closed: 12/25. **Features:** Drop a quarter in the jukebox for a trip down memory lane at this nostalgic 1950s-
American style diner. The friendly, fun and casual atmosphere attracts plenty of families who enjoy the burgers, nachos, sandwiches and wings, plus the efficient service. Cocktails. **Parking:** on-site. **Cards:** AX, MC, VI.

OUTBACK STEAKHOUSE **Lunch:** $9-$21 **Dinner:** $12-$21 **Phone:** 905/665-4587

Location: Hwy 401, exit 412 (Thickson Rd). 75 Consumer Dr L1N 9S2. **Hours:** 4:30 pm-10 pm, Fri noon-11 pm,
Sat 3 pm-11 pm, Sun 3 pm-10 pm. Closed: 12/25. **Features:** The restaurant sustains a fun, casual mood in
Steak House a loud and bustling Aussie atmosphere. Huge portions of freshly grilled and barbecued foods—including well-spiced steaks, chicken and ribs dinners—are a challenge to finish but are too good to leave. Fresh bread, tasty salads and the ever-popular bloomin' onion starter bring back locals and tourists alike. Service is friendly. Cocktails.
Parking: on-site. **Cards:** AX, MC, VI.

WILNO

——— **WHERE TO DINE** ———

WILNO TAVERN RESTAURANT **Lunch:** $4-$12 **Dinner:** $4-$12 **Phone:** 613/756-2029

Location: Centre. 17589 Hwy 60 K0J 2N0. **Hours:** 11 am-10 pm. Closed: 4/17, 12/25. **Reservations:** accepted.
Features: Established in 1896, the restaurant continues to be a friendly meeting spot. Although hearty
Polish Canadian fare is the focus, the menu also reflects local Polish heritage in such dishes as Polish sausage, sledzie (pickled herring), pierogi and golabki (cabbage rolls). Tempting desserts are made in-house. Casual dress; cocktails. **Parking:** on-site. **Cards:** AX, MC, VI.

WINDERMERE

——— **WHERE TO STAY** ———

WINDERMERE HOUSE RESORT-HOTEL **Phone:** 705/769-3611

6/25-9/5	1P: $165-$277	2P: $235-$395	XP: $75
9/6-10/10	1P: $137-$224	2P: $195-$320	XP: $75
5/6-6/24	1P: $125-$210	2P: $175-$300	XP: $75

Resort **Location:** In Windermere Village (Muskoka Rd 4). Located on Lake Rosseau. 2508 Windermere Rd P0B 1P0 (PO Box
Small-scale Hotel 68). **Fax:** 705/769-2168. **Facility:** Rustic cottage-style accommodations and elegantly appointed lodge rooms are offered at this property. 77 units. 68 one-bedroom standard units, some with whirlpools. 4 one- and 4 two-bedroom suites with kitchens, some with efficiencies. 1 vacation home. 3 stories, interior/exterior corridors. **Parking:** on-site.
Terms: open 5/6-10/10, check-in 4 pm, 2 night minimum stay - seasonal, 10 day cancellation notice-fee imposed, package plans. **Amenities:** voice mail, irons, hair dryers. *Some:* DVD players (fee). **Dining:** Rosseau Dining Room, see separate listing.
Pool(s): heated outdoor. **Leisure Activities:** sauna, whirlpool, steamrooms, canoeing, paddleboats, tennis court, recreation programs, bicycles, exercise room, spa, basketball, horseshoes, shuffleboard, volleyball. **Fee:** marina, waterskiing, golf-18 holes. **Guest Services:** gift shop, area transportation. **Business Services:** meeting rooms. **Cards:** AX, DC, MC, VI.

SOME UNITS

——— **WHERE TO DINE** ———

ROSSEAU DINING ROOM **Dinner:** $19-$42 **Phone:** 705/769-3611

Location: In Windermere Village (Muskoka Rd 4). In Windermere House Resort-Hotel. 2508 Windermere Rd P0B 1P0.
Hours: Open 5/8-10/15; 6 pm-9:30 pm. **Reservations:** required. **Features:** In a beautiful Muskoka setting,
International the dining room has a pleasant atmosphere, attentive service and a well-rounded menu offering fish, chicken, veal, steak and good desserts. Dressy casual; cocktails. **Parking:** on-site. **Cards:** AX, DC, MC, VI.

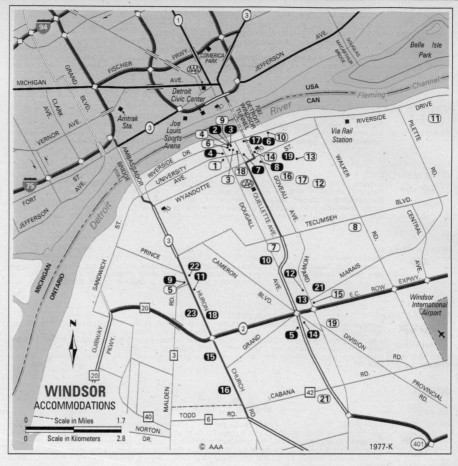

Windsor

This index helps you "spot" where approved accommodations and restaurants are located on the corresponding detailed maps. Lodging rate ranges are for comparison only and show the property's high season; rates are per night, unless only weekly (W) rates are available. Restaurant rate range is for dinner, unless only lunch (L) is served. Turn to the listing page for more detailed rate information and consult display ads for special promotions.

Spotter/Map Page Number	OA	WINDSOR - Lodgings	Diamond Rating	Rate Range High Season	Listing Page
2 / below		Hilton Windsor	▽▽▽	$149-$199	565
3 / below	CAA	Radisson Riverfront Hotel - see color ad p 566, p 521, on TourBookMark	▽▽▽	$119-$199 SAVE	566
4 / below	CAA	Quality Suites Windsor	▽▽▽	$129-$249 SAVE	566
5 / below		Comfort Inn	▽▽	$92-$150	564
6 / below	CAA	Casino Windsor Hotel	▽▽▽▽	$175-$300 SAVE	564
7 / below		Ramada Plaza Hotel and Suites	▽▽▽	$109-$139	566
8 / below		Days Inn Windsor	▽▽	$89-$199	565
9 / below	CAA	Holiday Inn Select Windsor (Ambassador Bridge) - see color ad card insert	▽▽▽	$139-$159 SAVE	565

Spotter/Map Page Number	OA	**WINDSOR - Lodgings (continued)**	Diamond Rating	Rate Range High Season	Listing Page
⑩ / p. 562	CAA	Cadillac Motel	◆◆◆	$85-$130 SAVE	564
⑪ / p. 562		Econo Lodge	◆◆	$75-$225	565
⑫ / p. 562		Towne and Country Motel	◆◆	$60-$125	567
⑬ / p. 562	CAA	Ivy Rose Motor Inn Ltd.	◆◆	$58-$175 SAVE	565
⑭ / p. 562	CAA	Stonecroft Inn	◆◆◆	$85-$112 SAVE	566
⑮ / p. 562	CAA	Comfort Inn	◆◆	$89-$150 SAVE	564
⑯ / p. 562	CAA	Best Western Continental Inn	◆◆◆	$85-$150 SAVE	564
⑰ / p. 562	CAA	Travelodge Hotel Downtown Windsor - see color ad on TourBookMark	◆◆◆	$119-$229 SAVE	567
⑱ / p. 562	CAA	Travelodge Windsor Ambassador Bridge	◆◆◆	$100-$180 SAVE	567
⑲ / p. 562	CAA	Comfort Suites Downtown	◆◆◆	$79-$349 SAVE	565
㉑ / p. 562		Royal Marquis Hotel	◆◆◆	$95-$120	566
㉒ / p. 562		Hampton Inn and Suites - see color ad p 4	◆◆◆	$139-$169	565
㉓ / p. 562	CAA	Super 8 Motel	◆◆◆	$89 SAVE	567
		WINDSOR - Restaurants			
① / p. 562		North of the Border	◆◆	$11-$17	568
③ / p. 562		Ye Olde Steak House	◆◆	$13-$28	569
④ / p. 562		The City Beer Market	◆◆◆	$15-$30	567
⑤ / p. 562		T BQ's Marketplace	◆◆	$15-$40	569
⑥ / p. 562		The Chatham Street Grill	◆◆◆	$20-$25	567
⑦ / p. 562		Bern Fondue & Wine Bar	◆◆	$12-$15	567
⑧ / p. 562		Franco's Restaurant	◆	$9-$17	568
⑨ / p. 562		The Park Terrace	◆◆◆	$12-$25	568
⑩ / p. 562		Riverside Grille	◆◆◆	$23-$55	569
⑪ / p. 562		Elaine's Bistro	◆◆	$17-$22	568
⑫ / p. 562		Nico Ristorante	◆◆◆	$15-$20	568
⑬ / p. 562		Il Boschetto Ristorante	◆◆◆	$12-$25	568
⑭ / p. 562		Tunnel Bar-B-Q	◆	$4-$34	569
⑮ / p. 562		Jose's Noodle Factory	◆◆	$8-$22	568
⑯ / p. 562		La Zingara Pizzeria Trattoria	◆◆	$10-$15	568
⑰ / p. 562		Spago Trattoria & Pizzeria	◆◆	$10-$18	569
⑱ / p. 562		Chanoso's Restaurant	◆◆	$6-$16	567
⑲ / p. 562		The Keg Steakhouse and Bar	◆◆	$15-$30	568
㉑ / p. 562		Porcino	◆◆◆	$15-$24	568

WINDSOR pop. 208,402 (See map and index starting on p. 562)

———— WHERE TO STAY ————

BEST WESTERN CONTINENTAL INN *Book at aaa.com*   Phone: (519)966-5541   **16**
(CAA) (SAVE)   All Year   1P: $85-$105   2P: $95-$150   XP: $10   F12
◆◆/◆◆   **Location:** 8 km sw from Detroit-Windsor Tunnel via Wyandotte St W; from Ambassador Bridge, 5 km s on Hwy 3A. 3345 Huron Church Rd N9E 4H5. Fax: 519/972-3384. **Facility:** 71 one-bedroom standard units. 2 stories (no elevator), interior corridors. **Parking:** on-site, winter plug-ins. **Terms:** [AP], [BP], [CP], [ECP] & [MAP] meal
Small-scale Hotel plans available. **Amenities:** voice mail, irons, hair dryers. **Dining:** 7 am-9 pm, Sun-8 pm, cocktails. **Pool(s):** heated outdoor. **Guest Services:** valet laundry. **Business Services:** meeting rooms, fax (fee). **Cards:** AX, DC, DS, MC, VI. **Special Amenities:** free local telephone calls and early check-in/late check-out.

SOME UNITS
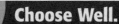

CADILLAC MOTEL   Phone: (519)969-9340   **10**
(CAA) (SAVE)   5/1-12/1   1P: $85-$95   2P: $95-$130   XP: $10
    12/2-4/30   1P: $80-$90   2P: $95-$120   XP: $10
◆◆/◆◆   **Location:** 4 km s on Hwy 3B from Detroit-Windsor Tunnel, just w on Eugenie, then just n. Located opposite Dorwin Plaza. 2498 Dougall Ave N8X 1T2. Fax: 519/969-9342. **Facility:** 71 one-bedroom standard units, some with
Motel   whirlpools. 2 stories (no elevator), exterior corridors. **Parking:** on-site, winter plug-ins. **Terms:** office hours 7 am-11 pm, 7 day cancellation notice. **Amenities:** voice mail, irons, hair dryers. **Pool(s):** heated outdoor.
Leisure Activities: whirlpool. **Guest Services:** valet laundry. **Business Services:** meeting rooms. **Cards:** AX, DC, DS, MC, VI. **Special Amenities:** free local telephone calls.

SOME UNITS

CASINO WINDSOR HOTEL   Phone: 519/258-7878   **6**
(CAA) (SAVE)   6/1-9/7   2P: $175-$300   XP: $20
    5/1-5/31 & 9/8-11/30   2P: $165-$300   XP: $20
◆◆/◆◆   12/1-4/30   2P: $155-$300   XP: $20
  Location: Jct McDougall Ave; downtown. 377 Riverside Dr E N9A 7H7. Fax: 519/985-5800. **Facility:** An indoor
Large-scale Hotel tropical waterfall and garden are featured at the hotel, which includes a spa, a fitness center, meeting facilities and a large casino. 389 units. 365 one-bedroom standard units, some with whirlpools. 24 one-bedroom suites ($250-$1000) with whirlpools. 22 stories, interior corridors. **Parking:** valet. **Terms:** check-in 4 pm, age restrictions may apply. **Amenities:** video games (fee), dual phone lines, voice mail, safes, irons, hair dryers. *Some:* CD players. **Dining:** 4 restaurants, 24 hours, also, Riverside Grille, see separate listing, entertainment. **Pool(s):** heated indoor. **Leisure Activities:** saunas, whirlpool, steamroom, exercise room, spa. **Guest Services:** gift shop, valet laundry, area transportation-downtown, beauty salon. **Business Services:** conference facilities, fax (fee). **Cards:** AX, DS, MC, VI.

SOME UNITS

COMFORT INN *Book at aaa.com*   Phone: (519)972-1331   **15**
(CAA) (SAVE)   5/1-10/31 & 1/1-4/30   1P: $89-$130   2P: $99-$150   XP: $10   F18
◆◆/◆◆   11/1-12/31   1P: $86-$117   2P: $96-$127   XP: $10   F18
  Location: 0.8 km s of EC Row Expwy; west side of Huron Church Rd. 2765 Huron Church Rd N9E 3Y7. Fax: 519/972-5574. **Facility:** 100 one-bedroom standard units. 2 stories (no elevator), interior corridors.
Small-scale Hotel **Parking:** on-site, winter plug-ins. **Terms:** 7 day cancellation notice, package plans, pets ($10 extra charge). **Amenities:** irons, hair dryers. *Some:* dual phone lines. **Dining:** 24 hours, cocktails. **Guest Services:** valet laundry. **Cards:** AX, DC, DS, MC, VI.

SOME UNITS
FEE

COMFORT INN *Book at aaa.com*   Phone: (519)966-7800   **5**
◆◆/◆◆   5/1-10/31 [CP]   1P: $92-$140   2P: $102-$150   XP: $10   F18
  11/1-4/30 [CP]   1P: $89-$130   2P: $99-$140   XP: $10   F18
Small-scale Hotel **Location:** 5.3 km s on Hwy 3B, off Hwy 401 via Detroit-Windsor Tunnel exit. 2955 Dougall Ave N9E 1S1. Fax: 519/966-0403. **Facility:** 80 one-bedroom standard units. 2 stories (no elevator), interior corridors.
Parking: on-site, winter plug-ins. **Terms:** pets ($10 extra charge). **Amenities:** voice mail, irons, hair dryers. *Some:* dual phone lines. **Guest Services:** valet laundry. **Cards:** AX, DC, DS, JC, MC, VI.

SOME UNITS
FEE

(AAA) (CAA) **Choose Well.**

Discover the secret to choosing well … **AAA/CAA Approved**.

From simple motels to luxury resorts, rest assured. **AAA/CAA's professional evaluators** have tested the locks and peeked under the beds, checking for qualities like cleanliness, service, and value — assigning a rating from one to five Diamonds.

Choose your Diamond rated accommodations from theTourBook® listings, in print and on aaa.com, and look for the bold red AAA/CAA logo on signage and billboards.

For more information on **AAA/CAA Lodging Diamond Ratings**, turn to page 16.

Show Your Card

(See map and index starting on p. 562)

COMFORT SUITES DOWNTOWN — Book at aaa.com
Phone: (519)971-0505   **19**

(AAA) (SAVE)

5/1-12/31	1P: $79-$349	2P: $79-$349	XP: $20 F18
1/1-4/30	1P: $79-$249	2P: $79-$249	XP: $20 F18

Location: Jct Glengary and Wyandotte sts E. 500 Tuscarora St N9A 3M2. Fax: 519/971-8444. **Facility:** 45 one-bedroom standard units, some with whirlpools. 3 stories, interior corridors. *Bath:* combo or shower only. **Small-scale Hotel** **Parking:** on-site. **Terms:** cancellation fee imposed. **Amenities:** high-speed Internet, voice mail, irons, hair dryers. **Leisure Activities:** pool table, game room. **Guest Services:** valet and coin laundry, area transportation-casino. **Cards:** AX, DC, DS, MC, VI. **Special Amenities: free continental breakfast and free local telephone calls.**

SOME UNITS

DAYS INN WINDSOR — Book at aaa.com
Phone: (519)258-8411   **8**

5/1-9/10 [CP]	1P: $89-$199	2P: $89-$199	XP: $20 F12
9/11-4/30 [CP]	1P: $74-$169	2P: $74-$169	XP: $20 F12

Small-scale Hotel **Location:** 1 km s of Detroit-Windsor Tunnel. 675 Goyeau St N9A 1H3. Fax: 519/258-6771. **Facility:** 117 one-bedroom standard units, some with whirlpools. 3 stories, interior corridors. **Parking:** on-site. **Terms:** cancellation fee imposed, weekly rates available, package plans. **Amenities:** hair dryers. *Some:* high-speed Internet, irons. **Guest Services:** area transportation. **Business Services:** meeting rooms. **Cards:** AX, DC, DS, JC, MC, VI.

SOME UNITS

FEE

ECONO LODGE — Book at aaa.com
Phone: 519/966-8811   **11**

All Year	1P: $75-$175	2P: $80-$225	XP: $5 F16

Motel   **Location:** 1 km n of EC Row Expwy. 2000 Huron Church Rd N9C 2L5. Fax: 519/966-3117. **Facility:** 33 one-bedroom standard units, some with whirlpools. 2 stories (no elevator), exterior corridors. *Bath:* combo or shower only. **Parking:** on-site, winter plug-ins. **Terms:** cancellation fee imposed. **Amenities:** hair dryers. **Cards:** AX, CB, DC, DS, JC, MC, VI.

SOME UNITS

HAMPTON INN AND SUITES — Book at aaa.com
Phone: (519)972-0770   **22**

1/1-4/30 [ECP]	1P: $139-$169	2P: $139-$169	XP: $10 F18
5/1-12/31 [ECP]	1P: $129-$159	2P: $129-$159	XP: $10 F18

Small-scale Hotel **Location:** 1.5 km n of EC Row Expwy. 1840 Huron Church Rd N9C 2L5. Fax: 519/972-0404. **Facility:** 147 one-bedroom standard units. 7 stories, interior corridors. *Bath:* combo or shower only. **Parking:** on-site. **Terms:** package plans. **Amenities:** video games (fee), high-speed Internet, dual phone lines, voice mail, irons, hair dryers. **Pool(s):** heated indoor. **Leisure Activities:** whirlpool, exercise room. **Guest Services:** sundries, valet laundry. **Business Services:** meeting rooms. **Cards:** AX, DC, JC, MC, VI. *(See color ad p 4)*

SOME UNITS

HILTON WINDSOR — Book at aaa.com
Phone: (519)973-5555   **2**

5/1-8/31	1P: $149-$199	2P: $149-$199	XP: $20 F18
9/1-4/30	1P: $129-$199	2P: $129-$199	XP: $20 F18

Large-scale Hotel **Location:** 1 km w of Detroit-Windsor Tunnel; 1 km e of Ambassador Bridge; downtown. 277 Riverside Dr W N9A 5K4. Fax: 519/973-1600. **Facility:** 305 units. 4 one-bedroom standard units, some with whirlpools. 22 stories, interior corridors. **Parking:** on-site (fee) and valet. **Terms:** package plans, small pets only. **Amenities:** video games (fee), dual phone lines, voice mail, irons, hair dryers. *Some:* high-speed Internet, honor bars. **Dining:** The Park Terrace, see separate listing. **Pool(s):** heated indoor. **Leisure Activities:** saunas, whirlpool, exercise room. **Guest Services:** gift shop, valet laundry, area transportation. **Business Services:** conference facilities, business center. **Cards:** AX, DC, DS, MC, VI.

SOME UNITS

HOLIDAY INN SELECT WINDSOR (AMBASSADOR BRIDGE) — Book at aaa.com
Phone: (519)966-1200   **9**

(AAA) (SAVE)

All Year	1P: $139-$159	2P: $139-$159

Location: Jct Huron Church and Malden rds; 1.5 km n of EC Row Expwy. 1855 Huron Church Rd N9C 2L6. Fax: 519/966-2521. **Facility:** 214 units. 208 one-bedroom standard units, some with whirlpools. 6 one-bedroom suites ($179) with whirlpools. 8 stories, interior corridors. **Parking:** on-site, winter plug-ins. **Large-scale Hotel** **Terms:** small pets only. **Amenities:** video games (fee), high-speed Internet, voice mail, irons, hair dryers. **Dining:** 6:30 am-11 pm, Fri & Sat-midnight, cocktails. **Pool(s):** heated indoor, wading. **Leisure Activities:** saunas, whirlpool, exercise room. **Guest Services:** valet and coin laundry. **Business Services:** conference facilities, business center. **Cards:** AX, DC, DS, MC, VI. *(See color ad card insert)*

SOME UNITS

IVY ROSE MOTOR INN LTD.
Phone: (519)966-1700   **13**

(AAA) (SAVE)

All Year	1P: $58-$175

Location: 4.8 km s of downtown; just n of Devonshire Shopping Mall. 2885 Howard Ave N8X 3Y4. Fax: 519/966-2874. **Facility:** 91 units. 90 one- and 1 two-bedroom standard units, some with whirlpools. 1-2 stories (no elevator), exterior corridors. *Bath:* combo or shower only. **Parking:** on-site, winter plug-ins. Motel   **Terms:** office hours 5:30 am-1 am. **Amenities:** *Some:* hair dryers. **Dining:** 7 am-10 pm, Sun-2:30 pm, cocktails. **Pool(s):** heated outdoor. **Leisure Activities:** playground. **Business Services:** meeting rooms, fax (fee). **Cards:** AX, DC, DS, MC, VI.

SOME UNITS

FEE

(See map and index starting on p. 562)

QUALITY SUITES WINDSOR   *Book at aaa.com*   Phone: (519)977-9707   **4**

CAA SAVE

5/1-9/30 & 12/31-4/30	1P: $129-$249	2P: $139-$249	XP: $10	F18
10/1-12/30	1P: $119-$249	2P: $129-$249	XP: $10	F18

Location: Jct Dougall Ave and Chatham St; downtown. 250 Dougall Ave N9A 7C6. Fax: 519/977-6404. **Facility:** 128 one-bedroom suites. 9 stories, interior corridors. **Parking:** on-site (fee). **Terms:** [BP] & [CP] meal plans available, package plans, pets ($50 fee). **Amenities:** irons, hair dryers. *Some:* honor bars. **Dining:** North of the Border, see separate listing. **Guest Services:** sundries, valet laundry, area transportation-casino.
Small-scale Hotel
Business Services: meeting rooms. **Cards:** AX, CB, DC, DS, JC, MC, VI.

SOME UNITS

FEE   FEE

RADISSON RIVERFRONT HOTEL   *Book at aaa.com*   Phone: (519)977-9777   **3**

CAA SAVE

All Year	1P: $119-$189	2P: $129-$199	XP: $10	F18

Location: 1 km w of Detroit-Windsor Tunnel; 1 km e of Ambassador Bridge. 333 Riverside Dr W N9A 5K4. Fax: 519/977-1411. **Facility:** 207 one-bedroom standard units. 19 stories, interior corridors. **Parking:** on-site (fee). **Terms:** package plans, small pets only. **Amenities:** video games (fee), voice mail, irons, hair dryers. *Some:* dual phone lines. **Dining:** The Park Terrace, see separate listing. **Pool(s):** heated indoor. **Leisure Activities:** saunas, whirlpool, exercise room. **Guest Services:** gift shop, valet laundry, area transportation-casino. **Business Services:** meeting rooms, fax (fee). **Cards:** AX, DC, DS, MC, VI.
Large-scale Hotel
(See color ad below, p 521 & on TourBookMark)

SOME UNITS

FEE

RAMADA PLAZA HOTEL AND SUITES   *Book at aaa.com*   Phone: 519/256-4656   **7**

All Year	1P: $109-$129	2P: $119-$139	XP: $10	F

Location: 0.5 km s of Riverside Dr at Park St W. 430 Ouellette Ave N9A 1B2. Fax: 519/256-9745. **Facility:** 145 one-bedroom standard units. 8 stories, interior corridors. **Parking:** on-site (fee). **Terms:** weekly rates available. **Amenities:** voice mail, irons, hair dryers. *Some:* dual phone lines. *Fee:* high-speed Internet.
Small-scale Hotel
Pool(s): heated indoor. **Leisure Activities:** exercise room. **Guest Services:** valet laundry, area transportation. **Business Services:** meeting rooms, business center. **Cards:** AX, DS, MC, VI.

SOME UNITS

FEE FEE

ROYAL MARQUIS HOTEL   Phone: (519)966-1900   **21**

All Year	1P: $95-$110	2P: $100-$120	XP: $10	F10

Location: Just n of Devonshire Mall and EC Row Expwy. 590 Grand Marais Rd E N8X 3H4. Fax: 519/966-4689. **Facility:** 99 one-bedroom standard units, some with whirlpools. 5 stories, interior corridors. **Parking:** on-site. **Terms:** 7 day cancellation notice-fee imposed, small pets only ($10 extra charge). **Amenities:** voice mail, hair dryers. **Pool(s):** heated indoor. **Leisure Activities:** saunas, whirlpool, exercise room. **Guest Services:** valet laundry.
Small-scale Hotel
Business Services: meeting rooms. **Cards:** AX, CB, DC, DS, JC, MC, VI.

SOME UNITS

FEE

STONECROFT INN   Phone: (519)969-7600   **14**

CAA SAVE

All Year	1P: $85-$95	2P: $95-$112	XP: $10	F16

Location: 0.5 km s of EC Row Expwy. 3032 Dougall Ave N9E 1S4. Fax: 519/969-7600. **Facility:** 59 units. 57 one-bedroom standard units, some with whirlpools. 2 one-bedroom suites. 2 stories (no elevator), interior corridors. **Parking:** on-site, winter plug-ins. **Terms:** [CP] meal plan available. **Amenities:** irons, hair dryers. **Dining:** 11 am-11 pm, Fri & Sat-midnight, Sun noon-10 pm. **Guest Services:** coin laundry. **Cards:** AX, CB, DC, MC, VI. **Special Amenities:** free continental breakfast and free local telephone calls.
Small-scale Hotel

SOME UNITS

STAY YOUR OWN WAY℠

Come to Canada South. Enjoy dining, festivals, gaming, horseracing, music, museums, shopping, and more. Downtown Windsor, minutes from the border.

Radisson

Radisson Riverfront Hotel • 333 Riverside Drive West • Windsor, ON, Canada
Ph: 1-519-977-9777 • Fax: 1-519-977-1411 • www.radisson.com/windsorca
Reservations Worldwide 1-800-333-3333

(See map and index starting on p. 562)

SUPER 8 MOTEL
Book at aaa.com — Phone: (519)966-8868 **23**
CAA SAVE — All Year — 1P: $89 — 2P: $89 — XP: $10 — F13
Location: Directly n of EC Row Expwy. 2265 Huron Church Rd N9C 2L5. Fax: 519/966-8814. **Facility:** 51 one-bedroom standard units, some with whirlpools. 2 stories (no elevator), interior corridors. *Bath:* combo or shower only. **Parking:** on-site. **Terms:** package plans. **Amenities:** high-speed Internet, irons, hair dryers.
Small-scale Hotel **Cards:** AX, DC, MC, VI. **Special Amenities:** free continental breakfast and free local telephone calls.

SOME UNITS

TOWNE AND COUNTRY MOTEL
Phone: 519/969-9120 **12**
All Year — 1P: $60-$95 — 2P: $65-$125 — XP: $10 — F12
Location: Just n of Devonshine Mall and EC Row Expwy. 2883 Howard Ave N8X 3Y4. Fax: 519/969-6362.
Motel — **Facility:** 51 one-bedroom standard units. 2 stories (no elevator), interior/exterior corridors. *Bath:* combo or shower only. **Parking:** on-site. **Amenities:** hair dryers. **Pool(s):** outdoor. **Cards:** AX, DC, MC, VI.

SOME UNITS

TRAVELODGE HOTEL DOWNTOWN WINDSOR
Book at aaa.com — Phone: (519)258-7774 **17**
CAA SAVE — 7/1-10/31 — 1P: $119-$219 — 2P: $129-$229 — XP: $10 — F18
5/1-6/30 & 11/1-4/30 — 1P: $99-$189 — 2P: $99-$189 — XP: $10 — F18
Location: Jct Ouellette Ave; downtown. 33 Riverside Dr E N9A 2S4. Fax: 519/258-0020. **Facility:** 160 one-bedroom standard units. 10 stories, interior corridors. **Parking:** on-site (fee). **Terms:** package plans.
Small-scale Hotel **Amenities:** voice mail, irons, hair dryers. **Dining:** 7-11 am, Sat & Sun-1 pm, cocktails. **Pool(s):** heated indoor. **Leisure Activities:** whirlpool. **Guest Services:** valet laundry, area transportation-casino. **Business Services:** meeting rooms. **Cards:** AX, DC, DS, MC, VI. *(See color ad on TourBookMark)*

SOME UNITS

TRAVELODGE WINDSOR AMBASSADOR BRIDGE
Book at aaa.com — Phone: (519)972-1100 **18**
CAA SAVE — 7/1-9/15 — 1P: $100-$180 — 2P: $100-$180 — XP: $10 — F12
9/16-4/30 — 1P: $90-$160 — 2P: $90-$160 — XP: $10 — F12
5/1-6/30 — 1P: $85-$150 — 2P: $85-$150 — XP: $10 — F12
Location: N of EC Row Expwy. 2330 Huron Church Rd N9E 3S6. Fax: 519/972-6310. **Facility:** 136 units. 129
Small-scale Hotel one-bedroom standard units. 7 one-bedroom suites ($150-$200). 2 stories (no elevator), interior corridors.
Parking: on-site. **Terms:** package plans, pets ($100 deposit). **Amenities:** video games (fee), voice mail.
Some: irons, hair dryers. **Pool(s):** heated indoor, wading. **Leisure Activities:** whirlpool, exercise room. *Fee:* game room. **Guest Services:** sundries, valet and coin laundry. **Business Services:** meeting rooms. **Cards:** AX, CB, DC, DS, JC, MC, VI.
Special Amenities: free expanded continental breakfast and free local telephone calls.

SOME UNITS

—— WHERE TO DINE ——

BERN FONDUE & WINE BAR
Dinner: $12-$15 — Phone: 519/973-3100 **7**
Location: Just w of Ouellette Ave. 122 Chatham St W N9A 5M7. **Hours:** 5 pm-11 pm. Closed major holidays; also Mon & Tues. **Reservations:** accepted. **Features:** Slightly seductive, the quietly upscale restaurant is a
Fondue — romantic retreat away from the hustle of downtown streets. Diners can choose among a variety of cheese and savory fondues designed to be shared but should definitely leave room for the sinful chocolate fondue and a glass of local iced wine. Casual dress; cocktails. **Parking:** street. **Cards:** AX, MC, VI.

CHANOSO'S RESTAURANT
Lunch: $6-$16 — Dinner: $6-$16 — Phone: 519/254-8530 **18**
Location: Between Chatham St and University. 255 Ouellette Ave N9A 4H9. **Hours:** 11 am-10 pm, Fri-11 pm, Sat noon-11 pm, Sun noon-9 pm. Closed: 12/25. **Features:** Often crowded, loud and bustling, the casual eatery
Asian — lets diners create their own customized stir-fries with a variety of sauces and degrees of spice. Starters include noodle rolls, pita and hummus, Asian soups and salads, which can be followed with a wide choice of stir-fries, rice noodle salads and Asian fajitas. This place is a hit with the locals. Selections from the extensive wine list complement the fare. Casual dress; cocktails. **Parking:** street. **Cards:** AX, MC, VI.

THE CHATHAM STREET GRILL
Lunch: $8-$10 — Dinner: $20-$25 — Phone: 519/256-2555 **6**
Location: Jct Ferry St. 149 Chatham St W N9A 5M7. **Hours:** noon-11 pm, Fri & Sat-midnight, Sun 4 pm-10 pm. Closed major holidays. **Reservations:** suggested, required weekends. **Features:** Pasta and grilled entree
American — specialties draw an eclectic crowd of special occasion, business and tourist diners. The creative menu features certified Angus beef, Australian sea bass and smoked duck. The decor is decidedly Mediterranean, with dim lighting. A large, outdoor patio is a popular draw in the summer months. Dressy casual; cocktails. **Parking:** street.
Cards: AX, DC, MC, VI.

THE CITY BEER MARKET
Lunch: $6-$12 — Dinner: $15-$30 — Phone: 519/253-3511 **4**
Location: Jct Pellisier. 119 Chatham St W N9A 5M7. **Hours:** 11:30 am-2 am, Mon & Tues from 4 pm. Closed major holidays; also Sun. **Reservations:** suggested. **Features:** A sophisticated ambience, complete with
Steak House — deep leather booths and candlelit tables, complements the traditional steak house menu at this club-like dining room. The menu features old-time favourites such as shrimp cocktail, bacon-wrapped scallops and hearty salads with a modern flair. Steaks and prime rib come in varied sizes to suit all appetites, and some lighter seafood options are also offered. A livelier atmosphere is found on the weekend when live jazz is featured in the upstairs lounge. Dressy casual; cocktails. **Parking:** on-site (fee). **Cards:** AX, MC, VI.

(See map and index starting on p. 562)

ELAINE'S BISTRO Lunch: $7-$9 Dinner: $17-$22 Phone: 519/948-0693 ⑪
French
Location: Located in Old Riverside Village. 5880 Wyandotte St E N8S 1M8. **Hours:** 11:30 am-2:30 & 5:30-9:30 pm, Fri & Sat-10 pm. Closed major holidays; also Sun & Mon. **Reservations:** suggested. **Features:** Serving a modest range of dishes, the small, informal bistro could have been pulled from the streets of Paris or Nice. Offering le plat du jour as well as other traditional and popular specialties, the chef/owners have created an authentic touch of France a short drive from downtown. Casual dress; cocktails. **Parking:** street. **Cards:** MC, VI. ✕

FRANCO'S RESTAURANT Lunch: $5-$8 Dinner: $9-$17 Phone: 519/258-3151 ⑧
Italian
Location: 2 km e of Ouellette Ave. 1545 Tecumseh Rd E N8W 1C3. **Hours:** 11 am-11 pm, Fri & Sat-2 am. Closed: 12/25. **Features:** Franco's friendly, casual, family-oriented eatery offers a varied menu and several house specialties such as tasty pizza, veal parmigiana, pasta and ribs. The lunch buffet is fresh and well stocked. The service staff is fast and efficient. Casual dress; cocktails. **Parking:** on-site. **Cards:** AX, MC, VI. ✕

IL BOSCHETTO RISTORANTE Lunch: $8-$15 Dinner: $12-$25 Phone: 519/252-4550 ⑬
Italian
Location: Jct Ellis St W. 1368 Ouellette Ave N8X 1J9. **Hours:** 11 am-3 & 5-10 pm. Closed major holidays; also Mon. **Reservations:** accepted. **Features:** With fractured Doric columns, arches and small lion heads along the stucco walls, the dining area evokes the feel of the courtyard of an Italian villa, complete with a small gazebo. The atmosphere is lively and casual. While offering an extensive menu of Italian standards, the kitchen reaches deep into its country roots to create dishes such as braised rabbit with root vegetables. Dressy casual; cocktails. **Parking:** on-site and street. **Cards:** AX, DC, MC, VI.

JOSE'S NOODLE FACTORY Lunch: $5-$9 Dinner: $8-$22 Phone: 519/972-1760 ⑮
American
Location: Just n of Devonshire Mall and EC Row Expwy. 2731 Howard Ave N9X 3X4. **Hours:** 11 am-1 am. Closed: 12/25. **Features:** The bustling eatery sustains a cantina feel in decor and menu offerings and features outdoor patio seating in season. The kitchen dishes hearty portions of Italian fare, including pasta, pizzas, sizzling burgers, ribs, tasty wings and a great selection of finger foods. Watch for the changing daily specials, which offer exceptional value and great taste. Casual dress; cocktails. **Parking:** on-site. **Cards:** AX, MC, VI. 🍸 ✕

THE KEG STEAKHOUSE AND BAR Dinner: $15-$30 Phone: 519/969-3146 ⑲
Steak House
Location: Jct Howard Ave; adjacent to Devonshire Mall. 490 Division Rd N9A 6K7. **Hours:** 4:30 pm-10:30 pm, Fri & Sat-11 pm, Sun 4 pm-9:30 pm. Closed: 12/25. **Features:** Well-known for its mesquite-grilled steaks and fun, laid-back atmosphere, the steak house is a longtime favourite with the local crowd. In addition to great beef, the traditional menu features seafood, grilled chicken, hickory ribs and pasta offerings. All meals come with a hot loaf of sourdough bread. Try a specialty coffee or tasty cheesecake for the perfect ending. Casual dress; cocktails. **Parking:** on-site. **Cards:** AX, DC, DS, MC, VI. 🍸 ✕

LA ZINGARA PIZZERIA TRATTORIA Lunch: $8-$12 Dinner: $10-$15 Phone: 519/258-7555 ⑯
Pizza
Location: Jct Howard Ave and Erie St. 555 Erie St E N9A 3X7. **Hours:** 11:30 am-2 & 5-10 pm, Fri & Sat-midnight, Sun 4 pm-10 pm. Closed major holidays. **Features:** Popular and well-known for its wood-fired pizzas and menu of Italian favorites, the sometimes boisterous restaurant has waiting lines on summer weekends. Several days a week, a musician adds a pleasant backdrop to the already comfortable atmosphere. Dressy casual; cocktails. **Parking:** street. **Cards:** MC, VI. ✕

NICO RISTORANTE Lunch: $10-$15 Dinner: $15-$20 Phone: 519/255-7548 ⑫
Italian
Location: Jct Elsmere and Erie sts; in Via Italia. 851 Erie St E N9A 3Y7. **Hours:** 11:30 am-2 & 5-10 pm, Sat-Mon from 5 pm. Closed major holidays. **Reservations:** accepted. **Features:** Fresh herbs, grown from window baskets outside the storefront windows, inevitably find their way into Italian dishes. Well-known for its fresh seafood, the upscale yet cozy restaurant can at once be both romantic and boisterous. Dressy casual; cocktails. **Parking:** street. **Cards:** AX, MC, VI. ✕

NORTH OF THE BORDER Lunch: $5-$8 Dinner: $11-$17 Phone: 519/258-1535 ①
Italian
Location: Jct Dougall Ave and Chatham St; downtown; in Quality Suites Windsor. 250 Dougall Ave N9A 7C6. **Hours:** 6:30 am-11 pm, Fri-4 am, Sat 7 am-4 am, Sun 7 am-11 pm. Closed: 12/25. **Features:** The casual eatery presents a fun menu of tasty fare, including burgers, ribs, steaks and pasta dishes. Portions are hearty. In warmer weather, diners unwind on the outdoor patio. This is a nice spot for relaxed downtown dining. Casual dress; cocktails. **Parking:** street. **Cards:** AX, DC, DS, MC, VI. ✕

THE PARK TERRACE Lunch: $9-$19 Dinner: $12-$25 Phone: 519/973-4225 ⑨
Continental
Location: 1 km w of Detroit-Windsor Tunnel; 1 km e of Ambassador Bridge; downtown; in Radisson Riverfront Hotel. 277 Riverside Dr W N9A 5K4. **Hours:** 6:30 am-2:30 & 6-10:30 pm. **Reservations:** suggested, weekends. **Features:** The relaxed, yet elegant, restaurant's large, open dining room affords an excellent view of the Detroit skyline. Diners are presented a menu of fine Continental cuisine, including selections of steak, rack of lamb, seafood, poultry and pasta. Among decadent desserts are such items as chocolate truffle mousse and New York-style cheesecake. Also offered are lighter items along the lines of sandwiches and salads, as well as a popular luncheon buffet. Dressy casual; cocktails. **Parking:** on-site. **Cards:** AX, DC, DS, MC, VI. 🍸 ✕

PORCINO Lunch: $8-$15 Dinner: $15-$24 Phone: 519/972-5699 ㉑
Continental
Location: Just s of jct Cabona Rd; in strip mall. 3891 Dougall Ave N9G 1X2. **Hours:** 11:30 am-2 & 5-10 pm, Sat from 5 pm. Closed major holidays; also Sun & Mon. **Reservations:** suggested. **Features:** On the south side of town, this contemporary, elegant dining room features a frosted glass window which allows diners to peek into the kitchen while the chefs prepare a globally influenced menu featuring items such as Asian spring rolls and duck confit with red cabbage slaw. Dressy casual; cocktails. **Parking:** on-site. **Cards:** AX, MC, VI. 🅼 🍸 ✕

(See map and index starting on p. 562)

RIVERSIDE GRILLE   **Dinner:** $23-$55   **Phone:** 519/258-7878   ⑩
▼▼▼▼   **Location:** Jct McDougall Ave; downtown; in Casino Windsor Hotel. 377 Riverside Dr E N9A 7H7. **Hours:** 6 pm-
midnight. **Reservations:** suggested. **Features:** The popular restaurant prepares hearty portions of
Continental   traditional fare with a Continental flair. Diners often enjoy a drink at the upscale lounge before moving to the
sophisticated dining room for their meal. Fine show plates and fresh flowers are an elegant touch at the
tables, many of which offer a commanding view of the Detroit skyline. Dressy casual; cocktails. **Parking:** on-site. **Cards:** AX,
DC, DS, MC, VI.

SPAGO TRATTORIA & PIZZERIA   **Lunch:** $8-$12   **Dinner:** $10-$18   **Phone:** 519/252-9099   ⑰
▼▼ ▼▼   **Location:** Jct Erie and St. Louis sts; in Via Italia. 614 Erie St E, Unit 1 N9A 3X9. **Hours:** 11:30 am-3 & 5-10 pm, Fri
& Sat-midnight, Sun 4 pm-9 pm. Closed major holidays. **Features:** Patrons who peek through storefront
Italian   windows will find that the large, wood-fired pizza oven hides the rustic and charming country-style
restaurant that awaits. Traditional favorites are prepared to order in the small, open kitchen. Casual dress;
cocktails. **Parking:** street. **Cards:** AX, DC, MC, VI.

T BQ'S MARKETPLACE   **Lunch:** $10-$25   **Dinner:** $15-$40   **Phone:** 519/250-3663   ⑤
▼▼ ▼▼   **Location:** Jct Huron Church and Maiden rds; 1.5 km n of EC Row Expwy; in Holiday Inn Select Windsor (Ambassador
Bridge). 1855 Huron Church Rd N9C 2L6. **Hours:** 6:30 am-11 pm, Fri-midnight, Sat 7 am-midnight, Sun 7 am-
American   10 pm. **Features:** If you're in the mood for "sink your teeth into ribs" or a fat, sizzling steak, T BQ's
MarketPlace is sure to please. Hearty portions of tasty fare are served up with a selection of tangy sauces
to perfectly finish off the barbecue taste. To end, make sure to try some of the fabulous freshly prepared desserts, including a
selection of decadent pies, cheesecakes and tortes. Casual dress; cocktails. **Parking:** on-site. **Cards:** AX, DC, MC, VI.

TUNNEL BAR-B-Q   **Lunch:** $4-$34   **Dinner:** $4-$34   **Phone:** 519/258-3663   ⑭
▼▼   **Location:** Across from Windsor-Detroit Tunnel exit. 58 Park St E N9A 3A7. **Hours:** 8 am-2 am, Fri & Sat-4 am.
Closed: 12/25. **Features:** A city landmark for more than 60 years, the old-time diner pleases patrons with its
American   no-frills atmosphere and hearty portions of barbecue ribs, chicken steaks and sandwiches. Save room for
dessert as the selection is extensive and the homemade taste irresistible. Casual dress; beer & wine only.
Parking: on-site. **Cards:** AX, DC, MC, VI.

YE OLDE STEAK HOUSE   **Lunch:** $6-$26   **Dinner:** $13-$28   **Phone:** 519/256-0222   ③
▼▼ ▼▼   **Location:** Just n of Detroit-Windsor Tunnel; between Ouellette Ave and Ferry St. 46 Chatham St W N9A 5M6.
Hours: 11:30 am-10 pm, Sat 4 pm-11 pm, Sun 4 pm-9 pm. **Reservations:** suggested. **Features:** An Old
Steak House   English theme, a comfortable atmosphere and a traditional steak house menu have made the restaurant
popular for years. Diners enjoy the distinct Tudor decor and a menu of such old-time favourites as shrimp
cocktail, French onion soup and fine cuts of filet, New York or rib-eye steak. Tasty accompaniments include baked potatoes and
sauteed mushrooms. Dressy casual; cocktails. **Parking:** street. **Cards:** AX, DC, MC, VI.

WOODSTOCK pop. 33,061

--- **WHERE TO STAY** ---

QUALITY HOTEL AND SUITES   *Book at aaa.com*   **Phone:** (519)537-5586
(AAA) (SAVE)   9/15-4/30   1P: $129-$236   2P: $129-$236   XP: $10   F18
5/1-9/14   1P: $124-$228   2P: $124-$228   XP: $10   F18
▼▼▼▼   **Location:** Hwy 401, exit 232, just n; w of Hwy 59. 580 Bruin Blvd N4V 1E5. **Fax:** 519/421-1304. **Facility:** 136 units.
Small-scale Hotel   131 one-bedroom standard units, some with whirlpools. 5 one-bedroom suites with whirlpools. 2-5 stories,
interior corridors. **Parking:** on-site, winter plug-ins. **Amenities:** video games (fee), voice mail, irons, hair
dryers. *Some:* dual phone lines. **Dining:** 6:30 am-11 pm, cocktails. **Pool(s):** outdoor. **Leisure
Activities:** saunas. *Fee:* aerobics instruction, pool table. **Guest Services:** valet laundry. *Fee:* tanning facility. **Business
Services:** conference facilities. **Cards:** AX, DC, DS, JC, MC, VI. **Special Amenities: free local telephone calls.**

SOME UNITS
FEE   FEE

SUPER 8 MOTEL   *Book at aaa.com*   **Phone:** 519/421-4588
▼▼ ▼▼   All Year   1P: $78-$83   2P: $86-$93   XP: $8   F12
Location: Jct Hwy 401 and 59, exit 232, just n. 560 Norwich Ave N4V 1C6. **Fax:** 519/421-4550. **Facility:** 72 one-
Small-scale Hotel   bedroom standard units. 2 stories (no elevator), interior corridors. **Parking:** on-site. **Guest Services:** coin
laundry. **Business Services:** meeting rooms. **Cards:** AX, DC, DS, MC, VI.

SOME UNITS
FEE   FEE

WYOMING pop. 2,200

--- **WHERE TO STAY** ---

**COUNTRY VIEW MOTEL AND RV CAMPING
RESORT**   **Phone:** 519-845-3394
(AAA) (SAVE)   5/1-9/30   1P: $54-$74   2P: $59-$89   XP: $10
10/1-4/30   1P: $49-$69   2P: $54-$84   XP: $10
▼▼ ▼▼   **Location:** Hwy 402, exit 25, 1 km s on Hwy 21 to Hwy 22, then just e. 4569 London Line N0N 1T0 (RR 1).
Fax: 519/845-0732. **Facility:** 16 one-bedroom standard units, some with kitchens (utensils extra charge). 1
Motel   story, exterior corridors. **Parking:** on-site, winter plug-ins. **Terms:** office hours 8 am-11 pm, 30 day
cancellation notice, weekly rates available, small pets only ($10 extra charge). **Pool(s):** outdoor. **Leisure
Activities:** rental paddleboats, fishing, playground. *Fee:* miniature golf, driving range. **Guest Services:** coin laundry. **Business
Services:** fax (fee). **Cards:** MC, VI.

SOME UNITS

FEE

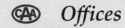

Offices

Cities with main offices are listed in **BOLD TYPE** and toll-free member service numbers in *ITALIC TYPE*. All are closed Saturdays, Sundays and holidays unless otherwise indicated.

The type of service provided is designated below the name of the city where the office is located:

✛ Auto travel services, including books/maps, marked maps and on-demand Triptik maps

● Auto travel services, including books/maps, marked maps, but no on-demand Triptik maps

■ Provides books/maps only. No marked maps or on-demand Triptik maps available

▲ Travel agency services

NATIONAL OFFICE: 1000 AAA DRIVE, HEATHROW, FLORIDA 32746-5063, (407) 444-7000

PROVINCE OF ONTARIO

BARRIE—CAA CENTRAL ONTARIO, 411 BAYFIELD ST, L4M 6E5. MON-FRI 9-6, THU 9-7, SAT 9:30-4:30. (705) 726-1803, *(800) 268-3750.*●▲

BELLEVILLE—CAA CENTRAL ONTARIO, HWY 2 AT WALLBDGE/LOYALST, K8N 4Z2. MON-FRI 9-5, SAT 10-2. (613) 968-9832, *(800) 268-3750.*●▲

BRAMPTON—CAA CENTRAL ONTARIO, 2925 HWY 7 E UNIT 2, L6T 3S1. MON-FRI 9-6, THU & FRI 9-9, SAT 9:30-4:30. (905) 793-4912.●▲

BRANTFORD—CAA SOUTH CENTRAL ONTARIO, 47 CHARING CROSS ST, N3R 2H4. MON-FRI 9-6, THU & FRI 9-7, SAT 9-5. (519) 756-6321.●▲

BURLINGTON—CAA SOUTH CENTRAL ONTARIO, 3480 FAIRVIEW ST, L7N 2R5. MON-FRI 9-6, THU & FRI 9-9, SAT 9-5. (905) 632-6772.●▲

CAMBRIDGE—CAA MID-WESTERN ONTARIO, 600 HESPELER RD UNIT 2, N1R 8H2. MON-FRI 9-5:30, THU 9-8, SAT 9-3. (519) 624-2582, *(800) 265-8975.*●▲

CHATHAM—CAA CENTRAL ONTARIO, 810 RICHMOND ST, N7M 5J5. MON-FRI 9-6, SAT 10-1. (519) 351-2222, *(800) 268-3750.*●

COBOURG—CAA CENTRAL ONTARIO, 975 ELGIN ST W, K9A 5J3. MON-FRI 9-5, SAT 9-12. (905) 372-8777, *(800) 268-3750.*●▲

ESPANOLA—CAA NORTH & EAST ONTARIO, 800 CENTRE ST, P5E 1J3. MON-FRI 9-5. (705) 869-3611, *(800) 461-7111.*●▲

GLOUCESTER—CAA NORTH & EAST ONTARIO, 2446 BANK ST, K1V 0Y7. MON-FRI 9-5:30, SAT 10-4. (613) 736-9696, *(800) 267-8713.*●▲

GRIMSBY—CAA NIAGARA, 155 MAIN ST E, L3M 1P2. MON-FRI 9-5, THU 9-6, SAT 9-12. (905) 945-5555, *(800) 263-7272.*●▲

GUELPH—CAA MID-WESTERN ONTARIO, 170 SILVERCREEK PKY N #6, N1H 7P7. MON-FRI 9-6, MON & THU & FRI 9-8, SAT 9-5. (519) 823-2582, *(800) 265-8975.*●▲

HAMILTON—CAA SOUTH CENTRAL ONTARIO, 163 CENTENNIAL PKY, L8E 1H8. MON-FRI 9-6, THU & FRI 9-7, SAT 9-5. (905) 525-1210, *(800) 263-8389.*✛▲

HAMILTON—CAA SOUTH CENTRAL ONTARIO, 990 UPPER WENTWORTH ST, L9A 5E9. MON-FRI 9-6, THU & FRI 9-9, SAT 9-5. (905) 385-8500.●▲

KINGSTON—CAA CENTRAL ONTARIO, 2300 PRINCESS ST, K7M 3G4. MON-FRI 9-6, SAT 9:30-4:30. (613) 546-2596, *(800) 268-3750.*●▲

KITCHENER—CAA MID-WESTERN ONTARIO, 148 MANITOU DR, N2C 1L3. MON-FRI 8:30-6, SAT 9-3. (519) 894-2582, *(800) 265-8975.*✛▲

KITCHENER—CAA MID-WESTERN ONTARIO, 645 WESTMOUNT RD E, N2E 3S3. MON-FRI 8:30-6, SAT 9-3. (519) 570-2582, *(800) 265-8975.*●▲

LEAMINGTON—CAA CENTRAL ONTARIO, 140 ERIE ST N, N8N 3A2. MON-FRI 9-6, SAT 10-1. (519) 322-2356, *(800) 268-3750.*●▲

LONDON—CAA MID-WESTERN ONTARIO, 841 WELLINGTON RD S, N6E 3R5. MON-FRI 9-6, THU & FRI 9-8, SAT 9-4. (519) 685-2582, *(800) 265-8975.*●▲

LONDON—CAA MID-WESTERN ONTARIO, 301 OXFORD ST W, N6H 1S6. MON-FRI 9-8, SAT 9-6. (519) 858-2582, *(800) 265-8975.*●▲

MISSISSAUGA—CAA CENTRAL ONTARIO, 5025 HEATHERLEIGH AVE #12, L5V 2Y7. MON-FRI 9-6, THU & FRI 9-7, SAT 9:30-4:30. (905) 275-2502.●▲

MISSISSAUGA—CAA CENTRAL ONTARIO, 1744 LAKESHORE RD W, L5J 1J5. MON-FRI 9-6, SAT 10-3. (905) 823-6801.●▲

NEWMARKET—CAA CENTRAL ONTARIO, 130 DAVIS DR UNIT 2, L3Y 2N1. MON-FRI 10-6, THU & FRI 10-7, SAT 10-4. (905) 836-5171, *(800) 268-3750.*●▲

NIAGARA FALLS—CAA NIAGARA, 4465 DRUMMOND RD, L2E 6C5. MON-FRI 9-5, THU 9-6, SAT 9-12. (905) 357-0001, *(800) 263-7272.*●▲

NORTH BAY—CAA NORTH & EAST ONTARIO, 300 LAKESHORE DR, P1A 3V2. MON-FRI 9-5. (705) 474-8230, *(800) 461-7111.*●▲

OAKVILLE—CAA SOUTH CENTRAL ONTARIO, 230 N SERVICE RD W, L6M 2Y4. MON-FRI 9-6, THU & FRI 9-9, SAT 9-5. (905) 845-9680.●▲

ORANGEVILLE—CAA CENTRAL ONTARIO, 78 FIRST ST, L9W 2E4. MON-FRI 9-6, SAT 10-1. (519) 941-8360, *(800) 268-3750.*●▲

ORILLIA—CAA CENTRAL ONTARIO, ORILLIA SQ SHOPPING CTR, L3V 6H4. MON-FRI 9:30-6, THU & FRI 9:30-7, SAT 9:30-4:30. (705) 325-7211, *(800) 268-3750.*●▲

ORLEANS—CAA NORTH & EAST ONTARIO, 3095 ST JOSEPH BLVD, K1E 3W6. MON-FRI 9-5:30, SAT 10-4. (613) 841-6441, *(800) 267-8713.*●▲

OSHAWA—CAA CENTRAL ONTARIO, 1050 SIMCOE ST N, L1G 4W5. MON-FRI 9-6, SAT 9:30-4:30. (905) 723-5203, *(800) 268-3750.*●▲

OTTAWA—CAA NORTH & EAST ONTARIO, 2525 CARLING AVE, K2B 7Z2. MON-FRI 9-5:30, SAT 10-4. (613) 820-1880, *(800) 267-8713.*✛▲

OWEN SOUND—CAA CENTRAL ONTARIO, 187 10TH ST W, N4K 3R1. MON-FRI 9-6, SAT 9-3. (519) 376-1940, *(800) 268-3750.*●▲

PARRY SOUND—CAA NORTH & EAST ONTARIO, 70 JOSEPH ST, P2A 2G5. MON-FRI 9-5. (705) 746-9305, *(800) 461-7111.*●▲

PETERBOROUGH—CAA CENTRAL ONTARIO, 680 THE QUEENSWAY, K9J 7X7. MON-FRI 8:30-5:30, SAT 9-3. (705) 743-4343, *(800) 268-3750.*●▲

PICKERING—CAA CENTRAL ONTARIO, 726 KINGSTON RD UNIT 2, L1V 1A8. MON-FRI 9:30-6, THU 9:30-8, FRI 9:30-7, SAT 9:30-4:30. (905) 831-5253.●▲

SARNIA—CAA CENTRAL ONTARIO, 1095 LONDON RD, N7S 1P2. MON-FRI 9-6, SAT 9:30-4:30. (519) 344-8686, *(800) 268-3750.*●▲

SAULT STE MARIE—CAA CENTRAL ONTARIO, 293 BAY ST, P6A 1X3. MON-FRI 9:30-6, THU & FRI 9:30-7, SAT 9:30-4:30. (705) 942-4600, *(800) 268-3750.*●

SCARBOROUGH—CAA CENTRAL ONTARIO, 3563 LAWRENCE AVE E, M1H 1B3. MON-FRI 9-6, THU & FRI 9-8, SAT 9-4:30. (416) 439-6371.●▲

SIMCOE—CAA MID-WESTERN ONTARIO, 8 QUEENSWAY DR E, N3Y 4M3. MON-FRI 9-5:30, SAT 10-2. (519) 426-7230.●▲

ST CATHARINES—CAA NIAGARA, 76 LAKE ST, L2R 5X4. MON-FRI 9-5, THU 9-6, SAT 9-12. (905) 688-0321, *(800) 263-7272.*●▲

ST THOMAS—CAA MID-WESTERN ONTARIO, 24 FIRST AVE UNIT 8, N5R 4M5. MON-FRI 9-5:30, SAT 10-2. (519) 631-6490, *(800) 265-8975.*●▲

SUDBURY—CAA NORTH & EAST ONTARIO, 2140 REGENT ST, P3E 5S8. MON-FRI 9-5:30, SAT 10-4. (705) 522-0000, *(800) 461-7111.*●▲

THORNHILL—CAA CENTRAL ONTARIO, 60 COMMERCE VALLEY DR E, L3T 7P9. MON-FRI 8:30-5. (905) 771-3000, *(800) 268-3750.*✚▲

THOROLD—CAA NIAGARA, 3271 SCHMON PKY, L2V 4Y6. MON-FRI 9-5, THU 9-6, SAT 9-12. (905) 984-8585, *(800) 263-7272.*✚▲

THUNDER BAY—CAA NORTH & EAST ONTARIO, 585 MEMORIAL AVE, P7B 3Z1. MON-FRI 9-5:30, SAT 10-4. (807) 345-1261, *(800) 267-8713.*●▲

TORONTO—CAA CENTRAL ONTARIO, 225 THE EAST MALL, M9B 6J1. MON-FRI 9-6, THU & FRI 9-8, SAT 9:30-4:30. (416) 231-4438.●▲

TORONTO—CAA CENTRAL ONTARIO, 6212 YONGE ST, M2M 3X4. MON-FRI 9-6, THU & FRI 9-8, SAT 9:30-4:30. (416) 223-1211.●▲

TORONTO—CAA CENTRAL ONTARIO, 3338 DUFFERIN ST UNIT 1&2, M6A 3A4. MON-FRI 9-6, THU & FRI 9-8, SAT 9:30-4:30. (416) 789-7467.●▲

TORONTO—CAA CENTRAL ONTARIO, 895 LAWRENCE AVE E, M3C 1P7. MON-FRI 9-6, THU & FRI 9-8, SAT 9:30-4:30. (416) 449-9442.●▲

TORONTO—CAA CENTRAL ONTARIO, 461 YONGE ST, M4Y 1X4. MON-FRI 8:30-6, SAT 9:30-4:30. (416) 593-7375.●▲

WATERLOO—CAA MID-WESTERN ONTARIO, 572 KING ST N UNIT A-1, N2L 6L3. MON-FRI 9-8, SAT 9-5. (519) 746-5562.●▲

WELLAND—CAA NIAGARA, 440 NIAGARA ST, L3C 1L5. MON-FRI 9-5, THU 9-6, SAT 9-12. (905) 735-1100, *(800) 263-7272.*●▲

WINDSOR—CAA CENTRAL ONTARIO, 1255 OUELLETTE AVE, N8X 1J3. MON-FRI 8:30-6, SAT 9-1. (519) 255-1212, *(800) 268-3750.*●▲

WOODSTOCK—CAA MID-WESTERN ONTARIO, 925 DUNDAS ST, N4S 8V3. MON-FRI 9-5:30, SAT 9-3. (519) 421-2582, *(800) 265-8975.*●▲

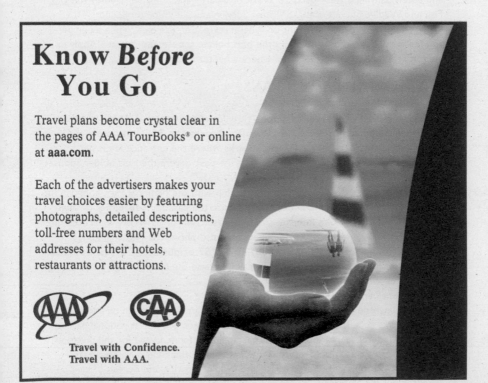

Know *Before* You Go

Travel plans become crystal clear in the pages of AAA TourBooks® or online at **aaa.com**.

Each of the advertisers makes your travel choices easier by featuring photographs, detailed descriptions, toll-free numbers and Web addresses for their hotels, restaurants or attractions.

**Travel with Confidence.
Travel with AAA.**

GOLDEN PASSPORTS

Golden Passports, available in three types, offer benefits and significant savings to individuals who plan to visit federal recreation sites.

The *Golden Eagle Passport*, available for a **$65** annual fee, is valid for entrance only to all federal recreation areas that have an entrance fee. Sites include those operated by the National Forest Service, National Park Service, Bureau of Land Management and the U.S. Fish and Wildlife Service. The passport admits all occupants of a private vehicle at locations where entrance is on a per vehicle basis. At locations where a per person fee is charged, the pass covers the pass holder, spouse, parents and children.

Citizens or permanent residents of the United States who are 62 and older can obtain *Golden Age Passports* for a one-time **$10** fee. Proof of age is required.

Golden Access Passports are free to citizens or permanent residents of the United States (regardless of age) who are medically blind or permanently disabled. Medical documention is required.

Both *Golden Age* and *Golden Access Passports* cover entrance fees for the holder and accompanying private party to all national parks and sites managed by the U.S. Fish and Wildlife Service, the U.S. Forest Service and the Bureau of Land Management, plus a 50% discount on federal recreation use fees. When a per person fee is imposed, the pass covers the pass holder, spouse and children. Apply in person at a federally operated area where an entrance fee is charged.

NATIONAL PARKS PASS

The *National Parks Pass*, valid for 1 year from its first use in a park, allows unlimited admissions to all U.S. national parks. The **$50** pass covers all occupants of a private vehicle at parks where the entrance fee is per vehicle. At parks with individual entry fees, the pass covers the pass holder, spouse, parents and children.

As a result of a partnership with the National Park Foundation, AAA members may purchase the pass for **$48**, either through AAA's internet site (www.aaa.com) or by visiting a participating AAA office. Members may also phone the National Park Foundation at **(888) 467-2757** or purchase the pass online at www.nationalparks.org. Non-members may purchase the pass through participating AAA offices for the full **$50** price or online at www.nationalparks.org.

For an upgrade fee of **$15**, a Golden Eagle Hologram sticker can be added to a *National Parks Pass*. The hologram covers entrance fees not just at national parks, but at any federal recreation area that has an admission fee. Valid for the duration of the *National Parks Pass* to which it is affixed, the Golden Eagle hologram is available at National Park Service, Fish and Wildlife Service and Bureau of Land Management fee stations.

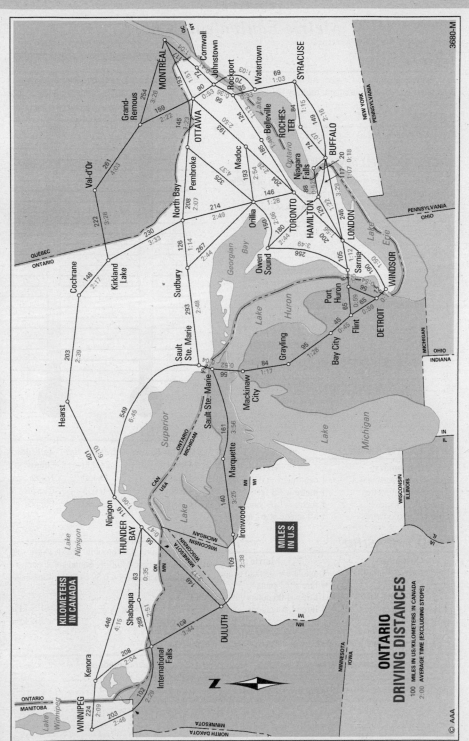

ONTARIO
DRIVING DISTANCES

100 MILES IN US/KILOMETERS IN CANADA
2:00 AVERAGE TIME (EXCLUDING STOPS)

© AAA

3680-M

Metric Equivalents Chart

TEMPERATURE

To convert Fahrenheit to Celsius, subtract 32 from the Fahrenheit temperature, multiply by 5 and divide by 9. To convert Celsius to Fahrenheit, multipy by 9, divide by 5 and add 32.

ACRES

1 acre = 0.4 hectare (ha)   1 hectare = 2.47 acres

MILES AND KILOMETRES

Note: A kilometre is approximately 5/8 or 0.6 of a mile. To convert kilometres to miles multiply by 0.6.

Miles/Kilometres		Kilometres/Miles	
15	24.1	30	18.6
20	32.2	35	21.7
25	40.2	40	24.8
30	48.3	45	27.9
35	56.3	50	31.0
40	64.4	55	34.1
45	72.4	60	37.2
50	80.5	65	40.3
55	88.5	70	43.4
60	96.6	75	46.6
65	104.6	80	49.7
70	112.7	85	52.8
75	120.7	90	55.9
80	128.7	95	59.0
85	136.8	100	62.1
90	144.8	105	65.2
95	152.9	110	68.3
100	160.9	115	71.4

Celsius ° / Fahrenheit °

Celsius °		Fahrenheit °
100	BOILING	212
37		100
35		95
32		90
29		85
27		80
24		75
21		70
18		65
16		60
13		55
10		50
7		45
4		40
2		35
0	FREEZING	32
-4		25
-7		20
-9		15
-12		10
-15		5
-18		0
-21		-5
-24		-10
-27		-15

LINEAR MEASURE

Customary	Metric
1 inch = 2.54 centimetres	1 centimetre = 0.4 inches
1 foot = 30 centimetres	1 metre = 3.3 feet
1 yard = 0.91 metres	1 metre = 1.09 yards
1 mile = 1.6 kilometres	1 kilometre = .62 miles

WEIGHT

If You Know:	Multiply By:	To Find:
Ounces	28.000	Grams
Pounds	0.450	Kilograms
Grams	0.035	Ounces
Kilograms	2.200	Pounds

LIQUID MEASURE

Customary	Metric
1 fluid ounce = 30 millilitres	1 millilitre = .03 fluid ounces
1 cup = .24 litres	1 litre = 2.1 pints
1 pint = .47 litres	1 litre = 1.06 quarts
1 quart = .95 litres	1 litre = .26 gallons
1 gallon = 3.8 litres	

PRESSURE

Air pressure in automobile tires is expressed in kilopascals. Multiply pound-force per square inch (psi) by 6.89 to find kilopascals (kPa).

24 psi = 165 kPa	28 psi = 193 kPa
26 psi = 179 kPa	30 psi = 207 kPa

GALLON AND LITRES

Gallons/Litres				Litres/Gallons			
5	19.0	12	45.6	10	2.6	40	10.4
6	22.8	14	53.2	15	3.9	50	13.0
7	26.6	16	60.8	20	5.2	60	15.6
8	30.4	18	68.4	25	6.5	70	18.2
9	34.2	20	76.0	30	7.8	80	20.8
10	38.0	25	95.0	35	9.1	90	23.4

Border Information

ENTERING CANADA AND RETURNING TO THE UNITED STATES

PASSPORTS to enter Canada or return to the United States are NOT required for native-born citizens of either country. However, proof of citizenship must be carried; a certified birth certificate accompanied by a photo ID usually will suffice. Proof of residence also may be required. Naturalized citizens should carry their naturalization certificate, and U.S. resident aliens must have an Alien Registration Receipt Card (Green Card). **A passport is the best proof of citizenship and its use is strongly suggested.**

Due to concerns over child abduction, single parents, grandparents or guardians traveling abroad with a minor should be prepared to document their legal custody and provide proof of citizenship for each child. Most common carriers, such as airlines, trains and buses, will demand proof and accept only the minor's passport or the parents' passport that includes the child. When the child is with only one parent, that parent should have a notarized letter of consent from the other parent or have legal custody documents. In other cases, the minor (if traveling alone) or the individual with the minor, should have a notarized letter of consent from both parents (including a telephone number) or a custody document.

THE CANADIAN GST: A 7 percent Goods and Services Tax (GST) is levied on most items sold and most services rendered in Canada. In Nova Scotia, New Brunswick and Newfoundland, a Harmonized Sales Tax (HST) of 15 percent (7 percent GST and 8 percent provincial) is charged on most goods and services. Visitors may apply for a GST/HST rebate on many items, including short-term accommodations (less than 1 month in one location). A rebate may be claimed on a minimum of $200 of eligible purchases prior to taxes, provided the goods are exported 60 days from date of purchase. Purchased items on which the GST/HST is not refundable include alcohol, food and beverages, tobacco, transportation, entertainment, automobile fuel and such services as dry cleaning. Original receipts must be submitted; each receipt must be for $50 or more before tax.

Free brochures explaining the GST and containing a rebate form are available in Canada at participating land border Duty Free shops, Tourist Information Centers, Customs Offices and at hotels. Allow 4 to 6 weeks for processing. For more information write: Visitor Rebate Program, Summerside Tax Centre, Canada Customs and Revenue Agency, 275 Pope Rd., Suite 104, Summerside, P.E., Canada C1N 6C6; phone (902) 432-5608 outside Can., or (800) 668-4748 in Can.

CANADIAN CUSTOMS REGULATIONS

EMPLOYMENT OF VISITORS and other non-immigrants is not permitted without employment authorization, usually obtained prior to entry into Canada. Permits authorizing paid employment at a specified job for a specified period of time must be obtained from the Human Resources Canada Centre. You will be denied entry if you intend to finance your visit by seeking a paying job.

FIREARMS are regulated by classification. All firearms must be declared and registered upon entry into Canada. The fee for a Firearms Declaration is $50. Visitors who borrow a firearm must obtain in advance a Non-Resident's Sixty-Day Possession License ($30); phone (800) 731-4000. It is advised that U.S. residents register weapons with U.S. Customs before departure. Upon return, U.S. residents may be asked to show proof that they had the weapon before departure. Under certain circumstances individuals and businesses may import firearms.

Prohibited (may not enter Canada): weapons with no legitimate sporting or recreational use, including weapons that discharge bullets in rapid succession during one pull of the trigger, such as a fully automatic rifle or machine gun (regardless of conversion); and rifles or shotguns designed or adapted so the barrel is less than 470 mm (18.5 in.) long or the overall length is less than 660 mm (26 in.); handguns with a barrel length of 105 mm (4.14 in.) or less, or using 25 or 32 calibre cartridges; and any other firearm prohibited by an Order in Council.

Other prohibited items include any large capacity cartridge magazines (limited to five rounds for semiautomatic rifles or shotguns and 10 rounds for handguns); tasers; any device designed to stop the sound of a firearm; any knife with a blade that opens by spring pressure, such as a switchblade; and any other weapons declared prohibited by an Order in Council, such as mace, tear gas (if designed for use against humans), throwing stars,

When You Travel In Canada

AAA-affiliated motor clubs form the Canadian Automobile Association, with its national office at 1145 Hunt Club Rd., Suite 200, Ottawa, ON, Canada K1V 0Y3. CAA clubs provide the same services for AAA members as do the AAA clubs in the United States. Establishments displaying the Official Appointment sign have met the rigid inspection requirements of the two associations.

SEAT BELTS: The use of seat belts by vehicle drivers and all passengers is required in Canada.

RADAR DETECTORS: The possession of radar detection devices is illegal in Manitoba, New Brunswick and Yukon Territory. The use of radar detectors is illegal in Newfoundland, Northwest Territories and Nunavut, Nova Scotia, Ontario, Prince Edward Island and Québec.

INSURANCE: In the event of an accident, if proper proof is not presented, a substantial fine may be imposed. If renting a vehicle, check with the rental car company regarding insurance.

CURRENCY: All prices and admission fees quoted are in Canadian dollars. Private establishments are under no obligation to accept, convert or pay a premium on the currencies of other countries. It is to your financial advantage to use Canadian currency when traveling in Canada. The only means of obtaining the official exchange rate is to change U.S. funds at a bank or purchase travelers checks in Canadian currency. If you plan to carry cash instead of travelers checks, be aware that some Canadian banks will not accept U.S. bills in large denominations for exchange.

PROVINCIAL REGULATIONS: Check the Fast Facts page for any additional regulations imposed by individual provinces or territories.

LEGAL ISSUES: Persons with felony convictions, driving while intoxicated records or other offenses may be denied admittance into Canada. Contact the Canadian Embassy or nearest Canadian Consulate before travel.

Nunchaku sticks, belt-buckle knives, spiked wristbands, blowguns, stun guns, finger rings with blades, brass knuckles, armor-piercing handgun cartridges, explosive projectiles for small arms cartridges, shotgun cartridges containing "flechettes," a "bull pup" stock for rifles and carbines, and trigger enhancement devices.

Restricted (admitted only for approved shooting competitions at which time an Authorization to Transport is required from the provincial chief firearms officer—phone (800) 731-4000 for addresses and phone numbers) semiautomatic firearms that have a barrel less than 470 mm (18.5 in.) and that discharge center-fire ammunition; and those that can be fired when reduced to less than 660 mm (26 in.) in length. Other restricted weapons include any firearm designed, altered or intended to be aimed and fired by the action of one hand, such as pistols and revolvers; and any firearm that is declared to be a restricted firearm by an Order in Council.

Non-restricted (regular hunting rifles or shotguns): You must be at least 18 to import and they may be imported only for legitimate purposes such as hunting or use during hunting season; use in approved competitions; protection against wildlife in Canadian wilderness areas; or in-transit movement through Canada.

Hunters may bring in, duty-free, 200 rounds of ammunition; participants in a competition, 1,500 rounds. **A valid license or declaration must be shown to purchase ammunition.** If you hunt in Canada's parks or game reserves, you may have to get a hunting license from each province or territory in which you plan to hunt.

For more information about parks and hunting regulations, contact the appropriate provincial or territorial tourism information office: Alberta, (800) 661-8888 or (780) 427-4321; British Columbia, (800) 663-6000 or (250) 387-1642; Manitoba, (800) 665-0040 or (204) 945-3777; New Brunswick, (800) 561-0123 or (506) 789-4982; Newfoundland and Labrador, (800) 563-6353 or (709) 729-2830; Northwest Territories (Western NWT), (800) 661-0788 or (867) 873-7200; Nova Scotia, (800) 565-0000 or (902) 425-5781; Nunavut (Eastern NWT), (800) 491-7910 or (867) 979-6551; Ontario, (800) 668-2746 or (416) 314-0944; Prince Edward Island, (888) 734-7529 or (902) 368-4444; Québec (800) 363-7777 or (514) 873-2015; Saskatchewan (877) 237-2273 or (306) 787-2300; Yukon, (867) 667-5340.

Most provinces and territories also have their own laws regulating the transportation of firearms through their area. Contact the provincial or territorial tourism information office listed above. For further information on the entry of firearms, contact Canada Customs and Revenue Agency at (506) 636-5064, or (800) 461-9999 inside Can.

PERSONAL BAGGAGE is admissible into Canada on a temporary basis without payment of duty and taxes; however, a refundable security deposit may be required by Customs at the time of entry. Deposits normally are not required when visits are made for health or pleasure, provided all items are exported at the end of your trip.

Personal baggage that may be taken into Canada on a duty- and tax-free basis includes clothing and personal effects, sporting goods, automobiles, vessels, aircraft, snowmobiles, cameras, personal computers, food products and other items appropriate for the purpose and duration of your visit. Tobacco products are limited per person to 50 cigars, 200 cigarettes, 200 grams (7 oz.) of tobacco, and 200 tobacco sticks. Alcoholic beverages are limited to 1.14 liters (40 oz.) of liquor, *or* 1.5 liters (1.6 qts.) of wine *or* 8.5 liters (9 qts.) of beer or ale (equivalent to 24 twelve-ounce bottles/cans). Generally, a minimum stay of 24 hours is required to transport any liquor or tobacco into Canada.

All articles above allowable quantities are subject to federal duty and taxes, as well as provincial liquor fees. Provincial fees can be paid at Customs at the time of entry in all provinces and the Yukon Territory. In the Northwest Territories and Nunavut, it is illegal to bring in more alcohol than specified above. The minimum legal age for the importation of alcoholic beverages or tobacco products is 18 or 19 years, depending on the province or territory; check the Fast Facts page.

Articles purchased at Canadian duty-free shops are subject to U.S. Customs exemptions and restrictions; those purchased at U.S. duty-free shops before entering Canada are subject to duty if brought back into the United States.

Persons who may require prescription drugs while visiting Canada are permitted to bring medication for their own use. Prescription drugs should be clearly identified and should be carried in the original packaging with the label listing the drug and its intended use. It also is good to bring a copy of the prescription and the contact number of the doctor.

GIFTS, excluding tobacco, alcoholic beverages and advertising matter, taken into or mailed to Canada are allowed free entry if the value of each gift does not exceed $60 (Canadian currency).

Gifts valued at more than $60 are subject to the regular duty and taxes on the excess amount.

PETS AND PLANTS: Dogs and cats 3 months of age and older must be accompanied by a certificate signed by a licensed veterinarian that clearly describes the animal and declares that the animal has been vaccinated against rabies within the past 12 or 36 months, depending upon the type of vaccine. Collar tags are not sufficient proof of immunization. This certificate also is needed to bring a dog back into the United States; be sure the vaccination does not expire while traveling in Canada. "Seeing Eye" dogs are exempt from these rules, as well as up to two healthy puppies and kittens under 3 months old; it is recommended that the owner obtain a certificate of health from a veterinarian indicating that an animal is too young to vaccinate. Puppies under 4 months will not be admitted into the U.S. before 30 days after their rabies vaccination.

Plants or plant material must be declared. For additional information about pets and plants, contact one of the following Canadian Food Inspection Agency (CFIA) Import Service Centres: eastern Canada (877) 493-0468; central Canada (800) 835-4486; or western Canada (888) 732-6222.

RADIO COMMUNICATION EQUIPMENT: You may bring your cellular or PCS phone or citizens band (CB) or Family Radio Service (FRS) radio into Canada without any prior registration. You may use your aircraft, marine or amateur radio in Canada without prior authorization. All other types of radio transmitting stations may only be used in Canada if accompanied by a letter of authorization from Industry Canada's Radiocommunication and Broadcasting Regulatory Branch. For additional information contact Industry Canada at (613) 990-4737.

SPECIAL PERMITS: A CITIES (Convention on International Trade in Endangered Species) permit is required for any endangered species brought into Canada, including those kept as pets and for any items made from them, such as coats, handbags or shoes. For further information contact Environment Canada, Canadian Wildlife Service; phone (819) 997-1840.

Canada has restrictions to keep objects that are of historical, cultural or scientific signification inside Canada. If you wish to take objects more than 50 years old, such as fossils, archeological artifacts,

National Park Entrance Fees

At Canada's national parks, the basic per person or per family entry fee gives visitors access to the park, scenic outlooks, picnic areas and a variety of facilities. Additional fees are charged for visitors who choose to use other recreational services such as campgrounds, special interpretation programs and golf courses

To receive a free Parks Canada vacation planner, phone (888) 773-8888. Detailed information on the services, benefits, entry fees and discounts at all national parks and historic sites is available by calling the following numbers:

(800) 748-7275 for Alberta;

(902) 426-3436 for the Atlantic provinces (Newfoundland and Labrador, New Brunswick, Nova Scotia and Prince Edward Island);

(604) 513-4777 for British Columbia;

(888) 748-2928 for Manitoba;

(800) 748-7275 for Northwest Territories and Nunavut

(800) 839-8221 for Ontario;

(800) 748-7275 for Saskatchewan;

(800) 463-6769 for Québec;

(800) 661-0486 for Yukon Territory.

fine and decorative art, technological objects or books and archival material, out of the country, you may need an export permit to do so. Contact the Moveable Cultural Property Program of Canadian Heritage, 15 Eddy St., 3rd floor, Hull, Québec, Canada K1A 0M5; phone (819) 997-7761.

Importation of clothing, textiles, steel and certain agricultural products in excess of minimum quantities may be subject to import permit requirements under the Export and Import Permits Act. For further information, write the Department of Foreign Affairs and International Trade, Export and Import Control Bureau, P.O. Box 481, Station A, Ottawa, ON Canada K1N 9K6. Goods originating in Iraq are not admissible.

VEHICLES, including trailers not exceeding 2.6 metres (8 ft., 6 in.) in width, entering Canada for touring are generally subject to quick and routine entry procedures. You may not leave or store a car, trailer or other goods in Canada while you leave the country without either paying import duty and taxes or presenting the necessary permit to leave the items in Canada. This and any other required permits are issued by Canadian Customs officials at the point of entry. Vacation trailers may not be stored in Canada during the off-season.

Vehicle registration cards are necessary for Canadian travel. If you are driving a car other than your own, you must get written permission from the owner for use of the car in Canada. A copy of the contract is required for rented cars. A valid U.S. driver's license is valid in Canada for varying periods of time as ruled by the individual provinces and territories.

Some provinces and territories have made it a statutory requirement that motorists drive with vehicle headlights on for extended periods after dawn and before dusk. In Alberta, British Columbia, New Brunswick and Prince Edward Island lights must be turned on when light conditions restrict visibility to 150 metres (500 ft.); in Manitoba, the restriction is 60 metres (200 ft.). Headlights must remain on at all times in the Yukon Territory and Northwest Territories and Nunavut.

In cases of accident involving death, injury or property damage, the Canadian provinces and territories require evidence of financial responsibility. In some provinces, you may be asked to show this evidence at any time. The penalties for not producing such evidence vary by province and territory and can result in costly and time-consuming problems if you are unprepared.

The minimum liability insurance requirement is $200,000 in all provinces and territories except Québec, which requires $50,000, and Northwest Territories and Nunavut, which requires $100,000. Should the courts' judgments exceed these figures, motorists held accountable are responsible for paying the full amount.

U.S. CUSTOMS REGULATIONS

EXEMPTIONS granted to returning U.S. residents include an $800 exemption, if not used within the past 30 days, for residents who have been in Canada **no less than 48 hours.** Any amount over the $800 exemption is subject to duty. The exemptions are based on fair retail value and apply to articles acquired for personal or household use or as gifts, but **not intended for sale.**

Exemptions for a family (related persons living in the same house) may be combined; thus, a family of 5 would be entitled to a duty-free $4,000 exemption on one declaration, even if the articles declared by one member of the family exceeded that individual's $800 exemption. **Sales slips should be kept; they are proof of fair retail value.** All articles for which the $800 exemption is claimed must accompany you at the time of return.

You may send *bona fide* gifts to friends and relatives in the United States free of duty and taxes provided the recipient does not receive more than $100 worth of gifts per day. Tobacco products, alcoholic beverages and perfume containing alcohol and valued at more than $5 retail are excluded from this provision. The package containing the gift must be marked "Unsolicited Gift," with the contents and retail value indicated on the outside. These gifts are not included in your $800 exemption and are not to be declared upon your return.

If you are entitled to the $800 exemption, you may include 100 cigars and 200 cigarettes duty free. Cigarettes may be subject to state or local tax. Persons 21 years of age or older may include liquor to the amount of 1 litre (33.8 fl. oz.) per person in their $800 resident's exemption from duty and tax. In all cases, state liquor laws are enforced by Customs.

If you have been in Canada for **less than 48 hours,** you may bring back merchandise valued at $200 or less, duty and tax free. Such an exemption must not include more than 10 cigars, 50 cigarettes, 150 milliliters (5 fl. oz.) of alcoholic beverage *or* 150 milliliters (5 fl. oz.) of perfume containing alcohol. If any article brought back is subject to duty or tax or if the total value of all articles exceeds $200, no article may be exempted from duty or tax. Members of a family unit may not combine the value of their purchases under this exemption. All goods must be declared.

CERTAIN ARTICLES considered injurious or detrimental to the general welfare of the United States are *prohibited* entry by law. Among these are such items as narcotics and dangerous drugs; drug paraphernalia; hazardous articles (e.g., fireworks, dangerous toys and toxic or poisonous substances), obscene articles and publications; lottery tickets; switchblade knives; seditious or treasonable matter; and merchandise originating in Afghanistan, Cuba, Iran, Iraq, Libya, Serbia and Sudan.

Prohibited also are endangered species of plants and wildlife, or products made of any part of such species. If you are considering the purchase or import of fur, animal skins other than cowhide or any product manufactured wholly or in part from wildlife, write to the U.S. Fish and Wildlife Service, Department of the Interior, Washington, DC 20240 for additional information.

RESTRICTED ITEMS often require special licenses or controls. While some agricultural products of Canadian origin (fruit, plants with phytosanitary certificates, meats, etc.) may be brought into the United States, many are restricted to prevent the introduction of plant and animal pests and diseases into the country. All must be declared to customs officials at the U.S. border. For specific information, write for the free booklet "Traveler's Tips," available in English, Spanish, Italian or Japanese from USDA-APHIS Public Affairs, 4700 River Road Unit 51, Riverdale, MD 20737, ATTN: AQI Publications.

If you require medicines containing narcotics or habit-forming drugs, including cough and headache remedies, you should have them properly identified and carry only such quantities as might normally be needed for a health problem. You should carry proof, either in prescription form or as a written statement from your physician, that the medicines are being used under a doctor's direction and are necessary for your well-being.

Other restricted items include imported automobiles; biological materials (disease organisms and vectors for research); cultural treasures; firearms and ammunition; articles bearing marks or names copying or simulating trademarked articles or trade names (e.g., watches, cameras, perfumes); pirated copies of copyrighted articles (e.g., books, CDs, DVDs, computer programs); and pets, wildlife and fish.

Additional helpful booklets such as "Visiting the U.S.: Requirements for Non-Residents," "Importing or Exporting a Car," "Know Before You Go" and "Pets, Wildlife and U.S. Customs," are available online and by writing Customs Service Center, 1300 Pennsylvania Ave. N.W., Room 3.4A, Washington, DC 20229; phone (202) 354-1000.

Points of Interest Index

Index Legend

NB.	national battlefield	NR.	national river
NBP.	national battlefield park	NS.	national seashore
NC.	national cemetery	NWR.	national wildlife refuge
NF.	national forest	PHP.	provincial historic(al) park
NHM.	national historic(al) monument	PHS.	provincial historic(al) site
NHP.	national historic(al) park	PP.	provincial park
NHS.	national historic(al) site	SF.	state forest
NL.	national lakeshore	SHM.	state historic(al) monument
NME.	national memorial	SHP.	state historic(al) park
NMO.	national monument	SHS.	state historic(al) site
NMP.	national military park	SME.	state memorial
NP.	national park	SP.	state park
NRA.	national recreation area	SRA.	state recreation area

⚱ GEM: Points of Interest Offering a *Great Experience for Members*®

HISTORIC DOCUMENTS, MANUSCRIPTS & RARE BOOKS

HISTORIC SITES

HORSE FARMS

INDIAN MOUNDS, REMAINS & RUINS

INDIAN BURIAL GROUNDS

INDIAN PICTOGRAPHS & PETROGLYPHS

INDIAN RESERVATIONS & VILLAGES

INDUSTRIAL TOURS

ISLANDS

JAILS

LAKES, PONDS & RESERVOIRS

LIBRARIES, ARCHIVES

🖫 *Attraction Admission Discount Index*

Travel Planning Your Way

Visit **aaa.com** and enjoy a whole new world of travel information.

AAA/CAA's Internet TripTik® provides interactive maps and search tools that make travel planning easy. Get hotel Diamond ratings, photos, and great room rates. Find the best in restaurants and attractions.

Trust AAA/CAA to simplify travel planning.

  **Travel with Confidence.
Travel with AAA/CAA.**

Bed & Breakfast Lodgings Index

Some bed and breakfasts listed below might have historical significance. Those properties are also referenced in the Historical index. The indication that continental [CP] or full breakfast [BP] is included in the room rate reflects whether a property is a Bed-and-Breakfast facility.

Country Inns Index

Some of the following country inns can also be considered as bed-and-breakfast operations. The indication that continental [CP] or full breakfast [BP] is included in the room rate reflects whether a property is a Bed-and-Breakfast facility.

Historical Lodgings & Restaurants Index

Some of the following historical lodgings can also be considered as bed-and-breakfast operations. The indication that continental [CP] or full breakfast [BP] is included in the room rate reflects whether a property is a Bed-and-Breakfast facility.

HISTORICAL LODGINGS & RESTAURANTS (CONT'D)

Resorts Index

Many establishments are located in resort areas; however, the following places have extensive on-premises recreational facilities:

What Does a Perfect Vacation Sound Like?

The non-stop rhythm of a big city? The soft caress of waves on pure white sand? No matter what vacation sounds best, visit **aaa.com** before you go.

Get an internet TripTik® and find TourBook® information:
- AAA/CAA Approved hotels and restaurants
- Destination descriptions and attraction information
- Interactive maps
- Complete driving directions

Make travel planning easy with **aaa.com**.
CLICK! Sounds like the start of a perfect vacation.

  Travel with Confidence.
Travel with AAA/CAA

Comprehensive City Index

Here is an alphabetical list of all cities appearing in this TourBook® guide. Cities are presented by state/province. Page numbers under the POI column indicate where points of interest text begins. Page numbers under the L&R column indicate where lodging and restaurant listings begin.

Comprehensive City Index (cont'd)

It's More Than a Gift …
It's a Companion for Life

ive a AAA Gift Membership. With top quality automotive, travel services, member savings programs, access to financial and insurance services, and more, a AAA Gift Membership is a companion for life. To purchase, contact your local AAA office, visit aaa.com, or call 1-800-Join-AAA.